UNIVERSITY CASEBOOK SERIES®

RACIAL JUSTICE AND LAW

CASES AND MATERIALS

RALPH RICHARD BANKS
Jackson Eli Reynolds Professor of Law
Stanford Law School

KIM FORDE-MAZRUI
Mortimer M. Caplin Professor of Law
University of Virginia School of Law

GUY-URIEL E. CHARLES
Charles S. Rhyne Professor of Law
Duke University School of Law

CRISTINA M. RODRÍGUEZ
Leighton Homer Surbeck Professor of Law
Yale Law School

FOUNDATION
PRESS

University Casebook Series is a trademark registered in the U.S. Patent and Trademark Office.

© 2016 LEG, Inc. d/b/a West Academic
    444 Cedar Street, Suite 700
    St. Paul, MN 55101
    1-877-888-1330

Printed in the United States of America

ISBN: 978-1-60930-230-6

ACKNOWLEDGEMENTS

We are indebted to many people for invaluable help with this project. We thank the following scholars (in alphabetical order) for substantive comments and suggestions: Margalynne Armstrong, Mario Barnes, Al Brophy, Devon Carbado, Sheryll Cashin, Jennifer Chacón, Bob Chang, Jack Chin, Justin Driver, Jennifer Eberhardt, Rich Ford, Risa Goluboff, Ariela Gross, Eisha Jain, Kevin Johnson, Olati Johnson, Bill Koski, Ian Haney-Lopez, Ken Mack, Rachel Moran, Camille Gear Rich, Stephen Rich, Daria Roithmayr, Rose Cuison Villazor, and Kimberly West-Faulcon.

We thank the following (then) students for their research assistance: Ana Apostoleris, Jeremy Bennie, Corrine Blalock, Jared Campbell, Evan Didier, Nina Goepfert, Aaron Gober-Sims, Amy Herrera, Grace Kao, Tim Lovelace, Chris Mincher, Amanda Oakes, Peter Park, Dana Rasmussen, Mike Raymond, Paul Ream, Yenisey Rodríguez, Hadi Sedigh, and Stephen Tagert.

Generations of Stanford Law School students inspired this book and helped to bring it to fruition. Those who played especially important roles in the process include those students in Professor Banks's Equal Protection classes during the 2008–2009 school year: Tamika Butler, Brad Chernin, Michael Correll, Orion Danjuma, Tim Fisher, Chris Grieco, James Hairston, Brad Hansen, Jana Hardy, Bobby Harrington, Laura Hurtado, Matt Jackson, Marina Jenkins, Gabe Martinez, Elizabeth McCrillis, Beverly Moore, Mike Powers, Tracy Rubin, Alberto Tovar, Sonia Valdez, Connor Williams, Allison Woo and Jodi Wu. Ling Lew also shaped these pages and, more recently, the assistance of Gilat Bachar has been indispensable.

We are grateful for the expert assistance from our reference librarians (too many to name) and for the dedicated and essential support of our administrative assistants Mary Ann Rundell, Sara Abarbanel, Ginny Smith, and Delores Clatterbuck. Finally, we are especially grateful to our Deans for their ongoing academic support: Larry Kramer, David Levi, Elizabeth Magill, Paul Mahoney, and Robert Post.

PREFACE

This book critically examines the role that law has played in creating, maintaining, and resisting a regime of white supremacy in America. It builds upon, expands, and is in conversation with prior theoretical explanations of our current racial order, including critical race theory. This book is borne of a desire to develop a law school course that reshapes and reinvigorates the conversation about law, race, and inequality. Contrary to assumptions that race is less significant today than it has been in the past, or that racial injustices arise only sporadically and as exceptions to an otherwise egalitarian system, this book makes the claim that race has been and remains central to American law, history, policy, culture, and society. Put differently, we cannot fully understand American law, history, society, or culture without coming to terms with the role that race has played in all segments of American life. Race shapes people's identities, experiences, opportunities, and life trajectories. It influences not only where people live, and where (and whether) they work, but also how they vote and who they love. It has done so in the past and it continues to do so today.

Indeed, it is difficult to find areas of American life that are untouched by race. Racial disparities pervade American society, from incarceration and victimization, to educational achievement, housing, employment, wealth, and immigration status. Despite the monumental legal, social, and cultural transformations of the second half of the 20th century—*Brown v. Board of Education*, the demise of Jim Crow, the enactment of wide-ranging federal civil rights laws, the disavowal of overt bigotry, and the election and (as importantly) re-election of our nation's first black President—race remains with us. From the glorious proclamations of the Declaration of Independence to the Constitution's sanction of slavery, from the enactment of the Thirteenth, Fourteenth, and Fifteenth Amendments, to the demise of Reconstruction, we have attempted to overcome race, only to be disappointed by the illusion that race had been overcome.

Because this is a legal text, we are primarily, though not by any means exclusively, interested in the relationship between law and race. Law is both an instrument of racial oppression and a tool of racial liberation. Law established the content and contours of white supremacy. Law established the racial caste system, which dictated the terms of social interactions between the races, such as who can marry whom, who can live next to whom, and even which races could and could not immigrate to this country.

Law is also a setting in which race-related controversies play out. Race-related conflicts arise in just about every area that touches people's lives, from housing and employment to education and child custody. Racial conflict generated a large body of statutory law that now shapes the lives of all Americans. The civil rights laws enacted as a result of racial justice efforts have provided the template for a wide array of federal, state, and local laws that guarantee an expansive set of rights. One cannot fully understand the development of American law and legal institutions without an appreciation of the centrality of racial conflict in that process.

Moreover, even contemporary legal controversies that are not ostensibly about race may nonetheless implicate race. Racial conflict has spawned generally applicable legal doctrines across many settings. For example, laws that block felons from voting or that prohibit loitering or that tie school funding to local property taxes cannot be sensibly assessed without consideration of their race-related dimensions. The rules that govern police officers, the death penalty, voting, the relation between federal and state governments, the state action requirement— constitutional doctrines in each of these areas have developed partly in response to race-related controversies.

Unfortunately, the intersection of race and the law has been unduly marginalized in many law school curricula and in legal scholarship. Not only is race and law not a required course at practically any law school, it is typically viewed as a specialized, boutique offering, a course the vast majority of students are not expected to take. One cause, and consequence, of this marginalization is that there are few teaching materials that reveal the pervasiveness, complexity, richness, and significance of racial controversies as they relate to the law.

Our creation of this casebook reflects our belief that the best and most effective way for students and scholars to study the intersection of race and the law is to do so in a sustained and systematic manner. It is important, of course, to recognize racial issues as they arise in courses such as contracts, torts, or property. But that sort of intermittent consideration cannot match the depth of engagement and understanding that flow from a more concerted examination of the intersection of race and law across a range of settings. In addition to being a good teaching tool, we hope that this book will help to further and deepen scholarship related to race and the law.

We hope that students benefit from this book in multiple ways. We want students to appreciate the range, depth and richness of those controversies at the intersection of law and race. Conflicts arise in varied settings, and before varied decision-makers, who, in turn, bring to bear a multiplicity of values and considerations. We want students to appreciate the difficulty of the changes that legal decision-makers confront. The legal controversies that we examine in this book are fraught and difficult to resolve because they are subject to legitimate disagreement about what racial justice should entail or about the capacity of legal institutions to realize racial justice goals. So too do legal decision-makers often rely on divergent assumptions about how society operates, and in particular about the extent and magnitude of racial discrimination. A primary goal then is for students to understand why cases are decided as they are, why controversies are handled in one way rather than another.

Our further hope is that students develop a perspective that is both critical and constructive. Students should be able to evaluate and critique the law. They should also help to make it better. We hope this book will help students to identify improvements in the law, articulate what the law should be, and what the law should do, and how to use the law to advocate effectively for change. For all the instances of injustice that are recounted in these pages, we want students to be able to envision a better future, and to chart a course toward it. We highlight problems to prompt students to think hard about solutions, not simply about how to craft a lawsuit, so much as about the wide range of avenues of reform that law school graduates might pursue. The law is multifaceted and ever changing, and we want students to feel empowered to take part in that process.

* * *

To realize these goals, we have made a number of pedagogical choices in constructing this casebook, some of which differentiate this book starkly from other race and law casebooks. First, we focus on contemporary controversies. Though we include a significant amount of historical material and legal developments, primarily for the purpose of illuminating present circumstances or framing contemporary debates, the casebook aims to confront the racial controversies of the twenty-first century. Thus, at the foreground of our inquiry is what's happening in American society today.

Second, of the many ways that a race and law casebook might be organized—by racial group, by historical period, by theme—we have chosen to structure this book by setting, to focus on one social context at a time. Inasmuch as legal conflicts and legal analysis are invariably fact specific, we consider controversies as they arise in particular social settings, from political participation and housing, to employment, education, and family relationships, among others. More than an organizational convenience, this approach reflects our conviction that the application of legal principles depends very much on the circumstances of particular settings and the myriad interests at stake within each.

Third, this book has a broad conception of law and the source of law. While we recognize the past and continued centrality of constitutional law in racial conflict (and therefore devote substantial space to such cases), we also look beyond that familiar setting. We feature a wide range of primary sources of law—cases, statutes, regulations—and also highlight the varied decision-makers that formulate and enact the rules and practices that shape our society. Law is not the province of judges alone. Federal, state, and local legislators, government lawyers, nonelected government officials, private sector lawyers and business owners, even private citizens—all play a role in giving content to law. We want students to consider the range of options and possibilities that confront these different decision-makers. We rely extensively on problems, role plays, and other exercises that require students to approach a controversy from the vantage point of different actors in the legal system. We emphasize these sources of law as well because law school graduates are less likely to produce social change through changing constitutional law than through one of the other mechanisms that our book identifies.

Finally, though this casebook recognizes that racial conflict in the United States has been historically understood primarily as the relationship between whites and blacks (or what scholars have called the black-white paradigm), we have also attempted to move beyond the black-white paradigm. The casebook takes into account the changing racial dynamics in the United States, which is the product of the increasing rates of miscegenation, interracial relationships, and immigration of the past few decades. We embrace a multi-racial approach that reflects the broad diversity of American society. We do not limit our focus to African Americans but neither do we treat different groups in distinct sections. Rather, we seek to integrate the similar and contrasting issues confronted by African Americans, Latinos, Asian Americans, Native peoples, and Whites within each of the settings studied. Issues related to immigration are woven throughout the book. We decided against devoting a separate chapter to immigration because we wanted to reflect the extent to which immigration and changing demographics have shaped racial conflict in multiple domains, from voting and employment to education and housing. The materials in this casebook present the myriad challenges that confront a range of legal decision-makers across a wide variety of settings. Our hope is that these materials are as rich and nuanced as the problems of race in contemporary American society.

RALPH RICHARD BANKS
KIM FORDE-MAZRUI
GUY-URIEL E. CHARLES
CRISTINA M. RODRÍGUEZ

May 13, 2016

EDITORIAL NOTE

Readers should be aware of two of our editorial choices. First, in editing cases and other materials for ease of reading and comprehension, we have not consistently indicated with ellipses where text has been omitted. Similarly, footnotes have been numbered consecutively within each chapter so that omission of footnotes from the original text is not always apparent, and the footnote numbers in the book typically do not match those contained in the original, excerpted materials.

Second, we have chosen to tolerate inconsistencies in our use of terms for particular groups, e.g., black and African American; Native American and Indian; Latino and Hispanic; white, Caucasian, and European; multi-racial and mixed race. This choice of terminology reflects that nomenclature is political and contested; we want this book to reflect divergent views regarding the characterization of self and others. Designations are historically situated as well; old cases may include terms that today would be considered passé or offensive, such as "Negro" or "Oriental." As with the book more generally, we hope that these editorial choices facilitate productive and thoughtful engagements in the classroom and beyond.

SUMMARY OF CONTENTS

TABLE OF CONTENTS

TABLE OF CASES

The principal cases are in bold type.

UNIVERSITY CASEBOOK SERIES®

RACIAL JUSTICE AND LAW

CASES AND MATERIALS

CHAPTER 1

SLAVERY AND THE FIRST RECONSTRUCTION: ESTABLISHING AND CONTESTING THE RACIAL ORDER

I.   LAW AND WHITE SUPREMACY

Our nation was founded in contradiction, ostensibly committed to liberty while countenancing slavery. The Declaration of Independence proclaimed "that all men are created equal, and endowed by their Creator with certain unalienable Rights." The Constitution purported to "establish Justice . . . and secure the Blessings of Liberty." James Madison, in Federalist 1, argued that the Constitution is "the safest" course for the preservation of dignity, liberty, and happiness.

Yet the Constitution also protected slavery, even as it avoided use of the term. By the time of the Constitution's drafting, some northern states in which slavery had waned would have supported its nationwide abolition, but the southern states, with their agricultural economies and continuing need for cheap labor, would not have entered any Union that prohibited slavery. The Constitution thus granted Congress the power to respond to slave insurrections; declared that slaves who escaped into free states remained slaves; and determined that, for purposes of state representation in the House of Representatives, each slave would count as three-fifths of a person. The Constitution not only prohibited congressional abolition of slavery for more than two decades, it also precluded any amendment to the Constitution during that same period that would impair the slave trade. The Constitution's treatment of slavery highlights the role of law in mediating the tension between our nation's noble aspirations and its White Supremacist foundations.

While the bulk of this book focuses on contemporary racial controversies, we begin with an examination of the historical role of law in the development and persistence of White Supremacy. During the course of our history, law has alternately moved us closer to the ideal of racial justice and entrenched White Supremacy, all the while remaining inextricably intertwined with both who we are and who we want to be as a society.

Though many historical developments contributed to White Supremacy—prominent among them the decimation of Native populations, colonialist and imperialist projects, and exclusionary immigration policies—slavery was especially integral to the development of White Supremacy and the law that enabled it. The early colonists initially met their need for cheap labor through indentured servitude, in which African and British people worked alongside each other for a term of years. By the 1600s, problems with the system of indentured servitude had become apparent; the freeing of servants created both potential competition for landowners and the need to continually purchase new servants. Servants who escaped could readily mix with a free population from whom they were indistinguishable.

Thus, in the 1600s, the system of indentured servitude gave way to the enslavement of Africans and, to some extent, Native peoples. All 13 colonies permitted slavery and, beginning in the seventeenth century, passed laws formally recognizing the institution. The enslavement of Africans became especially attractive—their dark skin disabled them from melding into the population of English settlers—and the enslavement of Native peoples became disfavored, partly due to the tensions it stoked with local tribes.

The justifications for slavery changed over time, as necessary to buttress the institution. The early colonists were Christian, and they justified slavery and the subjugation of Native peoples by highlighting that Africans and natives were not. That rationale eventually gave way to the belief that Africans and their descendants (many of whom became Christians) were subject to enslavement because, by virtue of their race, they were inherently inferior. The need for a stable ideological foundation for slavery thus produced the doctrine of racial inferiority.

White Supremacy ultimately came to be constituted both by material racial conditions (i.e., the institution and prevalence of slavery) and by racial consciousness (i.e., prevalent understandings of the meaning of race, and, in particular, belief in inherent racial inferiority). Racial conditions and racial consciousness reinforced each other. Slavery was defined in terms of race, and race was accepted as a sufficient justification for slavery. Subjugation came to seem normal, inevitable, and even desirable. Race became simultaneously a means of distributing rights and resources and of justifying that distribution. Even the poorest, most disadvantaged whites could take solace in the fact that they were not, and could not be, enslaved.

Then no less than now, law shapes racial conditions and racial consciousness. Through its allocation of legal entitlements, law shapes economic, social and political relationships and positions, distributing many of the burdens and the benefits of our collective life. Law also performs an expressive role; through communicating meanings, law helps to create our culture, to shape popular understandings of race and of racial justice. While the rule of law is popularly associated with justice, law may also underwrite injustice and bolster narratives that incline us to accept as desirable or inevitable practices or outcomes that we should in fact oppose.

Myriad sources and forms of law have contributed to the racial order. Though recognized by the Constitution and perpetuated by the Supreme Court, slavery was also a matter of state law and depended for its stability on the cooperation of all manner of public officials and private citizens. Southern jurisdictions prohibited slaves from reading, leaving their masters' property without permission, assembling to worship, smoking in public, making loud noises, or defending themselves against assault. Though free black populations existed in the South, the slave regime limited the scope of their rights. The laws of northern states also denied many rights to free blacks, even as some were voters, property owners, merchants, and professionals.

The overthrow of slavery through the Civil War brought forth three amendments to the Constitution, one outlawing slavery, the others making the newly freed slaves rights bearing citizens. But the practical significance of these rights was stunted not only by the Supreme Court, but also by the actions of state legislatures, other government officials, and even private property owners. Many southern states enacted so-called Black Codes meant to recreate the conditions and depredations of slavery. Even rights that the Supreme Court or other sources of law had recognized—the right to own property, for example, or to serve on a jury—were often nullified in practice. A formal system of segregation, known as Jim Crow, spread throughout the South, and depended not only on the support of state laws, but also on social norms and the untold numbers of people who accepted its logic.

History not only illuminates law's complicity in the creation of White Supremacy, it also offers insight into the challenges of dismantling that system. The racial controversies of the past offer a template for the analysis of contemporary problems. As distant and distinct as the past may sometimes seem, the ways that decision-makers confronted challenges then can inform our choices now. Their questions are ours: In the years following the Civil War, what would it have meant to dismantle White Supremacy? To eliminate laws that take account of race? To guarantee important substantive rights for everyone? Would it have been enough to limit government power alone, or must private power and social norms have been transformed as well? Who should bear responsibility for dismantling White Supremacy? Legislatures or courts? States and localities or the federal government?

The concept of racial justice does not have a settled meaning, and we do not purport to offer a single conception here. But the pursuit of racial justice has long been informed, and sometimes limited, by the following clusters of principles and concepts:

i) Capitalism, Property and Profit

ii) Privacy, Liberty, and Autonomy

    iii) Safety, Security, and Protection

    iv) Custom, Tradition, Culture, and Community

    v)   Identity and Dignity

These categories provide tools or frameworks for evaluating whether, when, and how we have achieved racial justice or fallen short of the mark. Each of these clusters has roots in American political, legal, and social thought, and therefore represents shared values that judges, politicians, activists, scholars, and other commentators may draw upon to shape understandings of racial justice.

II. RACE, SLAVERY, AND JUDICIAL POWER

The pre-Civil War cases that follow frame the question of racial justice by foregrounding its antithesis: slavery. These cases prompt us to ask: What was the essence of the freedom and equality that slavery denied? How did the judges of the era address the intertwining of law with the social structure and cultural meanings of slavery?

The following decision from a state court demonstrates how a person's condemnation to slavery or entitlement to freedom turned on official determinations of race.

Hudgins v. Wrights
Supreme Court of Appeals of Virginia, 1806.
11 Va. 134.

■ JUDGE TUCKER.

In this case, the paupers claim their freedom as being descended from Indians entitled to their freedom. They have set forth their pedigree in the bill, which the evidence proves to be fallacious. But as there is no *Herald's Office* in this country, nor even a *Register* of births for any but white persons, and those *Registers* are either all lost, or of all records probably the most imperfect, our Legislature has very justly dispensed with the old common law precision required in a *writ of right*, and the reason for dispensing with it in the present case, is a thousand times stronger. In a claim for freedom, like a claim for money had and received, the plaintiff may well be permitted to make out his case on the trial according to the evidence.

What then is the evidence in this case? Unequivocal proof adduced perhaps by the defendant, that the plaintiffs are in the maternal line descended from Butterwood Nan, an old Indian woman;—that she was 60 years old, or upwards, in the year 1755;—that it was always understood, as the witness Robert Temple says, that her father was an Indian, though he cautiously avoids saying he knew, or ever heard, who, or what, her mother was. The other witness Mary Wilkinson, the only one except Robert Temple who had ever seen her, describes her as an old

Indian: and her testimony is strengthened by that of the other witnesses, who depose that her daughter Hannah had long black hair, was of a copper complexion, and generally called an Indian among the neighbours;—a circumstance which could not well have happened, if her mother had not had an equal, or perhaps a larger portion of Indian blood in her veins.

In aid of the other evidence, the Chancellor decided upon his own view. This, with the principles laid down in the decree, has been loudly complained of. [The chancellor (i.e., the lower court) has declared the appellee's free, reasoning that whoever would attempt to hold another person in slavery always bears the burden of proof.]

As a preliminary to my opinion upon this subject, I shall make a few observations upon the laws of our country, as connected with natural history.

From the first settlement of the colony of Virginia to the year 1778, all negroes, Moors, and mulattoes, except Turks and Moors in amity with Great Britain, brought into this country by sea, or by land, were SLAVES. And by the uniform declarations of our laws, the descendants of the females remain slaves, to this day, unless they can prove a right to freedom, by actual emancipation, or by descent in the maternal line from an emancipated female.

By the adjudication of the General Court, in the case of Hannah and others against Davis, April term, 1777, all American Indians brought into this country, and their descendants in the maternal line, are free.

Consequently I draw this conclusion, that all American Indians are prima facie FREE: and that where the fact of their nativity and descent, in a maternal line, is satisfactorily established, the burthen of proof thereafter lies upon the party claiming to hold them as slaves. To effect which, according to my opinion, he must prove the progenitrix of the party claiming to be free, to have been brought into Virginia, and made a slave between the passage of the act of 1679 [treating Indians as slaves], and its repeal in 1691.

All white persons are and ever have been FREE in this country. If one evidently white, be notwithstanding claimed as a slave, the proof lies on the party claiming to make the other his slave.

Nature has stampt upon the African and his descendants two characteristic marks, besides the difference of complexion, which often remain visible long after the characteristic distinction of colour either disappears or becomes doubtful; a flat nose and woolly head of hair. The latter of these characteristics disappears the last of all: and so strong an ingredient in the African constitution is this latter character, that it predominates uniformly where the party is in equal degree descended from parents of different complexions, whether white or Indians; giving to the jet black lank hair of the Indian a degree of flexure, which never

fails to betray that the party distinguished by it, cannot trace his lineage purely from the race of native Americans. Its operation is still more powerful where the mixture happens between persons descended equally from European and African parents. So pointed is this distinction between the natives of Africa and the aborigines of America, that a man might as easily mistake the glossy, jetty cloathing of an American bear for the wool of a black sheep, as the hair of an American Indian for that of an African, or the descendant of an African. Upon these distinctions as connected with our laws, the burden of proof depends. Upon these distinctions not infrequently does the evidence given upon trials of such questions depend; as in the present case, where the witnesses concur in assigning to the hair of Hannah, the daughter of Butterwood Nan, the long, straight, black hair of the native aborigines of this country. That such evidence is both admissible and proper, I cannot doubt. That it may at sometimes be necessary for a Judge to decide upon his own view, I think the following case will evince.

Suppose three persons, a black or mulatto man or woman with a flat nose and woolly head; a copper-coloured person with long jetty black, straight hair; and one with a fair complexion, brown hair, not woolly nor inclining thereto, with a prominent Roman nose, were brought together before a Judge upon a writ of Habeas Corpus, on the ground of false imprisonment and detention in slavery: that the only evidence which the person detaining them in his custody could produce was an authenticated bill of sale from another person, and that the parties themselves were unable to produce any evidence concerning themselves, whence they came, & c. & c. How must a Judge act in such a case? I answer he must judge from his own view. He must discharge the white person and the Indian out of custody, taking surety, if the circumstances of the case should appear to authorise it, that they should not depart the state within a reasonable time, that the holder may have an opportunity of asserting and proving them to be lineally descended in the maternal line from a female African slave; and he must redeliver the black or mulatto person, with the flat nose and woolly hair to the person claiming to hold him or her as a slave, unless the black person or mulatto could procure some person to be bound for him, to produce proof of his descent, in the maternal line, from a free female ancestor.—But if no such caution should be required on either side, but the whole case be left with the Judge, he must deliver the former out of custody, and permit the latter to remain in slavery, until he could produce proofs of his right to freedom. This case shows my interpretation how far the onus probandi may be shifted from one party to the other.

■ Judge Roane, concurring.

The distinguishing characteristics of the different species of the human race are so visibly marked, that those species may be readily discriminated from each other by mere inspection only. This, at least, is emphatically true in relation to the negroes, to the Indians of North America, and the European white people. When, however, these races become intermingled, it is difficult, if not impossible, to say from inspection only, which race predominates in the offspring, and certainly impossible to determine whether the descent from a given race has been through the paternal or maternal line. In the case of a Propositus of unmixed blood, therefore, I do not see but that the fact may be as well ascertained by the Jury or the Judge, upon view, as by the testimony of witnesses, who themselves have no other means of information:—but where an intermixture has taken place in relation to the person in question, this criterion is not infallible; and testimony must be resorted to for the purpose of shewing through what line a descent from a given stock has been deduced; and also to ascertain, perhaps, whether the colouring of the complexion has been derived from a negro or an Indian ancestor.

In the case of a person visibly appearing to be a negro, the presumption is, in this country, that he is a slave, and it is incumbent on him to make out his right to freedom: but in the case of a person visibly appearing to be a white man, or an Indian, the presumption is that he is free, and it is necessary for his adversary to shew that he is a slave.

In the present case it is not and cannot be denied that the appellees have entirely the appearance of white people: and how does the appellant attempt to deprive them of the blessing of liberty to which all such persons are entitled? He brings no testimony to shew that any ancestor in the female line was a negro slave or even an Indian rightfully held in slavery. Length of time shall not bar the right to freedom of those who, prima facie, are free, and whose poverty and oppression, (to say nothing of the rigorous principles of former times on this subject,) has prevented an attempt to assert their rights. But in the case before us, there has been no acquiescence. It is proved that John, (a brother of Hannah,) brought a suit to recover his freedom; and that Hannah herself made an almost continual claim as to her right of freedom, insomuch that she was threatened to be whipped by her master for mentioning the subject. It is also proved by Francis Temple (perhaps the brother of Robert) that the people in the neighbourhood said "that if she would try for her freedom she would get it." This general reputation and opinion of the neighbourhood is certainly entitled to some credit: it goes to repel the idea that the given female ancestor of Hannah was a lawful slave; it goes to confirm the other strong testimony as to Hannah's appearance as an Indian. It is not to be believed but that some of the neighbours would have sworn to that concerning which they all agreed in opinion; and, if so, Hannah might, on their testimony, have perhaps obtained her freedom, had those times been as just and liberal on the subject of slavery as the present.

No testimony can be more complete and conclusive than that which exists in this cause to shew that Hannah had every appearance of an Indian.

That appearance, on the principle with which I commenced, will suffice for the claim of her posterity, unless it is opposed by counter-evidence showing that some female ancestor of her's was a negro slave, or that she or some female ancestor, was lawfully an Indian slave. As to the first, there is no kind of testimony going to establish it. Robert Temple is not only entirely silent as to the colour and appearance of the mother of Nan, the mother of Hannah, but also as to that of Nan herself. The testimony of this witness (to say nothing of his probable interest in the question) is not satisfactory. His memory seems only to serve him so far as the interest of the appellant required. If Hannah's grandmother (the mother of Nan) were a negro, it is impossible that Hannah should have had that entire appearance of an Indian which is proved by the witnesses.—If they tell the truth, therefore, Hannah's grandmother was not a negro slave. This is more especially the case, if the father of Hannah were other than an Indian, and it is not proved nor can be presumed, that, in this country, at that time, her father was an Indian: in that case, Hannah would have had so little Indian blood in her veins, as not to justify the character of her appearance given by the witnesses. The mother and grandmother of Hannah must therefore be taken to have been Indians: but this will not suffice for the appellant unless they (or one of them) be shewn to have been Indian slaves.

Judges FLEMING, CARRINGTON, and LYONS, President, concurring, the latter delivered the decree of the Court as follows:

"This Court, not approving of the Chancellor's principles and reasoning in his decree made in this cause, except so far as the same relates to white persons and native American Indians, but entirely disapproving thereof, so far as the same relates to native Africans and their descendants, who have been and are now held as slaves by the citizens of this state, and discovering no other error in the said decree, affirms the same."

NOTES AND QUESTIONS

1. *Racialization of Slavery.* Note that the Chancellor, whose decision is on appeal, would have ignored appearance and always put the burden of proof on the party who is claiming to hold the other as a slave. Why isn't the Chancellor's position—the argument that legal presumptions should cut against slavery and in favor of freedom—the correct one? As an empirical matter, is it sensible to presume that all blacks are slaves? Why did the judges in this case reject the Chancellor's approach?

2. *Liberty Versus Enslavement.* The presumptions about race and slavery set forth in *Hudgins* were enormously important, eventually becoming settled law in virtually every part of the slaveholding South. Cases

such as *Hudgins* necessarily involved two different types of errors: freeing people who should by law be slaves and making slaves of people who should by law be free. In determining the appropriate legal rule, how should a court have balanced these two types of errors? Is there any legitimate reason not to employ a strong presumption in favor of liberty?

3.   *Defining Race.* The law of most states in the period in which *Hudgins* was decided did not define race. Whites of that era generally believed that race was self-evident. But in 1705, in the course of prohibiting Native peoples, blacks, and mulattoes, as well as criminals, from holding any office of public power, the Virginia legislature defined a mulatto as "the child of an Indian, or the child, grandchild, or great grandchild of a Negro." In 1785, the legislature changed the definition of mulatto to include only those who had a quarter or more "of negro blood." Thus, Virginians who had one black great-grandparent and who were mulattos under the 1705 statute were now white under the 1785 statute. In 1910, a Virginia statute declared that anyone with one-sixteenth black ancestry was "colored." In 1930, anyone with any known black ancestry whatsoever was black. Why would the state have sought to enlarge the black population by making the definition of "colored" more capacious? What do these sorts of changes suggest to you about the meaning of race?

4.   *Identifying Race.* The opinions in *Hudgins* point to many different ways of assessing a person's race: through appearance, ancestry, social understandings, self-identification, or behavior. What factors, in your view, best define race? Does the answer change depending on the reason the definition is sought?

In the following case, the Court grapples with the obligations of officials and private parties in free states to cooperate with the efforts of slave owners or slave catchers to capture escaped slaves. Northern states had enacted personal liberty laws that favored individuals' claims to freedom, while Congress, seeking to protect the property of slave owners, passed two Fugitive Slave Laws, one in 1793 and another in 1850. The latter of the two substantially strengthened slave owners' ability to reclaim their escaped slaves and is often cited as one of the events that helped precipitate the Civil War. *Prigg v. Pennsylvania* addresses Congress's authority to adopt the 1793 law and considers whether it preempted the personal liberty law adopted by Pennsylvania.

Prigg v. Pennsylvania

Supreme Court of the United States, 1842.
41 U.S. 539.

■ MR. JUSTICE STORY delivered the opinion of the court:

The plaintiff in error was indicted in York county, for having, with force and violence, taken and carried away from that county, to the state of Maryland, a certain negro woman, named Margaret Morgan, with a

design and intention of selling and disposing of, and keeping her, as a slave or servant for life, contrary to a statute of Pennsylvania, passed on the 26th of March 1826. That statute, in the first section, in substance, provides, that if any person or persons shall, from and after the passing of the act, by force and violence, take and carry away, or cause to be taken and carried away, and shall, by fraud or false pretence, seduce, or cause to be seduced, or shall attempt to take, carry away or seduce, any negro or mulatto, from any part of that commonwealth, with a design and intention of selling and disposing of, or causing to be sold, or of keeping and detaining, or of causing to be kept and detained, such negro or mulatto, as a slave or servant for life, or for any term whatsoever; every such person or persons, his or their aiders or abettors, shall, on conviction thereof, be deemed guilty of felony, and shall forfeit and pay a sum not less than five hundred, nor more than one thousand dollars; and moreover, shall be sentenced to undergo servitude for any term or terms of years, not less than seven years nor exceeding twenty-one years; and shall be confined and kept to hard labor.

The plaintiff in error pleaded not guilty to the indictment; and at the trial, the jury found a special verdict, which, in substance, states, that the negro woman, Margaret Morgan, was a slave for life, and held to labor and service under and according to the laws of Maryland, to a certain Margaret Ashmore, a citizen of Maryland; that the slave escaped and fled from Maryland, into Pennsylvania, in 1832; that the plaintiff in error, being legally constituted the agent and attorney of the said Margaret Ashmore, in 1837, caused the said negro woman to be taken and apprehended as a fugitive from labor, by a state constable, under a warrant from a Pennsylvania magistrate; that the said negro woman was thereupon brought before the said magistrate, who refused to take further cognisance of the case; and thereupon, the plaintiff in error did remove, take and carry away the said negro woman and her children, out of Pennsylvania, into Maryland, and did deliver the said negro woman and her children into the custody and possession of the said Margaret Ashmore. The special verdict further finds, that one of the children was born in Pennsylvania, more than a year after the said negro woman had fled and escaped from Maryland. Upon this special verdict, the court adjudged that the plaintiff in error was guilty of the offence charged in the indictment.

The question arising in the case, as to the constitutionality of the statute of Pennsylvania, has been most elaborately argued at the bar. The counsel for the plaintiff in error has contended, that the statute of Pennsylvania is unconstitutional.

There are two clauses in the constitution upon the subject of fugitives, which stands in juxtaposition with each other, and have been thought mutually to illustrate each other. They are both contained in the second section of the fourth article, and are in the following words: 'A person charged in any state with treason, felony or other crime, who shall flee from justice, and be found in another state, shall, on demand of the executive authority of the state from which he fled, be delivered up, to be removed to the state having jurisdiction of the crime.' 'No person held to service or labor in one state, under the laws thereof, escaping into another, shall, in consequence of any law or regulation therein, be discharged from such service or labor; but shall be delivered up, on claim of the party to whom such service or labor may be due.'

The last clause is that, the true interpretation whereof is directly in judgment before us. Historically, it is well known, that the object of this clause was to secure to the citizens of the slave-holding states the complete right and title of ownership in their slaves, as property, in every state in the Union into which they might escape from the state where they were held in servitude. The full recognition of this right and title was indispensable to the security of this species of property in all the slave-holding states; and, indeed, was so vital to the preservation of their domestic interests and institutions, that it cannot be doubted, that it constituted a fundamental article, without the adoption of which the Union could not have been formed. Its true design was, to guard against the doctrines and principles prevalent in the non-slave-holding states, by preventing them from intermeddling with, or obstructing, or abolishing the rights of the owners of slaves.

The clause manifestly contemplates the existence of a positive, unqualified right on the part of the owner of the slave, which no state law or regulation can in any way qualify, regulate, control or restrain. The slave is not to be discharged from service or labor, in consequence of any state law or regulation. Now, certainly, without indulging in any nicety of criticism upon words, it may fairly and reasonably be said, that any state law or state regulation, which interrupts, limits, delays or postpones the right of the owner to the immediate possession of the slave, and the immediate command of his service and labor, operates, *pro tanto*, a discharge of the slave therefrom.

We have said, that the clause contains a positive and unqualified recognition of the right of the owner in the slave, unaffected by any state law or legislation whatsoever, because there is no qualification or restriction of it to be found therein; and we have no right to insert any, which is not expressed, and cannot be fairly implied. The owner must, therefore, have the right to seize and repossess the slave, which the local laws of his own state confer upon him, as property; and we all know that this right of seizure and recaption is universally acknowledged in all the slave-holding states. Upon this ground, we have not the slightest hesitation in holding, that under and in virtue of the constitution, the owner of a slave is clothed with entire authority, in every state in the Union, to seize and recapture his slave, whenever he can do it, without any breach of the peace or any illegal violence. In this sense, and to this extent, this clause of the constitution may properly be said to execute itself, and to require no aid from legislation, state or national.

But the clause of the constitution does not stop here; nor, indeed, consistently with its professed objects, could it do so.

It says, 'but he (the slave) shall be delivered up, on claim of the party to whom such service or labor may be due.' Now, we think it exceedingly difficult, if not impracticable, to read this language, and not to feel, that it contemplated some further remedial redress than that which might be administered at the hands of the owner himself.

If, indeed, the constitution guaranties the right, and if it requires the delivery upon the claim of the owner (as cannot well be doubted), the natural inference certainly is, that the national government is clothed with the appropriate authority and functions to enforce it.

Congress has taken this very view of the power and duty of the national government. The result of their deliberations was the passage of the act of the 12th of February 1793, ch. 51.

But it has been argued, that the act of congress is unconstitutional, because it does not fall within the scope of any of the enumerated powers of legislation confided to that body; and therefore, it is void. If this be the true interpretation of the constitution, it must, in a great measure, fail to attain many of its avowed and positive objects, as a security of rights, and a recognition of duties. Such a limited construction of the constitution has never yet been adopted as correct, either in theory or practice.

Our judgment would be the same, if the question were entirely new, and the act of congress were of recent enactment. We hold the act to be clearly constitutional, in all its leading provisions, and, indeed, with the exception of that part which confers authority upon state magistrates, to be free from reasonable doubt and difficulty, upon the grounds already stated. As to the authority so conferred upon state magistrates, while a difference of opinion has existed, and may exist still, on the point, in different states, whether state magistrates are bound to act under it, none is entertained by this court, that state magistrates may, if they choose, exercise that authority, unless prohibited by state legislation.

The remaining question is, whether the power of legislation upon this subject is exclusive in the national government, or concurrent in the states, until it is exercised by congress. In our opinion, it is exclusive.

In the first place, it is material to state (what has been already incidentally hinted at), that the right to seize and retake fugitive slaves and the duty to deliver them up, in whatever state of the Union they may be found, and, of course, the corresponding power in congress to use the appropriate means to enforce the right and duty, derive their whole validity and obligation exclusively from the constitution of the United States, and are there, for the first time, recognised and established in that peculiar character. Before the adoption of the constitution, no state had any power whatsoever over the subject, except within its own territorial limits, and could not bind the sovereignty or the legislation of other states.

It is scarcely conceivable, that the slave-holding states would have been satisfied with leaving to the legislation of the non-slave-holding states, a power of regulation, in the absence of that of congress, which would or might practically amount to a power to destroy the rights of the owner.

To guard, however, against any possible misconstruction of our views, it is proper to state, that we are by no means to be understood, in any manner whatsoever, to doubt or to interfere with the police power belonging to the states, in virtue of their general sovereignty. We entertain no doubt whatsoever, that the states, in virtue of their general police power, possesses full jurisdiction to arrest and restrain runaway slaves, and remove them from their borders, and otherwise to secure themselves against their depredations and evil example, as they certainly may do in cases of idlers, vagabonds and paupers. The rights of the owners of fugitive slaves are in no just sense interfered with, or regulated, by such a course; and in many cases, the operations of this police power, although designed generally for other purposes, for protection, safety and peace of the state, may essentially promote and aid the interests of the owners. But such regulations can never be permitted to interfere with, or to obstruct, the just rights of the owner to reclaim his slave, derived from the constitution of the United States, or with the remedies prescribed by congress to aid and enforce the same.

Upon these grounds, we are of opinion, that the act of Pennsylvania upon which this indictment is founded, is unconstitutional and void.

■ MR. JUSTICE MCLEAN, dissenting:

The seizure which the master has a right to make under the act of congress, is for the purpose of taking the slave before an officer. His possession the subject for which it was made. The certificate of right to the service the subject for which it was made. The important point is, shall the presumption of right set up by the master, unsustained by any proof, or the presumption which arises from the laws and institutions of the state, prevail; this is the true issue. The sovereignty of the state is on one side, and the asserted interest of the master on the other; that interest is protected by the paramount law, and a special, a summary, and an effectual, mode of redress is given. But this mode is not pursued, and the remedy is taken into his own hands by the master.

The presumption of the state that the colored person is free, may be erroneous in fact; and if so, there can be no difficulty in proving it. But may not the assertion of the master be erroneous also; and if so, how is his act of force to be remedied? The colored person is taken and forcibly conveyed beyond the jurisdiction of the state. This force, not being authorized by the act of congress nor by the constitution, may be prohibited by the state. As the act covers the whole power in the constitution and carries out, by special enactments, its provisions, we are, in my judgment bound by the act. We can no more, under such circumstances administer a remedy under the constitution, in disregard of the act, than we can exercise a commercial or other power in disregard of an act of congress on the same subject. This view respects the rights of the master and the rights of the state; it neither jeopardizes nor retards the reclamation of the slave; it removes all state action prejudicial to the rights of the master; and recognises in the state a power to guard and protect its own jurisdiction, and the peace of its citizen.

It appears, in the case under consideration, that the state magistrate before whom the fugitive was brought refused to act. In my judgment, he was bound to perform the duty required of him by a law paramount to any act, on the same subject, in his own state. But this refusal does not justify the subsequent action of the claimant; he should have taken the fugitive before a judge of the United States, two of whom resided within the state.

NOTES AND QUESTIONS

1. *Was* Prigg *Rightly Decided?* The Fugitive Slave Clause, Article IV, section 2, clause 3, guarantees the property interest of slave owners in the event that their slaves escape to a free state. But it does not explicitly grant Congress the power to enact legislation, such as the Fugitive Slave Act, enabling such recapture. Justice Story concluded nonetheless that the Constitution's Fugitive Slave Clause both deprived the states of any power to address the fugitive slave issue and authorized congressional legislation in furtherance of the Fugitive Slave Clause. Was he right on both counts?

2. *Federalism and States' Rights.* What do you make of the implication of Justice McLean's opinion—that states, if they wished, were entitled to create a presumption that all individuals within their jurisdiction were free? Under this view, the Pennsylvania statute could be justified as establishing a burden on the slave owner to prove that the person being apprehended was by law a slave. As not all black persons were slaves, imposing the burden on the slave catcher would protect the liberty interests of free persons of color, though at some cost to the slave owner. However just that approach, would it have been constitutional? Would the Constitution have justified states giving priority to the liberty interest of the black person over the property interest of the slave owner?

3. *Justice Story the Abolitionist.* Consider the fact that Justice Story was a staunch abolitionist. Does *Prigg* reflect the conscience of an abolitionist? What other motives could Justice Story have had in sustaining the constitutionality of the Fugitive Slave Act, despite his abolitionist views?

The Court's decision *in Prigg* did not resolve the fugitive slave controversy. After *Prigg*, some northern states simply declined to help enforce the Fugitive Slave Act, a possibility that the Supreme Court's *Prigg* decision had ironically highlighted. Even as it struck down the Pennsylvania law, the Court permitted states to decline to help enforce the federal law. In response, Congress passed the Fugitive Slave Act of 1850, as part of the Compromise of 1850, which also abolished the slave trade in the District of Columbia and admitted California as a free state, while admitting New Mexico and Utah as territories with the slavery question left to future legislation. The 1850 Fugitive Slave Act levied a substantial fine on any law enforcement official who declined to arrest an alleged runaway slave. It also subjected anyone who aided a runaway slave to both a hefty fine and imprisonment. Slave catchers needed only to provide an affidavit attesting that an individual was actually a slave; the alleged slave was not entitled to a trial to assert a claim for freedom.

———————

Dred Scott v. Sanford—perhaps the most infamous decision ever made by the Supreme Court—confronts the question whether state or federal law could alter the legal status of a slave who had departed the jurisdiction in which he was enslaved.

Dred Scott v. Sandford

Supreme Court of the United States, 1857.
60 U.S. 393.

[Dred Scott, admittedly once a slave but now claiming to be a citizen of Missouri, brought an action in federal court against John F.A. Sanford—whose name was apparently misspelled in the official case reports—a citizen of New York. Federal jurisdiction was premised on diversity of citizenship. In 1834, Scott's former owner had taken him from Missouri to Illinois, where they resided for two years before moving to Minnesota, which was then part of the Louisiana Territory. In 1838, they returned to Missouri, and Scott was sold as a slave to Sanford. Although slavery was legal in Missouri, it was prohibited in Illinois by the state constitution, and in the Louisiana Territory by the federal statute embodying the Missouri Compromise. Scott argued that these provisions made him a free man. In response, Sanford contended that the court lacked diversity jurisdiction over Scott's claim because, as a black man, Scott could not be a citizen of Missouri; moreover, he argued that Scott's time in Illinois and Minnesota could not deprive his owner of his property interest in Scott when he returned to Missouri.]

■ MR. CHIEF JUSTICE TANEY delivered the opinion of the Court.

There are two leading questions presented by the record:

1. Had the Circuit Court of the United States jurisdiction to hear and determine the case between these parties? And

2. If it had jurisdiction, is the judgment it has given erroneous or not?

The plaintiff in error, who was also the plaintiff in the court below, was, with his wife and children, held as slaves by the defendant, in the State of Missouri; and he brought this action in the Circuit Court of the United States for that district, to assert the title of himself and his family to freedom.

The declaration is in the form usually adopted in that State to try questions of this description, and contains the averment necessary to give the court jurisdiction; that he and the defendant are citizens of different States; that is, that he is a citizen of Missouri, and the defendant a citizen of New York.

The defendant pleaded in abatement to the jurisdiction of the court, that the plaintiff was not a citizen of the State of Missouri, as alleged in his declaration, being a negro of African descent, whose ancestors were of pure African blood, and who were brought into this country and sold as slaves.

The question is simply this: Can a negro, whose ancestors were imported into this country, and sold as slaves, become a member of the political community formed and brought into existence by the Constitution of the United States, and as such become entitled to all the rights, and privileges, and immunities, guarantied by that instrument to the citizen? One of which rights is the privilege of suing in a court of the United States in the cases specified in the Constitution.

It will be observed, that the plea applies to that class of persons only whose ancestors were negroes of the African race, and imported into this country, and sold and held as slaves. The only matter in issue before the court, therefore, is, whether the descendants of such slaves, when they shall be emancipated, or who are born of parents who had become free before their birth, are citizens of a State, in the sense in which the word citizen is used in the Constitution of the United States. And this being the only matter in dispute on the pleadings, the court must be understood as speaking in this opinion of that class only, that is, of those persons who are the descendants of Africans who were imported into this country, and sold as slaves.

The situation of this population was altogether unlike that of the Indian race. The latter, it is true, formed no part of the colonial communities, and never amalgamated with them in social connections or in government. But although they were uncivilized, they were yet a free and independent people, associated together in nations or tribes, and governed by their own laws. Many of these political communities were situated in territories to which the white race claimed the ultimate right of dominion. But that claim was acknowledged to be subject to the right of the Indians to occupy it as long as they thought proper, and neither the English nor colonial Governments claimed or exercised any dominion over the tribe or nation by whom it was occupied, nor claimed the right to the possession of the territory, until the tribe or nation consented to cede it. These Indian Governments were regarded and treated as foreign Governments, as much so as if an ocean had separated the red man from the white; and their freedom has constantly been acknowledged, from the time of the first emigration to the English colonies to the present day, by the different Governments which succeeded each other. Treaties have been negotiated with them, and their alliance sought for in war; and the people who compose these Indian political communities have always been treated as foreigners not living under our Government. It is true that the course of events has brought the Indian tribes within the limits of the United States under subjection to the white race; and it has been found necessary, for their sake as well as our own, to regard them as in a state of pupilage, and to legislate to a certain extent over them and the territory they occupy. But they may, without doubt, like the subjects of any other foreign Government, be naturalized by the authority of Congress, and become citizens of a State, and of the United States; and if an individual should leave his nation or tribe, and take up his abode among the white population, he would be entitled to all the rights and privileges which would belong to an emigrant from any other foreign people.

Re Native Am.

We proceed to examine the case as presented by the pleadings.

The words 'people of the United States' and 'citizens' are synonymous terms, and mean the same thing. They both describe the political body who, according to our republican institutions, form the sovereignty, and who hold the power and conduct the Government through their representatives. They are what we familiarly call the 'sovereign people,' and every citizen is one of this people, and a constituent member of this sovereignty. The question before us is, whether the class of persons described in the plea in abatement compose a portion of this people, and are constituent members of this sovereignty? We think they are not, and that they are not included, and were not intended to be included, under the word 'citizens' in the Constitution, and can therefore claim none of the rights and privileges which that instrument provides for and secures to citizens of the United States. On the contrary, they were at that time considered as a subordinate and inferior class of beings, who had been subjugated by the dominant race, and, whether emancipated or not, yet remained subject to their authority, and had no rights or privileges but such as those who held the power and the Government might choose to grant them.

people = citizens

It is not the province of the court to decide upon the justice or injustice, the policy or impolicy, of these laws. The decision of that question belonged to the political or law-making power; to those who formed the sovereignty and framed the Constitution. The duty of the court is, to interpret the instrument they have framed, with the best lights we can obtain on the subject, and to administer it as we find it, according to its true intent and meaning when it was adopted.

In discussing this question, we must not confound the rights of citizenship which a State may confer within its own limits, and the rights of citizenship as a member of the Union. It does not by any means follow, because he has all the rights and privileges of a citizen of a State, that he must be a citizen of the United States. He may have all of the rights and privileges of the citizen of a State, and yet not be entitled to the rights and privileges of a citizen in any other State. For, previous to the adoption of the Constitution of the United States, every State had the undoubted right to confer on whomsoever it pleased the character of citizen, and to endow him with all its rights. But this character of course was confined to the boundaries of the State, and gave him no rights or privileges in other States beyond those secured to him by the laws of nations and the comity of States. Nor have the several States surrendered the power of conferring these rights and privileges by adopting the Constitution of the United States. Each State may still confer them upon an alien, or any one it thinks proper, or upon any class or description of persons; yet he would not be a citizen in the sense in which that word is used in the Constitution of the United States, nor entitled to sue as such in one of its courts, nor to the privileges and immunities of a citizen in the other States. The rights which he would acquire would be restricted to the State which gave them. The Constitution has conferred on Congress the right to establish an uniform rule of naturalization, and this right is evidently exclusive, and has always been held by this court to be so. Consequently, no State, since the adoption of the Constitution, can by naturalizing an alien invest him with the rights and privileges secured to a citizen of a State under the Federal Government, although, so far as the State alone was concerned, he would undoubtedly be entitled to the rights of a citizen, and clothed with all the rights and immunities which the Constitution and laws of the State attached to that character.

It is very clear, therefore, that no State can, by any act or law of its own, passed since the adoption of the Constitution, introduce a new member into the political community created by the Constitution of the United States. It cannot make him a member of this community by making him a member of its own. And for the same reason it cannot introduce any person, or description of persons, who were not intended to be embraced in this new political family, which the Constitution brought into existence, but were intended to be excluded from it.

The question then arises, whether the provisions of the Constitution, in relation to the personal rights and privileges to which the citizen of a State should be entitled, embraced the negro African race, at that time in this country, or who might afterwards be imported, who had then or should afterwards be made free in any State; and to put it in the power of a single State to make him a citizen of the United States, and endue him with the full rights of citizenship in every other State without their consent? Does the Constitution of the United States act upon him whenever he shall be made free under the laws of a State, and raised there to the rank of a citizen, and immediately clothe him with all the privileges of a citizen in every other State, and in its own courts?

The court think the affirmative of these propositions cannot be maintained. And if it cannot, the plaintiff in error could not be a citizen of the State of Missouri, within the meaning of the Constitution of the United States, and, consequently, was not entitled to sue in its courts.

It is true, every person, and every class and description of persons, who were at the time of the adoption of the Constitution recognized as citizens in the several States, became also citizens of this new political body; but none other; it was formed by them, and for them and their posterity, but for no one else. And the personal rights and privileges guaranteed to citizens of this new sovereignty were intended to embrace those only who were then members of the several State communities, or who should afterwards by birthright or otherwise become members, according to the provisions of the Constitution and the principles on which it was founded. It was the union of those who were at that time members of distinct and separate political communities into one political family, whose power, for certain specified purposes, was to extend over the whole territory of the United States. And it gave to each citizen rights and privileges outside of his State which he did not before possess, and placed him in every other State upon a perfect equality with its own citizens as to rights of person and rights of property; it made him a citizen of the United States.

It becomes necessary, therefore, to determine who were citizens of the several States when the Constitution was adopted. And in order to do this, we must recur to the Governments and institutions of the thirteen colonies, when they separated from Great Britain and formed new sovereignties, and took their places in the family of independent nations. We must inquire who, at that time, were recognized as the people or citizens of a State, whose rights and liberties had been outraged by the English Government; and who declared their independence, and assumed the powers of Government to defend their rights by force of arms.

In the opinion of the court, the legislation and histories of the times, and the language used in the Declaration of Independence, show, that neither the class of persons who had been imported as slaves, nor their descendants, whether they had become free or not, were then acknowledged as a part of the people, nor intended to be included in the general words used in that memorable instrument.

It is difficult at this day to realize the state of public opinion in relation to that unfortunate race, which prevailed in the civilized and enlightened portions of the world at the time of the Declaration of Independence, and when the Constitution of the United States was

framed and adopted. But the public history of every European nation
displays it in a manner too plain to be mistaken.

They had for more than a century before been regarded as beings of
an inferior order, and altogether unfit to associate with the white race,
either in social or political relations; and so far inferior, that they had no
rights which the white man was bound to respect; and that the negro
might justly and lawfully be reduced to slavery for his benefit. He was
bought and sold, and treated as an ordinary article of merchandise and
traffic, whenever a profit could be made by it. This opinion was at that
time fixed and universal in the civilized portion of the white race. It was
regarded as an axiom in morals as well as in politics, which no one
thought of disputing, or supposed to be open to dispute; and men in every
grade and position in society daily and habitually acted upon it in their
private pursuits, as well as in matters of public concern, without
doubting for a moment the correctness of this opinion.

And in no nation was this opinion more firmly fixed or more
uniformly acted upon than by the English Government and English
people. They not only seized them on the coast of Africa, and sold them
or held them in slavery for their own use; but they took them as ordinary
articles of merchandise to every country where they could make a profit
on them, and were far more extensively engaged in this commerce than
any other nation in the world.

The opinion thus entertained and acted upon in England was
naturally impressed upon the colonies they founded on this side of the
Atlantic. And, accordingly, a negro of the African race was regarded by
them as an article of property, and held, and bought and sold as such, in
every one of the thirteen colonies which united in the Declaration of
Independence, and afterwards formed the Constitution of the United
States. The slaves were more or less numerous in the different colonies,
as slave labor was found more or less profitable. But no one seems to have
doubted the correctness of the prevailing opinion of the time.

We proceed, therefore, to inquire whether the facts relied on by the
plaintiff entitled him to his freedom.

The case, as he himself states it, on the record brought here by his
writ of error, is this:

The plaintiff was a negro slave, belonging to Dr. Emerson, who was
a surgeon in the army of the United States. In the year 1834, he took the
plaintiff from the State of Missouri to the military post at Rock Island, in
the State of Illinois, and held him there as a slave until the month of
April or May, 1836. At the time last mentioned, said Dr. Emerson
removed the plaintiff from said military post at Rock Island to the
military post at Fort Snelling, situate on the west bank of the Mississippi
river, in the Territory known as Upper Louisiana, acquired by the United
States of France, and situate north of the latitude of thirty-six degrees
thirty minutes north, and north of the State of Missouri. Said Dr.

Emerson held the plaintiff in slavery at said Fort Snelling, from said last-mentioned date until the year 1838.

In the year 1835, Harriet, who is named in the second count of the plaintiff's declaration, was the negro slave of Major Taliaferro, who belonged to the army of the United States. In that year, 1835, said Major Taliaferro took said Harriet to said Fort Snelling, a military post, situated as hereinbefore stated, and kept her there as a slave until the year 1836, and then sold and delivered her as a slave, at said Fort Snelling, unto the said Dr. Emerson hereinbefore named. Said Dr. Emerson held said Harriet in slavery at said Fort Snelling until the year 1838.

In the year 1836, the plaintiff and Harriet intermarried, at Fort Snelling, with the consent of Dr. Emerson, who then claimed to be their master and owner. Eliza and Lizzie, named in the third count of the plaintiff's declaration, are the fruit of that marriage. Eliza is about fourteen years old, and was born on board the steamboat Gipsey, north of the north line of the State of Missouri, and upon the river Mississippi. Lizzie is about seven years old, and was born in the State of Missouri, at the military post called Jefferson Barracks.

In the year 1838, said Dr. Emerson removed the plaintiff and said Harriet, and their said daughter Eliza, from said Fort Snelling to the State of Missouri, where they have ever since resided.

Before the commencement of this suit, said Dr. Emerson sold and conveyed the plaintiff, and Harriet, Eliza, and Lizzie, to the defendant, as slaves, and the defendant has ever since claimed to hold them, and each of them, as slaves.

In considering this part of the controversy, two questions arise: 1. Was he, together with his family, free in Missouri by reason of the stay in the territory of the United States hereinbefore mentioned? And 2. If they were not, is Scott himself free by reason of his removal to Rock Island, in the State of Illinois, as stated in the above admissions?

We proceed to examine the first question.

The act of Congress, upon which the plaintiff relies, declares that slavery and involuntary servitude, except as a punishment for crime, shall be forever prohibited in all that part of the territory ceded by France, under the name of Louisiana, which lies north of thirty-six degrees thirty minutes north latitude, and not included within the limits of Missouri. And the difficulty which meets us at the threshold of this part of the inquiry is, whether Congress was authorized to pass this law under any of the powers granted to it by the Constitution; for if the authority is not given by that instrument, it is the duty of this court to declare it void and inoperative, and incapable of conferring freedom upon any one who is held as a slave under the have of any one of the States.

There is certainly no power given by the Constitution to the Federal Government to establish or maintain colonies bordering on the United States or at a distance, to be ruled and governed at its own pleasure; nor to enlarge its territorial limits in any way, except by the admission of new States. That power is plainly given; and if a new State is admitted, it needs no further legislation by Congress, because the Constitution itself defines the relative rights and powers, and duties of the State, and the citizens of the State, and the Federal Government. But no power is given to acquire a Territory to be held and governed permanently in that character.

But the power of Congress over the person or property of a citizen can never be a mere discretionary power under our Constitution and form of Government. The powers of the Government and the rights and privileges of the citizen are regulated and plainly defined by the Constitution itself. And when the Territory becomes a part of the United States, the Federal Government enters into possession in the character impressed upon it by those who created it. It enters upon it with its powers over the citizen strictly defined, and limited by the Constitution, from which it derives its own existence, and by virtue of which alone it continues to exist and act as a Government and sovereignty. It has no power of any kind beyond it; and it cannot, when it enters a Territory of the United States, put off its character, and assume discretionary or despotic powers which the Constitution has denied to it. It cannot create for itself a new character separated from the citizens of the United States, and the duties it owes them under the provisions of the Constitution. The Territory being a part of the United States, the Government and the citizen both enter it under the authority of the Constitution, with their respective rights defined and marked out; and the Federal Government can exercise no power over his person or property, beyond what that instrument confers, nor lawfully deny any right which it has reserved.

The powers over person and property of which we speak are not only not granted to Congress, but are in express terms denied, and they are forbidden to exercise them. And this prohibition is not confined to the States, but the words are general, and extend to the whole territory over which the Constitution gives it power to legislate, including those portions of it remaining under Territorial Government, as well as that covered by States. It is a total absence of power everywhere within the dominion of the United States, and places the citizens of a Territory, so far as these rights are concerned, on the same footing with citizens of the States, and guards them as firmly and plainly against any inroads which the General Government might attempt, under the plea of implied or incidental powers. And if Congress itself cannot do this-if it is beyond the powers conferred on the Federal Government-it will be admitted, we presume, that it could not authorize a Territorial Government to exercise them. It could confer no power on any local Government, established by its authority, to violate the provisions of the Constitution.

Now, as we have already said in an earlier part of this opinion, upon a different point, the right of property in a slave is distinctly and expressly affirmed in the Constitution. The right to traffic in it, like an ordinary article of merchandise and property, was guarantied to the citizens of the United States, in every State that might desire it, for twenty years. And the Government in express terms is pledged to protect it in all future time, if the slave escapes from his owner. This is done in plain words-too plain to be misunderstood. And no word can be found in the Constitution which gives Congress a greater power over slave property, or which entitles property of that kind to less protection that property of any other description. The only power conferred is the power coupled with the duty of guarding and protecting the owner in his rights.

Upon these considerations, it is the opinion of the court that the act of Congress which prohibited a citizen from holding and owning property of this kind in the territory of the United States north of the line therein mentioned, is not warranted by the Constitution, and is therefore void; and that neither Dred Scott himself, nor any of his family, were made free by being carried into this territory; even if they had been carried there by the owner, with the intention of becoming a permanent resident.

We have so far examined the case, as it stands under the Constitution of the United States, and the powers thereby delegated to the Federal Government.

But there is another point in the case which depends on State power and State law. And it is contended, on the part of the plaintiff, that he is made free by being taken to Rock Island, in the State of Illinois, independently of his residence in the territory of the United States; and being so made free, he was not again reduced to a state of slavery by being brought back to Missouri.

Our notice of this part of the case will be very brief; for the principle on which it depends was decided in this court, upon much consideration, in the case of Strader et al. *v.* Graham, reported in 10th Howard, 82. In that case, the slaves had been taken from Kentucky to Ohio, with the consent of the owner, and afterwards brought back to Kentucky. And this court held that their *status* or condition, as free or slave, depended upon the laws of Kentucky, when they were brought back into that State, and not of Ohio; and that this court had no jurisdiction to revise the judgment of a State court upon its own laws. This was the point directly before the court, and the decision that this court had not jurisdiction turned upon it, as will be seen by the report of the case.

So in this case. As Scott was a slave when taken into the State of Illinois by his owner, and was there held as such, and brought back in that character, his *status*, as free or slave, depended on the laws of Missouri, and not of Illinois.

It has, however, been urged in the argument, that by the laws of Missouri he was free on his return, and that this case, therefore, cannot be governed by the case of Strader et al. *v.* Graham, where it appeared, by the laws of Kentucky, that the plaintiffs continued to be slaves on their return from Ohio. But whatever doubts or opinions may, at one time, have been entertained upon this subject, we are satisfied, upon a careful examination of all the cases decided in the State courts of Missouri referred to, that it is now firmly settled by the decisions of the highest court in the State, that Scott and his family upon their return were not free, but were, by the laws of Missouri, the property of the defendant; and that the Circuit Court of the United States had no jurisdiction, when, by the laws of the State, the plaintiff was a slave, and not a citizen.

Moreover, the plaintiff, it appears, brought a similar action against the defendant in the State court of Missouri, claiming the freedom of himself and his family upon the same grounds and the same evidence upon which he relies in the case before the court. The case was carried before the Supreme Court of the State; was fully argued there; and that court decided that neither the plaintiff nor his family were entitled to freedom, and were still the slaves of the defendant; and reversed the judgment of the inferior State court, which had given a different decision. If the plaintiff supposed that this judgment of the Supreme Court of the State was erroneous, and that this court had jurisdiction to revise and reverse it, the only mode by which he could legally bring it before this court was by writ of error directed to the Supreme Court of the State, requiring it to transmit the record to this court. If this had been done, it is too plain for argument that the writ must have been dismissed for want of jurisdiction in this court. The case of Strader and others *v.* Graham is directly in point; and, indeed, independent of any decision, the language of the 25th section of the act of 1789 is too clear and precise to admit of controversy.

Upon the whole, therefore, it is the judgment of this court, that it appears by the record before us that the plaintiff in error is not a citizen of Missouri, in the sense in which that word is used in the Constitution; and that the Circuit Court of the United States, for that reason, had no jurisdiction in the case, and could give no judgment in it. Its judgment for the defendant must, consequently, be reversed, and a mandate issued, directing the suit to be dismissed for want of jurisdiction.

■ MR. JUSTICE MCLEAN dissenting.

In the argument, it was said that a colored citizen would not be an agreeable member of society. This is more a matter of taste than of law. Several of the States have admitted persons of color to the right of suffrage, and in this view have recognized them as citizens; and this has been done in the slave as well as the free States. On the question of citizenship, it must be admitted that we have not been very fastidious. Under the late treaty with Mexico, we have made citizens of all grades, combinations, and colors. The same was done in the admission of Louisiana and Florida. No one ever doubted, and no court ever held, that the people of these Territories did not become citizens under the treaty. They have exercised all the rights of citizens, without being naturalized under the acts of Congress.

There are several important principles involved in this case, which have been argued, and which may be considered under the following heads:

1.   The locality of slavery, as settled by this court and the courts of the States.

2.   The relation which the Federal Government bears to slavery in the States.

3.   The power of Congress to establish Territorial Governments, and to prohibit the introduction of slavery therein.

4.   The effect of taking slaves into a new State or Territory, and so holding them, where slavery is prohibited.

5.   Whether the return of a slave under the control of his master, after being entitled to his freedom, reduces him to his former condition.

6.   Are the decisions of the Supreme Court of Missouri, on the questions before us, binding on this court, within the rule adopted.

In the course of my judicial duties, I have had occasion to consider and decide several of the above points.

1.   As to the locality of slavery. The civil law throughout the Continent of Europe, it is believed, without an exception, is, that slavery can exist only within the territory where it is established; and that, if a slave escapes, or is carried beyond such territory, his mater cannot reclaim him, unless by virtue of some express stipulation.

I will now consider the relation which the Federal Government bears to slavery in the States:

Slavery is emphatically a State institution. In the ninth section of the first article of the Constitution, it is provided 'that the migration or importation of such persons as any of the States now existing shall think proper to admit, shall not be prohibited by the Congress prior to the year 1808, but a tax or duty may be imposed on such importation, not exceeding ten dollars for each person.'

In the Convention, it was proposed by a committee of eleven to limit the importation of slaves to the year 1800, when Mr. Pinckney moved to extend the time to the year 1808. This motion was carried-New Hampshire, Massachusetts, Connecticut, Maryland, North Carolina, South Carolina, and Georgia, voting in the affirmative; and New Jersey,

Pennsylvania, and Virginia, in the negative. In opposition to the motion, Mr. Madison said: 'Twenty years will produce all the mischief that can be apprehended from the liberty to import slaves; so long a term will be more dishonorable to the American character than to say nothing about it in the Constitution.' (Madison Papers.)

The provision in regard to the slave trade shows clearly that Congress considered slavery a State institution, to be continued and regulated by its individual sovereignty; and to conciliate that interest, the slave trade was continued twenty years, not as a general measure, but for the 'benefit of such States as shall think proper to encourage it.'

The only connection which the Federal Government holds with slaves in a State, arises from that provision of the Constitution which declares that 'No person held to service or labor in one State, under the laws thereof, escaping into another, shall, in consequence of any law or regulation therein, be discharged from such service or labor, but shall be delivered up, on claim of the party to whom such service or labor may be due.'

This being a fundamental law of the Federal Government, it rests mainly for its execution, as has been held, on the judicial power of the Union; and so far as the rendition of fugitives from labor has become a subject of judicial action, the Federal obligation has been faithfully discharged.

In the formation of the Federal Constitution, care was taken to confer no power on the Federal Government to interfere with this institution in the States. In the provision respecting the slave trade, in fixing the ratio of representation, and providing for the reclamation of fugitives from labor, slaves were referred to as persons, and in no other respect are they considered in the Constitution.

We need not refer to the mercenary spirit which introduced the infamous traffic in slaves, to show the degradation of negro slavery in our country. This system was imposed upon our colonial settlements by the mother country, and it is due to truth to say that the commercial colonies and States were chiefly engaged in the traffic. But we know as a historical fact, that James Madison, that great and good man, a leading member in the Federal Convention, was solicitous to guard the language of that instrument so as not to convey the idea that there could be property in man.

I prefer the lights of Madison, Hamilton, and Jay, as a means of construing the Constitution in all its bearings, rather than to look behind that period, into a traffic which is now declared to be piracy, and punished with death by Christian nations. I do not like to draw the sources of our domestic relations from so dark a ground. Our independence was a great epoch in the history of freedom; and while I admit the Government was not made especially for the colored race, yet many of them were citizens of the New England States, and exercised, the rights of suffrage when the Constitution was adopted, and it was not doubted by any intelligent person that its tendencies would greatly ameliorate their condition.

Many of the States, on the adoption of the Constitution, or shortly afterward, took measures to abolish slavery within their respective jurisdictions; and it is a well-known fact that a belief was cherished by the leading men, South as well as North, that the institution of slavery would gradually decline, until it would become extinct. The increased value of slave labor, in the culture of cotton and sugar, prevented the realization of this expectation. Like all other communities and States, the South were influenced by what they considered to be their own interests.

But if we are to turn our attention to the dark ages of the world, why confine our view to colored slavery? On the same principles, white men were made slaves. All slavery has its origin in power, and is against right.

The power of Congress to establish Territorial Governments, and to prohibit the introduction of slavery therein, is the next point to be considered.

Under the fifth head, we were to consider whether the status of slavery attached to the plaintiff and wife, on their return to Missouri . . . This doctrine is not asserted in the late opinion of the Supreme Court of Missouri, and up to 1852 the contrary doctrine was uniformly maintained by that court.

In its late decision, the court say that it will not give effect in Missouri to the laws of Illinois, or the law of Congress called the Missouri compromise. This was the effect of the decision, though its terms were, that the court would not take notice, judicially, of those laws.

In 1851, the Court of Appeals of South Carolina recognized the principle, that a slave, being taken to a free State, became free. (Commonwealth *v.* Pleasants, 10 Leigh Rep., 697.) In Betty *v.* Horton, the Court of Appeals held that the freedom of the slave was acquired by the action of the laws of Massachusetts, by the said slave being taken there. (5 Leigh Rep., 615.)

The slave States have generally adopted the rule, that where the master, by a residence with his slave in a State or Territory where slavery is prohibited, the slave was entitled to his freedom everywhere. This was the settled doctrine of the Supreme Court of Missouri. It has been so held in Mississippi, in Virginia, in Louisiana, formerly in Kentucky, Maryland, and in other States.

The law, where a contract is made and is to be executed, governs it. This does not depend upon comity, but upon the law of the contract. And if, in the language of the Supreme Court of Missouri, the master, by taking his slave to Illinois, and employing him there as a slave, emancipates him as effectually as by a deed of emancipation, is it possible that such an act is not matter for adjudication in any slave State where the master may take him? Does not the master assent to the law, when he places himself under it in a free State?

The States of Missouri and Illinois are bounded by a common line. The one prohibits slavery, the other admits it. This has been done by the exercise of that sovereign power which appertains to each. We are bound to respect the institutions of each, as emanating from the voluntary action of the people. Have the people of either any right to disturb the relations of the other? Each State rests upon the basis of its own sovereignty, protected by the Constitution. Our Union has been the foundation of our prosperity and national glory. Shall we not cherish and maintain it? This can only be done by respecting the legal rights of each State.

If a citizen of a free State shall entice or enable a slave to escape from the service of his master, the law holds him responsible, not only for the loss of the slave, but he is liable to be indicted and fined for the misdemeanor. And I am bound here to say, that I have never found a jury in the four States which constitute my circuit, which have not sustained this law, where the evidence required them to sustain it. And it is proper that I should also say, that more cases have arisen in my circuit, by reason of its extent and locality, than in all other parts of the Union. This has been done to vindicate the sovereign rights of the Southern States, and protect the legal interests of our brethren of the South.

Let these facts be contrasted with the case now before the court. Illinois has declared in the most solemn and impressive form that there shall be neither slavery nor involuntary servitude in that State, and that any slave brought into it, with a view of becoming a resident, shall be emancipated. And effect has been given to this provision of the Constitution by the decision of the Supreme Court of that State. With a full knowledge of these facts, a slave is brought from Missouri to Rock Island, in the State of Illinois, and is retained there as a slave for two years, and then taken to Fort Snelling, where slavery is prohibited by the Missouri compromise act, and there he is detained two years longer in a state of slavery. Harriet, his wife, was also kept at the same place four years as a slave, having been purchased in Missouri. They were then removed to the State of Missouri, and sold as slaves, and in the action before us they are not only claimed as slaves, but a majority of my brethren have held that on their being returned to Missouri the status of slavery attached to them.

I am not able to reconcile this result with the respect due to the State of Illinois. Having the same rights of sovereignty as the State of Missouri in adopting a Constitution, I can perceive no reason why the institutions of Illinois should not receive the same consideration as those of Missouri. Allowing to my brethren the same right of judgment that I exercise myself, I must be permitted to say that it seems to me the principle laid down will enable the people of a slave State to introduce slavery into a free State, for a longer or shorter time, as may suit their convenience; and by returning the slave to the State whence he was brought, by force or otherwise, the status of slavery attaches, and protects the rights of the master, and defies the sovereignty of the free State. There is no evidence before us that Dred Scott and his family returned to Missouri voluntarily. The contrary is inferable from the agreed case: 'In the year 1838, Dr. Emerson removed the plaintiff and said Harriet, and their daughter Eliza, from Fort Snelling to the State of Missouri, where they have ever since resided.' This is the agreed case; and can it be inferred from this that Scott and family returned to Missouri voluntarily? He was removed; which shows that he was passive, as a slave, having exercised no volition on the subject. He did not resist the master by absconding or force. But that was not sufficient to bring him within Lord Stowell's decision; he must have acted voluntarily. It would be a mockery of law and an outrage on his rights to coerce his return, and then claim that it was voluntary, and on that ground that his former status of slavery attached.

If the decision be placed on this ground, it is a fact for a jury to decide, whether the return was voluntary, or else the fact should be distinctly admitted. A presumption against the plaintiff in this respect, I say with confidence, is not authorized from the facts admitted.

The Supreme Court of Missouri refused to notice the act of Congress or the Constitution of Illinois, under which Dred Scott, his wife and children, claimed that they are entitled to freedom. . . . The Missouri court disregards the express provisions of an act of Congress and the Constitution of a sovereign State, both of which laws for twenty-eight years it had not only regarded, but carried into effect.

If a State court may do this, on a question involving the liberty of a human being, what protection do the laws afford? So far from this being a Missouri question, it is a question, as it would seem, within the twenty-fifth section of the judiciary act, where a right to freedom being set up under the act of Congress, and the decision being against such right, it may be brought for revision before this court, from the Supreme Court of Missouri.

■ MR. JUSTICE CURTIS dissenting.

The plaintiff alleged that he was a citizen of the State of Missouri, and that the defendant was a citizen of the State of New York. It is not doubted that it was necessary to make each of these allegations, to sustain the jurisdiction of the Circuit Court. The defendant denied that the plaintiff was a citizen of the State of Missouri. The plaintiff demurred to that plea. The Circuit Court adjudged the plea insufficient, and the first question for our consideration is, whether the sufficiency of that plea is before this court for judgment, upon this writ of error. The part of the judicial power of the United States, conferred by Congress on the Circuit Courts, being limited to certain described cases and controversies, the question whether a particular case is within the cognizance of a Circuit Court, may be raised by a plea to the jurisdiction of such court. When that question has been raised, the Circuit Court must, in the first instance, pass upon and determine it. Whether its determination be final, or subject to review by this appellate court, must depend upon the will of Congress; upon which body the Constitution has conferred the power, with certain restrictions, to establish inferior courts, to determine their jurisdiction, and to regulate the appellate power of this court. The twenty-second section of the judiciary act of 1789, which allows a writ of error from final judgments of Circuit Courts, provides that there shall be no reversal in this court, on such writ of error, for error in ruling any plea in abatement, *other than a plea to the jurisdiction of the court*. Accordingly it has been held, from the origin of the court to the present day, that Circuit Courts have not been made by Congress the final judges of their own jurisdiction in civil cases. And that when a record comes here and it appears to this court that the Circuit Court had not jurisdiction, its judgment must be reversed, and the cause remanded, to be dismissed for want of jurisdiction.

To determine whether any free persons, descended from Africans held in slavery, were citizens of the United States under the Confederation, and consequently at the time of the adoption of the Constitution of the United States, it is only necessary to know whether any such persons were citizens of either of the States under the Confederation, at the time of the adoption of the Constitution.

Of this there can be no doubt. At the time of the ratification of the Articles of Confederation, all free native-born inhabitants of the States of New Hampshire, Massachusetts, New York, New Jersey, and North Carolina, though descended from African slaves, were not only citizens of those States, but such of them as had the other necessary qualifications possessed the franchise of electors, on equal terms with other citizens.

The conclusions at which I have arrived on this part of the case are:

First. That the free native-born citizens of each State are citizens of the United States.

Second. That as free colored persons born within some of the States are citizens of those States, such persons are also citizens of the United States.

Third. That every such citizen, residing in any State, has the right to sue and is liable to be sued in the Federal courts, as a citizen of that State in which he resides.

Fourth. That as the plea to the jurisdiction in this case shows no facts, except that the plaintiff was of African descent, and his ancestors were sold as slaves, and as these facts are not inconsistent with his citizenship of the United States, and his residence in the State of

Missouri, the plea to the jurisdiction was bad, and the judgment of the Circuit Court overruling it was correct.

I dissent, therefore, from that part of the opinion of the majority of the court, in which it is held that a person of African descent cannot be a citizen of the United States; and I regret I must go further, and dissent both from what I deem their assumption of authority to examine the constitutionality of the act of Congress commonly called the Missouri compromise act, and the grounds and conclusions announced in their opinion.

NOTES AND QUESTIONS

1.   *What's the Injustice?* How exactly did the Court err in *Dred Scott*? Was the problem that the Justices were racist, and imposed their own (outdated) moral views? Or was the problem simply their willingness to give effect to the racist views of the Founders? More succinctly, is the problem the racist of the Justices or the racism embedded in our history? Either way, does *Dred Scott* suggest that the Civil War was inevitable, that the slavery issue could not have been resolved any other way?

2.   *What Could Have Been Done Differently?* Given the existing state and federal law, could the Court have justifiably declared Scott free as the result of the time he spent in Illinois or Minnesota? Or would the Court have overstepped its role by doing so? How might Justice Taney have written a narrower opinion rejecting Scott's claim? Is there anything the Court could have done to eliminate slavery while avoiding the Civil War?

3.   *Are You Persuaded?* Were the opinions of the dissenting judges persuasive as a matter of law? Is it even possible to decide a politically controversial case based simply on "the law"? Or must a Justice necessarily consider his own moral views, the potential reactions to any decision, and various policy considerations?

III. FROM SLAVERY, TO CIVIL WAR, TO SEGREGATION

Chief Justice Taney may have hoped his opinion in *Dred Scott* would resolve the conflict over slavery. It did not. It inflamed tensions and helped to precipitate the Civil War. Southern states began to secede from the Union shortly after Lincoln's election in 1860. Congress, in an effort to lure them back, proposed a Thirteenth Amendment to the Constitution that would have precluded the abolition of slavery, either by legislation or constitutional amendment. Lincoln referred favorably to the amendment in his first inaugural address, and it was submitted to the states for ratification. The outbreak of the Civil War ended the deliberation.

President Lincoln's January 1863 issuance of the Emancipation Proclamation is often thought to have freed the slaves. But it did no such thing. Indeed, it did not even accomplish what it purported to do, which was to free the slaves only in those states then in rebellion against the

Union. The Emancipation Proclamation did, however, transform a war to preserve the Union into a war to end slavery. In January 1865, Congress proposed a Thirteenth Amendment to ban slavery, and by December 1865, after the conclusion of the war, it had been ratified.

Southerners lost the war, but they didn't stop fighting. The Ku Klux Klan formed throughout the South to use violence and intimidation to assert white supremacy. Almost all the states in the former Confederacy soon passed the Black Codes aimed at recreating the conditions of slavery. Among numerous other restrictions, the Black Codes imposed travel and movement restrictions on former slaves, precluded them from any employment other than as tenant farmers or laborers, punished vagrancy harshly, and limited the rights of the former slaves to own property. A Mississippi statute, for example, prohibited blacks' intermarriage with whites, restricted their rental of property to certain areas, and required that they have employment and a place to live and proof of such. The law also provided that "if a freedman, free negro or mulatto quits . . . the service of his or her employer before the expiration of his or her term of service without good cause . . . , any person may arrest him, and bring him back at an expense to be deducted from the employee's pay." Another provision provided that "all freemen, free negroes and mulattoes in this State . . . found . . . with no lawful employment or business, or found unlawfully assembling themselves together either in the day or night time . . . shall be deemed vagrants, and on conviction thereof, shall be fined and imprisoned at the discretion of the court."

Congress passed the Civil Rights Act of 1866 largely in response to the Black Codes. The Act conferred citizenship on all "persons" born in the United States. The Act also guaranteed the right of all citizens, without respect to race, color, or previous condition of servitude, "to make and enforce contracts, to sue, be parties, and give evidence, to inherit, purchase, lease, sell, hold, and convey real and personal property, and to full and equal benefit of all laws and proceedings for the security of person and property, as is enjoyed by white citizens."

As Congress debated the 1866 Act, many, including some of the Act's supporters, raised the question whether Congress had the power to promulgate the Act. As a result, Ohio Congressman John Bingham introduced a first draft of what would become the Fourteenth Amendment. The text of the Amendment went through numerous iterations, and in late April 1866, the Joint Committee on Reconstruction proposed the text that was eventually added to the Constitution: "No state shall make or enforce any law which shall abridge the privileges and immunities of citizens of the United States; nor shall any state deprive any person of life, liberty, and property without due process of law, nor deny to any person within its jurisdiction the equal protection of the laws." The language that is now the first sentence of the Fourteenth

Amendment—"all persons born or naturalized in the United States and subject to the jurisdiction thereof, are citizens of the United States and the state wherein they reside"—was added to overrule *Dred Scott* and reinforce the rights of citizenship provided in the 1866 Act. The Amendment was ratified in 1868. Like the Thirteenth Amendment (and the Fifteenth Amendment), the Fourteenth Amendment also contains a clause that grants Congress the power to enforce its substantive provisions—a triumph of federal power in the wake of the Civil War.

After the Civil War, Congress enacted a slew of statutes in an effort to bolster blacks' citizenship. In addition to the Civil Rights Act of 1866, Congress passed the Reconstruction Act of 1867, which put the South under military control, banned confederate leaders from voting, compelled southern states to adopt new constitutions, and required the ratification of the Fourteenth Amendment as a condition for readmission to the Union. Congress also passed the Enforcement Act of 1870 (also known as the Civil Rights Act of 1870), which protected the right to vote for black males against unlawful state action and private violence. The Civil Rights Act of 1871 (also known as the Ku Klux Klan Act) authorized the President to use military force to address racial violence by the Klan and other white supremacist organizations. The Civil Rights Act of 1875 guaranteed equal access to public accommodations, such as inns and public conveyances.

But Reconstruction was short-lived. Andrew Johnson (who had ascended to the presidency following Lincoln's death) opposed much of what Congress sought to accomplish, including the establishment of the Freedman's Bureau established to aid former slaves. He and his Democratic Party believed it encroached upon states' rights and would impede slaves' self-reliance by offering them too much assistance. Crippled by political stalemate, the Freedman's Bureau closed in 1872. By 1876, federal troops withdrew from the South as part of the Compromise of 1876, which resolved the contested presidential election of that year, awarding the presidency to Republican candidate Rutherford B. Hayes in exchange for his ending Reconstruction.

In the decades after the war, the Supreme Court also interpreted the Reconstruction Amendments narrowly, even as the Court itself recognized that they were intended to secure the freedom and political equality of the freed slaves. In the *Slaughter-House Cases*, 83 U.S. 36 (1873), the Court first interpreted both the Thirteenth and Fourteenth Amendments. Louisiana butchers had filed a lawsuit challenging as a violation of the Reconstruction Amendments a statute that granted a monopoly to engage in the business of slaughtering to a single company. In rejecting the plaintiffs' arguments, the Court stated that the "one pervading purpose" of the Reconstruction Amendments is "the freedom of the slave race, the security and firm establishment of that freedom, and the protection of the newly-made freeman and citizen from the oppressions of those who had formerly exercised unlimited dominion over him." The Court described the Equal Protection Clause as remedying the "evil" of racial discrimination represented by the "existence of laws in the States where the newly emancipated negroes resided, which discriminated with gross injustice and hardship against them as a class."

But perhaps more consequential was the Court's rejection of the butchers' claim that the grant of the monopoly violated the privileges and immunities of citizenship. The Court interpreted that Clause exceedingly narrowly to protect only a limited set of rights of "national" citizenship, which did not include the sorts of economic or labor rights the butchers sought to advance. The case thus rendered a central component of the Fourteenth Amendment—the Privileges and Immunities Clause—a dead letter. The Court emphasized that the Reconstruction Amendments did not displace the states as guarantors of civil rights, observing that "[u]nder the pressure of all the excited feeling growing out of the war, our statesmen have still believed that the existence of the State with powers for domestic and local government, including the regulation of civil rights—the rights of persons and property—were essential to the perfect working of our complex form of government, though they have thought proper to impose additional limitations on the states." A later ruling in *The Civil Rights Cases* reveals the devastating implications of that view.

The Civil Rights Cases

Supreme Court of the United States, 1883.
109 U.S. 3.

■ BRADLEY, J.

These cases are all founded on the first and second sections of the act of congress known as the 'Civil Rights Act,' passed March 1, 1875, entitled 'An act to protect all citizens in their civil and legal rights.' Two of the cases, are indictments for denying to persons of color the accommodations and privileges of an inn or hotel; two of them are for denying to individuals the privileges and accommodations of a theater. The case against the Memphis & Charleston Railroad Company was [for] the refusal by the conductor of the railroad company to allow the wife to ride in the ladies' car, for the reason, as stated in one of the counts, that she was a person of African descent.

It is obvious that the primary and important question in all the cases is the constitutionality of the law; for if the law is unconstitutional none of the prosecutions can stand.

The sections of the law referred to provide as follows:

'Section 1. That all persons within the jurisdiction of the United States shall be entitled to the full and equal enjoyment of the accommodations, advantages, facilities, and privileges of inns, public conveyances on land or water, theaters, and other places of public amusement; subject only to the conditions and limitations established by law, and applicable alike to citizens of every race and color, regardless of any previous condition of servitude.

'Sec. 2. That any person who shall violate the foregoing section by denying to any citizen, except for reasons by law applicable to citizens of every race and color, and regardless of any previous condition of servitude, the full enjoyment of any of the accommodations, advantages, facilities, or privileges in said section enumerated, or by aiding or inciting such denial, shall, for every such offense, forfeit and pay the sum of $500 to the person aggrieved thereby, to be recovered in an action of debt, with full costs; and shall, also, for every such offense, be deemed guilty of a misdemeanor, and upon conviction thereof shall be fined not less than $500 nor more than $1,000, or shall be imprisoned not less than 30 days nor more than one year.

Are these sections constitutional? The essence of the law is, not to declare broadly that all persons shall be entitled to the full and equal enjoyment of the accommodations, advantages, facilities, and privileges of inns, public conveyances, and theaters; but that such enjoyment shall not be subject to any conditions applicable only to citizens of a particular race or color, or who had been in a previous condition of servitude. In other words, it is the purpose of the law to declare that, in the enjoyment of the accommodations and privileges of inns, public conveyances, theaters, and other places of public amusement, no distinction shall be made between citizens of different race or color, or between those who have, and those who have not, been slaves. Its effect is to declare that in all inns, public conveyances, and places of amusement, colored citizens, whether formerly slaves or not, and citizens of other races, shall have the same accommodations and privileges in all inns, public conveyances, and places of amusement, as are enjoyed by white citizens; and vice versa. The second section makes it a penal offense in any person to deny to any citizen of any race or color, regardless of previous servitude, any of the accommodations or privileges mentioned in the first section.

Has congress constitutional power to make such a law? Of course, no one will contend that the power to pass it was contained in the constitution before the adoption of the last three amendments. The power is sought, first, in the fourteenth amendment, and the views and arguments of distinguished senators, advanced while the law was under consideration, claiming authority to pass it by virtue of that amendment, are the principal arguments adduced in favor of the power.

The first section of the fourteenth amendment,—which is the one relied on,—after declaring who shall be citizens of the United States, and of the several states, is prohibitory in its character, and prohibitory upon the states. It declares that "no state shall make or enforce any law which shall abridge the privileges or immunities of citizens of the United States; nor shall any state deprive any person of life, liberty, or property without due process of law; nor deny to any person within its jurisdiction the equal protection of the laws." It is state action of a particular character that is prohibited. Individual invasion of individual rights is not the subject-matter of the amendment. It nullifies and makes void all state legislation, and state action of every kind, which impairs the privileges and immunities of citizens of the United States, or which injures them in life, liberty, or property without due process of law, or which denies to any of them the equal protection of the laws. It not only does this, but, in order that the national will, thus declared, may not be a mere *brutum fulmen*, the last section of the amendment invests congress with power to enforce it by appropriate legislation. To enforce what? To enforce the prohibition. To adopt appropriate legislation for correcting the effects of such prohibited state law and state acts, and thus to render them effectually null, void, and innocuous. This is the legislative power conferred upon congress, and this is the whole of it. It does not invest congress with power to legislate upon subjects which are within the domain of state legislation; but to provide modes of relief against state legislation, or state action, of the kind referred to. It does not authorize congress to create a code of municipal law for the regulation of private rights; but to provide modes of redress against the operation of state laws, and the action of state officers, executive or judicial, when these are subversive of the fundamental rights specified in the amendment. Positive rights and privileges are undoubtedly secured by the fourteenth amendment; but they are secured by way of prohibition against state laws and state proceedings affecting those rights and privileges, and by power given to congress to legislate for the purpose of carrying such prohibition into effect; and such legislation must necessarily be predicated upon such supposed state laws or state proceedings, and be directed to the correction of their operation and effect.

And so in the present case, until some state law has been passed, or some state action through its officers or agents has been taken, adverse to the rights of citizens sought to be protected by the fourteenth amendment, no legislation of the United States under said amendment, nor any proceeding under such legislation, can be called into activity, for the prohibitions of the amendment are against state laws and acts done under state authority.

An inspection of the law shows that it makes no reference whatever to any supposed or apprehended violation of the fourteenth amendment on the part of the states. It is not predicated on any such view. It proceeds *ex directo* to declare that certain acts committed by individuals shall be deemed offenses, and shall be prosecuted and punished by proceedings in the courts of the United States. It does not profess to be corrective of any constitutional wrong committed by the states; it does not make its operation to depend upon any such wrong committed.

If this legislation is appropriate for enforcing the prohibitions of the amendment, it is difficult to see where it is to stop. Why may not congress, with equal show of authority, enact a code of laws for the enforcement and vindication of all rights of life, liberty, and property? The assumption is certainly unsound. It is repugnant to the tenth amendment of the constitution, which declares that the powers not delegated to the United States by the constitution, nor prohibited by it to the states, are reserved to the states respectively or to the people.

Of course, these remarks do not apply to those cases in which congress is clothed with direct and plenary powers of legislation over the whole subject, accompanied with an express or implied denial of such power to the states, as in the regulation of commerce with foreign nations, among the several states, and with the Indian tribes, the coining of money, the establishment of post-offices and post-roads, the declaring of war, etc. In these cases congress has power to pass laws for regulating the subjects specified, in every detail, and the conduct and transactions of individuals respect thereof. But where a subject is not submitted to the general legislative power of congress, but is only submitted thereto for the purpose of rendering effective some prohibition against particular state legislation or state action in reference to that subject, the power given is limited by its object, and any legislation by congress in the matter must necessarily be corrective in its character, adapted to counteract and redress the operation of such prohibited state laws or proceedings of state officers.

If the principles of interpretation which we have laid down are correct, as we deem them to be,—and they are in accord with the principles laid down in the cases before referred to, as well as in the recent case of U. S. v. Harris, decided at the last term of this court,—it is clear that the law in question cannot be sustained by any grant of legislative power made to congress by the fourteenth amendment. That amendment prohibits the states from denying to any person the equal protection of the laws, and declares that congress shall have power to enforce, by appropriate legislation, the provisions of the amendment. The law in question, without any reference to adverse state legislation on the subject, declares that all persons shall be entitled to equal accommodation and privileges of inns, public conveyances, and places of public amusement, and imposes a penalty upon any individual who shall deny to any citizen such equal accommodations and privileges. This is not corrective legislation; it is primary and direct; it takes immediate and absolute possession of the subject of the right of admission to inns, public conveyances, and places of amusement. It supersedes and displaces state legislation on the same subject, or only allows it permissive force. It ignores such legislation, and assumes that the matter is one that belongs to the domain of national regulation. Whether it would not have been a more effective protection of the rights of citizens to have clothed congress with plenary power over the whole subject, is not now the question. What we have to decide is, whether such plenary power has been conferred upon congress by the fourteenth amendment, and, in our judgment, it has not.

But the power of congress to adopt direct and primary, as distinguished from corrective, legislation on the subject in hand, is sought, in the second place, from the thirteenth amendment, which abolishes slavery. This amendment declares 'that neither slavery, nor involuntary servitude, except as a punishment for crime, whereof the party shall have been duly convicted, shall exist within the United States, or any place subject to their jurisdiction;' and it gives congress power to enforce the amendment by appropriate legislation.

This amendment, as well as the fourteenth, is undoubtedly self-executing without any ancillary legislation, so far as its terms are applicable to any existing state of circumstances. By its own unaided force it abolished slavery, and established universal freedom. Still, legislation may be necessary and proper to meet all the various cases and circumstances to be affected by it, and to prescribe proper modes of redress for its violation in letter or spirit. And such legislation may be primary and direct in its character; for the amendment is not a mere prohibition of state laws establishing or upholding slavery, but an absolute declaration that slavery or involuntary servitude shall not exist in any part of the United States.

It is true that slavery cannot exist without law any more than property in lands and goods can exist without law, and therefore the thirteenth amendment may be regarded as nullifying all state laws which establish or uphold slavery. But it has a reflex character also, establishing and decreeing universal civil and political freedom throughout the United States; and it is assumed that the power vested in congress to enforce the article by appropriate legislation, clothes congress with power to pass all laws necessary and proper for abolishing all badges and incidents of slavery in the United Stated; and upon this assumption it is claimed that this is sufficient authority for declaring by law that all persons shall have equal accommodations and privileges in all inns, public conveyances, and places of public amusement; the argument being that the denial of such equal accommodations and privileges is in itself a subjection to a species of servitude within the meaning of the amendment. Conceding the major proposition to be true, that that congress has a right to enact all necessary and proper laws for the obliteration and prevention of slavery, with all its badges and incidents, is the minor proposition also true, that the denial to any person of admission to the accommodations and privileges of an inn, a public conveyance, or a theater, does subject that person to any form of servitude, or tend to fasten upon him any badge of slavery? If it does not, then power to pass the law is not found in the thirteenth amendment.

In a very able and learned presentation of the cognate question as to the extent of the rights, privileges, and immunities of citizens which cannot rightfully be abridged by state laws under the fourteenth amendment, made in a former case, a long list of burdens and disabilities of a servile character, incident to feudal vassalage in France, and which were abolished by the decrees of the national assembly, was presented for the purpose of showing that all inequalities and observances exacted by one man from another, were servitudes or badges of slavery, which a great nation, in its effort to establish universal liberty, made haste to wipe out and destroy. But these were servitudes imposed by the old law, or by long custom which had the force of law, and exacted by one man from another without the latter's consent. Should any such servitudes be imposed by a state law, there can be no doubt that the law would be repugnant to the fourteenth, no less than to the thirteenth, amendment; nor any greater doubt that congress has adequate power to forbid any such servitude from being exacted.

But is there any similarity between such servitudes and a denial by the owner of an inn, a public conveyance, or a theater, of its accommodations and privileges to an individual, even though the denial be founded on the race or color of that individual? Where does any slavery or servitude, or badge of either, arise from such an act of denial? Whether it might not be a denial of a right which, if sanctioned by the state law, would be obnoxious to the prohibitions of the fourteenth amendment, is another question. But what has it to do with the question of slavery?

The long existence of African slavery in this country gave us very distinct notions of what it was, and what were its necessary incidents. Compulsory service of the slave for the benefit of the master, restraint of his movements except by the master's will, disability to hold property, to make contracts, to have a standing in court, to be a witness against a white person, and such like burdens and incapacities were the inseparable incidents of the institution. Severer punishments for crimes were imposed on the slave than on free persons guilty of the same offenses. Congress, by the civil rights bill of 1866, passed in view of the thirteenth amendment, before the fourteenth was adopted, undertook to wipe out these burdens and disabilities, the necessary incidents of slavery, constituting its substance and visible from; and to secure to all citizens of every race and color, and without regard to previous servitude, those fundamental rights which are the essence of civil freedom, namely, the same right to make and enforce contracts, to sue, be parties, give evidence, and to inherit, purchase, lease, sell, and convey property, as is enjoyed by white citizens. Whether this legislation was fully authorized by the thirteenth amendment alone, without the support which it afterwards received from the fourteenth amendment, after the adoption of which it was re-enacted with some additions, it is not necessary to inquire. It is referred to for the purpose of showing that at that time (in 1866) congress did not assume, under the authority given by the

*Social
Rights v
Fund.
Rights*

thirteenth amendment, to adjust what may be called the social rights of
men and races in the community; but only to declare and vindicate those
fundamental rights which appertain to the essence of citizenship, and the
enjoyment or deprivation of which constitutes the essential distinction
between freedom and slavery.

We must not forget that the province and scope of the thirteenth and
fourteenth amendments are different: the former simply abolished
slavery: the latter prohibited the states from abridging the privileges or
immunities of citizens of the United States, from depriving them of life,
liberty, or property without due process of law, and from denying to any
the equal protection of the laws. The amendments are different, and the
powers of congress under them are different. What congress has power
to do under one, it may not have power to do under the other. Under the
thirteenth amendment, it has only to do with slavery and its incidents.
Under the fourteenth amendment, it has power to counteract and render
nugatory all state laws and proceedings which have the effect to abridge
any of the privileges or immunities which have the effect to abridge any
deprive them of life, liberty, or property without due process of law, or to
deny to any of them the equal protection of the laws. Under the thirteenth
amendment the legislation, so far as necessary or proper to eradicate all
forms and incidents of slavery and involuntary servitude, may be direct
and primary, operating upon the acts of individuals, whether sanctioned
by state legislation or not; under the fourteenth, as we have already
shown, it must necessarily be, and can only be, corrective in its character,
addressed to counteract and afford relief against state regulations or
proceedings.

The only question under the present head, therefore, is, whether the
refusal to any persons of the accommodations of an inn, or a public
conveyance, or a place of public amusement, by an individual, and
without any sanction or support from any state law or regulation, does
inflict upon such persons any manner of servitude, or form of slavery, as
those terms are understood in this country? Many wrongs may be
obnoxious to the prohibitions of the fourteenth amendment which are
not, in any just sense, incidents or elements of slavery. Such, for example,
would be the taking of private property without due process of law; or
allowing persons who have committed certain crimes (horse-stealing, for
example) to be seized and hung by the *posse comitatus* without regular
trial; or denying to any person, or class of persons, the right to pursue
any peaceful avocations allowed to others. What is called class legislation
would belong to this category, and would be obnoxious to the prohibitions
of the fourteenth amendment, but would not to the prohibitions of the
fourteenth when not involving the idea of any subjection of one man to
another. The thirteenth amendment has respect, not to distinctions of
race, or class, or color, but to slavery. The fourteenth amendment extends
its protection to races and classes, and prohibits any state legislation

which has the effect of denying to any race or class, or to any individual, the equal protection of the laws.

Now, conceding, for the sake of the argument, that the admission to an inn, a public conveyance, or a place of public amusement, on equal terms with all other citizens, is the right of every man and all classes of men, is it any more than one of those rights which the states by the fourteenth amendment are forbidden to deny to any person? And is the constitution violated until the denial of the right has some state sanction or authority? Can the act of a mere individual, the owner of the inn, the public conveyance, or place of amusement, refusing the accommodation, be justly regarded as imposing any badge of slavery or servitude upon the applicant, or only as inflicting an ordinary civil injury, properly cognizable by the laws of the state, and presumably subject to redress by those laws until the contrary appears?

After giving to these questions all the consideration which their importance demands, we are forced to the conclusion that such an act of refusal has nothing to do with slavery or involuntary servitude, and that if it is violative of any right of the party, his redress is to be sought under the laws of the state; or, if those laws are adverse to his rights and do not protect him, his remedy will be found in the corrective legislation which congress has adopted, or may adopt, for counteracting the effect of state laws, or state action, prohibited by the fourteenth amendment. It would be running the slavery argument into the ground to make it apply to every act of discrimination which a person may see fit to make as to the guests he will entertain, or as to the people he will take into his coach or cab or car, or admit to his concert or theater, or deal with in other matters of intercourse or business. Innkeepers and public carriers, by the laws of all the states, so far as we are aware, are bound, to the extent of their facilities, to furnish proper accommodation to all unobjectionable persons who in good faith apply for them. If the laws themselves make any unjust discrimination, amenable to the prohibitions of the fourteenth amendment, congress has full power to afford a remedy under that amendment and in accordance with it.

When a man has emerged from slavery, and by the aid of beneficent legislation has shaken off the inseparable concomitants of that state, there must be some stage in the progress of his elevation when he takes the rank of a mere citizen, and ceases to be the special favorite of the laws, and when his rights as a citizen, or a man, are to be protected in the ordinary modes by which other men's rights are protected. There were thousands of free colored people in this country before the abolition of slavery, enjoying all the essential rights of life, liberty, and property the same as white citizens; yet no one, at that time, thought that it was any invasion of their personal status as freemen because they were not admitted to all the privileges enjoyed by white citizens, or because they were subjected to discriminations in the enjoyment of accommodations in inns, public conveyances, and places of amusement. Mere discriminations on account of race or color were not regarded as badges of slavery. If, since that time, the enjoyment of equal rights in all these respects has become established by constitutional enactment, it is not by force of the thirteenth amendment, (which merely abolishes slavery,) but by force of the fourteenth and fifteenth amendments.

On the whole, we are of opinion that no countenance of authority for the passage of the law in question can be found in either the thirteenth or fourteenth amendment of the constitution; and no other ground of authority for its passage being suggested, it must necessarily be declared void, at least so far as its operation in the several states is concerned.

This conclusion disposes of the cases now under consideration. In the cases of United States v. Ryan, and of Robinson v. Memphis & C.R. Co., the judgments must be affirmed. In the other cases, the answer to be given will be, that the first and second sections of the act of congress of March 1, 1875, entitled 'An act to protect all citizens in their civil and legal rights,' are unconstitutional and void, and that judgment should be rendered upon the several indictments in those cases accordingly. And it is so ordered.

■ HARLAN, J., dissenting.

The opinion in these cases proceeds, as it seems to me, upon grounds entirely too narrow and artificial. The substance and spirit of the recent amendments of the constitution have been sacrificed by a subtle and ingenious verbal criticism. . . . By this . . . I mean only, in this form, to express an earnest conviction that the court has departed from the familiar rule requiring, in the interpretation of constitutional provisions, that full effect be given to the intent with which they were adopted.

The thirteenth amendment, my brethren concede, did something more than to prohibit slavery as an institution, resting upon distinctions of race, and upheld by positive law. They admit that it established and decreed universal civil freedom throughout the United States. But did the freedom thus established involve nothing more than exemption from actual slavery? . . . Had the thirteenth amendment stopped with the sweeping declaration, in its first section, against the existence of slavery and involuntary servitude, except for crime, congress would have had the power, by implication, according to the doctrines of *Prigg v. Com.*, repeated in *Strauder v. West Virginia*, to protect the freedom thus established, and consequently to secure the enjoyment of such civil rights as were fundamental in freedom. But that it can exert its authority to that extent is now made clear, and was intended to be made clear, by the express grant of power contained in the second section of that amendment.

That there are burdens and disabilities which constitute badges of slavery and servitude, and that the express power delegated to congress to enforce, by appropriate legislation, the thirteenth amendment, may be exerted by legislation of a direct and primary character, for the eradication, not simply of the institution, but of its badges and incidents, are propositions which ought to be deemed indisputable. They lie at the very foundation of the civil rights act of 1866. Whether that act was fully authorized by the thirteenth amendment alone, without the support which it afterwards received from the fourteenth amendment, after the adoption of which it was re-enacted with some additions, the court, in its opinion, says it is unnecessary to inquire. But I submit, with all respect to my brethren, that its constitutionality is conclusively shown by other portions of their opinion. It is expressly conceded by them that the thirteenth amendment established freedom; that there are burdens and disabilities, the necessary incidents of slavery, which constitute its substance and visible form; that congress, by the act of 1866, passed in view of the thirteenth amendment, before the fourteenth was adopted, undertook to remove certain burdens and disabilities, the necessary incidents of slavery, and to secure to all citizens of every race and color, and without regard to previous servitude, those fundamental rights which are the essence of civil freedom, namely, the same right to make and enforce contracts, to sue, be parties, give evidence, and to inherit, purchase, lease, sell, and convey property as is enjoyed by white citizens; that under the thirteenth amendment congress has to do with slavery and its incidents; and that legislation, so far as necessary or proper to eradicate all forms and incidents of slavery and involuntary servitude, may be direct and primary, operating upon the acts of individuals, whether sanctioned by state legislation or not. These propositions being conceded, it is impossible, as it seems to me, to question the constitutional validity of the civil rights act of 1866. It remains now to inquire what are the legal rights of colored persons in respect of the accommodations, privileges, and facilities of public conveyances, inns, and places of public amusement.

1.   As to public conveyances on land and water. The sum of the adjudged cases is that a railroad corporation is a governmental agency, created primarily for public purposes, and subject to be controlled for the public benefit.

Such being the relations these corporations hold to the public, it would seem that the right of a colored person to use an improved public highway, upon the terms accorded to freemen of other races, is as fundamental in the state of freedom, established in this country, as are any of the rights which my brethren concede to be so far fundamental as to be deemed the essence of civil freedom.

2.   As to inns. The same general observations which have been made as to railroads are applicable to inns. . . . The[ ] authorities are sufficient to show a keeper of an inn is in the exercise of a quasi public employment. The law gives him special privileges, and he is charged with certain duties and responsibilities to the public. The public nature of his

employment forbids him from discriminating against any person asking admission as a guest on account of the race or color of that person.

3.   As to places of public amusement. [P]laces of public amusement, within the meaning of the act of 1875, are such as are established and maintained under direct license of the law. The authority to establish and maintain them comes from the public. The colored race is a part of that public. The local government granting the license represents them as well as all other races within its jurisdiction. A license from the public to establish a place of public amusement, imports, in law, equality of right, at such places, among all the members of that public. This must be so, unless it be—which I deny—that the common municipal government of all the people may, in the exertion of its powers, conferred for the benefit of all, discriminate or authorize discrimination against a particular race, solely because of its former condition of servitude.

Congress has not, in these matters, entered the domain of state control and supervision. It does not assume to prescribe the general conditions and limitations under which inns, public conveyances, and places of public amusement shall be conducted or managed. It simply declares in effect that since the nation has established universal freedom in this country for all time, there shall be no discrimination, based merely upon race or color, in respect of the legal rights in the accommodations and advantages of public conveyances, inns, and places of public amusement.

It remains now to consider these cases with reference to the power congress has possessed since the adoption of the fourteenth amendment.

[U]nder what circumstances, and to what extent may congress, by means of legislation, exert its power to enforce the provisions of this amendment?

The assumption that this amendment consists wholly of prohibitions upon state laws and state proceedings in hostility to its provisions, is unauthorized by its language. The first clause of the first section . . . created and granted, as well citizenship of the United States, as citizenship of the state in which they respectively resided. It introduced all of that race, whose ancestors had been imported and sold as slaves, at once, into the political community known as the 'People of the United States.' Further, they were brought, by this supreme act of the nation, within the direct operation of that provision of the constitution which declares that 'the citizens of each state shall be entitled to all privileges and immunities of citizens in the several states.' Article 4, § 2.

The citizenship thus acquired by that race, in virtue of an affirmative grant by the nation, may be protected, not alone by the judicial branch of the government, but by congressional legislation of a primary direct character; this, because the power of congress is not restricted to the enforcement of prohibitions upon state laws or state action. It is, in terms distinct and positive, to enforce 'the provisions of this article' of amendment; not simply those of a prohibitive character, but the provisions,—all of the provisions,—affirmative and prohibitive, of the amendment. It is, therefore, a grave misconception to suppose that the fifth section of the amendment has reference exclusively to express prohibitions upon state laws or state action. If any right was created by that amendment, the grant of power, through appropriate legislation, to enforce its provisions authorizes congress, by means of legislation operating throughout the entire Union, to guard, secure, and protect that right.

It is, therefore, an essential inquiry what, if any, right, privilege, or immunity was given by the nation to colored persons when they were made citizens of the state in which they reside? . . . That they became entitled, upon the adoption of the fourteenth amendment, 'to all privileges and immunities of citizens in the several states,' within the meaning of section 2 of article 4 of the constitution, no one, I suppose, will for a moment question. What are the privileges and immunities to which, by that clause of the constitution, they became entitled? To this it may be answered, generally, upon the authority of the adjudged cases, that they are those which are fundamental in citizenship in a free government, 'common to the citizens in the latter states under their constitutions and laws by virtue of their being citizens.'

There is one, if there be no others—exemption from race discrimination in respect of any civil right belonging to citizens of the white race in the same state. That, surely, is their constitutional privilege when within the jurisdiction of other states. And such must be their constitutional right, in their own state. . . . It is fundamental in American citizenship that, in respect of such rights, there shall be no discrimination by the state, or its officers, or by individuals, or corporations exercising public functions or authority, against any citizen because of his race or previous condition of servitude.

If, then, exemption from discrimination in respect of civil rights is a new constitutional right, secured by the grant of state citizenship to colored citizens of the United States, why may not the nation, by means of its own legislation of a primary direct character, guard, protect, and enforce that right? . . . The legislation congress may enact, in execution of its power to enforce the provisions of this amendment, is that which is appropriate to protect the right granted. Under given circumstances, that which the court characterizes as corrective legislation might be sufficient. Under other circumstances primary direct legislation may be required. But it is for congress, not the judiciary, to say which is best adapted to the end to be attained.

My brethren say that when a man has emerged from slavery, and by the aid of beneficent legislation has shaken off the inseparable concomitants of that state, there must be some stage in the progress of his elevation when he takes the rank of a mere citizen, and ceases to be the special favorite of the laws, and when his rights as a citizen, or a man, are to be protected in the ordinary modes by which other men's rights are protected. It is, I submit, scarcely just to say that the colored race has been the special favorite of the laws. What the nation, through congress, has sought to accomplish in reference to that race is, what had already been done in every state in the Union for the white race, to secure and protect rights belonging to them as freemen and citizens; nothing more. The one underlying purpose of congressional legislation has been to enable the black race to take the rank of mere citizens. The difficulty has been to compel a recognition of their legal right to take that rank, and to secure the enjoyment of privileges belonging, under the law, to them as a component part of the people for whose welfare and happiness government is ordained. At every step in this direction the nation has been confronted with class tyranny, which a contemporary English historian says is, of all tyrannies, the most intolerable, 'for it is ubiquitous in its operation, and weighs, perhaps, most heavily on those whose obscurity or distance would withdraw them from the notice of a single despot.' Today it is the colored race which is denied, by corporations and individuals wielding public authority, rights fundamental in their freedom and citizenship. At some future time it may be some other race that will fall under the ban. If the constitutional amendments be enforced, according to the intent with which, as I conceive, they were adopted, there cannot be, in this republic, any class of human beings in practical subjection to another class, with power in the latter to dole out to the former just such privileges as they may choose to grant. The supreme law of the land has decreed that no authority shall be exercised in this country upon the basis of discrimination, in respect of civil rights, against freemen and citizens because of their race, color, or previous condition of servitude. To that decree—for the due enforcement of which, by appropriate legislation, congress has been invested with express power—every one must bow, whatever may have been, or whatever now are, his individual views as to the wisdom or policy, either of the recent changes in the fundamental law, or of the legislation which has been enacted to give them effect.

For the reasons stated I feel constrained to withhold my assent to the opinion of the court.

NOTES AND QUESTIONS

1.   **The Civil Rights Cases.** The *Civil Rights Cases* are a consolidation of five cases alleging violations of the Civil Rights Act of 1875: *U.S. v. Stanley*, out of Kansas; *U.S. v. Ryan*, out of California, *U.S. v. Nichols*, out of Missouri; *U.S. v. Singleton*, out of New York; and *Robinson and Wife v. Memphis & Charleston Rail Company*, out of Tennessee. The *Stanley* and *Nichols* cases were prosecutions by the United States for denying nondiscriminatory hotel accommodations. The *Ryan* and *Singleton* cases were federal criminal prosecutions for failure to provide nondiscriminatory access to theatres. The

Robinson case was an action to recover the statutory penalty against the Charleston Rail Company for denying Sallie Robinson the right to ride in the "ladies car" of the train.

In the wake of the Act, many African Americans seized the opportunity to access services previously denied them. For instance, "in Wilmington, North Carolina, a saloon customer demanded that a barkeep be arrested for refusing to serve him." Such attempts to exercise newly guaranteed rights did not sit well with many whites. *See* A. K. Sandoval-Strausz, Travelers, Strangers, and Jim Crow: Law, Public Accommodations, and Civil Rights in America, 23 L. & Hist. Review 53 (2005). How might these dynamics highlight the importance of courts in the protection of rights? What might be the limits of law and judicial intervention in the face of entrenched prejudice?

2.   *What Did the Civil Rights Act of 1875 Mean?* The Court noted, "it is the purpose of the law to declare that, in the enjoyment of the accommodations and privileges of inns, public conveyances, theaters, and other places of public amusement, no distinction shall be made between citizens of different race or color." The Court then went on to argue that Congress did not have the power under the Fourteenth Amendment to create substantive rights "which are within the domain of state legislation." In the view of the Court, did the Civil Rights Act create a right of access for African Americans, or merely preclude the denial of rights on the basis of race? How significant is the difference between these two formulations?

3.   *The State Action Doctrine and Limits on Congressional Power.* Notwithstanding section 5 of the Fourteenth Amendment, which grants Congress the "power to enforce, by appropriate legislation, the provisions of this article," the Court concluded in the *Civil Rights Cases* that Congress did not have the power to pass the Civil Rights Act of 1875. The Court declared that Section 1 of the Fourteenth Amendment applies only to "state action" and that Section 5 only permits Congress to regulate "state action," not the behavior of private actors. The Court wrote that Congress could police "state laws and acts done under state authority." Did the defendants—innkeepers, theatre owners, railroad operators and the like—not operate their establishment "under state authority"? The Court could have found state action. As Professor Joseph Singer has noted, before the Civil War, the common law "probably required all businesses that held themselves out as open to the public to serve anyone who sought service." Joseph William Singer, *No Right to Exclude: Public Accommodations and Private Property*, 90 Northwestern L. Rev. 1283, 1292 (1996). The common law began to allow denials of service only when African Americans started to demand the right to access public accommodations. So, two questions arise: Should the court have limited Congress's Section 5 power to state action? Should the Court have found that the law did target actions taken under "state authority"? How would you construct a decision upholding the 1875 Act?

4.   *The   Thirteenth   Amendment.* The   Court   concluded   that   the Fourteenth Amendment did not grant Congress the power to enact the Civil Rights Act because that Amendment did not authorize Congress to adopt "direct and primary, as distinguished from corrective, legislation on the

subject in hand." But as the Court acknowledged, the Thirteenth Amendment does not contain any such limitations. Nevertheless, the Court argues that discrimination in public accommodations does not constitute a badge of slavery under the Thirteenth Amendment. Why? Professors Jack Balkin and Sanford Levinson argue that, "[t]he colonial vision that opposed slavery to republican liberty held that slavery meant more than simply being free from compulsion to labor by threats or physical coercion. Rather, the true marker of slavery was that slaves were always potentially subject to domination and to the arbitrary will of another person." *The Dangerous Thirteenth Amendment*, 112 Colum. L. Rev. 1459, 1484 (2012). How are the sorts of exclusions at issue in the *Civil Rights Cases* tantamount to "domination" or otherwise so egregious as to come within the purview of the Thirteenth Amendment? What do you make of Justice Harlan's argument that discrimination by common carriers, inns, and places of amusement constitutes a badge of servitude?

5. *Federalism and* **The Civil Rights Cases.** The Court found the statute unconstitutional in part because Congress had legislated on matters reserved to the states. The Court also pointed out that the Act applied indiscriminately to states, regardless of the extent to which they protected the rights of black citizens. Are these federalism arguments consistent with the essence of the Reconstruction Amendments, which made the federal government the guarantors of political equality for people of color? Is the Court's assumption that the states, particularly the states of the former Confederacy, would protect the rights of black citizens realistic? Should proof of state violations of section 1 of the Fourteenth Amendment have been required to justify congressional action? What would count as a state violation? What if states guaranteed rights, but then did not provide effective remedies? What if state law were silent as to the rights of blacks?

6. *The Aftermath of* **The Civil Rights Cases.** The effect of the Court's decision was mixed. Some states reacted by taking up the mantle of protection. "Within two years of the ruling, eleven state legislatures in the North and West passed civil rights statutes of their own, and by century's end a total of eighteen states had mandated racial equality in public accommodations." Sandoval-Strausz, *supra*, at 78. For the most part, the federal government did not attempt to protect citizens of color from racial discrimination in public accommodations in a robust way until 1964, when it passed Title II of the Civil Rights Act of 1964, relying on its power to regulate interstate commerce. The Interstate Commerce Act of 1887, which established the Interstate Commerce Commission, contained a promising provision, but it was interpreted so narrowly by the Court that it did not provide any relief to black citizens. Professor Sandoval-Strausz notes that, in the wake of the *Civil Rights Cases*, access to public accommodations by blacks in the South was uncertain and highly dependent on local custom and even the individual preferences of proprietors. By the beginning of the twentieth century, almost all Southern states had laws requiring segregation on common carriers, in public accommodations, and in other public spaces. The very state laws that mandated access for blacks thus became the basis of de jure segregation.

The post-Reconstruction retrenchment by the Court, Congress, and southern states limited the radical potential of the Reconstruction Amendments. But in the late nineteenth and early twentieth centuries, that status of blacks within the polity was complex, and the Court's treatment of the rights protected by the Fourteenth Amendment distinguished among the spheres into which its protections reached; whereas the Court applied the Fourteenth Amendment to the realms of political and civil rights, it did not extend the Amendment to the private and social spheres. In the cases that follow, the Court simultaneously offered a vigorous defense of the rights of freedmen and of the legal justifications for segregation and inequality.

Strauder v. West Virginia

Supreme Court of the United States, 1879.
100 U.S. 303.

■ MR. JUSTICE STRONG delivered the opinion of the court.

The plaintiff in error, a colored man, was indicted for murder in the Circuit Court of Ohio County, in West Virginia, on the 20th of October, 1874, and upon trial was convicted and sentenced. The record was then removed to the Supreme Court of the State, and there the judgment of the Circuit Court was affirmed. The present case is a writ of error to that court, and it is now, in substance, averred that at the trial in the State court the defendant (now plaintiff in error) was denied rights to which he was entitled under the Constitution and laws of the United States.

In the Circuit Court of the State, before the trial of the indictment was commenced, the defendant presented his petition, verified by his oath, praying for a removal of the cause into the Circuit Court of the United States, assigning, as ground for the removal, that 'by virtue of the laws of the State of West Virginia no colored man was eligible to be a member of the grand jury or to serve on a petit jury in the State; that white men are so eligible, and that by reason of his being a colored man and having been a slave, he had reason to believe, and did believe, he could not have the full and equal benefit of all laws and proceedings in the State of West Virginia for the security of his person as is enjoyed by white citizens, and that he had less chance of enforcing in the courts of the State his rights on the prosecution, as a citizen of the United States, and that the probabilities of a denial of them to him as such citizen on every trial which might take place on the indictment in the courts of the State were much more enhanced than if he was a white man.' This petition was denied by the State court, and the cause was forced to trial.

The law of the State to which reference was made in the petition for removal and in the several motions was enacted on the 12th of March, 1873 and it is as follows: 'All white male persons who are twenty-one years of age and who are citizens of this State shall be liable to serve as jurors, except as herein provided.' The persons excepted are State officials.

In this court, several errors have been assigned, and the controlling questions underlying them all are, first, whether, by the Constitution and laws of the United States, every citizen of the United States has a right to a trial of an indictment against him by a jury selected and impanelled without discrimination against his race or color, because of race or color; and, second, if he has such a right, and is denied its enjoyment by the State in which he is indicted, may he cause the case to be removed into the Circuit Court of the United States?

It is to be observed that the first of these questions is not whether a colored man, when an indictment has been preferred against him, has a right to a grand or a petit jury composed in whole or in part of persons of his own race or color, but it is whether, in the composition or selection of jurors by whom he is to be indicted or tried, all persons of his race or color may be excluded by law, solely because of their race or color, so that by no possibility can any colored man sit upon the jury.

The questions are important, for they demand a construction of the recent amendments of the Constitution. If the defendant has a right to have a jury selected for the trial of his case without discrimination against all persons of his race or color, because of their race or color, the right, if not created, is protected by those amendments, and the legislation of Congress under them. The Fourteenth Amendment ordains that 'all persons born or naturalized in the United States and subject to the jurisdiction thereof are citizens of the United States and of the State wherein they reside. No State shall make or enforce any laws which shall abridge the privileges or immunities of citizens of the United States, nor shall any State deprive any person of life, liberty, or property, without due process of law, nor deny to any person within its jurisdiction the equal protection of the laws.'

This is one of a series of constitutional provisions having a common purpose; namely, securing to a race recently emancipated, a race that through many generations had been held in slavery, all the civil rights that the superior race enjoy. The true spirit and meaning of the amendments, as we said in the *Slaughter-House Cases (16 Wall. 36)*, cannot be understood without keeping in view the history of the times when they were adopted, and the general objects they plainly sought to accomplish. At the time when they were incorporated into the Constitution, it required little knowledge of human nature to anticipate that those who had long been regarded as an inferior and subject race would, when suddenly raised to the rank of citizenship, be looked upon with jealousy and positive dislike, and that State laws might be enacted or enforced to perpetuate the distinctions that had before existed. Discriminations against them had been habitual. It was well known that in some States laws making such discriminations then existed, and others might well be expected. The colored race, as a race, was abject and ignorant, and in that condition was unfitted to command the respect of those who had superior intelligence. Their training had left them mere children, and as such they needed the protection which a wise government extends to those who are unable to protect themselves. They especially needed protection against unfriendly action in the States where they were resident. It was in view of these considerations the Fourteenth Amendment was framed and adopted. It was designed to assure to the colored race the enjoyment of all the civil rights that under the law are enjoyed by white persons, and to give to that race the protection of the general government, in that enjoyment, whenever it should be denied by the States. It not only gave citizenship and the privileges of citizenship to persons of color, but it denied to any State the power to withhold from them the equal protection of the laws, and authorized Congress to enforce its provisions by appropriate legislation. To quote the language used by us in the *Slaughter-House Cases*, 'No one can fail to be impressed with the one pervading purpose found in all the amendments, lying at the foundation of each, and without which none of them would have been suggested,—we mean the freedom of the slave race, the security and firm establishment of that freedom, and the protection of the newly made freeman and citizen from the oppressions of those who had formerly exercised unlimited dominion over them.' So again: 'The existence of laws in the States where the newly emancipated negroes resided, which discriminated with gross injustice and hardship against them as a class, was the evil to be remedied, and by it [the Fourteenth Amendment] such laws were forbidden. If, however, the States did not conform their laws to its requirements, then, by the fifth section of the article of amendment, Congress was authorized to enforce it by suitable legislation.' And it was added, 'We doubt very much whether any action of a State, not directed by way of discrimination against the negroes, as a class, will ever be held to come within the purview of this provision.'

If this is the spirit and meaning of the amendment, whether it means more or not, it is to be construed liberally, to carry out the purposes of its framers. It ordains that no State shall make or enforce any laws which shall abridge the privileges or immunities of citizens of the United States (evidently referring to the newly made citizens, who, being citizens of the United States, are declared to be also citizens of the State in which they reside). It ordains that no State shall deprive any person of life, liberty, or property, without due process of law, or deny to any person within its jurisdiction the equal protection of the laws. What is this but declaring that the law in the States shall be the same for the black as for the white; that all persons, whether colored or white, shall stand equal before the laws of the States, and, in regard to the colored race, for whose protection the amendment was primarily designed, that no discrimination shall be made against them by law because of their color? The words of the

Positive immunity or right

amendment, it is true, are prohibitory, but they contain a necessary implication of a positive immunity, or right, most valuable to the colored race,—the right to exemption from unfriendly legislation against them distinctively as colored,—exemption from legal discriminations, implying inferiority in civil society, lessening the security of their enjoyment of the rights which others enjoy, and discriminations which are steps towards reducing them to the condition of a subject race.

That the West Virginia statute respecting juries—the statute that controlled the selection of the grand and petit jury in the case of the plaintiff in error—is such a discrimination ought not to be doubted. Nor would it be if the persons excluded by it were white men. If in those States where the colored people constitute a majority of the entire population a law should be enacted excluding all white men from jury service, thus denying to them the privilege of participating equally with the blacks in the administration of justice, we apprehend no one would be heard to claim that it would not be a denial to white men of the equal protection of the laws. Nor if a law should be passed excluding all naturalized Celtic Irishmen, would there by any doubt of its inconsistency with the spirit of the amendment. The very fact that colored people are singled out and expressly denied by a statute all right to participate in the administration of the law, as jurors, because of their color, though they are citizens, and may be in other respects fully qualified, is practically a brand upon them, affixed by the law, an assertion of their inferiority, and a stimulant to that race prejudice which is an impediment to securing to individuals of the race that equal justice which the law aims to secure to all others.

The right to a trial by jury is guaranteed to every citizen of West Virginia by the Constitution of that State, and the constitution of juries is a very essential part of the protection such a mode of trial is intended to secure. The very idea of a jury is a body of men composed of the peers or equals of the person whose rights it is selected or summoned to determine; that is, of his neighbors, fellows, associates, persons having the same legal status in society as that which he holds. Blackstone, in his Commentaries, says, 'The right of trial by jury, or the country, is a trial by the peers of every Englishman, and is the grand bulwark of his liberties, and is secured to him by the Great Charter.' It is also guarded by statutory enactments intended to make impossible what Mr. Bentham called 'packing juries.' It is well known that prejudices often exist against particular classes in the community, which sway the judgment of jurors, and which, therefore, operate in some cases to deny to persons of those classes the full enjoyment of that protection which others enjoy. Prejudice in a local community is held to be a reason for a change of venue. The framers of the constitutional amendment must have known full well the existence of such prejudice and its likelihood to continue against the manumitted slaves and their race, and that knowledge was doubtless a motive that led to the amendment. By their manumission and citizenship the colored race became entitled to the equal protection of the laws of the States in which they resided; and the apprehension that through prejudice they might be denied that equal protection, that is, that there might be discrimination against them, was the inducement to bestow upon the national government the power to enforce the provision that no State shall deny to them the equal protection of the laws. Without the apprehended existence of prejudice that portion of the amendment would have been unnecessary, and it might have been left to the States to extend equality of protection.

In view of these considerations, it is hard to see why the statute of West Virginia should not be regarded as discriminating against a colored man when he is put upon trial for an alleged criminal offence against the State. It is not easy to comprehend how it can be said that while every white man is entitled to a trial by a jury selected from persons of his own race or color, or, rather, selected without discrimination against his color, and a negro is not, the latter is equally protected by the law with the former. Is not protection of life and liberty against race or color prejudice, a right, a legal right, under the constitutional amendment? And how can it be maintained that compelling a colored man to submit to a trial for his life by a jury drawn from a panel from which the State has expressly excluded every man of his race, because of color alone, however well qualified in other respects, is not a denial to him of equal legal protection?

We do not say that within the limits from which it is not excluded by the amendment a State may not prescribe the qualifications of its jurors, and in so doing make discriminations. It may confine the selection to males, to freeholders, to citizens, to persons within certain ages, or to persons having educational qualifications. We do not believe the Fourteenth Amendment was ever intended to prohibit this. Looking at its history, it is clear it had no such purpose. Its aim was against discrimination because of race or color. As we have said more than once, its design was to protect an emancipated race, and to strike down all possible legal discriminations against those who belong to it. To quote further from 16 Wall., *supra:* 'In giving construction to any of these articles [amendments], it is necessary to keep the main purpose steadily in view.' 'It is so clearly a provision for that race and that emergency, that a strong case would be necessary for its application to any other.' We are not now called upon to affirm or deny that it had other purposes.

The Fourteenth Amendment makes no attempt to enumerate the rights it designed to protect. It speaks in general terms, and those are as comprehensive as possible. Its language is prohibitory; but every prohibition implies the existence of rights and immunities, prominent among which is an immunity from inequality of legal protection, either for life, liberty, or property. Any State action that denies this immunity to a colored man is in conflict with the Constitution.

Concluding, therefore, that the statute of West Virginia, discriminating in the selection of jurors, as it does, against negroes because of their color, amounts to a denial of the equal protection of the laws to a colored man when he is put upon trial for an alleged offence against the State, it remains only to be considered whether the power of Congress to enforce the provisions of the Fourteenth Amendment by appropriate legislation is sufficient to justify the enactment of sect. 641 of the Revised Statutes.

A right or an immunity, whether created by the Constitution or only guaranteed by it, even without any express delegation of power, may be protected by Congress. Prigg v. The Commonwealth of Pennsylvania, 16 Pet. 539. So in *United States* v. *Reese* (92 (U. S. 214), it was said by the Chief Justice of this court: 'Rights and immunities created by or dependent upon the Constitution of the United States can be protected by Congress. The form and manner of the protection may be such as Congress in the legitimate exercise of its legislative discretion shall provide. These may be varied to meet the necessities of the particular right to be protected.' But there is express authority to protect the rights and immunities referred to in the Fourteenth Amendment, and to enforce observance of them by appropriate congressional legislation. And one very efficient and appropriate mode of extending such protection and securing to a party the enjoyment of the right or immunity, is a law providing for the removal of his case from a State court, in which the right is denied by the State law, into a Federal court, where it will be upheld. This is an ordinary mode of protecting rights and immunities conferred by the Federal Constitution and laws. Sect. 641 is such a provision. It enacts that 'when any civil suit or criminal prosecution is commenced in any State court for any cause whatsoever against any person who is denied, or cannot enforce, in the judicial tribunals of the State, or in the part of the State where such prosecution is pending, any right secured to him by any law providing for the equal civil rights of citizens of the United States, or of all persons within the jurisdiction of the United States, such suit or prosecution may, upon the petition of such defendant, filed in said State court at any time before the trial, or final hearing of the case, stating the facts, and verified by oath, be removed before trial into the next Circuit Court of the United States to be held in the district where it is pending.'

This act plainly has reference to sects. 1977 and 1978 of the statutes which partially enumerate the rights and immunities intended to be guaranteed by the Constitution, the first of which declares that 'all persons within the jurisdiction of the United States shall have the same right in every State and Territory to make and enforce contracts, to sue, be parties, give evidence, and to the full and equal benefit of all laws and proceedings for the security of persons and property, as is enjoyed by white citizens, and shall be subject to like punishment, pains, penalties, taxes, licenses, and exactions of every kind, and to no other.' This act puts in the form of a statute what had been substantially ordained by the constitutional amendment. It was a step towards enforcing the constitutional provisions. Sect. 641 was an advanced step, fully warranted, we think, by the fifth section of the Fourteenth Amendment.

We have heretofore considered and affirmed the constitutional power of Congress to authorize the removal from State courts into the circuit courts of the United States, before trial, of criminal prosecutions for alleged offences against the laws of the State, when the defence presents a Federal question, or when a right under the Federal Constitution or laws is involved.

That the petition of the plaintiff in error, filed by him in the State court before the trial of his case, made a case for removal into the Federal Circuit Court, under sect. 641, is very plain, if, by the constitutional amendment and sect. 1977 of the Revised Statutes, he was entitled to immunity from discrimination against him in the selection of jurors, because of their color, as we have endeavored to show that he was. It set forth sufficient facts to exhibit a denial of that immunity, and a denial by the statute law of the State.

There was error, therefore, in proceeding to the trial of the indictment against him after his petition was filed. The judgment of the Supreme Court of West Virginia will be reversed.

NOTES AND QUESTIONS

1. ***Conceptions of Equal Protection.*** How exactly did the West Virginia statute violate equal protection? Consider some possibilities. (A) The statute denied to black citizens the right to perform their civic duty by serving on juries, a right that is available to white citizens. (B) The statute denied to all defendants the right to have a jury process unaffected by race. (C) The statute denied to black defendants the right to have a jury process that is unaffected by racial discrimination in jury selection. (D) The statute denied to black defendants the right to a fair criminal procedure because white jurors are unlikely to give black defendants a fair hearing. (E) The statute communicates an expressive and unconstitutional message that blacks are not full citizens. (F) The statute contains an express racial classification on its face. (G) The statute contains an express racial classification on its face and singles out black citizens for disfavored treatment. Which of the above possibilities best represents the Court's understanding of the constitutional violation in *Strauder*?

2. ***Universality Versus Particularity.*** How does the Court characterize the purposes of the Fourteenth Amendment? On the one hand, the Court states that the Fourteenth Amendment "was primarily designed" to protect black citizens. On the other hand, the Court notes that, "the spirit of the amendment" would be violated by a statute that excluded "all naturalized Celtic Irishmen" from jury service. How should we understand the purpose of the Fourteenth Amendment and should that understanding matter today when interpreting its reach?

3. ***Reconciling*** **Strauder** ***with the*** **Civil Rights Cases.** Is *Strauder* consistent with the *Civil Rights Cases*? Which of these factors most helps to justify the Court's ruling in *Strauder*, given the precedent of the Civil Rights cases: the distinction between federal and state law, the type of rights at issue, or the distinction between affirmative and negative rights?

4. ***White Supremacy.*** What do you make of the Court's characterization of blacks as "abject and ignorant" and as "mere children" who were "unfitted to command the respect of those who had superior intelligence"? What work, if any, do these views do in the opinion? Should we dismiss these views as the product of the times? Are they harmless in light of the fact that the Court reached the "right" result? Consider these questions as you read *Plessy v. Ferguson* below.

Plessy v. Ferguson

Supreme Court of the United States, 1896.
163 U.S. 537.

■ MR. JUSTICE BROWN, delivered the opinion of the court.

This case turns upon the constitutionality of an act of the general assembly of the state of Louisiana, passed in 1890, providing for separate railway carriages for the white and colored races.

The first section of the statute enacts 'that all railway companies carrying passengers in their coaches in this state, shall provide equal but separate accommodations for the white, and colored races, by providing two or more passenger coaches for each passenger train, or by dividing the passenger coaches by a partition so as to secure separate accommodations: provided, that this section shall not be construed to apply to street railroads. No person or persons shall be permitted to occupy seats in coaches, other than the ones assigned to them, on account of the race they belong to.'

The information filed in the criminal district court charged, in substance, that Plessy, being a passenger between two stations within the state of Louisiana, was assigned by officers of the company to the coach used for the race to which he belonged, but he insisted upon going into a coach used by the race to which he did not belong. Neither in the information nor plea was his particular race or color averred.

The petition for the writ of prohibition averred that petitioner was seven-eighths Caucasian and one-eighth African blood; that the mixture of colored blood was not discernible in him; and that he was entitled to every right, privilege, and immunity secured to citizens of the United States of the white race; and that, upon such theory, he took possession of a vacant seat in a coach where passengers of the white race were accommodated, and was ordered by the conductor to vacate said coach, and take a seat in another, assigned to persons of the colored race, and, having refused to comply with such demand, he was forcibly ejected, with the aid of a police officer, and imprisoned in the parish jail to answer a charge of having violated the above act.

The constitutionality of this act is attacked upon the ground that it conflicts both with the thirteenth amendment of the constitution, abolishing slavery, and the fourteenth amendment, which prohibits certain restrictive legislation on the part of the states.

1.   That it does not conflict with the thirteenth amendment, which abolished slavery and involuntary servitude, except as a punishment for crime, is too clear for argument. Slavery implies involuntary servitude,—a state of bondage; the ownership of mankind as a chattel, or, at least, the control of the labor and services of one man for the benefit of another, and the absence of a legal right to the disposal of his own person, property, and services. This amendment was said in the *Slaughter-House Cases,* 16 Wall. 36, to have been intended primarily to abolish slavery, as it had been previously known in this country, and that it equally forbade Mexican peonage or the Chinese coolie trade, when they amounted to slavery or involuntary servitude, and that the use of the word 'servitude' was intended to prohibit the use of all forms of involuntary slavery, of whatever class or name. It was intimated, however, in that case, that this amendment was regarded by the statesmen of that day as insufficient to protect the colored race from certain laws which had been enacted in the Southern states, imposing upon the colored race onerous disabilities and burdens, and curtailing their rights in the pursuit of life, liberty, and property to such an extent that their freedom was of little value; and that the fourteenth amendment was devised to meet this exigency.

So, too, in the *Civil Rights Cases,* 109 U. S. 3, it was said that the act of a mere individual, the owner of an inn, a public conveyance or place of amusement, refusing accommodations to colored people, cannot be justly regarded as imposing any badge of slavery or servitude upon the applicant, but only as involving an ordinary civil injury, properly cognizable by the laws of the state, and presumably subject to redress by those laws until the contrary appears. 'It would be running the slavery question into the ground,' said Mr. Justice Bradley, 'to make it apply to every act of discrimination which a person may see fit to make as to the guests he will entertain, or as to the people he will take into his coach or cab or car, or admit to his concert or theater, or deal with in other matters of intercourse or business.'

A statute which implies merely a legal distinction between the white and colored races—a distinction which is founded in the color of the two races, and which must always exist so long as white men are distinguished from the other race by color—has no tendency to destroy the legal equality of the two races, or re-establish a state of involuntary servitude. Indeed, we do not understand that the thirteenth amendment is strenuously relied upon by the plaintiff in error in this connection.

2.   By the fourteenth amendment, all persons born or naturalized in the United States, and subject to the jurisdiction thereof, are made citizens of the United States and of the state wherein they reside; and the states are forbidden from making or enforcing any law which shall abridge the privileges or immunities of citizens of the United States, or shall deprive any person of life, liberty, or property without due process of law, or deny to any person within their jurisdiction the equal protection of the laws.

The proper construction of this amendment was first called to the attention of this court in the *Slaughter-House Cases,* 16 Wall. 36, which involved, however, not a question of race, but one of exclusive privileges. The case did not call for any expression of opinion as to the exact rights it was intended to secure to the colored race, but it was said generally that its main purpose was to establish the citizenship of the negro, to give definitions of citizenship of the United States and of the states, and to protect from the hostile legislation of the states the privileges and immunities of citizens of the United States, as distinguished from those of citizens of the states.

The object of the amendment was undoubtedly to enforce the absolute equality of the two races before the law, but, in the nature of things, it could not have been intended to abolish distinctions based upon color, or to enforce social, as distinguished from political, equality, or a commingling of the two races upon terms unsatisfactory to either. Laws permitting, and even requiring, their separation, in places where they are liable to be brought into contact, do not necessarily imply the inferiority of either race to the other, and have been generally, if not universally, recognized as within the competency of the state legislatures in the exercise of their police power. The most common instance of this is connected with the establishment of separate schools for white and colored children, which have been held to be a valid exercise of the legislative power even by courts of states where the political rights of the colored race have been longest and most earnestly enforced.

One of the earliest of these cases is that of *Roberts v. City of Boston,* 5 Cush. 198, in which the supreme judicial court of Massachusetts held that the general school committee of Boston had power to make provision for the instruction of colored children in separate schools established exclusively for them, and to prohibit their attendance upon the other schools. 'The great principle,' said Chief Justice Shaw, 'advanced by the learned and eloquent advocate for the plaintiff [Mr. Charles Sumner], is that, by the constitution and laws of Massachusetts, all persons, without distinction of age or sex, birth or color, origin or condition, are equal before the law. * * * But, when this great principle comes to be applied to the actual and various conditions of persons in society, it will not warrant the assertion that men and women are legally clothed with the same civil and political powers, and that children and adults are legally to have the same functions and be subject to the same treatment; but only that the rights of all, as they are settled and regulated by law, are equally entitled to the paternal consideration and protection of the law for their maintenance and security.' It was held that the powers of the committee extended to the establishment of separate schools for children of different ages, sexes and colors, and that they might also establish special schools for poor and neglected children, who have become too old to attend the primary school, and yet have not acquired the rudiments of learning, to enable them to enter the ordinary schools. Similar laws have been enacted by congress under its general power of legislation over the District of Columbia (sections 281–283, 310, 319, Rev. St. D. C.), as well as by the legislatures of many of the states, and have been generally, if not uniformly, sustained by the courts.

Laws forbidding the intermarriage of the two races may be said in a technical sense to interfere with the freedom of contract, and yet have been universally recognized as within the police power of the state.

The distinction between laws interfering with the political equality of the negro and those requiring the separation of the two races in schools, theaters, and railway carriages has been frequently drawn by this court. Thus, in *Strauder v. West Virginia,* 100 U.S. 303, it was held that a law of West Virginia limiting to white male persons 21 years of age, and citizens of the state, the right to sit upon juries, was a discrimination which implied a legal inferiority in civil society, which lessened the security of the right of the colored race, and was a step towards reducing them to a condition of servility.

It is claimed by the plaintiff in error that, in any mixed community, the reputation of belonging to the dominant race, in this instance the white race, is 'property,' in the same sense that a right of action or of inheritance is property. Conceding this to be so, for the purposes of this case, we are unable to see how this statute deprives him of, or in any way affects his right to, such property. If he be a white man, and assigned to a colored coach, he may have his action for damages against the company for being deprived of his so-called 'property.' Upon the other hand, if he be a colored man, and be so assigned, he has been deprived of no property, since he is not lawfully entitled to the reputation of being a white man.

In this connection, it is also suggested by the learned counsel for the plaintiff in error that the same argument that will justify the state legislature in requiring railways to provide separate accommodations for the two races will also authorize them to require separate cars to be provided for people whose hair is of a certain color, or who are aliens, or who belong to certain nationalities, or to enact laws requiring colored people to walk upon one side of the street, and white people upon the other, or requiring white men's houses to be painted white, and colored men's black, or their vehicles or business signs to be of different colors, upon the theory that one side of the street is as good as the other, or that a house or vehicle of one color is as good as one of another color. The reply to all this is that every exercise of the police power must be reasonable, and extend only to such laws as are enacted in good faith for the promotion of the public good, and not for the annoyance or oppression of a particular class. Thus, in *Yick Wo v. Hopkins,* 118 U. S. 356, it was held by this court that a municipal ordinance of the city of San Francisco, to regulate the carrying on of public laundries within the limits of the municipality, violated the provisions of the constitution of the United States, if it conferred upon the municipal authorities arbitrary power, at their own will, and without regard to discretion, in the legal sense of the term, to give or withhold consent as to persons or places, without regard to the competency of the persons applying or the propriety of the places selected for the carrying on of the business. It was held to be a covert attempt on the part of the municipality to make an arbitrary and unjust discrimination against the Chinese race. While this was the case of a municipal ordinance, a like principle has been held to apply to acts of a state legislature passed in the exercise of the police power.

So far, then, as a conflict with the fourteenth amendment is concerned, the case reduces itself to the question whether the statute of Louisiana is a reasonable regulation, and with respect to this there must necessarily be a large discretion on the part of the legislature. In determining the question of reasonableness, it is at liberty to act with reference to the established usages, customs, and traditions of the people, and with a view to the promotion of their comfort, and the preservation of the public peace and good order. Gauged by this standard, we cannot say that a law which authorizes or even requires the separation of the two races in public conveyances is unreasonable, or more obnoxious to the fourteenth amendment than the acts of congress requiring separate schools for colored children in the District of Columbia, the constitutionality of which does not seem to have been questioned, or the corresponding acts of state legislatures.

We consider the underlying fallacy of the plaintiff's argument to consist in the assumption that the enforced separation of the two races stamps the colored race with a badge of inferiority. If this be so, it is not by reason of anything found in the act, but solely because the colored race chooses to put that construction upon it. The argument necessarily assumes that if, as has been more than once the case, and is not unlikely to be so again, the colored race should become the dominant power in the state legislature, and should enact a law in precisely similar terms, it would thereby relegate the white race to an inferior position. We imagine that the white race, at least, would not acquiesce in this assumption. The argument also assumes that social prejudices may be overcome by legislation, and that equal rights cannot be secured to the negro except by an enforced commingling of the two races. We cannot accept this proposition. If the two races are to meet upon terms of social equality, it must be the result of natural affinities, a mutual appreciation of each other's merits, and a voluntary consent of individuals. As was said by the court of appeals of New York in *People v. Gallagher,* 93 N. Y. 438, 448: 'This end can neither be accomplished nor promoted by laws which conflict with the general sentiment of the community upon whom they are designed to operate. When the government, therefore, has secured to each of its citizens equal rights before the law, and equal opportunities for improvement and progress, it has accomplished the end for which it was organized, and performed all of the functions respecting social advantages with which it is endowed.' Legislation is powerless to eradicate racial instincts, or to abolish distinctions based upon physical differences, and the attempt to do so can only result in accentuating the difficulties of the present situation. If the civil and political rights of both races be equal, one cannot be inferior to the other civilly or politically. If one race be inferior to the other socially, the constitution of the United States cannot put them upon the same plane.

It is true that the question of the proportion of colored blood necessary to constitute a colored person, as distinguished from a white person, is one upon which there is a difference of opinion in the different states; some holding that any visible admixture of black blood stamps the person as belonging to the colored race; others, that it depends upon the preponderance of blood; and still others, that the predominance of white blood must only be in the proportion of three-fourths. But these are questions to be determined under the laws of each state, and are not properly put in issue in this case. Under the allegations of his petition, it may undoubtedly become a question of importance whether, under the laws of Louisiana, the petitioner belongs to the white or colored race.

■ MR. JUSTICE BREWER did not hear the argument or participate in the decision of this case.

■ MR. JUSTICE HARLAN dissenting.

By the Louisiana statute the validity of which is here involved, all railway companies (other than street-railroad companies) carry passengers in that state are required to have separate but equal accommodations for white and colored persons, 'by providing two or more passenger coaches for each passenger train, or by dividing the passenger coaches by a partition so as to secure separate accommodations.'

Only 'nurses attending children of the other race' are excepted from the operation of the statute. No exception is made of colored attendants traveling with adults. A white man is not permitted to have his colored servant with him in the same coach, even if his condition of health requires the constant personal assistance of such servant. If a colored maid insists upon riding in the same coach with a white woman whom she has been employed to serve, and who may need her personal attention while traveling, she is subject to be fined or imprisoned for such an exhibition of zeal in the discharge of duty.

However apparent the injustice of such legislation may be, we have only to consider whether it is consistent with the constitution of the United States.

That a railroad is a public highway, and that the corporation which owns or operates it is in the exercise of public functions, is not, at this day, to be disputed. Mr. Justice Strong, delivering the judgment of this court in *Olcott v. Supervisors,* 16 Wall. 678, 694, said: 'That railroads, though constructed by private corporations, and owned by them, are public highways, has been the doctrine of nearly all the courts ever since such conveniences for passage and transportation have had any existence. So, in *Township of Pine Grove v. Talcott,* 19 Wall. 666, 676: 'Though the corporation [a railroad company] was private, its work was public, as much so as if it were to be constructed by the state.' So, in Inhabitants of *Worcester v. Western R. Corp.*, 4 Metc. (Mass.) 564: 'The establishment of that great thoroughfare is regarded as a public work, established by public authority, intended for the public use and benefit, the use of which is secured to the whole community, and constitutes, therefore, like a canal, turnpike, or highway, a public easement.' 'It is true that the real and personal property, necessary to the establishment and management of the railroad, is vested in the corporation; but it is in trust for the public.'

In respect of civil rights, common to all citizens, the constitution of the United States does not, I think, permit any public authority to know the race of those entitled to be protected in the enjoyment of such rights. Every true man has pride of race, and under appropriate circumstances, when the rights of others, his equals before the law, are not to be affected, it is his privilege to express such pride and to take such action based upon it as to him seems proper. But I deny that any legislative body or judicial tribunal may have regard to the race of citizens when the civil rights of those citizens are involved. Indeed, such legislation as that here in question is inconsistent not only with that equality of rights which pertains to citizenship, national and state, but with the personal liberty enjoyed by every one within the United States.

The thirteenth amendment does not permit the withholding or the deprivation of any right necessarily inhering in freedom. It not only struck down the institution of slavery as previously existing in the United States, but it prevents the imposition of any burdens or disabilities that constitute badges of slavery or servitude. It decreed universal civil freedom in this country. This court has so adjudged. But, that amendment having been found inadequate to the protection of the rights of those who had been in slavery, it was followed by the fourteenth amendment, which added greatly to the dignity and glory of American citizenship, and to the security of personal liberty, by declaring that 'all persons born or naturalized in the United States, and subject to the jurisdiction thereof, are citizens of the United States and of the state wherein they reside,' and that 'no state shall make or enforce any law which shall abridge the privileges or immunities of citizens of the United States; nor shall any state deprive any person of life, liberty or property without due process of law, nor deny to any person within its jurisdiction the equal protection of the laws.' These two amendments, if enforced according to their true intent and meaning, will protect all the civil rights that pertain to freedom and citizenship. Finally, and to the end that no citizen should be denied, on account of his race, the privilege of participating in the political control of his country, it was declared by the fifteenth amendment that 'the right of citizens of the United States to vote shall not be denied or abridged by the United States or by any state on account of race, color or previous condition of servitude.'

These notable additions to the fundamental law were welcomed by the friends of liberty throughout the world. They removed the race line from our governmental systems. They had, as this court has said, a common purpose, namely, to secure 'to a race recently emancipated, a race that through many generations have been held in slavery, all the civil rights that the superior race enjoy.' They declared, in legal effect, this court has further said, 'that the law in the states shall be the same for the black as for the white; that all persons, whether colored or white, shall stand equal before the laws of the states; and in regard to the colored race, for whose protection the amendment was primarily designed, that no discrimination shall be made against them by law because of their color.' We also said: 'The words of the amendment, it is true, are prohibitory, but they contain a necessary implication of a positive immunity or right, most valuable to the colored race,—the right to exemption from unfriendly legislation against them distinctively as colored; exemption from legal discriminations, implying inferiority in civil society, lessening the security of their enjoyment of the rights which others enjoy; and discriminations which are steps towards reducing them to the condition of a subject race.' It was, consequently, adjudged that a state law that excluded citizens of the colored race from juries, because of their race, however well qualified in other respects to discharge the duties of jurymen, was repugnant to the fourteenth amendment. At the present term, referring to the previous adjudications, this court declared that 'underlying all of those decisions is the principle that the constitution of the United States, in its present form, forbids, so far as civil and political rights are concerned, discrimination by the general government or the states against any citizen because of his race. All citizens are equal before the law.' *Gibson v. State,* 162 U. S. 565, 16 Sup. Ct. 904.

It was said in argument that the statute of Louisiana does not discriminate against either race, but prescribes a rule applicable alike to white and colored citizens. But this argument does not meet the difficulty. Every one knows that the statute in question had its origin in the purpose, not so much to exclude white persons from railroad cars occupied by blacks, as to exclude colored people from coaches occupied by or assigned to white persons. Railroad corporations of Louisiana did not make discrimination among whites in the matter of accommodation for travelers. The thing to accomplish was, under the guise of giving equal accommodation for whites and blacks, to compel the latter to keep to themselves while traveling in railroad passenger coaches. No one would be so wanting in candor as to assert the contrary. The fundamental objection, therefore, to the statute, is that it interferes with the personal freedom of citizens. 'Personal liberty,' it has been well said, 'consists in the power of locomotion, of changing situation, or removing one's person to whatsoever places one's own inclination may direct, without imprisonment or restraint, unless by due course of law.' If a white man and a black man choose to occupy the same public conveyance on a public highway, it is their right to do so; and no government, proceeding alone on grounds of race, can prevent it without infringing the personal liberty of each.

It is one thing for railroad carriers to furnish, or to be required by law to furnish, equal accommodations for all whom they are under a legal duty to carry. It is quite another thing for government to forbid citizens of the white and black races from traveling in the same public conveyance, and to punish officers of railroad companies for permitting persons of the two races to occupy the same passenger coach. If a state can prescribe, as a rule of civil conduct, that whites and blacks shall not travel as passengers in the same railroad coach, why may it not so regulate the use of the streets of its cities and towns as to compel white citizens to keep on one side of a street, and black citizens to keep on the other? Why may it not, upon like grounds, punish whites and blacks who ride together in street cars or in open vehicles on a public road *558 or street? Why may it not require sheriffs to assign whites to one side of a court room, and blacks to the other? And why may it not also prohibit the commingling of the two races in the galleries of legislative halls or in public assemblages convened for the consideration of the political questions of the day? Further, if this statute of Louisiana is consistent with the personal liberty of citizens, why may not the state require the separation in railroad coaches of native and naturalized citizens of the United States, or of Protestants and Roman Catholics?

The white race deems itself to be the dominant race in this country. And so it is, in prestige, in achievements, in education, in wealth, and in power. So, I doubt not, it will continue to be for all time, if it remains true to its great heritage, and holds fast to the principles of constitutional liberty. But in view of the constitution, in the eye of the law, there is in this country no superior, dominant, ruling class of citizens. There is no caste here. Our constitution is color-blind, and neither knows nor tolerates classes among citizens. In respect of civil rights, all citizens are equal before the law. The humblest is the peer of the most powerful. The law regards man as man, and takes no account of his surroundings or of his color when his civil rights as guaranteed by the supreme law of the land are involved. It is therefore to be regretted that this high tribunal, the final expositor of the fundamental law of the land, has reached the conclusion that it is competent for a state to regulate the enjoyment by citizens of their civil rights solely upon the basis of race.

In my opinion, the judgment this day rendered will, in time, prove to be quite as pernicious as the decision made by this tribunal in the Dred Scott Case.

It was adjudged in that case that the descendants of Africans who were imported into this country, and sold as slaves, were not included nor intended to be included under the word 'citizens' in the constitution, and could not claim any of the rights and privileges which that instrument provided for and secured to citizens of the United States; that, at time of the adoption of the constitution, they were 'considered as a subordinate and inferior class of beings, who had been subjugated by the dominant race, and, whether emancipated or not, yet remained subject to their authority, and had no rights or privileges but such as those who held the power and the government might choose to grant them.' 19 How. 393, 404. The recent amendments of the constitution, it was supposed, had eradicated these principles from our institutions. But it seems that we have yet, in some of the states, a dominant race,—a superior class of citizens,—which assumes to regulate the enjoyment of civil rights, common to all citizens, upon the basis of race. The present decision, it may well be apprehended, will not only stimulate aggressions, more or less brutal and irritating, upon the admitted rights of colored citizens, but will encourage the belief that it is possible, by means of state enactments, to defeat the beneficent purposes which the people of the United States had in view when they adopted the recent amendments of the constitution, by one of which the blacks of this country were made citizens of the United States and of the states in which they respectively reside, and whose privileges and immunities, as citizens, the states are forbidden to abridge. Sixty millions of whites are in no danger from the presence here of eight millions of blacks. The destinies of the two races, in this country, are indissolubly linked together, and the interests of both require that the common government of all shall not permit the seeds of race hate to be planted under the sanction of law. What can more certainly arouse race hate, what more certainly create and perpetuate a feeling of distrust between these races, than state enactments which, in fact, proceed on the ground that colored citizens are so inferior and degraded that they cannot be allowed to sit in public coaches occupied by white citizens? That, as all will admit, is the real meaning of such legislation as was enacted in Louisiana.

There is a race so different from our own that we do not permit those belonging to it to become citizens of the United States. Persons belonging to it are, with few exceptions, absolutely excluded from our country. I allude to the Chinese race. But, by the statute in question, a Chinaman can ride in the same passenger coach with white citizens of the United States, while citizens of the black race in Louisiana, many of whom, perhaps, risked their lives for the preservation of the Union, who are entitled, by law, to participate in the political control of the state and nation, who are not excluded, by law or by reason of their race, from public stations of any kind, and who have all the legal rights that belong to white citizens, are yet declared to be criminals, liable to imprisonment, if they ride in a public coach occupied by citizens of the white race. It is scarcely just to say that a colored citizen should not object to occupying a public coach assigned to his own race. He does not object, nor, perhaps, would he object to separate coaches for his race if his rights under the law were recognized. But he does object, and he ought never to cease objecting, that citizens of the white and black races can be adjudged criminals because they sit, or claim the right to sit, in the same public coach on a public highway.

The arbitrary separation of citizens, on the basis of race, while they are on a public highway, is a badge of servitude wholly inconsistent with the civil freedom and the equality before the law established by the constitution. It cannot be justified upon any legal grounds.

The result of the whole matter is that while this court has frequently adjudged, and at the present term has recognized the doctrine, that a state cannot, consistently with the constitution of the United States, prevent white and black citizens, having the required qualifications for jury service, from sitting in the same jury box, it is now solemnly held that a state may prohibit white and black citizens from sitting in the same passenger coach on a public highway, or may require that they be separated by a 'partition' when in the same passenger coach. May it not now be reasonably expected that astute men of the dominant race, who affect to be disturbed at the possibility that the integrity of the white race may be corrupted, or that its supremacy will be imperiled, by contact on public highways with black people, will endeavor to procure statutes requiring white and black jurors to be separated in the jury box by a 'partition,' and that, upon retiring from the court room to consult as to their verdict, such partition, if it be a movable one, shall be taken to their consultation room, and set up in such way as to prevent black jurors from coming too close to their brother jurors of the white race. If the 'partition' used in the court room happens to be stationary, provision could be made for screens with openings through which jurors of the two races could confer as to their verdict without coming into personal contact with each other. I cannot see but that, according to the principles this day announced, such state legislation, although conceived in hostility to, and enacted for the purpose of humiliating, citizens of the United States of a particular race, would be held to be consistent with the constitution.

I do not deem it necessary to review the decisions of state courts to which reference was made in argument. Some, and the most important, of them, are wholly inapplicable, because rendered prior to the adoption of the last amendments of the constitution, when colored people had very few rights which the dominant race felt obliged to respect. Others were made at a time when public opinion, in many localities, was dominated by the institution of slavery; when it would not have been safe to do justice to the black man; and when, so far as the rights of blacks were concerned, race prejudice was, practically, the supreme law of the land. Those decisions cannot be guides in the era introduced by the recent amendments of the supreme law, which established universal civil freedom, gave citizenship to all born or naturalized in the United States, and residing here, obliterated the race line from our systems of governments, national and state, and placed our free institutions upon the broad and sure foundation of the equality of all men before the law.

I am of opinion that the state of Louisiana is inconsistent with the personal liberty of citizens, white and black, in that state, and hostile to both the spirit and letter of the constitution of the United States. If laws of like character should be enacted in the several states of the Union, the effect would be in the highest degree mischievous. Slavery, as an institution tolerated by law, would, it is true, have disappeared from our country; but there would remain a power in the states, by sinister legislation, to interfere with the full enjoyment of the blessings of freedom, to regulate civil rights, common to all citizens, upon the basis of race, and to place in a condition of legal inferiority a large body of American citizens, now constituting a part of the political community, called the 'People of the United States,' for whom, and by whom through representatives, our government is administered. Such a system is inconsistent with the guaranty given by the constitution to each state of a republican form of government, and may be stricken down by congressional action, or by the courts in the discharge of their solemn duty to maintain the supreme law of the land, anything in the constitution or laws of any state to the contrary notwithstanding.

NOTES AND QUESTIONS

1. *Equality.* What is the most persuasive basis for Plessy's challenge to the law that forbade him from sitting in a railcar assigned to whites: a denial of equality, liberty, or property? The case is best known for its holding that Plessy was not denied equality. In what way was Plessy denied equality? Consider some possibilities:

One argument is that the railcars were unequal. This was true to some extent. The so-called colored passengers were assigned to the cars that were closer to the engine and therefore more exposed to smoke and soot. Was the Court's error in failing to acknowledge the unequal quality of the railcars? If the railcars were truly identical, would Plessy have no basis to complain?

Why might Plessy have declined to argue that the railroad cars were, in fact, unequal?

Another argument on Plessy's behalf is that, even if the cars were equal, the state's motivation was premised on a belief in black inferiority. Justice Harlan characterizes the segregation law as rooted in the view "that colored citizens are so inferior and degraded that they cannot be allowed to sit in public coaches occupied by white citizens." How could the majority convince itself otherwise? In other words, it seems obvious to us that, while the law at issue was formally equal in that it prohibited whites from sitting with blacks and vice versa, but the legislature that passed the law was clearly attempting to keep blacks away from whites. Professor Jamal Greene points out that the court in *Plessy* may simply have been following a strong tradition of refusing to look into the motives of legislatures. *See The Anticanon*, 125 Harv. L. Rev. 379, 416 (2011). Greene argues that *Plessy* was well within the mainstream of legal thought at the time it was decided, and that it is therefore a mistake to see it as an example of poor legal reasoning.

Moreover, even accepting Harlan's view of the state's motives, how can racist motives make a law that otherwise treats people the same a denial of equality? If a company creates separate restrooms for men and women, believing one sex is inferior, but the restrooms are identical in quality and quantity, what is the harm? Perhaps the harm is in the message sent by the law. That seems to be how the Court characterizes Plessy's argument, as based on "the assumption that the enforced separation of the two races stamps the colored race with a badge of inferiority." The Court counters that, "[i]f this be so, it is not by reason of anything found in the act, but solely because the colored race chooses to put that construction upon it." Is the Court wrong in its assessment of the law's message? Even if the law does stigmatize blacks, is the message of a segregating law really its principal harm?

Equally important, ought courts be in the business of judging whether laws that are formally equal on their face carry implicit messages? Is it realistic to expect courts to perceive the messages expressed by laws differently from the legislatures who enact them or the public subject to them? Professor Michael Klarman argues that the *Plessy* decision was completely understandable in light of prevailing economic and social conditions, including the "dominant racial norms of the period," with which the majority opinion was "fully congruent." *Rethinking the Civil Rights and Civil Liberties Revolutions*, 82 Va. L. Rev. 1, 27 (1996).

Finally, consider the Court's distinction between equality with respect to civil and political rights, on the one hand, and social rights, on the other. Civil and political rights, which include the right to serve on juries, to own and dispose of property, and to enter into contracts, receive strong constitutional protection. Thus the Court in *Strauder* invalidated the exclusion of minorities from jury service because the implicated the civil right to a fair trial. However, the Court explained, the Fourteenth Amendment does not ensure social equality, which includes the ability to attend integrated schools, marry someone of a different race, and ride in an integrated railcar. In the realm of social rights, the Court reasoned, the question of legality is whether the regulation is "reasonable," for which "there must necessarily be a large discretion on the part of the legislature . . . [which] is at liberty to act with reference to the established usages, customs, and traditions of the people, and with a view to the promotion of their comfort, and the preservation of the public peace and good order."

The Court in *Plessy* thus affirmed its commitment to uphold "absolute equality of the two races before the law" with respect to civil and political rights, and reasonable separations with respect to social rights, at least where the separate facilities are "equal but separate." Is that really such an implausible interpretation of equality sufficient to accuse the *Plessy* Court of racism? Again, is it realistic to expect the Court to have a view of rights radically different from the culture of the time? As Professor Klarman observes, a "generally consistent body of state and lower federal court precedents had sustained the 'separate but equal' doctrine for a quarter century before the Supreme Court provided its imprimatur in *Plessy." Id.* So, how exactly did the *Plessy* Court err when it rejected Plessy's equality claim?

2.   *Liberty.* Perhaps the Court erred by failing to protect Plessy's liberty, a point that Justice Harlan's dissent endorses emphatically: "The fundamental objection, therefore, to the statute, is that it interferes with the personal freedom of citizens." What freedom or liberty was Plessy denied? He could still travel by rail and do so in a car that, at least by statute, was of equal quality. Did his constitutional freedom include the right to sit with white passengers? If so, then was the law equally liberty-denying to white people, at least those who would want to sit with black passengers? Do you believe most black passengers wanted to sit with white passengers? And what if white or black passengers did not want to sit with passengers of the other race? Do they have a liberty interest at stake that the law protected? Is liberty a more or less persuasive way to understand the harm of the law in *Plessy* than a denial of equality?

3.   *Property?* Another argument Plessy made was that he was denied a property right. This claim is not against the segregation in the law but in its application to him. He claimed he had a property interest in his race, namely, his whiteness. The Court describes Plessy as "seven-eighths Caucasian and one-eighth African blood; that the mixture of colored blood was not discernible in him." Does he have a legitimate claim that his reputation of being white is a kind of property interest that Plessy was unjustly denied as a result of being deemed black? Albion Tourgée, one of Plessy attorneys, made this argument in his Brief:

> How much would it be *worth* to a young man entering upon the practice of law, to be regarded as a *white* man rather than a colored one? Six-sevenths of the population are white. Nineteen-twentieths of the property of the country is owned by white people. Ninety-nine hundredths of the business opportunities are in the control of white people. These propositions are rendered even more startling by the intensity of feeling which excludes the colored man from the friendship and companionship of the white man. Probably

most white persons if given a choice, would prefer death to life in the United States *as colored persons*. Under these conditions, is it possible to conclude that the *reputation of being white* is not property? Indeed, is it not the most valuable sort of property, being the master-key that unlocks the golden door of opportunity?

Brief for Plaintiff in Error at 9, *Plessy* (No. 210).

Are you persuaded that racial identity is a property right, or at least something analogous? Does such a conception make sense today, when the market for legal and other services is no longer racially segregated by law? The Court seems to accept the premise that whiteness is a property interest that deserves protection in a case in which a white man is mistakenly deemed black. But the Court simply accepts that Homer Plessy is black because that is how Louisiana state law designated him. How can a state define away a property interest that the Constitution protects? For an influential account of whiteness as a property interest, *see* Cheryl I. Harris, *Whiteness as Property*, 106 Harv. L. Rev. 1707 (1993).

4. *What Is Race?* Although Plessy was 87.5% white and 12.5% black, Louisiana defined him as colored, *i.e.*, black. Was Plessy black, or was he just considered to be black? What's the difference? If most of Homer Plessy's ancestors were white, why wasn't he white? The Court notes that states differed in the proportion of "colored blood" a person must have to be considered colored, ranging from requiring a preponderance of colored heritage to having any "visible admixture" of colored heritage. The Court defers to Louisiana's definition, stating that, "these are questions to be determined under the laws of each state, and are not properly put in issue in this case." Notice then that Plessy's race would vary between colored and white as he travels from state to state. Does that make sense that a state legislature can define, and presumably re-define, different meanings of race for people with identical ancestry and appearance? For a discussion of racial categorization during the Plessy era, see R. Richard Banks and Jennifer L. Eberhardt, Social Psychological Principles and the Legal Bases of Racial Categorization, in Racism: The Problem and the Response (1998) (Jennifer L. Eberhardt and Susan T. Fiske, eds.).

5. *Colorblindness.* Justice Harlan's dissent is famous for arguing that the Constitution is "colorblind." Harlan specifies that the rights that the Constitution secures to all regardless of color are the civil rights mentioned in the majority opinion (e.g., the rights to vote, enter contracts, sue, serve on juries, and own and dispose of property). Does this suggest that Harlan believed, as did the majority, that the Fourteenth Amendment does not mandate social equality between the races? Harlan seems to endorse white supremacy in the following passage: "The white race deems itself to be the dominant race in this country. And so it is, in prestige, in achievements, in education, in wealth, and in power. So, I doubt not, it will continue to be for all time, if it remains true to its great heritage, and holds fast to the principles of constitutional liberty." What is the relation, then, between law and social equality? Does the maintenance of a social caste system require a racially discriminatory legal system? Or might caste be compatible with a

colorblind legal regime? For an argument that colorblindness is compatible with continued racial inequality, see R. Richard Banks, "Nondiscriminatory" Perpetuation of Racial Subordination, 76 Boston University Law Review, 669 (1996). Further complicating things, Harlan seems to argue that people of Chinese ancestry are rightly denied the protections of the Fourteenth Amendment: "There is a race [the Chinese] so different from our own that we do not permit those belonging to it to become citizens of the United States." Is Harlan suggesting that the Chinese are not entitled to the basic civil rights that African Americans and whites are entitled to? If so, doesn't that mean that Harlan's commitment to colorblindness is, at best, unevenly applied, with some racial minorities (blacks) receiving constitutional protection and others (Chinese) being denied this protection?

6. ***Racial Symmetry.*** Recall that the Court places responsibility exclusively with the colored race for perceiving the segregation law as stigmatizing. It supports this point by "reversing the groups," *i.e.,* hypothesizing what would happen if blacks and whites were in each other's position. The Court says whites would not feel stigmatized by a similar law if it were passed by a black legislature: "The argument necessarily assumes that if, as has been more than once the case, and is not unlikely to be so again, the colored race should become the dominant power in the state legislature, and should enact a law in precisely similar terms, it would thereby relegate the white race to an inferior position. We imagine that the white race, at least, would not acquiesce in this assumption." Is that true? If a black dominated legislature passed a law separating blacks and whites, would whites not feel stamped with a badge of inferiority? If not, why not?

7. ***The Effect of Law on Racial Attitudes.*** The Court suggests that it is misguided to attempt to legislate equality, writing: "Legislation is powerless to eradicate racial instincts, or to abolish distinctions based upon physical differences, and the attempt to do so can only result in accentuating the difficulties of the present situation." Is the Court correct about the limited effect of law? How, precisely, does law shape our society? How would you assess the relative importance of law's effects on racial conditions versus racial consciousness? In Chapter 2, you will study the legal reforms of the Civil Rights Movement of the 1960s. Ask yourself, did changes in the law help diminish the racism in American society? How so?

8. ***The Practical Effect of*** Plessy. During the early decades of the twentieth century, de jure segregation spread throughout the South. Facilities of all sorts were legally and formally segregated on the basis of race—theaters, parks, schools, trains, bathrooms, even drinking fountains. White supremacy operated under the guise of the system described, misleadingly, as "separate but equal." In a series of cases following *Plessy* and until about 1930, the Court reaffirmed *Plessy* and sanctioned segregation in numerous settings. In *Cumming v. Richmond County Bd. of Educ.,* 175 U.S. 528 (1899), Justice Harlan wrote for the Court upholding a county's decision to extend free public education to white schools only. He wrote:

If, in some appropriate proceeding instituted directly for that purpose, the plaintiffs had sought to compel the board of education, out of the funds in its hands or under its control, to establish and maintain a high school for colored children, and if it appeared that the board's refusal to maintain such a school was in fact an abuse of its discretion and in hostility to the colored population because of their race, different questions might have arisen in the state court.

[W]hile all admit that the benefits and burdens of public taxation must be shared by citizens without discrimination against any class on account of their race, the education of the people in schools maintained by state taxation is a matter belonging to the respective states, and any interference on the part of Federal authority with the management of such schools cannot be justified except in the case of a clear and unmistakable disregard of rights secured by the supreme law of the land. We have here no such case to be determined.

How do you reconcile this decision with Harlan's dissent in *Plessy* (and also his dissent in *Berea College v. Kentucky*, 211 U.S. 45 (1908), in which the Court upheld a state law requiring segregation of private schools chartered by the state)?

The Reconstruction Amendments and the extensive civil rights legislation enacted in the years after the Civil War offered vehicles for upending unequal legal and social structures. But in the decades immediately following their enactment, their reach proved limited, and between the 1880s and 1950s, Congress passed no civil rights legislation, and the courts did little to spur reform.

IV. COLONIALISM, IMMIGRATION, AND THE COMPLEXITIES OF THE RACIAL ORDER

The American racial order has long pivoted on the black/white divide, but it has also been shaped by the presence, exclusions, and mobilizations of numerous other groups. In the words of the late historian Aristide Zolberg, the United States, since its inception, has been a "Nation by Design."

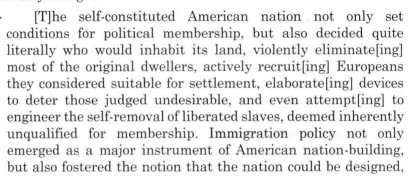

[T]he self-constituted American nation not only set conditions for political membership, but also decided quite literally who would inhabit its land, violently eliminate[ing] most of the original dwellers, actively recruit[ing] Europeans they considered suitable for settlement, elaborate[ing] devices to deter those judged undesirable, and even attempt[ing] to engineer the self-removal of liberated slaves, deemed inherently unqualified for membership. Immigration policy not only emerged as a major instrument of American nation-building, but also fostered the notion that the nation could be designed, stimulating the elevation of that belief into an article of national faith.

Aristide Zolberg, *A Nation by Design: Immigration Policy in the Fashioning of America* 1–2 (Russell Sage Foundation: New York (2006)). Nation building occurred as well through our nation's pursuit of Manifest Destiny, including the acquisition of vast territories in the Southwest and colonies in the Caribbean and Pacific that once belonged to Spain and Mexico. These imperial undertakings led to the United States dominion over many indigenous inhabitants, including millions of people we today call Latinos or Hispanics.

While no single casebook could do justice to the complexities generated by our history, we do intend this project as the beginnings of an effort to situate studies of Racial Justice in the context of a variegated understanding of this country's history and demography. What follows is a brief survey of some of the Supreme Court's nineteenth century precedents that reflect a young nation's efforts to situate some of these racialized groups in the constitutional order, even as it violently subjugated or excluded them.

A. NATIVE PEOPLES AND THE FORMATION OF THE UNITED STATES

Neither the colonies nor the United States could have taken shape without the subjugation and near elimination of the Continent's indigenous populations. Though scholars debate the numbers, by one estimate, when European explorers first "discovered" what is now known as the Americas, approximately 20 million people comprising hundreds of tribes inhabited the territory. *See* Jared Diamond, Guns, Germs and Steel 211 (1997); Angela R. Riley, *Indians and Guns*, 100 Geo. L.J. 1675, 1684 (2012). Within what would become the United States, colonists both slaughtered and enslaved indigenous peoples.

Independent indigenous societies survived the formation of the United States nonetheless, but their status has been fraught from the beginning. Congress and the Supreme Court repeatedly have been forced to grapple with the tension between colonialism and principles of republican constitutionalism, including the commitments to "limited government, democracy, inclusion, and fairness." Philip Frickey, *Marshalling Past and Present: Colonialism, Constitutionalism, and Interpretation in Federal Indian Law*, 107 Harv. L. Rev. 381, 383 (1993). In the words of the renowned Indian law scholar Philip Frickey, the Constitution was a document for "the colonizers" and treated "Indians and tribes as outsiders," mentioning them only three times and establishing Congress's plenary authority to regulate them. Frickey, Marshalling Past and Present, at 383.

In the first significant Indian law case heard by the Supreme Court, Chief Justice Marshall's opinion reflects this distance between

Europeans and Natives, as well as his opening attempt to reconcile colonialism with constitutionalism. In *Johnson v. M'Intosh*, 21 U.S. (8 Wheat.) at 572–73, in the course of resolving a dispute between two non-Indians to a piece of land a tribe had sold to the federal government, he defined the consequences of discovery and concluded that the European sovereign could extinguish a tribe's title to the land "either by purchase or conquest." *Id.* at 57. In describing the theory of discovery, he wrote:

> [T]he tribes of Indians inhabiting this country were fierce savages, whose occupation was war, and whose subsistence was drawn chiefly from the forest. To leave them in possession of their country, was to leave the country a wilderness; to govern them as a distinct people, was impossible, because they were as brave and as high spirited as they were fierce, and were ready to repel by arms every attempt on their independence.

> What was the inevitable consequence of this state of things?

> Frequent and bloody wars, in which the whites were not always the aggressors, unavoidably ensued. European policy, numbers, and skill, prevailed.

> However extravagant the pretension of converting the discovery of an inhabited country into conquest may appear; if the principle has been asserted in the first instance, and afterwards sustained; if a country has been acquired and held under it; if the property of the great mass of the community originates in it, it becomes the law of the land, and cannot be questioned.

Id. at 590.

But Marshall also wrote that tribes' "rights to complete sovereignty, as independent nations, were necessarily diminished" but not extinguished entirely, *id.* at 574. In later cases he developed the concept of tribal sovereignty to protect native interests in self-government. In *Cherokee Nation v. Georgia*, 30 U.S. (5 Pet.) 1 (1831), for example, he characterized tribes as "a distinct political society, separated from others, capable of managing its own affairs and governing itself." Yet he also described them as "domestic dependent nations," *id.* at 16, whose relations to the United States resembled "that of a ward to his guardian." *Id.* at 17. *See also Worcester v. Georgia*, 31 U.S. (6 Pet.) 515 (1832) (holding that a Georgia law requiring state permission for presence on a Cherokee reservation was preempted by the "sovereign-to-sovereign" relationship between the tribe and the federal government).

But even as the Supreme Court recognized a semblance of tribal sovereignty, the federal government continued to exercise its authority over tribes in ways designed to arguably continue the conquest. Seven years after the Court's judgment in *Johnson v. M'Intosh*, Congress enacted the Indian Removal Act, which was designed to force Native peoples living east of the Mississippi to relocate west. The justification for their removal included the belief that Native peoples did not know how to cultivate their land properly and therefore were not entitled to it—a conclusion based on familiar Lockean understandings of property ownership that then justified federal seizure. *See* Lindsay Glauner, The Need for Accountability and Reparation: 1830–1976 The United States Government's Role in the Promotion, Implementation, and Execution of the Crime of Genocide against Native Americans, 51 DePaul L. Rev. 911 (2002). The Act led to the uprooting of tens of thousands of Southern Native peoples from their homes. The infamous Cherokee "Trail of Tears," which produced severe misery and privation on the populations forced West, stemmed from this Act. Despite Cherokee efforts to adapt to the U.S. constitutional order—the tribe adopted a constitution that resembled the American one, for example—nineteenth century federal Indian policy resulted in ongoing efforts to marginalize and even destroy tribes.

The U.S. government today recognizes Indian tribes as sovereign entities entitled to exercise authority over their members. Tribes may relinquish aspects of their sovereignty by agreement with the United States government, but the basic principle of tribal autonomy remains the key component of relations between the United States and Native peoples. For an illuminating discussion of tribal sovereignty, *see* Felix Cohen, *Handbook of Federal Indian Law* § 4.01 (2012 ed.). But what exactly does tribal sovereignty mean in a context in which the federal government has the power to regulate tribes and extinguish tribal claims to land? Does tribal sovereignty reflect a respect for Native peoples' autonomy and self-determination? Or does tribal sovereignty reflect a refusal to incorporate Native peoples within the American polity? Is it possible to recognize simultaneously Native peoples' sovereignty and citizenship?

Consider the fact that before the passage of the Indian Citizenship Act of 1924, which made all native-born Native peoples citizens of the United States, Native peoples were not considered United States citizens. In *Elk v. Wilkins*, 112 U.S. 94 (1884), the Supreme Court considered whether the Fourteenth Amendment's Citizenship Clause, intended to overturn *Dred Scott*, also granted birthright citizenship to Native peoples, such that the petitioner had been denied his constitutional rights by a local registrar in Omaha who refused to recognize him as a qualified voter. Despite the fact that the petitioner had severed relations with his tribe, the Court concluded that, because he was born a member of the tribe, he could become a citizen of the United States only through naturalization. Citing Justice Marshall's foundational opinions, the Court wrote that the Indian tribes were "alien nations, distinct political communities . . . with whom the United States might and habitually did deal . . . either through treaties . . . or acts of congress . . . and were not part of the people of the United States." *Id.* at

99. Citizens at birth had to be "completely subject to [the political jurisdiction of the United States], owing them direct and immediate allegiance." *Id.* at 102. Although Indians were born within the geographical boundaries of the United States, they were "no more born into the United States and subject to the jurisdiction thereof" as the Fourteenth Amendment stipulates than "children born within the United States, of ambassadors or other public ministers of foreign nations." *Id.*

Today, Native peoples are citizens both of the United States and of their tribes. It is worth noting that not all Native peoples approve of the conferral of United States citizenship. Some activists and commentators have argued that Native peoples should focus their energies on internal tribal affairs rather than participating in American politics, and that those who do not participate in tribal government are betraying the principle of indigenous self-government. A variant of this argument is that the desire to exercise American citizenship rights at the expense of engagement with tribal politics reflects mainstream American values and thus the rejection of indigenous values. For a provocative discussion of the perils of neglecting tribal self-government, *see* Robert B. Porter, The Demise of the Ongwehoweh and the Rise of the Native Americans: Redressing the Genocidal Act of Forcing American Citizenship upon Indigenous Peoples, 15 Harv. Black Letter L. Rev. 107 (1999). Should Native peoples assimilate into the American political community? Or should they maintain and seek to broaden a separate political identity?

The Supreme Court today maintains a steady diet of federal Indian law cases. In addition to intricate questions of statutory interpretation, the Court has grappled with the reach of tribal jurisdiction and the implications of the recognition of tribal sovereignty for the constitutional rights of members and non-members alike. For instance, in 2008, the Court framed the issue in this way:

> The ability of nonmembers to know where tribal jurisdiction begins and ends, it should be stressed, is a matter of real, practical consequence given "[t]he special nature of [Indian] tribunals," *Duro v. Reina,* 495 U.S. 676, 693, 110 S.Ct. 2053, 109 L.Ed.2d 693 (1990), which differ from traditional American courts in a number of significant respects. To start with the most obvious one, it has been understood for more than a century that the Bill of Rights and the Fourteenth Amendment do not of their own force apply to Indian tribes. *See Talton v. Mayes,* 163 U.S. 376, 382–385, 16 S.Ct. 986, 41 L.Ed. 196 (1896); F. Cohen, Handbook of Federal Indian Law 664–665 (1982 ed.) (hereinafter Cohen) ("Indian tribes are not states of the union within the meaning of the Constitution, and the constitutional limitations on states do not apply to tribes"). Although the Indian Civil Rights Act of 1968 (ICRA) makes a handful of analogous safeguards enforceable in tribal courts, 25

U.S.C. § 1302, "the guarantees are not identical," *Oliphant*, 435 U.S., at 194, 98 S.Ct. 1011, and there is a "definite trend by tribal courts" toward the view that they "ha[ve] leeway in interpreting" the ICRA's due process and equal protection clauses and "need not follow the U.S. Supreme Court precedents 'jot-for-jot,'" Newton, *Tribal Court Praxis: One Year in the Life of Twenty Indian Tribal Courts*, 22 Am. Indian L.Rev. 285 (1998) . . . In any event, a presumption against tribal-court civil jurisdiction squares with one of the principal policy considerations underlying *Oliphant*, namely, an overriding concern that citizens who are not tribal members be "protected . . . from unwarranted intrusions on their personal liberty," 435 U.S., at 210, 98 S.Ct. 1011.

Tribal courts also differ from other American courts (and often from one another) in their structure, in the substantive law they apply, and in the independence of their judges. Although some modern tribal courts "mirror American courts" and "are guided by written codes, rules, procedures, and guidelines," tribal law is still frequently unwritten, being based instead "on the values, mores, and norms of a tribe and expressed in its customs, traditions, and practices," and is often "handed down orally or by example from one generation to another." Melton, *Indigenous Justice Systems and Tribal Society*, 79 Judicature 126, 130–131 (1995). The resulting law applicable in tribal courts is a complex "mix of tribal codes and federal, state, and traditional law," National American Indian Court Judges Assn., Indian Courts and the Future 43 (1978), which would be unusually difficult for an outsider to sort out.

Plains Commerce Bank v. Long Family Land & Cattle Co., 554 U.S. 316, 337, 128 S. Ct. 2709, 2724 (2008).

Quite apart from these persistent legal questions, and the debate over whether tribal sovereignty is too thin on the one hand or provides too much insulation from the requirements and benefits of the Constitution on the other, Native peoples in the United States today face many of the inequalities and exclusions experienced by other racial minorities, often in acute form. One in four Native peoples lives below the poverty line, compared to one in ten non-Hispanic Whites. *See* American Community Survey Reports, The American Community— American Indians and Alaska Natives (May 2007). Native peoples are much less likely to have high school diplomas and bachelor's degrees than their white counterparts, and they are incarcerated at a disproportionate rate. In addition, rates of violent crime on reservations are double the national average, and rates of violence against women are high. *See* James Anaya, Report of the Special Rapporteur on the rights of indigenous peoples 9–10 (30 August 2012). Just as we grapple with the extent to which our histories of slavery and segregation remain responsible for institutional racism and the material inequalities faced by African Americans, the United States' history as a colonial power weighs heavily in contemporary struggles for equality and justice for Native peoples.

B. IMMIGRATION, CITIZENSHIP, AND EXCLUSION

Until 1965, race and national origin were explicit criteria in the selection of immigrants to the United States. The immigration reforms of that year ended the national origins quotas that had favored European migrants from Northern and Western nations over those from Southern and Eastern European nations. The reforms also eliminated the final vestiges of the outright exclusion of Asians (which had started in the late 19th century with laws barring the entry of Chinese immigrants).

In part because race arguably remains a factor in the construction and operation of our nation's immigration policy, it is important to understand the history of race-based exclusions and of efforts to reconcile them with our national identity. The cases discussed below reveal still more of the fraught origins of our multi-racial society.

In the 1860's, the United States entered into treaties with China that facilitated the arrival of immigrant laborers, primarily to assist in the construction of the trans-continental railroad. The California gold rush fueled westward movement and development of the United States and thus the need for immigrant labor. By the 1880's, growing anti-Chinese sentiment in the West, coupled with a nationwide depression, gave rise to numerous discriminatory state laws in California and eventually led Congress to enact the Chinese Exclusion Act of 1882, which suspended the entry of all Chinese laborers. A subsequent enactment required Chinese laborers present in the United States to obtain and carry certificates proving their entitlement to be in the country.

In *Chae Chan Ping v. United States*, 130 U.S. 581 (1889), the Supreme Court concluded that the Chinese Exclusion Act was a valid exercise of federal power. The Court reasoned:

> To preserve its independence, and give security against foreign aggression and encroachment, is the highest duty of every nation, and to attain these ends nearly all other considerations are to be subordinated. . . . It matters not in what form such aggression and encroachment come, whether from the foreign nation acting in its national character or from vast hordes of its people crowding in upon us. . . . If, therefore, the government of the United States, through its legislative department, considers the presence of foreigners of a different race in this country, who will not assimilate with us, to be dangerous to its peace and security, their exclusion is not to be

stayed because at the time there are no actual hostilities with the nation of which the foreigners are subjects.

What do you make of this sort of national security argument, which perceives a threat to the nation in the presence of supposedly unassimilable migrants? Recall that Justice Harlan, in his dissent in *Plessy* rejecting the logic and constitutionality of black-white segregation, nonetheless appears to accept without question the exclusion of Chinese people from U.S. citizenship, noting that they are a race "so different from our own." He points to the irony of permitting the Chinese to share railcars with whites while prohibiting black citizens from doing the same.

But the question of Chinese citizenship and status under the Constitution has always been more complex than this commentary taken on its own would suggest. In *Yick Wo v. Hopkins*, 118 U.S. 356 (1886), for example, the Court held that a local San Francisco ordinance that gave municipal authorities discretion to determine who could operate a public laundry amounted to arbitrary discrimination against the Chinese. Most important for our purposes, the Court interpreted the Equal Protection Clause to include Chinese immigrants, noting that "[t]he rights of petitioners, as affected by the proceedings of which they complain, are not less because they are aliens and subjects of the emperor of China." 118 U.S. 368, 369. And even though the Chinese in particular, and later Asians in general, were prohibited from becoming naturalized citizens until 1952, the Court also gave effect to the Clause's universalistic language in a seminal case construing the reach of the Fourteenth Amendment's Citizenship Clause.

In the 1898 case of *United States v. Wong Kim Ark*, 169 U.S. 649 (1898), the Supreme Court confronted the question "whether a child born in the United States, of parents of Chinese descent, who, at the time of his birth, are subjects of the Emperor of China, but have a permanent domicil[e] and residence in the United States, and are there carrying on business, and are not employed in any diplomatic or official capacity under the Emperor of China, becomes at the time of his birth a citizen of the United States, by virtue of the first clause of the fourteenth amendment of the constitution: 'All persons born or naturalized in the United States, and subject to the jurisdiction thereof, are citizens of the United States and of the state wherein they reside.' " The Court wrote of the Citizenship Clause:

> It is declaratory in form, and enabling and extending in effect. Its main purpose doubtless was, as has been often recognized by this court, to establish the citizenship of free negroes, which had been denied in the opinion delivered by Chief Justice Taney in *Scott v. Sandford*; and to put it beyond doubt that all blacks, as well as whites, born or naturalized within the jurisdiction of the United States, are citizens of the United States. But the opening words, "All persons born," are

general, not to say universal, restricted only by place and jurisdiction, and not be color or race.

Id. at 467. The Court spelled out the logical conclusion of holding that the Fourteenth Amendment did not reach the children of parents who were citizens or subjects of other countries: it would be "to deny citizenship to thousands of persons of English, Scotch, Irish, German, or other European parentage, who have always been considered and treated as citizens of the United States." *Id.* at 474.

How do you reconcile the Court's willingness to protect the constitutional rights of Chinese immigrants and acknowledge the citizenship status of children born to Chinese parents with its acceptance of racially exclusionary immigration and naturalization laws? Is it consistent as a matter of political theory to exclude Chinese from naturalization but to understand them as included within the terms of birthright citizenship?

Despite these cases incorporating Chinese immigrants and their children into the political order, racial restrictions on naturalization remained in place until 1952. An immigrant hoping to become a naturalized United States citizen had to be either of "African descent" or a "free white person." Some Asian immigrants seeking to naturalize sought to claim whiteness, giving rise to two Supreme Court cases, excerpted below, that sought to define that category. These cases highlight a fluid understanding of whiteness and underscore how courts and other legal actors have manipulated its meaning to re-enforce racial exclusion.

In thinking about what these cases suggest about the construction of racial identity, it is also important to understand that, during the 1920's, whiteness (or what we would consider whiteness today) was not enough to entitle someone to entrance into the polity. In the early twentieth century, Congress enacted immigration quotas to significantly limit the entrance of undesirable peoples from Southern and Eastern Europe whose racial status was either ambiguous or beside the point, at the same time that it enacted outright prohibitions of Asian immigration. These laws reflected the culmination of decades of debate over the desirability of different immigrant stock, and they effectively implemented the recommendations of the Dillingham Commission, a joint House-Senate Commission that met from 1907–1910 to study the state of immigration to the United States. In its more than 40 volume report, the Commission constructed a dichotomy between "old" (good and Northern European) and "new" (bad and Southern and Eastern Europeans) immigrants—the former assimilated seamlessly and the latter remained mired in ethnic enclaves.

Throughout the first decades of the twentieth century, Congress had attempted to block the entry of "lower-quality" immigrants through devices such as literacy tests. Presidents Wilson and Roosevelt both

vetoed these bills (Congress eventually enacted a literacy
Wilson's veto), though both Presidents also wrote tracts with
racialized overtones, about the low quality of certain immigra
importance of assimilation. But the system's ethnic ideolog
complemented by economic compromises. Congress, for examp
subject Western Hemisphere immigration to quotas, and large nu.
of Mexicans entered during this period to satisfy labor needs.

Among the important conceptual questions raised by the
immigration and naturalization laws of this period are: to what extent
were they about race, or the production of race, and to what extent did
they implicate the intersection of ethnicity and class? Rogers Smith has
argued that the immigration laws of this period helped re-enforce the
segregationist ideologies used to subjugate the black population. Rogers
Smith, *Civic Ideals* (1999). In tracing the effects of the immigration laws,
Desmond King has highlighted the failure of the 1924 quota regime to
produce the racial make-up desired by Congress, as well as the gradual
assimilation of once undesirable white Europeans and the corresponding
disappearance of ethnic enclaves. According to King, the "complex system
of races" reflected in the immigration debates of this period eventually
gave way to "a strict scheme of black and white," according to which the
assimilation experience of European immigrants came to be the standard
against which "blacks were measured—and found wanting." Desmond
King, *Making Americans: Immigration, Race, and the Origins of Diverse
Democracy* (2002).

Takao Ozawa v. United States

Supreme Court of the United States, 1922.
260 U.S. 178.

■ MR. JUSTICE SUTHERLAND delivered the opinion of the Court.

The appellant is a person of the Japanese race born in Japan. He
applied, on October 16, 1914, to the United States District Court for the
Territory of Hawaii to be admitted as a citizen of the United States.
Including the period of his residence in Hawaii appellant had
continuously resided in the United States for 20 years. He was a graduate
of the Berkeley, Cal., high school, had been nearly three years a student
in the University of California, had educated his children in American
schools, his family had attended American churches and he had
maintained the use of the English language in his home. That he was
well qualified by character and education for citizenship is conceded.

The District Court of Hawaii, however, held that, having been born
in Japan and being of the Japanese race, he was not eligible to
naturalization under section 2169 of the Revised Statutes, and denied
the petition.

[We must] inquire whether, under section 2169, the appellant is eligible to naturalization. The language of the naturalization laws from 1790 to 1870 had been uniformly such as to deny the privilege of naturalization to an alien unless he came within the description 'free white person.' By section 7 of the act of July 14, 1870 (16 Stat. 254, 256 [Comp. St. § 4358]), the naturalization laws were 'extended to aliens of African nativity and to persons of African descent.' Is appellant, therefore, a 'free white person,' within the meaning of that phrase as found in the statute?

On behalf of the appellant it is urged that we should give to this phrase the meaning which it had in the minds of its original framers in 1790 and that it was employed by them for the sole purpose of excluding the black or African race and the Indians then inhabiting this country. It may be true that those two races were alone thought of as being excluded, but to say that they were the only ones within the intent of the statute would be to ignore the affirmative form of the legislation. The provision is not that Negroes and Indians shall be excluded, but it is, in effect, that only free white persons shall be included. The intention was to confer the privilege of citizenship upon that class of persons whom the fathers knew as white, and to deny it to all who could not be so classified. It is not enough to say that the framers did not have in mind the brown or yellow races of Asia. It is necessary to go farther and be able to say that had these particular races been suggested the language of the act would have been so varied as to include them within its privileges.

If it be assumed that the opinion of the framers was that the only persons who would fall outside the designation 'white' were Negroes and Indians, this would go no farther than to demonstrate their lack of sufficient information to enable them to foresee precisely who would be excluded by that term in the subsequent administration of the statute. It is not important in construing their words to consider the extent of their ethnological knowledge or whether they thought that under the statute the only persons who would be denied naturalization would be Negroes and Indians. It is sufficient to ascertain whom they intended to include and having ascertained that it follows, as a necessary corollary, that all others are to be excluded.

The question then is: Who are comprehended within the phrase 'free white persons'? Undoubtedly the word 'free' was originally used in recognition of the fact that slavery then existed and that some white persons occupied that status. The word, however, has long since ceased to have any practical significance and may now be disregarded.

We have been furnished with elaborate briefs in which the meaning of the words 'white person' is discussed with ability and at length, both from the standpoint of judicial decision and from that of the science of ethnology. It does not seem to us necessary, however, to follow counsel in their extensive researches in these fields. It is sufficient to note the fact that these decisions are, in substance, to the effect that the words import a racial and not an individual test, and with this conclusion, fortified as it is by reason and authority, we entirely agree. Manifestly the test afforded by the mere color of the skin of each individual is impracticable, as that differs greatly among persons of the same race, even among Anglo-Saxons, ranging by imperceptible gradations from the fair blond to the swarthy brunette, the latter being darker than many of the lighter hued persons of the brown or yellow races. Hence to adopt the color test alone would result in a confused overlapping of races and a gradual merging of one into the other, without any practical line of separation. Beginning with the decision of Circuit Judge Sawyer, *In re Ah Yup,* 5 Sawy. 155, Fed. Cas. No. 104 (1878), the federal and state courts, in an almost unbroken line, have held that the words 'white person' were meant to indicate only a person of what is popularly known as the Caucasian race.

The determination that the words 'white person' are synonymous with the words 'a person of the Caucasian race' simplifies the problem, although it does not entirely dispose of it. Controversies have arisen and will no doubt arise again in respect of the proper classification of individuals in border line cases. The effect of the conclusion that the words 'white person' means a Caucasian is not to establish a sharp line of demarcation between those who are entitled and those who are not entitled to naturalization, but rather a zone of more or less debatable ground outside of which, upon the one hand, are those clearly eligible, and outside of which, upon the other hand, are those clearly ineligible for citizenship. Individual cases falling within this zone must be determined as they arise from time to time by what this court has called, in another connection 'the gradual process of judicial inclusion and exclusion.'

The appellant, in the case now under consideration, however, is clearly of a race which is not Caucasian and therefore belongs entirely outside the zone on the negative side. A large number of the federal and state courts have so decided and we find no reported case definitely to the contrary. These decisions are sustained by numerous scientific authorities, which we do not deem it necessary to review. We think these decisions are right and so hold.

The briefs filed on behalf of appellant refer in complimentary terms to the culture and enlightenment of the Japanese people, and with this estimate we have no reason to disagree; but these are matters which cannot enter into our consideration of the questions here at issue. We have no function in the matter other than to ascertain the will of Congress and declare it. Of course there is not implied—either in the legislation or in our interpretation of it—any suggestion of individual unworthiness or racial inferiority. These considerations are in no manner involved.

United States v. Bhagat Singh Thind

Supreme Court of the United States, 1923.
261 U.S. 204.

■ MR. JUSTICE SUTHERLAND delivered the opinion of the Court.

This cause is here upon a certificate from the Circuit Court of appeals requesting the instruction of this Court in respect of the following questions:

1. Is a high-caste Hindu, of full Indian blood, born at Amritsar, Punjab, India, a white person within the meaning of section 2169, Revised Statutes?

2. Does the Act of February 5, 1917, disqualify from naturalization as citizens those Hindus now barred by that act, who had lawfully entered the United States prior to the passage of said act?'

No question is made in respect of the individual qualifications of the appellee. The sole question is whether he falls within the class designated by Congress as eligible.

Section 2169, provides that the provisions of the Naturalization Act 'shall apply to aliens being free white persons and to aliens of African nativity and to persons of African descent.'

If the applicant is a white person within the meaning of this section, he is entitled to naturalization; otherwise not. Mere ability on the part of an applicant for naturalization to establish a line of descent from a Caucasian ancestor will not ipso facto to and necessarily conclude the inquiry. 'Caucasian' is a conventional word of much flexibility, as a study of the literature dealing with racial questions will disclose, and while it and the words 'white persons' are treated as synonymous for the purposes of that case, they are not of identical meaning.

In the endeavor to ascertain the meaning of the statute we must not fail to keep in mind that it does not employ the word 'Caucasian,' but the words 'white persons,' and these are words of common speech and not of scientific origin. The word 'Caucasian,' [is by no] means clear, and the use of it in its scientific sense probably wholly unfamiliar to the original framers of the statute in 1790. When we employ it, we do so as an aid to the ascertainment of the legislative intent and not as an invariable substitute for the statutory words. Indeed, as used in the science of ethnology, the connotation of the word is by no means clear, and the use of it in its scientific sense as an equivalent for the words of the statute, other considerations aside, would simply mean the substitution of one perplexity for another. But in this country, during the last half century especially, the word by common usage has acquired a popular meaning, not clearly defined to be sure, but sufficiently so to enable us to say that its popular as distinguished from its scientific application is of appreciably narrower scope. It is in the popular sense of the word, therefore, that we employ it as an aid to the construction of the statute, for it would be obviously illogical to convert words of common speech used in a statute into words of scientific terminology when neither the latter nor the science for whose purposes they were coined was within the contemplation of the framers of the statute or of the people for whom it was framed. The words of the statute are to be interpreted in accordance with the understanding of the common man from whose vocabulary they were taken.

They imply, as we have said, a racial test; but the term 'race' is one which, for the practical purposes of the statute, must be applied to a group of living persons now possessing in common the requisite characteristics, not to groups of persons who are supposed to be or really are descended from some remote, common ancestor, but who, whether they both resemble him to a greater or less extent, have, at any rate, ceased altogether to resemble one another. It may be true that the blond Scandinavian and the brown Hindu have a common ancestor in the dim reaches of antiquity, but the average man knows perfectly well that there are unmistakable and profound differences between them to-day; and it is not impossible, if that common ancestor could be materialized in the flesh, we should discover that he was himself sufficiently differentiated from both of his descendants to preclude his racial classification with either. The question for determination is not, therefore, whether by the speculative processes of ethnological reasoning we may present a probability to the scientific mind that they have the same origin, but whether we can satisfy the common understanding that they are now the same or sufficiently the same to justify the interpreters of a statute—written in the words of common speech, for common understanding, by unscientific men—in classifying them together in the statutory category as white persons.

The eligibility of this applicant for citizenship is based on the sole fact that he is of high-caste Hindu stock, born in Punjab, one of the extreme northwestern districts of India, and classified by certain scientific authorities as of the Caucasian or Aryan race. The Aryan theory as a racial basis seems to be discredited by most, if not all, modern writers on the subject of ethnology. A review of their contentions would serve no useful purpose.

The term 'Aryan' has to do with linguistic, and not at all with physical characteristics, and it would seem reasonably clear that mere resemblance in language, indicating a common linguistic root buried in remotely ancient soil, is altogether inadequate to prove common racial origin. There is, and can be, no assurance that the so-called Aryan language was not spoken by a variety of races living in proximity to one another. Our own history has witnessed the adoption of the English tongue by millions of negroes, whose descendants can never be classified racially with the descendants of white persons, notwithstanding both may speak a common root language.

The word 'Caucasian' is in scarcely better repute. It is at best a conventional term, with an altogether fortuitous origin,[1] which under scientific manipulation, has come to include far more than the unscientific mind suspects. According to Keane, for example, it includes not only the Hindu, but some of the Polynesians (that is, the Maori, Tahitians, Samoans, Hawaiians, and others), the Hamites of Africa, upon the ground of the Caucasic cast of their features, though in color they range from brown to black. We venture to think that the average well-informed white American would learn with some degree of astonishment that the race to which he belongs is made up of such heterogeneous elements.[2]

The various authorities are in irreconcilable disagreement as to what constitutes a proper racial division. For instance, Blumenbach has 5 races; Keane following Linnaeus, 4; Deniker, 29. The explanation probably is that 'the innumerable varieties of mankind run into one another by insensible degrees,' and to arrange them in sharply bounded divisions is an undertaking of such uncertainty that common agreement is practically impossible.

It may be, therefore, that a given group cannot be properly assigned to any of the enumerated grand racial divisions. The type may have been so changed by intermixture of blood as to justify an intermediate classification. Something very like this has actually taken place in India. Thus, in Hindustan and Berar there was such an intermixture of the 'Aryan' invader with the dark skinned Dravidian.

In the Punjab and Rajputana, while the invaders seem to have met with more success in the effort to preserve their racial purity, intermarriages did occur producing an intermingling of the two and

---

[1] 2 Encyclopaedia Britannica (11th Ed.) p. 113: 'The ill-chosen name of Caucasian, invented by Blumenbach in allusion to a South Caueasian skull of specially typical proportions, and applied by him to the so-called white races, is still current; it brings into one race peoples such as the Arabs and Swedes, although these are scarcely less different than the Americans and Malays, who are set down as two distinct races. Again, two of the best marked varieties of mankind are the Australians and the Bushmen, neither of whom, however, seems to have a natural place in Blumenbach's series.'

[2] Keane himself says that the Caucasic division of the human family is 'in point of fact the most debatable field in the whole range of anthropological studies.'

And again: 'Hence it seems to require a strong mental effort to sweep into a single category, however elastic, so many different peoples-Europeans, North Africans, West Asiatics, Iranians, and others all the way to the Indo-Gangetic plains and uplands, whose complexion presents every shade of color, except yellow, from white to the deepest brown or even black.

'But they are grouped together in a single division, because their essential properties are one, * * * their substantial uniformity speaks to the eye that sees below the surface * * * we recognize a common racial stamp in the facial expression, the structure of the hair, partly also the bodily proportions, in all of which points they agree more with each other than with the other main divisions. Even in the case of certain black or very dark races, such as the Bejas, Somali, and a few other Eastern Hamites, we are reminded instinctively more of Europeans or Berbers thanks to their more regular features and brighter expression.'

destroying to a greater or less degree the purity of the 'Aryan' blood. The rules of caste, while calculated to prevent this intermixture, seem not to have been entirely successful.

It does not seem necessary to pursue the matter of scientific classification further. We are unable to agree with the District Court, or with other lower federal courts, in the conclusion that a native Hindu is eligible for naturalization under section 2169. The words of familiar speech, which were used by the original framers of the law, were intended to include only the type of man whom they knew as white. The immigration of that day was almost exclusively from the British Isles and Northwestern Europe, whence they and their forebears had come. When they extended the privilege of American citizenship to 'any alien being a free white person' it was these immigrants—bone of their bone and flesh of their flesh—and their kind whom they must have had affirmatively in mind. The succeeding years brought immigrants from Eastern, Southern and Middle Europe, among them the Slavs and the dark-eyed, swarthy people of Alpine and Mediterranean stock, and these were received as unquestionably akin to those already here and readily amalgamated with them. It was the descendants of these, and other immigrants of like origin, who constituted the white population of the country when section 2169, re-enacting the naturalization test of 1790, was adopted, and, there is no reason to doubt, with like intent and meaning.

What, if any, people of Primarily Asiatic stock come within the words of the section we do not deem it necessary now to decide.

What we now hold is that the words 'free white persons' are words of common speech, to be interpreted in accordance with the understanding of the common man, synonymous with the word 'Caucasian' only as that word is popularly understood. As so understood and used, whatever may be the speculations of the ethnologist, it does not include the body of people to whom the appellee belongs. It is a matter of familiar observation and knowledge that the physical group characteristics of the Hindus render them readily distinguishable from the various groups of persons in this country commonly recognized as white. The children of English, French, German, Italian, Scandinavian, and other European parentage, quickly merge into the mass of our population and lose the distinctive hallmarks of their European origin. On the other hand, it cannot be doubted that the children born in this country of Hindu parents would retain indefinitely the clear evidence of their ancestry. It is very far from our thought to suggest the slightest question of racial superiority or inferiority. What we suggest is merely racial difference, and it is of such character and extent that the great body of our people instinctively recognize it and reject the thought of assimilation.

It is not without significance in this connection that Congress, has now excluded from admission into this country all natives of Asia within designated limits of latitude and longitude, including the whole of India.

This not only constitutes conclusive evidence of the congressional attitude of opposition to Asiatic immigration generally, but is persuasive of a similar attitude toward Asiatic naturalization as well, since it is not likely that Congress would be willing to accept as citizens a class of persons whom it rejects as immigrants.

NOTES AND QUESTIONS

1. ***Statutory Interpretation.*** On what does the Court rest its decision in these two cases? Precedent? Science? Current social understandings? Legislative intent? If the Court is to decide such a case based on legislative intent, is it more sensible to consider who was intended to be excluded from citizenship, or who was intended to be included? Is the Court's reasoning in *Ozawa* and *Thind* consistent?

2. ***The Fluidity of Race.*** Does the meaning of "free white person" in the naturalization statute necessarily remain the same across time? If not, what causes its meaning to shift? Moreover, if the Court is to determine the meaning of naturalization laws by looking to the intent of their framers, doesn't that create problems for members of racial groups that today are considered "white" but that 200 years ago were perhaps not so regarded?

3. ***Are Race-Based Restrictions Necessarily Racist?*** The Court says at the end of *Thind* and also at the end of *Ozawa* that its decision and the naturalization statute have nothing to do with racism. Is it possible for a Court, in interpreting this type of statute, to engage in any type of racial classification *without* entrenching racial hierarchies? What would have been the least racist, legitimate approach the Court could have taken?

4. ***Race and National Identity.*** *Ozawa* and *Thind* reflect a time when our nation thought of itself as white. Notwithstanding the demise of overtly race-based naturalization laws, and the changing demographics of our own nation, one might ask: is our national identity still shaped by race? Is there any sense in which America remains a "white nation"? Or in which the experiences of racial minorities remain marginalized? For a discussion of this issue in the context of gender relations, see R. Richard Banks, *Are African Americans Us?* 93 Boston Univ.L.Rev. 681 (2103).

V. A TWENTIETH-CENTURY RECKONING

One lesson of our history is that, as one form of racial subordination is (seemingly) vanquished, another may arise. Racial conflict is less resolved than relocated. In part, our inability to attain racial justice reflects the indeterminacy of our ideals, the inevitable interplay of competing conceptions of what racial justice demands. How should we treat people now? And, also, how should we respond to the acknowledged injustices of the past? The final case in this chapter, *Korematsu v. United States*, raises both issues.

After the Japanese attack on Pearl Harbor, the government interned more than 110,000 people of Japanese descent (nearly 2/3 of them United

States citizens). In *Korematsu*, the Court upheld the conviction of a Japanese citizen for violating a military order excluding Japanese on the West Coast from certain zones, thus condoning their internment. Ironically, *Korematsu* was also the first case in which the Supreme Court held that racial classifications were to be subject to the most stringent form of judicial scrutiny, an approach that continues to shape the law today.

Korematsu v. United States

Supreme Court of the United States, 1944.
323 U.S. 214.

■ MR. JUSTICE BLACK delivered the opinion of the Court.

The petitioner, an American citizen of Japanese descent, was convicted in a federal district court for remaining in San Leandro, California, a 'Military Area', contrary to Civilian Exclusion Order No. 34 of the Commanding General of the Western Command, U.S. Army, which directed that after May 9, 1942, all persons of Japanese ancestry should be excluded from that area. No question was raised as to petitioner's loyalty to the United States.

It should be noted, to begin with, that all legal restrictions which curtail the civil rights of a single racial group are immediately suspect. That is not to say that all such restrictions are unconstitutional. It is to say that courts must subject them to the most rigid scrutiny. Pressing public necessity may sometimes justify the existence of such restrictions; racial antagonism never can.

Exclusion Order No. 34, which the petitioner knowingly and admittedly violated was one of a number of military orders and proclamations, all of which were substantially based upon Executive Order No. 9066. That order, issued after we were at war with Japan, declared that "the successful prosecution of the war requires every possible protection against espionage and against sabotage to national-defense material, national-defense premises, and national-defense utilities. * * * "

One of the series of orders and proclamations, a curfew order, which like the exclusion order here was promulgated pursuant to Executive Order 9066, subjected all persons of Japanese ancestry in prescribed West Coast military areas to remain in their residences from 8 p.m. to 6 a.m. As is the case with the exclusion order here, that prior curfew order was designed as a "protection against espionage and against sabotage." In *Kiyoshi v. United States*, we sustained a conviction obtained for violation of the curfew order. The Hirabayashi conviction and this one thus rest on the same 1942 Congressional Act and the same basic executive and military orders, all of which orders were aimed at the twin dangers of espionage and sabotage.

We upheld the curfew order as an exercise of the power of the government to take steps necessary to prevent espionage and sabotage in an area threatened by Japanese attack.

In the light of the principles we announced in the Hirabayashi case, we are unable to conclude that it was beyond the war power of Congress and the Executive to exclude those of Japanese ancestry from the West Coast war area at the time they did. True, exclusion from the area in which one's home is located is a far greater deprivation than constant confinement to the home from 8 p.m. to 6 a.m. Nothing short of apprehension by the proper military authorities of the gravest imminent danger to the public safety can constitutionally justify either. But exclusion from a threatened area, no less than curfew, has a definite and close relationship to the prevention of espionage and sabotage. The military authorities, charged with the primary responsibility of defending our shores, concluded that curfew provided inadequate protection and ordered exclusion. They did so, as pointed out in our Hirabayashi opinion, in accordance with Congressional authority to the military to say who should, and who should not, remain in the threatened areas.

Here, as in the Hirabayashi case . . . , " * * * we cannot reject as unfounded the judgment of the military authorities and of Congress that there were disloyal members of that population, whose number and strength could not be precisely and quickly ascertained. We cannot say that the war-making branches of the Government did not have ground for believing that in a critical hour such persons could not readily be isolated and separately dealt with, and constituted a menace to the national defense and safety, which demanded that prompt and adequate measures be taken to guard against it."

Like curfew, exclusion of those of Japanese origin was deemed necessary because of the presence of an unascertained number of disloyal members of the group, most of whom we have no doubt were loyal to this country. It was because we could not reject the finding of the military authorities that it was impossible to bring about an immediate segregation of the disloyal from the loyal that we sustained the validity of the curfew order as applying to the whole group. In the instant case, temporary exclusion of the entire group was rested by the military on the same ground. The judgment that exclusion of the whole group was for the same reason a military imperative answers the contention that the exclusion was in the nature of group punishment based on antagonism to those of Japanese origin. That there were members of the group who retained loyalties to Japan has been confirmed by investigations made subsequent to the exclusion. Approximately five thousand American citizens of Japanese ancestry refused to swear unqualified allegiance to the United States and to renounce allegiance to the Japanese Emperor, and several thousand evacuees requested repatriation to Japan.

We uphold the exclusion order as of the time it was made and when the petitioner violated it. . . . In doing so, we are not unmindful of the hardships imposed by it upon a large group of American citizens. . . . But hardships are part of war, and war is an aggregation of hardships. All citizens alike, both in and out of uniform, feel the impact of war in greater or lesser measure. Citizenship has its responsibilities as well as its privileges, and in time of war the burden is always heavier. Compulsory exclusion of large groups of citizens from their homes, except under circumstances of direst emergency and peril, is inconsistent with our basic governmental institutions. But when under conditions of modern warfare our shores are threatened by hostile forces, the power to protect must be commensurate with the threatened danger.

It is said that we are dealing here with the case of imprisonment of a citizen in a concentration camp solely because of his ancestry, without evidence or inquiry concerning his loyalty and good disposition towards the United States. Our task would be simple, our duty clear, were this a case involving the imprisonment of a loyal citizen in a concentration camp because of racial prejudice. Regardless of the true nature of the assembly and relocation centers—and we deem it unjustifiable to call them concentration camps with all the ugly connotations that term implies—we are dealing specifically with nothing but an exclusion order. To cast this case into outlines of racial prejudice, without reference to the real military dangers which were presented, merely confuses the issue. Korematsu was not excluded from the Military Area because of hostility to him or his race. He was excluded because we are at war with the Japanese Empire, because the properly constituted military authorities feared an invasion of our West Coast and felt constrained to take proper security measures, because they decided that the military urgency of the situation demanded that all citizens of Japanese ancestry be segregated from the West Coast temporarily, and finally, because Congress, reposing its confidence in this time of war in our military leaders—as inevitably it must—determined that they should have the power to do just this. There was evidence of disloyalty on the part of some, the military authorities considered that the need for action was great, and time was short. We cannot—by availing ourselves of the calm perspective of hindsight—now say that at that time these actions were unjustified.

■ MR. JUSTICE FRANKFURTER, concurring.

[T]he validity of action under the war power must be judged wholly in the context of war. That action is not to be stigmatized as lawless because like action in times of peace would be lawless. To talk about a military order that expresses an allowable judgment of war needs by those entrusted with the duty of conducting war as 'an unconstitutional order' is to suffuse a part of the Constitution with an atmosphere of unconstitutionality. The respective spheres of action of military authorities and of judges are of course very different. But within their sphere, military authorities are no more outside the bounds of obedience to the Constitution than are judges within theirs. To recognize that military orders are 'reasonably expedient military precautions' in time of war and yet to deny them constitutional legitimacy makes of the Constitution an instrument for dialectic subtleties not reasonably to be attributed to the hard-headed Framers, of whom a majority had had actual participation in war. If a military order such as that under review does not transcend the means appropriate for conducting war, such action by the military is as constitutional as would be any authorized action by the Interstate Commerce Commission within the limits of the constitutional power to regulate commerce. And being an exercise of the war power explicitly granted by the Constitution for safeguarding the national life by prosecuting war effectively, I find nothing in the Constitution which denies to Congress the power to enforce such a valid military order by making its violation an offense triable in the civil courts.

■ MR. JUSTICE ROBERTS, dissenting.

[T]he indisputable facts exhibit a clear violation of Constitutional rights.

This is not a case of keeping people off the streets at night as was *Kiyoshi Hirabayashi v. United States*, nor a case of temporary exclusion of a citizen from an area for his own safety or that of the community, nor a case of offering him an opportunity to go temporarily out of an area where his presence might cause danger to himself or to his fellows. On the contrary, it is the case of convicting a citizen as a punishment for not submitting to imprisonment in a concentration camp, based on his ancestry, and solely because of his ancestry, without evidence or inquiry concerning his loyalty and good disposition towards the United States.

The predicament in which the petitioner thus found himself was this: He was forbidden, by Military Order, to leave the zone in which he lived; he was forbidden, by Military Order, after a date fixed, to be found within that zone unless he were in an Assembly Center located in that zone. General DeWitt's report to the Secretary of War concerning the programme of evacuation and relocation of Japanese makes it entirely clear . . . that an Assembly Center was a euphemism for a prison. No person within such a center was permitted to leave except by Military Order.

■ MR. JUSTICE MURPHY, dissenting.

This exclusion of "all persons of Japanese ancestry, both alien and non-alien," from the Pacific Coast area on a plea of military necessity in the absence of martial law ought not to be approved. Such exclusion goes over "the very brink of constitutional power" and falls into the ugly abyss of racism.

The judicial test of whether the Government, on a plea of military necessity, can validly deprive an individual of any of his constitutional rights is whether the deprivation is reasonably related to a public danger that is so 'immediate, imminent, and impending' as not to admit of delay and not to permit the intervention of ordinary constitutional processes to alleviate the danger. Yet no reasonable relation to an 'immediate, imminent, and impending' public danger is evident to support this racial restriction which is one of the most sweeping and complete deprivations of constitutional rights in the history of this nation in the absence of martial law.

It must be conceded that the military and naval situation in the spring of 1942 was such as to generate a very real fear of invasion of the Pacific Coast, accompanied by fears of sabotage and espionage in that area. The military command was therefore justified in adopting all reasonable means necessary to combat these dangers. In adjudging the military action taken in light of the then apparent dangers, we must not erect too high or too meticulous standards; it is necessary only that the action have some reasonable relation to the removal of the dangers of invasion, sabotage and espionage. But the exclusion, either temporarily or permanently, of all persons with Japanese blood in their veins has no such reasonable relation. And that relation is lacking because the exclusion order necessarily must rely for its reasonableness upon the assumption that all persons of Japanese ancestry may have a dangerous tendency to commit sabotage and espionage and to aid our Japanese enemy in other ways. It is difficult to believe that reason, logic or experience could be marshalled in support of such an assumption.

That this forced exclusion was the result in good measure of this erroneous assumption of racial guilt rather than bona fide military necessity is evidenced by the Commanding General's Final Report on the evacuation from the Pacific Coast area. In it he refers to all individuals of Japanese descent as 'subversive,' as belonging to 'an enemy race' whose 'racial strains are undiluted,' and as constituting "over 112,000 potential enemies * * * at large today" along the Pacific Coast.[3] In support of this blanket condemnation of all persons of Japanese descent, however, no reliable evidence is cited to show that such individuals were generally

---

[3]   Further evidence of the Commanding General's attitude toward individuals of Japanese ancestry is revealed in his voluntary testimony on April 13, 1943, in San Francisco before the House Naval Affairs Subcommittee to Investigate Congested Areas, Part 3, pp. 739–40 (78th Cong., 1st Sess.):

I don't want any of them (persons of Japanese ancestry) here. They are a dangerous element. There is no way to determine their loyalty. The west coast contains too many vital installations essential to the defense of the country to allow any Japanese on this coast. * * * The danger of the Japanese was, and is now-if they are permitted to come back-espionage and sabotage. It makes no difference whether he is an American citizen, he is still a Japanese. American citizenship does not necessarily determine loyalty. * * * But we must worry about the Japanese all the time until he is wiped off the map. Sabotage and espionage will make problems as long as he is allowed in this area. * * * '

disloyal, or had generally so conducted themselves in this area as to constitute a special menace to defense installations or war industries, or had otherwise by their behavior furnished reasonable ground for their exclusion as a group.

Justification for the exclusion is sought, instead, mainly upon questionable racial and sociological grounds not ordinarily within the realm of expert military judgment, supplemented by certain semi-military conclusions drawn from an unwarranted use of circumstantial evidence. Individuals of Japanese ancestry are condemned because they are said to be "a large, unassimilated, tightly knit racial group, bound to an enemy nation by strong ties of race, culture, custom and religion." They are claimed to be given to 'emperor worshipping ceremonies' and to 'dual citizenship.' Japanese language schools and allegedly pro-Japanese organizations are cited as evidence of possible group disloyalty, together with facts as to certain persons being educated and residing at length in Japan. It is intimated that many of these individuals deliberately resided 'adjacent to strategic points,' thus enabling them "to carry into execution a tremendous program of sabotage on a mass scale should any considerable number of them have been inclined to do so." The need for protective custody is also asserted. The report refers without identity to 'numerous incidents of violence' as well as to other admittedly unverified or cumulative incidents. From this, plus certain other events not shown to have been connected with the Japanese Americans, it is concluded that the "situation was fraught with danger to the Japanese population itself" and that the general public "was ready to take matters into its own hands." Finally, it is intimated, though not directly charged or proved, that persons of Japanese ancestry were responsible for three minor isolated shellings and bombings of the Pacific Coast area, as well as for unidentified radio transmissions and night signalling.

The main reasons relied upon by those responsible for the forced evacuation, therefore, do not prove a reasonable relation between the group characteristics of Japanese Americans and the dangers of invasion, sabotage and espionage. The reasons appear, instead, to be largely an accumulation of much of the misinformation, half-truths and insinuations that for years have been directed against Japanese Americans by people with racial and economic prejudices—the same people who have been among the foremost advocates of the evacuation. A military judgment based upon such racial and sociological considerations is not entitled to the great weight ordinarily given the judgments based upon strictly military considerations. Especially is this so when every charge relative to race, religion, culture, geographical location, and legal and economic status has been substantially discredited by independent studies made by experts in these matters.

The military necessity which is essential to the validity of the evacuation order thus resolves itself into a few intimations that certain individuals actively aided the enemy, from which it is inferred that the entire group of Japanese Americans could not be trusted to be or remain loyal to the United States. No one denies, of course, that there were some disloyal persons of Japanese descent on the Pacific Coast who did all in their power to aid their ancestral land. Similar disloyal activities have been engaged in by many persons of German, Italian and even more pioneer stock in our country. But to infer that examples of individual disloyalty prove group disloyalty and justify discriminatory action against the entire group is to deny that under our system of law individual guilt is the sole basis for deprivation of rights. Moreover, this inference, which is at the very heart of the evacuation orders, has been used in support of the abhorrent and despicable treatment of minority groups by the dictatorial tyrannies which this nation is now pledged to destroy. To give constitutional sanction to that inference in this case, however well-intentioned may have been the military command on the Pacific Coast, is to adopt one of the cruelest of the rationales used by our enemies to destroy the dignity of the individual and to encourage and open the door to discriminatory actions against other minority groups in the passions of tomorrow.

No adequate reason is given for the failure to treat these Japanese Americans on an individual basis by holding investigations and hearings to separate the loyal from the disloyal, as was done in the case of persons of German and Italian ancestry. It is asserted merely that the loyalties of this group "were unknown and time was of the essence." Yet nearly four months elapsed after Pearl Harbor before the first exclusion order was issued; nearly eight months went by until the last order was issued; and the last of these 'subversive' persons was not actually removed until almost eleven months had elapsed. Leisure and deliberation seem to have been more of the essence than speed. And the fact that conditions were not such as to warrant a declaration of martial law adds strength to the belief that the factors of time and military necessity were not as urgent as they have been represented to be.

Moreover, there was no adequate proof that the Federal Bureau of Investigation and the military and naval intelligence services did not have the espionage and sabotage situation well in hand during this long period. Nor is there any denial of the fact that not one person of Japanese ancestry was accused or convicted of espionage or sabotage after Pearl Harbor while they were still free, a fact which is some evidence of the loyalty of the vast majority of these individuals and of the effectiveness of the established methods of combatting these evils. It seems incredible that under these circumstances it would have been impossible to hold loyalty hearings for the mere 112,000 persons involved—or at least for the 70,000 American citizens—especially when a large part of this number represented children and elderly men and women.[4] Any

---

[4]   During a period of six months, the 112 alien tribunals or hearing boards set up by the British Government shortly after the outbreak of the present war summoned and examined

inconvenience that may have accompanied an attempt to conform to procedural due process cannot be said to justify violations of constitutional rights of individuals.

I dissent, therefore, from this legalization of racism. Racial discrimination in any form and in any degree has no justifiable part whatever in our democratic way of life. It is unattractive in any setting but it is utterly revolting among a free people who have embraced the principles set forth in the Constitution of the United States. All residents of this nation are kin in some way by blood or culture to a foreign land. Yet they are primarily and necessarily a part of the new and distinct civilization of the United States. They must accordingly be treated at all times as the heirs of the American experiment and as entitled to all the rights and freedoms guaranteed by the Constitution.

■ MR. JUSTICE JACKSON, dissenting.

Had Korematsu been one of four—the others being, say, a German alien enemy, an Italian alien enemy, and an [American] convicted of treason but out on parole—only Korematsu's presence would have violated the order. The difference between their innocence and his crime would result, not from anything he did, said, or thought, different than they, but only in that he was born of different racial stock.

Now, if any fundamental assumption underlies our system, it is that guilt is personal and not inheritable. . . . [H]ere is an attempt to make an otherwise innocent act a crime merely because this prisoner is the son of parents as to whom he had no choice, and belongs to a race from which there is no way to resign. If Congress in peace-time legislation should enact such a criminal law, I should suppose this Court would refuse to enforce it.

[Perhaps we cannot]confine military expedients by the Constitution, but neither would I distort the Constitution to approve all that the military may deem expedient. This is what the Court appears to be doing, whether consciously or not. I cannot say, from any evidence before me, that the orders of General DeWitt were not reasonably expedient military precautions, nor could I say that they were. But even if they were permissible military procedures, I deny that it follows that they are constitutional. If, as the Court holds, it does follow, then we may as well say that any military order will be constitutional and have done with it.

The limitation under which courts always will labor in examining the necessity for a military order are illustrated by this case. How does the Court know that these orders have a reasonable basis in necessity? No evidence whatever on that subject has been taken by this or any other court. There is sharp controversy as to the credibility of the DeWitt

approximately 74,000 German and Austrian aliens. These tribunals determined whether each individual enemy alien was a real enemy of the Allies or only a 'friendly enemy.' About 64,000 were freed from internment and from any special restrictions, and only 2,000 were interned.

report. So the Court, having no real evidence before it, has no choice but to accept General DeWitt's own unsworn, self-serving statement, untested by any cross-examination, that what he did was reasonable. And thus it will always be when courts try to look into the reasonableness of a military order.

In the very nature of things military decisions are not susceptible of intelligent judicial appraisal. They do not pretend to rest on evidence, but are made on information that often would not be admissible and on assumptions that could not be proved. Information in support of an order could not be disclosed to courts without danger that it would reach the enemy. Neither can courts act on communications made in confidence. Hence courts can never have any real alternative to accepting the mere declaration of the authority that issued the order that it was reasonably necessary from a military viewpoint.

Much is said of the danger to liberty from the Army program for deporting and detaining these citizens of Japanese extraction. But a judicial construction of the due process clause that will sustain this order is a far more subtle blow to liberty than the promulgation of the order itself. A military order, however unconstitutional, is not apt to last longer than the military emergency. Even during that period a succeeding commander may revoke it all. But once a judicial opinion rationalizes such an order to show that it conforms to the Constitution, or rather rationalizes the Constitution to show that the Constitution sanctions such an order, the Court for all time has validated the principle of racial discrimination in criminal procedure and of transplanting American citizens. The principle then lies about like a loaded weapon ready for the hand of any authority that can bring forward a plausible claim of an urgent need. Every repetition imbeds that principle more deeply in our law and thinking and expands it to new purposes.

I should hold that a civil court cannot be made to enforce an order which violates constitutional limitations even if it is a reasonable exercise of military authority.

NOTES AND QUESTIONS

1.   *Who Was Fred Korematsu?* Born in Oakland, California in 1919, Korematsu was the third of four sons of Japanese parents who immigrated to the United States in 1905. When Korematsu's family packed up to leave their home to comply with the evacuation order, Korematsu, who had a good-paying welder's job and an Italian-American girlfriend, refused to go. He and his girlfriend instead moved to Nevada, where Korematsu underwent plastic surgery on his eyelids to make him look less Japanese. He changed his name to Clyde Serra and claimed to be of Spanish and Hawaiian heritage. But he was eventually arrested and jailed for violating the order. An ACLU lawyer asked him to be the named plaintiff in a case challenging the Japanese exclusion orders. Korematsu agreed, and the case made its way to the

Supreme Court while Fred himself remained confined in an internment camp in Utah. Annie Nakao, "Overturning a wartime act decades later," *San Francisco Chronicle*, December 12, 2004. What relevance, if any, do these particular facts have in your understanding or assessment of the case?

2. **Korematsu's Precursors.** After the outbreak of World War I, German immigrants, and even American-born citizens of German descent, fell under suspicion of being disloyal. Wendy McElroy, *WWI, Xenophobia and Suppressing Political Opposition*, History News Network (Apr. 11, 2010), *available at*: http://historynewsnetwork.org/blog/125397. In the name of national security, the U.S government required 250,000 immigrants from Germany (who had not become United States citizens) to register at their local post office, to carry their registration cards at all times, and to report any change of address or employment. Of those aliens, 6,300 were also arrested. Thousands more were interrogated and investigated. More than 2000 were interned for the duration of the war in two camps in Utah and in Georgia. Arnold Krammer, *Undue Process: The Untold Story of America's German Alien Internees*. Rowman & Littlefield Pub Incorporated, 1997. For more on nationalistic fervor and xenophobia during World War I, *see*: John Higham, *Strangers in the land: Patterns of American nativism*, 1860–1925. Rutgers University Press, 2002. Does this historical background make the internment of Japanese Americans during World War II seem more understandable? Less objectionable? Or more outrageous?

3. **The Case of Italians and Germans.** During World War II, more than 11,000 people of German ancestry (along with a smaller number of Italians) were interned, pursuant to the same Executive Order that authorized the internment of Japanese Americans. Most of those interned were non-citizens, either long-term residents in the case of Germans, or people in the country temporarily in the case of Italians. Although General DeWitt (the same Commander who ordered the removal of people with Japanese ancestry) did press for the large-scale removal of Germans and Italians, President Roosevelt and his Secretary of War rejected the proposal, in part due to political opposition to mass detention of Germans. Immigrants from Germany and their children constituted a sizeable portion of the U.S. population. Instead, Germans and Italians received individualized hearings adjudicating their loyalty before being interned. Do you think anything other than racism can account for the differential treatment of Europeans and Japanese? In light of the way Germans and Italians were treated, would you say that a less restrictive order against Japanese—that all Japanese Americans report for individual questioning, so that their loyalty could be determined—would have been permissible? Would the Japanese internment have been less objectionable if it (or the individualized questioning) had been limited to Japanese non-citizens? Would the fact that the law at the time precluded Japanese immigrants from becoming naturalized citizens figure into your analysis?

4. **Judicial Review.** The majority in *Korematsu* expressed reluctance about second-guessing military officials' judgments during wartime. When a race classification so clearly burdens a particular racial group, is such

deference ever appropriate? What exactly does strict scrutiny mean in the hands of the *Korematsu* majority?

5.   *Making Amends for Internment.* In four related steps, the federal government has attempted to make amends for the internment of Japanese Americans. First, in 1948, President Truman signed the Japanese-American Claims Act, which provided compensation to Japanese Americans for economic losses due to their forced evacuation from their homes. Congress appropriated $38 million to settle 23,000 claims for damage to property and businesses. The final claim was adjudicated in 1965.

Second, in 1980, President Jimmy Carter appointed the Commission on Wartime Relocation and Internment of Civilians (CWRIC) to investigate the internment. The Commission's report, titled *Personal Justice Denied*, found little evidence of Japanese disloyalty at the time and attributed the internment to racism. According to the report, "the record does not permit the conclusion that military necessity warranted the exclusion of ethnic Japanese from the West Coast." The evidence on which General DeWitt supposedly relied—signaling from shore to enemy submarines, and arms and contraband found by the FBI during raids on ethnic Japanese homes and businesses—was deemed not credible. An investigation by the Federal Communications Commission found no substantiated cases of shore-to-ship signaling. And the arms and contraband confiscated by the FBI from ethnic Japanese were items normally in the possession of law-abiding civilians. The FBI concluded that their searches had uncovered no dangerous persons that "we could not otherwise know about." (*Personal Justice Denied*, Summary, p. 7).

Third, in 1984 a federal district court overturned Fred Korematsu's conviction, noting that the government had "knowingly withheld information from the courts when they were considering the critical questions of military necessity." *Korematsu v. United States*, 584 F. Supp. 1406 (N.D. Cal. 1984). The government had not made available to the courts documents and reports in its possession that undermined the claim that the people of Japanese descent represented a credible threat to the United States. The court ruled that the submission of the withheld evidence likely would have changed the Court's decision in *Korematsu*.

Fourth, Congress passed the Civil Liberties Act of 1988, officially acknowledging the "fundamental injustice" of the evacuation and paying reparations of $20,000 to each internee. The Act noted that "the evacuation, relocation, and internment of civilians during World War II . . . were carried out without adequate security reasons and without any acts of espionage or sabotage documented by the Commission, and were motivated largely by racial prejudice, wartime hysteria, and a failure of political leadership." The Act went on: "For these fundamental violations of the basic civil liberties and constitutional rights of these individuals of Japanese ancestry, the Congress apologizes on behalf of the Nation." For more on Japanese Americans' reparations, *see* Eric K. Yamamoto, Margaret Chon, Carol L. Izumi, Jerry Kang & Frank H. Wu, *Race, rights, and reparation: Law and the Japanese American internment*. Aspen Law & Business (2nd Ed., 2013).

None of these efforts to make amends encompassed the Germans and Italians who were interned. In *Jacobs v. Barr*, 959 F.2d 313 (D.C. Cir. 1992), the court of appeals considered an equal protection challenge to the Civil Liberties Act of 1988 by a German American who alleged that he was interned along with his German father during the war, even though neither was ever found to have engaged in any wrongdoing. Rejecting the claim, the court found ample evidence in the legislative history of the Civil Liberties Act of 1988 that Japanese American internees (but not their German American counterparts) were the victims of racial prejudice. The court noted no mass exclusion or detention of German (or Italian) Americans was ordered, and those detained, including the plaintiff and his father in *Jacobs*, were first given due process hearings to establish their threat to national security. Are you persuaded by these distinctions? Is it sensible and justifiable to compensate one set of innocent internees but not another?

6.   *Native Peoples and Reparations.* In addition to the internment, the U.S. government has also paid reparations to Indian tribes to redress a wide range of claims, including violations of treaties for which a judicial remedy was denied, and the loss of lands under treaties signed under duress. The total cost of the program, created by Congress in 1946, is estimated at $800 million. *See* Final Report of the United States Indian Claims Commission, H.R. Doc. No. 96–383 (1980). How is the case of Native peoples in the U.S. different from that of Japanese Americans?

7.   *African Americans and Reparations.* The question of reparations for African Americans is longstanding. During Reconstruction, freedmen were promised "40 acres and a mule"—a refrain that has been used since to invoke the idea that blacks ought to be compensated. In fact, no such reparations have ever been made on account of slavery. Slave owners were required to relinquish their slaves, but not their land. Various institutions, however, have extended reparations to African Americans for other wrongs. After reviewing these examples, consider what you think offers the best means of making amends for the past, and in what contexts, if any, such amends should be made.

a.   *The Tuskegee Syphilis Experiment.* Between 1932 and 1972 the U.S. Public Health Service studied the progression of untreated syphilis in hundreds of rural African-American men in Alabama. The aim was to document the dire effects of the disease. Officials told the men that they were receiving free healthcare from the government, and in fact did receive free medical exams, meals and burial insurance. But the government did not provide the men appropriate medical treatment for syphilis, even after penicillin became a widely used and effective treatment in the 1940s. The federal government, the American Medical Association and National Medical Association (a nationwide group of black doctors) continued to officially support the study as late as 1969.

An Associated Press story in 1972 prompted a public outcry about the study. A government panel subsequently concluded that the study was "ethically unjustified." In the mid-1970s, the U.S. government settled a class action lawsuit brought on behalf of the heirs of the deceased study participants, agreeing to contribute approximately $10,000,000 to a settlement fund, which was used to create the Tuskegee Health Benefit Program (THBP). THBP provided lifetime medical benefits and burial services to all study participants, widows and offspring. In 1997, President Bill Clinton, in a White House ceremony that included Tuskegee study participants and their families, formally apologized for the study. The federal government also contributed to establishing the National Center for Bioethics in Research and Health Care at Tuskegee, which opened in 1999 to explore issues that underlie research and medical care of African Americans and other underserved people.

b. ***Tulsa Race Riots Lawsuit.*** In 1921, after a black man was accused of sexually assaulting a white woman, whites rioted and decimated the black community of Tulsa, Oklahoma. Hundreds of armed white men gathered outside the courthouse where the man was being held, and a group of armed black men arrived to prevent his lynching. After a shot was fired, the black men fled to Greenwood, a wealthy black neighborhood popularly known as "black Wall Street," and the white men chased them. The Tulsa police chief apparently enabled the ensuing battle by deputizing hundreds of white men and commandeering gun shops to arm them. A state government report estimated that roughly 300 people were killed and more than 8,000 left homeless as a result of the attack. No one was convicted or compensated. Not until decades later was a state commission formed that investigated the episode and recommended payments to the survivors. A lawsuit filed on behalf of the survivors in 2003 was dismissed due to the statute of limitations having run.

c. ***Truth and Reconciliation Commission.*** On November 3, 1979, in Greensboro, North Carolina, members of the Ku Klux Klan and the American Nazi Party shot and killed five protest marchers at a rally organized by communists intended to demonstrate opposition to the Klan. In 2004, a private organization, the "Greensboro Truth and Reconciliation Commission," declared that it would take public testimony and examine the causes and consequences of the Greensboro massacre. This private group (which lacked any government recognition or authority) was patterned after the state-created Truth and Reconciliation Commissions in post-apartheid South Africa. The Greensboro TRC aimed to give hope to victims "who have waited in vain for their governments to show the political will to address past injustices." *See* Magarrell, Lisa, Joya Wesley, and Bongani Finca. *Learning from Greensboro: Truth and reconciliation in the United States*. University of Pennsylvania Press, 2010. When might a public discussion to air out controversies be useful as a way to reckon with past wrongs? Does the fact that the North Carolina Truth and Reconciliation Commission was not officially recognized by the state matter? Should claims for past injustices be made before a committee, a court, a governmental agency, Congress?

d. ***Brown University Steering Committee on Slavery and Justice and Subsequent University Actions.*** In 2003, Brown University President Ruth Simmons appointed a committee of faculty, students, and administrators to investigate and report on the University's involvement with slavery and the trans-Atlantic slave trade. The Committee's final report, presented to President Simmons in October 2006, led to a number of changes; the University i) took steps to recast its official history to present a more complete picture of its origins, ii) established a major research and teaching initiative on slavery and justice, which included strengthening and expanding the Department of Africana Studies; iii) raised a permanent endowment in the amount of $10 million to establish a Fund for the Education of the Children of Providence, and iv) expanded support to Historically Black Colleges and Universities. How effective are these efforts as a means of making amends for the past?

Following campus protests against racial injustices in November 2015, the president of Princeton University agreed to consider the demands of student protesters, including opening a debate about Woodrow Wilson's legacy at Princeton. This would potentially include removing the name of Woodrow Wilson, the 28th U.S. president, a segregationist who some believe supported the ideas of the Ku Klux Klan, from a residential college, from the Woodrow Wilson School of Public Policy and International Affairs, and from any other buildings. Mary Hui, "After protests, Princeton debates Woodrow Wilson's legacy," The Washington Post, Nov 23, 2015. Should Universities "cleanse" themselves of their connection to our slave past by changing names of buildings named after slave-owners or racists? What are the drawbacks of such moves?

8. *Reparations and Slavery.* Let's consider now how the United States should make amends for the wrong of slavery, if at all. One form of making amends would be a simple apology. On a visit to Africa in 1998, President Bill Clinton apologized for the slave trade. Congressional resolutions apologizing for slavery were passed separately by the House of Representatives in 2008 and by the Senate in 2009. The nonbinding Senate resolution sponsored by Sen. Tom Harkin, D-Iowa, was similar to the House resolution, acknowledging the wrongs of slavery without offering any reparations. These resolutions were never reconciled or signed by the President. Consider the following excerpt from the 2009 Senate resolution (S. Con. Res. 26):

> "(1) APOLOGY FOR THE ENSLAVEMENT AND SEGREGATION OF AFRICAN-AMERICANS.—The Congress— (A) acknowledges the fundamental injustice, cruelty, brutality, and inhumanity of slavery and Jim Crow laws; (B) apologizes to African-Americans on behalf of the people of the United States, for the wrongs committed against them and their ancestors who suffered under slavery and Jim Crow laws; and (C) expresses its recommitment to the principle that all people are created equal and endowed with inalienable rights to life, liberty, and the pursuit of happiness, and calls on all people of the United States to work toward eliminating racial prejudices, injustices, and discrimination from our society. (2) DISCLAIMER.—Nothing in this resolution— (A) authorizes or supports any claim against the United States; or (B) serves as a settlement of any claim against the United States."

Every year since 1989, Rep. John Conyers has introduced some version of the "Commission to Study Reparation Proposals for African Americans Act" (H.R. 40), portions of which are reproduced below:

"A BILL

To acknowledge the fundamental injustice, cruelty, brutality, and inhumanity of slavery in the United States and the 13 American colonies between 1619 and 1865 and to establish a commission to examine the institution of slavery, subsequently de jure and de facto racial and economic discrimination against African-Americans, and the impact of these forces on living African-Americans, to make recommendations to the Congress on appropriate remedies, and for other purposes.

Sec. 3 ESTABLISHMENT AND DUTIES

The Commission shall perform the following duties:

(7) Recommend appropriate remedies in consideration of the Commission's findings. In making such recommendations, the Commission shall address among other issues, the following questions:

(A) Whether the Government of the United States should offer a formal apology on behalf of the people of the United States for the perpetration of gross human rights violations on African slaves and their descendants.

(B) Whether African-Americans still suffer from the lingering effects of [slavery].

(C) Whether, in consideration of the Commission's findings, any form of compensation to the descendants of African slaves is warranted.

(D) If the Commission finds that such compensation is warranted, what should be the amount of compensation, what form of compensation should be awarded, and who should be eligible for such compensation."

Do you think the Act is a good idea? Is there a benefit to studying the issue of reparations for past harm? Why do you think the bill never passes in Congress? Do you think it would ever pass? Should it?

For more on African-American reparations, *see* Kim Forde-Mazrui, *Taking conservatives seriously: a moral justification for affirmative action and reparations*, 92(3) Cal. L. Rev. 683 (2004); Keith B. Hylton, *A Framework for Reparations Claims*, 24 BC Third World LJ 31 (2004).

CHAPTER 2

CIVIL RIGHTS, THE SECOND RECONSTRUCTION, AND THE ASCENDANCE OF COLORBLINDNESS

"The world is before you, and you need not take it or leave it as it was when you came in."

—James Baldwin

Historians and legal scholars sometimes characterize the middle decades of the twentieth century as the Second Reconstruction—a period of dramatic legal developments targeting the institutional manifestations of white supremacy. In 1954, the Supreme Court decided *Brown v. Board of Education*, overruling *Plessy v. Ferguson* and declaring Jim Crow segregation in public education a violation of the Fourteenth Amendment. In a series of per curiam opinions, the Court also ordered the dismantling of formal, legally mandated segregation in other public facilities. In 1964, 1965, and 1968, Congress enacted sweeping civil rights legislation that prohibited race discrimination, among private and public actors alike, in public accommodations, employment, voting, and housing.

But as with the first Reconstruction, these developments were contested, subject to popular mobilization both for and against civil rights. The South resisted *Brown's* injunction to desegregate the schools—so much so that President Eisenhower eventually sent federal troops to Little Rock, Arkansas, in 1957 to integrate its Central High School. In 1956, most members of Congress from the South signed the Southern Manifesto, proclaiming *Brown* an unprincipled assertion of the preferences of the Supreme Court in derogation of the long-standing and legally sanctioned mores of the people of the South. President Johnson's signing of the civil rights statutes, in effect, yielded the South to the Republican Party. Republican politicians—most famously Richard Nixon—used white resentment of school busing and other racial remedies as weapons during campaigns.

The battle over the meaning of the Second Reconstruction continues to this day, and we can trace competing conceptions of racial justice through the jurisprudence and legal developments of the last sixty years. Though overt racial bigotry is now less acceptable than it once was, the disadvantages experienced by blacks and other racial minorities relative to whites, along with other forms of bias, remain serious social problems.

Disagreements over how to define, much less combat, racial injustices have persisted and taken the form of debates over how to implement the legal achievements of the civil rights movement. Two major organizing principles have come to dominate scholarly and legal understandings of the pursuit of racial justice. One focuses on outcomes (i.e., Racial Conditions) and the other on decision-making processes (i.e., Racial Consciousness). While both stand opposed to Jim Crow, they embody divergent accounts of the path to racial justice.

The anti-subordination approach calls for ongoing attention to the status and conditions of historically disadvantaged racial groups. Its objectives include narrowing racial gaps in opportunities and outcomes throughout society. The anti-subordination principle justifies race-conscious efforts to enhance disadvantaged groups' welfare, as well as prohibitions on public and private practices that even inadvertently aggravate minority groups' disadvantage. The colorblindness approach, in contrast, focuses on decision-making processes rather than outcomes; it eschews race conscious decision-making, by the state and (many) private actors as well, regarding any use of race as potentially pernicious, given our nation's sordid history of race discrimination.

The central question posed by these theories—whether racial justice requires policing race-consciousness or ameliorating unequal conditions (or some combination of the two)—plays out throughout this book, and throughout our society. Should we prohibit any individual from being treated differently from others on account of race? Or, instead, should we attend to the racial group consequences of even purportedly race-blind decisions? To what extent are these goals mutually exclusive? In what ways is each attractive, or incomplete?

While initially elaborated in the constitutional setting, the principles of anti-subordination and colorblindness can also be used to understand different strategies for regulating private institutions and actors. Indeed, a central question of the Second Reconstruction concerns the extent to which nondiscrimination mandates can and should extend beyond the government. Does the eradication of White Supremacy, and the realization of racial justice, require something more than the enforcement of equality principles against the government? If so, how are we to decide what realms of social life to remake? And on the basis of what principle?

While both anti-subordination and colorblindness continue to play a role in our law and in our intuitions about racial justice, the story of the last half-century has been the ascendance of colorblindness as a dominant cultural and legal norm. The Supreme Court has come increasingly close to interpreting the Fourteenth Amendment's equal protection clause to mandate governmental colorblindness. That approach is also reflected in the Court's interpretation of federal statutes. Beyond the courts, colorblindness has attracted support as a moral principle that should guide not only governmental action but, ostensibly, private decision-making as well. We therefore pay special attention to how colorblindness has evolved as a legal norm and challenge you to consider whether the doctrines that embody it advance, or impede, racial justice.

As we begin consideration of the Second Reconstruction, pause and ask: how has the meaning of white supremacy evolved since slavery and the First Reconstruction? How, why and in what ways did White Supremacy survive the First Reconstruction? What tools did reformers and activists of the Second Reconstruction devise to dismantle it, and how did those tools differ from those that emerged after the Civil War? While Jim Crow is unquestionably different from slavery, can you identify continuities in the forms of racial injustice across the two periods? How and why have attitudes toward regulation of the private sphere changed? These same questions will recur as you explore the contemporary settings throughout this book.

I. THE SECOND RECONSTRUCTION

The Supreme Court's momentous decision in *Brown v. Board of Education* is typically and understandably accorded primacy in accounts of the legal demise of Jim Crow. Here we situate *Brown* as part of a quartet of Court decisions, and as a significant moment in a wide-ranging Civil Rights Movement that culminated in transformative federal legislation a decade after the Court's judgment. The Supreme Court handed down the first decision—*Hernandez v. Texas*, 347 U.S. 475 (1954)—two weeks before *Brown* and made clear that the Equal Protection Clause extended to all racial groups in the United States. Segregation in the decades before *Brown* was widespread and not limited to African Americans. Latinos and Asian Americans were often relegated to separate schools. In *Gong Lum v. Rice*, for example, the Supreme Court upheld a ruling by the Mississippi Supreme Court that classified Chinese American plaintiff as "colored" and therefore not permitted to attend the local school for white children. In *Hernandez*, the Court grapples with the exclusion of Mexican Americans from jury service.

Hernandez v. Texas

Supreme Court of the United States, 1954.
347 U.S. 475.

■ MR. CHIEF JUSTICE WARREN delivered the opinion of the Court.

The petitioner, Pete Hernandez, was indicted for the murder of one Joe Espinosa by a grand jury in Jackson County, Texas. He was convicted and sentenced to life imprisonment. . . . Prior to the trial, the petitioner, by his counsel, offered timely motions to quash the indictment and the jury panel. He alleged that persons of Mexican descent were systematically excluded from service as jury commissioners, grand jurors, and petit jurors, although there were such persons fully qualified to serve residing in Jackson County. The petitioner asserted that exclusion of this class deprived him, as a member of the class, of the equal protection of the laws guaranteed by the Fourteenth Amendment of the Constitution. After a hearing, the trial court denied the motions. . . . In affirming the judgment of the trial court, the Texas Court of Criminal Appeals considered and passed upon the substantial federal question raised by the petitioner. We granted a writ of certiorari to review that decision.

In numerous decisions, this Court has held that it is a denial of the equal protection of the laws to try a defendant of a particular race or color under an indictment issued by a grand jury, or before a petit jury, from which all persons of his race or color have, solely because of that race or color, been excluded by the State, whether acting through its legislature, its courts, or its executive or administrative officers. Although the Court has had little occasion to rule on the question directly, it has been recognized since *Strauder v. West Virginia* that the exclusion of a class of persons from jury service on grounds other than race or color may also deprive a defendant who is a member of that class of the constitutional guarantee of equal protection of the laws. The State of Texas would have us hold that there are only two classes—white and Negro—within the contemplation of the Fourteenth Amendment. The decisions of this Court do not support that view.

Throughout our history differences in race and color have defined easily identifiable groups which have at times required the aid of the courts in securing equal treatment under the laws. But community prejudices are not static, and from time to time other differences from the community norm may define other groups which need the same protection. Whether such a group exists within a community is a question of fact. When the existence of a distinct class is demonstrated, and it is further shown that the laws, as written or as applied, single out that class for different treatment not based on some reasonable classification, the guarantees of the Constitution have been violated. The Fourteenth Amendment is not directed solely against discrimination due to a "two-class theory"—that is, based upon differences between "white" and Negro.

As the petitioner acknowledges, the Texas system of selecting grand and petit jurors by the use of jury commissions is fair on its face and capable of being utilized without discrimination. But as this Court has held, the system is susceptible to abuse and can be employed in a discriminatory manner. The exclusion of otherwise eligible persons from jury service solely because of their ancestry or national origin is discrimination prohibited by the Fourteenth Amendment. The Texas statute makes no such discrimination, but the petitioner alleges that those administering the law do.

The petitioner's initial burden in substantiating his charge of group discrimination was to prove that persons of Mexican descent constitute a separate class in Jackson County, distinct from "whites." One method by which this may be demonstrated is by showing the attitude of the community. Here the testimony of responsible officials and citizens contained the admission that residents of the community distinguished between "white" and "Mexican." The participation of persons of Mexican descent in business and community groups was shown to be slight. Until very recent times, children of Mexican descent were required to attend a segregated school for the first four grades. At least one restaurant in town prominently displayed a sign announcing "No Mexicans Served." On the courthouse grounds at the time of the hearing, there were two men's toilets, one unmarked, and the other marked "Colored Men" and "Hombres Aqui" ("Men Here"). No substantial evidence was offered to rebut the logical inference to be drawn from these facts, and it must be concluded that petitioner succeeded in his proof.

Having established the existence of a class, petitioner was then charged with the burden of proving discrimination. To do so, he relied on the pattern of proof established by *Norris v. Alabama*. In that case, proof that Negroes constituted a substantial segment of the population of the jurisdiction, that some Negroes were qualified to serve as jurors, and that none had been called for jury service over an extended period of time, was held to constitute prima facie proof of the systematic exclusion of Negroes from jury service. This holding, sometimes called the "rule of exclusion," has been applied in other cases, and it is available in supplying proof of discrimination against any delineated class.

The petitioner established that 14% of the population of Jackson County were persons with Mexican or Latin-American surnames, and that 11% of the males over 21 bore such names. The County Tax Assessor testified that 6 or 7 percent of the freeholders on the tax rolls of the County were persons of Mexican descent. The State of Texas stipulated that "for the last twenty-five years there is no record of any person with a Mexican or Latin American name having served on a jury commission, grand jury or petit jury in Jackson County." The parties also stipulated that "there are some male persons of Mexican or Latin American descent in Jackson County who, by virtue of being citizens, householders, or freeholders, and having all other legal prerequisites to jury service, are eligible to serve as members of a jury commission, grand jury and/or petit jury."

The petitioner met the burden of proof imposed in *Norris v. Alabama*. To rebut the strong prima facie case of the denial of the equal protection of the laws guaranteed by the Constitution thus established, the State offered the testimony of five jury commissioners that they had not discriminated against persons of Mexican or Latin-American descent in selecting jurors. They stated that their only objective had been to select those whom they thought were best qualified. This testimony is not enough to overcome the petitioner's case. As the Court said in *Norris v. Alabama*:

> That showing as to the long-continued exclusion of negroes from jury service, and as to the many negroes qualified for that service, could not be met by mere generalities. If, in the presence of such testimony as defendant adduced, the mere general assertions by officials of their performance of duty were to be accepted as an adequate justification for the complete exclusion of negroes from jury service, the constitutional provision . . . would be but a vain and illusory requirement. [294 U. S., at 598.]

The same reasoning is applicable to these facts.

Circumstances or chance may well dictate that no persons in a certain class will serve on a particular jury or during some particular period. But it taxes our credulity to say that mere chance resulted in there being no members of this class among the over six thousand jurors called in the past 25 years. The result bespeaks discrimination, whether or not it was a conscious decision on the part of any individual jury commissioner. The judgment of conviction must be reversed.

To say that this decision revives the rejected contention that the Fourteenth Amendment requires proportional representation of all the component ethnic groups of the community on every jury ignores the facts. The petitioner did not seek proportional representation, nor did he claim a right to have persons of Mexican descent sit on the particular juries which he faced. His only claim is the right to be indicted and tried by juries from which all members of his class are not systematically excluded—juries selected from among all qualified persons regardless of national origin or descent. To this much, he is entitled by the Constitution.

NOTES AND QUESTIONS

1. ***The Status of Mexican-Americans.*** Why did the Court hold that the Equal Protection Clause protects Mexican-American status? Is Mexican-American a race? If not, why treat it as such? What if Mexican Americans had not been the objects of pervasive prejudice in the local community? Does the racial status of a group result from the attitudes of the community? What conception of equality and equal protection does the Court's approach seem to reflect?

2. ***Outcome Discrimination.*** Describing the statistical under-representation of Mexican Americans summoned for jury service, the Court in *Hernandez* said that "[t]he result bespeaks discrimination, whether or not it was a conscious decision on the part of any individual jury commissioner." What does this mean? Is it legitimate to describe the under-selection of

Mexican Americans from jury service as "discrimination" if it was not conscious? Why or why not?

A. THE ROAD TO BROWN V. BOARD OF EDUCATION

During the early decades of the 20th century, the NAACP adopted a litigation strategy designed to prompt courts to enforce the "equal" prong of "separate but equal." But eventually the leadership of the organization concluded that Jim Crow was simply too powerful a symbol of racism to leave unchallenged. Litigation over equalization of individual institutions was simply too piecemeal and costly to pursue. The litigation that culminated in *Brown* began with NAACP challenges to segregation in higher education. In *Missouri ex rel. Gaines v. Canada*, 305 U.S. 337 (1938), the Supreme Court held that the State University of Missouri Law School could not deny admission to Lloyd Gaines, an African American, on the basis of his race. The Fourteenth Amendment required that if Missouri provided legal education, it either had to furnish a substantially equivalent school for black students, or it had to admit Gaines to the existing law school.

In response to a similar legal challenge, Texas attempted to follow the Supreme Court's suggestion of creating a separate law school for black students. But in *Sweatt v. Painter*, 339 U.S. 629 (1950), the Supreme Court held that the hastily-created school was not substantially equal in quality to the University of Texas Law School, where the plaintiff had been denied admission. Chief Justice Vinson noted inadequacies in the school's library and its thin staffing. Of the greatest precedential value, however, was the following observation: "What is more important, the University of Texas Law School possesses to a far greater degree those qualities which are incapable of objective measurement but which make for greatness in a law school. Such qualities, to name but a few, include reputation of the faculty, experience of the administration, position and influence of the alumni, standing in the community, traditions and prestige. It is difficult to believe that one who had a free choice between these law schools would consider the question close."

On the same day it decided *Sweatt*, the Supreme Court decided *McLaurin v. Oklahoma State Regents*, 339 U.S. 637 (1950). G.W. McLaurin was enrolled in a doctoral program at the University of Oklahoma, but school officials required him to sit in a separate part of the classroom, to study in a designated area in the library, and to eat his meals at a designated table in the cafeteria. Chief Justice Vinson concluded: "[These restrictions] signify that the State, in administering the facilities it affords for professional and graduate study, sets McLaurin apart from the other students. The result is that appellant is handicapped in his pursuit of effective graduate instruction. Such restrictions impair and inhibit his ability to study, to engage in discussions and exchange views with other students, and, in general, to learn his profession. . . . State imposed restrictions which produce such inequalities cannot be sustained."

With the precedent from the higher education cases, the NAACP mounted a direct challenge to segregation in primary and secondary schools, well aware of the heightened threat it would pose to norms and customs in the Jim Crow South. In explaining the strategy of targeting graduate schools first, Thurgood Marshall had said: "Those racial supremacy boys somehow think that little kids of six or seven are going to get funny ideas about sex and marriage just from going to school together, but for some equally funny reason youngsters in law school aren't supposed to feel that way." In 1952, the Court heard arguments in a set of consolidated cases from five different school districts around the country. The Court did not decide the case until 1954, however. It had been held over for re-argument, purportedly because the Court was badly divided. The Court asked the parties to brief how the history of the Fourteenth Amendment should affect the outcome of the case. But before the Court could hear the new arguments, Chief Justice Vinson—a likely vote against the NAACP—died suddenly. President Eisenhower replaced him with Governor Earl Warren of California, who eventually oversaw a unanimous decision in this most controversial of cases.

Brown v. Board of Education

Supreme Court of the United States, 1954.
347 U.S. 483.

■ MR. CHIEF JUSTICE WARREN delivered the opinion of the Court.

These cases come to us from the States of Kansas, South Carolina, Virginia, and Delaware. They are premised on different facts and different local conditions, but a common legal question justifies their consideration together in this consolidated opinion.

In each of the cases, minors of the Negro race, through their legal representatives, seek the aid of the courts in obtaining admission to the public schools of their community on a nonsegregated basis. In each instance, they have been denied admission to schools attended by white children under laws requiring or permitting segregation according to race. This segregation was alleged to deprive the plaintiffs of the equal protection of the laws under the Fourteenth Amendment. In each of the cases other than the Delaware case, a three-judge federal district court denied relief to the plaintiffs on the so-called "separate but equal" doctrine announced by this Court in Plessy v. Ferguson. Under that doctrine, equality of treatment is accorded when the races are provided substantially equal facilities, even though these facilities be separate. In the Delaware case, the Supreme Court of Delaware adhered to that doctrine, but ordered that the plaintiffs be admitted to the white schools because of their superiority to the Negro schools.

The plaintiffs contend that segregated public schools are not "equal" and cannot be made "equal," and that hence they are deprived of the equal protection of the laws. Because of the obvious importance of the question presented, the Court took jurisdiction. Argument was heard in the 1952 Term, and reargument was heard this Term on certain questions propounded by the Court.

Reargument was largely devoted to the circumstances surrounding the adoption of the Fourteenth Amendment in 1868. It covered exhaustively consideration of the Amendment in Congress, ratification by the states, then existing practices in racial segregation, and the views of proponents and opponents of the Amendment. This discussion and our own investigation convince us that, although these sources cast some light, it is not enough to resolve the problem with which we are faced. At best, they are inconclusive. The most avid proponents of the post-War Amendments undoubtedly intended them to remove all legal distinctions among "all persons born or naturalized in the United States." Their opponents, just as certainly, were antagonistic to both the letter and the spirit of the Amendments and wished them to have the most limited effect. What others in Congress and the state legislatures had in mind cannot be determined with any degree of certainty.

An additional reason for the inconclusive nature of the Amendment's history, with respect to segregated schools, is the status of public education at that time. In the South, the movement toward free common schools, supported by general taxation, had not yet taken hold. Education of white children was largely in the hands of private groups. Education of Negroes was almost nonexistent, and practically all of the race were illiterate. In fact, any education of Negroes was forbidden by law in some states. Today, in contrast, many Negroes have achieved outstanding success in the arts and sciences as well as in the business and professional world. It is true that public school education at the time of the Amendment had advanced further in the North, but the effect of the Amendment on Northern States was generally ignored in the congressional debates. Even in the North, the conditions of public education did not approximate those existing today. The curriculum was usually rudimentary; ungraded schools were common in rural areas; the school term was but three months a year in many states; and compulsory school attendance was virtually unknown. As a consequence, it is not surprising that there should be so little in the history of the Fourteenth Amendment relating to its intended effect on public education.

In the first cases in this Court construing the Fourteenth Amendment, decided shortly after its adoption, the Court interpreted it as proscribing all state-imposed discriminations against the Negro race.[1]

---

[1] *In re Slaughter-House Cases,* 1873, 16 Wall. 36, 67–72, 21 L.Ed. 394; *Strauder v. West Virginia,* 1880, 100 U.S. 303, 307–308, 25 L.Ed. 664:

It ordains that no State shall deprive any person of life, liberty, or property, without due process of law, or deny to any person within its jurisdiction the equal protection of

The doctrine of "separate but equal" did not make its appearance in this court until 1896 in the case of Plessy v. Ferguson, *supra*, involving not education but transportation.[2] American courts have since labored with the doctrine for over half a century. In this Court, there have been six cases involving the "separate but equal" doctrine in the field of public education.[3] In Cumming v. Board of Education of Richmond County and Gong Lum v. Rice, the validity of the doctrine itself was not challenged.[4] In more recent cases, all on the graduate school level, inequality was found in that specific benefits enjoyed by white students were denied to Negro students of the same educational qualifications. In none of these cases was it necessary to re-examine the doctrine to grant relief to the Negro plaintiff. And in Sweatt v. Painter, *supra*, the Court expressly reserved decision on the question whether Plessy v. Ferguson should be held inapplicable to public education.

In the instant cases, that question is directly presented. Here, unlike Sweatt v. Painter, there are findings below that the Negro and white schools involved have been equalized, or are being equalized, with respect to buildings, curricula, qualifications and salaries of teachers, and other "tangible" factors.[5] Our decision, therefore, cannot turn on merely a comparison of these tangible factors in the Negro and white schools

----

the laws. What is this but declaring that the law in the States shall be the same for the black as for the white; that all persons, whether colored or white, shall stand equal before the laws of the States, and, in regard to the colored race, for whose protection the amendment was primarily designed, that no discrimination shall be made against them by law because of their color? The words of the amendment, it is true, are prohibitory, but they contain a necessary implication of a positive immunity, or right, most valuable to the colored race,—the right to exemption from unfriendly legislation against them distinctively as colored,—exemption from legal discriminations, implying inferiority in civil society, lessening the security of their enjoyment of the rights which others enjoy, and discriminations which are steps towards reducing them to the condition of a subject race.

See also State of Virginia v. Rives, 1879, 100 U.S. 313, 318, 25 L.Ed. 667; *Ex parte Virginia,* 1879, 100 U.S. 339, 344–345, 25 L.Ed. 676.

[2]   The doctrine apparently originated in *Roberts v. City of Boston,* 1850, 5 Cush. 198, 59 Mass. 198, 206, upholding school segregation against attack as being violative of a state constitutional guarantee of equality. Segregation in Boston public schools was eliminated in 1855. Mass. Acts 1855, c. 256. But elsewhere in the North segregation in public education has persisted in some communities until recent years. It is apparent that such segregation has long been a nationwide problem, not merely one of sectional concern.

[3]   *See also Berea College v. Kentucky,* 1908, 211 U.S. 45, 29 S.Ct. 33, 53 L.Ed. 81.

[4]   In the Cumming case, Negro taxpayers sought an injunction requiring the defendant school board to discontinue the operation of a high school for white children until the board resumed operation of a high school for Negro children. Similarly, in the Gong Lum case, the plaintiff, a child of Chinese descent, contended only that state authorities had misapplied the doctrine by classifying him with Negro children and requiring him to attend a Negro school.

[5]   In the Kansas case, the court below found substantial equality as to all such factors. 98 F.Supp. 797, 798.In the South Carolina case, the court below found that the defendants were proceeding 'promptly and in good faith to comply with the court's decree.' 103 F.Supp. 920, 921.In the Virginia case, the court below noted that the equalization program was already 'afoot and progressing,' 103 F.Supp. 337, 341; since then, we have been advised, in the Virginia Attorney General's brief on reargument, that the program has now been completed. In the Delaware case, the court below similarly noted that the state's equalization program was well under way. 91 A.2d 137, 139.

involved in each of the cases. We must look instead to the effect of segregation itself on public education.

In approaching this problem, we cannot turn the clock back to 1868 when the Amendment was adopted, or even to 1896 when Plessy v. Ferguson was written. We must consider public education in the light of its full development and its present place in American life throughout the Nation. Only in this way can it be determined if segregation in public schools deprives these plaintiffs of the equal protection of the laws.

Today, education is perhaps the most important function of state and local governments. Compulsory school attendance laws and the great expenditures for education both demonstrate our recognition of the importance of education to our democratic society. It is required in the performance of our most basic public responsibilities, even service in the armed forces. It is the very foundation of good citizenship. Today it is a principal instrument in awakening the child to cultural values, in preparing him for later professional training, and in helping him to adjust normally to his environment. In these days, it is doubtful that any child may reasonably be expected to succeed in life if he is denied the opportunity of an education. Such an opportunity, where the state has undertaken to provide it, is a right which must be made available to all on equal terms. We come then to the question presented: Does segregation of children in public schools solely on the basis of race, even though the physical facilities and other "tangible" factors may be equal, deprive the children of the minority group of equal educational opportunities? We believe that it does.

In Sweatt v. Painter, in finding that a segregated law school for Negroes could not provide them equal educational opportunities, this Court relied in large part on "those qualities which are incapable of objective measurement but which make for greatness in a law school." In McLaurin v. Oklahoma State Regents, the Court, in requiring that a Negro admitted to a white graduate school be treated like all other students, again resorted to intangible considerations: " . . . his ability to study, to engage in discussions and exchange views with other students, and, in general, to learn his profession." Such considerations apply with added force to children in grade and high schools. To separate them from others of similar age and qualifications solely because of their race generates a feeling of inferiority as to their status in the community that may affect their hearts and minds in a way unlikely ever to be undone. The effect of this separation on their educational opportunities was well stated by a finding in the Kansas case by a court which nevertheless felt compelled to rule against the Negro plaintiffs:

> Segregation of white and colored children in public schools has a detrimental effect upon the colored children. The impact is greater when it has the sanction of the law; for the policy of separating the races is usually interpreted as denoting the

inferiority of the negro group. A sense of inferiority affects the motivation of a child to learn. Segregation with the sanction of law, therefore, has a tendency to (retard) the educational and mental development of Negro children and to deprive them of some of the benefits they would receive in a racial(ly) integrated school system.

Whatever may have been the extent of psychological knowledge at the time of Plessy v. Ferguson, this finding is amply supported by modern authority.[6] Any language in Plessy v. Ferguson contrary to this finding is rejected.

We conclude that in the field of public education the doctrine of "separate but equal' has no place. Separate educational facilities are inherently unequal.

Bolling v. Sharpe

Supreme Court of the United States, 1954.
347 U.S. 497.

■ MR. CHIEF JUSTICE WARREN delivered the opinion of the Court.

This case challenges the validity of segregation in the public schools of the District of Columbia. The petitioners, minors of the Negro race, allege that such segregation deprives them of due process of law under the Fifth Amendment. They were refused admission to a public school attended by white children solely because of their race.

We have this day held that the Equal Protection Clause of the Fourteenth Amendment prohibits the states from maintaining racially segregated public schools. The legal problem in the District of Columbia is somewhat different, however. The Fifth Amendment, which is applicable in the District of Columbia, does not contain an equal protection clause, as does the Fourteenth Amendment, which applies only to the states. But the concepts of equal protection and due process, both stemming from our American ideal of fairness, are not mutually exclusive. The "equal protection of the laws" is a more explicit safeguard of prohibited unfairness than "due process of law," and, therefore, we do not imply that the two are always interchangeable phrases. But, as this Court has recognized, discrimination may be so unjustifiable as to be violative of due process.

---

[6]   K.B. Clark, Effect of Prejudice and Discrimination on Personality Development (Midcentury White House Conference on Children and Youth, 1950); Witmer and Kotinsky, Personality in the Making (1952), c. VI; Deutscher and Chein, The Psychological Effects of Enforced Segregation: A Survey of Social Science Opinion, 26 J.Psychol. 259 (1948); Chein, What are the Psychological Effects of Segregation Under Conditions of Equal Facilities?, 3 Int. J. Opinion and Attitude Res. 229 (1949); Brameld, Educational Costs, in Discrimination and National Welfare (MacIver, ed., 1949), 44–48; Frazier, The Negro in the United States (1949), 674–681. And see generally Myrdal, An American Dilemma (1944).

Classifications based solely upon race must be scrutinized with particular care, since they are contrary to our traditions, and hence constitutionally suspect. As long ago as 1896, this Court declared the principle that the Constitution of the United States, in its present form, forbids, so far as civil and political rights are concerned, discrimination by the General Government, or by the States, against any citizen because of his race.

And in *Buchanan v. Warley*, [1917] the Court held that a statute which limited the right of a property owner to convey his property to a person of another race was, as an unreasonable discrimination, a denial of due process of law.

Although the Court has not assumed to define "liberty" with any great precision, that term is not confined to mere freedom from bodily restraint. Liberty under law extends to the full range of conduct which the individual is free to pursue, and it cannot be restricted except for a proper governmental objective. Segregation in public education is not reasonably related to any proper governmental objective, and thus it imposes on Negro children of the District of Columbia a burden that constitutes an arbitrary deprivation of their liberty in violation of the Due Process Clause.

In view of our decision that the Constitution prohibits the states from maintaining racially segregated public schools, it would be unthinkable that the same Constitution would impose a lesser duty on the Federal Government. We hold that racial segregation in the public schools of the District of Columbia is a denial of the due process of law guaranteed by the Fifth Amendment to the Constitution.

NOTES AND QUESTIONS

1.   *Is Separate Necessarily Unequal?* What did the Court mean in saying that "separate educational facilities are *inherently* unequal?" If, as the parties had stipulated in *Brown*, the facilities, supplies and so forth in white and negro schools were equal or were being made so, in what way would the segregated schools still be unequal?

2.   *Clark's Doll Studies.* The Court reasoned that segregated education "generates a feeling of inferiority . . . that may affect [black students'] hearts and minds in a way unlikely ever to be undone." The court supported that conclusion by reference to "modern authority," and cited the so-called doll studies conducted by the famed psychologist Kenneth Clark. Those studies of black children in the North and South presented the children with white dolls and black dolls and asked the children to identify the "good doll" and the "bad doll." The Court cited the findings to support the conclusion that segregation leads to self-hatred and low esteem among segregated black children in the south. Some of the findings from the doll studies are reproduced below. Do you agree with the Court's interpretation of the findings? What conclusions do you draw?

Doll Choices of Black Children in Southern (Segregated) and Northern (Integrated) Schools

	"Nice Doll"		"Looks Bad"	
	South	North	South	North
Black Doll	46	30	49	71
White Doll	52	68	16	17
No Choice	2	2	35	12

3. *Justifying the Court's Ruling in* **Brown.** Putting aside the question of psychological harm, what other justifications might there be for the Court's conclusion that segregation is "inherently unequal"? What social, political, or economic developments might have made segregation seem less justifiable to the mid-20th century Justices than it had to their late 19th century forebears?

4. *Only Segregation by Law?* In future cases, the Court would confront the question of how broadly to construe its ruling in *Brown.* Had the Court concluded that the mere fact of segregation was unconstitutional, or that segregation was unconstitutional only when legally mandated? That is, if segregation was to occur without laws requiring it, would that be permissible? And, to what other settings beyond the public schools did the decision apply?

5. *The Southern Manifesto.* Consider this response to the Court's decision in *Brown*:

B. DECLARATION OF CONSTITUTIONAL PRINCIPLES

[T]he increasing gravity of the situation following the decision of the Supreme Court in the so-called segregation cases, and the peculiar stress in sections of the country where this decision has created many difficulties, unknown and unappreciated, perhaps, by many people residing in other parts of the country, have led some Senators and some Members of the House of Representatives to prepare a statement of the position which they have felt and now feel to be imperative.

. . . We regard the decisions of the Supreme Court in the school cases as a clear abuse of judicial power. It climaxes a trend in the Federal Judiciary undertaking to legislate, in derogation of the authority of Congress, and to encroach upon the reserved rights of the States and the people.

The original Constitution does not mention education. Neither does the Fourteenth Amendment nor any other amendment. The debates preceding the submission of the Fourteenth Amendment clearly show that there was no intent that it should affect the system of education maintained by the States. The very Congress which proposed the amendment subsequently provided for segregated schools in the District of Columbia. When the amendment was adopted in 1868, there were 37 States of the Union. . . . Every one of the 26 States that had any substantial racial differences among its people, either approved the operation of segregated schools already in existence or subsequently established such schools by action of the same law-making body which considered the Fourteenth Amendment.

This constitutional doctrine began in the North, not in the South, and it was followed not only in Massachusetts, but in Connecticut, New York, Illinois, Indiana, Michigan, Minnesota, New Jersey, Ohio, Pennsylvania and other northern states until they, exercising their rights as states through the constitutional processes of local self-government, changed their school systems.

It is notable that the Supreme Court, speaking through Chief Justice Taft, a former President of the United States, unanimously declared in 1927 in *Gong Lum v. Rice* that the "separate but equal" principle is "within the discretion of the State in regulating its public schools and does not conflict with the Fourteenth Amendment." This interpretation, restated time and again, became a part of the life of the people of many of the States and confirmed their habits, traditions, and way of life. It is founded on elemental humanity and commonsense, for parents should not be deprived by Government of the right to direct the lives and education of their own children.

This unwarranted exercise of power by the Court, contrary to the Constitution, is creating chaos and confusion in the States principally affected. It is destroying the amicable relations between the white and Negro races that have been created through 90 years of patient effort by the good people of both races. It has planted hatred and suspicion where there has been heretofore friendship and understanding.

Without regard to the consent of the governed, outside mediators are threatening immediate and revolutionary changes in our public schools systems. If done, this is certain to destroy the system of public education in some of the States. With the gravest concern for the explosive and dangerous condition created by this decision and inflamed by outside meddlers:

We reaffirm our reliance on the Constitution as the fundamental law of the land. We decry the Supreme Court's encroachment on the rights reserved to the States and to the people, contrary to established law, and to the Constitution. We commend the motives of those States which have declared the intention to resist forced integration by any lawful means. We appeal to the States and people who are not directly affected by these decisions to consider the constitutional principles involved against the time when they too, on issues vital to them may be the victims of judicial encroachment.

> We pledge ourselves to use all lawful means to bring about a
> reversal of this decision which is contrary to the Constitution and
> to prevent the use of force in its implementation. In this trying
> period, as we all seek to right this wrong, we appeal to our people
> not to be provoked by the agitators and troublemakers invading our
> States and to scrupulously refrain from disorder and lawless acts.

102 Cong. Rec. H3948, 4004 (May 12, 1956).

What, if any, arguments can you make to defend the legitimacy of the
Southern Manifesto? Does that legitimacy depend on the plausibility of its
legal claims regarding judicial review, federalism, and original
understanding of the Constitution? Or, does its defense of segregation render
irrelevant its constitutional principles?

6.   **Brown II.** The vehemence of the opposition made clear that enforcing
the mandate of *Brown* across the many hundreds of school districts
throughout the South would not be easy. In *Brown II*, 349 US. 294 (1955),
the Court declined to order the immediate admission of black students to
previously all white schools and instead remanded the cases to the lower
courts for the "solution of varied local school problems" that would require "a
practical flexibility in shaping . . . remedies and . . . adjusting and reconciling
public and private needs." While admonishing "that the vitality of
constitutional principles cannot be allowed to yield simply because of
disagreement with them," the Court nonetheless directed only "that the
defendants make a prompt and reasonable *start* toward full compliance" with
Brown [Italics added]: "Once such a start has been made, the courts may find
that additional time is necessary to carry out the ruling in an effective
manner." Does this approach to the remedial question reflect capitulation to
Southern resistance or judicial pragmatism? How, if at all, should the
Supreme Court take account of likely opposition to a potential ruling? Should
the expectation of resistance influence the Court's proclamation of a right or
its fashioning of a remedy?

7.   **Cooper v. Aaron.** *Brown II* did little to quell resistance to
desegregation. Some border states desegregated, as did the District of
Columbia. But in the Deep South, massive resistance prevailed. School
boards, state legislatures, and even lower courts evaded the Supreme Court's
rulings. In *Cooper v. Aaron*, 358 U.S. 1 (1958), the Supreme Court confronted
directly the opposition to *Brown* that prevented the desegregation of the
schools in Little Rock, Arkansas. It commanded:

> The constitutional rights of respondents are not to be sacrificed or
> yielded to the violence and disorder which have followed upon the
> actions of the Governor and Legislature. Law and order are not
> here to be preserved by depriving the Negro children of their
> constitutional rights. The record before us clearly establishes that
> the growth of the Board's difficulties to a magnitude beyond its
> unaided power to control is the product of state action. Those
> difficulties, as counsel for the Board forthrightly conceded on the
> oral argument in this Court, can also be brought under control by
> state action. . . . The principles announced in [Brown] and the

obedience of the States to them, according to the command of the Constitution, are indispensable for the protection of the freedoms guaranteed by our fundamental charter for all of us. Our constitutional ideal of equal justice under law is thus made a living truth.

Are *Cooper* and *Brown II* consistent with one another? Is it possible for the Court to enforce its ruling without the cooperation of other branches of government, state and federal? If not, how might the Court generate support for its rulings?

8.   **Bolling v. Sharpe.** Recall that in *Bolling v. Sharpe*, decided the same day as *Brown*, the Court said it would be "unthinkable" to permit de jure segregation in Washington, D.C., schools while striking it down elsewhere. But why would that have been "unthinkable"? After all, different constitutional provisions governed the two situations—the equal protection clause of the Fourteenth Amendment for states, and the due process clause of the 5th amendment for the federal government and the District of Columbia. Did the Court explain why different constitutional standards could not apply to states and the federal government?

B. THE CIVIL RIGHTS MOVEMENT AND CONGRESSIONAL ACTION

The factors that propelled the Second Reconstruction were not limited to the strategies of NAACP lawyers and the pronouncements of the courts. During World War II, over 900,000 black soldiers served in the military, fighting a war against Nazism, only to return home to Jim Crow segregation. The war thus diminished African Americans' tolerance for segregation, heightening their expectations for equal treatment. Indeed, in 1948, pressure from civil rights activists led to President Harry Truman's order to desegregate the armed forces.

At the same time that litigation challenging Jim Crow wended its way through the courts, the civil rights movement took shape, influencing not only the litigation strategy, but also spurring legislative developments and helping to transform public opinion. A pivotal event in the movement occurred December 1, 1955, when Rosa Parks, a 42-year-old black seamstress and active member of the NAACP in Montgomery, Alabama, refused (contrary to the norms of segregation) to give up her seat on a city bus to a white man who did not have a seat. She was arrested and convicted of civil disobedience in violation of Alabama's segregation laws. Fed up with the indignities of Jim Crow, local activists met to discuss a boycott of the Montgomery bus system. The risks were high, including the difficulty of getting to work and the predictable reprisals that would befall many activists for challenging white rule. Organized as the Montgomery Improvement Association (MIA), the activists asked the new young Baptist minister in town, Martin Luther King, Jr., to lead the effort.

The boycott lasted 381 days. The boycotters suffered many costs, including losing their jobs with outraged white employers; criminal prosecutions for the crime of boycotting without "just cause" and for providing transportation without a license (car pools); and violent attacks. Several activists had their homes bombed, including Martin Luther King, Jr., and Robert Graetz, the sole white board member of the MIA. During the boycott, the MIA initiated a federal lawsuit challenging bus segregation policies. That suit ultimately reached the Supreme Court, which, applying Brown, ruled that segregation on city buses was unconstitutional. *See Browder v. Gayle,* 352 U.S. 903 (1956).

Although the desegregation of buses might not have occurred without the lawsuit, it was the boycott that inspired people across the country to challenge Jim Crow. On February 1, 1960, activists began "sit ins" and other forms of direct action across the South and elsewhere. News coverage of these events captured white police officers brutalizing non-violent protestors with clubs, dogs, and fire hoses. The media also highlighted the jails filling with young adults and children who simply sought service at lunch counters, and the news coverage brought the bombings of black homes and churches to the country's attention. The publicizing of these events pressured politicians in Washington to act.

President John F. Kennedy, who was initially reluctant to push for civil rights legislation, eventually became a champion of the cause and proposed civil rights legislation in 1963. Support for the bill gained momentum from the March on Washington for Jobs and Freedom on August 28, 1963. After Kennedy was assassinated in November of that year, President Lyndon Johnson, who hailed from Texas, took up the civil rights cause, though legislation was met with strong opposition from southern members of Congress. But on July 2, 1964, Johnson signed the Civil Rights Act of 1964, after the longest filibuster in Senate history: 82 days, 10 million words, and 6,300 pages in the Congressional Record. President Johnson reportedly lamented to an aide later that day, "I think we just delivered the South to the Republican Party for a long time to come." Dr. King described the Civil Rights Act as a "second emancipation."

The Civil Rights Act of 1964 prohibits discrimination in several important respects. First, its Title II bars discrimination by places of public accommodation, providing that "[a]ll persons shall be entitled to the full and equal enjoyment of the goods, services, facilities, privileges, advantages, and accommodations of any place of public accommodation [defined to include inns, motels, hotels, restaurants, lunch counters, gas stations, theaters, sports arenas, etc.] without discrimination or segregation on the ground of race, color, religion, or national origin." 42 U.S.C. § 2000a. Second, its Title VII prohibits discrimination on the basis of race, color, national origin, religion, and sex by employers and labor unions, and the law created the Equal Employment Opportunity

Commission with the power to file lawsuits on behalf of aggrieved workers. Third, the Civil Rights Act involved Congress and the President more directly in enforcing school desegregation. Title IV authorizes the Department of Justice to bring desegregation lawsuits, and Title VI prohibits racial discrimination in any program receiving federal funds. The Elementary and Secondary Education Act of 1965 provides federal funds to school districts, with the stipulation (from the 1964 Act) that segregated districts could not receive any funds. The Department of Health, Education, and Welfare implemented strict guidelines for receiving funding, inducing greater compliance by school districts than had been achieved through litigation.

The Civil Rights Act of 1964 did not, however, contain adequate protections of voting rights. States, especially in the South, continued to utilize a variety of "neutral" qualifications and procedures that were adopted and administered with the purpose of suppressing the black vote. Civil rights activists called for federal legislation to protect the franchise. On March 7, 1965, known as "Bloody Sunday," over 500 civil rights activists marched from Selma to Montgomery, Alabama. They walked just six blocks to the Edmund Pettus Bridge when they were attacked by state and local police officers on horseback wielding billy clubs and spraying tear gas. Several marchers were seriously injured, including John Lewis—now a long-time member of the House of Representatives. These and other political protests motivated Congress to pass the Voting Rights Act (VRA), which President Johnson signed on August 6, 1965. Observing that the VRA "reflects Congress' firm intention to rid the country of racial discrimination in voting," the Supreme Court summarized the Act's principal provisions:

> The heart of the Act is a complex scheme of stringent remedies aimed at areas where voting discrimination has been most flagrant. . . . The first of the remedies, contained in s. 4(a), is the suspension of literacy tests and similar voting qualifications for a period of five years from the last occurrence of substantial voting discrimination. Section 5 prescribes a second remedy, the suspension of all new voting regulations pending review by federal authorities to determine whether their use would perpetuate voting discrimination. The third remedy . . . is the assignment of federal examiners on certification by the Attorney General to list qualified applicants who are thereafter entitled to vote in all elections.

> The remaining remedial portions of the Act are aimed at voting discrimination in any area of the country where it may occur. Section 2 broadly prohibits the use of voting rules to abridge exercise of the franchise on racial grounds. Sections 3, 6(a), and 13(b) strengthen existing procedures for attacking voting discrimination by means of litigation. Section 4(e) excuses

citizens educated in American schools conducted in a foreign language from passing English-language literacy tests. Section 10(a)–(c) facilitates constitutional litigation challenging the imposition of all poll taxes for state and local elections. Sections 11 and 12(a)–(d) authorize civil and criminal sanctions against interference with the exercise of rights guaranteed by the Act.

South Carolina v. Katzenbach, 383 U.S. 301, 315–316 (1966).

As you will see in detail in Chapter 10, section 5 remains the most controversial part of the VRA, as it brought the states of the South, along with several other jurisdictions, under a form of direct federal supervision. The section precludes certain jurisdictions—primarily those with a history of discriminating against minority voters—from enforcing any new voting qualifications or rules unless they first "preclear" the new requirements with the Attorney General or the United States District Court for the District of Columbia. Section 2 of the Act, by contrast, applies nationwide and precludes any state or political subdivision from applying a voting qualification or prerequisite to voting that denies a voter the right to vote on the basis of race. Congress amended section 2 in 1982, making clear that a voting qualification denies the vote on the basis of race if it has the purpose or effect of inhibiting or diluting the vote of a racial group.

In 1968, Congress passed the Fair Housing Act (FHA). Prior laws had failed to include significant restrictions on housing discrimination, and the Supreme Court's important equal protection precedent in *Shelley v. Kraemer,* 224 U.S. 1 (1948), concerned only racially explicit covenants and did not address other means of discrimination in the sale or rental of housing. Civil rights protests between 1965 and 1968 focused on issues of both racial and economic disadvantage and included demonstrations in northern cities against impoverished slums. Providing access to affordable housing became part of President Johnson's War on Poverty. The assassination of Dr. King in April of 1968 helped to push the FHA to enactment. The Act prohibited discrimination on the basis of race, color, national origin, and religion (and sex as of 1974) in the sale, rental, or financing of residential dwellings. The Act also prohibited certain specific practices, such as steering, redlining, quoting different terms to persons in a protected class, and using discriminatory advertisements.

The same year Congress enacted the FHA, the Supreme Court re-interpreted a Reconstruction-era statute, the Civil Rights Act of 1866, currently 42 U.S.C. § 1982, to prohibit private discrimination in the sale or rental of real property. *See Jones v. Alfred H. Mayer Co.,* 392 U.S. 409 (1968). In the 19th century, the Court had interpreted the 1866 Act as only applying to state-sponsored race discrimination in property transactions, but in *Jones,* the Court concluded that Congress intended for the Thirteenth Amendment to reach private discrimination. Eight years later, the Court similarly interpreted another provision of the 1866

Act, currently 42 U.S.C. § 1981, to prohibit private race discrimination in making contracts, including by private employers and schools. *See Runyon v. McCrary,* 427 U.S. 160 (1976).

In the midst of these landmark civil rights achievements, Congress also dramatically reformed the nation's immigration laws. When Congress enacted the Immigration and Nationality Act of 1952 (INA), it had already taken a substantial step in ridding the immigration code of racial classifications. In that Act, Congress finally abolished all race-based prohibitions on naturalization and opened up wider channels for immigrants from Asia to come to the United States. President Harry Truman vetoed the bill nonetheless (Congress overrode the veto), citing the unfair treatment of Asian immigrants embodied in the still limited quotas for Asian immigrants. In his veto message, he adopted the civil rights mantle, as well as the Cold War imperative:

> The end to certain discriminations come] before me embedded in a mass of legislation which would perpetuate injustices of long standing against many other nations of the world, hamper the efforts we are making to rally the men of East and West alike to the cause of freedom, and intensify the repressive and inhumane aspects of our immigration procedures. The price is too high, and in good conscience I cannot agree to pay it.

> I want all our residents of Japanese ancestry, and all our friends throughout the far East, to understand this point clearly. I cannot take the step I would like to take, and strike down the bars that prejudice has erected against them, without, at the same time, establishing new discriminations against the peoples of Asia and approving harsh and repressive measures directed at all who seek a new life within our boundaries. I am sure that with a little more time and a little more discussion in this country the public conscience and the good sense of the American people will assert themselves, and we shall be in a position to enact an immigration and naturalization policy that will be fair to all.

> The idea behind this discriminatory policy was, to put it baldly, that Americans with English or Irish names were better people and better citizens than Americans with Italian or Greek or Polish names.

> Today, we are "protecting" ourselves, as we were in 1924, against being flooded by immigrants from Eastern Europe. This is fantastic. The countries of Eastern Europe have fallen under the communist yoke—they are silenced, fenced off by barbed wire and minefields—no one passes their borders but at the risk of his life. We do not need to be protected against immigrants from these countries—on the contrary we want to stretch out a helping hand, to save those who have managed to flee into

Western Europe, to succor those who are brave enough to escape from barbarism, to welcome and restore them against the day when their countries will, as we hope, be free again.

In no other realm of our national life are we so hampered and stultified by the dead hand of the past, as we are in this field of immigration. We do not limit our cities to their 1920 boundaries—we do not hold our corporations to their 1920 capitalizations—we welcome progress and change to meet changing conditions in every sphere of life, except in the field of immigration.

HARRY S. TRUMAN

Harry S. Truman, *Veto of Bill To Revise the Laws Relating to Immigration, Naturalization, and Nationality* (June 25, 1952), http://www.presidency.ucsb.edu/ws/?pid=14175.

Like President Truman, Presidents Eisenhower, Kennedy, and Johnson each drew an express link between immigration reform and civil rights objectives and targeted the national origins quotas as inconsistent with the animating values of the civil rights legislation they also championed. In 1965, Congress eventually enacted the major reforms to the INA Truman had sought, eliminating the national origins quotas from the law and adopting a selection system based on family relationships and employment preferences. The Act also imposed a worldwide ceiling on immigration, but it was to be implemented without regard to national origin. The Act's timing, and the rhetoric used by the immigration reform's advocates, re-enforced the connection between the pursuit of racial equality and the rejection of national origins-based selection of new immigrants. At the very least, then, the 1965 immigration Act advanced a vision of nation building that eschewed formal racial categories, and in this sense, it amounted to an important civil rights victory.

NOTES AND QUESTIONS

1.   While the Civil Rights era laws may now seem to have been eminently sensible and necessary, at the time there was disagreement about their desirability and constitutionality. Consider first the Civil Rights Act of 1964. It prohibits privately owned businesses from discriminating on their own property and in their choice of employees, an area traditionally left to states to regulate by balancing property rights and personal liberty concerns. The Supreme Court ultimately rejected constitutional challenges to the Act, holding that Congress could regulate private discrimination in the marketplace through the Interstate Commerce Clause, which authorizes Congress to "regulate Commerce with foreign Nations, and among the several States, and with the Indian Tribes." Const. art. 1, sec. 8. *See Heart of Atlanta Motel, Inc. v. United States*, 379 U.S. 241 (1964). Eighty years earlier, in the Civil Rights Cases, in which the Supreme Court held that

Congress could not prohibit private discrimination in the marketplace through the Fourteenth Amendment, no one thought Congress's commerce power reached such local practices. *See The Civil Rights Cases*, 109 U.S. 3, 20–21 (1993) (stating that "no one will contend that the power to pass [the Civil Rights Act of 1876] was contained in the Constitution before the adoption of the [Reconstruction] amendments."). Assuming race discrimination in hiring and serving the public is immoral, should it nonetheless be within the personal liberty of private business owners? And even if that liberty is subject to being regulated, should regulation come from state or local governments, not from Washington?

2. How satisfying is it that the body blow to Jim Crow by the Civil Rights Act was legally justified in the name of regulating commerce? In *Heart of Atlanta*, the Court upheld the prohibitions on race discrimination as applied to a hotel by the fact that the hotel catered to interstate travelers. Similarly, in *Katzenbach v. McClung*, 379 U.S. 294 (1964), the Court upheld application of the Act to a small, local restaurant on the ground that "Congress has determined for itself that refusals of service to Negroes have imposed burdens both upon the interstate flow of food and upon the movement of products generally." Id. at 303. Justice Goldberg, in contrast, understood the problem of discrimination in public accommodation as a matter of human dignity "and not mere economics." Why might the Court have turned to the Commerce Clause, rather than section 5 of the Fourteenth Amendment, which gives Congress the power to enforce the Equal Protection Clause, to uphold the Civil Rights Act? Are there downsides to relying on the commerce power instead of the Thirteenth and Fourteenth Amendments, which were specifically designed to promote racial equality?

3. Debate about the Voting Rights Act persists. Did it go too far in requiring covered states and local jurisdictions to request approval from the federal government before enacting any new voting procedures? In Chapter 10, you will consider these questions in detail, as well as whether elements of the Voting Rights Act have become outdated today and ought to be repealed or struck down.

4. There were also arguments against the Fair Housing Act. Isn't one's choice over to whom to rent or sell one's property a core liberty or property right? Should we treat housing as a quintessential matter of local concern such that the federal government has no business intruding even if states do not wish to prohibit discrimination? Do people ever have a legitimate interest, through property sale or rental, in creating or joining a community of people with similar racial or ethnic backgrounds?

5. If you believe Congress and the Court were justified in expanding broad federal power over local and personal matters through the Civil Rights Acts and Voting Rights Acts of the 1960s, is it because you do not believe that federalism and personal autonomy are that important? Whatever your assessment, what interests should be taken into account and what weight do you give to each?

6. How much of a civil rights victory were the 1965 reforms to the Immigration and Nationality Act? The high-flying rhetoric by powerful lawmakers notwithstanding, they were not accompanied by a broad popular social movement resembling anything like the sustained mobilization of blacks and other Americans who fought through public protest, litigation, and multi-level legislative advocacy to bring an end to Jim Crow. Instead, the immigration reforms were arguably triumphs of the ordinary pluralist legislative process, with Italian and Jewish ethnic lobbies advocating on behalf of co-ethnics and family members, and the State Department advocating for reform for foreign policy reasons. How should these aspects of the reforms shape our understanding of them?

7.   Whatever the motivations of the lawmakers who passed it, the Immigration Act of 1965 created a legal framework that would eventually contribute to a demographic re-making of America. Between 1970 and 1990, for example, the Asian-American population of the United States went from 1.5 million to 7.3 million. Scholars debate whether lawmakers who adopted the reforms were aware of this possibility. The conventional wisdom is that Congress did not intend to increase immigration substantially in 1965. In a best-selling tract of 1982, *America in Search of Itself*, Theodore White observed that the Act changed "all previous patterns, and in so doing, probably changed the future of America." He described the immigration law as "noble, revolutionary" and also "probably the most thoughtless of the many acts of the Great Society." Theodore White, America in Search of Itself 363 (1982). Revisionist accounts, by contrast, highlight parts of the legislative history that ostensibly reveal lawmakers' awareness and implicit acceptance of the demographic change that would come from the reforms. *See* Gabriel J. Chin, *The Civil Rights Revolution Comes to American Immigration Law: A New Look at the Immigration and Nationality Act of 1965*, 75 N. Carolina L. Rev. 273 (1996). What exactly is at stake in this debate?

8.   Even as Congress eradicated national origins distinctions from the immigration laws, it found other ways to restrict immigration, including by imposing a ceiling on immigration from Mexico, Central and South America, and the Caribbean—immigration that had not been subject to formal numerical restrictions before (even though Latin American immigrants throughout the twentieth century were subject to deportation). Some legislators regarded the ceiling as a trade-off for the liberalization of the system as a whole, and the debate over whether to adopt the ceiling surfaced a great deal of concern about the growth of Latin American immigration and a desire among some lawmakers to curtail it. Regardless of the motivations behind the ceilings, their incorporation into the law produced arguably pernicious effects. Congress opted for a regime of formal equality by applying the same numerical ceiling to all countries of the world, but its actions had a disparate impact on Mexicans, in particular, by suddenly reducing the number of legal channels for migration from Mexico to the United States. This impact arose from the fact that Mexican migration historically had been motivated by strong ties between the people of the two countries and the logic of the region's shared labor market, making the "supply" of Mexican immigrants far greater in number than from most other countries of the world. Some scholars trace the rise of illegal immigration in the late

twentieth century to this change in the law, given that the "natural" ebb and flow of migration across our southern border, once relatively unrestricted, had become subject to tight control. *See* Douglas Massey, Jorge Durand, and Nolan Malone, Beyond Smoke and Mirrors: Mexican Immigration in an Era of Economic Integration (2002). Should Mexicans, Central Americans, and immigrants from the Caribbean be given preferences over immigrants from other parts of the world to account for these dynamics?

C. ANTI-MISCEGENATION LAWS AND SEGREGATION IN THE PRIVATE SPHERE

The civil rights legislation of the 1960s attacked segregation and racial distinctions across the public sphere. But Congress left intact a set of laws and norms instrumental in the promotion of white supremacy— bans on inter-racial marriage. Even some states that did not otherwise segregate by race had such bans on the books. Historically, opponents of racial equality employed the threat of interracial marriage as a tactic to stymie reform. In the years following the Civil War, for example, opponents of civil rights laws would ask, rhetorically, "do you want your daughter to marry a Negro?" Perhaps even in the 1960s, politicians did not want to be viewed as advocating for interracial marriage. Segregationists commonly invoked the specter of inter-racial marriage as a reason to oppose *Brown*. *See*, e.g., Randall Kennedy, Interracial Intimacies: Sex, Marriage, Identity, and Adoption 22 (2012).

Why might Congress have declined to prohibit state laws against interracial marriage during the civil rights era? Should it have done so? Anti-miscegenation statutes easily satisfy the state action doctrine, so the *Civil Rights Cases* would not seem to have precluded Congress from addressing those statutes through the Fourteenth Amendment. Also, don't restrictions on marriage affect commerce? The bans on interracial marriage also restricted personal choice, and autonomy interests thus weighed in favor of abolishing them. In the decade after *Brown*, the Supreme Court similarly avoided addressing anti-miscegenation laws, despite rejecting segregation in schools and elsewhere. But in 1967, the Court finally grappled with whether state marriage bans violated the Fourteenth Amendment.

Loving v. Virginia

Supreme Court of the United States, 1967.
388 U.S. 1.

■ MR. CHIEF JUSTICE WARREN delivered the opinion of the Court.

This case presents a constitutional question never addressed by this Court: whether a statutory scheme adopted by the State of Virginia to prevent marriages between persons solely on the basis of racial classifications violates the Equal Protection and Due Process Clauses of the Fourteenth Amendment. For reasons which seem to us to reflect the central meaning of those constitutional commands, we conclude that these statutes cannot stand consistently with the Fourteenth Amendment.

In June 1958, two residents of Virginia, Mildred Jeter, a Negro woman, and Richard Loving, a white man, were married in the District of Columbia pursuant to its laws. Shortly after their marriage, the Lovings returned to Virginia and established their marital abode in Caroline County. A grand jury issued an indictment charging the Lovings with violating Virginia's ban on interracial marriages. [T]he Lovings pleaded guilty to the charge and were sentenced to one year in jail; however, the trial judge suspended the sentence for a period of 25 years on the condition that the Lovings leave the State and not return to Virginia together for 25 years. He stated in an opinion that:

> 'Almighty God created the races white, black, yellow, malay and red, and he placed them on separate continents. And but for the interference with his arrangement there would be no cause for such marriages. The fact that he separated the races shows that he did not intend for the races to mix.'

After their convictions, the Lovings took up residence in the District of Columbia [and] filed a motion in the state trial court to vacate the judgment and set aside the sentence.

The two statutes under which appellants were convicted and sentenced are part of a comprehensive statutory scheme aimed at prohibiting and punishing interracial marriages. The Lovings were convicted of violating [a section] of the Virginia Code:

> 'Leaving State to evade law.—If any white person and colored person shall go out of this State, for the purpose of being married, and with the intention of returning, and be married out of it, and afterwards return to and reside in it, cohabiting as man and wife, they shall be punished as provided in § 20–59, and the marriage shall be governed by the same law as if it had been solemnized in this State. The fact of their cohabitation here as man and wife shall be evidence of their marriage.'

Section 20–59, which defines the penalty for miscegenation, provides: "Punishment for marriage.—If any white person intermarry with a colored person, or any colored person intermarry with a white person, he shall be guilty of a felony and shall be punished by confinement in the penitentiary for not less than one nor more than five years."

Other provisions in the Virginia statutory scheme . . . automatically voids all marriages between 'a white person and a colored person' without any judicial proceeding [like a divorce or annulment], and [others] . . . define 'white persons' and 'colored persons and Indians' for purposes of the statutory prohibitions. The Lovings have never disputed in the course of this litigation that Mrs. Loving is a 'colored person' or that Mr. Loving is a 'white person' within the meanings given those terms by the Virginia statutes.

Virginia is now one of 16 States which prohibit and punish marriages on the basis of racial classifications. Penalties for miscegenation arose as an incident to slavery and have been common in Virginia since the colonial period. The present statutory scheme dates from the adoption of the Racial Integrity Act of 1924, passed during the period of extreme nativism which followed the end of the First World War. The central features of this Act, and current Virginia law, are the absolute prohibition of a 'white person' marrying other than another 'white person,' a prohibition against issuing marriage licenses until the issuing official is satisfied that the applicants' statements as to their race are correct, certificates of 'racial composition' to be kept by both local and state registrars, and the carrying forward of earlier prohibitions against racial intermarriage.

I.

In upholding the constitutionality of these provisions in the decision below, the Supreme Court of Appeals of Virginia referred to its 1955 decision in *Naim v. Naim*, 197 Va. 80, 87 S.E.2d 749, as stating the reasons supporting the validity of these laws. In *Naim*, the state court concluded that the State's legitimate purposes were 'to preserve the racial integrity of its citizens,' and to prevent 'the corruption of blood,' 'a mongrel breed of citizens,' and 'the obliteration of racial pride,' obviously an endorsement of the doctrine of White Supremacy. The court also reasoned that marriage has traditionally been subject to state regulation without federal intervention, and, consequently, the regulation of marriage should be left to exclusive state control by the Tenth Amendment.

While the state court is no doubt correct in asserting that marriage is a social relation subject to the State's police power, *Maynard v. Hill*, 125 U.S. 190 (1888), the State does not contend in its argument before this Court that its powers to regulate marriage are unlimited notwithstanding the commands of the Fourteenth Amendment. Instead, the State argues that the meaning of the Equal Protection Clause, as illuminated by the statements of the Framers, is only that state penal laws containing an interracial element as part of the definition of the offense must apply equally to whites and Negroes in the sense that members of each race are punished to the same degree. Thus, the State contends that, because its miscegenation statutes punish equally both the white and the Negro participants in an interracial marriage, these statutes, despite their reliance on racial classifications do not constitute an invidious discrimination based upon race. The second argument advanced by the State assumes the validity of its equal application theory. The argument is that, if the Equal Protection Clause does not outlaw miscegenation statutes because of their reliance on racial classifications, the question of constitutionality would thus become whether there was any rational basis for a State to treat interracial marriages differently from other marriages. On this question, the State argues, the scientific evidence is substantially in doubt and, consequently, this Court should defer to the wisdom of the state legislature in adopting its policy of discouraging interracial marriages.

Because we reject the notion that the mere 'equal application' of a statute containing racial classifications is enough to remove the classifications from the Fourteenth Amendment's proscription of all invidious racial discriminations, we do not accept the State's contention that these statutes should be upheld if there is any possible basis for concluding that they serve a rational purpose. The mere fact of equal application does not mean that our analysis of these statutes should follow the approach we have taken in cases involving no racial discrimination where the Equal Protection Clause has been arrayed against a statute discriminating between the kinds of advertising which may be displayed on trucks in New York City, or an exemption in Ohio's *ad valorem* tax for merchandise owned by a non-resident in a storage warehouse. In these cases, involving distinctions not drawn according to race, the Court has merely asked whether there is any rational foundation for the discriminations, and has deferred to the wisdom of the state legislatures. In the case at bar, however, we deal with statutes containing racial classifications, and the fact of equal application does not immunize the statute from the very heavy burden of justification which the Fourteenth Amendment has traditionally required of state statutes drawn according to race.

The State argues that statements in the Thirty-ninth Congress about the time of the passage of the Fourteenth Amendment indicate that the Framers did not intend the Amendment to make unconstitutional state miscegenation laws. Many of the statements alluded to by the State concern the debates over the Freedmen's Bureau Bill, which President Johnson vetoed, and the Civil Rights Act of 1866, enacted over his veto. While these statements have some relevance to the intention of Congress in submitting the Fourteenth Amendment, it must be understood that they pertained to the passage of specific statutes and not to the broader, organic purpose of a constitutional amendment. As for the various statements directly concerning the Fourteenth Amendment, we have said in connection with a related problem, that although these historical sources 'cast some light' they are not sufficient to resolve the problem; [a]t best, they are inconclusive. The most avid proponents of the post-War Amendments undoubtedly intended them to remove all legal distinctions among 'all persons born or naturalized in the United States.' Their opponents, just as certainly, were antagonistic to both the letter and the spirit of the Amendments and wished them to have the most limited effect.

We have rejected the proposition that the debates in the Thirty-ninth Congress or in the state legislatures which ratified the Fourteenth Amendment supported the theory advanced by the State, that the requirement of equal protection of the laws is satisfied by penal laws defining offenses based on racial classifications so long as white and Negro participants in the offense were similarly punished. *McLaughlin v. State of Florida*, 379 U.S. 184 (1964).

The State finds support for its 'equal application' theory in the decision of the Court in *Pace v. State of Alabama*, 106 U.S. 583 (1883). In that case, the Court upheld a conviction under an Alabama statute forbidding adultery or fornication between a white person and a Negro which imposed a greater penalty than that of a statute proscribing similar conduct by members of the same race. The Court reasoned that the statute could not be said to discriminate against Negroes because the punishment for each participant in the offense was the same. However, as recently as the 1964 Term, in rejecting the reasoning of that case, we stated 'Pace represents a limited view of the Equal Protection Clause which has not withstood analysis in the subsequent decisions of this Court.' *McLaughlin v. Florida*, 379 U.S. at 188. As we there demonstrated, the Equal Protection Clause requires the consideration of whether the classifications drawn by any statute constitute an arbitrary and invidious discrimination. The clear and central purpose of the Fourteenth Amendment was to eliminate all official state sources of invidious racial discrimination in the States.

There can be no question but that Virginia's miscegenation statutes rest solely upon distinctions drawn according to race. The statutes proscribe generally accepted conduct if engaged in by members of different races. Over the years, this Court has consistently repudiated "[d]istinctions between citizens solely because of their ancestry" as being "odious to a free people whose institutions are founded upon the doctrine of equality." *Hirabayashi v. United States*, 320 U.S. 81, 100 (1943). At the very least, the Equal Protection Clause demands that racial classifications, especially suspect in criminal statutes, be subjected to the "most rigid scrutiny," *Korematsu v. United States*, 323 U.S. 214, 216 (1944), and, if they are ever to be upheld, they must be shown to be necessary to the accomplishment of some permissible state objective, independent of the racial discrimination which it was the object of the Fourteenth Amendment to eliminate. Indeed, two members of this Court have already stated that they 'cannot conceive of a valid legislative purpose . . . which makes the color of a person's skin the test of whether his conduct is a criminal offense.' *McLaughlin v. Florida*, 379 U.S. at 198 (Stewart, J., joined by Douglas, J., concurring).

There is patently no legitimate overriding purpose independent of invidious racial discrimination which justifies this classification. The fact that Virginia prohibits only interracial marriages involving white persons demonstrates that the racial classifications must stand on their own justification, as measures designed to maintain White Supremacy.[7] We have consistently denied the constitutionality of measures which restrict the rights of citizens on account of race. There can be no doubt that restricting the freedom to marry solely because of racial classifications violates the central meaning of the Equal Protection Clause.

II.

These statutes also deprive the Lovings of liberty without due process of law in violation of the Due Process Clause of the Fourteenth Amendment. The freedom to marry has long been recognized as one of the vital personal rights essential to the orderly pursuit of happiness by free men.

Marriage is one of the 'basic civil rights of man,' fundamental to our very existence and survival. To deny this fundamental freedom on so unsupportable a basis as the racial classifications embodied in these statutes, classifications so directly subversive of the principle of equality at the heart of the Fourteenth Amendment, is surely to deprive all the State's citizens of liberty without due process of law. The Fourteenth Amendment requires that the freedom of choice to marry not be restricted by invidious racial discriminations. Under our Constitution, the freedom to marry, or not marry, a person of another race resides with the individual and cannot be infringed by the State.

NOTES AND QUESTIONS

1.   Following *Loving*, lower federal and state courts invalidated remaining anti-miscegenation laws. A few courts went further and on the basis of *Loving* invalidated state laws that prohibited the placement of children for adoption across racial lines, an issue that will be taken up in Chapter 3. Based on the reasoning of *Loving*, how would you construct the argument that prohibitions on inter-racial adoption violate the Fourteenth Amendment?

2.   In *Loving*, the Court rejects the state's reliance on *Pace v. Alabama*, 106 U.S. 583 (1883), in which the Court upheld a law that treated inter-racial fornication more harshly than intra-racial fornication. The state's rationale was that the law punished equally the black and white members of the inter-racial couple. The Court's rejection in *Loving* of the symmetry argument reflects changes over time in understandings of race. In the 19th century,

---

[7]   Appellants point out that the State's concern in these statutes, as expressed in the words of the 1924 Act's title, 'An Act to Preserve Racial Integrity,' extends only to the integrity of the white race. While Virginia prohibits whites from marrying any nonwhite (subject to the exception for the descendants of Pocahontas), Negroes, Orientals, and any other racial class may intermarry without statutory interference. Appellants contend that this distinction renders Virginia's miscegenation statutes arbitrary and unreasonable even assuming the constitutional validity of an official purpose to preserve 'racial integrity.' We need not reach this contention because we find the racial classifications in these statutes repugnant to the Fourteenth Amendment, even assuming an even-handed state purpose to protect the 'integrity' of all races.

racial groups were believed to be biologically distinct and ineradicably different; some races were "better" than others. By the middle of the 20th century, in the aftermath of the Holocaust, such thinking had been discredited. Indeed, the term "racism" first came into being during the Nazi era in Germany to discredit racial ideas that had once been accepted as common sense. As a result, race came to seem an artificial rather than natural basis on which to regulate marriage.

3. The Court in *Loving* states that: "the Equal Protection Clause requires the consideration of whether the classifications drawn by any statute constitute an arbitrary and invidious discrimination." In what way was the Virginia law "arbitrary and invidious"? Is the problem more that such laws restricted individual freedom to marry or that they contributed to group-based inequality? Does the Court's decision mean that the state has no interest in the racial composition of families, or simply that that interest is outweighed by the harms of the statute?

4. The *Loving* Court also stated a test for when it would apply a more stringent form of judicial review to certain racial classifications. The Court rejected the state's argument that the equal application of the law to different races meant that only rational basis review should apply to it. Instead, the Court explained, "the Equal Protection Clause demands that racial classifications, especially suspect in criminal statutes, be subjected to the 'most rigid scrutiny,' and, if they are ever to be upheld, they must be shown to be necessary to the accomplishment of some permissible state objective." Applying this test, the Court concluded that the anti-miscegenation law was not necessary to a legitimate end but rather was intended to preserve white supremacy, an illegitimate state objective. Can you think of a compelling interest that an otherwise invidious racial classification might serve? Post-*Brown* and *Loving*, do you think the national security justification accepted in *Korematsu* for the racial classifications behind the internment of Japanese Americans would suffice as a justification for other race-based exclusions or burdens?

II. IMPLEMENTING THE SECOND RECONSTRUCTION AND THE RISE OF COLORBLINDNESS

The Second Reconstruction promised nothing less than the re-ordering of American society. Not surprisingly, then, the meaning of its achievements has been fiercely contested, in court and in the political process. How far can the state go in its efforts to dismantle the vestiges of white supremacy and address racial inequalities? What sorts of inequalities are cognizable under the law? Are race-conscious laws designed to help disadvantaged minorities as constitutionally problematic as those designed to subjugate them? Here we focus on two battlegrounds that arose around these questions and in reaction to the remedies developed to end Jim Crow and its effects: (1) the debate over whether the law should be concerned only with the intent to discriminate, or whether it reaches the discriminatory effects of state and private action; and (2) whether and under what circumstances the state can engage in race-conscious affirmative action to help elevate the status of disadvantaged racial minorities in institutions such as schools and the commercial sphere. The way each of these debates has unfolded captures a core ideological disagreement about the civil rights movement's meaning. Should the law first and foremost seek to prevent race consciousness or classification, or should its animating purpose be to combat unequal conditions and status among different racial groups?

A. DISCRIMINATORY INTENT VERSUS DISCRIMINATORY EFFECTS

The debate over whether the law prohibits only intentional racial discrimination or also holds the state and other actors accountable for the racially disparate effects of their policies has played out along two dimensions—the constitutional and the statutory. Even if the Fourteenth Amendment only reaches racial inequalities or disparities intended by the state, the landmark statutes of the civil rights era might hold other actors to a higher standard. Consider first the constitutional question.

Washington v. Davis

Supreme Court of the United States, 1976.
426 U.S. 229.

■ MR. JUSTICE WHITE delivered the opinion of the Court.

This case involves the validity of a qualifying test administered to applicants for positions as police officers in the District of Columbia Metropolitan Police Department.

This action began on April 10, 1970, when two Negro police officers filed suit against the then Commissioner of the District of Columbia, the Chief of the District's Metropolitan Police Department, and the Commissioners of the United States Civil Service Commission. An amended complaint . . . alleged that the promotion policies of the Department were racially discriminatory, . . . that the Department's recruiting procedures discriminated on the basis of race against black applicants by a series of practices including, but not limited to, a written personnel test which excluded a disproportionately high number of Negro applicants.

[T]o be accepted by the Department and to enter an intensive 17-week training program, the police recruit was required to satisfy certain physical and character standards, to be a high school graduate or its equivalent, and to receive a grade of at least 40 out of 80 on "Test 21," which is "an examination that is used generally throughout the federal service," which "was developed by the Civil Service Commission, not the Police Department," and which was "designed to test verbal ability, vocabulary, reading and comprehension."

The validity of Test 21 was the sole issue before the court on the motions for summary judgment. The District Court noted that there was no claim of "an intentional discrimination or purposeful discriminatory acts" but only a claim that Test 21 bore no relationship to job performance and "has a highly discriminatory impact in screening out black candidates." Ibid. Respondents' evidence, the District Court said, warranted three conclusions: "(a) The number of black police officers, while substantial, is not proportionate to the population mix of the city. (b) A higher percentage of blacks fail the Test than whites. (c) The Test has not been validated to establish its reliability for measuring subsequent job performance." Ibid. This showing was deemed sufficient to shift the burden of proof to the defendants in the action, petitioners here; but the court nevertheless concluded that on the undisputed facts respondents were not entitled to relief. The District Court relied on several factors. Since August 1969, 44% Of new police force recruits had been black; that figure also represented the proportion of blacks on the total force and was roughly equivalent to 20- to 29-year-old blacks in the 50-mile radius in which the recruiting efforts of the Police Department had been concentrated. It was undisputed that the Department had systematically and affirmatively sought to enroll black officers many of whom passed the test but failed to report for duty. The District Court rejected the assertion that Test 21 was culturally slanted to favor whites and was "satisfied that the undisputable facts prove the test to be reasonably and directly related to the requirements of the police recruit training program and that it is neither so designed nor operates [sic] to discriminate against otherwise qualified blacks' Id., at 17. It was thus not necessary to show that Test 21 was not only a useful indicator of training school performance but had also been validated in terms of job performance—"The lack of job performance validation does not defeat the Test, given its direct relationship to recruiting and the valid part it plays in this process." Ibid. The District Court ultimately concluded that "(t)he proof is wholly lacking that a police officer qualifies on the color of his skin rather than ability" and that the Department "should not be required on this showing to lower standards or to abandon efforts to achieve excellence." Id., at 18.

The Court of Appeals, addressing that issue, announced that it would be guided by *Griggs v. Duke Power Co.,* 401 U.S. 424 (1971), a case involving the interpretation and application of Title VII of the Civil Rights Act of 1964, and held that the statutory standards elucidated in that case were to govern the due process question tendered in this one. The court went on to declare that lack of discriminatory intent in designing and administering Test 21 was irrelevant; the critical fact was rather that a far greater proportion of blacks—four times as many—failed the test than did whites. This disproportionate impact, standing alone and without regard to whether it indicated a discriminatory purpose, was held sufficient to establish a constitutional violation, absent proof by petitioners that the test was an adequate measure of job performance in addition to being an indicator of probable success in the training program, a burden which the court ruled petitioners had failed to discharge.

As the Court of Appeals understood Title VII, employees or applicants proceeding under it need not concern themselves with the employer's possibly discriminatory purpose but instead may focus solely on the racially differential impact of the challenged hiring or promotion practices. This is not the constitutional rule. We have never held that the constitutional standard for adjudicating claims of invidious racial discrimination is identical to the standards applicable under Title VII, and we decline to do so today.

The central purpose of the Equal Protection Clause of the Fourteenth Amendment is the prevention of official conduct discriminating on the basis of race. It is also true that the Due Process Clause of the Fifth Amendment contains an equal protection component prohibiting the United States from invidiously discriminating between individuals or groups. But our cases have not embraced the proposition that a law or other official act, without regard to whether it reflects a racially discriminatory purpose, is unconstitutional Solely because it has a racially disproportionate impact.

Almost 100 years ago, *Strauder v. West Virginia,* 100 U.S. 303 (1880), established that the exclusion of Negroes from grand and petit juries in criminal proceedings violated the Equal Protection Clause, but the fact that a particular jury or a series of juries does not statistically reflect the racial composition of the community does not in itself make out an invidious discrimination forbidden by the Clause. "A purpose to discriminate must be present which may be proven by systematic exclusion of eligible jurymen of the proscribed race or by unequal application of the law to such an extent as to show intentional discrimination." *Akins v. Texas,* 325 U.S. 398, 403–404 (1945). A defendant in a criminal case is entitled "to require that the State not deliberately and systematically deny to members of his race the right to participate as jurors in the administration of justice." *Alexander v. Louisiana,* 405 U.S. 625, 628–629 (1972).

The school desegregation cases have also adhered to the basic equal protection principle that the invidious quality of a law claimed to be racially discriminatory must ultimately be traced to a racially discriminatory purpose. That there are both predominantly black and predominantly white schools in a community is not alone violative of the Equal Protection Clause. The essential element of De jure segregation is "a current condition of segregation resulting from intentional state action. The differentiating factor between De jure segregation and so-called De facto segregation . . . is Purpose or Intent to segregate."

This is not to say that the necessary discriminatory racial purpose must be express or appear on the face of the statute, or that a law's disproportionate impact is irrelevant in cases involving Constitution-based claims of racial discrimination. A statute, otherwise neutral on its face, must not be applied so as invidiously to discriminate on the basis of race. *Yick Wo v. Hopkins,* 118 U.S. 356 (1886). It is also clear from the cases dealing with racial discrimination in the selection of juries that the systematic exclusion of Negroes is itself such an "unequal application of the law . . . as to show intentional discrimination."

Necessarily, an invidious discriminatory purpose may often be inferred from the totality of the relevant facts, including the fact, if it is true, that the law bears more heavily on one race than another. It is also not infrequently true that the discriminatory impact in the jury cases for example, the total or seriously disproportionate exclusion of Negroes from jury venires may for all practical purposes demonstrate unconstitutionality because in various circumstances the discrimination is very difficult to explain on nonracial grounds. Nevertheless, we have not held that a law, neutral on its face and serving ends otherwise within the power of government to pursue, is invalid under the Equal Protection Clause simply because it may affect a greater proportion of one race than of another. Disproportionate impact is not irrelevant, but it is not the sole touchstone of an invidious racial discrimination forbidden by the Constitution. Standing alone, it does not trigger the rule that racial classifications are to be subjected to the strictest scrutiny and are justifiable only by the weightiest of considerations.

[H]owever, various Courts of Appeals have held in several contexts . . . that the substantially disproportionate racial impact of a statute or official practice standing alone and without regard to discriminatory purpose, suffices to prove racial discrimination violating the Equal Protection Clause absent some justification going substantially beyond what would be necessary to validate most other legislative classifications. The cases impressively demonstrate that there is another side to the issue; but, with all due respect, to the extent that those cases rested on or expressed the view that proof of discriminatory racial purpose is unnecessary in making out an equal protection violation, we are in disagreement.

As an initial matter, we have difficulty understanding how a law establishing a racially neutral qualification for employment is nevertheless racially discriminatory and denies "any person . . . equal protection of the laws" simply because a greater proportion of Negroes fail to qualify than members of other racial or ethnic groups. Had respondents, along with all others who had failed Test 21, whether white or black, brought an action claiming that the test denied each of them equal protection of the laws as compared with those who had passed with high enough scores to qualify them as police recruits, it is most unlikely that their challenge would have been sustained. Test 21, which is administered generally to prospective Government employees, concededly seeks to ascertain whether those who take it have acquired a particular level of verbal skill; and it is untenable that the Constitution prevents the Government from seeking modestly to upgrade the communicative abilities of its employees rather than to be satisfied with some lower level of competence, particularly where the job requires special ability to communicate orally and in writing. Respondents, as Negroes, could no more successfully claim that the test denied them equal protection than could white applicants who also failed. The conclusion would not be different in the face of proof that more Negroes than whites had been disqualified by Test 21. That other Negroes also failed to score well would, alone, not demonstrate that respondents individually were being denied equal protection of the laws by the application of an otherwise valid qualifying test being administered to prospective police recruits.

Nor on the facts of the case before us would the disproportionate impact of Test 21 warrant the conclusion that it is a purposeful device to discriminate against Negroes and hence an infringement of the constitutional rights of respondents as well as other black applicants. As we have said, the test is neutral on its face and rationally may be said to serve a purpose the Government is constitutionally empowered to pursue. Even agreeing with the District Court that the differential racial effect of Test 21 called for further inquiry, we think the District Court correctly held that the affirmative efforts of the Metropolitan Police Department to recruit black officers, the changing racial composition of the recruit classes and of the force in general, and the relationship of the test to the training program negated any inference that the Department discriminated on the basis of race or that "a police officer qualifies on the color of his skin rather than ability." 348 F.Supp., at 18.

Under Title VII, Congress provided that when hiring and promotion practices disqualifying substantially disproportionate numbers of blacks are challenged, discriminatory purpose need not be proved, and that it is an insufficient response to demonstrate some rational basis for the challenged practices. It is necessary, in addition, that they be "validated" in terms of job performance in any one of several ways, perhaps by ascertaining the minimum skill, ability, or potential necessary for the position at issue and determining whether the qualifying tests are appropriate for the selection of qualified applicants for the job in question. However this process proceeds, it involves a more probing judicial review of, and less deference to, the seemingly reasonable acts of administrators and executives than is appropriate under the Constitution where special racial impact, without discriminatory purpose, is claimed. We are not disposed to adopt this more rigorous standard for the purposes of applying the Fifth and the Fourteenth Amendments in cases such as this.

A rule that a statute designed to serve neutral ends is nevertheless invalid, absent compelling justification, if in practice it benefits or burdens one race more than another would be far-reaching and would raise serious questions about, and perhaps invalidate, a whole range of tax, welfare, public service, regulatory, and licensing statutes that may be more burdensome to the poor and to the average black than to the more affluent white.

■ MR. JUSTICE STEVENS, concurring.

Frequently the most probative evidence of intent will be objective evidence of what actually happened rather than evidence describing the subjective state of mind of the actor. For normally the actor is presumed to have intended the natural consequences of his deeds. This is particularly true in the case of governmental action which is frequently the product of compromise, of collective decisionmaking, and of mixed motivation. It is unrealistic, on the one hand, to require the victim of alleged discrimination to uncover the actual subjective intent of the decisionmaker or, conversely, to invalidate otherwise legitimate action simply because an improper motive affected the deliberation of a participant in the decisional process. A law conscripting clerics should not be invalidated because an atheist voted for it.

My point in making this observation is to suggest that the line between discriminatory purpose and discriminatory impact is not nearly as bright, and perhaps not quite as critical, as the reader of the Court's opinion might assume. I agree, of course, that a constitutional issue does not arise every time some disproportionate impact is shown. On the other hand, when the disproportion is as dramatic as in *Gomillion v. Lightfoot,* 364 U.S. 339, 81 S.Ct. 125, 5 L.Ed.2d 110 or *Yick Wo v. Hopkins,* 118 U.S. 356, 6 S.Ct. 1064, 30 L.Ed. 220 (1886), it really does not matter whether the standard is phrased in terms of purpose or effect.

[The dissenting opinion of Justice Brennan, joined by Justice Marshall, addressing the statutory issues is omitted.]

NOTES AND QUESTIONS

1.   The Court held, without dissent, that a government employment policy constitutes race discrimination under the Due Process Clause of the Fifth Amendment (and by extension the Equal Protection Clause of the Fourteenth) only if the plaintiff proves the policy was adopted for a racially discriminatory purpose. Proof that a policy has a significant racial impact, even if the impact is known to the government, does not require the government to show the policy is job-related unless the government intended the racial impact. The Court states that, "[a]s an initial matter, we have difficulty understanding how a law establishing a racially neutral qualification for employment is nevertheless racially discriminatory and denies 'any person . . . equal protection of the laws' simply because a greater proportion of Negroes fail to qualify than members of other racial or ethnic

groups." Why might the Court have adopted an intent standard as the measure of constitutional liability? Are you persuaded by the Court's reasoning? In a world of unequal conditions, it might be difficult to imagine government policies that wouldn't have a disparate impact based on race. Can you think of a constitutional effects standard that wouldn't turn the Equal Protection Clause into a source of unlimited liability for the government?

2.   The Court asserts that "[t]he central purpose of the Equal Protection Clause of the Fourteenth Amendment is the prevention of official conduct discriminating on the basis of race." What does the Court mean by discrimination on the basis of race? Note that in the next sentence, the Court states that the United States is prohibited from "*invidiously* discriminating between individuals or groups." (Emphasis added). Are all racially motivated laws or policies "invidious"? If Congress purposely imposes liability on employers based on the racial impact of their policies, has Congress acted with an invidious racial purpose? What if a government employer purposely recruits minority employees? What does the Court's opinion in *Davis* suggest about the lawfulness of these approaches to increasing minority access to the workplace?

3.   In *Personnel Administrator v. Feeney,* 442 U.S. 256 (1979), the Court upheld a state law giving a preference to veterans for civil service employment, which had a significant discriminatory effect on female applicants. Notwithstanding the obvious impact of such a preference, the Court upheld it on the ground that no discriminatory purpose had been proven, explaining that "'[d]iscriminatory purpose,' . . . implies more than intent as volition or intent as awareness of consequences. It implies that the decisionmaker . . . selected or reaffirmed a particular course of action at least in part 'because of,' not merely 'in spite of,' its adverse effects upon an identifiable group." 442 U.S. at 279 (citation omitted). Although *Feeney* involved a claim of sex-based discrimination, its definition of discriminatory purpose has been applied to claims of racial discrimination as well. As a consequence of *Davis,* constitutional challenges to laws that have significant discriminatory effects against blacks or other subordinated racial groups are virtually immune from challenge unless the challenging party can prove that the government adopted the laws because of the racially disparate impact they would have.

4.   Just one year after *Washington v. Davis,* the Court made clear that the discriminatory effects of state action were not irrelevant to the equal protection inquiry. In *Arlington Heights v. Metropolitan Housing Development Corp.,* 429 U.S. 252 (1977), the Court rejected a Fourteenth Amendment challenge to a municipality's decision to reject the re-zoning request of a developer seeking to build low and moderate-income housing. In so doing, however, it explained how racially disparate impacts would have evidentiary relevance in the effort to meet the constitutional intent standard:

> Our decision last Term in Washington v. Davis made it clear that official action will not be held unconstitutional solely because it results in a racially disproportionate impact.

Davis does not require a plaintiff to prove that the challenged action rested solely on racially discriminatory purposes. Rarely can it be said that a legislature or administrative body operating under a broad mandate made a decision motivated solely by a single concern, or even that a particular purpose was the "dominant" or "primary" one. In fact, it is because legislators and administrators are properly concerned with balancing numerous competing considerations that courts refrain from reviewing the merits of their decisions, absent a showing of arbitrariness or irrationality. But racial discrimination is not just another competing consideration. When there is a proof that a discriminatory purpose has been a motivating factor in the decision, this judicial deference is no longer justified.

Determining whether invidious discriminatory purpose was a motivating factor demands a sensitive inquiry into such circumstantial and direct evidence of intent as may be available. The impact of the official action whether it "bears more heavily on one race than another," may provide an important starting point. Sometimes a clear pattern, unexplainable on grounds other than race, emerges from the effect of the state action even when the governing legislation appears neutral on its face. The evidentiary inquiry is then relatively easy. But such cases are rare. Absent a pattern as stark as that in Gomillion [v. Lightfoot] or Yick Wo [v. Hopkins], impact alone is not determinative, and the Court must look to other evidence.

The historical background of the decision is one evidentiary source, particularly if it reveals a series of official actions taken for invidious purposes. The specific sequence of events leading up to the challenged decision also may shed some light on the decisionmaker's purposes. For example, if the property involved here always had been zoned R-5 but suddenly was changed to R-3 when the town learned of MHDC's plans to erect integrated housing, we would have a far different case. Departures from the normal procedural sequence also might afford evidence that improper purposes are playing a role. Substantive departures too may be relevant, particularly if the factors usually considered important by the decisionmaker strongly favor a decision contrary to the one reached.

The legislative or administrative history may be highly relevant, especially where there are contemporary statements by members of the decisionmaking body, minutes of its meetings, or reports.

If disparate effects can serve as proof of discriminatory intent, how significant is the Court's holding in *Washington v. Davis*? What are the pros and cons of a disparate impact rule versus a discriminatory purpose rule that allows impact as evidence of purpose? Given the stringency of the intent standard as advanced in *Feeney*—just two years after *Arlington Heights*—

would you expect evidence of disparate effects to often be sufficient to prove discriminatory purpose?

B. DISPARATE IMPACT AND THE CIVIL RIGHTS STATUTES

Washington v. Davis set the parameters for state accountability under the Constitution. Congress has legislated more broadly, however, imposing liability on a variety of actors for the racially disparate impacts of their actions. The Civil Rights Act of 1964, the Voting Rights Act of 1965, and the Fair Housing Act of 1968 all establish that a law or policy with a racially disparate impact is not per se invalid, but such impact does require the government or private defendant to justify its law or policy. The disparate impact standard has not gone uncontested, however. In 1971, for example, the Supreme Court was called upon to interpret Title VII of the Civil Rights Act of 1964, and the remedial reach of that statute remains contested today. In *Griggs v. Duke Power Company*, 401 U.S. 424 (1971), the Court held that supposedly neutral employment tests could nonetheless violate Title VII by having a disparate impact on black applicants and workers. In Chapter 6, you will consider the legal framework this foundational case launched. Here, consider the Court's justification for reading Title VII to encompass disparate impact liability. After noting that blacks long have received inferior educations as the result of segregation in North Carolina, where the case arose, the Court observed:

> The facts of this case demonstrate the inadequacy of broad and general testing devices as well as the infirmity of using diplomas or degrees as fixed measures of capability. History is filled with examples of men and women who rendered highly effective performance without the conventional badges of accomplishment in terms of certificates, diplomas, or degrees. Diplomas and tests are useful servants, but Congress has mandated the commonsense proposition that they are not to become masters of reality.

> Nothing in the Act precludes the use of testing or measuring procedures; obviously they are useful. What Congress has forbidden is giving these devices and mechanisms controlling force unless they are demonstrably a reasonable measure of job performance. Congress has not commanded that the less qualified be preferred over the better qualified simply because of minority origins. Far from disparaging job qualifications as such, Congress has made such qualifications the controlling factor, so that race, religion, nationality, and sex become irrelevant. What Congress has commanded is that any tests used must measure the person for the job and not the person in the abstract.

Griggs v. Duke Power Company, 401 U.S. at 433.

NOTES AND QUESTIONS

1. What justifies reading Title VII to reach neutral acts that nonetheless have a disparate impact on certain racial groups? If it's the history of unequal educational opportunities for blacks and other groups, for how long should such a justification be valid?

2. The Court's decision in *Griggs* was on the books when it decided the constitutional question in *Washington v. Davis*. Why do you think its reasoning in the former didn't affect the outcome of the latter? Was it simply because *Griggs* involved a question of statutory interpretation? Should employers be held to a higher standard than the state?

3. The reach of liability articulated by the Court in *Griggs* did not last for long. In *Wards Cove v. Atonio*, 490 U.S. 642 (1989), the Court redefined the meaning of "business necessity"—the test it required employers to meet to justify a policy with a discriminatory impact—to a standard far more deferential to the employer. Under *Wards Cove*, an employer need only show that the challenged employment practice serves in some "significant way" its "legitimate employment goals," 490 U.S. at 659, rather than that the practice is essential or indispensable.

In the Civil Rights Act of 1991, Congress responded by expressly defining the disparate impact liability standard. Section 105(a)(k)(1)(A)(i) of the statute reads as follows:

> [An unlawful employment practice based on disparate impact is established if] a complaining party demonstrates that a respondent uses a particular employment practice that causes a disparate impact on the basis of race, color, religion, sex, or national origin and the respondent fails to demonstrate that the challenged practice is job related for the position in question and consistent with business necessity. . . .

> The legislative history of the statute suggests that Congress sought to return the meaning of business necessity to the *Griggs* standard. What, exactly, is at stake in the interpretation of business necessity? Do the two standards reflect different conceptions of what Title VII should be understood to accomplish?

4. In *Ricci v. DeStefano*, 557 U.S. 557 (2009), the Court addressed a potential conflict between the two forms of liability authorized by Title VII— disparate impact and disparate treatment. The City of New Haven had administered a test for promotion of fire fighters. After certifying the results of the test, the City decided not to use them to promote the firefighters who performed best. Under the various civil service rules and collective bargaining agreements in play, the City would only have been able to promote one minority candidate. The city stated it was suspending the promotion process due to its concern that it could face disparate impact liability for using the tests. A group of white and one Latino firefighter sued the City, arguing that its rejection of the test results constituted disparate treatment on the basis of race.

The Court held that discarding test results after the test had been administered constituted race discrimination against the firefighters who would have been promoted. Four dissenters would have held that discarding the test results was a lawful way to comply with the disparate impact obligations of Title VII of the Civil Rights Act of 1964. You do not have the reasoning of the opinions here, but what is your intuitive assessment of whether discarding test results because of their disparate impact is discriminatory against those who would have benefited from the results? Should it have been permissible for the City to have taken an employment action based on the race of those who would have been affected by its decision to do otherwise? Does it matter that all but one of the firefighters who would have been promoted was white? The white firefighters would have been permitted to take any new test or go through any subsequent assessment procedure for promotion devised by the City. Would it amount to disparate treatment if the City had chosen in the first place a method of assessment based on evidence that minority candidates fare better using that tool as opposed to alternative methods?

Justice Scalia would have gone further than the Court. In his concurrence, he suggests that any time an employer or institution changes a policy in order to avoid a racial impact, it engages in racially discriminatory action. His analysis would call into question Congress's authority to require employers and other institutions to justify policies that have a racially disparate impact. Consider his reasoning:

> [I]f the Federal Government is prohibited from discriminating on the basis of race, then surely it is also prohibited from enacting laws mandating that third parties—e.g., employers, whether private, State, or municipal—discriminate on the basis of race. . . . Title VII's disparate-impact provisions place a racial thumb on the scales, often requiring employers to evaluate the racial outcomes of their policies, and to make decisions based on (because of) those racial outcomes. That type of racial decisionmaking is, as the Court explains, discriminatory.

> To be sure, the disparate-impact laws do not mandate imposition of quotas, but it is not clear why that should provide a safe harbor. Would a private employer not be guilty of unlawful discrimination if he refrained from establishing a racial hiring quota but intentionally designed his hiring practices to achieve the same end? Surely he would. Intentional discrimination is still occurring, just one step up the chain. Government compulsion of such design would therefore seemingly violate equal protection principles. Nor would it matter that Title VII requires consideration of race on a wholesale, rather than retail, level. "[T]he Government must treat citizens as individuals, not as simply components of a racial, religious, sexual or national class." And of course the purportedly benign motive for the disparate-impact provisions cannot save the statute (citing Adarand). . . . [T]he war between disparate impact and equal protection will be waged sooner or later, and it behooves

us to begin thinking about how—and on what terms—to make
peace between them.

Ricci v. De Stefano, 557 U.S. at 594–595 (Scalia, J., concurring) (citations
omitted).

Are you persuaded by Justice Scalia that modifying facially neutral
policies that have a racially disparate impact is the same as purposely
discriminating against the group that benefited from the existing policy?

5.   The disparate impact standards of other civil rights statutes have met
mixed fates in the hands of the Supreme Court. In 2001, for example, in
Alexander v. Sandoval, 532 U.S. 275 (2001), the Court considered the
availability of a disparate impact cause of action under Title VI of the 1964
Civil Rights Act. Title VI prohibits racial discrimination by any entity that
receives funding from the federal government. The Court concluded that
Title VI includes no private right of action to enforce the disparate impact
regulations issued pursuant to the statute. The statute only authorized the
government to bring such claims. In 2015, the Court surprised many
observers by upholding disparate impact under the Fair Housing Act. *See
Tex. Dept. Housing & Comm'n. Affairs v. Inclusive Comtys Project*, 135 S.Ct.
2507 (2015). The Court relied on its interpretation of *Griggs* to reach this
result, concluding that the imposition of harms "because of race" in both Title
VII and the FHA encompassed disparate impact. Are these cases different or
similar? In what ways? Could you come up with a persuasive, coherent
explanation for the Court's mixed approach towards disparate impact
standards?

C.   THE CASE OF AFFIRMATIVE ACTION

Recall that *Loving v. Virginia* stated, in reviewing anti-
miscegenation laws, that strict scrutiny applies to racial classifications.
In the 1970s, it became increasingly apparent to many Americans that
simply ending de jure segregation would not eliminate the consequences
of centuries of intergenerational oppression. Racial disparities were
blatant and stark across virtually all aspects of social and economic life.
Some governmental institutions began to use race-conscious policies to
increase opportunities for blacks and other disadvantaged racial
minorities.

One such institution was the University of California at Davis
Medical School, which decided to reserve 16 out of 100 seats in its
entering class for blacks, Mexican Americans, Asians and Native
Americans. Alan Bakke, a white applicant who had been denied
admission, challenged the policy, arguing that it violated the Equal
Protection Clause. The Supreme Court decided his claim in 1978. The
case presented a conflict between the goal of eschewing racial categories
altogether in government decision-making and the reality that, without
affirmative action, schools of higher education and the professions they
served would remain overwhelmingly white. The question facing the
Court was what state interests, if any, could justify race-conscious

admissions, and what form could such race consciousness take. In the course of answering these questions, the Court also grappled with the level of scrutiny that should apply to the race-based admissions policy designed to benefit minorities.

The Justices' answer in *Regents of the Univ. of Cal. v. Bakke*, 438 U.S. 265 (1978), was as fractured as the political debate surrounding the case. The Court invalidated the medical school's policy of reserving a fixed number of seats in the entering class for racial minorities. Four justices concluded that all uses of race, including the racial quota, were invalid as a matter of federal statutory law, while another four justices would have upheld the quota, as well as other kinds of racial preferences. Justice Powell split the difference, holding that the use of a racial quota was unconstitutional, but that giving some weight in the admission process to race, among other factors, was permissible. Thus, a majority, including Justice Powell, voted to invalidate the quota, while a different majority, also including Justice Powell, voted to permit consideration of race in admissions.

Further complicating *Bakke* is that the Justices who approved the use of race disagreed as to the purposes that could legally justify an affirmative action program. Justice Powell alone endorsed the use of race to achieve a diverse student body, while the other four justices, in an opinion by Justice Brennan, concluded that state institutions could use affirmative action to remedy the effects of past societal discrimination.

Powell's opinion, which has come to be regarded as the controlling one in *Bakke*, gave voice to two positions that have been instrumental in the "colorblind" theory of equal protection. First, he concluded that any differential treatment based upon race should be subject to strict scrutiny. Justice Powell wrote:

> The guarantees of the Fourteenth Amendment extend to all persons. The guarantee of equal protection cannot mean one thing when applied to one individual and something else when applied to a person of another color. If both are not accorded the same protection, then it is not equal.

> Racial and ethnic distinctions of any sort are inherently suspect and thus call for the most exacting judicial examination.

> As the Nation filled with the stock of many lands, the reach of the Clause was gradually extended to all ethnic groups seeking protection from official discrimination. *See* Strauder v. West Virginia (Celtic Irishmen) (dictum); Yick Wo v. Hopkins (Chinese); Truax v. Raich (Austrian resident aliens); Korematsu, (Japanese); Hernandez v. Texas (Mexican-Americans).

> It suffices to say that "[o]ver the years, this Court has consistently repudiated '[d]istinctions between citizens solely

because of their ancestry' as being 'odious to a free people whose institutions are founded upon the doctrine of equality.' "

Petitioner urges us to adopt for the first time a more restrictive view of the Equal Protection Clause and hold that discrimination against members of the white "majority" cannot be suspect if its purpose can be characterized as "benign." The clock of our liberties, however, cannot be turned back to 1868. It is far too late to argue that the guarantee of equal protection to all persons permits the recognition of special wards entitled to a degree of protection greater than that accorded others. "The Fourteenth Amendment is not directed solely against discrimination due to a 'two-class theory'—that is, based upon differences between 'white' and Negro."

Once the artificial line of a "two-class theory" of the Fourteenth Amendment is put aside, the difficulties entailed in varying the level of judicial review according to a perceived "preferred" status of a particular racial or ethnic minority are intractable. The concepts of "majority" and "minority" necessarily reflect temporary arrangements and political judgments. As observed above, the white "majority" itself is composed of various minority groups, most of which can lay claim to a history of prior discrimination at the hands of the State and private individuals. Not all of these groups can receive preferential treatment and corresponding judicial tolerance of distinctions drawn in terms of race and nationality, for then the only "majority" left would be a new minority of white Anglo-Saxon Protestants. There is no principled basis for deciding which groups would merit "heightened judicial solicitude" and which would not. Courts would be asked to evaluate the extent of the prejudice and consequent harm suffered by various minority groups. Those whose societal injury is thought to exceed some arbitrary level of tolerability then would be entitled to preferential classifications at the expense of individuals belonging to other groups. Those classifications would be free from exacting judicial scrutiny. As these preferences began to have their desired effect, and the consequences of past discrimination were undone, new judicial rankings would be necessary. The kind of variable sociological and political analysis necessary to produce such rankings simply does not lie within the judicial competence—even if they otherwise were politically feasible and socially desirable.[8]

---

[8]   Mr. Justice Douglas has noted the problems associated with such inquiries:

"The reservation of a proportion of the law school class for members of selected minority groups is fraught with . . . dangers, for one must immediately determine which groups are to receive such favored treatment and which are to be excluded, the proportions of the class that are to be allocated to each, and even the criteria by which to determine

Bakke, 438 U.S. at 289–291.

A second salient feature of Justice Powell's opinion is his rejection of societal discrimination as a justification for race-based remedial action:

> The State certainly has a legitimate and substantial interest in ameliorating, or eliminating where feasible, the disabling effects of identified discrimination. The line of school desegregation cases, commencing with Brown, attests to the importance of this state goal and the commitment of the judiciary to affirm all lawful means toward its attainment. In the school cases, the States were required by court order to redress the wrongs worked by specific instances of racial discrimination. That goal was far more focused than the remedying of the effects of "societal discrimination," an amorphous concept of injury that may be ageless in its reach into the past.

> We have never approved a classification that aids persons perceived as members of relatively victimized groups at the expense of other innocent individuals in the absence of judicial, legislative, or administrative findings of constitutional or statutory violations. After such findings have been made, the governmental interest in preferring members of the injured groups at the expense of others is substantial, since the legal rights of the victims must be vindicated. In such a case, the extent of the injury and the consequent remedy will have been judicially, legislatively, or administratively defined. Also, the remedial action usually remains subject to continuing oversight to assure that it will work the least harm possible to other innocent persons competing for the benefit. Without such findings of constitutional or statutory violations, it cannot be

---

whether an individual is a member of a favored group. [Cf. Plessy v. Ferguson.] There is no assurance that a common agreement can be reached, and first the schools, and then the courts, will be buffeted with the competing claims. The University of Washington included Filipinos, but excluded Chinese and Japanese; another school may limit its program to blacks, or to blacks and Chicanos. Once the Court sanctioned racial preferences such as these, it could not then wash its hands of the matter, leaving it entirely in the discretion of the school, for then we would have effectively overruled Sweatt v. Painter, and allowed imposition of a 'zero' allocation. But what standard is the Court to apply when a rejected applicant of Japanese ancestry brings suit to require the University of Washington to extend the same privileges to his group? The Committee might conclude that the population of Washington is now 2% Japanese, and that Japanese also constitute 2% of the Bar, but that had they not been handicapped by a history of discrimination, Japanese would now constitute 5% of the Bar, or 20%. Or, alternatively, the Court could attempt to assess how grievously each group has suffered from discrimination, and allocate proportions accordingly; if that were the standard the current University of Washington policy would almost surely fall, for there is no Western State which can claim that it has always treated Japanese and Chinese in a fair and evenhanded manner.

"Nor obviously will the problem be solved if next year the Law School included only Japanese and Chinese, for then Norwegians and Swedes, Poles and Italians, Puerto Ricans and Hungarians, and all other groups which form this diverse Nation would have just complaints." DeFunis v. Odegaard, (dissenting opinion) (footnotes omitted).

said that the government has any greater interest in helping one individual than in refraining from harming another. Thus, the government has no compelling justification for inflicting such harm.

Petitioner does not purport to have made, and is in no position to make, such findings. Its broad mission is education, not the formulation of any legislative policy or the adjudication of particular claims of illegality. [I]solated segments of our vast governmental structures are not competent to make those decisions, at least in the absence of legislative mandates and legislatively determined criteria.[9] Before relying upon these sorts of findings in establishing a racial classification, a governmental body must have the authority and capability to establish, in the record, that the classification is responsive to identified discrimination. Lacking this capability, petitioner has not carried its burden of justification on this issue.

Id. at 307–310.

Because of the fractured opinion in *Bakke*, the Court did not fully resolve the question of the appropriate standard of review for affirmative action programs. And though Justice Powell rejected societal discrimination, as well as the cultivation of minority role models, as justifications for race-conscious decision-making in admissions decisions, the case hardly resolved whether other justifications would be valid, whether in the educational setting or otherwise. In Chapter 5 you will study in detail how Powell's conception of diversity has evolved in the educational setting. But in 1989, the Court issued a crucial precedent for the development of affirmative action more generally—commanding a majority and settling the standard of review for virtually all uses of racial classifications by state and local actors.

City of Richmond v. J.A. Croson Co.
Supreme Court of the United States, 1989.
488 U.S. 469.

■ JUSTICE O'CONNOR announced the judgment of the Court.

In this case, we confront once again the tension between the Fourteenth Amendment's guarantee of equal treatment to all citizens, and the use of race-based measures to ameliorate the effects of past discrimination on the opportunities enjoyed by members of minority groups in our society.

---

[9] For example, the University is unable to explain its selection of only the four favored groups—Negroes, Mexican-Americans, American-Indians, and Asians—for preferential treatment. The inclusion of the last group is especially curious in light of the substantial numbers of Asians admitted through the regular admissions process.

I

On April 11, 1983, the Richmond City Council adopted the Minority Business Utilization Plan (the Plan). The Plan required prime contractors to whom the city awarded construction contracts to subcontract at least 30% of the dollar amount of the contract to one or more Minority Business Enterprises (MBE's). The 30% set-aside did not apply to city contracts awarded to minority-owned prime contractors. The Plan defined an MBE as "[a] business at least fifty-one (51) percent of which is owned and controlled . . . by minority group members." "Minority group members" were defined as "[c]itizens of the United States who are Blacks, Spanish-speaking, Orientals, Indians, Eskimos, or Aleuts." There was no geographic limit to the Plan; an otherwise qualified MBE from anywhere in the United States could avail itself of the 30% set-aside. The Plan declared that it was "remedial" in nature, and enacted "for the purpose of promoting wider participation by minority business enterprises in the construction of public projects." The Plan expired on June 30, 1988, and was in effect for approximately five years.

The Plan was adopted by the Richmond City Council after a public hearing. Proponents of the set-aside provision relied on a study which indicated that, while the general population of Richmond was 50% black, only 0.67% of the city's prime construction contracts had been awarded to minority businesses in the 5-year period from 1978 to 1983. It was also established that a variety of contractors' associations, whose representatives appeared in opposition to the ordinance, had virtually no minority businesses within their membership. There was no direct evidence of race discrimination on the part of the city in letting contracts or any evidence that the city's prime contractors had discriminated against minority-owned subcontractors.

II

The parties and their supporting amici fight an initial battle over the scope of the city's power to adopt legislation designed to address the effects of past discrimination. Relying on our decision in *Wygant,* appellee argues that the city must limit any race-based remedial efforts to eradicating the effects of its own prior discrimination. Appellant argues that our decision in *Fullilove* is controlling, and that as a result the city of Richmond enjoys sweeping legislative power to define and attack the effects of prior discrimination in its local construction industry. We find that neither of these two rather stark alternatives can withstand analysis.

It would seem equally clear, however, that a state or local subdivision (if delegated the authority from the State) has the authority to eradicate the effects of private discrimination within its own legislative jurisdiction. This authority must, of course, be exercised within the constraints of § 1 of the Fourteenth Amendment. As a matter of state law, the city of Richmond has legislative authority over its procurement policies, and can use its spending powers to remedy private discrimination, if it identifies that discrimination with the particularity required by the Fourteenth Amendment. Thus, if the city could show that it had essentially become a "passive participant" in a system of racial exclusion practiced by elements of the local construction industry, we think it clear that the city could take affirmative steps to dismantle such a system. It is beyond dispute that any public entity, state or federal, has a compelling interest in assuring that public dollars drawn from the tax contributions of all citizens, do not serve to finance the evil of private prejudice.

III

The Richmond Plan denies certain citizens the opportunity to compete for a fixed percentage of public contracts based solely upon their race. To whatever racial group these citizens belong, their "personal rights" to be treated with equal dignity and respect are implicated by a rigid rule erecting race as the sole criterion in an aspect of public decision-making.

Absent searching judicial inquiry into the justification for such race-based measures, there is simply no way of determining what classifications are "benign" or "remedial" and what classifications are in fact motivated by illegitimate notions of racial inferiority or simple racial politics. Indeed, the purpose of strict scrutiny is to "smoke out" illegitimate uses of race by assuring that the legislative body is pursuing a goal important enough to warrant use of a highly suspect tool. The test also ensures that the means chosen "fit" this compelling goal so closely that there is little or no possibility that the motive for the classification was illegitimate racial prejudice or stereotype. Classifications based on race carry a danger of stigmatic harm. Unless they are strictly reserved for remedial settings, they may in fact promote notions of racial inferiority and lead to a politics of racial hostility.

Even were we to accept a reading of the guarantee of equal protection under which the level of scrutiny varies according to the ability of different groups to defend their interests in the representative process, heightened scrutiny would still be appropriate in the circumstances of this case. One of the central arguments for applying a less exacting standard to "benign" racial classifications is that such measures essentially involve a choice made by dominant racial groups to disadvantage themselves. If one aspect of the judiciary's role under the Equal Protection Clause is to protect "discrete and insular minorities" from majoritarian prejudice or indifference, *see* United States v. Carolene Products Co. (1938), some maintain that these concerns are not implicated when the "white majority" places burdens upon itself. *See* J. Ely, Democracy and Distrust 170 (1980).

In this case, blacks constitute approximately 50% of the population of the city of Richmond. Five of the nine seats on the city council are held by blacks. The concern that a political majority will more easily act to the disadvantage of a minority based on unwarranted assumptions or incomplete facts would seem to militate for, not against, the application of heightened judicial scrutiny in this case.

The District Court found the city council's "findings sufficient to ensure that, in adopting the Plan, it was remedying the present effects of past discrimination in the construction industry." Like the "role model" theory employed in *Wygant*, a generalized assertion that there has been past discrimination in an entire industry provides no guidance for a legislative body to determine the precise scope of the injury it seeks to remedy. It "has no logical stopping point." "Relief" for such an ill-defined wrong could extend until the percentage of public contracts awarded to MBE's in Richmond mirrored the percentage of minorities in the population as a whole.

Appellant argues that it is attempting to remedy various forms of past discrimination that are alleged to be responsible for the small number of minority businesses in the local contracting industry. Among these the city cites the exclusion of blacks from skilled construction trade unions and training programs. The city also lists a host of nonracial factors which would seem to face a member of any racial group attempting to establish a new business enterprise, such as deficiencies in working capital, inability to meet bonding requirements, unfamiliarity with bidding procedures, and disability caused by an inadequate track record.

While there is no doubt that the sorry history of both private and public discrimination in this country has contributed to a lack of opportunities for black entrepreneurs, this observation, standing alone, cannot justify a rigid racial quota in the awarding of public contracts in Richmond, Virginia. Like the claim that discrimination in primary and secondary schooling justifies a rigid racial preference in medical school admissions, an amorphous claim that there has been past discrimination in a particular industry cannot justify the use of an unyielding racial quota.

It is sheer speculation how many minority firms there would be in Richmond absent past societal discrimination, just as it was sheer speculation how many minority medical students would have been admitted to the medical school at Davis absent past discrimination in educational opportunities. Defining these sorts of injuries as "identified discrimination" would give local governments license to create a patchwork of racial preferences based on statistical generalizations about any particular field of endeavor.

These defects are readily apparent in this case. The 30% quota cannot in any realistic sense be tied to any injury suffered by anyone.

None of [the district court's] "findings," singly or together, provide the city of Richmond with a "strong basis in evidence for its conclusion that remedial action was necessary." There is nothing approaching a prima facie case of a constitutional or statutory violation by *anyone* in the Richmond construction industry.

The District Court accorded great weight to the fact that the city council designated the Plan as "remedial." But the mere recitation of a "benign" or legitimate purpose for a racial classification is entitled to little or no weight. Racial classifications are suspect, and that means that simple legislative assurances of good intention cannot suffice.

In sum, none of the evidence presented by the city points to any identified discrimination in the Richmond construction industry. We, therefore, hold that the city has failed to demonstrate a compelling interest in apportioning public contracting opportunities on the basis of race. To accept Richmond's claim that past societal discrimination alone can serve as the basis for rigid racial preferences would be to open the door to competing claims for "remedial relief" for every disadvantaged group. The dream of a Nation of equal citizens in a society where race is irrelevant to personal opportunity and achievement would be lost in a mosaic of shifting preferences based on inherently unmeasurable claims of past wrongs. "Courts would be asked to evaluate the extent of the prejudice and consequent harm suffered by various minority groups. Those whose societal injury is thought to exceed some arbitrary level of tolerability then would be entitled to preferential classifications. . . ." We think such a result would be contrary to both the letter and spirit of a constitutional provision whose central command is equality.

The foregoing analysis applies only to the inclusion of blacks within the Richmond set-aside program. There is absolutely no evidence of past discrimination against Spanish-speaking, Oriental, Indian, Eskimo, or Aleut persons in any aspect of the Richmond construction industry. It may well be that Richmond has never had an Aleut or Eskimo citizen. The random inclusion of racial groups that, as a practical matter, may never have suffered from discrimination in the construction industry in Richmond suggests that perhaps the city's purpose was not in fact to remedy past discrimination.

If a 30% set-aside was "narrowly tailored" to compensate black contractors for past discrimination, one may legitimately ask why they are forced to share this "remedial relief" with an Aleut citizen who moves to Richmond tomorrow? The gross overinclusiveness of Richmond's racial preference strongly impugns the city's claim of remedial motivation.

As noted by the court below, it is almost impossible to assess whether the Richmond Plan is narrowly tailored to remedy prior discrimination since it is not linked to identified discrimination in any way. We limit ourselves to two observations in this regard.

First, there does not appear to have been any consideration of the use of race-neutral means to increase minority business participation in city contracting. Many of the barriers to minority participation in the construction industry relied upon by the city to justify a racial classification appear to be race neutral. If MBE's disproportionately lack capital or cannot meet bonding requirements, a race-neutral program of city financing for small firms would, a fortiori, lead to greater minority participation. There is no evidence in this record that the Richmond City Council has considered any alternatives to a race-based quota.

Second, the 30% quota cannot be said to be narrowly tailored to any goal, except perhaps outright racial balancing. It rests upon the "completely unrealistic" assumption that minorities will choose a particular trade in lockstep proportion to their representation in the local population. Since the city must already consider bids and waivers on a case-by-case basis, it is difficult to see the need for a rigid numerical quota. Based upon proper findings, such programs are less problematic from an equal protection standpoint because they treat all candidates individually, rather than making the color of an applicant's skin the sole relevant consideration. Unlike the program upheld in *Fullilove,* the Richmond Plan's waiver system focuses solely on the availability of MBE's; there is no inquiry into whether or not the particular MBE seeking a racial preference has suffered from the effects of past discrimination by the city or prime contractors.

Nothing we say today precludes a state or local entity from taking action to rectify the effects of identified discrimination within its jurisdiction. If the city of Richmond had evidence before it that nonminority contractors were systematically excluding minority businesses from subcontracting opportunities it could take action to end the discriminatory exclusion. Where there is a significant statistical disparity between the number of qualified minority contractors willing and able to perform a particular service and the number of such contractors actually engaged by the locality or the locality's prime contractors, an inference of discriminatory exclusion could arise. Under such circumstances, the city could act to dismantle the closed business system by taking appropriate measures against those who discriminate on the basis of race or other illegitimate criteria. In the extreme case, some form of narrowly tailored racial preference might be necessary to break down patterns of deliberate exclusion.

Even in the absence of evidence of discrimination, the city has at its disposal a whole array of race-neutral devices to increase the accessibility of city contracting opportunities to small entrepreneurs of all races. Simplification of bidding procedures, relaxation of bonding requirements, and training and financial aid for disadvantaged entrepreneurs of all races would open the public contracting market to all those who have suffered the effects of past societal discrimination or neglect. Many of the formal barriers to new entrants may be the product of bureaucratic inertia more than actual necessity, and may have a disproportionate effect on the opportunities open to new minority firms. Their elimination or modification would have little detrimental effect on the city's interests and would serve to increase the opportunities available to minority business without classifying individuals on the basis of race. The city may also act to prohibit discrimination in the provision of credit or bonding by local suppliers and banks. Business as usual should not mean business pursuant to the unthinking exclusion of certain members of our society from its rewards.

In the case at hand, the city has not ascertained how many minority enterprises are present in the local construction market nor the level of their participation in city construction projects. The city points to no evidence that qualified minority contractors have been passed over for city contracts or subcontracts, either as a group or in any individual case. Under such circumstances, it is simply impossible to say that the city has demonstrated "a strong basis in evidence for its conclusion that remedial action was necessary."

Proper findings in this regard are necessary to define both the scope of the injury and the extent of the remedy necessary to cure its effects. Such findings also serve to assure all citizens that the deviation from the norm of equal treatment of all racial and ethnic groups is a temporary matter, a measure taken in the service of the goal of equality itself. Absent such findings, there is a danger that a racial classification is merely the product of unthinking stereotypes or a form of racial politics. "[I]f there is no duty to attempt either to measure the recovery by the wrong or to distribute that recovery within the injured class in an evenhanded way, our history will adequately support a legislative preference for almost any ethnic, religious, or racial group with the political strength to negotiate 'a piece of the action' for its members." Because the city of Richmond has failed to identify the need for remedial action in the awarding of its public construction contracts, its treatment of its citizens on a racial basis violates the dictates of the Equal Protection Clause.

■ JUSTICE STEVENS, concurring in part and concurring in the judgment.

I believe the Constitution requires us to evaluate our policy decisions—including those that govern the relationships among different racial and ethnic groups—primarily by studying their probable impact on the future. I therefore do not agree with the premise that seems to underlie today's decision, that a governmental decision that rests on a racial classification is never permissible except as a remedy for a past wrong. I do, however, agree with the Court's explanation of why the Richmond ordinance cannot be justified as a remedy for past discrimination.

■ JUSTICE SCALIA, concurring in the judgment.

I agree with Justice O'Connor's conclusion that strict scrutiny must be applied to all governmental classification by race, whether or not its asserted purpose is "remedial" or "benign." I do not agree, however, with Justice O'Connor's dictum suggesting that state and local governments may in some circumstances discriminate on the basis of race in order (in a broad sense) "to ameliorate the effects of past discrimination." The benign purpose of compensating for social disadvantages, whether they have been acquired by reason of prior discrimination or otherwise, can no more be pursued by the illegitimate means of racial discrimination than can other assertedly benign purposes we have repeatedly rejected.

I share the view expressed by Alexander Bickel that "[t]he lesson of the great decisions of the Supreme Court and the lesson of contemporary history have been the same for at least a generation: discrimination on the basis of race is illegal, immoral, unconstitutional, inherently wrong, and destructive of democratic society." A. Bickel, The Morality of Consent 133 (1975). At least where state or local action is at issue, only a social emergency rising to the level of imminent danger to life and limb—for example, a prison race riot, requiring temporary segregation of inmates, can justify an exception to the principle embodied in the Fourteenth Amendment that "[o]ur Constitution is colorblind, and neither knows nor tolerates classes among citizens."

In my view there is only one circumstance in which the States may act by race to "undo the effects of past discrimination": where that is necessary to eliminate their own maintenance of a system of unlawful racial classification. If, for example, a state agency has a discriminatory pay scale compensating black employees in all positions at 20% less than their nonblack counterparts, it may assuredly promulgate an order raising the salaries of "all black employees" to eliminate the differential.

■ JUSTICE MARSHALL, with whom JUSTICE BRENNAN and JUSTICE BLACKMUN join, dissenting.

It is a welcome symbol of racial progress when the former capital of the Confederacy acts forthrightly to confront the effects of racial discrimination in its midst. In my view, nothing in the Constitution can be construed to prevent Richmond, Virginia, from allocating a portion of its contracting dollars for businesses owned or controlled by members of minority groups. Indeed, Richmond's set-aside program is indistinguishable in all meaningful respects from—and in fact was patterned upon—the federal set-aside plan which this Court upheld in Fullilove v. Klutznick (1980).

A majority of this Court holds today, however, that the Equal Protection Clause of the Fourteenth Amendment blocks Richmond's initiative. The essence of the majority's position is that Richmond has failed to catalog adequate findings to prove that past discrimination has impeded minorities from joining or participating fully in Richmond's construction contracting industry. I find deep irony in second-guessing Richmond's judgment on this point. As much as any municipality in the United States, Richmond knows what racial discrimination is; a century of decisions by this and other federal courts has richly documented the city's disgraceful history of public and private racial discrimination. In any event, the Richmond City Council has supported its determination that minorities have been wrongly excluded from local construction contracting. Its proof includes statistics showing that minority-owned businesses have received virtually no city contracting dollars and rarely if ever belonged to area trade associations; testimony by municipal officials that discrimination has been widespread in the local construction industry; and the same exhaustive and widely publicized federal studies relied on in *Fullilove,* studies which showed that pervasive discrimination in the Nation's tight-knit construction industry had operated to exclude minorities from public contracting. These are precisely the types of statistical and testimonial evidence which, until today, this Court had credited in cases approving of race-conscious measures designed to remedy past discrimination.

More fundamentally, today's decision marks a deliberate and giant step backward in this Court's affirmative-action jurisprudence. Cynical of one municipality's attempt to redress the effects of past racial discrimination in a particular industry, the majority launches a grapeshot attack on race-conscious remedies in general. The majority's unnecessary pronouncements will inevitably discourage or prevent governmental entities, particularly States and localities, from acting to rectify the scourge of past discrimination. This is the harsh reality of the majority's decision, but it is not the Constitution's command.

[T]he majority downplays the fact that the city council had before it a rich trove of evidence that discrimination in the Nation's construction industry had seriously impaired the competitive position of businesses owned or controlled by members of minority groups. The city council's members also heard testimony that, although minority groups made up half of the city's population, only 0.67% of the $24.6 million which Richmond had dispensed in construction contracts during the five years ending in March 1983 had gone to minority-owned prime contractors. They heard testimony that the major Richmond area construction trade associations had virtually no minorities among their hundreds of members. Finally, they heard testimony from city officials as to the exclusionary history of the local construction industry. As the District Court noted, not a single person who testified before the city council denied that discrimination in Richmond's construction industry had been widespread. So long as one views Richmond's local evidence of discrimination against the backdrop of systematic nationwide racial discrimination which Congress had so painstakingly identified in this very industry, this case is readily resolved.

Richmond has two powerful interests in setting aside a portion of public contracting funds for minority-owned enterprises. The first is the city's interest in eradicating the effects of past racial discrimination. It is far too late in the day to doubt that remedying such discrimination is a compelling, let alone an important, interest.

Richmond has a second compelling interest in setting aside, where possible, a portion of its contracting dollars. That interest is the prospective one of preventing the city's own spending decisions from reinforcing and perpetuating the exclusionary effects of past discrimination.

Today, for the first time, a majority of this Court has adopted strict scrutiny as its standard of Equal Protection Clause review of race-conscious remedial measures. This is an unwelcome development. A profound difference separates governmental actions that themselves are racist, and governmental actions that seek to remedy the effects of prior racism or to prevent neutral governmental activity from perpetuating the effects of such racism. Racial classifications "drawn on the presumption that one race is inferior to another or because they put the weight of government behind racial hatred and separatism" warrant the strictest judicial scrutiny because of the very irrelevance of these rationales. By contrast, racial classifications drawn for the purpose of remedying the effects of discrimination that itself was race-based have a highly pertinent basis: the tragic and indelible fact that discrimination against blacks and other racial minorities in this Nation has pervaded our Nation's history and continues to scar our society.

In concluding that remedial classifications warrant no different standard of review under the Constitution than the most brutal and repugnant forms of state-sponsored racism, a majority of this Court signals that it regards racial discrimination as largely a phenomenon of the past, and that government bodies need no longer preoccupy themselves with rectifying racial injustice. I, however, do not believe this Nation is anywhere close to eradicating racial discrimination or its vestiges. In constitutionalizing its wishful thinking, the majority today does a grave disservice not only to those victims of past and present racial discrimination in this Nation whom government has sought to assist, but also to this Court's long tradition of approaching issues of race with the utmost sensitivity.

The majority today sounds a full-scale retreat from the Court's longstanding solicitude to race-conscious remedial efforts "directed toward deliverance of the century-old promise of equality of economic opportunity." Fullilove, 448 U.S., at 463. The new and restrictive tests it applies scuttle one city's effort to surmount its discriminatory past, and imperil those of dozens more localities. I, however, profoundly disagree with the cramped vision of the Equal Protection Clause which the majority offers today and with its application of that vision to Richmond,

Virginia's, laudable set-aside plan. The battle against pernicious racial discrimination or its effects is nowhere near won. I must dissent.

NOTES AND QUESTIONS

1. In his opinion of *Bakke*, Powell rejects the idea that any particular group should be a perpetual "ward" of the state. What does he mean by that? He also would treat "discrimination" against whites the same as "discrimination" against blacks and other disadvantaged minorities. What justifies that equivalence? In your estimation, does it matter to you, as it seems to have mattered to Powell, that the white population is itself quite diverse in terms of its origins and status in American history and society?

2. What, precisely, is the harm of classifying someone on the basis of his or her race? Does the classification itself impose a cost, or does the definition of the nature of harm depend on what follows from the classification? In *Croson*, both Justice O'Connor and Scalia talk about the dangers of racial classifications. In particular, Justice O'Connor writes that racial classifications "carry a danger of stigmatic harm." What is that stigmatic harm? Is this an empirical claim or a normative conclusion? Do race-based policies that ostensibly favor minorities in fact harm them? Does the stigmatic harm to minority firms outweigh the benefit to them of being awarded the contract? Are minorities harmed more than the white construction contractors who lose out because of the quota? If stigmatic harm to minorities should be considered in assessing the costs of race-based policies, should the message of superior status sent by such policies about white contractors also be considered in assessing the white contractors' claimed harm?

3. What is "societal" discrimination? Can it be used to justify affirmative action in a way that would not entrench such policies for the foreseeable future and in relation to all markets and institutions, regardless of their particular histories of exclusion?

4. In *Croson*, the City of Richmond attempted to use governmental power to redress what it believed to be private discrimination in the marketplace, in this case the construction market. The City relied in part on the fact that minorities received 0.67% of prime contracts from the City, even though they constituted about 50% of the City's population. In your view, is this statistical disparity evidence of a skewed market? Justice O'Connor does not think so. She writes that it is "completely unrealistic" to assume "that minorities will choose a particular trade in lockstep proportion to their representation." Justice O'Connor's intimation is that maybe minorities are not interested in the contracting market. In order to figure out whether a market is functioning properly we need a baseline. If the population of the City is not a relevant baseline, what should our baseline be to determine whether the market is skewed?

5. Assuming that the market is skewed, we would need to show that the skew is either because of present discrimination or the continued effects of past discrimination. One would also need to identify the discriminator: either the government or private actors. Though the opinions in *Croson* are not crystal clear on this point, we have four categories: (a) past discrimination by the government; (b) present discrimination by the government; (c) past discrimination by private actors; and (d) present discrimination by private actors. Of the four categories, pursuant to which of the four, if any, is the state allowed to draw a racial classification?

6. The majority rejects the City's reasons for promulgating a set-aside program by arguing against each reason as if it "stood alone." Disaggregated, the individual reasons are insufficient to sustain Richmond's remedial plan. This point does not go unnoticed by Justice Marshall: "The majority also takes the disingenuous approach of disaggregating Richmond's local evidence, attacking it piecemeal, and thereby concluding that no *single* piece of evidence adduced by the city, 'standing alone,' . . . suffices to prove past discrimination. But items of evidence do not, of course, 'stan[d] alone' or exist in alien juxtaposition; they necessarily work together, reinforcing or contradicting each other." Would or should the aggregated reasons support the plan under the majority's strict scrutiny review?

7. A theme of Justice O'Connor's opinion is distrust of the government's use of race. For example, Justice O'Connor argues that one cannot believe that the City was using race for remedial purposes because the City's set-aside program included other minority groups such as Indians, Eskimos, and Aleuts. Justice O'Connor also expressed some distrust of the City council's decision because a majority of the city council was black. Justice O'Connor's observation prompted a stinging rebuke from Justice Marshall, who intimated that the Court was making it harder for black elected officials in numerous cities to improve the lot of their constituents by undoing decades of economic deprivations as a consequence of racial discrimination. Who has the better of the argument here? Can legislative bodies that are controlled by elected officials of color able to take remedial action without being seen as trying to "even the score"?

8. *Exercise 1.* You are counsel to the City following *Croson*. The city council believes that some reliance on race in the awarding of construction contracts is necessary to meaningfully increase the number and viability of construction contractors of color. The council has asked you to draft the most aggressive race-based program possible, within the confines of *Croson*. What are the distinctive features of your plan? How likely is it that it would withstand scrutiny under Croson?

9. *Exercise 2.* You are counsel to the City. Assume that the difficulty of a race-based set aside program satisfying strict scrutiny under *Croson* leads you to recommend the use of race-neutral criteria in awarding construction contracts. What criteria would you recommend and how effective do you believe they would be at increasing participation by minority-owned firms? Note that both Justices O'Connor and Scalia advised in Croson that the city could use race-neutral means to accomplish its goals without running afoul of the Constitution or even having to satisfy strict scrutiny. Query: why would seeking to increase minority participation in city construction escape strict scrutiny just because the policy used race-neutral means to achieve the racial goal? What if the city chose race-neutral means that favored white-owned firms for the purpose of excluding minority-owned businesses? Should that also escape strict scrutiny?

10. In *Croson*, the Justices debate whether the states ought to be held to a stricter standard when engaging in affirmative action than the federal government. At the time *Croson* was decided, existing precedent applied only intermediate scrutiny to federal affirmative action programs. *See Fullilove v. Klutznick*, 448 U.S. 448 (1980). Justice Scalia argued that states were to be uniquely distrusted when it came to race. Justice O'Connor contended that the Reconstruction Amendments changed the balance of power between the states and the federal government, in favor of the federal government. Justice Marshall, by contrast, insisted that the Reconstruction Amendments did not forbid the states from engaging in remedial action to remedy past discrimination. Should the federal government have more, less, or the same latitude in employing race-based policies than the states?

The Court decided this question in *Adarand Constructors, Inc. v. Pena*, 515 U.S. 200 (1995), holding that strict scrutiny applied to federal affirmative action programs. The argument in defense of a less stringent standard of review for federal classifications had been based in section 5 of the Fourteenth Amendment, which granted Congress authority to enforce section 1 of the Amendment. But in her opinion reviewing minority set asides in federal contracting, Justice O'Connor rejected this line of thinking.

> We hold today that all racial classifications, imposed by whatever federal, state, or local governmental actor, must be analyzed by a reviewing court under strict scrutiny. In other words, such classifications are constitutional only if they are narrowly tailored measures that further compelling governmental interests.

> [In dissent,] Justice Stevens chides us for our "supposed inability to differentiate between 'invidious' and 'benign' discrimination," because it is in his view sufficient that "people understand the difference between good intentions and bad." But, [the] point of strict scrutiny is to "differentiate between" permissible and impermissible governmental use of race. And Justice Stevens himself has already explained in his dissent in *Fullilove* why "good intentions" alone are not enough to sustain a supposedly "benign" racial classification: "Even though it is not the actual predicate for this legislation, a statute of this kind inevitably is perceived by many as resting on an assumption that those who are granted this special preference are less qualified in some respect that is identified purely by their race. Because that perception—especially when fostered by the Congress of the United States—can only exacerbate rather than reduce racial prejudice, it will delay the time when race will become a truly irrelevant, or at least insignificant, factor. Unless Congress clearly articulates the need and basis for a racial classification, and also tailors the classification to its justification, the Court should not uphold this kind of statute." *Fullilove* (dissenting opinion).

Perhaps it is not the standard of strict scrutiny itself, but our use of the concepts of "consistency" and "congruence" in conjunction with it, that leads Justice Stevens to dissent. According to Justice Stevens, our view of consistency "equates remedial preferences with invidious discrimination," and ignores the difference between "an engine of oppression" and an effort "to foster equality in society," or, more colorfully, "between a 'No Trespassing' sign and a welcome mat." It does nothing of the kind. The principle of consistency simply means that whenever the government treats any person unequally because of his or her race, that person has suffered an injury that falls squarely within the language and spirit of the Constitution's guarantee of equal protection. It says nothing about the ultimate validity of any particular law; that determination is the job of the court applying strict scrutiny.

Finally, we wish to dispel the notion that strict scrutiny is "strict in theory, but fatal in fact." The unhappy persistence of both the practice and the lingering effects of racial discrimination against minority groups in this country is an unfortunate reality, and government is not disqualified from acting in response to it. When race-based action is necessary to further a compelling interest, such action is within constitutional constraints if it satisfies the "narrow tailoring" test this Court has set out in previous cases. *Adarand*, 515 U.S. at 227–37.

D. THE UNITED STATES CENSUS AND THE CHANGING MEANINGS OF RACE

The United States Constitution requires that an "enumeration" of the nation's population be conducted every 10 years. U.S. Const. Art. 1, § 2. The immediate constitutional purpose of the Census is to enable apportionment for the House of Representatives. But from its inception in 1790, the federal government also has used the Census to collect demographic information about the nation's inhabitants. In this sense, the Census acts as a repudiation of the colorblind ideal because it stands for the proposition that racial categories matter to the government.

The amount and type of demographic information the Census Bureau, located in the Department of Commerce, collects have changed considerably over the centuries. The Census simultaneously reflects and constructs our national identity and our sense of how and why race matters. The 1790 Census contained only three race-related categories: "slaves," "free white females and males," and "All other free persons." By 1820, the Bureau had added a category for "free Colored persons." Subsequent enumerations included such categories as Chinese, Japanese, Hindu, Filipino, and Korean.

In the 1970s, the federal government attempted to standardize the classifications it used for government programs, reporting, and record keeping. Published by the Office of Management and Budget (OMB) in

1977, Directive No. 15: Race and Ethnic Standards for Federal Statistics and Administrative Reporting, required that the Census Bureau collect information that could be aggregated into four racial groups and one ethnic group, though OMB did not prohibit the collection of other, more detailed information. Those categories were defined as follows:

a.   *American Indian or Alaskan Native.* A person having origins in any of the original peoples of North America, and who maintains cultural identification through tribal affiliation or community recognition.

b.   *Asian or Pacific Islander.* A person having origins in any of the original peoples of the Far East, Southeast Asia, the Indian subcontinent, or the Pacific Islands. This area includes, for example, China, India, Japan, Korea, the Philippine Islands, and Samoa.

c.   *Black.* A person having origins in any of the black racial groups of Africa.

d.   *Hispanic.* A person of Mexican, Puerto Rican, Cuban, Central or South American or other Spanish culture or origin, regardless of race.

e.   *White.* A person having origins in any of the original peoples of Europe, North Africa, or the Middle East.

In 1997, the OMB revised Directive 15 to add "Latino" to the Hispanic category and separate out Native Hawaiians from the Asian or Pacific Islander Category, in response to claims by Hawaiians that lumping them together with all Asians impeded assessment of their social and economic status. In both its original and revised versions, Directive 15 contained a version of this caveat: "[t]he categories represent a social-political construct designed for collecting data on the race and ethnicity of broad population groups in this country, and are not anthropologically or scientifically based."

The evolution of efforts to count the Hispanic/Latino population over time reveals some of the challenges and political choices associated with collecting this demographic data. The 1930 Census included the one-time category Mexican. In 1970, the Census attempted its first large-scale counting of the Hispanic population, asking recipients of the long-form Census (received by only a small sample of the population) whether their origin was "Mexican, Puerto Rican, Cuban, Central or South American, Other Spanish." This question was not regarded as a success, including because hundreds of thousands of people who lived in the central or southern regions of the United States answered that they were part of the category. In 1980, the short form Census sent to all households included the Hispanic question and expressly asked whether the person was of Hispanic/Spanish origin. It then asked those who answered "yes" whether they were Mexican, Puerto Rican, Cuban, or other Hispanic. By

2000, the Bureau added the term "Latino" alongside Hispanic; the question of Hispanic identity preceded rather than succeeded the race question; and the form instructed respondents to respond to both, though 43% of Hispanics declined to specify a race.

For the 2020 Census, the Census Bureau is considering combining the race and ethnicity questions. Roughly 1 in 3 people who identify as Hispanic/Latino also check "some other race," rather than any of the available racial categories, thus stymieing efforts to categorize Latinos along the racial lines of the rest of the population. Research indicates that combining the race/ethnicity questions would dramatically reduce the percentage of Hispanic/Latinos checking "some other race" and also reduce the percentage of Latinos who check "white." What might be the costs and benefits of this proposed change? What do these developments over time suggest to you about the meaning of "Hispanic" or "Latino"?

Census data have been used historically for a wide variety of purposes and by a wide range of government agencies, including the Departments of Education and Labor, the National Center for Education Statistics, the National Center for Health Statistics, the Bureau of Justice Statistics, and the Bureau of Labor Statistics. The Census categories are also used by state and local governmental agencies (e.g., school districts, health departments, and so forth) and even private institutions (e.g., universities, banks, and hospitals), which may be required to report to federal agencies about the populations they serve. Census data are used as part of civil rights enforcement and monitoring, including in the administration of the Voting Rights Act, the Fair Housing Act, and employment discrimination and fair lending laws. The data are also used to monitor health disparities and in medical research and policy formulation in the health sciences by the Veterans Administration and the Department of Health and Human Services. The information collected through the Census and the categories it uses thus shape policy and identity both.

In 2000, a group of recipients of the Census questionnaire brought a constitutional challenge to the race and ethnicity questions, arguing that they violated the equal protection guarantees of the Constitution. In *Morales v. Daley,* 116 F. Supp. 2d 801 (S.D. Tex. 2000), a federal district court in Texas rejected the challenge:

> Plaintiffs argue that only by eliminating the race question on the census can governmental bodies be deprived of the resource to continue a race-ridden society. They argue that Americans can never achieve a "color-blind kind of race neutral society," until the government sheds all the vestiges of racial classification.

> The government's response is to point out that plaintiffs make no claim that Census 2000 discriminates against any protected group. Rather, the argument is that the prohibition against

disparate treatment precludes the compilation of demographic data regarding protected groups. The government's position is that case law is clear that it is differential treatment, not classification, that implicates equal protection. "The equal protection clause does not forbid classification. It simply keeps decision makers from treating differently persons who are in all relevant respects alike."

Plaintiffs' position is based upon a misunderstanding of the distinction between collecting demographic data so that the government may have the information it believes at a given time it needs in order to govern, and governmental use of suspect classifications without a compelling interest. The plaintiffs' position, particularly on the race and ethnicity questions, is one that attempts to strike at the root of the problem of racial and ethnic classifications. Their argument is that racial and ethnic self-classification that is mandated by the government itself can do nothing to propel this country toward a society in which race and ethnicity do not matter. Many would agree with their argument, but the issue here is not social, moral, or political. The issue is whether requiring a person to self-classify racially or ethnically, knowing to what use such classifications have been put in the past, can violate the due process implications of the Fifth Amendment. This court holds that such self-classifications do not. The Bureau has stated for each of the challenged questions the statutory mandate, other reasons, or both why this demographic information is needed. The Constitution requires nothing more.

* * *

Below are the 2010 Census questions about race and ethnicity. Also described below are the federal criminal penalties for failing to answer or for providing false answers to Census questions.

5. Is this person of Hispanic, Latino, or Spanish origin?

☐ **No,** not of Hispanic, Latino, or Spanish origin
☐ Yes, Mexican, Mexican Am., Chicano
☐ Yes, Puerto Rican
☐ Yes, Cuban
☐ Yes, another Hispanic, Latino, or Spanish origin — *Print origin, for example, Argentinean, Colombian, Dominican, Nicaraguan, Salvadoran, Spaniard, and so on.* ↘

6. What is this person's race? *Mark* [X] *one or more boxes.*

☐ White

☐ Black, African Am., or Negro

☐ American Indian or Alaska Native — *Print name of enrolled or principal tribe.* ↗

[blank boxes]

☐ Asian Indian   ☐ Japanese   ☐ Native Hawaiian
☐ Chinese   ☐ Korean   ☐ Guamanian or Chamorro
☐ Filipino   ☐ Vietnamese ☐ Samoan
☐ Other Asian — *Print race, for*   ☐ Other Pacific Islander — *Print*
   example, Hmong, Laotian, Thai,   *race, for example, Fijian, Tongan,*
   Pakistani, Cambodian, and so on. ↗   *and so on.* ↗

[blank boxes]

☐ Some other race — *Print race.* ↗

[blank boxes]

Note that 13 U.S.C. § 221(a) and (b) provide that a person who does not answer or who provides a false answer can be fined up to $100 or $500 respectively for each unanswered or falsely answered question. In addition, the False Statements Act, 18 U.S.C. § 1001, makes it a crime to knowingly make a false statement to the United States or to any department or agency thereof. A violator shall be fined, imprisoned not more than 5 years, or both (In 1994, Congress removed the $10,000 upper limit on the possible fine).

NOTES AND QUESTIONS

[handwritten margin note: Do we wanta colorblind society?]

1.   What do you think of the constitutional challenge to the Census? Should the race and ethnicity questions be subjected to strict scrutiny? Does the Census thwart the achievement of a colorblind society? What might be the perils of the effort to classify the American population by race and ethnicity?

2.   Until 1950, the Census Bureau workers who went door to door recorded the race of respondents. In 1960, the Bureau mailed out its forms, permitting respondents to identify themselves—a practice that continues to this day. What do you think precipitated this change? Are there any downsides to a self-identification model?

3.   What do you think of the OMB's decision in 1997 to treat Pacific Islanders and Native Hawaiians as distinct from Asians? What considerations should be relevant to increasing, or decreasing, the number of recognized racial groups?

4. Note that the 1977 OMB standard directed that racial classification should "most closely reflect ... the individual's recognition in his community," whereas the 2000 Census referred to the race or races that a "person considers himself/herself to be." Is one approach preferable to the other? To what extent is race a matter of how others perceive you as opposed to how you perceive yourself? Should the goal of the Census be to capture how people self-identify or how they are identified by others?

5. The appropriate classification of individuals, especially immigrants, within the Census categories is not always clear. Consider how each of these immigrants should classify themselves:

> a.   A person from Jamaica, whose grandparents were born in India.
>
> b.   A person from Peru who speaks Spanish and maintains an affiliation with an indigenous tribe.
>
> c.   A Muslim person from Yemen with dark skin and thick curly hair

6. Individuals make choices about how to categorize themselves racially when they respond to Census questions. Consider the hypothetical cases below:

> a.   Suppose that a 42-year-old man who has always thought of himself as white discovers that his father was not a curly haired Italian (as the son had always been led to believe) but instead had a black mother. Should the son now think of himself as black? As biracial (insofar as his mother was white)? Or continue to think of himself as white? What if, instead, the son's identity was shaken by a genetic test that traced a significant portion of his lineage to western Africa?
>
> b.   Suppose that two twin boys, children of the same parents, a black mother and white father, consider themselves to be of different races. One twin checks black, and the other checks black and white. Are both responses legitimate? What if one of the twins simply checks white?

7. Partly in response to a perceived increase in multi-raciality, the 2000 Census permitted respondents to check more than one box for race. An alternative approach considered was to create a separate designation "multiracial." Is it preferable to allow respondents to check i) multiple boxes, ii) a multiracial box, or iii) both?

8. For American Indians, Asians, and Pacific Islanders, the Census provides for subracial designations based on either national origin or tribal affiliation. But the Census does not allow for any comparable sorts of designation for whites (e.g., German, English) or blacks/African Americans (e.g., Jamaican, Nigerian). Should it? How should the Census officials decide which subracial designations to list?

9. Would it be desirable to eliminate the race category entirely and simply allow people to indicate the national origin of their ancestors? What purposes would be served by doing so?

10. As noted above, for the 2020 Census, the Bureau is considering combining the race and ethnicity question, primarily to address the fact that 1 in 3 people who identify as Hispanic/Latino also check "some other race." In addition, the Bureau is considering adding a new check box for the race question: Middle Eastern or North African (MENA). The OMB standard lists MENA as illustrative of the racial category "white," which, formally, they would still be, even with the Census change. Would you support the proposed addition of a MENA check box? Do you agree with the OMB's characterization of MENA's as white?

11. The Census form contemplates that some answers provided by individuals would be "false." On what basis might a response be deemed "false"? What evidence would be relevant to that determination?

12. Some social science researchers argue that race is fluid, and that at different times the same individual may be perceived differently and think of himself differently with respect to race. For example, there is evidence that imprisonment or prolonged unemployment may make a "white" person more likely to be perceived as, and to think of oneself as, black. Could unemployment and incarceration really make one black? Or would those experiences merely cause one to be mistakenly perceived as black? What other factors, if any, might change how one is perceived and how they think of themselves?

13. If you were doing research about, say, racial differences in earnings, or about the racially disparate impact of government policies, how would you categorize people who either check Latino and a racial category, or who check more than one racial category? Would you apportion an individual who checks more than one category among different groups? Would you create intersectional or hybrid groups? If you would place each individual in only one of the existing groups, how would you determine which group? In particular, how would you treat the individuals below and how would you justify your decisions:

a. A person who answers yes to the Spanish/Hispanic/Latino question and checks the box for White;

b. A person who answers yes to the Spanish/Hispanic/Latino question and checks the box for Black/African American

c. A person who answers no to the Spanish/Hispanic/Latino question and checks the boxes for African American and White;

d. A person who answers no to the Spanish/Hispanic/Latino question and checks the boxes for Asian American and White.

e. A person who answers no to the Spanish/Hispanic/Latino question and checks the boxes for Asian American and Black.

E. CHANGE AND CONTINUITY IN THE RACIAL ORDER

As the Census Bureau's continual re-evaluation of its demographic questions highlights, the racial order of the United States has always been in flux. Before your study of racial justice moves into specific settings in the next chapter, we pause to take account of the racial landscape of our nation. That landscape is shaped by myriad factors, including: i) the composition of our peoples; ii) their relative economic and material circumstances; and iii) the dominant psychological understandings of race and racism.

Immigration has long shaped our diverse nation. The arrival of different groups of Europeans throughout the nineteenth and early twentieth centuries certainly contributed to the ethnic diversity and strife that has marked American history. But perhaps most important today, the immigration reforms of 1965 opened the door to dramatic immigration from Asia, in particular. These developments have occurred along with unprecedented movement (both lawful and unlawful) to the United States from Latin America and the Caribbean. In large part because of immigration, Latinos now constitute the largest minority group in the country, and Asians represent the fastest growing minority group.

Immigration has produced a new kind of race-based "competition," between African Americans (and to a lesser extent native-born Hispanics) on the one hand and immigrant groups, particularly new Latinos, on the other. These inter-group dynamics have given rise to questions such as whether and how to foster cross-racial coalitions to achieve equality and economic justice, as well as more sensitive questions, such as whether ongoing immigration actually undermines the interests of disadvantaged blacks.

Marriage across racial and ethnic lines also contributes to the scrambling of familiar racial categories, and to the dramatic increase in the number of people who now identify as multi-racial. Since the Supreme Court's 1967 decision in *Loving*, rates of interracial dating and romance have risen substantially among all races. Asian Americans and Latinos are the most likely to marry outside their group, with roughly half of them doing so in recent years. African Americans and whites are the least likely to marry outside their group. Overall, about 1 in 6 marriages now occurs across group lines, which means that most Americans have *someone* in their extended family who is married outside the group.

Despite the reforms of the Second Reconstruction, stark economic inequalities persist across racial groups. Across multiple dimensions, African Americans fare the least well. Unemployment remains roughly twice as high among blacks as whites, as has been the case for as long as official records have been kept. Relatedly, the median income of black households is only about 60% of that of white households. And the racial gap in wealth is even starker, with white households having 20 times as much wealth as their black counterparts. While Latinos also fare poorly relative to whites (with higher unemployment rates, lower household earnings, and wealth holdings not much higher than blacks), Asian Americans, in contrast, do better than whites. Average earnings and employment rates for Asian Americans exceed those of their white counterparts.

These economic outcomes are mirrored in educational outcomes. While rates of high school graduation and college enrollment have risen nationwide during the last half century, Latinos and, especially, African Americans, still lag behind whites in rates of academic performance and college graduation. Asian Americans, in contrast, achieve higher levels of academic performance and rates of college graduation than whites.

The problem of poverty is particularly stark among African Americans. African Americans between the ages of 13 and 28 are *ten times* as likely as their white counterparts to live in poor neighborhoods. And those black children who grow up in poor neighborhoods are less likely than their white counterparts to move out of poverty. Forty-eight percent of black families have lived in poor neighborhoods for at least two generations, compared to seven percent of white families. Richard Rothstein, "Modern Segregation," Economic Policy Institute (Mar. 6, 2014).

These economic disparities are reflected in rates of imprisonment. Though incarceration rates in the United States have recently begun to decline from unprecedented highs, not long ago estimates were that a startling one in three black men will spend time in prison during their lives, as compared to one in 17 white men. Blacks and Latinos account for 30 percent of the population as a whole, but they make up 58 percent of prisoners. Even black women, who are not incarcerated at nearly the same rate as men, do end up in prison at more than twice the rate of white women.[10]

Just as it is important to take account of the relative economic positions of groups, it is also crucial to attend to diversity within groups. While many African Americans, for example, remain mired in poverty and isolated in decaying inner-cities, others have been able to take advantage of newly available opportunities, enter high status professions, move to comfortable or affluent neighborhoods, and the like. By some measures, economic inequality *within* minority groups is actually greater than for the United States population as a whole. The internal differentiation among African Americans is so great that, according to one national survey, a substantial minority of African

---

[10]   Bureau of Justice Statistics, Correctional Populations in the U.S., 2010 and U.S. Census 2010 Summary File 1, Ian Bremmer, "These 5 Facts Explain America's Enduring Racial Divide," Time (Jun. 29, 2015), available at: http://time.com/3931216/these–5–facts–explain–americas–enduring-racial-divide/.

Americans think that blacks no longer share the same race. One axis of division is between black immigrants and their children on one hand, and those blacks whose ancestors were held as slaves on the other. Other groups too may experience similar divisions.

Given this variegated racial landscape, how should we think about race? One consequence of the civil rights era's disavowal of overt bigotry has been the ascendance of color blindness. Not just a constitutional principle, colorblindness is now also a cultural ideal, an aspirational social norm. Even as we laud the value of diversity, many people think they are, or should be, colorblind. How should the law respond when disparities persist despite professed disavowal of racism, and when so many people believe they should not see what it is almost impossible to ignore? More generally, how should our efforts to promote racial justice evolve as the social and cultural terrain shifts?

CHAPTER 3

INTIMACY AND CHILD PLACEMENT

I. INTRODUCTION

Intimate and familial relationships are often assumed to be beyond the scope of racial equality considerations. Yet such relationships have long been a locus of racial conflict. Even the most private of relationships carries public significance, as a means through which the racial order of society is constructed, and understandings of race enacted.

Historically, the law has regulated the construction of family and intimate relationships so as to maintain the primacy of whiteness. Now, in the wake of the civil rights era, laws no longer prohibit, much less criminalize, interracial intimacy. We now laud the freedom to choose one's sexual partners or spouses. Yet, this new regime of choice does not eclipse racial equality concerns.

Individual choice operates in some areas but not others. It is the state that must choose, for example, with whom to place a child when there is a custody dispute or an adoption. In such situations, the preferences of adults often conflict, and the preferences of children may be unformed and uninformed. Thus, deferring to individuals' choice will not resolve the dispute. Judges and social workers resolve such disputes, guided and limited by statutory and constitutional law.

In placing children with families, governmental decision-makers must adhere to the best interests of the child standard, the guiding principle of child welfare law. But that principle is far from determinate: Does it demand, or preclude, considerations of race? And if race is to be considered, how, precisely, should it be incorporated into the decision-making calculus? The placement of children may also entail consideration of the interests of the group of which the child is a part. For example, how do the best interests of a minority group relate, if at all, to the best interests of minority children?

The resolution of these disputes raises a question about competing sources of law. Child placement is typically a matter of state law, but with respect to race, federal statutes have been enacted and constitutional law interpreted, so as to supplant or constrain the decisions of state legislators, judges, and social workers. Is that displacement of state authority legitimate? What are the obligations of state decision-makers, including legislators but in particular judges and social workers, to "comply" with federal law with which they may disagree? Is their judgment any less, or more, legitimate and valuable than that of federal officials?

Whatever the law, adults remain race conscious in their choice of intimate partners and also in their choice of children to adopt. That fact prompts us to think critically about how and why race remains salient in American society. Why do we all take account of race? And to what ends? Should racial difference be celebrated as a consideration in choosing our friends, lovers, and family members? Or should we hope and expect that our awareness of race will gradually wither? Why?

In influencing family formation, race also shapes the racial order of American society. The persistence of racial patterns raises enduring questions: Is racial justice compatible with continued racial separation in the family context? Is some degree of racial separation innocuous or even desirable? And how will the racial order be transformed by increasing rates of interracial family formation.

This chapter raises these broad questions by examining the formation of adult intimate relationships within and across racial lines and by describing the government regulation of child custody disputes and adoption with respect to race.

II. Marriage and Intimate Coupling

Race has long been a basis for intimate relationships and family formation, and the history of the intersection of race and intimacy is essential background for thinking about current patterns of family formation.

The system of slavery underpinned the racial order of American society. Slavery defined blackness as a basis of enslavement and whiteness as an entitlement to freedom. Yet the sorting of individuals into one category or the other was not a simple process.

From the earliest days of our society, sexual relationships have occurred across the race line. As some of the cases in the Introduction highlight, the maintenance of the racial order demanded that rules and practices be developed to classify people as either black or white. At common law, children followed the status of their father. Because this rule would have granted whiteness and, thus, freedom to those children sired by white men with slave women, the rule was changed, so that the child's status followed that of the mother. Any child born to a slave woman would remain a slave—by definition black. Sexual relations between black men and white women were policed through lynchings or other forms of violence.

The Civil War and Reconstruction destabilized the racial order of American society. The Thirteenth Amendment prohibited slavery. The Fourteenth Amendment overthrew Justice Taney's proclamation in *Dred Scott v. Sanford*, 60 U.S. 393 (1857), that the descendants of Africans could not be United States citizens. And the Fifteenth Amendment prohibited the denial of the right to vote on account of race. Congress established the Freedmen's Bureau and embarked upon (an unfortunately short lived) Reconstruction to promote the adjustment of the freed slaves. Federal legislation granted the freed slaves the same civil rights as whites and equal access to public accommodations.

One product of this period was the spread of so-called anti-miscegenation laws—state statutes that prohibited sex or marriage between whites and non-whites. Forty-one states (and all southern states) at one time or another had a law prohibiting marriage or sexual relations across racial lines. Some laws barred "Mongolians" or Native Americans from intermarrying with whites, and nearly every miscegenation law prohibited blacks from intermarrying with whites. State laws requiring the segregation of blacks and whites in public spread throughout the South.

While the doctrine of separate-but-equal is widely associated with *Plessy v. Ferguson*, 163 U.S. 537 (1896), the Supreme Court first blessed the logic of that doctrine more than a decade prior to *Plessy*, in the Court's 1883 decision in *Pace v. Alabama*, 106 U.S. 583 (1883). In *Pace*, the Court upheld an Alabama statute that penalized adultery and fornication more harshly when committed by an interracial black/white couple than by a same-race couple. While acknowledging that the purpose of the recently enacted Fourteenth Amendment was "to prevent hostile and discriminating state legislation against any person or class of persons," the Court nonetheless upheld the law because it "applies the same punishment to both offenders, the white and the black. The punishment of each offending person, whether white or black, is the same." The Court's reasoning thus perfectly embodied the logic that would later come to be associated with *Plessy v. Ferguson*.

Pace also highlights then-common views about race. The Supreme Court of Alabama had upheld the law to thwart the possibility of "the amalgamation of the two races, producing a mongrel population and a degraded civilization, the prevention of which is dictated by a sound public policy affecting the highest interests of society and government." Miscegenation statutes were gradually repealed in some states during the middle of the 20th century, but *Pace* remained good law until the 1960s. Then, the Court, in its 1964 decision in *McLaughlin v. Florida*, 379 U.S. 184 (1964), invalidated a law that, in punishing fornication and adultery, included especially harsh provisions applicable to unmarried interracial couples.

As you saw in Chapter 2, it was not until 1967 that the Court did for intimate relationships what *Brown v. Board of Education*, 347 U.S. 483 (1954), did for public places: retire the doctrine of separate but equal. In *Loving v. Virginia*, 388 U.S. 1 (1967), the Supreme Court struck down Virginia's ban on interracial marriage. It wrote:

[T]he Equal Protection Clause requires the consideration of whether the classifications drawn by any statute constitute an arbitrary and invidious discrimination. The clear and central purpose of the Fourteenth Amendment was to eliminate all official state sources of invidious racial discrimination in the States.

There can be no question but that Virginia's miscegenation statutes rest solely upon distinctions drawn according to race. The statutes proscribe generally accepted conduct if engaged in by members of different races. Over the years, this Court has consistently repudiated "[d]istinctions between citizens solely because of their ancestry" as being "odious to a free people whose institutions are founded upon the doctrine of equality." Hirabayashi v. United States (1943). At the very least, the Equal Protection Clause demands that racial classifications, especially suspect in criminal statutes, be subjected to the "most rigid scrutiny," Korematsu v. United States (1944), and, if they are ever to be upheld, they must be shown to be necessary to the accomplishment of some permissible state objective, independent of the racial discrimination which it was the object of the Fourteenth Amendment to eliminate. Indeed, two members of this Court have already stated that they 'cannot conceive of a valid legislative purpose . . . which makes the color of a person's skin the test of whether his conduct is a criminal offense.' McLaughlin v. Florida, (Stewart, J., joined by Douglas, J., concurring).

There is patently no legitimate overriding purpose independent of invidious racial discrimination which justifies this classification. The fact that Virginia prohibits only interracial marriages involving white persons demonstrates that the racial classifications must stand on their own justification, as measures designed to maintain White Supremacy. We have consistently denied the constitutionality of measures which restrict the rights of citizens on account of race. There can be no doubt that restricting the freedom to marry solely because of racial classifications violates the central meaning of the Equal Protection Clause.

388 U.S. at 10–12.

The Court also concluded that the Virginia laws violated the Due Process Clause of the Fourteenth Amendment by abridging the freedom to marry, which the Court understood as having "long been recognized as one of the vital personal rights essential to the orderly pursuit of happiness by free men." Id. at 12.

NOTES AND QUESTIONS

1.   *From* Pace *to* Loving. The transition from *Pace* to *Loving* partly reflects changes in understandings of race. Through the early twentieth century, racial groups were believed to be biologically distinct and ineradicably different. By the middle of the 20th century, in the aftermath of the Holocaust, such thinking had been discredited, and race came to be seen as morally irrelevant, an artificial rather than natural basis on which to regulate marriage.

2.   *White Supremacy.* The *Loving* case is noteworthy in that it, alone among Supreme Court decisions, refers disparagingly to White Supremacy. How, precisely, does the statute "maintain White Supremacy"? Would it still do so even if it were re-drafted so as "to protect the 'integrity' of all races"?

3.   *Marriage and State Interests.* Does the Court's opinion suggest that the assertion of any state interest in the racial composition of marriages would be "arbitrary and invidious"? Did the *Loving* court mean that the state has no interest in the marital status of its citizens, or simply that marriage choices could not be restricted on the basis of race?

4.   *Racial Differences in Marriage Rates.* There are dramatic differences in rates of marriage, divorce and unwed childbearing across groups. Asian Americans have the lowest rate of unwed childbearing, the highest rate of marriage, and the lowest rate of divorce. African Americans, in contrast, have the lowest rate of marriage, highest rate of divorce, and highest rate of unwed childbearing. President George W. Bush's administration funded a Healthy Marriage Initiatives for various groups, African Americans in particular. Is it appropriate for the government to take account of, and perhaps respond to, racial differences in rates of marriage, divorce or unwed childbearing? For a discussion of changing patterns of family life, see R. Richard Banks, *Intimacy and Inequality: The Changing Contours of Family Life*, 1 Indiana J.L. and Soc. Inequality 150 (2013)

5.   *Marriage and Racial Discourse.* During the last half century, marriage rates have diverged substantially by both class and race. Educationally and economically disadvantaged people have become much less likely to marry or stay married than their more affluent peers. African Americans too are now less likely to marry and stay married than are other groups, even controlling for socioeconomic differences in marriage rates. *See* R. Richard Banks, *Is Marriage for White People? How the African American Marriage Decline Affects Everyone* (2011). The racial gap in marriage has often figured in discourse about racial inequality. As claims of inherent racial inferiority became socially unacceptable during the twentieth century, the discourse of racial inequality shifted, often, to discussions of culture. Commentators began to argue that African Americans were deficient not due to their genetics so much as their culture, of which the family was the primary repository. Many progressives have rejected claims of cultural deficiency as pernicious victim-blaming—a socially acceptable way of asserting the same condemnation that overtly racist arguments about genetics had previously performed. So, the question arises: is it necessarily racist to identify cultural deficiency and to associate it with family structure?

Do you think that discussions about the high incidence of single parent families among African Americans are typically racist? Or would it be racist not to discuss such issues? Do you think that people tend to explain group patterns (e.g., the marriage decline) differently depending on whether they are discussing African Americans or whites?

6. *Interracial Relationships Now.* In the decades since the Supreme Court's 1967 decision in *Loving v. Virginia*, rates of interracial dating and romance have risen substantially, if unevenly across groups. While it is still the case that 90% of existing marriages are within group, new marriages reflect substantially more mixing. Nearly 20% of new marriages occur across group lines. How should we evaluate the rise of interracial marriage? To what extent is increasing interracial marriage a positive social development? Is it legitimate to worry that interracial marriage will precipitate the loss of group solidarity and culture? Is increasing interracial marriage a sign that racial conflict and injustice are diminishing? Is increasing interracial intimacy a welcome sign of the waning of racial aversion and stereotypes?

7. *Group Differences in Intermarriage.* Rates of interracial marriage have risen for all groups, though unevenly. Asian Americans and Latinos are the most likely to marry outside their group, with roughly half of them doing so in recent years. African Americans and whites are the least likely to marry outside their group. What do you think are some of the factors that contribute to these differences in rates of interracial marriage? For a discussion, see R. Richard Banks, *Is Marriage for White People? How the African American Marriage Decline Affects Everyone* (2011).

8. *Personal Preferences.* *Loving* characterizes state restrictions on interracial intimacy as "arbitrary and invidious." What about those restrictions on interracial intimacy that individuals impose on themselves— are self-imposed restrictions on interracial intimacy "arbitrary and invidious" as well? In seeking an intimate partner (e.g., through an Internet dating website or otherwise), most people take account of race. Consider these ads taken from Internet dating websites:

    a.   Single black female looking for an intelligent educated man. I prefer black men but I keep my options open;

    b.   32-year-old Latino Puerto Rican seeking a Latina woman that's sweet, honest, full of love and affection;

    c.   Pretty, fit, intelligent, blond SWF, is seeking WM, who is 45– 55, smart, thin, educated, successful.

9. *Explaining Same-Race Preferences.* Why might Internet daters so frequently state a preference for someone of their own race? Why and how do people use race in their search for a partner?

10. *Evaluating Same-Race Preferences.* Even as it is legally permissible to express or act upon racial preferences in the selection of intimate partners, some sorts of racial preference might nonetheless be morally objectionable or otherwise problematic. Are there reasons for same-race preferences that strike you as morally objectionable? Which reasons would be perfectly justifiable? Are there any justifications for expressing racial dating

preferences that, if held by a close friend of yours, you would criticize or endorse? Do individuals ever have a moral obligation to marry or to prefer to marry someone from their own race? Is the desire for racial solidarity a legitimate basis for preferring to marry within one's own race?

11. *Symmetry?* Does your assessment of same race preferences vary depending on whether it is expressed by a white person or by a minority? For example, is a same-race preference expressed by a white person more morally objectionable than a same-race preference expressed by a black or Asian person? If so, why?

12. *Other Race Preferences.* Not all preferences are for a member of one's own race; sometimes people state preferences for other races. Why would people do so? Consider these ads taken from Internet dating websites:

   a.   SBF in search of friendship and possible LTR with Latin man;

   b.   42-year-old SWM in search of petite SBF;

   c.   40-year-old single white female (SWF) looking for an educated single black male (SBM) for friendship and possible LTR [long term relationship];

   d.   SWM looking for feminine SAF

13. *Evaluating Other-Race Preferences.* How would you compare the moral justifiability of preferences for other races with preferences for a person of one's own race? Are other-race preferences generally more, or less, morally objectionable (or permissible) than own-race preferences?

14. *Family Preferences.* Sometimes, an individual's expressed relationship preference may reflect the views of family, friends, or other community members. Many families approve or disapprove of prospective marital partners on the basis of race. Do parents or other family members have any legitimate interest in wanting one of their own to marry someone of the same race? Or in believing that marriage to an individual of a particular race is undesirable? For example, what if Chinese immigrants think that their child should marry a white person rather than a black or Latino person in order to avoid prejudice? What if the Chinese parents want their child to "marry up" and believe that marrying a white person is the way to do that? Is their assessment of the racial order inaccurate? Is it morally troubling even if accurate? Or is it perfectly legitimate? Alternatively, what if say a Latino or African-American couple wanted their adult child to marry within the group in order to preserve the group's culture or identity? Or if a black mother, aware of the shortage of stable and successful black men, urges her son to marry a black woman. Is that sensible?

15. *African-American Intermarriage.* African Americans exhibit the starkest gender disparity in outmarriage. About 1 in 5 black men, but only 1 in 10 black women, marry someone of a different race. Considering that outmarriage rates are influenced both by the individuals' preferences and the social pressures they confront, what do you think are some of the explanations for the gender disparity in outmarriage among African Americans?

16. ***Communicating Across Racial Lines.*** One possible impediment to interracial relationships is the difficulty of communication across group lines. For example, people may find it difficult to read the signals or expressions of interest from someone of another group. Or they may lack friends in common who can function as a go between to facilitate the relationship or convey the interest of one person in the other. To what extent do you think this sort of communication disconnect impedes the formation of relationships across group lines?

17. ***Colorism.*** Many people express intimate preferences based on complexion. What if someone states that they prefer a pale partner with blond hair and blue eyes? Or a black person who is copper colored or lighter? Are these preferences morally objectionable? Does your assessment depend at all on the race of the person expressing the preference? For example, is it any different for a white man to prefer a dark skinned black woman than for a black man to state a similar preference?

18. ***Evaluating Intermarriage and the Racial Order.*** What do these patterns of interracial marriage suggest about the racial order in American society? To what extent do they signify change versus continuity? Will the high intermarriage rate of Latinos and Asian Americans result in their merging or assimilating into the white majority? If so, how will that transform the racial order? Note that some commentators contend that we could transition to a society in which the racial divide is black/nonblack, rather than either multiple groups (as now), or white/nonwhite as it has been in the past. What do you think?

PROBLEMS

1.   You are the president of E-love, an online dating website and singles matching service. Like almost all online dating services, participants often describe themselves in terms of race and express whether they are open to dating someone of a particular race. When individuals sign up to use the site, they are required to enter information about themselves and the characteristics or qualities they are seeking in a partner. Currently, the site allows, but does not require, users to describe their own race as well the races they either want to date or do not want to date. Although some users decline to state their own race or any racial preferences, the overwhelming majority of users, especially African Americans, both describe their race and state a preference for members of their own race. African Americans are the most frequently   excluded   group   of   potential   daters.   This   racial disclosure/preference policy has generated a great deal of controversy. Two lower level managers each object to the current policy but for different reasons.

One manager believes that the site should require people to state their own race, even if they do not have any preference as to the race of their ideal partner. He contends that most of the site's users will have a racial preference and that if the goal is to generate as many good matches as possible, then users should be able to access all available information about the site's other members. Disclosing race, he argues, will enable people to make the best decisions about who to contact and pursue. He calls his proposal one for "mandated disclosure" and "optional preferences."

The other manager takes the opposite tack. He believes that the site should not require people to disclose their own race; it should prohibit them from doing so. Nor should the site allow users to state any preference as to the race of their desired partners. To enforce this policy, he believes that the site should encourage users to "flag" references to race that violate the policy so that the site could remove any such references. The manager acknowledges that this solution is not perfect—as sometimes users will be able to infer a person's race based on their photograph or self-description—but he thinks it is much better than the current policy. The manager refers to his proposed policy as the "nondiscrimination approach."

As the president of the company, you must resolve this controversy and devise a policy for the website. Which policy would you support? Why? Do you think that the company's policy would actually influence members' relationship choices?

2. Race can also play a role in relationships that are not romantic or sexual. Imagine that you are the housing coordinator for a large, predominantly white university. One of your tasks is to assign freshmen to rooms. All freshmen are required to live on campus, and each will have one or two roommates (depending on the room configuration). You confront a simple question: should the matching process take race into account? Currently, the process matches on the basis of gender; female freshman, for example, are only assigned female roommates. For many other characteristics, the process matches so as to produce diverse roommate combinations. Students who live in-state, for example, are almost invariably matched with students from out-of-state. Students are unlikely to be placed with a roommate with the same academic interest or prospective major. For other characteristics, though, the housing coordinators strive for similarity. Students who describe themselves as night owls, for example, are not matched with students who like to go to bed early. So too are self-described "slobs" not matched with self-described "neat freaks." So how, if at all, should race enter into this process? As with the Internet dating website, there are some members of your staff who think that students should be able to express a preference as to the race of their roommate.

3. Your university does not consider race in the placement of students into campus housing, but on-campus housing is segregated nonetheless because current students advise incoming students which houses to choose. If you were in charge of on-campus housing assignments, would you regard students' segregated living patterns as innocuous? Or would you take action to promote more racially integrated on-campus housing?

III. CHILD PLACEMENTS

A. CUSTODY DETERMINATIONS

The most common child placement controversy arises when two parents, typically after divorce, vie for custody of their child. Such cases are governed by state statutes, which generally embody the best interest of the child standard, and are usually heard in state courts. Only rarely, as in the following case, has the Supreme Court applied the Constitution to invalidate a state child custody decision under the nondiscrimination mandate of the equal protection clause. *Palmore v. Sidoti* concerns the interplay of the best interest of the child standard and the nondiscrimination mandate. In reading this case, consider: Does the nondiscrimination mandate further the child's best interest? Or does it trump it?

Palmore v. Sidoti

Supreme Court of the United States, 1984.
466 U.S. 429.

■ CHIEF JUSTICE BURGER delivered the opinion of the Court.

We granted certiorari to review a judgment of a state court divesting a natural mother of the custody of her infant child because of her remarriage to a person of a different race. . . . When petitioner Linda Sidoti Palmore and respondent Anthony J. Sidoti, both Caucasians, were divorced in May 1980 in Florida, the mother was awarded custody of their 3-year-old daughter.

In September 1981 the father sought custody of the child by filing a petition to modify the prior judgment because of changed conditions. The change was that the child's mother was then cohabiting with a Negro, Clarence Palmore, Jr., whom she married two months later. Additionally, the father made several allegations of instances in which the mother had not properly cared for the child.

After hearing testimony from both parties and considering a court counselor's investigative report, the court noted that the father had made allegations about the child's care, but the court made no findings with respect to these allegations. On the contrary, the court made a finding that "there is no issue as to either party's devotion to the child, adequacy of housing facilities, or respectability of the new spouse of either parent."

The court . . . concluded that the best interests of the child would be served by awarding custody to the father. The court's rationale is contained in the following:

> "The father's evident resentment of the mother's choice of a black partner is not sufficient to wrest custody from the mother. It is of some significance, however, that the mother did see fit to

bring a man into her home and carry on a sexual relationship with him without being married to him. Such action tended to place gratification of her own desires ahead of her concern for the child's future welfare. This Court feels that despite the strides that have been made in bettering relations between the races in this country, it is inevitable that Melanie will, if allowed to remain in her present situation and attains school age and thus becomes more vulnerable to peer pressures, suffer from the social stigmatization that is sure to come." . . .

The judgment of a state court determining or reviewing a child custody decision is not ordinarily a likely candidate for review by this Court. However, the court's opinion, after stating that the "father's evident resentment of the mother's choice of a black partner is not sufficient" to deprive her of custody, then turns to what it regarded as the damaging impact on the child from remaining in a racially mixed household. This raises important federal concerns arising from the Constitution's commitment to eradicating discrimination based on race.

The Florida court did not focus directly on the parental qualifications of the natural mother or her present husband, or indeed on the father's qualifications to have custody of the child. The court found that "there is no issue as to either party's devotion to the child, adequacy of housing facilities, or respectability of the new spouse of either parent." This, taken with the absence of any negative finding as to the quality of the care provided by the mother, constitutes a rejection of any claim of petitioner's unfitness to continue the custody of her child.

The court correctly stated that the child's welfare was the controlling factor. But that court was entirely candid and made no effort to place its holding on any ground other than race. Taking the court's findings and rationale at face value, it is clear that the outcome would have been different had petitioner married a Caucasian male of similar respectability.

A core purpose of the Fourteenth Amendment was to do away with all governmentally imposed discrimination based on race. *See Strauder v. West Virginia*, 100 U.S. 303, 307–308, 310 (1880). Classifying persons according to their race is more likely to reflect racial prejudice than legitimate public concerns; the race, not the person, dictates the category. Such classifications are subject to the most exacting scrutiny; to pass constitutional muster, they must be justified by a compelling governmental interest and must be "necessary . . . to the accomplishment" of their legitimate purpose, *McLaughlin v. Florida*, 379 U.S. 184, 196 (1964).

The State, of course, has a duty of the highest order to protect the interests of minor children, particularly those of tender years. In common with most states, Florida law mandates that custody determinations be made in the best interests of the children involved. The goal of granting custody based on the best interests of the child is indisputably a substantial governmental interest for purposes of the Equal Protection Clause.

It would ignore reality to suggest that racial and ethnic prejudices do not exist or that all manifestations of those prejudices have been eliminated. There is a risk that a child living with a stepparent of a different race may be subject to a variety of pressures and stresses not present if the child were living with parents of the same racial or ethnic origin.

The question, however, is whether the reality of private biases and the possible injury they might inflict are permissible considerations for removal of an infant child from the custody of its natural mother. We have little difficulty concluding that they are not. The Constitution cannot control such prejudices but neither can it tolerate them. Private biases may be outside the reach of the law, but the law cannot, directly or indirectly, give them effect. "Public officials sworn to uphold the Constitution may not avoid a constitutional duty by bowing to the hypothetical effects of private racial prejudice that they assume to be both widely and deeply held." *Palmer v. Thompson,* 403 U.S. 217. 260–261 (1971) (WHITE, J., dissenting).

This is by no means the first time that acknowledged racial prejudice has been invoked to justify racial classifications. In *Buchanan v. Warley,* 245 U.S. 60 (1917), for example, this Court invalidated a Kentucky law forbidding African Americans to buy homes in white neighborhoods: "It is urged that this proposed segregation will promote the public peace by preventing race conflicts. Desirable as this is, and important as is the preservation of the public peace, this aim cannot be accomplished by laws or ordinances which deny rights created or protected by the Federal Constitution."

Whatever problems racially mixed households may pose for children in 1984 can no more support a denial of constitutional rights than could the stresses that residential integration was thought to entail in 1917. The effects of racial prejudice, however real, cannot justify a racial classification removing an infant child from the custody of its natural mother found to be an appropriate person to have such custody.

NOTES AND QUESTIONS

1. ***The Aftermath.*** The mother in *Palmore* never did regain custody of her child. While the Supreme Court decision was pending, the father moved with the daughter to Texas. The Florida state court agreed to transfer the case there, based on the father's continued residence there with the child. Do you think the Florida court's decision to transfer the case to Texas was consistent with the Supreme Court's ruling? What about the Texas court's determination that the time the daughter spent with her father and the bond

they developed justified leaving the Florida custodial order in place, notwithstanding the Supreme Court's criticism of the Florida court?

2.   **The Rationale.** Although observers and commentators generally support the *Palmore* decision itself, its normative basis remains unclear. The central tension in the case can be stated directly: Did the Supreme Court enforce the nondiscrimination mandate because it furthered the child's best interest? Or was the Supreme Court saying that the nondiscrimination mandate should trump the child's best interest? In other words, did the Court make a legal determination that race cannot be considered? Or did the Court's ruling rest on a factual determination that the trial judge had clearly erred in his assessment of the child's best interest? If the latter, what could have been the Supreme Court's basis for second guessing the trial judge who had conducted a trial at which the testimony of the parents and expert evidence was presented? Was the trial court's order so unquestionably contrary to the child's best interest as to warrant reversal?

3.   **Private Bias?** The *Palmore* Court wrote, "The Constitution cannot control such prejudices but neither can it tolerate them. Private biases may be outside the reach of the law, but the law cannot, directly or indirectly, give them effect." As you read the following materials, ask what, specifically, counts as private biases? What would it mean for the law to not "directly or indirectly, give them effect"? If you were a Supreme Court Justice, how would you have decided *Palmore*? Why?

APPLYING *PALMORE*

Although decided three decades ago, *Palmore* remains the only Supreme Court decision to address directly the constitutionality of courts' use of race in child custody decisions. The case has been subject to a variety of interpretations by federal and state courts, as the discussion below indicates.

1.   **Per Se Prohibition.** Some lower courts have interpreted the *Palmore* prohibition in absolute terms. For example, in *In re Marriage of Olson*, 344 Mont. 385 (Mont. 2008), the Supreme Court of Montana declared that "Constitutional requirements of equal protection prohibit courts from relying on race to make decisions regarding child custody. This Court cannot and will not condone the consideration of race or national origin in establishing a parenting plan." 344 Mont., at 391. Likewise, in *Parker v. Parker*, 986 S.W.2d 557 (1999), the Supreme Court of Tennessee held that the "appropriate factors governing child custody . . . exclude race." 986 S.W.2d, at 562. What's the best argument that *Palmore* should be read to preclude any and all consideration of race? How persuasive is that argument?

2.   **Race as the Sole Consideration.** A common, and especially narrow, interpretation of *Palmore* is that it only prohibits the consideration of race as the *sole* factor in a custody determination. Consider, for example, the case of *In re Marriage of Gambla and Woodson*, 853 N.E.2d 847 (Ill. 2006), in which a white father and African-American mother of a six-month-old biracial child had an especially acrimonious split. When the couple filed for divorce, each sought sole custody of the child, Kira. Although the trial court found both the father and the mother would be fine parents, it was

determined to make a sole custody award due to their inability to co-parent. The court considered the prescribed statutory factors:

    a.   the wishes of the child's parent or parents as to his custody;

    b.   the wishes of the child as to his custodian;

    c.   the interaction and interrelationship of the child with his parent or parents, his siblings and any other person who may significantly affect the child's best interest;

    d.   the child's adjustment to his home, school and community;

    e.   the mental and physical health of all individuals involved;

    f.   the physical violence or threat of physical violence by the child's potential custodian, whether directed against the child or directed against another person;

    g.   the occurrence of ongoing . . . abuse . . . ; and

    h.   the willingness and ability of each parent to facilitate and encourage a close and continuing relationship between the other parent and the child."

The trial court found that not one of these factors favored placement with one parent over the other. The trial court noted that, although each parent had a very different outlook on what was best for Kira, neither Christopher's nor Kimberly's parenting approach was wrong. The trial court also found the fact that Kira was a biracial child to be a relevant factor. The trial court stated that it did not believe in a "broad stroke" approach under which Kimberly would be awarded custody *solely* because she was African American. However, the trial court *did* find that Kimberly would be able to provide Kira with a "breadth of cultural knowledge and experience that Christopher will not be able to do." The trial court noted that Kira would have to learn to exist as a biracial individual in a society that is sometimes hostile toward people of different races and that Kimberly would be better equipped to provide for this emotional need of Kira's. Thus, the court granted custody to the mother, and visitation to the father.

The father contended that the trial court's decision violated *Palmore*. The appeals court ruled that consideration of Kira's race was permissible so long as it was not the sole factor considered. The appeals court's interpretation of *Palmore* was that "[t]he Supreme Court [had] determined that the custody award was unconstitutional, not because the trial court considered race, but because the trial court considered solely race. Indeed, the Supreme Court was careful to premise its holding with the following statement: 'But that court was entirely candid and made no effort to place its holding on any ground other than race.' " *Gambla*, 853 N.E.2d at 869. For the *Gambla* court, the fact that the trial court "carefully weighed each of the statutory factors," before looking to *other* relevant factors, meant that, though "Kira's racial status did play a role in the trial court's decision to award custody to Kimberly . . . it was not the sole factor." Thus, the trial court did not run afoul of *Palmore*.

In support of its conclusion, the appeals court referenced a number of other decisions, both before and since *Palmore*, in which courts approved of the consideration of race as one factor of many. The court stated that "[v]olumes of cases from other jurisdictions have interpreted *Palmore* as not prohibiting the consideration of race in matters of child custody."

The *Gambla* court is unquestionably correct in its characterization of post-*Palmore* decisions. Yet, if *Palmore* is read to apply only to cases in which race is the sole consideration, then its application would be very narrow indeed. The only cases that would satisfy the sole consideration standard are those where race functions as an absolute bar to a cross racial placement. Statutes that prohibit the placement of children across racial lines, for example, would meet that standard. But these are the very sorts of statutes that no longer exist, victims of the civil rights era ascendance of the antidiscrimination principle. It is difficult to imagine the type of discretionary decision at issue in *Gambla* or, for that matter, *Palmore* as meeting the sole factor criterion. For a judge to violate *Palmore*, on the sole factor interpretation, he would have to be committed to awarding custody to the father in *Palmore* and the mother in *Gambla* wholly irrespective of the characteristics of the other parent. Such a circumstance is rather unlikely. And it's not even clear that the trial judge's decision in *Palmore* met that standard. Is the court's reasoning in *Gambla* an appropriate interpretation of *Palmore*?

3.   *Speculative Harm and the Child's Best Interest.* A broader interpretation of *Palmore* is that it prohibits considerations of race that do not further the child's best interest. On this account the lower court judge erred because the change of custody order was not, in fact, justified by a consideration of the child's best interest. Note that the Supreme Court in *Palmore* observes that no actual harm to the child had been documented. The Court's decision referred to the "possible injury" that might result from private biases. The father in *Palmore* made sweeping generalizations about how the mother's interracial marriage would cause harm to their daughter. But there was never any evidence that anything bad actually happened to the child, and there was no specific reason to believe that anything would, other than the existence of general racist attitudes in the surrounding community. There are both substantive and pragmatic reasons for only allowing a custody change in the face of actual harm. The substantive reason would be that such discrimination is only justified when necessary to further a child's best interest by averting concrete and verifiable harm. The pragmatic reason has to do with judicial discretion, and the need to constrain it. If "potential harm" is sufficient to order a change in custody, a judge would have too much leeway to decide the case based on his own prejudices and biases with respect to race. One might imagine, for example, that the *Palmore* judge himself was opposed to interracial relationships and would all too readily find that being raised in such a setting would harm a child. How does the speculative nature of the asserted harm cast doubt on the contention that the best interest of the child warranted the change in custody?

4.   *The Disregard of Actual Harm.* A still broader view of *Palmore*'s nondiscrimination mandate does not turn on the speculative nature of the harm. Neither the court nor the mother seemed to take issue with the extent of racism in southern Florida. The harm in the case then might be better viewed as non-speculative and, in fact, quite likely. If there had been uncontroverted evidence that the child was teased and taunted a result of her mother's interracial relationship, would a judge still have been obligated not to order a change in custody?

In *Holt v. Chenault*, 722 S.W.2d 897 (Ky. 1987), the Supreme Court of Kentucky considered a case in which there was actual harm. Danny Holt and Barbara Chenault—both white—were the parents of Dawn Holt. When Danny and Barbara divorced, custody of Dawn, who was then an infant, was granted to Barbara. Four years after her separation from Danny, Barbara remarried an African-American man, and following the marriage, Danny sought a change in custody. At the time the suit was filed, Barbara was pregnant with a biracial child. At trial, Dawn testified that she had been taunted by schoolmates when her mother married a black man. Dawn was further taunted about her mother's "black" baby. Dawn complained to her father about her home situation and stated her intent to leave her mother's home. Later, Dawn left school to go to her father's house instead of taking the bus home to her mother's house. Another time, Dawn was left with her stepfather's mother when her mother went to work. While the older woman slept, Dawn left and walked to her father's workplace. Though the trial court specifically found the mother to be a suitable parent, it granted the modification of custody.

The Supreme Court of Kentucky overturned the trial court ruling, holding that the trial court's consideration of the mother's subsequent interracial marriage was impermissible because it "[gave] effect to private racial biases." *Chenault*, 722 S.W.2d, at 898. The Kentucky Supreme Court thus seemed to say that even actual harm does not justify a change of custody, at least when the actual harm is a result of private racial biases. This is a broader view of the nondiscrimination mandate, one that arguably puts it in tension with the best interests of the individual child.

5.   *Child's Reaction.* *Holt v. Chenault* raises another issue as well. The court also noted that "the child's emotional reaction to her mother's marital circumstances may enter into deciding what is in the best interest of the child if it is significant and severe, and, if it does, this is a consideration whatever the cause." *Chenault*, 722 S.W.2d, at 898. Can these two statements—that the interracial marriage should not be considered but that the child's emotional reaction to her mother's "marital circumstances" must be considered—be reconciled? Is the court drawing a substantive distinction, or just telling lower courts to frame their rationales not in terms of race, but instead in terms of the child's reaction? Under *Chenault*, if the child wants to live with her father because she is teased and taunted by her peers, can the court take the child's preference into account, given the fact that courts often consider the wishes of children old enough to state preferences about who they would like as their custodians? Should equal protection doctrine prohibit a change in custody even when that is what the child wants?

EXERCISE

It is clear enough that there are certain biases courts *cannot* consider when making custody decisions. But what, precisely, counts as a private bias to which a court may not defer? For the following scenario, consider how you would argue if you were counsel for the mother. What if you were the counsel for the father? The facts are as follows:

> A black mother and a white father divorce, and are granted joint legal and physical custody of their two children. Two years later, the mother petitions for sole legal and physical custody of the children so she can move with them from Lincoln, Nebraska, where the father also resides, to New York City. The mother contends that the children, as members of a racial and ethnic minority, would be better off in the more racially diverse population of New York City than the less diverse community of Lincoln. Should the court hearing this custody case be permitted to consider the effects of community racial diversity on the emotional, physical, and social development of the child, or is consideration of the child's race and racial diversity in the community strictly forbidden?

These facts are taken from *Brown v. Brown*, 621 N.W.2d 70 (Ne. 2000), in which the Nebraska Supreme Court confronted these facts and allowed consideration of the diversity of the community. However, the court required evidence that greater diversity would provide a specific advantage for the children. In this case, the court found that "[t]he record indicates that with respect to diversity, the living conditions of the children are satisfactory in Lincoln, given that there is no evidence of discrimination and that their local school is ethnically diverse. Based on the record presented, we cannot conclude that the greater racial diversity of the New York City metropolitan area would improve the living conditions for the children." The court was unwilling to assume that just because the children would be perceived as black or biracial that the more diverse community in New York City would be advantageous.

Is the consideration of the racial diversity of a community any less objectionable than the consideration of the racial attitudes at issue in *Palmore*? What sort of evidence might the mother produce to show the benefits of racial diversity for the child?

Given that the diverse community consideration can be applied equally to both parents, in that either could reside in a more diverse community than the other, it may be completely outside the bounds of *Palmore*. Seemingly if the court found that a particular child's needs would be best served in a more diverse community, either parent could be found to better situated in that respect. But even in that case, the consideration of race might still turn on the race of the child; it is unlikely that a judge would give community diversity as much weight in the case of a white child as a black child. Would it be discriminatory not to? Should the jurisprudence of child custody strive for race-blindness, both as to the race of the parents *and* the children? Or is it sensible to consider race more with racial minority children than with white children?

B. Adoption and Foster Care of Black and Biracial Children

Child placement decisions may concern custody with one or the other parent, as in *Palmore*, or the adoptive or foster care placement of a child with someone other than a parent. *Palmore* is generally interpreted not to apply to adoptive or foster care placements. As the court observed in *J.H.H. v. O'Hara*, 878 F.2d 240 (1989), "*Palmore's* holding that an otherwise fit natural parent may not be deprived of permanent custody based solely on race did not clearly establish that race may never be taken into account in determining the best interests of a child in a foster care placement decision." On what distinctions could the court be relying here?

As with custody determinations, adoption is generally subject to state law. State adoption laws have historically reinforced the monoracial family, just as miscegenation statutes once did. But adoption policy with respect to race was also shaped by broader assumptions about adoption. Traditionally, children in need of adoption were placed with adoptive families that resembled as closely as possible the biological families into which the children were born. Through the middle decades of the 20th century, policymakers thought that the adoptive family should mimic the biological family. Religion, race, nationality, social class, even intelligence, all were characteristics that were taken into account in the placement of children into adoptive families. Thus, black children in need of adoption were placed only with black families, and white children were placed only with white families. Bi-racial children were placed with mixed race couples. In some states, cross-racial adoptions were precluded, either by statute or social work practice or judicial decision-making. As the desire for the adoptive family to mimic the biological family diminished during the 1960s, so too did race matching become less pervasive. Increasing numbers of black children were placed with white families.

As you read the following case, ask yourself: should decision makers be permitted to consider race in child placement? If so, how so?

Petition of R.M.G.

District of Columbia Court of Appeals, 1982.
454 A.2d 776.

■ FERREN, ASSOCIATE JUDGE:

I.   STATEMENT OF FACTS AND PROCEEDINGS

D. was born September 22, 1977, to unwed, teenage, black parents. By that time, her father lived in Cleveland, Ohio; her mother, in Washington, D.C. In early January 1978, D.'s mother decided to give her up for adoption and signed papers relinquishing parental rights. She did not tell the natural father. Nor did she tell his mother and stepfather, appellees R.M.G. and E.M.G.

On January 6, 1978, the Department of Human Resources placed D. with foster parents, appellants J.H. and J.H., who are white. The foster mother realized almost immediately that D. was not healthy. D. was suffering from nausea and diarrhea and, although more than three months old, weighed only 10 pounds. D., moreover, was extremely lethargic and, according to Dr. Robert Ganter, a child psychiatrist, showed signs of mental retardation. During the next year, however, D.'s foster parents nurtured her to good physical and mental health.

On April 26, 1978, a few months after D. came to live with them, J.H. and J.H. filed a petition for adoption. Initially, the Department of Human Resources recommended approval. At the foster mother's insistence, however, the Department notified the child's natural father of the proposed adoption. He objected. His own mother and stepfather, R.M.G. and E.M.G., then filed a petition to adopt D. The natural father consented. The Department of Human Resources studied the grandparents' home and, withdrawing its earlier support of the foster parents' petition, recommended approval of the grandparents' petition.

At the hearing on both petitions beginning on April 27, 1979, the court received the following evidence: The foster parents have four other children—three natural and a fourth, a black male, by adoption. They are a military family, living on a racially integrated military base with racially integrated schools. When asked about the problems of raising a child of another race, the foster mother testified that she and her husband had begun "an affirmative program" with their adopted male child. For example, she had obtained pre-school black history and coloring books for their son. She testified, "I make sure he knows that he's not white. I don't care how long he lives with us, he's black, and he's beautiful, and he's ours."

The child's natural grandmother and her husband also testified at the hearing. The grandmother has eight children (all by a previous marriage) of whom the youngest was 14 at the time of the hearing. She also has nine grandchildren, two of whom reside at her home (one is a few months younger than D.). Although the grandmother is employed outside the home, she testified that she would take a leave of absence to be with the child. Both the grandmother and her husband added that they wanted to raise D., that they were able to care for her, and that they desired to show her their love.

Doris Kirksey, a social worker, testified on behalf of the Department of Human Resources. She recommended D.'s placement with her grandparents "based on the premise that the best place for a child is . . . with blood relatives." Ms. Kirksey discounted any harm that might come to D. from removal from her foster family. She based her assessment, in part, on the advice of her agency psychiatrist, Dr. Frances Welsing.

The trial court asked Dr. Welsing to testify in person. Her position, in a nutshell, was that cross-racial adoption always will be harmful to a child and—at the very least—should be discouraged. She emphasized that a non-white child would encounter particular difficulties in a white home upon reaching adolescence. Dr. Welsing made her recommendation to the Department of Human Resources without having met the J.H. family. Most of Dr. Welsing's testimony concerned the problems of cross-racial adoption in a broad societal context.

In response to Dr. Welsing, the foster parents called their own expert, Dr. F. Jay Pepper. He identified several factors germane to adoption. He agreed that race should be considered, but only with respect to the attitudes of the particular family petitioning for adoption. Like Dr. Welsing, Dr. Pepper had not met J.H. and J.H.

The trial court made the following findings and conclusions:

Colonel H and his wife, Caucasians, presently have four children, one of whom is a Black adopted child. They are a stable, middle-income, affectionate family unit who will likely travel to some degree because of the father's military career. They clearly love the child in question.

The G family is a stable Black family of modest means. Mr. G is the second husband of Mrs. G, her first husband having died. She has raised eight children and also has nine grandchildren. At least two of the grandchildren reside in the G home. Mr. and Mrs. G are both employed. If the baby is placed in her care, she plans to take a leave of absence to be with the child. The Court is impressed with the affectionate nature and willingness of the G family to sacrifice.

In any adoption, the paramount concern is the best interest of the child. In that regard, the Court should consider an array of factors. Among them are:

1.   The age of the child.

2.   The stability of the adopting family and reasons for seeking an adoption.

3.   Financial and other resources available to the adopting family.

4. Existence of love and affection between the persons involved.

5. Blood relationships, if any.

6. Race.

7. Any other significant factors.

It is equally important that the Court weigh these factors in terms of past, present and future.

It is seen that the child is very young—less than two years old. In her young life she has already undergone significant and probably traumatic changes. Having regard for the history of this case, it is predictable that another change in the life of this child will cause some degree of injury or harm to her.

The pivotal question becomes, given the available alternatives, evaluated now and for the future, what decision is prudent as being in the child's best interests? Some aspects of this case are clear. Both families have shown love and concern for the child. Both families are reasonably stable; the H family has greater financial resources.

With regard to blood relationships, the evidence indicates that it is a factor but certainly not conclusive. Thus, in the absence of love, affection, stability, and other supportive traits, blood relationship alone confers no special right of parenting. Yet the question should also be weighed in the interest of family tradition, culture and other intangibles.

The question of race is important. It is interesting that all the experts who appeared in this matter agreed that not enough work has been done on the subject as it pertains to adoption. However unpleasant, it would seem that race is a problem which must be considered and should not be ignored or minimized. Conversely, there are not conclusive absolutes to be drawn on the basis of race. It would seem, however, entirely reasonable that as a child grows older the ramifications of this problem would increase. At a later stage, notwithstanding love and affection, severe questions of identity arising from the adoption and race most probably would evolve. In the world at large, as the circle of contacts and routines widens, there are countless adjustments which must be made. Given the circumstances in this case, the child's present status is relatively secure and carefree. The future, in each of its stages—childhood, adolescence, young adulthood, etc.—would likely accentuate these vulnerable points. The Court does not conclude such a family could not sustain itself. Rather the question is, is there not a better alternative? The Court is concerned that little medical or scientific attention has been devoted to this problem. The Court is concerned that, without fault, the Hs stand to lose a beloved member of their family. However, our test remains the best interest of the child.

On June 1, 1979, the trial court [ruled in favor of] the grandparents, E.M.G. and R.M.G.

II.   THE STATUTE: ITS CONSTRUCTION
AND APPLICATION

The adoption statute permits the court to take race into account, although it does not provide any guidance as to how the court is to do it. Nor does the legislative history.

The statute does not bar cross-racial adoption, which of course would be fatal. Thus, the racial classification is sustainable, if at all, only because it is one among a number of relevant factors.

There is, however, an important caveat: if race is to be a relevant factor, the court cannot properly weight it, either automatically or presumptively—*i.e.*, without regard to evidence—for or against cross-racial adoption. To do so would add a racially discriminatory policy to evaluation of the child's best interest. As a consequence, in an adoption contest, petitioners of a particular race would receive a head start, contrary to the constitutional requirement that the use of race—which is "presumptively invalid"—must be affirmatively justified.

The question thus becomes: whether statutory authority to consider race among the factors relevant to adoption, without preference for the race of any party, can ever be "necessary" for a determination of the child's best interest. . . .

Whether adopted by parents of their own or another race, adoptees often find it difficult to establish a sense of identity. "Identity," in this context, has at least three components: (1) a sense of "belonging" in a stable family and community; (2) a feeling of self-esteem and confidence; and (3) "survival skills" that enable the child to cope with the world outside the family. One's sense of identity, therefore, includes perceptions of oneself as both an individual and a social being. While adoptive parents' attitudes toward the adoption and their child are not the only influence on that child, these parental attitudes do affect, to a significant extent, whether the child will feel secure and confident in the family and community. Because race may be highly relevant to these parental attitudes, as the expert witnesses of both parties confirmed—it is relevant to the larger issue of the child's best interest.

I conclude, accordingly, that in a significant number of instances where prospects for adoption are evaluated, those who are responsible for a recommendation and decision—social workers from the Department of Human Resources, expert witnesses at trial, and the trial court itself—will not be able to focus adequately on an adoptive child's sense of identity, and thus on the child's best interest, without considering race.

B.   *Judicial Application of the Race Factor*

When race is relevant in an adoption contest, the court must make a three-step evaluation: (1) how each family's race is likely to affect the child's development of a sense of identity, including racial identity; (2) how the families compare in this regard; and (3) how significant the racial differences between the families are when all the factors relevant to adoption are considered together.

In taking the first step concerning identity, the court must evaluate the probable effect of each family's race and related attitudes on the child's sense of belonging in the family and community, the child's self-esteem and confidence, and the child's ability to cope with problems outside the family. Relevant questions bearing on one or more of these concerns, for example, would be: To what extent would the family expose the child to others of her own race through the immediate family? Through family friendships? Through the neighborhood? Through school? What other efforts will the family most likely make to foster the child's sense of identity—including racial and cultural [identity]—and self-esteem? To what extent has the family associated itself with efforts to enhance respect for the child's race and culture? To what extent has the family reflected any prejudice against the race of the child it proposes to adopt?

When the court takes the second step in the analysis—comparing the families—it hardly would be surprising if the answers to these questions favor prospective parents of the same race as the child. But even when that is true, it is also possible that prospective parents of a different race may receive very positive ratings on these questions. If so, the third analytic step—how significant the racial differences are when all relevant factors are taken together—becomes especially important; for in that situation the racial factor may present such a close question that it will not have the significant, perhaps determinative, impact that it would if racial differences between parent and child simply were deemed a wholly negative factor.

In the present case, the trial court obviously was conscientious and thorough, properly treating race as only one of several relevant considerations. . . . In examining the trial court's decision, I note the following: First, the court conducted a three-day hearing during which it observed the demeanor of witnesses and assured a thorough presentation of evidence, including expert testimony on the general aspects of the racial issue (neither expert was familiar with the families seeking to adopt). Thus, presumably the court had before it each family's best possible personal presentation on the racial issue, as well as the best possible case for each family based on expert views concerning the effects of race on adoption generally.

Second, the court expressly disclaimed that it could draw on "conclusive absolutes" as to race; it referred to "the total circumstances in this case," while "applying all of the factors to be considered" (each of which the court discussed) "and evaluating the question in terms of past, present, and future." In sum, the court specifically eschewed a dogmatic concentration on race, openly discussed all the relevant factors (age of child, stability of family, financial and other resources, love and affection, blood relationship, race), did not rely on an irrelevant factor, and manifested a thoughtful weighing process. The fact that race apparently tipped the decision in favor of appellees, does not, in itself, suggest a discriminatory result.

Third, the court's analysis, as far as it goes, is supported by testimony of record.

Issues

Nonetheless, while correctly beginning with the first analytical step as to race focusing on growth of the child's sense of identity, the court made no specific findings (reflecting the kinds of questions listed above) as to how race would be likely to affect this particular black child growing up, respectively, in the families of J.H. and J.H. and of E.M.G. and R.M.G. Furthermore, aside from reciting facts about the racial makeup of each family, the court did not articulate the comparative analysis required by steps two and three: how the families compare in their respective abilities to accommodate race, and how significant racial differences between the families are when all factors relevant to the adoption are considered together.

Because the race factor is determinative here, I conclude that the trial court's analysis did not provide the reasoning and detail necessary to assure a reviewing court that the evaluation of race was precisely tailored to the best interest of the child. . . .

In a case such as this, where there is every indication from the trial court's analysis that, but for considerations of race, the decision might have been different, any determination as to race that is not precisely articulated on a comparative basis will fail to survive strict scrutiny. Given the trial court's opinion, which could be read to say that appellants—the J.H. family—were slightly favored but for race, an articulation of how close the race question is will be necessary to assure this court that the result is constitutionally justifiable. Otherwise, the risk that race will be misused is too high, even when there is no reason to believe the trial court is intentionally discriminatory.

V. CONCLUSION

In summary, the statute, with its explicit recognition of race among the factors relevant to adoption, does not deny equal protection of the laws. However, the trial court, in granting the petition of R.M.G. and E.M.G. to adopt D., did not articulate its analysis of the race factor in sufficient detail to assure a reviewing court that the application of that factor, in conjunction with the other relevant considerations, was precisely tailored to the best interest of the child.

■ MACK, ASSOCIATE JUDGE, concurring . . .

I think that reversal is required in this case because the trial court, unwittingly, employed the factor of race as an impermissible *presumption*. . . . I do not think, moreover, that the fact that the trial court did not speak in terms of a presumption, or the fact that it might have relied upon the testimony of an "expert" (who had never met the parties) made its ruling rest on more than a presumption. . . .

■ NEWMAN, CHIEF JUDGE, dissenting . . .

I think it is clear that the Constitution does *not* require a court to ignore racial differences between prospective parent and child.

It is clear from the opinion and trial record, however, that there was no improper consideration of race to be remedied, and it is unlikely that a wordier opinion will make it easier to detect and overturn abuses if and when they occur in the future.

I.   THE NATURE OF THE TRIAL COURT'S DECISION

In the trial court, both sets of prospective adoptive parents had an opportunity to present any and all available evidence bearing on how the child's best interest would be affected by either of the alternative placements, including potential effects of racial differences, and any factors mitigating those risks. After a thorough hearing, the trial court was able to judge such factors as the families' respective financial resources, blood relationships with the child, the effect of a shift in custody away from the family with temporary custody, family stability, and the sort of love and care that each family could be expected to provide. The court was in an unusually good position to judge with respect to the H. family, for they had already had custody for some time on a temporary basis. Moreover, they have another adopted child, who, unlike the parents, is black. The court thus had before it evidence of affirmative steps taken by the parents to mitigate some of the potential problems arising in an interracial adoption.

Q.   Have you made particular efforts to cultivate his black heritage, and maintain the presence of that in your household?

A.   We definitely began an affirmative program when Jeff came to live with us.

Q.   How long has Jeff been with you?

A.   Jeff came to live with us when he was eight days old, so he has been with us almost six years. He'll be six in August.

Needless to say, being in the military, we live in a thoroughly integrated society, and much more accepting than you would find in most civilian communities. Through guidance of friends and associates of my husband, the chaplain at the chapel where we go to church—one of our chaplains is black—I have gotten in magazines, and I have some pre-school black history books for my son, a black coloring book for children, put out by Ebony Jr. I make sure he knows that he's not white. I don't care how long he lives with us, he's black, and he's beautiful, and he's ours.

Having weighed all this evidence, the court found as a fact that considerations other than the difference in race between the child and one set of adoptive parents were in equipoise.

The court then turned to a consideration of the possible effects of racial differences between parents and child, and concluded that the possibility of adverse effects in the H. family tipped the balance in favor of the G. family. This conclusion was based on considerable expert testimony, which the majority opinion recites in part. It is evident that neither the parties nor the court approached this issue lightly. Indeed, when a social worker indicated that her testimony was largely based on the views of Dr. Welsing, the agency psychiatrist, the court requested that Dr. Welsing testify in person. After weighing facts and expert opinion on both sides, the court observed that conclusive data on the efficacy of interracial adoption is lacking.

While there is a debate among social scientists about the viability of interracial adoption, no one—including the parties herein and their expert witnesses—contends that such adoptions tend to be *superior* to intraracial adoptions, all other factors equal. Rather, the dispute concerns the degree to which the fact of a racial difference presents risks which are not otherwise present, and the extent to which those risks may be reduced by affirmative steps on the part of the parents.

Most authorities agree that intraracial adoption is preferable.

The hazards of interracial adoption should not be exaggerated, but neither should they be ignored. An inevitably imprecise prediction about the effects of an interracial placement must be made in the context of all relevant circumstances, including any mitigating efforts by the parents. But *when all other factors are in equipoise*, the *possibility* of an adverse effect, no matter how small or how unlikely, would suffice to permit the trial judge to tip the balance in the direction of the intraracial alternative.

Accordingly, the result below can be upset only if it is constitutionally impermissible to give any weight whatsoever to adverse effects on the child related to racial differences between herself and her parents.

II. THE CONSTITUTIONALITY OF THE TRIAL COURT'S DECISION

A. *The Level of Scrutiny*

[T]he use of race in this case does not require application of the strict scrutiny standard. . . . First, the use of the racial factor does not stigmatize a particular racial group. In other words, the use of race in this adoption proceeding was not based on the presumption that one race is inferior to another, nor does it place the weight of the court behind racial bigotry and separatism. The trial judge used race as one of many factors to be weighed in calculating the child's best interests, not as a means of insuring racial purity or separation.

Secondly, though the consideration of race was not purposefully remedial, neither were its purpose and effect pernicious with respect to the distribution of burdens and benefits among racial groups. . . . Here, the consideration of race seeks not to improve the position of any particular racial group, but simply to protect the best interests of the child, of whatever race. . . .

[T]he purpose and predominant effect of the court's action is legitimate and compelling: protection of the child's best interests. It is also significant that only one side of the proposed interracial adoption consists of consenting parties: the H. family. The child is not of consenting age, and therefore it is the *court* which is in the difficult position of standing in her shoes and judging what is in her interest. If the child had capacity to decide for herself, she would certainly not be prevented from taking note of the different race of those proposing to adopt her. When the court does the same on her behalf, there is no indication of invidiousness that necessitates the strictest level of scrutiny. . . .

B.   *Constitutional Scrutiny of the Court's Decision . . .*

Some of the risks of interracial adoption involve the child's development of identity (including racial and cultural identity), self-esteem, and a sense of belonging in the family—relevant considerations which the majority recognizes as legitimate and important. One problem is the possibility that the child may not perceive herself as black or develop an identity as a black person. There was evidence at trial that the foster parents would make efforts to alleviate this possibility. Even if the child is made aware of her black identity, however, other problems might develop. The child would then have to cope with the fact that she is different from her parents.

Another aspect of the identity problem is the possibility that the child may experience a "conflict of loyalties" as she grows older. If she identifies with the culture of her heritage, she may feel isolated from her family. If she identifies with her family, her skin color will always be there to remind her and others of her origins. In other words, the child may be caught between two cultures and accepted by neither. Even if the white foster parents were able to nurture the child's ability to perceive herself as black, there is little they could do to prevent the ambivalent feelings and rejection she may experience later in life.

In addition to a strong sense of identity, the black child must learn to develop certain survival skills. Regardless of how she is identified by herself or her family, she will be identified as a black person by society and will inevitably experience racism. Blacks and other minorities develop survival skills for coping with such racism, which they can pass to their children expressly, or more importantly, by unconscious example.

Parents of interracial families may attempt to learn these lessons and then teach them, but most authorities recognize that this is an inferior substitute for learning directly from minority role models. Few white parents even claim they can teach such skills. In one study, a third of interracial parents did not undertake affirmative efforts to teach them. The two thirds who did, did so predominately through secondary materials like books, rather than by example, which is the normal method of socialization.

The racism experienced by blacks in this society may be encountered even more often by blacks in interracial families. Those with racist attitudes are undoubtedly opposed to interracial families. Acts of bigotry may be visited upon a child of a different race than his adoptive parents, regardless of the child's own race. Other children in the family may also become the targets of slurs. Certainly the possibility of such traumatic experiences, with their attendant psychological effects, bears on the child's best interest. However, it cannot be emphasized too strongly that the desires of those opposing racial mixing are *not* to be weighed in the balance. The existence of such desires is significant only in that they may lead to acts directed against the child that adversely affect *his or her* interest. There is no reason for failing to weigh the effect of prejudice on the child's best interest as one factor among a multitude.

Since black children in interracial families may be even more exposed to racist attitudes than other blacks, their need for survival skills is more acute. White parents, however, tend to be less equipped to pass on those skills. It is ironic and unfortunate that those black children most in need of survival skills are in environments which are the least able to provide them.

Racial slurs are not the only kinds of public reaction that pose problems for the child and his family. The range of responses is wide, and serves as a recurrent reminder that the child is "different" from his family. When some people see a child whose race is different from that of his parents, they assume he is an illegitimate child or the product of a multi-racial marriage—circumstances they may disapprove of. Other people overreact in a well-meaning way, commenting on how wonderful it is to adopt a minority child. But however well-intentioned, such reactions have the effect of emphasizing to the child that he is "different" and can lead to a sense of isolation. Thus, while *all* adopted children have to cope with the fact that they are adopted, the interracial adoptee may have an even more difficult experience since his status is evident to the world at large.

In sum, consciousness of a racial difference between the adoptive parents and the child is necessitated by society's compelling interest in fostering the child's best interest.

III. FLAWS IN THE MAJORITY'S APPROACH

A. *An Overly Narrow View of the Relevance of Racial Differences to the Child's Best Interest . . .*

[T]he question that social scientists, the expert witnesses, and ultimately the courts have to grapple with is whether, *notwithstanding the very best of intentions and efforts on the part of the parents*, there are potential problems in the interracial context of a kind not expected in the intraracial case. The court should be permitted to conclude, as it did in this case, that such risks persist to some degree even when parental attitudes and the external environment are favorable. In other words, the issue is not exhausted simply by consideration of attitudes and environment; a difference in race between parents and child is of independent significance.

Yet the majority comes close to saying that differences in the relative viability of interracial and uniracial families are only coincidentally or indirectly related to racial differences, due to a possible statistical correlation between the race and favorable attitudes or external environment. However, there is no basis for excluding from consideration the more direct influence of race.

If an approach taking account of potential problems associated with interracial adoption amounts to a "preference" for intraracial adoption, it is an entirely permissible one. Such a preference is no less legitimate than a preference for a two parent family or for parents with adequate resources to raise the child. If, in the guise of neutrality, the majority's framework rules out of order a preference for intraracial adoption that is supported by evidence, it introduces a bias against adoption [of a black child] by a black family. It is just as prejudicial to eliminate a legitimate consideration as it is to introduce an illegitimate one.

The majority finds the [trial court's] lack of "specific findings . . . as to how race would be likely to affect this *particular* black child" in the H. & G. families to be fatal. However, the effort to distinguish a "generalized" judgment from a "particularized" inquiry concerning the individual family before it is misleading. This approach seems quite plausible on the surface, but the supposed distinction blurs considerably on closer examination. Of course, the statement that "this family is of a different race than D.G." would be true of a great many potential adoptive families. But the same is true of virtually any other relevant fact including those emphasized by the majority (e.g., living in an integrated neighborhood, attending an integrated school). That such factors may have positive effects is no less a "generalization" than the type of inference that the majority criticizes. Indeed, where the goal is prediction of future conditions such as how a child's interests will be served by a given adoption, no piece of evidence has any probative value unless it is possible to relate it to the past experience of other adoptive families. Only then can one infer (generalize) therefrom that the experience of this family is likely to be similar. Thus there is nothing suspect about reliance on testimony based on "generalization" from the experience of other families who are similarly situated in relevant ways, including racial differences between parent and child. . . .

CONCLUSION

The Constitution does not require a court to blind itself to realities affecting a child's best interest, even when those facts depend on the respective races of the parents and child. What is in the best interest of a child is a *factual* question to be resolved by the trial court. [There is a] relatively straightforward issue posed by this case: whether it is constitutionally permissible and appropriate for a court to give *any* weight to evidence that an interracial adoption presents certain risks to a child's welfare, which may be mitigated though not eliminated by special efforts on the part of the parents. I think that this factor may and should be included among the many others relevant to the child's best interest. It follows that, in a case such as this, where other factors are in equipoise, the interracial factor may sway the result. Since race-consciousness in this limited context is permissible, and the court's judgment as to the child's best interest is supported by the evidence and not clearly erroneous, the result should be affirmed.

We must live in the world as it *is* while we strive to make it as it should be.

NOTES AND QUESTIONS

1. ***Level of Scrutiny.*** In *R.M.G.*, the majority and dissent disagree on whether strict or intermediate scrutiny should apply. At the time that *RMG* was decided, the Supreme Court had not yet declared that strict scrutiny applied to *all* racial classifications. Should the Court have applied strict scrutiny? If not, why not?

2. ***Articulating the Race Factor.*** Does the court's mandate that the trial court "articulate its analysis of the race factor" in more detail serve any sensible purpose? Would the trial court likely reach a different conclusion on remand? Would the trial judge find it difficult to justify his decision?

3. ***Best Interest of the Child.*** Did the trial court, as the concurring judge asserts, rely on a presumption in favor of same-race placement? If it did, what is so bad about that? Is the precise tailoring to the best interest of the child, which the majority calls for, even possible?

4. ***The Court's Final Statement.*** Consider the final statement of the dissent: "We must live in the world as it *is* while we strive to make it as it should be." Is the judge saying that the state of society sometimes justifies racial discrimination? If so, isn't that acquiescing to social attitudes in a manner contrary to the spirit of *Palmore*? If we acquiesce to racial attitudes, doesn't that allow them to persist? Finally, what precisely is it that society "should be"?

5.   Palmore *Revisited.* Despite intense controversy about the role of race in adoptive placements during the 1970s and 1980s, the Supreme Court has never clarified the constitutional standard. Not since *Palmore* has the Court issued any opinion concerning the constitutionality of considering race in child placement. State statutes continued to direct or allow judges to consider race. Statutes no longer categorically prohibited placement across race lines, but they do contemplate the consideration of race as one factor of many. Are state statutes that permit a judge to consider race in the adoption context consistent with the Supreme Court's current insistence that strict scrutiny apply to all racial classifications? Would such statutes pass strict scrutiny? What compelling interest would they further?

EXERCISES

1.   The majority in *R.M.G.* distinguishes between considering racial attitudes and considering the race of the parties, and concludes that to consider the prospective adoptive families' racial attitudes and circumstances would be "to consider race . . . without preference for the race of any party." Do you agree that taking account of racial attitudes is different than considering the race of the parties? Is it possible, or desirable, to consider adoptive parents' racial attitude without considering their race? Is that distinction conceptually coherent? Practically feasible? Think about how you would argue either side of the following contention: taking account of racial attitudes is meaningfully different from relying on a presumption in favor of same race placement. Is there a distinction between considering potential parents' race and considering their racial attitudes? Should the law rely on that distinction and treat those forms of race consciousness differently?

2.   If social workers are to consider racial attitudes, how precisely should they do so? If, for example, a prospective white adoptive family says that they would teach their black child that "race doesn't matter," and that the only race is the human race, should that be held against them? If so, what about a black adoptive family who says the same thing?

In one case, *DeWees v. Stevenson*, 779 F. Supp. 25 (E.D. Pa. 1991), a social worker and psychiatrist who had responsibility for placing a black child denied the foster family's adoption application because the foster parents said "that race had no impact on the raising of a child" and that they would not prepare the child for racial discrimination unless, and until, a problem with discrimination occurred. Based on the interview, the social worker denied the foster parents' request for adoption, concluding that the foster parents would not "be sufficiently sensitive to the needs of a bi-racial child during the critical period of socialization, self-identification and personality development of age two through six years." Did the social worker and psychiatrist discriminate against the foster family on the basis of race?

The court upheld their decision, reasoning that the social worker "is currently prepared to place [the child] for adoption with any suitable couple, regardless of race, who appear to her to have the awareness, sensitivity and skills to address adequately the needs of a bi-racial child in his formative years. Her decision was based on the perceived best interests of the child, and not on the color of plaintiffs' skins. . . . The state's responsibility to protect the best interests of a child in its custody is a compelling interest for purposes of the equal protection clause. . . . Because of the potential difficulties inherent in a trans-racial adoption, a state agency may consider race and racial attitudes in assessing prospective adoptive parents."

C. THE RACE MATCHING CONTROVERSY

R.M.G. usefully highlights broader issues about the propriety of taking account of race in the adoption process. As racial attitudes became more liberal in the late 1960s, and as adoption policy became less centered on mimicking the biological family, rates of transracial adoption increased. That increase was also spurred by another demographic development: the precipitous decline in the number of white children available for adoption. As the stigma associated with unwed childbearing diminished, unmarried women who decades earlier would have placed their newborn for adoption became increasingly likely to raise the child. Also, the availability of birth control and abortion resulted in lower rates of childbearing by teenage girls, who had been especially likely to place a child for adoption.

1. NATIONAL ASSOCIATION OF BLACK SOCIAL WORKERS STATEMENT

One of the most vociferous opponents of transracial adoption has been the National Association of Black Social Workers, which in the early 1970s issued a strongly worded position paper critical of the placement of black children with white families. The position paper read, in part:

> The National Association of Black Social Workers has taken a vehement stand against the placement of black children in white homes for any reason. We affirm the inviolable position of black children in black families where they belong physically, psychologically and culturally in order that they receive the total sense of themselves and develop a sound projection of their future.
>
> In our society, the developmental needs of Black children are significantly different from those of white children. Black children are taught, from an early age, highly sophisticated coping techniques to deal with racist practices perpetrated by individuals and institutions. These coping techniques become successfully integrated into ego functions and can be incorporated only through the process of developing positive identification with significant black others. Only a black family can transmit the emotional and sensitive subtleties of perception and reaction essential for a black child's survival in a racist society.

Identity

We fully recognize the phenomenon of transracial adoption as an expedient for white folk, not as an altruistic humane concern for black children. The supply of white children for adoption has all but vanished and adoption agencies, having always catered to middle class whites developed an answer to their desire for parenthood by motivating them to consider black children. This has brought about a re-definition of some black children. Those born of black-white alliances are no longer black as decreed by immutable law and social custom for centuries. They are now black-white, inter-racial, bi-racial, emphasizing the whiteness as the adoptable quality; a further subtle, but vicious design to further diminish black and accentuate white. We resent this high-handed arrogance and are insulted by this further assignment of chattel status to black people.

White parents of black children seek out special help with their parenting; help with acquiring the normal and usually instinctual parental behaviors inherent in the cultural and psychological development of children. It is tantamount to having to be taught to do what comes naturally.

Special programming in learning to handle black children's hair, learning black culture, "trying to become black," puts normal family activities in the form of special family projects to accommodate the odd member of the family. This is accentuated by the white parents who had to *prepare* their neighbors for their forthcoming black child and those who hasten, even struggle, to make acquaintance with black persons. These actions highlight the unnatural character of trans racial adoption, giving rise to artificial conditions, logically lacking in substance. Superficialities convey nothing of worth and are more damaging than helpful.

We know there are numerous alternatives to the placement of black children with white families and challenge all agencies and organizations to commit themselves to the basic concept of black families for black children. With such commitment all else finds its way to successful realization of that concept. Black families can be found when agencies alter their requirements, methods of approach, definition of suitable family and tackle the legal machinery to facilitate inter-state placements. Additionally, the proposed commitment invokes the social work profession to a re-orientation to the black family permitting sight of the strengths therein. Exploration for resources within a child's biological family can reveal possibilities for permanent planning. The extended family of grandparents, aunts, cousins, etc. may well be viable resources if agencies will legitimize them; make them their area for initial exploration and work first to develop and cement their potential. This is valid and preferable even if financial assistance is necessary.

We denounce the assertions that blacks will not adopt; we affirm the fact that black people, in large number, cannot maneuver the obstacle course of the traditional adoption process. This process has long been a screening out device. The emphasis on high income, educational achievement, residential status and other accoutrements of a white middle class life style eliminates black applicants by the score.

The National Association of Black Social Workers asserts the conviction that children should not remain in foster homes or institutions when adoption can be a reality. We stand firmly, though, on conviction that a white home is not a suitable placement for black children and contend it is totally unnecessary.

* * *

NOTES AND QUESTIONS

1.   *Evaluating the NABSW Position.* What do you think of the NABSW statement? Which of its concerns do you think were justified then? Which concerns do you think are still justified today?

While the NABSW position paper may seem uncomfortably strident from a contemporary vantage point, it is important to understand the context in which it arose and the problems to which it responded. The paper reflects the black power movement and a racial consciousness that was much more widespread in the late 1960s and early 70s than now. Black had only recently become beautiful, and many interpreted transracial adoption as negating or denying the value of black families and black culture. That cultural and social context partly explains the tone and style of the position paper.

The NABSW paper's assertion that black children are best served by black families reflects many of the intuitions that continue to shape the debate about race and child placement, issues that will be more fully discussed below.

In addition, the NABSW paper rests on two broad claims about racial inequity:

   a.   That black families were systematically excluded from the adoption process due either to biased outreach practices or selection standards that favored whites.

   b.   That black children were disproportionately brought into the child welfare system due to culturally biased standards of child rearing.

2.   *The NABSW Statement Impact.* Whatever the merits of the NABSW's position, its paper influenced adoption practice during the 1970s and 80s, as social work organizations became less supportive of, and more cautious in,

making transracial placements. The number of transracial placements declined during that period. Assuming that the NABSW's claims were correct, and that it caused a decline in transracial placements, how would you evaluate that development?

2.   EVALUATING RACE MATCHING

There has been a considerable amount of research concerning transracial adoption, but many of the key issues remain unresolved. Some of the central questions are empirical, while others are normative, in the sense that they entail a vision of what should be.

Most studies have found that transracially adopted black children fare no worse than their in-racially adopted counterparts in terms of educational, employment, and health outcomes. The chief difference between the two groups of adoptees relates to racial identity. Perhaps unsurprisingly, black children adopted by white families are less likely to have "strong racial identity," and in the view of some researchers are more likely to have "identity issues." Studies of children adopted both transracially and internationally have found that those adoptees are more likely to express discomfort with their appearance or to profess a desire to be white.

Consider the following rationales for race matching, and the questions posed with respect to each:

1.   ***Identity.*** That black children raised by black parents are more likely to develop a strong racial identity than had they been raised by white parents.

> Granted, a child may develop stronger racial identity with a black family, but why is it important for a child to have a strong racial identity? How does a strong racial identity further a child's best interests? Is there anything wrong with a child dismissing the relevance of race and identifying only as a member of the human race? Can one have a healthy identity without having a strong racial identity?

2.   ***Coping Skills.*** That black parents are generally better able to impart the coping mechanisms or survival skills that black children will need to thrive in American society.

> Given the absence of any evidence that transracially adopted black children fare any less well overall than other adopted black children, isn't the assumption that black parents are uniquely able to teach coping skills simply an ungrounded stereotype?

> To the extent that succeeding in American society entails interacting with whites, why aren't white parents *better* able to teach the necessary skills than black parents?

After all, wouldn't white parents know more about how white people view African Americans than would black parents?

3. ***Stigma.*** That transracially adopted children experience a unique stigma as a result of their visible difference from their adopted parents.

> This may have been the case generations ago, but is it still true today?

> Isn't it a positive for the fact of adoption to be more open than hidden, as in prior eras?

> Doesn't the child's experience of stigma depend primarily on how the parents explain the fact of the adoption to the child?

4. ***Culture.*** That black children are more likely to be connected to black culture, and the black community, if they are raised by black parents.

> What is black culture?

> Is it necessary to be raised by black parents to be connected to it? Given the prevalence of black culture in American society, can't a child access black culture without having black parents?

> Given that no child will grow to maturity without any culture, why is it beneficial for a black child to have a tie to black culture in particular? Is there anything wrong with a black child simply partaking of American culture?

> Can a black child become a healthy adult without feeling a part of the black community?

EXERCISE

Divide into groups and each take a side—pro or con—with respect to each race matching argument above. For each issue consider whether it is possible to substantiate, or refute, the claim factually. If so, what sort of evidence would need to be collected in order to do so? If it is not possible to resolve the empirical question, on what assumptions or intuitions should policy rely?

3.   THE MULTI-ETHNIC PLACEMENT ACT

The Multi-Ethnic Placement Act (known as MEPA) was passed in 1994 (and amended in 1996) in response to the disproportionate representation of black children in foster care awaiting adoption. Black children were roughly 13% of the youth population yet constituted more than 1/3 of those children in foster care awaiting adoption. Black children both waited longer to be placed with an adoptive family (two years compared to an average of one for whites) and also were less likely to be placed at all. One study from the late 1980s found that race was a more powerful determinant in the placement process than any other factor. Elizabeth Bartholet, *Where Do Black Children Belong? The Politics of Race Matching in Adoption*, 139 U. Pa. L. Rev. 1163 (1991).

Professor Elizabeth Bartholet has been one of the harshest critics of race matching. She has argued that the costs of race matching are in practice substantial. Race matching, she has contended, harms black children by delaying or denying their placement with an adoptive family, because social workers often decline to place a child with a waiting white family, and instead continue to search for a black family. Delaying placement, in turn, results in fewer placements because many adoptive parents prefer to adopt a younger child, and consequently older children are substantially harder to place.

MEPA is reprinted below:

Sec. 552. FINDINGS AND PURPOSE.

(a)   Findings.—The Congress finds that—

(1)   nearly 500,000 children are in foster care in the United States;

(2)   tens of thousands of children in foster care are waiting for adoption;

(3)   2 years and 8 months is the median length of time that children wait to be adopted;

(4)   child welfare agencies should work to eliminate racial, ethnic, and national origin discrimination and bias in adoption and foster care recruitment, selection, and placement procedures; and

(5)   active, creative, and diligent efforts are needed to recruit foster and adoptive parents of every race, ethnicity, and culture in order to facilitate the placement of children in foster and adoptive homes which will best meet each child's needs.

(b)   Purpose.—It is the purpose of this subpart to promote the best interests of children by—

(1)   decreasing the length of time that children wait to be adopted;

(2)   preventing discrimination in the placement of children on the basis of race, color, or national origin; and

(3)   facilitating the identification and recruitment of foster and adoptive families that can meet children's needs.

Sec. 553. MULTIETHNIC PLACEMENTS.

(a) Activities.—

(1) Prohibition.—An agency, or entity, that receives Federal assistance and is involved in adoption or foster care placements may not—

(A) categorically deny to any person the opportunity to become an adoptive or a foster parent, solely on the basis of the race, color, or national origin of the adoptive or foster parent, or the child, involved; or

(B) delay or deny the placement of a child for adoption or into foster care, or otherwise discriminate in making a placement decision, solely on the basis of the race, color, or national origin of the adoptive or foster parent, or the child, involved.

(2) Permissible consideration.—An agency or entity to which paragraph (1) applies may consider the cultural, ethnic, or racial background of the child and the capacity of the prospective foster or adoptive parents to meet the needs of a child of this background as one of a number of factors used to determine the best interests of a child.

(3) Definition.—As used in this subsection, the term "placement decision" means the decision to place, or to delay or deny the placement of, a child in a foster care or an adoptive home, and includes the decision of the agency or entity involved to seek the termination of birth parent rights or otherwise make a child legally available for adoptive placement.

Sec. 554. REQUIRED RECRUITMENT EFFORTS FOR CHILD WELFARE SERVICES PROGRAMS.

Section 422(b) of the Social Security Act (42 U.S.C. 622(b)) is amended—

(3) by adding at the end the following:

"(9) provide for the diligent recruitment of potential foster and adoptive families that reflect the ethnic and racial diversity of children in the State for whom foster and adoptive homes are needed."

Only 2 years after its enactment, MEPA was amended by the Interethnic Adoption Provisions of the 1996 Small Business Protection Act (called the IEP).

4.   1996 AMENDMENT, INTERETHNIC ADOPTION PROVISIONS

Sec.   1808.   REMOVAL   OF   BARRIERS   TO   INTERETHNIC ADOPTION. . . .

> [N]either the State nor any other entity in the State that receives funds from the Federal Government and is involved in adoption or foster care placements may—
>
> > "(A) deny to any person the opportunity to become an adoptive or a foster parent, on the basis of the race, color, or national origin of the person, or of the child, involved; or
> >
> > "(B) delay or deny the placement of a child for adoption or into foster care, on the basis of the race, color, or national origin of the adoptive or foster parent, or the child, involved."
>
> (d) Conforming Amendment.—Section 553 of the ... Multiethnic Placement Act of 1994 is repealed.

NOTES AND QUESTIONS

1.   *The 1996 Amendment.* How exactly did the 1996 amendment change MEPA? Look back to the previous pages in order to remind yourself of what was included in Section 553 of MEPA, which was repealed by the IEP. What concerns might have motivated the changes made by the IEP? Were the changes sensible? Necessary? Which version of MEPA, the original 1994 enactment or the 1996 Amendment, do you think best furthers the interests of children in need of adoption?

2.   R.M.G. *After MEPA.* In *R.M.G.*, would the trial judge's decision have violated MEPA, as amended? What about the approach advocated by the court of appeals judge?

3.   *Interpreting MEPA.* Although MEPA unquestionably was intended to restrict race matching, many social work professionals—from front line case workers to those administrators who set policy—continue to believe that minority children benefit by being placed with families from their own racial or ethnic group.

Because there are very few litigated challenges brought by private plaintiffs, the enforcement of MEPA has fallen to the Office of Civil Rights (OCR), in the Department of Health and Human Services. The OCR has interpreted MEPA's nondiscrimination mandate in an expansive manner. The following scenarios illustrate practices that OCR has deemed to be prohibited by MEPA. For each scenario, consider whether you think the practice: i) furthers the best interests of the child, and ii) whether, on balance, the practice should be prohibited as a matter of policy. In doing so, you should consider the goals of MEPA, as well as the specific language of the statute.

> a.   An adoption agency formally prohibits the consideration of race in child placement, but the standard practice among

social workers is to initially seek a same-race placement, and only if they cannot find one to consider transracial placements. The social workers justify this by saying that being removed from their family members and placed into a home with total strangers can be difficult for children, and that placing them with a family of another race makes this transition even harder.

b.   Two sets of prospective parents, one black couple and one white couple, have indicated a desire to adopt the same black child. Following a home study, background check, and family assessment, the adoption agency determines that both families are matches for the child. Regardless of the family chosen, the placement will take the same amount of time. The committee in charge of the placement agrees to use race as a tiebreaker, reasoning that, all else being equal, "black babies are best in black families." They place the child with the black family.

c.   The adoption agency committee declares that it will place a black child with a particular white couple only if the white couple completes a two-week course specifically designed around the potential problems facing transracially adopted children, including trouble establishing identity and learning to cope with racism. Otherwise, the child will be placed with a black couple (whom the agency did not require to complete any class).

d.   The adoption agency declined one white couple's application to adopt a black child (even though they had already adopted a biracial child and were foster parents to a three year-old African-American child) due to the couple's lack of contact with the African-American community and the low percentage of African Americans in their local school system as either teachers or students. Instead, the agency placed the child with a single white women who lived in an "integrated neighborhood and had bi-racial brothers."

e.   As part of the interview process, Adoption Specialists routinely ask children (whose consent to the adoption is not legally required) what sort of family they want to be placed with. If the child states a preference for the race of the adoptive family, the Adoption Specialists will usually accommodate that request and work to match the race of the child with the adoptive parent. However, if the child expresses another preference, such as a desire to be placed in a family with a large home or to be placed near his friends, the Adoption Specialist may attempt to encourage the child be more flexible or, in some cases, may dismiss the child's request as unrealistic.

4.   *Assessing MEPA.* In which, if any, of the preceding cases, did the Office of Civil Rights go too far by treating it as prohibited?

    a.   Are OCR's prohibitions consistent with the text of the statute? Its intent?

    b.   How might such expansive reach of MEPA be justified?

    c.   Do each of the prohibitions further the best interests of children in need of adoption?

    d.   Or, instead, can the prohibitions only be understood in terms of protecting the interests of adults in the adoption process? If so, is it appropriate for a law governing the placement of children to grant adults a right not to be discriminated against? Do, or should, prospective adoptive parents have a right to be free of racial discrimination in the adoption process?

    e.   In any of the above circumstances did an adult's right not to be discriminated against conflict with the furtherance of the child's best interests? If so, which should prevail?

    f.   Which, if any, of these practices should be held unconstitutional when undertaken by a state agency?

5.   *Cultural Competency Training.* A continued source of controversy is MEPA's prohibition of so-called cultural competency training for parents who adopt transracially. Some critics contend that prohibiting such cultural competency training harms children. Consider the statement below from the Evan B. Donaldson Adoption Institute:

> When families who adopt transracially do not receive preparation and training that promote racial awareness and competence, they and their children are not well-served. Families lose critical opportunities to assess their own preparedness to adopt transracially and to develop the awareness and skills that are essential to meeting their children's racial/ethnic identity and socialization needs. Failing to provide families with this preparation is contrary to sound and ethical social work practice and is not in the best interest of the child. (Finding Families for African American Children report, p. 41).

Do you agree with this statement?

6.   *Recruitment.* The San Diego California Children Services Bureau is aggressively recruiting prospective families from the black and Latino communities (children from each of which are overrepresented in foster care), and has established two units to facilitate this research: Tayari and Nuestros Niños.

The Tayari unit specializes in recruiting African-American families to adopt. In assigning children to the Tayari unit, the Bureau assigns cases based on geography, caseload, and race. Adoption cases for African-American children are generally assigned to Tayari, unless the unit is full. Most social workers in the unit are African American and the Bureau assigns only African-American children to the unit.

The Bureau assigns cases to the Nuestros Niños unit based on geography, caseload, and language need. Because Nuestros Niños is located in a geographical area with a significant Hispanic population, most of the children and applicants served by the unit are Hispanic. The unit also serves non-Hispanic clients who live in the service area. Most social workers assigned to the unit speak Spanish, but some do not. The racial and ethnic composition of the unit's staff is mixed. The Bureau assigns Hispanic children and applicants who are bilingual to workers who speak only English. If the unit has additional space on its caseload, the Bureau will assign English only speaking clients to bilingual workers.

Does either of these efforts to fulfill the county's obligation to diligently recruit underrepresented minorities constitute an impermissible use of race?

OCR found that the Bureau's "placements of children within Tayari were not neutral with regard to race" and expressed concern that "the practice of segregating African-American children and applicants in one unit could present a ready opportunity for race matching and for bypassing applicants of other races from consideration." As a result of OCR's investigation, the Bureau stopped assigning adoption cases to the Tayari unit, so that Tayari functioned "only as a recruitment and applicant approval unit that seeks to address the shortage of African-American applicants," and does not place children. In contrast, despite the fact that most of the children and applicants dealt with by Nuestros Niños are Hispanic, OCR found that "the language needs of clients and the language abilities of workers are legitimate factors for case assignments," and thus did not require the Bureau to separate the recruitment and placement functions.

7. *Judicial Enforcement of MEPA.* Imagine that you are a Federal District Court Judge. The state legislature passed a bill 10 years ago that amends the factors to be considered in the placement of children, which created a preference for keeping children over the age of three in the city or town in which they live. The bill's supporters cite the benefits of maintaining continuity with the community, of not severing the relationships that children have formed with peers, adults, and church communities. In the years since the law's passage, the percentage of same-race placements has increased and transracial adoptions decreased, largely because many cities and towns are highly segregated. At the same time, the average time that black children remain in foster care has risen by six months, and the percentage of children that never achieve placement has increased by 8%. Prospective foster and adoptive parents from a predominantly white suburban town have challenged the law as a violation of MEPA. Does this policy violate MEPA? Why? Does this policy violate the Equal Protection Clause? Should it?

8. *Ethics of Opposing MEPA.* Imagine that you are a social worker at an agency subject to MEPA. Your supervisor has made clear that MEPA aims to eliminate race matching. But you think that the law is misguided. You firmly believe that, for a child, a family of a different race is better than no family. But you also think that, other things being equal, black children fare better when placed in a black family. What steps would you take to place children consistent with your own professional views? How would you define the line that divides legitimate from irresponsible efforts to resist MEPA?

9.   *Evaluating MEPA.* The empirical evidence about the effects of MEPA is equivocal. Since the passage of MEPA, adoption rates of black children from foster care have increased, but black children are still less likely than white children to be adopted. According to data from 2006 (ten years after the amendment to MEPA), black children represent 35% of those awaiting adoption, yet only 27% of those adopted. *See* Donaldson Institute Report, Finding Families for African American Children: The Role of Race and Law in Adoption from Foster Families (May 2008), http://adoptioninstitute.org/old/publications/MEPApaper20080527.pdf. Transracial adoptions of black children have increased, but it is not clear the extent to which the increase in transracial adoption has led to an increase in the adoption of black children. According to a report by the Evan B. Donaldson Adoption Institute, some of the states that most improved the adoption rates of black children also had relatively low rates of transracial adoption. Increased adoption rates may have been spurred by other policy changes—e.g., the Adoption and Safe Families Act, which prompted states to more quickly move children from foster care to adoption.

Whether MEPA has contributed significantly to the increased adoption of black children is thus unclear. It does seem likely that the law has redistributed from black to white adoptive parents many children who would have been adopted anyway. The black children who are hardest to place—those who are older and have been in the system awhile—are not ideal for either a transracial or in-racial adoption. Most parents seek to adopt younger children, and that is no less true for transracial adopters.

Does such evidence weigh in favor of repeal of MEPA, as some advocates contend? Or does it indicate that the law is successful in eliminating racial discrimination from the adoption process? A more normative question arises as well: What is the standard for the success of MEPA? Is the law successful if it ends discrimination in the placement of children? Or must the law also lead to more and better placements for black children?

Some commentators contend that MEPA has not been more effective in increasing the adoption of black children because the practice of race matching persists. Judges often still consider race as a relevant factor in child custody decisions. Many courts take the position that the legislation applies only to child welfare agencies, and not to judges. Another problem is the ease with which agencies can avoid enforcement by implicitly using race when weighing any of the myriad other factors that go into the best interest analysis. This is further compounded by the fact that there is no institutional incentive for agencies and government to follow the spirit of the law. Many DHHS officials support race matching and opposed the amendment to the law in the first place. Do these factors suggest that MEPA should be enforced more vigorously? Or perhaps it is simply not possible to fully remove race from the adoption process. Or perhaps the resistance of social work professionals to MEPA suggests that a colorblind adoption process isn't really in children's best interest.

Given the practical difficulties of removing race from the adoption process, would it be preferable to expand recruitment of racial minority families to adopt racial minority children? Should the MEPA provision concerning recruitment be enforced more vigorously?

10. *Institutional Competency.* The MEPA materials raise a broad question that often arises in race-related controversies: Who is the best and most appropriate decision maker? Should courts extend the constitutional mandate of nondiscrimination to the placement of children? Or should legislatures be free to set bounds on the consideration of race? Or should social workers be granted wide discretion to consider race, along with other factors, as they see fit? Who is the best situated to assess the best interests of the children? What are the costs and benefits of allowing discretion on the part of a judge or a social worker? Will either consider race too much or too little? Although judges do not want to sit as super adoption agencies, why would a judge be any less qualified to examine racial issues in this context than other areas such as education?

11. *Your MEPA.* Given all that you have read, is race matching a defensible policy? If you had to draft a race matching policy, what would it be? Would you amend MEPA? If so, how?

D. PERSONAL PREFERENCES REVISITED

Just as *Loving v. Virginia* invalidated governmentally imposed restrictions on marrying across racial lines, MEPA invalidates governmentally imposed restrictions on the adoptive placement of children across racial lines. But whereas *Loving* left people free to choose whether, and how much, to value race in their choice of an intimate partner, the prohibition of race matching is more equivocal with respect to personal racial preferences. Adults can choose partners and form relationships beyond the reach of the state. In a state-managed adoption process, in contrast, the government is more closely connected to, and implicated by, the operation of private preferences. The preferences of prospective adoptive parents for a child of a specific race, for example, are given effect within a state-managed process and according to the rules of that process.

Most state laws and policies typically defer to the preferences of prospective adoptive parents. Those who want to adopt a boy, for example, are only presented with boys who are available for adoption. Adoption agencies typically take account of a wide array of prospective parent preferences. Such a process seems neutral and sensible. Yet it can also become tantamount to race matching. *See* R. Richard Banks, *The Multiethnic Placement Act and the Troubling Persistence of Race Matching*, 38 Capital Univ.L.Rev. 271 (2009)

In one widely noted enforcement action, the Department of Health and Human Services concluded that the South Carolina Department of Social Services had violated MEPA by granting prospective adoptive parents' racial preferences greater deference than other sorts of preferences (e.g., preferences related to the age or sex of the child). Given that most prospective adoptive parents who express a racial preference want a child of the same race as they are, granting deference to such preferences could function as an indirect or covert means of race matching. The adoption agency might defer to and indeed facilitate such preferences precisely because they tend to lead to same-race families. The agency would be attempting to evade MEPA by claiming, in essence, that "we only place children with parents of the same race because that is what the parents want." The Department of Health and Human Services made clear that such covert forms of race matching are no more permissible than more overt practices.

But what about a preference policy that is not implemented as an indirect means of race matching? Should it be permissible for an agency to treat prospective adoptive parents' racial preferences the same as any other characteristics they would desire in a child? Would such a policy be consistent with MEPA, even if it results in very few children being placed across racial lines? For an examination of adoption agencies' facilitation of adoptive parents' racial preferences, *see* R. Richard Banks, *The Color of Desire: Fulfilling Adoptive Parents' Racial Preferences through Discriminatory State Action*, 107 Yale L.J. 875 (1998).

There is also a question about the moral permissibility of parents' wanting a child of a particular race. As was discussed in the dating context, preferences may be both legally permissible and morally objectionable. The fact that one is free to embrace an ethos of, say, white supremacy in one's private life does not mean that one should do so, or should be free from moral censure if one chooses to do so.

Is there anything morally objectionable about a couple wanting to adopt a child that is the same race as they are? Consider, for example, the case of Chief Justice John Roberts, who, along with his wife, adopted two white children who were born in Ireland, notwithstanding the fact that there were likely many African American children in Washington D.C. who were available for adoption at the time. Assuming that Chief Justice Roberts actually preferred to adopt a white child, is there any tension between that desire and his frequently expressed commitment to color blindness?

Race preferences may also run in the other direction as well. A number of white celebrities, for example, Sandra Bullock and Angelina Jolie, have received substantial publicity around their decisions to adopt black or other non-white children. What should we make of the role of race in such stories? Does adopting a black child make the parent seem "cool" or "hip"? Should it?

Finally, prospective parents sometimes express a preference not about race so much as complexion. How do such preferences compare to racial preferences? Is there anything troubling, say, about a black couple that wants to adopt a black child provided the child isn't "too dark"? Or too light? What are the various reasons why a couple might accord weight to a child's complexion? Which reasons seem okay to you, and which are troubling?

* * *

Individuals' preferences for particular types of children are also expressed and regulated through the processes of assisted reproduction. Commercial establishments provide eggs and sperm to enable childbearing. Prospective parents select eggs or sperm based on the characteristics of the donor. Donor traits that are typically considered include height, weight, education, occupation, religion, ethnic origin, facial features, eye and hair color, hair texture, skin tone, and race. While prospective parent preferences vary, some traits are generally more valued than others. Most prospective parents prefer the eggs or sperm of donors who are well educated and white. How should sperm/egg banks treat race in this process? Consider 3 possibilities:

1: Race is prohibited as a basis for decision-making. Prospective parents cannot select on the basis of race and are not given information about race.

2: Race is treated the same as other characteristics that are of primary importance to prospective parents. For example, clients would be able to conduct searches and sort results on the basis of key characteristics, including race.

3: Race is treated the same as other characteristics that are of secondary importance to prospective parents. Clients would not be able to conduct searches or sort results on the basis of such characteristics, but they would be given information about those characteristics.

Which of these approaches seems preferable to you? For a provocative discussion of race and assisted reproduction, *see* Dov Fox, *Racial Classification and Assisted Reproduction*, 118 Yale L.J. 1844 (2009).

E. THE PLACEMENT OF INDIAN CHILDREN

In 1978 Congress enacted the Indian Child Welfare Act (ICWA) to govern the placement of Indian children (defined as "any unmarried person who is under age eighteen and is either (a) a member of an Indian tribe or (b) is eligible for membership in an Indian tribe and is the biological child of a member of an Indian tribe."). ICWA, like MEPA, aims to further the best interests of minority children, but it takes an approach precisely counter to the nondiscrimination mandate of MEPA. ICWA establishes a set of placement preferences to govern the selection of adoptive or foster parents for Indian children in state court proceedings. Absent good cause to the contrary, ICWA directs that adoptive placements be made preferentially to (1) a member of the child's extended family, (2) other members of the same tribe, or (3) other Indian families. A similar preference scheme applies for foster care placements. ICWA's placement preferences are not absolute. A state court can decline to apply them if there is "good cause to the contrary," which may be satisfied by the request of the biological parents, as well as other reasons.

Nonetheless, in prescribing the same sort of matching policy that MEPA prohibits, ICWA is similar to race matching, and raises an analogous issue: Are children best served by being placed within "their" group? As you work through the rest of the chapter, you should consider whether the arguments in favor of a matching policy are stronger, weaker, or the same with Indian children as compared to black and biracial children.

ICWA is premised explicitly on two additional concerns that are often implicit in much of the debate about race matching. One is the risk that children from Indian families will be removed without adequate cause. Prior governmental policies had resulted in the disproportionate removal of children from Indian families and their placement with white families. The other concern is to bolster the group to which Indian children "belong," tribes whose survival has been jeopardized by the removal of so many children.

In enacting MEPA, Congress found:

(3)   that there is no resource that is more vital to the continued existence and integrity of Indian tribes than their children;

(4)   that an alarmingly high percentage of Indian families are broken up by the removal, often unwarranted, of their children from them by nontribal public and private agencies and that an alarmingly high percentage of such children are placed in non-Indian foster and adoptive homes and institutions; and

(5)   that the States, exercising their recognized jurisdiction over Indian child custody proceedings through administrative and judicial bodies, have often failed to recognize the essential tribal relations of Indian people and the cultural and social standards prevailing in Indian communities and families.

The Congressional Declaration of policy accompanying the law stated that:

The Congress hereby declares that it is the policy of this Nation to protect the best interests of Indian children and to promote the stability and security of Indian tribes and families by the establishment of minimum Federal standards for the removal of Indian children from their families and the placement of such children in foster or adoptive homes which will reflect the unique values of Indian culture, and by providing for assistance to Indian tribes in the operation of child and family service programs.

Similarly, the House Report accompanying the law stated that ICWA "seeks to protect the rights of the Indian child as an Indian and the rights of the Indian community and tribe in retaining its children in its society."

Research had shown that as many as 1/3 of Indians had been separated from their families and placed with adoptive or foster families or in institutions. Ninety percent of the children were placed in non-Indian settings. The wholesale removal of Indian children from their families also undermined the stability of Indian tribes, in some cases threatening their very existence. In Congress's view, the removal of Indian children from their families in many cases reflected a failure to appreciate distinctive Indian values, in which, for example, children learned to look after themselves earlier than children raised in white communities, and were more often than white children cared for by people who were not members of their biological family.

In addition to the preference scheme, ICWA governs the placement of Indian children in two other ways. ICWA accords tribes either exclusive or concurrent jurisdiction over cases involving the placement of Indian children. And for proceedings in state courts, the Act creates special, more difficult to satisfy, standards for the involuntary removal of Indian children from their parents and placement with foster or adoptive families.

The Supreme Court has only heard two cases under ICWA, both of which are examined below. The first case, *Mississippi Band of Choctaw Indians v. Holyfield*, concerns the jurisdictional provision of the statute.

1.   TRIBAL JURISDICTION

Mississippi Band of Choctaw Indians v. Holyfield

Supreme Court of the United States, 1989.
490 U.S. 30.

■ JUSTICE BRENNAN delivered the opinion of the Court.

This appeal requires us to construe the provisions of the Indian Child Welfare Act that establish exclusive tribal jurisdiction over child custody proceedings involving Indian children domiciled on the tribe's reservation.

* * *

The Indian Child Welfare Act of 1978 (ICWA), was the product of rising concern in the mid-1970's over the consequences to Indian children, Indian families, and Indian tribes of abusive child welfare practices that resulted in the separation of large numbers of Indian children from their families and tribes through adoption or foster care placement, usually in non-Indian homes. Senate oversight hearings in 1974 yielded numerous examples, statistical data, and expert testimony documenting what one witness called "[t]he wholesale removal of Indian children from their homes, . . . the most tragic aspect of Indian life today." Studies undertaken by the Association on American Indian Affairs in 1969 and 1974, and presented in the Senate hearings, showed that 25 to 35% of all Indian children had been separated from their families and placed in adoptive families, foster care, or institutions. Adoptive placements counted significantly in this total: in the State of Minnesota, for example, one in eight Indian children under the age of 18 was in an adoptive home, and during the year 1971–1972 nearly one in every four infants under one year of age was placed for adoption. The adoption rate of Indian children was eight times that of non-Indian children. Approximately 90% of the Indian placements were in non-Indian homes. A number of witnesses also testified to the serious adjustment problems encountered by such children during adolescence, as well as the impact of the adoptions on Indian parents and the tribes themselves . . . there was also considerable emphasis [in Congressional testimony] on the impact on the tribes themselves of the massive removal of their children. For example, Mr. Calvin Isaac, Tribal Chief of the Mississippi Band of Choctaw Indians and representative of the National Tribal Chairmen's Association, testified as follows:

> "Culturally, the chances of Indian survival are significantly reduced if our children, the only real means for the transmission of the tribal heritage, are to be raised in non-Indian homes and denied exposure to the ways of their People. Furthermore, these practices seriously undercut the tribes' ability to continue as self-governing communities. Probably in no area is it more important that tribal sovereignty be respected than in an area as socially and culturally determinative as family relationships."

Chief Isaac also summarized succinctly what numerous witnesses saw as the principal reason for the high rates of removal of Indian children:

> "One of the most serious failings of the present system is that Indian children are removed from the custody of their natural parents by nontribal government authorities who have no basis for intelligently evaluating the cultural and social premises underlying Indian home life and childrearing. Many of the individuals who decide the fate of our children are at best ignorant of our cultural values; and at worst contemptful of the Indian way and convinced that removal, usually to a non-Indian household or institution, can only benefit an Indian child."

. . . At the heart of the ICWA are its provisions concerning jurisdiction over Indian child custody proceedings. Section 1911 lays out a dual jurisdictional scheme. Section 1911(a) establishes exclusive jurisdiction in the tribal courts for proceedings concerning an Indian child "who resides or is domiciled within the reservation of such tribe". [The statute] creates concurrent but presumptively tribal jurisdiction in the case of children not domiciled on the reservation: on petition of either parent or the tribe, state-court proceedings for foster care placement or termination of parental rights are to be transferred to the tribal court, except in cases of "good cause," objection by either parent, or declination of jurisdiction by the tribal court.

* * *

This case involves the status of twin babies, known for our purposes as B. B. and G. B., who were born out of wedlock on December 29, 1985. Their mother, J. B., and father, W. J., were both enrolled members of appellant Mississippi Band of Choctaw Indians (Tribe), and were residents and domiciliaries of the Choctaw Reservation in Neshoba County, Mississippi. J. B. gave birth to the twins in Gulfport, Harrison County, Mississippi, some 200 miles from the reservation. On January 10, 1986, J. B. executed a consent-to-adoption form before the Chancery Court of Harrison County. W. J. signed a similar form. On January 16, appellees Orrey and Vivian Holyfield filed a petition for adoption in the same court, and the chancellor issued a Final Decree of Adoption on January 28. Despite the court's apparent awareness of the ICWA, the adoption decree contained no reference to it, nor to the infants' Indian background.

Two months later the Tribe moved in the Chancery Court to vacate the adoption decree on the ground that under the ICWA exclusive jurisdiction was vested in the tribal court. On July 14, 1986, the court overruled the motion, holding that the Tribe "never obtained exclusive jurisdiction over the children involved herein. . . . " The court's one-page opinion relied on two facts in reaching that conclusion. The court noted first that the twins' mother "went to some efforts to see that they were born outside the confines of the Choctaw Indian Reservation" and that the parents had promptly arranged for the adoption by the Holyfields. Second, the court stated: "At no time from the birth of these children to the present date have either of them resided on or physically been on the Choctaw Indian Reservation."

The Supreme Court of Mississippi affirmed. The sole issue in this case is, as the Supreme Court of Mississippi recognized, whether the twins were "domiciled" on the reservation.

A

The meaning of "domicile" in the ICWA is, of course, a matter of Congress' intent. The ICWA itself does not define it. The initial question we must confront is whether there is any reason to believe that Congress intended the ICWA definition of "domicile" to be a matter of state law. . . .

First, and most fundamentally, the purpose of the ICWA gives no reason to believe that Congress intended to rely on state law for the definition of a critical term; quite the contrary. It is clear from the very text of the ICWA, not to mention its legislative history and the hearings that led to its enactment, that Congress was concerned with the rights of Indian families and Indian communities vis-a-vis state authorities. More specifically, its purpose was, in part, to make clear that in certain situations the state courts did *not* have jurisdiction over child custody proceedings. Indeed, the congressional findings that are a part of the statute demonstrate that Congress perceived the States and their courts as partly responsible for the problem it intended to correct.

Second, Congress could hardly have intended the lack of nationwide uniformity that would result from state-law definitions of domicile. . . . We therefore think it beyond dispute that Congress intended a uniform federal law of domicile for the ICWA.

B

The holding of the Supreme Court of Mississippi that the twin babies were not domiciled on the Choctaw Reservation appears to have rested on two findings of fact by the trial court: (1) that they had never been physically present there, and (2) that they were "voluntarily surrendered" by their parents. . . .

. . . "Domicile" is not necessarily synonymous with "residence," and one can reside in one place but be domiciled in another. For adults, domicile is established by physical presence in a place in connection with a certain state of mind concerning one's intent to remain there. . . . Since most minors are legally incapable of forming the requisite intent to establish a domicile, their domicile is determined by that of their parents. In the case of an illegitimate child, that has traditionally meant the domicile of its mother. . . .

It is undisputed in this case that the domicile of the mother (as well as the father) has been, at all relevant times, on the Choctaw Reservation. Thus, it is clear that at their birth the twin babies were also domiciled on the reservation, even though they themselves had never been there. . . .

Nor can the result be any different simply because the twins were "voluntarily surrendered" by their mother. Tribal jurisdiction under § 1911(a) was not meant to be defeated by the actions of individual members of the tribe, for Congress was concerned not solely about the interests of Indian children and families, but also about the impact on the tribes themselves of the large numbers of Indian children adopted by non-Indians. The numerous prerogatives accorded the tribes through the ICWA's substantive provisions, must, accordingly, be seen as a means of protecting not only the interests of individual Indian children and families, but also of the tribes themselves.

In addition, it is clear that Congress' concern over the placement of Indian children in non-Indian homes was based in part on evidence of the detrimental impact on the children themselves of such placements outside their culture. . . .

. . . The appellees in this case argue strenuously that the twins' mother went to great lengths to give birth off the reservation so that her children could be adopted by the Holyfields. But that was precisely part of Congress' concern. Permitting individual members of the tribe to avoid tribal exclusive jurisdiction by the simple expedient of giving birth off the reservation would, to a large extent, nullify the purpose the ICWA was intended to accomplish. . . .

We are not unaware that over three years have passed since the twin babies were born and placed in the Holyfield home, and that a court deciding their fate today is not writing on a blank slate in the same way it would have in January 1986. Three years' development of family ties cannot be undone, and a separation at this point would doubtless cause considerable pain.

Whatever feelings we might have as to where the twins should live, however, it is not for us to decide that question. We have been asked to decide the legal question of *who* should make the custody determination concerning these children—not what the outcome of that determination should be. The law places that decision in the hands of the Choctaw tribal court. . . .

■ JUSTICE STEVENS, with whom THE CHIEF JUSTICE and JUSTICE KENNEDY join, dissenting.

The parents of these twin babies unquestionably expressed their intention to have the state court exercise jurisdiction over them. J. B. gave birth to the twins at a hospital 200 miles from the reservation, even though a closer hospital was available. Both parents gave their written advance consent to the adoption and, when the adoption was later challenged by the Tribe, they reaffirmed their desire that the Holyfields adopt the two children. . . .

. . . To preclude parents domiciled on a reservation from deliberately invoking the adoption procedures of state court, the Court gives "domicile" a meaning that Congress could not have intended and distorts the delicate balance between individual rights and group rights recognized by the ICWA.

The Act gives Indian tribes certain rights, not to restrict the rights of parents of Indian children, but to complement and help effect them. The Indian tribe may petition to transfer an action in state court to the tribal court, but the Indian parent may veto the transfer. The Act provides for a tribal right of notice and intervention in involuntary proceedings but not in voluntary ones. Finally, the tribe may petition the court to set aside a parental termination action upon a showing that the provisions of the ICWA that are designed to protect parents and Indian children have been violated.

While the Act's substantive and procedural provisions effect a major change in state child custody proceedings, its jurisdictional provision is designed primarily to preserve tribal sovereignty over the domestic relations of tribe members and to confirm a developing line of cases which held that the tribe's exclusive jurisdiction could not be defeated by the temporary presence of an Indian child off the reservation. . . .

If J. B. and W. J. had established a domicile off the reservation, the state courts would have been required to give effect to their choice of jurisdiction; there should not be a different result when the parents have not changed their own domicile, but have expressed an unequivocal intent to establish a domicile for their children off the reservation. . . .

The interpretation of domicile adopted by the Court . . . renders any custody decision made by a state court forever suspect, susceptible to challenge at any time as void for having been entered in the absence of jurisdiction. Finally, it forces parents of Indian children who desire to invoke state-court jurisdiction to establish a domicile off the reservation. Only if the custodial parent has the wealth and ability to establish a domicile off the reservation will the parent be able to use the processes of [the] state court. . . .

NOTES AND QUESTIONS

1. *Applying the Child's Best Interest Standard.* Can *Holyfeld* plausibly be justified in terms of the best interest of the child standard? Notwithstanding the parents' desire to have their child raised by a non-Indian family, is it plausibly in the child's best interest for the tribe to exercise jurisdiction over the placement decision? Would the children suffer if they were raised off the reservation?

2. *Children as Resources.* As Professor Solangel Maldonado has noted, the Choctaw tribe litigated this case to the Supreme Court in part because of its belief that its survival was at risk:

> The Tribe was also concerned that allowing the twins to be adopted by a non-Choctaw family could compromise its ability to sustain itself. The Tribe's requirements for tribal membership are stricter than those of most tribes. Tribal members must have at least fifty percent Mississippi Choctaw blood; indeed, most enrolled members are full-blooded Choctaws. As a result of its stringent enrollment requirements, the Tribe's membership is relatively small (less than 5000 members) . . . [T]he loss of two full-blooded Choctaws to a non-Indian family would have had a greater impact on the Choctaw Tribe than a similar loss to nations without a minimum blood quantum, since those nations are open to a significantly larger potential membership.

Solangel Maldonado, *Race, Culture, and Adoption: Lessons from* Mississippi Band of Choctaw Indians v. Holyfield, 17 Colum. J. Gender & L. 1, 13–14 (2008). Is it appropriate to view children as a "resource" of Indian tribes?

Should the law permit the tribe to use a child to further its interest in sustaining itself?

3. ***Birth Parents Versus Adoptive Parents.*** Even supposing the legitimacy of the tribe's interest, how should that interest be balanced against the unquestionably legitimate interest of the birth parents in selecting an adoptive parent? On the one hand, the parents clearly wanted their child to be adopted off the reservation, by a non-Indian family, and drove 200 miles partly in furtherance of that desire. Yet, on the other hand, as the Supreme Court noted, the parents remained subject to the exclusive jurisdiction of the tribal court because they had not established domicile off the reservation. Does the Court's resolution strike the right balance? Is it fair to the parents to circumscribe their parental authority in that fashion? Would it matter whether the parents remained on the reservation because they could not afford to leave, or because they preferred that life for themselves (though not for their children)?

4.   While the exclusive jurisdiction provision at issue in *Holyfeld* turned on whether the child resided or was domiciled on the reservation, the statute also grants tribal courts concurrent jurisdiction when the Indian child is not domiciled or residing on the reservation. The tribe can petition for a transfer of the case to the tribal court, but the state court may decline to transfer the case, if there is good cause not to do so or if either parent objects to the transfer. Does this arrangement seem justified to you? Why or why not?

EXERCISE

Guidelines from the Bureau of Indian Affairs (BIA) state that good cause not to transfer a proceeding may exist if:

a.   [T]he Indian child's tribe does not have a tribal court as defined by the Act to which the case can be transferred,

b.   if any of the following circumstances exists:

   i.   The proceeding was at an advanced stage when the petition to transfer was received and the petitioner did not file the petition promptly after receiving notice of the hearing.

   ii.   The Indian child is over twelve years of age and objects to the transfer.

   iii.   The evidence necessary to decide the case could not be adequately presented in the tribal court without undue hardship to the parties or the witnesses.

   iv.   The parents of a child over five years of age are not available and the child has had little or no contact with the child's tribe or members of the child's tribe.

c.   Socio-economic conditions and the perceived adequacy of tribal or Bureau of Indian Affairs social services or judicial systems may not be considered in a determination that good cause exists.

d.   The burden of establishing good cause to the contrary shall be on the party opposing the transfer.

Consider the following scenario (drawn from an actual case):

On November 29, 1982, the Indian tribal court filed a motion in district court to transfer to its jurisdiction a proceeding concerning an Indian child born to a mother who did not live on the reservation. The state social work agency was placing the child for adoption. The child's mother had a history of drug and alcohol abuse. She had been placed in jail on approximately fifteen occasions and had attempted to commit suicide at least four times. She had also been divorced from the same man twice for reasons relating to his alcohol use and physical abuse of her, and she now intended to remarry him. Testimony by a psychologist and child protective child service worker for the county indicated that, beyond a reasonable doubt, the custody of the child by the mother would likely result in serious emotional and physical harm to the child.

The district court judge is considering both an adoption petition by a stable non-Indian family and the transfer motion. Is it permissible for the judge to decline the transfer in this case, based on her view of the best interests of the child? You are the law clerk handling this case. How would you construct a memo to your judge on this issue?

2.   THE TERMINATION OF PARENTAL RIGHTS

The only other ICWA case to be decided by the Supreme Court, which is examined below, concerns the termination of parental rights.

Adoptive Couple v. Baby Girl

Supreme Court of the United States, 2013.
133 S.Ct. 2552.

■ JUSTICE ALITO delivered the opinion of the Court.

This case is about a little girl (Baby Girl) who is classified as an Indian because she is 1.2% (3/256) Cherokee. Because Baby Girl is classified in this way, the South Carolina Supreme Court held that certain provisions of the federal Indian Child Welfare Act of 1978 required her to be taken, at the age of 27 months, from the only parents she had ever known and handed over to her biological father, who had attempted to relinquish his parental rights and who had no prior contact with the child. The provisions of the federal statute at issue here do not demand this result.

In this case, Birth Mother (who is predominantly Hispanic) and Biological Father (who is a member of the Cherokee Nation) became engaged in December 2008. One month later, Birth Mother informed Biological Father, who lived about four hours away, that she was pregnant. After learning of the pregnancy, Biological Father asked Birth Mother to move up the date of the wedding. He also refused to provide any financial support until after the two had married. The couple's relationship deteriorated, and Birth Mother broke off the engagement in May 2009. In June, Birth Mother sent Biological Father a text message asking if he would rather pay child support or relinquish his parental rights. Biological Father responded via text message that he relinquished his rights.

Birth Mother then decided to put Baby Girl up for adoption. Because Birth Mother believed that Biological Father had Cherokee Indian heritage, her attorney contacted the Cherokee Nation to determine whether Biological Father was formally enrolled. The inquiry letter misspelled Biological Father's first name and incorrectly stated his birthday, and the Cherokee Nation responded that, based on the information provided, it could not verify Biological Father's membership in the tribal records.

Working through a private adoption agency, Birth Mother selected Adoptive Couple, non-Indians living in South Carolina, to adopt Baby Girl. Adoptive Couple supported Birth Mother both emotionally and financially throughout her pregnancy. Adoptive Couple was present at Baby Girl's birth in Oklahoma on September 15, 2009, and Adoptive Father even cut the umbilical cord. The next morning, Birth Mother signed forms relinquishing her parental rights and consenting to the adoption. Adoptive Couple initiated adoption proceedings in South Carolina a few days later, and returned there with Baby Girl. After returning to South Carolina, Adoptive Couple allowed Birth Mother to visit and communicate with Baby Girl.

It is undisputed that, for the duration of the pregnancy and the first four months after Baby Girl's birth, Biological Father provided no financial assistance to Birth Mother or Baby Girl, even though he had the ability to do so. Indeed, Biological Father "made no meaningful attempts to assume his responsibility of parenthood" during this period. App. to Pet. for Cert. 122a (Sealed; internal quotation marks omitted).

Approximately four months after Baby Girl's birth, Adoptive Couple served Biological Father with notice of the pending adoption. (This was the first notification that they had provided to Biological Father regarding the adoption proceeding.) Biological Father signed papers stating that he accepted service and that he was "not contesting the adoption." But Biological Father later testified that, at the time he signed the papers, he thought that he was relinquishing his rights to Birth Mother, not to Adoptive Couple.

Biological Father contacted a lawyer the day after signing the papers, and subsequently requested a stay of the adoption proceedings. In the adoption proceedings, Biological Father sought custody and stated that he did not consent to Baby Girl's adoption. Moreover, Biological Father took a paternity test, which verified that he was Baby Girl's biological father.

A trial took place in the South Carolina Family Court in September 2011, by which time Baby Girl was two years old. The Family Court concluded that Adoptive Couple had not carried the heightened burden under [ICWA] § 1912(f) of proving that Baby Girl would suffer serious emotional or physical damage if Biological Father had custody. The Family Court therefore denied Adoptive Couple's petition for adoption and awarded custody to Biological Father. On December 31, 2011, at the age of 27 months, Baby Girl was handed over to Biological Father, whom she had never met.

The South Carolina Supreme Court affirmed the Family Court's denial of the adoption and the award of custody to Biological Father. The court held that two separate provisions of the ICWA barred the termination of Biological Father's parental rights. *First*, the court held that Adoptive Couple had not shown that "active efforts ha[d] been made to provide remedial services and rehabilitative programs designed to prevent the breakup of the Indian family." § 1912(d); *Second*, the court concluded that Adoptive Couple had not shown that Biological Father's "custody of Baby Girl would result in serious emotional or physical harm to her beyond a reasonable doubt."

A

Section 1912(f) addresses the involuntary termination of parental rights with respect to an Indian child. Specifically, § 1912(f) provides that "[n]o termination of parental rights may be ordered in such proceeding in the absence of a determination, supported by evidence beyond a reasonable doubt, . . . that the *continued custody* of the child by the parent or Indian custodian is likely to result in serious emotional or physical damage to the child." (Emphasis added.) The South Carolina Supreme Court held that Adoptive Couple failed to satisfy § 1912(f) because they did not make a heightened showing that Biological Father's "*prospective* legal and physical custody" would likely result in serious damage to the child. That holding was error.

Section 1912(f) conditions the involuntary termination of parental rights on a showing regarding the merits of "*continued* custody of the child by the parent." (Emphasis added.) The adjective "continued" plainly refers to a pre-existing state. . . . The phrase "continued custody" therefore refers to custody that a parent already has (or at least had at some point in the past). As a result, § 1912(f) does not apply in cases where the Indian parent *never* had custody of the Indian child.

Our reading of § 1912(f) comports with the statutory text demonstrating that the primary mischief the ICWA was designed to counteract was the unwarranted *removal* of Indian children from Indian families due to the cultural insensitivity and biases of social workers and state courts. The statutory text expressly highlights the primary problem that the statute was intended to solve: "an alarmingly high percentage of Indian families [were being] broken up by the *removal*, often unwarranted, of their children from them by nontribal public and private agencies." § 1901(4) (emphasis added); In sum, when, as here, the adoption of an Indian child is voluntarily and lawfully initiated by a non-

Indian parent with sole custodial rights, the ICWA's primary goal of preventing the unwarranted removal of Indian children and the dissolution of Indian families is not implicated.

Under our reading of § 1912(f), Biological Father should not have been able to invoke § 1912(f) in this case, because he had never had legal or physical custody of Baby Girl as of the time of the adoption proceedings.

Section 1912(d) provides that "[a]ny party" seeking to terminate parental rights to an Indian child under state law "shall satisfy the court that active efforts have been made to provide remedial services and rehabilitative programs designed *to prevent the breakup of the Indian family* and that these efforts have proved unsuccessful." (Emphasis added.) The South Carolina Supreme Court found that Biological Father's parental rights could not be terminated because Adoptive Couple had not demonstrated that Biological Father had been provided remedial services in accordance with § 1912(d). We disagree.

Consistent with the statutory text, we hold that § 1912(d) applies only in cases where an Indian family's "breakup" would be precipitated by the termination of the parent's rights. The term "breakup" refers in this context to "[t]he discontinuance of a relationship." . . . [W]hen an Indian parent abandons an Indian child prior to birth and that child has never been in the Indian parent's legal or physical custody, there is no "relationship" that would be "discontinu[ed]"—and no "effective entity" that would be "end[ed]"—by the termination of the Indian parent's rights. In such a situation, the "breakup of the Indian family" has long since occurred, and § 1912(d) is inapplicable.

Our interpretation of § 1912(d) is, like our interpretation of § 1912(f), consistent with the explicit congressional purpose of providing certain "standards for the *removal* of Indian children from their families." § 1902

Section 1912(d) is a sensible requirement when applied to state social workers who might otherwise be too quick to remove Indian children from their Indian families. It would, however, be unusual to apply § 1912(d) in the context of an Indian parent who abandoned a child prior to birth and who never had custody of the child. The decision below illustrates this point. The South Carolina Supreme Court held that § 1912(d) mandated measures such as "attempting to stimulate [Biological] Father's desire to be a parent." 398 S. C., at 647, 731 S. E. 2d, at 562. But if prospective adoptive parents were required to engage in the bizarre undertaking of "stimulat[ing]" a biological father's "desire to be a parent," it would surely dissuade some of them from seeking to adopt Indian children. And this would, in turn, unnecessarily place vulnerable Indian children at a unique disadvantage in finding a permanent and loving home, even in cases where neither an Indian parent nor the relevant tribe objects to the adoption.

In sum, the South Carolina Supreme Court erred in finding that § 1912(d) barred termination of Biological Father's parental rights.

* * *

The Indian Child Welfare Act was enacted to help preserve the cultural identity and heritage of Indian tribes, but under the State Supreme Court's reading, the Act would put certain vulnerable children at a great disadvantage solely because an ancestor—even a remote one— was an Indian. As the State Supreme Court read §§ 1912(d) and (f), a biological Indian father could abandon his child *in utero* and refuse any support for the birth mother—perhaps contributing to the mother's decision to put the child up for adoption—and then could play his ICWA trump card at the eleventh hour to override the mother's decision and the child's best interests. If this were possible, many prospective adoptive parents would surely pause before adopting any child who might possibly qualify as an Indian under the ICWA. Such an interpretation would raise equal protection concerns, but the plain text of §§ 1912(f) and (d) makes clear that neither provision applies in the present context. We therefore reverse the judgment of the South Carolina Supreme Court and remand the case for further proceedings not inconsistent with this opinion.

■ JUSTICE THOMAS, concurring. [Omitted.] [Justice Thomas questioned the legitimacy of the Indian Child Welfare Act under the Constitution, and concurred in the judgement because it avoided the constitutional question.]

■ JUSTICE BREYER, concurring.

[T]he statute does not directly explain how to treat an absentee Indian father who had next-to-no involvement with his child in the first few months of her life. That category of fathers may include some who would prove highly unsuitable parents, some who would be suitable, and a range of others in between. Most of those who fall within that category seem to fall outside the scope of the language of 25 U.S.C. §§ 1912(d) and (f). Thus, while I agree that the better reading of the statute is, as the majority concludes, to exclude most of those fathers, I also understand the risk that, from a policy perspective, the Court's interpretation could prove to exclude too many.

Second, we should decide here no more than is necessary. Thus, this case does not involve a father with visitation rights or a father who has paid "all of his child support obligations." Neither does it involve special circumstances such as a father who was deceived about the existence of the child or a father who was prevented from supporting his child. The Court need not, and in my view does not, now decide whether or how §§ 1912(d) and (f) apply where those circumstances are present.

■ JUSTICE SCALIA, dissenting.

The Court's opinion, it seems to me, needlessly demeans the rights of parenthood. It has been the constant practice of the common law to respect the entitlement of those who bring a child into the world to raise that child. We do not inquire whether leaving a child with his parents is "in the best interest of the child." It sometimes is not; he would be better off raised by someone else. But parents have their rights, no less than children do. This father wants to raise his daughter, and the statute amply protects his right to do so. There is no reason in law or policy to dilute that protection.

■ JUSTICE SOTOMAYOR, with whom JUSTICE GINSBURG and JUSTICE KAGAN join, and with whom JUSTICE SCALIA joins in part, dissenting.

[I]n the majority's view, a family bond that does not take custodial form is not a family bond worth preserving from "breakup."

[N]otwithstanding the majority's focus on the perceived parental shortcomings of Birth Father, its reasoning necessarily extends to *all* Indian parents who have never had custody of their children, no matter how fully those parents have embraced the financial and emotional responsibilities of parenting. The majority thereby transforms a statute that was intended to provide uniform federal standards for child custody proceedings involving Indian children and their biological parents into an illogical piecemeal scheme.

ICWA commences with express findings. Congress recognized that "there is no resource that is more vital to the continued existence and integrity of Indian tribes than their children," 25 U.S.C. § 1901(3), and it found that this resource was threatened. State authorities insufficiently sensitive to "the essential tribal relations of Indian people and the cultural and social standards prevailing in Indian communities and families" were breaking up Indian families and moving Indian children to non-Indian homes and institutions.

Consistent with these findings, Congress declared its purpose "to protect the best interests of Indian children and to promote the stability and security of Indian tribes and families by the establishment of minimum Federal standards" applicable to child custody proceedings involving Indian children.

The majority asserts baldly that "when an Indian parent abandons an Indian child prior to birth and that child has never been in the Indian parent's legal or physical custody, there is no 'relationship' that would be 'discontinu[ed]' . . . by the termination of the Indian parent's rights." Says who? Certainly not the statute. Section 1903 recognizes Birth Father as Baby Girl's "parent," and, in conjunction with ICWA's other provisions, it further establishes that their "parent-child relationship" is protected under federal law. In the face of these broad definitions, the majority has no warrant to substitute its own policy views for Congress' by saying that "no 'relationship' " exists between Birth Father and Baby Girl simply because, based on the hotly contested facts of this case, it views their family bond as insufficiently substantial to deserve protection.

[S]ubsection (f), the relevant provision here, is headed "Parental rights termination orders." Subsection (f) reads in its entirety,

> "No termination of parental rights may be ordered in such proceeding in the absence of a determination, supported by evidence beyond a reasonable doubt, including testimony of qualified expert witnesses, that the continued custody of the child by the parent or Indian custodian is likely to result in serious emotional or physical damage to the child." § 1912(f).

The text of the subsection begins by announcing, "[n]o termination of parental rights may be ordered" unless the specified evidentiary showing is made. To repeat, a "termination of parental rights" includes "*any* action resulting in the termination of the parent-child relationship," 25 U.S.C. § 1903(1)(ii) (emphasis added), including the relationship Birth Father, as an ICWA "parent," has with Baby Girl. The majority's reading disregards the Act's sweeping definition of "termination of parental rights," which is not limited to terminations of custodial relationships.

The entire foundation of the majority's argument that subsection (f) does not apply is the lonely phrase "continued custody." It simply cannot bear the interpretive weight the majority would place on it.

With respect to § 1912(d), the majority states that it would be "unusual" to apply a rehabilitation requirement where a natural parent has never had custody of his child. The majority does not support this bare assertion, and in fact state child welfare authorities can and do provide reunification services for biological fathers who have not previously had custody of their children. And notwithstanding the South Carolina Supreme Court's imprecise interpretation of the provision, § 1912(d) does not require the prospective adoptive family to themselves undertake the mandated rehabilitative efforts. Rather, it requires the party seeking termination of parental rights to "satisfy the court that active efforts have been made" to provide appropriate remedial services.

In other words, the prospective adoptive couple have to make an evidentiary showing, not undertake person-to-person remedial outreach. The services themselves might be attempted by the Indian child's Tribe, a state agency, or a private adoption agency. Such remedial efforts are a familiar requirement of child welfare law, including federal child welfare policy.

B

On a more general level, the majority intimates that ICWA grants Birth Father an undeserved windfall: in the majority's words, an "ICWA trump card" he can "play . . . at the eleventh hour to override the mother's decision and the child's best interests." The implicit argument is that Congress could not possibly have intended to recognize a parent-child relationship between Birth Father and Baby Girl that would have to be legally terminated (either by valid consent or involuntary termination) before the adoption could proceed.

But this supposed anomaly is illusory. In fact, the law of at least 15 States did precisely that at the time ICWA was passed. And the law of a number of States still does so.

Without doubt, laws protecting biological fathers' parental rights can lead—even outside the context of ICWA—to outcomes that are painful and distressing for both would-be adoptive families, who lose a much wanted child, and children who must make a difficult transition. On the other hand, these rules recognize that biological fathers have a valid interest in a relationship with their child. And children have a reciprocal interest in knowing their biological parents. These rules also reflect the understanding that the biological bond between a parent and a child is a strong foundation on which a stable and caring relationship may be built. Many jurisdictions apply a custodial preference for a fit natural parent over a party lacking this biological link.

Balancing the legitimate interests of unwed biological fathers against the need for stability in a child's family situation is difficult, to be sure, and States have, over the years, taken different approaches to the problem. Some States, like South Carolina, have opted to hew to the constitutional baseline established by this Court's precedents and do not require a biological father's consent to adoption unless he has provided financial support during pregnancy. Other States, however, have decided to give the rights of biological fathers more robust protection and to afford them consent rights on the basis of their biological link to the child. At the time that ICWA was passed, as noted, over one-fourth of States did so.

ICWA, on a straightforward reading of the statute, is consistent with the law of those States that protected, and protect, birth fathers' rights more vigorously. This reading can hardly be said to generate an anomaly. ICWA, as all acknowledge, was "the product of rising concern . . . [about] abusive child welfare practices that resulted in the separation of large numbers of Indian children from their families." *Holyfield*, 490 U. S., at 32. It stands to reason that the Act would not render the legal status of an Indian father's relationship with his biological child fragile, but would instead grant it a degree of protection commensurate with the more robust state-law standards.

C

The majority also protests that a contrary result to the one it reaches would interfere with the adoption of Indian children. This claim is the most perplexing of all. A central purpose of ICWA is to "promote the stability and security of Indian . . . families," 25 U.S.C. § 1902, in part by countering the trend of placing "an alarmingly high percentage of [Indian] children . . . in non-Indian foster and adoptive homes and institutions." § 1901(4). The Act accomplishes this goal by, first, protecting the familial bonds of Indian parents and children; and, second, establishing placement preferences should an adoption take place, *see* § 1915(a). ICWA does not interfere with the adoption of Indian children except to the extent that it attempts to avert the necessity of adoptive placement and makes adoptions of Indian children by non-Indian families less likely.

The majority may consider this scheme unwise. But no principle of construction licenses a court to interpret a statute with a view to averting the very consequences Congress expressly stated it was trying to bring about. Instead, it is the " 'judicial duty to give faithful meaning to the language Congress adopted in the light of the evident legislative purpose in enacting the law in question.' "

The majority further claims that its reading is consistent with the "primary" purpose of the Act, which in the majority's view was to prevent the dissolution of "intact" Indian families. We may not, however, give effect only to congressional goals we designate "primary" while casting aside others classed as "secondary"; we must apply the entire statute Congress has written. While there are indications that central among Congress' concerns in enacting ICWA was the removal of Indian children from homes in which Indian parents or other guardians had custody of them, Congress also recognized that "there is no resource that is more vital to the continued existence and integrity of Indian tribes than their children," § 1901(3). A tribe's interest in its next generation of citizens is adversely affected by the placement of Indian children in homes with no connection to the tribe, whether or not those children were initially in the custody of an Indian parent.

Moreover, the majority's focus on "intact" families, begs the question of what Congress set out to accomplish with ICWA. In an ideal world, perhaps all parents would be perfect. They would live up to their parental responsibilities by providing the fullest possible financial and emotional support to their children. They would never suffer mental health problems, lose their jobs, struggle with substance dependency, or encounter any of the other multitudinous personal crises that can make it difficult to meet these responsibilities. In an ideal world parents would never become estranged and leave their children caught in the middle. But we do not live in such a world. Even happy families do not always fit the custodial-parent mold for which the majority would reserve IWCA's substantive protections; unhappy families all too often do not. They are families nonetheless. Congress understood as much. ICWA's definitions of "parent" and "termination of parental rights" provided in § 1903 sweep broadly. They should be honored.

* * *

The majority opinion turns § 1912 upside down, reading it from bottom to top in order to reach a conclusion that is manifestly contrary to Congress' express purpose in enacting ICWA: preserving the familial bonds between Indian parents and their children and, more broadly, Indian tribes' relationships with the future citizens who are "vital to [their] continued existence and integrity." § 1901(3).

The majority casts Birth Father as responsible for the painful circumstances in this case, suggesting that he intervened "at the eleventh hour to override the mother's decision and the child's best interests." I have no wish to minimize the trauma of removing a 27-month-old child from her adoptive family. It bears remembering, however, that Birth Father took action to assert his parental rights when Baby Girl was four months old, as soon as he learned of the impending adoption. As the South Carolina Supreme Court recognized, " '[h]ad the mandate of . . . ICWA been followed [in 2010], . . . much potential anguish might have been avoided[;] and in any case the law cannot be applied so as automatically to "reward those who obtain custody, whether lawfully or otherwise, and maintain it during any ensuing (and protracted) litigation." ' "

The majority's hollow literalism distorts the statute and ignores Congress' purpose in order to rectify a perceived wrong that, while heartbreaking at the time, was a correct application of federal law and that in any case cannot be undone. Baby Girl has now resided with her father for 18 months. However difficult it must have been for her to leave Adoptive Couple's home when she was just over 2 years old, it will be equally devastating now if, at the age of 3½, she is again removed from her home and sent to live halfway across the country. Such a fate is not foreordained, of course. But it can be said with certainty that the anguish this case has caused will only be compounded by today's decision.

NOTES AND QUESTIONS

1. **Best Interest of the Child.** A central issue in any child placement case concerns the best interest of the child standard. Does the Court's decision further the best interests of Baby Girl? Of Indian children more generally? Would the dissent's approach do so? More specifically, does the effort to keep children within the Indian community further the interests of those individual children?

2. **Parental Rights.** A central issue in the Baby Girl case concerns the legal rights of the unwed father. As even the dissent notes, states vary in the protection they accord an unwed father who has never fulfilled any of the duties of a parent. The Court's decision denies the unwed father much protection, while the dissent's position would grant the father legal rights much stronger than if he was not an Indian. (Under state law, the biological father's consent to the adoption would not have been required.) Which decision do you think is the more justifiable interpretation of ICWA? Which is the better policy? Justice Scalia suggests that the father's parental rights should be respected even if doing so is not in the best interests of the child. Do you agree?

3.   *Tribal Group Interests.* The dissent gives great weight to the goal of keeping Indian children with Indian parents, while the majority is disinclined create rules that would discourage families from adopting Indian children. Which interpretation of ICWA is more justifiable? Which would you embrace?

4.   *Clashing Interests.* The guardian ad litem for the child recommended that the child be placed with the adoptive parents. Based on the guardian's investigation and interviews with the parties, the guardian determined that placement with the adoptive parents would further the child's best interest. If, as the guardian believed, the interests of the child, on the one hand, and of the parents and tribe on the other, were incompatible, how should the competing interests be balanced?

5.   *Existing Indian Family Exception.* The majority's approach—in emphasizing that no existing Indian family was disrupted—is consistent with a means of limiting the reach of ICWA that a number of courts have explicitly invoked: the Existing Indian Family Exception. Some courts use this judicially created doctrine to justify not applying ICWA to children who do not have cultural links to a tribe or to an Indian way of life, reasoning that the goals of the statute would not be furthered by application of ICWA in such circumstances. While the majority of states do not apply the exception, some states, including California, Alabama, Louisiana, Kentucky, Indiana, and Missouri, still allow it. Is it appropriate for judges to create this exception to the reach of ICWA?

EXERCISE

If you were a state court judge, would you apply ICWA in the following situation?

> An unwed mother voluntarily placed her child for adoption but then had second thoughts. After the placement of the child with a family, but prior to the adoption being finalized, the mother discovers her Indian heritage, applies for and is granted tribal membership, and then petitions the court to revoke her consent to adoption, which is allowed under ICWA so long as a permanent adoption has not been finalized. The mother has had no contact with the tribe whatsoever other than enrolling and has given no indication that she would raise Baby O. any differently than if she had never learned of her Indian heritage. (State law does not permit non-Indian mothers to revoke consent in similar circumstances.)

3.   RACE AND SOVEREIGNTY

Congress exercises plenary power to legislate with respect to Indian tribes, yet a lingering question about ICWA is whether the application of the statute in certain circumstances may constitute a racial classification, which would be subject to strict scrutiny if challenged as unconstitutional.

The basis for treating the classification of Indians as nonracial is that Indian tribes are semi-sovereign political entities with an interest in self-government and regulating their internal affairs. Thus, in *Morton v. Mancari*, 417 U.S. 535 (1974), the Court rejected the claim that hiring preferences for tribal Indians at the Bureau of Indian Affairs constituted a racial classification. Not only were the preferences limited to the BIA, which itself promoted self-government among the tribes, "[t]he preference, as applied, is granted to Indians not as a discrete racial group, but, rather, as members of quasi-sovereign tribal entities whose lives and activities are governed by the BIA in a unique fashion." The Court went on to observe that "[t]he preference is not directed towards a 'racial' group consisting of 'Indians'; instead, it applies only to members of 'federally recognized' tribes. This operates to exclude many individuals who are racially to be classified as 'Indians.' In this sense, the preference is political rather than racial in nature."

This distinction between a political classification and a racial classification has persisted as a basis for exempting ICWA from the heightened scrutiny applicable to racial classifications. Yet, in the context of ICWA, the two types of classifications are intertwined rather than neatly separable. ICWA defines Indian child with reference to eligibility for tribal membership, yet tribes define eligibility with reference to descent from a tribal member or a specified percentage of Indian "blood," which arguably sounds even more racial. Indeed, the federal government requires tribes to limit membership on the basis of descent. 25 CFR § 83.7(e) (2012).

While most courts have declined to invoke the racial classification rule, in some cases California judges have held ICWA unconstitutional when applied to families in which neither the parents nor the child have any connection to the tribe other than genetically. In *In re Bridget R.*, a California Appeals court ruled that, "[a]ny application of ICWA triggered by an Indian child's genetic heritage, without substantial social, cultural or political affiliations between the child's family and a tribal community, is an application based solely, or at least predominantly, upon race and is subject to strict scrutiny under the equal protection clause." *In re Bridget R.*, 41 Cal. App. 4th 1483, 1492 (Ct. App. 1996).

In *In re Santos Y.*, another California appeals court affirmed the holding of *In re Bridget R.*, holding that,

> Absent social, cultural, and political relationships, or where the relationships are very attenuated, the only basis for applying ICWA rather than state law in dependency proceedings is the child's genetic heritage" . . . a determination based on "blood," on its face invokes strict scrutiny to determine whether the classification serves a compelling governmental interest and is narrowly tailored to achieve that interest.

112 Cal. Rptr. 2d 692, 727, 730 (Cal. 2002).

This issue arises obliquely in the Baby Girl case, where the majority begins its opinion by noting: "This case is about a little girl (Baby Girl) who is classified as an Indian because she is 1.2% (3/256) Cherokee." Although the Court's opinion does not invoke equal protection analysis, it repeatedly mentions the classification of the child as 1.2% Cherokee, as if to emphasize the irrationality of applying the statute in that circumstance. The Court notes, for example, that "under the State Supreme Court's reading, the Act would put certain vulnerable children at a great disadvantage solely because an ancestor—even a remote one—was an Indian." Justice Sotomayor, in dissent, takes issue with "[t]he majority's repeated, analytically unnecessary references to the fact that Baby Girl is 3/256 Cherokee by ancestry [which] do nothing to elucidate its intimation that the statute may violate the Equal Protection Clause as applied here."

In the Baby Girl case, the guardian ad litem for the child had argued that treating her as an Indian child would have amounted to a racial classification. As the guardian ad litem argued in its brief: "The key to whether legislation involving Indians triggers the relaxed review of *Mancari*, or the exacting scrutiny traditionally demanded of classifications based on race, is whether the challenged legislation "relates to Indian land, tribal status, self-government or culture." Williams v. Babbitt, 115 F.3d 657, 664–65 (9th Cir. 1997). When tribal preferences are untethered from tribal land or tribal self-government and simply provide a naked preference based on race, strict scrutiny is imperative. . . . Conferring special privileges on the biological father—or more to the point, special disabilities on a child—simply because of race serves no purpose relating to "Indian self-government," *Mancari*, 417 U.S. at 555.

Do you think that the application of ICWA in the Baby Girl case amounts to a racial classification?

EXERCISES

1.   A.W. and S.W. are the children of Tina, an enrolled Winnebago Indian with 1/4 Winnebago ancestry, and Anthony, a Caucasian. Due to a history of substance abuse, the state removed A.W. and S.W. from the home and began proceedings to terminate their parental rights.

The Winnebago Tribe, a federally recognized tribe, filed a motion to intervene in the proceeding on the grounds that A.W. and S.W. were "Indian Children," under the Iowa ICWA, state legislation complementary to the federal ICWA.

Passed in order to "clarify state policies and procedures regarding implementation" of the federal ICWA, Iowa ICWA provides greater protection to Indian families and tribes, including a broader definition of "Indian Child." The Iowa ICWA defines an "Indian child" as "an unmarried Indian person who is under eighteen years of age or a child who is under eighteen years of age that an Indian tribe identifies as a child of the tribe's community." The state ICWA applies the jurisdictional and substantive preferences of the federal ICWA to all children in this class, without applying the eligibility for tribal membership criterion of the federal law.

Neither A.W. nor S.W. is eligible for membership in the Winnebago Tribe because they are only 1/8 Winnebago, and the Tribe's eligibility policies require 1/4 or more. As such, they do not meet the "Indian Child" standard of the federal ICWA. However, a Winnebago Tribe resolution states: "[F]or purposes of determining the applicability of the Iowa ICWA, any child of an enrolled Winnebago tribal member shall be included as a child of the Winnebago tribal community." Under these criteria, A.W. and S.W. are "Indian Children," due to their enrolled mother, for state ICWA, and thus subject to the provisions of the federal ICWA.

The Guardian At Litem for the children argues that the Iowa ICWA constitutes an impermissible racial classification.

You are a Judge on the Iowa State Supreme Court. Is applying the Iowa ICWA to A.W. and S.W. constitutional?

In the actual case, the Iowa Supreme Court found that application of the Iowa ICWA unconstitutional because it turned on ancestry rather than tribal membership. As such, the classification was not "political," applying only to tribal Indians, but rather racial. Furthermore, the classification "bears insufficient relation to the traditional rationale for upholding federal Indian legislation—advancement of tribal self-government—to be considered a 'political' classification." *In re A.W., 741 N.W.2d 793, 810 (Iowa, 2007).* Since tribes can alter their membership standards, the Winnebago Tribe could have lowered its standard to 1/8 Winnebago blood, making A.W. and S.W. eligible for federal ICWA. Is this significantly different from what happened? Significant enough to justify completely opposite results?

2.   Consider the following scenario:

> Crystal is the daughter of John and Jane. The family lives in New York City. Crystal goes to public school. The family is not religiously observant, but they celebrate holidays like Christmas and Thanksgiving. Both John and Jane are vaguely aware that their grandparents were Indians but have never researched the issue.

> Things went downhill for the family when John lost his job, began drinking, and became abusive to Jane, and once shoved Crystal. Jane in turn became addicted to painkillers to the point at which she was allegedly unable to care for Crystal. State social workers removed Crystal from the home, and three months later moved to terminate the parental rights of both parents. Informed that ICWA makes it more difficult for the state to terminate a parent's rights to an Indian child (compared to a non-Indian child), both parents began researching their ancestral past. Both found that they were eligible for tribal membership, applied, and were enrolled, at which point the parents and tribe moved to intervene.

Would designation of Crystal as an "Indian Child" constitute a racial classification? Should the court apply the Existing Indian Family Exception?

F.   INTERNATIONAL ADOPTION

Two international adoption treaties establish the rights of children up for adoption and set standards for governments to follow to protect these rights. The Convention on the Rights of the Child (CRC) was approved by the United Nations in 1989 and ratified by more than 175 countries. Only the United States and Somalia have failed to adopt the treaty. The CRC recognizes the right to "identity" and creates obligations for the government to protect a child's cultural background, mandating that "when considering [placement] solutions, due regard shall be paid to the desirability of continuity in a child's upbringing and to the child's ethnic, religious, cultural and linguistic background."

The second major international adoption treaty is the Hague Convention on Protection of Children and Cooperation in Respect of Intercountry Adoption. Adopted in 1993 at the Hague Conference, the treaty has been ratified by 75 countries, including the United States. The treaty is intended to protect the rights of children, birth parents, and adoptive parents through the regulation of international adoptions. It acknowledges the importance of a child's identity, requiring that a child's birth country must "give due consideration to the child's upbringing and to his or her ethnic, religious and cultural background" and "determine, on the basis of in particular of the reports relating to the child and the prospective adoptive parents, whether the envisaged placement is in the best interest of the child."

In order to bring the country into compliance with the Hague Convention standards, Congress enacted the Intercountry Adoption Act of 2000. Regulations issued by the State Department, as the designated authority for international adoptions, require that prospective adoptive parents receive ten hours of pre-adoption training on the long-term implications of multi-cultural adoptions, as well as counseling from service providers about their child's cultural, racial, religious, and linguistic background. Thus, while the U.S. government requires consideration of a child's racial and ethnic identity for inter-country adoptions and for the adoption of Indian children, it has expressly prohibited similar considerations for adoptions of racial minority children within the United States. Is the inconsistency of these rules troubling? Or do the different circumstances call for different approaches?

International adoption is subject to an even more fundamental dispute. While some proponents of the practice argue that it performs the vital function of matching children in need to loving and stable families, and should therefore be promoted, others are less sanguine about international adoption. They contend that international adoption is fraught with corruption, improper financial inducements, and misrepresentations or fraud, and argue for more stringent regulation or moratoria to prevent illegal or unethical practices, even if this means suspending or curtailing the opportunity for legal adoptions. Given these contrary perspectives, how would you evaluate the phenomenon of international adoption? What additional information will you require in order to assess the advantages and the disadvantages of it?

CHAPTER 4

PRIMARY EDUCATION AND INTEGRATION

I. INTRODUCTION

In 1954, the Supreme Court proclaimed that "[s]eparate educational facilities are inherently unequal." With its decision in *Brown v. Board of Education*, the Court rejected the system of *de jure* segregation known as Jim Crow. *Brown* represented the crowning achievement of the decades-long effort by the NAACP Legal Defense Fund to topple the regime that had developed in the aftermath of Reconstruction.

Yet, in African Americans' quest for quality schooling, their commitment to integration has long been equivocal. The question of the relationship between integration and quality education has been the subject of debate at least as far back as the early nineteenth century. At that time, for example, the Boston, Massachusetts schools were integrated, but some black parents petitioned for the establishment of separate schools for their children, to circumvent the unfair treatment and outright racism their children suffered at the hands of white teachers and white classmates. Separate schools opened for black students in 1806. But by the 1830s, black parents began to advocate for integrated schools, citing the inferior facilities and ineffective teachers in the black schools, as well as the general absence of state concern for the quality of those schools. A lawsuit brought to end segregated schooling in Boston failed, but in 1855 the Massachusetts governor signed a law prohibiting race as a criterion for school assignment.

Decades later, in the 1930s, renowned scholar W.E.B. DuBois posed the question: Does the Negro need Separate Schools? He answered yes, because "race prejudice in the United States is such that most Negroes cannot receive proper education in white institutions." Aware, and hopeful, that racism might abate, DuBois concluded, "theoretically, the Negro needs neither segregated schools nor mixed schools. What he needs is Education. What he must remember is that there is no magic, either in mixed schools or in segregated schools. . . . Other things being equal, the mixed school is the broader, more natural basis for the education of all youth . . . . But other things are seldom equal." W.E.B. DuBois, *Does the Negro need Separate Schools?*, 4 J. of Negro Education 328 (1935).

Today, our nation's schools are no longer formally segregated, but neither are they fully integrated. Roughly 4 in 10 black and Latino students, for example, attend highly segregated schools, where fewer than 10% of the students are white. Moreover, school integration, once a central goal of social reform and racial justice efforts, has been relegated to the margins of contemporary legal and policy debate.

This chapter traces the rise and fall of the ideal of school integration and asks: Is our inability to realize the integration ideal a tragic failure or a practical accommodation of political realities and personal preferences? What alternatives for promoting educational equality exist, and are they superior to integration?

II. THE USE AND LIMITATIONS OF JUDICIAL POWER TO PROMOTE INTEGRATION

As discussed in Chapter 2, massive resistance arose in response to *Brown*. The Court's decision in *Brown II* ordering lower courts to devise remedies with "all deliberate speed" was understood as permitting jurisdictions to take their time. And the Court allowed them to. As southern districts variously resisted and adopted tepid remedies to achieve integration, the Supreme Court stayed mostly silent, though in *Cooper v. Aaron*, 358 U.S. 1 (1958), it famously ordered officials in Little Rock, Arkansas to desegregate their schools—an order President Eisenhower followed up by calling in the National Guard to secure compliance. The Civil Rights Act of 1964 authorized the federal government to withhold funding from school districts that did not comply with court orders to eliminate segregation, and by the late 1960s, litigation to compel districts to desegregate resumed in earnest.

In *Green v. New Kent County* (1968), the Court confronted a two-school North Carolina district whose only effort to desegregate in response to a lawsuit was to implement a freedom-of-choice plan that assigned every student to attend the (previously segregated) school they had attended the previous year, unless they elected to attend the other school. The Court, in an opinion by Justice Brennan, declared emphatically that school boards operating de jure segregated schools were "clearly charged with the affirmative duty to take whatever steps might be necessary to convert to a unitary system in which racial discrimination would be eliminated root and branch." The Court had little trouble rejecting the district's "freedom-of-choice" plan as insufficient to "effectuate a transition" to a unitary system. "In three years of operation not a single white child has chosen to attend [the black] school and . . . 85% of the Negro children in the system still attend the all-Negro school. In other words, the school system remains a dual system. Rather than further the dismantling of the dual system, the plan has operated simply to burden children and their parents with a responsibility which *Brown II* placed squarely on the School Board." The Court explained: "The burden on a school board today is to come forward with a plan that promises realistically to work, and promises realistically to work *now*." The Court directed the school board to "fashion steps which promise realistically to convert promptly to a system without a "white" school and a "Negro" school, but just schools."

In later decisions, the Court expanded the reach of the desegregation mandate and gave lower courts the power to implement it. In *Swann v. Charlotte-Mecklenburg Board of Education*, 402 U.S. 1 (1971), the Court approved a far-reaching order entered by the district court for the Charlotte metropolitan area. The Court-approved plan rezoned the high school districts so as to promote integration, requiring the busing of African American high school students to a previously all- white high school. The plan also created new attendance zones for elementary and junior high schools, which grouped inner city black schools with outlying white schools.

In order to eliminate "all vestiges of state-imposed segregation," the Court granted the district court substantial remedial power, noting that "the scope of a district court's equitable powers to remedy past wrongs is broad, for breadth and flexibility are inherent in equitable remedies." The Court permitted the district court to use mathematical ratios regarding racial balance as "a starting point in the process of shaping a remedy." The Court reasoned that, in the desegregation process, "[t]he district judge or school authorities should make every effort to achieve the greatest possible degree of actual desegregation and will thus necessarily be concerned with the elimination of one-race schools," perhaps through the use of "an optional majority-to-minority transfer provision." In its effort to desegregate a district, the court may further alter attendance zones "deliberately to accomplish the transfer of Negro students out of formerly segregated Negro schools and transfer of white students to formerly all-Negro schools." In furtherance of that end, the court may order busing of students.

But the Court's endorsement of expansive judicial remedies to create integrated schools came to a halt in the Court's 1974 decision in *Milliken v. Bradley*.

Milliken v. Bradley (Milliken I)

Supreme Court of the United States, 1974.
418 U.S. 717.

■ MR. CHIEF JUSTICE BURGER delivered the opinion of the Court.

The trial of the issue of segregation in the Detroit school system consum[ed] some 41 trial days.

The District Court found that the Detroit Board of Education created and maintained optional attendance zones[1] within Detroit neighborhoods undergoing racial transition and between high school attendance areas of opposite predominant racial compositions. These

---

[1]   Optional zones, sometimes referred to as dual zones or dual overlapping zones, provide pupils living within certain areas a choice of attendance at one of two high schools.

zones, the court found, had the "natural, probable, foreseeable and actual effect" of allowing white pupils to escape identifiably Negro schools. Similarly, the District Court found that Detroit school attendance zones had been drawn along north-south boundary lines despite the Detroit Board's awareness that drawing boundary lines in an east-west direction would result in significantly greater desegregation. Again, the District Court concluded, the natural and actual effect of these acts was the creation and perpetuation of school segregation within Detroit.

The District Court found that in the operation of its school transportation program, which was designed to relieve overcrowding, the Detroit Board had admittedly bused Negro Detroit pupils to predominantly Negro schools which were beyond or away from closer white schools with available space. This practice was found to have continued in recent years despite the Detroit Board's avowed policy, adopted in 1967, of utilizing transportation to increase desegregation.

With respect to the Detroit Board of Education's practices in school construction, the District Court found that Detroit school construction generally tended to have a segregative effect with the great majority of schools being built in either overwhelmingly all-Negro or all-white neighborhoods so that the new schools opened as predominantly one-race schools. Thus, of the 14 schools which opened for use in 1970–1971, 11 opened over 90% Negro and one opened less than 10% Negro.

The District Court also found that the State of Michigan had committed several constitutional violations with respect to the exercise of its general responsibility for, and supervision of, public education.[2] The State, for example, was found to have failed, until the 1971 Session of the Michigan Legislature, to provide authorization or funds for the transportation of pupils within Detroit regardless of their poverty or distance from the school to which they were assigned; during this same period the State provided many neighboring, mostly white, suburban districts the full range of state-supported transportation.

The District Court also held that the acts of the Detroit Board of Education, as a subordinate entity of the State, were attributable to the State of Michigan, thus creating a vicarious liability on the part of the State.

---

[2]   School districts in the State of Michigan are instrumentalities of the State and subordinate to its State Board of Education and legislature. The Constitution of the State of Michigan, Art. 8, § 2, provides in relevant part:

"The legislature shall maintain and support a system of free public elementary and secondary schools as defined by law."

Similarly, the Michigan Supreme Court has stated: "The school district is a State agency. Moreover, it is of legislative creation. . . ." *Attorney General ex rel. Kies v. Lowrey,* 131 Mich. 639, 644, 92 N. W. 289, 290 (1902); " 'Education in Michigan belongs to the State. It is no part of the local self-government inherent in the township or municipality, except so far as the legislature may choose to make it such. The Constitution has turned the whole subject over to the legislature. . . .' " *Attorney General ex rel. Zacharias v. Detroit Board of Education,* 154 Mich. 584, 590, 118 N. W. 606, 609 (1908).

[T]he District Court . . . designated 53 of 85 suburban school districts plus Detroit as the "desegregation area" and appointed a panel to prepare and submit "an effective desegregation plan" for the Detroit schools that would encompass the entire desegregation area.

The Court of Appeals agreed with the District Court that "any less comprehensive a solution than a metropolitan area plan would result in an all black school system immediately surrounded by practically all white suburban school systems, with an overwhelmingly white majority population in the total metropolitan area." The court went on to state that it could "not see how such segregation can be any less harmful to the minority students than if the same result were accomplished within one school district."

Accordingly, the Court of Appeals concluded that "the only feasible desegregation plan involves the crossing of the boundary lines between the Detroit School District and adjacent or nearby school districts for the limited purpose of providing an effective desegregation plan." It reasoned that such a plan would be appropriate because of the State's violations, and could be implemented because of the State's authority to control local school districts. Without further elaboration, and without any discussion of the claims that no constitutional violation by the outlying districts had been shown and that no evidence on that point had been allowed, the Court of Appeals held:

> [The] State has committed de jure acts of segregation and . . . the State controls the instrumentalities whose action is necessary to remedy the harmful effects of the State acts.

An interdistrict remedy was thus held to be "within the equity powers of the District Court."

II

Viewing the record as a whole, it seems clear that the District Court and the Court of Appeals shifted the primary focus from a Detroit remedy to the metropolitan area only because of their conclusion that total desegregation of Detroit would not produce the racial balance which they perceived as desirable. Both courts proceeded on an assumption that the Detroit schools could not be truly desegregated—in their view of what constituted desegregation—unless the racial composition of the student body of each school substantially reflected the racial composition of the population of the metropolitan area as a whole. The metropolitan area was then defined as Detroit plus 53 of the outlying school districts.

The court's analytical starting point was its conclusion that school district lines are no more than arbitrary lines on a map drawn "for political convenience." Boundary lines may be bridged where there has been a constitutional violation calling for interdistrict relief, but the notion that school district lines may be casually ignored or treated as a mere administrative convenience is contrary to the history of public education in our country. No single tradition in public education is more deeply rooted than local control over the operation of schools; local autonomy has long been thought essential both to the maintenance of community concern and support for public schools and to quality of the educational process.

The Michigan educational structure involved in this case, in common with most States, provides for a large measure of local control,[3] and a review of the scope and character of these local powers indicates the extent to which the interdistrict remedy approved by the two courts could disrupt and alter the structure of public education in Michigan. The metropolitan remedy would require, in effect, consolidation of 54 independent school districts historically administered as separate units into a vast new super school district. Entirely apart from the logistical and other serious problems attending large-scale transportation of students, the consolidation would give rise to an array of other problems in financing and operating this new school system. Some of the more obvious questions would be: What would be the status and authority of the present popularly elected school boards? Would the children of Detroit be within the jurisdiction and operating control of a school board elected by the parents and residents of other districts? What board or boards would levy taxes for school operations in these 54 districts constituting the consolidated metropolitan area? What provisions could be made for assuring substantial equality in tax levies among the 54 districts, if this were deemed requisite? What provisions would be made for financing? Would the validity of long-term bonds be jeopardized unless approved by all of the component districts as well as the State? What body would determine that portion of the curricula now left to the discretion of local school boards? Who would establish attendance zones, purchase school equipment, locate and construct new schools, and indeed attend to all the myriad day-to-day decisions that are necessary to school operations affecting potentially more than three-quarters of a million pupils?

---

[3] Under the Michigan School Code of 1955, the local school district is an autonomous political body corporate, operating through a Board of Education popularly elected. *Mich. Comp. Laws §§ 340.27, 340.55, 340.107, 340.148, 340.149, 340.188.* As such, the day-to-day affairs of the school district are determined at the local level in accordance with the plenary power to acquire real and personal property, §§ 340.26, 340.77, 340.113, 340.165, 340.192, 340.352; to hire and contract with personnel, §§ 340.569, 340.574; to levy taxes for operations, § 340.563; to borrow against receipts, § 340.567; to determine the length of school terms, § 340.575; to control the admission of nonresident students, *§ 340.582*; to determine courses of study, § 340.583; to provide a kindergarten program, § 340.584; to establish and operate vocational schools, § 340.585; to offer adult education programs, § 340.586; to establish attendance areas, § 340.589; to arrange for transportation of nonresident students, § 340.591; to acquire transportation equipment, § 340.594; to receive gifts and bequests for educational purposes, § 340.605; to employ an attorney, § 340.609; to suspend or expel students, § 340.613; to make rules and regulations for the operation of schools, § 340.614; to cause to be levied authorized millage, § 340.643a; to acquire property by eminent domain, § 340.711 *et seq.*; and to approve and select textbooks, § 340.882.

[These are] tasks which few, if any, judges are qualified to perform and one which would deprive the people of control of schools through their elected representatives.

The controlling principle consistently expounded in our holdings is that the scope of the remedy is determined by the nature and extent of the constitutional violation. *Swann, 402 U.S., at 16.* Before the boundaries of separate and autonomous school districts may be set aside by consolidating the separate units for remedial purposes or by imposing a cross-district remedy, it must first be shown that there has been a constitutional violation within one district that produces a significant segregative effect in another district. Specifically, it must be shown that racially discriminatory acts of the state or local school districts, or of a single school district have been a substantial cause of interdistrict segregation. Thus an interdistrict remedy might be in order where the racially discriminatory acts of one or more school districts caused racial segregation in an adjacent district, or where district lines have been deliberately drawn on the basis of race. In such circumstances an interdistrict remedy would be appropriate to eliminate the interdistrict segregation directly caused by the constitutional violation. Conversely, without an interdistrict violation and interdistrict effect, there is no constitutional wrong calling for an interdistrict remedy.

The record before us, voluminous as it is, contains evidence of *de jure* segregated conditions only in the Detroit schools; indeed, that was the theory on which the litigation was initially based and on which the District Court took evidence. With no showing of significant violation by the 53 outlying school districts and no evidence of any interdistrict violation or effect, the court went beyond the original theory of the case as framed by the pleadings and mandated a metropolitan area remedy. To approve the remedy ordered by the court would impose on the outlying districts, not shown to have committed any constitutional violation, a wholly impermissible remedy based on a standard not hinted at in *Brown I* and *II* or any holding of this Court.

Disparate treatment of white and Negro students occurred within the Detroit school system, and not elsewhere, and on this record the remedy must be limited to that system.

III

The Court of Appeals . . . held the State derivatively responsible for the Detroit Board's violations on the theory that actions of Detroit as a political subdivision of the State were attributable to the State. Accepting, *arguendo*, the correctness of this finding of state responsibility for the segregated conditions within the city of Detroit, it does not follow that an interdistrict remedy is constitutionally justified or required. With a single exception, discussed later, there has been no showing that either the State or any of the 85 outlying districts engaged in activity that had a cross-district effect. The boundaries of the Detroit School District, which are coterminous with the boundaries of the city of Detroit, were established over a century ago by neutral legislation when the city was incorporated; there is no evidence in the record, nor is there any suggestion by the respondents, that either the original boundaries of the Detroit School District, or any other school district in Michigan, were established for the purpose of creating, maintaining, or perpetuating segregation of races. There is no claim and there is no evidence hinting that petitioner outlying school districts and their predecessors, or the 30-odd other school districts in the tricounty area—but outside the District Court's "desegregation area"—have ever maintained or operated anything but unitary school systems. Unitary school systems have been required for more than a century by the Michigan Constitution as implemented by state law. Where the schools of only one district have been affected, there is no constitutional power in the courts to decree relief balancing the racial composition of that district's schools with those of the surrounding districts.

We conclude that the relief ordered by the District Court and affirmed by the Court of Appeals was based upon an erroneous standard and was unsupported by record evidence that acts of the outlying districts effected the discrimination found to exist in the schools of Detroit.

■ MR. JUSTICE STEWART, concurring.

The basic issue now before the Court concerns the appropriate exercise of federal equity jurisdiction.

The courts were in error for the simple reason that the remedy they thought necessary was not commensurate with the constitutional violation found.

The opinion of the Court convincingly demonstrates that traditions of local control of schools, together with the difficulty of a judicially supervised restructuring of local administration of schools, render improper and inequitable such an interdistrict response to a constitutional violation found to have occurred only within a single school district.

By approving a remedy that would reach beyond the limits of the city of Detroit to correct a constitutional violation found to have occurred solely within that city the Court of Appeals thus went beyond the governing equitable principles established in this Court's decisions.

■ MR. JUSTICE DOUGLAS, dissenting.

When we rule against the metropolitan area remedy we take a step that will likely put the problems of the blacks and our society back to the period that antedated the "separate but equal" regime of *Plessy v. Ferguson,* 163 U.S. 537. The reason is simple.

The inner core of Detroit is now rather solidly black; and the blacks, we know, in many instances are likely to be poorer, just as were the

Chicanos in *San Antonio School District v. Rodriguez,* 411 U.S. 1. By that decision the poorer school districts must pay their own way. It is therefore a foregone conclusion that we have now given the States a formula whereby the poor must pay their own way.

Today's decision, given *Rodriguez,* means that there is no violation of the *Equal Protection Clause* though the schools are segregated by race and though the black schools are not only "separate" but "inferior."

So far as equal protection is concerned we are now in a dramatic retreat from the 7-to-1 decision in 1896 that blacks could be segregated in public facilities, provided they received equal treatment.

As I indicated in *Keyes v. School District No. 1 Denver, Colorado, 413 U.S. 189, 214–217,* there is so far as the school cases go no constitutional difference between *de facto* and *de jure* segregation. Each school board performs state action for *Fourteenth Amendment* purposes when it draws the lines that confine it to a given area, when it builds schools at particular sites, or when it allocates students. The creation of the school districts in Metropolitan Detroit either maintained existing segregation or caused additional segregation. Restrictive covenants maintained by state action or inaction build black ghettos. It is state action when public funds are dispensed by housing agencies to build racial ghettos. Where a community is racially mixed and school authorities segregate schools, or assign black teachers to black schools or close schools in fringe areas and build new schools in black areas and in more distant white areas, the State creates and nurtures a segregated school system, just as surely as did those States involved in *Brown v. Board of Education,* 347 U.S. 483 when they maintained dual school systems.

Given the State's control over the educational system in Michigan, the fact that the black schools are in one district and the white schools are in another is not controlling—either constitutionally or equitably.

■ MR. JUSTICE WHITE, with whom MR. JUSTICE DOUGLAS, MR. JUSTICE BRENNAN, and MR. JUSTICE MARSHALL join, dissenting.

This Court now reverses the Court of Appeals. It does not question the District Court's findings that *any* feasible Detroit-only plan would leave many schools 75 to 90 percent black and that the district would become progressively more black as whites left the city. Neither does the Court suggest that including the suburbs in a desegregation plan would be impractical or infeasible because of educational considerations, because of the number of children requiring transportation, or because of the length of their rides. Indeed, the Court leaves unchallenged the District Court's conclusion that a plan including the suburbs would be physically easier and more practical and feasible than a Detroit-only plan. Whereas the most promising Detroit-only plan, for example, would have entailed the purchase of 900 buses, the metropolitan plan would involve the acquisition of no more than 350 new vehicles.

Despite the fact that a metropolitan remedy, if the findings of the District Court accepted by the Court of Appeals are to be credited, would more effectively desegregate the Detroit schools, would prevent resegregation, and would be easier and more feasible from many standpoints, the Court fashions out of whole cloth an arbitrary rule that remedies for constitutional violations occurring in a single Michigan school district must stop at the school district line. Apparently, no matter how much less burdensome or more effective and efficient in many respects, such as transportation, the metropolitan plan might be, the school district line may not be crossed. Otherwise, it seems, there would be too much disruption of the Michigan scheme for managing its educational system, too much confusion, and too much administrative burden.

I am even more mystified as to how the Court can ignore the legal reality that the constitutional violations, even if occurring locally, were committed by governmental entities for which the State is responsible and that it is the State that must respond to the command of the *Fourteenth Amendment*. An interdistrict remedy for the infringements that occurred in this case is well within the confines and powers of the State, which is the governmental entity ultimately responsible for desegregating its schools. The Michigan Supreme Court has observed that "[the] school district is a State agency," *Attorney General ex rel. Kies v. Lowrey,* 131 Mich. 639, 644, 92 N. W. 289, 290 (1902), and that " '[education] in Michigan belongs to the State. It is no part of the local self-government inherent in the township or municipality, except so far as the legislature may choose to make it such. The Constitution has turned the whole subject over to the legislature. . . .' " *Attorney General ex rel. Zacharias v. Detroit Board of Education,* 154 Mich. 584, 590, 118 N. W. 606, 609 (1908).

The Court draws the remedial line at the Detroit school district boundary, even though the *Fourteenth Amendment* is addressed to the State and even though the *State* denies equal protection of the laws when its public agencies, acting in its behalf, invidiously discriminate. The State's default is "the condition that offends the Constitution," *Swann v. Charlotte-Mecklenburg Board of Education, supra,* at 16, and state officials may therefore be ordered to take the necessary measures to completely eliminate from the Detroit public schools "all vestiges of state-imposed segregation." *Id., at 15.* I cannot understand, nor does the majority satisfactorily explain, why a federal court may not order an appropriate interdistrict remedy, if this is necessary or more effective to accomplish this constitutionally mandated task. As the Court unanimously observed in *Swann:* "Once a right and a violation have been shown, the scope of a district court's equitable powers to remedy past wrongs is broad, for breadth and flexibility are inherent in equitable remedies." In this case, both the right and the State's *Fourteenth Amendment* violation have concededly been fully established, and there is no acceptable reason for permitting the party responsible for the constitutional violation to contain the remedial powers of the federal court within administrative boundaries over which the transgressor itself has plenary power.

Nor does the Court's conclusion follow from the talismanic invocation of the desirability of local control over education. Local autonomy over school affairs, in the sense of the community's participation in the decisions affecting the education of its children, is, of course, an important interest. But presently constituted school district lines do not delimit fixed and unchangeable areas of a local educational community. If restructuring is required to meet constitutional requirements, local authority may simply be redefined in terms of whatever configuration is adopted, with the parents of the children attending schools in the newly demarcated district or attendance zone continuing their participation in the policy management of the schools with which they are concerned most directly. The majority's suggestion that judges should not attempt to grapple with the administrative problems attendant on a reorganization of school attendance patterns is wholly without foundation. It is precisely this sort of task which the district courts have been properly exercising to vindicate the constitutional rights of Negro students since *Brown I* and which the Court has never suggested they lack the capacity to perform. Intradistrict revisions of attendance zones, and pairing and grouping of schools, are techniques unanimously approved in *Swann* v. *Charlotte-Mecklenburg Board of Education* which entail the same sensitivity to the interest of parents in the education their children receive as would an interdistrict plan which is likely to employ the very same methods. There is no reason to suppose that the District Court, which has not yet adopted a final plan of desegregation, would not be as capable of giving or as likely to give sufficient weight to the interest in community participation in schools in an interdistrict setting, consistent with the dictates of the *Fourteenth Amendment*. The majority's assumption that the District Court would act otherwise is a radical departure from the practical flexibility previously left to the equity powers of the federal judiciary.

[T]he majority's arbitrary limitation on the equitable power of federal district courts, based on the invisible borders of local school districts, is unrelated to the State's responsibility for remedying the constitutional wrongs visited upon the Negro schoolchildren of Detroit. It is oblivious to the potential benefits of metropolitan relief, to the noneducational communities of interest among neighborhoods located in and sometimes bridging different school districts, and to the considerable interdistrict cooperation already existing in various educational areas. Ultimately, it is unresponsive to the goal of attaining the utmost actual desegregation consistent with restraints of practicability and thus augurs the frequent frustration of the remedial powers of the federal courts.

Here the District Court will be forced to impose an intracity desegregation plan more expensive to the district, more burdensome for many of Detroit's Negro students, and surely more conducive to white flight than a metropolitan plan would be—all of this merely to avoid what the Detroit School Board, the District Court, and the en banc Court of Appeals considered to be the very manageable and quite surmountable difficulties that would be involved in extending the desegregation remedy to the suburban school districts.

■ MR. JUSTICE MARSHALL, with whom MR. JUSTICE DOUGLAS, MR. JUSTICE BRENNAN, and MR. JUSTICE WHITE join, dissenting.

[T]he Court today takes a giant step backwards . . . Our precedents, in my view, firmly establish that where, as here, state-imposed segregation has been demonstrated, it becomes the duty of the State to eliminate root and branch all vestiges of racial discrimination and to achieve the greatest possible degree of actual desegregation. I agree with both the District Court and the Court of Appeals that, under the facts of this case, this duty cannot be fulfilled unless the State of Michigan involves outlying metropolitan area school districts in its desegregation remedy. Furthermore, I perceive no basis either in law or in the practicalities of the situation justifying the State's interposition of school district boundaries as absolute barriers to the implementation of an effective desegregation remedy. Under established and frequently used Michigan procedures, school district lines are both flexible and permeable for a wide variety of purposes, and there is no reason why they must now stand in the way of meaningful desegregation relief.

The rights at issue in this case are too fundamental to be abridged on grounds as superficial as those relied on by the majority today. We deal here with the right of all of our children, whatever their race, to an equal start in life and to an equal opportunity to reach their full potential as citizens. Those children who have been denied that right in the past deserve better than to see fences thrown up to deny them that right in the future. Our Nation, I fear, will be ill served by the Court's refusal to remedy separate and unequal education, for unless our children begin to learn together, there is little hope that our people will ever learn to live together.

[T]he District Court's decision to expand its desegregation decree beyond the geographical limits of the city of Detroit rested in large part on its conclusions (A) that the State of Michigan was ultimately responsible for curing the condition of segregation within the Detroit city schools, and (B) that a Detroit-only remedy would not accomplish this task. In my view, both of these conclusions are well supported by the facts of this case and by this Court's precedents.

A

To begin with, the record amply supports the District Court's findings that the State of Michigan, through state officers and state agencies, had engaged in purposeful acts which created or aggravated segregation in the Detroit schools. The State Board of Education, for example, prior to 1962, exercised its authority to supervise local schoolsite selection in a manner which contributed to segregation. *484 F.2d 215, 238 (CA6 1973).* Furthermore, the State's continuing authority, after 1962, to approve school building construction plans had intertwined the State with site-selection decisions of the Detroit Board of Education which had the purpose and effect of maintaining segregation.

The State had also stood in the way of past efforts to desegregate the Detroit city schools. In 1970, for example, the Detroit School Board had begun implementation of its own desegregation plan for its high schools, despite considerable public and official resistance. The State Legislature intervened by enacting Act 48 of the Public Acts of 1970, specifically prohibiting implementation of the desegregation plan and thereby continuing the growing segregation of the Detroit school system. Adequate desegregation of the Detroit system was also hampered by discriminatory restrictions placed by the State on the use of transportation within Detroit. While state aid for transportation was provided by statute for suburban districts, many of which were highly urbanized, aid for intracity transportation was excepted. One of the effects of this restriction was to encourage the construction of small walk-in neighborhood schools in Detroit, thereby lending aid to the intentional policy of creating a school system which reflected, to the greatest extent feasible, extensive residential segregation. Indeed, that one of the purposes of the transportation restriction was to impede desegregation was evidenced when the Michigan Legislature amended the State Transportation Aid Act to cover intracity transportation but expressly prohibited the allocation of funds for cross-busing of students within a school district to achieve racial balance. Cf. *North Carolina State Board of Education v. Swann,* 402 U.S. 43 (1971).

Also significant was the State's involvement during the 1950's in the transportation of Negro high school students from the Carver School District past a closer white high school in the Oak Park District to a more distant Negro high school in the Detroit system. Certainly the District Court's finding that the State Board of Education had knowledge of this action and had given its tacit or express approval was not clearly erroneous. Given the comprehensive statutory powers of the State Board of Education over contractual arrangements between school districts in the enrollment of students on a nonresident tuition basis, including certification of the number of pupils involved in the transfer and the amount of tuition charged, over the review of transportation routes and distances, and over the disbursement of transportation funds, the State Board inevitably knew and understood the significance of this discriminatory act.

Aside from the acts of purposeful segregation committed by the State Legislature and the State Board of Education, the District Court also concluded that the State was responsible for the many intentional acts of segregation committed by the Detroit Board of Education, an agency of the State. The majority is only willing to accept this finding *arguendo*. *See ante*, at 748. I have no doubt, however, as to its validity under the *Fourteenth Amendment*.

"The command of the *Fourteenth Amendment*," it should be recalled, "is that no 'State' shall deny to any person within its jurisdiction the equal protection of the laws." *Cooper v. Aaron,* 358 U.S. 1, 16 (1958). While a State can act only through "the officers or agents by whom its powers are exerted," *Ex parte Virginia,* 100 U.S. 339, 347 (1880), actions by an agent or officer of the State are encompassed by the *Fourteenth Amendment* for, "as he acts in the name and for the State, and is clothed with the State's power, his act is that of the State." *Ibid. See also Cooper v. Aaron, supra; Virginia v. Rives,* 100 U.S. 313, 318 (1880); *Shelley v. Kraemer,* 334 U.S. 1, 14 (1948).

Under Michigan law a "school district is an agency of the State government." Racial discrimination by the school district, an agency of the State, is therefore racial discrimination by the State itself, forbidden by the *Fourteenth Amendment*.

Vesting responsibility with the State of Michigan for Detroit's segregated schools is particularly appropriate as Michigan, unlike some other States, operates a single statewide system of education rather than several separate and independent local school systems. The majority's emphasis on local governmental control and local autonomy of school districts in Michigan will come as a surprise to those with any familiarity with that State's system of education. School districts are not separate and distinct sovereign entities under Michigan law, but rather are " 'auxiliaries of the State,' " subject to its "absolute power." *Attorney General of Michigan ex rel. Kies v. Lowrey,* 199 U.S. 233, 240 (1905).

The State's control over education is reflected in the fact that, contrary to the Court's implication, there is little or no relationship between school districts and local political units. To take the 85 outlying local school districts in the Detroit metropolitan area as examples, 17 districts lie in two counties, two in three counties. One district serves five municipalities; other suburban municipalities are fragmented into as many as six school districts. Nor is there any apparent state policy with regard to the size of school districts, as they now range from 2,000 to 285,000 students.

Centralized state control manifests itself in practice as well as in theory. The State controls the financing of education in several ways. The legislature contributes a substantial portion of most school districts' operating budgets with funds appropriated from the State's General Fund revenues raised through statewide taxation. The State's power over the purse can be and is in fact used to enforce the State's powers over local districts. In addition, although local districts obtain funds through local property taxation, the State has assumed the responsibility to ensure equalized property valuations throughout the State. The State also establishes standards for teacher certification and teacher tenure; determines part of the required curriculum; sets the minimum school term; approves bus routes, equipment, and drivers; approves textbooks; and establishes procedures for student discipline. The State Superintendent of Public Instruction and the State Board of Education have the power to remove local school board members from office for neglect of their duties.

Most significantly for present purposes, the State has wide-ranging powers to consolidate and merge school districts, even without the consent of the districts themselves or of the local citizenry. Indeed, recent years have witnessed an accelerated program of school district consolidations, mergers, and annexations, many of which were state imposed. Furthermore, the State has broad powers to transfer property from one district to another, again without the consent of the local school districts affected by the transfer. *See, e.g., School District of the City of Lansing v. State Board of Education, supra; Imlay Township District v. State Board of Education*, 359 Mich. 478, 102 N. W. 2d 720 (1960).

Whatever may be the history of public education in other parts of our Nation, it simply flies in the face of reality to say, as does the majority, that in Michigan, "[no] single tradition in public education is more deeply rooted than local control over the operation of schools. . . ."

In sum, several factors in this case coalesce to support the District Court's ruling that it was the State of Michigan itself, not simply the Detroit Board of Education, which bore the obligation of curing the condition of segregation within the Detroit city schools. The actions of the State itself directly contributed to Detroit's segregation. Under the *Fourteenth Amendment*, the State is ultimately responsible for the actions of its local agencies. And, finally, given the structure of Michigan's educational system, Detroit's segregation cannot be viewed as the problem of an independent and separate entity. Michigan operates a single statewide system of education, a substantial part of which was shown to be segregated in this case.

B

Under our decisions, it was clearly proper for the District Court to take into account the so-called "white flight" from the city schools which would be forthcoming from any Detroit-only decree. The court's prediction of white flight was well supported by expert testimony based on past experience in other cities undergoing desegregation relief. We ourselves took the possibility of white flight into account in evaluating the effectiveness of a desegregation plan in *Wright, supra*, where we relied on the District Court's finding that if the city of Emporia were allowed to withdraw from the existing system, leaving a system with a higher proportion of Negroes, it " 'may be anticipated that the proportion of whites in county schools may drop as those who can register in private academies'. . . ." 407 U.S., at 464. One cannot ignore the white-flight problem, for where legally imposed segregation has been established, the District Court has the responsibility to see to it not only that the dual system is terminated at once but also that future events do not serve to perpetuate or re-establish segregation.

Because of the already high and rapidly increasing percentage of Negro students in the Detroit system, as well as the prospect of white flight, a Detroit-only plan simply has no hope of achieving actual desegregation. Under such a plan white and Negro students will not go to school together. Instead, Negro children will continue to attend all-Negro schools. The very evil that *Brown I* was aimed at will not be cured, but will be perpetuated for the future.

Nor can it be said that the State is free from any responsibility for the disparity between the racial makeup of Detroit and its surrounding suburbs. The State's creation, through *de jure* acts of segregation, of a growing core of all-Negro schools inevitably acted as a magnet to attract Negroes to the areas served by such schools and to deter them from settling either in other areas of the city or in the suburbs. By the same token, the growing core of all-Negro schools inevitably helped drive whites to other areas of the city or to the suburbs.

The rippling effects on residential patterns caused by purposeful acts of segregation do not automatically subside at the school district border. With rare exceptions, these effects naturally spread through all the residential neighborhoods within a metropolitan area.

The State must also bear part of the blame for the white flight to the suburbs which would be forthcoming from a Detroit-only decree and would render such a remedy ineffective. Having created a system where whites and Negroes were intentionally kept apart so that they could not become accustomed to learning together, the State is responsible for the fact that many whites will react to the dismantling of that segregated system by attempting to flee to the suburbs. Indeed, by limiting the District Court to a Detroit-only remedy and allowing that flight to the suburbs to succeed, the Court today allows the State to profit from its own wrong and to perpetuate for years to come the separation of the races it achieved in the past by purposeful state action.

Nor should it be of any significance that the suburban school districts were not shown to have themselves taken any direct action to promote segregation of the races. Given the State's broad powers over local school districts, it was well within the State's powers to require those districts surrounding the Detroit school district to participate in a metropolitan remedy.

It is the State, after all, which bears the responsibility under *Brown* of affording a nondiscriminatory system of education. The State, of course, is ordinarily free to choose any decentralized framework for education it wishes, so long as it fulfills that *Fourteenth Amendment* obligation.

III

Desegregation is not and was never expected to be an easy task. Racial attitudes ingrained in our Nation's childhood and adolescence are not quickly thrown aside in its middle years. But just as the inconvenience of some cannot be allowed to stand in the way of the rights of others, so public opposition, no matter how strident, cannot be permitted to divert this Court from the enforcement of the constitutional principles at issue in this case. Today's holding, I fear, is more a reflection of a perceived public mood that we have gone far enough in enforcing the Constitution's guarantee of equal justice than it is the product of neutral principles of law. In the short run, it may seem to be the easier course to allow our great metropolitan areas to be divided up each into two cities— one white, the other black—but it is a course, I predict, our people will ultimately regret. I dissent.

NOTES AND QUESTIONS

1. More than one-third of the students in the Detroit city school district were white. Why wouldn't a desegregation remedy limited to the Detroit schools have been adequate?

2. Should the obligation to create integrated schools depend on whether the state or district previously intentionally segregated its schools? In *Milliken*, is there evidence that the state intentionally racially segregated the Detroit schools? Given that school districts, along with other local government agencies, are instrumentalities of the state, what is the justification for treating the districts as legally separate and autonomous?

3. In crafting a remedy, what weight, if any, should the district court accord parents' opposition to the busing of their children? Does is matter whether the opposition to busing comes from white suburban residents or from black Detroit residents?

4. Segregated neighborhoods have been and continue to be a serious impediment to integrating schools. The Supreme Court invalidated de jure segregated housing decades before it invalidated de jure segregated schools. In its 1917 decision in *Buchanan v. Warley*, 245 U.S. 60 (1917), the Court considered the constitutionality of a city ordinance that precluded sales of residential property that would increase racial integration. Titled "An ordinance to prevent conflict and ill-feeling between the white and colored races in the city of Louisville, and to preserve the public peace and promote the general welfare," the law prohibited either race from acquiring property in a neighborhood in which the other race predominated. While conceding "[t]hat there exists a serious and difficult problem arising from a feeling of race hostility which the law is powerless to control, and to which it must give a measure of consideration," the Court nonetheless invalidated the ordinance, concluding that "promot[ing] the public peace by preventing race conflicts, [d]esirable as this is . . . cannot be accomplished by laws or ordinances which deny rights created or protected by the federal Constitution." *Buchanan*, 245 U.S. at 80–81.

Yet with the demise of statutes mandating segregation, neighborhoods did not become racially integrated. Once local ordinances could no longer impose segregation by law, racially restrictive covenants became even more popular. These ostensibly private agreements among homeowners precluded the purchase or use of property by members of disfavored races. Far from being viewed as pernicious discrimination, such covenants were viewed by many, including federal regulators, as a sensible means of promoting racial homogeneity and neighborhood stability. Through the 1930s, federal regulators recommended that properties be subject to restrictive covenants "[p]rohibit[ing] occupancy except by the race for which they are intended." Richard Rothstein, Racial Segregation and Black Student Achievement, in *Education, Justice and Democracy*, Danielle Allen & Rob Reich, eds. 180 (2013). Real estate agents and brokers steered prospective home buyers only to neighborhoods in which people of their own race predominated. Banks and other mortgage lenders preferred to extend loans for property in segregated neighborhoods and often did not extend loans in black neighborhoods at all. Thus did segregation persist with the aid of private, institutional, and governmental actors.

In the landmark case, *Shelley v. Kraemer*, 334 U.S. 1 (1948), the Court considered the constitutional status of racially restrictive covenants— private agreements that prohibited the ownership or occupancy of property "by people of the Negro or Mongolian race." While observing "that the restrictive agreements standing alone cannot be regarded as a violation of any rights guaranteed to petitioners by the Fourteenth Amendment," 334 U.S. at 13, the Court nonetheless held that the judicial enforcement of such agreements violated the Equal Protection Clause of the Fourteenth Amendment.

Given these Supreme Court decisions, why might racial segregation have persisted within cities? In school desegregation cases, should cities and states be held responsible for the residential segregation that gives rise to segregated schools? What degree of responsibility must the state bear to hold it accountable?

5.   The Court's decision in *Milliken* made it extraordinarily difficult for lower courts to impose effective desegregation plans. Throughout the 1970s and 80s, middle class families, often white, left the urban areas of our nation's metropolises for suburbs that offered newer housing and better schools. So-called white flight from the inner cities meant that, in many urban areas, there were decreasing numbers of whites to integrate with the racial minorities who remained within the city. As two commentators have observed:

Virtually every metropolitan area in the land includes ghettos of blacks (and increasingly Latinos), ringed by affluent white neighborhoods or suburbs. The central city black ghettos are studies in urban decay, mired in poor jobs, poor schools, and poor public services, breeders of an American underclass. The outlying neighborhoods and suburbs (though some of them have become extensions of the black city ghetto) often remain bastions of white exclusivity, and racial exclusion.

William M. Leiter and Samuel Leiter, *Affirmative Action in Antidiscrimination Law and Policy* 232 (2011).

———————

Having been deprived of the power to order inter-district remedies, and confronted with inferior inner city schools, some federal judges explored alternative means of remedying segregation, as the following case exemplifies.

Missouri v. Jenkins
Supreme Court of the United States, 1995.
515 U.S. 70.

■ CHIEF JUSTICE REHNQUIST delivered the opinion of the Court.

As this school desegregation litigation enters its 18th year, we are called upon again to review the decisions of the lower courts. In this case, the State of Missouri has challenged the District Court's order of salary increases for virtually all instructional and noninstructional staff within the Kansas City, Missouri, School District (KCMSD) and the District Court's order requiring the State to continue to fund remedial "quality education" programs because student achievement levels were still "at or below national norms at many grade levels."

In June 1985, the District Court determined that "segregation had caused a system wide *reduction* in student achievement in the schools of the KCMSD." The District Court made no particularized findings regarding the extent that student achievement had been reduced or what portion of that reduction was attributable to segregation. The District Court also identified 25 schools within the KCMSD that had enrollments of 90% or more black students.

The District Court, pursuant to plans submitted by the KCMSD and the State, ordered a wide range of quality education programs for all students attending the KCMSD. First, the District Court ordered that the KCMSD be restored to an AAA classification, the highest classification awarded by the State Board of Education. Second, it ordered that the number of students per class be reduced so that the student-to-teacher ratio was below the level required for AAA standing. The District Court justified its reduction in class size as

An essential part of any plan to remedy the vestiges of segregation in the KCMSD. Reducing class size will serve to remedy the vestiges of past segregation by increasing individual attention and instruction, as well as increasing the potential for desegregative educational experiences for KCMSD students by maintaining and attracting non-minority enrollment.

The District Court also ordered programs to expand educational opportunities for all KCMSD students: full-day kindergarten; expanded summer school; before- and after-school tutoring; and an early childhood development program. Finally, the District Court implemented a state-funded "effective schools" program that consisted of substantial yearly cash grants to each of the schools within the KCMSD. Under the "effective schools" program, the State was required to fund programs at both the 25 racially identifiable schools as well as the 43 other schools within the KCMSD.

The total cost for these quality education programs has exceeded $220 million.

The District Court determined that "achievement of AAA status, improvement of the quality of education being offered at the KCMSD schools, magnet schools, as well as other components of this desegregation plan can serve to maintain and hopefully attract non-minority student enrollment."

In November 1986, the District Court approved a comprehensive magnet school and capital improvements plan and held the State and the KCMSD jointly and severally liable for its funding. Under the District Court's plan, every senior high school, every middle school, and one-half of the elementary schools were converted into magnet schools. The District Court adopted the magnet-school program to "provide a greater educational opportunity to all KCMSD students," id., at 131–132, and because it believed "that the proposed magnet plan [was] so attractive that it would draw non-minority students from the private schools who have abandoned or avoided the KCMSD, and draw in additional non-minority students from the suburbs." The District Court felt that "the long-term benefit of all KCMSD students of a greater educational opportunity in an integrated environment is worthy of such an investment." Since its inception, the magnet school program has operated at a cost, including magnet transportation, in excess of $448 million.

In June 1985, the District Court ordered substantial capital improvements to combat the deterioration of the KCMSD's facilities. In formulating its capital-improvements plan, the District Court dismissed as "irrelevant" the "State's argument that the present condition of the facilities [was] not traceable to unlawful segregation." Instead, the District Court focused on its responsibility to "remedy the vestiges of segregation" and to "implement a desegregation plan which would maintain and attract non-minority enrollment." I. The initial phase of the capital improvements plan cost $37 million. The District Court also required the KCMSD to present further capital improvements proposals "in order to bring its facilities to a point comparable with the facilities in neighboring suburban school districts." In November 1986, the District Court approved further capital improvements in order to remove the vestiges of racial segregation and "to . . . attract non-minority students back to the KCMSD."

In September 1987, the District Court adopted, for the most part, KCMSD's long-range capital improvements plan at a cost in excess of $187 million. The plan called for the renovation of approximately 55 schools, the closure of 18 facilities, and the construction of 17 new schools.

As part of its desegregation plan, the District Court has ordered salary assistance to the KCMSD. In 1987, the District Court initially ordered salary assistance only for teachers within the KCMSD. Since that time, however, the District Court has ordered salary assistance to all but three of the approximately 5,000 KCMSD employees. The total cost of this component of the desegregation remedy since 1987 is over $200 million.

The District Court's desegregation plan has been described as the most ambitious and expensive remedial program in the history of school desegregation. The KCMSD, which has pursued a "friendly adversary" relationship with the plaintiffs, has continued to propose ever more expensive programs. As a result, the desegregation costs have escalated and now are approaching an annual cost of $200 million. These massive expenditures have financed:

> high schools in which every classroom will have air conditioning, an alarm system, and 15 microcomputers; a 2,000-square-foot planetarium; green houses and vivariums; a 25-acre farm with an air-conditioned meeting room for 104 people; a Model United Nations wired for language translation; broadcast capable radio and television studios with an editing and animation lab; a temperature controlled art gallery; movie editing and screening rooms; a 3,500-square-foot dust-free diesel mechanics room; 1,875-square-foot elementary school animal rooms for use in a zoo project; swimming pools; and numerous other facilities.

Not surprisingly, the cost of this remedial plan has "far exceeded KCMSD's budget, or for that matter, its authority to tax." The State, through the operation of joint-and-several liability, has borne the brunt of these costs. The District Court candidly has acknowledged that it has "allowed the District planners to dream" and "provided the mechanism for those dreams to be realized." In short, the District Court "has gone to great lengths to provide KCMSD with facilities and opportunities not available anywhere else in the country."

First, the State has challenged the District Court's requirement that it fund salary increases for KCMSD instructional and noninstructional staff. The State claimed that funding for salaries was beyond the scope of the District Court's remedial authority. Second, the State has challenged the District Court's order requiring it to continue to fund the remedial quality education programs for the 1992–1993 school year.

The District Court rejected the State's arguments. It first determined that the salary increases were warranted because "high quality personnel are necessary not only to implement specialized desegregation programs intended to 'improve educational opportunities and reduce racial isolation', but also to 'ensure that there is no diminution in the quality of its regular academic program.'" Its "ruling [was] grounded in remedying the vestiges of segregation by improving the desegregative attractiveness of the KCMSD."

It rejected the State's argument that the salary increases did not directly address and relate to the State's constitutional violation and that "low teacher salaries did not flow from any earlier constitutional violations by the State." In doing so, it observed that "in addition to compensating the victims, the remedy in this case was also designed to reverse white flight by offering superior educational opportunities."

III

The District Court's pursuit of the goal of "desegregative attractiveness" results in so many imponderables and is so far removed from the task of eliminating the racial identifiability of the schools within the KCMSD that we believe it is beyond the admittedly broad discretion of the District Court. In this posture, we conclude that the District Court's order of salary increases, which was "grounded in remedying the vestiges of segregation by improving the desegregative attractiveness of the KCMSD," is simply too far removed from an acceptable implementation of a permissible means to remedy previous legally mandated segregation.

Similar considerations lead us to conclude that the District Court's order requiring the State to continue to fund the quality education programs because student achievement levels were still "at or below national norms at many grade levels" cannot be sustained. The basic task of the District Court is to decide whether the reduction in achievement by minority students attributable to prior *de jure* segregation has been remedied to the extent practicable. Under our precedents, the State and the KCMSD are "entitled to a rather precise statement of [their] obligations under a desegregation decree." Although the District Court has determined that "segregation has caused a system wide *reduction* in achievement in the schools of the KCMSD," it never has identified the incremental effect that segregation has had on minority student achievement or the specific goals of the quality education programs.

On remand, the District Court must bear in mind that its end purpose is not only "to remedy the violation" to the extent practicable, but also "to restore state and local authorities to the control of a school system that is operating in compliance with the Constitution."

■ JUSTICE O'CONNOR, concurring. [omitted]

■ JUSTICE THOMAS, concurring.

It never ceases to amaze me that the courts are so willing to assume that anything that is predominantly black must be inferior. Instead of focusing on remedying the harm done to those black schoolchildren injured by segregation, the District Court sought to convert the Kansas City, Missouri, School District (KCMSD) into a "magnet district" that would reverse the "white flight" caused by desegregation.

Two threads in our jurisprudence have produced this unfortunate situation, in which a District Court has taken it upon itself to experiment with the education of the KCMSD's black youth. First, the court has read our cases to support the theory that black students suffer an unspecified psychological harm from segregation that retards their mental and educational development. This approach not only relies upon questionable social science research rather than constitutional principle, but it also rests on an assumption of black inferiority. Second, we have permitted the federal courts to exercise virtually unlimited equitable powers to remedy this alleged constitutional violation. The exercise of this authority has trampled upon principles of federalism and the separation of powers and has freed courts to pursue other agendas unrelated to the narrow purpose of precisely remedying a constitutional harm.

I

A

The mere fact that a school is black does not mean that it is the product of a constitutional violation. A "racial imbalance does not itself establish a violation of the Constitution "The differentiating factor between *de jure* segregation and so-called *de facto* segregation . . . is *purpose* or *intent* to segregate."

B

Brown I did not say that "racially isolated" schools were inherently inferior; the harm that it identified was tied purely to *de jure* segregation, not *de facto* segregation. Indeed, *Brown I* itself did not need to rely upon any psychological or social-science research in order to announce the simple, yet fundamental, truth that the government cannot discriminate among its citizens on the basis of race.

Segregation was not unconstitutional because it might have caused psychological feelings of inferiority. Public school systems that separated blacks and provided them with superior educational resources—making blacks "feel" superior to whites sent to lesser schools—would violate the *Fourteenth Amendment*, whether or not the white students felt stigmatized, just as do school systems in which the positions of the races are reversed. Psychological injury or benefit is irrelevant to the question whether state actors have engaged in intentional discrimination—the critical inquiry for ascertaining violations of the *Equal Protection Clause*. The judiciary is fully competent to make independent determinations concerning the existence of state action without the unnecessary and misleading assistance of the social sciences.

Regardless of the relative quality of the schools, segregation violated the Constitution because the State classified students based on their race. Of course, segregation additionally harmed black students by relegating them to schools with substandard facilities and resources. But neutral policies, such as local school assignments, do not offend the Constitution when individual private choices concerning work or residence produce schools with high black populations. *See Keyes* v. *School Dist. No. 1,* 413 U.S. at 211. The Constitution does not prevent individuals from choosing to live together, to work together, or to send their children to school together, so long as the State does not interfere with their choices on the basis of race.

Given that desegregation has not produced the predicted leaps forward in black educational achievement, there is no reason to think that black students cannot learn as well when surrounded by members of their own race as when they are in an integrated environment. Indeed, it may very well be that what has been true for historically black colleges is true for black middle and high schools. Despite their origins in "the shameful history of state-enforced segregation," these institutions can be " 'both a source of pride to blacks who have attended them and a source of hope to black families who want the benefits of . . . learning for their children.' " *Fordice, 505 U.S. at 748* (THOMAS, J., concurring) (citation omitted). Because of their "distinctive histories and traditions," *ibid.,* black schools can function as the center and symbol of black communities, and provide examples of independent black leadership, success, and achievement.

C

Two clear restraints on the use of the equity power—federalism and the separation of powers—derive from the very form of our Government. Federal courts should pause before using their inherent equitable powers to intrude into the proper sphere of the States. We have long recognized that education is primarily a concern of local authorities. "Local autonomy of school districts is a vital national tradition." A structural reform decree eviscerates a State's discretionary authority over its own program and budgets and forces state officials to reallocate state resources and funds to the desegregation plan at the expense of other citizens, other government programs, and other institutions not represented in court. *See* Dwyer, *supra,* at 163. When district courts seize complete control over the schools, they strip state and local governments of one of their most important governmental responsibilities, and thus deny their existence as independent governmental entities.

Federal courts do not possess the capabilities of state and local governments in addressing difficult educational problems. State and local school officials not only bear the responsibility for educational decisions, they also are better equipped than a single federal judge to make the day-to-day policy, curricular, and funding choices necessary to bring a school district into compliance with the Constitution. Federal courts simply cannot gather sufficient information to render an effective decree, have limited resources to induce compliance, and cannot seek political and public support for their remedies. *See* generally P. Schuck, Suing Government 150–181 (1983). When we presume to have the institutional ability to set effective educational, budgetary, or administrative policy, we transform the least dangerous branch into the most dangerous one.

The separation of powers imposes additional restraints on the judiciary's exercise of its remedial powers. To be sure, this is not a case of one branch of Government encroaching on the prerogatives of another, but rather of the power of the Federal Government over the States. Nonetheless, what the federal courts cannot do at the federal level they cannot do against the States; in either case, Article III courts are constrained by the inherent constitutional limitations on their powers. There simply are certain things that courts, in order to remain courts, cannot and should not do. There is no difference between courts running school systems or prisons and courts running Executive Branch agencies.

D

III

This Court should never approve a State's efforts to deny students, because of their race, an equal opportunity for an education. But the federal courts also should avoid using racial equality as a pretext for solving social problems that do not violate the Constitution. It seems apparent to me that the District Court undertook the worthy task of providing a quality education to the children of KCMSD. As far as I can tell, however, the District Court sought to bring new funds and facilities into the KCMSD by finding a constitutional violation on the part of the State where there was none. Federal courts should not lightly assume that States have caused "racial isolation" in 1984 by maintaining a segregated school system in 1954. We must forever put aside the notion that simply because a school district today is black, it must be educationally inferior.

Even if segregation were present, we must remember that a deserving end does not justify all possible means. The desire to reform a school district, or any other institution, cannot so captivate the Judiciary that it forgets its constitutionally mandated role. Usurpation of the traditionally local control over education not only takes the judiciary beyond its proper sphere, it also deprives the States and their elected officials of their constitutional powers. At some point, we must recognize that the judiciary is not omniscient, and that all problems do not require a remedy of constitutional proportions.

■ JUSTICE SOUTER, with whom JUSTICE STEVENS, JUSTICE GINSBURG, and JUSTICE BREYER join, dissenting. [omitted]

■ JUSTICE GINSBURG, dissenting.

The Court stresses that the present remedial programs have been in place for seven years. But compared to more than two centuries of firmly entrenched official discrimination, the experience with the desegregation remedies ordered by the District Court has been evanescent.

In 1724, Louis XV of France issued the Code Noir, the first slave code for the Colony of Louisiana, an area that included Missouri. When Missouri entered the Union in 1821, it entered as a slave State. Before the Civil War, Missouri law prohibited the creation or maintenance of schools for educating blacks: "No person shall keep or teach any school for the instruction of negroes or mulattoes, in reading or writing, in this State."

Beginning in 1865, Missouri passed a series of laws requiring separate public schools for blacks. The Missouri Constitution first permitted, then required, separate schools.

Today, the Court declares illegitimate the goal of attracting nonminority students to the Kansas City, Missouri, School District, and thus stops the District Court's efforts to integrate a school district that was, in the 1984/1985 school year, sorely in need and 68.3% black. Given the deep, inglorious history of segregation in Missouri, to curtail desegregation at this time and in this manner is an action at once too swift and too soon.

NOTES AND QUESTIONS

1. *The Harm of Segregation.* The district court had determined that the racially segregated schools resulted in a district-wide reduction in student achievement. Is that the harm of segregation with which the courts should be concerned? If so, then was the remedy of increased funding sufficiently tailored to the harm? Why should attracting white students to the district be a goal if the concern is with student achievement?

2. *Funding as Remedy to Segregation.* If increased funding is accepted as a remedy for prior unconstitutional segregation, how might a court determine when the vestiges of segregation have been eliminated to the extent practicable? Should the court focus on whether the formerly segregated school now receives equal funding with non-segregated schools? Equality of facilities? Equality of achievement among students? And to what should a court compare the district under court order: comparable urban districts, neighboring suburban districts, some other benchmark?

3. Is equitable funding a sensible remedy for prior segregation even if it does not bring about integration? Even if it does not increase student achievement, as was the case in *Jenkins*? Why might racial integration improve student achievement?

Throughout the 1980s and 90s, the federal district courts subjected few new school districts to desegregation decrees, and an ever-growing number of districts were found to have satisfied the court orders that governed them by virtue of having desegregated "in good faith" and "to the extent practicable." But some schools adopted voluntary integration plans, giving rise to the central question in the next case: to what extent may school districts and other state actors rely on race in order to promote integration in their schools?

Parents Involved in Community Schools v. Seattle School District No. 1
Supreme Court of the United States, 2007.
551 U.S. 701.

■ CHIEF JUSTICE ROBERTS announced the judgment of the Court, and delivered the opinion of the Court with respect to Parts I, II, III-A, and III-C, and an opinion with respect to Parts III-B and IV, in which JUSTICES SCALIA, THOMAS, and ALITO join.

The school districts in these cases voluntarily adopted student assignment plans that rely upon race to determine which public schools certain children may attend. The Seattle school district classifies children as white or nonwhite; the Jefferson County school district as black or "other." In Seattle, this racial classification is used to allocate slots in oversubscribed high schools. In Jefferson County, it is used to make certain elementary school assignments and to rule on transfer requests. In each case, the school district relies upon an individual student's race in assigning that student to a particular school, so that the racial balance at the school falls within a predetermined range based on the racial composition of the school district as a whole.

I

Both cases present the same underlying legal question—whether a public school that had not operated legally segregated schools or has been found to be unitary may choose to classify students by race and rely upon that classification in making school assignments. Although we examine the plans under the same legal framework, the specifics of the two plans, and the circumstances surrounding their adoption, are in some respects quite different.

A

Seattle School District No. 1 operates 10 regular public high schools. In 1998, it adopted the plan at issue in this case for assigning students to these schools. The plan allows incoming ninth graders to choose from among any of the district's high schools, ranking however many schools they wish in order of preference.

Some schools are more popular than others. If too many students list the same school as their first choice, the district employs a series of "tiebreakers" to determine who will fill the open slots at the oversubscribed school. The first tiebreaker selects for admission students who have a sibling currently enrolled in the chosen school. The next tiebreaker depends upon the racial composition of the particular school and the race of the individual student. In the district's public schools approximately 41 percent of enrolled students are white; the remaining 59 percent, comprising all other racial groups, are classified by Seattle for assignment purposes as nonwhite.[4] If an oversubscribed school is not within 10 percentage points of the district's overall white/nonwhite racial balance, it is what the district calls "integration positive," and the district employs a tiebreaker that selects for assignment students whose race "will serve to bring the school into balance."

Seattle has never operated segregated schools—legally separate schools for students of different races—nor has it ever been subject to court-ordered desegregation. It nonetheless employs the racial tiebreaker in an attempt to address the effects of racially identifiable housing patterns on school assignments. Most white students live in the northern part of Seattle, most students of other racial backgrounds in the southern part.

B

Jefferson County Public Schools operates the public school system in metropolitan Louisville, Kentucky. In 1973 a federal court found that Jefferson County had maintained a segregated school system . . . and in 1975 the District Court entered a desegregation decree. . . . Jefferson County operated under this decree until 2000, when the District Court dissolved the decree after finding that the district had achieved unitary status by eliminating "[t]o the greatest extent practicable" the vestiges of its prior policy of segregation.

In 2001, after the decree had been dissolved, Jefferson County adopted the voluntary student assignment plan at issue in this case. . . . Approximately 34 percent of the district's 97,000 students are black; most of the remaining 66 percent are white. . . . The plan requires all nonmagnet schools to maintain a minimum black enrollment of 15

---

[4]   The racial breakdown of this nonwhite group is approximately 23.8 percent Asian-American, 23.1 percent African-American, 10.3 percent Latino, and 2.8 percent Native-American.

percent, and a maximum black enrollment of 50 percent. "Decisions to assign students to schools within each cluster are based on available space within the schools and the racial guidelines in the District's current student assignment plan." If a school has reached the "extremes of the racial guidelines," a student whose race would contribute to the school's racial imbalance will not be assigned there. Transfers may be requested for any number of reasons, and may be denied because of lack of available space or on the basis of the racial guidelines.

III

A

[I]t suffices to note that our prior cases, in evaluating the use of racial classifications in the school context, have recognized two interests that qualify as compelling. The first is the compelling interest of remedying the effects of past intentional discrimination. We have emphasized that the harm being remedied by mandatory desegregation plans is the harm that is traceable to segregation, and that "the Constitution is not violated by racial imbalance in the schools, without more." *Milliken v. Bradley*, 433 U.S. 267, 280, n.14 (1977).

The second government interest we have recognized as compelling for purposes of strict scrutiny is the interest in diversity in higher education upheld in *Grutter*. The specific interest found compelling in *Grutter* was student body diversity "in the context of higher education." The diversity interest was not focused on race alone but encompassed "all factors that may contribute to student body diversity." In upholding the admissions plan in *Grutter* . . . this Court relied upon considerations unique to institutions of higher education, noting that in light of "the expansive freedoms of speech and thought associated with the university environment, universities occupy a special niche in our constitutional tradition." 539 U.S., at 329. The present cases are not governed by *Grutter*.

B

Perhaps recognizing that reliance on *Grutter* cannot sustain their plans, both school districts assert additional interests, distinct from the interest upheld in *Grutter,* to justify their race-based assignments. Seattle contends that its use of race helps to reduce racial concentration in schools and to ensure that racially concentrated housing patterns do not prevent nonwhite students from having access to the most desirable schools. Jefferson County has articulated a similar goal, phrasing its interest in terms of educating its students "in a racially integrated environment." Each school district argues that educational and broader socialization benefits flow from a racially diverse learning environment, and each contends that because the diversity they seek is racial diversity—not the broader diversity at issue in *Grutter*—it makes sense to promote that interest directly by relying on race alone.

The parties and their *amici* dispute whether racial diversity in schools in fact has a marked impact on test scores and other objective yardsticks or achieves intangible socialization benefits. The debate is not one we need to resolve, however, because it is clear that the racial classifications employed by the districts are not narrowly tailored to the goal of achieving the educational and social benefits asserted to flow from racial diversity. In design and operation, the plans are directed only to racial balance, pure and simple, an objective this Court has repeatedly condemned as illegitimate.

The plans are tied to each district's specific racial demographics, rather than to any pedagogic concept of the level of diversity needed to obtain the asserted educational benefits. In Seattle, the district seeks white enrollment of between 31 and 51 percent (within 10 percent of "the district white average" of 41 percent), and nonwhite enrollment of between 49 and 69 percent (within 10 percent of "the district minority average" of 59 percent). In Jefferson County, by contrast, the district seeks black enrollment of no less than 15 or more than 50 percent, a range designed to be "equally above and below Black student enrollment system wide," based on the objective of achieving at "all schools . . . an African-American enrollment equivalent to the average district-wide African-American enrollment" of 34 percent. In Seattle, then, the benefits of racial diversity require enrollment of at least 31 percent white students; in Jefferson County, at least 50 percent. There must be at least 15 percent nonwhite students under Jefferson County's plan; in Seattle, more than three times that figure. This comparison makes clear that the racial demographics in each district—whatever they happen to be—drive the required "diversity" numbers. The plans here are not tailored to achieving a degree of diversity necessary to realize the asserted educational benefits; instead the plans are tailored, in the words of Seattle's Manager of Enrollment Planning, Technical Support, and Demographics, to "the goal established by the school board of attaining a level of diversity within the schools that approximates the district's overall demographics."

The districts offer no evidence that the level of racial diversity necessary to achieve the asserted educational benefits happens to coincide with the racial demographics of the respective school districts— or rather the white/nonwhite or black/"other" balance of the districts, since that is the only diversity addressed by the plans. . . . When asked for "a range of percentage that would be diverse," however, Seattle's expert said it was important to have "sufficient numbers so as to avoid students feeling any kind of specter of exceptionality." The district did not attempt to defend the proposition that anything outside its range posed the "specter of exceptionality." Nor did it demonstrate in any way how the educational and social benefits of racial diversity or avoidance of racial isolation are more likely to be achieved at a school that is 50 percent white and 50 percent Asian-American, which would qualify as diverse under Seattle's plan, than at a school that is 30 percent Asian-American, 25 percent African-American, 25 percent Latino, and 20 percent white, which under Seattle's definition would be racially concentrated.

Similarly, Jefferson County's expert referred to the importance of having "at least 20 percent" minority group representation for the group "to be visible enough to make a difference," and noted that "small isolated minority groups in a school are not likely to have a strong effect on the overall school." The Jefferson County plan, however, is based on a goal of replicating at each school "an African-American enrollment equivalent to the average district-wide African-American enrollment."

In fact, in each case the extreme measure of relying on race in assignments is unnecessary to achieve the stated goals, even as defined by the districts. For example, at Franklin High School in Seattle, the racial tiebreaker was applied because nonwhite enrollment exceeded 69 percent, and resulted in an incoming ninth-grade class in 2000–2001 that was 30.3 percent Asian-American, 21.9 percent African-American, 6.8 percent Latino, 0.5 percent Native-American, and 40.5 percent Caucasian. Without the racial tiebreaker, the class would have been 39.6 percent Asian-American, 30.2 percent African-American, 8.3 percent Latino, 1.1 percent Native-American, and 20.8 percent Caucasian. When the actual racial breakdown is considered, enrolling students without regard to their race yields a substantially diverse student body under any definition of diversity.

This working backward to achieve a particular type of racial balance, rather than working forward from some demonstration of the level of diversity that provides the purported benefits, is a fatal flaw under our existing precedent. We have many times over reaffirmed that "[r]acial balance is not to be achieved for its own sake."

Accepting racial balancing as a compelling state interest would justify the imposition of racial proportionality throughout American society, contrary to our repeated recognition that "[a]t the heart of the Constitution's guarantee of equal protection lies the simple command that the Government must treat citizens as individuals, not as simply components of a racial, religious, sexual or national class."

[I]n Seattle the plans are defended as necessary to address the consequences of racially identifiable housing patterns. The sweep of the mandate claimed by the district is contrary to our rulings that remedying past societal discrimination does not justify race-conscious government action.

The principle that racial balancing is not permitted is one of substance, not semantics. Racial balancing is not transformed from "patently unconstitutional" to a compelling state interest simply by relabeling it "racial diversity." While the school districts use various verbal formulations to describe the interest they seek to promote—racial diversity, avoidance of racial isolation, racial integration—they offer no definition of the interest that suggests it differs from racial balance.

[T]he costs [of the school districts' racial classifications] are undeniable. "[D]istinctions between citizens solely because of their ancestry are by their very nature odious to a free people whose institutions are founded upon the doctrine of equality." *Adarand*, (internal quotation marks omitted). Government action dividing us by race is inherently suspect because such classifications promote "notions of racial inferiority and lead to a politics of racial hostility," *Croson*, "reinforce the belief, held by too many for too much of our history, that individuals should be judged by the color of their skin," *Shaw v. Reno*, and "endorse race-based reasoning and the conception of a Nation divided into racial blocs, thus contributing to an escalation of racial hostility and conflict." *Metro Broadcasting*, (O'Connor, J., dissenting). As the Court explained in *Rice v. Cayetano,* (2000), "[o]ne of the principal reasons race is treated as a forbidden classification is that it demeans the dignity and worth of a person to be judged by ancestry instead of by his or her own merit and essential qualities."

All this is true enough in the contexts in which these statements were made—government contracting, voting districts, allocation of broadcast licenses, and electing state officers—but when it comes to using race to assign children to schools, history will be heard. In *Brown v. Board of Education*, we held that segregation deprived black children of equal educational opportunities regardless of whether school facilities and other tangible factors were equal, because government classification and separation on grounds of race themselves denoted inferiority. It was not the inequality of the facilities but the fact of legally separating children on the basis of race on which the Court relied to find a constitutional violation ("The impact [of segregation] is greater when it has the sanction of the law"). The next Term, we accordingly stated that "full compliance" with *Brown I* required school districts "to achieve a system of determining admission to the public schools *on a nonracial basis*." *Brown II*, (emphasis added).

The parties and their *amici* debate which side is more faithful to the heritage of *Brown*, but the position of the plaintiffs in *Brown* was spelled out in their brief and could not have been clearer: "[T]he Fourteenth Amendment prevents states from according differential treatment to American children on the basis of their color or race." What do the racial classifications at issue here do, if not accord differential treatment on the basis of race? As counsel who appeared before this Court for the plaintiffs in *Brown* put it: "We have one fundamental contention which we will seek to develop in the course of this argument, and that contention is that no State has any authority under the equal-protection clause of the Fourteenth Amendment to use race as a factor in affording educational opportunities among its citizens." Tr. of Oral Arg. in *Brown I*, p. 7 (Robert

L. Carter, Dec. 9, 1952). There is no ambiguity in that statement. And it was that position that prevailed in this Court, which emphasized in its remedial opinion that what was "[a]t stake is the personal interest of the plaintiffs in admission to public schools as soon as practicable *on a nondiscriminatory basis*," and what was required was "determining admission to the public schools *on a nonracial basis*." What do the racial classifications do in these cases, if not determine admission to a public school on a racial basis?

Before *Brown*, schoolchildren were told where they could and could not go to school based on the color of their skin. The school districts in these cases have not carried the heavy burden of demonstrating that we should allow this once again—even for very different reasons. . . . The way to stop discrimination on the basis of race is to stop discriminating on the basis of race.

■ JUSTICE THOMAS, concurring.

None of [the] elements [identified by Justice Breyer] is compelling. And the combination of the three unsubstantiated elements does not produce an interest any more compelling than that represented by each element independently.

[T]he records in these cases do not demonstrate that either school board's plan is supported by an interest in remedying past discrimination. Moreover, the school boards have no interest in remedying the sundry consequences of prior segregation unrelated to schooling, such as "housing patterns, employment practices, economic conditions, and social attitudes." General claims that past school segregation affected such varied societal trends are "too amorphous a basis for imposing a racially classified remedy," *Wygant*, (plurality opinion), because "[i]t is sheer speculation" how decades-past segregation in the school system might have affected these trends, *see Croson*. Consequently, school boards seeking to remedy those societal problems with race-based measures in schools today would have no way to gauge the proper scope of the remedy. Indeed, remedial measures geared toward such broad and unrelated societal ills have " 'no logical stopping point,' " and threaten to become "ageless in their reach into the past, and timeless in their ability to affect the future," *Wygant*, (plurality opinion). *See Grutter*, (stating the "requirement that all governmental use of race must have a logical end point").

In reality, it is far from apparent that coerced racial mixing has any educational benefits, much less that integration is necessary to black achievement. Scholars have differing opinions as to whether educational benefits arise from racial balancing. Some have concluded that black students receive genuine educational benefits. *See, e.g.,* Crain & Mahard, Desegregation and Black Achievement: A Review of the Research, 42 L. & Contemp. Probs. 17, 48 (1978). Others have been more circumspect. *See, e.g.,* Henderson, Greenberg, Schneider, Uribe, & Verdugo, High

Quality Schooling for African American Students, in Beyond Desegregation 166 (M. Shujaa ed. 1996) ("Perhaps desegregation does not have a single effect, positive or negative, on the academic achievement of African American students, but rather some strategies help, some hurt, and still others make no difference whatsoever. It is clear to us that focusing simply on demographic issues detracts from focusing on improving schools"). And some have concluded that there are no demonstrable educational benefits. *See, e.g.,* Armor & Rossell, Desegregation and Resegregation in the Public Schools, in Beyond the Color Line: New Perspectives on Race and Ethnicity in America 239, 251 (A. Thernstrom & S. Thernstrom eds.2002).

The *amicus* briefs in the cases before us mirror this divergence of opinion. Supporting the school boards, one *amicus* has assured us that "both early desegregation research and recent statistical and econometric analyses . . . indicate that there are positive effects on minority student achievement scores arising from diverse school settings." Brief for American Educational Research Association as *Amicus Curiae* 10. Another brief claims that "school desegregation has a modest positive impact on the achievement of African-American students." App. to Brief for 553 Social Scientists as *Amici Curiae* 13–14 (footnote omitted). Yet neither of those briefs contains specific details like the magnitude of the claimed positive effects or the precise demographic mix at which those positive effects begin to be realized. Indeed, the social scientists' brief rather cautiously claims the existence of any benefit at all, describing the "positive impact" as "modest," acknowledging that "there appears to be little or no effect on math scores," and admitting that the "underlying reasons for these gains in achievement are not entirely clear," *id.,* at 15.FN11

Add to the inconclusive social science the fact of black achievement in "racially isolated" environments. *See* T. Sowell, Education: Assumptions Versus History 7–38 (1986). Before *Brown,* the most prominent example of an exemplary black school was Dunbar High School. *Id.,* at 29 ("[I]n the period 1918–1923, Dunbar graduates earned fifteen degrees from Ivy League colleges, and ten degrees from Amherst, Williams, and Wesleyan"). Dunbar is by no means an isolated example.

The Seattle school board itself must believe that racial mixing is not necessary to black achievement. Seattle operates a K–8 "African-American Academy," which has a "nonwhite" enrollment of 99%. That school was founded in 1990 as part of the school board's effort to "increase academic achievement." According to the school's most recent annual report, "[a]cademic excellence" is its "primary goal." This racially imbalanced environment has reportedly produced test scores "higher across all grade levels in reading, writing and math." Contrary to what the dissent would have predicted, the children in Seattle's African

American Academy have shown gains when placed in a "highly segregated" environment.

Finally, the dissent asserts a "democratic element" to the integration interest. [T]he dissent argues that the racial balancing in these plans is not an end in itself but is instead intended to "teac[h] children to engage in the kind of cooperation among Americans of all races that is necessary to make a land of three hundred million people one Nation." These "generic lessons in socialization and good citizenship" are too sweeping to qualify as compelling interests. And they are not "uniquely relevant" to schools or "uniquely 'teachable' in a formal educational setting. Therefore, if governments may constitutionally use racial balancing to achieve these aspirational ends in schools, they may use racial balancing to achieve similar goals at every level—from state-sponsored 4-H clubs, to the state civil service.

Moreover, the democratic interest has no durational limit, contrary to *Grutter*'s command. In other words, it will always be important for students to learn cooperation among the races. If this interest justifies race-conscious measures today, then logically it will justify race-conscious measures forever. Thus, the democratic interest, limitless in scope and "timeless in [its] ability to affect the future," cannot justify government race-based decisionmaking.

By the dissent's account, improvements in racial attitudes depend upon the increased contact between black and white students thought to occur in more racially balanced schools. There is no guarantee, however, that students of different races in the same school will actually spend time with one another. Schools frequently group students by academic ability as an aid to efficient instruction, but such groupings often result in classrooms with high concentrations of one race or another. In addition to classroom separation, students of different races within the same school may separate themselves socially. Therefore, even supposing interracial contact leads directly to improvements in racial attitudes and race relations, a program that assigns students of different races to the same schools might not capture those benefits. Simply putting students together under the same roof does not necessarily mean that the students will learn together or even interact.

Furthermore, it is unclear whether increased interracial contact improves racial attitudes and relations. One researcher has stated that "the reviews of desegregation and intergroup relations were unable to come to any conclusion about what the probable effects of desegregation were . . . [;] virtually all of the reviewers determined that few, if any, firm conclusions about the impact of desegregation on intergroup relations could be drawn." Schofield, School Desegregation and Intergroup Relations: A Review of the Literature, in 17 Review of Research in Education 356 (G. Grant ed.1991). Some studies have even found that a deterioration in racial attitudes seems to result from racial mixing in schools. *See* N. St. John, School Desegregation Outcomes for Children 67–68 (1975) ("A glance at [the data] shows that for either race positive findings are less common than negative findings"); Stephan, The Effects of School Desegregation: An Evaluation 30 Years After Brown, in Advances in Applied Social Psychology 183–186 (M. Saks & L. Saxe eds.1986). Therefore, it is not nearly as apparent as the dissent suggests that increased interracial exposure automatically leads to improved racial attitudes or race relations.

Given our case law and the paucity of evidence supporting the dissent's belief that these plans improve race relations, no democratic element can support the integration interest.

What was wrong in 1954 cannot be right today. Whatever else the Court's rejection of the segregationists' arguments in *Brown* might have established, it certainly made clear that state and local governments cannot take from the Constitution a right to make decisions on the basis of race by adverse possession. The fact that state and local governments had been discriminating on the basis of race for a long time was irrelevant to the *Brown* Court. The fact that racial discrimination was preferable to the relevant communities was irrelevant to the *Brown* Court. And the fact that the state and local governments had relied on statements in this Court's opinions was irrelevant to the *Brown* Court. The same principles guide today's decision. None of the considerations trumpeted by the dissent is relevant to the constitutionality of the school boards' race-based plans because no contextual detail—or collection of contextual details, can "provide refuge from the principle that under our Constitution, the government may not make distinctions on the basis of race." *Adarand*, 515 U.S., at 240, 115 S.Ct. 2097 (THOMAS, J., concurring in part and concurring in judgment).

■ JUSTICE KENNEDY, concurring in part and concurring in the judgment.

That the school districts consider these plans to be necessary should remind us our highest aspirations are yet unfulfilled. But the solutions mandated by these school districts must themselves be lawful. To make race matter now so that it might not matter later may entrench the very prejudices we seek to overcome. In my view the state-mandated racial classifications at issue . . . are unconstitutional as the cases now come to us.

The plurality opinion is too dismissive of the legitimate interest government has in ensuring all people have equal opportunity regardless of their race. . . . The plurality opinion is at least open to the interpretation that the Constitution requires school districts to ignore the problem of *de facto* resegregation in schooling. I cannot endorse that conclusion. To the extent the plurality opinion suggests the Constitution mandates that state and local school authorities must accept the status quo of racial isolation in schools, it is, in my view, profoundly mistaken.

In the administration of public schools by the state and local authorities it is permissible to consider the racial makeup of schools and to adopt general policies to encourage a diverse student body, one aspect of which is its racial composition. If school authorities are concerned that the student-body compositions of certain schools interfere with the objective of offering an equal educational opportunity to all of their students, they are free to devise race-conscious measures to address the problem in a general way and without treating each student in different fashion solely on the basis of a systematic, individual typing by race.

School boards may pursue the goal of bringing together students of diverse backgrounds and races through other means, including strategic site selection of new schools; drawing attendance zones with general recognition of the demographics of neighborhoods; allocating resources for special programs; recruiting students and faculty in a targeted fashion; and tracking enrollments, performance, and other statistics by race. These mechanisms are race conscious but do not lead to different treatment based on a classification that tells each student he or she is to be defined by race, so it is unlikely any of them would demand strict scrutiny to be found permissible. Executive and legislative branches, which for generations now have considered these types of policies and procedures, should be permitted to employ them with candor and with confidence that a constitutional violation does not occur whenever a decisionmaker considers the impact a given approach might have on students of different races. Assigning to each student a personal designation according to a crude system of individual racial classifications is quite a different matter; and the legal analysis changes accordingly.

III

C

[There are] dangers presented by individual classifications, dangers that are not as pressing when the same ends are achieved by more indirect means. When the government classifies an individual by race, it must first define what it means to be of a race. Who exactly is white and who is nonwhite? To be forced to live under a state-mandated racial label is inconsistent with the dignity of individuals in our society. And it is a label that an individual is powerless to change. Governmental classifications that command people to march in different directions based on racial typologies can cause a new divisiveness. The practice can lead to corrosive discourse, where race serves not as an element of our diverse heritage but instead as a bargaining chip in the political process. On the other hand race-conscious measures that do not rely on differential treatment based on individual classifications present these problems to a lesser degree.

The idea that if race is the problem, race is the instrument with which to solve it cannot be accepted as an analytical leap forward. And if this is a frustrating duality of the Equal Protection Clause it simply reflects the duality of our history and our attempts to promote freedom in a world that sometimes seems set against it. Under our Constitution the individual, child or adult, can find his own identity, can define her own persona, without state intervention that classifies on the basis of his race or the color of her skin.

'This Nation has a moral and ethical obligation to fulfill its historic commitment to creating an integrated society that ensures equal opportunity for all of its children. A compelling interest exists in avoiding racial isolation, an interest that a school district, in its discretion and expertise, may choose to pursue. Likewise, a district may consider it a compelling interest to achieve a diverse student population. Race may be one component of that diversity, but other demographic factors, plus special talents and needs, should also be considered. What the government is not permitted to do, absent a showing of necessity not made here, is to classify every student on the basis of race and to assign each of them to schools based on that classification. Crude measures of this sort threaten to reduce children to racial chits valued and traded according to one school's supply and another's demand.

That statement, to be sure, invites this response: A sense of stigma may already become the fate of those separated out by circumstances beyond their immediate control. But to this the replication must be: Even so, measures other than differential treatment based on racial typing of individuals first must be exhausted.

The decision today should not prevent school districts from continuing the important work of bringing together students of different racial, ethnic, and economic backgrounds. Due to a variety of factors— some influenced by government, some not—neighborhoods in our communities do not reflect the diversity of our Nation as a whole. Those entrusted with directing our public schools can bring to bear the creativity of experts, parents, administrators, and other concerned citizens to find a way to achieve the compelling interests they face without resorting to widespread governmental allocation of benefits and burdens on the basis of racial classifications.

■ JUSTICE STEVENS, dissenting.

There is a cruel irony in THE CHIEF JUSTICE's reliance on our decision in Brown v. Board of Education. The first sentence in the concluding paragraph of his opinion states: "Before Brown, schoolchildren were told where they could and could not go to school based on the color of their skin." This sentence reminds me of Anatole France's observation: "[T]he majestic equality of the la[w], . . . forbid[s] rich and poor alike to sleep under the bridges, to beg in the streets, and to steal their bread." THE CHIEF JUSTICE fails to note that it was only black schoolchildren who were so ordered; indeed, the history books do not tell stories of white children struggling to attend black schools. In this and other ways, THE CHIEF JUSTICE rewrites the history of one of this Court's most important decisions.

■ JUSTICE BREYER, with whom JUSTICE STEVENS, JUSTICE SOUTER, and JUSTICE GINSBURG join, dissenting.

These cases consider the longstanding efforts of two local school boards to integrate their public schools. The school board plans before us resemble many others adopted in the last 50 years by primary and secondary schools throughout the Nation. All of those plans represent local efforts to bring about the kind of racially integrated education that *Brown v. Board of Education*, long ago promised—efforts that this Court has repeatedly required, permitted, and encouraged local authorities to undertake. . . . [We] have understood that the Constitution *permits* local communities to adopt desegregation plans even where it does not *require* them to do so.

I

Facts

[Throughout the nation, school] districts—some acting under court decree, some acting in order to avoid threatened lawsuits, some seeking to comply with federal administrative orders, some acting purely voluntarily, some acting after federal courts had dissolved earlier orders—adopted, modified, and experimented with hosts of different kinds of plans, including race-conscious plans, all with a similar objective: greater racial integration of public schools. The techniques that different districts have employed range "from voluntary transfer programs to mandatory reassignment." And the design of particular plans has been "dictated by both the law and the specific needs of the district."

Overall these efforts brought about considerable racial integration. More recently, however, progress has stalled. Between 1968 and 1980, the number of black children attending a school where minority children constituted more than half of the school fell from 77% to 63% in the Nation (from 81% to 57% in the South) but then reversed direction by the year 2000, rising from 63% to 72% in the Nation (from 57% to 69% in the South). Similarly, between 1968 and 1980, the number of black children attending schools that were more than 90% minority fell from 64% to 33% in the Nation (from 78% to 23% in the South), but that too reversed direction, rising by the year 2000 from 33% to 37% in the Nation (from 23% to 31% in the South). As of 2002, almost 2.4 million students, or over 5% of all public school enrollment, attended schools with a white population of less than 1%. Of these, 2.3 million were black and Latino students, and only 72,000 were white. Today, more than one in six black children attend a school that is 99–100% minority. In light of the evident risk of a return to school systems that are in fact (though not in law) resegregated, many school districts have felt a need to maintain or to extend their integration efforts.

No one here disputes that Louisville's segregation was *de jure*. But what about Seattle's? Was it *de facto*? *De jure*? A mixture? Opinions differed. Or is it that a prior federal court had not adjudicated the matter? Does that make a difference? Is Seattle free on remand to say that its schools were *de jure* segregated, just as in 1956 a memo for the School Board admitted? The plurality does not seem confident as to the answer.

A court finding of *de jure* segregation cannot be the crucial variable. After all, a number of school districts in the South that the Government or private plaintiffs challenged as segregated *by law* voluntarily desegregated their schools *without a court order*—just as Seattle did. Moreover, Louisville's history makes clear that a community under a court order to desegregate might submit a race-conscious remedial plan *before* the court dissolved the order, but with every intention of following that plan even *after* dissolution. How could such a plan be lawful the day before dissolution but then become unlawful the very next day? On what legal ground can the majority rest its contrary view?

Are courts really to treat as merely *de facto* segregated those school districts that avoided a federal order by voluntarily complying with *Brown*'s requirements? This Court has previously done just the opposite, permitting a race-conscious remedy without any kind of court decree. Because the Constitution emphatically does not forbid the use of race-conscious measures by districts in the South that voluntarily desegregated their schools, on what basis does the plurality claim that the law forbids Seattle to do the same?

II

The Legal Standard

Here, the context is one in which school districts seek to advance or to maintain racial integration in primary and secondary schools. . . . This context is *not* a context that involves the use of race to decide who will receive goods or services that are normally distributed on the basis of merit and which are in short supply. It is not one in which race-conscious limits stigmatize or exclude; the limits at issue do not pit the races against each other or otherwise significantly exacerbate racial tensions. They do not impose burdens unfairly upon members of one race alone but instead seek benefits for members of all races alike. The context here is one of racial limits that seek, not to keep the races apart, but to bring them together.

III

The principal interest advanced in these cases to justify the use of race-based criteria goes by various names. Sometimes a court refers to it as an interest in achieving racial "diversity." Other times a court, like the plurality here, refers to it as an interest in racial "balancing." I have used more general terms to signify that interest, describing it, for example, as an interest in promoting or preserving greater racial "integration" of public schools. By this term, I mean the school districts' interest in eliminating school-by-school racial isolation and increasing the degree to which racial mixture characterizes each of the district's schools and each individual student's public school experience.

Regardless of its name, however, the interest at stake possesses three essential elements. First, there is a historical and remedial element: an interest in setting right the consequences of prior conditions of segregation. This refers back to a time when public schools were highly segregated, often as a result of legal or administrative policies that facilitated racial segregation in public schools. It is an interest in continuing to combat the remnants of segregation caused in whole or in part by these school-related policies, which have often affected not only schools, but also housing patterns, employment practices, economic conditions, and social attitudes. It is an interest in maintaining hard-won gains. And it has its roots in preventing what gradually may become the *de facto* resegregation of America's public schools.

Second, there is an educational element: an interest in overcoming the adverse educational effects produced by and associated with highly segregated schools. Studies suggest that children taken from those schools and placed in integrated settings often show positive academic gains. *See, e.g.,* Powell, Living and Learning: Linking Housing and Education, in Pursuit of a Dream Deferred: Linking Housing and Education Policy 15, 35 (J. Powell, G. Kearney, & V. Kay eds.2001) (hereinafter Powell); Hallinan, Diversity Effects on Student Outcomes: Social Science Evidence, 59 Ohio St. L.J. 733, 741–742 (1998) (hereinafter Hallinan).

Other studies reach different conclusions. But the evidence supporting an educational interest in racially integrated schools is well established and strong enough to permit a democratically elected school board reasonably to determine that this interest is a compelling one.

Research suggests, for example, that black children from segregated educational environments significantly increase their achievement levels once they are placed in a more integrated setting. Indeed in Louisville itself the achievement gap between black and white elementary school students grew substantially smaller (by seven percentage points) after the integration plan was implemented in 1975. Conversely, to take another example, evidence from a district in Norfolk, Virginia, shows that resegregated schools led to a decline in the achievement test scores of children of all races.

One commentator, reviewing dozens of studies of the educational benefits of desegregated schooling, found that the studies have provided "remarkably consistent" results, showing that: (1) black students' educational achievement is improved in integrated schools as compared to racially isolated schools, (2) black students' educational achievement is improved in integrated classes, and (3) the earlier that black students are removed from racial isolation, the better their educational outcomes. *See* Hallinan 741–742. Multiple studies also indicate that black alumni of integrated schools are more likely to move into occupations traditionally closed to African-Americans, and to earn more money in those fields.

Third, there is a democratic element: an interest in producing an educational environment that reflects the "pluralistic society" in which our children will live. It is an interest in helping our children learn to work and play together with children of different racial backgrounds. It is an interest in teaching children to engage in the kind of cooperation among Americans of all races that is necessary to make a land of three hundred million people one Nation.

[T]he evidence supporting a democratic interest in racially integrated schools is firmly established and sufficiently strong to permit a school board to determine, as this Court has itself often found, that this interest is compelling. For example, one study documented that "black and white students in desegregated schools are less racially prejudiced than those in segregated schools," and that "interracial contact in desegregated schools leads to an increase in interracial sociability and friendship." Hallinan 745. *See also* Quillian & Campbell 541. Cf. Bowen & Bok 155. Other studies have found that both black and white students who attend integrated schools are more likely to work in desegregated companies after graduation than students who attended racially isolated schools. Dawkins & Braddock 401–403; Wells & Crain 550. Further research has shown that the desegregation of schools can help bring adult communities together by reducing segregated housing. Cities that have implemented successful school desegregation plans have witnessed increased interracial contact and neighborhoods that tend to become less racially segregated. These effects not only reinforce the prior gains of integrated primary and secondary education; they also foresee a time when there is less need to use race-conscious criteria.

Moreover, this Court from *Swann* to *Grutter* has treated these civic effects as an important virtue of racially diverse education.

The compelling interest at issue here, then, includes an effort to eradicate the remnants, not of general "societal discrimination," but of primary and secondary school segregation, it includes an effort to create school environments that provide better educational opportunities for all children; it includes an effort to help create citizens better prepared to know, to understand, and to work with people of all races and backgrounds, thereby furthering the kind of democratic government our Constitution foresees. If an educational interest that combines these three elements is not "compelling," what is?

B

[P]lans that are less explicitly race-based are unlikely to achieve the board's "compelling" objectives. The wide variety of different integration plans that school districts use throughout the Nation suggests that the problem of racial segregation in schools, including *de facto* segregation, is difficult to solve.

[D]e facto resegregation is on the rise. It is reasonable to conclude that such resegregation can create serious educational, social, and civic problems. Given the conditions in which school boards work to set policy, they may need all of the means presently at their disposal to combat those problems. Yet the plurality would deprive them of at least one tool that some districts now consider vital—the limited use of broad race-conscious student population ranges.

I fear the consequences of doing so for the law, for the schools, for the democratic process, and for America's efforts to create, out of its diversity, one Nation.

VI

Conclusions

[S]egregation policies did not simply tell schoolchildren "where they could and could not go to school based on the color of their skin"; they perpetuated a caste system rooted in the institutions of slavery and 80 years of legalized subordination. The lesson of history is not that efforts to continue racial segregation are constitutionally indistinguishable from efforts to achieve racial integration. Indeed, it is a cruel distortion of history to compare Topeka, Kansas, in the 1950's to Louisville and Seattle in the modern day—to equate the plight of Linda Brown (who was ordered to attend a Jim Crow school) to the circumstances of Joshua McDonald (whose request to transfer to a school closer to home was initially declined). This is not to deny that there is a cost in applying "a state-mandated racial label." But that cost does not approach, in degree or in kind, the terrible harms of slavery, the resulting caste system, and 80 years of legal racial segregation.

Brown held out a promise. It was a promise embodied in three Amendments designed to make citizens of slaves. It was the promise of true racial equality—not as a matter of fine words on paper, but as a matter of everyday life in the Nation's cities and schools. It was about the nature of a democracy that must work for all Americans. It sought one law, one Nation, one people, not simply as a matter of legal principle but in terms of how we actually live.

The last half-century has witnessed great strides toward racial equality, but we have not yet realized the promise of *Brown*. To invalidate the plans under review is to threaten the promise of *Brown*. The plurality's position, I fear, would break that promise. This is a decision that the Court and the Nation will come to regret.

NOTES AND QUESTIONS

1.   *The Remedial Rationale.* Prior doctrine dictates, and all the Justices agree, that race-based student assignments can be justified as a response to a history of segregation within the school district. Why, in the view of a majority of the Justices, isn't that standard met in either of these cases? Does it make sense to limit districts' use of race-based student assignment plans to circumstances in which they are under judicial supervision? Doesn't that standard create perverse incentives for a district that wants to racially integrate its schools: either not to settle a lawsuit prior to judgment, or not to fully comply with a judgment that has been entered so that judicial supervision can continue? Why then does the majority impose such a stringent standard on race-based student assignment plans?

2.   *The Educational Interest.* How and why does Justice Breyer think that racial integration would improve education? What precisely is the basis of his disagreement with Justice Thomas? Why and how might the racial composition of a school influence student achievement?

3.   *The Democratic Interest.* Putting aside the educational and remedial interests, is the democratic interest in integration alone sufficient to justify a race-based school assignment plan? Is it proper for school district officials to take into account these larger societal goals?

4.   *The Meaning of Integration.* The Seattle and Louisville districts use different racial categories and hence different definitions of integration. Seattle classifies children as white or nonwhite, and Louisville as black or "other." Is there any rationale for these different categorization schemes? In Seattle, would a school that is 60% white, 30% Asian and 10% black count as integrated? Should it?

5.   *Shifting Demographics.* As the demographic composition of the nation and local communities has shifted and become more diverse, it has become less obvious what "integration" means or should require. In the 1960s, 4 out of every 5 students in public schools were white. Today, white students constitute barely half the national public school population. Latinos, at roughly 25% of the student population, have become the largest minority group in the public schools, while the previously miniscule representation of Asian American students has increased to approximately 5% of the school population. African Americans remain between 15 and 20% of the public school population. How should these changes affect one's conception of integration?

6.   *Harms of Race-Based Student Selection.* In the view of the *Parents Involved* majority, what is the harm of assigning students to schools in part on the basis of race? Why wouldn't the fact that every student is ultimately assigned to a school mean that no one is harmed by such a process?

7.   *The Kennedy Alternative.* Justice Kennedy both accords importance to integration and finds race-based assignment schemes objectionable. He thus advocates for race-conscious integration efforts that do not distinguish among students on the basis of race. How effective do you think these aspects of his proposed approach would be at promoting integrated schools: "strategic

site selection of new schools; drawing attendance zones with general recognition of the demographics of neighborhoods; allocating resources for special programs; recruiting students and faculty in a targeted fashion; and tracking enrollments, performance, and other statistics by race"?

8. *Socioeconomic Segregation.* Schools are segregated not only by race, but by class as well. On average, white students attend schools where about 30% of their classmates are low income. Blacks and Latinos, in contrast, attend schools were nearly 60% of their classmates are low income. Asian Americans attend schools where about 35% of the students are low income. More striking, 40% of black and Latino children attend schools where more than 70% of their classmates are poor. Only a few percent of whites and less than 10% of Asian Americans attend such schools. Do these patterns indicate that we should strive for socioeconomic integration rather than racial integration?

9.   *Race-Neutral Alternatives.* Suppose that, rather than rely on race in assigning students to schools, the Seattle district had developed a "disadvantage profile" for each student based on the following factors:

   a.   Economic Disadvantage: Does the student live in public housing? Is the student a foster youth? Does the family participate in a homelessness program? Does the student or his or her family receive any means-tested public benefits programs, such as free/reduced lunch, food stamps, or TANF? Is the student's family income at or near the poverty line?

   b.   Home Language: Is English the student's home language? If not, what is the home language?

   c.   Academic Performance Rank of Sending School: How is the student's current school ranked by the state department of education?

   d.   Academic Achievement Status:

      i.   Incoming Kindergartners: Did the student attend preschool?

      ii. Students Entering Grades 1–12: Did the student score above or below the thirtieth (30th) percentile on the most recent state standardized test?

   In considering requests to transfer out of a neighborhood school, the district considers each student's "disadvantage profile" and assigns students to its schools by taking into account these profiles to achieve diversity in individual schools along these various dimensions. Is such a policy constitutional after *Parents Involved*? Would any of the factors listed above be more suspect than others? Would you deem the policy a success even if the schools remain racially identifiable? If the district had, in fact, enacted the policy in order to create more racially integrated schools, would the policy still be constitutional? Are such racially motivated practices less objectionable than the sort of individual racial classifications used by the districts in the *Parents Involved* case?

10. ***Assignment Schemes and State Law.*** The Berkeley, California school district developed an assignment scheme in which it sought to integrate students from neighborhoods of different racial compositions. The scheme was challenged as a violation of Proposition 209, which had amended the California constitution in 1996, to state:

> "The state shall not discriminate against, or grant preferential treatment to, any individual or group on the basis of race, sex, color, ethnicity, or national origin in the operation of public employment, public education, or public contracting."

The California Court of Appeal ruled on the challenge in March 2009. *American Civil Rights Found. v. Berkeley Unified Sch. Dist.*, 172 Cal.App.4th 207 (2009). The court held that the school district's policy did not violate Proposition 209, because the policy did not treat an individual or group differently based on the race of *that* individual or group:

> [Proposition 209] prohibits using the race of an individual or group in order to give preference to, or to discriminate against, that individual or group. Here, the School District does not use the race of a student or student group to give preference to that student or student group. Instead, the School District reviews the racial composition of a neighborhood (which includes multiple races) to assess the neighborhood's level of social diversity and, based on that diversity rating, assigns students to various schools and programs. While the race of an individual student may be included within this composite diversity rating (along with the race of all students in the neighborhood), any preference given to the student is not based on the student's race. White and African-American students from the same neighborhood receive the same diversity rating and the same treatment.

Imagine that you are on the California Supreme Court and the case comes up for appeal. Do you agree with the lower court's assessment?

III. ALTERNATIVES TO INTEGRATION

The struggle to achieve equality in the public schools has not been limited to the *Brown*-inspired battles over desegregation. Particularly as courts' appetite for mandating integration waned, and as segregation became less clearly traceable to overt or intentional state policies, education reformers began pursuing other avenues for improving the quality of the education for minority students. In this section, we explore two of those strategies: efforts to equalize funding and promote educational adequacy, and efforts to draw attention to race-related discrimination and inequities within schools themselves.

A. THE PURSUIT OF EQUAL FUNDING AND EDUCATIONAL ADEQUACY

Minority groups have opposed segregated schools in part because they have almost invariably been inferior schools—less well funded, with lower-quality facilities and teachers. As an alternative to integration strategies, then, education reformers and activists have turned to the courts to seek increased funding for education, particularly in school districts composed mostly of racial minorities. In *San Antonio v. Rodriguez*, a group of Mexican-American parents challenged the constitutionality of the funding scheme adopted by the state of Texas.

San Antonio Independent School District v. Rodriguez

Supreme Court of the United States, 1973.
411 U.S. 1.

■ MR. JUSTICE POWELL delivered the opinion of the Court.

This suit attacking the Texas system of financing public education was initiated by Mexican-American parents whose children attend the elementary and secondary schools in the Edgewood Independent School District, an urban school district in San Antonio, Texas. They brought a class action on behalf of schoolchildren throughout the State who are members of minority groups or who are poor and reside in school districts having a low property tax base.

I

[The state has recently increased funding for the lowest funded districts, but] [d]espite these recent increases, substantial interdistrict disparities in school expenditures found by the District Court to prevail in San Antonio and in varying degrees throughout the State still exist. And it was these disparities, largely attributable to differences in the amounts of money collected through local property taxation, that led the District Court to conclude that Texas' system of public school financing violated the Equal Protection Clause. The District Court held that the Texas system discriminates on the basis of wealth in the manner in which education is provided for its people. Finding that wealth is a 'suspect' classification and that education is a 'fundamental' interest, the District Court held that the Texas system could be sustained only if the State could show that it was premised upon some compelling state interest. On this issue the court concluded that '(n)ot only are defendants unable to demonstrate compelling state interests . . . they fail even to establish a reasonable basis for these classifications.'

The system of alleged discrimination and the class it defines have none of the traditional indicia of suspectness: the class is not saddled with such disabilities, or subjected to such a history of purposeful unequal treatment, or relegated to such a position of political powerlessness as to command extraordinary protection from the majoritarian political process.

We thus conclude that the Texas system does not operate to the peculiar disadvantage of any suspect class.

We are in complete agreement with the conclusion of the three-judge panel below that 'the grave significance of education both to the individual and to our society' cannot be doubted. But the importance of a service performed by the State does not determine whether it must be regarded as fundamental for purposes of examination under the Equal Protection Clause.

It is not the province of this Court to create substantive constitutional rights in the name of guaranteeing equal protection of the laws.

Education, of course, is not among the rights afforded explicit protection under our Federal Constitution. Nor do we find any basis for saying it is implicitly so protected. As we have said, the undisputed importance of education will not alone cause this Court to depart from the usual standard for reviewing a State's social and economic legislation.

Even if it were conceded that some identifiable quantum of education is a constitutionally protected prerequisite to the meaningful exercise of either right, we have no indication that the present levels of educational expenditures in Texas provide an education that falls short. Whatever merit appellees' argument might have if a State's financing system occasioned an absolute denial of educational opportunities to any of its children, that argument provides no basis for finding an interference with fundamental rights where only relative differences in spending levels are involved and where—as is true in the present case—no charge fairly could be made that the system fails to provide each child with an opportunity to acquire the basic minimal skills necessary for the enjoyment of the rights of speech and of full participation in the political process.

C

We need not rest our decision, however, solely on the inappropriateness of the strict-scrutiny test. A century of Supreme Court adjudication under the Equal Protection Clause affirmatively supports the application of the traditional standard of review, which requires only that the State's system be shown to bear some rational relationship to legitimate state purposes. This case represents far more than a challenge to the manner in which Texas provides for the education of its children. We have here nothing less than a direct attack on the way in which Texas has chosen to raise and disburse state and local tax revenues. We are asked to condemn the State's judgment in conferring on political subdivisions the power to tax local property to supply revenues for local interests. In so doing, appellees would have the Court intrude in an area in which it has traditionally deferred to state legislatures.

Thus, we stand on familiar grounds when we continue to acknowledge that the Justices of this Court lack both the expertise and the familiarity with local problems so necessary to the making of wise decisions with respect to the raising and disposition of public revenues. Yet, we are urged to direct the States either to alter drastically the present system or to throw out the property tax altogether in favor of some other form of taxation. No scheme of taxation, whether the tax is imposed on property, income, or purchases of goods and services, has yet been devised which is free of all discriminatory impact. In such a complex arena in which no perfect alternatives exist, the Court does well not to impose too rigorous a standard of scrutiny lest all local fiscal schemes become subjects of criticism under the Equal Protection Clause.

In addition to matters of fiscal policy, this case also involves the most persistent and difficult questions of educational policy, another area in which this Court's lack of specialized knowledge and experience counsels against premature interference with the informed judgments made at the state and local levels. Education, perhaps even more than welfare assistance, presents a myriad of 'intractable economic, social, and even philosophical problems.' The very complexity of the problems of financing and managing a statewide public school system suggests that 'there will be more than one constitutionally permissible method of solving them,' and that, within the limits of rationality, 'the legislature's efforts to tackle the problems' should be entitled to respect. On even the most basic questions in this area the scholars and educational experts are divided. Indeed, one of the major sources of controversy concerns the extent to which there is a demonstrable correlation between educational expenditures and the quality of education—an assumed correlation underlying virtually every legal conclusion drawn by the District Court in this case. Related to the questioned relationship between cost and quality is the equally unsettled controversy as to the proper goals of a system of public education. And the question regarding the most effective relationship between state boards of education and local school boards, in terms of their respective responsibilities and degrees of control, is now undergoing searching re-examination. The ultimate wisdom as to these and related problems of education is not likely to be divined for all time even by the scholars who now so earnestly debate the issues. In such circumstances, the judiciary is well advised to refrain from imposing on the States inflexible constitutional restraints that could circumscribe or handicap the continued research and experimentation so vital to finding even partial solutions to educational problems and to keeping abreast of ever-changing conditions.

It must be remembered, also, that every claim arising under the Equal Protection Clause has implications for the relationship between national and state power under our federal system. Questions of federalism are always inherent in the process of determining whether a State's laws are to be accorded the traditional presumption of constitutionality, or are to be subjected instead to rigorous judicial scrutiny. While '(t)he maintenance of the principles of federalism is a foremost consideration in interpreting any of the pertinent constitutional provisions under which this Court examines state action,' it would be difficult to imagine a case having a greater potential impact on our federal system than the one now before us, in which we are urged to abrogate systems of financing public education presently in existence in virtually every State.

III

[Appellees]   attack the school-financing system precisely because, in their view, it does not provide the same level of local control and fiscal flexibility in all districts. Appellees suggest that local control could be preserved and promoted under other financing systems that resulted in more equality in education expenditures ... [T]he existence of 'some inequality' in the manner in which the State's rationale is achieved is not alone a sufficient basis for striking down the entire system. It may not be condemned simply because it imperfectly effectuates the State's goals. Nor must the financing system fail because, as appellees suggest, other methods of satisfying the State's interest, which occasion 'less drastic' disparities in expenditures, might be conceived. Only where state action impinges on the exercise of fundamental constitutional rights or liberties must it be found to have chosen the least restrictive alternative.

Appellees further urge that the Texas system is unconstitutionally arbitrary because it allows the availability of local taxable resources to turn on 'happenstance.' . . . But any scheme of local taxation—indeed the very existence of identifiable local governmental units—requires the establishment of jurisdictional boundaries that are inevitably arbitrary. It is equally inevitable that some localities are going to be blessed with more taxable assets than others. Nor is local wealth a static quantity. Changes in the level of taxable wealth within any district may result from any number of events, some of which local residents can and do influence.

Moreover, if local taxation for local expenditures were an unconstitutional method of providing for education then it might be an equally impermissible means of providing other necessary services customarily financed largely from local property taxes, including local police and fire protection, public health and hospitals, and public utility facilities of various kinds. . . . It has simply never been within the constitutional prerogative of this Court to nullify statewide measures for financing public services merely because the burdens or benefits thereof fall unevenly depending upon the relative wealth of the political subdivisions in which citizens live.

[T]o the extent that the Texas system of school financing results in unequal expenditures between children who happen to reside in different districts, we cannot say that such disparities are the product of a system that is so irrational as to be invidiously discriminatory. . . . In giving substance to the presumption of validity to which the Texas system is entitled, it is important to remember that at every stage of its development it has constituted a 'rough accommodation' of interests in an effort to arrive at practical and workable solutions. One also must remember that the system here challenged is not peculiar to Texas or to any other State. In its essential characteristics, the Texas plan for financing public education reflects what many educators for a half century have thought was an enlightened approach to a problem for which there is no perfect solution. We are unwilling to assume for ourselves a level of wisdom superior to that of legislators, scholars, and educational authorities in 50 States, especially where the alternatives proposed are only recently conceived and nowhere yet tested. The constitutional standard under the Equal Protection Clause is whether the challenged state action rationally furthers a legitimate state purpose or interest. We hold that the Texas plan abundantly satisfies this standard.

IV

The complexity of these problems is demonstrated by the lack of consensus with respect to whether it may be said with any assurance that the poor, the racial minorities, or the children in over-burdened core-city school districts would be benefited by abrogation of traditional modes of financing education. Unless there is to be a substantial increase in state expenditures on education across the board—an event the likelihood of which is open to considerable question these groups stand to realize gains in terms of increased per-pupil expenditures only if they reside in districts that presently spend at relatively low levels, i.e., in those districts that would benefit from the redistribution of existing resources. Yet, recent studies have indicated that the poorest families are not invariably clustered in the most impecunious school districts. Nor does it now appear that there is any more than a random chance that racial minorities are concentrated in property-poor districts. Additionally, several research projects have concluded that any financing alternative designed to achieve a greater equality of expenditures is likely to lead to higher taxation and lower educational expenditures in the major urban centers, a result that would exacerbate rather than ameliorate existing conditions in those areas.

These practical considerations, of course, play no role in the adjudication of the constitutional issues presented here. But they serve to highlight the wisdom of the traditional limitations on this Court's function. The consideration and initiation of fundamental reforms with respect to state taxation and education are matters reserved for the legislative processes of the various States, and we do no violence to the values of federalism and separation of powers by staying our hand. We hardly need add that this Court's action today is not to be viewed as placing its judicial imprimatur on the status quo. The need is apparent for reform in tax systems which may well have relied too long and too heavily on the local property tax. And certainly innovative thinking as to public education, its methods, and its funding is necessary to assure both a higher level of quality and greater uniformity of opportunity. These matters merit the continued attention of the scholars who already have contributed much by their challenges. But the ultimate solutions must come from the lawmakers and from the democratic pressures of those who elect them.

■ MR. JUSTICE BRENNAN, dissenting.

Here, there can be no doubt that education is inextricably linked to the right to participate in the electoral process and to the rights of free speech and association guaranteed by the First Amendment. . . . [A]ny classification affecting education must be subjected to strict judicial scrutiny, and since even the State concedes that the statutory scheme now before us cannot pass constitutional muster under this stricter standard of review, I can only conclude that the Texas school-financing scheme is constitutionally invalid.

■ MR. JUSTICE WHITE, with whom MR. JUSTICE DOUGLAS and MR. JUSTICE BRENNAN join, dissenting.

The Texas public schools are financed through a combination of state funding, local property tax revenue, and some federal funds. Concededly, the system yields wide disparity in per-pupil revenue among the various districts. In a typical year, for example, the Alamo Heights district had total revenues of $594 per pupil, while the Edgewood district had only $356 per pupil. The majority and the State concede, as they must, the existence of major disparities in spendable funds.

I cannot disagree with the proposition that local control and local decisionmaking play an important part in our democratic system of government. Much may be left to local option, and this case would be quite different if it were true that the Texas system, while insuring minimum educational expenditures in every district through state funding, extended a meaningful option to all local districts to increase their per-pupil expenditures and so to improve their children's education to the extent that increased funding would achieve that goal. The system would then arguably provide a rational and sensible method of achieving the stated aim of preserving an area for local initiative and decision.

The difficulty with the Texas system, however, is that it provides a meaningful option to Alamo Heights and like school districts but almost none to Edgewood and those other districts with a low per-pupil real estate tax base. In these latter districts, no matter how desirous parents are of supporting their schools with greater revenues, it is impossible to do so through the use of the real estate property tax. In these districts, the Texas system utterly fails to extend a realistic choice to parents because the property tax, which is the only revenue-raising mechanism extended to school districts, is practically and legally unavailable.

Local school districts in Texas raise their portion of the Foundation School Program—the Local Fund Assignment—by levying ad valorem taxes on the property located within their boundaries. In addition, the districts are authorized, by the state constitution and by statute, to levy ad valorem property taxes in order to raise revenues to support educational spending over and above the expenditure of Foundation School Program funds.

Both the Edgewood and Alamo Heights districts are located in Bexar County, Texas. Student enrollment in Alamo Heights is 5,432, in Edgewood 22,862. The per-pupil market value of the taxable property in Alamo Heights is $49,078, in Edgewood $5,960.

In order to equal the highest yield in any other Bexar County district, Alamo Heights would be required to tax at the rate of 68 cents per $100 of assessed valuation. Edgewood would be required to tax at the prohibitive rate of $5.76 per $100. But state law places a $1.50 per $100 ceiling on the maintenance tax rate, a limit that would surely be reached long before Edgewood attained an equal yield. Edgewood is thus precluded in law, as well as in fact, from achieving a yield even close to that of some other districts.

If the State aims at maximizing local initiative and local choice, by permitting school districts to resort to the real property tax if they choose to do so, it utterly fails in achieving its purpose in districts with property tax bases so low that there is little if any opportunity for interested parents, rich or poor, to augment school district revenues. Requiring the State to establish only that unequal treatment is in furtherance of a permissible goal, without also requiring the State to show that the means chosen to effectuate that goal are rationally related to its achievement, makes equal protection analysis no more than an empty gesture.

This does not, of course, mean that local control may not be a legitimate goal of a school financing system. Nor does it mean that the State must guarantee each district an equal per-pupil revenue from the state school-financing system. Nor does it mean, as the majority appears to believe, that, by affirming the decision below, this Court would be "imposing on the States inflexible constitutional restraints that could circumscribe or handicap the continued research and experimentation so vital to finding even partial solutions to educational problems and to keeping abreast of ever-changing conditions." On the contrary, it would merely mean that the State must fashion a financing scheme which provides a rational basis for the maximization of local control, if local control is to remain a goal of the system, and not a scheme with "different treatment be[ing] accorded to persons placed by a statute into different classes on the basis of criteria wholly unrelated to the objective of that statute."

There is no difficulty in identifying the class that is subject to the alleged discrimination and that is entitled to the benefits of the *Equal Protection Clause*. I need go no farther than the parents and children in the Edgewood district, who are plaintiffs here and who assert that they are entitled to the same choice as Alamo Heights to augment local expenditures for schools but are denied that choice by state law. This group constitutes a class sufficiently definite to invoke the protection of the Constitution. [I]n the present case we would blink reality to ignore the fact that school districts, and students in the end, are differentially affected by the Texas school-financing scheme with respect to their capability to supplement the Minimum Foundation School Program. At the very least, the law discriminates against those children and their parents who live in districts where the per-pupil tax base is sufficiently low to make impossible the provision of comparable school revenues by resort to the real property tax which is the only device the State extends for this purpose.

■ MR. JUSTICE MARSHALL, with whom MR. JUSTICE DOUGLAS concurs, dissenting.

The right of every American to an equal start in life, so far as the provision of a state service as important as education is concerned, is far too vital to permit state discrimination on grounds as tenuous as those presented by this record. Nor can I accept the notion that it is sufficient to remit these appellees to the vagaries of the political process which, contrary to the majority's suggestion, has proved singularly unsuited to the task of providing a remedy for this discrimination. I, for one, am unsatisfied with the hope of an ultimate "political" solution sometime in the indefinite future while, in the meantime, countless children unjustifiably receive inferior educations that "may affect their hearts and minds in a way unlikely ever to be undone."

I

[H]owever praiseworthy Texas' equalizing efforts, the issue in this case is not whether Texas is doing its best to ameliorate the worst features of a discriminatory scheme but, rather, whether the scheme itself is in fact unconstitutionally discriminatory in the face of the *Fourteenth Amendment's* guarantee of equal protection of the laws. When the Texas financing scheme is taken as a whole, I do not think it can be doubted that it produces a discriminatory impact on substantial numbers of the school-age children of the State of Texas.

A

B

Appellants reject the suggestion that the quality of education in any particular district is determined by money—beyond some minimal level of funding which they believe to be assured every Texas district by the Minimum Foundation School Program.

It is an inescapable fact that if one district has more funds available per pupil than another district, the former will have greater choice in educational planning than will the latter. In this regard, I believe the question of discrimination in educational quality must be deemed to be an objective one that looks to what the State provides its children, not to what the children are able to do with what they receive. That a child forced to attend an underfunded school with poorer physical facilities, less experienced teachers, larger classes, and a narrower range of courses than a school with substantially more funds—and thus with greater choice in educational planning—may nevertheless excel is to the credit of the child, not the State. Indeed, who can ever measure for such a child the opportunities lost and the talents wasted for want of a broader, more enriched education? Discrimination in the opportunity to learn that is afforded a child must be our standard.

In my view, then, it is inequality—not some notion of gross inadequacy—of educational opportunity that raises a question of denial of equal protection of the laws. I find any other approach to the issue unintelligible and without directing principle.

C

[W]hile on its face the Texas scheme may merely discriminate between local districts, the impact of that discrimination falls directly upon the children whose educational opportunity is dependent upon where they happen to live. Consequently, the District Court correctly concluded that the Texas financing scheme discriminates, from a constitutional perspective, between schoolchildren on the basis of the amount of taxable property located within their local districts.

II

A

I cannot accept the majority's labored efforts to demonstrate that fundamental interests, which call for strict scrutiny of the challenged classification, encompass only established rights which we are somehow bound to recognize from the text of the Constitution itself.

I would like to know where the Constitution guarantees the right to procreate, *Skinner v. Oklahoma,* 316 U.S. 535, 541 (1942), or the right to vote in state elections, e.g., *Reynolds v. Sims,* 377 U.S. 533 (1964), or the right to an appeal from a criminal conviction, e.g., *Griffin v. Illinois,* 351 U.S. 12 (1956). These are instances in which, due to the importance of the interests at stake, the Court has displayed a strong concern with the existence of discriminatory state treatment. But the Court has never said or indicated that these are interests which independently enjoy full-blown constitutional protection.

[T]his Court has consistently adjusted the care with which it will review state discrimination in light of the constitutional significance of the interests affected and the invidiousness of the particular classification. In the context of economic interests, we find that discriminatory state action is almost always sustained, for such interests are generally far removed from constitutional guarantees. But the situation differs markedly when discrimination against important individual interests with constitutional implications and against particularly disadvantaged or powerless classes is involved.

It is true that this Court has never deemed the provision of free public education to be required by the Constitution. Nevertheless, the fundamental importance of education is amply indicated by the prior decisions of this Court, by the unique status accorded public education by our society, and by the close relationship between education and some of our most basic constitutional values.

[I]t seems to me that discrimination on the basis of group wealth in this case likewise calls for careful judicial scrutiny. First, it must be recognized that while local district wealth may serve other interests, it bears no relationship whatsoever to the interest of Texas school children in the educational opportunity afforded them by the State of Texas. Given the importance of that interest, we must be particularly sensitive to the invidious characteristics of any form of discrimination that is not clearly intended to serve it, as opposed to some other distinct state interest. Discrimination on the basis of group wealth may not, to be sure, reflect the social stigma frequently attached to personal poverty. Nevertheless, insofar as group wealth discrimination involves wealth over which the disadvantaged individual has no significant control, it represents in fact a more serious basis of discrimination than does personal wealth. For such discrimination is no reflection of the individual's characteristics or his abilities. And thus—particularly in the context of a disadvantaged class composed of children—we have previously treated discrimination on a basis which the individual cannot control as constitutionally disfavored. Cf. *Weber v. Aetna Casualty & Surety Co.,* 406 U.S. 164 (1972); *Levy v. Louisiana,* 391 U.S. 68 (1968).

The disability of the disadvantaged class in this case extends as well into the political processes upon which we ordinarily rely as adequate for the protection and promotion of all interests. Here legislative reallocation of the State's property wealth must be sought in the face of inevitable opposition from significantly advantaged districts that have a strong vested interest in the preservation of the status quo, a problem not completely dissimilar to that faced by underrepresented districts prior to the Court's intervention in the process of reapportionment.

Nor can we ignore the extent to which, in contrast to our prior decisions, the State is responsible for the wealth discrimination in this instance. Griffin, Douglas, Williams, Tate, and our other prior cases have dealt with discrimination on the basis of indigency which was attributable to the operation of the private sector. But we have no such simple de facto wealth discrimination here. The means for financing public education in Texas are selected and specified by the State. It is the State that has created local school districts, and tied educational funding to the local property tax and thereby to local district wealth. At the same time, governmentally imposed land use controls have undoubtedly encouraged and rigidified natural trends in the allocation of particular areas for residential or commercial use, and thus determined each district's amount of taxable property wealth. In short, this case, in contrast to the Court's previous wealth discrimination decisions, can only be seen as "unusual in the extent to which governmental action is the cause of the wealth classifications."

D

The nature of our inquiry into the justifications for state discrimination is essentially the same in all equal protection cases: We must consider the substantiality of the state interests sought to be served, and we must scrutinize the reasonableness of the means by which the State has sought to advance its interests. Here, both the nature of the interest and the classification dictate close judicial scrutiny of the purposes which Texas seeks to serve with its present educational financing scheme and of the means it has selected to serve that purpose.

The only justification offered by appellants to sustain the discrimination in educational opportunity caused by the Texas financing scheme is local educational control. Presented with this justification, the District Court concluded that "[n]ot only are defendants unable to demonstrate compelling state interests for their classifications based upon wealth, they fail even to establish a reasonable basis for these classifications." *337 F. Supp., at 284.* I must agree with this conclusion.

I do not question that local control of public education, as an abstract matter, constitutes a very substantial state interest. But here the State's purported concern with local control is offered primarily as an excuse rather than as a justification for interdistrict inequality.

In Texas, statewide laws regulate in fact the minutest details of local public education. For example, the State prescribes required courses. All textbooks must be submitted for state approval, and only approved textbooks may be used. The State has established the qualifications necessary for teaching in Texas public schools and the procedures for obtaining certification. The State has even legislated on the length of the school day. Texas' own courts have said: "As a result of the acts of the

Legislature our school system is not of mere local concern but it is statewide. While a school district is local in territorial limits, it is an integral part of the vast school system which is coextensive with the confines of the State of Texas."

Moreover, even if we accept Texas' general dedication to local control in educational matters, it is difficult to find any evidence of such dedication with respect to fiscal matters. It ignores reality to suggest—as the Court does, ante, at 49–50—that the local property tax element of the Texas financing scheme reflects a conscious legislative effort to provide school districts with local fiscal control. If Texas had a system truly dedicated to local fiscal control, one would expect the quality of the educational opportunity provided in each district to vary with the decision of the voters in that district as to the level of sacrifice they wish to make for public education. In fact, the Texas scheme produces precisely the opposite result. Local school districts cannot choose to have the best education in the State by imposing the highest tax rate. Instead, the quality of the educational opportunity offered by any particular district is largely determined by the amount of taxable property located in the district—a factor over which local voters can exercise no control.

Because of the difference in taxable local property wealth, Edgewood would have to tax itself almost nine times as heavily to obtain the same yield as Alamo Heights. At present, then, local control is a myth for many of the local school districts in Texas.

If, for the sake of local education control, this Court is to sustain interdistrict discrimination in the educational opportunity afforded Texas school children, it should require that the State present something more than the mere sham now before us.

III

In conclusion, it is essential to recognize that an end to the wide variations in taxable district property wealth inherent in the Texas financing scheme would entail none of the untoward consequences suggested by the Court or by the appellants.

First, affirmance of the District Court's decisions would hardly sound the death knell for local control of education. It would mean neither centralized decision making nor federal court intervention in the operation of public schools. Clearly, this suit has nothing to do with local decisionmaking with respect to educational policy or even educational spending. It involves only a narrow aspect of local control—namely, local control over the raising of educational funds.

Nor does the District Court's decision even necessarily eliminate local control of educational funding. No one in the course of this entire litigation has ever questioned the constitutionality of the local property tax as a device for raising educational funds. The District Court's decision, at most, restricts the power of the State to make educational funding dependent exclusively upon local property taxation so long as there exists interdistrict disparities in taxable property wealth. But it hardly eliminates the local property tax as a source of educational funding or as a means of providing local fiscal control.

The Court seeks solace for its action today in the possibility of legislative reform. The Court's suggestions of legislative redress and experimentation will doubtless be of great comfort to the schoolchildren of Texas' disadvantaged districts, but considering the vested interests of wealthy school districts in the preservation of the status quo, they are worth little more. The possibility of legislative action is, in all events, no answer to this Court's duty under the Constitution to eliminate unjustified state discrimination.

NOTES AND QUESTIONS

1. **Wealth as a Suspect Classification.** Why was the Court reluctant to treat "wealth" or "poverty" as a suspect classification? What practical problems would such a distinction raise? To what extent was "wealth" or "poverty" different from suspect classifications that the Court had recognized already, such as national origin or race? Are you persuaded by the distinctions the Court drew?

2. **Education as a Fundamental Right.** The Court discussed the importance of education at length but then failed to deem it a "fundamental" right under the Constitution. How much weight should be assigned to a key fact emphasized by the Court—that the students in the case had not been denied an education altogether? What would constitute a complete denial of education?

3. **Local Funding and State Responsibility.** Should the state be responsible for funding levels for the myriad schools districts within its jurisdiction by virtue of the fact that it has designed the entire educational system? Or do the property taxes raised in particular districts belong to those districts? Why isn't the state obligated to redistribute money from richer districts to poorer ones? How would districts response to such mandated redistribution? Might voters decide not to tax themselves if they know that their tax dollars will go elsewhere?

4. **Hypothetical.** You are a litigator in a state court case in which the plaintiffs challenge the state's school funding scheme which is based largely on local property taxes and which has resulted in substantial differences in per-pupil expenditure between districts. The plaintiffs rely only on the state constitution's equal protection clause. The case arises shortly after *San Antonio Independent School District v. Rodriguez* was handed down. As a litigator for the plaintiffs, what are your best arguments? In particular, how could you most effectively overcome the reasoning in the majority opinion in *San Antonio*? As a litigator for the defendants, what are your best arguments? How would you answer plaintiffs' attempts to distinguish *San Antonio*?

5. ***State Court Funding Litigation.*** After it became clear that litigation under the United States Constitution would not succeed, advocates for more funding for poor school districts began to look to state courts and to seek remedies under state constitutional provisions. The first wave of state claims focused on funding inequalities within states, which litigants argued were prohibited by provisions in state constitutions. Although litigants were sometimes successful in these claims, efforts to remedy the constitutional violation were impeded by the politics of school funding. Equal funding, in effect, imposed a ceiling on how much money wealthy suburban districts could contribute to their schools. That limitation gave such districts strong incentives to oppose reform. Advocates then shifted from equality to adequacy, arguing that educational funding must be equal across all districts but instead that the education provided in each district must be at least adequate. State constitutions provided a basis for this claim as well, and the prospect of the state ensuring that all schools provide an "adequate" education was not nearly so threatening to affluent districts. Yet, whether this litigation has had a positive impact on the academic achievement of racial minority students remains unclear.

6. ***Market-Based Approaches.*** An alternative means of reform looks to the market. Some commentators have argued that schools serving poor black children are inadequate because the teachers and administrators at those schools have no incentive to provide a quality education. They have a monopoly and are therefore not disciplined by market forces. One way to improve education, under this view, would be to allow poor families to choose their schools, just as their affluent counterparts have long been able to do.

While the advent of vouchers, charter schools, and other choice-based reform efforts implicate many issues, the central question is whether choice will improve academic outcomes? Consider the excerpt below from a seminal school choice article, John E. Chubb and Terry Moe, Choice *Is* a Panacea, *Brookings Review* (1990):

> People who make decisions about education would behave differently if their institutions were different.
>
> A market system is not built to enable the imposition of higher-order values on the schools, nor is it driven by a democratic struggle to exercise public authority. Instead, the authority to make educational choices is radically decentralized to those most immediately involved. Schools compete for the support of parents and students, and parents and students are free to choose among schools. The system is built on decentralization, competition, and choice.
>
> Of course, not all schools in the market will respond equally well to incentives. But those that falter will find it more difficult to attract support, and they will tend to be weeded out in favor of schools that are better organized. This process of natural selection complements the incentives of the marketplace in propelling and supporting a population of autonomous, effectively organized schools.

How would you evaluate the authors' argument? Do you think the dissolution of public education as we know it would likely improve educational outcomes for disadvantaged students? What practical or political impediments do you think might impede the creation of such a system?

B. SEGREGATION 2.0: WITHIN SCHOOL SEGREGATION

While integration programs throughout the country have led to placing students from various racial groups in the same school environments, this has not resulted in complete racial integration. Instead, segregation seems to have reemerged *within* the school, through a host of ostensibly benign or non-race dependent educational policies. This phenomenon—dubbed "resegregation" or "second-generation segregation"—involves the stratification of students into different types or levels of educational experiences within a given school. It can take the form of tracking (including into special education) or racially disparate disciplinary referrals. In this section, we examine how these mechanisms operate to recreate racial segregation within schools and contemplate different ways to challenge them.

1. TRACKING

Tracking is an educational practice that designates students for separate educational paths based on assessments of their prior academic performance or of their potential. *See* Kevin G. Welner, Tracking in an Era of Standards: Low-expectation Classes Meet High-expectation Laws." 28 *Hastings Const. LQ* 699 (2000). High achievement or high potential students are provided a different educational experience than those students who are identified as low performers or as having low potential. Students may be segregated based on perceived ability either within or across classes. At the elementary school level, teachers may provide different educational experiences to different types of students within a classroom. Or students may be placed with different teachers, with some students placed into gifted classes, and others into remedial, or special education, classes. At the high school level, perceptions of student ability become a basis for offering different curricula, with some students preparing for college, and others not. Whether in elementary school or high school, different academic groups receive vastly different educations, with the greatest resources and the highest-quality education typically provided for the highest academic groups.

Proponents of tracking and of ability grouping maintain that these practices allow students to learn at their own pace and prevent a difficult situation for teachers: large classes where children with a wide range of different needs and skill levels are mixed together. In many districts, the higher-level instruction in "gifted and talented" or advanced placement classes is what keeps wealthier families from entirely abandoning the public school system. Yet, according to its opponents, the ill effects of tracking for students in the lower-skilled classes outweigh the advantages that students in the advanced classes gain. Many education researchers have argued that tracking perpetuates class inequality and is partially to blame for the stubborn achievement gap in the U.S. educational system—between white and Asian students on one side, and black and Latino students on the other. Sonali Kohli, "Modern-Day Segregation in Public Schools," The Atlantic (Nov. 18, 2014), available at: http://www.theatlantic.com/education/archive/2014/11/modern-day-segregation-in-public-schools/382846/.

Some research has shown that tracking, or academic sorting, practices are significantly associated with racial disparities. Consider, too, the data below, based on information gathered by the Department of Education in 2013:

Racial Distribution in South Orange Maplewood School District's 8th Grade

U.S. Department of Education

Racial Distribution in AP Courses at Columbia High School

U.S. Department of Education

While tracking is facially race neutral, the data noted above indicate it disparately impacts racial minorities. According to Daniel Losen and Gary Orfield, tracking is more likely to be used in a racially diverse district than in a district that is either exclusively white or exclusively black. And when employed in a diverse district, students become racially segregated, with white students being placed disproportionally in "fast or advanced" tracks and students of color being largely relegated to "slow or remedial" tracks. This, Losen and Orfield contend, creates a separate and explicitly unequal system. Daniel J. Losen & Gary Orfield, Racial Inequity in Special Education (2002).

EXERCISE

Parents of black and Latino students in a racially integrated school turn to you, a public interest lawyer, complaining that their sons and daughters have been placed in lower-level classes and steered towards vocational training rather than college preparation classes. To support their claims, they provide information showing that the lower-level classes at their children's schools are composed almost exclusively of black and Latino students, while the higher-level classes are almost entirely populated by white students. They argue that their children are being discriminated against based on their race and that tracking unfairly holds back African American and Latino students.

1. How would you determine whether tracking is indeed a discriminatory practice? What exactly is wrong with it? What additional data would you need about the specific schools in question?

2. How would you frame the parents' arguments for the purpose of legally challenging the schools' tracking practices?

3. If a suit were to be filed, what arguments would you raise in it? What remedy would you demand?

2. DISCIPLINARY REFERRALS

School disciplinary practices can also function to sort students in racially disparate ways. Disciplinary interventions, ranging from office referrals to corporal punishment, suspension, and expulsion, are ostensibly intended to preserve order and safety by removing students who break school rules and disrupt the learning environment. Discipline might also function as a deterrent to other students.

Disciplinary referrals, like tracking, have a well-documented disparate impact on racial minorities, particularly Black students. This conclusion has been drawn for a wide array of sanctions (e.g., suspensions, office discipline referrals). The Children's Defense Fund, in 1975, first brought the issue of racial disproportionality to national attention, showing that Black students were two to three times overrepresented in school suspensions compared with their enrollment rates in localities across the nation. National and state data show consistent patterns of Black disproportionality in school discipline over the past 30 years, specifically in suspension, expulsion, and office discipline referrals.

According to a 2003 nationally representative study utilizing parent reports, Black students were significantly more likely to be suspended than White or Asian students. Specifically, almost one in five Black students (19.6%) were suspended, compared with fewer than 1 in 10 White students (8.8%) and Asian and Pacific Islanders. A nationally representative survey of 74,000 10th graders found that about 50% of Black students reported that they had ever been suspended or expelled compared with about 20% of White students. The study further showed that, unlike the pattern for other racial and ethnic groups, suspensions and expulsions of Black students increased from 1991 to 2005 (Wallace et al., 2008). Most recently, Daniel Losen and Jon Gillespie, of the Center for Civil Rights Remedies at The Civil Rights Project at UCLA, have composed a national report on suspensions of students in K–12 grades. In their report, Losen and Gillespie note that, while students from every racial group can be found to have a high risk for suspension in some school districts, African-American children are at far greater risk than others. For example, one out of every six enrolled Black students was suspended, compared with about one in twenty white students. *See generally* Daniel J. Losen & Jonathan Gillespie, Opportunities Suspended: The Disparate Impact of Disciplinary Exclusion from School (2012).

Are there better alternatives to the frequent use of arguably extreme disciplinary sanctions, such as suspension and expulsion? Losen and Gillespie point to many such available options. One alternative path has been applied in the Los Angeles Unified School District, the nation's second-largest school system. The L.A. Unified School District was the first in California to ban suspensions for defiance and announced plans to roll out "restorative justice" programs, which seek to resolve conflicts through talking circles and other trust building methods. According to a recent report in the *Los Angeles Times*, this shift has brought dramatic changes: Suspensions districtwide plummeted to 0.55% in 2015 compared with 8% in 2007–08, and days lost to suspension also plunged, to 5,024 from 75,000 during that same period, according to the most recent data. Yet the change has also created new challenges for teachers in the district, who say their classrooms are now reeling from unruly students who are escaping consequences for their actions. Teachers blame the district for failing to provide the staff and training needed to effectively shift to the new approach. *See* Teresa Watanabe and Howard Blume, Why some LAUSD teachers are balking at a new approach to discipline problems, *L.A. Times* (Nov. 7, 2015).

NOTES AND QUESTIONS

1.   What might account for the disparate disciplinary referrals of Black students in particular? Is this disparity necessarily the result of racial bias? Are there any alternative explanations you might be able to think of?

2.   How would you legally challenge disciplinary referrals in schools that have a disparate impact on Black students? What evidence would you look for to substantiate your claim? How would you frame your arguments and what remedy would you ask for?

3. What alternatives, in addition to the Los Angeles strategy described above, might be available to the current disciplinary sanctions used in schools across the country? Which alternatives do you think would be less prone to racial biases? What obstacles, if any, would schools face in attempting to implement such policies?

CHAPTER 5

HIGHER EDUCATION

I. FORMAL EQUALITY

Just as racial minorities have long been denied quality primary and secondary education, so too have they faced barriers in higher education. Through the early decades of the twentieth century, many institutions voluntarily restricted enrollment to white students, and some states (including every southern state) prohibited racially integrated education.

Yet minorities were not wholly without access to higher education. During the decades after the Civil War, more than 100 colleges (some of which have since closed) were established to serve African Americans. Although typically less well funded than those colleges and universities that were limited to whites, Historically Black Colleges and Universities (HBCUs) served African Americans well. Now, with the demise of de jure segregation and the entry of black students into historically white institutions, many HBCUs struggle, both financially and in attracting students. Still, HBCUs continue to produce a substantial percentage of black college graduates, as well as a disproportionate number of black doctors and engineers.

Cases challenging racial exclusion in higher education figured prominently in the battle against de jure segregation. In *Missouri ex rel. Gaines v. Canada*, 305 U.S. 337 (1938), the Supreme Court required Missouri to either furnish a substantially equivalent law school for black students or admit Gaines, the black plaintiff, to its existing law school. In response to a similar legal challenge, Texas created a separate law school for black students. However, in *Sweatt v. Painter*, 339 U.S. 629 (1950), the Supreme Court held that the hastily-created school was not substantially equal in quality to the University of Texas Law School, where the plaintiff had been denied admission. The Court noted inadequacies in the school's library and in its thin staffing. Of the greatest precedential value, however, was the following observation: "What is more important, the University of Texas Law School possesses to a far greater degree those qualities which are incapable of objective measurement but which make for greatness in a law school. Such qualities, to name but a few, include reputation of the faculty, experience of the administration, position and influence of the alumni, standing in the community, traditions and prestige. It is difficult to believe that one who had a free choice between these law schools would consider the question close."

On the same day as *Sweatt*, the Supreme Court decided *McLaurin v. Oklahoma State Regents*, 339 U.S. 637 (1950). G.W. McLaurin was enrolled in a doctoral program at the University of Oklahoma, but school officials required him to sit in a separate part of the classroom, to study in a designated area in the library, and to eat his meals at a designated table in the cafeteria. The Court concluded: "[These restrictions] signify that the State ... sets McLaurin apart from the other students. The result is that appellant is handicapped in his pursuit of effective graduate instruction. Such restrictions impair and inhibit his ability to study, to engage in discussions and exchange views with other students, and, in general, to learn his profession. . . . State imposed restrictions which produce such inequalities cannot be sustained." These successful challenges to the exclusion of racial minorities from higher education ultimately helped set the stage for the Supreme Court's decision in *Brown v. Board of Education*, 347 U.S. 483 (1954).

These formal, express racial barriers have been dismantled by the triumphs of the Second Reconstruction. Today, no public or private university can bar its doors to students of any race. But impediments to equal access remain, as do efforts to promote the inclusion in institutions of higher learning of members of historically disadvantaged groups. Much of the recent effort to promote equal access to higher education has focused on selective colleges and universities. While access to post high school education is desirable, admission to a selective institution is particularly coveted. Selective schools invest much more in the educational process than their open enrollment counterparts. They have more accomplished faculty, higher achieving students, and better facilities. Even though the academic environment is more demanding than at non-selective schools, their graduation rates are higher. And, finally, for low-income students, the financial aid elite schools provide may mean that more elite institutions provide more affordable educations than those with fewer resources. Elite schools, in turn, lead to elite jobs, which are higher paying and provide a pathway to the upper echelons of business and government. These benefits are arguably greater now than in past eras. Due to changes in the labor market as a result of technology and globalization, the economic premium associated with a college or professional school degree has grown. While college graduates have long earned more than their high school educated counterparts, the earnings gap is now nearly two to one.

II. AFFIRMATIVE ACTION AS RACIAL REMEDY

Beginning in the late 1960s and early 1970s, many universities began affirmative action programs as a means of boosting the admission and enrollment of underrepresented racial minority students. Even today, much of the debate about affirmative action remains shaped by the Supreme Court's 1978 decision in which it first ruled on the constitutionality of affirmative action in university admissions: *Regents of the University of California v. Allan Bakke*, 438 U.S. 265 (1978). The *Bakke* case highlights many of the central issues of debate: whether affirmative action should be viewed as skeptically as discrimination against racial minorities; what rationales are sufficient to justify affirmative action; and what forms affirmative action can take in the admissions process.

The Court produced six opinions in *Bakke*. The fractured decision thus did not resolve many of the central issues that the case raised. By a vote of five-to-four, the Court struck down the specific admissions policy of the U.C. Davis medical school at issue, but also by a five-to-four vote allowed universities to engage in some form of race-based affirmative action. Four Justices (the Stevens contingent) would have both struck down the Davis program and imposed a stringent prohibition on affirmative action admissions policies generally. Four other Justices (the Brennan/Marshall contingent) would have upheld the Davis program and accorded universities substantial leeway to engage in affirmative action in admissions. Justice Powell proved to be the swing vote. He wrote an opinion striking down the Davis program yet allowing universities to practice some forms of affirmative action in order to achieve diversity among the student body. Because of Justice Powell's pivotal role, it is his opinion that has received the most attention and with which *Bakke* is most associated.

We include below selections from the opinions focused on the constitutional issues. (The Title VI discussion is omitted, inasmuch as the Court determined that "[i]n view of the clear legislative intent, Title VI must be held to proscribe only those racial classifications that would violate the Equal Protection Clause or the Fifth Amendment.") In the excerpt of *Bakke* below, we first present the Court's treatment of two general issues central to the affirmative action debate: i) whether affirmative action is benign and therefore should be subject to a more lenient standard of scrutiny than racial classifications intended to disadvantage minority groups, and ii) whether any rationales other than promoting diversity constitute a constitutionally sufficient justification for affirmative action.

Regents of the University of California v. Bakke

Supreme Court of the United States, 1978.
438 U.S. 265.

■ MR. JUSTICE POWELL announced the judgment of the Court.

I

The Medical School of the University of California at Davis opened in 1968 with an entering class of 50 students. In 1971, the size of the entering class was increased to 100 students, a level at which it remains. No admissions program for disadvantaged or minority students existed when the school opened, and the first class contained three Asians but no blacks, no Mexican-Americans, and no American Indians. Over the next two years, the faculty devised a special admissions program to increase the representation of "disadvantaged" students in each Medical School class. The special program consisted of a separate admissions system operating in coordination with the regular admissions process.

Under the regular admissions procedure, a candidate could submit his application to the Medical School beginning in July of the year preceding the academic year for which admission was sought. Because of the large number of applications,[1] the admissions committee screened each one to select candidates for further consideration. Candidates whose overall undergraduate grade point averages fell below 2.5 on a scale of 4.0 were summarily rejected. About one out of six applicants was invited for a personal interview. Following the interviews, each candidate was rated on a scale of 1 to 100 by his interviewers and other members of the admissions committee. The rating embraced the interviewers' summaries, the candidate's overall grade point average, grade point average in science courses, scores on the Medical College Admissions Test (MCAT), letters of recommendation, extracurricular activities, and other biographical data. The ratings were added together to arrive at each candidate's "benchmark" score. The full committee then reviewed the file and scores of each applicant and made offers of admission on a "rolling" basis. The chairman was responsible for placing names on the waiting list. They were not placed in strict numerical order; instead, the chairman had discretion to include persons with "special skills."

The special admissions program operated with a separate committee, a majority of whom were members of minority groups. On the 1973 application form, candidates were asked to indicate whether they wished to be considered as "economically and/or educationally disadvantaged" applicants; on the 1974 form the question was whether they wished to be considered as members of a "minority group," which the Medical School apparently viewed as "Blacks," "Chicanos," "Asians," and "American Indians." If these questions were answered affirmatively, the application was forwarded to the special admissions committee. No formal definition of "disadvantaged" was ever produced, but the chairman of the special committee screened each application to see whether it reflected economic or educational deprivation.[2] Having passed this initial hurdle, the applications then were rated by the special committee in a fashion similar to that used by the general admissions committee, except that special candidates did not have to meet the 2.5 grade point average cutoff applied to regular applicants. About one-fifth of the total number of special applicants were invited for interviews in

---

[1] For the 1973 entering class of 100 seats, the Davis Medical School received 2,464 applications. For the 1974 entering class, 3,737 applications were submitted.

[2] The chairman normally checked to see if, among other things, the applicant had been granted a waiver of the school's application fee, which required a means test; whether the applicant had worked during college or interrupted his education to support himself or his family; and whether the applicant was a member of a minority group.

1973 and 1974.[3] Following each interview, the special committee assigned each special applicant a benchmark score. The special committee then presented its top choices to the general admissions committee. The latter did not rate or compare the special candidates against the general applicants, but could reject recommended special candidates for failure to meet course requirements or other specific deficiencies. The special committee continued to recommend special applicants until a number prescribed by faculty vote were admitted. While the overall class size was still 50, the prescribed number was 8; in 1973 and 1974, when the class size had doubled to 100, the prescribed number of special admissions also doubled, to 16.

From the year of the increase in class size—1971—through 1974, the special program resulted in the admission of 21 black students, 30 Mexican-Americans, and 12 Asians, for a total of 63 minority students. Over the same period, the regular admissions program produced 1 black, 6 Mexican-Americans, and 37 Asians, for a total of 44 minority students. Although disadvantaged whites applied to the special program in large numbers, none received an offer of admission through that process. Indeed, in 1974, at least, the special committee explicitly considered only "disadvantaged" special applicants who were members of one of the designated minority groups.

Allan Bakke is a white male who applied to the Davis Medical School in both 1973 and 1974. In both years Bakke's application was considered under the general admissions program, and he received an interview. Despite a strong benchmark score of 468 out of 500, Bakke was rejected. His application had come late in the year, and no applicants in the general admissions process with scores below 470 were accepted after Bakke's application was completed. There were four special admissions slots unfilled at that time however, for which Bakke was not considered.

[The next year] Bakke's application was rejected [again]. In neither year did the chairman of the admissions committee, exercise his discretion to place Bakke on the waiting list. In both years, applicants were admitted under the special program with grade point averages, MCAT scores, and benchmark scores significantly lower than Bakke's. After the second rejection, Bakke filed the instant suit.

III

A

The special admissions program is undeniably a classification based on race and ethnic background. To the extent that there existed a pool of at least minimally qualified minority applicants to fill the 16 special admissions seats, white applicants could compete only for 84 seats in the entering class, rather than the 100 open to minority applicants. Whether

---

[3]   For the class entering in 1973, the total number of special applicants was 297, of whom 73 were white. In 1974, 628 persons applied to the special committee, of whom 172 were white.

this limitation is described as a quota or a goal, it is a line drawn on the basis of race and ethnic status.

The guarantees of the Fourteenth Amendment extend to all persons. The guarantee of equal protection cannot mean one thing when applied to one individual and something else when applied to a person of another color. If both are not accorded the same protection, then it is not equal.

Nevertheless, petitioner argues that the court below erred in applying strict scrutiny to the special admissions program because white males, such as respondent, are not a "discrete and insular minority" requiring extraordinary protection from the majoritarian political process. Carolene Products Co. This rationale, however, has never been invoked in our decisions as a prerequisite to subjecting racial or ethnic distinctions to strict scrutiny.

Racial and ethnic distinctions of any sort are inherently suspect and thus call for the most exacting judicial examination.

B

This perception of racial and ethnic distinctions is rooted in our Nation's constitutional and demographic history. The Court's initial view of the Fourteenth Amendment was that its "one pervading purpose" was "the freedom of the slave race, the security and firm establishment of that freedom, and the protection of the newly-made freeman and citizen from the oppressions of those who had formerly exercised dominion over him." Slaughter-House Cases. The Equal Protection Clause, however, was "[v]irtually strangled in infancy by post-civil-war judicial reactionism." It was relegated to decades of relative desuetude while the Due Process Clause of the Fourteenth Amendment, after a short germinal period, flourished as a cornerstone in the Court's defense of property and liberty of contract. In that cause, the Fourteenth Amendment's "one pervading purpose" was displaced. See, e.g., Plessy v. Ferguson. It was only as the era of substantive due process came to a close, that the Equal Protection Clause began to attain a genuine measure of vitality.

By that time it was no longer possible to peg the guarantees of the Fourteenth Amendment to the struggle for equality of one racial minority. During the dormancy of the Equal Protection Clause, the United States had become a Nation of minorities. Each had to struggle— and to some extent struggles still—to overcome the prejudices not of a monolithic majority, but of a "majority" composed of various minority groups of whom it was said—perhaps unfairly in many cases—that a shared characteristic was a willingness to disadvantage other groups. As the Nation filled with the stock of many lands, the reach of the Clause was gradually extended to all ethnic groups seeking protection from official discrimination. See Strauder v. West Virginia (Celtic Irishmen) (dictum); Yick Wo v. Hopkins (Chinese); Truax v. Raich (Austrian resident aliens); Korematsu, (Japanese); Hernandez v. Texas (Mexican-Americans).

Although many of the Framers of the Fourteenth Amendment conceived of its primary function as bridging the vast distance between members of the Negro race and the white "majority," Slaughter-House Cases, the Amendment itself was framed in universal terms, without reference to color, ethnic origin, or condition of prior servitude. Indeed, it is not unlikely that among the Framers were many who would have applauded a reading of the Equal Protection Clause that states a principle of universal application and is responsive to the racial, ethnic, and cultural diversity of the Nation.

Because the landmark decisions in this area arose in response to the continued exclusion of Negroes from the mainstream of American society, they could be characterized as involving discrimination by the "majority" white race against the Negro minority. But they need not be read as depending upon that characterization for their results. It suffices to say that "[o]ver the years, this Court has consistently repudiated '[d]istinctions between citizens solely because of their ancestry' as being 'odious to a free people whose institutions are founded upon the doctrine of equality.'" Loving v. Virginia, quoting Hirabayashi.

Petitioner urges us to adopt for the first time a more restrictive view of the Equal Protection Clause and hold that discrimination against members of the white "majority" cannot be suspect if its purpose can be characterized as "benign." The clock of our liberties, however, cannot be turned back to 1868. It is far too late to argue that the guarantee of equal protection to all persons permits the recognition of special wards entitled to a degree of protection greater than that accorded others. "The Fourteenth Amendment is not directed solely against discrimination due to a 'two-class theory'—that is, based upon differences between 'white' and Negro." Hernandez.

Once the artificial line of a "two-class theory" of the Fourteenth Amendment is put aside, the difficulties entailed in varying the level of judicial review according to a perceived "preferred" status of a particular racial or ethnic minority are intractable. The concepts of "majority" and "minority" necessarily reflect temporary arrangements and political judgments. As observed above, the white "majority" itself is composed of various minority groups, most of which can lay claim to a history of prior discrimination at the hands of the State and private individuals. Not all of these groups can receive preferential treatment and corresponding judicial tolerance of distinctions drawn in terms of race and nationality, for then the only "majority" left would be a new minority of white Anglo-Saxon Protestants. There is no principled basis for deciding which groups would merit "heightened judicial solicitude" and which would not. Courts would be asked to evaluate the extent of the prejudice and consequent harm suffered by various minority groups. Those whose societal injury is thought to exceed some arbitrary level of tolerability then would be entitled to preferential classifications at the expense of individuals belonging to other groups. Those classifications would be free from exacting judicial scrutiny. As these preferences began to have their desired effect, and the consequences of past discrimination were undone, new judicial rankings would be necessary. The kind of variable sociological and political analysis necessary to produce such rankings simply does not lie within the judicial competence—even if they otherwise were politically feasible and socially desirable.[4]

Moreover, there are serious problems of justice connected with the idea of preference itself. First, it may not always be clear that a so-called preference is in fact benign. Courts may be asked to validate burdens imposed upon individual members of a particular group in order to advance the group's general interest. Nothing in the Constitution supports the notion that individuals may be asked to suffer otherwise impermissible burdens in order to enhance the societal standing of their ethnic groups. Second, preferential programs may only reinforce common stereotypes holding that certain groups are unable to achieve success without special protection based on a factor having no relationship to individual worth. Third, there is a measure of inequity in forcing innocent persons in respondent's position to bear the burdens of redressing grievances not of their making.

By hitching the meaning of the Equal Protection Clause to these transitory considerations, we would be holding, as a constitutional principle, that judicial scrutiny of classifications touching on racial and ethnic background may vary with the ebb and flow of political forces. Disparate constitutional tolerance of such classifications well may serve

---

[4]   Mr. Justice Douglas has noted the problems associated with such inquiries:

"The reservation of a proportion of the law school class for members of selected minority groups is fraught with . . . dangers, for one must immediately determine which groups are to receive such favored treatment and which are to be excluded, the proportions of the class that are to be allocated to each, and even the criteria by which to determine whether an individual is a member of a favored group. [Cf. Plessy v. Ferguson.] There is no assurance that a common agreement can be reached, and first the schools, and then the courts, will be buffeted with the competing claims. The University of Washington included Filipinos, but excluded Chinese and Japanese; another school may limit its program to blacks, or to blacks and Chicanos. Once the Court sanctioned racial preferences such as these, it could not then wash its hands of the matter, leaving it entirely in the discretion of the school, for then we would have effectively overruled Sweatt v. Painter, and allowed imposition of a 'zero' allocation. But what standard is the Court to apply when a rejected applicant of Japanese ancestry brings suit to require the University of Washington to extend the same privileges to his group? The Committee might conclude that the population of Washington is now 2% Japanese, and that Japanese also constitute 2% of the Bar, but that had they not been handicapped by a history of discrimination, Japanese would now constitute 5% of the Bar, or 20%. Or, alternatively, the Court could attempt to assess how grievously each group has suffered from discrimination, and allocate proportions accordingly; if that were the standard the current University of Washington policy would almost surely fall, for there is no Western State which can claim that it has always treated Japanese and Chinese in a fair and evenhanded manner.

"Nor obviously will the problem be solved if next year the Law School included only Japanese and Chinese, for then Norwegians and Swedes, Poles and Italians, Puerto Ricans and Hungarians, and all other groups which form this diverse Nation would have just complaints." DeFunis v. Odegaard, (dissenting opinion) (footnotes omitted).

to exacerbate racial and ethnic antagonisms rather than alleviate them. Also, the mutability of a constitutional principle, based upon shifting political and social judgments, undermines the chances for consistent application of the Constitution from one generation to the next, a critical feature of its coherent interpretation. In expounding the Constitution, the Court's role is to discern "principles sufficiently absolute to give them roots throughout the community and continuity over significant periods of time, and to lift them above the level of the pragmatic political judgments of a particular time and place." A. Cox, The Role of the Supreme Court in American Government 114 (1976).

If it is the individual who is entitled to judicial protection against classifications based upon his racial or ethnic background because such distinctions impinge upon personal rights, rather than the individual only because of his membership in a particular group, then constitutional standards may be applied consistently. Political judgments regarding the necessity for the particular classification may be weighed in the constitutional balance, Korematsu v. United States, but the standard of justification will remain constant. This is as it should be, since those political judgments are the product of rough compromise struck by contending groups within the democratic process. When they touch upon an individual's race or ethnic background, he is entitled to a judicial determination that the burden he is asked to bear on that basis is precisely tailored to serve a compelling governmental interest. The Constitution guarantees that right to every person regardless of his background.

C

The Courts of Appeals have fashioned various types of racial preferences as remedies for constitutional or statutory violations resulting in identified, race-based injuries to individuals held entitled to the preference. Such preferences also have been upheld where a legislative or administrative body charged with the responsibility made determinations of past discrimination by the industries affected, and fashioned remedies deemed appropriate to rectify the discrimination. But we have never approved preferential classifications in the absence of proved constitutional or statutory violations. [T]he operation of petitioner's special admissions program ... prefers the designated minority groups at the expense of other individuals who are totally foreclosed from competition for the 16 special admissions seats in every Medical School class. Because of that foreclosure, some individuals are excluded from enjoyment of a state-provided benefit—admission to the Medical School—they otherwise would receive. When a classification denies an individual opportunities or benefits enjoyed by others solely because of his race or ethnic background, it must be regarded as suspect.

IV

The special admissions program purports to serve the purposes of: (i) "reducing the historic deficit of traditionally disfavored minorities in medical schools and in the medical profession," (ii) countering the effects of societal discrimination;[5] (iii) increasing the number of physicians who will practice in communities currently underserved; and (iv) obtaining the educational benefits that flow from an ethnically diverse student body. It is necessary to decide which, if any, of these purposes is substantial enough to support the use of a suspect classification.

A

If petitioner's purpose is to assure within its student body some specified percentage of a particular group merely because of its race or ethnic origin, such a preferential purpose must be rejected not as insubstantial but as facially invalid. Preferring members of any one group for no reason other than race or ethnic origin is discrimination for its own sake.

B

The State certainly has a legitimate and substantial interest in ameliorating, or eliminating where feasible, the disabling effects of identified discrimination. The line of school desegregation cases, commencing with Brown, attests to the importance of this state goal and the commitment of the judiciary to affirm all lawful means toward its attainment. In the school cases, the States were required by court order to redress the wrongs worked by specific instances of racial discrimination. That goal was far more focused than the remedying of the effects of "societal discrimination," an amorphous concept of injury that may be ageless in its reach into the past.

---

[5] A number of distinct subgoals have been advanced as falling under the rubric of "compensation for past discrimination." For example, it is said that preferences for Negro applicants may compensate for harm done them personally, or serve to place them at economic levels they might have attained but for discrimination against their forebears. Another view of the "compensation" goal is that it serves as a form of reparation by the "majority" to a victimized group as a whole. That justification for racial or ethnic preference has been subjected to much criticism. Finally, it has been argued that ethnic preferences "compensate" the group by providing examples of success whom other members of the group will emulate, thereby advancing the group's interest and society's interest in encouraging new generations to overcome the barriers and frustrations of the past. For purposes of analysis these subgoals need not be considered separately.

Racial classifications in admissions conceivably could serve a fifth purpose, one which petitioner does not articulate: fair appraisal of each individual's academic promise in the light of some cultural bias in grading or testing procedures. To the extent that race and ethnic background were considered only to the extent of curing established inaccuracies in predicting academic performance, it might be argued that there is no "preference" at all. Nothing in this record, however, suggests either that any of the quantitative factors considered by the Medical School were culturally biased or that petitioner's special admissions program was formulated to correct for any such biases. Furthermore, if race or ethnic background were used solely to arrive at an unbiased prediction of academic success, the reservation of fixed numbers of seats would be inexplicable.

We have never approved a classification that aids persons perceived as members of relatively victimized groups at the expense of other innocent individuals in the absence of judicial, legislative, or administrative findings of constitutional or statutory violations. After such findings have been made, the governmental interest in preferring members of the injured groups at the expense of others is substantial, since the legal rights of the victims must be vindicated. In such a case, the extent of the injury and the consequent remedy will have been judicially, legislatively, or administratively defined. Also, the remedial action usually remains subject to continuing oversight to assure that it will work the least harm possible to other innocent persons competing for the benefit. Without such findings of constitutional or statutory violations, it cannot be said that the government has any greater interest in helping one individual than in refraining from harming another. Thus, the government has no compelling justification for inflicting such harm.

Petitioner does not purport to have made, and is in no position to make, such findings. Its broad mission is education, not the formulation of any legislative policy or the adjudication of particular claims of illegality. [I]solated segments of our vast governmental structures are not competent to make those decisions, at least in the absence of legislative mandates and legislatively determined criteria.[6] Before relying upon these sorts of findings in establishing a racial classification, a governmental body must have the authority and capability to establish, in the record, that the classification is responsive to identified discrimination. Lacking this capability, petitioner has not carried its burden of justification on this issue.

Hence, the purpose of helping certain groups whom the faculty of the Davis Medical School perceived as victims of "societal discrimination" does not justify a classification that imposes disadvantages upon persons like respondent, who bear no responsibility for whatever harm the beneficiaries of the special admissions program are thought to have suffered. To hold otherwise would be to convert a remedy heretofore reserved for violations of legal rights into a privilege that all institutions throughout the Nation could grant at their pleasure to whatever groups are perceived as victims of societal discrimination. That is a step we have never approved. Cf. Pasadena City Board of Education v. Spangler.

Petitioner identifies, as another purpose of its program, improving the delivery of health-care services to communities currently underserved. It may be assumed that in some situations a State's interest in facilitating the health care of its citizens is sufficiently compelling to support the use of a suspect classification. But there is virtually no

---

[6]   For example, the University is unable to explain its selection of only the four favored groups—Negroes, Mexican-Americans, American-Indians, and Asians—for preferential treatment. The inclusion of the last group is especially curious in light of the substantial numbers of Asians admitted through the regular admissions process.

evidence in the record indicating that petitioner's special admissions program is either needed or geared to promote that goal.[7]

Petitioner simply has not carried its burden of demonstrating that it must prefer members of particular ethnic groups over all other individuals in order to promote better health-care delivery to deprived citizens. Indeed, petitioner has not shown that its preferential classification is likely to have any significant effect on the problem.

■ Opinion of MR. JUSTICE BRENNAN, MR. JUSTICE WHITE, MR. JUSTICE MARSHALL, and MR. JUSTICE BLACKMUN, concurring in the judgment in part and dissenting in part.

I

Our Nation was founded on the principle that "all Men are created equal." Yet candor requires acknowledgment that the Framers of our Constitution, to forge the 13 Colonies into one Nation, openly compromised this principle of equality with its antithesis: slavery. The consequences of this compromise are well known and have aptly been called our "American Dilemma." Still, it is well to recount how recent the time has been, if it has yet come, when the promise of our principles has flowered into the actuality of equal opportunity for all regardless of race or color.

The Fourteenth Amendment, the embodiment in the Constitution of our abiding belief in human equality, has been the law of our land for only slightly more than half its 200 years. And for half of that half, the Equal Protection Clause of the Amendment was largely moribund so that, as late as 1927, Mr. Justice Holmes could sum up the importance of that Clause by remarking that it was the "last resort of constitutional arguments." Buck v. Bell. Worse than desuetude, the Clause was early turned against those whom it was intended to set free, condemning them to a "separate but equal" status before the law, a status always separate but seldom equal. Not until 1954—only 24 years ago—was this odious doctrine interred by our decision in Brown v. Board of Education and its progeny, which proclaimed that separate schools and public facilities of all sorts were inherently unequal and forbidden under our Constitution. Even then inequality was not eliminated with "all deliberate speed."

---

[7]   The only evidence in the record with respect to such underservice is a newspaper article. "The University concedes it cannot assure that minority doctors who entered under the program, all of whom expressed an 'interest' in practicing in a disadvantaged community, will actually do so. It may be correct to assume that some of them will carry out this intention, and that it is more likely they will practice in minority communities than the average white doctor. Nevertheless, there are more precise and reliable ways to identify applicants who are genuinely interested in the medical problems of minorities than by race. An applicant of whatever race who has demonstrated his concern for disadvantaged minorities in the past and who declares that practice in such a community is his primary professional goal would be more likely to contribute to alleviation of the medical shortage than one who is chosen entirely on the basis of race and disadvantage. In short, there is no empirical data to demonstrate that any one race is more selflessly socially oriented or by contrast that another is more selfishly acquisitive." 18 Cal.3d, at 56, 132 Cal.Rptr., at 695, 553 P.2d, at 1167.

[Brown II] In 1968 and again in 1971, for example, we were forced to remind school boards of their obligation to eliminate racial discrimination root and branch. And a glance at our docket and at dockets of lower courts will show that even today officially sanctioned discrimination is not a thing of the past.

Against this background, claims that law must be "color-blind" or that the datum of race is no longer relevant to public policy must be seen as aspiration rather than as description of reality. This is not to denigrate aspiration; for reality rebukes us that race has too often been used by those who would stigmatize and oppress minorities. Yet we cannot let color blindness become myopia which masks the reality that many "created equal" have been treated within our lifetimes as inferior both by the law and by their fellow citizens.

IV

Davis' articulated purpose of remedying the effects of past societal discrimination is, sufficiently important to justify the use of race-conscious admissions programs where there is a sound basis for concluding that minority underrepresentation is substantial and chronic, and that the handicap of past discrimination is impeding access of minorities to the Medical School.

[T]he requirement of a judicial determination of a constitutional or statutory violation as a predicate for race-conscious remedial actions would be self-defeating. Such a requirement would severely undermine efforts to achieve voluntary compliance with the requirements of law. And our society and jurisprudence have always stressed the value of voluntary efforts to further the objectives of the law. Judicial intervention is a last resort to achieve cessation of illegal conduct or the remedying of its effects rather than a prerequisite to action.

[T]he presence or absence of past discrimination by universities or employers is largely irrelevant to resolving respondent's constitutional claims. If it was reasonable to conclude—as we hold that it was—that the failure of minorities to qualify for admission at Davis under regular procedures was due principally to the effects of past discrimination, then there is a reasonable likelihood that, but for pervasive racial discrimination, respondent would have failed to qualify for admission even in the absence of Davis' special admissions program.

B

Properly construed, our prior cases unequivocally show that a state government may adopt race-conscious programs if the purpose of such programs is to remove the disparate racial impact its actions might otherwise have and if there is reason to believe that the disparate impact is itself the product of past discrimination, whether its own or that of society at large. There is no question that Davis' program is valid under this test.

Certainly, on the basis of the undisputed factual submissions before this Court, Davis had a sound basis for believing that the problem of underrepresentation of minorities was substantial and chronic and that the problem was attributable to handicaps imposed on minority applicants by past and present racial discrimination. Until at least 1973, the practice of medicine in this country was, in fact, if not in law, largely the prerogative of whites. Moreover, Davis had very good reason to believe that the national pattern of underrepresentation of minorities in medicine would be perpetuated if it retained a single admissions standard. For example, the entering classes in 1968 and 1969, the years in which such a standard was used, included only 1 Chicano and 2 Negroes out of the 50 admittees for each year. Nor is there any relief from this pattern of underrepresentation in the statistics for the regular admissions program in later years.

Davis clearly could conclude that the serious and persistent underrepresentation of minorities in medicine depicted by these statistics is the result of handicaps under which minority applicants labor as a consequence of a background of deliberate, purposeful discrimination against minorities in education and in society generally, as well as in the medical profession. From the inception of our national life, Negroes have been subjected to unique legal disabilities impairing access to equal educational opportunity. Under slavery, penal sanctions were imposed upon anyone attempting to educate Negroes. After enactment of the Fourteenth Amendment the States continued to deny Negroes equal educational opportunity, enforcing a strict policy of segregation that itself stamped Negroes as inferior, that relegated minorities to inferior educational institutions, and that denied them intercourse in the mainstream of professional life necessary to advancement. Segregation was not limited to public facilities, moreover, but was enforced by criminal penalties against private action as well.

The generation of minority students applying to Davis Medical School since it opened in 1968—most of whom were born before or about the time Brown I was decided—clearly have been victims of this discrimination. Judicial decrees recognizing discrimination in public education in California testify to the fact of widespread discrimination suffered by California-born minority applicants; many minority group members living in California, moreover, were born and reared in school districts in Southern States segregated by law. Since separation of school-children by race "generates a feeling of inferiority as to their status in the community that may affect their hearts and minds in a way unlikely ever to be undone," Brown I, the conclusion is inescapable that applicants to medical school must be few indeed who endured the effects of de jure segregation, the resistance to Brown I, or the equally debilitating pervasive private discrimination fostered by our long history of official discrimination, and yet come to the starting line with an education equal to whites.

■ MR. JUSTICE MARSHALL.

[I]it must be remembered that, during most of the past 200 years, the Constitution as interpreted by this Court did not prohibit the most ingenious and pervasive forms of discrimination against the Negro. Now, when a State acts to remedy the effects of that legacy of discrimination, I cannot believe that this same Constitution stands as a barrier.

I

Three hundred and fifty years ago, the Negro was dragged to this country in chains to be sold into slavery. Uprooted from his homeland and thrust into bondage for forced labor, the slave was deprived of all legal rights. It was unlawful to teach him to read; he could be sold away from his family and friends at the whim of his master; and killing or maiming him was not a crime. The system of slavery brutalized and dehumanized both master and slave.

The status of the Negro as property was officially erased by his emancipation at the end of the Civil War. But the long-awaited emancipation, while freeing the Negro from slavery, did not bring him citizenship or equality in any meaningful way. Slavery was replaced by a system of "laws which imposed upon the colored race onerous disabilities and burdens, and curtailed their rights in the pursuit of life, liberty, and property to such an extent that their freedom was of little value." Slaughter-House Cases. Despite the passage of the Thirteenth, Fourteenth, and Fifteenth Amendments, the Negro was systematically denied the rights those Amendments were supposed to secure. The combined actions and inactions of the State and Federal Governments maintained Negroes in a position of legal inferiority for another century after the Civil War.

II

The position of the Negro today in America is the tragic but inevitable consequence of centuries of unequal treatment. Measured by any benchmark of comfort or achievement, meaningful equality remains a distant dream for the Negro.

A Negro child today has a life expectancy which is shorter by more than five years than that of a white child. The Negro child's mother is over three times more likely to die of complications in childbirth, and the infant mortality rate for Negroes is nearly twice that for whites. The median income of the Negro family is only 60% that of the median of a white family, and the percentage of Negroes who live in families with incomes below the poverty line is nearly four times greater than that of whites.

When the Negro child reaches working age, he finds that America offers him significantly less than it offers his white counterpart. For Negro adults, the unemployment rate is twice that of whites, and the unemployment rate for Negro teenagers is nearly three times that of white teenagers. A Negro male who completes four years of college can expect a median annual income of merely $110 more than a white male who has only a high school diploma. Although Negroes represent 11.5% of the population, they are only 1.2% of the lawyers, and judges, 2% of the physicians, 2.3% of the dentists, 1.1% of the engineers and 2.6% of the college and university professors.

The relationship between those figures and the history of unequal treatment afforded to the Negro cannot be denied. At every point from birth to death the impact of the past is reflected in the still disfavored position of the Negro. In light of the sorry history of discrimination and its devastating impact on the lives of Negroes, bringing the Negro into the mainstream of American life should be a state interest of the highest order. To fail to do so is to ensure that America will forever remain a divided society.

III

I do not believe that the Fourteenth Amendment requires us to accept that fate. Neither its history nor our past cases lend any support to the conclusion that a university may not remedy the cumulative effects of society's discrimination by giving consideration to race in an effort to increase the number and percentage of Negro doctors.

It is plain that the Fourteenth Amendment was not intended to prohibit measures designed to remedy the effects of the Nation's past treatment of Negroes. The Congress that passed the Fourteenth Amendment is the same Congress that passed the 1866 Freedmen's Bureau Act, an Act that provided many of its benefits only to Negroes. Although the Freedmen's Bureau legislation provided aid for refugees, thereby including white persons within some of the relief measures, the bill was regarded, to the dismay of many Congressmen, as "solely and entirely for the freedmen, and to the exclusion of all other persons. . . ." Indeed, the bill was bitterly opposed on the ground that it "undertakes to make the negro in some respects . . . superior . . . and gives them favors that the poor white boy in the North cannot get." The bill's supporters defended it—not by rebutting the claim of special treatment—but by pointing to the need for such treatment:

"The very discrimination it makes between 'destitute and suffering' negroes, and destitute and suffering white paupers, proceeds upon the distinction that, in the omitted case, civil rights and immunities are already sufficiently protected by the possession of political power, the absence of which in the case provided for necessitates governmental protection."

Despite the objection to the special treatment the bill would provide for Negroes, it was passed by Congress. President Johnson vetoed this bill and also a subsequent bill that contained some modifications; one of his principal objections to both bills was that they gave special benefits to Negroes. Rejecting the concerns of the President and the bill's opponents, Congress overrode the President's second veto.

Since the Congress that considered and rejected the objections to the 1866 Freedmen's Bureau Act concerning special relief to Negroes also proposed the Fourteenth Amendment, it is inconceivable that the Fourteenth Amendment was intended to prohibit all race-conscious relief measures. It "would be a distortion of the policy manifested in that amendment, which was adopted to prevent state legislation designed to perpetuate discrimination on the basis of race or color." Railway Mail Assn. v. Corsi, to hold that it barred state action to remedy the effects of that discrimination. Such a result would pervert the intent of the Framers by substituting abstract equality for the genuine equality the Amendment was intended to achieve.

IV

While I applaud the judgment of the Court that a university may consider race in its admissions process, it is more than a little ironic that, after several hundred years of class-based discrimination against Negroes, the Court is unwilling to hold that a class-based remedy for that discrimination is permissible. In declining to so hold, today's judgment ignores the fact that for several hundred years Negroes have been discriminated against, not as individuals, but rather solely because of the color of their skins. It is unnecessary in 20th-century America to have individual Negroes demonstrate that they have been victims of racial discrimination; the racism of our society has been so pervasive that none, regardless of wealth or position, has managed to escape its impact. The experience of Negroes in America has been different in kind, not just in degree, from that of other ethnic groups. It is not merely the history of slavery alone but also that a whole people were marked as inferior by the law. And that mark has endured. The dream of America as the great melting pot has not been realized for the Negro; because of his skin color he never even made it into the pot.

It is because of a legacy of unequal treatment that we now must permit the institutions of this society to give consideration to race in making decisions about who will hold the positions of influence, affluence, and prestige in America. For far too long, the doors to those positions have been shut to Negroes. If we are ever to become a fully integrated society, one in which the color of a person's skin will not determine the opportunities available to him or her, we must be willing to take steps to open those doors. I do not believe that anyone can truly look into America's past and still find that a remedy for the effects of that past is impermissible.

■ MR. JUSTICE BLACKMUN.

The number of qualified, indeed highly qualified, applicants for admission to existing medical schools in the United States far exceeds the number of places available. Wholly apart from racial and ethnic considerations, therefore, the selection process inevitably results in the denial of admission to many qualified persons, indeed, to far more than the number of those who are granted admission. Obviously, it is a denial to the deserving.

It is somewhat ironic to have us so deeply disturbed over a program where race is an element of consciousness, and yet to be aware of the fact, as we are, that institutions of higher learning, albeit more on the undergraduate than the graduate level, have given conceded preferences up to a point to those possessed of athletic skills, to the children of alumni, to the affluent who may bestow their largess on the institutions, and to those having connections with celebrities, the famous, and the powerful.

Programs of admission to institutions of higher learning are basically a responsibility for academicians and for administrators and the specialists they employ. The judiciary, in contrast, is ill-equipped and poorly trained for this. The administration and management of educational institutions are beyond the competence of judges and are within the special competence of educators, provided always that the educators perform within legal and constitutional bounds. For me, therefore, interference by the judiciary must be the rare exception and not the rule.

It is worth noting, perhaps, that governmental preference has not been a stranger to our legal life. We see it in veterans' preferences. We see it in the aid-to-the-handicapped programs. We see it in the progressive income tax. We see it in the Indian programs. We may excuse some of these on the ground that they have specific constitutional protection or, as with Indians, that those benefited are wards of the Government. Nevertheless, these preferences exist and may not be ignored. And in the admissions field, as I have indicated, educational institutions have always used geography, athletic ability, anticipated financial largess, alumni pressure, and other factors of that kind.

I suspect that it would be impossible to arrange an affirmative-action program in a racially neutral way and have it successful. To ask that this be so is to demand the impossible. In order to get beyond racism, we must first take account of race. There is no other way. And in order to treat some persons equally, we must treat them differently. We cannot—we dare not—let the Equal Protection Clause perpetuate racial supremacy.

So the ultimate question, as it was at the beginning of this litigation, is: Among the qualified, how does one choose?

NOTES AND QUESTIONS

1. *Standard of Review.* Why does Powell think that affirmative action should be subject to the same standard of scrutiny as policies intended to exclude racial minorities? What is his worry about "judicial rankings"? Is Powell correct that they are necessary and that they do "not lie within the

judicial competence"? What reasons do Justices Marshall, Brennan and Blackmun offer for applying a less stringent standard of scrutiny?

2. *Harm of Affirmative Action.* Part of the disagreement among the justices is about the harm of affirmative action. According to Justice Powell, what are the harms of affirmative action? How weighty are they? How would the other Justices respond to his concerns?

3. *The Harm to* **Bakke.** What was the nature of the harm that Allan Bakke suffered: was it merely that the University considered his race; that he was not allowed to compete for those slots reserved for minorities; or that he was denied acceptance on the basis of race? In ordering Bakke's admission, did the Court find that he was denied admission on the basis of race? Or was the mere fact that the University considered his race a sufficient harm to warrant his admission?

4. *The Racial Order.* Justice Powell also writes that the United States has become a "nation of minorities." What does he mean by that and how does it, in his view, undermine the case for viewing affirmative action as "benign" and therefore subject to a less stringent standard of review? Do you agree with Powell's characterization of America as a "nation of minorities"? Would Justice Marshall agree with Powell's view?

5. *The Role of History.* Justice Marshall, in particular, emphasizes the historical oppression of African Americans. Is that relevant to the meaning of the equal protection mandate today? Do Justice Marshall and Powell view history differently? Or do they simply understand equal protection differently? Who gets the better of the argument?

6. *Remedial Rationales.* While most current debate about affirmative action centers on the wisdom and limits of the diversity rationale, it is important to recognize that the University in *Bakke* put forth a variety of non-diversity based justifications for its affirmative action policy. Justice Powell rejects societal discrimination as a sufficient predicate for affirmative action. Why? What requirements would Justice Powell impose on a remedial justification for affirmative action? Why does he reject the more permissive approach proposed by Justice Marshall?

7. *Remedial Justifications in Court.* In the aftermath of *Bakke*, the courts have imposed restrictive requirements on remedial justifications for race-based affirmative action. In its 1996 decision in *Hopwood v. Texas*, for example, the Fifth Circuit rejected the University of Texas's argument that the desire to remedy discrimination in primary and secondary education within the state provided a basis for affirmative action in admissions policy. The Court wrote:

> [T]he law school has no comparative advantage in measuring the present effects of discrimination in primary and secondary schools in Texas. Such a task becomes even more improbable where, as here, benefits are conferred on students who attended out-of-state or private schools for such education. Such boundless 'remedies' raise a constitutional concern beyond mere competence. In this

situation, an inference is raised that the program was the result of racial social engineering rather a desire to implement a remedy.

Justice Scalia has been among the most strident critics of remedial justifications for affirmative action. Consider this section of his opinion from the 1995 case *Adarand Constructors v. Pena*, 515 U.S. 200 (1995):

> In my view, government can never have a compelling interest in discriminating on the basis of race in order to make up for past racial discrimination in the opposite direction. Individuals who have been wronged by unlawful racial discrimination should be made whole; but under our Constitution there can be no such thing as either a creditor or a debtor race. That concept is alien to the Constitution's focus upon the individual. To pursue the concept of racial entitlement even for the most admirable and benign of purposes is to reinforce and preserve for future mischief the way of thinking that produced race slavery, race privilege and race hatred. In the eyes of government, we are just one race here. It is American.

How would you respond to Justice Scalia? Note that he does recognize the importance of compensating individuals who have been harmed by racial discrimination. How expansive should the remedial justification for affirmative action be? Should it reach societal discrimination, judicially or administratively identified discrimination, or only discrimination perpetrated by the institution seeking to adopt an affirmative action policy?

8. ***Defining Beneficiary Groups.*** A remedial justification for affirmative action also raises the question of beneficiary groups: how tight should the link between discrimination and beneficiaries of affirmative action be? Should recent immigrants from Africa or the Caribbean be counted as "black/African American" for purposes of a remedially justified affirmative action program? Does it matter that first or second generation immigrants are dramatically overrepresented among black students at selective colleges and universities? Roughly 40% of black students at Ivy League colleges are first or second generation immigrants, even as immigrants are only about 13% of the black population in the United States. Immigrants comprise more than one-third of black students at highly selective colleges generally. *See* generally, Douglas Massey et. al., *Black immigrants and Black Natives Attending Selective Colleges and Universities in the United States*, 113 Am. J. Educ. (Feb. 2007). Given this information, should universities count African or Caribbean immigrants as "black" for purposes of affirmative action?

III. THE DIVERSITY RATIONALE

The excerpts from Bakke below focus on the diversity rationale for affirmative action and on what form an affirmative action policy must take to pass constitutional muster. Justice Powell, as the swing vote, embraces diversity yet rejects the use of quotas.

Regents of the University of California v. Bakke

Supreme Court of the United States, 1978.
438 U.S. 265.

■ MR. JUSTICE POWELL announced the judgment of the Court.

D

The fourth goal asserted by petitioner is the attainment of a diverse student body. This clearly is a constitutionally permissible goal for an institution of higher education. Academic freedom, though not a specifically enumerated constitutional right, long has been viewed as a special concern of the First Amendment. The freedom of a university to make its own judgments as to education includes the selection of its student body. Mr. Justice Frankfurter summarized the "four essential freedoms" that constitute academic freedom:

" 'It is the business of a university to provide that atmosphere which is most conducive to speculation, experiment and creation. It is an atmosphere in which there prevail "the four essential freedoms" of a university—to determine for itself on academic grounds who may teach, what may be taught, how it shall be taught, and who may be admitted to study.' "

The atmosphere of "speculation, experiment and creation"—so essential to the quality of higher education—is widely believed to be promoted by a diverse student body.[8]

Thus, in arguing that its universities must be accorded the right to select those students who will contribute the most to the "robust exchange of ideas," petitioner invokes a countervailing constitutional interest, that of the First Amendment. In this light, petitioner must be viewed as seeking to achieve a goal that is of paramount importance in the fulfillment of its mission.

Ethnic diversity, however, is only one element in a range of factors a university properly may consider in attaining the goal of a heterogeneous

---

[8] The president of Princeton University has described some of the benefits derived from a diverse student body:

"[A] great deal of learning occurs informally. It occurs through interactions among students of both sexes; of different races, religions, and backgrounds; who come from cities and rural areas, from various states and countries; who have a wide variety of interests, talents, and perspectives; and who are able, directly or indirectly, to learn from their differences and to stimulate one another to reexamine even their most deeply held assumptions about themselves and their world. As a wise graduate of ours observed in commenting on this aspect of the educational process, 'People do not learn very much when they are surrounded only by the likes of themselves.'

"In the nature of things, it is hard to know how, and when, and even if, this informal 'learning through diversity' actually occurs. It does not occur for everyone. For many, however, the unplanned, casual encounters with roommates, fellow sufferers in an organic chemistry class, student workers in the library, teammates on a basketball squad, or other participants in class affairs or student government can be subtle and yet powerful sources of improved understanding and personal growth." Bowen, Admissions and the Relevance of Race, Princeton Alumni Weekly 7, 9 (Sept. 26, 1977).

student body. Although a university must have wide discretion in making the sensitive judgments as to who should be admitted, constitutional limitations protecting individual rights may not be disregarded. Respondent urges—and the courts below have held—that petitioner's dual admissions program is a racial classification that impermissibly infringes his rights under the Fourteenth Amendment. As the interest of diversity is compelling in the context of a university's admissions program, the question remains whether the program's racial classification is necessary to promote this interest.

V

A

It may be assumed that the reservation of a specified number of seats in each class for individuals from the preferred ethnic groups would contribute to the attainment of considerable ethnic diversity in the student body. But petitioner's argument that this is the only effective means of serving the interest of diversity is seriously flawed. In a most fundamental sense the argument misconceives the nature of the state interest that would justify consideration of race or ethnic background. It is not an interest in simple ethnic diversity, in which a specified percentage of the student body is in effect guaranteed to be members of selected ethnic groups, with the remaining percentage an undifferentiated aggregation of students. The diversity that furthers a compelling state interest encompasses a far broader array of qualifications and characteristics of which racial or ethnic origin is but a single though important element. Petitioner's special admissions program, focused solely on ethnic diversity, would hinder rather than further attainment of genuine diversity.

Nor would the state interest in genuine diversity be served by expanding petitioner's two-track system into a multitrack program with a prescribed number of seats set aside for each identifiable category of applicants. Indeed, it is inconceivable that a university would thus pursue the logic of petitioner's two-track program to the illogical end of insulating each category of applicants with certain desired qualifications from competition with all other applicants.

The experience of other university admissions programs, which take race into account in achieving the educational diversity valued by the First Amendment, demonstrates that the assignment of a fixed number of places to a minority group is not a necessary means toward that end. An illuminating example is found in the Harvard College program:

> "In recent years Harvard College has expanded the concept of diversity to include students from disadvantaged economic, racial and ethnic groups. Harvard College now recruits not only Californians or Louisianans but also blacks and Chicanos and other minority students. . . .

"In practice, this new definition of diversity has meant that race has been a factor in some admission decisions. When the Committee on Admissions reviews the large middle group of applicants who are 'admissible' and deemed capable of doing good work in their courses, the race of an applicant may tip the balance in his favor just as geographic origin or a life spent on a farm may tip the balance in other candidates' cases. A farm boy from Idaho can bring something to Harvard College that a Bostonian cannot offer. Similarly, a black student can usually bring something that a white person cannot offer. [*See* Appendix hereto.] . . .

"In Harvard College admissions the Committee has not set target-quotas for the number of blacks, or of musicians, football players, physicists or Californians to be admitted in a given year. . . . But that awareness [of the necessity of including more than a token number of black students] does not mean that the Committee sets a minimum number of blacks or of people from west of the Mississippi who are to be admitted. It means only that in choosing among thousands of applicants who are not only 'admissible' academically but have other strong qualities, the Committee, with a number of criteria in mind, pays some attention to distribution among many types and categories of students."

App. to Brief for Columbia University, Harvard University, Stanford University, and the University of Pennsylvania, as Amici Curiae 2–3.

In such an admissions program,[9] race or ethnic background may be deemed a "plus" in a particular applicant's file, yet it does not insulate the individual from comparison with all other candidates for the available seats. The file of a particular black applicant may be examined for his potential contribution to diversity without the factor of race being decisive when compared, for example, with that of an applicant identified as an Italian-American if the latter is thought to exhibit qualities more likely to promote beneficial educational pluralism. Such qualities could include exceptional personal talents, unique work or service experience, leadership potential, maturity, demonstrated compassion, a history of overcoming disadvantage, ability to communicate with the poor, or other qualifications deemed important. In short, an admissions program operated in this way is flexible enough to consider all pertinent elements

---

[9]   The admissions program at Princeton has been described in similar terms:

"While race is not in and of itself a consideration in determining basic qualifications, and while there are obviously significant differences in background and experience among applicants of every race, in some situations race can be helpful information in enabling the admission officer to understand more fully what a particular candidate has accomplished—and against what odds. Similarly, such factors as family circumstances and previous educational opportunities may be relevant, either in conjunction with race or ethnic background (with which they may be associated) or on their own." Bowen, *supra* n.48, at 8–9.

of diversity in light of the particular qualifications of each applicant, and to place them on the same footing for consideration, although not necessarily according them the same weight. Indeed, the weight attributed to a particular quality may vary from year to year depending upon the "mix" both of the student body and the applicants for the incoming class.

This kind of program treats each applicant as an individual in the admissions process. The applicant who loses out on the last available seat to another candidate receiving a "plus" on the basis of ethnic background will not have been foreclosed from all consideration for that seat simply because he was not the right color or had the wrong surname. It would mean only that his combined qualifications, which may have included similar nonobjective factors, did not outweigh those of the other applicant. His qualifications would have been weighed fairly and competitively, and he would have no basis to complain of unequal treatment under the Fourteenth Amendment.

It has been suggested that an admissions program which considers race only as one factor is simply a subtle and more sophisticated—but no less effective—means of according racial preference than the Davis program. A facial intent to discriminate, however, is evident in petitioner's preference program and not denied in this case. No such facial infirmity exists in an admissions program where race or ethnic background is simply one element—to be weighed fairly against other elements—in the selection process. [A] court would not assume that a university, professing to employ a facially nondiscriminatory admissions policy, would operate it as a cover for the functional equivalent of a quota system. In short, good faith would be presumed in the absence of a showing to the contrary.

B

In summary, it is evident that the Davis special admissions program involves the use of an explicit racial classification never before countenanced by this Court. It tells applicants who are not Negro, Asian, or Chicano that they are totally excluded from a specific percentage of the seats in an entering class. No matter how strong their qualifications, quantitative and extracurricular, including their own potential for contribution to educational diversity, they are never afforded the chance to compete with applicants from the preferred groups for the special admissions seats. At the same time, the preferred applicants have the opportunity to compete for every seat in the class.

With respect to respondent's entitlement to an injunction directing his admission to the Medical School, petitioner has conceded that it could not carry its burden of proving that, but for the existence of its unlawful special admissions program, respondent still would not have been admitted. Hence, respondent is entitled to the injunction, and that portion of the judgment must be affirmed.

APPENDIX TO OPINION OF POWELL, J.

Harvard College Admissions Program[10]

For the past 30 years Harvard College has received each year applications for admission that greatly exceed the number of places in the freshman class. The number of applicants who are deemed to be not "qualified" is comparatively small. The vast majority of applicants demonstrate through test scores, high school records and teachers' recommendations that they have the academic ability to do adequate work at Harvard, and perhaps to do it with distinction. Faced with the dilemma of choosing among a large number of "qualified" candidates, the Committee on Admissions could use the single criterion of scholarly excellence and attempt to determine who among the candidates were likely to perform best academically. But for the past 30 years the Committee on Admissions has never adopted this approach. The belief has been that if scholarly excellence were the sole or even predominant criterion, Harvard College would lose a great deal of its vitality and intellectual excellence and that the quality of the educational experience offered to all students would suffer. The belief that diversity adds an essential ingredient to the educational process has long been a tenet of Harvard College admissions. Fifteen or twenty years ago, however, diversity meant students from California, New York, and Massachusetts; city dwellers and farm boys; violinists, painters and football players; biologists, historians and classicists; potential stockbrokers, academics and politicians. The result was that very few ethnic or racial minorities attended Harvard College. In recent years Harvard College has expanded the concept of diversity to include students from disadvantaged economic, racial and ethnic groups. Harvard College now recruits not only Californians or Louisianans but also blacks and Chicanos and other minority students. Contemporary conditions in the United States mean that if Harvard College is to continue to offer a first-rate education to its students, minority representation in the undergraduate body cannot be ignored by the Committee on Admissions.

In practice, this new definition of diversity has meant that race has been a factor in some admission decisions. When the Committee on Admissions reviews the large middle group of applicants who are "admissible" and deemed capable of doing good work in their courses, the race of an applicant may tip the balance in his favor just as geographic origin or a life spent on a farm may tip the balance in other candidates' cases. A farm boy from Idaho can bring something to Harvard College that a Bostonian cannot offer. Similarly, a black student can usually bring something that a white person cannot offer. The quality of the educational experience of all the students in Harvard College depends in

---

[10] This statement appears in the Appendix to the Brief for Columbia University, Harvard University, Stanford University, and the University of Pennsylvania, as Amici Curiae.

part on these differences in the background and outlook that students bring with them.

■ Opinion of MR. JUSTICE BRENNAN, MR. JUSTICE WHITE, MR. JUSTICE MARSHALL, and MR. JUSTICE BLACKMUN, concurring in the judgment in part and dissenting in part.

It is not even claimed that Davis' program in any way operates to stigmatize or single out any discrete and insular, or even any identifiable, nonminority group. Nor will harm comparable to that imposed upon racial minorities by exclusion or separation on grounds of race be the likely result of the program. It does not, for example, establish an exclusive preserve for minority students apart from and exclusive of whites. Rather, its purpose is to overcome the effects of segregation by bringing the races together. True, whites are excluded from participation in the special admissions program, but this fact only operates to reduce the number of whites to be admitted in the regular admissions program in order to permit admission of a reasonable percentage—less than their proportion of the California population—of otherwise underrepresented qualified minority applicants.[11]

Nor was Bakke in any sense stamped as inferior by the Medical School's rejection of him. Indeed, it is conceded by all that he satisfied those criteria regarded by the school as generally relevant to academic performance better than most of the minority members who were admitted. Moreover, there is absolutely no basis for concluding that Bakke's rejection as a result of Davis' use of racial preference will affect him throughout his life in the same way as the segregation of the Negro schoolchildren in Brown I would have affected them. Unlike discrimination against racial minorities, the use of racial preferences for remedial purposes does not inflict a pervasive injury upon individual whites in the sense that wherever they go or whatever they do there is a significant likelihood that they will be treated as second-class citizens because of their color. This distinction does not mean that the exclusion of a white resulting from the preferential use of race is not sufficiently serious to require justification; but it does mean that the injury inflicted

---

[11] The constitutionality of the special admissions program is buttressed by its restriction to only 16% of the positions in the Medical School, a percentage less than that of the minority population in California, and to those minority applicants deemed qualified for admission and deemed likely to contribute to the Medical School and the medical profession. This is consistent with the goal of putting minority applicants in the position they would have been in if not for the evil of racial discrimination. Accordingly, this case does not raise the question whether even a remedial use of race would be unconstitutional if it admitted unqualified minority applicants in preference to qualified applicants or admitted, as a result of preferential consideration, racial minorities in numbers significantly in excess of their proportional representation in the relevant population. Such programs might well be inadequately justified by the legitimate remedial objectives. Our allusion to the proportional percentage of minorities in the population of the State administering the program is not intended to establish either that figure or that population universe as a constitutional benchmark. In this case, even respondent, as we understand him, does not argue that, if the special admissions program is otherwise constitutional, the allotment of 16 places in each entering class for special admittees is unconstitutionally high.

by such a policy is not distinguishable from disadvantages caused by a wide range of government actions, none of which has ever been thought impermissible for that reason alone.

In addition, there is simply no evidence that the Davis program discriminates intentionally or unintentionally against any minority group which it purports to benefit. The program does not establish a quota in the invidious sense of a ceiling on the number of minority applicants to be admitted. Nor can the program reasonably be regarded as stigmatizing the program's beneficiaries or their race as inferior. The Davis program does not simply advance less qualified applicants; rather, it compensates applicants, who it is uncontested are fully qualified to study medicine, for educational disadvantages which it was reasonable to conclude were a product of state-fostered discrimination. Once admitted, these students must satisfy the same degree requirements as regularly admitted students; they are taught by the same faculty in the same classes; and their performance is evaluated by the same standards by which regularly admitted students are judged. Under these circumstances, their performance and degrees must be regarded equally with the regularly admitted students with whom they compete for standing. Since minority graduates cannot justifiably be regarded as less well qualified than nonminority graduates by virtue of the special admissions program, there is no reasonable basis to conclude that minority graduates at schools using such programs would be stigmatized as inferior by the existence of such programs.

[T]he Davis admissions program does not simply equate minority status with disadvantage. Rather, Davis considers on an individual basis each applicant's personal history to determine whether he or she has likely been disadvantaged by racial discrimination. The record makes clear that only minority applicants likely to have been isolated from the mainstream of American life are considered in the special program; other minority applicants are eligible only through the regular admissions program. True, the procedure by which disadvantage is detected is informal, but we have never insisted that educators conduct their affairs through adjudicatory proceedings, and such insistence here is misplaced. A case-by-case inquiry into the extent to which each individual applicant has been affected, either directly or indirectly, by racial discrimination, would seem to be, as a practical matter, virtually impossible, despite the fact that there are excellent reasons for concluding that such effects generally exist. When individual measurement is impossible or extremely impractical, there is nothing to prevent a State from using categorical means to achieve its ends, at least where the category is closely related to the goal. And it is clear from our cases that specific proof that a person has been victimized by discrimination is not a necessary predicate to offering him relief where the probability of victimization is great. *See* Teamsters v. United States.

Finally, Davis' special admissions program cannot be said to violate the Constitution simply because it has set aside a predetermined number of places for qualified minority applicants rather than using minority status as a positive factor to be considered in evaluating the applications of disadvantaged minority applicants. For purposes of constitutional adjudication, there is no difference between the two approaches. In any admissions program which accords special consideration to disadvantaged racial minorities, a determination of the degree of preference to be given is unavoidable, and any given preference that results in the exclusion of a white candidate is no more or less constitutionally acceptable than a program such as that at Davis. Furthermore, the extent of the preference inevitably depends on how many minority applicants the particular school is seeking to admit in any particular year so long as the number of qualified minority applicants exceeds that number. There is no sensible, and certainly no constitutional, distinction between, for example, adding a set number of points to the admissions rating of disadvantaged minority applicants as an expression of the preference with the expectation that this will result in the admission of an approximately determined number of qualified minority applicants and setting a fixed number of places for such applicants as was done here.

The "Harvard" program, as those employing it readily concede, openly and successfully employs a racial criterion for the purpose of ensuring that some of the scarce places in institutions of higher education are allocated to disadvantaged minority students. That the Harvard approach does not also make public the extent of the preference and the precise workings of the system while the Davis program employs a specific, openly stated number, does not condemn the latter plan for purposes of Fourteenth Amendment adjudication. It may be that the Harvard plan is more acceptable to the public than is the Davis "quota." If it is, any State, including California, is free to adopt it in preference to a less acceptable alternative, just as it is generally free, as far as the Constitution is concerned, to abjure granting any racial preferences in its admissions program. But there is no basis for preferring a particular preference program simply because in achieving the same goals that the Davis Medical School is pursuing, it proceeds in a manner that is not immediately apparent to the public.

■ MR. JUSTICE BLACKMUN.

I am not convinced, as Mr. Justice POWELL seems to be, that the difference between the Davis program and the one employed by Harvard is very profound or constitutionally significant. The line between the two is a thin and indistinct one. In each, subjective application is at work. Because of my conviction that admission programs are primarily for the educators, I am willing to accept the representation that the Harvard program is one where good faith in its administration is practiced as well as professed. I agree that such a program, where race or ethnic background is only one of many factors, is a program better formulated than Davis' two-track system. The cynical, of course, may say that under a program such as Harvard's one may accomplish covertly what Davis concedes it does openly. I need not go that far, for despite its two-track aspect, the Davis program, for me, is within constitutional bounds, though perhaps barely so. It is surely free of stigma, and, I am not willing to infer a constitutional violation.

NOTES AND QUESTIONS

1.   *The Application of Strict Scrutiny.* Although Powell purports to apply strict scrutiny in *Bakke*, does he actually do so? Why does the Court in *Bakke* defer to the University? Is that deference justified?

2.   *The Benefits of Diversity.* In Powell's view, what are the benefits of diversity? Is the consideration of race necessary to realize those benefits?

3.   *Why Diversity?* Why do you think Justice Powell accepts diversity as a basis for affirmative action but rejects the societal discrimination rationale? Is his decision a sensible or defensible one?

4.   *Other Prospective Rationales.* Although Powell embraces the diversity rationale, he rejects another prospective rationale that the university also asserted. In particular, the University argued that training more minority doctors was necessary to provide services to minority communities. To what extent is Powell's rejection of this rationale consistent with his acceptance of the diversity rationale? Does it suggest any limit on Powell's understanding of diversity?

5.   *The Quota Prohibition.* Justice Powell invalidates the UC Davis program, in part, because it relies on a quota. But this raises a question: what is so bad about a quota? As some of the Justices suggest, isn't there a difference between a quota that aims to keep a historically disfavored group out of a school, as opposed to one that aims to bring them in? Does it make sense to view the two types of quotas as equally objectionable? Even if quotas intended to admit disadvantaged minorities are less concerning than those intended to exclude them, are there still reasons to prohibit use of the former?

6.   *The Quota-Holistic Distinction.* How significant is the distinction between the use of race in the UC Davis program and the way Harvard takes account of race in its admissions program cited favorably by Justice Powell?

A.   THE RE-AFFIRMATION OF DIVERSITY

After the Supreme Court's decision in *Bakke*, the Court did not revisit the issue of affirmative action in university admissions for 25 years. During that period, hundreds of selective colleges and universities throughout the nation crafted affirmative action policies premised on the diversity rationale. Inasmuch as the diversity rationale in *Bakke* was endorsed only by Justice Powell, a great deal of uncertainty and anxiety greeted the Court's decision to grant certiorari in 2003 in two cases challenging affirmative action at the University of Michigan. As you will see, in *Grutter v. Bollinger*, 539 U.S. 306 (2003), and *Gratz v. Bollinger*, 539 U.S. 244 (2003), the Supreme Court embraced Powell's reasoning in some respects, and extended or modified it in others.

Grutter v. Bollinger
Supreme Court of the United States, 2003.
539 U.S. 306.

■ JUSTICE O'CONNOR delivered the opinion of the Court.

The [University of Michigan] Law School ranks among the Nation's top law schools. It receives more than 3,500 applications each year for a class of around 350 students. Seeking to "admit a group of students who individually and collectively are among the most capable," the Law School looks for individuals with "substantial promise for success in law school" and "a strong likelihood of succeeding in the practice of law and contributing in diverse ways to the well-being of others." More broadly, the Law School seeks "a mix of students with varying backgrounds and experiences who will respect and learn from each other."

[T]he [admissions] policy requires admissions officials to look beyond grades and test scores to other criteria that are important to the Law School's educational objectives. So-called "'soft' variables" such as "the enthusiasm of recommenders, the quality of the undergraduate institution, the quality of the applicant's essay, and the areas and difficulty of undergraduate course selection" are all brought to bear in assessing an "applicant's likely contributions to the intellectual and social life of the institution."

The policy aspires to "achieve that diversity which has the potential to enrich everyone's education and thus make a law school class stronger than the sum of its parts." The policy does not restrict the types of diversity contributions eligible for "substantial weight" in the admissions process, but instead recognizes "many possible bases for diversity admissions." The policy does, however, reaffirm the Law School's longstanding commitment to "one particular type of diversity," that is, "racial and ethnic diversity with special reference to the inclusion of students from groups which have been historically discriminated against, like African-Americans, Hispanics and Native Americans, who without this commitment might not be represented in our student body in meaningful numbers." By enrolling a "'critical mass' of [underrepresented] minority students," the Law School seeks to "ensure their ability to make unique contributions to the character of the Law School."

The policy does not define diversity "solely in terms of racial and ethnic status." Nor is the policy "insensitive to the competition among all students for admission to the Law School." Rather, the policy seeks to guide admissions officers in "producing classes both diverse and academically outstanding, classes made up of students who promise to continue the tradition of outstanding contribution by Michigan Graduates to the legal profession."

B

III

A

Before this Court, as they have throughout this litigation, respondents assert only one justification for their use of race in the admissions process: obtaining "the educational benefits that flow from a diverse student body."

As part of its goal of "assembling a class that is both exceptionally academically qualified and broadly diverse," the Law School seeks to "enroll a 'critical mass' of minority students." The Law School's interest is not simply "to assure within its student body some specified percentage of a particular group merely because of its race or ethnic origin. That would amount to outright racial balancing, which is patently unconstitutional. Rather, the Law School's concept of critical mass is defined by reference to the educational benefits that diversity is designed to produce.

These benefits are substantial. As the District Court emphasized, the Law School's admissions policy promotes "cross-racial understanding," helps to break down racial stereotypes, and "enables [students] to better understand persons of different races." These benefits are "important and laudable," because "classroom discussion is livelier, more spirited, and simply more enlightening and interesting" when the students have "the greatest possible variety of backgrounds."

The Law School's claim of a compelling interest is further bolstered by its *amici*, who point to the educational benefits that flow from student body diversity. In addition to the expert studies and reports entered into evidence at trial, numerous studies show that student body diversity promotes learning outcomes, and "better prepares students for an increasingly diverse workforce and society, and better prepares them as professionals."

These benefits are not theoretical but real, as major American businesses have made clear that the skills needed in today's increasingly global marketplace can only be developed through exposure to widely diverse people, cultures, ideas, and viewpoints. What is more, high-ranking retired officers and civilian leaders of the United States military assert that, "based on [their] decades of experience," a "highly qualified, racially diverse officer corps . . . is essential to the military's ability to fulfill its principle mission to provide national security." The primary sources for the Nation's officer corps are the service academies and the

Reserve Officers Training Corps (ROTC), the latter comprising students already admitted to participating colleges and universities. At present, "the military cannot achieve an officer corps that is *both* highly qualified *and* racially diverse unless the service academies and the ROTC used limited race-conscious recruiting and admissions policies." To fulfill its mission, the military "must be selective in admissions for training and education for the officer corps, *and* it must train and educate a highly qualified, racially diverse officer corps in a racially diverse setting." We agree that "it requires only a small step from this analysis to conclude that our country's other most selective institutions must remain both diverse and selective."

We have repeatedly acknowledged the overriding importance of preparing students for work and citizenship, describing education as pivotal to "sustaining our political and cultural heritage" with a fundamental role in maintaining the fabric of society. This Court has long recognized that "education . . . is the very foundation of good citizenship." For this reason, the diffusion of knowledge and opportunity through public institutions of higher education must be accessible to all individuals regardless of race or ethnicity. The United States, as *amicus curiae*, affirms that "ensuring that public institutions are open and available to all segments of American society, including people of all races and ethnicities, represents a paramount government objective." And, "nowhere is the importance of such openness more acute than in the context of higher education." Effective participation by members of all racial and ethnic groups in the civic life of our Nation is essential if the dream of one Nation, indivisible, is to be realized.

Moreover, universities, and in particular, law schools, represent the training ground for a large number of our Nation's leaders. Individuals with law degrees occupy roughly half the state governorships, more than half the seats in the United States Senate, and more than a third of the seats in the United States House of Representatives. The pattern is even more striking when it comes to highly selective law schools. A handful of these schools accounts for 25 of the 100 United States Senators, 74 United States Courts of Appeals judges, and nearly 200 of the more than 600 United States District Court judges.

In order to cultivate a set of leaders with legitimacy in the eyes of the citizenry, it is necessary that the path to leadership be visibly open to talented and qualified individuals of every race and ethnicity. All members of our heterogeneous society must have confidence in the openness and integrity of the educational institutions that provide this training. As we have recognized, law schools "cannot be effective in isolation from the individuals and institutions with which the law interacts." Access to legal education (and thus the legal profession) must be inclusive of talented and qualified individuals of every race and ethnicity, so that all members of our heterogeneous society may participate in the educational institutions that provide the training and education necessary to succeed in America.

The Law School does not premise its need for critical mass on "any belief that minority students always (or even consistently) express some characteristic minority viewpoint on any issue." To the contrary, diminishing the force of such stereotypes is both a crucial part of the Law School's mission, and one that it cannot accomplish with only token numbers of minority students. Just as growing up in a particular region or having particular professional experiences is likely to affect an individual's views, so too is one's own, unique experience of being a racial minority in a society, like our own, in which race unfortunately still matters. The Law School has determined, based on its experience and expertise, that a "critical mass" of underrepresented minorities is necessary to further its compelling interest in securing the educational benefits of a diverse student body.

B

We are satisfied that the Law School's admissions program, like the Harvard plan described by Justice Powell, does not operate as a quota. Properly understood, a "quota" is a program in which a certain fixed number or proportion of opportunities are "reserved exclusively for certain minority groups." Quotas " 'impose a fixed number or percentage which must be attained, or which cannot be exceeded,' " and "insulate the individual from comparison with all other candidates for the available seats." In contrast, "a permissible goal . . . requires only a good-faith effort . . . to come within a range demarcated by the goal itself," and permits consideration of race as a "plus" factor in any given case while still ensuring that each candidate "competes with all other qualified applicants."

The Law School's goal of attaining a critical mass of underrepresented minority students does not transform its program into a quota.

The Chief Justice believes that the Law School's policy conceals an attempt to achieve racial balancing, and cites admissions data to contend that the Law School discriminates among different groups within the critical mass. But, as the Chief Justice concedes, the number of underrepresented minority students who ultimately enroll in the Law School differs substantially from their representation in the applicant pool and varies considerably for each group from year to year.

With respect to the use of race itself, all underrepresented minority students admitted by the Law School have been deemed qualified. By virtue of our Nation's struggle with racial inequality, such students are both likely to have experiences of particular importance to the Law School's mission, and less likely to be admitted in meaningful numbers on criteria that ignore those experiences.

The Law School does not, however, limit in any way the broad range of qualities and experiences that may be considered valuable contributions to student body diversity. To the contrary, the school's policy makes clear "there are many possible bases for diversity admissions," and provides examples of admittees who have lived or traveled widely abroad, are fluent in several languages, have overcome personal adversity and family hardship, have exceptional records of extensive community service, and have had successful careers in other fields. The Law School seriously considers each "applicant's promise of making a notable contribution to the class by way of a particular strength, attainment, or characteristic—*e.g.*, an unusual intellectual achievement, employment experience, nonacademic performance, or personal background." All applicants have the opportunity to highlight their own potential diversity contributions through the submission of a personal statement, letters of recommendation, and an essay describing the ways in which the applicant will contribute to the life and diversity of the Law School.

What is more, the Law School actually gives substantial weight to diversity factors besides race. The Law School frequently accepts nonminority applicants with grades and test scores lower than underrepresented minority applicants (and other nonminority applicants) who are rejected. This shows that the Law School seriously weighs many other diversity factors besides race that can make a real and dispositive difference for nonminority applicants as well. By this flexible approach, the Law School sufficiently takes into account, in practice as well as in theory, a wide variety of characteristics besides race and ethnicity that contribute to a diverse student body. Petitioner and the United States argue that the Law School's plan is not narrowly tailored because race-neutral means exist to obtain the educational benefits of student body diversity that the Law School seeks. We disagree. Narrow tailoring does not require exhaustion of every conceivable race-neutral alternative. Nor does it require a university to choose between maintaining a reputation for excellence or fulfilling a commitment to provide educational opportunities to members of all racial groups. Narrow tailoring does, however, require serious, good faith consideration of workable race-neutral alternatives that will achieve the diversity the university seeks.

IV

In summary, the *Equal Protection Clause* does not prohibit the Law School's narrowly tailored use of race in admissions decisions to further a compelling interest in obtaining the educational benefits that flow from a diverse student body.

■ JUSTICE SCALIA, with whom JUSTICE THOMAS joins, concurring in part and dissenting in part.

I add the following: The "educational benefit" that the University of Michigan seeks to achieve by racial discrimination consists, according to the Court, of " 'cross-racial understanding,' " and " 'better prepar[ation of] students for an increasingly diverse workforce and society,' " ibid., all of which is necessary not only for work, but also for good "citizenship." This is not, of course, an "educational benefit" on which students will be graded on their law school transcript (Works and Plays Well with Others: B+) or tested by the bar examiners (Q: Describe in 500 words or less your cross-racial understanding). For it is a lesson of life rather than law—essentially the same lesson taught to (or rather learned by, for it cannot be "taught" in the usual sense) people three feet shorter and 20 years younger than the full-grown adults at the University of Michigan Law School, in institutions ranging from Boy Scout troops to public-school kindergartens. If properly considered an "educational benefit" at all, it is surely not one that is either uniquely relevant to law school or uniquely "teachable" in a formal educational setting. And therefore: If it is appropriate for the University of Michigan Law School to use racial discrimination for the purpose of putting together a "critical mass" that will convey generic lessons in socialization and good citizenship, surely it is no less appropriate—indeed, particularly appropriate—for the civil service system of the State of Michigan to do so. There, also, those exposed to "critical masses" of certain races will presumably become better Americans, better Michiganders, better civil servants. And surely private employers cannot be criticized—indeed, should be praised—if they also "teach" good citizenship to their adult employees through a patriotic, all-American system of racial discrimination in hiring. The nonminority individuals who are deprived of a legal education, a civil service job, or any job at all by reason of their skin color will surely understand.

■ JUSTICE THOMAS, with whom JUSTICE SCALIA joins as to Parts I–VII, concurring in part and dissenting in part.

The Court relies heavily on social science evidence to justify its deference. The Court never acknowledges, however, the growing evidence that racial (and other sorts) of heterogeneity actually impairs learning among black students. *See*, e.g., Flowers & Pascarella, Cognitive Effects of College Racial Composition on African American Students After 3 Years of College, 40 J. of College Student Development 669, 674 (1999) (concluding that black students experience superior cognitive development at Historically Black Colleges (HBCs) and that, even among blacks, "a substantial diversity moderates the cognitive effects of attending an HBC"); Allen, The Color of Success: African-American College Student Outcomes at Predominantly White and Historically Black Public Colleges and Universities, 62 Harv. Educ. Rev. 26, 35 (1992) (finding that black students attending HBCs report higher academic achievement than those attending predominantly white colleges).

The majority grants deference to the Law School's "assessment that diversity will, in fact, yield educational benefits." It follows, therefore, that an HBC's assessment that racial homogeneity will yield educational benefits would similarly be given deference. An HBC's rejection of white applicants in order to maintain racial homogeneity seems permissible, therefore, under the majority's view of the Equal Protection Clause. Contained within today's majority opinion is the seed of a new constitutional justification for a concept I thought long and rightly rejected—racial segregation.

[N]o modern law school can claim ignorance of the poor performance of blacks, relatively speaking, on the Law School Admissions Test (LSAT). Nevertheless, law schools continue to use the test and then attempt to "correct" for black underperformance by using racial discrimination in admissions so as to obtain their aesthetic student body. The Law School's continued adherence to measures it knows produce racially skewed results is not entitled to deference by this Court. The Law School itself admits that the test is imperfect, as it must, given that it regularly admits students who score at or below 150 (the national median) on the test. *See* App. 156–203 (showing that, between 1995 and 2000, the Law School admitted 37 students—27 of whom were black; 31 of whom were "underrepresented minorities"—with LSAT scores of 150 or lower). And the Law School's *amici* cannot seem to agree on the fundamental question whether the test itself is useful. Compare Brief for Law School Admission Council as *Amicus Curiae* 12 ("LSAT scores . . . are an effective predictor of students' performance in law school") with Brief for Harvard Black Law Students Association et al. as *Amici Curiae* 27 ("Whether [the LSAT] measures objective merit . . . is certainly questionable"). An infinite variety of admissions methods are available to the Law School. Considering all of the radical thinking that has historically occurred at this country's universities, the Law School's intractable approach toward admissions is striking.

It is uncontested that each year, the Law School admits a handful of blacks who would be admitted in the absence of racial discrimination. Who can differentiate between those who belong and those who do not? The majority of blacks are admitted to the Law School because of discrimination, and because of this policy all are tarred as undeserving. This problem of stigma does not depend on determinacy as to whether those stigmatized are actually the "beneficiaries" of racial discrimination. When blacks take positions in the highest places of government, industry, or academia, it is an open question today whether their skin color played a part in their advancement. The question itself is the stigma—because either racial discrimination did play a role, in which case the person may be deemed "otherwise unqualified," or it did not, in which case asking the question itself unfairly marks those blacks who would succeed without discrimination.

"[T]he very existence of racial discrimination of the type practiced by the Law School may impede the narrowing of the LSAT testing gap. An applicant's LSAT score can improve dramatically with preparation, but such preparation is a cost, and there must be sufficient benefits attached to an improved score to justify additional study. Whites scoring between 163 and 167 on the LSAT are routinely rejected by the Law School, and thus whites aspiring to admission at the Law School have every incentive to improve their score to levels above that range. Blacks, on the other hand, are nearly guaranteed admission if they score above 155. As admission prospects approach certainty, there is no incentive for the black applicant to continue to prepare for the LSAT once he is reasonably assured of achieving the requisite score. It is far from certain that the LSAT test-taker's behavior is responsive to the Law School's admissions policies. Nevertheless, the possibility remains that this racial discrimination will help fulfill the bigot's prophecy about black underperformance—just as it confirms the conspiracy theorist's belief that "institutional racism" is at fault for every racial disparity in our society.

■ CHIEF JUSTICE REHNQUIST, with whom JUSTICE SCALIA, JUSTICE KENNEDY, and JUSTICE THOMAS join, dissenting.

The Law School claims it must take the steps it does to achieve a 'critical mass' of underrepresented minority students. But its actual program bears no relation to this asserted goal. Stripped of its "critical mass" veil, the Law School's program is revealed as a naked effort to achieve racial balancing.

Respondents and school administrators explain generally that "critical mass" means a sufficient number of underrepresented minority students to achieve several objectives: To ensure that these minority students do not feel isolated or like spokespersons for their race; to provide adequate opportunities for the type of interaction upon which the educational benefits of diversity depend; and to challenge all students to think critically and reexamine stereotypes. These objectives indicate that "critical mass" relates to the size of the student body.

In practice, the Law School's program bears little or no relation to its asserted goal of achieving "critical mass." Respondents explain that the Law School seeks to accumulate a "critical mass" of each underrepresented minority group. But the record demonstrates that the Law School's admissions practices with respect to these groups differ dramatically and cannot be defended under any consistent use of the term "critical mass."

From 1995 through 2000, the Law School admitted between 1,130 and 1,310 students. Of those, between 13 and 19 were Native American, between 91 and 108 were African-American, and between 47 and 56 were

Hispanic. If the Law School is admitting between 91 and 108 African-Americans in order to achieve "critical mass," thereby preventing African-American students from feeling "isolated or like spokespersons for their race," one would think that a number of the same order of magnitude would be necessary to accomplish the same purpose for Hispanics and Native Americans. Similarly, even if all of the Native American applicants admitted in a given year matriculate, which the record demonstrates is not at all the case, how can this possibly constitute a "critical mass" of Native Americans in a class of over 350 students? In order for this pattern of admission to be consistent with the Law School's explanation of "critical mass," one would have to believe that the objectives of "critical mass" offered by respondents are achieved with only half the number of Hispanics and one-sixth the number of Native Americans as compared to African-Americans.

These statistics have a significant bearing on petitioner's case. Respondents have never offered any race-specific arguments explaining why significantly more individuals from one underrepresented minority group are needed in order to achieve "critical mass" or further student body diversity. . . . [T]he Law School's disparate admissions practices with respect to these minority groups demonstrate that its alleged goal of "critical mass" is simply a sham. Petitioner may use these statistics to expose this sham, which is the basis for the Law School's admission of less qualified underrepresented minorities in preference to her. Surely strict scrutiny cannot permit these sorts of disparities without at least some explanation.

Only when the "critical mass" label is discarded does a likely explanation for these numbers emerge. The percentage of admitted applicants who were members of these minority groups closely tracked the percentage of individuals in the school's applicant pool who were from the same groups. The tight correlation between the percentage of applicants and admittees of a given race, therefore, must result from careful race-based planning by the Law School. It suggests a formula for admission based on the aspirational assumption that all applicants are equally qualified academically, and therefore that the proportion of each group admitted should be the same as the proportion of that group in the applicant pool. . . . [T]he ostensibly flexible nature of the Law School's admissions program that the Court finds appealing, appears to be, in practice, a carefully managed program designed to ensure proportionate representation of applicants from selected minority groups.

Before the Court's decision today, we consistently applied the same strict scrutiny analysis regardless of the government's purported reason for using race and regardless of the setting in which race was being used. We rejected calls to use more lenient review in the face of claims that race was being used in "good faith" because " '[m]ore than good motives should be required when government seeks to allocate its resources by way of an explicit racial classification system.' " Adarand, Fullilove, (STEVENS, J., dissenting) ("Racial classifications are simply too pernicious to permit any but the most exact connection between justification and classification"). We likewise rejected calls to apply more lenient review based on the particular setting in which race is being used. Indeed, even in the specific context of higher education, we emphasized that "constitutional limitations protecting individual rights may not be disregarded." Bakke.

Although the Court recites the language of our strict scrutiny analysis, its application of that review is unprecedented in its deference.

■ JUSTICE KENNEDY, dissenting.

The Court confuses deference to a university's definition of its educational objective with deference to the implementation of this goal. In the context of university admissions the objective of racial diversity can be accepted based on empirical data known to us, but deference is not to be given with respect to the methods by which it is pursued. Preferment by race, when resorted to by the State, can be the most divisive of all policies, containing within it the potential to destroy confidence in the Constitution and in the idea of equality. The majority today refuses to be faithful to the settled principle of strict review designed to reflect these concerns

NOTES AND QUESTIONS

1. **Standard of Review.** The majority purports to apply strict scrutiny, but Chief Justice Rehnquist, in dissent, contends that the majority does not do so. Is Rehnquist's critique accurate? Persuasive? If so, why doesn't the majority either actually apply strict scrutiny or admit that it is not doing so?

2. **Identifying the Harm.** What harm, if any, did Barbara Grutter suffer as a result of the school's affirmative action policy? Consider these possibilities: i) she was denied admission due to the affirmative action program; ii) she suffered a significantly decreased likelihood of admission due to the affirmative action program; iii) she was stigmatized by the mere fact that her race was considered in the admissions process; iv) she was treated less favorably than underrepresented minority applicants with credentials comparable to hers. Which of these harms best fits the case? What weight would you give these various types of harms?

3. **Harms and Beneficiaries.** As Justice Thomas' opinion suggests, there are claims that affirmative action actually harms its supposed beneficiary groups. One claim is that it undermines minority students' incentives to achieve at a high level. Consider this observation from linguist and commentator John McWhorter:

> For even the most highly motivated of students, school work is often dull and demanding. If a talented black or Hispanic student knows that he need not work as hard or perform as well in the classroom as an equally talented—or more talented—white or Asian student

to get into the same college or graduate school, the black and Hispanic student will have every reason to work less hard and devote more time to more fun-producing activities than school work. . . . [O]ne could think of few better ways to depress a race's propensity for pushing itself to do its best in school than a policy ensuring that less-than-best efforts will have a disproportionately high yield.

Another contention, which Justice Thomas emphasizes, is that affirmative action stigmatizes beneficiary groups as undeserving, as unable to succeed without special treatment. According to this view, the existence of affirmative action suggests that students from underrepresented minority groups were admitted less because of their own efforts and achievements than because of a racial preference. The perniciousness of the resulting stigma, in Justice Thomas' view, is that even those minority students who would have been admitted in the absence of affirmative action are viewed as undeserving. A final criticism is that affirmative action harms beneficiaries by placing them in competitive academic environments for which they are ill prepared. According to this view, affirmative action beneficiaries may become overwhelmed academically and consequently will learn less than if they had attended less challenging and less prestigious schools. The primary proponent of this view is UCLA law professor Richard Sander, who argues that many minority students attend schools where they find themselves "overmatched" and thus become demoralized and disengaged from their studies. According to Sander, students who are overmatched in law school, for example, receive lower grades, learn less than their peers, and in turn are more likely to fail the bar exam than if they had attended a less competitive school. Sander contends that affirmative action in law school admission has ironically reduced the number of black lawyers by rendering black students less likely to pass the bar than if they had attended a less challenging school. See, e.g., Richard Sander & Stuart Taylor, *Mismatch: How Affirmative Action Hurts Students it's intended to Help, and Why Universities Won't Admit it* (2012); Richard Sander, *A Systemic Analysis of Affirmative Action in American Law Schools*, 57 Stan.L.Rev.367 (2004).

Other empirical analyses cast doubt on Sander's claims. William Bowen and Derek Bok have conducted the most long-term and comprehensive study of university affirmative action and have found that racial minority students have benefitted, in terms of likelihood of graduation, future earnings, and other outcomes, from attending more rather than less prestigious universities. William G. Bowen and Derek Bok, The Shape of the River: Long-Term Consequences of Considering Race in College and University Admissions (2000). More recently, other analyses of law school data by experts in empirical research have undermined Sander's key claims. *See, e.g.*, Daniel Ho, *Why Affirmative Action Does Not Cause Black Students To Fail the Bar*, 114 YaleL.J. 1997 (2005)

What do you make of Sander's criticisms of affirmative action? Which seem most empirically plausible? How much weight, if any, should each be accorded in evaluating affirmative action policy?

4.   *Race and Culture.* If one aspect of diversity's benefits is cultural difference, is race a good proxy for that cultural difference? Does the Court suggest that it is? See Kim Forde-Mazrui, *Does Racial Diversity Promote Cultural Diversity?: The Missing Question in Fisher v. Texas,* 17 Lewis & ClarkL.Rev. 987 (2013)

5.   *The Benefits of Diversity.* Is Justice O'Connor's articulation of the benefits of diversity consistent with Powell's opinion in *Bakke*? In what ways do their descriptions of the benefits of diversity differ?

6.   *Diversity and Society.* O'Connor's articulation of the benefits of diversity drew upon two of the highest profile amicus briefs submitted in *Grutter:* from military officers and business leaders. The amicus in the military brief included "former high-ranking officers and civilian leaders of the Army, Navy, Air Force, and Marine Corps, including former military-academy superintendents, Secretaries of Defense, and present and former members of the U.S. Senate." The brief noted that ROTC cadets were the primary source for military officers and that eliminating the pipeline of diverse officers from universities threatened the military's ability to fight effectively:

> Plainly, the missions of the United States military services cannot be accomplished without the minority men and women who constitute almost 40% of the active duty armed forces. Moreover: the current leadership views complete racial integration as a military necessity—that is, as a prerequisite to a cohesive, and therefore effective, fighting force. In short, *success with the challenges of diversity is critical to national security.* Experience during the 1960s and 1970s with racial conflict in the ranks was an effective lesson in the importance of inclusion and equal opportunity. As a senior Pentagon official told us, 'Doing affirmative action the right way is deadly serious for us—people's lives depend on it.' (citation omitted).

Business leaders made a similar argument. A brief on behalf of 65 corporations, including Boeing, GE, Coke, Shell, and Microsoft among others, highlighted the global marketplace that students will enter into from college or law school. The brief argued:

> [I]ndividuals who have been educated in a diverse setting are more likely to succeed, because they can make valuable contributions to the workforce in several important and concrete ways. First, a diverse group of individuals educated in a cross-cultural environment has the ability to facilitate unique and creative approaches to problem-solving arising from the integration of different perspectives. Second, such individuals are better able to develop products and services that appeal to a variety of consumers and to market offerings in ways that appeal to those consumers. Third, a racially diverse group of managers with cross-cultural experience is better able to work with business partners, employees, and clientele in the United States and around the world. Fourth, individuals who have been educated in a diverse

setting are likely to contribute to a positive work environment, by decreasing incidents of discrimination and stereotyping. Overall, an educational environment that ensures participation by diverse people, viewpoints and ideas will help produce the most talented workforce.

Do you find convincing the argument that diversity in the university setting helps businesses, the military, or American society more generally? How precisely might it do so?

7.   *The Critique of Diversity.* Justice Scalia criticizes the "educational benefits" of diversity as akin to a socialization process that is not the province of professional schools. Is he correct that such socialization should not be viewed as a compelling interest for a professional school that trains lawyers? What about with respect to undergraduate education?

8.   *Diversity and Race.* Assuming that there are educational benefits to diversity, is it necessary to consider race to attain each of those benefits? In the Court's view, is racial diversity an end in itself, or is it a means of realizing some other sort of diversity? If the latter, then why not select for those characteristics directly (e.g., political views, interests, unusual experiences, cultural background) without relying on race? Isn't the use of race as a proxy for other, relevant characteristics simply the form of stereotyping that antidiscrimination law has often condemned? More generally, do the arguments made by the business and military leaders conflate diversity and racial difference?

9.   *The Role of Social Science.* Justice Thomas criticizes the Court's reliance on social science in accepting diversity as a compelling state interest. But is social science really the basis for the Court's embrace of diversity? If social science research demonstrated that there are benefits to racial homogeneity, would the Court accept that as a sufficient justification for a race-based admissions policy? Should it? See R. Richard Banks, *The Benign-Invidious Asymmetry in Equal Protection Analysis*, 31 Hasting Const.L.Q. 573 (2003). If the Court would not recognize homogeneity as a compelling interest on the basis of social science evidence, is it justifiable for the Court to rely on social science in pronouncing diversity compelling?

10.   *The Utility of the LSAT.* Justice Thomas also raises an important question about the role of testing in the admissions process. He notes, correctly, that affirmative action is necessary, in part, due to law schools' heavy reliance on the LSAT, a test on which black and Latino applicants do not typically perform as well as their white and Asian American counterparts. The LSAT has been shown to predict, modestly, law students' first year grades and maybe bar passage. It is not clear how well the LSAT predicts the likelihood of one's success as a lawyer. In addition, research has shown that African Americans perform less well on a test if they experience anxiety about confirming the stereotype of African Americans as intellectually inferior. Given this evidence, is it justifiable for universities to place such heavy reliance on test scores? How strong is the argument that the LSAT creates an unjustified disparate impact on black and Latino applicants?

11. *Racial Balancing.* Chief Justice Rehnquist contends that Michigan Law School's supposed pursuit of critical mass is actually a form of racial balancing. How does he reach that conclusion? Is he correct?

12. *The Goal of Racial Balance.* Supposing that Chief Justice Rehnquist is correct and that the law school was seeking to reflect the racial demographics of, say, the state of Michigan. Should it be permitted to attempt to do so? What if it already attempts to reflect, say, the proportion of rural vs. urban residents within the state? Or attempts, as many schools unquestionably do, to maintain a certain gender balance? Is the goal of racial balance any less beneficial or more harmful than other sorts of demographic representation?

IV. THE MEANS OF AFFIRMATIVE ACTION

In *Gratz v. Bollinger*, 529 U.S. 244 (2003), the companion case to *Grutter*, the Court considered the affirmative action program used as part of the University of Michigan's undergraduate admissions process. While the undergraduate admissions policy was also premised on the diversity rationale, it operated differently than did the law school policy—a fact that resulted in its invalidation.

Gratz v. Bollinger
Supreme Court of the United States, 2003.
539 U.S. 244.

■ CHIEF JUSTICE REHNQUIST delivered the opinion of the Court.

OUA [the Office of Undergraduate Admissions] considers a number of factors in making admissions decisions, including high school grades, standardized test scores, high school quality, curriculum strength, geography, alumni relationships, and leadership. OUA also considers race. During all periods relevant to this litigation, the University has considered African-Americans, Hispanics, and Native Americans to be "underrepresented minorities," and it is undisputed that the University admits "virtually every qualified . . . applicant" from these groups.

* * *

Beginning with the 1998 academic year, the OUA [instituted] a "selection index," on which an applicant could score a maximum of 150 points. This index was divided linearly into ranges generally calling for admissions dispositions as follows: 100–150 (admit); 95–99 (admit or postpone); 90–94 (postpone or admit); 75–89 (delay or postpone); 74 and below (delay or reject).

Each application received points based on high school grade point average, standardized test scores, academic quality of an applicant's high school, strength or weakness of high school curriculum, in-state residency, alumni relationship, personal essay, and personal achievement or leadership. Of particular significance here, under a "miscellaneous" category, an applicant was entitled to 20 points based upon his or her membership in an underrepresented racial or ethnic minority group.

Starting in 1999, the University established an Admissions Review Committee (ARC), to provide an additional level of consideration for some applications. Under the new system, counselors may, in their discretion, "flag" an application for the ARC to review after determining that the applicant (1) is academically prepared to succeed at the University, (2) has achieved a minimum selection index score, and (3) possesses a quality or characteristic important to the University's composition of its freshman class, such as high class rank, unique life experiences, challenges, circumstances, interests or talents, socioeconomic disadvantage, and underrepresented race, ethnicity, or geography. After reviewing "flagged" applications, the ARC determines whether to admit, defer, or deny each applicant.

* * *

We find that the University's policy, which automatically distributes 20 points, or one-fifth of the points needed to guarantee admission, to every single "underrepresented minority" applicant solely because of race, is not narrowly tailored to achieve the interest in educational diversity that respondents claim justifies their program.

In Bakke, Justice Powell reiterated that "[p]referring members of any one group for no reason other than race or ethnic origin is discrimination for its own sake." He then explained, however, that in his view it would be permissible for a university to employ an admissions program in which "race or ethnic background may be deemed a 'plus' in a particular applicant's file." Such a system, in Justice Powell's view, would be "flexible enough to consider all pertinent elements of diversity in light of the particular qualifications of each applicant."

Justice Powell's opinion in Bakke emphasized the importance of considering each particular applicant as an individual, assessing all of the qualities that individual possesses, and in turn, evaluating that individual's ability to contribute to the unique setting of higher education. The admissions program Justice Powell described, however, did not contemplate that any single characteristic automatically ensured a specific and identifiable contribution to a university's diversity. Instead, under the approach Justice Powell described, each characteristic of a particular applicant was to be considered in assessing the applicant's entire application.

The current [undergraduate admissions] policy does not provide such individualized consideration. The policy automatically distributes 20 points to every single applicant from an "underrepresented minority" group, as defined by the University. The only consideration that accompanies this distribution of points is a factual review of an application to determine whether an individual is a member of one of these minority groups. Moreover, unlike Justice Powell's example, where the race of a "particular black applicant" could be considered without being decisive, the automatic distribution of 20 points has the effect of making "the factor of race . . . decisive" for virtually every minimally qualified underrepresented minority applicant.

Also instructive in our consideration of the [undergraduate admissions] system is the example provided in the description of the Harvard College Admissions Program, which Justice Powell both discussed in, and attached to, his opinion in Bakke. The example was included to "illustrate the kind of significance attached to race" under the Harvard College program. It provided as follows:

> "The Admissions Committee, with only a few places left to fill, might find itself forced to choose between A, the child of a successful black physician in an academic community with promise of superior academic performance, and B, a black who grew up in an inner-city ghetto of semi-literate parents whose academic achievement was lower but who had demonstrated energy and leadership as well as an apparently abiding interest in black power. If a good number of black students much like A but few like B had already been admitted, the Committee might prefer B; and vice versa. If C, a white student with extraordinary artistic talent, were also seeking one of the remaining places, his unique quality might give him an edge over both A and B. Thus, the critical criteria are often individual qualities or experience *not dependent upon race but sometimes associated with it.*" (emphasis added).

This example further demonstrates the problematic nature of the university's [undergraduate] admissions system. Even if student C's "extraordinary artistic talent" rivaled that of Monet or Picasso, the applicant would receive, at most, five points under the [Michigan] system. At the same time, every single underrepresented minority applicant, including students A and B, would automatically receive 20 points for submitting an application. Clearly, the LSA's system does not offer applicants the individualized selection process described in Harvard's example. Instead of considering how the differing backgrounds, experiences, and characteristics of students A, B, and C might benefit the University, admissions counselors reviewing [undergraduate] applications would simply award both A and B 20 points because their applications indicate that they are African-American, and student C would receive up to 5 points for his "extraordinary talent."

Respondents emphasize the fact that the [undergraduate admissions process] has created the possibility of an applicant's file being flagged for individualized consideration. We think that the flagging program only emphasizes the flaws of the University's system as a whole when compared to that described by Justice Powell. Again, students A, B, and C illustrate the point. First, student A would never be flagged. This is because, as the University has conceded, the effect of automatically awarding 20 points is that virtually every qualified underrepresented minority applicant is admitted. Student A, an applicant "with promise of superior academic performance," would certainly fit this description. Thus, the result of the automatic distribution of 20 points is that the University would never consider student A's individual background, experiences, and characteristics to assess his individual "potential contribution to diversity." Instead, every applicant like student A would simply be admitted.

It is possible that students B and C would be flagged and considered as individuals. This assumes that student B was not already admitted because of the automatic 20-point distribution, and that student C could muster at least 70 additional points. But the fact that the "review committee can look at the applications individually and ignore the points," once an application is flagged is of little comfort under our strict scrutiny analysis. The record does not reveal precisely how many applications are flagged for this individualized consideration, but it is undisputed that such consideration is the exception and not the rule in the operation of the LSA's admissions program. Additionally, this individualized review is only provided *after* admissions counselors automatically distribute the University's version of a "plus" that makes race a decisive factor for virtually every minimally qualified underrepresented minority applicant.

Respondents contend that "[t]he volume of applications and the presentation of applicant information make it impractical for [LSA] to use the . . . admissions system" upheld by the Court today in *Grutter*. But the fact that the implementation of a program capable of providing individualized consideration might present administrative challenges does not render constitutional an otherwise problematic system.

We conclude, therefore, that because the University's use of race in its current freshman admissions policy is not narrowly tailored to achieve respondents' asserted compelling interest in diversity, the admissions policy violates the Equal Protection Clause of the Fourteenth Amendment.

■ JUSTICE O'CONNOR, concurring.

Unlike the law school admissions policy the Court upholds today in *Grutter v. Bollinger,* the procedures employed by the University of Michigan's Office of Undergraduate Admissions do not provide for a meaningful individualized review of applicants. The law school considers the various diversity qualifications of each applicant, including race, on a case-by-case basis. By contrast, the Office of Undergraduate Admissions relies on the selection index to assign *every* underrepresented minority applicant the same, *automatic* 20-point bonus without consideration of the particular background, experiences, or qualities of each individual applicant. And this mechanized selection index score, by and large, automatically determines the admissions decision for each applicant. The selection index thus precludes admissions counselors from conducting the type of individualized consideration the Court's opinion in *Grutter* requires: consideration of each applicant's individualized qualifications, including the contribution each individual's race or ethnic identity will make to the diversity of the student body, taking into account diversity within and among all racial and ethnic groups.

* * *

Although the Office of Undergraduate Admissions does assign 20 points to some "soft" variables other than race, the points available for other diversity contributions, such as leadership and service, personal achievement, and geographic diversity, are capped at much lower levels. Even the most outstanding national high school leader could never receive more than five points for his or her accomplishments—a mere quarter of the points automatically assigned to an underrepresented minority solely based on the fact of his or her race. Of course, as Justice Powell made clear in *Bakke,* a university need not "necessarily accor[d]" all diversity factors "the same weight," and the "weight attributed to a particular quality may vary from year to year depending upon the 'mix' both of the student body and the applicants for the incoming class." But the selection index, by setting up automatic, predetermined point allocations for the soft variables, ensures that the diversity contributions of applicants cannot be individually assessed.

The only potential source of individualized consideration appears to be the Admissions Review Committee. The evidence in the record, however, reveals very little about how the review committee actually functions. And what evidence there is indicates that the committee is a kind of afterthought, rather than an integral component of a system of individualized review. As the Court points out, it is undisputed that the " '[committee] reviews only a portion of all of the applications. The bulk of admissions decisions are executed based on selection index score parameters set by the [Enrollment Working Group].' " Review by the committee thus represents a necessarily limited exception to the Office of Undergraduate Admissions' general reliance on the selection index. Indeed, the record does not reveal how many applications admissions counselors send to the review committee each year, and the University has not pointed to evidence demonstrating that a meaningful percentage of applicants receives this level of discretionary review. In addition, eligibility for consideration by the committee is itself based on automatic cutoff levels determined with reference to selection index scores. And there is no evidence of how the decisions are actually made—what type of individualized consideration is or is not used. Given these circumstances, the addition of the Admissions Review Committee to the admissions process cannot offset the apparent absence of individualized consideration from the Office of Undergraduate Admissions' general practices.

■ JUSTICE SOUTER, dissenting.

The cases now contain two pointers toward the line between the valid and the unconstitutional in race-conscious admissions schemes. *Grutter* reaffirms the permissibility of individualized consideration of race to achieve a diversity of students, at least where race is not assigned a preordained value in all cases. On the other hand, Justice Powell's opinion in *Bakke,* rules out a racial quota or set-aside, in which race is the sole fact of eligibility for certain places in a class. Although the freshman admissions system here is subject to argument on the merits, I think it is closer to what *Grutter* approves than to what *Bakke* condemns, and should not be held unconstitutional on the current record.

The record does not describe a system with a quota like the one struck down in *Bakke,* which "insulate[d]" all nonminority candidates from competition from certain seats. The *Bakke* plan "focused *solely* on ethnic diversity" and effectively told nonminority applicants that "[n]o matter how strong their qualifications, quantitative and extracurricular, including their own potential for contribution to educational diversity, they are never afforded the chance to compete with applicants from the preferred groups for the [set-aside] special admissions seats."

The plan here lets all applicants compete for all places and values an applicant's offering for any place not only on grounds of race, but on grades, test scores, strength of high school, quality of course of study, residence, alumni relationships, leadership, personal character, socioeconomic disadvantage, athletic ability, and quality of a personal essay. A nonminority applicant who scores highly in these other categories can readily garner a selection index exceeding that of a minority applicant who gets the 20-point bonus.

[T]his scheme of considering, through the selection index system, all of the characteristics that the college thinks relevant to student diversity for every one of the student places to be filled fits Justice Powell's description of a constitutionally acceptable program: one that considers "all pertinent elements of diversity in light of the particular qualifications of each applicant" and places each element "on the same footing for consideration, although not necessarily according them the same weight." In the Court's own words, "each characteristic of a particular applicant [is] considered in assessing the applicant's entire application." An unsuccessful nonminority applicant cannot complain that he was rejected "simply because he was not the right color"; an applicant who is rejected because "his combined qualifications . . . did not outweigh those of the other applicant" has been given an opportunity to compete with all other applicants.

The one qualification to this description of the admissions process is that membership in an underrepresented minority is given a weight of 20 points on the 150-point scale. On the face of things, however, this assignment of specific points does not set race apart from all other weighted considerations. Nonminority students may receive 20 points for athletic ability, socioeconomic disadvantage, attendance at a socioeconomically disadvantaged or predominantly minority high school, or at the Provost's discretion; they may also receive 10 points for being residents of Michigan, 6 for residence in an underrepresented Michigan county, 5 for leadership and service, and so on.

The very nature of a college's permissible practice of awarding value to racial diversity means that race must be considered in a way that increases some applicants' chances for admission. Since college admission is not left entirely to inarticulate intuition, it is hard to see what is inappropriate in assigning some stated value to a relevant characteristic, whether it be reasoning ability, writing style, running speed, or minority race. Justice Powell's plus factors necessarily are assigned some values. The college simply does by a numbered scale what the law school accomplishes in its "holistic review," the distinction does not imply that applicants to the undergraduate college are denied individualized consideration or a fair chance to compete on the basis of all the various merits their applications may disclose.

Nor is it possible to say that the 20 points convert race into a decisive factor comparable to reserving minority places as in *Bakke*. Of course we can conceive of a point system in which the "plus" factor given to minority applicants would be so extreme as to guarantee every minority applicant a higher rank than every nonminority applicant in the university's admissions system. But petitioners do not have a convincing argument that the freshman admissions system operates this way. The present record obviously shows that nonminority applicants may achieve higher selection point totals than minority applicants owing to characteristics other than race, and the fact that the university admits "virtually every qualified under-represented minority applicant," may reflect nothing more than the likelihood that very few qualified minority applicants apply, as well as the possibility that self-selection results in a strong minority applicant pool. It suffices for me that there are no *Bakke*-like set-asides and that consideration of an applicant's whole spectrum of ability is no more ruled out by giving 20 points for race than by giving the same points for athletic ability or socioeconomic disadvantage.

The point system cannot operate as a *de facto* set-aside if the greater admissions process, including review by the committee, results in individualized review sufficient to meet the Court's standards. Since the record is quiet, if not silent, on the case-by-case work of the committee, the Court would be on more defensible ground by vacating and remanding for evidence about the committee's specific determinations.

Without knowing more about how the Admissions Review Committee actually functions, it seems especially unfair to treat the candor of the admissions plan as an Achilles' heel.

■ JUSTICE GINSBERG, dissenting.

[A]s I see it, government decision-makers may properly distinguish between policies of exclusion and inclusion.

Our jurisprudence ranks race a "suspect" category, "not because [race] is inevitably an impermissible classification, but because it is one which usually, to our national shame, has been drawn for the purpose of maintaining racial inequality." But where race is considered "for the purpose of achieving equality," no automatic proscription is in order. For, as insightfully explained: "The Constitution is both color blind and color conscious. To avoid conflict with the equal protection clause, a classification that denies a benefit, causes harm, or imposes a burden must not be based on race. In that sense, the Constitution is color blind. But the Constitution is color conscious to prevent discrimination being perpetuated and to undo the effects of past discrimination." *United States v. Jefferson County Bd. of Ed.,* (C.A.5 1966) (Wisdom, J.).

Like other top-ranking institutions, the College has many more applicants for admission than it can accommodate in an entering class. Every applicant admitted under the current plan, petitioners do not here dispute, is qualified to attend the College. The racial and ethnic groups to which the College accords special consideration (African-Americans, Hispanics, and Native-Americans) historically have been relegated to inferior status by law and social practice; their members continue to experience class-based discrimination to this day. There is no suggestion that the College adopted its current policy in order to limit or decrease enrollment by any particular racial or ethnic group, and no seats are reserved on the basis of race. Nor has there been any demonstration that the College's program unduly constricts admissions opportunities for students who do not receive special consideration based on race.

The stain of generations of racial oppression is still visible in our society and the determination to hasten its removal remains vital. One can reasonably anticipate, therefore, that colleges and universities will seek to maintain their minority enrollment—and the networks and opportunities thereby opened to minority graduates—whether or not they can do so in full candor through adoption of affirmative action plans of the kind here at issue. Without recourse to such plans, institutions of higher education may resort to camouflage. For example, schools may encourage applicants to write of their cultural traditions in the essays they submit, or to indicate whether English is their second language. Seeking to improve their chances for admission, applicants may highlight the minority group associations to which they belong, or the Hispanic surnames of their mothers or grandparents. In turn, teachers' recommendations may emphasize who a student is as much as what he or she has accomplished. If honesty is the best policy, surely Michigan's accurately described, fully disclosed College affirmative action program is preferable to achieving similar numbers through winks, nods, and disguises.

NOTES AND QUESTIONS

1.   *Extending the* **Bakke** *Prohibition.* In *Bakke*, Justice Powell criticized the use of quotas. In *Gratz*, the Court condemned the use of the mechanical, points-based admissions scheme. In what way, if any, does the mechanical, points-based approach of *Gratz* violate the quota prohibition of *Bakke*? Is the Gratz approach tantamount to a quota? Or does it fail narrow tailoring for other reasons? To what extent is the *Gratz* approach in tension with the Court's emphasis in *Grutter* that applicants be given individualized consideration?

2.   *Utility of Points-Based Systems.* As Justice Souter notes, given that some weight will be accorded race in the admissions process, why should a university be precluded from making that process uniform across different categories of applicants? Rather than relying on individual admissions officers to determine how much weight race should be given in any particular case, why shouldn't the university be free to take the administratively attractive approach of determining how much weight race should have across the board? Put differently, should the university be precluded from assuming, say, that all unrepresented racial groups (and all individuals within each particular group) would contribute equally to the diversity of the student body?

3.   *Transparency and Accountability.* The points-based approach of the undergraduate admissions office is unquestionably more transparent than the holistic approach of the law school. The advantage of transparency is that it facilitates government institutions being held accountable. Should this consideration have weighed in the Court's calculus? Does the Court, as Justice Ginsberg suggests, encourage schools to rely on "winks, nods and disguises"? Why would the Court do so? Which approach facilitates holding a University accountable for its admissions policy: the holistic approach or the points-based approach?

4.   *Fairness.* To what extent is the majority concerned that the points-based system is less fair than the holistic approach because the points-based system accords too much weight to race? Reproduced below is the worksheet used by the University of Michigan in evaluating applicants for the undergraduate program. The "school factor" was derived from the number of AP/IB courses offered at the school, the percentage of the school's students attending two and four year colleges, and average SAT/ACT scores. The higher these numbers, the higher the school factor. The "curriculum factor" was based on the difficulty of the student's choice of curriculum within the context of what the high school offered. This factor could have resulted in either adding or deducting points from the student's overall Selection Index. Applications with scores above a certain threshold were sent for a second layer of more individualized review, which did not guarantee admission, but

did guarantee a closer look. Notice the number of points awarded for race versus other personal characteristics. How would you evaluate the fairness of the points scheme? What about as compared to the holistic approach adopted by Michigan Law School? Does the mechanical points-based system necessarily entail greater reliance on race than the holistic process that the Court approved in *Grutter*?

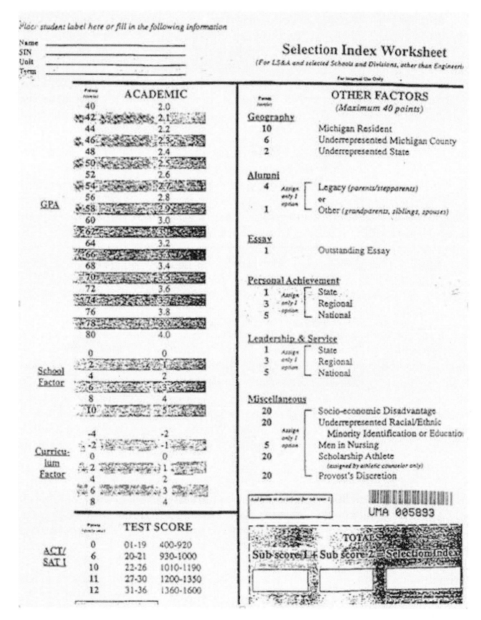

5.   *The Incentives for Applicants.* Some commentators have argued that diversity-based individualized consideration encourages admissions officers to stereotype applicants, and encourages applicants to conform to stereotypes. Consider the following critique by Professor Cristina Rodríguez:

> The ultimate effect of individualized consideration is to augment rather than limit the harms of race-conscious decision making by the state, because individualized consideration gives state actors the power to make authenticity judgments concerning the identities of both individuals and groups, subsequently creating incentives for groups to define themselves using authenticity as a metric.

> Individualized consideration gives state actors the power not just to notice race, as mechanical interpretation does, but also to define race, on a case-by-case basis. This power means that race will be treated as more relevant to some applicants than to others.

> By permitting admissions officers to decide "who counts," individualized consideration opens the door to stereotypical decision making, because it gives admissions officers the power to determine which applicants' races or ethnicities will contribute to the representation of those races or ethnicities. The ways in which non-Latinos (who probably make up the majority of university admissions officers) define Latino are more likely to be beset by expectations that particular narratives be present in the life of the applicant. Admissions officers may, for example, look for a narrative of discrimination and disadvantage, re-enforcing the social tendency to see Latinos through one lens—as those who have overcome obstacles, experienced poverty, come from uneducated stock, or speak accented English.

> [I]ndividualized consideration [also] demands that people perform their ethnicity for admissions officers, either through their personal statements or in entrance interviews.

> [N]ot only does the mechanical version of this process have the advantage of restraining the state from assigning value to the content or substance of race, it also ensures that all members of a given racial grouping are treated equally. In this sense, mechanical interpretation is substantially less race-conscious than individualized consideration.

Cristina M. Rodríguez, *Against Individualized Consideration*, 83 Indiana Law Journal 1415 (2008).

––––––––––––––––

In her opinion in *Grutter*, Justice O'Connor observed that 25 years had passed since the Court's decision in *Bakke* and "[w]e expect that 25 years from now, the use of racial preferences will no longer be necessary to further the interest approved today." *Grutter*, 539 U.S. at 343. Only a decade later, with the composition of the Court having changed, the

Court decided another affirmative action case that did not overrule *Grutter* but that arguably called for more rigorous scrutiny of affirmative action in admissions. Below are brief excerpts from the Supreme Court's initial decision in the case, *Fisher v. the University of Texas*, and the Fifth Circuit's opinion on remand. [As this book goes to press the Supreme Court is rehearing *Fisher*.]

Fisher v. University of Texas at Austin et al.
Supreme Court of the United States, 2013.
570 U.S. ___, 133 S.Ct. 2411.

Petitioner, who is Caucasian, sued the University after her application was rejected. She contends that the University's use of race in the admissions process violated the Equal Protection Clause of the Fourteenth Amendment.

Located in Austin, Texas, on the most renowned campus of the Texas state university system, the University is one of the leading institutions of higher education in the Nation. Admission is prized and competitive. In 2008, when petitioner sought admission to the University's entering class, she was 1 of 29,501 applicants. From this group 12,843 were admitted, and 6,715 accepted and enrolled. Petitioner was denied admission.

In recent years the University has used three different programs to evaluate candidates for admission. The first is the program it used for some years before 1997, when the University considered two factors: a numerical score reflecting an applicant's test scores and academic performance in high school (Academic Index or AI), and the applicant's race. In 1996, this system was held unconstitutional by the United States Court of Appeals for the Fifth Circuit. It ruled the University's consideration of race violated the Equal Protection Clause because it did not further any compelling government interest.

The second program was adopted to comply with the Hopwood decision. The University stopped considering race in admissions and substituted instead a new holistic metric of a candidate's potential contribution to the University, to be used in conjunction with the Academic Index. This "Personal Achievement Index" (PAI) measures a student's leadership and work experience, awards, extra-curricular activities, community service, and other special circumstances that give insight into a student's background. These included growing up in a single-parent home, speaking a language other than English at home, significant family responsibilities assumed by the applicant, and the general socioeconomic condition of the student's family. Seeking to address the decline in minority enrollment after Hopwood, the University also expanded its outreach programs.

The Texas State Legislature also responded to the Hopwood decision. It enacted a measure known as the Top Ten Percent Law, [which] grants automatic admission to any public state college, including the University, to all students in the top 10% of their class at high schools in Texas that comply with certain standards.

The University's revised admissions process, coupled with the operation of the Top Ten Percent Law, resulted in a more racially diverse environment at the University. Before the admissions program at issue in this case, in the last year under the post-Hopwood AI/PAI system that did not consider race, the entering class was 4.5% African-American and 16.9% Hispanic. This is in contrast with the 1996 pre-Hopwood and [pre-]Top Ten Percent regime, when race was explicitly considered, and the University's entering freshman class was 4.1% African-American and 14.5% Hispanic.

Following this Court's decisions in Grutter v. Bollinger, and Gratz v. Bollinger, the University adopted a third admissions program, the 2004 program in which the University reverted to explicit consideration of race. This is the program here at issue.

The University's plan to resume race-conscious admissions was given formal expression in June 2004 in an internal document entitled Proposal to Consider Race and Ethnicity in Admissions (Proposal). The Proposal relied in substantial part on a study of a subset of undergraduate classes containing between 5 and 24 students. It showed that few of these classes had significant enrollment by members of racial minorities. In addition the Proposal relied on what it called "anecdotal" reports from students regarding their "interaction in the classroom." The Proposal concluded that the University lacked a "critical mass" of minority students and that to remedy the deficiency it was necessary to give explicit consideration to race in the undergraduate admissions program.

To implement the Proposal the University included a student's race as a component of the PAI score, beginning with applicants in the fall of 2004. The University asks students to classify themselves from among five predefined racial categories on the application. Race is not assigned an explicit numerical value, but it is undisputed that race is a meaningful factor.

Once applications have been scored, they are plotted on a grid with the Academic Index on the x-axis and the Personal Achievement Index on the y-axis. On that grid students are assigned to so-called cells based on their individual scores. All students in the cells falling above a certain line are admitted. All students below the line are not. Each college—such as Liberal Arts or Engineering—admits students separately. So a student is considered initially for her first-choice college, then for her second choice, and finally for general admission as an undeclared major.

Petitioner applied for admission to the University's 2008 entering class and was rejected. She sued the University. The District Court granted summary judgment to the University. The United States Court of Appeals for the Fifth Circuit affirmed. It held that Grutter required courts to give substantial deference to the University, both in the definition of the compelling interest in diversity's benefits and in deciding whether its specific plan was narrowly tailored to achieve its stated goal. Applying that standard, the court upheld the University's admissions plan.

According to Grutter, a university's "educational judgment that such diversity is essential to its educational mission is one to which we defer." Grutter concluded that the decision to pursue "the educational benefits that flow from student body diversity," that the University deems integral to its mission is, in substantial measure, an academic judgment to which some, but not complete, judicial deference is proper under Grutter. A court, of course, should ensure that there is a reasoned, principled explanation for the academic decision. On this point, the District Court and Court of Appeals were correct in finding that Grutter calls for deference to the University's conclusion, " 'based on its experience and expertise,' " that a diverse student body would serve its educational goals.

Once the University has established that its goal of diversity is consistent with strict scrutiny, however, there must still be a further judicial determination that the admissions process meets strict scrutiny in its implementation. The University must prove that the means chosen by the University to attain diversity are narrowly tailored to that goal. On this point, the University receives no deference. Grutter made clear that it is for the courts, not for university administrators, to ensure that "[t]he means chosen to accomplish the [government's] asserted purpose must be specifically and narrowly framed to accomplish that purpose." True, a court can take account of a university's experience and expertise in adopting or rejecting certain admissions processes. But, as the Court said in Grutter, it remains at all times the University's obligation to demonstrate, and the Judiciary's obligation to determine, that admissions processes "ensure that each applicant is evaluated as an individual and not in a way that makes an applicant's race or ethnicity the defining feature of his or her application."

Narrow tailoring also requires that the reviewing court verify that it is "necessary" for a university to use race to achieve the educational benefits of diversity. This involves a careful judicial inquiry into whether a university could achieve sufficient diversity without using racial classifications. Although "[n]arrow tailoring does not require exhaustion of every conceivable race-neutral alternative," strict scrutiny does require a court to examine with care, and not defer to, a university's "serious, good faith consideration of workable race-neutral alternatives."

Consideration by the university is of course necessary, but it is not sufficient to satisfy strict scrutiny: The reviewing court must ultimately be satisfied that no workable race-neutral alternatives would produce the educational benefits of diversity. If " 'a nonracial approach . . . could promote the substantial interest about as well and at tolerable administrative expense,' " then the university may not consider race. A plaintiff, of course, bears the burden of placing the validity of a university's adoption of an affirmative action plan in issue. But strict scrutiny imposes on the university the ultimate burden of demonstrating, before turning to racial classifications, that available, workable race-neutral alternatives do not suffice.

Rather than perform this searching examination, however, the Court of Appeals held petitioner could challenge only "whether [the University's] decision to reintroduce race as a factor in admissions was made in good faith." And in considering such a challenge, the court would "presume the University acted in good faith" and place on petitioner the burden of rebutting that presumption. The Court of Appeals held that to "second-guess the merits" of this aspect of the University's decision was a task it was "ill-equipped to perform" and that it would attempt only to "ensure that [the University's] decision to adopt a race-conscious admissions policy followed from [a process of] good faith consideration." The Court of Appeals thus concluded that "the narrow-tailoring inquiry— like the compelling-interest inquiry—is undertaken with a degree of deference to the Universit[y]." Because "the efforts of the University have been studied, serious, and of high purpose," the Court of Appeals held that the use of race in the admissions program fell within "a constitutionally protected zone of discretion."

These expressions of the controlling standard are at odds with Grutter's command that "all racial classifications imposed by government 'must be analyzed by a reviewing court under strict scrutiny.' In Grutter, the Court approved the plan at issue upon concluding that it was not a quota, was sufficiently flexible, was limited in time, and followed "serious, good faith consideration of workable race-neutral alternatives." As noted above, the parties do not challenge, and the Court therefore does not consider, the correctness of that determination.

Grutter did not hold that good faith would forgive an impermissible consideration of race. It must be remembered that "the mere recitation of a 'benign' or legitimate purpose for a racial classification is entitled to little or no weight." Croson. Strict scrutiny does not permit a court to accept a school's assertion that its admissions process uses race in a permissible way without a court giving close analysis to the evidence of how the process works in practice.

■ JUSTICE KAGAN took no part in the consideration or decision of this case.

■ JUSTICE SCALIA, concurring. [omitted]

■ JUSTICE GINSBURG, dissenting. [omitted]

■ JUSTICE THOMAS, concurring. [omitted]

NOTES AND QUESTIONS

1.   ***Limiting*** Grutter ***Deference.*** In calling for less deference to the University's means of pursuing diversity, the Court embraces the argument of the dissent in *Grutter*, where Justice Kennedy wrote, "[t]he Court confuses deference to a university's definition of its educational objective with deference to the implementation of this goal. In the context of university admissions the objective of racial diversity can be accepted based on empirical data known to us, but deference is not to be given with respect to the methods by which it is pursued. Preferment by race, when resorted to by the State, can be the most divisive of all policies, containing within it the potential to destroy confidence in the Constitution and in the idea of equality. The majority today refuses to be faithful to the settled principle of strict review designed to reflect these concerns." Is it sensible for the Court to defer to a university's selection of goals, but not to its selection of means? What would be the rationale for that sort of asymmetry in the doctrine?

2.   ***Defining Critical Mass.*** How might a court determine whether a university, as the Court says, "could achieve sufficient diversity without using racial classifications"? What amount of diversity is "sufficient"?

3.   ***Proving Necessity.*** According to the Court's opinion, the University actually enrolled more African-American and Hispanic students when it relied on the Top Ten Percent Plan and did not consider race than prior to the Fifth Circuit's decision in *Hopwood* when the University did consider race in admissions. If this is correct, how could the University plausibly show that an affirmative action plan was "necessary" to achieving racial diversity? Doesn't the evidence that the Top Ten Percent Plan produced more diversity than the prior affirmative action policy fatally undermine any such claim? Isn't the Ten Percent plan an obviously "workable alternative" to race-based affirmative action in admissions, at least for undergraduate admissions in a segregated state such as Texas? Consequently, should universities be required to use a race-neutral approach such as the Top Ten Percent Plan prior to implementing a conventional affirmative action plan? Is Texas' Ten Percent Plan, in fact, neutral?

4.   ***Interpreting*** Fisher. What's the best way to understand the Supreme Court's opinion in *Fisher*? Is it an effort to hold the university accountable or an indirect means of ending affirmative action in university admissions? To the extent the Court restricts race-based affirmative action, it encourages schools to rely on class-based affirmative action. For a discussion of how to reconcile a class-based scheme with racial justice, see R. Richard Banks, Meritocratic Values and Racial Outcomes: Defending Class-based College Admissions 79 N.Carolina L.Rev. 1029 (2001).

5. *Admissions Options.* In addition to the consideration of the race of individual applicants, the University of Texas had relied on three different types of admissions schemes: i) the Academic Achievement Index, ii) the Personal Achievement Index, and iii) the Top Ten Percent Plan. How would you compare the benefits and drawbacks of each of these approaches? Should admissions be based primarily on academic achievement, as indicated by the Academic Achievement Index? Or should the sort of personal, non-academic factors captured by the Personal Achievement Index also play an important role? Note that two effects of the Top Ten Percent Plan have been to increase the numbers of low-income (and mostly minority) urban students, as well as rural students at the University of Texas. Should a goal of admissions policy be to increase the representation of such students, even at the cost of excluding affluent students from competitive high schools who, objectively, are higher achieving? Should the flagship campus of a public university have any obligation to admit students from all parts of the state? Or even from all high schools within the state?

6. *Grades, Test Scores, and Privilege.* An important feature of the admissions landscape is that test scores and grades are very much correlated with both socioeconomic status and race. The more educated and affluent a child's parents, the more likely that child is to achieve high grades and test scores. Children of white and (especially) Asian-American parents tend to have higher grades and test scores than children of black and Latino parents. With these patterns in mind, if you were the admissions dean for a selective undergraduate university, what criteria would you use to evaluate applicants? Here are some possibilities:

1: Rank order admission based on standardized test scores

2: Rank order admission based on a combination of grades and test scores

3: Test scores (and grades) relative to socioeconomic status peers

4: Test scores (and grades) relative to race peers

5: Lottery, for students above a minimum test scores/grades threshold

6: Lottery, with chances weighted by test scores and grades, for students above a certain threshold

7: Admissions officer discretion, based on grades/test scores and wide range of diversity factors, including race

---

On remand, the Fifth Circuit again upheld the University of Texas affirmative action policy.

Fisher v. Texas

Court of Appeals, Fifth Circuit, 2014.
758 F.3d 633.

In language from which it has not retreated, the Supreme Court explained that the educational goal of diversity must be "defined by reference to the educational benefits that diversity is designed to produce." Recognizing that universities do more than download facts from professors to students, the Supreme Court recognized three distinct educational objectives served by diversity: (i) increased perspectives, meaning that diverse perspectives improve educational quality by making classroom discussion "livelier, more spirited, and simply more enlightening and interesting when the students have the greatest possible variety of backgrounds"; (ii) professionalism, meaning that "student body diversity . . . better prepares [students] as professionals," because the skills students need for the "increasingly global marketplace can only be developed through exposure to widely diverse people, cultures, ideas, and viewpoints"; and, (iii) civic engagement, meaning that a diverse student body is necessary for fostering "[e]ffective participation by members of all racial and ethnic groups in the civil life of our Nation[, which] is essential if the dream of one Nation, indivisible, is to be realized." All this the Supreme Court reaffirmed, leaving for this Court a "further judicial determination that the admissions process meets strict scrutiny in its implementation"; that is, its means of achieving the goal of diversity are narrowly tailored.

A university "must prove that the means chosen by the University to attain diversity are narrowly tailored to that goal." And a university "receives no deference" on this point because it is the courts that must ensure that the "means chosen to accomplish the [university's] asserted purpose . . . be specifically and narrowly framed to accomplish that purpose." Although "a court can take account of a university's experience and expertise in adopting or rejecting certain admissions processes," it remains a university's burden to demonstrate and the court's obligation to determine whether the "admissions processes ensure that each applicant is evaluated as an individual, and not in a way that makes an applicant's race or ethnicity the defining feature of his or her application."

Narrow tailoring requires that the court "verify that it is 'necessary' for a university to use race to achieve the educational benefits of diversity." Such a verification requires a "careful judicial inquiry into whether a university could achieve sufficient diversity without using racial classifications."

Thus, the reviewing court must "ultimately be satisfied that no workable race-neutral alternatives would produce the educational benefits of diversity." It follows, therefore, that if "a nonracial approach . . . could promote the substantial interest about as well and at tolerable expenses, . . . then the university may not consider race." And it is the university that bears "the ultimate burden of demonstrating, before turning to racial classifications, that available, workable race-neutral alternatives do not suffice."

UT Austin's holistic review program—a program nearly indistinguishable from the University of Michigan Law School's program in *Grutter*—was a necessary and enabling component of the Top Ten Percent Plan by allowing UT Austin to reach a pool of minority and non-minority students with records of personal achievement, higher average test scores, or other unique skills. A variety of perspectives, that is differences in life experiences, is a distinct and valued element of diversity. Yet a significant number of students excelling in high-performing schools are passed over by the Top Ten Percent Plan although they could bring a perspective not captured by admissions along the sole dimension of class rank. For example, the experience of being a minority in a majority-white or majority-minority school and succeeding in that environment offers a rich pool of potential UT Austin students with demonstrated qualities of leadership and sense of self. Efforts to draw from this pool do not demean the potential of Top Ten admittees. Rather it complements their contribution to diversity—mitigating in an important way the effects of the single dimension process

UT Austin persuades that this reach into the applicant pool is not a further search for numbers but a search for students of unique talents and backgrounds who can enrich the diversity of the student body in distinct ways including test scores, predicting higher levels of preparation and better prospects for admission to UT Austin's more demanding colleges and ultimately graduation. It also signifies that this is a draw from a highly competitive pool, a mix of minority and non-minority students who would otherwise be absent from a Top Ten Percent pool selected on class rank, a relative and not an independent measure across the pool of applicants.

VI

These realities highlight the difficulty of an approach that seeks to couch the concept of critical mass within numerical terms. The numbers support UT Austin's argument that its holistic use of race in pursuit of diversity is not about quotas or targets, but about its focus upon individuals, an opportunity denied by the Top Ten Percent Plan. Achieving the critical mass requisite to diversity goes astray when it drifts to numerical metrics. UT Austin urges that it has made clear that looking to numbers, while relevant, has not been its measure of success; and that its goals are not captured by population ratios. We find this contention proved, mindful that by 2011, Texas high school graduates were majority-minority.

UT Austin urges that its first step in narrow tailoring was the admission of over 80% of its Texas students though a facially race-neutral process, and that Fisher's embrace of the sweep of the Top Ten Percent Plan as a full achievement of diversity reduces critical mass to a numerical game and little more than a cover for quotas. Fisher refuses to acknowledge this distinction between critical mass—the tipping point of diversity—and a quota. And in seeking to quantify "critical mass" as a rigid numerical goal, Fisher misses the mark. Fisher is correct that if UT Austin defined its goal of diversity by the numbers only, the Top Ten Percent Plan could be calibrated to meet that mark. To do so, however, would deny the role of holistic review as a necessary complement to Top Ten Percent admissions. We are persuaded that holistic review is a necessary complement to the Top Ten Percent Plan, enabling it to operate without reducing itself to a cover for a quota system; that in doing so, its limited use of race is narrowly tailored to this role—as small a part as possible for the Plan to succeed.

In sum, Fisher points to the numbers and nothing more in arguing that race-conscious admissions were no longer necessary because a "critical mass" of minority students had been achieved by the time Fisher applied for admission—a head count by skin color or surname that is not the diversity envisioned by *Bakke* and a measure it rejected. In 2007, Fisher emphasizes, there were 5.8% African-American and 19.7% Hispanic enrolled students, which exceeds pre-*Hopwood* levels and the minority enrollment at the University of Michigan Law School examined in *Grutter*. But an examination that looks exclusively at the percentage of minority students fails before it begins. Indeed, as *Grutter* teaches, an emphasis on numbers in a mechanical admissions process is the most pernicious of discriminatory acts because it looks to race alone, treating minority students as fungible commodities that represent a single minority viewpoint. Critical mass, the tipping point of diversity, has no fixed upper bound of universal application, nor is it the minimum threshold at which minority students do not feel isolated or like spokespersons for their race. *Grutter* defines critical mass by reference to a broader view of diversity rather than by the achievement of a certain quota of minority students. Here, UT Austin has demonstrated a permissible goal of achieving the educational benefits of diversity within that university's distinct mission, not seeking a percentage of minority students that reaches some arbitrary size.

We are satisfied that UT Austin has demonstrated that race-conscious holistic review is necessary to make the Top Ten Percent Plan workable by patching the holes that a mechanical admissions program leaves in its ability to achieve the rich diversity that contributes to its academic mission—as described by *Bakke* and *Grutter*.

[I]t is suggested that while holistic review may be a necessary and ameliorating complement to the Top Ten Percent Plan, UT Austin has not shown that its holistic review need include any reference to race, this because the Plan produces sufficient numbers of minorities for critical mass. This contention views minorities as a group, abjuring the focus upon individuals—each person's unique potential. Race is relevant to minority and non-minority, notably when candidates have flourished as a minority in their school—whether they are white or black. *Grutter* reaffirmed that "[j]ust as growing up in a particular region or having particular professional experiences is likely to affect an individual's views, so too is one's own, unique experience of being a racial minority in a society, like our own, in which race still matters."

We are persuaded that to deny UT Austin its limited use of race in its search for holistic diversity would hobble the richness of the educational experience in contradiction of the plain teachings of *Bakke* and *Grutter*. The need for such skill sets to complement the draws from majority-white and majority-minority schools flows directly from an understanding of what the Court has made plain diversity is not. To conclude otherwise is to narrow its focus to a tally of skin colors produced in defiance of Justice Kennedy's opinion for the Court which eschewed the narrow metric of numbers and turned the focus upon individuals. This powerful charge does not deny the relevance of race.

We find force in the argument that race here is a necessary part, albeit one of many parts, of the decisional matrix where being white in a minority-majority school can set one apart just as being a minority in a majority-white school—not a proffer of societal discrimination in justification for use of race, but a search for students with a range of skills, experiences, and performances—one that will be impaired by turning a blind eye to the differing opportunities offered by the schools from whence they came.

■ EMILIO M. GARZA, CIRCUIT JUDGE, dissenting:

In vacating our previous opinion, *Fisher v. Univ. of Tex. at Austin*, 631 F.3d 213 (5th Cir. 2011), the Supreme Court clarified the strict scrutiny standard as it applies to cases involving racial classifications in higher education admissions: Now, reviewing courts cannot defer to a state actor's argument that its consideration of race is narrowly tailored to achieve its diversity goals. Although the University has articulated its diversity goal as a "critical mass," surprisingly, it has failed to define this term in any objective manner. Accordingly, it is impossible to determine whether the University's use of racial classifications in its admissions process is narrowly tailored to its stated goal—essentially, its ends remain unknown.

By holding that the University's use of racial classifications is narrowly tailored, the majority continues to defer impermissibly to the University's claims. This deference is squarely at odds with the central lesson of *Fisher*. A proper strict scrutiny analysis, affording the University "no deference" on its narrow tailoring claims, compels the conclusion that the University's race-conscious admissions process does not survive strict scrutiny.

In *Fisher*, the Supreme Court modified the narrow tailoring calculus applied in higher education affirmative action cases. While the overarching principles from *Bakke*, *Gratz*, and *Grutter*—that a university can have a compelling interest in attaining the educational benefits of diversity, and that its admissions program must be narrowly tailored to serve this interest—were taken "as given,", the *Fisher* Court altered the application of those principles in a critical way. Now, courts must give "no deference," to a Thus, under the current principles governing review of race-conscious admissions programs, providing any deference to a state actor's claim that its use of race is narrowly tailored is "antithetical to strict scrutiny, not consistent with it." *Grutter*, (Kennedy, J., dissenting).

The majority entirely overlooks the University's failure to define its "critical mass" objective for the purposes of assessing narrow tailoring. This is the crux of this case—absent a meaningful explanation of its desired ends, the University cannot prove narrow tailoring under its strict scrutiny burden. Indeed, the majority repeatedly invokes the term "critical mass" without even questioning its definition.

The University's failure to define meaningfully its "critical mass" objective is manifest in its various strict scrutiny arguments. The University claims that its use of racial classifications is necessary and narrowly tailored because (1) quantitative metrics reflect an inadequate minority presence; (2) qualitative diversity is lacking; (3) certain selective colleges are insufficiently diverse; (4) its periodic review demonstrates that its goals have not yet been achieved; and (5) its use of racial classifications is almost identical to that approved in *Grutter*. Each of these arguments falls short—either overlooking a more narrowly tailored alternative or eliding any articulation of *how* this specific use of racial classification advances the University's objective.

The Top Ten Percent Law matters only insofar as it causes the University to admit a large number of minority students separate and apart from the holistic review process. That is, the Law creates a separate admissions channel for many minority students, which then calls into question the necessity of using race as a factor in the holistic review process for filling the remaining seats. Whether, in light of the Top Ten Percent Law, race-conscious holistic review is more or less necessary is an open question, and it is *the University* that bears the burden of explaining how the Law impacts its achievement of its diversity goal. Here, it has failed to do so, under any theory of "critical mass" it has proffered.

NOTES AND QUESTIONS

1.   ***The Meaning of Critical Mass.*** A central question in *Fisher* concerns the meaning of critical mass. The University contends that the affirmative action program will admit students with different diversity attributes than

those students admitted under the Top Ten Percent Plan. In terms of educational, economic, political, cultural, and social characteristics, what would distinguish those black and Latino students under the race-conscious affirmative action plan from those admitted under the Top Ten Percent Plan? Are these differences legitimate considerations in the critical mass calculus? Are they sufficient to justify the use of race to achieve critical mass? Or, as the dissent argues, must the University offer and defend some numerical definition of critical mass? If the University were required to do so, could it?

2.   *Varieties of Race Consciousness. Fisher* concerns two different types of race-conscious policies: individualized vs. categorical. The affirmative action policy at issue in the case considers race in an individualized fashion, whereas the Top Ten Percent Plan was motivated in part by racial considerations, namely finding a means of promoting racial diversity. Does one or the other type of policy seem preferable to you? What, in your view, are the benefits and drawbacks of each?

3.   *Constitutional Analysis.* The Top Ten Percent plan does not treat individual applicants differently on the basis of race, but isn't such a policy animated by a racial purpose no less than a race-conscious affirmative action policy? More specifically, is the Top Ten Percent Plan animated by a racially discriminatory purpose? How would you make, and rebut, the argument that the Ten Percent Plan itself is unconstitutional?

4.   *Politics and Policy.* Putting aside constitutional law, which policy do you think is preferable: The Top Ten Percent Plan or conventional affirmative action?

5.   *State Prohibitions.* Affirmative action also has been restricted by state law. States such as Michigan, California, Arizona, Washington, and Florida, have passed initiatives prohibiting race-based affirmative action by state institutions. California was the first state to enact such a measure, when voters approved Proposition 209 in 1996. Its passage amended the California constitution to include a new section (Section 31 of Article I), whose key provision now reads:

> *(a) The state shall not discriminate against, or grant preferential treatment to, any individual or group on the basis of race, sex, color, ethnicity, or national origin in the operation of public employment, public education, or public contracting.*

Other states have adopted similar bans. The only state where an anti-affirmative action initiative has failed at the ballot was Colorado, where voters narrowly rejected Amendment 46 in 2008.

Court challenges to such state prohibitions have been repeatedly unsuccessful. In April 2012, the U.S. Court of Appeals for the Ninth Circuit affirmed the district court's dismissal of a challenge to California's Proposition 209. More recently, in 2014, the question landed at the doorstep of the U.S. Supreme Court, after Michigan adopted Proposal 2, prohibiting state and local agencies from granting preferential treatment to any individual or group on the basis of race, sex, color, ethnicity or national origin in public education, public employment, or public contracting. In 2011, a panel of the Sixth Circuit ruled that Michigan's Proposal 2 was unconstitutional, thus overturning the ban on affirmative action in college admissions in Michigan. The court sitting en banc upheld the ruling in 2012. However, in April 2014, the Supreme Court ruled in a 6–2 decision that voters could prohibit affirmative action in public universities, thus upholding Proposition 2. *Schuette v. Coalition to Defend Affirmative Action*, 572 U.S. ___ (2014).

The American public as a whole, however, appears to strongly support affirmative action policies, at least when it comes to higher education. In a Pew Research Center survey conducted in March 2014, 63% of people said that programs aimed at increasing the number of black and minority students on college campuses were a good thing, versus just 30% who called them a bad thing. *See* Drew Desilver, "Supreme Court says states can ban affirmative action; 8 already have," Pew Research Center (Apr. 22, 2014), *available at*: http://www.pewresearch.org/fact-tank/2014/04/22/supreme-court-says-states-can-ban-affirmative-action–8–already-have/.

V. INTER-MINORITY CONFLICT

The increasingly multiracial character of American society highlights the potential for conflict between different minority groups when it comes to affirmative action. In recent years, for example, Asian Americans have begun to object that affirmative action admissions policies unfairly disadvantage them. Asian-American groups have filed complaints with the U.S. Department of Education and have taken their complaints to court. To date, no court has ruled on the merits of such a suit, but some remain pending. We include below portions of the complaint filed against Harvard University, alleging that its admissions process unfairly discriminates against Asian American applicants.

Students for Fair Admissions, Inc. v. Harvard College

Complaint available at https://studentsforfairadmissions.org/wp-content/uploads/2014/11/SFFA-v.-Harvard-Complaint.pdf.

Plaintiff Students for Fair Admissions, Inc. brings this action to obtain, a declaratory judgment that "Harvard" [has] employed and [is] employing racially and ethnically discriminatory policies and procedures in administering the undergraduate admissions program at Harvard College in violation of Title VI of the Civil Rights Act of 1964, ("Title VI"). Harvard's undergraduate admissions policies and procedures have injured and continue to injure Plaintiff's members by intentionally and improperly discriminating against them on the basis of their race and ethnicity in violation of Title VI. [Note: The Court has held that Title VI prohibits admissions policies that are prohibited under the Equal Protection Clause.]

The admissions plan Harvard advocated for in Bakke (the "Harvard Plan") that promised to treat each applicant as an individual has always been an elaborate mechanism for hiding Harvard's systematic campaign of racial and ethnic discrimination against certain disfavored classes of applicants. Indeed, the Harvard Plan was created for the specific purpose of discriminating against Jewish applicants. Put simply, Bakke "legitimated an admissions process that is inherently capable of gross abuse and that . . . has in fact been deliberately manipulated for the specific purpose of perpetuating religious and ethnic discrimination in college admissions." Alan Dershowitz and Laura Hanft, Affirmative Action and the Harvard College Diversity-Discretion Model: Paradigm or Pretext, 1 Cardozo L. Rev. 379, 385 (1979). Today it is used to hide intentional discrimination against Asian Americans. Harvard is using the same "holistic" code words to discriminate for the same invidious reasons and it is relying on the same pretextual excuses to justify its disparate treatment of another high-achieving racial and ethnic minority group.

In any event, even if the Harvard Plan at some point outgrew its discriminatory roots, Harvard has long since abandoned an admissions policy that purported to merely use race contextually to fill the last few seats in the entering freshman class. Harvard now labels every applicant by race on the claim that it is pursuing the so-called "critical mass" diversity objective. That creates two problems for Harvard. First, as it has abandoned the very "plan" that led the Supreme Court to permit the use of racial admissions preferences, Harvard has deprived the Court of any continuing "authority to approve the use of race in pursuit of student diversity." Grutter, 539 U.S. at 394 (Kennedy, J., dissenting). Second, Harvard's new diversity interest—critical mass—should never have been endorsed and should be outlawed once and for all. "[T]he concept of critical mass is a delusion used . . . to mask [an] attempt to make race an automatic factor in most instances and to achieve numerical goals indistinguishable from quotas." Id. at 389.

Worse still, Harvard is not even pursuing its claimed "critical mass" interest. Rather, even under governing Supreme Court precedent, Harvard is violating Title VI for at least four reasons. First, Harvard is using racial classifications to engage in the same brand of invidious discrimination against Asian Americans that it formerly used to limit the number of Jewish students in its student body. Statistical evidence reveals that Harvard uses "holistic" admissions to disguise the fact that it holds Asian Americans to a far higher standard than other students and essentially forces them to compete against each other for admission. There is nothing high-minded about this campaign of invidious discrimination. It is "illegitimate racial prejudice or stereotype." Croson, 488 U.S. at 493.

Second, Harvard is engaging in racial balancing. Over an extended period, Harvard's admission and enrollment figures for each racial category have shown almost no change. Each year, Harvard admits and enrolls essentially the same percentage of African Americans, Hispanics, whites, and Asian Americans even though the application rates and qualifications for each racial group have undergone significant changes over time. This is not the coincidental byproduct of an admissions system that treats each applicant as an individual; indeed, the statistical evidence shows that Harvard modulates its racial admissions preference whenever there is an unanticipated change in the yield rate of a particular racial group in the prior year. Harvard's remarkably stable admissions and enrollment figures over time are the deliberate result of systemwide intentional racial discrimination designed to achieve a predetermined racial balance of its student body.

Third, Harvard is failing to use race merely as a "plus factor" in admissions decisions. Rather, Harvard's racial preference for each student (which equates to a penalty imposed upon Asian-American applicants) is so large that race becomes the "defining feature of his or her application." Grutter, 539 U.S. at 337. Only using race or ethnicity as a dominant factor in admissions decisions could, for example, account for the remarkably low admission rate for high-achieving Asian-American applicants. Harvard's admissions decisions simply are not explainable on grounds other than race. High-achieving Asian-American applicants are as broadly diverse and eclectic in their abilities and interests as any other group seeking admission to Harvard. They compete in interscholastic sports, are members of the school band, work part-time jobs after school, travel, and engage in volunteer work just like everyone else. It is not a lack of non-academic achievement that is keeping them from securing admission. It is Harvard's dominant use of racial preferences to their detriment.

Fourth, and last, Harvard is using race in admissions decisions when race-neutral alternatives can achieve diversity. As other elite universities have shown, increased utilization of non-race-based criteria, such as socioeconomic preferences, can promote diversity about as well as racial preferences. This approach is particularly effective when combined with increased use of financial aid, scholarships, and recruitment to attract and enroll minority applicants and the elimination of admissions policies and practices, such as legacy preferences and early admission, which operate to the disadvantage of minority applicants. Further, eliminating racial preferences at Harvard will alleviate the substantial harm these discriminatory policies cause to those minority applicants who receive such admissions preferences, the Harvard community, and society as a whole. Racial preferences are a dangerous tool and may only be used as a last resort. There is now overwhelming evidence that race-neutral alternatives render reliance on racial preferences unnecessary. It is incumbent on Harvard to take full advantage of these preferred alternatives.

Accordingly, there is no doubt that Harvard is in violation of Title VI. The only question is the proper judicial response. Given what is occurring at Harvard and at other schools, the proper response is the outright prohibition of racial preferences in university admissions—period. Allowing this issue to be litigated in case after case will only "perpetuate the hostilities that proper consideration of race is designed to avoid." Grutter, 539 U.S. at 394 (Kennedy, J., dissenting). Harvard and other academic institutions cannot and should not be trusted with the awesome and historically dangerous tool of racial classification. As in the past, they will use any leeway the Supreme Court grants them to use racial preferences in college admissions—under whatever rubric—to engage in racial stereotyping, discrimination against disfavored minorities, and quota-setting to advance their social-engineering agenda. Strict scrutiny has proven to be no match for concerted discrimination hidden behind the veil of "holistic" admissions.

THE PARTIES

A. Plaintiff

Plaintiff, Students for Fair Admissions, Inc. ("SFFA") is a coalition of prospective applicants and applicants to higher education institutions who were denied admission to higher education institutions, their parents, and other individuals who support the organization's purpose and mission of eliminating racial discrimination in higher education admissions. SFFA has members throughout the country.

Discrimination on the basis of race or ethnicity is longstanding at Harvard. The "Harvard Plan" itself—and the concept of an admissions system based on a "holistic" review of applicants instead of admission based on academic qualifications—was formulated for the specific purpose of discriminating against disfavored minority groups. "Indeed, the historical evidence points inexorably to the conclusion that the current Harvard College admissions system was born out of one of the most shameful episodes in the history of American higher education in general, and of Harvard college in particular." Alan Dershowitz and Laura Hanft, Affirmative Action and the Harvard College Diversity-Discretion Model: Paradigm or Pretext, 1 Cardozo L. Rev. 379, 385 (1979).

B. 1900s to 1920s: Before "Selective Admissions"

Until the early 1920s, Harvard, like all other Ivy League schools, selected its students by admitting applicants who passed a required examination. Because Harvard's entrance examination was not especially demanding, an applicant for undergraduate admission with average intelligence from a prominent school could usually pass with ease. Though the performance of some students placed them in a gray zone from which they could be admitted "with conditions," most applicants were admitted based solely on objective academic criteria. Under this system, the number of students entering Harvard fluctuated, sometimes quite widely, from year to year. Harvard's student body during this time period was fairly homogenous in terms of class, race, religion, and ethnicity. Students during this time period were overwhelmingly from affluent backgrounds, almost exclusively white, and composed largely of graduates of elite private secondary schools. Harvard was considered somewhat open to African Americans, immigrants, and foreigners, though the numerical presence of each of these groups of students on campus was relatively small.

C.   1920s to 1930s: Harvard's "Jewish Problem"

Ivy League schools began to reevaluate their admissions systems when students deemed socially "undesirable"—most prominently, Jewish applicants—started to pass the examinations and enroll in greatly increasing numbers. In or around the late 1910s, the number of Jewish students enrolling at Harvard began to increase, and Harvard administrator determined that the college had a "Jewish problem" that it needed to address. By 1918, Harvard's freshman class was 20 percent Jewish, three times the percentage at Yale and six times that at Princeton. The President of Harvard, A. Lawrence Lowell, was deeply troubled by this rising Jewish population. President Lowell feared that the enrollment of too many Jewish students would cause students from Protestant upper and upper-middle class families to choose other elite colleges over Harvard. In 1920, in a letter to William Hocking, a Harvard philosophy professor, President Lowell wrote that the increasing number of Jewish students enrolling at Harvard would ultimately "ruin the college." To combat this "Jewish problem," President Lowell sought to institute a cap on Jewish enrollment in each entering class. In his letter to Hocking, President Lowell stated that the best approach would be "to state frankly that we thought we could do the most good by not admitting more than a certain proportion of men in a group that did not intermingle with the rest, and give our reasons for it to the public." According to Lowell, "[e]xperience seems to place that proportion at about 15%." Yet President Lowell knew that such overt discrimination would meet resistance. He believed that the faculty, and probably the governing boards, would prefer to make a rule whose motive was less obvious on its face, such as giving to the Committee on Admission authority to refuse admittance to persons who possessed particular qualities believed to be characteristic of Jewish applicants. If such a system was instituted, however, President Lowell wished to ensure that the faculty knew "perfectly well what they are doing, and that any vote passed with the intent of limiting the number of Jews should not be supposed by anyone to be passed as a measurement of character really applicable to Jews and Gentiles alike." By the spring of 1922, the proportion of Jewish students had reached 21.5 percent. President Lowell warned that unless immediate measures were taken "the danger would seem to be imminent." President Lowell made clear that absent the rise in Jewish enrollment, no change in Harvard's admissions policies would be needed. The problem was not with the academic method of selection *per se*, but with its results: it was now yielding too many Jewish students at Harvard.

In a 1922 letter President Lowell wrote: "We can reduce the number of Jews by talking about other qualifications than those of admission examinations. If the object is simply to diminish the Jews, this is merely an indirect method of avoiding a problem in American life which is really important. This is the feeling of the most thoughtful people here, both gentile and Jew. On the other hand, we are in no present danger of having more students in college than we can well take care of; nor, apart from the Jews, is there any real problem of selection, the present method of examination giving us, for the Gentile, a satisfactory result."

In May 1922, Professor Ropes proposed that the Committee on Admission "take into account the proportionate size of racial and national groups in the membership of Harvard College," declaring that "it is not desirable that the number of students in any group which is not easily assimilated into the common life of the College should exceed 15 percent of the whole college." As one Harvard alumnus noted, "I am fully prepared to accept the judgment of the Harvard authorities that a concentration of Jews in excess of fifteen percent will produce a segregation of culture rather than a fusion."

At the same time, Harvard was beginning to gather the information that would permit it to identify which applicants were Jewish. Starting in the fall of 1922, applicants were required to answer questions on "Race and Color," "Religious Preference," "Maiden Name of Mother," and "Birthplace of Father," as well as the question, "What change, if any, has been made since birth in your own name or that of your father? (Explain fully.)" In addition, Harvard asked high school principals and private school headmasters to fill out a form indicating "by a check [the applicant's] religious preference so far as known . . . Protestant . . . Roman Catholic . . . Hebrew . . . Unknown."

Harvard also created a committee tasked with counting the number of Jewish students at Harvard. After analyzing all the student information it could obtain, the committee began classifying each Harvard student into one of four categories: "J1," "J2," "J3," and "other." A "J1" was assigned "when the evidence pointed conclusively to the fact that the student was Jewish;" a "J2" was assigned when a "preponderance of evidence" suggested the student was Jewish; and a "J3" was assigned when "the evidence suggested the possibility that the student might be Jewish."

During this time period, Harvard also adopted a "one-seventh plan," which purported to target "a new group of men from the West and South" who were in the top seventh of their graduating class. In reality, however, it was a "thinly disguised attempt to lower the Jewish proportion of the student body by bringing in boys—some of them academically ill equipped for Harvard—from regions of the country where there were few Jews."

By 1924, Harvard's Jewish enrollment had risen to 25 percent. According to President Lowell, Harvard's "reputation of having so many Jews" was hurting its ability to "attract applicants from western cities and the great preparatory schools."

By 1925, the dean's office reported that the proportion of known Jewish freshmen (the J1s and J2s) had risen to 27.6 percent, with an additional 3.6 percent in the J3 category. As President Lowell was contemplating these figures, he was receiving letters from alumni castigating the school for being overrun by Jewish students. Among these letters was one from W.F. Williams '01, who had attended a recent Harvard-Yale football game. Williams recommended using the school's admissions program to discretely limit the number of Jewish students enrolling at Harvard: "Naturally, after twenty-five years, one expects to find many changes but to find that one's University had become so Hebrewized was a fearful shock. There were Jews to the right of me, Jews to the left of me, in fact they were so obviously everywhere that instead of leaving the Yard with pleasant memories of the past I left with a feeling of utter disgust of the present and grave doubts about the future of my Alma Mater. . . . The Jew is undoubtedly of high mental order, desires the best education he can get CHEAPEST, and is more persistent than other races in his endeavors to get what he wants. It is self evident, therefore, that by raising the standard of marks he can't be eliminated from Harvard, whereas by the same process of raising the standard 'White' boys ARE eliminated. And is this to go on? Why the Psychology Test if not to bar those not wanted? Are the Overseers so lacking in genius that they can't devise a way to bring Harvard back to the position it always held as a 'white man's' college?"

President Lowell agreed with Williams' assessment, responding that he "had foreseen the peril of having too large of a number of an alien race and had tried to prevent it," but that "not one of the alumni ventured to defend the policy publicly." President Lowell was "glad to see from your letter, as I have from many other signs, that the alumni are beginning to appreciate that I was not wholly wrong three years ago in trying to limit the proportion of Jews."

Despite increasing alumni approval, President Lowell still faced significant obstacles to his plan. He needed Harvard's "Special Committee on the Limitation of the Size of the Freshman Class" to approve his new admissions plan.

In a letter to the chairman of the committee, President Lowell wrote that "questions of race," though "delicate and disagreeable," were not solved by ignoring them. The solution was a new admissions system giving the school wide discretion to limit the admission of Jewish applicants: "To prevent a dangerous increase in the proportion of Jews, I know at present only one way which is at the same time straightforward and effective, and that is a selection by a personal estimate of character on the part of the Admissions authorities, based upon the probable value to the candidate, to the college and to the community of his admission. Now a selection of this kind can be carried out only in case the numbers are limited. If there is no limit, it is impossible to reject a candidate who passes the admissions examinations without proof of defective character, which practically cannot be obtained. The only way to make a selection is to limit the numbers, accepting those who appear to be the best."

Anticipating pushback, President Lowell insisted that he was not proposing to discriminate against Jewish applicants. Instead, he sought "discrimination among individuals in accordance with the probable value of a college education to themselves, to the University, and the community," carefully adding that "a very large proportion of the less desirable, upon this basis, are at the present time the Jews." The committee's chairman was initially opposed, stating that "[e]verything in my education and bringing up makes me shrink from a proposal to begin a racial discrimination at Harvard—there's no use my pretending this isn't the case." In the end, however, the chairman agreed with President Lowell's notion of "a sound and discerning 'discrimination' among individuals" and expressed confidence that "such a discrimination would inevitably eliminate most of the Jewish element which is making trouble." Nevertheless, the chairman refused to endorse "a candid regulation excluding all but so many or such a proportion of 'Jews.'" Instead, he advised President Lowell that more subtle measures to exclude Jewish applicants would be a wiser approach.

In its report, the Committee made multiple recommendations along these lines. First, the committee recommended that Harvard limit its incoming class to just 1,000 students. Second, it recommended that "the application of the rule concerning candidates from the first seventh of their school be discretionary with the Committee on Admission." This modification would allow the committee to eliminate from the program high schools that sent too many Jewish students to Harvard.

Finally, and most important, the committee rejected an admissions policy that would select the 1,000 students on the basis of scholarship alone. According to the committee, it was "neither feasible nor desirable to raise the standards of the College so high that none but brilliant scholars can enter" and "the standards ought never to be too high for serious and ambitious students of average intelligence."

Not only did the faculty adopt these proposals, but it also approved measures making the admissions process even more subjective. In particular, the faculty called on the admissions committee to interview as many applicants as possible to gather additional information on "character and fitness and the promise of the greatest usefulness in the future as a result of a Harvard education." In addition, Harvard began requiring a passport-sized photo "as an essential part of the application for admissions." Harvard also began using "legacy" preferences for the children of alumni as a strategy for reducing the admission of Jewish students. President Lowell was elated by these changes, realizing that they "provided a tremendous opportunity to impose, at long last, the policy of restriction he had favored since 1922."

The reduction in Jewish enrollment at Harvard was immediate. The Jewish portion of Harvard's entering class dropped from over 27 percent in 1925 to 15 percent the following year. For the next 20 years, this percentage (15 percent) remained virtually unchanged. Harvard's new system of selection was far more complicated than the exam-based system that had preceded it, and implementing it required a new bureaucratic apparatus of information gathering and assessment.

In addition to expanding its administrative staffing apparatus, the new Office of Admissions needed to collect vast quantities of data formerly unnecessary. The development of a procedure for identifying Jewish applicants was only the first step. For the first time, candidates were asked to fill out lengthy applications that included demographic information, a personal essay, and a detailed description of extracurricular activities that might demonstrate "leadership" and reveal something about their "character." The centerpiece of the new system was the personal letter of recommendation, especially those from trusted sources such as alumni and headmasters or teachers from the leading feeder schools. Finally, to ensure that "undesirables" were identified and to assess important but subtle indicators of background and breeding such as speech, dress, deportment, and physical appearance, a personal interview was required, a final screening device usually conducted by the Director of Admissions or a trusted alumnus.

The new policy permitted the rejection of scholastically brilliant students considered "undesirable," and it granted the director of admissions broad latitude to admit those of good background with weaker academic records. The key code word used was "character"—a quality thought to be frequently lacking among Jewish applicants, but present congenitally among affluent Protestants. By emphasizing the inherently subjective character of admissions decisions, Harvard's new system of selection left it free to adapt to changing circumstances by admitting—and rejecting—whomever it wished. These tools gave admissions officials the power to discriminate, ostensibly on the basis of "objective" evidence. Any number of reasons could be invoked to deny an applicant. "Selective admissions deflected much criticism precisely because it singled out no single status as 'key.'" As a consequence, university leaders could deny the existence of any racial or religious quotas, while still managing to reduce Jewish enrollment to a much lower level, and thereafter hold it essentially constant during the decades that followed.

D.   1930s to 1960s: A Continuation of Policies

In the 1930s, Harvard continued the discriminatory admissions policies instituted during the previous decade. In the late 1940s and early 1950s, following World War II, American public sentiment turned against anti-Semitism, and Harvard began to gradually reduce its discrimination against Jewish applicants.

In the early 1960's, Harvard began actively seeking to increase the number of African-American students on its campus. Notwithstanding this concerted effort, African-American enrollment stagnated until 1968. In 1968, Harvard altered its admissions policies and practices to admit more African Americans by taking into greater account the limitations of background and schooling that shaped the qualification of many African-American applicants. Under this new policy, an applicant who had "survived the hazards of poverty" and showed that he or she "is clearly intellectually thirsty" and "still has room for more growth" was given an admissions preference.

In 1969, one year after this policy change, Harvard's African-American enrollment increased 76 percent over the prior year to 7 percent of the enrolled freshman class. Although Harvard denied that it had instituted a quota, the enrollment rate consistently averaged 7 percent over the next several years. In 1969, a majority of the African-American applicants admitted to Harvard came from socioeconomically challenged backgrounds. By 1973, however, this number had decreased dramatically, with 75 to 80 percent of the African Americans admitted to Harvard coming from backgrounds that did not include "the hazards of poverty." According to Dean Peterson, Harvard diminished its focus on applicants with disadvantaged backgrounds because African Americans from relatively privileged backgrounds allegedly made the transition to Harvard more easily than those from working class and poor backgrounds: "We have learned" that "we cannot accept the victims of social disaster, however deserving of promise they once might have been, or however romantically or emotionally an advocate (or a society) might plead for him."

Harvard started considering Asian-American students a discrete subset of its undergraduate applicant pool in the early 1970s. At that juncture, Harvard took the position that Asian Americans students were not "under represented" on its campus and therefore were not in need of "affirmative action." Harvard nevertheless included Asian Americans in its affirmative-action compliance reports to the Federal government. Like Jewish applicants, Asian-American applicants tended to have superior academic records, and were well represented among the most successful students.

Harvard came to the conclusion that Asian Americans were "over-represented" in its student body. According to Henry Rosovsky, Harvard's Dean of the Faculty of Arts and Sciences (and later Acting President), Asian-American students were "no doubt the most over-represented group in the university." In 1974, a group calling itself the Coalition of Asian Americans ("CAA") formed at Harvard. For at least two years, Harvard refused to recognize the CAA as a minority student organization. In 1976, Harvard continued to refuse to recognize Asian Americans as a minority and barred those Asian Americans that had accepted admission to the college from participating in its Freshman Minority Orientation. By 1977, the CAA had become the Asian-American Association ("AAA"). The AAA demanded, among other things, that Harvard expand Asian-American recruitment and include Asian Americans within the college's "affirmative action" program.

Between 1976 and 1978, the proportion of Asian Americans increased from 3.6 percent to 6.5 percent of the freshman class—a result of the successful mobilization of Asian-American students at Harvard. These events coincided with a massive increase in Asian Americans applying to Harvard for undergraduate admission. Despite these increases, Harvard held Asian Americans to a higher standard than other applicants. In 1983, Margaret Chin, a Harvard undergraduate who had worked in the college's admissions office, co-authored a report entitled "Admissions Impossible." Surveying data from 25 universities, the report found that while Asian-American applications to Harvard and other universities were soaring, enrollments were barely increasing.

Although Harvard claimed that the lower admission rate for Asian-American applicants was attributable to weaker academic qualifications, the "Admissions Impossible" report found that, on average, Asian Americans were *more* qualified than other applicants and that Harvard had set an informal ceiling on Asian-American enrollment. In the wake of this report, Harvard abandoned the argument that Asian-American applicants had weaker qualifications. Former Dean of Admissions Fred Jewett instead claimed, on behalf of Harvard, that "arguments over numbers ignore a whole range of personal qualities," and that Harvard's official policy favored "choosing people who bring talents underrepresented in the applicant pool."

In 1987, a study found that Asian-American students admitted to Harvard had an average SAT score of 1467, whereas white students admitted to Harvard had an average SAT score of 1355—a 112-point difference. In a 1987 *New York Times* article, Berkeley professor Ling-Chi Wang compared the way Asian Americans are considered in college admissions to the earlier treatment of Jews: "I think all of the elite universities in America suddenly realized they had what used to be called a 'Jewish problem' before World War II, and they began to look for ways of slowing down the admissions of Asians." Robert Lindsey, *Colleges Accused of Bias to Stem Asians' Gains*, New York Times (Jan. 19, 1987).

In 1988, Harvard rejected Ling-Chi Wang's claim of discrimination against Asian-American applicants just as it had rejected the "Admissions Impossible" study's findings of discrimination. Dean of Admissions William Fitzsimmons—who remains Dean of Admissions today—acknowledged that "Asian Americans are slightly stronger than whites on academic criteria," but blamed the disparity in admissions on Asian Americans, as a group, being "slightly less strong on extracurricular criteria."

In July 1988, the Office of Civil Rights ("OCR") of the U.S. Department of Education began investigating the treatment of Asian-American applicants at Harvard to determine whether Harvard was engaging in discrimination in violation of Title VI of the Civil Rights Act. However, the investigation was strictly limited to the treatment of Asian-American applicants as compared to white applicants. The OCR investigation lasted more than two years. Under the pressure of the investigation, Harvard began to increase its enrollment of Asian Americans. By the end of the investigation, the percentage of Asian Americans admitted to Harvard increased from 10.8 percent in 1988 to 16.1 percent in 1991.

OCR announced its findings in October 1990. Focusing on ten groups admitted from 1979 through 1988, it found that Asian Americans had been admitted at a significantly lower rate for each of the past seven years, even though they were "similarly qualified" to white applicants. OCR nevertheless blamed the differential on legacy preferences and found that the differential admission rates were not the product of racial or ethnic discrimination.

E. Harvard's Admissions Process

1. The Application.

During an admissions cycle, the Harvard Admissions Committee reviews each student's admissions materials. Those materials include: (1) the Common Application or Universal College Application, including an essay, and the required parts of the Harvard Supplement; (2) the high school transcript, school report, and mid-year school report—all submitted by a student's guidance counselor; (3) standardized test scores—submitted by the College Board; (4) teacher and guidance counselor recommendations; (5) optional on-campus and/or off-campus interviewer evaluation; (6) optional personal statements (found on the Harvard Supplement) in addition to the required essays; and (7) optional music tapes, artwork slides, or samples of academic work.

Harvard gathers information about the race and ethnicity of its applicants through numerous ways. An applicant filling out a Common Application has the option of disclosing his or her racial identity. The

Common Application asks two questions to identify an applicant's race and ethnicity: (1) "Are you Hispanic/Latino?" and (2) "Regardless of your answer to the prior question, please indicate how you identify yourself. (Check one or more and describe your background.) American Indian or Alaska Native (including all Original Peoples of the Americas); Asian (including Indian subcontinent and Philippines); Black or African American (including Africa and Caribbean); Native Hawaiian or Other Pacific Islander (Original People); or White (including Middle Eastern)."

The Common Application requires applicants to identify their parents' first and last name, the parents' former last names, and their country of birth. Similarly, the Universal College Application gives the applicant the option of disclosing his or her racial identity. The Universal College Application asks two questions to identify an applicant's race and ethnicity: "Are you Hispanic or Latino?" and "How would you describe your racial background? (select one or more of the following categories): Asian ([if so, identify] country of family origin); Black or African American; American Indian or Alaska Native ([if so, identify where] enrolled [and] Tribal affiliation; Native Hawaiian or Other Pacific Islander; or White." The Universal College Application requires applicants to identify their parents' first and last names. The Universal College Application also requires applicants to identify, if it is not English, the "language spoken in your home."

Harvard also encourages students to emphasize their race and ethnicity through their essays. According to Monica Del Toro, a Harvard Admissions Officer, the essay "is the most important part of the application." The biggest rule, she says, "is to stand out," and a good way "to truly stand out from the rest of the pack is to discuss your culture."

F.   There Is Decisive Statistical Evidence That Harvard Discriminates Against Asian-American Applicants

Each year, Harvard publishes a significant amount of data concerning its application process. Among other things, Harvard releases admitted student data and enrolled student data broken down by racial category. Harvard used to allow the public to examine admission rates by race as well. More recently, however, Harvard began keeping these figures secret. Harvard has never offered an explanation for this decision. By contrast, the prestigious University of California system routinely releases information about its applicant pool broken down by racial category, which allows the public to examine admission rates by race. Nonetheless, significant data regarding Harvard's applicant pool has been made publicly available.

This statistical evidence establishes that Harvard is intentionally discriminating against Asian Americans by making it far more difficult for Asian Americans than for any other racial and ethnic group of students to gain admission to Harvard. Princeton professor Thomas J. Espenshade and his coauthor, Alexandra Radford, conducted an authoritative study of the role of race in elite American undergraduate admissions for their book *No Longer Separate, Not Yet Equal,* which was published in 2009. Espenshade and Radford gathered exhaustive application data on a group of three elite public and four elite private colleges. Controlling for a wide variety of academic, demographic, and personal characteristics, Espenshade and Radford found that Asian-American students were dramatically less likely to be admitted than otherwise similar students who identified themselves as white or Caucasian. In fact, Espenshade and Radford's analysis showed that the negative odds-ratio affecting Asian Americans relative to Whites was larger than the positive odds-ratio affecting African Americans relative to Whites.

The Espenshade-Radford study also expressed the admissions penalty facing Asian Americans in terms of SAT-point equivalents. The authors reported that Asian Americans needed SAT scores that were about 140 points higher than white students, all other quantifiable variables being equal, to get into elite schools. Thus, if a white student needed a 1320 SAT score to be admitted to one of these schools, an Asian American needed a 1460 SAT score to be admitted. That is a massive penalty given that marginal differences in SAT scores are magnified among those students competing for admission to the most elite universities, as there is less room at the very top of the SAT scale to differentiate between applicants.

Recent statistical evidence reveals that discrimination against Asian Americans at Harvard is even more severe than the Espenshade-Radford study found. In recent years, *The Harvard Crimson* has been surveying incoming freshmen. In 2013, nearly 80% of the incoming class of 2017 responded to its survey. According to the survey, the average SAT of respondents was 2237 (on a 2400-scale), while the average SAT of individual ethnic groups varied widely: 2299 for East Asians and Indians, 2107 for African-Americans, and 2142 for Native Americans). Given this reporting, the average SAT for non-Hispanic Whites is at or somewhat below the overall median.

This class average (2237) corresponds to roughly the 99.5 percentile of the SAT, meaning that Harvard draws half of its class from students scoring in the top 1/2 of 1 percent of the SAT I distribution. The "East Asian and Indian" average of 2299 corresponds to the 99.9 percentile of the SAT, meaning that Harvard draws about half of this ethnic group from the top 1/10 of 1 percent of the SAT I distribution. That is a dramatically higher standard of academic performance. Harvard requires much more of its Asian-American applicants than it requires of other races and ethnicities.

Dr. Richard Sander, a professor of law at UCLA, and Medha Uppala, a graduate student in statistics at UCLA, recently co-authored a working paper titled *The Evolution of SES Diversity in the Applicant Pool of*

Highly Selective Universities, 1994–2012. In this working paper, Dr. Sander and Ms. Uppala examine data on several Ivy League colleges that shed valuable light on the admissions practices at these schools. The paper examines the degree to which elite colleges, including Harvard, have expanded their access in recent years to students with low socioeconomic status. The primary data source is a widely used database from the College Board, which biannually compiles anonymized data on 100,000 SAT-takers nationwide. The paper reveals startling application patterns from the aggregated data that it reports, which, in conjunction with other data sources, make manifest Harvard's massive intentional discrimination against Asian Americans.

As an initial matter, the paper finds that Asian Americans are being admitted to these schools at a far lower rate than the rate at which they apply. The paper notes that for "three of the most selective Ivy League colleges," the average racial makeup of all domestic score senders between 2008 and 2012 is 27.3 percent Asian American, 11.3 percent African American, 12.5 percent Hispanic, 40.4 percent non-Hispanic White, and 8.5 percent other race or non-identified. Over this same time period, however, Asian Americans represented only 17–20 percent of the admitted students. No other racial or ethnic group at these schools is as underrepresented relative to its application numbers as are Asian Americans. Indeed, no other racial or ethnic group comes even remotely close to this level of underrepresentation. Thus, if Harvard admitted randomly from its applicant pool, the number of Asian Americans in its entering freshman class would be far higher than it actually is.

These data alone provide strong evidence that Harvard is engaging in intentional discrimination against Asian-American applicants absent some factor that makes this gross disparity explainable on non-discriminatory grounds. Moreover, the paper's data shows that Asian-American applicants have, on average, stronger qualifications for admission than any other racial or ethnic group applying to top Ivy League schools. Ironically, then, the most *underrepresented* group of admitted students relative to the applicant pool is the most *overrepresented* racial or ethnic group among top academic performers. Among "three of the most selective Ivy League colleges," the paper's data shows that, during the 2008, 2010, and 2012 admissions cycles, Asian Americans, on average, constituted nearly 39 percent of all domestic SAT-takers who (a) had scores of 2100 or higher and (b) sent their scores to these schools.

The Harvard Crimson survey, as does every other available public source, confirms that the vast majority of Harvard's students come from this pool of applicants (with SAT scores of 2100 or higher). Remarkably, students with higher test scores were even more likely to be Asian Americans. In 2008, Asian Americans made up 46 percent of domestic Harvard score-senders with SAT scores above 2200 (a range from which

Harvard draws more than half of its students). In addition, Asian Americans made up an even higher percentage of the very top students; they accounted for 55 percent of domestic Harvard score-senders with SAT scores above 2300. These patterns are very similar across all of the top Ivy League schools. In 2008–12, for the three Ivy League schools analyzed by Dr. Sander and Ms. Uppala, Asian Americans made up 38.9 percent of all domestic score-senders with SAT scores above 2100; 45 percent of domestic score-senders with SAT scores above 2200; and over 51 percent of domestic score-senders with SAT scores above 2300. These data, in combination with other publicly available data, demonstrate that Asian Americans admitted to Harvard are vastly underrepresented—by a factor of half or even two-thirds—relative to the number of applications from Asian Americans that Harvard receives.

A report by the Consortium on Financing Higher Education, in the Harvard Class of 1995, also showed that Asian Americans are held to a higher standard than any other group of applicants. *See* Melissa Lee, *Report Discloses SATs, Admit Rate*, The Harvard Crimson (May 7, 1993). Responding to this study, Dean Fitzsimmons stated that race is "only one factor in deciding whether a candidate is admitted," but that certain minority groups, particularly African Americans, are "highly sought after" and that, "[s]tatistically, one could make the argument that it's easier for certain minorities [to be admitted]." Dean Fitzsimmons added: "It's true that admission rates for Asian Americans and whites are lower than the admission rates for Hispanics and African American students and Native American students as well. But it's more complicated than that. . . . The question we look at is how much more likely will white and Asian American students have access to the kind of preparation that will make one an outstanding college candidate here."

No non-discriminatory factor justifies the gross disparity in Asian American admissions relative to their presence in Harvard's applicant pool. One non-discriminatory factor that theoretically could justify this gross disparity would be if a disproportionally high percentage of Asian-American students were clustered at the low end of the applicant pool with regard to academic qualifications as compared to other racial groups. But as Dr. Sander's and Ms. Uppala's paper and other data show, the opposite is in fact true. A disproportionally high percentage of Asian-American students are clustered at the high end of the applicant pool with regard to academic qualifications.

Another non-discriminatory factor that theoretically could justify this gross disparity would be if a disproportionally high percentage of Asian-American students were lacking with regard to non-academic criteria as compared to other racial groups. But there is no data to support that theory. *See, e.g.*, Esteban M. Aucejo, Hanming Fang, and Ken Spenner, "Does Affirmative Action Lead to Mismatch? A New Test and Evidence," 2 Quantitative Economics 303 (2011). This study found no racial advantage for underrepresented minority applicants in levels of personal achievement.

Studies also have shown that high-achieving Asian-American students are equally, if not more, qualified than other racial groups with regard to non-academic criteria. At the University of California, Los Angeles (UCLA), over several years, undergraduate admissions readers assigned each applicant three types of scores: "academic achievement" (principally high school grades, AP courses, and standardized test scores); "life challenges" (mainly socioeconomic background); and "personal achievement" (such as leadership, musical ability, and community service). These three scores jointly determined virtually all admissions decisions. *See* Peter Arcidiacono, Thomas Espenshade, Stacy Hawkins, and Richard Sander, *A Conversation on the Nature, Effects, and Future of Affirmative Action in Higher Education Admissions*, Pennsylvania Journal of Constitutional Law (Fall 2014).

The data cover over 100,000 undergraduate applicants to UCLA over three years and show absolutely no correlation between race and "personal achievement." Rather, the data show that the only strong predictor of personal-achievement scores is academic achievement; applicants with high test scores and grades tended to have personal achievement scores that were about one standard deviation higher than applicants with low test scores and grades. There is no evidence that Asian Americans applying to UCLA have personal achievement credentials that Asian Americans applying to Harvard uniformly lack. Rather, all available evidence points in the opposite direction. Moreover, notwithstanding Harvard's public relations emphasis on non-academic factors in reviewing applications, academic performance is the principal criteria for admission—except when it comes to minority groups that are either preferred or discriminated against based on their race and ethnicity.

Academic analyses of dozens of application processes at colleges and law schools around the country demonstrate that selective schools give far more weight to academic achievement and preparation than to other types of accomplishment and activity. *See* Richard Sander, *Why Strict Scrutiny Requires Transparency: The Practical Effects of Bakke, Gratz, and Grutter* (2011). In general, academic factors alone explain about 80 percent of admissions decisions at selective schools.

The gross disparity between the percentage of Asian-American students in the applicant pool and those in the admitted pool therefore are not explainable on any grounds other than intentional discrimination on the basis of race.

Not only does Harvard discriminate against Asian Americans, it racially balances its entering freshman class to ensure proportional representation of the various racial and ethnic groups present in Harvard's student body. As shown in Table C, the racial demographics of

Harvard's admitted class have remained stable across all racial groups at least over the last 9 years.

Table C

Harvard Admissions
(Percentage of Admitted Students by Race/Ethnicity)

	2014	2013	2012	2011	2010	2009	2008	2007	2006
African American	11.9%	11.5%	10.2%	11.8%	11.3%	10.8%	11.0%	10.7%	10.5%
Hispanic	13.0%	11.5%	11.2%	12.1%	10.3%	10.9%	9.7%	10.1%	9.8%
Asian American	19.7%	19.9%	20.7%	17.8%	18.2%	17.6%	18.5%	19.6%	17.7%
Native American	1.9%	2.2%	1.7%	1.9%	2.7%	1.3%	1.3%	1.5%	1.4%
White and Other	53.5%	54.9%	56.2%	56.4%	57.5%	59.4%	59.5%	58.1%	60.6%

No factor or criteria for admission—other than racial balancing—could explain these admissions patterns and the overall consistency of Harvard's admissions, enrollment, and overall student body figures across all racial groups. As the Unz study found, "ethnic enrolment levels which widely diverge from academic performance data or applications rates and which remain remarkably static over time provide obvious circumstantial evidence for at least a *de facto* quota system."

WHEREFORE, Plaintiff, Students for Fair Admissions, Inc., prays for the following relief as to all counts:

(a) A declaratory judgment that Harvard's admissions policies and procedures violate Title VI of the Civil Rights Act of 1964, 42 U.S.C. § 2000d *et seq.*;

(b) A declaratory judgment, that any use of race or ethnicity in the educational setting violates the Fourteenth Amendment and Title VI of the Civil Rights Act of 1964, 42

(c) A permanent injunction prohibiting Harvard from using race as a factor in future undergraduate admissions decisions;

(d) A permanent injunction requiring Harvard to conduct all admissions in a manner that does not permit those engaged in the decisional process to be aware of or learn the race or ethnicity of any applicant for admission.

NOTES AND QUESTIONS

1. Assuming that the factual claims in the complaint are correct, is the University's admissions process permissible? More specifically, should the complaint be dismissed under F.R.C.P. 12(b)(6), for failure to state a claim on which relief can be granted?

2. Again, assuming the facts in the complaint are correct, what are the relevant points of similarity and difference between the treatment of Asian Americans now and Jewish applicants in the first half of the 20th century? How would the university attempt to distinguish the two?

3. How does the complaint of Asian American students compare to that of the white students who assert that they are disadvantaged by affirmative action? How, if at all, should that difference influence the constitutional analysis of the plaintiffs' claim?

4. How much weight should be accorded the evidence offered in the complaint? Does it persuade you that the university is intentionally capping the enrollment of Asian Americans? What alternative explanations, if any, could the university offer?

5. If the court were to rule in favor of the plaintiffs, what remedy should be imposed? Should the university simply be prohibited from implementing a quota? Barred from learning the race of applicants? Be required to admit applicants on the basis of grades and test scores? What remedies would be desirable? Feasible?

VI. RETHINKING INTEGRATION

Racial justice advocates have devoted considerable energy to the effort to gain access to selective, predominantly white (and now Asian) universities. Less attention has been focused on institutions specifically intended to serve members of minority groups, such as Historically Black Colleges and Universities (HBCUs). Ironically, HBCUs, which were founded when elite institutions did not accept African Americans, have been remarkably successful with African-American students. HBCUs have long produced a disproportionate share of our nation's black engineers and scientists, important fields where African Americans remain underrepresented.

The following case, *United States v. Fordice*, 505 U.S. 717 (1992), highlights questions about the constitutionality and viability of HBCUs. Private plaintiffs filed the case arguing that Mississippi continued to maintain a racially segregated system of higher education. The United States intervened as a plaintiff.

United States v. Fordice

Supreme Court of the United States, 1992.
505 U.S. 717.

■ JUSTICE WHITE delivered the opinion of the Court.

In 1954, this Court held that the concept of " 'separate but equal' " has no place in the field of public education. Since [Brown], the Court has had many occasions to evaluate whether a public school district has met its affirmative obligation to dismantle its prior de jure segregated system in elementary and secondary schools. In these cases we decide what standards to apply in determining whether the State of Mississippi has met this obligation in the university context.

I

Mississippi launched its public university system in 1848 by establishing the University of Mississippi, an institution dedicated to the higher education exclusively of white persons. In succeeding decades, the State erected additional postsecondary, single-race educational facilities. Alcorn State University opened its doors in 1871 as "an agricultural college for the education of Mississippi's black youth." Creation of four more exclusively white institutions followed: Mississippi State University (1880), Mississippi University for Women (1885), University of Southern Mississippi (1912), and Delta State University (1925). The State added two more solely black institutions in 1940 and 1950: Jackson State University, which was charged with training "black teachers for the black public schools," and Mississippi Valley State University, whose functions were to educate teachers primarily for rural and elementary schools and to provide vocational instruction to black students.

The first black student was not admitted to the University of Mississippi until 1962, and then only by court order. For the next 12 years the segregated public university system in the State remained largely intact. Mississippi State University, Mississippi University for Women, University of Southern Mississippi, and Delta State University [remained] almost completely white. During this period, Jackson State and Mississippi Valley State were exclusively black; Alcorn State had admitted five white students by 1968.

[Beginning in 1969, the United States government and private plaintiffs undertook various efforts to compel the State to desegregate its system of higher education.]

By the mid-1980's, 30 years after Brown, more than 99 percent of Mississippi's white students were enrolled at [the five historically white institutions]. The student bodies at these universities remained predominantly white, averaging between 80 and 91 percent white students. Seventy-one percent of the State's black students attended [one of the three historically black schools], where the racial composition ranged from 92 to 99 percent black.

II

By 1987, the parties concluded that they could not agree on whether the State had taken the requisite affirmative steps to dismantle its prior de jure segregated system. They proceeded to trial. [The trial court ruled in favor of the state, finding that the State had sufficiently fulfilled its affirmative duty to dismantle its prior system of de jure segregated education.]

III

[T]he primary issue in these cases is whether the State has met its affirmative duty to dismantle its prior dual university system.

Our decisions establish that a State does not discharge its constitutional obligations until it eradicates policies and practices traceable to its prior de jure dual system that continue to foster segregation. Thus we have consistently asked whether existing racial identifiability is attributable to the State, and examined a wide range of factors to determine whether the State has perpetuated its formerly de jure segregation in any facet of its institutional system.

We do not agree with the Court of Appeals or the District Court, however, that the adoption and implementation of race-neutral policies alone suffice to demonstrate that the State has completely abandoned its prior dual system. That college attendance is by choice and not by assignment does not mean that a race-neutral admissions policy cures the constitutional violation of a dual system. In a system based on choice, student attendance is determined not simply by admissions policies, but also by many other factors. Although some of these factors clearly cannot be attributed to state policies, many can be. Thus, even after a State dismantles its segregative admissions policy, there may still be state action that is traceable to the State's prior de jure segregation and that continues to foster segregation. The Equal Protection Clause is offended by "sophisticated as well as simple-minded modes of discrimination." If policies traceable to the de jure system are still in force and have discriminatory effects, those policies too must be reformed to the extent practicable and consistent with sound educational practices.

If the State perpetuates policies and practices traceable to its prior system that continue to have segregative effects—whether by influencing student enrollment decisions or by fostering segregation in other facets of the university system—and such policies are without sound educational justification and can be practically eliminated, the State has not satisfied its burden of proving that it has dismantled its prior system. Such policies run afoul of the Equal Protection Clause, even though the State has abolished the legal requirement that whites and blacks be educated separately and has established racially neutral policies not animated by a discriminatory purpose.

IV

[T]here are several surviving aspects of Mississippi's prior dual system which are constitutionally suspect; for even though such policies may be race neutral on their face, they substantially restrict a person's choice of which institution to enter, and they contribute to the racial identifiability of the eight public universities. Mississippi must justify these policies or eliminate them.

. . . [W]e address four policies of the present system: admission standards, program duplication, institutional missions' assignments, and continued operation of all eight public universities.

We deal first with the current admissions policies of Mississippi's public universities. As the District Court found, the three flagship historically white universities in the system—University of Mississippi, Mississippi State University, and University of Southern Mississippi— enacted policies in 1963 requiring all entrants to achieve a minimum composite score of 15 on the test administered by the American College Testing Program (ACT). The court described the "discriminatory taint" of this policy, an obvious reference to the fact that, at the time, the average ACT score for white students was 18 and the average score for blacks was 7.

The present admissions standards are not only traceable to the de jure system and were originally adopted for a discriminatory purpose, but they also have present discriminatory effects. Every Mississippi resident under 21 seeking admission to the university system must take the ACT test. Any applicant who scores at least 15 qualifies for automatic admission to any of the five historically white institutions except Mississippi University for Women, which requires a score of 18 for automatic admission unless the student has a 3.0 high school grade average. Those scoring less than 15 but at least 13 automatically qualify to enter [only the historically black school]. Those scoring 13 or 14, with some exceptions, are excluded from the five historically white universities and if they want a higher education must go to one of the historically black institutions or attend junior college. Proportionately more blacks than whites face this choice: In 1985, 72 percent of Mississippi's white high school seniors achieved an ACT composite score of 15 or better, while less than 30 percent of black high school seniors earned that score. It is not surprising then that Mississippi's universities remain predominantly identifiable by race.

The segregative effect of this automatic entrance standard is especially striking in light of the differences in minimum automatic entrance scores among the regional universities in Mississippi's system. The minimum score for automatic admission to Mississippi University for Women is 18; it is 13 for the historically black universities. Yet Mississippi University for Women is assigned the same institutional mission as two other regional universities, Alcorn State and Mississippi Valley State—that of providing quality undergraduate education. The effects of the policy fall disproportionately on black students who might wish to attend Mississippi University for Women; and though the disparate impact is not as great, the same is true of the minimum standard ACT score of 15 at Delta State University—the other "regional" university—as compared to the historically black "regional" universities where a score of 13 suffices for automatic admission. The courts below made little, if any, effort to justify in educational terms those particular disparities in entrance requirements or to inquire whether it was practicable to eliminate them.

Another constitutionally problematic aspect of the State's use of the ACT test scores is its policy of denying automatic admission if an applicant fails to earn the minimum ACT score specified for the particular institution, without also resorting to the applicant's high school grades as an additional factor in predicting college performance. The United States produced evidence that the American College Testing Program (ACTP), the administering organization of the ACT, discourages use of ACT scores as the sole admissions criterion on the ground that it gives an incomplete "picture" of the student applicant's ability to perform adequately in college. One ACTP report presented into evidence suggests that "it would be foolish" to substitute a 3- or 4-hour test in place of a student's high school grades as a means of predicting college performance. The record also indicated that the disparity between black and white students' high school grade averages was much narrower than the gap between their average ACT scores, thereby suggesting that an admissions formula which included grades would increase the number of black students eligible for automatic admission to all of Mississippi's public universities.[12]

The District Court observed that the board of trustees was concerned with grade inflation and the lack of comparability in grading practices and course offerings among the State's diverse high schools. Both the District Court and the Court of Appeals found this concern ample justification for the failure to consider high school grade performance along with ACT scores. In our view, such justification is inadequate because the ACT requirement was originally adopted for discriminatory purposes, the current requirement is traceable to that decision and seemingly continues to have segregative effects, and the State has so far failed to show that the "ACT-only" admissions standard is not susceptible to elimination without eroding sound educational policy.]

A second aspect of the present system that necessitates further inquiry is the widespread duplication of programs. The District Court found that 34.6 percent of the 29 undergraduate programs at historically

---

[12] In 1985, 72 percent of white students in Mississippi scored 15 or better on the ACT test, whereas only 30 percent of black students achieved that mark, a difference of nearly 2 1/2 times. By contrast, the disparity among grade averages was not nearly so wide. 43.8 percent of white high school students and 30.5 percent of black students averaged at least a 3.0, and 62.2 percent of whites and 49.2 percent of blacks earned at least a 2.5 grade point average.

black institutions are "unnecessarily duplicated" by the historically white universities, and that 90 percent of the graduate programs at the historically black institutions are unnecessarily duplicated at the historically white institutions. . . .

It can hardly be denied that such duplication was part and parcel of the prior dual system of higher education—the whole notion of "separate but equal" required duplicative programs in two sets of schools—and that the present unnecessary duplication is a continuation of that practice.

We next address Mississippi's scheme of institutional mission classification, and whether it perpetuates the State's formerly de jure dual system. The District Court found that, throughout the period of de jure segregation, University of Mississippi, Mississippi State University, and University of Southern Mississippi were the flagship institutions in the state system. They received the most funds, initiated the most advanced and specialized programs, and developed the widest range of curricular functions. At their inception, each was restricted for the education solely of white persons. When they were founded, the three exclusively black universities were more limited in their assigned academic missions than the five all-white institutions. Alcorn State, for example, was designated to serve as "an agricultural college for the education of Mississippi's black youth." Jackson State and Mississippi Valley State were established to train black teachers.

In 1981, the State assigned certain missions to Mississippi's public universities as they then existed. It classified University of Mississippi, Mississippi State, and Southern Mississippi as "comprehensive" universities having the most varied programs and offering graduate degrees. Two of the historically white institutions, Delta State University and Mississippi University for Women, along with two of the historically black institutions, Alcorn State University and Mississippi Valley State University, were designated as "regional" universities with more limited programs and devoted primarily to undergraduate education. Jackson State University was classified as an "urban" university whose mission was defined by its urban location.

The institutional mission designations adopted in 1981 have as their antecedents the policies enacted to perpetuate racial separation during the de jure segregated regime. . . . That different missions are assigned to the universities surely limits to some extent an entering student's choice as to which university to seek admittance.

Fourth, the State attempted to bring itself into compliance with the Constitution by continuing to maintain and operate all eight higher educational institutions. The existence of eight instead of some lesser number was undoubtedly occasioned by state laws forbidding the mingling of the races. And as the District Court recognized, continuing to maintain all eight universities in Mississippi is wasteful and irrational. The District Court pointed especially to the facts that Delta

State and Mississippi Valley State are only 35 miles apart and that only 20 miles separate Mississippi State and Mississippi University for Women.

Unquestionably, a larger rather than a smaller number of institutions from which to choose in itself makes for different choices, particularly when examined in the light of other factors present in the operation of the system, such as admissions, program duplication, and institutional mission designations. Though certainly closure of one or more institutions would decrease the discriminatory effects of the present system, based on the present record we are unable to say whether such action is constitutionally required. Elimination of program duplication and revision of admissions criteria may make institutional closure unnecessary. However, on remand this issue should be carefully explored by inquiring and determining whether retention of all eight institutions itself affects student choice and perpetuates the segregated higher education system, whether maintenance of each of the universities is educationally justifiable, and whether one or more of them can be practicably closed or merged with other existing institutions.

Because the former de jure segregated system of public universities in Mississippi impeded the free choice of prospective students, the State in dismantling that system must take the necessary steps to ensure that this choice now is truly free. The full range of policies and practices must be examined with this duty in mind. That an institution is predominantly white or black does not in itself make out a constitutional violation. But surely the State may not leave in place policies rooted in its prior officially segregated system that serve to maintain the racial identifiability of its universities if those policies can practicably be eliminated without eroding sound educational policies.

If we understand private petitioners to press us to order the upgrading of Jackson State, Alcorn State, and Mississippi Valley State solely so that they may be publicly financed, exclusively black enclaves by private choice, we reject that request. The State provides these facilities for all its citizens and it has not met its burden under Brown to take affirmative steps to dismantle its prior de jure system when it perpetuates a separate, but "more equal" one. Whether such an increase in funding is necessary to achieve a full dismantlement under the standards we have outlined, however, is a different question, and one that must be addressed on remand.

■ JUSTICE O'CONNOR, concurring.

In light of the State's long history of discrimination, and the lost educational and career opportunities and stigmatic harms caused by discriminatory educational systems, the courts below must carefully examine Mississippi's proffered justifications for maintaining a remnant of de jure segregation to ensure that such rationales do not merely mask the perpetuation of discriminatory practices. Where the State can accomplish legitimate educational objectives through less segregative means, the courts may infer lack of good faith; "at the least it places a heavy burden upon the [State] to explain its preference for an apparently less effective method." In my view, it also follows from the State's obligation to prove that it has "take[n] all steps" to eliminate policies and practices traceable to de jure segregation, that if the State shows that maintenance of certain remnants of its prior system is essential to accomplish its legitimate goals, then it still must prove that it has counteracted and minimized the segregative impact of such policies to the extent possible. Only by eliminating a remnant that unnecessarily continues to foster segregation or by negating insofar as possible its segregative impact can the State satisfy its constitutional obligation to dismantle the discriminatory system that should, by now, be only a distant memory.

■ JUSTICE THOMAS, concurring.

A challenged policy does not survive under the standard we announce today if it began during the prior de jure era, produces adverse impacts, and persists without sound educational justification.

. . . I find most encouraging the Court's emphasis on "sound educational practices." From the beginning, we have recognized that desegregation remedies cannot be designed to ensure the elimination of any remnant at any price, but rather must display "a practical flexibility" and "a facility for adjusting and reconciling public and private needs." Quite obviously, one compelling need to be considered is the educational need of the present and future students in the Mississippi university system, for whose benefit the remedies will be crafted.

In particular, we do not foreclose the possibility that there exists "sound educational justification" for maintaining historically black colleges as such. Despite the shameful history of state-enforced segregation, these institutions have survived and flourished. Indeed, they have expanded as opportunities for blacks to enter historically white institutions have expanded. Between 1954 and 1980, for example, enrollment at historically black colleges increased from 70,000 to 200,000 students, while degrees awarded increased from 13,000 to 32,000. These accomplishments have not gone unnoticed: "The colleges founded for Negroes are both a source of pride to blacks who have attended them and a source of hope to black families who want the benefits of higher learning for their children. They have exercised leadership in developing educational opportunities for young blacks at all levels of instruction, and, especially in the South, they are still regarded as key institutions for enhancing the general quality of the lives of black Americans."

I think it undisputable that these institutions have succeeded in part because of their distinctive histories and traditions; for many, historically black colleges have become "a symbol of the highest attainments of black culture." Obviously, a State cannot maintain such traditions by closing particular institutions, historically white or historically black, to particular racial groups. Nonetheless, it hardly follows that a State cannot operate a diverse assortment of institutions—including historically black institutions—open to all on a race-neutral basis, but with established traditions and programs that might disproportionately appeal to one race or another. No one, I imagine, would argue that such institutional diversity is without "sound educational justification," or that it is even remotely akin to program duplication, which is designed to separate the races for the sake of separating the races. Although I agree that a State is not constitutionally required to maintain its historically black institutions as such, I do not understand our opinion to hold that a State is forbidden to do so. It would be ironic, to say the least, if the institutions that sustained blacks during segregation were themselves destroyed in an effort to combat its vestiges.

■ JUSTICE SCALIA, concurring in the judgment in part and dissenting in part.

I reject the effectively unsustainable burden the Court imposes on Mississippi, and all States that formerly operated segregated universities, to demonstrate compliance with Brown I. That requirement, which resembles what we prescribed for primary and secondary schools in *Green v. School Bd. of New Kent County*, 391 U.S. 430 (1968), has no proper application in the context of higher education, provides no genuine guidance to States and lower courts, and is as likely to subvert as to promote the interests of those citizens on whose behalf the present suit was brought.

The Court is essentially applying to universities the amorphous standard adopted for primary and secondary schools in Green v. School Bd. of New Kent County. Like that case, today's decision places upon the State the ordinarily unsustainable burden of proving the negative proposition that it is not responsible for extant racial disparity in enrollment. Green requires school boards to prove that racially identifiable schools are not the consequence of past or present discriminatory state action; today's opinion requires state university administrators to prove that racially identifiable schools are not the consequence of any practice or practices (in such impromptu "aggregation" as might strike the fancy of a district judge) held over from the prior de jure regime. This will imperil virtually any practice or program plaintiffs decide to challenge—just as Green has—so long as racial imbalance remains. And just as under Green, so also under today's decision, the only practicable way of disproving that "existing racial identifiability is attributable to the State," is to eliminate extant segregation, i.e., to assure racial proportionality in the schools. Failing that, the State's only defense will be to establish an excuse for each challenged practice—either impracticability of elimination, which is also a theoretical excuse under the *Green* regime or sound educational value, which (presumably) is not much different from the "important and legitimate ends" excuse available under *Green*.

In the context of higher education, a context in which students decide whether to attend school and if so where, the only unconstitutional derivations of [segregation] are those that limit access on discriminatory bases; for only they have the potential to generate the harm Brown I condemned, and only they have the potential to deny students equal access to the best public education a State has to offer. Legacies of the dual system that permit (or even incidentally facilitate) free choice [among] racially identifiable schools—while still assuring each individual student the right to attend whatever school he wishes—do not have these consequences.

It is my view that the requirement of compelled integration (whether by student assignment, as in *Green* itself, or by elimination of nonintegrated options, as the Court today effectively decrees) does not apply to higher education. Only one aspect of a historically segregated university system need be eliminated: discriminatory admissions standards. The burden is upon the formerly de jure system to show that that has been achieved. A State is in compliance with Brown I once it establishes that it has dismantled all discriminatory barriers to its public universities.

That analysis brings me to agree with the judgment that the Court of Appeals must be reversed in part—for the reason (quite different from the Court's) that Mississippi has not borne the burden of demonstrating that intentionally discriminatory admissions standards have been eliminated. It has been established that Mississippi originally adopted ACT assessments as an admissions criterion because that was an effective means of excluding blacks from the HWI's. Given that finding, the District Court should have required Mississippi to prove that its continued use of ACT requirements does not have a racially exclusionary purpose and effect—a not insubstantial task.

I must add a few words about the unanticipated consequences of today's decision. Among petitioners' contentions is the claim that the Constitution requires Mississippi to correct funding disparities between its HBI's and HWI's. The Court rejects that—as I think it should, since it is students and not colleges that are guaranteed equal protection of the laws. But to say that the Constitution does not require equal funding is not to say that the Constitution prohibits it. The citizens of a State may conclude that if certain of their public educational institutions are used predominantly by whites and others predominantly by blacks, it is desirable to fund those institutions more or less equally.

Ironically enough, however, today's decision seems to prevent adoption of such a conscious policy. What the Court says about duplicate programs is as true of equal funding: The requirement "was part and parcel of the prior dual system." Moreover, equal funding, like program duplication, facilitates continued segregation—enabling students to attend schools where their own race predominates without paying a penalty in the quality of education. Nor could such an equal-funding policy be saved on the basis that it serves what the Court calls a "sound educational justification." The only conceivable educational value it furthers is that of fostering schools in which blacks receive their education in a "majority" setting; but to acknowledge that as a "value" would contradict the compulsory-integration philosophy that underlies Green. Just as vulnerable, of course, would be all other programs that have the effect of facilitating the continued existence of predominantly black institutions.

But this predictable impairment of HBI's should come as no surprise: for incidentally facilitating—indeed, even tolerating—the continued existence of HBI's is not what the Court's test is about, and has never been what Green is about. What the Court's test is designed to achieve is the elimination of predominantly black institutions. While that may be good social policy, the present petitioners, I suspect, would not agree; . . . But whether or not the Court's antagonism to unintegrated schooling is good policy, it is assuredly not good constitutional law. There is nothing unconstitutional about a "black" school in the sense, not of a school that blacks must attend and that whites cannot, but of a school that, as a consequence of private choice in residence or in school selection, contains, and has long contained, a large black majority. In a perverse way, in fact, the insistence, whether explicit or implicit, that such institutions not be permitted to endure perpetuates the very stigma of black inferiority that Brown I sought to destroy. Not only Mississippi, but Congress itself, seems out of step with the drum that the Court beats today, judging by its passage of an Act entitled "Strengthening Historically Black Colleges and Universities," which authorizes the Education Department to provide money grants to historically black colleges. The implementing regulations designate Alcorn State University, Jackson State University, and Mississippi Valley State University as eligible recipients.

NOTES AND QUESTIONS

1. *The Primary Education Standard.* The Court evaluated the Mississippi state university system under the same standards applicable to primary and secondary schools. Was it appropriate to do so? Students are typically assigned by the state, often based on where they live, to elementary schools. But college students choose which schools to attend. Given this difference, is there still justification for attributing current de facto segregation of universities to prior de jure segregation?

2. **Bazemore v. Friday.** The higher education system exists midway between primary schools, where the state assigns students to a particular school, and the 4H clubs considered by the Supreme Court in *Bazemore v. Friday*, 478 U.S. 385 (1986). In *Bazemore*, a divided court held that continuing racial imbalance in local agricultural clubs funded and promoted

by the state of North Carolina was not a violation of the Fourteenth Amendment, distinguishing the case from primary school rulings that required affirmative efforts to desegregate. Justice White wrote:

> The mere continued existence of single-race clubs does not make out a constitutional violation. As the District Court found, one's choice of a Club is entirely voluntary.... Even if the Service in effect assigned blacks and whites to separate clubs prior to 1965, it did not do so after that time. While schoolchildren must go to school, there is no compulsion to join [the local club], and while school boards customarily have the power to create school attendance areas and otherwise designate the school that particular students may attend, there is no statutory or regulatory authority to deny a young person the right to join any Club he or she wishes to join.

3.   ***Dismantling Segregation.*** If the elimination of formally discriminatory admissions standards is insufficient to dismantle the prior de jure segregated system, then what must the State do? In saying that no practice or policy that contributes to segregated colleges can be maintained, unless the state can prove that a particular practice has a "sound educational justification," is the Court attempting to promote integration? Should it do so? Or is the Court simply insuring that no practice or policy is maintained for a discriminatory purpose?

4.   ***Elements of Reform.*** The Court addressed four issues: admission standards, program duplication, institutional mission assignments, and continued operation of all eight universities. If you were the head of the university system, which of these issues would you first address and how?

5.   ***Funding.*** The private plaintiffs in *Fordice* filed suit primarily to force the state to upgrade its black colleges, which had always received substantially less funding than the white state universities. Should the Court have more clearly focused on the issue of funding? Should the Court have ordered equalization of funding? Wouldn't that approach have also promoted integration? Does the Court's opinion, as Justice Scalia contends, prohibit equal funding of black and white institutions?

6.   ***The Value of Integration.*** If the black and white schools in Mississippi were consolidated, which schools do you think would be closed? Would the consolidation of black and white colleges in Mississippi constitute a social gain, even if it meant that predominantly black institutions in the state ceased to exist?

7.   ***Choosing a Black College.*** Are there legitimate reasons for black students to want to attend an historically (and predominantly) black college? What are they? It is fair for black students not to have a predominantly black college available to them given that numerous predominantly white colleges exist for white students who wish to attend one?

8.   ***Preservation of HBCUs.*** If the state decided to maintain predominantly black colleges "as such," (to use Justice Thomas' phrase) so that black students could receive a college education in a predominantly

black setting, would that count as a "sound educational justification" for not consolidating the schools? Or would the desire to maintain historically black colleges "as such" constitute a discriminatory purpose? An intentional continuation of segregation?

9.   *Colorblindness.* Is Justice Thomas' position in *Fordice* consistent with his stated commitments to colorblindness in other cases? Similarly, is Justice Scalia as committed to colorblindness in this setting as in other cases? How would you reconcile their views in *Fordice* to their positions in *Grutter* or *Fisher*?

10. *Recently   Established   Minority-Serving   Institutions.* The University of Florida Law School is the flagship program in the state. It is home to roughly 1,200 students and 120 faculty members, and is ranked in the first tier of law schools, according to US News and World Report. Its entering class for 2012 was 25% minority. Florida has two other state law schools, both of which were established in 2000—the same year that the "One Florida Initiative" was passed to outlaw the use of race-based affirmative action. Florida A&M University College of Law was founded for black law students, and Florida International University College of Law was founded for Latinos. Florida A&M's web site notes that part of the school's mission is to "increase representation of minorities within the legal profession." US News currently ranks both schools as fourth-tier institutions, and both have a fraction of the faculty members that the University of Florida boasts. Does this state of affairs present any legal concerns? Does the establishment of these minority-serving institutions further or retard the cause of racial justice?

CHAPTER 6

EMPLOYMENT DISCRIMINATION

I. INTRODUCTION

If you own or manage a company, should you have the right to hire, promote, and discharge employees as you see fit, free from governmental oversight? Should the government be entitled to second-guess the qualifications that you genuinely believe would produce the best person for the job? Should the government be permitted to place any restrictions on your personnel decisions?

The legal answer to the last question for most of American history was—no. The American tradition is of "employment at will," *i.e.,* employers have absolute discretion over whether and whom to hire or fire. This tradition reflects both respect for the individual liberty of employers in managing their property and company and a societal commitment to *laissez faire* capitalism rooted in the belief that free markets best promote innovation, efficiency, and productivity.

The "at will" aspect of employment doctrine, however, historically has applied only to employers. Individuals have faced significant restrictions throughout history on their own labor. Slavery required black people to work for their "owners" for life, and indentured servants were bound to work for their masters for a period of years. Vagrancy laws made it a crime to be unemployed, and peonage laws held people in forced labor to pay off a debt or to serve a criminal sentence.

The rights of individuals over their labor have expanded over the course of American history, especially during three "constitutional moments."[1] The first moment was Reconstruction following the Civil War, during which the Thirteenth, Fourteenth, and Fifteenth Amendments were added to the Constitution. The Thirteenth Amendment prohibited slavery and involuntary servitude, and the Fourteenth Amendment prohibited states from depriving persons of due process and equal protection. Congress also passed civil rights laws during Reconstruction, including the Civil Rights Act of 1866, which guaranteed to all persons the same right to contract, including for employment, held by whites. These laws were critically important in liberating blacks from legal slavery. They were, however, limited in effect. States and private employers continued to discriminate by race,

---

[1] We borrow the term "constitutional moments" from Professor Bruce Ackerman, who used it to refer to periods of American history during which social and political upheaval is so momentous as to bring about a new constitutional order, whether or not reflected in formal amendments to the Constitution. See Bruce Ackerman, We the People: Foundations (Harvard University Press, 1991).

aided by Supreme Court decisions permitting state-sponsored segregation and protecting private discrimination from constitutional and congressional restriction. As a consequence, state and private discrimination against blacks and other people of color in employment and elsewhere remained prevalent.

The second constitutional moment occurred during the New Deal, when Congress legislated expansively into new areas of the national economy, including by creating rights for workers with respect to minimum compensation and maximum work hours, and by protecting workers' right to organize and bargain collectively to secure additional rights and benefits. After some initial resistance, the New Deal Court came to interpret congressional power broadly, upholding the federal government's unprecedented regulation of contexts traditionally regulated, if at all, by state and local governments. Despite gains for workers' rights brought by these legal reforms, however, racial discrimination by employers and unions, especially but not only in the South, remained widespread and legal.

The third constitutional moment was the Civil Rights Movement of the 1960s, which produced landmark civil rights and voting rights legislation that explicitly prohibited, among other things, racial discrimination by private employers—prohibitions Congress extended to state and federal employers by 1972. The Supreme Court upheld these laws and, by the mid-1970s, provided new interpretations of Reconstruction-era civil rights statutes that extended their reach to discrimination by private actors with respect to employment contracts.

This third constitutional moment sets the stage for this chapter. We will examine a range of race-related controversies in the employment setting and how three federal legal frameworks apply to them. The Equal Protection Clause of the Fourteenth Amendment provides that "[n]o State shall . . . deny to any person within its jurisdiction the equal protection of the laws." (The Fifth Amendment's Due Process Clause imposes an identical duty on the federal government.) Second, Section 1981 of the Civil Rights Act of 1866, 42 U.S.C. § 1981, provides in relevant part, "[a]ll persons within the jurisdiction of the United States shall have the same right in every State and Territory to make and enforce contracts . . . as is enjoyed by white citizens," a right which extends to employment contracts. Third, Title VII of the Civil Rights Act of 1964 is the law most explicitly addressed to employment discrimination and is the most comprehensive in its coverage. Section 703(a) of the Act provides:

> (a) It shall be an unlawful employment practice for an employer—
>
> > (1) to fail or refuse to hire or to discharge any individual, or otherwise to discriminate against any individual with respect to his compensation, terms, conditions, or privileges

of employment, because of such individual's race, color, religion, sex, or national origin; or

(2) to limit, segregate, or classify his employees or applicants for employment in any way which would deprive or tend to deprive any individual of employment opportunities or otherwise adversely affect his status as an employee, because of such individual's race, color, religion, sex, or national origin.

42 U.S.C. § 2000e–2(a). Other provisions of Title VII apply similar prohibitions to unions, employment agencies, and joint labor-management committees.

The cases and notes in this chapter examine a range of situations in which employees have claimed that an adverse employment decision constituted unlawful race discrimination under the laws outlined above, especially Title VII. For each situation, we invite students to ask three questions: (1) do the adverse employment decisions constitute wrongful racial discrimination; (2) how effectively does the law respond to such decisions; and (3) how *should* the law respond to such decisions? More specific questions include what employer practices constitute "discrimination"; what traits should qualify as "race" for the purpose of defining race discrimination; what *conduct* by employees should be protected from discrimination; whether the interaction of race and other characteristics creates unique forms of discrimination; whether race discrimination should ever be permitted; and to what extent should the law focus on the impact of employment decisions on racial groups rather than on individuals only?

Answering the foregoing questions requires asking a more fundamental question. What should be the goal of the law? Should the law seek only to eliminate individual acts of (invidious) discrimination? Or should the law aim to narrow persistent disparities in income and employment across racial groups? And if law should aim to eliminate group-based disparities, should it also seek to eliminate racially identifiable workplaces? That is, what if workers across racial groups achieve equal income and career success but self-select into different occupations or businesses so that individual workplaces might be predominantly one race or another? Is that a problem that law should address?

These questions, in turn, spark a threshold question. To what extent do we need the law at all to address race discrimination in employment? Why not rely on the market to address the problem of racial discrimination? Some prominent economists have argued that, to the extent race discrimination is irrational, the free market will punish employers who discriminate because those employers who do *not* discriminate will be able to hire the most qualified employees for each job, whatever their race may be, and will therefore function better in the marketplace. The free-market approach may have particular purchase now that segregation laws compelling employers to hire only whites have been invalidated. Is there reason to believe that, today, when employers are free to hire the best employee regardless of race, employers would profit from discriminating by race? What types of businesses, if any, would benefit from discriminatory hiring practices? And if businesses do benefit from race-conscious practices, why should employers not be permitted to use them? Should rational race-conscious practices by employers be subject to prohibition?

II. TWO THEORIES OF DISCRIMINATION: TREATMENT AND IMPACT

A. DISPARATE TREATMENT

All three sources of employment discrimination law discussed in this chapter were intended to attack purposeful discrimination, that is, when an employer intentionally subjects an employee to an adverse employment action, such as refusing to hire or promote, because of the employee's race. This form of discrimination is called racially "disparate treatment" under the employment discrimination statutes (Title VII and § 1981) and race discrimination under the Equal Protection Clause. But the reach of these constitutional and statutory provisions is distinct, in two principal ways. First and most significantly, the Equal Protection Clause only applies to government employers. Second, the procedure for proving intentional discrimination is somewhat more employee-friendly and complicated under the statutes than under the Equal Protection Clause.

To make out a claim under the Equal Protection Clause, a government employee must prove by a preponderance of the evidence that her employer acted with a racially discriminatory purpose. Relevant proof includes any direct or circumstantial evidence giving rise to an inference of discriminatory purpose, including the racial impact of the government's employment practices and any other historical or contemporary facts that bear on the employer's motivation. If the employee succeeds in proving that the government employer acted with a discriminatory purpose, the employer must prove it had a compelling interest for discriminating by race and that such discrimination was necessary to advance that interest. Outside the affirmative action context, in which reliance on race is overt, the most challenging issue in winning a case of purposeful discrimination against a government employer is proving that the employer acted with a discriminatory purpose.

Under Title VII and Section 1981, the employee must prove that her employer was motivated by race. The Supreme Court initially set forth the relative burdens of production and persuasion on the part of employee and employer in a Title VII case, *McDonnell Douglas Corp. v. Green*, 411 U.S. 792 (1973). The following case explains these burdens as the Court currently interprets them:

St. Mary's Honor Center v. Hicks
Supreme Court of the United States, 1993.
509 U.S. 502.

■ JUSTICE SCALIA delivered the opinion of the Court.

We granted certiorari to determine whether, in a suit against an employer alleging intentional racial discrimination in violation of § 703(a)(1) of Title VII of the Civil Rights Act of 1964, the trier of fact's rejection of the employer's asserted reasons for its actions mandates a finding for the plaintiff.

I

Petitioner St. Mary's Honor Center (St. Mary's) is a halfway house operated by the Missouri Department of Corrections and Human Resources (MDCHR). Respondent Melvin Hicks, a black man, was hired as a correctional officer at St. Mary's in August 1978 and was promoted to shift commander, one of six supervisory positions, in February 1980.

In 1983 MDCHR conducted an investigation of the administration of St. Mary's, which resulted in extensive supervisory changes in January 1984. Respondent retained his position, but John Powell became the new chief of custody (respondent's immediate supervisor) and petitioner Steve Long the new superintendent. Prior to these personnel changes respondent had enjoyed a satisfactory employment record, but soon thereafter became the subject of repeated, and increasingly severe, disciplinary actions. He was suspended for five days for violations of institutional rules by his subordinates on March 3, 1984. He received a letter of reprimand for alleged failure to conduct an adequate investigation of a brawl between inmates that occurred during his shift on March 21. He was later demoted from shift commander to correctional officer for his failure to ensure that his subordinates entered their use of a St. Mary's vehicle into the official log book on March 19, 1984. Finally, on June 7, 1984, he was discharged for threatening Powell during an exchange of heated words on April 19.

Respondent brought this suit in the United States District Court for the Eastern District of Missouri, alleging that petitioner St. Mary's violated § 703(a)(1) of Title VII . . . by demoting and then discharging him because of his race. After a full bench trial, the District Court found for petitioners. The United States Court of Appeals for the Eighth Circuit reversed and remanded, and we granted certiorari.

II

With the goal of "progressively . . . sharpen[ing] the inquiry into the elusive factual question of intentional discrimination," *Texas Dept. of Community Affairs v. Burdine,* 450 U.S. 248, 255, n.8 (1981), our opinion in McDonnell Douglas Corp. v. Green, 411 U.S. 792 (1973), established an allocation of the burden of production and an order for the presentation of proof in Title VII discriminatory-treatment cases. The plaintiff in such a case, we said, must first establish, by a preponderance of the evidence, a "prima facie" case of racial discrimination. Petitioners do not challenge the District Court's finding that respondent satisfied the minimal requirements of such a prima facie case (set out in *McDonnell Douglas*) by proving (1) that he is black, (2) that he was qualified for the position of shift commander, (3) that he was demoted from that position and ultimately discharged, and (4) that the position remained open and was ultimately filled by a white man.

Under the *McDonnell Douglas* scheme, "[e]stablishment of the prima facie case in effect creates a presumption that the employer unlawfully discriminated against the employee." *Burdine.* To establish a "presumption" is to say that a finding of the predicate fact (here, the prima facie case) produces "a required conclusion in the absence of explanation" (here, the finding of unlawful discrimination). 1 D. Louisell & C. Mueller, Federal Evidence § 67, p.536 (1977). Thus, the *McDonnell Douglas* presumption places upon the defendant the burden of producing an explanation to rebut the prima facie case—i.e., the burden of "producing evidence" that the adverse employment actions were taken "for a legitimate, nondiscriminatory reason." *Burdine.* "[T]he defendant must clearly set forth, through the introduction of admissible evidence," reasons for its actions which, *if believed by the trier of fact,* would support a finding that unlawful discrimination was not the cause of the employment action. Id. It is important to note, however, that although the *McDonnell Douglas* presumption shifts the burden of production to the defendant, "[t]he ultimate burden of persuading the trier of fact that the defendant intentionally discriminated against the plaintiff remains at all times with the plaintiff," Id.

Respondent does not challenge the District Court's finding that petitioners sustained their burden of production by introducing evidence of two legitimate, nondiscriminatory reasons for their actions: the severity and the accumulation of rules violations committed by respondent. Our cases make clear that at that point the shifted burden of production became irrelevant: "If the defendant carries this burden of production, the presumption raised by the prima facie case is rebutted," *Burdine,* and "drops from the case," Id. The plaintiff then has "the full and fair opportunity to demonstrate," through presentation of his own case and through cross-examination of the defendant's witnesses, "that the proffered reason was not the true reason for the employment decision," Id., and that race was. He retains that "ultimate burden of persuading the [trier of fact] that [he] has been the victim of intentional discrimination."

The District Court, acting as trier of fact in this bench trial, found that the reasons petitioners gave were not the real reasons for respondent's demotion and discharge. It found that respondent was the only supervisor disciplined for violations committed by his subordinates; that similar and even more serious violations committed by respondent's coworkers were either disregarded or treated more leniently; and that Powell manufactured the final verbal confrontation in order to provoke respondent into threatening him. It nonetheless held that respondent had failed to carry his ultimate burden of proving that his race was the determining factor in petitioners' decision first to demote and then to dismiss him.[2]

In short, the District Court concluded that "although [respondent] has proven the existence of a crusade to terminate him, he has not proven that the crusade was racially rather than personally motivated."

The Court of Appeals set this determination aside on the ground that "[o]nce [respondent] proved all of [petitioners'] proffered reasons for the adverse employment actions to be pretextual, [respondent] was entitled to judgment as a matter of law." The Court of Appeals reasoned:

> Because all of defendants' proffered reasons were discredited, defendants were in a position of having offered no legitimate reason for their actions. In other words, defendants were in no better position than if they had remained silent, offering no rebuttal to an established inference that they had unlawfully discriminated against plaintiff on the basis of his race.

That is not so. By producing *evidence* (whether ultimately persuasive or not) of nondiscriminatory reasons, petitioners sustained their burden of production, and thus placed themselves in a "better position than if they had remained silent."

In the nature of things, the determination that a defendant has met its burden of production (and has thus rebutted any legal presumption of intentional discrimination) can involve no credibility assessment. For the burden-of-production determination necessarily *precedes* the credibility-assessment stage. At the close of the defendant's case, the court is asked to decide whether an issue of fact remains for the trier of fact to determine. None does if, on the evidence presented, (1) any rational person would have to find the existence of facts constituting a prima facie case, and (2) the defendant has failed to meet its burden of production— i.e., has failed to introduce evidence which, *taken as true*, would *permit*

---

[2]   Various considerations led it to this conclusion, including the fact that two blacks sat on the disciplinary review board that recommended disciplining respondent, that respondent's black subordinates who actually committed the violations were not disciplined, and that "the number of black employees at St. Mary's remained constant."

the conclusion that there was a nondiscriminatory reason for the adverse action. In that event, the court must award judgment to the plaintiff as a matter of law under Federal Rule of Civil Procedure 50(a)(1) (in the case of jury trials) or Federal Rule of Civil Procedure 52(c) (in the case of bench trials). If the defendant has failed to sustain its burden but reasonable minds could *differ* as to whether a preponderance of the evidence establishes the facts of a prima facie case, then a question of fact *does* remain, which the trier of fact will be called upon to answer.

If, on the other hand, the defendant has succeeded in carrying its burden of production, the *McDonnell Douglas* framework—with its presumptions and burdens—is no longer relevant. To resurrect it later, after the trier of fact has determined that what was "produced" to meet the burden of production is not credible, flies in the face of our holding in *Burdine* that to rebut the presumption "[t]he defendant need not persuade the court that it was actually motivated by the proffered reasons." The presumption, having fulfilled its role of forcing the defendant to come forward with some response, simply drops out of the picture. The defendant's "production" (whatever its persuasive effect) having been made, the trier of fact proceeds to decide the ultimate question: whether plaintiff has proven "that the defendant intentionally discriminated against [him]" because of his race. The factfinder's disbelief of the reasons put forward by the defendant (particularly if disbelief is accompanied by a suspicion of mendacity) may, together with the elements of the prima facie case, suffice to show intentional discrimination. Thus, rejection of the defendant's proffered reasons, will permit the trier of fact to infer the ultimate fact of intentional discrimination, and the Court of Appeals was correct when it noted that, upon such rejection, "[n]o additional proof of discrimination is *required*," 970 F.2d, at 493 (emphasis added). But the Court of Appeals' holding that rejection of the defendant's proffered reasons *compels* judgment for the plaintiff disregards the fundamental principle of Rule 301 that a presumption does not shift the burden of proof, and ignores our repeated admonition that the Title VII plaintiff at all times bears the "ultimate burden of persuasion."

III

Only one unfamiliar with our case-law will be upset by the dissent's alarum that we are today setting aside "settled precedent," "two decades of stable law in this Court," "a framework carefully crafted in precedents as old as 20 years," which "Congress is [aware]" of and has implicitly approved. Panic will certainly not break out among the courts of appeals, whose divergent views concerning the nature of the supposedly "stable law in this Court" are precisely what prompted us to take this case—a divergence in which the dissent's version of "settled precedent" cannot remotely be considered the "prevailing view." [Citations omitted.] We mean to answer the dissent's accusations in detail, by examining our cases, but at the outset it is worth noting the utter implausibility that we would ever have held what the dissent says we held.

As we have described, Title VII renders it unlawful "for an employer . . . to fail or refuse to hire or to discharge any individual, or otherwise to discriminate against any individual with respect to his compensation, terms, conditions, or privileges of employment, because of such individual's race, color, religion, sex, or national origin." 42 U.S.C. § 2000e–2(a)(1). Here (in the context of the now-permissible jury trials for Title VII causes of action) is what the dissent asserts we have held to be a proper assessment of liability for violation of this law: Assume that 40% of a business' work force are members of a particular minority group, a group which comprises only 10% of the relevant labor market. An applicant, who is a member of that group, applies for an opening for which he is minimally qualified, but is rejected by a hiring officer of that *same minority group*, and the search to fill the opening continues. The rejected applicant files suit for racial discrimination under Title VII, and before the suit comes to trial, the supervisor who conducted the company's hiring is fired. Under *McDonnell Douglas*, the plaintiff has a prima facie case, and under the dissent's interpretation of our law not only must the company come forward with some explanation for the refusal to hire (which it will have to try to confirm out of the mouth of its now antagonistic former employee), but the jury must be instructed that, if they find that explanation to be incorrect, they must assess damages against the company, *whether or not they believe the company was guilty of racial discrimination*. The disproportionate minority makeup of the company's work force and the fact that its hiring officer was of the same minority group as the plaintiff will be irrelevant, because the plaintiff's case can be proved "indirectly by showing that the employer's proffered explanation is unworthy of credence." Surely nothing short of inescapable prior *holdings* (the dissent does not pretend there are any) should make one assume that this is the law we have created.

We have no authority to impose liability upon an employer for alleged discriminatory employment practices unless an appropriate factfinder determines, according to proper procedures, *that the employer has unlawfully discriminated*. We may, according to traditional practice, establish certain modes and orders of proof, including an initial rebuttable presumption of the sort we described earlier in this opinion, which we believe *McDonnell Douglas* represents. But nothing in law would permit us to substitute for the required finding that the employer's action was the product of unlawful discrimination, the much different (and much lesser) finding that the employer's explanation of its action was not believable. The dissent's position amounts to precisely this, *unless* what is required to establish the *McDonnell Douglas* prima facie case is a degree of proof so high that it would, in absence of rebuttal, require a directed verdict for the plaintiff (for in that case proving the employer's rebuttal noncredible would leave the plaintiff's directed-verdict case in place, and compel a judgment in his favor). Quite obviously, however, what is required to establish the *McDonnell Douglas* prima facie case is infinitely less than what a directed verdict demands. The dissent is thus left with a position that has no support in the statute, no support in the reason of the matter, no support in any holding of this Court (that is not even contended), and support, if at all, only in the dicta of this Court's opinions. It is to those that we now turn—begrudgingly, since we think it generally undesirable, where holdings of the Court are not at issue, to dissect the sentences of the United States Reports as though they were the United States Code.

The principal case on which the dissent relies is *Burdine*. While there are some statements in that opinion that could be read to support the dissent's position, all but one of them bear a meaning consistent with our interpretation, and the one exception is simply incompatible with other language in the case. *Burdine* describes the situation that obtains after the employer has met its burden of adducing a nondiscriminatory reason as follows: "Third, should the defendant carry this burden, the plaintiff must then have an opportunity to prove by a preponderance of the evidence that the legitimate reasons offered by the defendant were not its true reasons, but were a pretext for discrimination." The dissent takes this to mean that if the plaintiff proves the asserted reason to be *false*, the plaintiff wins. But a reason cannot be proved to be "a pretext *for discrimination*" unless it is shown *both* that the reason was false, and that discrimination was the real reason. *Burdine*'s later allusions to proving or demonstrating simply "pretext" are reasonably understood to refer to the previously described pretext, i.e., "pretext for discrimination."

Burdine also says that when the employer has met its burden of production "the factual inquiry proceeds to a new level of specificity." The dissent takes this to mean that the factual inquiry reduces to whether the employer's asserted reason is true or false—if false, the defendant loses. But the "new level of specificity" may also (as we believe) refer to the fact that the inquiry now turns from the few generalized factors that establish a prima facie case to the specific proofs and rebuttals of discriminatory motivation the parties have introduced.

In the next sentence, *Burdine* says that "[p]lacing this burden of production on the defendant thus serves . . . to frame the factual issue with sufficient clarity so that the plaintiff will have a full and fair opportunity to demonstrate pretext." The dissent thinks this means that the only factual issue remaining in the case is whether the employer's reason is false. But since in our view "pretext" means "pretext for discrimination," we think the sentence must be understood as addressing the form rather than the substance of the defendant's production burden: The requirement that the employer "clearly set forth" its reasons gives the plaintiff a "full and fair" rebuttal opportunity.

A few sentences later, *Burdine* says: "[The plaintiff] now must have the opportunity to demonstrate that the proffered reason was not the true reason for the employment decision. This burden now merges with the ultimate burden of persuading the court that she has been the victim of intentional discrimination." Id. at 256. The dissent takes this "merger" to mean that the "the ultimate burden of persuading the court that she has been the victim of intentional discrimination" is *replaced* by the mere burden of "demonstrat[ing] that the proffered reason was not the true reason for the employment decision." But that would be a merger in which the little fish swallows the big one. Surely a more reasonable reading is that proving the employer's reason false becomes part of (and often considerably assists) the greater enterprise of proving that the real reason was intentional discrimination.

Finally, in the next sentence *Burdine* says: "[The plaintiff] may succeed in this [i.e., in persuading the court that she has been the victim of intentional discrimination] either directly by persuading the court that a discriminatory reason more likely motivated the employer or indirectly by showing that the employer's proffered explanation is unworthy of credence. *See McDonnell Douglas,* 411 U.S., at 804–805." We must agree with the dissent on this one: The words bear no other meaning but that the falsity of the employer's explanation is *alone enough* to compel judgment for the plaintiff. The problem is that that dictum contradicts or renders inexplicable numerous other statements, both in *Burdine* itself and in our later case-law—commencing with the very citation of authority *Burdine* uses to support the proposition. *McDonnell Douglas* does not say, at the cited pages or elsewhere, that all the plaintiff need do is disprove the employer's asserted reason. In fact, it says just the opposite: "[O]n the retrial respondent must be given a full and fair opportunity to demonstrate by competent evidence that the presumptively valid reasons for his rejection *were in fact a coverup for a racially discriminatory decision.*" 411 U.S., at 805 (emphasis added). "We . . . insist that respondent under § 703(a)(1) must be given a full and fair opportunity to demonstrate by competent evidence *that whatever the stated reasons for his rejection, the decision was in reality racially premised.*" Id. at 805, n.18 (emphasis added). The statement in question also contradicts *Burdine*'s repeated assurance (indeed, its holding) regarding the burden of persuasion: "The ultimate burden of persuading the trier of fact that the defendant intentionally discriminated against the plaintiff remains at all times with the plaintiff. . . . The plaintiff retains the burden of persuasion." And lastly, the statement renders inexplicable *Burdine*'s explicit reliance, in describing the shifting burdens of *McDonnell Douglas*, upon authorities setting forth the classic law of presumptions we have described earlier, including Wigmore's Evidence, 450 U.S., at 253, 254, n.7, 255, n.8, James' and Hazard's Civil Procedure, Id. at 255, n.8, Federal Rule of Evidence 301, Maguire's Evidence, Common Sense and Common Law, and Thayer's Preliminary

Treatise on Evidence, Id. at 255, n.10. In light of these inconsistencies, we think that the dictum at issue here must be regarded as an inadvertence, to the extent that it describes disproof of the defendant's reason as a totally independent, rather than an auxiliary, means of proving unlawful intent.

In sum, our interpretation of *Burdine* creates difficulty with one sentence; the dissent's interpretation causes many portions of the opinion to be incomprehensible or deceptive. But whatever doubt *Burdine* might have created was eliminated by *Aikens*. There we said, in language that cannot reasonably be mistaken, that "the ultimate question [is] discrimination vel non." 460 U.S., at 714. Once the defendant "responds to the plaintiff's proof by offering evidence of the reason for the plaintiff's rejection, the factfinder must then decide" *not* (as the dissent would have it) whether that evidence is credible, but "whether the rejection was discriminatory within the meaning of Title VII." At that stage, we said, "[t]he District Court was . . . in a position to decide the ultimate factual issue in the case," which is "whether the defendant intentionally discriminated against the plaintiff." Id. at 715 (brackets and internal quotation marks omitted). The *McDonnell Douglas* methodology was "never intended to be rigid, mechanized, or ritualistic." 460 U.S., at 715 (quoting *Furnco*, 438 U.S., at 577). Rather, once the defendant has responded to the plaintiff's prima facie case, "the district court has before it all the evidence it needs to decide" *not* (as the dissent would have it) whether defendant's response is credible, but "whether the defendant intentionally discriminated against the plaintiff. . . . On the state of the record at the close of the evidence, the District Court in this case should have proceeded to this specific question directly, just as district courts decide disputed questions of fact in other civil litigation." Id. at 715–716. *In confirmation of this* (rather than in contradiction of it), the Court then quotes the problematic passage from *Burdine*, which says that the plaintiff may carry her burden either directly "or indirectly by showing that the employer's proffered explanation is unworthy of credence." It then characterizes that passage as follows: "In short, the district court must decide which party's explanation of the employer's motivation it believes." It is not enough, in other words, to disbelieve the employer; the factfinder must *believe* the plaintiff's explanation of intentional discrimination. It is noteworthy that Justice Blackmun, although joining the Court's opinion in *Aikens*, wrote a separate concurrence for the sole purpose of saying that he understood the Court's opinion to be saying what the dissent today asserts. That concurrence was joined only by Justice Brennan. Justice Marshall would have none of that, but simply refused to join the Court's opinion, concurring without opinion in the judgment. We think there is little doubt what *Aikens* meant.

IV

We turn, finally, to the dire practical consequences that the respondents and the dissent claim our decision today will produce. What appears to trouble the dissent more than anything is that, in its view, our rule is adopted "for the benefit of employers who have been found to have given false evidence in a court of law," whom we "favo[r]" by "exempting them from responsibility for lies." As we shall explain, our rule in no way gives special favor to those employers whose evidence is disbelieved. But initially we must point out that there is no justification for assuming (as the dissent repeatedly does) that those employers whose evidence is disbelieved are perjurers and liars . . . even if these were typically cases in which an individual defendant's sworn assertion regarding a physical occurrence was pitted against an individual plaintiff's sworn assertion regarding the same physical occurrence, surely it would be imprudent to call the party whose assertion is (by a mere preponderance of the evidence) disbelieved, a perjurer and a liar. And in these Title VII cases, the defendant is ordinarily not an individual but a company, which must rely upon the statement of an employee—often a relatively low-level employee—as to the central fact; and that central fact is not a physical occurrence, but rather that employee's state of mind. To say that the company which in good faith introduces such testimony, or even the testifying employee himself, becomes a liar and a perjurer when the testimony is not believed, is nothing short of absurd. . . .

We reaffirm today what we said in *Aikens*:

[T]he question facing triers of fact in discrimination cases is both sensitive and difficult. The prohibitions against discrimination contained in the Civil Rights Act of 1964 reflect an important national policy. There will seldom be 'eyewitness' testimony as to the employer's mental processes. But none of this means that trial courts or reviewing courts should treat discrimination differently from other ultimate questions of fact. Nor should they make their inquiry even more difficult by applying legal rules which were devised to govern 'the basic allocation of burdens and order of presentation of proof,' *Burdine*, 450 U.S., at 252, in deciding this ultimate question. 460 U.S., at 716.

The judgment of the Court of Appeals is reversed, and the case is remanded for further proceedings consistent with this opinion.

It is so ordered.

■ JUSTICE SOUTER, with whom JUSTICE WHITE, JUSTICE BLACKMUN, and JUSTICE STEVENS join, dissenting.

. . . Proof of a prima facie case thus serves as a catalyst obligating the employer to step forward with an explanation for its actions. St. Mary's, in this case, used this opportunity to provide two reasons for its treatment of Hicks: the severity and accumulation of rule infractions he had allegedly committed.

The Court emphasizes that the employer's obligation at this stage is only a burden of production, and that, if the employer meets the burden, the presumption entitling the plaintiff to judgment "drops from the case." This much is certainly true, but the obligation also serves an important function neglected by the majority, in requiring the employer "to frame the factual issue with sufficient clarity so that the plaintiff will have a full and fair opportunity to demonstrate pretext." The employer, in other words, has a "burden of production" that gives it the right to choose the scope of the factual issues to be resolved by the factfinder. But investing the employer with this choice has no point unless the scope it chooses binds the employer as well as the plaintiff. Nor does it make sense to tell the employer, as this Court has done, that its explanation of legitimate reasons "must be clear and reasonably specific," if the factfinder can rely on a reason not clearly articulated, or on one not articulated at all, to rule in favor of the employer. Id. at 258; *see* id. at 255, n.9 ("An articulation not admitted into evidence will not suffice").

Once the employer chooses the battleground in this manner, "the factual inquiry proceeds to a new level of specificity." Id. at 255. During this final, more specific inquiry, the employer has no burden to prove that its proffered reasons are true; rather, the plaintiff must prove by a preponderance of the evidence that the proffered reasons are pretextual. *McDonnell Douglas* makes it clear that if the plaintiff fails to show "pretext," the challenged employment action "must stand." 411 U.S., at 807. If, on the other hand, the plaintiff carries his burden of showing "pretext," the court "must order a prompt and appropriate remedy." Or, as we said in *Burdine*: "[The plaintiff] now must have the opportunity to demonstrate that the proffered reason was not the true reason for the employment decision. This burden now merges with the ultimate burden of persuading the court that [the plaintiff] has been the victim of intentional discrimination." 450 U.S., at 256. *Burdine* drives home the point that the case has proceeded to "a new level of specificity" by explaining that the plaintiff can meet his burden of persuasion in either of two ways: "either directly by persuading the court that a discriminatory reason more likely motivated the employer or indirectly by showing that the employer's proffered explanation is unworthy of credence." Ibid.; *see Aikens*, 460 U.S., at 716 (quoting this language from *Burdine*); id. at 717–718 (Blackmun, J., joined by Brennan, J., concurring); *see also Price Waterhouse v. Hopkins,* 490 U.S. 228, 287–289 (1989) (Kennedy, J., dissenting) (discussing these "two alternative methods" and relying on Justice Blackmun's concurrence in *Aikens*). That the plaintiff can succeed simply by showing that "the employer's proffered explanation is unworthy of credence" indicates that the case has been narrowed to the question whether the employer's proffered reasons are pretextual. Thus, because Hicks carried his burden of persuasion by showing that St. Mary's proffered reasons were "unworthy of credence," the Court of Appeals properly concluded that he was entitled to judgment.

The majority's scheme greatly disfavors Title VII plaintiffs without the good luck to have direct evidence of discriminatory intent. The Court repeats the truism that the plaintiff has the "ultimate burden" of proving discrimination without ever facing the practical question of how the plaintiff without such direct evidence can meet this burden. *Burdine* provides the answer, telling us that such a plaintiff may succeed in meeting his ultimate burden of proving discrimination "indirectly by showing that the employer's proffered explanation is unworthy of credence." 450 U.S. at 256; *see Aikens, supra,* at 716; id. at 717–718 (Blackmun, J., joined by Brennan, J., concurring). The possibility of some practical procedure for addressing what *Burdine* calls indirect proof is crucial to the success of most Title VII claims, for the simple reason that employers who discriminate are not likely to announce their discriminatory motive. And yet, under the majority's scheme, a victim of discrimination lacking direct evidence will now be saddled with the tremendous disadvantage of having to confront, not the defined task of proving the employer's stated reasons to be false, but the amorphous requirement of disproving all possible nondiscriminatory reasons that a factfinder might find lurking in the record. In the Court's own words, the plaintiff must "disprove all other reasons suggested, no matter how vaguely, in the record."

While the Court appears to acknowledge that a plaintiff will have the task of disproving even vaguely suggested reasons, and while it recognizes the need for "[c]larity regarding the requisite elements of proof," it nonetheless gives conflicting signals about the scope of its holding in this case. In one passage, the Court states that although proof of the falsity of the employer's proffered reasons does not "compe[l] judgment for the plaintiff," such evidence, without more, "will permit the trier of fact to infer the ultimate fact of intentional discrimination." (emphasis omitted). The same view is implicit in the Court's decision to remand this case, keeping Hicks's chance of winning a judgment alive although he has done no more (in addition to proving his prima facie case) than show that the reasons proffered by St. Mary's are unworthy of credence. But other language in the Court's opinion supports a more extreme conclusion, that proof of the falsity of the employer's articulated reasons will not even be sufficient to sustain judgment for the plaintiff. For example, the Court twice states that the plaintiff must show "both that the reason was false, and that discrimination was the real reason." In addition, in summing up its reading of our earlier cases, the Court states that "[I]t is not enough . . . to disbelieve the employer." (emphasis omitted). This "pretext-plus" approach would turn *Burdine* on its head, and it would result in summary judgment for the employer in the many cases where the plaintiff has no evidence beyond that required to prove a prima facie case and to show that the employer's articulated reasons are unworthy of credence. Cf. *Carter v. Duncan-Huggins, Ltd.,* 727 F.2d 1225, 1245 (1984) (Scalia, J., dissenting) ("[I]n order to get to the jury the plaintiff would . . . have to introduce some evidence . . . that the *basis* for [the] discriminatory treatment was race") (emphasis in original). *See* generally Lanctot, The Defendant Lies and the Plaintiff Loses: The Fallacy of the "Pretext-Plus" Rule in Employment Discrimination Cases, 43 Hastings L. J. 57 (1991) (criticizing the "pretext-plus" approach).

The Court fails to explain, moreover, under either interpretation of its holding, why proof that the employer's articulated reasons are "unpersuasive, or even obviously contrived," falls short. Under *McDonnell Douglas* and *Burdine*, there would be no reason in this situation to question discriminatory intent. The plaintiff has raised an inference of discrimination (though no longer a presumption) through proof of his prima facie case, and as we noted in *Burdine*, this circumstantial proof of discrimination can also be used by the plaintiff to show pretext. Such proof is merely strengthened by showing, through use of further evidence, that the employer's articulated reasons are false, since "common experience" tells us that it is "more likely than not" that the employer who lies is simply trying to cover up the illegality alleged by the plaintiff. *Furnco*, 438 U.S., at 577. Unless *McDonnell Douglas*'s command to structure and limit the case as the employer chooses is to be rendered meaningless, we should not look beyond the employer's lie by assuming the possible existence of other reasons the employer might have proffered without lying. By telling the factfinder to keep digging in cases where the plaintiff's proof of pretext turns on showing the employer's reasons to be unworthy of credence, the majority rejects the very point of the *McDonnell Douglas* rule requiring the scope of the factual inquiry to be limited, albeit in a manner chosen by the employer. What is more, the Court is throwing out the rule for the benefit of employers who have been found to have given false evidence in a court of law. There is simply no justification for favoring these employers by exempting them from responsibility for lies. It may indeed be true that such employers have nondiscriminatory reasons for their actions, but ones so shameful that they wish to conceal them. One can understand human frailty and the natural desire to conceal it, however, without finding in it a justification to dispense with an orderly procedure for getting at "the elusive factual question of intentional discrimination." *Burdine*, 450 U.S., at 255, n.8.

With no justification in the employer's favor, the consequences to actual and potential Title VII litigants stand out sharply. To the extent that workers like Melvin Hicks decide not to sue, given the uncertainties they would face under the majority's scheme, the legislative purpose in adopting Title VII will be frustrated. To the extent such workers nevertheless decide to press forward, the result will likely be wasted time, effort, and money for all concerned. Under the scheme announced today, any conceivable explanation for the employer's actions that might be suggested by the evidence, however unrelated to the employer's articulated reasons, must be addressed by a plaintiff who does not wish to risk losing. Since the Court does not say whether a trial court may limit the introduction of evidence at trial to what is relevant to the employer's articulated reasons, and since the employer can win on the possibility of an unstated reason, the scope of admissible evidence at trial presumably includes any evidence potentially relevant to "the ultimate question" of discrimination, unlimited by the employer's stated reasons. If so, Title VII trials promise to be tedious affairs. But even if, on the contrary, relevant evidence is still somehow to be limited by reference to the employer's reasons, however "vaguely" articulated, the careful plaintiff will have to anticipate all the side issues that might arise even in a more limited evidentiary presentation. Thus, in either case, pretrial discovery will become more extensive and wide-ranging (if the plaintiff can afford it), for a much wider set of facts could prove to be both relevant and important at trial. The majority's scheme, therefore, will promote longer trials and more pre-trial discovery, threatening increased expense and delay in Title VII litigation for both plaintiffs and defendants, and increased burdens on the judiciary.

The enhancement of a Title VII plaintiff's burden wrought by the Court's opinion is exemplified in this case. Melvin Hicks was denied any opportunity, much less a full and fair one, to demonstrate that the supposedly nondiscriminatory explanation for his demotion and termination, the personal animosity of his immediate supervisor, was unworthy of credence. In fact, the District Court did not find that personal animosity (which it failed to recognize might be racially motivated) was the true reason for the actions St. Mary's took; it adduced this reason simply as a possibility in explaining that Hicks had failed to prove "that the crusade [to terminate him] was racially rather than personally motivated." It is hardly surprising that Hicks failed to prove anything about this supposed personal crusade, since St. Mary's never articulated such an explanation for Hicks's discharge, and since the person who allegedly conducted this crusade denied at trial any personal difficulties between himself and Hicks. While the majority may well be troubled about the unfair treatment of Hicks in this instance and thus remands for review of whether the District Court's factual conclusions were clearly erroneous, the majority provides Hicks with no opportunity to produce evidence showing that the District Court's hypothesized explanation, first articulated six months after trial, is unworthy of credence. Whether Melvin Hicks wins or loses on remand, many plaintiffs in a like position will surely lose under the scheme adopted by the Court today, unless they possess both prescience and resources beyond what this Court has previously required Title VII litigants to employ.

Because I see no reason why Title VII interpretation should be driven by concern for employers who are too ashamed to be honest in court, at the expense of victims of discrimination who do not happen to have direct evidence of discriminatory intent, I respectfully dissent.

NOTES AND QUESTIONS

1.   ***The*** McDonnell Douglas ***Proof Framework.*** The Court in *St. Mary's Honor Center v. Hicks* (hereinafter *Hicks*) explains the *McDonnell Douglas* proof framework, which sets forth a three-step approach for the presentation of evidence in disparate treatment cases under Title VII (and which courts also apply to Section 1981). First, the plaintiff must establish a prima facie case, *i.e.,* sufficient facts to support an inference of discrimination. In *McDonnell Douglas* the Court held that an employee who claims he was not hired because of his race can establish a prima facie case by showing:

> (i) that he belongs to a racial minority group; (ii) that he applied and was qualified for a job for which the employer was seeking applicants; (iii) that, despite his qualifications, he was rejected; and (iv) that, after his rejection, the position remained open and the employer continued to seek applicants from persons of complainant's qualifications.

If the plaintiff-employee satisfies the prima facie case, the burden of production shifts to the employer to articulate a nondiscriminatory explanation for the adverse employment decision. If the employer does so, then the case goes to the fact-finder, whether a jury or court in a bench trial, to decide whether the employee has proven by a preponderance of the evidence that the employer's explanation is a pretext for race discrimination.

2.   ***The Court's Holding.*** In *Hicks*, the plaintiff satisfied his prima facie case (it having been modified to fit the circumstances of a discriminatory discharge claim rather than a failure to hire claim). The defendant then offered nondiscriminatory explanations for discharging him, and the plaintiff ultimately convinced the trial judge that the defendant's offered explanations were false. The trial judge nonetheless ruled against Hicks because, although the judge disbelieved the defendant's explanations, he did not believe Hicks was discharged because of his race but rather because his boss, John Powell, had a personal grudge against him. The judge's finding, moreover, was contrary to the position of the defendant, St. Mary's Honor Center, which had denied at trial that Powell bore any personal animosity toward Hicks. The Supreme Court upheld the trial court's ruling, holding that a plaintiff who meets his prima facie case and also proves the defendant's explanations are false is still not entitled to prevail if the trier of fact finds that the reason for the discharge was some other, nonracial reason supported by evidence in the record. Four dissenting justices agreed with the Court of Appeals that the plaintiff's proof that the defendant's explanations were false entitled him to a ruling that the actual reason was race.

What's your reaction to the Court's holding and reasoning? Should Hicks have won given that he persuasively disproved all of the defendant's proffered explanations for Hicks' discharge? Why or why not?

On the specific facts of *Hicks*, was the trial judge right in concluding that Powell's personal animosity toward Hicks was a nonracial reason? Note also, in footnote 2 of the opinion, that the trial judge's finding that Hicks was not discharged because of race was based on the presence of blacks on the review board that had recommended disciplining Hicks, and because "the number of black employees at St. Mary's remained constant." To what extent do these facts undermine Hicks' claim that Powell's adverse treatment of him was motivated by race?

3.   *Exercise: If You Were the Trial Judge.* In the *Hicks* case, the trial judge determined that it was the employer's personal animus, not racial prejudice, which precipitated Hicks' dismissal. If you were the finder of fact, what evidence would you look for to determine whether the defendant's explanation was pretextual? What facts would you emphasize? How would they apply in the three-step process in this case to determine the legitimacy of the claim?

4.   *The Relevance of Statistics.* Justice Scalia's hypothetical in *Hicks* relied on statistics:

> Assume that 40% of a business' work force are members of a particular minority group, a group which comprises only 10% of the relevant labor market. An applicant, who is a member of that group, applies for an opening for which he is minimally qualified, but is rejected by a hiring officer of that same minority group, and the search to fill the opening continues.

Scalia believes that these hypothetical statistics indicate that the employer is unlikely to have discriminated against a black employee. Is his assumption sound? To what extent can group-based statistics demonstrate that an employer has not discriminated against a particular employee? Also, doesn't Scalia's hypothetical assume that black people are less likely to discriminate against black people? Isn't that the kind of stereotype he typically criticizes?

Conversely, to what extent can statistics prove that an employer *did* discriminate? The Court first addressed this question in *Int'l Brotherhood of Teamsters v. United States*, 431 U.S. 324 (1977). The United States sued a trucking company and its union for intentional discrimination in hiring drivers for long distance hauls. The company had substantial numbers of black and Latino drivers in the units that made short hauls, consistent with the composition of the general population, but it had virtually no drivers of color in the higher paying, long-distance units. The company had no explicit policy of segregating drivers. It argued that it was improper for the court to permit statistical disparities to support an inference of discrimination because, first, such disparities need not result from discrimination and, second, permitting statistics to prove discrimination would force companies to use racial quotas, something Title VII explicitly does not require. Rejecting this argument, the Supreme Court permitted statistics to support a prima facie case of discrimination, subject to rebuttal by the company, reasoning that:

Statistics showing racial or ethnic imbalance are probative . . . only because such imbalance is often a telltale sign of purposeful discrimination; absent explanation, it is ordinarily to be expected that nondiscriminatory hiring practices will in time result in a work force more or less representative of the racial and ethnic composition of the population in the community from which employees are hired. Evidence of longlasting and gross disparity between the composition of a work force and that of the general population thus may be significant even though . . . Title VII imposes no requirement that a work force mirror the general population.

Id. at 339, n.20. The Court in *Teamsters* did not provide much guidance on how to properly use statistics in the employment context because the disparities were so stark, with some long-haul units having (in the words of one of the Justices) the "inexorable zero" drivers of color despite the diversity of the short-haul units and of the local population. In contrast, the statistical disparities in the next case were not as stark so the Court needed to grapple more thoroughly with their relevance and probative value.

Hazelwood School District v. United States

Supreme Court of the United States, 1977.
433 U.S. 299.

■ JUSTICE STEWART delivered the opinion of the Court.

The petitioner Hazelwood School District covers 78 square miles in the northern part of St. Louis County, Mo. In 1973 the Attorney General brought this lawsuit against Hazelwood and various of its officials, alleging that they were engaged in a "pattern or practice" of employment discrimination in violation of Title VII of the Civil Rights Act of 1964. The complaint asked for an injunction requiring Hazelwood to cease its discriminatory practices, to take affirmative steps to obtain qualified Negro faculty members, and to offer employment and give backpay to victims of past illegal discrimination.

Hazelwood was formed from 13 rural school districts between 1949 and 1951 by a process of annexation. By the 1967–1968 school year, 17,550 students were enrolled in the district, of whom only 59 were Negro; the number of Negro pupils increased to 576 of 25,166 in 1972–1973, a total of just over 2%.

From the beginning, Hazelwood followed relatively unstructured procedures in hiring its teachers. Every person requesting an application for a teaching position was sent one, and completed applications were submitted to a central personnel office, where they were kept on file. During the early 1960's the personnel office notified all applicants whenever a teaching position became available, but as the number of applications on file increased in the late 1960's and early 1970's, this practice was no longer considered feasible. The personnel office thus began the practice of selecting anywhere from 3 to 10 applicants for interviews at the school where the vacancy existed. The personnel office did not substantively screen the applicants in determining which of them to send for interviews, other than to ascertain that each applicant, if selected, would be eligible for state certification by the time he began the job. Generally, those who had most recently submitted applications were most likely to be chosen for interviews.

Interviews were conducted by a department chairman, program coordinator, or the principal at the school where the teaching vacancy existed. Although those conducting the interviews did fill out forms rating the applicants in a number of respects, it is undisputed that each school principal possessed virtually unlimited discretion in hiring teachers for his school. The only general guidance given to the principals was to hire the "most competent" person available, and such intangibles as "personality, disposition, appearance, poise, voice, articulation, and ability to deal with people" counted heavily. The principal's choice was routinely honored by Hazelwood's Superintendent and the Board of Education.

In the early 1960's Hazelwood found it necessary to recruit new teachers, and for that purpose members of its staff visited a number of colleges and universities in Missouri and bordering States. All the institutions visited were predominantly white, and Hazelwood did not seriously recruit at either of the two predominantly Negro four-year colleges in Missouri. As a buyer's market began to develop for public school teachers, Hazelwood curtailed its recruiting efforts. For the 1971–1972 school year, 3,127 persons applied for only 234 teaching vacancies; for the 1972–1973 school year, there were 2,373 applications for 282 vacancies. A number of the applicants who were not hired were Negroes.

Hazelwood hired its first Negro teacher in 1969. The number of Negro faculty members gradually increased in successive years: 6 of 957 in the 1970 school year; 16 of 1,107 by the end of the 1972 school year; 22 of 1,231 in the 1973 school year. By comparison, according to 1970 census figures, of more than 19,000 teachers employed in that year in the St. Louis area, 15.4% were Negro. That percentage figure included the St. Louis City School District, which in recent years has followed a policy of attempting to maintain a 50% Negro teaching staff. Apart from that school district, 5.7% of the teachers in the county were Negro in 1970.

Drawing upon these historic facts, the Government mounted its "pattern or practice" attack in the District Court upon four different fronts. It adduced evidence of (1) a history of alleged racially discriminatory practices, (2) statistical disparities in hiring, (3) the standardless and largely subjective hiring procedures, and (4) specific instances of alleged discrimination against 55 unsuccessful Negro applicants for teaching jobs. Hazelwood offered virtually no additional evidence in response, relying instead on evidence introduced by the

Government, perceived deficiencies in the Government's case, and its own officially promulgated policy "to hire all teachers on the basis of training, preparation and recommendations, regardless of race, color or creed."

The District Court ruled that the Government had failed to establish a pattern or practice of discrimination. The court was unpersuaded by the alleged history of discrimination, noting that no dual school system had ever existed in Hazelwood. The statistics showing that relatively small numbers of Negroes were employed as teachers were found nonprobative, on the ground that the percentage of Negro pupils in Hazelwood was similarly small. The court found nothing illegal or suspect in the teacher-hiring procedures that Hazelwood had followed. Finally, the court reviewed the evidence in the 55 cases of alleged individual discrimination, and after stating that the burden of proving intentional discrimination was on the Government, it found that this burden had not been sustained in a single instance. Hence, the court entered judgment for the defendants.

The Court of Appeals for the Eighth Circuit reversed. After suggesting that the District Court had assigned inadequate weight to evidence of discriminatory conduct on the part of Hazelwood before the effective date of Title VII, the Court of Appeals rejected the trial court's analysis of the statistical data as resting on an irrelevant comparison of Negro teachers to Negro pupils in Hazelwood. The proper comparison, in the appellate court's view, was one between Negro teachers in Hazelwood and Negro teachers in the relevant labor market area. Selecting St. Louis County and St. Louis City as the relevant area, the Court of Appeals compared the 1970 census figures, showing that 15.4% of teachers in that area were Negro, to the racial composition of Hazelwood's teaching staff. In the 1972–1973 and 1973–1974 school years, only 1.4% and 1.8%, respectively, of Hazelwood's teachers were Negroes. This statistical disparity, particularly when viewed against the background of the teacher-hiring procedures that Hazelwood had followed, was held to constitute a prima facie case of a pattern or practice of racial discrimination.

In addition, the Court of Appeals reasoned that the trial court had erred in failing to measure the 55 instances in which Negro applicants were denied jobs against the four-part standard for establishing a prima facie case of individual discrimination set out in this Court's opinion in *McDonnell Douglas Corp. v. Green,* 411 U.S. 792, 802. Applying that standard, the appellate court found 16 cases of individual discrimination which "buttressed" the statistical proof. Because Hazelwood had not rebutted the Government's prima facie case of a pattern or practice of racial discrimination, the Court of Appeals directed judgment for the Government and prescribed the remedial order to be entered.

We granted certiorari to consider a substantial question affecting the enforcement of a pervasive federal law.

The petitioners primarily attack the judgment of the Court of Appeals for its reliance on "undifferentiated work force statistics to find an unrebutted prima facie case of employment discrimination." The question they raise, in short, is whether a basic component in the Court of Appeals' finding of a pattern or practice of discrimination—the comparatively small percentage of Negro employees in Hazelwood's teaching staff—was lacking in probative force.

This Court's recent consideration in *International Brotherhood of Teamsters v. United States,* 431 U.S. 324, of the role of statistics in pattern-or-practice suits under Title VII provides substantial guidance in evaluating the arguments advanced by the petitioners. In that case we stated that it is the Government's burden to "establish by a preponderance of the evidence that racial discrimination was the (employer's) standard operating procedure—the regular rather than the unusual practice." We also noted that statistics can be an important source of proof in employment discrimination cases, since,

> absent explanation, it is ordinarily to be expected that nondiscriminatory hiring practices will in time result in a work force more or less representative of the racial and ethnic composition of the population in the community from which employees are hired. Evidence of long-lasting and gross disparity between the composition of a work force and that of the general population thus may be significant even though § 703(j) makes clear that Title VII imposes no requirement that a work force mirror the general population. *Id.* at 340 n.20

Where gross statistical disparities can be shown, they alone may in a proper case constitute prima facie proof of a pattern or practice of discrimination. *Teamsters, supra,* 431 U.S., at 339.

There can be no doubt, in light of the *Teamsters* case, that the District Court's comparison of Hazelwood's teacher work force to its student population fundamentally misconceived the role of statistics in employment discrimination cases. The Court of Appeals was correct in the view that a proper comparison was between the racial composition of Hazelwood's teaching staff and the racial composition of the qualified public school teacher population in the relevant labor market. *See Teamsters, supra,* at 337–338, and n.17. The percentage of Negroes on Hazelwood's teaching staff in 1972–1973 was 1.4% and in 1973–1974 it was 1.8%. By contrast, the percentage of qualified Negro teachers in the area was, according to the 1970 census, at least 5.7%.[3] Although these

---

[3] As is discussed below, the Government contends that a comparative figure of 15.4%, rather than 5.7% is the appropriate one. But even assuming arguendo that the 5.7% figure urged by the petitioners is correct, the disparity between that figure and the percentage of Negroes on Hazelwood's teaching staff would be more than fourfold for the 1972–1973 school year, and

430   EMPLOYMENT DISCRIMINATION   CHAPTER 6

differences were on their face substantial, the Court of Appeals erred in
substituting its judgment for that of the District Court and holding that
the Government had conclusively proved its "pattern or practice" lawsuit.

The Court of Appeals totally disregarded the possibility that this
prima facie statistical proof in the record might at the trial court level be
rebutted by statistics dealing with Hazelwood's hiring after it became
subject to Title VII. Racial discrimination by public employers was not
made illegal under Title VII until March 24, 1972. A public employer who
from that date forward made all its employment decisions in a wholly
nondiscriminatory way would not violate Title VII even if it had formerly
maintained an all-white work force by purposefully excluding Negroes.
For this reason, the Court cautioned in the *Teamsters* opinion that once
a prima facie case has been established by statistical work-force
disparities, the employer must be given an opportunity to show that "the
claimed discriminatory pattern is a product of pre-Act hiring rather than
unlawful post-Act discrimination." 431 U.S., at 360.

The record in this case showed that for the 1972–1973 school year,
Hazelwood hired 282 new teachers, 10 whom (3.5%) were Negroes; for
the following school year it hired 123 new teachers, 5 of whom (4.1%)
were Negroes. Over the two-year period, Negroes constituted a total of
15 of the 405 new teachers hired (3.7%). Although the Court of Appeals
briefly mentioned these data in reciting the facts, it wholly ignored them
in discussing whether the Government had shown a pattern or practice
of discrimination. And it gave no consideration at all to the possibility
that post-Act data as to the number of Negroes hired compared to the
total number of Negro applicants might tell a totally different story.

The difference between these figures may well be important; the
disparity between 3.7% (the percentage of Negro teachers hired by
Hazelwood in 1972–1973 and 1973–1974) and 5.7% may be sufficiently
small to weaken the Government's other proof, while the disparity
between 3.7% and 15.4% may be sufficiently large to reinforce it.[4] In

---

threefold for the 1973–1974 school year. A precise method of measuring the significance of such
statistical disparities was explained in *Castaneda v. Partida,* 430 U.S. 482, 496–97 n.17. It
involves calculation of the "standard deviation" as a measure of predicted fluctuations from the
expected value of a sample. Using the 5.7% figure as the basis for calculating the expected value,
the expected number of Negroes on the Hazelwood teaching staff would be roughly 63 in 1972–
1973 and 70 in 1973–1974. The observed number in those years was 16 and 22, respectively.
The difference between the observed and expected values was more than six standard deviations
in 1972–1973 and more than five standard deviations in 1973–1974. The Court in *Castaneda*
noted that "[a]s a general rule for such large samples, if the difference between the expected
value and the observed number is greater than two or three standard deviations," then the
hypothesis that teachers were hired without regard to race would be suspect.

[4] Indeed, under the statistical methodology explained in *Castaneda v. Partida,* involving
the calculation of the standard deviation as a measure of predicted fluctuations, the difference
between using 15.4% and 5.7% as the areawide figure would be significant. If the 15.4% figure
is taken as the basis for comparison, the expected number of Negro teachers hired by Hazelwood
in 1972–1973 would be 43 (rather than the actual figure of 10) of a total of 282, a difference of
more than five standard deviations; the expected number of 1973–1974 would be 19 (rather than
the actual figure 5) of a total of 123, a difference of more than three standard deviations. For
the two years combined, the difference between the observed number of 15 Negro teachers hired

determining which of the two figures—or, very possibly, what intermediate figure—provides the most accurate basis for comparison to the hiring figures at Hazelwood, it will be necessary to evaluate such considerations as (i) whether the racially based hiring policies of the St. Louis City School District were in effect as far back as 1970, the year in which the census figures were taken; (ii) to what extent those policies have changed the racial composition of that district's teaching staff from what it would otherwise have been; (iii) to what extent St. Louis' recruitment policies have diverted to the city, teachers who might otherwise have applied to Hazelwood; (iv) to what extent Negro teachers employed by the city would prefer employment in other districts such as Hazelwood; and (v) what the experience in other school districts in St. Louis County indicates about the validity of excluding the City School District from the relevant labor market.

It is thus clear that a determination of the appropriate comparative figures in this case will depend upon further evaluation by the trial court. As this Court admonished in *Teamsters*: "[S]tatistics . . . come in infinite variety. . . . [T]heir usefulness depends on all of the surrounding facts and circumstances." Only the trial court is in a position to make the appropriate determination after further findings. And only after such a determination is made can a foundation be established for deciding whether or not Hazelwood engaged in a pattern or practice of racial discrimination in its employment practices in violation of the law.

We hold, therefore, that the Court of Appeals erred in disregarding the post-Act hiring statistics in the record, and that it should have remanded the case to the District Court for further findings as to the relevant labor market area and for an ultimate determination of whether Hazelwood engaged in a pattern or practice of employment discrimination after March 24, 1972. Accordingly, the judgment is vacated, and the case is remanded to the District Court for further proceedings consistent with this opinion.

It is so ordered.

■ JUSTICE BRENNAN, concurring.

I join the Court's opinion. Similarly to our decision in *Dayton Board of Education v. Brinkman,* 433 U.S. 406, today's opinion revolves around

---

(of a total of 405) would vary from the expected number of 62 by more than six standard deviations. Because a fluctuation of more than two or three standard deviations would undercut the hypothesis that decisions were being made randomly with respect to race, 430 U.S., at 497 n.17, each of these statistical comparisons would reinforce rather than rebut the Government's other proof. If, however, the 5.7% areawide figure is used, the expected number of Negro teachers hired in 1972–1973 would be roughly 16, less than two standard deviations from the observed number of 10; for 1973–1974, the expected value would be roughly seven, less than one standard deviation from the observed value of 5; and for the two years combined, the expected value of 23 would be less than two standard deviations from the observed total of 15. A more precise method of analyzing these statistics confirms the results of the standard deviation analysis. See F. Mosteller, R. Rourke, & G. Thomas, Probability with Statistical Applications 494 (2d ed. 1970).

the relative factfinding roles of district courts and courts of appeals. It should be plain, however, that the liberal substantive standards for establishing a Title VII violation, including the usefulness of statistical proof, are reconfirmed.

In the present case, the District Court had adopted a wholly inappropriate legal standard of discrimination, and therefore did not evaluate the factual record before it in a meaningful way. This remand in effect orders it to do so. It is my understanding, as apparently it is Mr. Justice STEVENS', that the statistical inquiry mentioned by the Court and accompanying text, can be of no help to the Hazelwood School Board in rebutting the Government's evidence of discrimination. Indeed, even if the relative comparison market is found to be 5.7% rather than 15.4% black, the applicable statistical analysis at most will not serve to bolster the Government's case. This obviously is of no aid to Hazelwood in meeting its burden of proof. Nonetheless I think that the remand directed by the Court is appropriate and will allow the parties to address these figures and calculations with greater care and precision. I also agree that given the misapplication of governing legal principles by the District Court, Hazelwood reasonably should be given the opportunity to come forward with more focused and specific applicant-flow data in the hope of answering the Government's prima facie case. If, as presently seems likely, reliable applicant data are found to be lacking, the conclusion reached by my Brother Stevens will inevitably be forthcoming.

■ JUSTICE WHITE, concurring.

I join the Court's opinion . . . but with reservations with respect to the relative neglect of applicant pool data in finding a prima facie case of employment discrimination and heavy reliance on the disparity between the areawide percentage of black public school teachers and the percentage of blacks on Hazelwood's teaching staff. Since the issue is whether Hazelwood discriminated against blacks in hiring after Title VII became applicable to it in 1972, perhaps the Government should have looked initially to Hazelwood's hiring practices in the 1972–1973 and 1973–1974 academic years with respect to the available applicant pool, rather than to history and to comparative work-force statistics from other school districts. Indeed, there is evidence in the record suggesting that Hazelwood, with a black enrollment of only 2%, hired a higher percentage of black applicants than of white applicants for these two years. The Court's opinion, of course, permits Hazelwood to introduce applicant pool data on remand in order to rebut the prima facie case of a discriminatory pattern or practice. This may be the only fair and realistic allocation of the evidence burden, but arguably the United States should have been required to adduce evidence as to the applicant pool before it was entitled to its prima facie presumption. At least it might have been required to present some defensible ground for believing that the racial composition of Hazelwood's applicant pool was roughly the same as that for the school districts in the general area, before relying on comparative work-force data to establish its prima facie case.

■ JUSTICE STEVENS, dissenting.

The basic framework in a pattern-or-practice suit brought by the Government under Title VII of the Civil Rights Act of 1964 is the same as that in any other lawsuit. The plaintiff has the burden of proving a prima facie case; if he does so, the burden of rebutting that case shifts to the defendant. In this case, since neither party complains that any relevant evidence was excluded, our task is to decide (1) whether the Government's evidence established a prima facie case; and (2), if so, whether the remaining evidence is sufficient to carry Hazelwood's burden of rebutting that prima facie case.

I

The first question is clearly answered by the Government's statistical evidence, its historical evidence, and its evidence relating to specific acts of discrimination.

One-third of the teachers hired by Hazelwood resided in the city of St. Louis at the time of their initial employment. As Mr. Justice Clark explained in his opinion for the Court of Appeals, it was therefore appropriate to treat the city, as well as the county, as part of the relevant labor market. In that market, 15% of the teachers were black. In the Hazelwood District at the time of trial less than 2% of the teachers were black. An even more telling statistic is that after Title VII became applicable to it, only 3.7% of the new teachers hired by Hazelwood were black. Proof of these gross disparities was in itself sufficient to make out a prima facie case of discrimination. *See International Brotherhood of Teamsters v. United States,* 431 U.S. 324, 339 (1977); *Castaneda v. Partida,* 430 U.S. 482, 494–498.

As a matter of history, Hazelwood employed no black teachers until 1969. Both before and after the 1972 amendment making the statute applicable to public school districts, petitioner used a standardless and largely subjective hiring procedure. Since "relevant aspects of the decisionmaking process had undergone little change," it is proper to infer that the pre-Act policy of preferring white teachers continued to influence Hazelwood's hiring practices.

The inference of discrimination was corroborated by post-Act evidence that Hazelwood had refused to hire 16 qualified black applicants for racial reasons. Taking the Government's evidence as a whole, there can be no doubt about the sufficiency of its prima facie case.

II

Hazelwood "offered virtually no additional evidence in response." It challenges the Government's statistical analysis by claiming that the city of St. Louis should be excluded from the relevant market and pointing out that only 5.7% of the teachers in the county (excluding the city) were black. It further argues that the city's policy of trying to maintain a 50% black teaching staff diverted teachers from the county to the city. There are two separate reasons why these arguments are insufficient: they are not supported by the evidence; even if true, they do not overcome the Government's case.

The petitioners offered no evidence concerning wage differentials, commuting problems, or the relative advantages of teaching in an inner-city school as opposed to a suburban school. Without any such evidence in the record, it is difficult to understand why the simple fact that the city was the source of a third of Hazelwood's faculty should not be sufficient to demonstrate that it is a part of the relevant market. The city's policy of attempting to maintain a 50/50 ratio clearly does not undermine that conclusion, particularly when the record reveals no shortage of qualified black applicants in either Hazelwood or other suburban school districts. Surely not all of the 2,000 black teachers employed by the city were unavailable for employment in Hazelwood at the time of their initial hire.

But even if it were proper to exclude the city of St. Louis from the market, the statistical evidence would still tend to prove discrimination. With the city excluded, 5.7% of the teachers in the remaining market were black. On the basis of a random selection, one would therefore expect 5.7% of the 405 teachers hired by Hazelwood in the 1972–1973 and 1973–1974 school years to have been black. But instead of 23 black teachers, Hazelwood hired only 15, less than two-thirds of the expected number. Without the benefit of expert testimony, I would hesitate to infer that the disparity between 23 and 15 is great enough, in itself, to prove discrimination. It is perfectly clear, however, that whatever probative force this disparity has, it tends to prove discrimination and does absolutely nothing in the way of carrying Hazelwood's burden of overcoming the Government's prima facie case.

Absolute precision in the analysis of market data is too much to expect. We may fairly assume that a nondiscriminatory selection process would have resulted in the hiring of somewhere between the 15% suggested by the Government and the 5.7% suggested by petitioners, or perhaps 30 or 40 black teachers, instead of the 15 actually hired. On that assumption, the Court of Appeals' determination that there were 16 individual cases of discriminatory refusal to hire black applicants in the post-1972 period seems remarkably accurate.

In sum, the Government is entitled to prevail on the present record. It proved a prima facie case, which Hazelwood failed to rebut. Why, then, should we burden a busy federal court with another trial? Hazelwood had an opportunity to offer evidence to dispute the 16 examples of racially motivated refusals to hire; but as the Court notes, the Court of Appeals has already "held that none of the 16 prima facie cases of individual discrimination had been rebutted by the petitioners." Hazelwood also had an opportunity to offer any evidence it could muster to show a change in hiring practices or to contradict the fair inference to be drawn from the statistical evidence. Instead, it "offered virtually no additional evidence in response."

Perhaps "a totally different story" might be told by other statistical evidence that was never presented. No lawsuit has ever been tried in which the losing party could not have pointed to a similar possibility. It is always possible to imagine more evidence which could have been offered, but at some point litigation must come to an end.

Rather than depart from well-established rules of procedure, I would affirm the judgment of the Court of Appeals. Since that judgment reflected a correct appraisal of the record, I see no reason to prolong this litigation with a remand neither side requested.

NOTES AND QUESTIONS

1. *The Relevant Statistical Disparity: Labor Market and Employer's Workforce.* In *Hazelwood*, the parties and Justices all agree that determining whether an employer discriminated in hiring entails an assessment of any disparity between the racial composition of the employer's work force (i.e., the pool of employees holding the particular job with respect to which the plaintiff alleges hiring discrimination) and the racial composition of the labor market (i.e., the pool of people who would be interested in, qualified for, and able to fill the job during the relevant time period). A work force composition that differs dramatically from that of the labor market could support an inference of discrimination. The parties and the Justices disagreed about how to define the labor market and the employer's work force. The following two Notes explore these questions.

2. *The Labor Market for* Hazelwood. The strategy for each party in a statistical case is clear. The employer seeks to define the labor market in a way that minimizes the percentage of racial minorities, thus decreasing the likelihood that minorities will be sufficiently underrepresented in the employer's work force to support an inference of discrimination. The plaintiff's incentive is the opposite: to define the labor market in a way that maximizes the percentage of minorities, and thereby increase the likelihood that minorities will seem suspiciously under-represented in the employer's work force. The main dispute in *Hazelwood* on this question was whether the labor market should include St. Louis, which is adjacent to Hazelwood. If St. Louis is included, as the United States argued, the percentage of minorities would be 15.4%. If St. Louis is excluded, as Hazelwood argued, the percentage of blacks in the labor market would be 5.7%. What arguments favor including St. Louis and what arguments favor excluding it? Are there reasons to believe that the percentage of black teachers in the St. Louis work force is related to the percentage of black teachers that would be interested in, qualified for, and able to work in the Hazelwood School District? As Justice Stevens observes, "[o]ne-third of the teachers hired by Hazelwood resided in the city of St. Louis at the time of their initial employment," *id.* at

315, and thus commuting distance is not a significant obstacle to working in Hazelwood. What else might explain why black teachers would work in St. Louis but not in Hazelwood other than discrimination by Hazelwood? How do the parties and justices define the labor market and why? How would you define the labor market?

3.   Hazelwood's *Work Force*. As, with the labor market, the strategy for the parties in defining the work force is equally clear. The employer seeks to define the work force in a way that *maximizes* the percentage of minorities, and the plaintiff seeks to define the work force in a way that *minimizes* the percentage of minorities. By this strategy, the employer and plaintiff seek, respectively, to minimize and maximize the disparity between the percentage of minorities in the labor market and the employer's work force. Based on the facts revealed in the opinions, what percentage best reflects the appropriate work force measure? What are the approaches suggested by the Justices and what justifies each approach? What concerns does each approach raise?

4.   *Exercise*. Divide into two groups, one that represents the United States and one that represents Hazelwood School District. Make arguments about how to define the labor market and the employer's work force. Anchor your arguments by the facts revealed in the case but also speculate about the facts that plausibly could justify defining the labor market and work force in a particular way. For example, if you represent the school district, offer plausible hypotheses as to why the disparity between black teachers in St. Louis and Hazelwood need not reflect discrimination by Hazelwood. Or, if you represent the United States, hypothesize why looking at the percentage of applications that Hazelwood received from black applicants does not fairly represent the percentage of willing and able blacks in the labor market.

B. DISPARATE IMPACT

Although the laws we are examining clearly prohibit most forms of *intentional* discrimination, it was initially unclear whether these laws also prohibited employment practices that had a discriminatory effect or "disparate impact" on a racial group without proof that the racial impact was intentional. Before reading the following case, pause to consider whether an employment practice or policy with a racially disparate impact should be unlawful, even if it is not racially motivated. Should the law at least require the employer to justify such practices as job-related? What if the racial impact of an employer's practice is foreseeable but the employer does not take reasonable steps to avoid the impact? What if the adverse racial impact of the employer's practice is known to the employer and could easily be avoided without compromising the employer's hiring goals?

Griggs v. Duke Power Co.

Supreme Court of the United States, 1971.
401 U.S. 424.

■ MR. CHIEF JUSTICE BURGER delivered the opinion of the Court.

We granted the writ in this case to resolve the question whether an employer is prohibited by the Civil Rights Act of 1964, Title VII, from requiring a high school education or passing of a standardized general intelligence test as a condition of employment in or transfer to jobs when (a) neither standard is shown to be significantly related to successful job performance, (b) both requirements operate to disqualify Negroes at a substantially higher rate than white applicants, and (c) the jobs in question formerly had been filled only by white employees as part of a longstanding practice of giving preference to whites.

[T]his proceeding was brought by a group of incumbent Negro employees against Duke Power Company. All the petitioners are employed at the Company's Dan River Steam Station, a power generating facility located at Draper, North Carolina. At the time this action was instituted, the Company had 95 employees at the Dan River Station, 14 of whom were Negroes; 13 of these are petitioners here.

The District Court found that prior to July 2, 1965, the effective date of the Civil Rights Act of 1964, the Company openly discriminated on the basis of race in the hiring and assigning of employees at its Dan River plant. The plant was organized into five operating departments: (1) Labor, (2) Coal Handling, (3) Operations, (4) Maintenance, and (5) Laboratory and Test. Negroes were employed only in the Labor Department where the highest paying jobs paid less than the lowest paying jobs in the other four 'operating' departments in which only whites were employed. Promotions were normally made within each department on the basis of job seniority. Transferees into a department usually began in the lowest position.

In 1955 the Company instituted a policy of requiring a high school education for initial assignment to any department except Labor, and for transfer from the Coal Handling to any 'inside' department (Operations, Maintenance, or Laboratory). When the Company abandoned its policy of restricting Negroes to the Labor Department in 1965, completion of high school also was made a prerequisite to transfer from Labor to any other department. From the time the high school requirement was instituted to the time of trial, however, white employees hired before the time of the high school education requirement continued to perform satisfactorily and achieve promotions in the 'operating' departments.

The Company added a further requirement for new employees on July 2, 1965, the date on which Title VII became effective. To qualify for placement in any but the Labor Department it become necessary to register satisfactory scores on two professionally prepared aptitude tests, as well as to have a high school education. Completion of high school alone continued to render employees eligible for transfer to the four desirable departments from which Negroes had been excluded if the incumbent had been employed prior to the time of the new requirement. In September 1965 the Company began to permit incumbent employees who lacked a high school education to qualify for transfer from Labor or Coal Handling to an 'inside' job by passing two tests—the Wonderlic Personnel Test, which purports to measure general intelligence, and the Bennett Mechanical Comprehension Test. Neither was directed or intended to measure the ability to learn to perform a particular job or category of jobs. The requisite scores used for both initial hiring and transfer approximated the national median for high school graduates.

The objective of Congress in the enactment of Title VII is plain from the language of the statute. It was to achieve equality of employment opportunities and remove barriers that have operated in the past to favor an identifiable group of white employees over other employees. Under the Act, practices, procedures, or tests neutral on their face, and even neutral in terms of intent, cannot be maintained if they operate to 'freeze' the status quo of prior discriminatory employment practices.

[On] the record in the present case, 'whites register far better on the Company's alternative requirements' than Negroes.[5] 420 F.2d 1225, 1239 n.6. This consequence would appear to be directly traceable to race. Basic intelligence must have the means of articulation to manifest itself fairly in a testing process. Because they are Negroes, petitioners have long received inferior education in segregated schools and this Court expressly recognized these differences in *Gaston County v. United States,* 395 U.S. 285 (1969). There, because of the inferior education received by Negroes in North Carolina, this Court barred the institution of a literacy test for voter registration on the ground that the test would abridge the right to vote indirectly on account of race. Congress did not intend by Title VII, however, to guarantee a job to every person regardless of qualifications. In short, the Act does not command that any person be hired simply because he was formerly the subject of discrimination, or because he is a member of a minority group. Discriminatory preference for any group, minority or majority, is precisely and only what Congress has proscribed. What is required by Congress is the removal of artificial, arbitrary, and unnecessary barriers to employment when the barriers operate invidiously to discriminate on the basis of racial or other impermissible classification.

Congress has now provided that tests or criteria for employment or promotion may not provide equality of opportunity merely in the sense of

---

[5]   In North Carolina, 1960 census statistics show that, while 34% of white males had completed high school, only 12% of Negro males had done so. Similarly, with respect to standardized tests, the EEOC in one case found that use of a battery of tests, including the Wonderlic and Bennett tests used by the Company in the instant case, resulted in 58% of whites passing the tests, as compared with only 6% of the blacks.

the fabled offer of milk to the stork and the fox. On the contrary, Congress has now required that the posture and condition of the job-seeker be taken into account. It has—to resort again to the fable—provided that the vessel in which the milk is proffered be one all seekers can use. The Act proscribes not only overt discrimination but also practices that are fair in form, but discriminatory in operation. The touchstone is business necessity. If an employment practice which operates to exclude Negroes cannot be shown to be related to job performance, the practice is prohibited.

On the record before us, neither the high school completion requirement nor the general intelligence test is shown to bear a demonstrable relationship to successful performance of the jobs for which it was used. Both were adopted, as the Court of Appeals noted, without meaningful study of their relationship to job-performance ability. Rather, a vice president of the Company testified, the requirements were instituted on the Company's judgment that they generally would improve the overall quality of the work force.

The evidence, however, shows that employees who have not completed high school or taken the tests have continued to perform satisfactorily and make progress in departments for which the high school and test criteria are now used. The promotion record of present employees who would not be able to meet the new criteria thus suggests the possibility that the requirements may not be needed even for the limited purpose of preserving the avowed policy of advancement within the Company. In the context of this case, it is unnecessary to reach the question whether testing requirements that take into account capability for the next succeeding position or related future promotion might be utilized upon a showing that such language requirements fulfill a genuine business need. In the present case the Company has made no such showing.

The Court of Appeals held that the Company had adopted the diploma and test requirements without any 'intention to discriminate against Negro employees.' 420 F.2d, at 1232. We do not suggest that either the District Court or the Court of Appeals erred in examining the employer's intent; but good intent or absence of discriminatory intent does not redeem employment procedures or testing mechanisms that operate as 'built-in headwinds' for minority groups and are unrelated to measuring job capability.

The Company's lack of discriminatory intent is suggested by special efforts to help the undereducated employees through Company financing of two-thirds the cost of tuition for high school training. But Congress directed the thrust of the Act to the consequences of employment practices, not simply the motivation. More than that, Congress has placed on the employer the burden of showing that any given requirement must have a manifest relationship to the employment in question.

The facts of this case demonstrate the inadequacy of broad and general testing devices as well as the infirmity of using diplomas or degrees as fixed measures of capability. History is filled with examples of men and women who rendered highly effective performance without the conventional badges of accomplishment in terms of certificates, diplomas, or degrees. Diplomas and tests are useful servants, but Congress has mandated the commonsense proposition that they are not to become masters of reality.

Nothing in the Act precludes the use of testing or measuring procedures; obviously they are useful. What Congress has forbidden is giving these devices and mechanisms controlling force unless they are demonstrably a reasonable measure of job performance. Congress has not commanded that the less qualified be preferred over the better qualified simply because of minority origins. Far from disparaging job qualifications as such, Congress has made such qualifications the controlling factor, so that race, religion, nationality, and sex become irrelevant. What Congress has commanded is that any tests used must measure the person for the job and not the person in the abstract.

NOTES AND QUESTIONS

1. ***The Court's Reasoning.*** The *Griggs* Court concluded the trial court's finding—that Duke Power Company did not intentionally discriminate against black employees when it adopted the test score and high school diploma requirements—was not clearly erroneous. Yet the Court held that the employment policy discriminated on the basis of race in violation of Title VII. How did the policy discriminate by race? What purposes are served by a theory of liability based on disparate impact? What purposes does it serve on the facts of *Griggs*? What conception of equality does the Court seem to envision?

2. ***Proof Framework.*** Claims against employment policies or practices that have a racially disparate impact follow a three-step procedure, albeit one that differs from the *McDonnell Douglas* framework for disparate treatment claims. First, a plaintiff alleging disparate impact bears the burdens of production and persuasion to establish that a specific employment practice has a significant racially disparate impact. If he fails, the employer wins. If he succeeds, the burdens of production and persuasion shift to the employer, who must demonstrate that the practice is "job related and consistent with business necessity"—a standard codified by Congress in 1991. If the employer fails, the plaintiff wins. If the employer succeeds, the plaintiff loses unless he can demonstrate that the employer's interests could be served equally effectively by an alternative employment practice with less of a racial impact.

3. ***Tests, Degrees, and Other "Objective" Qualifications.*** *Griggs* illustrates that tests and other qualifications can harm racial minorities. At

the same time, such criteria can minimize the risk of discrimination by requiring employers to hire based on explicit measures of knowledge and aptitude rather than relying on discretionary judgment or an "old boy's" network. Recall in *Hazelwood*, for example, that the subjective, discretionary nature of the school district's hiring process heightened the risk of discrimination. Yet no test can perfectly predict an employee's qualifications. If *Griggs* makes the use of tests, degrees, and other measures too difficult for employers to justify, they will inevitably resort to more impressionistic, subjective hiring decisions.

The legal standard required by Congress is that employment qualifications must be "job related and consistent with business necessity." What might this mean? How strict should the Court construe this standard when evaluating an employer's test or other job qualifications? For example, should an employer, acting in good faith, be permitted to take account of an applicant's level of education; her grade point average, class rank, and other scholastic honors; or her years of relevant work experience, even if these criteria have a significant racial impact? What harm could result from requiring employers to justify policies that have racially disparate impacts?

4.   *Criminal Records.* Many employment applications ask about the applicant's criminal record. Questions might range from whether the applicant has been convicted of a felony or any crime to simply whether the applicant has ever been arrested or charged with a crime. The application typically provides space to explain if the answer is yes. Sometimes applications make an exception for traffic offenses so that an applicant need not report such charges, even if the state defines such infractions as crimes. Are such questions legitimate?

Given the correlation between race and involvement with the criminal justice system, questions about an applicant's criminal record tend to have a significant discriminatory impact. As such, employers would need to justify them as adequately job related. Are they? Does it depend on the position applied for? Does it depend on whether the questions ask about convictions, charges, or arrests?

The EEOC has promulgated detailed guidelines addressing the use of criminal history by employers. It summarizes its approach as follows:

> An employer's use of an individual's criminal history in making employment decisions may, in some instances, violate the prohibition against employment discrimination under Title VII.
>
> The fact of an arrest does not establish that criminal conduct has occurred, and an exclusion based on an arrest, in itself, is not job related and consistent with business necessity. However, an employer may make an employment decision based on the conduct underlying an arrest if the conduct makes the individual unfit for the position in question.
>
> In contrast, a conviction record will usually serve as sufficient evidence that a person engaged in particular conduct.

> [T]he Commission believes employers will consistently meet the "job related and consistent with business necessity" defense when . . . [t]he employer develops a targeted screen considering at least the nature of the crime, the time elapsed, and the nature of the job. . . . The employer's policy then provides an opportunity for an individualized assessment for those people identified by the screen, to determine if the policy as applied is job related and consistent with business necessity.

EEOC Guidance No. 915.002, April 25, 2012, Consideration of Arrest and Conviction Records in Employment Decisions Under Title VII of the Civil Rights Act of 1964. Do these general principles seem sensible to you or do they give too little or too much weight to an employer's concerns over an applicant's criminal history? If you worked for the EEOC, what standards would you propose for assessing whether employment policies with a racially disparate impact were justified?

5. ***Problem.*** Alberto, a Latino man, has worked successfully at a public relations agency as the Director of Marketing for three years. Under new management, the agency adopts a policy requiring all high-level administrative positions, such as director, vice president, and president, to be held by someone with a four-year college degree. They also adopt a policy that bars employing anyone with a criminal conviction. The management team, which is highly respected in the industry, believes that these policies are necessary to ensure that the agency's reputation for professional skill and ethical standards remains beyond question.

Twenty years earlier, as a teenager, Alberto pled guilty to a charge of possession of crack cocaine and resisting arrest, both arising from the same incident in which he was stopped and frisked while walking to school. During the intervening years, Alberto graduated from high school and obtained a two-year degree in communications from a community college, and he worked successfully in advertising and public relations without further contact with the criminal justice system. At the agency, all of Alberto's supervisors assessed him as a talented, reliable, and trustworthy employee, and he has never posed a risk to people or property at work. However, once the new management learned of Alberto's criminal and education history, it terminated his employment.

If you represented Alberto, what arguments could you make to challenge the two policies of the agency? If you represented the agency, what justifications would you offer to support them? Would the criminal record policy by permissible under the EEOC guidelines? Should it be permissible?

———

As seen above, Congress and the Court have concluded, through Title VII, that equality in the workplace requires tests and other employment practices with significant racial impacts to either be job related or abandoned. The Constitution also prohibits government employers from denying equal protection of the laws. Should the duty imposed by Title VII on employers (both private and public) be stronger, weaker, or the same as the duty imposed by the Equal Protection Clause? What if, for example, a test by a police or fire department has a significant negative impact on black applicants? Should the Constitution require the department to ensure that the test is job related? The following case takes up that question.

Washington v. Davis
Supreme Court of the United States, 1976.
426 U.S. 229.

[Editors' Note: *Washington v. Davis* is a main case for this chapter that should be read at this point. Read the case and the Notes and Questions following it in Chapter 2, and then the Note below.]

NOTES AND QUESTIONS

1. ***The Relevance of Disparate Effects for Constitutional and Statutory Claims.*** Among the laws we are examining in this chapter, only Title VII imposes liability for employment practices with a racially disparate impact without proof of a discriminatory purpose. The Equal Protection Clause (and its federal counterpart in the Fifth Amendment), as well as Section 1981 of the Civil Rights Act of 1866, require a plaintiff to prove an employer's adverse action was intentionally based on race. For claims of intentional discrimination under any of these laws, however, the racial impact of an employer's practice is relevant evidence of the employer's intent.

III. CONCEPTUAL CONTROVERSIES OVER RACE AND DISCRIMINATION

This section examines controversies over the meaning of race and discrimination that potentially implicate employment discrimination laws. In determining whether race discrimination has occurred, we must have an account of what constitutes race and what kinds of adverse employment decisions constitute discrimination. Should discrimination be prohibited only when it is based on an immutable trait, or should discrimination based on conduct also be actionable?

A. IMMUTABLE TRAITS: ANCESTRY AND COLOR

In America today, racial groups are generally divided into five categories, Black, White, Native American, Asian, and Latino. Identities such as Jewish, Chinese, Arab, or Middle Eastern are not racial categories by contemporary standards, although some such categories can fall into other protected classifications, such as religion and national origin. Section 1981 of the Civil Rights Act of 1866, 42 U.S.C. § 1981, prohibits discrimination in employment, but only on account of race. The following case asks whether discrimination against someone because he is Arab is actionable as race discrimination under Section 1981.

Saint Francis College v. Al-Khazraji

Supreme Court of the United States, 1987.
481 U.S. 604.

■ JUSTICE WHITE delivered the opinion of the Court.

Respondent, a citizen of the United States born in Iraq, was an associate professor at St. Francis College, [who filed a claim of discrimination against the college based on the nonrenewal of his position.] The claimant's Title VII claims were time barred and the District Court ruled that § 1981 does not reach claims of discrimination based on Arabian ancestry.

Section 1981 provides:

"All persons within the jurisdiction of the United States shall have the same right in every State and Territory to make and enforce contracts, to sue, be parties, give evidence, and to the full and equal benefit of all laws and proceedings for the security of persons and property as is enjoyed by white citizens, and shall be subject to like punishment, pains, penalties, taxes, licenses, and exactions of every kind, and to no other."

Although § 1981 does not itself use the word "race," the Court has construed the section to forbid all "racial" discrimination in the making of private as well as public contracts. The issue is whether respondent has alleged racial discrimination within the meaning of § 1981.

Petitioners contend that respondent is a Caucasian and cannot allege the kind of discrimination § 1981 forbids.

Petitioner's submission rests on the assumption that all those who might be deemed Caucasians today were thought to be of the same race when § 1981 became law in the 19th century; and it may be that a variety of ethnic groups, including Arabs, are now considered to be within the Caucasian race.[6] The understanding of "race" in the 19th century, however, was different. Plainly, all those who might be deemed Caucasian today were not thought to be of the same race at the time § 1981 became law.

In the middle years of the 19th century, dictionaries commonly referred to race as a "continued series of descendants from a parent who

---

[6] There is a common popular understanding that there are three major human races—Caucasoid, Mongoloid, and Negroid. Many modern biologists and anthropologists, however, criticize racial classifications as arbitrary and of little use in understanding the variability of human beings. It is said that genetically homogeneous populations do not exist and traits are not discontinuous between populations; therefore, a population can only be described in terms of relative frequencies of various traits. Clear-cut categories do not exist. The particular traits which have generally been chosen to characterize races have been criticized as having little biological significance. It has been found that differences between individuals of the same race are often greater than the differences between the "average" individuals of different races. These observations and others have led some, but not all, scientists to conclude that racial classifications are for the most part sociopolitical, rather than biological, in nature. S. Molnar, Human Variation (2d ed. 1983); S. Gould, The Mismeasure of Man (1981).

is called the stock," N. Webster, An American Dictionary of the English Language 666 (New York 1830) (emphasis in original), "[t]he lineage of a family," 2 N. Webster, A Dictionary of the English Language 411 (New Haven 1841), or "descendants of a common ancestor," J. Donald, Chambers' Etymological Dictionary of the English Language 415 (London 1871). The 1887 edition of Webster's expanded the definition somewhat: "The descendants of a common ancestor; a family, tribe, people or nation, believed or presumed to belong to the same stock." N. Webster, Dictionary of the English Language 589 (W. Wheeler ed. 1887). It was not until the 20th century that dictionaries began referring to the Caucasian, Mongolian, and Negro races, 8 The Century Dictionary and Cyclopedia 4926 (1911), or to race as involving divisions of mankind based upon different physical characteristics. Webster's Collegiate Dictionary 794 (3d ed. 1916). Even so, modern dictionaries still include among the definitions of race "a family, tribe, people, or nation belonging to the same stock."

Encyclopedias of the 19th century also described race in terms of ethnic groups, which is a narrower concept of race than petitioners urge. Encyclopedia Americana in 1858, for example, referred to various races such as Finns, vol. 5, p. 123, gypsies, 6 id., at 123, Basques, 1 id., at 602, and Hebrews, 6 id., at 209. The 1863 version of the New American Cyclopaedia divided the Arabs into a number of subsidiary races, vol. 1, p. 739; represented the Hebrews as of the Semitic race, 9 id., at 27, and identified numerous other groups as constituting races, including Swedes, 15 id., at 216, Norwegians, 12 id., at 410, Germans, 8 id., at 200, Greeks, 8 id., at 438, Finns, 7 id., at 513, Italians, 9 id., at 644–645 (referring to mixture of different races), Spanish, 14 id., at 804, Mongolians, 11 id., at 651, Russians, 14 id., at 226, and the like. The Ninth edition of the Encyclopedia Britannica also referred to Arabs, vol. 2, p. 245 (1878), Jews, 13 id., at 685 (1881), and other ethnic groups such as Germans, 10 id., at 473 (1879), Hungarians, 12 id., at 365 (1880), and Greeks, 11 id., at 83 (1880), as separate races.

These dictionary and encyclopedic sources are somewhat diverse, but it is clear that they do not support the claim that for the purposes of § 1981, Arabs, Englishmen, Germans, and certain other ethnic groups are to be considered a single race. We would expect the legislative history of § 1981, which the Court held in Runyon v. McCrary had its source in the Civil Rights Act of 1866 as well as the Voting Rights Act of 1870 to reflect this common understanding, which it surely does. The debates are replete with references to the Scandinavian races, Cong.Globe, 39th Cong., 1st Sess., 499 (1866) (remarks of Sen. Cowan), as well as the Chinese, id., at 523 (remarks of Sen. Davis), Latin, id., at 238 (remarks of Rep. Kasson during debate of home rule for the District of Columbia), Spanish, id., at 251 (remarks of Sen. Davis during debate of District of Columbia suffrage), and Anglo-Saxon races, id., at 542 (remarks of Rep. Dawson). Jews, ibid., Mexicans, *see* ibid., (remarks of Rep. Dawson), blacks, passim, and Mongolians, id., at 498 (remarks of Sen. Cowan), were similarly categorized. Gypsies were referred to as a race. Ibid. (remarks of Sen. Cowan). Likewise, the Germans:

> "Who will say that Ohio can pass a law enacting that no man of the German race . . . shall ever own any property in Ohio, or shall ever make a contract in Ohio, or ever inherit property in Ohio, or ever come into Ohio to live, or even to work? If Ohio may pass such a law, and exclude a German citizen . . . because he is of the German nationality or race, then may every other State do so." Id., at 1294 (remarks of Sen. Shellabarger).

There was a reference to the Caucasian race, but it appears to have been referring to people of European ancestry. Id., at 523 (remarks of Sen. Davis).

The history of the 1870 Act reflects similar understanding of what groups Congress intended to protect from intentional discrimination. It is clear, for example, that the civil rights sections of the 1870 Act provided protection for immigrant groups such as the Chinese. This view was expressed in the Senate.

Based on the history of § 1981, we have little trouble in concluding that Congress intended to protect from discrimination identifiable classes of persons who are subjected to intentional discrimination solely because of their ancestry or ethnic characteristics. Such discrimination is racial discrimination that Congress intended § 1981 to forbid, whether or not it would be classified as racial in terms of modern scientific theory. . . . [A] distinctive physiognomy is not essential to qualify for § 1981 protection. If respondent on remand can prove that he was subjected to intentional discrimination based on the fact that he was born an Arab, rather than solely on the place or nation of his origin, or his religion, he will have made out a case under § 1981.

The judgment of the Court of Appeals is accordingly affirmed.

■ JUSTICE BRENNAN, concurring.

I write separately only to point out that the line between discrimination based on "ancestry or ethnic characteristics," and discrimination based on "place or nation of . . . origin," ibid., is not a bright one. It is true that one's ancestry—the ethnic group from which an individual and his or her ancestors are descended—is not necessarily the same as one's national origin—the country "where a person was born, or, more broadly, the country from which his or her ancestors came." Often, however, the two are identical as a factual matter: one was born in the nation whose primary stock is one's own ethnic group. Moreover, national origin claims have been treated as ancestry or ethnicity claims in some circumstances. . . . I therefore read the Court's opinion to state only that discrimination based on birthplace alone is insufficient to state a claim under § 1981.

NOTES AND QUESTIONS

1.   *"Race" Under Section 1981.* Prior to *St. Francis College*, Section 1981 only applied to race discrimination, not national origin or the other traits protected by Title VII (color, sex, and religion). Does the Court in *St. Francis College* change that? Does discrimination on the basis of national origin necessarily come within the ambit of section 1981? What exactly does the Court mean by *race* in *St. Francis College*? To what degree is its conception of race consistent with contemporary understandings?

In a case decided the same day as *St. Francis College*, the Court held that Jews constitute a race under 42 U.S.C. § 1982 (part of the Civil Rights Act of 1866 prohibiting race discrimination in relation to property). *See Shaare Tefila Congregation v. Cobb*, 481 U.S. 615 (1987). The Court applied its definition of race from *St. Francis College* to find that, even if Jews were today considered white, they were considered a distinct race in 1866 based on their ancestry and ethnic characteristics. Does this mean that a religion is a race? Do Jews have common ancestry or discernable characteristics? Should that matter?

2.   *Race Under Title VII and the Constitution.* Must the definition of race under Section 1981, as defined in *St. Francis College*, apply to claims of discrimination under Title VII or the Equal Protection Clause? Does it make sense to have race mean different things depending on which employment discrimination law is invoked? What if a lawsuit for employment discrimination relies, as is common, on two or three different sources of law, depending on the circumstances of the case?

3.   *Colorism.* What if an employer's workforce is racially diverse but the skin color of minority employees tends to be on the lighter, or darker, side? Within racial groups, people vary in their appearance, in terms of hair texture, skin tone and shape of eyes, nose and lips. In some settings, social significance is given to such differences. The blond hair and blue eyes inherited from Scandinavia, for example, might be more desirable among some whites than the darker complexions and hair of South or Eastern Europe. And there is a long tradition in America of black people with "whiter" features, such as lighter skin and a straighter nose, having higher status among whites than their darker skinned counterparts. During slavery, the "house nigger," who served in the Master's house under less onerous conditions than the "field hand," was often lighter skinned (sometimes owing to his or her being the progeny of the Master). Among blacks themselves, more Caucasian features could cut in either direction, sometimes enhancing status and sometimes generating resentment based on the belief that the fairer skinned are arrogant or think themselves racially superior. Light-skinned blacks known to have a white parent might also experience what sociologists call "social marginality," a lack of full acceptance by either parent's racial group.

The question arises, should the law attempt to address *colorism*, or discrimination toward members of a racial group based on the lightness or darkness of their skin? If so, is it because colorism is a form of racial discrimination, or is it a distinct form of discrimination? Note that "color" is explicitly mentioned in Title VII as a prohibited basis of discrimination. Are there nonetheless reasons why the law should not address color-based discrimination? How plausible is it that an employer would discriminate on the basis of color as distinct from race? What if the employer is the same race as the employee? Consider, for example, *Walker v. I.R.S.,* 713 F.Supp. 403, 405 (N.D. Ga. 1989):

> The plaintiff, Ms. Walker, was a permanent clerk typist in the Internal Revenue Service's Atlanta office. Ms. Walker is a light-skinned black person. Her supervisor was Ruby Lewis. Ms. Lewis is a dark-skinned black person. The employees in the office in which Ms. Walker and Ms. Lewis worked were predominantly black. In fact, following her termination, Ms. Walker was replaced by a black person. According to the record the working relationship between Ms. Walker and Ms. Lewis was strained from the very beginning. . . . Ms. Walker contends that Ms. Lewis singled her out for close scrutiny and reprimanded her for many things that were false or insubstantial. Ms. Walker's relationship with her former supervisor, Virginia Fite, was a cordial one. In fact, Ms. Walker received a favorable recommendation from Ms. Fite.

> Ms. Walker was terminated. The reasons given for her termination were: 1) tardiness to work; 2) laziness; 3) incompetence; and 4) attitude problems. It is Ms. Walker's belief that the reasons were fabricated and were the result of Ms. Lewis's personal hostility towards Ms. Walker because of Ms. Walker's light skin.

> Ms. Walker has not presented any direct evidence that Ms. Lewis was prejudiced against light-colored skinned blacks. There is evidence that Ms. Lewis might have harbored resentful feelings towards white people, and therefore by inference, possibly towards light-skinned black people.

How plausible an inference do these facts raise that Ms. Walker was discriminated against because of her color? What concerns do colorism claims raise? If you represented Ms. Walker, what evidence could you plausibly obtain that would support your claim? If you represented the I.R.S., how could you defend against such a claim if the fact of employment of other blacks (including the one who replaced Walker) is itself an insufficient defense? Would each party call the other employees to the stand to compare their skin to that of Ms. Walker's? Should courts be in the "unsavory business of measuring skin color and determining whether the skin pigmentation of the parties is sufficiently different to form the basis of a lawsuit." *Sere v. Board of Trustees, University of Illinois,* 628 F.Supp. 1543, 1546 (N.D. Ill. 1986). For an academic treatment of colorism see Trina Jones, *Shades of Brown: The Law of Skin Color,* 49 Duke L.J. 1487 (2000).

4.   *Proving Race.* Should one ever have to prove one's race. If so, how should he or she be expected to do so? Consider, for example, *Malone v. Civil Service Commission,* 646 N.E.2d 150 (Mass. 1995). Two brothers initially claimed they were white in applications to the Boston Fire Department. But after failing to get hired, they listed their race as black in a subsequent application and were hired as part of an affirmative action hiring plan. After ten years on the job, the department administrator discovered the racial designation and referred the matter to a hearing officer to determine whether the Malone brothers committed fraud on their application. The officer held a hearing at the conclusion of which she determined that the Malones' racial designation as black was false. She applied three criteria: "(i) visual observation of physical features; (ii) documentary evidence establishing black ancestry, such as birth certificates; and (iii) evidence that the Malones or their families held themselves out to be black and are considered black in the community." Id. at 151, n.3. She found that the Malones failed to satisfy any of the criteria. Instead, three generations of birth certificates listed the Malones as white, and the only contrary evidence was a "questionable and inconclusive photograph of a woman they claimed to be Sarah Carroll, their maternal great-grandmother," Id. at 152, n.5 (upholding the hearing officer's decision).

Was it legitimate for the Fire Department to require the Malone brothers to prove their race? Were the criteria employed by the hearing officer appropriate? How do they compare to the understanding of race reflected in other cases you have read in this book, historical or contemporary? Which cases employed the most accurate or normatively attractive conceptions of race?

5.   ***Problem: Achieving a Diverse Law Firm.*** If you were managing partner of a law firm committed to having a racially diverse workforce, including among attorneys and staff, how would you propose treating applicants who do not appear to be the race they claim? If someone claimed to be black, Latino, or Native American, for example, but looked white, would you require proof? What kinds of evidence would be relevant? Would you scrutinize their physical appearance, their spoken expression, the organizations they belong to or causes they contribute to, the race of their community, friends, spouse? What if, instead, an applicant clearly looks black or Asian but sounds "white," grew up in an exclusively white neighborhood, attended predominantly white schools, and otherwise seems completely assimilated into mainstream or "white" culture? What if that applicant had also been adopted as a young child by a white couple?

6.   ***Exercise: Prove Your Race.*** If you were required to prove your race, how could you? Come to class prepared to explain your race and how you would prove it. What kinds of evidence could you rely on? What cases that we have read or other sources provide support for your definition of race and the kind of evidence that tends to establish it?

B. CONDUCT: ACCENT AND LANGUAGE

Many employees have experienced discrimination based on accent. Some cases have involved college instructors or employees who serve the public who have been terminated or not hired because their accents were purportedly incomprehensible to students or customers. In *Fragante v. City & County of Honolulu*, 888 F.2d 591 (9th Cir. 1989), for example, the court upheld a city's refusal to hire a Filipino man for a clerk position in the Division of Motor Vehicles and Licensing, despite his achieving the highest score on the civil service exam, because his "heavy Filipino accent" would undermine his ability to communicate with the public at the information counter and over the phone.

Other cases involve employees who have been terminated because of language, such as for failing to speak English in a government agency or private company that requires English in the workplace. The question arises whether discrimination based on language or accent is discrimination based on race. If you represented a client who believes she was not hired, not promoted, or was fired because of her accent or language, how would you frame the claim of discrimination?

Although accent and language are distinct issues, they are included together in this subsection because they overlap in important ways. They both could be characterized as expressive conduct and are arguably more mutable than the physical features associated with race. At the same time, changing one's accent or gaining fluency in another language can be very difficult, and perhaps unachievable. Compliance with language-related employment policies, therefore, could present an insurmountable burden. One's accent and linguistic profile are also aspects of one's identity learned at an early age, typically from one's family, and are often characteristic of being foreign born. Indeed, the great majority of accent and language discrimination cases involve foreign-born employees, often of Latin American, Asian, or African origin.

The following case presents an unusual twist on the typical case of discrimination against a foreign-born employee. It involves discrimination against a white American employee justified by the employer on the ground that the employee's accent was not sufficiently "black."

Chaline v. KCHO

Court of Appeals, Fifth Circuit, 1982.
693 F.2d 477.

■ GOLDBERG, CIRCUIT JUDGE:

PROLOGUE

In this appeal of an employment discrimination dispute we are the audience for a real life radio drama produced and directed by defendant-appellant Michael P. Petrizzo. The action is set in Houston, Texas, at the offices of defendant-appellant KCOH, Inc. ("KCOH"), the black-oriented radio station where Petrizzo is executive vice president and general manager. In the leading role of the discharged employee is plaintiff-appellee Clarence Chaline, Jr., the former production manager at KCOH. Chaline, a white male, brought this action to challenge the allegedly racially discriminatory employment practices at KCOH. The district court held that Chaline was discharged from his position because of his race, and ordered that he be awarded back pay and reinstated as production manager. KCOH and Petrizzo now appeal to this court. We affirm.

ACT I: ON THE RADIO

For twenty-eight years radio station KCOH has broadcast black-oriented programming to listeners in the Houston area. The KCOH format mixes rhythm and blues or soul music with "rap" time during which the disc jockey communicates with the listening audience. The disc jockey's "rap" is characterized by the idiom and voice quality popular with the station's primarily black audience. KCOH has never had a white disc jockey.

Appellee Chaline was hired as production manager at KCOH in 1979 at a salary of $1200 per month. As production manager, Chaline was responsible for preparing commercial advertisements and community service announcements for air play. His job entailed writing and recording commercials as well as coordinating their broadcast. Chaline never served as a KCOH disc jockey during his tenure at the station.

In late 1979, KCOH faced decreasing ratings and a low volume of billings. In order to reduce costs, appellant Petrizzo decided to make the station's production manager a permanent part-time disc jockey as well. Instead of casting Chaline in this newly created dual role, however, Petrizzo asked Chaline to make a lateral move into the station's sales department. Chaline objected to the proposed transfer, because it involved a decrease in salary and because his wardrobe and transportation were inadequate for sales work, and asked to be retained as production manager and part-time disc jockey. Upon Chaline's refusal to move into sales, his employment was terminated. Exit Chaline, stage left.

Prior to Chaline's termination, Don Samuels, a black male, had auditioned for the part of production manager and part-time disc jockey. Samuels was well-known in the Houston area as a disc jockey at radio station KYOK, where he also performed production work. Petrizzo eventually hired Samuels to replace Chaline at a salary of $1200 per month.

ACT II: IN THE DISTRICT COURT

Chaline brought this action in the United States District Court for the Southern District of Texas under the Civil Rights Act of 1866, 42 U.S.C. § 1981 (1976). Following a bench trial, the district court found that Chaline was well qualified to be a KCOH disc jockey based upon his experience and demonstrated ability, and that Don Samuels was not more qualified than Chaline to fill the dual position of production manager and part-time disc jockey. Accordingly, the court concluded that Chaline's employment was terminated because he was white. In response to the appellants' suggestion that Chaline lacked the black "voice" and the sensitivity to black listening tastes necessary for the job, the court determined that this asserted justification for Chaline's termination was merely pretextual. Based on these findings, the court awarded Chaline back pay of $6000 and reinstatement as production manager. KCOH and Petrizzo appeal from the judgment in favor of Chaline.

INTERMISSION: ISSUES ON APPEAL

The district court held that Chaline proved by a preponderance of the evidence that he was the victim of purposeful racial discrimination at KCOH. The appellants, KCOH and Petrizzo, attack this conclusion on two basic grounds. First, they assert that Chaline failed to establish a prima facie case of racial discrimination because he was not qualified for the position as part-time disc jockey. Second, they contend that legitimate, nondiscriminatory business reasons prompted Chaline's dismissal.

ACT III: THE APPEAL

Scene 1—Order of Proof

In *McDonnell Douglas Corp. v. Green,* 411 U.S. 792 (1973), the Supreme Court established the basic allocation of burdens and order of presentation of proof to be used in cases alleging discriminatory treatment under Title VII of the Civil Rights Act of 1964. The elements of a case of racial discrimination as articulated in *McDonnell Douglas* and *Burdine* apply to cases brought under section 1981 as well. The plaintiff initially has the burden of showing a prima facie case of discrimination. If the plaintiff succeeds in raising a prima facie case, the burden shifts to the defendant "to articulate some legitimate, nondiscriminatory reason for the employee's rejection." *McDonnell Douglas,* 93 S.Ct. at 1824. Should the defendant carry this burden, the plaintiff then must establish by a preponderance of the evidence that the reasons offered by the defendant were merely a pretext for discrimination. This formulation is simply a division of intermediate evidentiary burdens; "[t]he ultimate burden of persuading the trier of fact that the defendant intentionally discriminated against the plaintiff remains at all time with the plaintiff." *Texas Department of Community Affairs v. Burdine,* 101 S.Ct. 1089, 1093 (1981).

Scene 2—Standard of Review

[O]ur inquiry on this appeal is limited to the question of whether the district court was clearly erroneous in finding that KCOH purposefully discriminated against Chaline on account of his race.

Scene 3—Examining the Findings

a.   Prima Facie Case

Under *McDonnell Douglas* and *Burdine*, the initial question is whether the plaintiff has established a prima facie case of racial discrimination. The plaintiff may discharge the burden by showing: (1) that he belongs to a protected class; (2) that he was qualified for a particular position; (3) that, despite his qualifications, he was rejected or discharged; and (4) that he was replaced by a nonminority. The prima facie case serves an important function in the litigation by eliminating the most common nondiscriminatory reasons for the plaintiff's discharge or rejection. By establishing the prima facie case, the plaintiff raises the presumption that the employer unlawfully discriminated against the employee.

The district court in this case determined that Chaline fulfilled all four of the *McDonnell Douglas* requirements. In particular, the court found that Chaline, a white male, was well qualified to be a KCOH disc jockey based upon his twenty years' experience in radio and his demonstrated ability. The court further found that Samuels, the black male who replaced Chaline, was not more qualified than Chaline to fill the dual position of production manager and part-time disc jockey. The court concluded from these findings that Chaline had established a prima facie case of purposeful racial discrimination.

We are not prepared to say that these findings are clearly erroneous. The record indicates that Chaline has been active in the radio industry in Houston since 1961. His experience has included work at eight different radio stations and in many capacities: disc jockey, general manager, operations manager, production manager, news director, and news editor. Chaline has also taught broadcasting. Samuels has worked for seven years at another Houston radio station. While he has served primarily as a disc jockey, he also has performed some production work.

b.   Employers' Rebuttal

Having found that Chaline carried his initial burden, we now move to the second stage of the *McDonnell Douglas-Burdine* order of proof. At this juncture the employer must set forth a legally sufficient explanation for the discharge of the aggrieved employee in order to rebut the prima facie showing.

KCOH and Petrizzo seek to justify Chaline's termination on the grounds that he does not have the proper "voice" to serve as a disc jockey on a black-oriented radio station. Additionally, the appellants claim that Chaline is not sensitive to the listening tastes of a black audience. The district court apparently found these arguments a sufficiently clear and specific rebuttal to require the plaintiff to move forward with his case. For purposes of disposing of this case, we too will assume the legitimacy of this asserted job qualification. We are not here to judge whether a characteristic black "voice" or idiom in truth exists; such a determination we leave to those far more schooled than we in linguistics, lexicography, and anthropological idioms. We note in passing, however, that such a subjective job qualification provides a "ready mechanism for racial discrimination." *Johnson v. Uncle Ben's, Inc.,* 628 F.2d 419, 426 (5th

Cir.1980). The more subjective the qualification sought and the more subjective its measurement, the more difficult it will be for the employer to satisfy *Burdine*'s requirement that the legitimate reasons for the discharge be "clear and reasonably specific." *Burdine,* 101 S.Ct. at 1096.

    c.   Pretext

    Assuming, then, that KCOH and Petrizzo have presented a question of fact concerning the decision to discharge Chaline, *McDonnell Douglas* and *Burdine* require Chaline to demonstrate that the proffered reason was pretextual. Chaline must prove by a preponderance of the evidence that the asserted justifications advanced by KCOH and Petrizzo were not the true reasons for his discharge. This burden merges with Chaline's ultimate burden of persuasion that he was the victim of intentional discrimination.

    In this case, Chaline's evidence persuaded the trial court that KCOH and Petrizzo were masking intentional racial discrimination when they raised objections to Chaline's voice quality and sensitivity to black listening tastes. Specifically, the court noted that Chaline's idiom and voice quality were sufficiently similar to those of black audience disc jockeys that such an excuse was a mere pretext. The court additionally found that the assertion that Chaline was insensitive to black radio listeners was unpersuasive in light of his prior experience and duties at KCOH. Accordingly, the court determined that Chaline had proved by a preponderance of the evidence that he was discharged because of his race.

    When examined under the appropriate "clearly erroneous" standard, the district court's findings must be affirmed. Chaline testified that on occasion he used a black voice in preparing commercial spots for broadcast; the record reflects that he demonstrated his mastery of the voice and idiom during the course of trial. Furthermore, Chaline's performance in scripting and recording commercials, which the appellees conceded was satisfactory at all times, indicates an awareness of the tastes and preferences of the KCOH listening audience.

EPILOGUE

    Under the highly individualized facts of this case, the district court found that Chaline had proved by a preponderance of the evidence that his discharge from radio station KCOH was the result of purposeful racial discrimination. The accents of *McDonnell Douglas, Burdine,* and *Pullman-Standard* highlight the basic idiom that this court should enunciate. Because our review of the record indicates that the district court was not clearly erroneous in its determinations, we must affirm.

NOTES AND QUESTIONS

1.   *The Court's Reasoning.* The court upholds the trial court's finding that KCOH discriminated against Chaline because he was white and not because he lacked a "black voice" or because he would not be adequately sensitive to a black-oriented radio audience. The fact that Chaline had recorded commercial spots for the station was given significant weight by the court against the employer. How plausible is KCOH's claim that it wanted a DJ with a black voice who was relatable to the station's black audience? How much does the fact that Chaline did commercial recordings undermine the station's claim that he would not meet their needs as much as the black DJ they hired?

Notice also that the court assumed that the station's proffered reasons for not hiring Chaline—that it desired a DJ with a black voice and sensitivity to a black audience—were legitimate, nondiscriminatory reasons, but the trial court just didn't believe they were the actual reasons. Are those reasons really nondiscriminatory? What is a "black voice" and, if there is such a voice, why is it a nonracial hiring criterion? If a "black voice" is not a race-based qualification, then, presumably, an employer could refuse to hire someone because they spoke with a "black voice." Should an employer be permitted to reject an applicant because he "sounds black"? If not, is that because such a reason is racial and thus the rejection would constitute "disparate treatment"? Or, is it because, though not racial, it would have a racially disparate impact on black applicants? If it is nonracial but has a disparate impact, then the employer would be permitted to justify the policy if it was "job related and consistent with business necessity." When, if ever, would having employees without a "black voice" be legitimately job related?

2.   *Race as a Bona Fide Occupational Qualification (BFOQ)?* Title VII provides:

> [I]t shall not be an unlawful employment practice for an employer to hire . . . employees . . . on the basis of his religion, sex, or national origin in those certain instances where religion, sex, or national origin is a bona fide occupational qualification reasonably necessary to the normal operation of that particular business or enterprise.

42 U.S.C. § 2000e–2 (e). The Court interprets this provision as permitting an employer to exclude from certain jobs people of a particular sex, religion, or national origin when almost all members of the excluded group could not perform the central purpose of the job or when it would be highly impractical to determine on an individualized basis which members of the excluded group would be qualified. Although the Court reads the BFOQ exception very narrowly, it has upheld male-only prison guards for an especially dangerous maximum-security prison. To respect privacy, courts also have allowed women-only nurse positions for maternity wards. The Supreme Court has also suggested, in dicta, that foreign corporations could reserve high-level management positions in U.S. branches for citizens of the home country. The legislative history to Title VII also suggests that an ethnic restaurant, to maintain authenticity, might reserve the head chef position for a national of the country of the cuisine's origin. Courts have also upheld women-only strippers in adult nightclubs, reasoning that sex appeal is central to such businesses (even as they have rejected an analogous rationale for women-

only flight attendant policies by commercial airlines, whose central purpose, courts have held, is safe air travel not sexual titillation).

Congress decided, however, not to permit race ever to serve as a BFOQ. Why might Congress have decided not to allow race to be a job qualification while allowing it for the other generally proscribed traits? Was that a mistake?

Whatever the legal standard, government and private employers alike unquestionably take account of race for reasons that are neither clearly remedial nor clearly invidious. Media companies cast certain roles in movies, TV shows, and advertisements with race in mind. Police departments unquestionably take race into account when selecting officers to serve undercover, perhaps to infiltrate a gang that is itself monoracial (as most gangs are). So too do principals of schools in heavily minority urban areas consider the race of teacher candidates, in the hope of avoiding having an all-white teaching corps responsible for educating a largely minority student body. These are only a few of the many circumstances in which employers are likely to rely on race, notwithstanding the absence of a race BFOQ. Can you think of other circumstances in which employers likely take account of race for non-remedial and non-invidious reasons? Should Congress amend Title VII to permit filling certain jobs based on race? Which jobs?

3.   *Framing   Claims   of   Accent   Discrimination.* Most accent discrimination cases involve foreign-born employees in which the employer justifies an adverse employment decision on the ground that the employee's accent is difficult to understand. Pause and consider, if you represented an employee discriminated against because of her accent, how you would frame her legal claim. On what theory of discrimination would you rely—disparate treatment or impact—and what evidence would support your claim?

There are at least three possible ways to frame a claim of accent discrimination. First, you could argue that accent discrimination constitutes race or national origin disparate treatment because it is inherently part of someone's racial or national-origin identity. Second, accent discrimination could reflect disparate treatment because, even if it is not inherently based on race or national origin, it is very likely that the employer is using accent as a pretext for race or national-origin discrimination. Third, accent discrimination could constitute disparate-impact discrimination, without any intent to discriminate by race or national origin, because it disproportionately burdens people of certain races and national origins. Which claim makes the most sense to you?

Courts have typically treated accent discrimination claims as viable, if at all, on the basis of disparate impact. Employers have justified discriminating on the basis of accent as serving the interest of communication with members of the public or with students in the case of college instructors. For accent discrimination to be justified as job-related, courts have usually required that the employee's accent be difficult to understand for an average person served by the employer. Most cases, but not all, have been decided in the employer's favor.

———————————

Many employees with accents grew up speaking a language other than English. Should employers be able to require that their employees speak only English at work? What if the employees have no contact with the public? Consider the following analysis.

Garcia v. Spun Steak Co.
Court of Appeals, Ninth Circuit, 1993.
998 F.2d 1480.

We are called upon to decide whether an employer violates Title VII of the Civil Rights Act of 1964 in requiring its bilingual workers to speak only English while working on the job.

Spun Steak Company ("Spun Steak") is a California corporation that produces poultry and meat products in South San Francisco for wholesale distribution. Spun Steak employs thirty-three workers, twenty-four of whom are Spanish-speaking. Virtually all of the Spanish-speaking employees are Hispanic. While two employees speak no English, the others have varying degrees of proficiency in English. Spun Steak has never required job applicants to speak or to understand English as a condition of employment.

Approximately two-thirds of Spun Steak's employees are production line workers or otherwise involved in the production process. Appellees Garcia and Buitrago are production line workers; they stand before a conveyor belt, remove poultry or other meat products from the belt and place the product into cases or trays for resale. Their work is done individually. Both Garcia and Buitrago are fully bilingual, speaking both English and Spanish.

Prior to September 1990, these Spun Steak employees spoke Spanish freely to their co-workers during work hours. After receiving complaints that some workers were using their bilingual capabilities to harass and to insult other workers in a language they could not understand, Spun Steak began to investigate the possibility of requiring its employees to speak only English in the workplace. Specifically, Spun Steak received complaints that Garcia and Buitrago made derogatory, racist comments in Spanish about two co-workers, one of whom is African-American and the other Chinese-American.

The company's president, Kenneth Bertelson, concluded that an English-only rule would promote racial harmony in the workplace. In addition, he concluded that the English-only rule would enhance worker safety because some employees who did not understand Spanish claimed that the use of Spanish distracted them while they were operating machinery, and would enhance product quality because the U.S.D.A. inspector in the plant spoke only English and thus could not understand if a product-related concern was raised in Spanish. Accordingly, the following rule was adopted:

> [I]t is hereafter the policy of this Company that only English will
> be spoken in connection with work. During lunch, breaks, and
> employees' own time, they are obviously free to speak Spanish
> if they wish. However, we urge all of you not to use your fluency
> in Spanish in a fashion which may lead other employees to
> suffer humiliation.

In addition to the English-only policy, Spun Steak adopted a rule forbidding offensive racial, sexual, or personal remarks of any kind.

It is unclear from the record whether Spun Steak strictly enforced the English-only rule. According to the plaintiffs-appellees, some workers continued to speak Spanish without incident. Spun Steak issued written exceptions to the policy allowing its clean-up crew to speak Spanish, allowing its foreman to speak Spanish, and authorizing certain workers to speak Spanish to the foreman at the foreman's discretion. One of the two employees who speak only Spanish is a member of the clean-up crew and thus is unaffected by the policy.

In November 1990, Garcia and Buitrago received warning letters for speaking Spanish during working hours. For approximately two months thereafter, they were not permitted to work next to each other. Local 115 protested the English-only policy and requested that it be rescinded but to no avail.

The Spanish-speaking employees do not contend that Spun Steak intentionally discriminated against them in enacting the English-only policy. Rather, they contend that the policy had a discriminatory impact on them because it imposes a burdensome term or condition of employment exclusively upon Hispanic workers and denies them a privilege of employment that non-Spanish-speaking workers enjoy.

It is beyond dispute that, in this case, if the English-only policy causes any adverse effects, those effects will be suffered disproportionately by those of Hispanic origin. The vast majority of those workers at Spun Steak who speak a language other than English—and virtually all those employees for whom English is not a first language—are Hispanic. It is of no consequence that not all Hispanic employees of Spun Steak speak Spanish; nor is it relevant that some non-Hispanic workers may speak Spanish. If the adverse effects are proved, it is enough under Title VII that Hispanics are disproportionately impacted.

The crux of the dispute between Spun Steak and the Spanish-speaking employees, however, is not over whether Hispanic workers will disproportionately bear any adverse effects of the policy; rather, the dispute centers on whether the policy causes any adverse effects at all, and if it does, whether the effects are significant. The Spanish-speaking employees argue that the policy adversely affects them in the following ways: (1) it denies them the ability to express their cultural heritage on the job; (2) it denies them a privilege of employment that is enjoyed by monolingual speakers of English; and (3) it creates an atmosphere of inferiority, isolation, and intimidation. We discuss each of these contentions in turn.

The employees argue that denying them the ability to speak Spanish on the job denies them the right to cultural expression. It cannot be gainsaid that an individual's primary language can be an important link to his ethnic culture and identity. Title VII, however, does not protect the ability of workers to express their cultural heritage at the workplace. Title VII is concerned only with disparities in the treatment of workers; it does not confer substantive privileges. It is axiomatic that an employee must often sacrifice individual self-expression during working hours. Just as a private employer is not required to allow other types of self-expression, there is nothing in Title VII which requires an employer to allow employees to express their cultural identity.

Next, the Spanish-speaking employees argue that the English-only policy has a disparate impact on them because it deprives them of a privilege given by the employer to native-English speakers: the ability to converse on the job in the language with which they feel most comfortable. It is undisputed that Spun Steak allows its employees to converse on the job. The ability to converse—especially to make small talk—is a privilege of employment, and may in fact be a significant privilege of employment in an assembly-line job. It is inaccurate, however, to describe the privilege as broadly as the Spanish-speaking employees urge us to do.

The employees have attempted to define the privilege as the ability to speak in the language of their choice. A privilege, however, is by definition given at the employer's discretion; an employer has the right to define its contours. Thus, an employer may allow employees to converse on the job, but only during certain times of the day or during the performance of certain tasks. The employer may proscribe certain topics as inappropriate during working hours or may even forbid the use of certain words, such as profanity.

Here, as is its prerogative, the employer has defined the privilege narrowly. When the privilege is defined at its narrowest (as merely the ability to speak on the job), we cannot conclude that those employees fluent in both English and Spanish are adversely impacted by the policy. Because they are able to speak English, bilingual employees can engage in conversation on the job. It is axiomatic that "the language a person who is multi-lingual elects to speak at a particular time is . . . a matter of choice." *Garcia v. Gloor,* 618 F.2d 264, 270 (5th Cir. 1980). The bilingual employee can readily comply with the English-only rule and still enjoy the privilege of speaking on the job. "There is no disparate impact" with respect to a privilege of employment "if the rule is one that the affected employee can readily observe and nonobservance is a matter of individual preference." Id.

This analysis is consistent with our decision in *Jurado v. Eleven-Fifty Corporation,* 813 F.2d 1406, 1412 (9th Cir.1987). In Jurado, a bilingual disc jockey was fired for disobeying a rule forbidding him from using an occasional Spanish word or phrase on the air. We concluded that Jurado's disparate impact claim failed "because Jurado was fluently bilingual and could easily comply with the order" and thus could not have been adversely affected.

The Spanish-speaking employees argue that fully bilingual employees are hampered in the enjoyment of the privilege because for them, switching from one language to another is not fully volitional. Whether a bilingual speaker can control which language is used in a given circumstance is a factual issue that cannot be resolved at the summary judgment stage. However, we fail to see the relevance of the assertion, even assuming that it can be proved. Title VII is not meant to protect against rules that merely inconvenience some employees, even if the inconvenience falls regularly on a protected class. Rather, Title VII protects against only those policies that have a significant impact. The fact that an employee may have to catch himself or herself from occasionally slipping into Spanish does not impose a burden significant enough to amount to the denial of equal opportunity. This is not a case in which the employees have alleged that the company is enforcing the policy in such a way as to impose penalties for minor slips of the tongue. The fact that a bilingual employee may, on occasion, unconsciously substitute a Spanish word in the place of an English one does not override our conclusion that the bilingual employee can easily comply with the rule. In short, we conclude that a bilingual employee is not denied a privilege of employment by the English-only policy.

By contrast, non-English speakers cannot enjoy the privilege of conversing on the job if conversation is limited to a language they cannot speak. As applied "[t]o a person who speaks only one tongue or to a person who has difficulty using another language than the one spoken in his home," an English-only rule might well have an adverse impact. *Garcia,* 618 F.2d at 270. Indeed, counsel for Spun Steak conceded at oral argument that the policy would have an adverse impact on an employee unable to speak English. There is only one employee at Spun Steak affected by the policy who is unable to speak any English. Even with regard to her, however, summary judgment was improper because a genuine issue of material fact exists as to whether she has been adversely affected by the policy. She stated in her deposition that she was not bothered by the rule because she preferred not to make small talk on the job, but rather preferred to work in peace. Furthermore, there is some evidence suggesting that she is not required to comply with the policy when she chooses to speak. For example, she is allowed to speak Spanish to her supervisor. Remand is necessary to determine whether she has suffered adverse effects from the policy. It is unclear from the record whether there are any other employees who have such limited proficiency in English that they are effectively denied the privilege of speaking on the job. Whether an employee speaks such little English as to be effectively denied the privilege is a question of fact for which summary judgment is improper.

Finally, the Spanish-speaking employees argue that the policy creates an atmosphere of inferiority, isolation, and intimidation. Under this theory, the employees do not assert that the policy directly affects a term, condition, or privilege of employment. Instead, the argument must be that the policy causes the work environment to become infused with ethnic tensions. The tense environment, the argument goes, itself amounts to a condition of employment.

[T]he employees urge us to adopt a per se rule that English-only policies always infect the working environment to such a degree as to amount to a hostile or abusive work environment. This we cannot do. Whether a working environment is infused with discrimination is a factual question, one for which a per se rule is particularly inappropriate. The dynamics of an individual workplace are enormously complex; we cannot conclude, as a matter of law, that the introduction of an English-only policy, in every workplace, will always have the same effect.

The Spanish-speaking employees in this case have presented no evidence other than conclusory statements that the policy has contributed to an atmosphere of "isolation, inferiority or intimidation." The bilingual employees are able to comply with the rule, and there is no evidence to show that the atmosphere at Spun Steak in general is infused with hostility toward Hispanic workers. Indeed, there is substantial evidence in the record demonstrating that the policy was enacted to prevent the employees from intentionally using their fluency in Spanish to isolate and to intimidate members of other ethnic groups. In light of the specific factual context of this case, we conclude that the bilingual employees have not raised a genuine issue of material fact that the effect is so pronounced as to amount to a hostile environment.

We do not foreclose the prospect that in some circumstances English-only rules can exacerbate existing tensions, or, when combined with other discriminatory behavior, contribute to an overall environment of discrimination. Likewise, we can envision a case in which such rules are enforced in such a draconian manner that the enforcement itself amounts to harassment. In evaluating such a claim, however, a court must look to the totality of the circumstances in the particular factual context in which the claim arises.

In holding that the enactment of an English-only while working policy does not inexorably lead to an abusive environment for those whose primary language is not English, we reach a conclusion opposite to the EEOC's [Equal Employment Opportunity Commission] long standing position. The EEOC Guidelines provide that an employee meets the prima facie case in a disparate impact cause of action merely by proving the existence of the English-only policy. *See* 29 C.F.R. § 1606.7(a) & (b) (1991). Under the EEOC's scheme, an employer must always provide a business justification for such a rule. The EEOC enacted this scheme in part because of its conclusion that English-only rules may "create an atmosphere of inferiority, isolation and intimidation based on national origin which could result in a discriminatory working environment." 29 C.F.R. § 1606.7(a).

NOTES AND QUESTIONS

1.   *The Court's Reasoning.* The *Spun Steak* court acknowledged that the English-only rule had a disparate impact on Latinos but ruled against the bilingual employees without requiring the employer to demonstrate that the policy was job related. The court held that the bilingual employees did not suffer a serious enough burden to qualify as an adverse employment action under Title VII. Title VII does not prohibit mere inconvenience. Thus, even if the policy was not job related, the employees have no case. What were the various burdens that the employees alleged? What's your assessment of the court's rejection thereof?

The court also held that the impact of the English-only rule on non-English speaking employees could be a significant enough burden to implicate Title VII and thereby require the company to justify the policy in light of its disparate impact. Does the policy impose a serious burden on non-English speakers? If so, does the employer have an adequate justification for the policy?

2.   *English-Only Policies.* EEOC guidelines treat all English-only policies as imposing a sufficiently burdensome disparate impact, such that employers with such policies should always have to justify them as job related. Most courts, however, have rejected claims against English-only rules, either because they are not unduly burdensome, as the court held in *Spun Steak*, or because the employers were found to have adequate, job-related justifications.

3.   *Cultural Assimilation Versus Pluralism.* Notice that the employer in *Spun Steak* readily hired Mexican Americans. There was no allegation that the employer intended to discriminate against Mexican Americans. Should such an employer be permitted to require its employees to speak in English to promote cultural assimilation? Does the United States have a legitimate interest in encouraging immigrants to learn and speak English in order to facilitate their integration into American society? Does Congress have an interest in the "cultivation of a shared commitment to the American values of liberty, democracy and equal opportunity"? 1997 Report to Congress of the U.S. Comm'n on Immigration Reform, Becoming an American: Immigration and Immigrant Policy, at 26. Does this interest include encouraging immigrants to learn common practices and values central to American heritage, culture, and identity? What might those practices and values be? To that end, should Congress and the courts tolerate English-only employment policies, not intended to discriminate by race or national origin, in order to encourage "Americanization"?

Barbara Jordan, the late civil rights leader and congresswoman, was a staunch advocate of citizenship for immigrants, stating that "[w]e are a nation of immigrants" and that "[n]aturalization is the most visible manifestation of Americanization," Leon Bouvier, Embracing America: A Look at Which Immigrants Become Citizens 7 (Ctr. for Immigration Studies Working Paper, 1996). Jordan acknowledged that the concept of Americanization has "earned a bad reputation when it was stolen by racists and xenophobes in the 1920's," but nonetheless believed that, done for inclusive purposes, Americanization benefits both immigrants and America as a whole. *See* Barbara Jordan, *The Americanization Ideal*, N.Y. Times, Sept. 11, 1995, at A14.

In your view, should we pursue the blurring or even erasure of ethnic and cultural differences, or should we foster cultural pluralism and the perpetuation of different ethnic identities and groups? Or, should our goal be a form of integration between these two options? Do the answers to these questions have relevance for employment policies that disfavor non-English languages and accents considered to be unacceptably foreign or difficult to understand?

4.   *Exercise: Advise a Client.* You have a bilingual client who has been affected by a rule that limits his or her use of a non-English language. How would you choose to argue this case? Would you analogize the case to disparate treatment based on race or national origin? Would you argue that the rule is a pretext for race or national origin discrimination? Or would you argue that the rule disproportionately burdens your client's race? Which strategy would work best? What factors would you take into account?

C. CULTURAL PERFORMANCE AND INTERSECTIONALITY

The previous section addressed discrimination based on accent and language, which are arguably more mutable than the biological features conventionally associated with race. At the same time, an employee's compliance with language and accent rules might require so much time and effort that language and accent ought to be considered quasi-immutable. This section radiates even further away from the physical features associated with race to conduct that is not very difficult to change, such as how one wears his or her hair or otherwise grooms oneself. Employees may nonetheless find rules requiring a change in such modes of presentation offensive because they conflict with aspects of their identity or cultural heritage. Such rules may also disproportionately burden one race more than another. Should rules governing this and other types of behavior, even if they are not employed as a pretext for race discrimination, nonetheless be considered race discrimination? Scholars who endorse such a move argue that some types of behavior constitute an integral part of the social definition of race. They refer to such behavioral aspects of race as "performance." *See*, e.g., Devon W. Carbado & Mitu Gulati, Acting White?: Rethinking Race in Post-Racial America (2013); Camille Gear Rich, *Performing Racial and*

Ethnic Identity: Discrimination by Proxy and the Future of Title VII, 79 NYU Law Rev. 1134 (2004). For a discussion of the challenges of applying the nondiscrimination mandate on the basis of behavior, see R. Richard Banks, *Class and Culture: The Indeterminacy of Nondiscrimination*, 5 Stan.Civ.Rts.-Civ. Liberties L.Rev.1 (2009)

A related concern with employment policies that regulate presentation or performance is that such policies often affect not only one race more than others, but will also differentially burden people based on the combination of their race and sex. As the next case reveals, for example, a challenged practice may affect black women differently than either women generally or blacks generally. For the original article proposing such a theory of discrimination, *see* Kimberle Crenshaw, *Demarginalizing the Intersection of Race and Sex: A Black Feminist Critique of Antidiscriminatory Doctrine, Feminist Theory and Antiracist Politics*, 1989 U. Chi. Legal F. 139.

Rogers v. American Airlines

Federal District Court of the Southern District of New York, 1981.
527 F. Supp. 229.

■ SOFAER, DISTRICT JUDGE.

Plaintiff is a black woman who seeks $10,000 damages, injunctive, and declaratory relief against enforcement of a grooming policy of the defendant American Airlines that prohibits employees in certain employment categories from wearing an all-braided hairstyle. Plaintiff has been an American Airlines employee for approximately eleven years, and has been an airport operations agent for over one year. Her duties involve extensive passenger contact, including greeting passengers, issuing boarding passes, and checking luggage. She alleges that the policy violates her rights under the Thirteenth Amendment of the United States Constitution, under Title VII of the Civil Rights Act, 42 U.S.C. s 2000e et seq. (1976), and under 42 U.S.C. s 1981 (1976), in that it discriminates against her as a woman, and more specifically as a black woman. She claims that denial of the right to wear her hair in the "corn row" style intrudes upon her rights and discriminates against her.

Defendants move to dismiss plaintiff's claims. Insofar as the motion is addressed to the claim under the Thirteenth Amendment, it is meritorious. That provision prohibits practices that constitute a "badge of slavery" and, unless a plaintiff alleges she does not have the option of leaving her job, does not support claims of racial discrimination in employment.

The motion is also meritorious with respect to the statutory claims insofar as they challenge the policy on its face. The statutory bases alleged, Title VII and section 1981, are indistinguishable in the circumstances of this case, and will be considered together. The policy is addressed to both men and women, black and white. Plaintiff's assertion that the policy has practical effect only with respect to women is not supported by any factual allegations. Many men have hair longer than many women. Some men have hair long enough to wear in braids if they choose to do so. Even if the grooming policy imposed different standards for men and women, however, it would not violate Title VII. It follows, therefore, that an even-handed policy that prohibits to both sexes a style more often adopted by members of one sex does not constitute prohibited sex discrimination. This is because this type of regulation has at most a negligible effect on employment opportunity. It does not regulate on the basis of any immutable characteristic of the employees involved. It concerns a matter of relatively low importance in terms of the constitutional interests protected by the Fourteenth Amendment and Title VII, rather than involving fundamental rights such as the right to have children or to marry. The complaint does not state a claim for sex discrimination.

The considerations with respect to plaintiff's race discrimination claim would clearly be the same except for plaintiff's assertion that the "corn row" style has a special significance for black women. She contends that it "has been, historically, a fashion and style adopted by Black American women, reflective of cultural, historical essence of the Black women in American society." Plaintiff's Memo. in Opposition to Motion to Dismiss, p. 4. "The style was 'popularized' so to speak, within the larger society, when Cicely Tyson adopted the same for an appearance on nationally viewed Academy Awards presentation several years ago. It was and is analogous to the public statement by the late Malcolm X regarding the Afro hair style. At the bottom line, the completely braided hair style, sometimes referred to as corn rows, has been and continues to be part of the cultural and historical essence of Black American women." Id. at 4–5. "There can be little doubt that, if American adopted a policy which foreclosed Black women/all women from wearing hair styled as an 'Afro/bush,' that policy would have very pointedly racial dynamics and consequences reflecting a vestige of slavery unwilling to die (that is, a master mandate that one wear hair divorced from ones historical and cultural perspective and otherwise consistent with the 'white master' dominated society and preference thereof)." Id. at 14–15.

Plaintiff is entitled to a presumption that her arguments, largely repeated in her affidavit, are true. But the grooming policy applies equally to members of all races, and plaintiff does not allege that an all-braided hair style is worn exclusively or even predominantly by black people. Moreover, it is proper to note that defendants have alleged without contravention that plaintiff first appeared at work in the all-braided hairstyle on or about September 25, 1980, soon after the style had been popularized by a white actress in the film "10." Affidavit of Robert Zurlo. Plaintiff may be correct that an employer's policy prohibiting the "Afro/bush" style might offend Title VII and section 1981.

But if so, this chiefly would be because banning a natural hairstyle would implicate the policies underlying the prohibition of discrimination on the basis of immutable characteristics. But cf. Smith v. Delta Air Lines, *supra*, (upholding no-mustache, short-sideburn policy despite showing that black males had more difficulty complying due to nature of hair growth). In any event, an all-braided hairstyle is a different matter. It is not the product of natural hair growth but of artifice. An all-braided hair style is an "easily changed characteristic," and, even if socioculturally associated with a particular race or nationality, is not an impermissible basis for distinctions in the application of employment practices by an employer. *Carswell v. Peachford Hospital,* 26 EPD P 32,012 (N.D.Ga.1981*)* (employee fired for wearing "corn row" style in violation of hospital policy not entitled to relief under Title VII). The Fifth Circuit recently upheld, without requiring any showing of business purpose, an employer's policy prohibiting the speaking of any language but English in the workplace, despite the importance of Spanish to the ethnic identity of Mexican-Americans. *Gloor v. Garcia, supra,* 618 F.2d 264, 267–69 (5th Cir. 1980). The court stated that Title VII

> is directed only at specific impermissible bases of discrimination—race, color, religion, sex, or national origin. National origin must not be confused with ethnic or sociocultural traits. . . . Save for religion, the discriminations on which the Act focuses its laser of prohibition are those that are either beyond the victim's power to alter, or that impose a burden on an employee on one of the prohibited bases. . . . "(A) hiring policy that distinguishes on some other ground, such as grooming codes or length of hair, is related more closely to the employer's choice of how to run his business than to equality of employment opportunity."

Id. at 269 (footnotes and citations omitted).

Although the Act may shield "employees' psychological as well as economic fringes" from employer abuse, *see Rogers v. EEOC,* 454 F.2d 234, 238 (5th Cir. 1971) (optical clinic's practice of segregating patients on the basis of national origin may create a "discriminatory atmosphere" in violation of minority employees' rights), plaintiff's allegations do not amount to charging American with "a practice of creating a working environment heavily charged with ethnic or racial discrimination," or one "so heavily polluted with discrimination as to destroy completely the emotional and psychological stability of minority group workers. . . ." Id. If an even-handed English-only policy that has the effect of prohibiting a Mexican-American from speaking Spanish during working hours is valid without a showing of business purpose, the policy at issue here, even if ill-advised, does not offend the law.

Moreover, the airline did not require plaintiff to restyle her hair. It suggested that she could wear her hair as she liked while off duty, and permitted her to pull her hair into a bun and wrap a hairpiece around the bun during working hours. A similar policy was approved in Carswell v. Peachford Hospital, *supra*. Plaintiff has done this, but alleges that the hairpiece has caused her severe headaches. A larger hairpiece would seem in order. But even if any hairpiece would cause such discomfort, the policy does not offend a substantial interest. Cf. *EEOC v. Greyhound Lines, Inc.*, 635 F.2d 188 (3d Cir. 1980) (upholding no-beard policy despite showing that some black men had difficulty complying due to racially-linked skin disease).

Plaintiff has failed to allege sufficient facts to require defendants to demonstrate that the policy has a bona fide business purpose. In this regard, however, plaintiff does not dispute defendant's assertion that the policy was adopted in order to help American project a conservative and business-like image, a consideration recognized as a bona fide business purpose. Rather she objects to its impact with respect to the "corn row" style, an impact not protected against by Title VII or section 1981.

Plaintiff also asserts in her complaint that the regulation has been applied in an uneven and discriminatory manner. She claims that white women in particular have been permitted to wear pony tails and shag cuts. She goes on to claim, in fact, that some black women are permitted to wear the same hairstyle that she has been prohibited from wearing. These claims seriously undercut her assertion that the policy discriminates against women, and her claim that it discriminates against black women in particular. Conceivably, however, the complaint could be construed as alleging that the policy has been applied in a discriminatory manner against plaintiff because she is black by some representative of the defendant. On its face, this allegation is sufficient, although it might be subject to dismissal on a summary judgment motion if it is not supplemented with some factual claims.

This remaining claim—of racially discriminatory application—by its nature is not appropriate for class action treatment. In light of plaintiff's assertions that both white and black women in the purported class have been permitted to wear the all-braided style, she seems to be saying, ultimately, that there are no similarly situated people, and she does not identify any. Therefore, the motion for class certification is denied. Indeed, even as broadly alleged, plaintiff's claims would not warrant certification of a class. Plaintiff seeks specific retroactive monetary relief only for herself and not for any class members. With respect to the class, plaintiff seeks a change in company policy, and a victory in plaintiff's case, with an injunctive and declaratory order, would afford relief to all similarly situated people.

This action is dismissed, except for plaintiff's claim of discriminatory treatment in the application of the grooming policy.

NOTES AND QUESTIONS

1.   *Potential Claims and the Court's Response.* As with accent and language discrimination, a policy banning braided hair could be challenged under various theories of discrimination. What were Rogers' claims? Were there any she failed to make or that she could have made more persuasively? Why did the court reject her claims? Were you persuaded?

2.   *Performance.* One basis for the court's decision was that it viewed one's hairstyle as a voluntary act rather than an immutable trait associated with race. A natural "Afrobush" might qualify as inextricably tied to one's race, but not corn-rows. Is the court right that the ability to choose not to braid one's hair makes policies against such hairstyles nonracial? How voluntary was Rogers' desire to braid her hair? Even if it was voluntary, does that mean it was not part of her race?

One conception of race is that it constitutes a social marker that identifies certain groups for stigmatic treatment. Physiognomy, such as skin color and facial features, is one type of marker. But conduct also can mark race, especially conduct reflecting one's ethnic heritage. By this account, Rogers was discriminated against for "performing" race. Speaking a non-English language could also be understood this way, especially if the language is that of one's family or national origin. Should the law be interpreted to prohibit, or at least require an employer to justify, bans on certain manners of appearance and conduct even if the employee could comply with the ban? What drawbacks might such a conception of race present, including for minority employees?

The decision in *Rogers* is over thirty years old. Courts continue to explicitly follow it, however, in upholding employer grooming and appearance policies, even when such policies have a racially disparate impact. For example, courts have in recent years upheld Abercrombie & Fitch's firing of a black female sales associate for having blonde streaks in her hair, *Burchette v. Abercrombie & Fitch Stores, Inc.*, 2010 WL 1948322 (S.D.N.Y. 2010); firing of a black female ticket sales-person at a theme park for wearing her hair in cornrows, *Pitts v. Wild Adventures, Inc.*, 2008 WL 1899306 (M.D. Ga. 2008); and refusal to hire a black female for the housekeeping staff of a hotel because she insisted on keeping her hair blonde, which the hotel viewed as "extreme," *Santee v. Windsor Court Hotel Ltd. P'ship*, 2000 WL 1610775 (E.D. La. 2000). In each of these cases, moreover, the court declined to require the employer to justify the policy, ruling instead that because the policies applied to voluntary conduct, they did not implicate race at all. Indeed, in *Santee*, the court assumed that a hotel could permit white but not black housekeeping staff to wear their hair blonde, without justification, because grooming policies simply don't involve race. Does that make sense? For more on law, race, and hair, see Paulette M. Caldwell, *A Hair Piece: Perspectives on the Intersection of Race and Gender*, 1991 Duke L.J. 365 and Angela Onwuachi-Willig, *Another Hair Piece: Exploring New Strands of Analysis under Title VII*, 98 Geo. L.J. 1079 (2010).

3.   *Intersectionality. Rogers* and the cases in the previous Note all involved black women. Rogers argued that she was discriminated against because she was a "black woman," not just because she was black or because she was a woman. As explained in the Notes preceding *Rogers*, scholars have termed her claim one of "intersectionality;" she was discriminated against because of the intersection or combination of two protected traits—race and sex—that together create a unique identity distinct from one's race or sex alone. How should courts treat claims of intersectionality?

Lam v. University of Hawai'i
Court of Appeals, Ninth Circuit, 1994.
40 F.3d 1551.

■ REINHARDT, CIRCUIT JUDGE:

Professor Maivan Clech Lam, a woman of Vietnamese descent, claims that the University of Hawai'i's Richardson School of Law ("the Law School") discriminated against her on the basis of her race, sex and national origin both times she applied for the position of Director of the Law School's Pacific Asian Legal Studies (PALS) Program. [After two extensive and rancorous searches, the faculty hiring committee for the position declined to hire anyone after their first offer to a white female was declined. The District Court granted summary judgment for the Law School.]

The district court found that Lam had established a *prima facie* case of discrimination under the four-part *McDonnell Douglas* test. It then found that defendants had met their burden of proffering legitimate reasons for not hiring Lam—specifically, Lam's lack of scholarship, and faculty disagreement regarding the desired characteristics of the PALS director—shifting the burden back to Lam to show the existence of a triable issue of fact.

Lam submitted evidence of discriminatory bias at two stages of the hiring process, with respect to at least two senior white male professors. Most significantly, [there was testimony] that Professor A., who headed the appointments committee for a month and disparaged Lam's abilities before the committee and the faculty as a whole, had a biased attitude toward women and Asians. Indeed, the district court specifically found that "the evidence suggests that Professor A. harbored prejudicial feelings towards Asians and women." There was also evidence that another white male professor had stated that, given Japanese cultural prejudices, the PALS director should be male. This evidence is, as a matter of law, sufficient to preclude the award of summary judgment for defendants.

The district court's second justification for granting summary judgment was based on the defendants' favorable consideration of two other candidates for the PALS position: one an Asian man, the other a white woman. In assessing the significance of these candidates, the court seemed to view racism and sexism as separate and distinct elements amenable to almost mathematical treatment, so that evaluating discrimination against an Asian woman became a simple matter of performing two separate tasks: looking for racism "alone" and looking for sexism "alone," with Asian men and white women as the corresponding model victims. The court questioned Lam's claim of racism in light of the fact that the Dean had been interested in the late application of an Asian male.[7] Similarly, it concluded that the faculty's subsequent offer of employment to a white woman indicated a lack of gender bias. We conclude that in relying on these facts as a basis for its summary judgment decision, the district court misconceived important legal principles.

As other courts have recognized, where two bases for discrimination exist, they cannot be neatly reduced to distinct components. Rather than aiding the decisional process, the attempt to bisect a person's identity at the intersection of race and gender often distorts or ignores the particular nature of their experiences. *Cf. Moore v. Hughes Helicopters, Inc.,* 708 F.2d 475, 480 (9th Cir. 1983) (black female not necessarily representative of interests of black males and white females). Like other subclasses under Title VII, Asian women are subject to a set of stereotypes and assumptions shared neither by Asian men nor by white women.[8] In consequence, they may be targeted for discrimination "even in the absence of discrimination against [Asian] men or white women." *Jefferies,* 615 F.2d at 1032 (discussing black women). Accordingly, we agree with the *Jefferies* court that, when a plaintiff is claiming race *and* sex bias, it is necessary to determine whether the employer discriminates on the basis of that *combination* of factors, not just whether it discriminates against people of the same race or of the same sex.

3.

[D]efendants argue that *Matsushita Elec. Industrial Co. v. Zenith Radio Corp.,* 475 U.S. 574 (1986), establishes a rule, triggered here, that if the factual context renders a plaintiff's claim implausible, she must come forward with more persuasive evidence to support her claim than would otherwise be necessary. They argue that because Professor A.'s alleged ethnic and gender biases would amount to professional suicide in today's politically correct academic climate, Lam's charges "simply make[ ] no economic sense," *id.,* thus justifying this more demanding evidentiary burden.

Antidiscrimination laws are not predicated upon the existence of economically "rational" discrimination; the problem that exists and

---

[7]   Aside from the difference in gender, it is significant that Lam and the Asian male candidate were of different national origins—Lam being Vietnamese-French, the male candidate, Chinese. Lam alleged not only race discrimination but also national origin discrimination, thereby raising this distinction as relevant under Title VII. Moreover, the particular geographic consciousness of the PALS program means that the distinction might be more salient than it otherwise might be.

[8]   *See, e.g.,* J. Hagedorn, *Asian Women in Film: No Joy, No Luck,* Ms., Jan./Feb. 1994, at 74 (listing stereotypes of Asian women such as geisha, dragon lady, concubine, lotus blossom).

which such laws target is, to a large extent, stubborn but irrational prejudice. Thus, we cannot say that Lam's charges are "implausible" simply because the discriminatory actions might have an adverse economic impact on Professor A. or the University. Nor are we persuaded by the University's assertion that Lam's claims are implausible in the present academic climate because acts that have even the appearance of bias would constitute professional suicide. To accept the University's argument would be to create a presumption that acts of academic employment discrimination are implausible and that the *Matsushita* burden applies to all such cases. This presumption is patently contrary to fact and we squarely reject it. There is no question that acts of bias and discrimination occur in university hirings today. The process of rooting out discrimination against women and minorities on our nation's faculties is far from ended.

We therefore reverse the district court's award of summary judgment. . . .

NOTES AND QUESTIONS

1. ***The Court's Reasoning.*** Why did the court recognize Lam's intersectionality or "combination" claim? Were you persuaded? What are potential drawbacks to recognizing intersectionality claims?

To the extent some courts have been reluctant to recognize intersectionality, the question arises whether such claims are necessary to prohibit the kinds of discrimination that Lam and Rogers alleged they experienced. Assuming the Law School did prefer Asian men or white women over Lam, could you frame a discrimination claim based simply on race or gender without intersectionality?

The court discounted the Law School's claim that the stigma associated with racism and sexism, especially in a liberal, academic institution, undermined Lam's claims. Is the Law School's argument plausible?

The court did not focus on the fact that the program for which the Law School was hiring was the Pacific Asian Legal Studies Program. Is that relevant to assessing whether the Law School likely discriminated against Lam? Is the Law School less likely to discriminate against an Asian applicant to run such a program? Would a preference for an Asian applicant be legitimate?

2. ***Asian and Other "Racial" Identities.*** If Lam was discriminated against because of her race and/or sex, was it because she was an Asian woman or a Vietnamese woman? In granting summary judgment to the University the district court cited the school's consideration of Chinese male candidate as a reason to doubt race discrimination had occurred. But the court of appeals rejected this basis for summary judgment, suggesting that national origin distinctions could be "salient" in the case. Is "Asian" a racial category? Asian Americans come from a wide variety of national origins, including Indian, Pakistani, Korean, Chinese, Japanese, Vietnamese, Laotian, Thai, and Hmong, which have distinctive languages, cultures,

histories, and socioeconomic circumstances. Is it accurate to group them together under the racial heading "Asian"? Similar questions could be raised about Latino/as and Indians. How accurate is black as a racial identity? Are differences between black communities purely economic? What about whiteness? Do white people constitute a single race?

3. *Class Exercise: De-Biasing Intersectional Stereotypes.* Empirical research suggests that stereotypes, including those unconsciously held, can be undermined by exposing those who hold them to people and situations inconsistent with their assumptions. The inconsistency cannot be too blatant or obvious, however, for then the observer tends to discount the situation as aberrational or contrived.

Break into small groups. Next, within each group, discuss stereotypes at the intersection of race and sex. Consider what stereotypes are commonly held in American society about, for example, "Asian women," "Latino men," "Native American women," etc. Discuss all the intersections of (1) White; (2) Native American; (3) Asian; (4) Latino/a; and (5) Black, combined with (A) Male and (B) Female. Third, write or design a play, skit, song, limerick, poem, story, PSA, television pilot, or video game that depicts one or more of these people in an employment setting, in a way inconsistent with the stereotypes associated with them. Present or describe it to the class. Do not, however, reveal the race or sex of the characters you are depicting. See if the class can guess which figures you are attempting to de-bias stereotypes about. This will suggest the extent to which intersectional stereotypes are recognized in common by your classmates. Finally, discuss as a class any stereotypes not adequately discussed during the exercise, including any differences among students' beliefs about the content of these stereotypes.

We recognize that these umbrella terms do not capture the full complexity of human identities, including, for example, intersections involving sub-groups within these racial categories and gender identities not adequately described by male/female terms. A goal of the exercise is to determine whether common, intersectional stereotypes exist in American society, and we believe the ones identified by this exercise are likely to illustrate the phenomenon.

D. AFFIRMATIVE ACTION

Affirmative action, i.e., granting favorable treatment to historically disadvantaged minority groups, arises in the employment setting, as well as in higher education and government contracting. The controversy over affirmative action typically involves debates over whether such policies are justified for the benefit of black people. The following case instead involves a preference for Native Americans. Do preferences for Indians raise different interests and values than a preference for other racial groups? The Supreme Court fails to apply strict scrutiny to the Indian preference, raising the question whether strict scrutiny is necessary to determine whether an affirmative action program is constitutionally justified.

Morton v. Mancari

Supreme Court of the United States, 1974.
417 U.S. 535.

■ JUSTICE BLACKMUN delivered the opinion of the Court.

The Indian Reorganization Act of 1934, also known as the Wheeler-Howard Act, accords an employment preference for qualified Indians in the Bureau of Indian Affairs (BIA or Bureau). Appellees, non-Indian BIA employees, challenged this preference as contrary to the anti-discrimination provisions of the Equal Employment Opportunity Act of 1972 and as violative of the Due Process Clause of the Fifth Amendment. A three-judge Federal District Court concluded that the Indian preference under the 1934 Act was impliedly repealed by the 1972 Act. We noted probable jurisdiction in order to examine the statutory and constitutional validity of this longstanding Indian preference.

I

Section 12 of the Indian Reorganization Act provides:

"The Secretary of the Interior is directed to establish standards of health, age, character, experience, knowledge, and ability for Indians who may be appointed, without regard to civil-service laws, to the various positions maintained, now or hereafter, by the Indian Office, in the administration of functions or services affecting any Indian tribe. Such qualified Indians shall hereafter have the preference to appointment to vacancies in any such positions."

In June 1972, pursuant to this provision, the Commissioner of Indian Affairs, with the approval of the Secretary of the Interior, issued a directive (Personnel Management Letter No. 72–12) stating that the BIA's policy would be to grant a preference to qualified Indians not only, as before, in the initial hiring stage, but also in the situation where an Indian and a non-Indian, both already employed by the BIA, were competing for a promotion within the Bureau. The record indicates that this policy was implemented immediately.

Shortly thereafter, appellees, who are non-Indian employees of the BIA at Albuquerque, instituted this class action, on behalf of themselves and other non-Indian employees similarly situated, in the United States District Court for the District of New Mexico, claiming that the "so-called 'Indian Preference Statutes,'" were repealed by the 1972 Equal Employment Opportunity Act and deprived them of rights to property without due process of law, in violation of the Fifth Amendment. Named as defendants were the Secretary of the Interior, the Commissioner of Indian Affairs, and the BIA Directors for the Albuquerque and Navajo Area Offices. Appellees claimed that implementation and enforcement of the new preference policy "placed and will continue to place [appellees] at a distinct disadvantage in competing for promotion and training programs with Indian employees, all of which has and will continue to subject the [appellees] to discrimination and deny them equal employment opportunity."

A three-judge court was convened pursuant to 28 U.S.C. § 2282 because the complaint sought to enjoin, as unconstitutional, the enforcement of a federal statute. Appellant Amerind, a nonprofit organization representing Indian employees of the BIA, moved to intervene in support of the preference; this motion was granted by the District Court and Amerind thereafter participated at all stages of the litigation.

After a short trial focusing primarily on how the new policy, in fact, has been implemented, the District Court concluded that the Indian preference was implicitly repealed by § 11 of the Equal Employment Opportunity Act of 1972 proscribing discrimination in most federal employment on the basis of race. Having found that Congress repealed the preference, it was unnecessary for the District Court to pass on its constitutionality. The court permanently enjoined appellants "from implementing any policy in the Bureau of Indian Affairs which would hire, promote, or reassign any person in preference to another solely for the reason that such person is an Indian."

II

The federal policy of according some hiring preference to Indians in the Indian service dates at least as far back as 1834. Since that time, Congress repeatedly has enacted various preferences of the general type here at issue. The purpose of these preferences, as variously expressed in the legislative history, has been to give Indians a greater participation in their own self-government; to further the Government's trust obligation toward the Indian tribes; and to reduce the negative effect of having non-Indians administer matters that affect Indian tribal life.

The preference directly at issue here was enacted as an important part of the sweeping Indian Reorganization Act of 1934. The overriding purpose of that particular Act was to establish machinery whereby Indian tribes would be able to assume a greater degree of self-government, both politically and economically. Congress was seeking to modify the then-existing situation whereby the primarily non-Indian-staffed BIA had plenary control, for all practical purposes, over the lives and destinies of the federally recognized Indian tribes. Initial congressional proposals would have diminished substantially the role of the BIA by turning over to federally chartered self-governing Indian communities many of the functions normally performed by the Bureau. Committee sentiment, however, ran against such a radical change in the role of the BIA. The solution ultimately adopted was to strengthen tribal government while continuing the active role of the BIA, with the understanding that the Bureau would be more responsive to the interests of the people it was created to serve.

One of the primary means by which self-government would be fostered and the Bureau made more responsive was to increase the participation of tribal Indians in the BIA operations. In order to achieve this end, it was recognized that some kind of preference and exemption from otherwise prevailing civil service requirements was necessary. Congressman Howard, the House sponsor, expressed the need for the preference:

> "The Indians have not only been thus deprived of civic rights and powers, but they have been largely deprived of the opportunity to enter the more important positions in the service of the very bureau which manages their affairs. Theoretically, the Indians have the right to qualify for the Federal civil service. In actual practice there has been no adequate program of training to qualify Indians to compete in these examinations, especially for technical and higher positions; and even if there were such training, the Indians would have to compete under existing law, on equal terms with multitudes of white applicants. . . .The various services on the Indian reservations are actually local rather than Federal services and are comparable to local municipal and county services, since they are dealing with purely local Indian problems. It should be possible for Indians with the requisite vocational and professional training to enter the service of their own people without the necessity of competing with white applicants for these positions. This bill permits them to do so." 78 Cong. Rec. 11729 (1934).

Congress was well aware that the proposed preference would result in employment disadvantages within the BIA for non-Indians. Not only was this displacement unavoidable if room were to be made for Indians, but it was explicitly determined that gradual replacement of non-Indians with Indians within the Bureau was a desirable feature of the entire program for self-government. Since 1934, the BIA has implemented the preference with a fair degree of success. The percentage of Indians employed in the Bureau rose from 34% in 1934 to 57% in 1972. This reversed the former downward trend, and was due, clearly, to the presence of the 1934 Act. The Commissioner's extension of the preference in 1972 to promotions within the BIA was designed to bring more Indians into positions of responsibility and, in that regard, appears to be a logical extension of the congressional intent.

III

It is against this background that we encounter the first issue in the present case: whether the Indian preference was repealed by the Equal Employment Opportunity Act of 1972. Title VII of the Civil Rights Act of 1964 was the first major piece of federal legislation prohibiting discrimination in *private* employment on the basis of "race, color, religion, sex, or national origin." 42 U.S.C. § 2000e–2(a).

Appellees assert, and the District Court held, that since the 1972 Act proscribed racial discrimination in Government employment, the Act necessarily, albeit sub silentio, repealed the provision of the 1934 Act that called for the preference in the BIA of one racial group, Indians, over non-Indians:

[The Supreme Court disagreed, concluding that Congress did not intend the 1972 Act to repeal the Indian preference authorized by the 1934 Act. The Court cited several reasons related to Congress's long-standing relationship to Indian tribes and a host of past and recent congressional laws intended to benefit Indians.]

IV

We still must decide whether, as the appellees contend, the preference constitutes invidious racial discrimination in violation of the Due Process Clause of the Fifth Amendment. Resolution of the instant issue turns on the unique legal status of Indian tribes under federal law and upon the plenary power of Congress, based on a history of treaties and the assumption of a "guardian-ward" status, to legislate on behalf of federally recognized Indian tribes. The plenary power of Congress to deal with the special problems of Indians is drawn both explicitly and implicitly from the Constitution itself. Article I, § 8, cl.3, provides Congress with the power to "regulate Commerce . . . with the Indian Tribes," and thus, to this extent, singles Indians out as a proper subject for separate legislation. Article II, § 2, cl.2, gives the President the power, by and with the advice and consent of the Senate, to make treaties. This has often been the source of the Government's power to deal with the Indian tribes. The Court has described the origin and nature of the special relationship:

> "In the exercise of the war and treaty powers, the United States overcame the Indians and took possession of their lands, sometimes by force, leaving them an uneducated, helpless and dependent people, needing protection against the selfishness of others and their own improvidence. Of necessity the United States assumed the duty of furnishing that protection, and with it the authority to do all that was required to perform that obligation and to prepare the Indians to take their place as independent, qualified members of the modern body politic. . . ." *Board of County Comm'rs v. Seber,* 318 U.S. 705, 715 (1943).

Literally every piece of legislation dealing with Indian tribes and reservations, and certainly all legislation dealing with the BIA, single out for special treatment a constituency of tribal Indians living on or near reservations. If these laws, derived from historical relationships and explicitly designed to help only Indians, were deemed invidious racial discrimination, an entire Title of the United States Code (25 U.S.C.)

would be effectively erased and the solemn commitment of the Government toward the Indians would be jeopardized.

It is in this historical and legal context that the constitutional validity of the Indian preference is to be determined. As discussed above, Congress in 1934 determined that proper fulfillment of its trust required turning over to the Indians a greater control of their own destinies. The overly paternalistic approach of prior years had proved both exploitative and destructive of Indian interests. Congress was united in the belief that institutional changes were required. An important part of the Indian Reorganization Act was the preference provision here at issue.

Contrary to the characterization made by appellees, this preference does not constitute "racial discrimination." Indeed, it is not even a 'racial' preference.[9] Rather, it is an employment criterion reasonably designed to further the cause of Indian self-government and to make the BIA more responsive to the needs of its constituent groups. It is directed to participation by the governed in the governing agency. The preference is similar in kind to the constitutional requirement that a United States Senator, when elected, be "an Inhabitant of that State for which he shall be chosen," Art. I, § 3, cl.3, or that a member of a city council reside within the city governed by the council. Congress has sought only to enable the BIA to draw more heavily from among the constituent group in staffing its projects, all of which, either directly or indirectly, affect the lives of tribal Indians. The preference, as applied, is granted to Indians not as a discrete racial group, but, rather, as members of quasi-sovereign tribal entities whose lives and activities are governed by the BIA in a unique fashion. *See* n.24, *supra.* In the sense that there is no other group of people favored in this manner, the legal status of the BIA is truly sui generis. Furthermore, the preference applies only to employment in the Indian service. The preference does not cover any other Government agency or activity, and we need not consider the obviously more difficult question that would be presented by a blanket exemption for Indians from all civil service examinations. Here, the preference is reasonably and directly related to a legitimate, nonracially based goal. This is the

---

[9] The preference is not directed towards a "racial" group consisting of "Indians"; instead, it applies only to members of "federally recognized" tribes. This operates to exclude many individuals who are racially to be classified as 'Indians.' In this sense, the preference is political rather than racial in nature. The eligibility criteria appear in 44 BIAM 335, 3.1:

> "1. Policy—An Indian has preference in appointment in the Bureau. To be eligible for preference in appointment, promotion, and training, an individual must be one-fourth or more degree Indian blood and be a member of a Federally-recognized tribe. It is the policy for promotional consideration that where two or more candidates who met the established qualification requirements are available for filling a vacancy, if one of them is an Indian, he shall be given preference in filling the vacancy. In accordance with the policy statement approved by the Secretary, the Commissioner may grant exceptions to this policy by approving the selection and appointment of non-Indians, when he considers it in the best interest of the Bureau.

> "This program does not restrict the right of management to fill positions by methods other than through promotion. Positions may be filled by transfers, reassignment, reinstatement, or initial appointment." App. 92.

principal characteristic that generally is absent from proscribed forms of racial discrimination.

On numerous occasions this Court specifically has upheld legislation that singles out Indians for particular and special treatment. As long as the special treatment can be tied rationally to the fulfillment of Congress' unique obligation toward the Indians, such legislative judgments will not be disturbed. Here, where the preference is reasonable and rationally designed to further Indian self-government, we cannot say that Congress' classification violates due process.

NOTES AND QUESTIONS

1. *The Court's Holding and Reasoning.* The Court's statutory and constitutional holdings are seemingly inconsistent on the question whether Indians are a race. The Court holds that the BIA's hiring and promotional preference for Indians is not prohibited by the 1972 Amendments to Title VII that extended prohibitions on race discrimination to the federal government. The Court reasons that Congress did not intend the 1972 Act to apply to Indians, at least not in the context of "special" legislation by Congress. Notice, however, that the Court's explication of the historical relationship between the federal government and Indian tribes in evaluating the statutory claim is premised on Indians constituting a race. Otherwise, the Court could simply have dismissed the suit as not involving race discrimination and therefore not implicating Title VII at all. In contrast, the portion of the opinion on the constitutional claim holds that the Indian hiring preference did not violate the equal protection component of the Fifth Amendment's Due Process Clause because the preference did *not* involve race. Are the two parts of the opinion reconcilable? If not, which is more accurate in describing the BIA preference, that is, does it involve race or not? If it does involve race, why might the Court have denied that fact?

2. *The Necessity of Strict Scrutiny.* Notice also that in the early part of the due process analysis, in which the Court viewed the preference as racial, it did not view it with the suspicion it typically accords government policies that classify by race, including for affirmative action purposes. Why might the Court have been unconcerned that this racially preferential hiring practice was rooted in the kinds of animus or stereotypes that have concerned the Court in other affirmative action cases? And why might the Court not have been concerned that the preference was racially divisive or might reinforce stereotypes in the same way as other preferential policies the Court has evaluated? Was the Court justified in finding the preference to be benign without subjecting it to strict scrutiny? In other affirmative action cases, the Court has explained that only by subjecting a racial preference to strict scrutiny can the Court know if it is, in fact, benign. Is this situation different, or is the Court's assumption about the need to subject other racial preferences to strict scrutiny questionable?

3. *Holding Current Society Responsible for Past Wrongs.* Consider also that the Court views with approval the federal government's

responsibility toward Indians in light of the government's extreme mistreatment of them in the past. But those atrocities were not committed during the lifetimes of Americans in power today or of the current taxpayers funding such federal programs for the benefit of Indians. Is it fair to hold the government and American people morally and financially responsible now for wrongs perpetrated against Indians during prior generations? If it is fair, would reparations to Native Americans paid from the federal government for past atrocities be fair to current Americans? What about reparations to blacks for past slavery and segregation? Recall your discussions of reparations in your study of Chapter 1.

4.   *Constitutionality of Affirmative Action.* As alluded to above and as revealed in other chapters of this book, the Supreme Court typically subjects racial preferences in government employment to strict scrutiny under the Fourteenth Amendment's Equal Protection Clause or the Fifth Amendment's Due Process Clause. Under such scrutiny, the Court will uphold an affirmative action policy only if the government proves that the racial preference is necessary or narrowly tailored to advance a compelling government interest. The test is very challenging, and the courts strike down the overwhelming number of laws subjected to it. In *Wygant v. Jackson Board of Education*, 476 U.S. 267 (19876), the Court held that remedying the effects of past societal discrimination was not sufficiently compelling to justify a racial preference used to protect minority school teachers from last-hired-first-fired lay-offs. The Court also rejected providing role models to minority school children as a justification for the lay-off preference. The Court does permit racial preferences to remedy "identified" racial discrimination but the need to identify the discrimination with particularity and to tailor the preference to the victims of discrimination makes this interest virtually impossible for a government entity to establish as a justification for race-based affirmative action. We saw in the higher education chapter that the Court has upheld the pursuit of diversity in higher education as compelling, at least in the law school setting. Whether that interest will survive the next Supreme Court case is uncertain. What is clear is that racial preferences by government employers are very unlikely to withstand constitutional scrutiny. To the extent *Mancari* suggests otherwise for Indian preferences, the case may be limited to contexts in which Congress is dealing with federally recognized Indian tribes as sovereign entities rather than when federal or state employers are acting in a more domestic capacity.

5.   *Exercise: Making Arguments.* If the Court did subject the Indian preference to strict scrutiny, how would it fare? If you were representing a tribe, what arguments would you make to prove that the statute discussed in *Mancari* withstands strict scrutiny? What is the compelling interest? Does the US government's unique relationship with Native American tribes have any impact on this? To what extent? Do similar historical considerations justify hiring preferences for African Americans? What about other racial groups?

6. *Affirmative Action Under Title VII.* In contrast to the Court's deferential approach to the BIA preference in *Morton*, the Court ordinarily subjects affirmative action policies by both public and private employers challenged under Title VII to a difficult but not insurmountable test. The Court will uphold racially preferential employment practices only if: (1) there is a manifest racial imbalance in a traditionally segregated job category, and (2) the preference does not unduly trammel the rights of other employees. *See United Steelworkers of America v. Weber*, 443 U.S. 193 (1979) (upholding voluntary preference for black apprentices for training program that traditionally admitted few blacks); *Johnson v. Transportation Agency*, 480 U.S. 616 (1987) (upholding mild preference for female promotion to position that was traditionally male). In devising the test in *Weber*, the Court had to respond to the argument that Title VII, more than the Equal Protection Clause, contains explicit text forbidding race discrimination and, moreover, has no exception for race, unlike the BFOQ exception we saw for sex, national origin, and religion. In rejecting this argument, the Court reasoned that the purpose of Title VII was to eliminate and redress employment discrimination against historically excluded racial groups, especially African Americans. Since affirmative action on behalf of such groups advanced the goal of Title VII, such policies are lawful despite the explicit language of Title VII to the contrary:

> It is a "familiar rule that a thing may be within the letter of the statute and yet not within the statute, because not within its spirit nor within the intention of its makers." The prohibition against racial discrimination in §§ 703(a) and (d) of Title VII must therefore be read against the background of the legislative history of Title VII and the historical context from which the Act arose. . . .
>
> Examination of those sources makes clear that an interpretation of the sections that forbade all race-conscious affirmative action would "bring about an end completely at variance with the purpose of the statute" and must be rejected.

Weber at 201–202 (internal citations omitted). *Weber* upheld a voluntary affirmative action plan by a company that had intentionally excluded blacks throughout the company's history. The following case illustrates a more contemporary application of the *Weber* standard.

Dix v. United Air Lines

District Court of the Northern District of Illinois, 2000.
No. 99 C 2597, 2000 WL 1230463.

■ KENNELY, J.

Plaintiff Christopher Dix, who filed this lawsuit *pro se,* claims that defendant United Air Lines, Inc. discriminated against him on the basis of his race (Caucasian) in violation of Title VII of the Civil Rights Act of 1964, 42 U.S.C. § 2000e–2(a) & (*l*), and 42 U.S.C. § 1981 in connection with Dix's application to become a flight attendant. Specifically, Dix says that United required Caucasian applicants to be bilingual but did not impose the same requirement on African-American applicants; he alleges that he was subjected to different terms and conditions of employment based on his race. Though Dix does not specifically allege in his complaint that he was not hired as a result of differential treatment, it is a fair inference that that is what he claims.

United has moved for summary judgment, arguing that the different requirements for Caucasian and African-American applicants had nothing to do with why Dix was not hired, and that even assuming it did, the policy was entirely legal. Dix has likewise moved for summary judgment, arguing that he was denied employment due to an illegally discriminatory hiring practice.

Facts

United periodically conducts "open interview" sessions for prospective flight attendants. During some periods, United seeks to hire flight attendants who are conversant in a second language besides English. During these periods, otherwise qualified applicants who are not conversant in a second language are advised that their applications will be kept on file for a year and will be considered when United is not seeking applicants with foreign language skills.

Since 1995, during periods when it is seeking bilingual flight attendants, United has excused African-Americans from the second-language requirement, in an effort to increase its minority hiring. Overall, however, a large number of non-bilingual applicants are selected to participate in United's training program for flight attendants. In 1997, 66% of the non-bilingual applicants selected (1303 of 1969) were white; in 1998, the figure was 65% (1175 of 1811).

In July 1998, Dix saw a newspaper advertisement placed by United seeking "bilingual flight attendants." The ad gave the time and place for several open interview sessions in Rosemont, Illinois. Dix, though not bilingual, attended one of the sessions. He says that at the outset of the session, a United representative stated to those present that "everybody here has to be conversant in another language unless you are African-American" and that "if you don't meet these requirements, you should leave." Dix was not bilingual or conversant in a second language, but he did not leave.

Dix and the forty or so other applicants who stayed were taken to another room where each was given a "Personal Information Sheet" and a "Flight Attendant Application Registration Form" to complete. On the form, Dix checked off that he was conversant in an "other" language, but did not say what language it was. (The form listed only foreign languages, not English; presumably Dix was indicating that English was the "other" language in which he was conversant.)

Following administration of a written test, the applicants were each asked to give an oral presentation on why he or she would be a good flight attendant. In his interview, Dix received poor scores, below the minimum acceptable for "professional image" and "oral communication skills." It is undisputed that it never came up that Dix was not conversant in any language other than English. After the presentations, United's representative announced that three people were being chosen to continue with the interview process; Dix was not one of the three, nor were any African-Americans.

In 1973, the Equal Employment Opportunity Commission sued United, alleging that it had engaged in a pattern and practice of discrimination on the basis of race in employment in a number of positions, including that of flight attendant. *EEOC v. United Air Lines, Inc.,* No. 73 C 972 (N.D.Ill.). In 1976, United entered into a consent decree requiring it to take affirmative measures to recruit African-American flight attendants and setting short-term and long-term goals for the representation of African-Americans in flight attendant positions. At that time, 10.3% of United's flight attendants were from minority groups; it is unclear what percentage of its flight attendants were African-American. The decree included a "long term" goal, which the parties hoped United would be able to meet within five years, that 17% of United's flight attendants would be members of minority groups.

United still maintains an affirmative action program with respect to the hiring of African-American flight attendants. As of January 1, 1998, 8.66% of its flight attendants were African-American, as compared with 15% in the qualified labor pool.

Discussion

We will deal with United's summary judgment motion first. In addressing that motion, we construe the facts in the light most favorable to Dix, the non-moving party, and draw reasonable inferences in his favor. *Celotex Corp. v. Catrett,* 417 U.S. 317, 322 (1986).

Assuming for purposes of discussion that United in fact had an unlawfully discriminatory policy, Dix must have evidence from which a reasonable fact finder could conclude that he was injured as a result of that policy. *See Melendez v. Illinois Bell Telephone Co.,* 79 F.3d 661, 668 (7th Cir.1995). He has none. Dix noted on the Personal Information Sheet that he *was* conversant in another language. Even though this was untrue, it is undisputed that Dix was not asked about this in his interview. In short, there is no evidence that his inability to speak a language other than English had anything to do with the fact that he was not hired. Indeed, there is no evidence that United's representatives had any idea that he lacked the ability to speak another language. Dix's alleged injury (the non-hiring) thus was not the result of the allegedly discriminatory policy. Rather, the evidence is undisputed that Dix was rejected because he performed poorly in his interview.

Dix's fallback position is that he was hampered in his interview because he was distressed by the fact that United's representative had started the session by announcing what Dix felt was a discriminatory policy. It is conceivable that a Title VII or § 1981 plaintiff could, in appropriate circumstances, sustain a claim on such a theory. To illustrate, imagine that United's representative had started the meeting by saying that black people don't have what it takes to be a flight attendant, or that any man who applies to be a flight attendant must be gay. A plaintiff who could show that he or she was chilled from proceeding, or that his performance at the ensuing job interview was affected, by such discriminatory statements might well be able to make out a claim under Title VII. But even if this is a viable theory in the abstract, a plaintiff making such a claim would have to show, at a minimum, that the employer's statements reflected *unlawfully* discriminatory attitudes or beliefs; otherwise an employer would be subject to suit for announcing a perfectly legal affirmative action plan. We turn, therefore, to United's justification for its differential treatment of Caucasians and African-Americans at the interview session.

United maintains that excusing the two-language requirement for African-Americans was part of a legal affirmative action plan. As noted earlier, United entered into a consent decree with the EEOC in 1976 requiring it to take affirmative steps to increase the percentage of African-American flight attendants. It maintains that its differential treatment of African-American and other applicants at the Rosemont interview session was one aspect of its continued pursuit of this policy. An affirmative action plan is valid under Title VII if it is adopted and designed to correct manifest racial imbalances in traditionally segregated job categories and does not unnecessarily trammel the interests of white employees. *Johnson v. Transportation Agency,* 480 U.S. 616, 628 (1987).

United has offered some evidence of a historical imbalance among African-Americans in flight attendant positions. As of January 1998, 8.66% of United's flight attendants were African-American; the general population is 15% African-American. Dix objects that the comparison is not relevant, as United hires only persons with a high school education as flight attendants; he says that United should have to demonstrate an imbalance between its work force and the percentage of African-Americans with a high school education. But *Johnson* makes clear that a perfect comparative fit of the type Dix seeks is not required when an employer is attempting to justify an affirmative action plan as a defense to a discrimination suit; the Supreme Court in *Johnson* noted that in *Steelworkers v. Weber,* 443 U.S. 193, 198–99 (1979), it had approved a comparison quite similar to the one that United has used here. *Johnson,* 480 U.S. at 633, nn.10 & 11.

United's evidence is somewhat thin on the question of whether the imbalance is "historic." It claims that the 1976 consent decree "recognized" a historic imbalance; however, it cites no particular provision of the decree to support this claim, and we see no such finding in the decree itself. But the attachments to the decree reflect that as of 1976, 10.3% of United's flight attendants were members of minority groups (a classification considerably broader than African-Americans), as compared with 17% in the population at large; the percentage of minorities in the general population was not materially lower in 1976 than in 1998. So United has succeeded, though by the skin of its teeth, in showing that a historic imbalance exists.

To determine whether an affirmative action plan unnecessarily trammels the interests of white employees, a court must consider whether the plan absolutely bars whites from employment, whether white workers are discharged because of the plan, and whether the plan is intended to last only until the company can achieve racial balance. *See Weber,* 443 U.S. at 208. United's plan certainly qualifies on the first two aspects of this test. The plan does not bar whites, not even non-bilingual whites, from employment as flight attendants. United has offered evidence, uncontradicted by Dix, that in 1997–98, fully two-thirds of the non-bilingual applicants selected by United were Caucasians. Moreover, the plan relates only to hiring, not to discharge; there is no indication that white workers are discharged because of the plan.

Though United has offered no evidence concerning the anticipated duration of the plan, this is not critical in this case, for three reasons. First, it appears that United is still operating pursuant to the 1976 consent decree, which means that its affirmative action program is subject to court supervision. Second, the burden of any uncertainty falls upon Dix, not United; when an employer articulates an affirmative action plan as the basis for the challenged employment decision or action, the burden lies with the plaintiff to show that the plan is invalid or that the employer's reliance on it is a pretext for discrimination. Dix has done neither. Finally, United's plan takes a gradual approach with a minimal intrusion on the legitimate expectations of other applicants; non-bilingual Caucasians like Dix still have ample opportunities for employment as United flight attendants. Under these circumstances, the longer duration of the plan is less significant.

In sum, Dix has offered no evidence from which a fact finder could conclude that United's affirmative action plan is invalid. He therefore cannot defeat United's motion for summary judgment.

NOTES AND QUESTIONS

1. *The Court's Reasoning.* What were the plaintiff's alternative arguments in *Dix*? Why did the court reject them? What weaknesses did the defendant's case involve and why were they overcome?

2. *Purposes of Affirmative Action.* As applied in *Dix*, the Supreme Court's test for affirmative action under Title VII requires that the job for which affirmative action is used must be one that has been historically or traditionally segregated in the employer's work force. But if minorities are underrepresented in a job classification only in recent years, why shouldn't an employer be able to use affirmative action to correct that underrepresentation? What purpose does the court's test seem to reflect? What purposes should be allowed as a justification for affirmative action under Title VII?

3.   *Harms of Affirmative Action.* What harms are plausibly caused by an employer's affirmative action program? What harms may result from that policy in *Dix*? Does the court's test for upholding affirmative action ameliorate those harms? How?

4.   *The Foreign Language Preference.* Why might United Airlines have relieved black applicants of speaking a foreign language? It obviously increases the number of black applicants who can be hired, but does it also serve any purpose similar to the purpose of the foreign language preference? Will black flight attendants be able to communicate with certain passengers better than the white flight attendants? Recall also our discussion in connection with *Spun Steak* case regarding whether language discrimination should be treated as race discrimination. Did United Airlines' policy discriminate against monolingual applicants in a way that should be viewed as a form of wrongful discrimination on the basis of language? Is United Airlines' policy of preferring English speakers who also speak a foreign language a form of affirmative action for bilinguals, a kind of reverse-*Spun Steak*?

5.   *The Anomalous Gap Between Title VII and Equal Protection Doctrine.* Typically, when a statute covers government action that also implicates constitutional concerns, courts interpret the statute, if reasonably possible, to permit the government to do only what the Constitution permits. Otherwise, the courts would have to invalidate the government's action on constitutional grounds, a move they prefer not to take. In the employment context, however, the Supreme Court has thus far interpreted Title VII to allow what the Constitution, as interpreted, forbids. As we saw in *Dix*, the Court's statutory test under Title VII permits government employers to engage in racially preferential employment practices provided there is a manifest racial imbalance in traditionally segregated jobs. While this standard is demanding, it is not as demanding as strict scrutiny under the Equal Protection Clause. For one thing, a manifest imbalance would not suffice as "identified discrimination" sufficient to withstand strict scrutiny. It is reasonable to expect that the anomalous situation in which Title VII permits what the Constitution forbids will be corrected in the near future. That is, the Court will likely narrow the range of permissible affirmative action under Title VII to the range permitted by the Equal Protection Clause. Such a move would also narrow the range of affirmative action permitted by private employers who are covered by Title VII but not the Constitution. The first case excerpted in the next section, while not directly involving affirmative action, likely has implications for its future lawfulness.

IV. THE UNCERTAIN FUTURE OF DISPARATE IMPACT CLAIMS (AND AFFIRMATIVE ACTION)

As set forth at the outset of this chapter, Title VII conceives of two kinds of discrimination claims: disparate treatment and disparate impact. The first involves a claim that race was a motivating factor in an employer's adverse treatment of an employee. The second involves a claim that an employer's decision or policy has a significant impact on a racial group, intentional or not, which the employer has to justify as adequately job related. As we have seen throughout this chapter, these two theories of discrimination plausibly support claims of discrimination for a variety of adverse employment decisions that occur in the workplace. But since the *Griggs* Court recognized disparate impact liability in 1971, that theory has remained controversial. Congress expressly authorized disparate impact liability in 1991, but as a matter of policy it remains subject to debate.

But what exactly is the relationship between disparate treatment and disparate impact claims? In some cases, both claims can prevail, as where a policy with a racially disparate impact is also shown to have been motivated by race. In other cases, disparate impact claims may establish liability where disparate treatment claims do not, such as when a claimant cannot prove that a policy with a disparate impact was motivated by race.

The Supreme Court has long assumed that an employer could safely avoid liability under Title VII by taking care not to utilize a test or other policy that has a racially disparate impact. It also has assumed, historically, that Congress can authorize disparate impact liability, irrespective of whether it should as a matter of policy. The following case puts both of these assumptions into doubt.

Ricci v. DeStefano

Supreme Court of the United States, 2009.
557 U.S. 557.

■ JUSTICE KENNEDY delivered the opinion of the Court.

In the fire department of New Haven, Connecticut—as in emergency-service agencies throughout the Nation—firefighters prize their promotion to and within the officer ranks. An agency's officers command respect within the department and in the whole community; and, of course, added responsibilities command increased salary and benefits. Aware of the intense competition for promotions, New Haven, like many cities, relies on objective examinations to identify the best qualified candidates.

In 2003, 118 New Haven firefighters took examinations to qualify for promotion to the rank of lieutenant or captain. Promotion examinations in New Haven (or City) were infrequent, so the stakes were high. The results would determine which firefighters would be considered for promotions during the next two years, and the order in which they would be considered. Many firefighters studied for months, at considerable personal and financial cost.

When the examination results showed that white candidates had outperformed minority candidates, the mayor and other local politicians opened a public debate that turned rancorous. Some firefighters argued the tests should be discarded because the results showed the tests to be discriminatory. They threatened a discrimination lawsuit if the City made promotions based on the tests. Other firefighters said the exams were neutral and fair. And they, in turn, threatened a discrimination lawsuit if the City, relying on the statistical racial disparity, ignored the test results and denied promotions to the candidates who had performed well. In the end the City took the side of those who protested the test results. It threw out the examinations.

Certain white and Hispanic firefighters who likely would have been promoted based on their good test performance sued the City and some of its officials . . . alleg[ing] that by discarding the test results, the City . . . discriminated against the plaintiffs based on their race, in violation of both Title VII of the Civil Rights Act of 1964, and the Equal Protection Clause of the Fourteenth Amendment.

Title VII of the Civil Rights Act of 1964 prohibits employment discrimination on the basis of race, color, religion, sex, or national origin. Title VII prohibits both intentional discrimination (known as "disparate treatment") as well as, in some cases, practices that are not intended to discriminate but in fact have a disproportionately adverse effect on minorities (known as "disparate impact").

Disparate-treatment cases present "the most easily understood type of discrimination," and occur where an employer has "treated [a] particular person less favorably than others because of" a protected trait. A disparate-treatment plaintiff must establish "that the defendant had a discriminatory intent or motive" for taking a job-related action. Under the disparate-impact statute, a plaintiff establishes a prima facie violation by showing that an employer uses "a particular employment practice that causes a disparate impact on the basis of race, color, religion, sex, or national origin." An employer may defend against liability by demonstrating that the practice is "job related for the position in question and consistent with business necessity." Even if the employer meets that burden, however, a plaintiff may still succeed by showing that the employer refuses to adopt an available alternative employment practice that has less disparate impact and serves the employer's legitimate needs.

B

Petitioners allege that when the CSB refused to certify the captain and lieutenant exam results based on the race of the successful candidates, it discriminated against them in violation of Title VII's disparate-treatment provision. The City counters that its decision was permissible because the tests "appear[ed] to violate Title VII's disparate-impact provisions."

Our analysis begins with this premise: The City's actions would violate the disparate-treatment prohibition of Title VII absent some valid defense. All the evidence demonstrates that the City chose not to certify the examination results because of the statistical disparity based on race—i.e., how minority candidates had performed when compared to white candidates. As the District Court put it, the City rejected the test results because "too many whites and not enough minorities would be promoted were the lists to be certified." (respondents' "own arguments . . . show that the City's reasons for advocating non-certification were related to the racial distribution of the results"). Without some other justification, this express, race-based decisionmaking violates Title VII's command that employers cannot take adverse employment actions because of an individual's race.

The District Court did not adhere to this principle, however. It held that respondents' "motivation to avoid making promotions based on a test with a racially disparate impact . . . does not, as a matter of law, constitute discriminatory intent." And the Government makes a similar argument in this Court. It contends that the "structure of Title VII belies any claim that an employer's intent to comply with Title VII's disparate-impact provisions constitutes prohibited discrimination on the basis of race." Brief for United States as Amicus Curiae 11. But both of those statements turn upon the City's objective—avoiding disparate-impact liability—while ignoring the City's conduct in the name of reaching that objective. Whatever the City's ultimate aim—however well intentioned or benevolent it might have seemed—the City made its employment decision because of race. The City rejected the test results solely because the higher scoring candidates were white. The question is not whether that conduct was discriminatory but whether the City had a lawful justification for its race-based action.

Courts often confront cases in which statutes and principles point in different directions. Our task is to provide guidance to employers and courts for situations when these two prohibitions could be in conflict absent a rule to reconcile them. In providing this guidance our decision must be consistent with the important purpose of Title VII—that the workplace be an environment free of discrimination, where race is not a barrier to opportunity.

With these principles in mind, we turn to the parties' proposed means of reconciling the statutory provisions. Petitioners take a strict approach, arguing that under Title VII, it cannot be permissible for an employer to take race-based adverse employment actions in order to avoid disparate-impact liability—even if the employer knows its practice violates the disparate-impact provision. Petitioners would have us hold that, under Title VII, avoiding unintentional discrimination cannot justify intentional discrimination. That assertion, however, ignores the fact that, by codifying the disparate-impact provision in 1991, Congress has expressly prohibited both types of discrimination. We must interpret the statute to give effect to both provisions where possible. We cannot accept petitioners' broad and inflexible formulation.

Petitioners next suggest that an employer in fact must be in violation of the disparate-impact provision before it can use compliance as a defense in a disparate-treatment suit. Again, this is overly simplistic and too restrictive of Title VII's purpose. The rule petitioners offer would run counter to what we have recognized as Congress's intent that "voluntary compliance" be "the preferred means of achieving the objectives of Title VII." Firefighters v. Cleveland; see also Wygant v. Jackson Bd. of Ed., (O'Connor, J., concurring in part and concurring in judgment). Forbidding employers to act unless they know, with certainty, that a practice violates the disparate-impact provision would bring compliance efforts to a near standstill. Even in the limited situations when this restricted standard could be met, employers likely would hesitate before taking voluntary action for fear of later being proven wrong in the course of litigation and then held to account for disparate treatment.

At the opposite end of the spectrum, respondents and the Government assert that an employer's good-faith belief that its actions are necessary to comply with Title VII's disparate-impact provision should be enough to justify race-conscious conduct. But the original, foundational prohibition of Title VII bars employers from taking adverse action "because of . . . race." And when Congress codified the disparate-impact provision in 1991, it made no exception to disparate-treatment liability for actions taken in a good-faith effort to comply with the new, disparate-impact provision in subsection (k). Allowing employers to violate the disparate-treatment prohibition based on a mere good-faith fear of disparate-impact liability would encourage race-based action at the slightest hint of disparate impact. A minimal standard could cause employers to discard the results of lawful and beneficial promotional examinations even where there is little if any evidence of disparate-impact discrimination. That would amount to a de facto quota system, in which a "focus on statistics . . . could put undue pressure on employers to adopt inappropriate prophylactic measures." Watson, (plurality opinion). Even worse, an employer could discard test results (or other employment practices) with the intent of obtaining the employer's preferred racial balance. That operational principle could not be justified, for Title VII is express in disclaiming any interpretation of its requirements as calling for outright racial balancing. The purpose of Title VII "is to promote hiring on the basis of job qualifications, rather than on the basis of race or color." Griggs.

In searching for a standard that strikes a more appropriate balance, we note that this Court has considered cases similar to this one, albeit in the context of the Equal Protection Clause of the Fourteenth Amendment. The Court has held that certain government actions to remedy past racial discrimination—actions that are themselves based on race—are constitutional only where there is a " 'strong basis in evidence' " that the remedial actions were necessary. Richmond v. J. A. Croson Co, (quoting Wygant (plurality opinion)). This suit does not call on us to consider whether the statutory constraints under Title VII must be parallel in all respects to those under the Constitution. That does not mean the constitutional authorities are irrelevant, however. Our cases discussing constitutional principles can provide helpful guidance in this statutory context.

Writing for a plurality in Wygant and announcing the strong-basis-in-evidence standard, Justice Powell recognized the tension between eliminating segregation and discrimination on the one hand and doing away with all governmentally imposed discrimination based on race on the other. The plurality stated that those "related constitutional duties are not always harmonious," and that "reconciling them requires . . . employers to act with extraordinary care." Ibid. The plurality required a strong basis in evidence because "[e]videntiary support for the conclusion that remedial action is warranted becomes crucial when the remedial program is challenged in court by nonminority employees." The Court applied the same standard in Croson, observing that "an amorphous claim that there has been past discrimination . . . cannot justify the use of an unyielding racial quota."

The same interests are at work in the interplay between the disparate-treatment and disparate-impact provisions of Title VII. Congress has imposed liability on employers for unintentional discrimination in order to rid the workplace of "practices that are fair in form, but discriminatory in operation." Griggs. But it has also prohibited employers from taking adverse employment actions "because of" race. Applying the strong-basis-in-evidence standard to Title VII gives effect to both the disparate-treatment and disparate-impact provisions, allowing violations of one in the name of compliance with the other only in certain, narrow circumstances. The standard leaves ample room for employers' voluntary compliance efforts, which are essential to the statutory scheme and to Congress's efforts to eradicate workplace discrimination. And the standard appropriately constrains employers' discretion in making race-based decisions: It limits that discretion to cases in which there is a strong basis in evidence of disparate-impact liability, but it is not so restrictive that it allows employers to act only when there is a provable, actual violation.

Resolving the statutory conflict in this way allows the disparate-impact prohibition to work in a manner that is consistent with other provisions of Title VII, including the prohibition on adjusting employment-related test scores on the basis of race. Examinations like those administered by the City create legitimate expectations on the part of those who took the tests. As is the case with any promotion exam, some of the firefighters here invested substantial time, money, and personal commitment in preparing for the tests. Employment tests can be an important part of a neutral selection system that safeguards against the very racial animosities Title VII was intended to prevent. Here, however, the firefighters saw their efforts invalidated by the City in sole reliance upon race-based statistics.

If an employer cannot rescore a test based on the candidates' race, § 2000e–2(l), then it follows a fortiori that it may not take the greater step of discarding the test altogether to achieve a more desirable racial distribution of promotion-eligible candidates—absent a strong basis in evidence that the test was deficient and that discarding the results is necessary to avoid violating the disparate-impact provision. Restricting an employer's ability to discard test results (and thereby discriminate against qualified candidates on the basis of their race) also is in keeping with Title VII's express protection of bona fide promotional examinations. "[N]or shall it be an unlawful employment practice for an employer to give and to act upon the results of any professionally developed ability test provided that such test, its administration or action upon the results is not designed, intended or used to discriminate because of race").

For the foregoing reasons, we adopt the strong-basis-in-evidence standard as a matter of statutory construction to resolve any conflict between the disparate-treatment and disparate-impact provisions of Title VII.

Our statutory holding does not address the constitutionality of the measures taken here in purported compliance with Title VII. We also do not hold that meeting the strong-basis-in-evidence standard would satisfy the Equal Protection Clause in a future case. As we explain below, because respondents have not met their burden under Title VII, we need not decide whether a legitimate fear of disparate impact is ever sufficient to justify discriminatory treatment under the Constitution.

Nor do we question an employer's affirmative efforts to ensure that all groups have a fair opportunity to apply for promotions and to participate in the process by which promotions will be made. But once that process has been established and employers have made clear their selection criteria, they may not then invalidate the test results, thus upsetting an employee's legitimate expectation not to be judged on the basis of race. Doing so, absent a strong basis in evidence of an impermissible disparate impact, amounts to the sort of racial preference that Congress has disclaimed and is antithetical to the notion of a workplace where individuals are guaranteed equal opportunity regardless of race.

Title VII does not prohibit an employer from considering, before administering a test or practice, how to design that test or practice in order to provide a fair opportunity for all individuals, regardless of their race. And when, during the test-design stage, an employer invites comments to ensure the test is fair, that process can provide a common ground for open discussions toward that end. We hold only that under Title VII, before an employer can engage in intentional discrimination for the asserted purpose of avoiding or remedying an unintentional disparate impact, the employer must have a strong basis in evidence to believe it will be subject to disparate-impact liability if it fails to take the race-conscious, discriminatory action.

On the record before us, there is no genuine dispute that the City lacked a strong basis in evidence to believe it would face disparate-impact liability if it certified the examination results. In other words, there is no evidence—let alone the required strong basis in evidence—that the tests were flawed because they were not job-related or because other, equally valid and less discriminatory tests were available to the City. Fear of litigation alone cannot justify an employer's reliance on race to the detriment of individuals who passed the examinations and qualified for promotions.

The record in this litigation documents a process that, at the outset, had the potential to produce a testing procedure that was true to the promise of Title VII: No individual should face workplace discrimination based on race. Respondents thought about promotion qualifications and relevant experience in neutral ways. They were careful to ensure broad racial participation in the design of the test itself and its administration. As we have discussed at length, the process was open and fair.

The problem, of course, is that after the tests were completed, the raw racial results became the predominant rationale for the City's refusal to certify the results. The injury arises in part from the high, and justified, expectations of the candidates who had participated in the testing process on the terms the City had established for the promotional process. Many of the candidates had studied for months, at considerable personal and financial expense, and thus the injury caused by the City's reliance on raw racial statistics at the end of the process was all the more severe. Confronted with arguments both for and against certifying the test results—and threats of a lawsuit either way—the City was required to make a difficult inquiry. But its hearings produced no strong evidence of a disparate-impact violation, and the City was not entitled to disregard the tests based solely on the racial disparity in the results.

Our holding today clarifies how Title VII applies to resolve competing expectations under the disparate-treatment and disparate-impact provisions. If, after it certifies the test results, the City faces a disparate-impact suit, then in light of our holding today it should be clear that the City would avoid disparate-impact liability based on the strong basis in evidence that, had it not certified the results, it would have been subject to disparate-treatment liability.

■ JUSTICE SCALIA, concurring.

I join the Court's opinion in full, but write separately to observe that its resolution of this dispute merely postpones the evil day on which the Court will have to confront the question: Whether, or to what extent, are the disparate-impact provisions of Title VII of the Civil Rights Act of 1964 consistent with the Constitution's guarantee of equal protection? The question is not an easy one.

The difficulty is this: Whether or not Title VII's disparate-treatment provisions forbid "remedial" race-based actions when a disparate-impact violation would not otherwise result—the question resolved by the Court today—it is clear that Title VII not only permits but affirmatively requires such actions when a disparate-impact violation would otherwise result. But if the Federal Government is prohibited from discriminating on the basis of race, then surely it is also prohibited from enacting laws mandating that third parties—e.g., employers, whether private, State, or municipal—discriminate on the basis of race. As the facts of these cases illustrate, Title VII's disparate-impact provisions place a racial thumb on the scales, often requiring employers to evaluate the racial outcomes of their policies, and to make decisions based on (because of) those racial outcomes. That type of racial decisionmaking is, as the Court explains, discriminatory.

To be sure, the disparate-impact laws do not mandate imposition of quotas, but it is not clear why that should provide a safe harbor. Would a private employer not be guilty of unlawful discrimination if he refrained from establishing a racial hiring quota but intentionally designed his hiring practices to achieve the same end? Surely he would. Intentional discrimination is still occurring, just one step up the chain. Government compulsion of such design would therefore seemingly violate equal protection principles. Nor would it matter that Title VII requires consideration of race on a wholesale, rather than retail, level. "[T]he Government must treat citizens as individuals, not as simply components of a racial, religious, sexual or national class." Miller v. Johnson. And of course the purportedly benign motive for the disparate-impact provisions cannot save the statute.

It might be possible to defend the law by framing it as simply an evidentiary tool used to identify genuine, intentional discrimination—to "smoke out," as it were, disparate treatment. Disparate impact is sometimes (though not always) a signal of something illicit, so a regulator might allow statistical disparities to play some role in the evidentiary process. But arguably the disparate-impact provisions sweep too broadly to be fairly characterized in such a fashion—since they fail to provide an affirmative defense for good-faith (i.e., nonracially motivated) conduct, or perhaps even for good faith plus hiring standards that are entirely reasonable. This is a question that this Court will have to consider in due course. It is one thing to free plaintiffs from proving an employer's illicit intent, but quite another to preclude the employer from proving that its motives were pure and its actions reasonable.

The Court's resolution of these cases makes it unnecessary to resolve these matters today. But the war between disparate impact and equal protection will be waged sooner or later, and it behooves us to begin thinking about how—and on what terms—to make peace between them.

■ JUSTICE ALITO, with whom JUSTICE SCALIA and JUSTICE THOMAS join, concurring. [omitted]

■ JUSTICE GINSBURG, with whom JUSTICE STEVENS, JUSTICE SOUTER, and JUSTICE BREYER join, dissenting.

In assessing claims of race discrimination, "[c]ontext matters." Grutter v. Bollinger. In 1972, Congress extended Title VII of the Civil Rights Act of 1964 to cover public employment. At that time, municipal fire departments across the country, including New Haven's, pervasively discriminated against minorities. The extension of Title VII to cover jobs in firefighting effected no overnight change. It took decades of persistent effort, advanced by Title VII litigation, to open firefighting posts to members of racial minorities.

The white firefighters who scored high on New Haven's promotional exams understandably attract this Court's sympathy. But they had no vested right to promotion. Nor have other persons received promotions in preference to them. New Haven maintains that it refused to certify the test results because it believed, for good cause, that it would be vulnerable to a Title VII disparate-impact suit if it relied on those results.

By order of this Court, New Haven, a city in which African-Americans and Hispanics account for nearly 60 percent of the population, must today be served—as it was in the days of undisguised discrimination—by a fire department in which members of racial and ethnic minorities are rarely seen in command positions.

Firefighting is a profession in which the legacy of racial discrimination casts an especially long shadow. In extending Title VII to state and local government employers in 1972, Congress took note of a U.S. Commission on Civil Rights (USCCR) report finding racial discrimination in municipal employment even "more pervasive than in the private sector." According to the report, overt racism was partly to blame, but so too was a failure on the part of municipal employers to apply merit-based employment principles. In making hiring and promotion decisions, public employers often "rel[ied] on criteria unrelated to job performance," including nepotism or political patronage.

Such flawed selection methods served to entrench preexisting racial hierarchies. The USCCR report singled out police and fire departments for having "[b]arriers to equal employment . . . greater . . . than in any other area of State or local government," with African-Americans "hold[ing] almost no positions in the officer ranks." *See also* National Commission on Fire Prevention and Control, America Burning 5 (1973) ("Racial minorities are under-represented in the fire departments in nearly every community in which they live.").

The city of New Haven (City) was no exception. In the early 1970's, African-Americans and Hispanics composed 30 percent of New Haven's population, but only 3.6 percent of the City's 502 firefighters. The racial disparity in the officer ranks was even more pronounced: "[O]f the 107 officers in the Department only one was black, and he held the lowest rank above private." Firebird Soc. of New Haven, Inc. v. New Haven Bd. of Fire Comm'rs, 66 F.R.D. 457, 460 (Conn. 1975).

Following a lawsuit and settlement agreement, *see* ibid., the City initiated efforts to increase minority representation in the New Haven Fire Department (Department). Those litigation-induced efforts produced some positive change. New Haven's population includes a greater proportion of minorities today than it did in the 1970's: Nearly 40 percent of the City's residents are African-American and more than 20 percent are Hispanic. Among entry-level firefighters, minorities are still underrepresented, but not starkly so. As of 2003, African-Americans and Hispanics constituted 30 percent and 16 percent of the City's firefighters, respectively. In supervisory positions, however, significant disparities remain. Overall, the senior officer ranks (captain and higher) are nine percent African-American and nine percent Hispanic. Only one of the Department's 21 fire captains is African-American. It is against this backdrop of entrenched inequality that the promotion process at issue in this litigation should be assessed.

B

By order of its charter, New Haven must use competitive examinations to fill vacancies in fire officer and other civil-service positions. Such examinations, the City's civil service rules specify, "shall be practical in nature, shall relate to matters which fairly measure the relative fitness and capacity of the applicants to discharge the duties of the position which they seek, and shall take into account character, training, experience, physical and mental fitness." The City may choose among a variety of testing methods, including written and oral exams and "[p]erformance tests to demonstrate skill and ability in performing actual work."

New Haven, the record indicates, did not closely consider what sort of "practical" examination would "fairly measure the relative fitness and capacity of the applicants to discharge the duties" of a fire officer. Instead, the City simply adhered to the testing regime outlined in its two-decades-old contract with the local firefighters' union: a written exam, which would account for 60 percent of an applicant's total score, and an oral exam, which would account for the remaining 40 percent. In soliciting bids from exam development companies, New Haven made clear that it would entertain only "proposals that include a written component that will be weighted at 60%, and an oral component that will be weighted at 40%." Chad Legel, a representative of the winning bidder, Industrial/Organizational Solutions, Inc. (IOS), testified during his deposition that the City never asked whether alternative methods might better measure the qualities of a successful fire officer, including leadership skills and command presence. ("I was under contract and had responsibility only to create the oral interview and the written exam.").

Pursuant to New Haven's specifications, IOS developed and administered the oral and written exams. The results showed significant racial disparities. On the lieutenant exam, the pass rate for African-American candidates was about one-half the rate for Caucasian candidates; the pass rate for Hispanic candidates was even lower. On the captain exam, both African-American and Hispanic candidates passed at about half the rate of their Caucasian counterparts. More striking still, although nearly half of the 77 lieutenant candidates were African-American or Hispanic, none would have been eligible for promotion to the eight positions then vacant. The highest scoring African-American candidate ranked 13th; the top Hispanic candidate was 26th. As for the seven then-vacant captain positions, two Hispanic candidates would have been eligible, but no African-Americans. The highest scoring African-American candidate ranked 15th.

Respondents were no doubt conscious of race during their decisionmaking process, the court acknowledged, but this did not mean they had engaged in racially disparate treatment. The conclusion they had reached and the action thereupon taken were race-neutral in this sense: "[A]ll the test results were discarded, no one was promoted, and firefighters of every race will have to participate in another selection process to be considered for promotion." New Haven's action, which gave no individual a preference, "was 'simply not analogous to a quota system or a minority set-aside where candidates, on the basis of their race, are not treated uniformly.'" For these and other reasons, the court also rejected petitioners' equal protection claim.

II

A

Title VII became effective in July 1965. Employers responded to the law by eliminating rules and practices that explicitly barred racial minorities from "white" jobs. But removing overtly race-based job classifications did not usher in genuinely equal opportunity. More subtle—and sometimes unconscious—forms of discrimination replaced once undisguised restrictions.

C

To "reconcile" the supposed "conflict" between disparate treatment and disparate impact, the Court offers an enigmatic standard. Employers may attempt to comply with Title VII's disparate-impact provision, the Court declares, only where there is a "strong basis in evidence" documenting the necessity of their action. The Court's standard, drawn from inapposite equal protection precedents, is not elaborated. One is left to wonder what cases would meet the standard and why the Court is so sure this case does not.

1

Until today, this Court has never questioned the constitutionality of the disparate-impact component of Title VII, and for good reason. By instructing employers to avoid needlessly exclusionary selection processes, Title VII's disparate-impact provision calls for a "race-neutral means to increase minority . . . participation"—something this Court's equal protection precedents also encourage.

2

As a result of today's decision, an employer who discards a dubious selection process can anticipate costly disparate-treatment litigation in which its chances for success—even for surviving a summary-judgment motion—are highly problematic. Concern about exposure to disparate-impact liability, however well grounded, is insufficient to insulate an employer from attack. Instead, the employer must make a "strong" showing that (1) its selection method was "not job related and consistent with business necessity," or (2) that it refused to adopt "an equally valid, less-discriminatory alternative." It is hard to see how these requirements differ from demanding that an employer establish "a provable, actual violation" against itself. There is indeed a sharp conflict here, but it is not the false one the Court describes between Title VII's core provisions. It is, instead, the discordance of the Court's opinion with the voluntary compliance ideal.

3

The Court's additional justifications for announcing a strong-basis-in-evidence standard are unimpressive. First, discarding the results of tests, the Court suggests, calls for a heightened standard because it "upset[s] an employee's legitimate expectation." This rationale puts the cart before the horse. The legitimacy of an employee's expectation depends on the legitimacy of the selection method. If an employer reasonably concludes that an exam fails to identify the most qualified individuals and needlessly shuts out a segment of the applicant pool, Title VII surely does not compel the employer to hire or promote based on the test, however unreliable it may be. Indeed, the statute's prime objective is to prevent exclusionary practices from "operat[ing] to 'freeze' the status quo." Griggs.

Second, the Court suggests, anything less than a strong-basis-in evidence standard risks creating "a de facto quota system, in which . . . an employer could discard test results . . . with the intent of obtaining the employer's preferred racial balance." Under a reasonableness standard, however, an employer could not cast aside a selection method based on a statistical disparity alone. The employer must have good cause to believe that the method screens out qualified applicants and would be difficult to justify as grounded in business necessity. Should an employer repeatedly reject test results, it would be fair, I agree, to infer that the employer is simply seeking a racially balanced outcome and is not genuinely endeavoring to comply with Title VII.

Applying what I view as the proper standard to the record thus far made, I would hold that New Haven had ample cause to believe its selection process was flawed and not justified by business necessity. Judged by that standard, petitioners have not shown that New Haven's failure to certify the exam results violated Title VII's disparate-treatment provision.

The City, all agree, "was faced with a prima facie case of disparate-impact liability,": The pass rate for minority candidates was half the rate for nonminority candidates, and virtually no minority candidates would have been eligible for promotion had the exam results been certified. Alerted to this stark disparity, the CSB heard expert and lay testimony, presented at public hearings, in an endeavor to ascertain whether the exams were fair and consistent with business necessity. Its investigation revealed grave cause for concern about the exam process itself and the City's failure to consider alternative selection devices.

Chief among the City's problems was the very nature of the tests for promotion. In choosing to use written and oral exams with a 60/40 weighting, the City simply adhered to the union's preference and apparently gave no consideration to whether the weighting was likely to identify the most qualified fire-officer candidates.[10] There is strong reason to think it was not.

---

[10] This alone would have posed a substantial problem for New Haven in a disparate-impact suit, particularly in light of the disparate results the City's scheme had produced in the past. See *supra*, at 7. Under the Uniform Guidelines on Employee Selection Procedures (Uniform Guidelines), employers must conduct "an investigation of suitable alternative selection procedures." *See also* Officers for Justice v. Civil Serv. Comm'n, ("before utilizing a procedure that has an adverse impact on minorities, the City has an obligation pursuant to the Uniform Guidelines to explore alternative procedures and to implement them if they have less adverse impact and are substantially equally valid"). It is no answer to "presume" that the two-decades-old 60/40 formula was adopted for a "rational reason" because it "was the result of a union-negotiated collective bargaining agreement." That the parties may have been "rational" says nothing about whether their agreed-upon selection process was consistent with business necessity. It is not at all unusual for agreements negotiated between employers and unions to run afoul of Title VII. See, e.g., Peters v. Missouri-Pacific R. Co (an employment practice "is not shielded [from the requirements of Title VII] by the facts that it is the product of collective bargaining and meets the standards of fair representation").

Relying heavily on written tests to select fire officers is a questionable practice, to say the least. Successful fire officers, the City's description of the position makes clear, must have the "[a]bility to lead personnel effectively, maintain discipline, promote harmony, exercise sound judgment, and cooperate with other officials." These qualities are not well measured by written tests. Testifying before the CSB, Christopher Hornick, an exam-design expert with more than two decades of relevant experience, was emphatic on this point: Leadership skills, command presence, and the like "could have been identified and evaluated in a much more appropriate way."

Hornick's commonsense observation is mirrored in case law and in Title VII's administrative guidelines. Courts have long criticized written firefighter promotion exams for being "more probative of the test-taker's ability to recall what a particular text stated on a given topic than of his firefighting or supervisory knowledge and abilities." Vulcan Pioneers, Inc. v. New Jersey Dep't of Civil Serv. A fire officer's job, courts have observed, "involves complex behaviors, good interpersonal skills, the ability to make decisions under tremendous pressure, and a host of other abilities—none of which is easily measured by a written, multiple choice test." Firefighters Inst. for Racial Equality v. St. Louis. Interpreting the Uniform Guidelines, EEOC and other federal agencies responsible for enforcing equal opportunity employment laws have similarly recognized that, as measures of "interpersonal relations" or "ability to function under danger (e.g., firefighters)," "[p]encil-and-paper tests . . . generally are not close enough approximations of work behaviors to show content validity."

It is indeed regrettable that the City's noncertification decision would have required all candidates to go through another selection process. But it would have been more regrettable to rely on flawed exams to shut out candidates who may well have the command presence and other qualities needed to excel as fire officers. Yet that is the choice the Court makes today. It is a choice that breaks the promise of Griggs that groups long denied equal opportunity would not be held back by tests "fair in form, but discriminatory in operation."

This case presents an unfortunate situation, one New Haven might well have avoided had it utilized a better selection process in the first place. But what this case does not present is race-based discrimination in violation of Title VII. I dissent from the Court's judgment, which rests on the false premise that respondents showed "a significant statistical disparity," but "nothing more."

NOTES AND QUESTIONS

1. **The Court's Holding and Reasoning.** The Court holds that the City of New Haven engaged in intentional racial discrimination, i.e., disparate treatment. In what way did the City discriminate by race? How does avoiding

use of a test that has a racially disparate impact amount to intentional discrimination? Given that the lower courts and the four dissenting justices denied that the city discriminated, the case is, presumably, debatable. What is the best argument that the City did not racially discriminate?

The Court purports to reconcile Title VII's prohibition of intentional disparate treatment with its prohibition of unintentional disparate impact. What test did it devise to achieve this? What were the various proposals by the plaintiffs and defendant and by the dissent? Which approach should the Court have adopted?

2.   *Implications for Disparate Impact Liability.* Disparate impact doctrine, which originated in *Griggs v. Duke Power Co.*, 401 U.S. 424 (1971), encourages employers to be race-conscious. It holds employers liable for employment practices that have a racially disparate impact if the employer cannot demonstrate that the practices are "job related and consistent with business necessity." To avoid the cost of litigation and liability, prudent employers will pay attention to the racial impact of their employment practices and avoid using those that are not adequately job related. Indeed, as Justice Ginsburg points out, employers taking the initiative voluntarily to design their practices to minimize their racial impact unless the job requires it is a process that Title VII is intended to encourage. The question after *Ricci* is whether disparate impact remains viable as a source of employer liability. Is it possible for an employer to intentionally avoid using policies with a disparate impact without engaging in intentional racial discrimination?

The Court did identify a potential "safe harbor" for employers: "[U]nder Title VII, before an employer can engage in intentional discrimination for the asserted purpose of avoiding or remedying an unintentional disparate impact, the employer must have a strong basis in evidence to believe it will be subject to disparate-impact liability if it fails to take the race-conscious, discriminatory action." Thus even if complying with disparate impact doctrine always involves intentional discrimination, it will not result in liability if the employer has a strong basis in evidence to believe it would lose a disparate impact claim.

But, as Justice Scalia's concurrence suggests, that might not be a safe harbor under the Constitution. First, cities like New Haven are state actors subject to the Equal Protection Clause. Race discrimination by state actors must satisfy strict scrutiny. The Court's endorsement of remedying "identified discrimination" in the affirmative action cases seems to mean remedying identified *intentional* discrimination, not a disparate impact. Moreover, although private employers covered by Title VII are not subject to the Constitution, the federal government is subject to equal protection constraints. If disparate impact liability cannot be imposed on state actors, then it presumably cannot be imposed by the federal government on private actors. Whether disparate impact liability will survive is thus in question if the Court continues its trend toward a colorblind interpretation of equal protection doctrine.

Are you persuaded that avoiding the use of tests or other employment practices with a disparate impact constitutes racial discrimination? Did the Court in *Griggs*, in finding liability for disparate impact, believe it was authorizing intentional discrimination under the newly enacted Title VII? Recall also *Washington v. Davis*, 426 U.S. 229 (1976). Did that Court believe that, when Congress imposes liability for employment practices with a disparate impact, it mandates intentional discrimination?

3.   *Implications for Affirmative Action.* The Court in *Ricci* holds that it was unlawful discrimination for the City to discard the promotional test results to avoid their racial impact, even though the City intended to redesign and administer the test without regard to the race of the test-takers. What if, instead of discarding the test results, the City had simply accorded favorable weight to the black applicants who scored less well on the test in order to promote a sufficient number of minority applicants? That is, what if the city had engaged in racially preferential promotions rather than discarding the test results and starting over? To the extent *Ricci* makes it very difficult for employers to discard test results to avoid a racially disparate impact, does it not follow that it should be at least as difficult, and arguably more so, for employers to outright favor the promotion of employees based on their race? The relatively lenient treatment the Court has accorded affirmative action under Title VII thus seems unlikely to continue after *Ricci*.

4.   *Is Disparate Treatment Liability Adequate?* Even if the Court is poised to prohibit affirmative action by employers through its interpretations of Title VII, and to eliminate disparate impact as a basis of liability, so what? It remains the case that employees can bring claims of disparate treatment to ensure access to the workplace. Is disparate treatment liability adequate to address the problem of race discrimination in the workplace? Is it adequate to ensure racial equality in the workplace? Whatever you think about affirmative action and disparate impact liability, should the Court or should Congress decide whether and how to use them? Based on the materials in this chapter, which institution do you think is doing a better job of ensuring racial equality in employment?

CHAPTER 7

POLICING

I. INTRODUCTION TO RACE AND CRIMINAL JUSTICE

"We really need to do something about the problem of white crime." What was your reaction to this statement? Make it to others and observe their reactions.[1] Did they think you were joking, or perhaps trying to make a point that white people commit crime? Did they want to confirm that you meant *white* crime? Did they think you meant white *collar* crime? Now try the same statement with someone else, only using the term "black crime." Was the reaction different? How? What about "brown," "yellow," or "red" crime? What associations do people commonly make between race and crime, and why might some of them be so prevalent?

American society has long promoted false stereotypes about racial minorities' propensities to commit certain crimes—stereotypes reinforced today, albeit in less blatant form, by films and other entertainment media. News broadcasters also focus almost obsessively on crime stories, often involving minority suspects, compounding public fears about race and crime. But no institution promotes a connection between race and crime more starkly than the criminal justice system. Rates of minority involvement therein are staggering.

Consider the racial demographics of the United States prison population, which consists of people whose incarceration resulted from conviction after trial or, more commonly, from a guilty plea. Blacks and Latinos represent a much higher proportion of inmates than their percentage of the general population. In 2010, according to Bureau of Justice Statistics, the rate of black men serving time in state and federal prison was 6.7 times the rate of white men, with Hispanic men serving 2.7 times the rate of white men. Black and Hispanic women were serving, respectively, at 2.8 and 1.6 times the rate of white women. *See* Paul Guerino et al., Bureau of Justice Statistics, Prisoners in 2010 at 27 (Table 14 (2011). Disparities among young prisoners, eighteen to nineteen years old, were especially pronounced, with black and Hispanic men incarcerated, respectively, at 10.4 and 3.8 times the rate of white men, and black and Hispanic women incarcerated at 3.6 and 2.8 times the rate of white women. *Id.* at table 15. In the most recent study of its kind, the Bureau of Justice Statistics examined imprisonment rates from 1974 to 2001 to estimate the likelihood of members of different groups going to prison. The study concluded that, if rates remain at 2001 levels, 1 in 3 black men, 1 in 6 Hispanic men, and 1 in 17 white men born in 2001 would be incarcerated during their lifetime. *See* Thomas P. Bonczar,

---

[1] See Michelle Alexander, The New Jim Crow 193 (suggesting this exercise).

Bureau of Justice Statistics, Prevalence of Imprisonment in the U.S. Population, 1974–2001, at 1 (2003). For white, Hispanic, and black females born in 2001, the likelihood of going to prison is approximately 1 in 111, 1 in 45, and 1 in 18, respectively. *Id.*

Marked racial disparities also exist among crime victims. Blacks, Latinos, and Indians are victims of violent crimes, such as assault, robbery, and murder, at significantly higher rates than non-Hispanic whites and Asians. According to the Bureau of Justice Statistics, between 2001 and 2005, Indians experienced violent crime almost twice as often as blacks, 2 1/2 times as often as whites, and more than five times as often as Asians. Blacks account for an exceedingly high proportion of homicide victims. In 2006, one out of eight Americans was black, but one of two murder victims was black—a rate approximately six times that of whites. Black males between the ages of 18 and 24 have had the highest homicide victimization rate among all racial groups for several decades. The vast majority of violent crime victims are the same race as their perpetrators. Without controlling for socioeconomic factors, crime victimization *and* perpetration rates thus vary significantly by race.

These correlations between race, incarceration and victimization raise difficult questions about the racial disparities in the criminal justice system. Are they objectionable? If so, why? Does your answer depend on what you believe causes the disparities? If you believe the system treats suspects and defendants equally, then these disparities may simply reflect that minorities commit a disproportionate amount of crime. That does not necessarily mean the disparities are not troubling, but it could suggest that responsibility for them lies outside the criminal justice system. Racial disparities in crime commission could, for example, result from differences in economic circumstances and educational opportunities. Alternatively, you might believe that the criminal justice system does not treat people equally, instead selectively arresting, convicting, and punishing some racial groups more than others for comparable conduct. And, of course, both explanations may be true.

Criminologists have not reached consensus about the exact causes of racial inequality in the criminal justice system. The evidence described above suggests that crime commission rates do vary among racial groups, with blacks, Latinos, and Indians committing a disproportionate number of certain serious crimes, such as robbery and murder. Evidence also supports the proposition that the criminal justice system contributes to racial disparities at every stage of the process for reasons unrelated to crime commission. With respect to drug offenses, for example, collected data suggest that crime commission rates across racial groups are much more similar than arrest and incarceration rates for each group, indicating that the criminal justice system itself probably plays a significant role in causing the disparities in outcomes.

As this is a text for students of law, not social science, the aim of this and the next chapter is to evaluate law's construction of and response to crime, criminal justice, and race. The chapters will proceed through each major stage of the criminal justice process—policing, prosecution, adjudication, and punishment—identifying important racial issues that arise at each stage and exploring how the law creates or responds to those issues. In examining the components of the criminal justice system, your attention also will be called to the role that the criminal laws themselves play in shaping the system. What impact do the laws enacted by the legislature have on the system through the discretion they give to police, prosecutors, judges, and juries?

Although each stage of the process raises distinct issues, several themes arise throughout the process and are worth keeping in mind as you read the following two chapters. These themes include the extent to which people are and ought to be treated as individuals versus groups; how best to manage the costs and benefits of discretion; whether race can and should be used as a sole or dominant factor, or only as one of many factors, in decision-making; and how to address the tension between racial equality and other societal values, such as individual liberty or the public interest in crime control. In addition, certain political controversies inform and shape the content of federal and state criminal laws and their administration and enforcement. The following two chapters implicate at least three major political agendas also at stake elsewhere in the book: the regulation of immigration, the War on Drugs, and counter-terrorism. Finally, these criminal justice materials implicate fundamental questions that arise across regulatory arenas: what would racial equality in the criminal justice system look like, what policies would best achieve those objectives, and which legal actors are best suited to carrying out such policies?

II. POLICING

A. INTRODUCTION

The role of police discretion in law enforcement gives rise to a central challenge. On one hand, police discretion is necessary for optimal enforcement of the law. Myriad decisions that officers make every day require careful and time-sensitive judgments, from whether to investigate a person or situation, to frisk a suspect for weapons, to conduct a search, to make an arrest and on what charge, and whether to use force. It would be impossible and undesirable to attempt to specify in advance exactly how an officer should respond to each situation. That law enforcement resources are limited further requires officers to prioritize and choose which enforcement actions to take from among many options.

On the other hand, police discretion contributes to some of the most vexing features of the criminal justice system. With discretion comes the risk of its abuse. Police are authorized by law to interfere with the liberty of individuals they investigate and arrest, and to use force if necessary. In making these decisions, police sometimes exercise their discretion against individuals in a manner that is unnecessarily time-consuming, humiliating, traumatic, injurious, and even deadly. The question thus becomes how to give police an adequate degree of discretion while ensuring that they are well supervised and held accountable.

The tension between the need for police intervention and the need to check police abuse is felt most acutely in poor, minority communities. Drugs and other vice crimes, as well as gun violence, ravage many such communities. Crime imposes devastating costs on the life chances of the adults and children in such places. They need police to proactively prevent crime and remove offenders to the criminal justice system. Police failure to investigate crimes in minority communities historically has been a serious problem.

At the same time, many residents of minority communities view the police with mistrust, as an invading force that harasses innocent people without legal basis and in an intrusive and abusive manner. They also believe that police selectively target people, especially young males, because of their race. And they are probably right. A growing body of empirical evidence suggests that, in the United States today, police stop, question, search, and arrest racial minorities at substantially higher rates than whites. Worse, police appear to subject black male suspects to force, including deadly force, more than other suspects. A pattern of such tragic encounters, too numerous to name here, has produced a nationwide movement around the declaration that "Black Lives Matter," with such rallying cries as "Hands Up, Don't Shoot!"

This chapter considers various approaches that civil rights activists and defense attorneys have developed for managing police discretion, especially to prevent its selective exercise against racial minorities. Their approaches have included constitutional litigation. Three doctrines constrain police discretion today. First, the void-for-vagueness doctrine under the Due Process Clause requires legislatures to define crimes with specificity in order to guide police as to what conduct is illegal and therefore a proper basis for investigation and arrest. Second, the Fourth Amendment requires that police have reasonable suspicion that a suspect has committed, is committing, or will commit a crime before they may coercively "stop and frisk" the suspect. Police must have probable cause of criminal activity before arresting and fully searching a suspect. Third, the Equal Protection Clause presumptively forbids police from selectively enforcing the law against suspects based on certain factors, such as race or ethnicity.

Activists turned to the courts and the Constitution rather than to legislative reform, not because they believed courts were better able to control police discretion, but because they believed courts would be more *willing* to do so. Explaining the need for constitutional protections from police abuse, Professor David Cole observes, "the political process will not adequately protect the interests of those targeted by the police. If the political process were sufficient, constitutional protections would be unnecessary." David Cole, *Foreword: Discretion and Discrimination Reconsidered: A Response to the New Criminal Justice Scholars*, 86 Geo. L.J. 1059 (1999).

In studying these constitutional protections, ask yourself how effective they are at preventing police from disproportionately targeting racial minorities for coercive investigation and arrest. What alternative approaches could, in theory, control police discretion more effectively? And how, in practice, can such alternative approaches gain the political support necessary to make them effective? Put another way, if the criminal justice system valued black and other lives equally, how, in the twenty-first century, would it protect the lives of its citizens from crime while treating the lives of suspects and defendants fairly?

B. APPROACH ONE: REQUIRE SPECIFICITY IN CRIME DEFINITION

The first approach to constraining discretion we consider conceives of the problem of police discretion as a product of crime definition. When legislatures define crimes in vague terms, the theory goes, it vests broad discretion in police to enforce the laws based on their own whims and predilections, including racial prejudice and bias. In the 1970s, the Supreme Court developed the "void for vagueness" doctrine to address this risk. Courts subsequently invalidated a broad range of laws across the country on these grounds, forcing legislatures to redraft their laws to be more precise.

Below you will encounter the Supreme Court's effort to constrain police discretion in *Chicago v. Morales,* 527 U.S. 41 (1999). As the notes following that case reveal, much of the debate over the case has revolved around whether the historical justifications for the vagueness doctrine are still relevant in the contemporary United States. Accordingly, in order to evaluate the vagueness doctrine's usefulness today, it is necessary to understand and evaluate its historical development.

Throughout American history, law enforcement officials have selectively targeted blacks and other minorities for investigation and arrest through the enforcement of vagrancy (chronic unemployment) and other so-called status crimes, such as loitering and acting suspiciously. Such laws criminalized behavior, or the lack thereof, that is so common and innocuous that police could arrest virtually anyone for any reason. Vagrancy laws date back to the decline of the feudal system in England when the laboring classes were dislocated from their traditional means of support. American states adopted similar laws and, following the Civil

War, used them to control the population of freed slaves. As the Supreme Court has explained:

> In 16th-century England . . . the "Slavery acts" provided for a 2-year enslavement period for anyone who "liveth idly and loiteringly, by the space of three days." . . . [M]any American vagrancy laws were patterned on these "Elizabethan poor laws." . . . In addition, vagrancy laws were used after the Civil War to keep former slaves in a state of quasi slavery. In 1865, for example, Alabama broadened its vagrancy statute to include "any runaway, stubborn servant or child" and "a laborer or servant who loiters away his time, or refuses to comply with any contract for a term of service without just cause."

Chicago v. Morales, 527 U.S. 41, 53 n.20 (1999). Also illustrative is Mississippi, which amended its vagrancy laws during Reconstruction to provide:

> Be it further enacted, That all freemen, free negroes and mulattoes in this State, over the age of eighteen years, found on the second Monday in January, 1866, or thereafter, with no lawful employment or business, or found unlawfully assembling themselves together either in the day or night time . . . shall be deemed vagrants, and on conviction thereof, shall be fined in the sum of not exceeding . . . fifty dollars . . . and imprisoned at the discretion of the court. Laws of Mississippi, Ch. VI, Sec. 2 (1865).

States throughout the South in the aftermath of the Civil War adopted similar laws as part of the system of "Black Codes," which required blacks to labor for whites under antebellum-like conditions, including as convict labor for a variety of minor crimes, such as vagrancy, "insulting gestures," and violating curfew. As the Supreme Court observed, freedom for blacks was strictly limited by "laws which imposed upon the colored race onerous disabilities and burdens, and curtailed their rights in the pursuit of life, liberty, and property to such an extent that their freedom was of little value." *Slaughter-House Cases*, 83 U.S. (16 Wall.) 36, 70 (1872). .

Despite significant gains in black rights in most regions of the country by the 1960s, vagrancy laws remained prevalent in the mid-twentieth century. Jacksonville, Florida's ordinance, typical of many such laws at the time, was sweeping in its enumeration of prohibited conduct. It made it a crime to be a "vagrant," defined as:

> Rogues and vagabonds, or dissolute persons who go about begging, common gamblers, persons who use juggling or unlawful games or plays, common drunkards, common night walkers, thieves, pilferers or pickpockets, traders in stolen property, lewd, wanton and lascivious persons, keepers of gambling places, common railers and brawlers, persons wandering or strolling around from place to place without any

lawful purpose or object, habitual loafers, disorderly persons, persons neglecting all lawful business and habitually spending their time by frequenting houses of ill fame, gaming houses, or places where alcoholic beverages are sold or served, persons able to work but habitually living upon the earnings of their wives or minor children.

Such laws enabled police to arrest people whose presence they considered unacceptable because of characteristics deemed undesirable, such as low economic status, unconventional appearance, boisterous behavior, and race. For example, police relied on the Jacksonville ordinance quoted above to arrest two white women and two black men seen driving together, on a charge of prowling by auto. In *Papachristou v. Jacksonville,* 405 U.S. 156, 161 (1972), the Supreme Court invalidated the Jacksonville ordinance under the Due Process Clause of the Fourteenth Amendment on grounds that it was void for vagueness, in that it "fails to give a person of ordinary intelligence fair notice that his contemplated conduct is forbidden by the statute, and because it encourages arbitrary and erratic arrests and convictions." The Court expressed concern that the vague and broad scope of the ordinance enabled police to discriminate based on arbitrary or invidious characteristics, including race:

> Those generally implicated by the imprecise terms of the ordinance—poor people, non-conformists, dissenters, idlers—may be required to comport themselves according to the lifestyle deemed appropriate by the Jacksonville police and the courts. Where, as here, there are no standards governing the exercise of the discretion granted by the ordinance, the scheme permits and encourages an arbitrary and discriminatory enforcement of the law. . . . It results in a regime in which the poor and the unpopular are permitted to "stand on a public sidewalk . . . only at the whim of any police officer."

> . . . Of course, vagrancy statutes are useful to the police. Of course, they are nets making easy the roundup of so-called undesirables. But the rule of law implies equality and justice in its application. Vagrancy laws of the Jacksonville type teach that the scales of justice are so tipped that even-handed administration of the law is not possible. The rule of law, evenly applied to minorities as well as majorities, to the poor as well as the rich, is the great mucilage that holds society together.

Papachristou, 405 U.S., at 170–71.

Although *Papachristou* is the best-known case from the early 1970s invalidating a status crime on vagueness grounds, it represented a culmination of other cases in which the Court began more aggressively applying the vagueness doctrine. For example, in *Coates v. City of Cincinnati*, 402 U.S. 611, 614–16 (1971), the Court found unconstitutionally vague and overbroad an ordinance that forbade congregating on sidewalks "in a manner annoying to persons passing by." Similarly, in *Palmer v. City of Euclid*, 402 U.S. 544, 545–46 (1971), the Court invalidated a conviction under a "suspicious person" ordinance, which prohibited being "without visible or lawful business." The Court found the phrase unconstitutionally vague as applied to the defendant whom police observed sitting in a parked car at night talking on a two-way radio.

Do you think the Court was justified in striking down the laws in *Papachristou, Coates*, and *Palmer*? Doesn't the law-abiding public have a legitimate interest in keeping public spaces free from people who are drunk, obnoxious, annoying, without lawful business, or potential thieves? Why can't we generally trust police to exercise discretion appropriately in investigating and, if necessary, moving along or arresting those persons who do pose a threat to public safety and the quality of life in public spaces? If you do believe these laws were problematic, is the problem their vagueness, or something else? Consider especially the ordinance invalidated in *Papachristou*. Was it really unclear who could be arrested under that ordinance? Would a law that was perfectly clear, such as one that defined a vagrant as someone who "walks upon a public street at night" or who "sleeps outside," be preferable? Also, if a major problem with vagrancy laws is that they were susceptible to being enforced in a discriminatory manner, why not simply invalidate arrests and convictions when the evidence indicates that the officer relied on race or some other impermissible factor?

In response to *Papachristou*, state legislatures returned to the drawing board to design laws that complied with the vagueness doctrine while giving police adequate discretion to investigate suspects believed to pose a threat to public safety. California, for example, passed a law that defined "disorderly conduct" to include one "who loiters or wanders upon the streets . . . without apparent reason . . . and who refuses to identify himself . . . when requested by any peace officer so to do, if the surrounding circumstances are such as to indicate to a reasonable man that the public safety demands such identification." As construed by a state court, the identification required by the law must be "credible and reliable," which meant "carrying reasonable assurance that the identification is authentic and providing means for later getting in touch with the person who has identified himself." The state court further held that a police officer could request identification only if he already had reasonable suspicion of criminal activity.

In *Kolender v. Lawson*, 461 U.S. 352 (1983), the Supreme Court invalidated the California law on the ground that the phrase "credible and reliable" was excessively vague and therefore created an undue risk that police would enforce it in an arbitrary or discriminatory manner. Edward Lawson challenged the law after having been stopped fifteen times in less than two years, prosecuted twice, and convicted once. His criminal record was otherwise clean. The Court did not mention in its opinion that Lawson was black, a civil rights activist, and unconventional in appearance, though these considerations may well have informed its ultimate decision. According to contemporaneous news reports, Lawson was tall and slender, with tightly coiled, shoulder-length hair. He enjoyed long walks in the evening through upscale, predominantly white San Diego neighborhoods. The law under which Lawson was repeatedly arrested failed to define identification with adequate specificity. Thus, as the Court observed, "an individual . . . is entitled to continue to walk the public streets 'only at the whim of any police officer' who happens to stop that individual." The vagueness doctrine, the Court explained, served to ensure that legislatures defined crimes with sufficient specificity to guide law enforcement and to give the public notice of what conduct was prohibited.

Was the Court in *Kolender* justified in holding that the identification statute was too vague and vested police with excessive discretion? The law required "credible and reliable" identification "carrying reasonable assurance that the identification is authentic and providing means for later getting in touch with the person." What forms of identification should meet the statutory requirement? Moreover, police were only authorized to request identification when they already had reasonable suspicion that the person had committed, is committing, or will commit a crime. Don't police have a legitimate interest in ascertaining the identity of someone they reasonably suspect of criminal activity? Didn't the law fairly well limit the scope of police authority to that purpose?

DRAFTING EXERCISE

The Court in *Kolender* believed that states could draft laws authorizing police to request identification without running afoul of the vagueness doctrine. "Although due process does not require 'impossible standards' of clarity," the Court explained, "this is not a case where further precision in the statutory language is either impossible or impractical." *Kolender*, 461 U.S. at 361. If you were advising the California legislature, how would you suggest that it redraft the identification statute to comply with the vagueness doctrine? Would the law you suggested necessarily survive a vagueness challenge? Would it adequately protect both individual rights and the public interest in crime control? Would another kind of law be preferable?

———————————

Numerous criminal laws ultimately satisfy the vagueness doctrine, including traditional common law crimes against violence and interference with property rights. Of more recent vintage, laws prohibiting the possession and distribution of controlled substances similarly satisfy this constitutional requirement. But the drug laws also implicate another set of issues that have given rise to contemporary vagueness concerns. The dramatic expansion of the scope of the drug laws and the penalties attached to them has been motivated at least in part by the interest in controlling urban gangs, many of which sell drugs and perpetrate gun-related violence to protect their commercial interests. By the 1990s in Chicago, for example, substantial areas of the city had become dominated by gangs that controlled streets and parks, intimidating law-abiding residents and killing members of rival gangs, innocent bystanders, and police officers. To address these problems, lawmakers relied not only on laws against drug dealing, assault, gun violence, and murder, but they also turned to crime control strategies that echoed the vagrancy laws of a pervious era. Consider the next case.

Chicago v. Morales

527 U.S. 41 (1999).

■ JUSTICE STEVENS announced the judgment of the Court and delivered the opinion of the Court with respect to Parts I, II, and V, and an opinion with respect to Parts III, IV, and VI, in which JUSTICE SOUTER and JUSTICE GINSBURG join.

In 1992, the Chicago City Council enacted the Gang Congregation Ordinance, which prohibits "criminal street gang members" from "loitering" with one another or with other persons in any public place. The question presented is whether the Supreme Court of Illinois correctly held that the ordinance violates the Due Process Clause of the Fourteenth Amendment to the Federal Constitution.

I.

Before the ordinance was adopted, the city council's Committee on Police and Fire conducted hearings to explore the problems created by the city's street gangs, and more particularly, the consequences of public loitering by gang members. Witnesses included residents of the neighborhoods where gang members are most active, as well as some of the aldermen who represent those areas. Based on that evidence, the council made a series of findings that are included in the text of the ordinance and explain the reasons for its enactment.

The council found that a continuing increase in criminal street gang activity was largely responsible for the city's rising murder rate, as well as an escalation of violent and drug related crimes. It noted that in many neighborhoods throughout the city, "the burgeoning presence of street gang members in public places has intimidated many law abiding citizens." Furthermore, the council stated that gang members "establish control over identifiable areas . . . by loitering in those areas and intimidating others from entering those areas; and . . . members of criminal street gangs avoid arrest by committing no offense punishable under existing laws when they know the police are present. . . ." It further found that "loitering in public places by criminal street gang members creates a justifiable fear for the safety of persons and property in the area" and that "aggressive action is necessary to preserve the city's streets and other public places so that the public may use such places without fear." Moreover, the council concluded that the city "has an interest in discouraging all persons from loitering in public places with criminal gang members."

The ordinance creates a criminal offense punishable by a fine of up to $500, imprisonment for not more than six months, and a requirement to perform up to 120 hours of community service. Commission of the offense involves four predicates. First, the police officer must reasonably believe that at least one of the two or more persons present in a "public place" is a "criminal street gang member." Second, the persons must be "loitering," which the ordinance defines as "remaining in any one place with no apparent purpose." Third, the officer must then order "all" of the persons to disperse and remove themselves "from the area." Fourth, a person must disobey the officer's order. If any person, whether a gang member or not, disobeys the officer's order, that person is guilty of violating the ordinance.

Two months after the ordinance was adopted, the Chicago Police Department promulgated General Order 92–4 to provide guidelines to govern its enforcement. That order purported to establish limitations on the enforcement discretion of police officers "to ensure that the anti-gang loitering ordinance is not enforced in an arbitrary or discriminatory way." The limitations confine the authority to arrest gang members who violate the ordinance to sworn "members of the Gang Crime Section" and certain other designated officers, and establish detailed criteria for defining street gangs and membership in such gangs. In addition, the order directs district commanders to "designate areas in which the presence of gang members has a demonstrable effect on the activities of law abiding persons in the surrounding community," and provides that the ordinance "will be enforced only within the designated areas." The city, however, does not release the locations of these "designated areas" to the public.

II.

During the three years of its enforcement, the police issued over 89,000 dispersal orders and arrested over 42,000 people for violating the ordinance. In the ensuing enforcement proceedings, two trial judges upheld the constitutionality of the ordinance, but eleven others ruled that it was invalid. In respondent Youkhana's case, the trial judge held that the "ordinance fails to notify individuals what conduct is prohibited, and it encourages arbitrary and capricious enforcement by police."

The Illinois Supreme Court affirmed. It held "that the gang loitering ordinance violates due process of law in that it is impermissibly vague on its face and an arbitrary restriction on personal liberties." The court did not reach the contentions that the ordinance "creates a status offense, permits arrests without probable cause or is overbroad."

. . . Like the Illinois Supreme Court, we conclude that the ordinance enacted by the city of Chicago is unconstitutionally vague.

III.

The basic factual predicate for the city's ordinance is not in dispute. As the city argues in its brief, "the very presence of a large collection of obviously brazen, insistent, and lawless gang members and hangers-on on the public ways intimidates residents, who become afraid even to leave their homes and go about their business. That, in turn, imperils community residents' sense of safety and security, detracts from property values, and can ultimately destabilize entire neighborhoods." The findings in the ordinance explain that it was motivated by these concerns. We have no doubt that a law that directly prohibited such intimidating conduct would be constitutional, but this ordinance broadly covers a significant amount of additional activity. Uncertainty about the scope of that additional coverage provides the basis for respondents' claim that the ordinance is too vague.

[T]he freedom to loiter for innocent purposes is part of the "liberty" protected by the Due Process Clause of the Fourteenth Amendment. We have expressly identified this "right to remove from one place to another according to inclination" as "an attribute of personal liberty" protected by the Constitution. Indeed, it is apparent that an individual's decision to remain in a public place of his choice is as much a part of his liberty as the freedom of movement inside frontiers that is "a part of our heritage," *Kent v. Dulles,* 357 U.S. 116, 126 (1958), or the right to move "to whatsoever place one's own inclination may direct" identified in Blackstone's Commentaries. 1 W. Blackstone, Commentaries on the Laws of England 130 (1765).

There is no need, however, to decide whether the impact of the Chicago ordinance on constitutionally protected liberty alone would suffice to support a facial challenge under the overbreadth doctrine. For it is clear that the vagueness of this enactment makes a facial challenge appropriate. This is not an ordinance that "simply regulates business behavior and contains a scienter requirement." It is a criminal law that contains no mens rea requirement, and infringes on constitutionally protected rights. When vagueness permeates the text of such a law, it is subject to facial attack.

Vagueness may invalidate a criminal law for either of two independent reasons. First, it may fail to provide the kind of notice that will enable ordinary people to understand what conduct it prohibits; second, it may authorize and even encourage arbitrary and discriminatory enforcement.

IV.

. . . The Illinois Supreme Court recognized that the term "loiter" may have a common and accepted meaning, but the definition of that term in this ordinance—"to remain in any one place with no apparent purpose"—does not. It is difficult to imagine how any citizen of the city of Chicago standing in a public place with a group of people would know if he or she had an "apparent purpose." If she were talking to another person, would she have an apparent purpose? If she were frequently checking her watch and looking expectantly down the street, would she have an apparent purpose?

Since the city cannot conceivably have meant to criminalize each instance a citizen stands in public with a gang member, the vagueness that dooms this ordinance is not the product of uncertainty about the normal meaning of "loitering," but rather about what loitering is covered by the ordinance and what is not. . . . The city's principal response to this concern about adequate notice is that loiterers are not subject to sanction until after they have failed to comply with an officer's order to disperse. . . . We find this response unpersuasive for at least two reasons.

First . . . [a]lthough it is true that a loiterer is not subject to criminal sanctions unless he or she disobeys a dispersal order, the loitering is the conduct that the ordinance is designed to prohibit. If the loitering is in fact harmless and innocent, the dispersal order itself is an unjustified impairment of liberty. . . . Because an officer may issue an order only after prohibited conduct has already occurred, it cannot provide the kind of advance notice that will protect the putative loiterer from being ordered to disperse. Such an order cannot retroactively give adequate warning of the boundary between the permissible and the impermissible applications of the law.

Second, the terms of the dispersal order compound the inadequacy of the notice afforded by the ordinance. It provides that the officer "shall order all such persons to disperse and remove themselves from the area." This vague phrasing raises a host of questions. After such an order issues, how long must the loiterers remain apart? How far must they move? If each loiterer walks around the block and they meet again at the same location, are they subject to arrest or merely to being ordered to disperse again? As we do here, we have found vagueness in a criminal statute exacerbated by the use of the standards of "neighborhood" and "locality." *Connally v. General Constr. Co.,* 269 U.S. 385 (1926). We remarked in Connally that "both terms are elastic and, dependent upon circumstances, may be equally satisfied by areas measured by rods or by miles."

Lack of clarity in the description of the loiterer's duty to obey a dispersal order might not render the ordinance unconstitutionally vague if the definition of the forbidden conduct were clear, but it does buttress our conclusion that the entire ordinance fails to give the ordinary citizen adequate notice of what is forbidden and what is permitted. The Constitution does not permit a legislature to "set a net large enough to catch all possible offenders, and leave it to the courts to step inside and say who could be rightfully detained, and who should be set at large." This ordinance is therefore vague "not in the sense that it requires a person to conform his conduct to an imprecise but comprehensible normative standard, but rather in the sense that no standard of conduct is specified at all."

V.

The broad sweep of the ordinance also violates " 'the requirement that a legislature establish minimal guidelines to govern law enforcement.' " There are no such guidelines in the ordinance. In any public place in the city of Chicago, persons who stand or sit in the company of a gang member may be ordered to disperse unless their purpose is apparent. The mandatory language in the enactment directs the police to issue an order without first making any inquiry about their possible purposes. It matters not whether the reason that a gang member and his father, for example, might loiter near Wrigley Field is to rob an unsuspecting fan or just to get a glimpse of Sammy Sosa leaving the ballpark; in either event, if their purpose is not apparent to a nearby police officer, she may—indeed, she "shall"—order them to disperse.

Recognizing that the ordinance does reach a substantial amount of innocent conduct, we turn, then, to its language to determine if it "necessarily entrusts lawmaking to the moment-to-moment judgment of the policeman on his beat." As we discussed in the context of fair notice, the principal source of the vast discretion conferred on the police in this case is the definition of loitering as "to remain in any one place with no apparent purpose."

As the Illinois Supreme Court interprets that definition, it "provides absolute discretion to police officers to determine what activities constitute loitering." . . .

It is true, as the city argues, that the requirement that the officer reasonably believe that a group of loiterers contains a gang member does place a limit on the authority to order dispersal. That limitation would no doubt be sufficient if the ordinance only applied to loitering that had an apparently harmful purpose or effect, or possibly if it only applied to loitering by persons reasonably believed to be criminal gang members. But this ordinance, for reasons that are not explained in the findings of the city council, requires no harmful purpose and applies to non-gang members as well as suspected gang members. It applies to everyone in the city who may remain in one place with one suspected gang member as long as their purpose is not apparent to an officer observing them. Friends, relatives, teachers, counselors, or even total strangers might unwittingly engage in forbidden loitering if they happen to engage in idle conversation with a gang member.

Ironically, the definition of loitering in the Chicago ordinance not only extends its scope to encompass harmless conduct, but also has the perverse consequence of excluding from its coverage much of the intimidating conduct that motivated its enactment. As the city council's findings demonstrate, the most harmful gang loitering is motivated either by an apparent purpose to publicize the gang's dominance of certain territory, thereby intimidating nonmembers, or by an equally apparent purpose to conceal ongoing commerce in illegal drugs. As the Illinois Supreme Court has not placed any limiting construction on the language in the ordinance, we must assume that the ordinance means what it says and that it has no application to loiterers whose purpose is apparent. The relative importance of its application to harmless loitering is magnified by its inapplicability to loitering that has an obviously threatening or illicit purpose.

Finally, in its opinion striking down the ordinance, the Illinois Supreme Court refused to accept the general order issued by the police department as a sufficient limitation on the "vast amount of discretion" granted to the police in its enforcement. We agree. That the police have adopted internal rules limiting their enforcement to certain designated areas in the city would not provide a defense to a loiterer who might be arrested elsewhere. Nor could a person who knowingly loitered with a well-known gang member anywhere in the city safely assume that they would not be ordered to disperse no matter how innocent and harmless their loitering might be.

VI.

[T]he ordinance does not provide sufficiently specific limits on the enforcement discretion of the police "to meet constitutional standards for definiteness and clarity." We recognize the serious and difficult problems testified to by the citizens of Chicago that led to the enactment of this ordinance. . . . However, in this instance the city has enacted an ordinance that affords too much discretion to the police and too little notice to citizens who wish to use the public streets.

■ JUSTICE O'CONNOR, with whom JUSTICE BREYER joins, concurring in part and concurring in the judgment.

As it has been construed by the [Illinois Supreme Court], Chicago's gang loitering ordinance is unconstitutionally vague because it lacks sufficient minimal standards to guide law enforcement officers. In particular, it fails to provide police with any standard by which they can judge whether an individual has an "apparent purpose." Indeed, because any person standing on the street has a general "purpose"—even if it is simply to stand—the ordinance permits police officers to choose which purposes are permissible. Under this construction the police do not have to decide that an individual is "threatening the public peace" to issue a dispersal order. *See* post, at 11 (THOMAS, J., dissenting). Any police officer in Chicago is free, under the Illinois Supreme Court's construction of the ordinance, to order at his whim any person standing in a public place with a suspected gang member to disperse. Further, as construed by the Illinois court, the ordinance applies to hundreds of thousands of persons who are not gang members, standing on any sidewalk or in any park, coffee shop, bar, or "other location open to the public, whether publicly or privately owned."

To be sure, there is no violation of the ordinance unless a person fails to obey promptly the order to disperse. But, a police officer cannot issue a dispersal order until he decides that a person is remaining in one place "with no apparent purpose," and the ordinance provides no guidance to the officer on how to make this antecedent decision. Moreover, the requirement that police issue dispersal orders only when they "reasonably believe" that a group of loiterers includes a gang member fails to cure the ordinance's vague aspects. If the ordinance applied only to persons reasonably believed to be gang members, this requirement might have cured the ordinance's vagueness because it would have directed the manner in which the order was issued by specifying to whom the order could be issued. But, the Illinois Supreme Court did not construe the ordinance to be so limited.

As the ordinance comes to this Court, it is unconstitutionally vague. Nevertheless, there remain open to Chicago reasonable alternatives to combat the very real threat posed by gang intimidation and violence. For example, the Court properly and expressly distinguishes the ordinance from laws that require loiterers to have a "harmful purpose," from laws that target only gang members, and from laws that incorporate limits on the area and manner in which the laws may be enforced. In addition, the ordinance here is unlike a law that "directly prohibits" the " 'presence of a large collection of obviously brazen, insistent, and lawless gang members and hangers-on on the public ways,' " that " 'intimidates residents.' " Indeed, as the plurality notes, the city of Chicago has several laws that do exactly this. . . . Chicago's general disorderly conduct provision allows the police to arrest those who knowingly "provoke, make or aid in making a breach of peace."

In my view, the gang loitering ordinance could have been construed more narrowly. The term "loiter" might possibly be construed in a more limited fashion to mean "to remain in any one place with no apparent purpose other than to establish control over identifiable areas, to intimidate others from entering those areas, or to conceal illegal activities." Such a definition would be consistent with the Chicago City Council's findings and would avoid the vagueness problems of the ordinance as construed by the Illinois Supreme Court. As noted above, so would limitations that restricted the ordinance's criminal penalties to gang members or that more carefully delineated the circumstances in which those penalties would apply to nongang members.

The Illinois Supreme Court did not choose to give a limiting construction to Chicago's ordinance.

■ [The concurring opinion of JUSTICE KENNEDY is omitted.]

■ JUSTICE BREYER, concurring in part and concurring in the judgment.

The ordinance before us creates more than a "minor limitation upon the free state of nature." Post, at 2 (SCALIA, J., dissenting). The law authorizes a police officer to order any person to remove himself from any "location open to the public, whether publicly or privately owned," i.e., any sidewalk, front stoop, public park, public square, lakeside promenade, hotel, restaurant, bowling alley, bar, barbershop, sports arena, shopping mall, etc., but with two, and only two, limitations: First, that person must be accompanied by (or must himself be) someone police reasonably believe is a gang member. Second, that person must have remained in that public place "with no apparent purpose."

The first limitation cannot save the ordinance. Though it limits the number of persons subject to the law, it leaves many individuals, gang members and nongang members alike, subject to its strictures. Nor does it limit in any way the range of conduct that police may prohibit. The second limitation is, as Justice Stevens and Justice O'Connor point out, not a limitation at all. Since one always has some apparent purpose, the so-called limitation invites, in fact requires, the policeman to interpret the words "no apparent purpose" as meaning "no apparent purpose except for. . . ." And it is in the ordinance's delegation to the policeman of open-ended discretion to fill in that blank that the problem lies. To grant to a policeman virtually standardless discretion to close off major portions of the city to an innocent person is, in my view, to create a major, not a "minor," "limitation upon the free state of nature."

Nor does it violate "our rules governing facial challenges," post, at 2 (SCALIA, J., dissenting), to forbid the city to apply the unconstitutional ordinance in this case. The reason why the ordinance is invalid explains how that is so. As I have said, I believe the ordinance violates the Constitution because it delegates too much discretion to a police officer to decide whom to order to move on, and in what circumstances. And I see no way to distinguish in the ordinance's terms between one application of that discretion and another. The ordinance is unconstitutional, not because a policeman applied this discretion wisely or poorly in a particular case, but rather because the policeman enjoys too much discretion in every case. And if every application of the ordinance represents an exercise of unlimited discretion, then the ordinance is invalid in all its applications. The city of Chicago may be able validly to apply some other law to the defendants in light of their conduct. But the city of Chicago may no more apply this law to the defendants, no matter how they behaved, than could it apply an (imaginary) statute that said, "It is a crime to do wrong," even to the worst of murderers. *See Lanzetta v. New Jersey,* 306 U.S. 451, 453 (1939).

■ JUSTICE SCALIA, dissenting.

The citizens of Chicago were once free to drive about the city at whatever speed they wished. At some point Chicagoans (or perhaps Illinoisans) decided this would not do, and imposed prophylactic speed limits designed to assure safe operation by the average (or perhaps even subaverage) driver with the average (or perhaps even subaverage) vehicle. This infringed upon the "freedom" of all citizens, but was not unconstitutional.

Similarly, the citizens of Chicago were once free to stand around and gawk at the scene of an accident. At some point Chicagoans discovered that this obstructed traffic and caused more accidents. They did not make the practice unlawful, but they did authorize police officers to order the crowd to disperse, and imposed penalties for refusal to obey such an order. Again, this prophylactic measure infringed upon the "freedom" of all citizens, but was not unconstitutional.

Until the ordinance that is before us today was adopted, the citizens of Chicago were free to stand about in public places with no apparent purpose—to engage, that is, in conduct that appeared to be loitering. In recent years, however, the city has been afflicted with criminal street gangs. As reflected in the record before us, these gangs congregated in public places to deal in drugs, and to terrorize the neighborhoods by demonstrating control over their "turf." Many residents of the inner city felt that they were prisoners in their own homes. Once again, Chicagoans decided that to eliminate the problem it was worth restricting some of the freedom that they once enjoyed. The means they took was similar to the second, and more mild, example given above rather than the first: Loitering was not made unlawful, but when a group of people occupied a public place without an apparent purpose and in the company of a known gang member, police officers were authorized to order them to disperse, and the failure to obey such an order was made unlawful. The minor limitation upon the free state of nature that this prophylactic arrangement imposed upon all Chicagoans seemed to them (and it seems to me) a small price to pay for liberation of their streets.

I.

Respondents' consolidated appeal presents a facial challenge to the Chicago Ordinance on vagueness grounds. When a facial challenge is successful, the law in question is declared to be unenforceable in all its applications, and not just in its particular application to the party in suit.

When our normal criteria for facial challenges are applied, it is clear that the Justices in the majority have transposed the burden of proof. Instead of requiring the respondents, who are challenging the Ordinance, to show that it is invalid in all its applications, they have required the petitioner to show that it is valid in all its applications. Both the plurality opinion and the concurrences display a lively imagination, creating hypothetical situations in which the law's application would (in their view) be ambiguous. But that creative role has been usurped from the petitioner, who can defeat the respondents' facial challenge by conjuring up a single valid application of the law. My contribution would go something like this: Tony, a member of the Jets criminal street gang, is standing alongside and chatting with fellow gang members while staking out their turf at Promontory Point on the South Side of Chicago; the group is flashing gang signs and displaying their distinctive tattoos to passersby. Officer Krupke, applying the Ordinance at issue here, orders the group to disperse. After some speculative discussion (probably irrelevant here) over whether the Jets are depraved because they are deprived, Tony and the other gang members break off further conversation with the statement—not entirely coherent, but evidently intended to be rude—"Gee, Officer Krupke, krup you." A tense standoff ensues until Officer Krupke arrests the group for failing to obey his dispersal order. Even assuming (as the Justices in the majority do, but I do not) that a law requiring obedience to a dispersal order is impermissibly vague unless it is clear to the objects of the order, before its issuance, that their conduct justifies it, I find it hard to believe that the Jets would not have known they had it coming. That should settle the matter of respondents' facial challenge to the Ordinance's vagueness.

Of course respondents would still be able to claim that the Ordinance was vague as applied to them. But the ultimate demonstration of the inappropriateness of the Court's holding of facial invalidity is the fact that it is doubtful whether some of these respondents could even sustain an as-applied challenge on the basis of the majority's own criteria. For instance, respondent Jose Renteria—who admitted that he was a member of the Satan Disciples gang—was observed by the arresting officer loitering on a street corner with other gang members. The officer issued a dispersal order, but when she returned to the same corner 15 to 20 minutes later, Renteria was still there with his friends, whereupon he was arrested. In another example, respondent Daniel Washington and several others—who admitted they were members of the Vice Lords gang—were observed by the arresting officer loitering in the street, yelling at passing vehicles, stopping traffic, and preventing pedestrians from using the sidewalks. The arresting officer issued a dispersal order, issued another dispersal order later when the group did not move, and finally arrested the group when they were found loitering in the same place still later. Finally, respondent Gregorio Gutierrez—who had previously admitted to the arresting officer his membership in the Latin Kings gang—was observed loitering with two other men. The officer issued a dispersal order, drove around the block, and arrested the men after finding them in the same place upon his return. Even on the majority's assumption that to avoid vagueness it must be clear to the object of the dispersal order ex ante that his conduct is covered by the Ordinance, it seems most improbable that any of these as-applied challenges would be sustained. Much less is it possible to say that the Ordinance is invalid in all its applications.

IV.

... A law is unconstitutionally vague if its lack of definitive standards either (1) fails to apprise persons of ordinary intelligence of the prohibited conduct, or (2) encourages arbitrary and discriminatory enforcement.

The plurality relies primarily upon the first of these aspects. Since, it reasons, "the loitering is the conduct that the ordinance is designed to prohibit," and "an officer may issue an order only after prohibited conduct has already occurred," the order to disperse cannot itself serve "to apprise persons of ordinary intelligence of the prohibited conduct." What counts for purposes of vagueness analysis, however, is not what the Ordinance is "designed to prohibit," but what it actually subjects to criminal penalty. As discussed earlier, that consists of nothing but the refusal to obey a dispersal order, as to which there is no doubt of adequate notice of the prohibited conduct. The plurality's suggestion that even the dispersal order itself is unconstitutionally vague, because it does not specify *how far to disperse (!)*, scarcely requires a response.

For its determination of unconstitutional vagueness, the Court relies secondarily—and Justice O'Connor's and Justice Breyer's concurrences exclusively—upon the second aspect of that doctrine, which requires sufficient specificity to prevent arbitrary and discriminatory law enforcement.

The criteria for issuance of a dispersal order under the Chicago Ordinance could hardly be clearer. First, the law requires police officers to "reasonably believe" that one of the group to which the order is issued is a "criminal street gang member." This resembles a probable-cause standard, and the Chicago Police Department's General Order 92–4 (1992)—promulgated to govern enforcement of the Ordinance—makes the probable cause requirement explicit. Under the Order, officers must have probable cause to believe that an individual is a member of a criminal street gang, to be substantiated by the officer's "experience and knowledge of the alleged offenders" and by "specific, documented and reliable information" such as reliable witness testimony or an individual's admission of gang membership or display of distinctive colors, tattoos, signs, or other markings worn by members of particular criminal street gangs.

Second, the Ordinance requires that the group be "remaining in one place with no apparent purpose." Justice O'Connor's assertion that this applies to "any person standing in a public place," is a distortion. The Ordinance does not apply to "standing," but to "remaining"—a term which in this context obviously means "[to] endure or persist," *see* American Heritage Dictionary 1525 (1992). There may be some ambiguity at the margin, but "remaining in one place" requires more than a temporary stop, and is clear in most of its applications, including all of those represented by the facts surrounding the respondents' arrests described *supra*.

As for the phrase "with no apparent purpose": Justice O'Connor's again distorts this adjectival phrase, by separating it from the word that it modifies. "Any person standing on the street," her concurrence says, "has a general 'purpose'—even if it is simply to stand," and thus "the ordinance permits police officers to choose which purposes are permissible." But Chicago police officers enforcing the Ordinance are not looking for people with no apparent purpose (who are regrettably in oversupply); they are looking for people who "remain in any one place with no apparent purpose"—that is, who remain there without any apparent reason for remaining there. That is not difficult to perceive.

[T]he fact that this clear instruction to the officers "encompasses a great deal of harmless behavior" would be invalidating if that harmless behavior were constitutionally protected against abridgment, such as speech or the practice of religion. Remaining in one place is not so protected, and so (as already discussed) it is up to the citizens of Chicago—not us—to decide whether the trade-off is worth it.

V.

The plurality points out that Chicago already has several laws that reach the intimidating and unlawful gang-related conduct the Ordinance was directed at. The problem, of course, well recognized by Chicago's City Council, is that the gang members cease their intimidating and unlawful behavior under the watchful eye of police officers, but return to it as soon as the police drive away. The only solution, the council concluded, was to clear the streets of congregations of gangs, their drug customers, and their associates.

Justice O'Connor's concurrence proffers the same empty solace of existing laws useless for the purpose at hand, but seeks to be helpful by suggesting some measures similar to this ordinance that would be constitutional. It says that Chicago could, for example, enact a law that "directly prohibits the presence of a large collection of obviously brazen, insistent, and lawless gang members and hangers-on on the public ways, that intimidates residents." Ibid., (internal quotation marks omitted). (If the majority considers the present ordinance too vague, it would be fun to see what it makes of "a large collection of obviously brazen, insistent, and lawless gang members.") This prescription of the concurrence is largely a quotation from the plurality—which itself answers the concurrence's suggestion that such a law would be helpful by pointing out that the city already "has several laws that serve this purpose." The problem, again, is that the intimidation and lawlessness do not occur when the police are in sight.

The fact is that the present ordinance is entirely clear in its application, cannot be violated except with full knowledge and intent, and vests no more discretion in the police than innumerable other measures authorizing police orders to preserve the public peace and safety. . . . The citizens of Chicago have decided that depriving themselves of the freedom to "hang out" with a gang member is necessary to eliminate pervasive gang crime and intimidation—and that the elimination of the one is worth the deprivation of the other. This Court has no business second-guessing either the degree of necessity or the fairness of the trade. . . .

■ JUSTICE THOMAS, with whom THE CHIEF JUSTICE and JUSTICE SCALIA join, dissenting.

The duly elected members of the Chicago City Council enacted the ordinance at issue as part of a larger effort to prevent gangs from establishing dominion over the public streets. By invalidating Chicago's ordinance, I fear that the Court has unnecessarily sentenced law-abiding citizens to lives of terror and misery.

I.

The human costs exacted by criminal street gangs are inestimable. In many of our Nation's cities, gangs have "virtually overtaken certain neighborhoods, contributing to the economic and social decline of these areas and causing fear and lifestyle changes among law-abiding residents." Gangs fill the daily lives of many of our poorest and most vulnerable citizens with a terror that the Court does not give sufficient consideration, often relegating them to the status of prisoners in their own homes. *See* U.S. Dept. of Justice, Attorney General's Report to the President, Coordinated Approach to the Challenge of Gang Violence: A Progress Report 1 (Apr. 1996) ("From the small business owner who is literally crippled because he refuses to pay 'protection' money to the neighborhood gang, to the families who are hostages within their homes, living in neighborhoods ruled by predatory drug trafficking gangs, the harmful impact of gang violence . . . is both physically and psychologically debilitating").

The city of Chicago has suffered the devastation wrought by this national tragedy. Last year, in an effort to curb plummeting attendance, the Chicago Public Schools hired dozens of adults to escort children to school. The youngsters had become too terrified of gang violence to leave their homes alone. In 1996, the Chicago Police Department estimated that there were 132 criminal street gangs in the city. Between 1987 and 1994, these gangs were involved in 63,141 criminal incidents, including 21,689 nonlethal violent crimes and 894 homicides. Id. at 4–5. Many of these criminal incidents and homicides result from gang "turf battles," which take place on the public streets and place innocent residents in grave danger.

Before enacting its ordinance, the Chicago City Council held extensive hearings on the problems of gang loitering. Concerned citizens appeared to testify poignantly as to how gangs disrupt their daily lives.

Ordinary citizens like Ms. D'Ivory Gordon explained that she struggled just to walk to work:

"When I walk out my door, these guys are out there. . . . They watch you. . . . They know where you live. They know what time you leave, what time you come home. I am afraid of them. I have even come to the point now that I carry a meat cleaver to work with me. . . . I don't want to hurt anyone, and I don't want to be hurt. We need to clean these corners up. Clean these communities up and take it back from them."

Eighty-eight-year-old Susan Mary Jackson echoed her sentiments, testifying, "We used to have a nice neighborhood. We don't have it anymore. . . . I am scared to go out in the daytime. . . . you can't pass because they are standing. I am afraid to go to the store. I don't go to the store because I am afraid. At my age if they look at me real hard, I be ready to holler." Id., at 93–95. Another long-time resident testified:

"I have never had the terror that I feel everyday when I walk down the streets of Chicago. . . . I have had my windows broken out. I have had guns pulled on me. I have been threatened. I get intimidated on a daily basis, and it's come to the point where I say, well, do I go out today. Do I put my ax in my briefcase. Do I walk around dressed like a bum so I am not looking rich or got any money or anything like that."

Following these hearings, the council found that "criminal street gangs establish control over identifiable areas . . . by loitering in those areas and intimidating others from entering those areas." It further found that the mere presence of gang members "intimidates many law abiding citizens" and "creates a justifiable fear for the safety of persons and property in the area." Ibid. It is the product of this democratic process—the council's attempt to address these social ills—that we are asked to pass judgment upon today.

II.

The ordinance does nothing more than confirm the well-established principle that the police have the duty and the power to maintain the public peace, and, when necessary, to disperse groups of individuals who threaten it.

The Court concludes that the ordinance is also unconstitutionally vague because it fails to provide adequate standards to guide police discretion and because, in the plurality's view, it does not give residents adequate notice of how to conform their conduct to the confines of the law. I disagree on both counts.

At the outset, it is important to note that the ordinance does not criminalize loitering per se. Rather, it penalizes loiterers' failure to obey a police officer's order to move along. A majority of the Court believes that this scheme vests too much discretion in police officers. Nothing could be further from the truth. Far from according officers too much discretion, the ordinance merely enables police officers to fulfill one of their traditional functions. Police officers are not, and have never been, simply enforcers of the criminal law. They wear other hats—importantly, they have long been vested with the responsibility for preserving the public peace. Nor is the idea that the police are also peace officers simply a quaint anachronism. In most American jurisdictions, police officers continue to be obligated, by law, to maintain the public peace.

In their role as peace officers, the police long have had the authority and the duty to order groups of individuals who threaten the public peace to disperse. . . . The authority to issue dispersal orders continues to play a commonplace and crucial role in police operations, particularly in urban areas. Even the ABA Standards for Criminal Justice recognize that "in day-to-day police experience there are innumerable situations in which police are called upon to order people not to block the sidewalk, not to congregate in a given place, and not to 'loiter'. . . . The police may suspect the loiterer of considering engaging in some form of undesirable conduct that can be at least temporarily frustrated by ordering him or her to 'move on.'" Standard 1–3.4(d), p. 1.88, and comments (2d ed. 1980, Supp. 1986).

In order to perform their peace-keeping responsibilities satisfactorily, the police inevitably must exercise discretion. Indeed, by empowering them to act as peace officers, the law assumes that the police will exercise that discretion responsibly and with sound judgment. That is not to say that the law should not provide objective guidelines for the police, but simply that it cannot rigidly constrain their every action. By directing a police officer not to issue a dispersal order unless he "observes a person whom he reasonably believes to be a criminal street gang member loitering in any public place." Chicago's ordinance strikes an appropriate balance between those two extremes. Just as we trust officers to rely on their experience and expertise in order to make spur-of-the-moment determinations about amorphous legal standards such as "probable cause" and "reasonable suspicion," so we must trust them to determine whether a group of loiterers contains individuals (in this case members of criminal street gangs) whom the city has determined threaten the public peace.

Today, the Court focuses extensively on the "rights" of gang members and their companions. It can safely do so—the people who will have to live with the consequences of today's opinion do not live in our neighborhoods. Rather, the people who will suffer from our lofty pronouncements are people like Ms. Susan Mary Jackson; people who have seen their neighborhoods literally destroyed by gangs and violence and drugs. They are good, decent people who must struggle to overcome their desperate situation, against all odds, in order to raise their families, earn a living, and remain good citizens. As one resident described, "There is only about maybe one or two percent of the people in the city causing these problems maybe, but it's keeping 98 percent of us in our houses and off the streets and afraid to shop." By focusing exclusively on the imagined "rights" of the two percent, the Court today has denied our most vulnerable citizens the very thing that Justice Stevens, elevates above all else—the "freedom of movement." And that is a shame. I respectfully dissent.

NOTES AND QUESTIONS

1. ***The Court's Reasoning.*** Was the Court justified in holding that the gang loitering ordinance was vague and vested police with excessive discretion? The ordinance was implicated only when police observed a congregation that included someone the police reasonably believed was a member of a criminal street gang, it only authorized arrest if the congregants refused to obey a police order to disperse, and the typical penalty for disobeying the order was a fine, with a maximum penalty of six months in jail. Was it not a moderate and fairly targeted response to a serious problem? More generally, while there will always be the occasional rogue cop who should be punished, why shouldn't we trust police to investigate persons they sincerely believe are engaging in criminal activity or posing a threat to public safety? *See* Craig S. Lerner, *Reasonable Suspicion and Mere* Hunches, 49 Vand. L. Rev. 405, 413 (2006) (describing claim by police that they have a "sixth sense" about potential suspects).

Consider the racial implications of the Court's holding in *Morales*. The Court worried that police might enforce the ordinance in a discriminatory manner. Harkening back to cases such as *Papachristou* and *Kolender*, the Court at least implicitly justified its application of the vagueness doctrine as protecting minority rights. Did the Court's decision accomplish that objective? By invalidating the anti-gang ordinance, did the Court, on balance, help or harm black people? Also, if you agree that the Court should have invalidated the ordinance, was the vagueness ground the most persuasive basis for doing so? Look back at the potential claims made earlier in the litigation before the Illinois Supreme Court. Are any of those a more satisfying account of what's objectionable about the ordinance? Reconsider these questions after reading the next two Notes.

2. ***Crime Control.*** The vagueness doctrine can be understood as balancing public and individual interests—crime control versus liberty. In holding that a law is too vague, the Court in effect determines that the cost to individual rights from broad police discretion outweighs the benefits of such discretion in controlling crime. Defenders of the Court's vagueness doctrine maintain that the rule of law requires that legislatures specify with clarity when police may coercively investigate or arrest members of the public. In contrast, critics of the Court's vagueness doctrine hold that police need broad discretion to protect law-abiding, often minority, residents in poor, urban communities from the dangers of gangs and serious crime. "Quality of life" or order-maintenance policing policies aim to preserve law and order in urban areas by proactive, aggressive enforcement of petty misdemeanor offenses. Underlying such policing is the "broken windows" theory, which posits that low-level misconduct in public areas, such as littering, urination,

graffiti, intoxication, and disorderly conduct breeds greater disorder and more serious crime by sending a signal to law-abiding residents and criminals that such areas are not well monitored. Law-abiding residents will avoid such areas while criminals take them over and become increasingly willing to commit serious and violent crimes. Broken windows theory suggests courts should tolerate some vagueness in the law where necessary to afford police adequate discretion to prevent and disrupt disorder. Identification and loitering laws, like those invalidated in *Kolender* and *Morales*, enable police to investigate, move along, and, if necessary, arrest potentially dangerous persons without having to catch them in the act of committing a more serious crime. Advocates of broken-windows policing criticize the Court's vagueness doctrine for undervaluing the public's interest in crime control.

3. *Individual Rights.* On the other side of the scale from the public's interest in crime control are the rights of individuals against abusive or discriminatory police treatment. Here again critics of the Court believe it has miscalculated the balance by being overly concerned that police will abuse individual rights if laws are not drafted precisely. These critics argue that the laws invalidated on vagueness grounds were specific enough to minimize the risk of discriminatory enforcement and note further that the laws imposed light penalties. The gang loitering ordinance, for example, typically resulted in a fine only, and gang members could avoid the penalty completely if they dispersed when ordered to by a police officer. In contrast, police will now have to arrest gang members on more serious crimes, such as conspiracy to distribute drugs, which can carry sentences of many years in prison. While catching the gang members in the act of these crimes requires more investigative work, the stop and frisk procedures that police have at their disposal (see the next section of this chapter) will enable them eventually to arrest and put many gang members away for a long time.

Professors Dan Kahan and Tracey Meares have further argued that the concerns over discriminatory law enforcement that animate the vagueness doctrine are anachronistic. The concerns are based on a past society in which whites held all of the political power and controlled the police, who therefore were not held accountable for abusive or discriminatory practices against disenfranchised minority communities. *See* Tracey L. Meares & Dan M. Kahan, *The Wages of Antiquated Procedural Thinking: A Critique of* Chicago v. Morales, 1998 U. Chi. Legal F. (1998). These conditions no longer obtain today, they argue, in the large cities with serious gang problems in which minorities exercise significant and sometimes controlling political power. They point out that much of the support for the Chicago ordinance came from black residents of the communities ravaged by gangs. They further note that the gang members are from the same communities and families as the law-abiding residents, sharing a "linked fate" with each other. In light of these contemporary social and political conditions, Meares and Kahan argue, police are unlikely to abuse their discretion in enforcing the ordinance because they are accountable to the law-abiding, minority residents of the communities who, in turn, would object to abusive or discriminatory police tactics toward their juvenile and young adult kin. For views contrary to

Meares and Kahan, *see* Albert W. Alschuler & Stephen J. Schulhofer, *Antiquated Procedures or Bedrock Rights?: A Response to Professors Meares and Kahan*, 1998 U. Chi. Legal F. 215 (1998); Dorothy E. Roberts, *Foreword: Race, Vagueness, and the Social Meaning of Order-Maintenance Policing*, 89 J. Crim. L. & Criminology 775 (1999); and David Cole, *Discretion and Discrimination Reconsidered: A Response to the New Criminal Justice Scholarship*, 87 Geo. L.J. 1059 (1999).

What's your assessment of Meares & Kahan's claim that police today in cities like Chicago are accountable to the law-abiding residents of poor, urban, minority communities? Is that accountability likely to inure to the protection of the young, typically black and Latino, males on the streets the police investigate? Do the interests of young minorities diverge from those of their parents? Do the interests of poor minorities diverge from those of their middle class counterparts? Is a conflict of interests between segments of the minority community relevant to assessing the relationship between policing practices and minority rights? How?

4.   *Advising Exercise.* The Court in *Morales* assumed that some form of anti-loitering law could be drafted to combat the problem of gang crime. If you were advising the Chicago City Council, how would you suggest that it draft a new anti-loitering ordinance to comply with the vagueness doctrine? Would it be as effective as the one struck down? Would an alternative to an anti-loitering ordinance be a better approach? If you were advising the police chief, what approach would you suggest that took adequate account of her agency's mission and officers' interests?

5.   *Design Exercise.* Compare this new statute with the one you drafted for the *Kolender* case. What elements do these statutes share? In what ways are they different? How would you draft a statute to address a different issue: the displaying of gang colors or hand gestures? What problems might you come across while designing a law to address these concerns? In thinking about these issues, it might be helpful refer back to the three statutes in the *Papachristou*, *Kolender*, and *Morales* cases to see how the various justices responded to similar concerns.

6.   *Evaluating the Vagueness Doctrine.* How effective is the vagueness doctrine at constraining law enforcement discretion, including at preventing racially discriminatory enforcement? Recall Edward Lawson, the black man with dreadlocks who was arrested repeatedly for not providing "credible and reliable" identification to police under the law invalidated in 1983 in *Kolender*. His run-ins with police continued. Ten years later, Lawson found himself in the news again. On March 29, 1993, Beverly Hills police received a phone call from a woman who reported a black man driving at a slow speed past an elementary school. Police stopped and questioned Lawson. After Lawson failed to produce his license, police arrested him and transported him to jail, where he spent two nights until arraignment. According to news reports, Lawson said that, "after being patted down by police officers, he raised his hands above his head, asked for a lawyer and declined to answer questions about his identity." Lawson insisted that he was "never asked to show identification, only if he had it." He eventually told officers his driver's license was in his car, where one of the policemen retrieved it. As before, he was stopped while traveling through an upper-class neighborhood, and, as before, he was arrested for failing to provide identification to police. This time, however, the police stopped him while driving and arrested him for the specific offense of failing to provide a driver's license. As to why Lawson had been driving slowly near a school, he explained that the law required it. "It's another Catch-22," Lawson complained, "[a] black man drives fast past a school . . . it's against the law. A black man drives slow past a school . . . that's against the law. I don't know what they expect us to do." *See* Kim Forde-Mazrui, *Ruling out the Rule of Law*, 60 Vand. L. Rev. 1497, 1499 (2007).

As Lawson's experience suggests, traffic laws afford police a substantial degree of discretion to stop motorists. Consider how often motorists violate traffic regulations every time they drive. Police routinely exploit such violations to investigate motorists they suspect are carrying or purchasing drugs, and empirical studies support the concern that race plays a role in such traffic stops. Yet traffic laws are, in most cases, specific enough to withstand a void-for-vagueness challenge.

Police have also engaged in aggressive order maintenance enforcement against people on foot notwithstanding the vagueness doctrine. Police rely on an array of specifically defined crimes, such as jay walking, littering, intoxication, public urination, pan handling, graffiti, trespass, and violating curfew, all of which enable police to investigate and arrest virtually anyone in public they deem undesirable. Such policing strategies raise similar concerns to those generated by vague laws but do not implicate the vagueness doctrine. *See* Debra Livingston, *Police Discretion and the Quality of Life in Public Places: Courts, Communities, and the New Policing*, 97 Colum. L. Rev. 551, 618 (1997) (arguing that specifically-defined laws that criminalize a large range of common conduct can afford police very broad discretion).

7.   *Turn to the Fourth Amendment.* The principal objective of the vagueness doctrine is to constrain police discretion by delineating with specificity the conduct that the law defines as criminal. Discretion also plays a role when a police officer decides whether he has observed conduct that gives rise to an inference that a criminal law has been or will be violated. People rarely engage in conduct defined as criminal in view of police. Accordingly, when police are deciding whether someone may have committed a crime or is intending to do so, they must rely on circumstantial evidence of criminal behavior that typically takes the form of behavior that is not itself illegal. The question arises: how probative of criminal behavior must the observed conduct be to justify police intervention? If police could arrest someone on the slightest suspicion of criminality, then even the most precise definitions of crimes would not meaningfully constrain police discretion, as almost any behavior could conceivably have some attenuated relationship to a crime. For police discretion to be adequately guided by the criminal law, then, the conduct sufficient to permit police intervention must be significantly probative of criminal behavior. Exactly how probative is the concern of the Fourth Amendment.

C. APPROACH TWO: REQUIRE OBJECTIVE EVIDENCE OF CRIMINALITY

The next approach to constraining discretion we examine requires police to have objective evidence that a suspect is engaged in criminal activity before subjecting the suspect to coercive investigation and arrest. The vagueness doctrine is of little use if police can target a suspect based simply on an officer's hunch that the suspect is violating a clearly defined law. Over time, litigants pressed courts to require police to have a substantial amount of objective evidence, or "probable cause," that a suspect is committing a crime before police could exercise coercive authority over the suspect. Courts also have grappled with whether the nature of the crime should affect how much evidence of suspicion police must have and whether race is a relevant factor in a police officer's assessment of suspiciousness. As you study this section, consider how the Supreme Court has addressed these questions.

The doctrinal home for this approach is the Fourth Amendment to the United States Constitution, which provides:

> The right of the people to be secure in their persons, houses, papers, and effects, against unreasonable searches and seizures, shall not be violated, and no Warrants shall issue, but upon probable cause, supported by Oath or affirmation, and particularly describing the place to be searched, and the persons or things to be seized.

U.S. CONST., AMEND 4. The Amendment applies to the states through the Due Process Clause of the Fourteenth Amendment.

1. *TERRY V. OHIO* AND STOP AND FRISK

Although the Fourth Amendment requires the police to have a warrant to conduct searches and arrests in a suspect's home, the Court has interpreted the amendment to allow police to conduct warrantless searches in certain circumstances. If they observe a suspect on the street or in an automobile, police may stop, search, and arrest the suspect without a warrant if the police officer has probable cause to believe the suspect is engaged in, will engage in, or has engaged in criminal activity. During the criminal procedure revolution of the 1960s, it remained unsettled whether police could subject suspects without probable cause to a "stop and frisk," that is, a detention and pat down more limited in time and scope than a full arrest and search. Supporters of a lower standard of suspicion contended that a stop-and-frisk did not constitute a "search" and "seizure" under the Fourth Amendment and hence no cause at all was required. They also stressed the need for police to maintain peace and order by questioning suspicious persons and frisking them for weapons while doing so. Those who argued that probable cause should apply to stop and frisks argued that they were searches and seizures for Fourth Amendment purposes. Opponents also raised concerns that police used stop and frisks to harass marginalized members of the public, such as the poor, minorities, and civil rights and anti-war protesters.

In *Terry v. Ohio,* 392 U.S. 1 (1968), the Court gave something to both sides. For potential suspects, the Court held that the Fourth Amendment's right against "unreasonable searches and seizures" is not limited to a full search and custodial arrest, but rather that any coercive police detention and pat down implicated the Amendment. For police, the Court held that an officer may frisk a suspect for weapons if he reasonably believed that person may be engaged in criminal activity and may be armed and dangerous. This "reasonable suspicion" standard, which is less demanding than probable cause, requires that the officer's suspicion be based on "articulable facts" and the "specific reasonable inferences which he is entitled to draw from the facts in light of his experience." The Court in later cases applied the reasonable suspicion standard to the brief detention or "stop" of a suspect. A person is "stopped" for Fourth Amendment purposes when he reasonably believes that he is not free to leave the encounter with the police. In sum, if a police officer reasonably suspects that someone is committing, has committed, or is going to commit a crime, the officer may stop the person and, if the officer reasonably suspects the person is armed and dangerous, may frisk the person for weapons.

Although the Court in *Terry* purported to give weight to the interests of both police and potential suspects, commentators have typically viewed the decision as more favorable to the police. Indeed, some have suggested that *Terry* served to compensate for the Court's invalidation of vagrancy and other status crimes under the vagueness doctrine. After *Papachristou*, police had to have have evidence of a specifically defined crime before they could search or seize a person. But because of *Terry*, that evidence need only create reasonable suspicion of the crime. *Terry* left for a later day the definition of what sorts of facts would be sufficient to create reasonable suspicion.

Terry has proven to be a very controversial decision, with the weight of criticism arguing that it affords police excessive discretion because the "reasonable suspicion" standard is too easily satisfied. A frequently voiced concern is that police can covertly discriminate by race in selecting people to stop, question, and frisk. The "stop and frisk" program of the New York City Police Department (NYPD) has generated significant controversy in large part for this reason. In 1971, New York State passed a law essentially codifying *Terry*. It authorized police to "stop a person in a public place . . . when he reasonably suspects that such person is committing, has committed or is about to commit either (a) a felony or (b) a misdemeanor . . . , and may demand of him his name, address and an explanation of his conduct." N.Y. CRIM. PRO. LAW § 140.50 (McKinney 2010). The law further provides that, if an officer conducting a stop "reasonably suspects that he is in danger of physical injury, he may search such person for a deadly weapon or any instrument, article or substance readily capable of causing serious physical injury." *Id.*

In 2002, after Michael Bloomberg was elected Mayor of New York, the police increased enforcement of the law, stopping over 4.4 million people between January 2004 and June 2012, the great majority black or Latino (87% in 2011 and 2012). *See Floyd v. City of New York*, No. 08 Civ. 1034 (SAS), 2013 WL 4046209 (S.D.N.Y., Aug. 12, 2013). As of 2010, New York City's resident population was roughly 23% black, 29% Hispanic, and 33% white. Eighty-eight percent of those stopped were released by the end of the encounter because evidence of wrongdoing was lacking. Fifty-two percent of people were frisked for weapons, and no weapons were found in 98.5% of frisks. A higher percentage of whites searched were carrying weapons and other contraband, while a lower percentage of whites were subjected to force.

While the stop-and-frisk program has long been a controversial topic, opposition to it intensified in recent years. On June 17, 2012, several thousand New Yorkers, including Reverend Al Sharpton, NAACP President Benjamin Jealous, and U.S. Representative Charles Rangel, marched silently down Fifth Avenue to Mayor Bloomberg's Upper East Side townhouse to protest the continuation of the program. *See* Chris Francescani, *Silent March to Protest NYPD's 'Stop-and-Frisk' Policy*, Reuters (June 17, 2012), http://www.reuters.com/article/2012/06/18/us-usa-newyork-march-idUSBRE85G0A920120618. Mayor Bloomberg defended the practice, claiming that recovering guns and other weapons contributed to a decline in crime. Denying that it involved any racial profiling, he explained that "the city would not 'deny reality' in order to stop different groups according to their relative proportions in the population." Kate Taylor, *Stop-and-Frisk Policy 'Saves Lives,' Mayor Tells Black Congregation*, N.Y. TIMES (June 10, 2012), http://www.ny times.com/2012/06/11/nyregion/at-black-church-in-brooklyn-bloomberg-defends-stop-and-frisk-policy.html/.

In 2008, a lawsuit was filed against the city, the mayor, and other officials, claiming that the stop-and-frisk program violated the Fourth and Fourteenth Amendments. The plaintiffs alleged that the defendants sanctioned "a policy and practice of stop and frisks by the New York Police Department ('NYPD') on the basis of race and ethnicity." *Floyd v. City of New York*, 2008 WL 4179210 at *1 (S.D.N.Y. Sept. 10, 2008). In May 2012, presiding Judge Shira Scheindlin granted the plaintiffs' motion for class certification, and on August 12, 2013, Judge Scheindlin issued a 195 page opinion holding that the police department's stop-and-frisk practices violated the Fourth Amendment and the Equal Protection

Clause. *Floyd v. City of New York*, No. 08 Civ. 1034 (SAS), 2013 WL 4046209 (S.D.N.Y., Aug. 12, 2013) (Liability Opinion). The opinion documents numerous incidents in which police confronted innocent people on the street, questioned them in a disrespectful manner, frisked or fully searched them, and physically handled them in a humiliating, invasive, and sometimes painful manner, often in view of passersby. During police stops, the court found, blacks and Hispanics "were more likely to be subjected to the use of force than whites, despite the fact that whites are more likely to be found with weapons or contraband." The court further found that the pattern of unlawful stops by individual officers was attributable to the NYPD for being "deliberately indifferent" to the practice: "[T]he city's highest officials have turned a blind eye to the evidence that officers are conducting stops in a racially discriminatory manner." The court also found that the city encouraged unlawful stops through inaccurate training on legal investigative tactics and by penalizing officers who failed to investigate a high number of pedestrians.

In a separate opinion, Judge Scheindlin ordered a variety of remedies. *Floyd v. City of New York*, No. 08 Civ. 1034 (SAS), 2013 WL 4046217 (S.D.N.Y., Aug. 12, 2013). She required that police in certain precincts wear cameras on their body to record street encounters with putative suspects. She also ordered the creation of a "joint remedial process," involving a series of community meetings to solicit input on how to reform the stop-and-frisk program from a range of interested constituencies, including local religious, advocacy, and other grassroots organizations; elected officials of the city; representatives of the NYPD; and prosecutors from the District Attorney's Office and the Department of Justice. The court also appointed an independent monitor, Peter Zimroth, a partner in the New York office of Arnold & Porter LLP, and a former corporation counsel and prosecutor in the Manhattan district attorney's office, to oversee the NYPD's compliance with the Constitution and the court's injunction.

Even before the court held the stop-and-frisk program unconstitutional, Mayor Bloomberg conceded that it needed to be "mended, not ended." Francescani, *supra*. Judge Scheindlin also denied ending the program altogether: "I am *not* ordering an end to the practice of stop and frisk. The purpose of the remedies addressed in this Opinion is to ensure that the practice is carried out in a manner that protects the rights and liberties of all New Yorkers, while still providing much needed police protection." Remedies Opinion (emphasis in original). If you were advising the court or Mayor Bloomberg, what policies would you recommend that would both keep the streets of New York sufficiently safe for law-abiding residents and tourists while avoiding the legal problems and social costs of aggressive stop-and-frisks? What, if anything, would you advise that the NYPD do in addition to or instead of the changes required by Judge Scheindlin?

2.   USE OF RACE AND RACIAL PROFILING

A principal criticism of *Terry*—that it encourages racially discriminatory law enforcement—assumes that racial discrimination by police is objectionable. Similarly, recall that the vagueness doctrine, by seeking to prevent discriminatory law enforcement enabled by vaguely drafted laws, also assumes that race-based enforcement is improper. Is it? Surely it is improper to focus on black and Latino suspects out of animosity toward them or on the assumption that, solely because of their race, they are more likely to commit crime. But could the race of a suspect be a relevant factor to a police officer attempting to gauge whether a suspect warrants scrutiny? Indeed, might responsible law enforcement sometimes *require* taking race into account in assessing the likelihood of criminal behavior? Consider the next case.

United States v. Brignoni-Ponce

Supreme Court of the United States, 1975.
422 U.S. 873.

■ MR. JUSTICE POWELL delivered the opinion of the Court.

This case raises questions as to the United States Border Patrol's authority to stop automobiles in areas near the Mexican border.

I

As part of its regular traffic-checking operations in southern California, the Border Patrol operates a fixed checkpoint on Interstate Highway 5 south of San Clemente. On the evening of March 11, 1973, the checkpoint was closed because of inclement weather, but two officers were observing northbound traffic from a patrol car parked at the side of the highway. The road was dark, and they were using the patrol car's headlights to illuminate passing cars. They pursued respondent's car and stopped it, saying later that their only reason for doing so was that its three occupants appeared to be of Mexican descent. The officers questioned respondent and his two passengers about their citizenship and learned that the passengers were aliens who had entered the country illegally. All three were then arrested, and respondent was charged with two counts of knowingly transporting illegal immigrants. At trial respondent moved to suppress the testimony of and about the two passengers, claiming that this evidence was the fruit of an illegal seizure. The trial court denied the motion, the aliens testified at trial, and respondent was convicted on both counts.

The Court of Appeals . . . held that the Fourth Amendment . . . forbids stopping a vehicle, even for the limited purpose of questioning its occupants, unless the officers have a "founded suspicion" that the occupants are aliens illegally in the country. The court refused to find that Mexican ancestry alone supported such a "founded suspicion" and held that respondent's motion to suppress should have been granted. . . .

The only issue presented for decision is whether a roving patrol may stop a vehicle in an area near the border and question its occupants when the only ground for suspicion is that the occupants appear to be of Mexican ancestry. For the reasons that follow, we affirm the decision of the Court of Appeals.

III

The Fourth Amendment applies to all seizures of the person, including seizures that involve only a brief detention short of traditional arrest. *Terry v. Ohio,* 392 U. S. 1, 16–19 (1968). "[W]henever a police officer accosts an individual and restrains his freedom to walk away, he has 'seized' that person," *id.,* at 16, and the Fourth Amendment requires that the seizure be "reasonable." As with other categories of police action subject to Fourth Amendment constraints, the reasonableness of such seizures depends on a balance between the public interest and the individual's right to personal security free from arbitrary interference by law officers. *Id.,* at 20–21.

The Government makes a convincing demonstration that the public interest demands effective measures to prevent the illegal entry of aliens at the Mexican border. Estimates of the number of illegal immigrants in the United States vary widely. A conservative estimate in 1972 produced a figure of about one million, but the INS now suggests there may be as many as 10 or 12 million aliens illegally in the country. Whatever the number, these aliens create significant economic and social problems, competing with citizens and legal resident aliens for jobs, and generating extra demand for social services. The aliens themselves are vulnerable to exploitation because they cannot complain of substandard working conditions without risking deportation.

The Government has estimated that 85% of the aliens illegally in the country are from Mexico. The Mexican border is almost 2,000 miles long, and even a vastly reinforced Border Patrol would find it impossible to prevent illegal border crossings. Many aliens cross the Mexican border on foot, miles away from patrolled areas, and then purchase transportation from the border area to inland cities, where they find jobs and elude the immigration authorities. Others gain entry on valid temporary border-crossing permits, but then violate the conditions of their entry. Most of these aliens leave the border area in private vehicles, often assisted by professional "alien smugglers." The Border Patrol's traffic-checking operations are designed to prevent this inland movement. They succeed in apprehending some illegal entrants and smugglers, and they deter the movement of others by threatening apprehension and increasing the cost of illegal transportation.

Against this valid public interest we must weigh the interference with individual liberty that results when an officer stops an automobile and questions its occupants. The intrusion is modest. The Government tells us that a stop by a roving patrol "usually consumes no more than a minute." There is no search of the vehicle or its occupants, and the visual inspection is limited to those parts of the vehicle that can be seen by anyone standing alongside. According to the Government, "[a]ll that is required of the vehicle's occupants is a response to a brief question or two and possibly the production of a document evidencing a right to be in the United States."

Because of the limited nature of the intrusion, stops of this sort may be justified on facts that do not amount to the probable cause required for an arrest. In *Terry* v. *Ohio*, the Court declined expressly to decide whether facts not amounting to probable cause could justify an "investigative 'seizure'" short of an arrest, 392 U. S., at 19 n.16, but it approved a limited search—a pat-down for weapons—for the protection of an officer investigating suspicious behavior of persons he reasonably believed to be armed and dangerous. The Court approved such a search on facts that did not constitute probable cause to believe the suspects guilty of a crime, requiring only that "the police officer . . . be able to point to specific and articulable facts which, taken together with rational inferences from those facts, reasonably warrant" a belief that his safety or that of others is in danger. *Id.*, at 21; *see id.*, at 27.

We elaborated on *Terry* in *Adams v. Williams,* 407 U. S. 143 (1972), holding that a policeman was justified in approaching the respondent to investigate a tip that he was carrying narcotics and a gun.

"The Fourth Amendment does not require a policeman who lacks the precise level of information necessary for probable cause to arrest to simply shrug his shoulders and allow a crime to occur or a criminal to escape. On the contrary, *Terry* recognizes that it may be the essence of good police work to adopt an intermediate response. . . . A brief stop of a suspicious individual, in order to determine his identity or to maintain the status quo momentarily while obtaining more information, may be most reasonable in light of the facts known to the officer at the time." *Id.*, at 145–146.

These cases together establish that in appropriate circumstances the Fourth Amendment allows a properly limited "search" or "seizure" on facts that do not constitute probable cause to arrest or to search for contraband or evidence of crime. In both *Terry* and *Adams* v. *Williams* the investigating officers had reasonable grounds to believe that the suspects were armed and that they might be dangerous. The limited searches and seizures in those cases were a valid method of protecting the public and preventing crime. In this case as well, because of the importance of the governmental interest at stake, the minimal intrusion of a brief stop, and the absence of practical alternatives for policing the border, we hold that when an officer's observations lead him reasonably to suspect that a particular vehicle may contain aliens who are illegally in the country, he may stop the car briefly and investigate the circumstances that provoke suspicion. As in *Terry,* the stop and inquiry must be "reasonably related in scope to the justification for their initiation." 392 U. S., at 29. The officer may question the driver and passengers about their citizenship and immigration status, and he may ask them to explain suspicious circumstances, but any further detention or search must be based on consent or probable cause.

We are unwilling to let the Border Patrol dispense entirely with the requirement that officers must have a reasonable suspicion to justify roving-patrol stops. In the context of border area stops, the reasonableness requirement of the Fourth Amendment demands something more than the broad and unlimited discretion sought by the Government. Roads near the border carry not only aliens seeking to enter the country illegally, but a large volume of legitimate traffic as well. San Diego, with a metropolitan population of 1.4 million, is located on the border. Texas has two fairly large metropolitan areas directly on the border: El Paso, with a population of 360,000, and the Brownsville-McAllen area, with a combined population of 320,000. We are confident that substantially all of the traffic in these cities is lawful and that relatively few of their residents have any connection with the illegal entry and transportation of aliens. To approve roving-patrol stops of all vehicles in the border area, without any suspicion that a particular vehicle is carrying illegal immigrants, would subject the residents of these and other areas to potentially unlimited interference with their use of the highways, solely at the discretion of Border Patrol officers. The only formal limitation on that discretion appears to be the administrative regulation defining the term "reasonable distance" in § 287 (a) (3) to mean within 100 air miles from the border. Thus, if we approved the Government's position in this case, Border Patrol officers could stop motorists at random for questioning, day or night, anywhere within 100 air miles of the 2,000-mile border, on a city street, a busy highway, or a desert road, without any reason to suspect that they have violated any law.

We are not convinced that the legitimate needs of law enforcement require this degree of interference with lawful traffic. As we discuss in Part IV, *infra,* the nature of illegal alien traffic and the characteristics of smuggling operations tend to generate articulable grounds for identifying violators. Consequently, a requirement of reasonable suspicion for stops allows the Government adequate means of guarding the public interest and also protects residents of the border areas from indiscriminate official interference. Under the circumstances, and even though the intrusion incident to a stop is modest, we conclude that it is not "reasonable" under the Fourth Amendment to make such stops on a random basis.

The Government also contends that the public interest in enforcing conditions on legal alien entry justifies stopping persons who may be aliens for questioning about their citizenship and immigration status.

Although we may assume for purposes of this case that the broad congressional power over immigration authorizes Congress to admit aliens on condition that they will submit to reasonable questioning about their right to be and remain in the country, this power cannot diminish the Fourth Amendment rights of citizens who may be mistaken for aliens. For the same reasons that the Fourth Amendment forbids stopping vehicles at random to inquire if they are carrying aliens who are illegally in the country, it also forbids stopping or detaining persons for questioning about their citizenship on less than a reasonable suspicion that they may be aliens.

IV

Except at the border and its functional equivalents, officers on roving patrol may stop vehicles only if they are aware of specific articulable facts, together with rational inferences from those facts, that reasonably warrant suspicion that the vehicles contain aliens who may be illegally in the country.

Any number of factors may be taken into account in deciding whether there is reasonable suspicion to stop a car in the border area. Officers may consider the characteristics of the area in which they encounter a vehicle. Its proximity to the border, the usual patterns of traffic on the particular road, and previous experience with alien traffic are all relevant. They also may consider information about recent illegal border crossings in the area. The driver's behavior may be relevant, as erratic driving or obvious attempts to evade officers can support a reasonable suspicion. Aspects of the vehicle itself may justify suspicion. For instance, officers say that certain station wagons, with large compartments for fold-down seats or spare tires, are frequently used for transporting concealed aliens. The vehicle may appear to be heavily loaded, it may have an extraordinary number of passengers, or the officers may observe persons trying to hide. The Government also points out that trained officers can recognize the characteristic appearance of persons who live in Mexico, relying on such factors as the mode of dress and haircut. In all situations the officer is entitled to assess the facts in light of his experience in detecting illegal entry and smuggling.

In this case the officers relied on a single factor to justify stopping respondent's car: the apparent Mexican ancestry of the occupants. We cannot conclude that this furnished reasonable grounds to believe that the three occupants were aliens. At best the officers had only a fleeting glimpse of the persons in the moving car, illuminated by headlights. Even if they saw enough to think that the occupants were of Mexican descent, this factor alone would justify neither a reasonable belief that they were aliens, nor a reasonable belief that the car concealed other aliens who were illegally in the country. Large numbers of native-born and naturalized citizens have the physical characteristics identified with Mexican ancestry, and even in the border area a relatively small proportion of them are aliens. The likelihood that any given person of Mexican ancestry is an alien is high enough to make Mexican appearance a relevant factor, but standing alone it does not justify stopping all Mexican-Americans to ask if they are aliens.

The judgment of the Court of Appeals is *Affirmed.*

■ MR. CHIEF JUSTICE BURGER, with whom MR. JUSTICE BLACKMUN joins, concurring in the judgment.

Like Mr. Justice WHITE I can, at most, do no more than concur in the judgment. As the Fourth Amendment now has been interpreted by the Court it seems that the Immigration and Naturalization Service is powerless to stop the tide of illegal aliens—and dangerous drugs—that daily and freely crosses our 2,000-mile southern boundary. Perhaps these decisions will be seen in perspective as but another example of a society seemingly impotent to deal with massive lawlessness. In that sense history may view us as prisoners of our own traditional and appropriate concern for individual rights, unable—or unwilling—to apply the concept of reasonableness explicit in the Fourth Amendment in order to develop a rational accommodation between those rights and the literal safety of the country.

Given today's decisions it would appear that, absent legislative action, nothing less than a massive force of guards could adequately protect our southern border. To establish hundreds of checkpoints with enlarged border forces so as to stop literally every car and pedestrian at every border checkpoint, however, would doubtless impede the flow of commerce and travel between this country and Mexico. Moreover, it is uncertain whether stringent penalties for employment of illegal aliens, and rigid requirements for proof of legal entry before employment, would help solve the problems, but those remedies have not been tried.

■ [Appendix to Opinion of BURGER, C.J., omitted.]

■ [The concurring opinions of JUSTICES WHITE AND REHNQUIST are omitted.]

■ MR. JUSTICE DOUGLAS, concurring in the judgment.

I join in the affirmance of the judgment. The stopping of respondent's automobile solely because its occupants appeared to be of Mexican ancestry was a patent violation of the Fourth Amendment. I cannot agree, however, with the standard the Court adopts to measure the lawfulness of the officers' action. The Court extends the "suspicion" test of *Terry v. Ohio,* 392 U. S. 1 (1968), to the stop of a moving automobile. I dissented from the adoption of the suspicion test in *Terry,* believing it an unjustified weakening of the Fourth Amendment's protection of citizens from arbitrary interference by the police. I remarked then:

"The infringement on personal liberty of any 'seizure' of a person can only be 'reasonable' under the Fourth Amendment if we require the police to possess 'probable cause' before they seize him. Only that line draws a meaningful distinction between an officer's mere inkling and the presence of facts within the officer's personal knowledge which would convince a reasonable man that the person seized has committed, is committing, or is about to commit a particular crime." *Id.,* at 38.

The fears I voiced in *Terry* about the weakening of the Fourth Amendment have regrettably been borne out by subsequent events. Hopes that the suspicion test might be employed only in the pursuit of violent crime—a limitation endorsed by some of its proponents—have now been dashed, as it has been applied in narcotics investigations, in apprehension of "illegal" aliens, and indeed has come to be viewed as a legal construct for the regulation of a general investigatory police power. The suspicion test has been warmly embraced by law enforcement forces and vigorously employed in the cause of crime detection. In criminal cases we see those for whom the initial intrusion led to the discovery of some wrongdoing. But the nature of the test permits the police to interfere as well with a multitude of law-abiding citizens, whose only transgression may be a nonconformist appearance or attitude. As one commentator has remarked:

> " 'Police power exercised without probable cause *is* arbitrary. To say that the police may accost citizens at their whim and may detain them upon reasonable suspicion is to say, in reality, that the police may both accost and detain citizens at their whim.' " Amsterdam, Perspectives on the Fourth Amendment, 58 Minn. L. Rev. 349, 395 (1974).

The uses to which the suspicion test has been put are illustrated in some of the cases cited in the Court's opinion. In *United States v. Wright,* 476 F. 2d 1027 (CA5 1973), for example, immigration officers stopped a station wagon near the border because there was a spare tire in the back seat. The court held that the officers reasonably suspected that the spare wheel well had been freed in order to facilitate the concealment of aliens. In *United States v. Bugarin-Cases,* 484 F. 2d 853 (CA9 1973), the Border Patrol officers encountered a man driving alone in a station wagon which was "riding low"; stopping the car was held reasonable because the officers suspected that aliens might have been hidden beneath the floorboards. The vacationer whose car is weighted down with luggage will find no comfort in these decisions; nor will the many law-abiding citizens who drive older vehicles that ride low because their suspension systems are old or in disrepair. The suspicion test has indeed brought a state of affairs where the police may stop citizens on the highway on the flimsiest of justifications.

The Court does, to be sure, disclaim approval of the particular decisions it cites applying the suspicion test. But by specifying factors to be considered without attempting to explain what combination is necessary to satisfy the test, the Court may actually induce the police to push its language beyond intended limits and to advance as a justification any of the enumerated factors even where its probative significance is negligible.

Ultimately the degree to which the suspicion test actually restrains the police will depend more upon what the Court does henceforth than upon what it says today. If my Brethren mean to give the suspicion test a new bite, I applaud the intention. But in view of the developments since the test was launched in *Terry,* I am not optimistic. This is the first decision to invalidate a stop on the basis of the suspicion standard. In fact, since *Terry* we have granted review of a case applying the test only once, in *Adams v. Williams,* 407 U. S. 143 (1972), where the Court found the standard satisfied by the tip from an informant whose credibility was not established and whose information was not shown to be based upon personal knowledge. If in the future the suspicion test is to provide any meaningful restraint of the police, its force must come from vigorous review of its applications, and not alone from the qualifying language of today's opinion.

NOTES AND QUESTIONS

1. ***The Court's Reasoning.*** The Court in *Brignoni-Ponce* held that reasonable suspicion was required before a roving patrol could stop and question motorists suspected of carrying undocumented immigrants. It also concluded that the Mexican appearance of motorists did not alone create reasonable suspicion that the motorists were undocumented. The Court added, however, that race can support reasonable suspicion when combined with other factors, explaining that "[t]he likelihood that any given person of Mexican ancestry is an alien is high enough to make Mexican appearance a relevant factor." Was the Court justified in holding that race can increase the likelihood that an observed vehicle is carrying undocumented aliens? If race is useful in predicting who is undocumented, does that necessarily make taking race into account "reasonable," or should the predictive value of race reach some minimum threshold. If so, what should that threshold be? Furthermore, is reasonable suspicion simply a matter of statistical probabilities, *i.e.,* whether the observed facts, including race, increase the probability that the person observed is engaged in criminal activity? Or, should reasonableness have a normative component, such that taking race into account might still be unreasonable even when race has predictive value?

2. **United States v. Martinez-Fuerte.** The next term after it decided *Brignoni-Ponce*, the Court held that no suspicion was required before border patrol agents could stop and investigate motorists at a fixed checkpoint within one hundred miles of the Mexican border. *See United States v. Martinez-Fuerte*, 428 U.S. 543 (1976). The Court balanced the government's interest in stopping illegal immigration against motorists' liberty interest in being shielded from coercive and intrusive investigations. The Court concluded that the stigma and anxiety imposed by a stop and brief questioning at a fixed checkpoint was significantly less than that caused by

a roving patrol. It also concluded that requiring border patrol agents to have reasonable suspicion before stopping motorists at fixed checkpoints would unduly undermine their effectiveness.

The Court in *Martinez-Fuerte* ultimately seemed to approve the use of race to a degree that went beyond the use recognized in *Brignoni-Ponce*. The Court suggested that cars could be ordered to a secondary area for additional inspection based largely or even solely on the basis of Mexican-appearance:

> We further believe that it is constitutional to refer motorists selectively to the secondary inspection area at the San Clemente checkpoint on the basis of criteria that would not sustain a roving-patrol stop. Thus, even if it be assumed that such referrals are made largely on the basis of apparent Mexican ancestry, as the intrusion here is sufficiently minimal that no particularized reason need exist to justify it, we think it follows that the Border Patrol officers must have wide discretion in selecting the motorists to be diverted for the brief questioning involved.

428 U.S. at 563.

Although the Court accepted the government's representation that border patrol agents did not rely exclusively on Mexican appearance, it suggested that agents have greater discretion to rely on race at fixed checkpoints than in roving patrols. The Court noted that the use of race appeared to be quite effective due to the proximity of the checkpoint to the Mexican border:

> Of the 820 vehicles referred to the secondary inspection area during the eight days surrounding the arrests involved in No. 74–1560, roughly 20% contained illegal aliens. Thus, to the extent that the Border Patrol relies on apparent Mexican ancestry at this checkpoint, . . . that reliance clearly is relevant to the law enforcement need to be served. . . . Different considerations would arise if, for example, reliance were put on apparent Mexican ancestry at a checkpoint operated near the Canadian border.

Id. at 554.

Was the Court justified in *Martinez-Fuerte* in permitting race to be a dominant factor in a stop? In a variety of contexts studied in this book, the courts have distinguished between taking race into account as the sole or dominant factor versus taking race into account as one of many factors, generally forbidding the first but sometimes allowing the second. Why do you think the Court failed to make that distinction here?

3. United States v. Montero-Camargo. At least one court of appeals has limited the reach of *Brignoni-Ponce* and *Martinez-Fuerte*, imposing its own constraints on police authority to rely on Mexican appearance in policing near the border. The Ninth Circuit has cited the demographic transformation of the country and developments in the Supreme Court's race jurisprudence since the 1970s, calling for heightened suspicion of race-based decision-making generally. In its en banc decision in *United States v. Montero-Camargo*, 208 F.3d 1122 (9th Cir. 2000), the Ninth Circuit rejected the relevance of race to the formation of reasonable suspicion for a stop. In so doing, it questioned the continuing relevance of the *Brignoni-Ponce* dictum. The court observed:

> *Brignoni-Ponce* was handed down in 1975, some twenty-five years ago. Current demographic data demonstrate that the statistical premises on which its dictum relies are no longer applicable. The Hispanic population of this nation, and of the Southwest and Far West in particular, has grown enormously—at least five-fold in the four states referred to in the Supreme Court's decision. According to the U.S. Census Bureau, as of January 1, 2000, that population group stands at nearly 34 million. Furthermore, Hispanics are heavily concentrated in certain states in which minorities are becoming if not the majority, then at least the single largest group, either in the state as a whole or in a significant number of counties. According to the same data, California has the largest Hispanic population of any state-estimated at 10,112,986 in 1998, while Texas has approximately 6 million. As of this year, minorities—Hispanics, Asians, blacks and Native Americans—comprise half of California's residents; by 2021, Hispanics are expected to be the Golden State's largest group, making up about 40% of the state's population. Today, in Los Angeles County, which is by far the state's biggest population center, Hispanics already constitute the largest single group.

> Moreover, the demographic changes we describe have been accompanied by significant changes in the law restricting the use of race as a criterion in government decision-making. The use of race and ethnicity for such purposes has been severely limited. *See Adarand Constructors v. Pena*, 515 U.S. 200 (1995). Relying on the principle that " '[o]ur Constitution is color-blind, and neither knows nor tolerates classes among citizens,' " the Supreme Court has repeatedly held that reliance "on racial or ethnic criteria must necessarily receive a most searching examination to make sure that it does not conflict with constitutional guarantees."

> The danger of stigmatic harm that the Court feared would flow from overbroad affirmative action programs is far more pronounced in the context of police stops in which race or ethnic appearance is a factor. So, too, are the consequences of "notions of racial inferiority" and the "politics of racial hostility" that the Court has pointed to in its affirmative action jurisprudence. Stops based on race or ethnicity can convey to the citizenry that those who are not white may often be judged by the color of their skin alone. Such stops also send a clear message that those who are not white enjoy a lesser degree of constitutional protection—that they have been assumed to be potential criminals first and individuals second. It would be anomalous to hold that race may be considered when it harms non-whites, but not when it helps them.

4. *Racial Profiling in Immigration Enforcement.* Historically, state and local police have assisted federal officials in the enforcement of immigration law by informally providing the federal government with information about potentially deportable non-citizens in their custody. In 1996, Congress added a provision to the Immigration and Nationality Act authorizing state and local police to enter into formal agreements with federal immigration authorities to participate in immigration policing. Pursuant to the these 287(g) agreements (so-called for their location in the Code), state and local law enforcement officials who have been trained by Immigration and Customs Enforcement may investigate immigration violations and make immigration arrests, effectively exercising federal immigration authority. Though this provision lay largely dormant when first enacted, after September 11, 2001, a handful of jurisdictions around the country entered into these agreements, to great fanfare and controversy. Today, the 287(g) program is small and shrinking, but the federal government still relies heavily on information gathered by state and local police during the ordinary course of law enforcement through a program called the Priority Enforcement Program (PEP) (formerly known as Secure Communities). Pursuant to the program, the arrest fingerprint data that police routinely send to the FBI is now shared with the Department of Homeland Security, enabling DHS to identify persons arrested for state and local violations for immigration purposes as well.

In recent years, the propriety of these various forms of state and local involvement in immigration policing has been challenged. One standard critique of police involvement in immigration enforcement, even indirectly through programs such as PEP, is that the practice compromises the trust of immigrant communities in law enforcement, making it harder for police to protect public safety, including because victims and witnesses afraid of deportation will be reluctant to report crimes. Critics also fear that local police will engage in racial profiling when enforcing immigration law, either because they are not adequately trained in the complexities of immigration law, or because they generally cannot be trusted. Perhaps the most significant cautionary tale on this front is Sheriff Joe Arpaio of Maricopa County, Arizona, who has become infamous for his sweeps of immigrant and Latino neighborhoods and the degrading treatment to which he subjects all arrestees. The Department of Homeland Security has rescinded the 287(g) agreement it signed with Maricopa County, and the Department of Justice has sued him for violations of the civil rights laws through the use of tactics such as racial profiling.

Some states and localities have even taken it upon themselves, outside the auspices of formal federal enforcement programs, to participate in immigration policing. The best-known example of these efforts is Arizona's 2010 Support Our Law Enforcement and Safe Neighborhoods Act, commonly known as S.B. 1070. Its most notorious provision—section 2(B) (sometimes referred to as the "show me your papers" provision)—requires, in some circumstances, that police conducting a stop, detention, or arrest of a person inquire into the immigration status of the person, if they have reason to believe he or she is present in the United States unlawfully. The state law requires police to make the inquiry only if it is "practicable." On its face the law prohibits the use of race in the formulation of reason to believe.

In *Arizona v. United States*, 567 U.S. ___, 132 S.Ct. 2492 (2012), the Supreme Court considered whether federal law preempted SB 1070. Despite striking down most of the law's provisions, it rejected the facial challenge to section 2(B), but left open the possibility of future as-applied challenges should the law result in constitutional violations, which could include detention beyond the time necessary for the legitimate local purpose, and racial profiling or harassment of immigrants and Latinos. As of yet, no systematic evidence about the law's application has emerged, state officials have not issued any clear guidance as to how section 2(B) should be enforced, and local jurisdictions appear to be conflicted about whether to engage in immigration questioning.

Do you believe that the Arizona law's prohibition of racial profiling is likely to be effective? Is it even constitutionally required? The immigration laws that lay out the criteria for entering or remaining in the United States lawfully are presumably sufficiently clear so as not to be void for vagueness. But the Fourth Amendment's requirement that law enforcement have reasonable suspicion that a crime has been or is being committed raises concerns similar to those raised by vague laws. What facts might give rise to reasonable suspicion that a person is not legally authorized to be in the United States? To the extent race is correlated with undocumented status, do *Brignoni-Ponce* and *Martinez-Fuerte* authorize state officials to rely on Mexican appearance as one factor in investigating a person's immigration status under laws such as Arizona's?

Recall that the Court in *Martinez-Fuerte* said that proximity to the Mexican border justified the use of race in a way that would not apply at the Canadian border. The point seems to be that the likelihood of a Mexican-appearing person near the Mexican border being undocumented is significantly higher than of a similar-looking person near the Canadian border. Is the interior of Arizona sufficiently far from the border to escape the permissible use of race, or is the number of undocumented Arizona residents sufficiently high to justify the use of race under the Fourth Amendment? Should it matter than the population of Arizona includes an ever-increasing number of legal residents of Mexican ancestry? *See* Montero-Carmargo, *supra*. Several states far from the Mexican border have experienced significant growth in their Latino populations in recent decades. If immigration and other law enforcement officials could not rely on Latino or other racial appearance, what facts could they rely on in these locations that would enable them effectively to identify undocumented immigrants?

Do you believe that state and local police are inherently more likely to engage in racial profiling, if given the authority to enforce the immigration law, than federal enforcement officials? What would be local officials' incentive to engage in racial profiling or to indirectly enforce federal immigration law? What might be the productive use of state and local police in immigration enforcement, and how can the dangers of racial profiling and community mistrust be alleviated?

5. ***Drug Courier Profiles.*** According to Professor Bernard Harcourt:

> *Brignoni-Ponce* and *Martinez-Fuerte* had an important impact not
> only on Fourth Amendment jurisprudence, but on border patrol and
> policing more generally. The decisions signaled a green light to
> criminal profiling—including racial profiling. The Court had given
> law enforcement a clear message that the use of a multiple factor
> profile, including as one factor race or ethnicity, were constitutional
> and legitimate police techniques.

Bernard Harcourt, *The Road to Racial Profiling, in* CRIMINAL PROCEDURE
STORIES 337 (Carol Steiker, ed., Foundation Press 2006). As Harcourt
observes, in the years following these cases, the federal Drug Enforcement
Agency went nationwide with the use of "drug courier profiles." These are
descriptions based on behavioral and demographic characteristics ostensibly
typical among people trafficking drugs, including by air travel. They include
such factors as whether the city of departure or arrival is a source city for
drugs, whether the plane ticket was bought with cash, whether the ticket
was one way, whether the passenger had only carry-on luggage, whether the
flight was early in the morning, whether the passenger was first or last off
the plane, whether he (or she) behaved nervously, how quickly he attempted
to exit the airport, and whether his race, age, or clothing were consistent
with known drug trafficking gangs. Criminal profiles were initially
developed in the early 1970s to identify airline hijackers but were expanded
in the '70s and '80s to target drug couriers at airports and bus stations. Both
courts and commentators have expressed concern that the profiles employed
across cases have often been inconsistent and contradictory.

Police use of drug courier profiles, including those that rely on race, have
been challenged in court. For example, in *United States v. Weaver*, 966 F.2d
391 (8th Cir. 1992), Arthur Weaver was convicted in the United States
District Court for the Western District of Missouri of possessing cocaine with
intent to distribute. He appealed the district court's refusal to suppress the
evidence, which he argued was seized in violation of the Fourth Amendment.
The Eighth Circuit described the facts as follows:

> In the early morning hours of March 8, 1989, Drug Enforcement
> Administration (DEA) agent Carl Hicks and Platte County
> Detectives Paul Carrill and Tully Kessler were at the Kansas City
> International Airport awaiting the arrival of Braniff Flight 650, a
> direct flight to Kansas City from Los Angeles due in at 6:45 a.m. As
> Weaver disembarked from Flight 650 he caught Officer Hick's [sic]
> attention because he was a "roughly dressed" young black male who
> was carrying two bags and walking rapidly, almost running, down
> the concourse toward a door leading to a taxi stand. Because Hicks
> was aware that a number of young roughly dressed black males
> from street gangs in Los Angeles frequently brought cocaine into
> the Kansas City area and that walking quickly towards a taxicab
> was a common characteristic of narcotics couriers at the airport, he
> became suspicious that Weaver was a drug trafficker.

Hicks and his fellow officers began running down the concourse after Weaver. Weaver stopped, turned around, saw the three men approaching him, and hesitated. Hicks displayed his badge and asked Weaver if he would answer some questions. In response to Hicks' question, Weaver said that he had been in Los Angeles trying to find his sister who had been missing for several years. Hicks requested to see Weaver's airline ticket, but after searching his pockets Weaver said that he must have left it on the plane. When Hicks asked Weaver if he had any identification, Weaver replied that he did not, but gave Hicks his name and Kansas City address. Hicks testified that while it is extremely uncommon for adults not to have identification, it is common for persons carrying narcotics not to have any. Hicks also testified that Weaver appeared to be very nervous: his voice was unsteady, his speech was rapid, his hands shook, and his body swayed. Officer Carrill testified that although people often become nervous when approached by a police officer, Weaver exhibited more nervousness than innocent people usually do.

Hicks again displayed his badge, identified himself as a DEA agent looking for drugs, and asked to search Weaver's bags. After telling Hicks that he did not have any drugs, Weaver initially assented to Hicks' searching his bags, but then changed his mind and told Hicks that he could not search the bags without a warrant. Weaver then said that he needed to catch a taxi to see his mother in the hospital, picked up his bags, and walked out of the terminal towards a taxicab.

Hicks decided at this point to detain Weaver's bags and apply for a search warrant. He and the other officers followed Weaver to the sidewalk outside the terminal, where Hicks told Weaver that he was going to detain his bags and attempt to get a search warrant. Weaver stopped, set down the bags, opened one of them and removed a sweater, saying, "[L]ook, there's no drugs in my bag," but would not let Hicks look in the bag. Weaver again picked up the bags and walked toward a taxi.

Hicks followed Weaver and again told him that he was going to seize his bags and attempt to get a search warrant. Hicks told Weaver that he was free to remove anything he needed in order to continue his trip. Weaver said he needed a coat out of the bag. Hicks told him that that was fine and that he would give Weaver a receipt for the bag. Nevertheless, Weaver got into the back seat of a taxi with both bags. Hicks grabbed one of the bags and tried to take it out of the taxi. When Weaver began hitting Hicks' hand in an attempt to pry it off his bag, Hicks placed him under arrest.

The officers then conducted a pat down search on Weaver. They found a plastic bag filled with crack cocaine and a smoking pipe, along with $2,532 in currency. Hicks obtained a warrant and searched both of Weaver's bags. One of the bags contained more than six pounds of crack cocaine.

Id. at 394–93.

Weaver pled guilty, preserving his right to appeal, and the district court sentenced him to 151 months imprisonment and a fine of ten thousand dollars. The Eighth Circuit upheld the conviction, holding that the totality of the circumstances gave the officers reasonable suspicion that Weaver was carrying drugs. The court limited its discussion of race to a footnote:

> Regarding the matter of race, Hicks testified that several different factors caused him to suspect that Weaver might be carrying drugs: 'Number one, we have intelligence information and also past arrest history on two black—all black street gangs from Los Angeles called the Crips and the Bloods. They are notorious for transporting cocaine into the Kansas City area from Los Angeles for sale. Most of them are young, roughly dressed male blacks.'

> We agree with the dissent that large groups of our citizens should not be regarded by law enforcement officers as presumptively criminal based upon their race. We would not hesitate to hold that a solely race-based suspicion of drug courier status would not pass constitutional muster. Accordingly, had Hicks relied solely upon the fact of Weaver's race as a basis for his suspicions, we would have a different case before us. As it is, however, facts are not to be ignored simply because they may be unpleasant—and the unpleasant fact in this case is that Hicks had knowledge, based upon his own experience and upon the intelligence reports he had received from the Los Angeles authorities, that young male members of black Los Angeles gangs were flooding the Kansas City area with cocaine. To that extent, then, race, when coupled with the other factors Hicks relied upon, was a factor in the decision to approach and ultimately detain Weaver. We wish it were otherwise, but we take the facts as they are presented to us, not as we would like them to be.

Id.

Chief Judge Richard Arnold issued a strong dissent. He considered the various behavioral facts relied on as insufficient to create reasonable suspicion, noting, for example, that young people often seem "roughly dressed" to older generations, many passengers limit their luggage to carry-on bags, and many innocent people presumably exhibit nervousness when questioned by law enforcement. He concluded on the issue of race:

> Finally, a word about the reliance placed on Weaver's race. This factor is repeated several times in the Court's opinion. I am not prepared to say that it could never be relevant. If, for example, we had evidence that young blacks in Los Angeles were more prone to drug offenses than young whites, the fact that a young person is black might be of some significance, though even then it would be dangerous to give it much weight. I do not know of any such

evidence. Use of race as a factor simply reinforces the kind of stereotyping that lies behind drug-courier profiles. When public officials begin to regard large groups of citizens as presumptively criminal, this country is in a perilous situation indeed.

Id. at 397 (Arnold, C.J., dissenting).

In your assessment, was Officer Hicks' use of race reasonable? Does the Eighth Circuit's acceptance of race in *Weaver* follow from *Brignoni-Ponce* and *Martinez-Fuerte* or is this case distinguishable? Does the fact that Weaver was carrying drugs affect your judgment as to whether the search was justified? Should it?

6. *Airport Security.* Following the catastrophic events of September 11, 2001, the United States dramatically increased its efforts to deter and capture terrorists before they carried out acts of terrorism. One focus of the effort has been on airport security, which was taken over by a new federal agency in 2002, the Transportation Security Administration (TSA). Following September 11, as David Rudovsky and Richard Banks have observed,

> [A]t airports and at the country's borders, it was apparent that Muslims and Arabs were being targeted for special attention for questioning, searches, and even for decisions prohibiting them from flying. The government insisted that it was not engaged in racial or ethnic profiling, but its practices spoke in far different terms.

David Rudovsky & R. Richard Banks, *Debate, Racial Profiling and the War on Terror*, 155 U. Pa. L. Rev. PENNumbra 173, 175 (2007). The TSA does not reveal its criteria for subjecting airline passengers to extra searches, but many observers believe that TSA personnel do, or should, take race into account. See R. Richard Banks, *Racial Profiling and Antiterrorism Efforts*, 89 Cornell L. Rev. 1201 (2004). Given that all the terrorists on September 11 were Arab and that the membership of the Al-Qaeda terrorist organization and other such groups is predominantly Muslim, is it reasonable for the Transportation Security Administration to take into account whether someone's name or appearance is likely Arab, Middle Eastern, or Muslim? One commentator contends it would be irresponsible not to:

> The odds that any Middle Eastern passenger is a terrorist are, of course, tiny. But if you make the plausible assumptions that Al Qaeda terrorists are at least 100 times as likely to be from the Middle East as to be native-born Americans, and that fewer than 5 percent of all passengers on domestic flights are Middle Eastern men, it would follow that a randomly chosen Middle Eastern male passenger is roughly 2,000 times as likely to be an Al Qaeda terrorist as a randomly-chosen native-born American. It is crazy to ignore such odds.

Stuart Taylor, Jr., *The Skies Won't be Safe Until We Use Commonsense Profiling*, The Nat'l J., March 16, 2002, at 11.

Do you agree? If you believe it is reasonable to take race into account in screening airline passengers, does it follow that it is reasonable in preventing illegal immigration, too? What about drug interdiction efforts that involve stopping cars or people on the street that police suspect are carrying contraband? If you believe it is more reasonable to use race to prevent terrorism, is that because race is more predictive of a likely terrorist than of a likely drug dealer or undocumented immigrant, or do you believe that the seriousness of the crime being investigated should affect the reasonableness calculation?

It turns out that the Fourth Amendment does not take account of the seriousness of the crime in determining whether reasonable suspicion of criminal activity exists. All that matters is the probability, based on observed facts, that the observed suspect is engaged in criminal activity. Reasonable suspicion to stop and frisk a potential terrorist need be no more probabilistically justified than reasonable suspicion to believe someone is not wearing a seatbelt. *See* William J. Stuntz, *Commentary, O.J. Simpson, Bill Clinton, and the Transsubstantive Fourth Amendment*, 114 HARV. L. REV. 842 (2001) (criticizing Fourth Amendment's failure to take account of the seriousness of a crime under investigation).

3. PRETEXTUAL INVESTIGATIONS

The foregoing cases and questions about the scope of reasonable suspicion under the Fourth Amendment have all involved situations in which law enforcement claimed to have reasonable suspicion of the crime they were investigating. But what if police lack reasonable suspicion of that crime but have reason to believe a person is committing a minor offense or civil infraction about which the police are indifferent? Should police be able to coercively investigate the person based on the minor offense as a pretext for investigating the crime they care about, even though they lack reasonable suspicion of the latter? What if the minor offense is merely a traffic violation, such as driving two miles over the posted limit or failing to wear a seatbelt? What if the police are also motivated by race? Consider the next case.

Whren v. United States

517 U.S. 806 (1996).

■ JUSTICE SCALIA, delivered the opinion of the Court.

In this case we decide whether the temporary detention of a motorist who the police have probable cause to believe has committed a civil traffic violation is inconsistent with the Fourth Amendment's prohibition against unreasonable seizures unless a reasonable officer would have been motivated to stop the car by a desire to enforce the traffic laws.

I

On the evening of June 10, 1993, plainclothes vice-squad officers of the District of Columbia Metropolitan Police Department were patrolling a "high drug area" of the city in an unmarked car. Their suspicions were aroused when they passed a dark Pathfinder truck with temporary license plates and youthful occupants waiting at a stop sign, the driver looking down into the lap of the passenger at his right. The truck remained stopped at the intersection for what seemed an unusually long time—more than 20 seconds. When the police car executed a U-turn in order to head back toward the truck, the Pathfinder turned suddenly to its right, without signaling, and sped off at an "unreasonable" speed. The policemen followed, and in a short while overtook the Pathfinder when it stopped behind other traffic at a red light. They pulled up alongside, and Officer Ephraim Soto stepped out and approached the driver's door, identifying himself as a police officer and directing the driver, petitioner Brown, to put the vehicle in park. When Soto drew up to the driver's window, he immediately observed two large plastic bags of what appeared to be crack cocaine in petitioner Whren's hands. Petitioners were arrested, and quantities of several types of illegal drugs were retrieved from the vehicle.

Petitioners were charged in a four-count indictment with violating various federal drug laws. At a pretrial suppression hearing, they challenged the legality of the stop and the resulting seizure of the drugs. They argued that the stop had not been justified by probable cause to believe, or even reasonable suspicion, that petitioners were engaged in illegal drug-dealing activity; and that Officer Soto's asserted ground for approaching the vehicle—to give the driver a warning concerning traffic violations—was pretextual. The District Court denied the suppression motion, concluding that "the facts of the stop were not controverted," and "[t]here was nothing to really demonstrate that the actions of the officers were contrary to a normal traffic stop."

Petitioners were convicted of the counts at issue here. The Court of Appeals affirmed the convictions, holding with respect to the suppression issue that, "regardless of whether a police officer subjectively believes that the occupants of an automobile may be engaging in some other illegal behavior, a traffic stop is permissible as long as a reasonable officer in the same circumstances *could have* stopped the car for the suspected traffic violation."

II

The Fourth Amendment guarantees "[t]he right of the people to be secure in their persons, houses, papers, and effects, against unreasonable searches and seizures." Temporary detention of individuals during the stop of an automobile by the police, even if only for a brief period and for a limited purpose, constitutes a "seizure" of "persons" within the meaning of this provision. *See United States v. Martinez-Fuerte,* 428 U. S. 543, 556 (1976); *United States v. Brignoni-Ponce,* 422 U. S. 873, 878 (1975). As a general matter, the decision to stop an automobile is reasonable where the police have probable cause to believe that a traffic violation has occurred.

Petitioners accept that Officer Soto had probable cause to believe that various provisions of the District of Columbia traffic code had been violated. *See* 18 D. C. Mun. Regs. §§ 2213.4 (1995) ("An operator shall . . . give full time and attention to the operation of the vehicle"); 2204.3 ("No person shall turn any vehicle . . . without giving an appropriate signal"); 2200.3 ("No person shall drive a vehicle . . . at a speed greater than is reasonable and prudent under the conditions"). They argue, however, that "in the unique context of civil traffic regulations" probable cause is not enough. Since, they contend, the use of automobiles is so heavily and minutely regulated that total compliance with traffic and safety rules is nearly impossible, a police officer will almost invariably be able to catch any given motorist in a technical violation. This creates the temptation to use traffic stops as a means of investigating other law violations, as to which no probable cause or even articulable suspicion exists. Petitioners, who are both black, further contend that police officers might decide which motorists to stop based on decidedly impermissible factors, such as the race of the car's occupants. To avoid this danger, they say, the Fourth Amendment test for traffic stops should be, not the normal one (applied by the Court of Appeals) of whether probable cause existed to justify the stop; but rather, whether a police officer, acting reasonably, would have made the stop for the reason given.

A

Petitioners' difficulty is not simply a lack of affirmative support for their position. Not only have we never held . . . that an officer's motive invalidates objectively justifiable behavior under the Fourth Amendment; but we have repeatedly held and asserted the contrary. In *United States v. Villamonte-Marquez,* 462 U. S. 579, 584, n.3 (1983), we held that an otherwise valid warrantless boarding of a vessel by customs officials was not rendered invalid "because the customs officers were accompanied by a Louisiana state policeman, and were following an informant's tip that a vessel in the ship channel was thought to be carrying marihuana." We flatly dismissed the idea that an ulterior motive might serve to strip the agents of their legal justification. In *United States v. Robinson,* 414 U. S. 218 (1973), we held that a traffic-violation arrest (of the sort here) would not be rendered invalid by the fact that it was "a mere pretext for a narcotics search," *id.,* at 221, n.1; and that a lawful postarrest search of the person would not be rendered invalid by the fact that it was not motivated by the officer-safety concern that justifies such searches, *see id.,* at 236. We think these cases foreclose any argument that the constitutional reasonableness of traffic stops depends on the actual motivations of the individual officers involved. We of course agree with petitioners that the Constitution prohibits selective enforcement of the law based on considerations such as race. But the constitutional basis for objecting to intentionally discriminatory application of laws is the Equal Protection Clause, not the Fourth

Amendment. Subjective intentions play no role in ordinary, probable-cause Fourth Amendment analysis.

B

Recognizing that we have been unwilling to entertain Fourth Amendment challenges based on the actual motivations of individual officers, petitioners disavow any intention to make the individual officer's subjective good faith the touchstone of "reasonableness." They insist that the standard they have put forward—whether the officer's conduct deviated materially from usual police practices, so that a reasonable officer in the same circumstances would not have made the stop for the reasons given—is an "objective" one.

But although framed in empirical terms, this approach is plainly and indisputably driven by subjective considerations. Its whole purpose is to prevent the police from doing under the guise of enforcing the traffic code what they would like to do for different reasons. Petitioners' proposed standard may not use the word "pretext," but it is designed to combat nothing other than the perceived "danger" of the pretextual stop, albeit only indirectly and over the run of cases. Instead of asking whether the individual officer had the proper state of mind, the petitioners would have us ask, in effect, whether (based on general police practices) it is plausible to believe that the officer had the proper state of mind.

Why one would frame a test designed to combat pretext in such fashion that the court cannot take into account *actual and admitted pretext* is a curiosity that can only be explained by the fact that our cases have foreclosed the more sensible option. If those cases were based only upon the evidentiary difficulty of establishing subjective intent, petitioners' attempt to root out subjective vices through objective means might make sense. But they were not based only upon that, or indeed even principally upon that. Their principal basis—which applies equally to attempts to reach subjective intent through ostensibly objective means—is simply that the Fourth Amendment's concern with "reasonableness" allows certain actions to be taken in certain circumstances, *whatever* the subjective intent. But even if our concern had been only an evidentiary one, petitioners' proposal would by no means assuage it. Indeed, it seems to us somewhat easier to figure out the intent of an individual officer than to plumb the collective consciousness of law enforcement in order to determine whether a "reasonable officer" would have been moved to act upon the traffic violation. While police manuals and standard procedures may sometimes provide objective assistance, ordinarily one would be reduced to speculating about the hypothetical reaction of a hypothetical constable— an exercise that might be called virtual subjectivity.

Moreover, police enforcement practices, even if they could be practicably assessed by a judge, vary from place to place and from time to time. We cannot accept that the search and seizure protections of the

Fourth Amendment are so variable and can be made to turn upon such trivialities. The difficulty is illustrated by petitioners' arguments in this case. Their claim that a reasonable officer would not have made this stop is based largely on District of Columbia police regulations which permit plainclothes officers in unmarked vehicles to enforce traffic laws "only in the case of a violation that is so grave as to pose an *immediate threat* to the safety of others." This basis of invalidation would not apply in jurisdictions that had a different practice. And it would not have applied even in the District of Columbia, if Officer Soto had been wearing a uniform or patrolling in a marked police cruiser.

III

In what would appear to be an elaboration on the "reasonable officer" test, petitioners argue that the balancing inherent in any Fourth Amendment inquiry requires us to weigh the governmental and individual interests implicated in a traffic stop such as we have here. That balancing, petitioners claim, does not support investigation of minor traffic infractions by plainclothes police in unmarked vehicles; such investigation only minimally advances the government's interest in traffic safety, and may indeed retard it by producing motorist confusion and alarm—a view said to be supported by the Metropolitan Police Department's own regulations generally prohibiting this practice. And as for the Fourth Amendment interests of the individuals concerned, petitioners point out that our cases acknowledge that even ordinary traffic stops entail "a possibly unsettling show of authority"; that they at best "interfere with freedom of movement, are inconvenient, and consume time" and at worst "may create substantial anxiety," *Prouse,* 440 U. S., at 657. That anxiety is likely to be even more pronounced when the stop is conducted by plainclothes officers in unmarked cars.

It is of course true that in principle every Fourth Amendment case, since it turns upon a "reasonableness" determination, involves a balancing of all relevant factors. With rare exceptions not applicable here, however, the result of that balancing is not in doubt where the search or seizure is based upon probable cause. That is why petitioners must rely upon cases like *Prouse* to provide examples of actual "balancing" analysis. There, the police action in question was a random traffic stop for the purpose of checking a motorist's license and vehicle registration, a practice that—like the practices at issue in the inventory search and administrative inspection cases upon which petitioners rely in making their "pretext" claim—involves police intrusion *without the probable cause that is its traditional justification.* Our opinion in *Prouse* expressly distinguished the case from a stop based on precisely what is at issue here: "probable cause to believe that a driver is violating any one of the multitude of applicable traffic and equipment regulations." *Id.,* at 661. It noted approvingly that "[t]he foremost method of enforcing traffic and vehicle safety regulations . . . is acting upon observed violations," *id.,* at 659, which afford the "'quantum of individualized suspicion'" necessary to ensure that police discretion is sufficiently constrained, *id.,* at 654–655.

Where probable cause has existed, the only cases in which we have found it necessary actually to perform the "balancing" analysis involved searches or seizures conducted in an extraordinary manner, unusually harmful to an individual's privacy or even physical interests—such as, for example, seizure by means of deadly force, unannounced entry into a home, entry into a home without a warrant, or physical penetration of the body. The making of a traffic stop out of uniform does not remotely qualify as such an extreme practice, and so is governed by the usual rule that probable cause to believe the law has been broken "outbalances" private interest in avoiding police contact.

Petitioners urge as an extraordinary factor in this case that the "multitude of applicable traffic and equipment regulations" is so large and so difficult to obey perfectly that virtually everyone is guilty of violation, permitting the police to single out almost whomever they wish for a stop. But we are aware of no principle that would allow us to decide at what point a code of law becomes so expansive and so commonly violated that infraction itself can no longer be the ordinary measure of the lawfulness of enforcement. And even if we could identify such exorbitant codes, we do not know by what standard (or what right) we would decide, as petitioners would have us do, which particular provisions are sufficiently important to merit enforcement.

Here the District Court found that the officers had probable cause to believe that petitioners had violated the traffic code. That rendered the stop reasonable under the Fourth Amendment, the evidence thereby discovered admissible, and the upholding of the convictions by the Court of Appeals for the District of Columbia Circuit correct. The judgment is

Affirmed.

NOTES AND QUESTIONS

1. ***The Court's Reasoning.*** Professor Kevin Johnson describes *Whren* as a case that "scholars almost universally love to hate." Kevin R. Johnson, *How Racial Profiling in America Became the 'Law of the Land':* United States v. Brignoni-Ponce *and* Whren v. United States *and the Need for Truly Rebellious Lawyering,* 98 Geo. L.J. 1005, 1009 (2010). Yet the decision was unanimous. Every Justice agreed that a search and seizure is reasonable under the Fourth Amendment if it is supported by probable cause of a crime or civil violation, no matter how trivial the violation and regardless of the subjective motivations of the police, including whether the police used the offense pretextually to investigate a different crime or relied on race. In contrast, a few states prohibit pretextual use of one crime to investigate another. What concerns led the Court to uphold pretextual stops under the Fourth Amendment? What concerns support an anti-pretext approach? If

you could introduce legislation to address whether police could engage in pretextual stops, arrests, and searches, what criteria, rules, or standards would you propose? Consider these questions as you read the following notes.

2.   *Implications for Fourth Amendment Doctrine.* Although *Wren* upheld a search and seizure based on probable cause, the reasoning also justifies a *Terry* stop and frisk, whether on the street or during a traffic stop, if police have reasonable suspicion of any crime, even if the officer is motivated by another crime for which he lacks reasonable suspicion. Moreover, in *Atwater v. City of Lago Vista*, 532 U.S. 318 (2001), a motorist was caught driving without wearing her seatbelt, an offense punishable by a fine only, yet the officer arrested her, in front of her young children, and took her into custody rather than issuing her a citation. A closely divided Court held that probable cause of the seatbelt offense made the custodial arrest reasonable under the Fourth Amendment, notwithstanding the fact that the crime, if proven, would not have resulted in any jail time. In *Virginia v. Moore*, 553 U.S. 164 (2008), the Court upheld an arrest as reasonable under the Fourth Amendment where there was probable cause of a seatbelt violation, even though state law prohibited arresting a person for that offense. The upshot is that a search and seizure under the Fourth Amendment is justified if objective facts create a sufficient degree of suspicion, regardless whether the officer is motivated by an unsubstantiated crime or by race, and regardless whether state law authorizes the police action.

3.   *Overcriminalization.* As described by the Court in *Wren*, the defendants contended that, "the 'multitude of applicable traffic and equipment regulations' is so large and so difficult to obey perfectly that virtually everyone is guilty of violation, permitting the police to single out almost whomever they wish for a stop." Are you persuaded by the defendants' claim? How difficult is it for a motorist to comply with traffic laws and motor vehicle regulations? If compliance is possible, then is not the motorist to blame for choosing not to comply, thereby assuming the risk that police may stop him for the traffic violation and may discover evidence of another crime in the process? Alternatively, to the extent complying with traffic laws is virtually impossible, is not the democratically elected legislature to blame for defining the laws so broadly as to make everyone a law-breaker, rather than the police for simply enforcing the laws on the books?

4.   *Insight from the Vagueness Doctrine.* Recall that the Court invalidated various vagrancy and loitering laws on the ground that their vagueness vested police with broad discretion, which, in turn, created an intolerable risk that police would enforce the law in an arbitrary or discriminatory manner. In one sense, traffic laws are very different as they are not vague. Indeed, laws that prohibit exceeding a particular speed, failing to stop completely at an intersection, failing to signal before turning or changing lanes, and failing to wear a seatbelt are considerably more specific than most laws. In another sense, however, traffic laws raise similar concerns as vague laws in the way in which they vest broad discretion in police. Like the vagrancy and loitering laws the Court has held invalid, traffic laws proscribe conduct which is commonly engaged in by law-abiding people and is often trivial or harmless. As such, police feel free to ignore minor violations. And yet, per *Whren*, they are entitled to investigate any violation so long as they have reasonable suspicion. If most motorists violate the traffic laws, then police have discretion to select from a large pool of motorists. As Professor Forde-Mazrui has observed:

> Speed limits alone cast a wide net for the police. The majority of motorists violate such laws, and law enforcement, often admittedly, ignores most drivers who exceed the limit by less than five miles per hour. Under-enforcement is not, moreover, merely a result of limited resources. For instance, a certain degree of non-compliance is probably desired to avoid the traffic burdens that would result from full compliance with posted speed limits. Indeed, the safest driving speeds on most highways exceed posted limits. However, because driving sixty-seven miles per hour in a zone posted at sixty-five violates the law, police can rely on the violation of a specific rule to justify stopping almost any motorist on the road. When the totality of traffic and vehicle regulations are considered, the great majority of motorists are in violation of the law within a relatively short period of driving, affording the police the discretion to pick virtually any car and follow it until a violation of the law is observed.

Kim Forde-Mazrui, *Ruling Out the Rule of Law*, 60 Vand. L. Rev. 1497, 1520–1521 (2007).

The insight from the vagueness doctrine is that broad discretion creates a risk of arbitrary and discriminatory enforcement. To the extent traffic laws vest broad discretion in police, they also create a substantial risk that such discretion may be exercised improperly, even if the language of the laws is specific. The risk exists, moreover, even if police are genuinely trying to stop serious crime. *Whren* holds that investigating a traffic violation can serve as a pretext for investigating an unsubstantiated, albeit good faith, suspicion of some other crime. The factors that might lead a particular police officer to suspect a motorist of another crime without reasonable suspicion is left to the assumptions of the officer, including his sincere but idiosyncratic hunches and stereotypical beliefs, conscious or not, based on a motorist's race. The concerns over arbitrary and discriminatory enforcement that animate the vagueness doctrine are thus implicated by the interaction between the broad scope of traffic laws and the Fourth Amendment as interpreted in *Whren*.

Consider also the implications of *Whren* for on-the-street encounters between police and the public. Police can exploit petty offenses to investigate people for evidence of more serious crimes, such as drugs or guns, despite lacking reasonable suspicion of these other crimes. Part of the aggressive policing employed in large urban areas over the past couple of decades has relied on minor offenses, such as littering, jay-walking, public intoxication, violating curfew, graffiti, and disorderly conduct, to investigate young, often minority, males in public places. Since all police need is reasonable suspicion of any minor offense to justify a stop and frisk, or probable cause to justify a full arrest and search, it is not difficult for police to investigate virtually anyone they choose for any reason.

5. ***Implications for Racial Profiling.*** Although the Court in *Whren* explained that "[s]ubjective intentions play no role in ordinary, probable-cause Fourth Amendment analysis," the Court did not deny that racial motivations by police raise constitutional concerns: "We of course agree with petitioners that the Constitution prohibits selective enforcement of the law based on considerations such as race. But the constitutional basis for objecting to intentionally discriminatory application of laws is the Equal Protection Clause, not the Fourth Amendment." Does the Court mean that it would have taken seriously the petitioners' allegations of possible race discrimination had petitioners cited the Equal Protection Clause rather than the Fourth Amendment? What difference does it make what constitutional provision a claim is raised under if the nature of the claim is clear? Also, to the extent the Court's statement appears to forbid race-based enforcement, does it mean that *Brignoni-Ponce* and *Martinez-Fuerte*, both of which approved some use of race in investigating motorists for undocumented immigrants, are no longer good law?

D. APPROACH THREE: PROHIBIT SUBJECTIVE RACIAL MOTIVATION

The Supreme Court's decision in *Whren* appears to signal that a motorist who believes he was selectively targeted for a traffic stop based on his race may challenge the stop, and presumably any resulting search or arrest, under the Equal Protection Clause. But how might the motorist prove that race played a role in his stop? Note that because *Whren* permits pretextual stops based on minor traffic violations, an officer could readily admit that he stopped a motorist based on an unsubstantiated hunch of drug trafficking, so the motorist would need to show more than that the traffic violation was not serious enough to have motivated the stop by itself. What other evidence would you present? How helpful would statistical evidence involving other traffic stops by the same officers be? The following case addresses issues related to proof of racial motivation.

Commonwealth v. Lora

Supreme Judicial Court of Massachusetts, 2008.
451 Mass. 425, 886.

■ CORDY, J.

In this case, in which we granted the defendant's application for direct appellate review, we conclude that evidence of racial profiling is relevant in determining whether a traffic stop is the product of selective enforcement violative of the equal protection guarantee of the Massachusetts Declaration of Rights; and that evidence seized in the course of a stop violative of equal protection should, ordinarily, be excluded at trial. We also conclude that statistical evidence demonstrating disparate treatment of persons based on their race may be offered to meet the defendant's burden to present sufficient evidence of impermissible discrimination so as to shift the burden to the Commonwealth to provide a race-neutral explanation for such a stop. Finally, we conclude that the evidence proffered by the defendant fell short of what is necessary to overcome the presumption that a law enforcement officer making a traffic stop, based on probable cause, has acted in good faith and without intent to discriminate. Consequently, the evidence seized in this case should not have been suppressed.

1. *Background.*

a. *Traffic stop.* On the evening of December 20, 2001, State Trooper Brendhan Shugrue was patrolling Interstate Route 290 in Auburn (Route 290). At approximately 9:10 P.M., he approached a motor vehicle traveling ahead of him in the left lane. At the time, there was no traffic in the center lane or the right lane. The vehicle traveled within the speed limit, did not swerve, and made no erratic movements. It did not pass any vehicles because there was no traffic at the time.

Shugrue followed the vehicle for three-quarters mile to an area within several hundred yards of the border between Auburn and Worcester. He observed that the two occupants of the vehicle were dark skinned (the defendant, Andres Lora, is Hispanic). He activated the cruiser's blue lights and stopped the vehicle for traveling in the left lane while the center and right lanes were unoccupied. Shugrue approached the vehicle from the passenger's side and asked the driver for his license and registration. The driver explained that his license had been suspended and that the vehicle belonged to the passenger, Lora. Lora then produced his license and the vehicle's registration.

Shugrue asked the driver to step out of the vehicle, and instructed him to sit in the back of his cruiser. Lora remained in the vehicle. Shugrue then checked the status of the driver's license, as well as the status of Lora's license and registration. He confirmed that the driver's license was, in fact, suspended, but that Lora's license and registration were both valid. As Shugrue was retrieving this information, he observed Lora getting out of his vehicle while talking on his cellular telephone. Shugrue got out of the cruiser intending to instruct Lora to get back into his vehicle; as Shugrue approached, Lora got back into the vehicle and shut the door. Shugrue then directed his flashlight inside the vehicle, where he observed a small glassine bag on the driver's side floor containing white powder.

Shugrue immediately asked Lora to step out of the vehicle and frisked him. He then retrieved the glassine bag, which appeared to contain cocaine, and radioed the State police barracks to request assistance. Trooper William Pinkes arrived at the scene ten to fifteen minutes later. The troopers then proceeded to search the vehicle. Shugrue discovered substantially more cocaine in the trunk. Pinkes then placed Lora and the driver under arrest.

A grand jury subsequently returned an indictment charging Lora with trafficking in cocaine.

b. *Motion to suppress.* On March 27, 2003, Lora filed a motion to suppress the cocaine as the fruit of an unconstitutional search. He contended that Shugrue initiated the traffic stop because the occupants of the vehicle were dark skinned, and not solely because the operator of the vehicle committed a traffic violation by driving in the left lane. In other words, he claimed that Shugrue impermissibly engaged in the practice of racial profiling. Thus, Lora asserted, the stop violated his right to equal protection under the law, as guaranteed by the Fourteenth Amendment to the United States Constitution and arts. 1 and 10 of the Massachusetts Declaration of Rights. He further asserted that a traffic stop predicated solely on the race of the passengers of a vehicle was inherently unreasonable and constitutionally infirm under the Fourth Amendment to the United States Constitution and art. 14 of the Massachusetts Declaration of Rights.

Lora sought to prove that the stop of the vehicle in which he was traveling was the product of racial profiling by establishing that Shugrue had a history of disproportionately stopping and citing nonwhite motorists for motor vehicle violations. To that end, defense counsel filed an affidavit stating that he had reviewed 256 citations issued by Trooper Shugrue between August 22, 2001, and February 18, 2002. The affidavit pointed out that during this time period, Shugrue cited the operators of fifty-one vehicles driving on the stretch of Route 290 that passes through Auburn. Sixteen of the operators cited (or 31.37 per cent) were identified as Hispanic, and six (or 11.76 per cent) as African-American.[2]

Defense counsel then compared the percentage of citations issued to each racial group with the racial composition of the town of Auburn, as tabulated by the 2000 United States census (census). White residents accounted for 97.5 per cent of the population of Auburn; Hispanic residents, one per cent; and African-American residents, .6 per cent. Implicitly assuming that the demographics of the town of Auburn mirror the demographics of those driving on Route 290 through Auburn, defense counsel argued that Shugrue cited minority drivers at a rate wildly disproportionate to their representation in the local Auburn population. This type of comparison is known as census benchmarking. Using this analytical framework, defense counsel contended that a Hispanic driver would be 31.37 times more likely to be cited than an average motorist[3]; and an African-American driver would be 19.60 times more likely to be

---

[2] One citation was given to an operator identified as Asian.

[3] The average motorist refers to a random motorist whose race cannot be ascertained by a patrolling officer. He or she is, therefore, race neutral.

cited than an average motorist. By contrast, white drivers were only .5631 times as likely to be pulled over as an average motorist (or, in other words, about one-half as likely).

Defense counsel's affidavit also included information regarding traffic citations issued by Shugrue along the stretch of Route 290 passing through the city of Worcester. In that same period, i.e., between August 22, 2001, and February 18, 2002, Shugrue cited eighty-nine motorists. Seventy-four, or 83.15 per cent, of the motorists cited were white; seven, or 7.87 per cent, were Hispanic; and six, or 6.74 per cent, were African-American. According to the census, white residents account for 77.1 per cent of the population of Worcester; Hispanic residents, 15.1 per cent; and African-American residents, 8.0 per cent. Defense counsel again used census benchmarking to compare the racial composition of the citations to the racial composition of the inhabitants of Worcester. Using the same implicit assumption that the demographics of Worcester accurately reflected the demographics of motorists driving on Route 290 in Worcester, defense counsel calculated that white motorists were 1.08 times more likely to be cited than an average motorist (that is, slightly *more* likely). Hispanic motorists were .52 times as likely to be cited as an average motorist (that is, about *one-half* as likely), while African-American drivers were .84 times as likely to be cited (that is, slightly *less* likely).

At the hearing on the motion to suppress, Lora introduced Shugrue's citation history, which was admitted de bene by the motion judge. Troopers Shugrue and Pinkes testified on behalf of the Commonwealth, contending that the traffic stop was motivated solely by the operator's failure to keep to the right, and that the subsequent search was justified by the cocaine-filled glassine bag within the passenger compartment of the vehicle. After taking the matter under advisement, the judge allowed Lora's motion to suppress. In his decision, the judge found that although "[a] strict reading of Massachusetts law supports that Shugrue was authorized to stop the [vehicle] for traveling in the left-hand lane," the record left "no reasonable conclusion but that Shugrue stopped the motor vehicle in which the Defendant was a passenger because of the race of the operator and the race of the Defendant." Therefore, the trooper "violated the Defendant's rights pursuant to the Fourteenth Amendment . . . and Articles 1 and 10 . . . when he stopped and searched his vehicle."

In reaching his conclusions, the judge noted that "Massachusetts appellate courts have yet to resolve the conflict that arises when a well-substantiated allegation of racial profiling is made within the context of a *legitimate* traffic stop" (emphasis in original). He ruled that the authorization approach to motor vehicle stops, under which a stop is deemed to be constitutionally valid as long as it is one that police are "legally permitted and objectively authorized" to make, *Commonwealth v. Santana,* 420 Mass. 205, 209 (1995), is inapplicable when a defendant is able to present objective evidence that the police officer who effectuated the stop has engaged in racial profiling. In this respect, the judge found that the evidence introduced by Lora, including Shugrue's past citations and the statistical evidence derived therefrom, was "both credible and relevant to the case at bar," creating an "inference of purposeful discrimination, which [was] not . . . rebutted by the Commonwealth" either with "a race-neutral explanation for the statistical disparities or [by] explain[ing] a compelling government interest in treating members of one race differently from another." The judge found that Lora had sustained his burden of proof of discrimination "both by a preponderance of the evidence as well as clear and convincing proof."

c.   *Motion for rehearing and the joint motion to vacate.* Following the judge's decision, the Commonwealth filed a motion for reconsideration. . . . The motion for reconsideration was allowed, and the judge ordered the scheduling of another evidentiary hearing.

At the rehearing, the defense called Scott Evans, a research scientist in the department of biostatistics at Harvard School of Public Health. In preparing for his testimony, Evans reviewed only the data regarding the citations issued by Shugrue in Auburn, and compared that information to the population demographics of that town. On the basis of that data, he concluded that the chance that race was not a factor in the disparate stop rates in Auburn was "very, very minute." On cross-examination by the Commonwealth, Evans admitted that the assumption underlying his conclusion was that the demographics of the town of Auburn reflected the demographics of motorists on Interstate Route 290, and admitted that he had not considered the stops that occurred in Worcester.

The Commonwealth called Bishop, who testified that the census benchmarking technique used by Lora is "outmoded and no longer accepted within the scientific community because . . . it is highly likely to yield misleading and erroneous conclusions." She testified that census benchmarking assumes that the "demographic profile of the community [is] nearly identical to the demographic profile of drivers on the road where the officer was patrolling," an assumption that is "not accurate." Bishop further testified that Shugrue's citations themselves demonstrate the flaw in census benchmarking: "I examined each of the citations that were given by Trooper Shugrue of [*sic*] motorists in Auburn . . . ninety per cent of those motorists were not from Auburn, which is conclusive evidence that a residential or a census benchmark coming from Auburn is totally inappropriate [as a point of comparison]." She went on to explain that an appropriate benchmark must include "a profile of the people who should be legitimately at more risk of being stopped and then compare that to the profile of who is actually stopped," and ideally "roadside observers [would be used to] develop a demographic profile of people who violate traffic laws in a particular location where police are patrolling and stops are being made. In that instance, the benchmark would represent fairly well the group of people who should be at risk for being stopped if no bias exists."[4]

The Commonwealth also called Joseph Petruccelli, a professor of mathematical sciences at Worcester Polytechnic Institute with a Ph.D. in statistics. Petruccelli testified that while the methodology used by Lora's expert is an established tool of statistical analysis, its results are valid only when the appropriate data are fed into it. The census data used here made the statistical study scientifically unacceptable.

On December 2, 2005, the judge issued his decision affirming the earlier suppression order and reiterating his conclusion that Lora "met his burden by offering evidence of an inference of selective law enforcement and that the Commonwealth has not sufficiently rebutted [that] evidence with a neutral explanation."

2. *Discussion.*

On appeal, the Commonwealth first argues that even assuming Lora could prove that Shugrue stopped the vehicle in which Lora was riding because of the race of its occupants, his subjective intent is irrelevant to the legality of the stop and the subsequent search. In support of its position, the Commonwealth points to our holding that "it is irrelevant whether a reasonable police officer would have made the stop but for [an] unlawful motive; the stop is valid 'so long as the police are doing no more than they are legally permitted and objectively authorized to do.'" *Commonwealth v. Santana,* 420 Mass. 205, 209 (1995). The Commonwealth also argues that the United States Supreme Court's decision in *Whren v. United States,* 517 U.S. 806, 813 (1996), "foreclose[s] any argument that the constitutional reasonableness of traffic stops depends on the actual motivations of the individual officers involved."

The Commonwealth reads too much into these cases. Both involved traffic stops that were objectively valid but motivated by an interest in investigating more serious crimes for which the officers had insufficient suspicion to justify an investigative stop. The defendants contended that if the traffic stops would not have been made by a reasonable police officer motivated to make the stop solely by a desire to enforce the traffic laws, they were "unreasonable" and therefore in violation of the Fourth Amendment right to be secure from unreasonable searches and seizures. Both courts rejected this argument, concluding essentially that the decision to stop an automobile is reasonable for Fourth Amendment purposes "where the police have probable cause to believe that a traffic violation has occurred." *Whren* at 810.

---

[4] Bishop also testified that in the Northeastern University study on racial profiling, "driving observation data" were used as the benchmark. The driving observation data were obtained by "post[ing] observers on the roadway at various times of day, at different roadways . . . and have them observe, as best they could, the race of the motorists at different times of day on each of those roadway segments." Although this data did not include observations of traffic law violators, Bishop testified the difference was only a "matter of degree."

Neither case involved a challenge to the traffic stops based on equal protection grounds. Indeed, in *Whren*, the Court specifically noted, "We of course agree with petitioners that the Constitution prohibits selective enforcement of the law based on considerations such as race. But the constitutional basis for objecting to intentionally discriminatory application of laws is the Equal Protection Clause, not the Fourth Amendment. Subjective intentions play no role in ordinary, probable cause Fourth Amendment analysis."

a.   *Selective enforcement.* It is well established that "[t]he equal protection principles of the Fourteenth Amendment . . . and arts. 1 and 10 . . . prohibit discriminatory application of impartial laws." *Commonwealth v. Franklin Fruit Co.,* 388 Mass. 228, 229–230 (1983). "It is equally well established, however, that prosecutors and other law enforcement officers enjoy considerable discretion in exercising some selectivity for purposes consistent with the public interest."

An arrest or prosecution based on probable cause is ordinarily cloaked with a presumption of regularity. "Because we presume that criminal prosecutions are undertaken in good faith, without intent to discriminate, the defendant bears the initial burden of demonstrating selective enforcement." *Commonwealth v. Franklin, supra* at 894. In order to meet this burden, the defendant must first "present evidence which raises at least a reasonable inference of impermissible discrimination," including evidence that "a broader class of persons than those prosecuted has violated the law, . . . that failure to prosecute was either consistent or deliberate, . . . and that the decision not to prosecute was based on an impermissible classification such as race, religion, or sex". *Commonwealth v. Franklin, supra.* at 894. Once a defendant has raised a reasonable inference of selective prosecution by presenting credible evidence that persons similarly situated to himself have been deliberately or consistently not prosecuted because of their race, "the Commonwealth must rebut that inference or suffer dismissal of the underlying complaint." *Commonwealth v. Franklin, supra* at 895.

b.   *Suppression as remedy.* The suppression of evidence under the exclusionary rule is a "judicially created remedy," whose "prime purpose is to deter future unlawful police conduct." *United States v. Calandra,* 414 U.S. 338, 347, 348 (1974). We conclude that the application of the exclusionary rule to evidence obtained in violation of the constitutional right to the equal protection of the laws is entirely consistent with the policy underlying the exclusionary rule, is properly gauged to deter intentional unconstitutional behavior, and furthers the protections guaranteed by the Massachusetts Declaration of Rights. *See State v. Segars,* 172 N.J. 481, 493 (2002) (rationales that support suppression of evidence, "namely, deterrence of impermissible investigatory behavior and maintenance of the integrity of the judicial system, apply equally, if not more so, to cases of racial targeting").[5]

c.   *Statistical evidence.* "Statistics may be used to make out a case of targeting minorities for prosecution of traffic offenses." *State v. Soto,* 324 N.J.Super. 66, 83 (1996) (unrebutted statistical evidence of disproportionate traffic stops of African-American motorists established de facto policy of targeting them for investigation and arrest). "Of course, parties may not prove discrimination merely by providing the court with statistical analyses. The statistics proffered must address the crucial question of whether one class is being treated differently from another class that is otherwise similarly situated." *Chavez v. Illinois State Police,* 251 F.3d 612, 638 (7th Cir. 2001). "Further, 'statistics are not irrefutable; they come in infinite variety and, like any other kind of evidence, they may be rebutted. In short, their usefulness depends on all of the surrounding facts and circumstances.' " *Id.*

In *State v. Soto, supra* at 69–73, a New Jersey case examining racial profiling in traffic stops, the judge was presented with rigorously prepared surveys regarding both the racial makeup of motorists traveling along a stretch of the New Jersey Turnpike encompassing three exits (traffic survey) and the racial makeup of motorists observed violating speeding and other moving violation laws along that same stretch of highway (violation survey). The data from these surveys demonstrated that the racial makeup of the motorists traveling the road was 13.5 per cent black, and that the observed violators were approximately fifteen per cent black. This data were used as the benchmark for comparison with the number of "race identified" traffic stops made by the State police along the same stretch of highway. The stop data showed that 46.2 per cent of the stops were of black motorists. This disparity was calculated to be more than sixteen standard deviations over the expected norm. Further expert testimony presented by the defendants established that the surveys were well designed and performed, and statistically reliable for the analysis, and that a similarly situated black motorist was 4.85 times as likely as a white motorist to be stopped on the roadway.

Ultimately, the judge concluded that the statistical data were sufficient to support the finding of a "de facto policy" on the part of certain State troopers of targeting black motorists, which was not adequately rebutted by the State. In reaching this conclusion, the judge found that the stark patterns revealed in the data established a prima facie case of selective enforcement, that is, that similarly situated motorists were intentionally treated differently because of their race. Accordingly, the

---

[5]   But see *United States v. Nichols,* 512 F.3d 789, 794 (6th Cir. 2008) ("While we, of course, agree with the general proposition that selective enforcement of the law based on a suspect's race may violate the Fourteenth Amendment, we do not agree that the proper remedy . . . is necessarily suppression of evidence . . . ").

judge granted the defendants' motions to suppress the evidence garnered as a result of their traffic stops.[6]

In contrast, in *Chavez v. Illinois State Police, supra,* the United States Court of Appeals for the Seventh Circuit concluded that the statistical data presented by the defendants against the Illinois State police failed to establish the elements of a "prima facie" case of selective enforcement of traffic laws based on race. The data in that case, which were drawn largely from field reports of traffic stops, were problematic for a number of reasons, but most importantly, the court found that the benchmark data used for comparison with the traffic stop data were census data for the entire State, which "can tell us very little about the numbers of Hispanics and African-Americans driving on [the] Illinois interstate highways [at issue], which is crucial to determining the population of motorists encountered by the . . . officers." *Id.* at 644.

We are of the view that statistical evidence may be used to meet a defendant's initial burden of producing sufficient evidence to raise a reasonable inference of impermissible discrimination. At a minimum, that evidence must establish that the racial composition of motorists stopped for motor vehicle violations varied significantly from the racial composition of the population of motorists making use of the relevant roadways, and who therefore could have encountered the officer or officers whose actions have been called into question.[7]

d. *Lora's evidence.* Lora has failed to present credible evidence establishing a reasonable inference of impermissible discrimination sufficient to rebut the presumption that the stop of his motor vehicle was "undertaken in good faith, without intent to discriminate." *Commonwealth v. Franklin,* 376 Mass. 885, 894 (1978).

An assessment of the evidence admitted at the rehearing on Lora's motion to suppress leads us to the inescapable conclusion that the use of

---

[6] The *Soto* decision had far-ranging effects within New Jersey. It led to a review of the law enforcement practices of the New Jersey State police (see, e.g., Interim Report of the State Police Review Team Regarding Racial Profiling Allegations, April, 1999), which led the New Jersey Attorney General to conclude "that defendants perceived to be African-American, Black or Hispanic are entitled to discovery [regarding racial profiling] for motor vehicle stops that originated as a result of observations made by [New Jersey] State Troopers." *State v. Lee,* 190 N.J. 270, 274–275, 280 (2007). In 2000, the Supreme Court of New Jersey issued an administrative order, at the request of the New Jersey Attorney General, assigning one judge to hear all motions for discovery relating to racial profiling by the New Jersey State police to ensure "centralized judicial management" of the rapidly emerging issue. *Id.* at 279.

The decision also became the center of attention in the ongoing legal debate about how to confront the problem of racial profiling. See, e.g., Garrett, Remedying Racial Profiling, 33 Colum. Hum. Rts. L.Rev. 41 (2001) (describing *Soto* case as "[t]he most dramatic example of a lawsuit drawing attention to the racial profiling problem"). Other litigants (criminal defendants and civil plaintiffs) sought to mirror the methodology used by the *Soto* defendants in their efforts to demonstrate selective enforcement. See Harris, The Stories, the Statistics, and the Law: Why "Driving While Black" Matters, 84 Minn. L.Rev. 265 (1999).

[7] While we do not presume that all races violate all laws equally, see *United States v. Armstrong,* 517 U.S. 456, 479–480 (1996), we are unaware of any reliable study establishing that motor vehicle violations are more frequently committed by any particular race of driver.

census benchmarking to compare the demographics of a small community with citation ratios on a major interstate highway, which happens to pass through it, is unreliable and not accepted in the scientific community. Such benchmarking data do not provide an adequate basis for assessing the racial composition of the drivers encountered by Shugrue on Route 290 and is inadequate to establish that similarly situated drivers of different races were treated differently. Indeed, Lora's own evidence disproves his premise of comparability: of the fifty-two motorists that Shugrue ticketed on Route 290 in Auburn, ninety per cent were not residents of Auburn. Lora therefore failed to present sufficient credible evidence of discriminatory effect. The judge's determination to the contrary was clearly erroneous, and the motion to suppress should not have been granted.

Even were we to consider census benchmarking data as providing some evidence of selective enforcement, the use of the population demographics of the inhabitants of the town of Auburn was too limited. The population of Auburn is 15,901; the population of Worcester is 172,648. Lora introduced evidence of Shugrue's citation history in both Worcester and Auburn, but compiled the data in isolation, comparing only the stops effectuated on Route 290 in Auburn with the demographics of Auburn, and the stops effectuated on Route 290 in Worcester with the demographics of Worcester. Logically, as Bishop testified, the combined census demographics of Worcester and Auburn are more likely to reflect the demographics of motorists on Route 290 near the border of Worcester and Auburn than the demographics of Auburn only. When the citations issued by Shugrue in Worcester and Auburn are compared to their combined demographics, a more balanced picture emerges. Shugrue cited 140 motorists in Worcester and Auburn during the relevant eight-month period, 102 of whom were white (72.9 per cent), twenty-three Hispanic (16.4 per cent), and twelve African-American (8.6 per cent). The combined demographics of the area reflect a population that is 77.2 per cent white, 13.7 per cent Hispanic, and 6.2 per cent African-American. Thus, when viewed through an appropriately broad lens, even the questionable census benchmarking methodology used by Lora fails to establish any significant disparity of treatment based on race.

3.   *Conclusion.*

Justices of this court have expressed considerable concern about the practice of racial profiling in prior decisions. *See Commonwealth v. Feyenord,* 445 Mass. 72, 88 (2005) (Greaney, J., concurring) ("A motorist must *never* be stopped based on his or her race or ethnicity without legally sufficient cause. Getting a traffic ticket is never a happy experience. Getting a traffic ticket if you are a black or Hispanic person who has committed a minor traffic violation and then been questioned in public view by an armed police officer determined to find a basis . . . to bring in a police dog, is humiliating, painful, and unlawful" [emphasis in original]); *Commonwealth v. Gonsalves,* 429 Mass. 658, 670 (1999) (Ireland, J., concurring) ("The widespread public concerns about police profiling, commonly referred to as 'DWB—driving while black,' has been the subject of much discussion and debate both across the country and within the Commonwealth"). *See also United States v. Montero-Camargo,* 208 F.3d 1122, 1135 (9th Cir.) (2000) ("Stops based on race or ethnic appearance send the underlying message to all our citizens that those who are not white are judged by the color of their skin alone"). These concerns would not be alleviated by a standard that nominally allows a defendant to make claim of selective enforcement of traffic laws, but forecloses such a claim in practice.

On the other hand, the standard must be sufficiently rigorous that its imposition does not unnecessarily intrude on the exercise of powers constitutionally delegated to other branches of government. Balance is therefore important. While racial profiling evidence is relevant to assessing the constitutionality of a traffic stop, and evidence seized during a traffic stop that violates the equal protection guarantees of the Massachusetts Declaration of Rights may be suppressed, the initial burden rests on the defendant to produce evidence that similarly situated persons were treated differently because of their race. The practical weight of this burden is admittedly daunting in some cases, but not impossible. It was done, and done well, in New Jersey. Data now being collected in Massachusetts,[8] and the work of academic and other institutions to develop more sophisticated analytic tools with which to identify and measure the use of race in the context of traffic stops may be of assistance in meeting this burden.

Of necessity, the important responsibility of eliminating racial considerations in the day-to-day enforcement of our laws lies principally with the executive branch of government, and no evidence was presented in this case to suggest that this is a responsibility that is being ignored. While the judicial branch shares the responsibility of ensuring that the protections of the Constitution are afforded to all residents, it can only

---

[8] See, e.g., "An Act providing for the collection of data relative to traffic stops," St. 2000, c. 228(Act), which empowers the registry of motor vehicles and the Secretary of the Executive Office of Public Safety (Secretary) to collect data to determine whether State and local police engage in the practice of racial profiling. Section 8 of the Act requires the registry to collect data from any issued Massachusetts uniform citation regarding the race and gender of the motorist, the traffic infraction, whether a search was initiated, and whether the stop resulted in a warning, citation, or arrest. The registry is then required to report the statistical information it collects every month to the Secretary.

Pursuant to § 10 of the Act, the Secretary shall transmit the collected data to a "university in the commonwealth with experience in the analysis of such data, for annual preparation of an analysis and report of its findings." If the analysis suggests that a State police barracks or a municipal police department "appears to have engaged in racial or gender profiling," that department or barracks is thereafter required to "collect information on all traffic stops, including those not resulting in a warning, citation, or arrest." *Id.* Individual police departments may mandate that police officers disclose additional information, including their identification, in order to allow those departments to "view data at the officer level" and "manage officers" accordingly.

exercise that responsibility when proper and sufficient evidence has been presented to it. The judge's order suppressing the evidence in this case is reversed.

So ordered.

■ [The concurring opinion of JUDGE IRELAND is omitted.]

NOTES AND QUESTIONS

1.   *The Court's Reasoning.* The court in *Lora* explained defendant's burden of proof: "the initial burden rests on the defendant to produce evidence that similarly situated persons were treated differently because of their race." Why did the court find defendant's evidence, which satisfied the trial judge, insufficient to meet this burden? Assume that you represent Lora and suspect that the officer acted based upon your client's race. What evidence could you present to prove it? How would you obtain it?

2.   *Defendant's Burden of Proof Under the Equal Protection Clause:* **United States v. Armstrong *and* McCleskey v. Kemp.** The *Lora* court's discrimination claim analysis was based on state constitutional law. The standards of proof it applied to proving race discrimination are, however, consistent with cases applying federal constitutional law, as the court's repeated citations to federal cases underscore. In *United States v. Armstrong*, 517 U.S. 456 (1996), and *McCleskey v. Kemp*, 481 U.S. 279 (1987), both of which you will study in detail in the next chapter, the United States Supreme Court explained the defendant's burden of proof under the Equal Protection Clause of the Fourteenth Amendment.

In *Armstrong*, the defendant was charged with distributing crack cocaine in violation of federal law. He proffered evidence at a suppression hearing that he was selected for federal prosecution because of his race, and he further sought discovery from the federal government regarding its criteria for prosecuting crack distribution. The defendant's evidence included hearsay testimony from a defense attorney and from a drug treatment counselor, which together suggested that whites and blacks both used crack cocaine at comparable rates but that only blacks were prosecuted in federal as opposed to state court. The district court found the evidence sufficiently probative of race discrimination that she ordered discovery from the government. When the government refused to comply with the discovery order, the district court dismissed the charges. The Supreme Court reversed, holding that the trial judge abused her discretion in ordering discovery from the government because the defendant had not first made a sufficient showing that the federal prosecutor failed to prosecute similarly situated white suspects. By "similarly situated," the Court apparently meant indistinguishable on any ground that might justify a prosecution of black defendants but not white defendants. After *Armstrong*, courts should not allow any inquiry into allegations of racial discrimination unless the defendant can already demonstrate that other similarly situated suspects of a different race were ignored.

In *McCleskey*, the Court reviewed allegations by a murder defendant that his death sentence was likely influenced by the race of his victim. The defendant introduced into evidence the "Baldus study," a sophisticated statistical study demonstrating that juries in the state systematically imposed the death penalty more often on defendants convicted of murdering white victims. The Baldus study also suggested that prosecutors sought the death penalty more often in cases involving white victims. Although the Court assumed the validity of the study, it rejected the defendant's claim, reasoning in part that, because the composition of each capital jury was unique, a study showing discrimination by past juries was not probative of the jury's motivations in the defendant's particular case. The Court also found the evidence of prosecutorial discrimination insufficient because it thought the sample was too small with respect to the particular prosecutor to show a statistically significant pattern of past discrimination.

3.   *Implications for Proving Racial Profiling.* Recall the *Lora* court's observation that the defendant's initial burden to show he was pulled over because of race is "admittedly daunting in some cases, but not impossible." Professor Forde-Mazrui explains why proving a police officer's traffic stop was racially motivated is, indeed, daunting under federal equal protection doctrine as set forth in *Armstrong* and *McCleskey*:

> [T]he broad array of traffic laws affords the officer, as an initial matter, the ability to readily identify a traffic violation as a justification for the stop. Furthermore, under *Whren*, the officer is permitted pretextually to single out motorists from observed traffic violators for objectives unrelated to the traffic violation, even without reasonable suspicion to support the ulterior objective. Accordingly, to prove a racial motive the defendant would have to establish that the officer ignored motorists of a different race who violated the same traffic laws, in the same or more egregious manner, and that there were no circumstances in defendant's case supporting an ulterior police motive for which the traffic stop served as a pretext. . . .

> Indeed, per *Armstrong*, the defendant would have to make a convincing showing that the officer ignored motorists similarly situated in all respects before a court would permit him to inquire, or otherwise discover from the officer, anything about the reasons he stopped the defendant or whether and why he had ignored other motorists. . . . Consider also that even if statistical evidence were available that suggested the police department for which the officer works has engaged in racial profiling, *McCleskey* suggests that courts would find such evidence inadequate unless it contained a sufficient sample of stops by the particular officer in question, and then only if non-racial grounds could be ruled out to explain the stop in the instant case. . . . [Moreover,] in determining the circumstances surrounding an allegedly discriminatory traffic stop, the trial judge would have to rely entirely on the respective accounts of the officer, who enjoys a presumption of good faith, and

a defendant, who is usually before the judge because evidence of more serious criminal activity was discovered during the traffic stop.

Kim Forde-Mazrui, *Ruling Out the Rule of Law*, 60 Vand. L. Rev. 1497, 1536–1537 (2007).

4.   *Compelling Interest.* If a defendant can prove that a police officer selected him for a stop or search based on race, then the police action is unconstitutional unless the government can demonstrate a sufficient justification for the discrimination. Recall that the Fourth Amendment only requires the use of race to be justified by "reasonable suspicion" or "probable cause," depending on the scope of the search and seizure. Under the Equal Protection Clause, in contrast, race discrimination by the state typically must satisfy the more demanding "strict scrutiny" test, which requires the government to prove that it was pursuing a compelling interest and that its use of race was necessary or narrowly tailored to achieve that interest. If a defendant can prove that the police stopped or searched him because of his race and the court applies strict scrutiny, can the government's interest in relying on race ever rise to the level of compelling?

The Supreme Court has upheld the use of race pursuant to strict scrutiny in only one context in which racial minorities have been the targets of racial profiling. In two cases decided during World War II, the Court upheld government policies targeting Japanese Americans, including their internment, explaining that "pressing public necessity"—namely national security—justified racial discrimination. *See Korematsu v. United States*, 343 U.S. 214 (1944); *Hirabayashi v. United States*, 320 U.S. 81 (1943).

The Court has also upheld the pursuit of a racially diverse student body as a compelling interest, and the Court has said in dicta that the state and its institutions have a compelling interest in remedying their own past discrimination. The Court has rejected as insufficiently compelling to justify race-based affirmative action the remedying of general societal discrimination and the provision of role models for school children. In view of these precedents, does the interest in crime control rise to the level of compelling? What if the crime being investigated is possession of marijuana or distribution of crack cocaine? What if the government's interest is in enforcing the immigration laws to protect border security by arresting unauthorized immigrants? What if the government's interest is to identify potential terrorists?

5.   *Narrow Tailoring.* Even if enforcing the criminal law were a compelling interest, could the government demonstrate that taking race into account was narrowly tailored to achieving that interest? In assessing whether the use of race is narrowly tailored, the Court considers whether the state could give less weight to race and still achieve the same goal without unduly sacrificing effectiveness. Thus, policies that use race as one of many factors are often regarded as better tailored than those that use race as the sole or predominant factor. Applying strict scrutiny, the Supreme Court also has placed the onus on state institutions to seriously consider race-neutral means of achieving their objectives. Would race-neutral factors alone adequately allow police to enforce laws against drug distribution, illegal immigration, or terrorism? Should courts ask how compelling the government interest is when deciding how narrowly tailored the use of race must be? *See* Kim Forde-Mazrui, The Constitutional Implications of Race-Neutral Affirmative Action, 88 Geo L.J. 2331 (2000) (arguing that courts applying strict scrutiny seem to adjust the strictness of the tailoring prong depending on how compelling the government's interest is, and vice versa).

6.   *Remedy for Equal Protection Violation?* If a court determines that a defendant's prosecution was brought about by evidence obtained by racially discriminatory police conduct that violated the Equal Protection Clause, what should the court do with the evidence? As the *Lora* court explained, when police violate the Fourth Amendment in discovering incriminating evidence, courts typically apply the exclusionary rule, precluding the evidence from being used in the prosecution. The result in many cases is that the charges must be dismissed. Although the exclusionary rule may not be constitutionally required, the Court has deemed it necessary to deter police from violating the Fourth Amendment and to protect the integrity of courts. The Supreme Court has never ruled on whether the exclusionary rule should apply in cases of evidence discovered from unlawful race discrimination, and lower courts have reached different conclusions. Compare *Commonwealth v. Lora, supra,* with *United States v. Nichols*, 512 F.3d 789, 794 (6th Cir. 2008) (doubting the propriety of the exclusionary rule for evidence resulting from equal protection violations). How should the Court resolve the question? Note that the exclusionary rule only protects people found in possession of incriminating evidence, whereas other remedies, such as civil lawsuits under 42 U.S.C. § 1983, allow innocent people subject to discriminatory stops to sue for damages. On the other hand, police officers enjoy qualified immunity when sued for damages, making lawsuits against them very difficult to win, even when a constitutional violation can be proven.

7.   *Data Collection.* A rare case in which a defendant successfully proved that a traffic stop was racially motivated was *State v. Soto*, 324 N.J. Super. 66 (1996), discussed in *Lora*. In *Soto*, defendants commissioned professionally designed surveys comparing the racial composition of traffic violators with that of motorists subjected to traffic stops along the particular stretch of highway on which the defendants had been stopped. The surveys, which the trial court found to be well designed and statistically reliable, demonstrated that blacks were stopped far in excess of what their driving patterns would predict, convincing the court that New Jersey State troopers had a "de facto policy" of stopping black motorists based on race. *Soto* shows that it is possible for a defendant to prove racial profiling if a police department systematically engages in the practice sufficient to generate an observable pattern on the specific road where the defendant was stopped, and if the defendant can afford to have that data documented. As *Lora* and the *Chavez* case it describes illustrate, however, proving that an individual officer discriminated by race on a particular occasion, even with statistical data, is a formidable task. For a discussion of controversies regarding the interpretation of stop/search data, see R. Richard Banks, *Beyond Profiling: Race, Policing and the Drug War*, 56 Stanford L. Rev. 571 (2004).

Notwithstanding the challenges of proving discrimination, the collection of demographic data on traffic stop patterns can nonetheless aid in a particular case or, perhaps more effectively, in generating political attention to the issue of racial profiling. Litigation has led to the generation of data in several states from consent decrees that settled lawsuits brought by private parties and the federal government, to orders by state attorneys general. In fact, the lawsuit challenging New York's stop and frisk program described previously was facilitated by court-mandated data collection by New York City police during *Terry* stops. Additionally, some state legislatures have enacted laws mandating data collection, including Massachusetts.

Does data collection seem like a promising approach to determining whether racial profiling is occurring? Is it reasonable to assume that police will accurately record the racial data of all motorists stopped, even when no arrest has been made? How should police determine a motorist's race if it is ambiguous? Assuming that police do record data as accurately as possible, what incentives does mandated data collection create for police conduct? If, for example, an officer knows his arrest records reveal a disproportionate number of black or Latino motorists charged with carrying drugs, would he have an incentive to selectively stop white motorists to search for drugs? Or to not stop black motorists when he otherwise would? Are these incentives troubling, irrelevant, or good?

8.   *Private Policing.* In February 2012, George Zimmerman pursued and shot and killed Trayvon Martin, an unarmed 17-year-old who was walking back to his father's home in a gated community in Sanford, Florida, after some sort of confrontation. Zimmerman claimed he pursued Martin in Zimmerman's capacity as the neighborhood watch coordinator. In July 2013, a criminal jury acquitted Zimmerman of murder and manslaughter charges. Although Zimmerman did not have reasonable suspicion of Martin, and evidence suggests he was motivated by Martin's race, no constitutional claims against Zimmerman for Martin's death were feasible under current constitutional law because Zimmerman acted in his personal capacity and was a private actor.

Non-state actors increasingly serve in quasi-formal law enforcement roles, however. The demand for the services of private security companies has steadily grown since the 1970s. "Today there are three times more private security guards as there are federal, state and local law-enforcement agents, said Dr. Simon Hakim, director of Temple University's Center for Competitive Government, adding that the estimate does not include corporate security." Jan Ransom, "More Residents Hiring Private Security as Police Budgets are Cut," Phila. Daily News (August 9, 2012) (2012 WLNR 16864890). The recent recession has required municipalities, large and small, to reduce their police forces, increasing demand among local residents to form voluntary watch programs and to hire private security firms to keep their neighborhoods safe. *Id.* Many of the security guards are off-duty police officers or former military. In one community in Illinois, private security guards even conduct traffic stops against resident motorists, a practice upheld by the Illinois Supreme Court. *See* "High Court's Disturbing Ruling on Private Cops," 1/31/13 Herald News (Joliet, Ill.) 12 (2013 WLNR 2417840). And, of course, private security firms have long provided security services to private businesses, such as office buildings and shopping malls.

The question arises whether the discretion of private actors that take on law enforcement-type responsibilities should be subject to constraints similar to those applicable to police. More specifically, should the law provide a remedy for a motorist, pedestrian, or customer who is selected for adverse treatment by a security guard without reasonable suspicion or because of race? To further explore this question, *see* Note 11 below.

9.   *Drafting Exercise.* Assume that Congress is considering a bill to prohibit some or all forms of racial profiling. Proponents of the law intend it to be comprehensive, applying to law enforcement agencies at the federal, state, and local levels, and addressing a range of contexts, including immigration enforcement, drug interdiction, and anti-terrorism efforts. You work for a civil rights organization that advocates for the interests of an ethnic community impacted by racial profiling, such as African Americans, Mexican Americans, Arabs, or South Asians. The Chair of the congressional committee holding hearings on the bill has asked your organization to submit a proposed draft, which your boss has asked you to help write. How would you define racial profiling? Would the statute allow for any exceptions? How would you design the law to be effective? What evidence would be sufficient for a defendant to prove racial profiling? What would the consequence be if profiling is proven? Explain your organizations' reasons for its drafting choices.

10. *Drafting Exercise.* Now consider instead that you work for an organization representing the relevant law enforcement agencies. How and why would the statute you draft differ, if at all? Would the statute you draft from this perspective be preferable as a matter of public policy to the one you would have drafted in response to Note 9?

11. *Advising Exercise.* Assume that, in the wake of the Trayvon Martin tragedy, Sanford, Florida (or another city of your choice) is considering enacting regulations for how security firms and voluntary watch programs conduct watches, security sweeps, and investigations. One proposed regulation would permit private actors to investigate or confront people only if they have the level of suspicion that would justify a *Terry* stop if conducted by the police. Another would forbid taking account of race in deciding whom to approach. Some local residents, businesses, and colleges oppose applying these provisions to private properties, such as shopping malls, office buildings, recreational facilities, apartment complexes, gated communities, and private college campuses, on the ground that a private property owner or association should have absolute discretion in deciding who can be on their property.

What would you advise the city council and why? If you would recommend placing some constraints on the discretion of private actors, would they be the same as the constitutional constraints on police discretion? Would they be stronger or weaker? What remedies should be available for violating the regulations?

E. THE PUZZLE OF RACE-BASED SUSPECT DESCRIPTIONS

We have seen that the Court has interpreted the Fourth Amendment to permit the use of race by police when it is probabilistically useful. In addition, existing doctrine places no limit on racial motivation if the observable non-racial facts establish sufficient suspicion or cause. We have also seen that courts now apply strict scrutiny under the Equal Protection Clause to racially discriminatory police actions, though it remains difficult for a defendant to prove that police acted with a racial motive. But are there any circumstances in which police reliance on race when deciding whom to stop, question, search, or arrest should not be subject to strict scrutiny? Consider the next case.

Brown v. City of Oneonta

221 F.3d 329 (2d. Cir. 2000).

■ JOHN M. WALKER, CIRCUIT JUDGE:

This case bears on the question of the extent to which law enforcement officials may utilize race in their investigation of a crime. We hold that under the circumstances of this case, where law enforcement officials possessed a description of a criminal suspect, even though that description consisted primarily of the suspect's race and gender, absent other evidence of discriminatory racial animus, they could act on the basis of that description without violating the Equal Protection Clause.

Police action is still subject to the constraints of the Fourth Amendment, however, and a description of race and gender alone will rarely provide reasonable suspicion justifying a police search or seizure. In this case, certain individual plaintiffs were subjected to seizures by defendant law enforcement officials, and those individuals may proceed with their claims under the Fourth Amendment.

BACKGROUND

I. *Factual Background*

Oneonta, a small town in upstate New York about sixty miles west of Albany, has about 10,000 full-time residents. In addition, some 7,500 students attend and reside at the State University of New York College at Oneonta ("SUCO"). The people in Oneonta are for the most part white. Fewer than three hundred blacks live in the town, and just two percent of the students at SUCO are black.

On September 4, 1992, shortly before 2:00 a.m., someone broke into a house just outside Oneonta and attacked a seventy-seven-year-old woman. The woman told the police who responded to the scene that she could not identify her assailant's face, but that he was wielding a knife; that he was a black man, based on her view of his hand and forearm; and that he was young, because of the speed with which he crossed her room.

She also told the police that, as they struggled, the suspect had cut himself on the hand with the knife. A police canine unit tracked the assailant's scent from the scene of the crime toward the SUCO campus, but lost the trail after several hundred yards.

The police immediately contacted SUCO and requested a list of its black male students. An official at SUCO supplied the list, and the police attempted to locate and question every black male student at SUCO. This endeavor produced no suspects. Then, over the next several days, the police conducted a "sweep" of Oneonta, stopping and questioning non-white persons on the streets and inspecting their hands for cuts. More than two hundred persons were questioned during that period, but no suspect was apprehended. Those persons whose names appeared on the SUCO list and those who were approached and questioned by the police, believing that they had been unlawfully singled out because of their race, decided to seek redress.

II. *Procedural History*

In early 1993, the SUCO students whose names appeared on the list and other persons questioned during the sweep of Oneonta filed this action in the district court against the City of Oneonta, the State of New York, SUCO, certain SUCO officials, and various police departments and police officers.

Plaintiffs asserted, under 42 U.S.C. § 1983, that defendants violated their rights under the Fourth Amendment and the Equal Protection Clause of the United States Constitution by questioning the black SUCO students and by conducting the sweep of Oneonta.

The district court dismissed one plaintiff's Fourth Amendment claim (because that plaintiff had not detailed the circumstances of his contact with law enforcement) and granted summary judgment for defendants on the remaining Fourth Amendment claims on the ground that the police encounters during the sweep were not seizures. The district court dismissed the equal protection claims, with leave to replead, on the ground that plaintiffs had not properly pleaded the existence of "a similarly-situated group of non-minority individuals [that] were treated differently by law enforcement officers during the investigation of a crime."

On July 18, 1994, the district court filed a second opinion. The district court granted defendants' motion to reconsider its ruling on the § 1981 claims, and dismissed those claims with leave to replead. As with the equal protection claims, the district court held that § 1981 claims "require a showing of specific instances . . . where the plaintiffs were singled out for unlawful oppression in contrast to others similarly situated."

DISCUSSION

I.   *Equal Protection Claims*

[Plaintiffs] contend that defendants utilized an express racial classification by stopping and questioning plaintiffs solely on the basis of their race. Plaintiffs assert that the district court erred in requiring them to plead the existence of a similarly situated group of non-minority individuals that were treated differently in the investigation of a crime.

When pleading a violation of the Equal Protection Clause, it is sometimes necessary to allege the existence of a similarly situated group that was treated differently. For example, if a plaintiff seeks to prove selective prosecution on the basis of his race, he "must show that similarly situated individuals of a different race were not prosecuted." *United States v. Armstrong,* 517 U.S. 456, 465 (1996).

Plaintiffs are correct, however, that it is not necessary to plead the existence of a similarly situated non-minority group when challenging a law or policy that contains an express, racial classification. These classifications are subject to strict judicial scrutiny, and strict scrutiny analysis in effect addresses the question of whether people of different races are similarly situated with regard to the law or policy at issue. This does not avail plaintiffs in this case, however, because they have not identified any law or policy that contains an express racial classification.

Plaintiffs do not allege that upon hearing that a violent crime had been committed, the police used an established profile of violent criminals to determine that the suspect must have been black. Nor do they allege that the defendant law enforcement agencies have a regular policy based upon racial stereotypes that all black Oneonta residents be questioned whenever a violent crime is reported. In short, plaintiffs' factual premise is not supported by the pleadings: they were not questioned solely on the basis of their race. They were questioned on the altogether legitimate basis of a physical description given by the victim of a crime. Defendants' policy was race-neutral on its face; their policy was to investigate crimes by interviewing the victim, getting a description of the assailant, and seeking out persons who matched that description. This description contained not only race, but also gender and age, as well as the possibility of a cut on the hand. In acting on the description provided by the victim of the assault—a description that included race as one of several elements—defendants did not engage in a suspect racial classification that would draw strict scrutiny. The description, which originated not with the state but with the victim, was a legitimate classification within which potential suspects might be found.

Plaintiffs cite to cases holding that initiating an investigation of a person based solely upon that person's race violates the Equal Protection Clause. In *United States v. Avery,* 137 F.3d 343 (6th Cir. 1997), the defendant claimed that he was stopped by law enforcement solely on the basis of his race. While the court affirmed his conviction, citing other factors utilized by the police in choosing to follow the defendant, the court stated that "[i]f law enforcement ... takes steps to initiate an investigation of a citizen based solely upon that citizen's race, without more, then a violation of the Equal Protection Clause has occurred." *Id.* at 355. Here, the police were not routinely patrolling an airport for possible drug smuggling, as in *Avery*.[9] Instead, it is alleged that they were searching for a particular perpetrator of a violent assault, relying in their search on the victim's description of the perpetrator as a young black man with a cut on his hand. As the police therefore are not alleged to have investigated "based solely upon ... race, without more," *id.*, plaintiffs have failed to state an actionable claim under the Equal Protection Clause. Police practices that mirror defendants' behavior in this case—attempting to question every person fitting a general description—may well have a disparate impact on small minority groups in towns such as Oneonta. If there are few black residents who fit the general description, for example, it would be more useful for the police to use race to find a black suspect than a white one. It may also be practicable for law enforcement to attempt to contact every black person who was a young male, but quite impossible to contact every such white person. If a community were primarily black with very few white residents and the search were for a young white male, the impact would be reversed. The Equal Protection Clause, however, has long been interpreted to extend to governmental action that has a disparate impact on a minority group only when that action was undertaken with discriminatory intent. Without additional evidence of discriminatory animus, the disparate impact of an investigation such as the one in this case is insufficient to sustain an equal protection claim.

In this case, plaintiffs do not sufficiently allege discriminatory intent. They do allege that at least one woman, Sheryl Champen, was stopped by law enforcement officials during their sweep of Oneonta. This allegation is significant because it may indicate that defendants considered race more strongly than other parts of the victim's description. However, this single incident, to the extent that it was

---

[9] The court's opinion in *Avery* also contained dicta to the effect that even if the police receive a "tip" consisting solely of a person's race, "and the officers pursue investigations of everyone of that race, their action may be found constitutionally impermissible." 137 F.3d at 354 n.5; *but cf. Buffkins v. City of Omaha*, 922 F.2d 465, 468 (8th Cir.1990) (holding that detention of black woman at an airport did not amount to racial discrimination under § 1981 because "her race matched the racial description of the person described in the tip"). We do not know if the "tip" contemplated by the *Avery* court is similar to a victim's description of an assailant; as the *Avery* court itself pointed out in somewhat contradictory fashion, where there is a tip from an outside source, "the officers obviously cannot control the race of the person they investigate and ultimately contact. Hence, their selection of that person as a target of investigation does not amount to an equal protection violation." 137 F.3d at 354 n.5. In any event, this non-binding dicta from a non-binding circuit court does not persuade us that the police action in this case violated the Equal Protection Clause.

related to the investigation, is not sufficient in our view to support an equal protection claim under the circumstances of this case.

We are not blind to the sense of frustration that was doubtlessly felt by those questioned by the police during this investigation. The actions of the police were understandably upsetting to the innocent plaintiffs who were stopped to see if they fit the victim's description of the suspect. The plaintiffs have argued that there is little difference between what occurred here and unlawful profiling based on a racial stereotype. While we disagree as a matter of law and believe that the conduct of the police in the circumstances presented here did not constitute a violation of the equal protection rights of the plaintiffs, we do not establish any rule that would govern circumstances giving rise to liability that are not present in this case. Any such rule will have to wait for the appropriate case. Nor do we hold that under no circumstances may the police, when acting on a description of a suspect, violate the equal protection rights of non-suspects, whether or not the police only stop persons conforming to the description of the suspect given by the victim.

We are also not unmindful of the impact of this police action on community relations. Law enforcement officials should always be cognizant of the impressions they leave on a community, lest distrust of law enforcement undermine its effectiveness. Yet our role is not to evaluate whether the police action in question was the appropriate response under the circumstances, but to determine whether what was done violated the Equal Protection Clause. We hold that it did not, and therefore affirm the district court's dismissal of plaintiffs' § 1983 claims alleging equal protection violations.

III. *Fourth Amendment Claims*

Plaintiffs' § 1983 claims also allege a violation of their Fourth Amendment rights during defendants' sweep of Oneonta. The district court dismissed many of these claims and granted summary judgment for defendants on other claims because, in its view, plaintiffs had not been subject to "seizures" under the Fourth Amendment. For the reasons that follow, we vacate the summary judgment against plaintiffs Jamel Champen, Jean Cantave, Ricky Brown, and Sheryl Champen, and affirm the district court's dismissal or grant of summary judgment with regard to the remaining claims.

In *Terry v. Ohio,* 392 U.S. 1, 24–27 (1968), the Supreme Court established that the Fourth Amendment does not prohibit the police from stopping a person for questioning when the police have a reasonable suspicion that a person may be armed and dangerous, even when that suspicion does not amount to the probable cause necessary to make an arrest. Defendants would have difficulty demonstrating reasonable suspicion in this case, and indeed, they do not attempt to do so. Defendants instead argue that the district court correctly determined that no reasonable suspicion was necessary, because no seizure—not even a *Terry* stop—occurred in this case.

To prevail on a § 1983 claim under the Fourth Amendment based on an allegedly unlawful *Terry* stop, a plaintiff first must prove that he was seized. "[A] seizure does not occur simply because a police officer approaches an individual and asks a few questions." *Florida v. Bostick,* 501 U.S. 429, 434 (1991). However, a seizure does occur when, "by means of physical force or show of authority," *United States v. Hooper,* 935 F.2d 484, 491 (2d Cir.1991) (quoting *Terry,* 392 U.S. at 19 n.16), a police officer detains a person such that "a reasonable person would have believed that he was not free to leave," *id*. Pertinent factors identifying a police seizure can include

> the threatening presence of several officers; the display of a weapon; physical touching of the person by the officer; language or tone indicating that compliance with the officer was compulsory; prolonged retention of a person's personal effects, such as airplane tickets or identification; and a request by the officer to accompany him to the police station or a police room.

Hooper, 935 F.2d at 491. Whether a seizure occurred is a question of law to be reviewed *de novo,* while the factual findings underlying that determination are reviewed for clear error.

Jamel Champen, in his affidavit, alleges that a police officer pointed a spotlight at him and said "What, are you stupid? Come here. I want to talk to you." He was then told to show his hands. While it is arguably a close case, we conclude that a reasonable person in Champen's circumstances would have considered the police officer's request to be compulsory. Accordingly, we hold that Champen was seized and vacate the summary judgment for defendants on his Fourth Amendment claim.

Jean Cantave avers that he was driving in Oneonta when he was pulled over by a police car with a siren and flashing lights. Cantave was ordered out of the car and instructed to place his hands on top of the car. The Supreme Court has stated that the "[t]emporary detention of individuals during the stop of an automobile by the police, even if only for a brief period and for a limited purpose, constitutes a 'seizure' of 'persons'" under the Fourth Amendment. *Whren v. United States,* 517 U.S. 806, 809 (1996). Under *Whren,* we have no doubt that Cantave was seized, and accordingly we vacate the summary judgment for defendants on Cantave's claim.

Ricky Brown's affidavit states that three police officers stopped him on the street. The police officers questioned him about whether he was a student and where he had been. They asked for his identification card, passed it around, and returned it to Brown. At one point, the officers "formed a circle around" Brown. When Brown asked if he had permission to leave, they told him that he was free to go. When Brown started to leave, however, one officer told him to come back and asked to see his hands. We conclude that a reasonable person in Brown's position—directed to return by one of the police officers who, just moments before, had encircled him—would not have felt free to leave. We therefore vacate the district court's grant of summary judgment on Brown's claim.

Sheryl Champen alleges that a police officer approached her at a bus station and told her that if she wanted to board the bus for which she was waiting, she would have to produce some identification. This contact is plainly a seizure under the caselaw because the police officer made it clear that he was detaining her. Accordingly, we vacate the summary judgment for defendants on Sheryl Champen's claim.

Raishawn Morris alleges that he encountered two police officers in his dorm lobby, and that they asked him to show them his hands. This does not rise to the level of a seizure, and we affirm the summary judgment for defendants on Morris's claim.

Finally, we also affirm the district court's dismissal of the remaining Fourth Amendment claims. The other plaintiffs did not submit any affidavits describing the details of their contacts with defendants, and the complaint fails to allege facts stating a claim that they were seized by defendants.

NOTES AND QUESTIONS

1. **Equal Protection Reasoning.** Why does the *Oneonta* court conclude that race in a suspect description does not constitute a "racial classification" subject to strict scrutiny under the Equal Protection Clause? The court also necessarily held that a race-based suspect description did not constitute a facially neutral policy applied with a discriminatory purpose. Did the police classify by race or act with a racially discriminatory purpose when they investigated black Oneonta residents regarding the alleged burglary? Why or why not?

2. **Fourth Amendment Reasoning.** The *Oneonta* court rejected the Fourth Amendment claims of most plaintiffs on the ground that being questioned and asked to voluntarily show one's hands did not generally constitute a search or seizure under the Fourth Amendment. For most plaintiffs, then, the court ruled that the police questioning posed no Fourth Amendment or equal protection concerns. Does this result make sense, especially given that the police questioned hundreds of black men? The court did remand a few Fourth Amendment claims for further proceedings on the ground that these few plaintiffs alleged facts supporting a claim that police had coercively detained them for a short period of time. If, on remand before the trial court, plaintiffs succeed on this part of the analysis, the next step for the court would be to determine whether the police had reasonable suspicion to stop and question these plaintiffs and to inspect their hands. Did they? Argue for the plaintiffs. Argue for the City of Oneonta. How should the trial court rule?

3. *Racial Profiles Versus Race-Based Suspect Descriptions.* The
Oneonta court's holding that race in a suspect description is not subject to
strict scrutiny under the Equal Protection Clause is consistent with other
courts that have confronted the issue. Indeed, no court, legislature, or scholar
(save one), has contended that race-based suspect descriptions should be
scrutinized as race discrimination for equal protection purposes. In contrast,
most courts and commentators today believe that police reliance on race as
a factor in predicting who might be committing a crime, whether as part of a
formal profile or an individual officer's suspicions, does constitute race
discrimination presumptively forbidden by the Equal Protection Clause. A
sharp distinction between racial profiles is also evidenced in police training
manuals and in state and federal legislation explaining the permissible use
of race in detaining or apprehending suspects. Such sources uniformly
permit law enforcement to rely on race in a suspect description and, almost
as uniformly, forbid any use of race as part of a criminal profile. Indeed,
police training manuals that prohibit racial profiling often *require* police to
solicit information about a suspect's race (and sex) when interviewing a
victim or witness to a crime. Why is profiling so widely condemned in law
and politics, whereas police reliance on race-based suspect descriptions is
accepted as so obviously legitimate as to scarcely require justification? In
what ways do racial profiles and race-based suspect descriptions differ from
one another such that their different treatment by the law is justified?
Consider the following possibilities:

a. *Accuracy:* Suspect descriptions are probably more accurate
than profiles because they are based on direct personal
observation of a particular perpetrator during a specific
incident known to have occurred, rather than on probabilistic
or statistical data that estimates the likelihood that a type of
person may have committed or will commit a certain crime.

b. *Individuals v. Groups:* Suspect descriptions treat suspects as
individuals, whereas profiles rely on generalizations that
involve gross stereotypes that stigmatize entire racial groups.

c. *Scope of Impact:* Profiles may impact more people by
promoting a wide-ranging, statistics-based investigation
intentionally applied to a broad swath of different people,
whereas suspect descriptions aim to identify a single assailant.
To the extent both practices result in false positives, *i.e.,*
investigating innocent people, profiles may tend to burden
more of them.

d. *Multiple Factors:* Suspect descriptions typically include race
among several factors, whereas profiles are often described as
targeting individuals solely on the basis of race. The *Oneonta*
court, for example, emphasized that the plaintiffs "were not
questioned solely on the basis of their race," and later observed
that the description also included "gender and age, as well as
the possibility of a cut on the hand," and finally that the
description "included race as one of several elements."

e.   *Appearance v. Criminal Propensity:* Suspect descriptions treat race purely as a physical trait, like hair color or height, whereas profiles accord a deeper meaning to race, positing how people of a certain race behave rather than just how they appear.

f.   *Witness as Source:* The racial information in a suspect description is not attributable to the state but rather derives from the victim or witness, a private party. The Oneonta court, for example, noted that the description "originated not with the state but with the victim." Profiles, by contrast, are typically developed by law enforcement.

g.   *Equal Application:* Race-based suspect descriptions are not discriminatory because they do not intentionally treat racial groups differently, provided that police use race in a suspect description in the same manner regardless of the race identified. Thus, in *Oneonta*, although the officers would probably not inspect the hands of virtually all the white men in town had the assailant been white, the court assumes that police would have done so if the town's racial demographics had been flipped: "If a community were primarily black with very few white residents and the search were for a young white male, the impact would be reversed."

Do the foregoing distinctions justify subjecting racial profiles to strict scrutiny while deeming race-based suspect descriptions virtually *per se* acceptable without any need for justification?

Professor Richard Banks has provided the most extensive examination of this question. *See* R. Richard Banks, *Race-Based Suspect Selection and Colorblind Equal Protection Doctrine and Discourse*, 48 UCLA L. Rev. 1075 (2001). Banks is also the one scholar who has seriously questioned the difference in the legal treatment accorded these two uses of race. First, Banks argues, both practices may be equally beneficial to law enforcement and harmful to innocent (and guilty) members of minority racial groups. In either case, a person is suspected of being a criminal in part because of his race. Profiles can also be highly accurate and rely on many factors, while suspect descriptions can be highly unreliable accounts of just a few factors. For example, a sophisticated profile based on reliable empirical data of criminal activity patterns, and which includes multiple appearance and behavioral factors in addition to race, can be more accurate in predicting whether an observed suspect is a criminal than an eye-witness description by a traumatized crime victim subject to well-documented forms of observational and recollection errors. With respect to the scope of impact, although a single profile might generally be used against more people than a single suspect description, there have been several cases in which one suspect description resulted in subjecting numerous innocent people to coercive investigation. Moreover, over time, police will often have many more suspect descriptions, including for crimes that remain unsolved, with which to justify stopping for questioning individuals on the street or in vehicles.

Police brutality and other mistreatment have also been linked in substantial number to both uses of race. With respect to stereotypes about criminal propensity, a suspect description may reflect a victim's biased but false conclusion that her assailant was black, or may lead a police officer to more readily accept her description because of his stereotypical assumptions. Conversely, a profile need not assume particular races have an inherent propensity to commit crime. As Banks observes:

> The stereotypes reflected in racial profiles are not clearly, and certainly not always, of the propensity type. For example, racial profiles are often based on the fact that specific criminal gangs dominate drug smuggling and that criminal gangs are almost always monoracial. A view that African Americans are disproportionately represented among drug couriers, in this account, would not imply that African Americans are more criminally minded than other groups, for example, but simply that the gangs known to smuggle drugs accept only African Americans as members.

Banks, *supra,* at 1098.

With respect to the court's equal protection analysis, are you persuaded that Oneonta's police would confront the town's white men in the same manner as the police confronted black men if whites were a minority of the town's population? Secondly, even if police would have behaved in that way, the claim that equal application of a race-based policy makes the policy nondiscriminatory would seem to be foreclosed by equal protection doctrine. *Loving v. Virginia,* 388 U.S. 1 (1967), for instance, rejected the state's argument that its anti-miscegenation law was not discriminatory because it applied equally to people of any race. Nor has the Court permitted states to act upon the racial intentions of private parties. For example, courts cannot enforce private racial covenants, public universities cannot administer "whites only" privately-funded scholarships, and state election boards cannot facilitate the racial preferences of voters by indicating candidates' race on ballots. Finally, both practices reinforce in police officers' minds an association between race and crime and, to the extent suspect descriptions are disseminated through the media, in the public's mind as well.

Banks also contends that the boundary between the use of profiles and suspect descriptions is not nearly as distinct as often assumed. The fuzziness of the boundary is highlighted by criminal enterprises, such as street gangs or terrorist organizations. Consider a crime police know was committed by a particular, monoracial gang (as most gangs are). If police only questioned people whose race matched that of gang members, would they be employing a suspect description or a gang profile? What if there is no particular crime being investigated but police know the gang has committed crimes in the past and is likely to do so again? Would police stops of people whose race fits the gang's race be employing a suspect description or a profile? Or consider if airline security personnel have intelligence that a particular individual, described as Arab, male, and bearded, is plotting to attack the United States. Would it be profiling or acting on a suspect description to subject every Arab-looking male coming through every airport to extra scrutiny? *See* R. Richard Banks, *Racial Profiling and Antiterrorism Efforts*, 89 Cornell L. Rev. 1201 (2004) Does the characterization matter?

Banks further observes that, even if race-based suspect descriptions can often be distinguished from profiles and may generally cause less harm, equal protection doctrine still requires subjecting them to strict scrutiny. R. Richard Banks, *Race-Based Suspect Selection and Color Blind Doctrine and Discourse*, 48 UCLA L. Rev 1075 (2001). The Court has insisted in other contexts that all government uses of race, however seemingly benign, must be subject to strict scrutiny to ensure that they are, in fact, benign. If the inclusion of race in a suspect description were indeed necessary to apprehend a dangerous criminal, then, according to the tenets of the doctrine, the court should review the description in question under strict scrutiny to confirm its necessity. Do you think race-based suspect descriptions should be prohibited or subject to strict scrutiny? What are the costs of exempting race-based suspect descriptions from strict scrutiny? What would the consequences be if they were subject to strict scrutiny?

4.   ***Applying Strict Scrutiny.*** If suspect descriptions were subject to strict scrutiny, would they survive? We considered in the Notes following *Commonwealth v. Lora* whether crime control was compelling, at least with respect to certain crimes, and whether some attention to race in a criminal profile could be narrowly tailored. Presumably, whether race-based suspect descriptions advance a compelling interest raises similar questions. What about tailoring? Are suspect descriptions narrowly tailored? What would make a description sufficiently tailored to withstand strict scrutiny? How tailored was the description in *Oneonta*? What if the crime in the town of Oneonta had been a murder but the description by an eye witness was the same? What if the crime had been underage drinking?

5.   ***Our Constitution Is Colorblind?*** Is it realistic to expect a victim not to report the race of her assailant or to prohibit a police officer who possesses a race-based description to ignore race in deciding whether someone is worth investigating? If apprehending criminals is one of government's most important functions, and taking account of race is necessary to achieve it, why do our legal and political systems refuse to acknowledge that police do classify suspects by race and that such a practice is important and necessary? Professor Banks offers this explanation:

> [R]ecognition of suspect description reliance as a racial classification, even if solely in an unusual case such as *Oneonta*, would undermine colorblindness as the animating principle of equal protection doctrine with respect to race. The primacy of colorblindness would be imperiled whatever the outcome of the strict scrutiny test. Conversely, the continued force of colorblindness as constitutional principle depends on suppression of awareness of the ways in which state actors use race and of the extent to which courts permit them to do so.

Banks, *supra,* at 1080.

Do you agree that subjecting race-based suspect descriptions to strict scrutiny would imperil the primacy of colorblindness in equal protection doctrine? Would it not just acknowledge that, although colorblindness is strongly preferred, some exceptions are justified? What effect might such an acknowledgement have on the legality of race-based policing more generally or race-based government action in other contexts? What effect might it have on our assessment of race-based decision-making by private actors? Would such effects be problematic or desirable?

6.   *Drafting Exercise.* Recall the first two exercises at the end of the prior section on equal protection asking you to draft legislation against racial profiling. Assume that the legislation should also include a section addressing the proper use of race in a suspect description. What should it say? Would it forbid police from using race in a suspect description, allow it without any restriction, or something in between? If the law should ban the use of race in a suspect description, how would it be enforced?

F.   CONCLUDING NOTES ON RACE AND POLICING

The court in *Commonwealth v. Lora*, 451 Mass. 425, 446 (2008), observed: "the important responsibility of eliminating racial considerations in the day-to-day enforcement of our laws lies principally with the executive branch of government." This acknowledgement of the limited capacity of courts in preventing discriminatory policing is consistent with the case law reviewed in this chapter. As we have seen, civil rights proponents have persuaded the courts to develop doctrines designed to limit the risk of arbitrary and discriminatory law enforcement by requiring legislatures to define crimes with adequate specificity; by requiring police to have objective justification to believe criminal activity is afoot before coercively investigating a person; and by presumptively prohibiting racial profiling. We have also seen, however, that despite these doctrines, the role of race in law enforcement remains a serious concern and one that courts are unable or unwilling to prevent absent clear evidence in a specific case. It is probably unrealistic to expect courts to be the principal safeguard of individual rights, including against race discrimination. Courts have limited competence and capacity to affect the behavior of police, at least without significant regulation and investment from the political branches of government to which police are most responsive. We saw, for example, how legislation and executive orders mandating racial data collection can aid in deterring racial profiling in ways that courts are ill-equipped to do on their own. For an argument that courts cannot meaningfully protect individual rights from police abuse without significant legislative and executive regulation, *see* Rachel Harmon, *The Problem of Policing*, 110 Mich. L. Rev. 761 (2012).

Based on the materials reviewed in this chapter, how would you grade the courts' performance in minimizing racially discriminatory policing? To the extent it has been inadequate, is the problem in the doctrines as conceived in theory or as implemented in practice? Or are courts simply incapable of adequately protecting minorities from racially discriminatory policing?

A primary concern of this chapter has been constraining police discretion in order to limit racially discriminatory law enforcement. The extent to which racially selective enforcement is responsible for the racially disparate impact of the criminal justice system, especially the War on Drugs, remains an open question, however. Professor Richard Banks, while acknowledging that racial profiling is objectionable, argues that "policymakers should abandon efforts to ferret out and eliminate racial profiling in drug interdiction. Instead, policy analyses should consider the race-related consequences of the drug war, without regard to whether officers engage in racial profiling." R. Richard Banks, *Beyond Profiling: Race, Policing, and the Drug War*, 56 Stan. L. Rev. 571, 572 (2004). Banks argues that legislative policies, such as the criminalization and heavy punishment of drug offenses, and abusive law enforcement tactics regardless of racial motivation, account for the racialization of the criminal justice system and the prisons it feeds, the instability of low-income minority communities, and the mistrust among residents of those communities toward police. If race were eliminated from the minds of police, Banks contends, the harmful racial consequences of the War on Drugs would largely persist. Conversely, if the substantive criminal law were narrower in scope and more just in its penalties, and if law enforcement practices were more respectful of the dignity and privacy of those investigated, the prospects for more order and stability in minority communities would be enhanced. "My primary purpose," Banks concludes, is "to counter the tendency to reduce questions of race, policing, and the drug war to questions of racial profiling. However politically appealing that approach, it may obscure rather than clarify potential remedies for problems that deserve immediate attention." *Id.* at 603.

What's your reaction to Banks' claim? Do you believe that judicial and legislative efforts to eliminate racially selective policing are misdirected or ineffective and therefore should be abandoned? Or should such efforts instead be strengthened? How?

CHAPTER 8

CRIMINAL TRIAL AND PUNISHMENT

I. INTRODUCTION

If you have not already done so, you should read the introduction to the previous chapter: "Introduction to Race and Criminal Justice". It details the stark racial disparities in America's prison population. That chapter also explores various ways in which policing practices plausibly contribute to those disparities and how law does and should address those practices. This chapter examines the adjudicative stage of the criminal justice process, from the initiation of charges by the prosecution through trial and sentencing. At every stage, the racial disparities that exist at the front end of the system increase.

Evaluating the role of race in the adjudicative process should begin with an understanding of the three principal goals of that process: securing accuracy, fairness, and legitimacy. How can the adjudicative process be designed to accurately determine the facts of an alleged crime and, ultimately, a defendant's factual guilt or innocence? Is the trial process fair—a standard that includes a variety of concerns, including whether the defendant has received a fair opportunity to participate in the trial process and challenge the prosecution's evidence, and whether the defendant has been treated humanely? Finally, to what degree do the defendant and the public regard the process as fair and impartial?

The question of race in this setting thus begins with an examination of how the system's treatment of race advances or impedes accuracy, fairness, and legitimacy in the trial and punishment of crime. But we must also ask whether achieving racial justice requires the system to deviate from these goals, or whether racial justice should be factored into our understanding of the goals? For example, does a prosecutor's attention to race in formulating charging decisions, or a defense attorney's attention to race in questioning or selecting juries advance or impede the principal goals of the adjudicative process? Regardless, does such attention to race otherwise advance or impede racial justice? If attention or inattention to race advances racial justice but conflicts with some other goal, such as accuracy, which value should the system privilege?

As with the previous chapter on policing, a principal theme of this chapter is how to manage the discretion of key decision-makers, such as prosecutors and jurors, so as to promote the legitimate goals of the criminal justice system while limiting the risk that such discretion will be exercised in a racially biased manner. Other more particular questions that will arise include whether the race of decision-makers influences or at least predicts their impartiality; whether the race of defendants and victims influences jury and legislative decision-making; whether racially biased decision-makers can be identified through individualized questioning; and whether the law should allow race to play a role in selecting jurors or in predicting the dangerousness of defendants and, if so, how. The chapter also considers whether the racially disparate impact of a penalty alone makes the penalty at least presumptively objectionable. The chapter begins with prosecutorial charging, then considers key aspects of jury selection and decision-making, and concludes with sentencing.

II. PROSECUTORIAL CHARGING

Prosecutors play an increasingly significant role in the criminal justice system. They are charged with representing the public, consistent with justice and the rule of law, by holding accountable those who commit crimes. They make critical decisions, such as whether to initiate prosecution and on what charges, whether to do so by complaint or grand jury indictment, whether to accept a plea to lesser charges or dismiss charges altogether, whether to recommend bail and for how much or whether to request pre-trial detention, and whether to seek the death penalty. Although, traditionally, sentencing was exclusively a judicial function, the rise of mandatory minimum sentences and guideline systems has shifted an increasingly large amount of power to prosecutors to determine a defendant's ultimate punishment. In the case of federal prosecutors, they also choose whether to bring charges in federal court against a defendant who is typically already eligible for prosecution in state court.

Empirical studies reveal that a variety of prosecutorial decisions have a racially disparate impact against black and Latino defendants. Such decisions include accepting pleas to lesser charges, entering diversion agreements, and dismissing charges altogether in the "interest of justice." Prosecutors are also more likely to seek higher bail or pre-trial detention for minority defendants. With respect to the death penalty, prosecutors are statistically more likely to bring capital charges against defendants who are black and, especially, against defendants accused of killing white victims.

Federal prosecutions also appear to have a racial tilt. Statistics demonstrate that the overwhelming majority of federal crack prosecutions are against black defendants. This is true despite studies indicating that the percentage of whites who use crack is much closer to that of blacks than conviction rates suggest, and that state prosecutions against whites for crack offenses are more common than federal prosecutions. From 1988 to 1994, for example, the United States Attorney's Office for Los Angeles and six surrounding counties prosecuted hundreds of black and Latino defendants, but no whites. During the same period, several hundred state crack prosecutions were brought against whites in California. Because federal law imposes much more severe penalties for drug crimes than state law does, the disproportionate racial impact of federal crack prosecutions means that, on average, more blacks are serving time for drug offenses than whites are, and they are serving more time for similar conduct.

The following case involves an attempt to address the risk of racial discrimination in the exercise of prosecutorial discretion.

United States v. Armstrong

Supreme Court of the United States, 1996.
517 U.S. 456.

■ CHIEF JUSTICE REHNQUIST delivered the opinion of the Court.

In this case, we consider the showing necessary for a defendant to be entitled to discovery on a claim that the prosecuting attorney singled him out for prosecution on the basis of his race. We conclude that respondents failed to satisfy the threshold showing: They failed to show that the Government declined to prosecute similarly situated suspects of other races.

In April 1992, respondents were indicted in the United States District Court for the Central District of California on charges of conspiring to possess with intent to distribute more than 50 grams of cocaine base (crack) and conspiring to distribute the same, in violation of 21 U.S.C. §§ 841 and 846, and federal firearms offenses. For three months prior to the indictment, agents of the Federal Bureau of Alcohol, Tobacco, and Firearms and the Narcotics Division of the Inglewood, California, Police Department had infiltrated a suspected crack distribution ring by using three confidential informants. On seven separate occasions during this period, the informants had bought a total of 124.3 grams of crack from respondents and witnessed respondents carrying firearms during the sales. The agents searched the hotel room in which the sales were transacted, arrested respondents Armstrong and Hampton in the room, and found more crack and a loaded gun. The agents later arrested the other respondents as part of the ring.

In response to the indictment, respondents filed a motion for discovery or for dismissal of the indictment, alleging that they were selected for federal prosecution because they are black. In support of their motion, they offered only an affidavit by a "Paralegal Specialist," employed by the Office of the Federal Public Defender representing one of the respondents. The only allegation in the affidavit was that, in every one of the 24 § 841 or § 846 cases closed by the office during 1991, the defendant was black. Accompanying the affidavit was a "study" listing the 24 defendants, their race, whether they were prosecuted for dealing cocaine as well as crack, and the status of each case.

The Government opposed the discovery motion, arguing, among other things, that there was no evidence or allegation "that the Government has acted unfairly or has prosecuted non-black defendants or failed to prosecute them." The District Court granted the motion. It ordered the Government (1) to provide a list of all cases from the last three years in which the Government charged both cocaine and firearms offenses, (2) to identify the race of the defendants in those cases, (3) to identify what levels of law enforcement were involved in the investigations of those cases, and (4) to explain its criteria for deciding to prosecute those defendants for federal cocaine offenses.

The Government moved for reconsideration of the District Court's discovery order. With this motion it submitted affidavits and other evidence to explain why it had chosen to prosecute respondents and why respondents' study did not support the inference that the Government was singling out blacks for cocaine prosecution. The federal and local agents participating in the case alleged in affidavits that race played no role in their investigation. An Assistant United States Attorney explained in an affidavit that the decision to prosecute met the general criteria for prosecution, because

> there was over 100 grams of cocaine base involved, over twice the threshold necessary for a ten year mandatory minimum sentence; there were multiple sales involving multiple defendants, thereby indicating a fairly substantial crack cocaine ring; . . . there were multiple federal firearms violations intertwined with the narcotics trafficking; the overall evidence in the case was extremely strong, including audio and videotapes of defendants; . . . and several of the defendants had criminal histories including narcotics and firearms violations.

The Government also submitted sections of a published 1989 Drug Enforcement Administration report which concluded that "[l]arge-scale, interstate trafficking networks controlled by Jamaicans, Haitians and Black street gangs dominate the manufacture and distribution of crack." J. Featherly & E. Hill, Crack Cocaine Overview 1989.

In response, one of respondents' attorneys submitted an affidavit alleging that an intake coordinator at a drug treatment center had told her that there are "an equal number of caucasian users and dealers to minority users and dealers." Respondents also submitted an affidavit from a criminal defense attorney alleging that in his experience many nonblacks are prosecuted in state court for crack offenses, and a newspaper article reporting that federal "crack criminals . . . are being punished far more severely than if they had been caught with powder cocaine, and almost every single one of them is black," Newton, Harsher

Crack Sentences Criticized as Racial Inequity, Los Angeles Times, Nov. 23, 1992, p. 1.

The District Court denied the motion for reconsideration. When the Government indicated it would not comply with the court's discovery order, the court dismissed the case.[1]

A divided three-judge panel of the Court of Appeals for the Ninth Circuit reversed, holding that, because of the proof requirements for a selective-prosecution claim, defendants must "provide a colorable basis for believing that 'others similarly situated have not been prosecuted' " to obtain discovery. The Court of Appeals voted to rehear the case en banc, and the en banc panel affirmed the District Court's order of dismissal, holding that "a defendant is not required to demonstrate that the government has failed to prosecute others who are similarly situated."

[The Supreme Court first held that Federal Rule of Criminal Procedure 16, which governs discovery in criminal cases, does not grant defendants discovery based on a claim of selective prosecution. The Court then proceeded to address whether the defendants' claim for discovery was properly upheld by the Court of Appeals as a matter of constitutional law.]

Our cases delineating the necessary elements to prove a claim of selective prosecution have taken great pains to explain that the standard is a demanding one. These cases afford a "background presumption," that the showing necessary to obtain discovery should itself be a significant barrier to the litigation of insubstantial claims.

In order to dispel the presumption that a prosecutor has not violated equal protection, a criminal defendant must present "clear evidence to the contrary." *Chemical Foundation, supra,* at 14–15. Judicial deference to the decisions of these executive officers rests in part on an assessment of the relative competence of prosecutors and courts. "Such factors as the strength of the case, the prosecution's general deterrence value, the Government's enforcement priorities, and the case's relationship to the Government's overall enforcement plan are not readily susceptible to the kind of analysis the courts are competent to undertake." *Wayte,* 470 U. S., at 607. It also stems from a concern not to unnecessarily impair the performance of a core executive constitutional function. "Examining the basis of a prosecution delays the criminal proceeding, threatens to chill law enforcement by subjecting the prosecutor's motives and decisionmaking to outside inquiry, and may undermine prosecutorial effectiveness by revealing the Government's enforcement policy." *Ibid.*

---

[1]   We have never determined whether dismissal of the indictment, or some other sanction, is the proper remedy if a court determines that a defendant has been the victim of prosecution on the basis of his race.

The requirements for a selective-prosecution claim draw on "ordinary equal protection standards." *Id.,* at 608. The claimant must demonstrate that the federal prosecutorial policy "had a discriminatory effect and that it was motivated by a discriminatory purpose." *Ibid.* To establish a discriminatory effect in a race case, the claimant must show that similarly situated individuals of a different race were not prosecuted.

The similarly situated requirement does not make a selective-prosecution claim impossible to prove. [In *Yick Wo v. Hopkins*, 118 U. S. 356, 374 (1886)], we invalidated a [San Francisco] ordinance . . . that prohibited the operation of laundries in wooden buildings The plaintiff in error successfully demonstrated that the ordinance was applied against Chinese nationals but not against other laundry-shop operators. The authorities had denied the applications of 200 Chinese subjects for permits to operate shops in wooden buildings, but granted the applications of 80 individuals who were not Chinese subjects to operate laundries in wooden buildings "under similar conditions." *Ibid.*

Having reviewed the requirements to prove a selective-prosecution claim, we turn to the showing necessary to obtain discovery in support of such a claim. If discovery is ordered, the Government must assemble from its own files documents which might corroborate or refute the defendant's claim. Discovery thus imposes many of the costs present when the Government must respond to a prima facie case of selective prosecution. It will divert prosecutors' resources and may disclose the Government's prosecutorial strategy. The justifications for a rigorous standard for the elements of a selective-prosecution claim thus require a correspondingly rigorous standard for discovery in aid of such a claim.

In this case we consider what evidence constitutes "some evidence tending to show the existence" of the discriminatory effect element. The Court of Appeals held that a defendant may establish a colorable basis for discriminatory effect without evidence that the Government has failed to prosecute others who are similarly situated to the defendant. We think it was mistaken in this view. As the three-judge panel explained, " '[s]elective prosecution' implies that a selection has taken place."[2]

The Court of Appeals reached its decision in part because it started "with the presumption that people of *all* races commit *all* types of crimes—not with the premise that any type of crime is the exclusive province of any particular racial or ethnic group." It cited no authority for this proposition, which seems contradicted by the most recent statistics of the United States Sentencing Commission. Those statistics show: More than 90% of the persons sentenced in 1994 for crack cocaine trafficking were black, United States Sentencing Comm'n, 1994 Annual

---

[2] We reserve the question whether a defendant must satisfy the similarly situated requirement in a case "involving direct admissions by [prosecutors] of discriminatory purpose." Brief for United States 15.

Report 107 (Table 45); 93.4% of convicted LSD dealers were white, *ibid.;* and 91% of those convicted for pornography or prostitution were white, *id.,* at 41 (Table 13). Presumptions at war with presumably reliable statistics have no proper place in the analysis of this issue.

The Court of Appeals also expressed concern about the "evidentiary obstacles defendants face." But all of its sister Circuits that have confronted the issue have required that defendants produce some evidence of differential treatment of similarly situated members of other races or protected classes. In the present case, if the claim of selective prosecution were well founded, it should not have been an insuperable task to prove that persons of other races were being treated differently than respondents. For instance, respondents could have investigated whether similarly situated persons of other races were prosecuted by the State of California and were known to federal law enforcement officers, but were not prosecuted in federal court. We think the required threshold—a credible showing of different treatment of similarly situated persons—adequately balances the Government's interest in vigorous prosecution and the defendant's interest in avoiding selective prosecution.

In the case before us, respondents' "study" did not constitute "some evidence tending to show the existence of the essential elements of" a selective-prosecution claim. The study failed to identify individuals who were not black and could have been prosecuted for the offenses for which respondents were charged, but were not so prosecuted. This omission was not remedied by respondents' evidence in opposition to the Government's motion for reconsideration. The newspaper article, which discussed the discriminatory effect of federal drug sentencing laws, was not relevant to an allegation of discrimination in decisions to prosecute. Respondents' affidavits, which recounted one attorney's conversation with a drug treatment center employee and the experience of another attorney defending drug prosecutions in state court, recounted hearsay and reported personal conclusions based on anecdotal evidence. The judgment of the Court of Appeals is therefore reversed, and the case is remanded for proceedings consistent with this opinion.

■ [The concurring opinions of JUSTICES SOUTER, GINSBURG and BREYER are omitted.]

■ JUSTICE STEVENS, dissenting.

Federal prosecutors are respected members of a respected profession. Nevertheless, the possibility that political or racial animosity may infect a decision to institute criminal proceedings cannot be ignored. For that reason, it has long been settled that the prosecutor's broad discretion to determine when criminal charges should be filed is not completely unbridled. As the Court notes, however, the scope of judicial review of particular exercises of that discretion is not fully defined.

The United States Attorney for the Central District of California is a member and an officer of the bar of that District Court. As such, she has a duty to the judges of that Court to maintain the standards of the profession in the performance of her official functions. If a District Judge has reason to suspect that she, or a member of her staff, has singled out particular defendants for prosecution on the basis of their race, it is surely appropriate for the judge to determine whether there is a factual basis for such a concern.

The Court correctly concludes that in this case the facts presented to the District Court in support of respondents' claim that they had been singled out for prosecution because of their race were not sufficient to prove that defense. Moreover, I agree with the Court that their showing was not strong enough to give them a *right* to discovery. . . . Like Chief Judge Wallace of the Court of Appeals, however, I am persuaded that the District Judge did not abuse her discretion when she concluded that the factual showing was sufficiently disturbing to require some response from the United States Attorney's Office. Perhaps the discovery order was broader than necessary, but I cannot agree with the Court's apparent conclusion that no inquiry was permissible.

The District Judge's order should be evaluated in light of three circumstances that underscore the need for judicial vigilance over certain types of drug prosecutions. First, the Anti-Drug Abuse Act of 1986 and subsequent legislation established a regime of extremely high penalties for the possession and distribution of so-called "crack" cocaine. Those provisions treat one gram of crack as the equivalent of 100 grams of powder cocaine. The distribution of 50 grams of crack is thus punishable by the same mandatory minimum sentence of 10 years in prison that applies to the distribution of 5,000 grams of powder cocaine. The Sentencing Guidelines extend this ratio to penalty levels above the mandatory minimums: For any given quantity of crack, the guideline range is the same as if the offense had involved 100 times that amount in powder cocaine. These penalties result in sentences for crack offenders that average three to eight times longer than sentences for comparable powder offenders.

Second, the disparity between the treatment of crack cocaine and powder cocaine is matched by the disparity between the severity of the punishment imposed by federal law and that imposed by state law for the same conduct. For a variety of reasons, often including the absence of mandatory minimums, the existence of parole, and lower baseline penalties, terms of imprisonment for drug offenses tend to be substantially lower in state systems than in the federal system. The difference is especially marked in the case of crack offenses. The majority of States draw no distinction between types of cocaine in their penalty schemes; of those that do, none has established as stark a differential as the Federal Government. For example, if respondent Hampton is found guilty, his federal sentence might be as long as a mandatory life term. Had he been tried in state court, his sentence could have been as short as 12 years, less worktime credits of half that amount.

Finally, it is undisputed that the brunt of the elevated federal penalties falls heavily on blacks. While 65% of the persons who have used crack are white, in 1993 they represented only 4% of the federal offenders convicted of trafficking in crack. Eighty-eight percent of such defendants were black. During the first 18 months of full guideline implementation, the sentencing disparity between black and white defendants grew from preguideline levels: Blacks on average received sentences over 40% longer than whites. *See* Bureau of Justice Statistics, Sentencing in the Federal Courts: Does Race Matter? 6–7 (Dec. 1993). Those figures represent a major threat to the integrity of federal sentencing reform, whose main purpose was the elimination of disparity (especially racial) in sentencing. The Sentencing Commission acknowledges that the heightened crack penalties are a "primary cause of the growing disparity between sentences for Black and White federal defendants."

The extraordinary severity of the imposed penalties and the troubling racial patterns of enforcement give rise to a special concern about the fairness of charging practices for crack offenses. Evidence tending to prove that black defendants charged with distribution of crack in the Central District of California are prosecuted in federal court, whereas members of other races charged with similar offenses are prosecuted in state court, warrants close scrutiny by the federal judges in that district. In my view, the District Judge, who has sat on both the federal and the state benches in Los Angeles, acted well within her discretion to call for the development of facts that would demonstrate what standards, if any, governed the choice of forum where similarly situated offenders are prosecuted.

Respondents submitted a study showing that of all cases involving crack offenses that were closed by the Federal Public Defender's Office in 1991, 24 out of 24 involved black defendants. To supplement this evidence, they submitted affidavits from two of the attorneys in the defense team. The first reported a statement from an intake coordinator at a local drug treatment center that, in his experience, an equal number of crack users and dealers were caucasian as belonged to minorities. The second was from David R. Reed, counsel for respondent Armstrong. Reed was both an active court-appointed attorney in the Central District of California and one of the directors of the leading association of criminal defense lawyers who practice before the Los Angeles County courts. Reed stated that he did not recall "ever handling a [crack] cocaine case involving non-black defendants" in federal court, nor had he even heard of one. He further stated that "[t]here are many crack cocaine sales cases prosecuted in state court that *do* involve racial groups other than blacks." (emphasis in original).

The majority discounts the probative value of the affidavits, claiming that they recounted "hearsay" and reported "personal conclusions based on anecdotal evidence." But the Reed affidavit plainly contained more than mere hearsay; Reed offered information based on his own extensive experience in both federal and state courts. Given the breadth of his background, he was well qualified to compare the practices of federal and state prosecutors. In any event, the Government never objected to the admission of either affidavit on hearsay or any other grounds. It was certainly within the District Court's discretion to credit the affidavits of two members of the bar of that Court, at least one of whom had presumably acquired a reputation by his frequent appearances there, and both of whose statements were made on pains of perjury.

The criticism that the affidavits were based on "anecdotal evidence" is also unpersuasive. I thought it was agreed that defendants do not need to prepare sophisticated statistical studies in order to receive mere discovery in cases like this one. Certainly evidence based on a drug counselor's personal observations or on an attorney's practice in two sets of courts, state and federal, can "'ten[d] to show the existence'" of a selective prosecution.

Even if respondents failed to carry their burden of showing that there were individuals who were not black but who could have been prosecuted in federal court for the same offenses, it does not follow that the District Court abused its discretion in ordering discovery. There can be no doubt that such individuals exist, and indeed the Government has never denied the same. In those circumstances, I fail to see why the District Court was unable to take judicial notice of this obvious fact and demand information from the Government's files to support or refute respondents' evidence. The presumption that some whites are prosecuted in state court is not "contradicted" by the statistics the majority cites, which show only that high percentages of blacks are *convicted* of certain federal crimes, while high percentages of whites are convicted of other federal crimes. Those figures are entirely consistent with the allegation of selective prosecution. The relevant comparison, rather, would be with the percentages of blacks and whites who *commit* those crimes. But, as discussed above, in the case of crack far greater numbers of whites are believed guilty of using the substance. The District Court, therefore, was entitled to find the evidence before it significant and to require some explanation from the Government.[3]

---

[3] Also telling was the Government's response to respondents' evidentiary showing. It submitted a list of more than 3,500 defendants who had been charged with federal narcotics violations over the previous three years. It also offered the names of 11 nonblack defendants whom it had prosecuted for crack offenses. All 11, however, were members of other racial or ethnic minorities. The District Court was authorized to draw adverse inferences from the Government's inability to produce a single example of a white defendant, especially when the very purpose of its exercise was to allay the court's concerns about the evidence of racially selective prosecutions.

NOTES AND QUESTIONS

1. ***Proof Standard.*** To prove a selective prosecution claim, the Court explains, a defendant "must demonstrate that the federal prosecutorial policy 'had a discriminatory effect and that it was motivated by a discriminatory purpose.'" Proving discriminatory effect, in turn, requires identifying similarly situated defendants who were not prosecuted. What function is the "discriminatory effect" element performing? If it is just to indicate a discriminatory purpose, why does the Court describe it as a separate element rather than as a means to prove purpose? If a defendant presents evidence supporting an inference that a prosecutor's charging decision was motivated by the defendant's race, why must similarly situated defendants of a different race also be identified?

The Court does qualify in a footnote that "[w]e reserve the question whether a defendant must satisfy the similarly situated requirement in a case 'involving direct admissions by [prosecutors] of discriminatory purpose.'" The Court thus concedes that it might relieve a defendant of identifying similarly situated suspects of a different race that were not prosecuted if the prosecution openly admits to racially discriminating. Absent such direct evidence, however, the defendant presumably must satisfy the similarly situated element even if circumstantial evidence of a discriminatory purpose is strong.

What kind of evidence would demonstrate that similarly situated persons were not prosecuted? If you were representing the defendants in *Armstrong*, how would you obtain such evidence?

2. ***Discovery Standard.*** The Court in *Armstrong* tied the standard for obtaining discovery to the standard for proving selective prosecution, stating that discovery should be granted only when the defendant presents "some evidence" supporting the elements of a selective prosecution claim. Defendants requested discovery from the government of documents relating to its strategy for prosecuting crack cocaine cases, a request that both the district court and the *en banc* court of appeals found convincing. The Supreme Court ruled, however, that the defendants' evidence was so inadequate that the trial judge abused her discretion in granting their discovery motion. Why? What concerns did the Court have? How valid are such concerns? What kind of evidence might satisfy the Court's discovery standard? How could defendants obtain such evidence?

3. ***Problem: Making Arguments.*** Assume you represent Armstrong. Argue that the evidence revealed in the Justices' opinions supports an inference of selective prosecution, at least sufficient to justify ordering discovery. If you were the government, what arguments would you make that the evidence was not sufficiently probative of selective prosecution? Consider Justice Stevens's dissent, which observed that "[w]hile 65% of the persons who have used crack are white, . . . they represented only 4% of the federal offenders convicted of trafficking in crack. Eighty eight percent . . . were black." How much does this support the defendants' claim? On the government's side, the Court majority relied on conviction-rate-by-race statistics from the Sentencing Commission as undermining Armstrong's

allegation of selective prosecution. Do they? What might explain the conviction-rate statistics of the Sentencing Commission other than actual crime commission rates? Indeed, to what extent is the Court's reliance on Sentencing Commission statistics consistent with the Court's demand that Armstrong present statistical evidence that is probative, precise, and convincing?

4. *Implications for Proving Selective Prosecution.* The Court believes its holding "adequately balances the Government's interest in vigorous prosecution and the defendant's interest in avoiding selective prosecution." Do you believe it does? Critics complain that *Armstrong's* discovery standard is too difficult. They contend, for example, that the "similarly situated" requirement almost requires a defendant to prove selective prosecution as a condition of obtaining discovery to prove selective prosecution. If presenting evidence of similarly situated persons of another race requires identifying people whose alleged crimes are indistinguishable on legitimate grounds from the defendants, then such evidence would already indicate that race or some other illegitimate factor explains the difference in treatment. Second, even if the showing needed to obtain discovery is less than what is required to prove selective prosecution, defendants are nonetheless placed in a Catch 22: to obtain discovery, a defendant must first make a showing of selective prosecution that would require discovery to substantiate.

The Court reassures that "[t]he similarly situated requirement does not make a selective-prosecution claim impossible." But the Court cites only one example of a successful claim: *Yick Wo v. Hopkins*, 118 U.S. 356 (1886). The facts of *Yick Wo*, however, were extreme. The San Francisco Board of Supervisors denied, without any stated reason, laundry permits to all 200 Chinese applicants, despite their compliance with all fire and health licensing requirements, while granting 80 applications from non-Chinese who were operating under similar circumstances. Indeed, the Court has on several occasions characterized *Yick Wo* as a case that was exceptional because discriminatory effect alone was sufficient to prove discriminatory intent. The discrimination in *Yick Wo*, moreover, was blatant because it took place at a time when overt discrimination was far more acceptable than today and when the reach of the Equal Protection Clause, especially to non-black, noncitizens was unclear. Thus, as Professor Richard McAdams observes:

> [T]oday, racist decisions are much more likely to be shrouded in plausible non-racial rationalizations than they were in 1886. If the Court's standard of proof actually permits defendants to prove selective prosecution where it exists, then it seems certain we would find cases since *Yick Wo*, some involving African Americans, in which the defendants met the required standard.

Richard H. McAdams, *Race and Selective Prosecution: Discovering the Pitfalls of Armstrong*, 73 Chi.-Kent L. Rev. 605, 615 (1998). McAdams' research found no such cases. The Court's citing of *Yick Wo* also supports the criticism that the threshold showing for discovery required by *Armstrong* is close to, if not identical with, the ultimate showing required to prove discrimination. The pattern of discrimination between similarly situated Chinese and non-Chinese in *Yick Wo* was sufficiently stark to prove intentional discrimination by the statistics alone.

Meeting the Court's discovery standard is likely to be even more challenging in state prosecutions, which comprise the vast majority of criminal cases. The Court in *Armstrong* suggested that the similarly situated requirement could be met by evidence of state prosecutions of white crack dealers that were known to federal prosecutors. How the defendants could prove, without the benefit of discovery, what federal prosecutors knew about state prosecutions is unclear, but at least the state prosecutions would be a matter of public record. With claims of selective prosecution against *state* prosecutors, in contrast, similarly situated persons of another race would typically be people who were not prosecuted at all, and no record likely would exist.

5.   *Federal Versus Local Prosecutors.* Are there reasons to suspect that local prosecutors are more likely to discriminate by race than federal prosecutors, or less so? Consider some common differences between the two positions. Local district attorneys, who hire line prosecutors, are typically elected and must run for re-election, whereas the President appoints (and the Senate confirms) U.S. Attorneys, who hire Assistant U.S. Attorneys. Federal prosecutors are likely to be more educated and to have graduated from more elite law schools than local prosecutors. Federal prosecutors are less dependent on particular law enforcement officers to gather evidence and testify for their cases. Federal prosecutors must seek indictment through a grand jury, whereas local prosecutors can typically just file a criminal complaint to initiate trial. If local prosecutors decline to prosecute, the crime will typically go unprosecuted, whereas federal prosecutors who decline a case typically leave the case in the hands of local prosecutors. Local prosecutors face more significant budgetary constraints than do federal prosecutors. Do these factors suggest reason to worry more about racial discrimination by one kind of prosecutor over the other? If so, should the discovery standard take account of such a difference? How?

6.   *Selective Death-Penalty Charging:* United States v. Bass. John Bass, a black male, was indicted for the intentional firearm killing of two individuals. The United States filed a notice of intent to seek the death penalty. Alleging that the Government charged him with a death-eligible offense based on his race, Bass moved to dismiss the death penalty notice and, in the alternative, moved for discovery regarding the Government's capital charging practices. Among other information, Bass requested all materials relating to his case; all policies or manuals used to determine whether to charge defendants federally; and a list of all death-eligible defendants, including the race of each defendant and the disposition of the case.

The evidence that Bass submitted in support of his discovery motion included a Department of Justice report, *The Federal Death Penalty System: A Statistical Survey*, which, as described by the Sixth Circuit Court of Appeals, shows that although whites make up the majority of all federal prisoners, they are only one-fifth of those charged by the United States with death-eligible offenses. The United States charges blacks with a death-eligible offense more than twice as often as it charges whites. . . . In addition, the United States charges blacks with racketeering murder one-and-a-half times as often as it charges whites, and with firearms murder (Bass's charge) more than twice as often as it charges blacks. Among death penalty defendants, the United States enters plea bargains with whites almost twice as often as it does with blacks.

United States v. Bass, 266 F.3d 532, 538–39 (6th Cir. 2001). With respect to the jurisdiction in which Bass was charged, he presented evidence that seventeen defendants were charged with death-eligible crimes. Fourteen of the defendants were black, three were Hispanic, and none was white. Bass supplemented the Survey with statistical evidence that blacks are no more likely than whites to commit violent federal crimes.

Bass also submitted comments by then-Attorney General Janet Reno and then-Deputy Attorney General Eric Holder expressing concern over the Survey's results and calling for more studies to determine if the disparities were caused by intentional racial discrimination. Holder testified, for example, that "no one reading this report can help but be disturbed, troubled, by this disparity. . . . I'm particularly struck by the facts that African-Americans and Hispanics are over-represented in those cases presented for consideration of the death penalty, and those cases where the defendant is actually sentenced to death," *id.* at 538. Reno said she was "sorely troubled" and that "[a]n even broader analysis must therefore be undertaken to determine if bias does in fact play any role in the federal death penalty system," *id.* John Ashcroft was asked about the survey during his confirmation hearings for Attorney General, and he said it "troubled [him] deeply," *id.* at 539, n.1.

7.   *Problem: You're the Judge.* Based on this evidence, if you were the trial judge, would you grant Bass's motion to dismiss the death penalty notice thereby removing the death penalty as a possible sentence? In the alternative, would you grant the motion for discovery, while perhaps reviewing *in camera* the Government's documents to protect work-product and other sensitive information of the government? If the trial judge did grant the discovery motion and you sat on the court of appeals, would you vote to affirm the trial judge's discovery order or reverse it as an abuse of discretion?

8.   *The Varying Court Decisions in* Bass. The District Court granted Bass's motion for discovery, and after the government refused to comply with the discovery order, the court dismissed the death penalty notice. The Sixth Circuit affirmed, concluding that, "the statistics presented by Bass constituted sufficient evidence of a discriminatory effect to warrant further discovery." That court further observed:

The United States concedes that the Survey shows a statistical disparity at the charging stage, but argues that Bass's evidence does not satisfy the "similarly situated" requirement because Bass has failed to identify white defendants who could have been charged with death-eligible crimes but were not. We find, however, that with the plea bargaining statistics, Bass has identified a pool of similarly situated defendants—those whose crimes shared sufficient aggravating factors that the United States chose to pursue the death penalty against each of them. Of those defendants, the United States enters plea bargains with one in two whites; it enters plea bargains with one in four blacks. Therefore, the United States' assertion that Bass has failed to show a discriminatory effect on similarly situated whites and blacks is simply wrong.

The Supreme Court summarily reversed the Court of Appeals and held for the government in a *per curium* decision, explaining that:

> Even assuming that the *Armstrong* requirement can be satisfied by a nationwide showing (as opposed to a showing regarding the record of the decisionmakers in respondent's case), raw statistics regarding overall charges say nothing about charges brought against *similarly situated defendants*. And the statistics regarding plea bargains are even less relevant, since respondent *was* offered a plea bargain but declined it. . . .

> The Sixth Circuit's decision is contrary to Armstrong and threatens the "performance of a core executive constitutional function." *United States v. Bass*, 536 U.S. 862, 863–64 (2002) (emphasis in original) (quoting *Armstrong*).

9.   *No Harm, No Foul?* As seen elsewhere in this casebook, proving the government covertly discriminated by race is challenging. Although the Court in *Armstrong* says it is applying conventional equal protection doctrine, many observers believe the standards for proving selective prosecution and obtaining discovery in support thereof are especially formidable. The deference the Court accords prosecutorial discretion seems especially strong. What is more, the evidence bearing on prosecutorial charging decisions is peculiarly within the prosecutor's possession, and a defendant's inability to obtain it through discovery therefore erects a virtually preclusive barrier.

To the extent *Armstrong* makes proving selective prosecution claims practically impossible, the question arises whether that result is, on balance, costly. The decision may not be costly if either of two propositions is true: (1) selective prosecutions are so unlikely as to make the cost of litigating them outweigh the benefit of finding the rare "needle in the haystack," or (2) selective prosecutions, even if numerous, do not cause harm because the "victims" of such prosecutions deserve to be prosecuted and society, including minority communities, benefits from their incapacitation.

How often selective prosecutions occur is difficult to determine in view of the difficulty of meeting the Court's discovery and proof standards. There is, however, reason to believe that they occur in non-trivial numbers and may be as likely as racial discrimination in other contexts in which courts and others take allegations of discrimination more seriously. First, prosecutors, whether federal, state, or local, are products of a society in which racial bias persists. Justice Stevens notes this possibility in his dissent in *Armstrong*. Second, assumptions that people of certain races are more likely to commit certain crimes or to lie in their defense are often unconsciously held even among people who sincerely profess to believe in racial equality. A prosecutor who denies making charging decisions based on race may not recognize his own unconscious biases that affect his judgment. Third, prosecutors' career advancement depends on the number and frequency of successful prosecutions. A prosecutor might hold no racial biases but recognize, consciously or unconsciously, that the race of a defendant or a victim can affect the likelihood of conviction at trial. Fourth, community reaction to certain crimes, such as murder and sexual assault, may be more intense when the perpetrator is black or the victim is white, creating pressure on prosecutors to prosecute such cases more aggressively.

Even assuming selective prosecutions occur in non-trivial numbers, the next question is whether they cause harm. If not, then failing to prevent them is arguably not a cause for concern. The defendant alleging selective prosecution is usually guilty. His complaint is, in fact, not that he is innocent but that prosecutors failed to proceed against someone of another race who may be equally guilty. If the consequence of proving selective prosecution is dismissal of the charges, as the Court in *Armstrong* assumes, might that do more harm than good by putting a dangerous person back on the street? Since most crime is intra-racial, selective prosecutions arguably benefit minority communities. Perhaps the ideal would be that prosecutors bring charges against similarly situated white suspects. Indeed, perhaps white communities burdened by drug and violent crime have the more legitimate complaint if prosecutors are ignoring white offenders. Courts have, however, consistently disclaimed authority to mandate prosecutions, which would raise serious constitutional concerns, and thus this solution is unrealistic. By effectively turning a blind eye to selective prosecution claims, then, the Court in *Armstrong* may be protecting the public from dangerous criminals while leaving it to political checks on prosecutorial charging to ensure that similarly situated criminals of other races are also prosecuted.

But several reasons nonetheless support allowing discovery if the allegation of selective prosecution is plausible, even if the defendant has not identified similarly situated individuals of other races. First, to the extent selective prosecution allegations usually lack merit, allowing discovery would substantiate the allegations only infrequently. Furthermore, discovery could occasionally lead to evidence of discrimination, and the burden of discovery might also deter selective prosecution claims more than the current regime in which such prosecutions can be pursued with impunity. Moreover, in cases in which racial selectivity is proven, the harm of dismissal need not be great because such cases are unlikely to involve serious crimes with direct victims. Even prosecutors harboring racial bias, trying to appease community outrage, or trying to maximize win-rates, are unlikely to ignore violent crimes against real victims perpetrated by white people. Selective prosecutions are thus likely to involve non-violent offenses. Moreover, even when a claim of selective prosecution involves a violent crime, such as the murders in *Bass*, the similarly situated defendants of other races probably receive a lesser punishment than the defendant, not freedom. Reducing the penalty of selectively prosecuted defendants charged with violent crimes would thus not result in putting them back on the street. For an elaboration of some of these points, *see* Richard H. McAdams, *Race and Selective Prosecution: Discovering the Pitfalls of Armstrong*, 73 Chi.-Kent L. Rev. 605, 624–66 (1998).

How would you assess the cost of selective prosecution claims? How much should the criminal justice system invest in protecting guilty criminals because some other guilty criminals got away with less or no punishment? How important is racial equality in a context in which the victims of discriminatory prosecutions, typically black and Latino defendants, probably deserve to be prosecuted? And how much might racial equality actually be advanced by the prosecution of those defendants who have victimized minority communities?

10. *Racial Identity of Prosecutors.* Historically, prosecutors have overwhelmingly been white and male. Today, although prosecutors remain disproportionately white males, they are increasingly nonwhite and female, especially in large, metropolitan areas. What effect is this likely to have? Are prosecutors of color more or less likely to act with racial bias? What about women? Also, do lawyers of color have any obligation to refrain from becoming prosecutors or at least to perform their duties with the interests of their racial group in mind? Does a Latino prosecutor who brings charges against Latino drug dealers betray her race or serve it?

The question whether a prosecutor of color can ethically prosecute his own race or even be a prosecutor at all, has been called the "Darden Dilemma," after Christopher Darden, the black prosecutor in the O.J. Simpson trial in 1994–95. Some critics of Darden called him a "token" or "sell out." Kenneth Nunn argues that black prosecutors cause serious and unavoidable damage to the black community by participating as lead players in a criminal justice system that oppresses black people. "[T]he best resolution of the 'Darden Dilemma'," Nunn writes, "is for African Americans to refrain from prosecuting crimes and to reject employment opportunities with prosecutors' offices." Kenneth B. Nunn, *The "Darden Dilemma": Should African Americans Prosecute Crimes?*, 68 Fordham L. Rev. 1473, 1474–75 (2000). By contrast, Angela Davis contends that black prosecutors have an important role to play in remedying injustices in the criminal justice system: "Prosecutors have been given more power and discretion than any other criminal justice official, so they have a greater ability to affect change where it is needed." Angela J. Davis, Prosecution and Race: The Power and Privilege of Discretion, 67 Fordham L. Rev. 13 (1998).

Which position do you lean toward and why? Is a black or Latino prosecutor a "sell out" or otherwise a traitor to the interests of their race? If the reason is that the criminal justice system is racist, then wouldn't white and Asian lawyers also be wrong to serve as prosecutors? Do you or any of your friends hope to become prosecutors? Would you or they betray or serve racial justice? Does it depend on how a prosecutor performs her job?

III. JURY SELECTION

Two types of criminal juries are provided for in the Constitution. First, the Fifth Amendment[4] requires that, in all federal prosecutions, a defendant must be indicted by a grand jury, a body of as many as twenty-three members empowered to investigate crimes and determine whether there is probable cause to proceed to trial on criminal charges. Second, under the Sixth Amendment,[5] a defendant to a federal prosecution has a right to be tried by a petit jury, a right made applicable to state and local prosecutions by the Due Process Clause of the Fourteenth Amendment. The petit (or trial) jury is typically composed of six to twelve laypersons who must find, before convicting a defendant, that the prosecution has proven every element of the charged crime beyond a reasonable doubt. Both juries are intended to guard against unjustified government power by interposing the judgment of ordinary citizens between the defendant and the potentially arbitrary, overzealous, or corrupt prosecutor or judge. To this end, they are staffed with lay citizens drawn from the surrounding community.

The following sections consider three stages of the jury selection process. Section A considers the selection of the venire for both grand and petit juries. The venire (or array) refers to the pool of people summoned to court and from which legally qualified individuals are identified and placed on individual juries. Section B examines the process of *voir dire* for petit juries, during which the judge and lawyers for each side question potential jurors to determine the likelihood that each juror will be impartial in the particular case.

Section C looks at the use of peremptory challenges (or "strikes") in selecting the petit jury. After voir dire, lawyers may make challenges to specific jurors. One type of challenge is "for cause," which means that some aspect of the juror's background or response to voir dire indicates that he or she is not, as a matter of law, impartial. The other type of challenge is "peremptory," which means the lawyer can challenge, without any reason, a juror because the lawyer believes the juror would be less favorable to his client than would other jurors.

---

[4] The Fifth Amendment provides in relevant part, "No person shall be held to answer for a capital, or otherwise infamous crime, unless on a presentment or indictment of a Grand Jury, except in cases arising in the land or naval forces, or in the Militia, when in actual service in time of War or public danger." U.S. Const. amend. V.

[5] The Sixth Amendment provides, "In all criminal prosecutions, the accused shall enjoy the right to a speedy and public trial, by an impartial jury of the State and district wherein the crime shall have been committed, which district shall have been previously ascertained by law." U.S. Const. amend. VI.

A. SELECTING THE VENIRE FOR GRAND AND PETIT JURIES

The first case to consider a race-based challenge to the selection of grand and petit jury venires was *Strauder v. West Virginia*, 100 U.S. 303 (1880). West Virginia state law explicitly limited service on all juries to white males. The black defendant argued that such exclusion violated the recently adopted Fourteenth Amendment's Equal Protection Clause. The Supreme Court agreed, explaining the harmful effect that excluding blacks from juries could have on the defendant's trial: "It is well known that prejudices often exist against particular classes in the community, which sway the judgment of jurors, and which, therefore, operate in some cases to deny to persons of those classes the full enjoyment of that protection which others enjoy." *Id*. at 309.

The Court in *Strauder* confronted the question whom does the Equal Protection Clause protect. It emphasized that the provision plainly protected black people. Its purpose, along with the other Reconstruction Amendments, was "securing to a race recently emancipated, a race that through many generations had been held in slavery, all the civil rights that the superior race enjoy," *id*. at 307, and that it "declar[es] that the law in the States shall be the same for the black as for the white." *Id*.

At points, the Court seemed to suggest that *only* black people had equal protection rights, stating that " '[w]e doubt very much whether any action of a State, not directed by way of discrimination against the negroes, as a class, will ever be held to come within the purview of this provision.' " *Id*. (quoting Slaughter House Cases). Elsewhere in the opinion, in contrast, the Court assumed that white people would be protected, at least if they were an ethnic or numerical minority:

> If in those States where the colored people constitute a majority of the entire population a law should be enacted excluding all white men from jury service, thus denying to them the privilege of participating equally with the blacks in the administration of justice, we apprehend no one would be heard to claim that it would not be a denial to white men of the equal protection of the laws. Nor if a law should be passed excluding all naturalized Celtic Irishmen, would there be any doubt of its inconsistency with the spirit of the amendment.

The Court also assumed that the Fourteenth Amendment did not prevent states from restricting jury service "to males, to freeholders, to citizens, to persons within certain ages, or to persons having educational qualifications." The Fourteenth Amendment's "aim was against discrimination because of race or color," the Court reiterated, while cautioning that "[w]e are not now called upon to affirm or deny that it had other purposes."

Strauder established that the Equal Protection Clause protected black people from statutory exclusion from jury service. The Court also assumed that white people would be protected if they were a minority. Though we might take *Strauder* to prohibit race discrimination in jury selection generally, it was not until 1954 that the Court again addressed the question with reference to a non-black or -white racial group.

Hernandez v. Texas

Supreme Court of the United States, 1954.
347 U.S. 475.

[Editors' Note: *Hernandez v. Texas* is a main case for this chapter that should be read at this point. Read the case and the Notes and Questions following it in Chapter 2, pp.107–111, and then proceed with the Notes and Questions below.]

NOTES AND QUESTIONS

1. *Problem:* **Castañeda v. Partida.** Consider the following case and assess whether you believe the defendant proved discrimination in grand jury selection. Rodrigo Partida was indicted in Hidalgo County, Texas, for burglary with intent to rape, and was subsequently tried and convicted. Following Texas's "key man" system of jury selection, the county judge had appointed five jury commissioners (or "key men") who compiled a list of twenty local residents. The judge summoned people on the list to court and, after screening them for statutory qualifications, appointed twelve to serve as the grand jury that indicted Partida.

The population of Hildalgo County was 79% Mexican-American, including a majority of elected officials and judges. Thirty-nine percent of grand jurors over an eleven-year period preceding Partida's indictment were Mexican-American. In the two-and-a-half years during which the judge who impaneled the grand jury that indicted Partida was in charge, 45.5% of grand jurors were Mexican-American. In the year in which Partida was indicted, 52.5% of people on the grand jury list were Mexican-American. The judge who appointed the jury commissioners for Partida's case and who later presided over Partida's criminal trial, was Mexican-American, as were three of the five commissioners who empanelled the grand jury that indicted him. On the list of people from which the grand jury that indicted Partida was selected, 10 of 20 were Mexican-American. The Sheriff who served the subpoena on those summoned for grand jury service was Mexican-American. Five of the 12 members of the grand jury that returned the indictment, including the foreman, and seven of the 12 members of the petit jury that ultimately convicted Partida were Mexican-American.

Hidalgo County's Mexican-American was socioeconomically disadvantaged and suffered from low income, substandard housing, and lower levels of education. It is unknown how many Mexican-American residents met statutory qualifications for grand jury service, such as citizenship, literacy, or lack of criminal record. It is also unknown how many Mexican Americans who were summoned for grand jury duty were excused due to age, health, or other legal reasons. Nor is it known how many of the women who served on the grand juries were in fact Mexican-American but were married to men with Anglo-American surnames

Partida challenged his conviction in post-trial proceedings at which the foregoing facts were adduced, alleging discrimination against Mexican Americans in grand jury selection. If you represented him, what arguments would you make that the facts supported an inference of intentional discrimination? If you represented the county, what arguments would you make that the evidence did not indicate discrimination? As a trial judge, how would you rule?

2.   *The Supreme Court's Decision.* The case eventually reached the Supreme Court. In *Castañeda v. Partida*, 430 U.S. 482 (1977), the Court held that the statistical under-representation of Mexican Americans in grand jury service, combined with the subjective nature of the "key man" selection system, sufficed to make a prima facie showing of discrimination that the County failed to rebut. The Court rejected the County's "governing majority" theory—that the dominance of Mexican Americans in positions of power in Hidalgo County refuted Partida's prima facie case of discrimination against Mexican Americans in grand jury selection. The Court explained that "[b]ecause of the many facets of human motivation, it would be unwise to presume as a matter of law that human beings of one definable group will not discriminate against other members of their group." *Id.* at 499.

Justice Powell's dissent gave greater credit to the governing majority theory: "[W]here Mexican-Americans control both the selection of jurors and the political process, rational inferences from the most basic facts in a democratic society render improbable respondent's claim of an intent to discriminate against him and other Mexican-Americans. As [trial] Judge Garza observed: 'If people in charge can choose whom they want, it is unlikely they will discriminate against themselves.' " *Id.* at 515.

That dissent drew a sharp response from Justice Marshall:

> Mr. Justice Powell's assumptions about human nature, plausible as they may sound, fly in the face of a great deal of social science theory and research. Social scientists agree that members of minority groups frequently respond to discrimination and prejudice by attempting to disassociate themselves from the group, even to the point of adopting the majority's negative attitudes towards the minority. Such behavior occurs with particular frequency among members of minority groups who have achieved some measure of economic or political success and thereby have gained some acceptability among the dominant group. *Id.* at 503.

What is your reaction to the governing majority theory? Aren't people who discriminate by race more likely to discriminate against a different race? Indeed, wasn't an assumption underlying the Court's holdings in *Strauder* and *Hernandez* that excluding, respectively, blacks and Mexican Americans from juries would harm defendants of those races because juries composed of other races would be more likely to discriminate against them? If, instead, racial groups will discriminate against their own race, what is the benefit, if any, to minority defendants of having people of their race on the juries that try them?

3.   *Method of Proof.* *Hernandez* and *Castañeda* applied the Equal Protection Clause to grand jury selection, which requires proof that the government intentionally discriminated on the basis of race. The Court in *Hernandez* and *Castañeda* accepted a method of proof called the "rule of exclusion." As the Court explained in *Castañeda*:

> The first step is to establish that the group is one that is a recognizable, distinct class, singled out for different treatment under the laws, as written or as applied. Next, the degree of underrepresentation must be proved, by comparing the proportion of the group in the total population to the proportion called to serve as grand jurors, over a significant period of time. . . . Finally, . . . a selection procedure that is susceptible of abuse or is not racially neutral supports the presumption of discrimination raised by the statistical showing. Once the defendant has shown substantial underrepresentation of his group, he has made out a prima facie case of discriminatory purpose, and the burden then shifts to the State to rebut that case. *Castañeda,* at 494–95.

Does this method of proof make sense? What are its virtues and vices? How does it compare with that employed in *Armstrong* or in cases you have read elsewhere in this casebook?

NOTES ON THE FAIR CROSS SECTION REQUIREMENT

1.   *The Fair Cross Section Requirement.* In addition to equal protection constraints, the Court developed a "fair cross section" requirement applicable to the selection of petit jury venires. The requirement derives from the Sixth Amendment's guarantee of an "impartial jury," which, the Court concluded, "requires that the jury be a 'body truly representative of the community,' and not the organ of any special group or class." *Glasser v. United States*, 315 U.S. 60, 86 (1942). To this end, the Court subsequently explained, it "is an essential component of the Sixth Amendment right to a jury trial" that the petit jury be drawn "from a representative cross section of the community." *Taylor v. Louisiana*, 419 U.S. 522, 528 (1975).

In cases applying the fair cross section requirement, the Court invalidated jury selection procedures that systematically excluded certain distinct groups or classes from the venire. In *Glasser*, the Court explained that if the defendant had proven that the only women's names in boxes from which jurors were drawn came from membership lists of the League of Women Voters, he would have been deprived of a representative jury. No matter how civic minded the members of the League of Women Voters may be, the Court explained, "[t]he deliberate selection of jurors from the membership of particular private organizations definitely does not conform to the traditional requirements of jury trial."

Another early case in the development of the fair cross section doctrine was *Thiel v. Southern Pacific Co.*, 328 U.S. 217 (1946). The Court invalidated a state court practice of automatically exempting from jury lists people who work for a daily wage, observing:

> The American tradition of trial by jury . . . necessarily contemplates an impartial jury drawn from a cross section of the community. This does not mean, of course, that every jury must contain representatives of all the economic, social, religious, racial, political and geographical groups of the community; frequently such complete representation would be impossible. But it does mean that prospective jurors shall be selected by court officials without systematic and intentional exclusion of any of these groups. *Id.* at 220.

In *Ballard v. United States*, 329 U.S. 187, 193–94 (1946), the Court offered this explanation as to why a selection process that excluded women impaired the jury's function:

> The thought is that the factors which tend to influence the action of women are the same as those which influence the action of men personality, background, economic status and not sex. Yet it is not enough to say that women when sitting as jurors neither act nor tend to act as a class. . . . The truth is that the two sexes are not fungible; a community made up exclusively of one is different from a community composed of both; the subtle interplay of influence one on the other is among the imponderables. To insulate the courtroom from either may not in a given case make an iota of difference. Yet a flavor, a distinct quality is lost if either sex is excluded.

In 1972, in a plurality decision in *Peters v. Kiff*, 407 U.S. 493, 503–504 (1972), Justice Marshall, joined by Justices Douglas and Stewart, relied on due process grounds to invalidate the exclusion of blacks from grand and petit jury pools, observing:

> [W]e are unwilling to make the assumption that the exclusion of Negroes has relevance only for issues involving race. When any large and identifiable segment of the community is excluded from jury service, the effect is to remove from the jury room qualities of human nature and varieties of human experience, the range of which is unknown and perhaps unknowable. It is not necessary to assume that the excluded group will consistently vote as a class in order to conclude, as we do, that its exclusion deprives the jury of a perspective on human events that may have unsuspected importance in any case that may be presented.

By 1975, a majority of the Court, in *Taylor v. Louisiana*, 419 U.S. 522 (1975), held that the Sixth Amendment's guarantee of an impartial jury in criminal trials, applied to the states by the Fourteenth Amendment, mandated a fair cross section. For a fuller discussion of the development of the fair cross section requirement, *see* Andrew D. Leipold, *Constitutionalizing Jury Selection in Criminal Cases: A Critical Evaluation*, 86 Georgetown L.J. 945, 949–60 (1998).

2.   *Elements and Burdens of Proof.* In *Duren v. Missouri*, 429 U.S. 357 (1979), a male defendant "contended that his right to trial by a jury chosen from a fair cross section of his community was denied by provisions of Missouri law granting women who so request an automatic exemption from jury service." In analyzing his claim, the Court set forth the elements and burdens of proof regarding the fair cross section requirement of the Sixth Amendment:

> In order to establish a prima facie violation of the fair cross section requirement, the defendant must show (1) that the group alleged to be excluded is a "distinctive" group in the community; (2) that the representation of this group in venires from which juries are selected is not fair and reasonable in relation to the number of such persons in the community; and (3) that this underrepresentation is due to systematic exclusion of the group in the jury selection process.
>
> However, once the defendant has made a prima facie showing of an infringement of his constitutional right to a jury drawn from a fair cross section of the community, it is the State that bears the burden of justifying this infringement by showing attainment of a fair cross section to be incompatible with a significant state interest. *Id.* at 364, 368.

The elements of a fair cross section challenge can be further clarified by contrasting them with those of an equal protection challenge. Unlike equal protection-based challenges to the selection of jury venires, a defendant making a fair cross section challenge need not prove that the exclusion of a distinct group was purposeful, nor need the defendant be a member of the excluded group. Thus, it was irrelevant for their fair cross section challenges that in *Taylor*, *Glasser* and *Duren*, the defendants challenging the exclusion of women were male, and that in *Peters* the exclusion of blacks was challenged by a white defendant.

Applying the fair cross section requirements in *Duren*, the Court found that the defendant had met all the elements of his prima facie case in challenging the state law automatically exempting women from petit jury service. Women, as the Court had held in *Taylor*, are sufficiently "numerous and distinct from men" to implicate the fair cross section requirement. The defendant also demonstrated that, although women made up 54% of the county's population, they represented only 14.5% of the venire from which jurors were drawn. The Court further held that the underrepresentation was systematic, *i.e.,* was not occasional but extended over a period of nearly a year and that it was caused by the automatic exemption for women. As to whether the exemption was justified by a significant state interest, the State claimed that many women had responsibilities toward home and family. While the Court acknowledged that exempting individuals who claimed hardship due to domestic responsibilities might be justified, granting an optional exemption to all woman without an individual showing of need was not.

Consider key elements of the fair cross section requirement in greater depth:

a.   "Distinctive" Groups. Does the fair cross section requirement that distinctive groups be included over time in jury venires make sense? Isn't every individual juror distinct? What benefits are gained from including a cross section of distinctive groups in jury service? What costs, if any, might result from the fair cross section requirement?

Assuming the value of representative juries, are you persuaded that the groups the Supreme Court has recognized as distinct are, in fact, distinct? The Court has recognized as distinct blacks, women (including women not members of the League of Women Voters), and daily wage earners. How is the inclusion of blacks in jury pools likely to affect the functioning of juries? Why would a white defendant be harmed by the exclusion of blacks? Is the Court plurality right in *Peters* that the inclusion of black jurors may have unsuspected importance in a case not involving racial issues? What non-racial issues would blacks tend to evaluate differently from whites or other racial groups? Do women bring a distinct "flavor" to jury deliberations, as the Court suggested in *Taylor*? Which group is least and most distinctive: blacks, women, or daily wage earners?

What other groups should be included in the fair cross section requirement? Consider (1) Latinos or subgroups thereof, such as Mexican or Cuban Americans; (2) Native Americans or particular Indian tribes, such as Cherokee or Navajo; (3) Asian Americans or subgroups thereof, such as Japanese or Vietnamese Americans. One way to think about the question of racial sub-groups is to consider whether a jury should be considered non-representative of a fair cross section if it contains a good number of Jamaican or Haitian Americans, but few or no several-generation black Americans. Or if Cuban Americans were represented in high numbers but Mexican Americans or Puerto Ricans were not? Would a jury with two Japanese Americans and a Pakistani American in a community with ten percent Asians represent a fair cross section of Asians if the jury had no Chinese or Korean Americans? To what extent does racial identity transcend ethnic or national-origin identity for fair cross section purposes?

What other groups defined by non-racial criteria should be recognized as "distinctive" for fair cross section purposes? Consider (1) low-income people; (2) college students; (3) persons under 25 years old or over the age of 65; (4) LGBT people; (5) people with loss of vision or mobility; (6) persons not registered to vote; or (7) people with a criminal record. Are these groups more or less distinctive than groups defined by race?

Although *Hernandez* and *Castañeda* were equal protection cases, the Court described Mexican Americans as a "distinct class," making it likely that they would be considered distinct for Sixth Amendment purposes as well. Indeed, it is fair to assume that the Sixth Amendment's fair cross section requirement comprehends as "distinct" those groups and characteristics that traditionally receive heightened protection under the Equal Protection Clause, such as race, including Latino identity, national origin, religion, and sex. We can also infer from the Court's inclusion of daily wage earners and women not members of the League of Women Voters that the fair cross section requirement includes a broader range of groups than equal protection doctrine. Most circuit courts follow a three-part test for determining whether a group is "distinct" for fair cross section purposes, asking whether:

> 1) the group is defined by a limiting quality (i.e., the group has a definite composition such as race or sex); 2) a common thread or basic similarity in attitude, idea, or experience runs through the group; and 3) a community of interests exists among members of the group such that the group's interest cannot be adequately represented if the group is excluded from the jury selection process.

United States v. Green, 435 F.3d 1265, 1265, 1271 (10th Cir. 2006). Does this test seem satisfactory? How would it apply to the groups identified in the previous paragraph? What test would you propose?

b. *Substantial Underrepresentation.* With respect to the second element, the defendant must demonstrate that a distinctive group is substantially underrepresented among people summoned or appearing for jury service compared to the group's percentage of the overall population. The Supreme Court has not identified a specific test or minimum disparity to constitute substantial underrepresentation, but the disparities seen in *Hernandez* and *Castañeda* would plainly suffice. Lower courts have most often employed a 10% "absolute disparity test" (ADT) by which a group's percentage of jury venires over time is *subtracted* from its percentage of the general population, and underrepresentation is found if the result is at least 10%. Thus, if Latinos represent 20% of a jurisdiction but constitute less than 10% of venirepersons, they would be underrepresented. If, however, they were 15% of the population and 10% of venirepersons, they would not be. An alternative, "comparative disparity test" (CDT), proposed by some scholars and litigants, determines what fraction of an underrepresented group is absent from jury venires. It takes the absolute disparity result and *divides* it by the group's percentage of the general population. In the first example above, the result would be (20–10)/20=50%. The second would yield (15–10)/15=33%. Both CDT results are significant. Notice, moreover, that a group comprising less than 10% of the general population could not be underrepresented under ADT but could be under CDT. The CDT is thus more favorable to finding a fair cross section violation, especially for small groups. It has not, however, been adopted as the determinative test by any court.

Why might courts be resistant to the CDT? Which test makes more sense? Also, why should a group's percentage of the general population be relevant under either test? Shouldn't the goal be to include a critical mass of any distinct group on juries so that their perspective is present in that unpredictable case where it might have unsuspected importance? The fair cross section requirement is supposed to promote the creation of impartial juries. Why are juries that are 10% Latino not impartial if Latinos are 20% of the general population but are impartial if Latinos are 15% of the population?

c.   ***Systematic Exclusion.*** The third element of a defendant's prima facie case is to show that "the cause of the underrepresentation was systematic—that is, inherent in the particular jury-selection process utilized." *Duren*, 439 U.S. at 366. This means that while the underrepresentation need not be intentional, it must be more than a one-time or haphazard occurrence, and it must not result from chance or factors unrelated to the jury selection process. Rather, the defendant must demonstrate that the challenged selection process caused the underrepresentation and that the underrepresentation persisted over time. In *Duren*, for example, the Court was persuaded that the exemption for women directly contributed to the underrepresentation of women on jury venires and that the underrepresentation continued for nearly a year, including the period during which the defendant was tried.

Even today, several common jury selection procedures contribute to the underrepresentation of racial minorities on jury venires:

> Courts commonly generate lists of potential jurors from voter registration records—a database that tends to under represent the minority population residing in a jury district. Also, because racial minorities are statistically more mobile than whites, a greater number fail to receive jury summonses mailed to outdated addresses. Even when they are contacted, minority residents are less likely to complete a jury questionnaire or to respond to a jury summons due to apathy or resentment toward a criminal justice system from which many feel alienated. Moreover, members of racial or ethnic minorities are more likely to be disqualified from service for reasons such as lack of English proficiency or having a criminal record. Minority jurors are more likely to be excused from jury service due to financial hardship, transportation difficulties, or child care responsibilities.

Kim Forde-Mazrui, *Jural Districting: Selecting Impartial Juries Through Community Representation*, 52 VAND. L. REV. 353, 356 (1999). As a consequence, notwithstanding the eradication of overt and covert discriminatory selection procedures, many jurisdictions throughout the nation continue to have jury venires with significantly fewer racial minorities than reside in the local population. Assuming these procedures result in substantial underrepresentation of distinct groups, do they "systematically exclude" them in violation of the Sixth Amendment's fair cross section requirement?

d.   ***Significant State Interest.*** Even if a court were to find that some or all of the above procedures systematically excluded minorities from jury service, the state, per *Duren*, would still have the opportunity to justify the excluding procedure by identifying a significant state interest served by the procedure. If you were the prosecutor and the defendant successfully demonstrated that the procedures described in the previous Note systematically excluded minorities, what state interests could you offer to justify the procedures? If you represented the defendant, how would you respond? As a judge, how would you rule?

The Supreme Court has decided only a few cases that shed light on what constitutes a sufficient state interest to justify the systematic exclusion of a distinct group. The Court acknowledged that hardship to an individual juror from lost wages or interference with domestic responsibilities could justify exemptions on an individual basis but not an automatic exemption for daily wage earners and women. *Glasser* also suggests that a well-intentioned effort to select civic-minded jurors could not justify limiting the women selected to members of the League of Women Voters. Lower court cases have grappled with a range of procedures that have excluded distinctive groups, often inadvertently. They have typically upheld the procedure if it would be costly to change, would impose hardship on the individual jurors, or would burden the community by depriving it of the juror's availability.

3. *Design Problem: Achieving Representative Venires.* If you were a state legislator or court administrator concerned about minority underrepresentation in jury service in your state or county, what procedures would you reform or propose to ensure that a fair cross section of qualified and available people was summoned for jury service? What procedures that tend to exclude minority jurors would you reform and why? What other procedures might be effective at convening a fair cross section on the venires from which jurors are drawn? What drawbacks, practical or legal, might such reforms present?

B. VOIR DIRE

After the venire is assembled, the prospective jurors are sworn in and subjected to *voir dire*. Latin for "to speak the truth," voir dire involves the examination of prospective jurors to identify those who might be biased against the defense or prosecution. The inquiry may include oral and written questions, may be conducted by the judge or counsel, and may be directed toward all jurors at once or to individual jurors. Voir dire typically opens with a statement about the case, the parties, and their lawyers. Questions are designed to uncover such issues as whether potential jurors have a personal interest in the case, are personally acquainted with the parties, witnesses or lawyers, or whether they have been exposed to news coverage that might bias their opinions. Questions can also be designed to elicit whether a juror has any prejudice that might impair their impartiality, such as negative attitudes about the race, ethnicity, or religion of any individuals in the case. Typically, the judge has broad discretion over the kind, scope, and number of voir dire questions that can be put to potential jurors, including about race. As the next case discusses, however, under certain circumstances the defendant has a right to ask jurors questions designed to reveal racial bias. Consider whether the Court has defined the scope of the right appropriately.

Turner v. Murray

Supreme Court of the United States, 1986.
476 U.S. 28.

■ JUSTICE WHITE announced the judgment of the Court and delivered the opinion of the Court with respect to Parts I and III, and an opinion with respect to Parts II and IV, in which JUSTICE BLACKMUN, JUSTICE STEVENS, and JUSTICE O'CONNOR join.

Petitioner is a black man sentenced to death for the murder of a white storekeeper. The question presented is whether the trial judge committed reversible error at *voir dire* by refusing petitioner's request to question prospective jurors on racial prejudice.

I

On July 12, 1978, petitioner entered a jewelry store in Franklin, Virginia, armed with a sawed-off shotgun. He demanded that the proprietor, W. Jack Smith, Jr., put jewelry and money from the cash register into some jewelry bags. Smith complied with petitioner's demand, but triggered a silent alarm, alerting the Police Department. When Alan Bain, a police officer, arrived to inquire about the alarm, petitioner surprised him and forced him to surrender his revolver.

Having learned that Smith had triggered a silent alarm, petitioner became agitated. He fired toward the rear wall of the store and stated that if he saw or heard any more police officers, he was going to start killing those in the store. When a police siren sounded, petitioner walked to where Smith was stationed behind a counter and without warning shot him in the head with Bain's pistol, wounding Smith and causing him to slump incapacitated to the floor.

Officer Bain attempted to calm petitioner, promising to take him anywhere he wanted to go and asking him not to shoot again. Petitioner angrily replied that he was going to kill Smith for "snitching," and fired two pistol shots into Smith's chest, fatally wounding him. As petitioner turned away from shooting Smith, Bain was able to disarm him and place him under arrest.

A Southampton County, Virginia, grand jury indicted petitioner on charges of capital murder, use of a firearm in the commission of a murder, and possession of a sawed-off shotgun in the commission of a robbery. Petitioner requested and was granted a change of venue to Northampton County, Virginia, a rural county some 80 miles from the location of the murder.

Prior to the commencement of *voir dire,* petitioner's counsel submitted to the trial judge a list of proposed questions, including the following:

"'The defendant, Willie Lloyd Turner, is a member of the Negro race. The victim, W. Jack Smith, Jr., was a white

Caucasian. Will these facts prejudice you against Willie Lloyd Turner or affect your ability to render a fair and impartial verdict based solely on the evidence?' "

The judge declined to ask this question. . . . The judge did ask the venire, who were questioned in groups of five in petitioner's presence, whether any person was aware of any reason why he could not render a fair and impartial verdict, to which all answered "no." At the time the question was asked, the prospective jurors had no way of knowing that the murder victim was white.

The jury that was empanelled, which consisted of eight whites and four blacks, convicted petitioner on all of the charges against him. After a separate sentencing hearing on the capital charge, the jury recommended that petitioner be sentenced to death, a recommendation the trial judge accepted.

[Petitioner appealed his death sentence to the Virginia Supreme Court, and subsequently sought habeas corpus relief from the District Court and the United States Court of Appeals for the Fourth Circuit, all of which rejected his claim.]

We granted certiorari to review the Fourth Circuit's decision that petitioner was not constitutionally entitled to have potential jurors questioned concerning racial prejudice. We reverse.

II

The Fourth Circuit's opinion correctly states the analytical framework for evaluating petitioner's argument: "The broad inquiry in each case must be . . . whether under all of the circumstances presented there was a constitutionally significant likelihood that, absent questioning about racial prejudice, the jurors would not be indifferent as [they stand] unsworn". The Fourth Circuit was correct, too, in holding that under *Ristaino* the mere fact that petitioner is black and his victim white does not constitute a "special circumstance" of constitutional proportions. What sets this case apart from *Ristaino,* however, is that in addition to petitioner's being accused of a crime against a white victim, the crime charged was a capital offense.

In a capital sentencing proceeding before a jury, the jury is called upon to make a "highly subjective, 'unique, individualized judgment regarding the punishment that a particular person deserves.' " *Caldwell v. Mississippi,* 472 U.S. 320, 340, n.7 (1985). The Virginia statute under which petitioner was sentenced is instructive of the kinds of judgments a capital sentencing jury must make. First, in order to consider the death penalty, a Virginia jury must find either that the defendant is likely to commit future violent crimes or that his crime was "outrageously or wantonly vile, horrible or inhuman in that it involved torture, depravity of mind or an aggravated battery to the victim." Second, the jury must consider any mitigating evidence offered by the defendant. Mitigating evidence may include, but is not limited to, facts tending to show that the defendant acted under the influence of extreme emotional or mental disturbance, or that at the time of the crime the defendant's capacity "to appreciate the criminality of his conduct or to conform his conduct to the requirements of law was significantly impaired." Finally, even if the jury has found an aggravating factor, and irrespective of whether mitigating evidence has been offered, the jury has discretion not to recommend the death sentence, in which case it may not be imposed.

Because of the range of discretion entrusted to a jury in a capital sentencing hearing, there is a unique opportunity for racial prejudice to operate but remain undetected. On the facts of this case, a juror who believes that blacks are violence prone or morally inferior might well be influenced by that belief in deciding whether petitioner's crime involved the aggravating factors specified under Virginia law. Such a juror might also be less favorably inclined toward petitioner's evidence of mental disturbance as a mitigating circumstance. More subtle, less consciously held racial attitudes could also influence a juror's decision in this case. Fear of blacks, which could easily be stirred up by the violent facts of petitioner's crime, might incline a juror to favor the death penalty.

The risk of racial prejudice infecting a capital sentencing proceeding is especially serious in light of the complete finality of the death sentence. "The Court, as well as the separate opinions of a majority of the individual Justices, has recognized that the qualitative difference of death from all other punishments requires a correspondingly greater degree of scrutiny of the capital sentencing determination." *California v. Ramos,* 463 U.S. 992, 998–999 (1983). We have struck down capital sentences when we found that the circumstances under which they were imposed "created an unacceptable risk that 'the death penalty [may have been] meted out arbitrarily or capriciously' or through 'whim . . . or mistake.'" *Caldwell, supra,* at 343 (O'CONNOR, J., concurring). In the present case, we find the risk that racial prejudice may have infected petitioner's capital sentencing unacceptable in light of the ease with which that risk could have been minimized. By refusing to question prospective jurors on racial prejudice, the trial judge failed to adequately protect petitioner's constitutional right to an impartial jury.

III

We hold that a capital defendant accused of an interracial crime is entitled to have prospective jurors informed of the race of the victim and questioned on the issue of racial bias. The rule we propose is minimally intrusive; as in other cases involving "special circumstances," the trial judge retains discretion as to the form and number of questions on the subject, including the decision whether to question the venire individually or collectively.

IV

The inadequacy of *voir dire* in this case requires that petitioner's death sentence be vacated. It is not necessary, however, that he be retried on the issue of guilt. Our judgment in this case is that there was an unacceptable risk of racial prejudice infecting the *capital sentencing proceeding*. This judgment is based on a conjunction of three factors: the fact that the crime charged involved interracial violence, the broad discretion given the jury at the death-penalty hearing, and the special seriousness of the risk of improper sentencing in a capital case. At the guilt phase of petitioner's trial, the jury had no greater discretion than it would have had if the crime charged had been noncapital murder. Thus, with respect to the guilt phase of petitioner's trial, we find this case to be indistinguishable from *Ristaino,* to which we continue to adhere.

■ THE CHIEF JUSTICE concurs in the judgment.

■ JUSTICE BRENNAN, concurring in part and dissenting in part.

I join only that portion of the Court's judgment granting petitioner a new sentencing proceeding, but dissent from that portion of the judgment refusing to vacate the conviction.

The Sixth Amendment guarantees criminal defendants an impartial jury. Among the most important of the means designed to insure an impartial jury is the right to strike those jurors who manifest an inability to try the case solely on the basis of the evidence. This right to exclude incompetent jurors cannot be exercised meaningfully or effectively unless counsel has sufficient information with which to evaluate members of the venire. As JUSTICE WHITE noted for the Court in *Rosales-Lopez v. United States,* 451 U.S. 182, 188 (1981), "lack of adequate *voir dire* impairs the defendant's right to exercise peremptory challenges where provided by statute or rule, as it is in the federal courts."

Recognizing this fact, we held long ago that "essential demands of fairness" may require a judge to ask jurors whether they entertain any racial prejudice. *Aldridge v. United States,* 283 U.S. 308 (1931). More recently, we attempted to refine the analysis, and declared that when there is a showing of a "likelihood" that racial or ethnic prejudice may affect the jurors, the Constitution requires a trial judge to honor a defendant's request to examine the jurors' ability to deal impartially with the evidence adduced at trial. Exercising our supervisory powers over the federal courts, we held in *Rosales-Lopez* that when a violent crime has been committed, and the victim and the accused are of different races, a *per se* inference of a "reasonable possibility" of prejudice is shown. In the present case, we deal with a criminal case from a state court involving an act of interracial violence, and are faced with the question of what factors and circumstances will elevate this presumptive "reasonable possibility" of prejudice into a constitutionally significant "likelihood" of prejudice.

The Court identifies three factors, the "conjunction" of which in its view entitled petitioner Turner as a matter of constitutional right to have the jury questioned on racial bias. These are (1) the fact that the crime committed involved interracial violence; (2) the broad discretion given the jury at the death penalty hearing; and (3) the "special seriousness of the risk of improper sentencing in a capital case." I agree with the Court that when these three factors are present, as they were at petitioner's sentencing hearing, the trial court commits constitutional error in refusing a defense request to ask the jurors if the race of either the victim or the accused will bear on their ability to render a decision based solely on the evidence. What I cannot accept is that the judge is released from this obligation to insure an impartial jury—or, to put it another way, that the defendant is stripped of this constitutional safeguard—when a capital jury is hearing evidence concerning a crime involving interracial violence but passing "only" on the issue of guilt/innocence, rather than on the appropriate sentence.

The Court's argument is simply untenable on its face. As best I can understand it, the thesis is that since there is greater discretion entrusted to a capital jury in the sentencing phase than in the guilt phase, "there is [in the sentencing hearing] a unique opportunity for racial prejudice to operate but remain undetected." *Ante.* However, the Court's own discussion of the issues demonstrates that the opportunity for racial bias to taint the jury process is not "uniquely" present at a sentencing hearing, but is equally a factor at the guilt phase of a bifurcated capital trial.

According to the Court, a prejudiced juror sitting at a sentencing hearing might be influenced by his racial bias in deciding whether the crime committed involved aggravating factors specified under state law; the Court notes that racial prejudice might similarly cause that juror to be less favorably inclined toward an accused's evidence of mitigating circumstances. Moreover, the Court informs us:

> "More subtle, less consciously held racial attitudes could also influence a juror's decision. . . . Fear of blacks, which could easily be stirred up by the violent facts of [a] crime, might incline a juror to favor the death penalty." *Ibid.*

The flaw in this "analysis" is that there is simply no connection between the proposition advanced, the support proffered for that thesis, and the conclusion drawn. In other words, it is certainly true, as the Court maintains, that racial bias inclines one to disbelieve and disfavor the object of the prejudice, and it is similarly incontestable that subconscious, as well as express, racial fears and hatreds operate to deny fairness to the person despised; that is why we seek to insure that the right to an impartial jury is a meaningful right by providing the defense with the opportunity to ask prospective jurors questions designed to expose even hidden prejudices. But the Court never explains why these biases should be of less concern at the guilt phase than at the sentencing phase. The majority asserts that "a juror who believes that blacks are violence prone or morally inferior might well be influenced by that belief in deciding whether petitioner's crime involved the aggravating factors specified under Virginia law." But might not that same juror be influenced by those same prejudices in deciding whether, for example, to credit or discredit white witnesses as opposed to black witnesses at the guilt phase? Might not those same racial fears that would incline a juror to favor death not also incline a juror to favor conviction?

A trial to determine guilt or innocence is, at bottom, nothing more than the sum total of a countless number of small discretionary decisions made by each individual who sits in the jury box. The difference between conviction and acquittal turns on whether key testimony is believed or rejected; on whether an alibi sounds plausible or dubious; on whether a character witness appears trustworthy or unsavory; and on whether the jury concludes that the defendant had a motive, the inclination, or the means available to commit the crime charged. A racially biased juror sits with blurred vision and impaired sensibilities and is incapable of fairly making the myriad decisions that each juror is called upon to make in the course of a trial. To put it simply, he cannot judge because he has prejudged. This is equally true at the trial on guilt as at the hearing on sentencing.

To sentence an individual to death on the basis of a proceeding tainted by racial bias would violate the most basic values of our criminal justice system. This the Court understands. But what it seems not to comprehend is that to permit an individual to be *convicted* by a prejudiced jury violates those same values in precisely the same way. The incongruity of the Court's split judgment is made apparent after it is appreciated that the opportunity for bias to poison decisionmaking operates at a guilt trial in the same way as it does at a sentencing hearing and after one returns to the context of the case before us. Implicit in the Court's judgment is the acknowledgment that there was a likelihood that the jury that pronounced the death sentence acted, in part, on the basis of racial prejudice. But the exact same jury convicted Turner. Does the Court really mean to suggest that the constitutional entitlement to an impartial jury attaches only at the sentencing phase? Does the Court really believe that racial biases are turned on and off in the course of one criminal prosecution?

My sense is that the Court has confused the *consequences* of an unfair trial with the *risk* that a jury is acting on the basis of prejudice. In other words, I suspect that what is really animating the Court's judgment is the sense of outrage it rightly experiences at the prospect of a man being sentenced to death on the basis of the color of his skin. Perhaps the Court is slightly less troubled by the prospect of a racially motivated conviction unaccompanied by the death penalty, and I suppose that if, for some unimaginable reason, I had to choose between the two cases, and could only rectify one, I would remedy the case where death had been imposed. But there is no need to choose between the two cases. To state what seems to me obvious, the constitutional right implicated is the right to be judged by an impartial jury, regardless of the sentence, and the constitutional focus thus belongs on whether there is a likelihood of bias, and not on what flows from that bias. In *Ham v. South Carolina,* 409 U.S. 524 (1973), we reversed the conviction of a young black man who was charged with and convicted of possession of marijuana; because the man was known in the community as a civil rights activist, and because we were persuaded that racial issues were inextricably bound up with the conduct of the trial, we concluded that it was likely that any prejudice that individual members of the jury might harbor would be intensified and held that under those circumstances the trial judge was required to oblige the defense request to inquire into the jury's possible racial bias. We did not reject the petitioner's claim in that case because he was sentenced only to 18 months' imprisonment. Surely one has a right to an impartial jury whether one is subject to punishment for a day or a lifetime.

The Court may believe that it is being Solomonic in "splitting the difference" in this case and granting petitioner a new sentencing hearing while denying him the other "half" of the relief demanded. Starkly put, petitioner "wins" in that he gets to be resentenced, while the State "wins" in that it does not lose its conviction. But King Solomon did not, in fact, split the baby in two, and had he done so, I suspect that he would be remembered less for his wisdom than for his hardheartedness. Justice is not served by compromising principles in this way. I would reverse the conviction as well as the sentence in this case to insure compliance with the constitutional guarantee of an impartial jury.

■ [JUSTICE MARSHALL's opinion concurring in part and dissenting in part is omitted.]

■ JUSTICE POWELL, with whom JUSTICE REHNQUIST joins, dissenting.

II

Until today a trial judge committed an unconstitutional abuse of discretion by refusing to inquire into racial prejudice only when the defendant showed that racial issues "were inextricably bound up with the conduct of the trial." *Ristaino,* 424 U.S., at 597. When a defendant makes such a showing, there is an unacceptable risk that racial prejudice will "distort the trial." *Ibid.* Under such circumstances, therefore, due process requires "a *voir dire* that include[s] questioning specifically directed to racial prejudice." *Ibid.* In *Ristaino,* however, the Court expressly declined to adopt a *per se* rule requiring *voir dire* inquiry into racial bias in every trial for an interracial crime. Neither the Constitution nor sound policy considerations supported such a *per se* approach. But today the Court decides that the Constitution does require a *per se* rule in capital cases because the capital jury exercises discretion at the sentencing phase. The Court's reasoning ignores the many procedural and substantive safeguards, similar to those governing the jury's decision on guilt or innocence, that circumscribe the capital jury's sentencing decision.

Under Virginia law, murder is a capital offense only if it is "willful, deliberate and premeditated" and is committed while the perpetrator is engaged in another crime or under specified aggravating circumstances. As in any criminal prosecution, of course, the State carries the burden of proving all elements of the capital offense beyond a reasonable doubt. Following a sentencing hearing, the death sentence may not be imposed unless the State proves beyond a reasonable doubt statutorily defined aggravating factors. Virginia law recognizes only two aggravating factors: whether, based on the defendant's criminal record, there is a probability that he would commit future crimes of violence, and whether the defendant's crime was "outrageously or wantonly vile, horrible or inhuman, in that it involved torture, depravity of mind or aggravated battery to the victim." The jury also is required to consider any relevant mitigating evidence offered by the defendant.

The existence of these significant limitations on the jury's exercise of sentencing discretion illustrates why the Court's *per se* rule is wholly unfounded. Just as the trial judge's charge at the guilt phase instructs the jurors that they may consider only the evidence in the case and that they must determine if the prosecution has established each element of the crime beyond a reasonable doubt, the charge at the penalty phase directs the jurors to focus solely on considerations relevant to determination of appropriate punishment and to decide if the prosecution has established beyond a reasonable doubt factors warranting imposition of death. Accordingly, just as there is no reason to presume racial bias on the part of jurors who determine the guilt of a defendant who has committed a violent crime against a person of another race, there is no reason to constitutionalize such a presumption with respect to the jurors who sit to recommend the penalty in a capital case.

Nor does anything in the circumstances of this jury's recommendation of the death penalty suggest a likelihood that sentencing decisions are being made on racial grounds so as to justify adoption of a *per se* rule. There is no question that the State proved the existence of the first aggravating factor beyond a reasonable doubt. As the Supreme Court of Virginia noted, since 1974 petitioner "has been convicted of malicious maiming, escape, unlawful wounding, malicious wounding, and second-degree murder. Four of these offenses occurred in the penal system." The court also expressly found that petitioner's criminal record was "one of the most extensive" it had reviewed in a capital case. The court further observed that, although the first aggravating factor plainly supported the recommendation of death, the circumstances of this crime were "vile" because petitioner had committed an aggravated battery on his victim.

Under the foregoing circumstances, there is no basis for concluding that the jury's sentencing decision was tainted by racial bias. The mere fact that the sentencing decision, after the jury had found guilt and the existence of aggravating factors beyond a reasonable doubt, involved an element of discretion provides no ground for this Court to presume that the decision was infected by racial prejudice. Instead, the rule that until today afforded due process required petitioner to establish that some special circumstances in *his* case, beyond the fact of an interracial crime, raised a constitutionally significant likelihood that racial prejudice would taint the proceedings. The Court rejects that rule, and adopts a singularly unwise and unjustified presumption that capital jurors harbor latent racial bias.

NOTES AND QUESTIONS

1. ***Competing Approaches.*** Three approaches emerged among the Justices in *Turner*. Justices Brennan and Marshall would have overturned both the defendant's conviction for capital murder and his death sentence on the ground that the jury that decided both issues could have been influenced by racial bias. Justices Powell and Rehnquist would have upheld both the conviction and sentence on the ground that the circumstances of the case did not raise a sufficient risk of prejudice. The Court majority split the difference, holding that the risk of prejudice at the sentencing phase was sufficient to entitle the defendant to racial voir dire but the risk of prejudice at the conviction stage was not. Which approach do you find most and least justified? What concerns weigh in favor and against racial voir dire in *Turner*? Do these considerations justify a distinction between the conviction and sentencing phase?

2. ***Supreme Court Cases on Racial Voir Dire.*** *Turner* represents the fourth Supreme Court case in modern times addressing racial voir dire. In *Ham v. South Carolina*, 409 U.S. 524 (1973), the Court held that a black defendant, charged with drug possession, who alleged that he was framed because of his race and widely-known civil rights activism was entitled as a matter of due process to racial voir dire. The Court determined that Ham's defense based on allegations of discrimination would make race inextricably bound up with the conduct of the trial and, moreover, would likely intensify any prejudice that individual jurors might harbor. In contrast, the Court in *Ristaino v. Ross*, 424 U.S. 589 (1976), ruled that a black defendant charged with assaulting with intent to murder a white security guard during the course of a robbery was not constitutionally entitled to racial voir dire, although the Court suggested that permitting it would have been the wiser course. The Court distinguished Ham as involving "special circumstances" creating a "significant likelihood" that, absent questioning about racial prejudice, the jury would be influenced by racial bias.

Then, in *Rosales-Lopez v. United States*, 451 U.S. 182 (1981), the Court applied a more defendant-friendly test to the federal-court trials over which it exerts supervisory powers, holding that, where the totality of the circumstances creates a "reasonable possibility" that prejudice could influence juror decisionmaking, federal judges should permit voir dire. The Court further specified that, when a defendant is charged with a violent crime and the victim is of a different race, a *per se* reasonable possibility of prejudice exists. Finally, *Turner v. Murray*, 476 U.S. 28 (1986), which involved a state trial, making only the constitutional standard applicable, held that interracial capital murder constituted a "special circumstance" under *Ham* for purposes of sentencing but not for purposes of conviction. If the prosecution seeks the death penalty in such a case, therefore, the defendant is entitled to conduct racial voir dire. Putting the cases together, a defendant is constitutionally entitled to racial voir dire in state and federal court when the case involves "special circumstances" that create a "significant likelihood" of racial bias, which includes imposition of the death penalty for interracial murder. In federal but not state court, a defendant is entitled to racial voir dire under the Court's supervisory power if the circumstances create a "reasonable possibility," though not necessarily a "significant likelihood," of racial bias, such as an interracial violent crime short of capital murder.

3.   *Problems.* For each of the three scenarios below, consider whether (1) the judge was required to allow racial voir dire as a matter of constitutional law under *Ham* and *Ristaino*; (2) whether the judge would have been required to allow racial voir dire if the case were in federal court under *Rosalez-Lopez*; and (3) whether, if you were the trial judge, you would grant defendant's request even if you were not required to.

a.   *Case 1: Interracial Couple.* Defendants, an interracial married couple, were tried in federal court for laundering profits from selling marijuana. The wife's defense lawyer sought permission to ask prospective jurors about their attitudes toward the defendants' interracial relationship. He was concerned "by the fact that the defendants are sitting there as an interracial couple." The question "lets [the jury] know race is not an issue. . . . It clears the air. . . . I'd like to clear [the jurors'] subconscious and agree that it is not an issue, a non-issue." *See United States v. Barber*, 80 F.3d 964 (4th Cir. 1996).

b.   *Case 2: Interracial Rape.* Defendant, a black male, was tried in state court on charges of rape, kidnapping, and assault with a deadly weapon. The prosecution alleged that he participated in a group of seven or eight black youths who robbed two young white couples at night and raped the two women at knifepoint. The trial judge asked jurors generally whether they were aware of any bias or prejudice they might have and admonished them that "they were not to consider the race of the defendants or victims in arriving at their verdict." He refused, however, to permit specific questions to jurors about their racial attitudes because, he explained, race was not a specific issue in the case. *See Dukes v. Waitkevitch*, 536 F.2d 469 (1st Cir. 1976).

c. ***Case 3: (Latino) Gang Member.*** Thaddeus Jimenez was 13 years old when he was tried for a murder that the prosecution alleged was gang-related. Jimenez's lawyer sought permission to ask prospective jurors: "Would the fact that an accused is allegedly a member of a street gang, prevent you from giving him a fair and impartial trial?" *See People v. Jimenez*, 672 N.E.2d 914 (1996). Consider also that Jimenez is Latino. Was he entitled to probe jurors' attitudes about race as a result?

Post-script: Jimenez was convicted and sentenced to 50 years in prison. After serving sixteen years, he was exonerated in 2009 by the Northwestern University Law School's Center on Wrongful Convictions.

4. ***Problem.*** Voir dire can involve asking potential jurors questions orally or through a questionnaire filled out by jurors prior to individualized voir dire. If you were a defense lawyer in any of the above cases, what questions would you pose to jurors, either through a questionnaire or live questions, to determine whether they harbor racial attitudes antagonistic (or favorable) to your client's case? How effective would those questions likely be in ferreting out racial bias? (Consider trying the questions out on an acquaintance or a fellow student in your class.) If you were to probe a juror's attitudes in a way that would reveal bias notwithstanding their likely denials, how might that juror feel toward you and by extension your client? If the judge, unpersuaded that the juror exhibited bias, refused to excuse the juror for cause, what could you do?

C. PEREMPTORY CHALLENGES

After conducting voir dire of eligible jurors, the next step in the jury selection process is to determine whether some jurors should be excused "for cause" because their answers to voir dire indicate that they probably cannot be impartial. After that, each party will have a certain number of "peremptory" challenges or strikes, that is, the right to strike potential jurors without giving any reason. The number of such challenges varies across jurisdictions and, typically, each party gets a higher number of peremptory challenges in more serious cases. Thus, each litigant might have three challenges in a larceny case and as many as twenty in a trial for murder.

The purpose of the peremptory challenge is to contribute to the selection of an impartial jury. Each party can be expected to peremptorily strike those jurors they believe are least sympathetic to their case. If each party strikes the jurors least favorable to their side, the remaining jurors should be relatively neutral compared to the jurors who were struck, resulting in an impartial jury. For-cause challenges should remove the most biased jurors in a venire and then peremptory challenges should remove the most biased of the jurors that remain. The rationale behind not requiring a reason for the peremptory challenge is that each litigant will have intuitive impressions about the attitudes of potential jurors that cannot be demonstrated but are nonetheless reliable. Requiring them to articulate the basis of the hunch may be unrealistic and, moreover, may be offensive as the hunch may be rational but nonetheless based on assumptions of a stereotypical nature. Peremptory challenges are also thought to give a sense of legitimacy to the jury in the eyes of the litigants and the public because both sides had a hand in selecting the jury.

Although the Court, in *Strauder* invalidated a state law excluding blacks from jury service, the exclusion of blacks and other racial groups through the use of peremptory challenges went unquestioned for nearly 100 years after the adoption of the Equal Protection Clause. Then, in *Swain v. Alabama*, 380 U.S. 202 (1965), the Court held that a prosecutor's use of peremptory challenges to strike black jurors could violate equal protection, but only if the defendant could demonstrate that the prosecutor struck blacks in case after case, reflecting an assumption by the prosecutor that blacks were unfit for jury service. The Court accepted, however, that it was lawful for a prosecutor to strike black jurors based on race if he did so only in cases in which the issues of the particular case led the prosecutor to suspect that black jurors would be unsympathetic.

In the case below, the defendant also claimed that the prosecutor peremptorily excluded all blacks from the jury because of their race. The defendant was unable to demonstrate the pattern of race-based challenges across cases required by *Swain* to make out a claim under the Equal Protection Clause. In addition, therefore, the defendant argued that the fair cross section requirement of the Sixth Amendment was violated by the prosecutor's intentional exclusion of blacks through the use of peremptory challenges. The Court, however, decided to revisit the equal protection proof standards of *Swain* rather than address the fair cross section claim.

Batson v. Kentucky

Supreme Court of the United States, 1986.
476 U.S. 79.

■ JUSTICE POWELL delivered the opinion of the Court.

I

Petitioner, a black man, was indicted in Kentucky on charges of second-degree burglary and receipt of stolen goods. On the first day of trial in Jefferson Circuit Court, the judge conducted *voir dire* examination of the venire, excused certain jurors for cause, and permitted the parties to exercise peremptory challenges. The prosecutor used his peremptory challenges to strike all four black persons on the venire, and a jury composed only of white persons was selected. Defense counsel moved to discharge the jury before it was sworn on the ground that the prosecutor's removal of the black veniremen violated petitioner's rights under the Sixth and Fourteenth Amendments to a jury drawn from a cross section of the community, and under the Fourteenth Amendment to equal protection of the laws. [T]he trial judge observed that the parties were entitled to use their peremptory challenges to "strike anybody they want to."

The Supreme Court of Kentucky affirmed. We granted certiorari and now reverse.

II

A

More than a century ago, the Court decided that the State denies a black defendant equal protection of the laws when it puts him on trial before a jury from which members of his race have been purposefully excluded. *Strauder* v. *West Virginia,* 100 U. S. 303 (1880).

In holding that racial discrimination in jury selection offends the Equal Protection Clause, the Court in *Strauder* recognized, however, that a defendant has no right to a "petit jury composed in whole or in part of persons of his own race." *Id.,* at 305. "The number of our races and nationalities stands in the way of evolution of such a conception" of the demand of equal protection. The Equal Protection Clause guarantees the defendant that the State will not exclude members of his race from the jury venire on account of race, or on the false assumption that members of his race as a group are not qualified to serve as jurors.

Purposeful racial discrimination in selection of the venire violates a defendant's right to equal protection because it denies him the protection that a trial by jury is intended to secure. "The very idea of a jury is a body . . . composed of the peers or equals of the person whose rights it is selected or summoned to determine; that is, of his neighbors, fellows, associates, persons having the same legal status in society as that which he holds." *Strauder,* at 308. The petit jury has occupied a central position in our system of justice by safeguarding a person accused of crime against the arbitrary exercise of power by prosecutor or judge. Those on the venire must be "indifferently chosen," to secure the defendant's right under the Fourteenth Amendment to "protection of life and liberty against race or color prejudice." *Strauder* at 309.

Racial discrimination in selection of jurors harms not only the accused whose life or liberty they are summoned to try. A person's race simply "is unrelated to his fitness as a juror." *Thiel* v. *Southern Pacific Co.,* 328 U. S. 217, 227 (1946) (Frankfurter, J., dissenting). As long ago as *Strauder,* therefore, the Court recognized that by denying a person participation in jury service on account of his race, the State unconstitutionally discriminated against the excluded juror.

The harm from discriminatory jury selection extends beyond that inflicted on the defendant and the excluded juror to touch the entire community. Selection procedures that purposefully exclude black persons from juries undermine public confidence in the fairness of our system of justice. Discrimination within the judicial system is most pernicious because it is "a stimulant to that race prejudice which is an impediment to securing to [black citizens] that equal justice which the law aims to secure to all others." *Strauder,* at 308.

B

In *Strauder,* the Court invalidated a state statute that provided that only white men could serve as jurors. We can be confident that no State now has such a law. The Constitution requires, however, that we look beyond the face of the statute defining juror qualifications and also consider challenged selection practices to afford "protection against action of the State through its administrative officers in effecting the prohibited discrimination." *Norris* v. *Alabama,* 294 U. S. 587, 589 (1935). While decisions of this Court have been concerned largely with discrimination during selection of the venire, the principles announced there also forbid discrimination on account of race in selection of the petit jury.

Accordingly, the component of the jury selection process at issue here, the State's privilege to strike individual jurors through peremptory challenges, is subject to the commands of the Equal Protection Clause. Although a prosecutor ordinarily is entitled to exercise permitted peremptory challenges "for any reason at all, as long as that reason is related to his view concerning the outcome" of the case to be tried, the Equal Protection Clause forbids the prosecutor to challenge potential jurors solely on account of their race or on the assumption that black jurors as a group will be unable impartially to consider the State's case against a black defendant.

III

A

Swain required the Court to decide, among other issues, whether a black defendant was denied equal protection by the State's exercise of peremptory challenges to exclude members of his race from the petit jury. The record in *Swain* showed that the prosecutor had used the State's peremptory challenges to strike the six black persons included on the petit jury venire. While rejecting the defendant's claim for failure to prove purposeful discrimination, the Court nonetheless indicated that the Equal Protection Clause placed some limits on the State's exercise of peremptory challenges.

The Court sought to accommodate the prosecutor's historical privilege of peremptory challenge free of judicial control and the constitutional prohibition on exclusion of persons from jury service on account of race. To preserve the peremptory nature of the prosecutor's challenge, the Court in *Swain* declined to scrutinize his actions in a particular case by relying on a presumption that he properly exercised the State's challenges.

A number of lower courts following the teaching of *Swain* reasoned that proof of repeated striking of blacks over a number of cases was necessary to establish a violation of the Equal Protection Clause. Since this interpretation of *Swain* has placed on defendants a crippling burden of proof, prosecutors' peremptory challenges are now largely immune from constitutional scrutiny. For reasons that follow, we reject this evidentiary formulation.

Old Standard

C

The standards for assessing a prima facie case in the context of discriminatory selection of the venire have been fully articulated since *Swain*. These principles support our conclusion that a defendant may establish a prima facie case of purposeful discrimination in selection of the petit jury solely on evidence concerning the prosecutor's exercise of peremptory challenges at the defendant's trial. To establish such a case, the defendant first must show that he is a member of a cognizable racial group and that the prosecutor has exercised peremptory challenges to remove from the venire members of the defendant's race. Second, the defendant is entitled to rely on the fact, as to which there can be no dispute, that peremptory challenges constitute a jury selection practice that permits "those to discriminate who are of a mind to discriminate." *Avery* v. *Georgia,* 345 U. S., at 562. Finally, the defendant must show that these facts and any other relevant circumstances raise an inference that the prosecutor used that practice to exclude the veniremen from the petit jury on account of their race.

New Standard

1

2

3

In deciding whether the defendant has made the requisite showing, the trial court should consider all relevant circumstances. For example, a "pattern" of strikes against black jurors included in the particular venire might give rise to an inference of discrimination. Similarly, the prosecutor's questions and statements during *voir dire* examination and in exercising his challenges may support or refute an inference of discriminatory purpose.

Once the defendant makes a prima facie showing, the burden shifts to the State to come forward with a neutral explanation for challenging black jurors. Though this requirement imposes a limitation in some cases on the full peremptory character of the historic challenge, we emphasize that the prosecutor's explanation need not rise to the level justifying exercise of a challenge for cause. But the prosecutor may not rebut the defendant's prima facie case of discrimination by stating merely that he challenged jurors of the defendant's race on the assumption—or his intuitive judgment—that they would be partial to the defendant because of their shared race. Just as the Equal Protection Clause forbids the States to exclude black persons from the venire on the assumption that blacks as a group are unqualified to serve as jurors, so it forbids the States to strike black veniremen on the assumption that they will be biased in a particular case simply because the defendant is black. The core guarantee of equal protection, ensuring citizens that their State will not discriminate on account of race, would be meaningless were we to approve the exclusion of jurors on the basis of such assumptions, which arise solely from the jurors' race. Nor may the prosecutor rebut the defendant's case merely by denying that he had a discriminatory motive or "affirm[ing] [his] good faith in making individual selections." *Alexander* v. *Louisiana,* 405 U. S., at 632. If these general assertions were accepted as rebutting a defendant's prima facie case, the Equal Protection Clause "would be but a vain and illusory requirement." *Norris* v. *Alabama, supra,* at 598. The prosecutor therefore must articulate a neutral explanation related to the particular case to be tried. The trial court then will have the duty to determine if the defendant has established purposeful discrimination.

IV

[W]e do not agree that our decision today will undermine the contribution the challenge generally makes to the administration of justice. The reality of practice, amply reflected in many state- and federal-court opinions, shows that the challenge may be, and unfortunately at times has been, used to discriminate against black jurors. By requiring trial courts to be sensitive to the racially discriminatory use of peremptory challenges, our decision enforces the mandate of equal protection and furthers the ends of justice. In view of the heterogeneous population of our Nation, public respect for our criminal justice system and the rule of law will be strengthened if we ensure that no citizen is disqualified from jury service because of his race.

V

In this case, petitioner made a timely objection to the prosecutor's removal of all black persons on the venire. Because the trial court flatly rejected the objection without requiring the prosecutor to give an explanation for his action, we remand this case for further proceedings. If the trial court decides that the facts establish, prima facie, purposeful discrimination and the prosecutor does not come forward with a neutral explanation for his action, our precedents require that petitioner's conviction be reversed.

■ [The concurring opinion of JUSTICE WHITE is omitted.]

■ JUSTICE MARSHALL, concurring.

I join JUSTICE POWELL's eloquent opinion for the Court, which takes a historic step toward eliminating the shameful practice of racial discrimination in the selection of juries. I nonetheless write separately to express my views. The decision today will not end the racial discrimination that peremptories inject into the jury-selection process. That goal can be accomplished only by eliminating peremptory challenges entirely.

I

Misuse of the peremptory challenge to exclude black jurors has become both common and flagrant. Black defendants rarely have been able to compile statistics showing the extent of that practice, but the few cases setting out such figures are instructive. *See United States* v. *Carter,* 528 F. 2d 844, 848 (CA8 1975) (in 15 criminal cases in 1974 in the Western District of Missouri involving black defendants, prosecutors peremptorily challenged 81% of black jurors); *United States* v. *McDaniels,* 379 F. Supp. 1243 (ED La. 1974) (in 53 criminal cases in 1972–1974 in the Eastern District of Louisiana involving black defendants, federal prosecutors used 68.9% of their peremptory challenges against black jurors, who made up less than one-quarter of the venire); *McKinney* v. *Walker,* 394 F. Supp. 1015, 1017–1018 (SC 1974) (in 13 criminal trials in 1970–1971 in Spartansburg County, South Carolina, involving black defendants, prosecutors peremptorily challenged 82% of black jurors). Prosecutors have explained to courts that they routinely strike black jurors. An instruction book used by the prosecutor's office in Dallas County, Texas, explicitly advised prosecutors that they conduct jury selection so as to eliminate " 'any member of a minority group.' " In 100 felony trials in Dallas County in 1983–1984, prosecutors peremptorily struck 405 out of 467 eligible black jurors; the chance of a qualified black sitting on a jury was 1 in 10, compared to 1 in 2 for a white.

Justice Rehnquist concedes [in his dissent] that exclusion of blacks from a jury, solely because they are black, is at best based upon "crudely stereotypical and . . . in many cases hopelessly mistaken" notions. Yet the Equal Protection Clause prohibits a State from taking any action based on crude, inaccurate racial stereotypes—even an action that does not serve the State's interests. Exclusion of blacks from a jury, solely because of race, can no more be justified by a belief that blacks are less likely than whites to consider fairly or sympathetically the State's case against a black defendant than it can be justified by the notion that blacks lack the "intelligence, experience, or moral integrity," *Neal, supra,* at 397, to be entrusted with that role.

II

I wholeheartedly concur in the Court's conclusion that use of the peremptory challenge to remove blacks from juries, on the basis of their race, violates the Equal Protection Clause. I would go further, however, in fashioning a remedy adequate to eliminate that discrimination. Merely allowing defendants the opportunity to challenge the racially discriminatory use of peremptory challenges in individual cases will not end the illegitimate use of the peremptory challenge.

Evidentiary analysis similar to that set out by the Court has been adopted as a matter of state law in States including Massachusetts and California. Cases from those jurisdictions illustrate the limitations of the approach. First, defendants cannot attack the discriminatory use of peremptory challenges at all unless the challenges are so flagrant as to establish a prima facie case. This means, in those States, that where only one or two black jurors survive the challenges for cause, the prosecutor need have no compunction about striking them from the jury because of their race. Prosecutors are left free to discriminate against blacks in jury selection provided that they hold that discrimination to an "acceptable" level.

Second, when a defendant can establish a prima facie case, trial courts face the difficult burden of assessing prosecutors' motives. Any prosecutor can easily assert facially neutral reasons for striking a juror, and trial courts are ill equipped to second-guess those reasons. How is the court to treat a prosecutor's statement that he struck a juror because the juror had a son about the same age as defendant, *see People* v. *Hall,* 672 P. 2d 854 (1983), or seemed "uncommunicative," *King* v. *County of Nassau,* 581 F. Supp. 493, 498 (EDNY 1984), or "never cracked a smile" and, therefore "did not possess the sensitivities necessary to realistically look at the issues and decide the facts in this case," *Hall, supra,* at 856? If such easily generated explanations are sufficient to discharge the prosecutor's obligation to justify his strikes on nonracial grounds, then the protection erected by the Court today may be illusory.

Nor is outright prevarication by prosecutors the only danger here. "[I]t is even possible that an attorney may lie to himself in an effort to convince himself that his motives are legal." *King, supra,* at 502. A prosecutor's own conscious or unconscious racism may lead him easily to the conclusion that a prospective black juror is "sullen," or "distant," a characterization that would not have come to his mind if a white juror had acted identically. A judge's own conscious or unconscious racism may lead him to accept such an explanation as well supported. As JUSTICE REHNQUIST concedes, prosecutors' peremptories are based on their "seat-of-the-pants instincts" as to how particular jurors will vote. Yet "seat-of-the-pants instincts" may often be just another term for racial prejudice. Even if all parties approach the Court's mandate with the best of conscious intentions, that mandate requires them to confront and overcome their own racism on all levels—a challenge I doubt all of them can meet.

III

The inherent potential of peremptory challenges to distort the jury process by permitting the exclusion of jurors on racial grounds should ideally lead the Court to ban them entirely from the criminal justice system.

Some authors have suggested that the courts should ban prosecutors' peremptories entirely, but should zealously guard the defendant's peremptory as "essential to the fairness of trial by jury," *Lewis* v. *United States,* 146 U. S. 370, 376 (1892), and "one of the most important of the rights secured to the accused," *Pointer* v. *United States,* 151 U. S. 396, 408 (1894). I would not find that an acceptable solution. Our criminal justice system "requires not only freedom from any bias against the accused, but also from any prejudice against his prosecution. Between him and the state the scales are to be evenly held." *Hayes* v. *Missouri,* 120 U. S. 68, 70 (1887). We can maintain that balance, not by permitting both prosecutor and defendant to engage in racial discrimination in jury selection, but by banning the use of peremptory challenges by prosecutors and by allowing the States to eliminate the defendant's peremptories as well.

■ [The concurring opinions of JUSTICES STEVENS and O'CONNOR are omitted.]

■ CHIEF JUSTICE BURGER, joined by JUSTICE REHNQUIST, dissenting.

II

Long ago it was recognized that "[t]he right of challenge is almost essential for the purpose of securing perfect fairness and impartiality in a trial." W. Forsyth, History of Trial by Jury 175 (1852). The peremptory challenge has been in use without scrutiny into its basis for nearly as long as juries have existed.

The Court's opinion, in addition to ignoring the teachings of history, also contrasts with *Swain* in its failure to even discuss the rationale of the peremptory challenge. *Swain* observed:

> The function of the challenge is not only to eliminate extremes of partiality on both sides, but to assure the parties that the jurors before whom they try the case will decide on the basis of the evidence placed for them, and not otherwise. In this way the peremptory satisfies the rule that 'to perform its high function in the best way, "justice must satisfy the appearance of justice." *Id.,* at 219.

Permitting unexplained peremptories has long been regarded as a means to strengthen our jury system in other ways as well. One commentator has recognized:

> The peremptory, made without giving any reason, avoids trafficking in the core of truth in most common stereotypes. . . . Common human experience, common sense, psychosociological studies, and public opinion polls tell us that it is likely that certain classes of people statistically have predispositions that would make them inappropriate jurors for particular kinds of cases. But to allow this knowledge to be expressed in the evaluative terms necessary for challenges for cause would undercut our desire for a society in which all people are judged as individuals and in which each is held reasonable and open to compromise. . . . [For example,] [a]lthough experience reveals that black males as a class can be biased against young

alienated blacks who have not tried to join the middle class, to enunciate this in the concrete expression required of a challenge for cause is societally divisive. Instead we have evolved in the peremptory challenge a system that allows the covert expression of what we dare not say but know is true more often than not. Babcock, Voir Dire: Preserving "Its Wonderful Power," 27 Stan. L. Rev. 545, 553–554 (1975).

Instead of even considering the history or function of the peremptory challenge, the bulk of the Court's opinion is spent recounting the well-established principle that intentional exclusion of racial groups from jury venires is a violation of the Equal Protection Clause. I too reaffirm that principle, which has been a part of our constitutional tradition since at least *Strauder* v. *West Virginia,* 100 U. S. 303 (1880). But if today's decision is nothing more than mere "application" of the "principles announced in *Strauder,*" as the Court maintains, some will consider it curious that the application went unrecognized for over a century. The Court in *Swain* had no difficulty in unanimously concluding that cases such as *Strauder* did not require inquiry into the basis for a peremptory challenge.

A moment's reflection quickly reveals the vast differences between the racial exclusions involved in *Strauder* and the allegations before us today:

> Exclusion from the venire summons process implies that the government (usually the legislative or judicial branch) . . . has made the general determination that those excluded are unfit to try *any* case. Exercise of the peremptory challenge, by contrast, represents the discrete decision, made by one of two or more opposed *litigants* in the trial phase of our adversary system of justice, that the challenged venireperson will likely be more unfavorable to that litigant in that *particular case* than others on the same venire.

> Thus, excluding a particular cognizable group from all venire pools is stigmatizing and discriminatory in several interrelated ways that the peremptory challenge is not. The former singles out the excluded group, while individuals of all groups are equally subject to peremptory challenge on any basis, including their group affiliation. Further, venire-pool exclusion bespeaks *a priori* across-the-board total unfitness, while peremptory-strike exclusion merely suggests potential partiality in a particular isolated case. Exclusion from venires focuses on the inherent attributes of the excluded group and infers its *inferiority,* but the peremptory does not. To suggest that a particular race is unfit to judge in any case necessarily is racially insulting. To suggest that each race may have its own

special concerns, or even may tend to favor its own, is not."
United States v. *Leslie,* 783 F. 2d 541, 554 (CA5 1986) (en banc).

That the Court is not applying conventional equal protection
analysis is shown by its limitation of its new rule to allegations of
impermissible challenge *on the basis of race;* the Court's opinion clearly
contains such a limitation. *See ante* (to establish a prima facie case, "the
defendant first must show that he is a member of a cognizable *racial
group*") (emphasis added); *ibid.* ("[F]inally, the defendant must show that
these facts and any other relevant circumstances raise an inference that
the prosecutor used that practice to exclude the veniremen from the petit
jury *on account of their race*") (emphasis added). But if conventional equal
protection principles apply, then presumably defendants could object to
exclusions on the basis of not only race, but also sex; age; religious or
political affiliation; mental capacity; number of children; living
arrangements; and employment in a particular industry or profession.

Rather than applying straightforward equal protection analysis, the
Court substitutes for the holding in *Swain* a curious hybrid. The
defendant must first establish a "prima facie case," of invidious
discrimination, then the "burden shifts to the State to come forward with
a neutral explanation for challenging black jurors."

Our system permits two types of challenges: challenges for cause and
peremptory challenges. Challenges for cause obviously have to be
explained; by definition, peremptory challenges do not. "It is called a
peremptory challenge, because the prisoner may challenge peremptorily,
on his own dislike, *without showing of any cause.*" H. Joy, On Peremptory
Challenge of Jurors 1 (1844) (emphasis added). Analytically, there is no
middle ground: A challenge either has to be explained or it does not. It is
readily apparent, then, that to permit inquiry into the basis for a
peremptory challenge would force "the peremptory challenge [to] collapse
into the challenge for cause." *United States* v. *Clark,* 737 F. 2d 679, 682
(CA7 1984).

An example will quickly demonstrate how today's holding, while
purporting to "further the ends of justice," *ante,* will not have that effect.
Assume an Asian defendant, on trial for the capital murder of a white
victim, asks prospective jury members, most of whom are white, whether
they harbor racial prejudice against Asians. *See Turner* v. *Murray.* The
basis for such a question is to flush out any "juror who believes that
[Asians] are violence-prone or morally inferior. . . ." *Ibid,* at 35. Assume
further that all white jurors deny harboring racial prejudice but that the
defendant, on trial for his life, remains unconvinced by these
protestations. Instead, he continues to harbor a hunch, an "assumption,"
or "intuitive judgment," that these white jurors will be prejudiced against
him, presumably based in part on race. The time-honored rule before
today was that peremptory challenges could be exercised on such a basis.

The effect of the Court's decision, however, will be to force the defendant to come forward and "articulate a neutral explanation," for his peremptory challenge, a burden he probably cannot meet. This example demonstrates that today's holding will produce juries that the parties do not believe are truly impartial. This will surely do more than "disconcert" litigants; it will diminish confidence in the jury system.

A further painful paradox of the Court's holding is that it is likely to interject racial matters back into the jury selection process, contrary to the general thrust of a long line of Court decisions and the notion of our country as a "melting pot." In *Avery* v. *Georgia,* 345 U. S. 559 (1953), for instance, the Court confronted a situation where the selection of the venire was done through the selection of tickets from a box; the names of whites were printed on tickets of one color and the names of blacks were printed on different color tickets. The Court had no difficulty in striking down such a scheme. Justice Frankfurter observed that "opportunity for working of a discriminatory system exists whenever the mechanism for jury selection *has a component part,* such as the slips here, *that differentiates between white and colored. . . ." Id.,* at 564 (concurring) (emphasis added).

Today we mark the return of racial differentiation as the Court accepts a positive evil for a perceived one. Prosecutors and defense attorneys alike will build records in support of their claims that peremptory challenges have been exercised in a racially discriminatory fashion by asking jurors to state their racial background and national origin for the record, despite the fact that "such questions may be offensive to some jurors and thus are not ordinarily asked on voir dire." *People* v. *Motton,* 704 P. 2d 176, 180. This process is sure to tax even the most capable counsel and judges since determining whether a prima facie case has been established will "require a continued monitoring and recording of the 'group' composition of the panel present and prospective. . . ." *People* v. *Wheeler,* 583 P. 2d 748, 773 (1978) (Richardson, J., dissenting).

Even after a "record" on this issue has been created, disputes will inevitably arise. In one case, for instance, a conviction was reversed based on the assumption that no blacks were on the jury that convicted a defendant. *See People* v. *Motton, supra.* However, after the court's decision was announced, Carolyn Pritchett, who had served on the jury, called the press to state that the court was in error and that she was black.

■ JUSTICE REHNQUIST, with whom THE CHIEF JUSTICE joins, dissenting.

In my view, there is simply nothing "unequal" about the State's using its peremptory challenges to strike blacks from the jury in cases involving black defendants, so long as such challenges are also used to exclude whites in cases involving white defendants, Hispanics in cases involving Hispanic defendants, Asians in cases involving Asian defendants, and so on. This case-specific use of peremptory challenges by the State does not single out blacks, or members of any other race for that matter, for discriminatory treatment. Such use of peremptories is at best based upon seat-of-the-pants instincts, which are undoubtedly crudely stereotypical and may in many cases be hopelessly mistaken. But as long as they are applied across-the-board to jurors of all races and nationalities, I do not see—and the Court most certainly has not explained—how their use violates the Equal Protection Clause.

The use of group affiliations, such as age, race, or occupation, as a "proxy" for potential juror partiality, based on the assumption or belief that members of one group are more likely to favor defendants who belong to the same group, has long been accepted as a legitimate basis for the State's exercise of peremptory challenges. Indeed, given the need for reasonable limitations on the time devoted to *voir dire,* the use of such "proxies" by both the State and the defendant may be extremely useful in eliminating from the jury persons who might be biased in one way or another.

NOTES AND QUESTIONS

1.   *Competing Approaches.* The majority in *Batson* stakes out a middle ground among the various justices. The majority holds that any time a prosecutor uses peremptory challenges to strike black jurors because of race in a criminal trial of a black defendant, he violates the defendant's equal protection rights. What harms does the majority believe are caused by the prosecutor's discriminatory peremptory challenges? Which harms seem most likely to result from racially discriminatory challenges? Which harms are most important to prevent?

The dissenting opinions would have held that peremptory challenges were completely unrestricted. They acknowledged that discriminatory selection of the *venire* from which jurors are drawn violated the Equal Protection Clause, but contended that discriminatory peremptory challenges in selecting the *petit jury* did not. Why not? Aren't such peremptory challenges racially discriminatory, and isn't the prosecutor a state actor? What concerns did they have with applying the Equal Protection Clause to peremptory challenges? Are such concerns legitimate?

Justice Marshall, in contrast, concurred in the result but argued that the Court should have gone further. He would have banned all peremptory challenges in any case by prosecutors and would have permitted states to deny them to defense counsel as well. Why? Which of the three approaches is preferable?

2.   *Proof Framework.* The Court in *Batson* set forth a three-step framework for reviewing a defendant's complaint that the prosecutor exercised racially discriminatory peremptory challenges. This procedure is typically referred to as a "*Batson* challenge."

a. ***Step One: Defendant's Prima Facie Case.*** In the first step, the defendant has the burden to make out a prima facie case of racial discrimination. This, in turn, involves three elements. First, the defendant must allege that he is a member of a cognizable racial group and that the prosecutor struck one or more jurors of the same group. Second, the defendant can rely on the fact that the discretionary nature of the peremptory challenge allows purposeful discrimination by one who is of a mind to discriminate. Third, the defendant must point to facts that support an inference that the prosecutor did discriminate by race. If the defendant fails to satisfy any of these elements, the trial judge must allow the prosecution's peremptory challenge and excuse the challenged juror.

Do these elements of the prima facie case make sense? Why must the juror whom the prosecutor struck be a member of the same racial group as the defendant? Are jurors of the defendant's race more likely to acquit?

b. ***Step Two: Prosecutor's Race-Neutral Explanation.*** If the defendant succeeds in his prima facie case, the next step requires the prosecutor to "articulate a neutral explanation related to the particular case" for his peremptory challenge. The prosecutor may not claim reliance on the assumption that the race of the struck juror inclined her to favor the defendant, nor may the prosecutor simply deny that he acted based on race. If the prosecutor fails to provide the requisite neutral explanation, the trial judge must hold the prosecutor's challenge violated the Equal Protection Clause.

What is your assessment of this step? Recall that step one's requirement that the defendant share the race of the struck juror appears premised on the assumption that jurors of the defendant's race are more likely to acquit. If that assumption is valid, why cannot prosecutors rely on that same assumption in step two as the explanation for the strike? Is not relying on realistic assumptions what peremptory challenges are for? What does the Court mean by a "neutral" explanation? What if the prosecutor says he struck a juror because his hair was short?

c. ***Step Three: Resolving the Conflict.*** If the defense and prosecution meet their burden of production in the first two steps, the trial court must decide which explanation for the prosecutor's peremptory challenge he believes. The burden of persuasion at this step rests with the defendant to prove that the prosecutor acted with a racially discriminatory purpose and thus that the prosecutor's race-neutral explanation is a pretext. If the trial judge finds in the defendant's favor by a preponderance of the evidence, he must invalidate the prosecutor's peremptory challenge. Otherwise, the peremptory challenge will stand and the juror will be excused.

3. ***Juror of a Different Race.*** In *Powers v. Ohio*, 499 U.S. 400 (1991), a white defendant objected that the prosecutor struck black jurors because of their race. The trial and lower appellate courts ruled against the defendant because the struck jurors did not share his race. The Supreme Court reversed, holding that defendants can object to race-based peremptory challenges by prosecutors even if the struck jurors are of a different race from the defendant. The Court did not, however, reverse its prior holding that a defendant's equal protection rights are only violated by peremptory strikes against jurors of his race. Instead, the Court held that *the jurors'* equal protection rights were violated and that the defendant had standing to raise the jurors' rights given the jurors' unlikely desire or ability to litigate the matter and given the defendant's interest in complaining on the jurors' behalf. By focusing on the jurors' rights instead of the defendant's, the Court did not need to address the question how a white defendant was harmed by the exclusion of blacks from his jury. In fact, the Court expressly denied that race indicated anything about juror disposition, emphasizing instead that race-based peremptory challenges harm the excluded jurors and cast doubt on the integrity of the judicial process.

Is the Court's denial in *Powers* that race is relevant to juror disposition consistent with assumptions underlying previous jury selection cases? If the Court's view has changed, is it justified in doing so? For a discussion of the contradictory position the Court has taken with respect to the relationship between race and juror disposition, see Eric L. Muller, Solving the Batson Paradox: Harmless Error, Jury Representation, and the Sixth Amendment, 106 Yale L.J. 93, 96–99 (1996).

4.   *Defendants' Peremptory Challenges.* In *Georgia v. McCollum*, 505 U.S. 42 (1992), three white people were indicted for assaulting two black people. "Shortly after the events, a leaflet was widely distributed in the local African-American community reporting the assault and urging community residents not to patronize [defendants'] business." *Id.* at 44. Prior to jury selection, the state moved to prohibit the defendants from using peremptory challenges on the basis of race, explaining that it expected to show that the victims' race was a motivating factor in the assault. The trial and lower courts rejected the motion. The Supreme Court reversed, holding that defendants could not exercise peremptory challenges in a racially discriminatory manner. The Court relied on *Edmonson v. Leesville Concrete Co.*, 500 U.S. 614 (1991), in which it had held that peremptory challenges by private litigants in a civil case constituted state action for equal protection purposes because the state was implicated by authorizing peremptory challenges, and because creating a jury is a quintessential government function.

Was the Court right to extend *Batson* to criminal defendants? What reasons, if any, justify allowing criminal defendants to use peremptory challenges in a race-based manner? Did the white defendants in *McCollum* have legitimate reasons to use race-based peremptories?

Dissenting in *McCollum*, Justice Thomas argued that defendants should be allowed to strike jurors based on race in part because it would help minority defendants secure minority representation on juries by reducing the number of whites in the venire. The NAACP Legal Defense Fund (LDF) also advocated this position in its *amicus* brief to the Court. Justice Thomas and LDF were thus in agreement, whereas Justice Marshall, the first Director-Counsel of LDF, had argued in his *Batson* concurrence that criminal defendants should not be permitted to use race-based challenges. What might explain LDF's break with its founding director and what might explain Justice Thomas's unusual agreement with LDF? Which is the better approach?

5.   *What Is Race?* The Court in *Batson* prohibited peremptory challenges against members of a "cognizable racial group." The Court has held that black and Latino constitute protected racial groups under *Batson*, and the Court presumably would so hold regarding Asian, Native American, and white. Whether the concept of race for *Batson* purposes will extend beyond these conventional racial categories remains to be seen. In *Hernandez v. New York*, 500 U.S. 352 (1991), a defendant complained that a prosecutor purposely struck jurors because they were Latino. The prosecutor said he struck them because they were fluent in Spanish and, based on their answers to voir dire questions, he doubted they would be able to accept the official translation of witnesses who testified in Spanish. The Court held that this explanation was "race-neutral" for purposes of step two of the *Batson* inquiry, despite its disproportionate impact on Latinos. The plurality explained:

> The prosecutor's articulated basis for these challenges divided potential jurors into two classes: those whose conduct during *voir dire* would persuade him they might have difficulty in accepting the translator's rendition of Spanish-language testimony and those potential jurors who gave no such reason for doubt. Each category would include both Latinos and non-Latinos. While the prosecutor's criterion might well result in the disproportionate removal of prospective Latino jurors, that disproportionate impact does not turn the prosecutor's actions into a *per se* violation of the Equal Protection Clause.

The plurality emphasized that the explanation was neutral on its face but that a trial judge could find, at stage three, that the explanation was a pretext for striking jurors because they were Latino. The plurality also suggested that striking potential jurors just because they were Spanish-speaking or bilingual might qualify as race discrimination under *Batson*:

> Language permits an individual to express both a personal identity and membership in a community, and those who share a common language may interact in ways more intimate than those without this bond. Bilinguals, in a sense, inhabit two communities, and serve to bring them closer. Indeed, some scholarly comment suggests that people proficient in two languages may not at times think in one language to the exclusion of the other. The analogy is that of a high-hurdler, who combines the ability to sprint and to jump to accomplish a third feat with characteristics of its own, rather than two separate functions. . . .

* * *

> Just as shared language can serve to foster community, language differences can be a source of division. Language elicits a response from others, ranging from admiration and respect, to distance and

alienation, to ridicule and scorn. Reactions of the latter type all too often result from or initiate racial hostility. In holding that a race-neutral reason for a peremptory challenge means a reason other than race, we do not resolve the more difficult question of the breadth with which the concept of race should be defined for equal protection purposes. We would face a quite different case if the prosecutor had justified his peremptory challenges with the explanation that he did not want Spanish-speaking jurors. It may well be, for certain ethnic groups and in some communities, that proficiency in a particular language, like skin color, should be treated as a surrogate for race under an equal protection analysis.

Do you agree that the prosecutor's explanation was race-neutral, at least on its face? Although the Court does not mention it, the trial record reveals that the only jurors whom the prosecutor questioned about their ability to accept the official translation had Latino surnames. Do you agree with the plurality that being fluent in Spanish or being bilingual should perhaps be treated as a race for *Batson* purposes?

6. *Juror Bias Toward Minority Dialects and Manners of Expression.* What if, instead of witnesses speaking in a foreign language, they spoke in a dialect of English common to a racial minority? For example, many black Americans speak in the dialect that linguists call African-American Vernacular English (AAVE) (also known as "Ebonics"). Could a prosecutor justify striking black jurors on the ground that they spoke AAVE in a case in which some witnesses would speak AAVE? Could defense counsel? In Florida v. Zimmerman, the case in which George Zimmerman, a white neighborhood watch-person, killed an unarmed black teenager named Trayvon Martin, it is likely that Zimmerman benefited at trial by there being no jurors who spoke AAVE. On the night of the fatal interaction between Martin and Zimmerman, Martin was on the phone with a friend when Zimmerman confronted him. The friend, Rachel Jeantel, who was on the phone throughout the altercation until just before Martin's death, testified that Zimmerman was the instigator. The jury, however, apparently did not believe Jeantel's testimony. As Linguistics Professor John Rickford observes, her testimony was likely misunderstood and stigmatized because she spoke AAVE, which is commonly and incorrectly viewed as "broken" English, when in fact it is a systematic dialect. According to Rickford:

> African Americans on the jury—especially fluent AAVE speakers—would have understood Jeantel, and the presence of even one such juror could have helped the others to understand what she was saying, . . . But the defense did a good job of making sure there were no African American jurors in this trial.

Marguerite Rigoglioso, *Stanford linguist Says Prejudice Toward African American Dialect Can Result in Unfair Rulings*, STANFORD REPORT, December 2, 2014, http://news.stanford.edu/news/2014/december/vernacular -trial-testimony–120214.html (last visited May 12, 2014).

Minority witnesses may also be discredited based on ignorance and prejudice toward their manner of expression. Trial witnesses of Asian ethnicity, for example, might speak in a more indirect way regarding events than a typical witness would, or they might avert their eyes from an interrogating lawyer out of cultural respect, both of which might be perceived by jurors as deceptive or evasive. As Chet Pager observes:

> [W]hite jurors may consciously or subconsciously ascribe a "distrustful" character to an inter-racial face, such as the association of "slanty eyes" (the Asian epicanthal fold) with deception and distrustfulness. [Second,] the cues being sent may differ among races. [A]lthough facial expressions can be controlled and rarely "leak" unintentional indicators of deception, jurors pay close attention to the face and have cohesive—but culturally-based—ideas of what an honest expression looks like. A less familiar witness, be she black or Chinese, may not present those honest expressions in her testimony.

Chet K.W. Pager, *Blind Justice, Colored Truths and the Veil of Ignorance*, 41 WILLAMETTE L. REV. 373, 397–398 (2005).

Minority witnesses might be more accurately understood and believed if the jury had members who shared the witnesses' ethnic background. If so, should litigants be prevented from striking jurors who share the cultural background of witnesses and thereby help the jury understand them better? How could such a rule be enforced? More generally, how can the justice system help to ensure that witnesses, including defendants, are not inaccurately discredited based on cultural ignorance about the witnesses' linguistic or expressive manner?

7.   *Beyond Race?* In a case subsequent to *Batson*, the Court held that the fair cross section requirement has no application to the use of peremptory challenges. *See Holland v. Illinois*, 493 U.S. 474 (1990). Accordingly, an equal protection claim remains the only basis on which to challenge the exclusion of jurors. Should groups defined by traits other than race be protected from peremptory challenges? One might expect the Court to recognize as "cognizable" any "suspect" group that receives special protection under the Equal Protection Clause. The Court has, however, extended *Batson* protection beyond race only to sex. *See J.E.B. v. Alabama*, 511 U.S. 127 (1994). It has not thus far extended it to other suspect classifications, such as national origin, religion, or political affiliation, and several lower courts have expressly declined to do so. Should the Court extend peremptory challenges to all suspect classifications under the Equal Protection Clause? Should it apply *Batson* to the increasingly protected classification of sexual orientation? Should *Batson* extend to groups that qualify as "distinctive" for fair cross section purposes, such as wage earners—an issue over which lower courts have divided. Why might the courts be reluctant to extend *Batson* to other groups typically protected by the Equal Protection Clause or the Sixth Amendment? Is it less objectionable to strike jurors because they are, for example, Catholic, Muslim, Italian, or Republican than because they are black, white, Asian, or male?

8.   *Proof Framework Revisited.* In addition to the modifications to *Batson* discussed in the foregoing Notes, the Court has clarified (or modified) the three steps of the *Batson* challenge process. In *Johnson v. California*, 545 U.S. 162 (2005), the Court explained that the prima facie case required by *Batson* need not prove a discriminatory purpose by a preponderance of the evidence. Rather, the burden on the defendant (or prosecutor after *McCollum*) is merely one of production and need only identify sufficient facts to raise a suspicion that would justify a finding of race discrimination *if* the party whose peremptory strike is being challenged failed to provide a race-neutral explanation.

In *Purkett v. Elem*, 514 U.S. 765 (1995), the Court explained that the party defending against a *Batson* challenge also has a light burden of production in step two—to articulate a legitimate, nondiscriminatory explanation. Step two is satisfied if the party offers any reason not inherently based on race (or other *Batson*-protected trait). The reason need not have anything to do with the issues in the case and need not otherwise make sense. Thus, in *Purkett*, a prosecutor explained his decision to peremptorily strike two black jurors on the ground that one had "long curly hair" and both had "facial hair," adding, "I don't like the way they looked, with the way the hair is cut, both of them. And the mustaches and the beards look suspicious to me." The Court held that this explanation was race-neutral, satisfying step two, because whether or not "silly or superstitious," "implausible or fantastic," the wearing of long, unkempt hair and facial hair is not peculiar to any race. Is this account of what constitutes a neutral explanation consistent with *Batson*?

In step three, the trial judge considers all the facts and circumstances including the competing explanations offered by the parties and decides whether he is persuaded by a preponderance of the evidence that the peremptory challenge under review was based on a prohibited trait, such as race. If not, the *Batson* challenge is rejected and the peremptory challenge stands. The Court also explained in *Purkett* that the determination at step three is a question of fact and thus should be reversed on appeal only if it is clearly erroneous.

9.   Batson *Reconsidered*. The *Batson* doctrine has generated an enormous amount of scholarship, mostly critical. Critics who agree that race-based peremptory challenges should be prohibited argue that the doctrine is too ineffective. Much of the criticism echoes Justice Marshall's concurrence in *Batson*. A prominent criticism of step one is that meeting the prima facie case requires, in practice, a pattern of strikes against a particular racial group, which may be very difficult to show, especially when certain minority groups are already underrepresented in the venire such that one or two peremptory challenges would be sufficient to completely remove that race from the trial jury. Step two has been criticized for allowing any nonracial explanation to suffice regardless of how implausible it seems, encouraging racially motivated litigants to fabricate pretextual explanations. Problems with step three are two-fold. First, the trial judge will often defer to a lawyer's explanation for a strike, especially by a prosecutor, out of a reluctance to accuse a fellow member of the bar of being both a racist and a liar. Second, appellate courts defer to trial judges even in cases where the explanation for the strike is implausible because it is very difficult to find that a trial judge's ruling based on in-person observations the appellate court can only evaluate with a cold record were clearly erroneous. These critics typically call for a more lenient proof standard or abolition of the peremptory challenge altogether, as suggested by Justice Marshall and which has been adopted in Great Britain.

Critics from the other side argue that the *Batson* doctrine burdens the ability of litigants to effectively eliminate jurors most partial to the other side. Some maintain, as did the dissents in *Batson*, that purposely striking based on race should be permitted because, rightly or wrongly, race is relevant to predicting a juror's inclination. Others complain that *Batson* has the effect of restricting *race-neutral* strikes because a litigant who believes for nonracial reasons that a juror is predisposed against his client may be blocked from striking her because he already struck a juror of the same race. Or he might just forego striking that juror because it's not worth the time and expense of litigating a *Batson* challenge. Also, if the court conducts a *Batson* hearing openly and finds an attempted strike to have been race-based, the seated juror may harbor resentment toward the litigant who tried to strike her.

In view of the developments since *Batson*, are you more or less persuaded of its value? If the Court were to revisit *Batson*, what approach would you recommend?

10. *Design Problem: Achieving Representative Trial Juries.* The Court has consistently denied that a defendant has an affirmative right to a representative jury in his trial. The Court has only mandated, under the Sixth Amendment, that selection processes not systematically exclude certain groups from venires and, under the Equal Protection Clause, that jurors not purposefully be excluded from venires or juries because of race or sex. At the same time, it is at least implicit in the Court's cases that, other things being equal, a representative jury is desirable. Why has the Court refused to constitutionalize a requirement that the jury that actually tries a defendant be representative in its composition? If you were a legislator or court administrator, what procedures could you propose to ensure or at least increase the chances that each jury was representative of the community or otherwise diverse? What practical or legal problems might such reforms face?

11. *Jural Districting.* Professor Kim Forde-Mazrui proposes a jury selection procedure he terms "jural districting." A jurisdiction would divide a jury district into twelve sub-districts of approximately equal population, designed around communities that likely share interests and experiences. Such communities would be identified according to electoral districting principles, taking account of geographical proximity, such as residential community or neighborhood, as well as common demographic factors such as race, ethnicity, religion, age, political affiliation, occupation, and socioeconomic status. Courts would then require that each trial jury contain a juror from each sub-district. By ensuring that each jury contains residents of different sub districts, jural districting would achieve demographic diversity through geographic diversity. Trial juries would tend to be more diverse in perspectives and experiences than juries selected by current procedures or even by proposals to select juries exclusively by race. For a fuller discussion of the proposal, *see* Kim Forde-Mazrui, *Jural Districting: Selecting Impartial Juries Through Community Representation*, 52 VAND. L. REV. 353 (1999).

How would you assess jural districting? What are its likely benefits and drawbacks? How does it compare to the other ideas for creating diverse juries that you generated in response to the previous Note?

In the spring of 2005, Senator Don Harmon introduced legislation entitled the "Fair Jury Act" in the Illinois Senate. The Act was modeled on Forde-Mazrui's proposal, with the exception that race was *not* included as a factor to be considered in drawing "subcircuits" (the Act's term for sub-districts). The Fair Jury Act would instead draw subcircuits primarily based on socioeconomic status in order to achieve more proportional representation on trial juries of low-income communities, which were also typically communities of color. The legislation would also apply only to counties of at least one hundred thousand residents. Is the Fair Jury Act's focus on economic communities without regard to race more or less preferable to Forde-Mazrui's proposal that would also include race as a factor in identifying communities of shared interest to include within jury sub-districts?

Although the Fair Jury Act made it out of committee with support from Democratic Illinois Senators, Republican senators blocked it. Why might lawmakers have objected to the Fair Jury Act and why might such opposition have fallen along partisan lines? If you worked for a legislator supporting the Act, what would you suggest your boss do to overcome likely objections to the Fair Jury Act? For an account of the Fair Jury Act and the problem of underrepresentative juries in Cook County to which it was responding, *see* Steve Bogira, "A Jury of Whose Peers?", *Chicago Reader*, Vol. 34, No. 33 (May 12, 2005).

IV. PUNISHMENT

A. THE DEATH PENALTY

According to Amnesty International, approximately two thirds of the world's nations have abolished the death penalty in law or practice. Among those that still impose it, the five jurisdictions that did so most frequently in 2013 were China, Iran, Iraq, Saudi Arabia, and the United States, which is the only country in the Americas that imposes the ultimate punishment. In the United States, thirty-two states and the federal government authorize execution.

Capital punishment in the United States is, of course, not new. The death penalty has always been legal, except for a five-year period in the 1970s. During the 1960s, the NAACP Legal Defense Fund brought several challenges against the death penalty, arguing that it was cruel and unusual, arbitrary, and racially discriminatory. In *Furman v.*

Georgia, 408 U.S. 238 (1972), the Supreme Court held that the death penalty was too arbitrary—as random as "being struck by lightning," remarked concurring Justice Potter Stewart. Many observers believed that *Furman* meant that the death penalty had been permanently abolished. Beginning in 1976, however, with *Gregg v. Georgia*, 428 U.S. 153 (1976), the Court upheld new capital-sentencing procedures, provided they involved certain guidelines, such as the requirement that juries find statutory aggravating factors and consider any mitigating factors before imposing execution.

Despite new safeguards, concerns over the death penalty have persisted, including over the extent to which the death penalty is imposed more often on black defendants and, especially, on defendants found guilty of killing white victims. In fact, the petitioner presented such evidence in our previous case on racial voir dire, *Turner v. Murray*, 476 U.S. 28 (1986), in support of his request to ask jurors about their racial attitudes. Recall that Justice Powell's dissent found the evidence wanting because it did not focus on the state in which the defendant was tried:

> As support for this proposed question, petitioner's counsel referred only to certain studies that were subsequently placed in the record. The studies purported to show that a black defendant who murders a white person is more likely to receive the death penalty than other capital defendants, but the studies included no statistics concerning administration of the death penalty in Virginia.

Turner, 476 U.S. at 49 (Powell, J., dissenting). What if, however, a black defendant accused of murdering a white victim produced reliable evidence that juries systematically imposed death more often in such cases *and* the evidence did focus on the state in which the defendant was tried?

McCleskey v. Kemp

Supreme Court of the United States, 1987.
481 U.S. 279.

■ JUSTICE POWELL delivered the opinion of the Court.

This case presents the question whether a complex statistical study that indicates a risk that racial considerations enter into capital sentencing determinations proves that petitioner McCleskey's capital sentence is unconstitutional under the Eighth or Fourteenth Amendment.

I

McCleskey, a black man, was convicted of two counts of armed robbery and one count of murder in the Superior Court of Fulton County, Georgia, on October 12, 1978. McCleskey's convictions arose out of the robbery of a furniture store and the killing of a white police officer during

SECTION IV   PUNISHMENT   **649**

the course of the robbery. The evidence at trial indicated that McCleskey and three accomplices planned and carried out the robbery. All four were armed. McCleskey entered the front of the store while the other three entered the rear. McCleskey secured the front of the store by rounding up the customers and forcing them to lie face down on the floor. The other three rounded up the employees in the rear and tied them up with tape. The manager was forced at gunpoint to turn over the store receipts, his watch, and $6. During the course of the robbery, a police officer, answering a silent alarm, entered the store through the front door. As he was walking down the center aisle of the store, two shots were fired. Both struck the officer. One hit him in the face and killed him.

Several weeks later, McCleskey was arrested in connection with an unrelated offense. He confessed that he had participated in the furniture store robbery, but denied that he had shot the police officer. At trial, the State introduced evidence that at least one of the bullets that struck the officer was fired from a .38 caliber Rossi revolver. This description matched the description of the gun that McCleskey had carried during the robbery. The State also introduced the testimony of two witnesses who had heard McCleskey admit to the shooting.

The jury convicted McCleskey of murder. At the penalty hearing, the jury heard arguments as to the appropriate sentence. Under Georgia law, the jury could not consider imposing the death penalty unless it found beyond a reasonable doubt that the murder was accompanied by one of the statutory aggravating circumstances. The jury in this case found two aggravating circumstances to exist beyond a reasonable doubt: the murder was committed during the course of an armed robbery and the murder was committed upon a peace officer engaged in the performance of his duties. In making its decision whether to impose the death sentence, the jury considered the mitigating and aggravating circumstances of McCleskey's conduct. McCleskey offered no mitigating evidence. The jury recommended that he be sentenced to death on the murder charge and to consecutive life sentences on the armed robbery charges. The court followed the jury's recommendation and sentenced McCleskey to death.

[McCleskey unsuccessfully exhausted direct appeal of his conviction.] McCleskey next filed a petition for a writ of habeas corpus in the Federal District Court for the Northern District of Georgia. His petition raised 18 claims, one of which was that the Georgia capital sentencing process is administered in a racially discriminatory manner in violation of the Eighth and Fourteenth Amendments to the United States Constitution. In support of his claim, McCleskey proffered a statistical study performed by Professors David C. Baldus, Charles Pulaski, and George Woodworth (the Baldus study) that purports to show a disparity in the imposition of the death sentence in Georgia based on the race of the murder victim and, to a lesser extent, the race of the defendant. The Baldus study is actually two sophisticated statistical studies that examine over 2,000 murder cases that occurred in Georgia during the 1970's.

Baldus subjected his data to an extensive analysis, taking account of 230 variables that could have explained the disparities on nonracial grounds. One of his models concludes that, even after taking account of 39 nonracial variables, defendants charged with killing white victims were 4.3 times as likely to receive a death sentence as defendants charged with killing blacks. According to this model, black defendants were 1.1 times as likely to receive a death sentence as other defendants. Thus, the Baldus study indicates that black defendants, such as McCleskey, who kill white victims have the greatest likelihood of receiving the death penalty.[6]

[The District Court and Court of Appeals denied McCleskey's petition for habeas corpus.] We granted certiorari and now affirm.

II

McCleskey's first claim is that the Georgia capital punishment statute violates the Equal Protection Clause of the Fourteenth Amendment. He argues that race has infected the administration of Georgia's statute in two ways: persons who murder whites are more likely to be sentenced to death than persons who murder blacks, and black murderers are more likely to be sentenced to death than white murderers. As a black defendant who killed a white victim, McCleskey claims that the Baldus study demonstrates that he was discriminated against because of his race and because of the race of his victim. In its broadest form, McCleskey's claim of discrimination extends to every actor in the Georgia capital sentencing process, from the prosecutor who sought the death penalty and the jury that imposed the sentence, to the State itself that enacted the capital punishment statute and allows it to remain in effect despite its allegedly discriminatory application.

A

[T]o prevail under the Equal Protection Clause, McCleskey must prove that the decisionmakers in *his* case acted with discriminatory purpose. He offers no evidence specific to his own case that would support an inference that racial considerations played a part in his sentence. Instead, he relies solely on the Baldus study. McCleskey argues that the Baldus study compels an inference that his sentence rests on purposeful discrimination. McCleskey's claim that these statistics are sufficient

---

[6]   Baldus' 230-variable model divided cases into eight different ranges, according to the estimated aggravation level of the offense. Baldus argued in his testimony to the District Court that the effects of racial bias were most striking in the midrange cases. "[W]hen the cases become tremendously aggravated so that everybody would agree that if we're going to have a death sentence, these are the cases that should get it, the race effects go away. It's only in the mid-range of cases where the decision makers have a real choice as to what to do. If there's room for the exercise of discretion, then the [racial] factors begin to play a role." According to Baldus, the facts of McCleskey's case placed it within the midrange.

proof of discrimination, without regard to the facts of a particular case, would extend to all capital cases in Georgia, at least where the victim was white and the defendant is black.

The Court has accepted statistics as proof of intent to discriminate in certain limited contexts. First, this Court has accepted statistical disparities as proof of an equal protection violation in the selection of the jury venire in a particular district. Second, this Court has accepted statistics in the form of multiple-regression analysis to prove statutory violations under Title VII of the Civil Rights Act of 1964.

But the nature of the capital sentencing decision, and the relationship of the statistics to that decision, are fundamentally different from the corresponding elements in the venire-selection or Title VII cases. Most importantly, each particular decision to impose the death penalty is made by a petit jury selected from a properly constituted venire. Each jury is unique in its composition, and the Constitution requires that its decision rest on consideration of innumerable factors that vary according to the characteristics of the individual defendant and the facts of the particular capital offense. Thus, the application of an inference drawn from the general statistics to a specific decision in a trial and sentencing simply is not comparable to the application of an inference drawn from general statistics to a specific venire-selection or Title VII case. In those cases, the statistics relate to fewer entities, and fewer variables are relevant to the challenged decisions.[7]

Another important difference between the cases in which we have accepted statistics as proof of discriminatory intent and this case is that, in the venire-selection and Title VII contexts, the decisionmaker has an opportunity to explain the statistical disparity. Here, the State has no practical opportunity to rebut the Baldus study. "[C]ontrolling considerations of . . . public policy," *McDonald v. Pless,* 238 U.S. 264, 267 (1915), dictate that jurors "cannot be called . . . to testify to the motives and influences that led to their verdict." *Chicago, B. & Q.R. Co. v. Babcock,* 204 U.S. 585, 593 (1907). Similarly, the policy considerations behind a prosecutor's traditionally "wide discretion" suggest the impropriety of our requiring prosecutors to defend their decisions to seek death penalties, "often years after they were made." *See Imbler v. Pachtman,* 424 U.S. 409, 425–426 (1976). Moreover, absent far stronger proof, it is unnecessary to seek such a rebuttal, because a legitimate and unchallenged explanation for the decision is apparent from the record:

---

[7]   It is also questionable whether any consistent policy can be derived by studying the decisions of prosecutors. The District Attorney is elected by the voters in a particular county. Since decisions whether to prosecute and what to charge necessarily are individualized and involve infinite factual variations, coordination among district attorney offices across a State would be relatively meaningless. Thus, any inference from statewide statistics to a prosecutorial "policy" is of doubtful relevance. Moreover, the statistics in Fulton County alone represent the disposition of far fewer cases than the statewide statistics. Even assuming the statistical validity of the Baldus study as a whole, the weight to be given the results gleaned from this small sample is limited.

McCleskey committed an act for which the United States Constitution and Georgia laws permit imposition of the death penalty.

Finally, McCleskey's statistical proffer must be viewed in the context of his challenge. McCleskey challenges decisions at the heart of the State's criminal justice system. "[O]ne of society's most basic tasks is that of protecting the lives of its citizens and one of the most basic ways in which it achieves the task is through criminal laws against murder." *Gregg v. Georgia,* 428 U.S. 153, 226 (1976) (WHITE, J., concurring). Implementation of these laws necessarily requires discretionary judgments. Because discretion is essential to the criminal justice process, we would demand exceptionally clear proof before we would infer that the discretion has been abused. The unique nature of the decisions at issue in this case also counsels against adopting such an inference from the disparities indicated by the Baldus study. Accordingly, we hold that the Baldus study is clearly insufficient to support an inference that any of the decisionmakers in McCleskey's case acted with discriminatory purpose.

B

McCleskey also suggests that the Baldus study proves that the State as a whole has acted with a discriminatory purpose. He appears to argue that the State has violated the Equal Protection Clause by adopting the capital punishment statute and allowing it to remain in force despite its allegedly discriminatory application. McCleskey would have to prove that the Georgia Legislature enacted or maintained the death penalty statute *because of* an anticipated racially discriminatory effect. In *Gregg v. Georgia,* this Court found that the Georgia capital sentencing system could operate in a fair and neutral manner. There was no evidence then, and there is none now, that the Georgia Legislature enacted the capital punishment statute to further a racially discriminatory purpose.

Nor has McCleskey demonstrated that the legislature maintains the capital punishment statute because of the racially disproportionate impact suggested by the Baldus study. As legislatures necessarily have wide discretion in the choice of criminal laws and penalties, and as there were legitimate reasons for the Georgia Legislature to adopt and maintain capital punishment, we will not infer a discriminatory purpose on the part of the State of Georgia.

IV

A

McCleskey also argued that Georgia's capital sentencing system violates the Eighth Amendment.] In light of our precedents under the Eighth Amendment, McCleskey cannot argue successfully that his sentence is "disproportionate to the crime in the traditional sense." *See Pulley v. Harris,* 465 U.S. 37, 43 (1984). He does not deny that he committed a murder in the course of a planned robbery, a crime for which this Court has determined that the death penalty constitutionally may be imposed. His disproportionality claim "is of a different sort." *Pulley v. Harris, supra,* 465 U.S., at 43. McCleskey argues that the sentence in his case is disproportionate to the sentences in other murder cases.

On the one hand, he cannot base a constitutional claim on an argument that his case differs from other cases in which defendants *did* receive the death penalty. On automatic appeal, the Georgia Supreme Court found that McCleskey's death sentence was not disproportionate to other death sentences imposed in the State. The court supported this conclusion with an appendix containing citations to 13 cases involving generally similar murders.

On the other hand, absent a showing that the Georgia capital punishment system operates in an arbitrary and capricious manner, McCleskey cannot prove a constitutional violation by demonstrating that other defendants who may be similarly situated did *not* receive the death penalty. . . . :

> . . . Nothing in any of our cases suggests that the decision to afford an individual defendant mercy violates the Constitution. *Furman* held only that, in order to minimize the risk that the death penalty would be imposed on a capriciously selected group of offenders, the decision to impose it had to be guided by standards so that the sentencing authority would focus on the particularized circumstances of the crime and the defendant. *Gregg v. Georgia,* 428 U.S. 153, 199 (1976)

Because McCleskey's sentence was imposed under Georgia sentencing procedures that focus discretion "on the particularized nature of the crime and the particularized characteristics of the individual defendant," *id.,* at 206, we lawfully may presume that McCleskey's death sentence was not "wantonly and freakishly" imposed, *id.,* at 207, and thus that the sentence is not disproportionate within any recognized meaning under the Eighth Amendment.

B

Although our decision in *Gregg* as to the facial validity of the Georgia capital punishment statute appears to foreclose McCleskey's disproportionality argument, he further contends that the Georgia capital punishment system is arbitrary and capricious in *application,* and therefore his sentence is excessive, because racial considerations may influence capital sentencing decisions in Georgia.

To evaluate McCleskey's challenge, we must examine exactly what the Baldus study may show. Even Professor Baldus does not contend that his statistics *prove* that race enters into any capital sentencing decisions or that race was a factor in McCleskey's particular case.[8] Statistics at

---

[8] According to Professor Baldus: "In an analysis of this type, obviously one cannot say that we can say to a moral certainty what it was that influenced the decision. We can't do that."

most may show only a likelihood that a particular factor entered into some decisions. There is, of course, some risk of racial prejudice influencing a jury's decision in a criminal case. There are similar risks that other kinds of prejudice will influence other criminal trials. The question "is at what point that risk becomes constitutionally unacceptable," *Turner v. Murray,* 476 U.S. 28, 36, n.8 (1986). McCleskey asks us to accept the likelihood allegedly shown by the Baldus study as the constitutional measure of an unacceptable risk of racial prejudice influencing capital sentencing decisions. This we decline to do.

The capital sentencing decision requires the individual jurors to focus their collective judgment on the unique characteristics of a particular criminal defendant. It is not surprising that such collective judgments often are difficult to explain. But the inherent lack of predictability of jury decisions does not justify their condemnation. On the contrary, it is the jury's function to make the difficult and uniquely human judgments that defy codification and that "buil[d] discretion, equity, and flexibility into a legal system." H. Kalven & H. Zeisel, The American Jury 498 (1966).

McCleskey's argument that the Constitution condemns the discretion allowed decisionmakers in the Georgia capital sentencing system is antithetical to the fundamental role of discretion in our criminal justice system. Discretion in the criminal justice system offers substantial benefits to the criminal defendant. Not only can a jury decline to impose the death sentence, it can decline to convict or choose to convict of a lesser offense. Whereas decisions against a defendant's interest may be reversed by the trial judge or on appeal, these discretionary exercises of leniency are final and unreviewable. Similarly, the capacity of prosecutorial discretion to provide individualized justice is "firmly entrenched in American law." 2 W. LaFave & D. Israel, Criminal Procedure § 13.2(a), p. 160 (1984). As we have noted, a prosecutor can decline to charge, offer a plea bargain, or decline to seek a death sentence in any particular case. Of course, "the power to be lenient [also] is the power to discriminate," K. Davis, Discretionary Justice 170 (1973), but a capital punishment system that did not allow for discretionary acts of leniency "would be totally alien to our notions of criminal justice." *Gregg v. Georgia,* 428 U.S., at 200, n.50.

C

At most, the Baldus study indicates a discrepancy that appears to correlate with race. Apparent disparities in sentencing are an inevitable part of our criminal justice system. Specifically, "there can be 'no perfect procedure for deciding in which cases governmental authority should be used to impose death.'" *Zant v. Stephens,* 462 U.S. 862, 884 (1983). Despite these imperfections, our consistent rule has been that constitutional guarantees are met when "the mode [for determining guilt or punishment] itself has been surrounded with safeguards to make it as fair as possible." *Singer v. United States,* 380 U.S., at 35. Where the discretion that is fundamental to our criminal process is involved, we decline to assume that what is unexplained is invidious.

V

Two additional concerns inform our decision in this case. First, McCleskey's claim, taken to its logical conclusion, throws into serious question the principles that underlie our entire criminal justice system. The Eighth Amendment is not limited in application to capital punishment, but applies to all penalties. Thus, if we accepted McCleskey's claim that racial bias has impermissibly tainted the capital sentencing decision, we could soon be faced with similar claims as to other types of penalty.[9] Moreover, the claim that his sentence rests on the irrelevant factor of race easily could be extended to apply to claims based on unexplained discrepancies that correlate to membership in other minority groups, and even to gender. Similarly, since McCleskey's claim relates to the race of his victim, other claims could apply with equally logical force to statistical disparities that correlate with the race or sex of other actors in the criminal justice system, such as defense attorneys, or judges. Also, there is no logical reason that such a claim need be limited to racial or sexual bias. If arbitrary and capricious punishment is the touchstone under the Eighth Amendment, such a claim could—at least in theory—be based upon any arbitrary variable, such as the defendant's facial characteristics, or the physical attractiveness of the defendant or the victim, that some statistical study indicates may be influential in jury decisionmaking. As these examples illustrate, there is no limiting principle to the type of challenge brought by McCleskey. The Constitution does not require that a State eliminate any demonstrable disparity that correlates with a potentially irrelevant factor in order to operate a criminal justice system that includes capital punishment.

Second, McCleskey's arguments are best presented to the legislative bodies. It is not the responsibility—or indeed even the right—of this Court to determine the appropriate punishment for particular crimes. It is the legislatures, the elected representatives of the people, that are "constituted to respond to the will and consequently the moral values of the people." *Furman v. Georgia,* 408 U.S., at 383 (Burger, C.J., dissenting). Legislatures also are better qualified to weigh and "evaluate the results of statistical studies in terms of their own local conditions and with a flexibility of approach that is not available to the courts," *Gregg v. Georgia, supra,* 428 U.S., at 186. Capital punishment is now the law in more than two-thirds of our States. It is the ultimate duty of courts to determine on a case-by-case basis whether these laws are applied consistently with the Constitution. Despite McCleskey's wide-ranging

---

[9]   Studies already exist that allegedly demonstrate a racial disparity in the length of prison sentences.

arguments that basically challenge the validity of capital punishment in our multiracial society, the only question before us is whether in his case, the law of Georgia was properly applied. We agree with the District Court and the Court of Appeals for the Eleventh Circuit that this was carefully and correctly done in this case.

■ JUSTICE BRENNAN, with whom JUSTICE MARSHALL joins, and with whom JUSTICE BLACKMUN and JUSTICE STEVENS join in all but Part I, dissenting.

I

Adhering to my view that the death penalty is in all circumstances cruel and unusual punishment forbidden by the Eighth and Fourteenth Amendments, I would vacate the decision below insofar as it left undisturbed the death sentence imposed in this case. The Court observes that "[t]he Gregg-type statute imposes unprecedented safeguards in the special context of capital punishment," which "ensure a degree of care in the imposition of the death penalty that can be described only as unique." Notwithstanding these efforts, murder defendants in Georgia with white victims are more than four times as likely to receive the death sentence as are defendants with black victims. Nothing could convey more powerfully the intractable reality of the death penalty: "that the effort to eliminate arbitrariness in the infliction of that ultimate sanction is so plainly doomed to failure that it—and the death penalty—must be abandoned altogether." *Godfrey v. Georgia,* 446 U.S. 420, 442 (1980) (MARSHALL, J., concurring in judgment).

Even if I did not hold this position, however, I would reverse the Court of Appeals, for petitioner McCleskey has clearly demonstrated that his death sentence was imposed in violation of the Eighth and Fourteenth Amendments. While I join Parts I through IV-A of Justice BLACKMUN's dissenting opinion discussing petitioner's Fourteenth Amendment claim, I write separately to emphasize how conclusively McCleskey has also demonstrated precisely the type of risk of irrationality in sentencing that we have consistently condemned in our Eighth Amendment jurisprudence.

II

At some point in this case, Warren McCleskey doubtless asked his lawyer whether a jury was likely to sentence him to die. A candid reply to this question would have been disturbing. First, counsel would have to tell McCleskey that few of the details of the crime or of McCleskey's past criminal conduct were more important than the fact that his victim was white. Furthermore, counsel would feel bound to tell McCleskey that defendants charged with killing white victims in Georgia are 4.3 times as likely to be sentenced to death as defendants charged with killing blacks. In addition, frankness would compel the disclosure that it was more likely than not that the race of McCleskey's victim would determine whether he received a death sentence: 6 of every 11 defendants convicted of killing a white person would not have received the death penalty if their victims had been black while, among defendants with aggravating and mitigating factors comparable to McCleskey's, 20 of every 34 would not have been sentenced to die if their victims had been black. Finally, the assessment would not be complete without the information that cases involving black defendants and white victims are more likely to result in a death sentence than cases featuring any other racial combination of defendant and victim. The story could be told in a variety of ways, but McCleskey could not fail to grasp its essential narrative line: there was a significant chance that race would play a prominent role in determining if he lived or died.

The Court today holds that Warren McCleskey's sentence was constitutionally imposed. It finds no fault in a system in which lawyers must tell their clients that race casts a large shadow on the capital sentencing process. The Court arrives at this conclusion by stating that the Baldus study cannot "*prove* that race enters into any capital sentencing decisions or that race was a factor in McCleskey's particular case." (emphasis in original). Since, according to Professor Baldus, we cannot say "to a moral certainty" that race influenced a decision, we can identify only "a likelihood that a particular factor entered into some decisions," and "a discrepancy that appears to correlate with race." This "likelihood" and "discrepancy," holds the Court, is insufficient to establish a constitutional violation. The Court's evaluation of the significance of petitioner's evidence is fundamentally at odds with our consistent concern for rationality in capital sentencing, and the considerations that the majority invokes to discount that evidence cannot justify ignoring its force.

III

A

It is important to emphasize at the outset that the Court's observation that McCleskey cannot prove the influence of race on any particular sentencing decision is irrelevant in evaluating his Eighth Amendment claim. Since *Furman v. Georgia,* 408 U.S. 238 (1972), the Court has been concerned with the *risk* of the imposition of an arbitrary sentence, rather than the proven fact of one. *Furman* held that the death penalty "may not be imposed under sentencing procedures that create a substantial risk that the punishment will be inflicted in an arbitrary and capricious manner." *Godfrey v. Georgia, supra,* 446 U.S., at 427. As Justice O'CONNOR observed in *Caldwell v. Mississippi,* 472 U.S. 320, 343 (1985), a death sentence must be struck down when the circumstances under which it has been imposed "creat[e] an unacceptable *risk* that 'the death penalty [may have been] meted out arbitrarily or capriciously' or through 'whim or mistake'" (emphasis added). This emphasis on risk acknowledges the difficulty of divining the jury's motivation in an individual case. In addition, it reflects the fact that concern for arbitrariness focuses on the rationality of the system as a whole, and that a system that features a significant probability that sentencing decisions are influenced by impermissible considerations cannot be regarded as rational.

As a result, our inquiry under the Eighth Amendment has not been directed to the validity of the individual sentences before us. In *Godfrey,* for instance, the Court struck down the petitioner's sentence because the vagueness of the statutory definition of heinous crimes created a *risk* that prejudice or other impermissible influences *might have infected* the sentencing decision.

McCleskey's claim does differ, however, in one respect from these earlier cases: it is the first to base a challenge not on speculation about how a system *might* operate, but on empirical documentation of how it *does* operate.

B

The Baldus study indicates that, after taking into account some 230 nonracial factors that might legitimately influence a sentencer, the jury *more likely than not* would have spared McCleskey's life had his victim been black. The study distinguishes between those cases in which (1) the jury exercises virtually no discretion because the strength or weakness of aggravating factors usually suggests that only one outcome is appropriate; and (2) cases reflecting an "intermediate" level of aggravation, in which the jury has considerable discretion in choosing a sentence. McCleskey's case falls into the intermediate range. In such cases, death is imposed in 34% of white-victim crimes and 14% of black-victim crimes, a difference of 139% in the rate of imposition of the death penalty. In other words, just under 59%—almost 6 in 10—defendants comparable to McCleskey would not have received the death penalty if their victims had been black.[10]

Furthermore, even examination of the sentencing system as a whole, factoring in those cases in which the jury exercises little discretion, indicates the influence of race on capital sentencing. For the Georgia system as a whole, race accounts for a six percentage point difference in the rate at which capital punishment is imposed. Since death is imposed in 11% of all white-victim cases, the rate in comparably aggravated black-victim cases is 5%. The rate of capital sentencing in a white-victim case is thus 120% greater than the rate in a black-victim case. Put another

---

[10] The considerable racial disparity in sentencing rates among these cases is consistent with the "liberation hypothesis" of H. Kalven and H. Zeisel in their landmark work, The American Jury (1966). These authors found that, in close cases in which jurors were most often in disagreement, "[t]he closeness of the evidence makes it possible for the jury to respond to sentiment by *liberating it* from the discipline of the evidence." *Id.,* at 165. While "the jury does not often consciously and explicitly yield to sentiment in the teeth of the law . . . it yields to sentiment in the apparent process of resolving doubts as to evidence. The jury, therefore, is able to conduct its revolt from the law within the etiquette of resolving issues of fact." *Ibid.* Thus, it is those cases in which sentencing evidence seems to dictate neither life imprisonment nor the death penalty that impermissible factors such as race play the most prominent role.

way, over half—55%—of defendants in white-victim crimes in Georgia would not have been sentenced to die if their victims had been black. Of the more than 200 variables potentially relevant to a sentencing decision, race of the victim is a powerful explanation for variation in death sentence rates—as powerful as nonracial aggravating factors such as a prior murder conviction or acting as the principal planner of the homicide.

These adjusted figures are only the most conservative indication of the risk that race will influence the death sentences of defendants in Georgia. Data unadjusted for the mitigating or aggravating effect of other factors show an even more pronounced disparity by race. The capital sentencing rate for all white-victim cases was almost *11 times* greater than the rate for black-victim cases. Furthermore, blacks who kill whites are sentenced to death at nearly *22 times* the rate of blacks who kill blacks, and more than *7 times* the rate of whites who kill blacks. In addition, prosecutors seek the death penalty for 70% of black defendants with white victims, but for only 15% of black defendants with black victims, and only 19% of white defendants with black victims. Since our decision upholding the Georgia capital sentencing system in *Gregg,* the State has executed seven persons. All of the seven were convicted of killing whites, and six of the seven executed were black. Such execution figures are especially striking in light of the fact that, during the period encompassed by the Baldus study, only 9.2% of Georgia homicides involved black defendants and white victims, while 60.7% involved black victims.

The statistical evidence in this case thus relentlessly documents the risk that McCleskey's sentence was influenced by racial considerations. This evidence shows that there is a better than even chance in Georgia that race will influence the decision to impose the death penalty: a majority of defendants in white-victim crimes would not have been sentenced to die if their victims had been black. In determining whether this risk is acceptable, our judgment must be shaped by the awareness that "[t]he risk of racial prejudice infecting a capital sentencing proceeding is especially serious in light of the complete finality of the death sentence," *Turner v. Murray,* 476 U.S. 28, 35 (1986), and that "[i]t is of vital importance to the defendant and to the community that any decision to impose the death sentence be, and appear to be, based on reason rather than caprice or emotion," *Gardner v. Florida,* 430 U.S. 349, 358 (1977). In determining the guilt of a defendant, a State must prove its case beyond a reasonable doubt. That is, we refuse to convict if the chance of error is simply less likely than not. Surely, we should not be willing to take a person's life if the chance that his death sentence was irrationally imposed is *more* likely than not.

C

Evaluation of McCleskey's evidence cannot rest solely on the numbers themselves. We must also ask whether the conclusion suggested by those numbers is consonant with our understanding of history and human experience. Georgia's legacy of a race-conscious criminal justice system, as well as this Court's own recognition of the persistent danger that racial attitudes may affect criminal proceedings, indicates that McCleskey's claim is not a fanciful product of mere statistical artifice.

For many years, Georgia operated openly and formally precisely the type of dual system the evidence shows is still effectively in place. The criminal law expressly differentiated between crimes committed by and against blacks and whites, distinctions whose lineage traced back to the time of slavery. During the colonial period, black slaves who killed whites in Georgia, regardless of whether in self-defense or in defense of another, were automatically executed. A. Higginbotham, In the Matter of Color: Race in the American Legal Process 256 (1978).

By the time of the Civil War, a dual system of crime and punishment was well established in Georgia. The state criminal code contained separate sections for "Slaves and Free Persons of Color," and for all other persons. The code provided, for instance, for an automatic death sentence for murder committed by blacks, but declared that anyone else convicted of murder might receive life imprisonment if the conviction were founded solely on circumstantial testimony *or* simply if the jury so recommended. The code established that the rape of a free white female by a black "shall be" punishable by death. However, rape by anyone else of a free white female was punishable by a prison term not less than 2 nor more than 20 years. The rape of *blacks* was punishable "by fine and imprisonment, at the discretion of the court." A black convicted of assaulting a free white person with intent to murder could be put to death at the discretion of the court, § 4708, but the same offense committed against a black, slave or free, was classified as a "minor" offense whose punishment lay in the discretion of the court, as long as such punishment did not "extend to life, limb, or health." Assault with intent to murder by a white person was punishable by a prison term of from 2 to 10 years.

In more recent times, some 40 years ago, Gunnar Myrdal's epochal study of American race relations produced findings mirroring McCleskey's evidence:

> As long as only Negroes are concerned and no whites are disturbed, great leniency will be shown in most cases. . . . The sentences for even major crimes are ordinarily reduced when the victim is another Negro.

> For offenses which involve any actual or potential danger to whites, however, Negroes are punished more severely than whites.

On the other hand, it is quite common for a white criminal to be set free if his crime was against a Negro." G. Myrdal, An American Dilemma 551–553 (1944).

This Court has invalidated portions of the Georgia capital sentencing system three times over the past 15 years. The specter of race discrimination was acknowledged by the Court in striking down the Georgia death penalty statute in *Furman.*

Five years later, the Court struck down the imposition of the death penalty in Georgia for the crime of rape. *Coker v. Georgia,* 433 U.S. 584 (1977). [E]vidence submitted to the Court indicated that black men who committed rape, particularly of white women, were considerably more likely to be sentenced to death than white rapists. For instance, by 1977 Georgia had executed 62 men for rape since the Federal Government began compiling statistics in 1930. Of these men, 58 were black and 4 were white.

This historical review of Georgia criminal law is not intended as a bill of indictment calling the State to account for past transgressions. Citation of past practices does not justify the automatic condemnation of current ones. But it would be unrealistic to ignore the influence of history in assessing the plausible implications of McCleskey's evidence. "[A]mericans share a historical experience that has resulted in individuals within the culture ubiquitously attaching a significance to race that is irrational and often outside their awareness." Lawrence, The Id, The Ego, and Equal Protection: Reckoning With Unconscious Racism, 39 Stan.L.Rev. 327 (1987). *See* generally *id.,* at 328–344 (describing the psychological dynamics of unconscious racial motivation). As we said in *Rose v. Mitchell,* 443 U.S. 545, 558–559 (1979).

> [W]e . . . cannot deny that, 114 years after the close of the War Between the States and nearly 100 years after *Strauder,* racial and other forms of discrimination still remain a fact of life, in the administration of justice as in our society as a whole. Perhaps today that discrimination takes a form more subtle than before. But it is not less real or pernicious."

The discretion afforded prosecutors and jurors in the Georgia capital sentencing system creates such opportunities. No guidelines govern prosecutorial decisions to seek the death penalty, and Georgia provides juries with no list of aggravating and mitigating factors, nor any standard for balancing them against one another. Once a jury identifies one aggravating factor, it has complete discretion in choosing life or death, and need not articulate its basis for selecting life imprisonment.

The majority thus misreads our Eighth Amendment jurisprudence in concluding that McCleskey has not demonstrated a degree of risk sufficient to raise constitutional concern. The determination of the significance of his evidence is at its core an exercise in human moral judgment, not a mechanical statistical analysis. It must first and foremost be informed by awareness of the fact that death is irrevocable, and that as a result "the qualitative difference of death from all other punishments requires a greater degree of scrutiny of the capital sentencing determination." *California v. Ramos,* 463 U.S., at 998–999. For this reason, we have demanded a uniquely high degree of rationality in imposing the death penalty. A capital sentencing system in which race more likely than not plays a role does not meet this standard. It is true that every nuance of decision cannot be statistically captured, nor can any individual judgment be plumbed with absolute certainty. Yet the fact that we must always act without the illumination of complete knowledge cannot induce paralysis when we confront what is literally an issue of life and death. Sentencing data, history, and experience all counsel that Georgia has provided insufficient assurance of the heightened rationality we have required in order to take a human life.

IV

The Court maintains that petitioner's claim "is antithetical to the fundamental role of discretion in our criminal justice system." It states that "[w]here the discretion that is fundamental to our criminal process is involved, we decline to assume that what is unexplained is invidious."

Reliance on race in imposing capital punishment, however, is antithetical to the very rationale for granting sentencing discretion. Discretion is a means, not an end. It is bestowed in order to permit the sentencer to "trea[t] each defendant in a capital case with that degree of respect due the uniqueness of the individual." *Lockett v. Ohio,* 438 U.S. 586, 605 (1978). Failure to conduct such an individualized moral inquiry "treats all persons convicted of a designated offense not as unique individual human beings, but as members of a faceless, undifferentiated mass to be subjected to the blind infliction of the penalty of death." *Woodson v. North Carolina,* 428 U.S., at 304.

Considering the race of a defendant or victim in deciding if the death penalty should be imposed is completely at odds with this concern that an individual be evaluated as a unique human being. Decisions influenced by race rest in part on a categorical assessment of the worth of human beings according to color, insensitive to whatever qualities the individuals in question may possess. Enhanced willingness to impose the death sentence on black defendants, or diminished willingness to render such a sentence when blacks are victims, reflects a devaluation of the lives of black persons.

Our desire for individualized moral judgments may lead us to accept some inconsistencies in sentencing outcomes. Since such decisions are not reducible to mathematical formulae, we are willing to assume that a certain degree of variation reflects the fact that no two defendants are completely alike. . . .

As we made clear in *Batson v. Kentucky,* 476 U.S. 79 (1986), however, that presumption is rebuttable. *Batson* dealt with another arena in which considerable discretion traditionally has been afforded, the exercise of peremptory challenges. Those challenges are normally exercised without any indication whatsoever of the grounds for doing so. The rationale for this deference has been a belief that the unique characteristics of particular prospective jurors may raise concern on the part of the prosecution or defense, despite the fact that counsel may not be able to articulate that concern in a manner sufficient to support exclusion for cause. As with sentencing, therefore, peremptory challenges are justified as an occasion for particularized determinations related to specific individuals, and, as with sentencing, we presume that such challenges normally are not made on the basis of a factor such as race. As we said in *Batson,* however, such features do not justify imposing a "crippling burden of proof," *id.,* at 92, in order to rebut that presumption. The Court in this case apparently seeks to do just that. On the basis of the need for individualized decisions, it rejects evidence, drawn from the most sophisticated capital sentencing analysis ever performed, that reveals that race more likely than not infects capital sentencing decisions. The Court's position converts a rebuttable presumption into a virtually conclusive one.

The Court also declines to find McCleskey's evidence sufficient in view of "the safeguards designed to minimize racial bias in the [capital sentencing] process." *Ante. Gregg v. Georgia,* 428 U.S., at 226, upheld the Georgia capital sentencing statute against a facial challenge which Justice WHITE described in his concurring opinion as based on "simply an assertion of lack of faith" that the system could operate in a fair manner (opinion concurring in judgment). It is clear that *Gregg* bestowed no permanent approval on the Georgia system. It simply held that the State's statutory safeguards were assumed sufficient to channel discretion without evidence otherwise.

It has now been over 13 years since Georgia adopted the provisions upheld in *Gregg.* Professor Baldus and his colleagues have compiled data on almost 2,500 homicides committed during the period 1973–1979. They have taken into account the influence of 230 nonracial variables, using a multitude of data from the State itself, and have produced striking evidence that the odds of being sentenced to death are significantly greater than average if a defendant is black or his or her victim is white. The challenge to the Georgia system is not speculative or theoretical; it is empirical. As a result, the Court cannot rely on the statutory safeguards in discounting McCleskey's evidence, for it is the very effectiveness of those safeguards that such evidence calls into question. While we may hope that a model of procedural fairness will curb the influence of race on sentencing, "we cannot simply assume that the model works as intended; we must critique its performance in terms of its results." Hubbard, "Reasonable Levels of Arbitrariness" in Death Sentencing Patterns: A Tragic Perspective on Capital Punishment, 18 U.C.D.L.Rev. 1113, 1162 (1985).

The Court next states that its unwillingness to regard petitioner's evidence as sufficient is based in part on the fear that recognition of McCleskey's claim would open the door to widespread challenges to all aspects of criminal sentencing. Taken on its face, such a statement seems to suggest a fear of too much justice. Yet surely the majority would acknowledge that if striking evidence indicated that other minority groups, or women, or even persons with blond hair, were disproportionately sentenced to death, such a state of affairs would be repugnant to deeply rooted conceptions of fairness. The prospect that there may be more widespread abuse than McCleskey documents may be dismaying, but it does not justify complete abdication of our judicial role. The Constitution was framed fundamentally as a bulwark against governmental power, and preventing the arbitrary administration of punishment is a basic ideal of any society that purports to be governed by the rule of law.

In fairness, the Court's fear that McCleskey's claim is an invitation to descend a slippery slope also rests on the realization that any humanly imposed system of penalties will exhibit some imperfection. Yet to reject McCleskey's powerful evidence on this basis is to ignore both the qualitatively different character of the death penalty and the particular repugnance of racial discrimination, considerations which may properly be taken into account in determining whether various punishments are "cruel and unusual." Furthermore, it fails to take account of the unprecedented refinement and strength of the Baldus study.

Certainly, a factor that we would regard as morally irrelevant, such as hair color, at least theoretically could be associated with sentencing results to such an extent that we would regard as arbitrary a system in which that factor played a significant role. As I have said above, however, the evaluation of evidence suggesting such a correlation must be informed not merely by statistics, but by history and experience. One could hardly contend that this Nation has on the basis of hair color inflicted upon persons deprivation comparable to that imposed on the basis of race.

The Court's projection of apocalyptic consequences for criminal sentencing is thus greatly exaggerated. The Court can indulge in such speculation only by ignoring its own jurisprudence demanding the highest scrutiny on issues of death and race. As a result, it fails to do justice to a claim in which both those elements are intertwined—an occasion calling for the most sensitive inquiry a court can conduct. Despite its acceptance of the validity of Warren McCleskey's evidence, the Court is willing to let his death sentence stand because it fears that we cannot successfully define a different standard for lesser punishments. This fear is baseless.

Finally, the Court justifies its rejection of McCleskey's claim by cautioning against usurpation of the legislatures' role in devising and monitoring criminal punishment. The Court is, of course, correct to emphasize the gravity of constitutional intervention and the importance that it be sparingly employed. The fact that "[c]apital punishment is now the law in more than two thirds of our States", *ante,* at 1781, however, does not diminish the fact that capital punishment is the most awesome act that a State can perform. The judiciary's role in this society counts for little if the use of governmental power to extinguish life does not elicit close scrutiny.

For these reasons, "[t]he methods we employ in the enforcement of our criminal law have aptly been called the measures by which the quality of our civilization may be judged." *Coppedge v. United States,* 369 U.S. 438, 449 (1962). Those whom we would banish from society or from the human community itself often speak in too faint a voice to be heard above society's demand for punishment. It is the particular role of courts to hear these voices, for the Constitution declares that the majoritarian chorus may not alone dictate the conditions of social life. The Court thus fulfills, rather than disrupts, the scheme of separation of powers by closely scrutinizing the imposition of the death penalty, for no decision of a society is more deserving of "sober second thought." Stone, The Common Law in the United States, 50 Harv.L.Rev. 4, 25 (1936).

V

Warren McCleskey's evidence confronts us with the subtle and persistent influence of the past. His message is a disturbing one to a society that has formally repudiated racism, and a frustrating one to a Nation accustomed to regarding its destiny as the product of its own will. Nonetheless, we ignore him at our peril, for we remain imprisoned by the past as long as we deny its influence in the present.

The Court's decision today will not change what attorneys in Georgia tell other Warren McCleskeys about their chances of execution. Nothing will soften the harsh message they must convey, nor alter the prospect that race undoubtedly will continue to be a topic of discussion. McCleskey's evidence will not have obtained judicial acceptance, but that will not affect what is said on death row. However many criticisms of today's decision may be rendered, these painful conversations will serve as the most eloquent dissents of all.

■ JUSTICE BLACKMUN, with whom JUSTICE MARSHALL and JUSTICE STEVENS join, and with whom JUSTICE BRENNAN joins in all but Part IV-B, dissenting.

McCleskey's case raises concerns that are central not only to the principles underlying the Eighth Amendment, but also to the principles underlying the Fourteenth Amendment.

B

The Court treats the case as if it is limited to challenges to the actions of two specific decisionmaking bodies—the petit jury and the state legislature. This self-imposed restriction enables the Court to distinguish this case from the venire-selection cases and cases under Title VII of the Civil Rights Act of 1964 in which it long has accepted statistical evidence and has provided an easily applicable framework for review. Considering McCleskey's claim in its entirety, however, reveals that the claim fits easily within that same framework. A significant aspect of his claim is that racial factors impermissibly affected numerous steps in the Georgia capital sentencing scheme between his indictment and the jury's vote to sentence him to death. The primary decisionmaker at each of the intervening steps of the process is the prosecutor, the quintessential state actor in a criminal proceeding.

II

A

Under *Batson v. Kentucky* and the framework established in *Castaneda v. Partida,* McCleskey must meet a three-factor standard. First, he must establish that he is a member of a group "that is a recognizable, distinct class, singled out for different treatment." 430 U.S., at 494. Second, he must make a showing of a substantial degree of differential treatment. Third, he must establish that the allegedly discriminatory procedure is susceptible to abuse or is not racially neutral.

B

There can be no dispute that McCleskey has made the requisite showing under the first prong of the standard. The Baldus study demonstrates that black persons are a distinct group that are singled out for different treatment in the Georgia capital sentencing system. The Court acknowledges, as it must, that the raw statistics included in the Baldus study and presented by petitioner indicate that it is much less likely that a death sentence will result from a murder of a black person than from a murder of a white person. White-victim cases are nearly 11 times more likely to yield a death sentence than are black-victim cases. The raw figures also indicate that even within the group of defendants who are convicted of killing white persons and are thereby more likely to receive a death sentence, black defendants are more likely than white defendants to be sentenced to death.

With respect to the second prong, McCleskey must prove that there is a substantial likelihood that his death sentence is due to racial factors. The Court of Appeals assumed the validity of the Baldus study and found that it "showed that systemic and substantial disparities existed in the penalties imposed upon homicide defendants in Georgia based on race of the homicide victim, that the disparities existed at a less substantial rate in death sentencing based on race of defendants, and that the factors of race of the victim and defendant were at work in Fulton County." The question remaining therefore is at what point does that disparity become constitutionally unacceptable.

McCleskey demonstrated the degree to which his death sentence was affected by racial factors by introducing multiple-regression analyses that explain how much of the statistical distribution of the cases analyzed is attributable to the racial factors. McCleskey established that because he was charged with killing a white person he was 4.3 times as likely to be sentenced to death as he would have been had he been charged with killing a black person. McCleskey also demonstrated that it was more likely than not that the fact that the victim he was charged with killing was white determined that he received a sentence of death—20 out of every 34 defendants in McCleskey's midrange category would not have been sentenced to be executed if their victims had been black. The most persuasive evidence of the constitutionally significant effect of racial factors in the Georgia capital sentencing system is McCleskey's proof that the race of the victim is more important in explaining the imposition of a death sentence than is the factor whether the defendant was a prime mover in the homicide. Similarly, the race-of-victim factor is nearly as crucial as the statutory aggravating circumstance whether the defendant had a prior record of a conviction for a capital crime.

McCleskey produced evidence concerning the role of racial factors at the various steps in the decisionmaking process, focusing on the prosecutor's decision as to which cases merit the death sentence. McCleskey established that the race of the victim is an especially significant factor at the point where the defendant has been convicted of murder and the prosecutor must choose whether to proceed to the penalty phase of the trial and create the possibility that a death sentence may be imposed or to accept the imposition of a sentence of life imprisonment. McCleskey demonstrated this effect at both the statewide level and in Fulton County where he was tried and sentenced. The statewide statistics indicated that black-defendant/white-victim cases advanced to the penalty trial at nearly five times the rate of the black-defendant/black-victim cases (70% v. 15%), and over three times the rate of white-defendant/black-victim cases (70% v. 19%). The multiple-regression analysis demonstrated that racial factors had a readily identifiable effect at a statistically significant level. The Fulton County statistics were consistent with this evidence although they involved fewer cases.

Individualized evidence relating to the disposition of the Fulton County cases that were most comparable to McCleskey's case was consistent with the evidence of the race-of-victim effect as well. Of the 17 defendants, including McCleskey, who were arrested and charged with homicide of a police officer in Fulton County during the 1973–1979 period, McCleskey, alone, was sentenced to death. The only other defendant whose case even proceeded to the penalty phase received a sentence of life imprisonment. That defendant had been convicted of killing a black police officer.

As to the final element of the prima facie case, McCleskey showed that the process by which the State decided to seek a death penalty in his case and to pursue that sentence throughout the prosecution was susceptible to abuse. There were no guidelines as to when [prosecutors] should seek an indictment for murder as opposed to lesser charges, when they should recommend acceptance of a guilty plea to murder, acceptance of a guilty plea to a lesser charge, reduction of charges, or dismissal of charges at the postindictment-preconviction stage, or when they should seek the death penalty.

As in the context of the rule of exclusion, McCleskey's showing is of sufficient magnitude that, absent evidence to the contrary, one must conclude that racial factors entered into the decisionmaking process that yielded McCleskey's death sentence. The burden, therefore, shifts to the State to explain the racial selections. It must demonstrate that legitimate racially neutral criteria and procedures yielded this racially skewed result.

III

The Court attempts to distinguish the present case from *Batson v. Kentucky,* in which we recently reaffirmed the fact that prosecutors' actions are not unreviewable. I agree with the Court's observation that this case is "quite different" from the *Batson* case. The irony is that McCleskey presented proof in this case that would have satisfied the more burdensome standard of *Swain v. Alabama,* 380 U.S. 202 (1965), a standard that was described in *Batson* as having placed on defendants a "crippling burden of proof." 476 U.S., at 92. As discussed above, McCleskey presented evidence of numerous decisions impermissibly affected by racial factors over a significant number of cases. The exhaustive evidence presented in this case certainly demands an inquiry into the prosecutor's actions.

■ JUSTICE STEVENS, with whom JUSTICE BLACKMUN joins, dissenting.

The Court's decision appears to be based on a fear that the acceptance of McCleskey's claim would sound the death knell for capital punishment in Georgia. If society were indeed forced to choose between a racially discriminatory death penalty (one that provides heightened protection against murder "for whites only") and no death penalty at all, the choice mandated by the Constitution would be plain. But the Court's fear is unfounded. One of the lessons of the Baldus study is that there exist certain categories of extremely serious crimes for which prosecutors consistently seek, and juries consistently impose, the death penalty without regard to the race of the victim or the race of the offender. If Georgia were to narrow the class of death-eligible defendants to those categories, the danger of arbitrary and discriminatory imposition of the death penalty would be significantly decreased, if not eradicated.

NOTES AND QUESTIONS

1. *The Baldus Study.* The Baldus study is a highly respected study that the Court was prepared to assume was valid. It found that the race of a murder victim was a significant factor in who received the death penalty, finding that, after controlling for other factors, killers of white victims were 4.3 times more likely to receive the death penalty than killers of black victims. Race of defendant was also found to be a factor, black defendants being 1.1 times more likely to be sentenced to death than white defendants. However, because the race-of-victim factor is more significant, a white killer of a white victim is more likely to receive the death penalty than a black killer of a black victim, with the most likely to be sentenced to death being a black killer of a white victim. Numerous studies conducted after Baldus have continued to find similar results in Georgia and other states. Why would juries in this day and age punish killers of white victims significantly more frequently than killers of black victims? Why would that effect be more pronounced than race of defendant? Some studies have also found a race-and-gender effect, with killers of white females having the highest likelihood of a death sentence. Why might murders of white females generate the most public outrage?

2. *Equal Protection.* Who had the better argument over whether McCleskey proved that his death sentence was more likely than not based on race, the majority or Justice Blackmun? Did his evidence at least justify requiring the state to rebut the evidence as we saw the Court require in cases like *Batson* and *Castañeda*? Indeed, recall *Armstrong*, in which the Court placed an especially high burden on a defendant claiming racially selective prosecution, requiring the defendant to present some evidence of similarly situated defendants of a different race who the federal prosecutor did not charge. The Court in *McCleskey* said, however, that "absent a showing that the Georgia capital punishment system operates in an arbitrary and capricious manner, McCleskey cannot prove a constitutional violation by demonstrating that other defendants who may be similarly situated did not receive the death penalty." How could a black defendant or defendant accused of killing a white victim ever prove that race played a role in his death sentence if it would be insufficient for him to identify similarly situated white defendants or defendants accused of killing black victims who were not sentenced to death? If race did play a role in McCleskey's ultimate sentence, which actor does the evidence suggest is most responsible: the legislature, the prosecutor, or the jury?

3. *The Eighth Amendment.* Who was more persuasive on the Eighth Amendment claim, the majority or Justice Brennan? Notice the similarity between Brennan's analysis and the void-for-vagueness doctrine covered in the previous chapter. Just as vague statutes are invalid because they create an intolerable *risk* of arbitrary or discriminatory law enforcement, the highly discretionary nature of capital sentencing creates an intolerable risk that a jury will impose the death penalty in an arbitrary or discriminatory manner. Consider also the majority's concern that recognizing McCleskey's claim could lead down a slippery slope to recognizing claims based on a risk of discrimination on the basis of other racial identities, or characteristics such as sex or attractiveness, and for punishments for crimes less serious than capital murder. What is Justice Brennan's response? How would you respond?

4.   ***Legislative Responses.*** The Court in *McCleskey* referred to the legislature as the proper forum for addressing the risk of racially disparate treatment in Georgia's capital sentencing scheme. How promising is looking to legislatures for reforming flaws in capital sentencing?

One effort at the national level has been the proposed Racial Justice Act ("RJA"). Advanced by Representative John Conyers (D-MI) and the late Senator Edward Kennedy (D-MA) in 1988, the RJA would have permitted the type of statistical evidence found in the Baldus study to serve as prima facie evidence of racial discrimination. As proposed, the act would not have required direct evidence of purposeful discrimination, but instead would create a rebuttable presumption that significant racial disparities in the death sentence, in the relevant jurisdiction, meant that there was racial discrimination in petitioner's case as well. The initial burden of proof, however, would be on the petitioner to substantiate a racially disparate pattern in capital sentencing.

Despite passing in the House of Representatives twice, the RJA has never passed the Senate. Some opposition came from groups that claim simply that it is necessary to be tough on crime, and that such toughness required support of capital punishment. Others argued that the RJA would inhibit the ability of jurisdictions to implement the death penalty, a necessary punishment for certain crimes. This argument stems from beliefs shared with the *McCleskey* majority that a murderer should not go free simply because of proof in cases other than his own.

Although these criticisms defeated the RJA at the national level, two states—Kentucky and North Carolina—passed legislation modeled on the RJA. The Kentucky state legislature commissioned a study in 1992 that found significant race-of-victim and race-of-defendant effects on capital sentencing analogous to those found by the Baldus study in Georgia. After being defeated in 1994 and 1996, the Kentucky Racial Justice Act (KRJA) passed in 1998. The KRJA creates the opportunity for a pre-trial hearing, before a judge, where the defendant may present statistical or other evidence that race was a significant factor in decisions to seek the death penalty within Kentucky. Although the defendant can rely exclusively on state-wide statistics, he ultimately bears the burden of persuading the judge, by clear and convincing evidence, that "racial considerations played a significant part in the decision to seek the death penalty in his or her case." The state can offer rebuttal evidence. If the court finds that the defendant met his burden, the court must forbid the death penalty in that case.

The effectiveness of the KRJA, however, is doubtful. Defendants must meet the "clear and convincing" standard, the challenge can only be raised in a pre-trial hearing, not post-conviction, and the defendant is limited to challenging the prosecutor's decision, not the jury's. A 2002 study of public defenders indicates that it was rarely invoked. Some did report that the law sometimes helped defendants secure a better plea agreement than they would have otherwise. Other public defenders, by contrast, reported that they noticed prosecutors seeking the death penalty in every eligible case to avoid claims of discrimination. Many of those surveyed reported reluctance to raise a claim at the only available opportunity, a pre-trial hearing, for fear that accusing a prosecutor of racial bias would sour the prosecutor's attitude toward the defense attorney for that case and others. A dominant observation among public defenders surveyed was that the KRJA was largely a symbolic gesture acknowledging the risk of racial bias by prosecutors.

North Carolina's law had more teeth than Kentucky's. The impetus for the North Carolina Racial Justice Act (NCRJA) was high-profile exonerations of death row inmates who were wrongfully convicted as a result of prosecutorial misconduct or grossly incompetent defense attorneys. The law gave defendants a claim where race has affected any aspect of the "decision to seek or impose the death penalty." It differed from Kentucky's RJA in that its scope was not limited to the prosecutor's decision to seek the death penalty; the law could also be used to challenge racial bias in the prosecutor's use of peremptory challenges and the jury's decision to impose the death penalty. It also allowed the claim to be raised either at a pretrial conference or in post-conviction proceedings.

As originally enacted, statistical or other evidence could be used from the county, district, or state to show either that death sentences were sought or imposed more frequently in cases with defendants or victims of a certain race, or else that race was a significant factor in jury selection. There was also no requirement that specific racial bias be shown in the defendant's case. If, after a hearing, the court found that race played a significant role (in the county, district, or state) at the time the death sentence was sought or imposed, a death sentence could no longer be sought or, if already imposed, would be commuted to life without parole.

In the first three years after the NCRJA's enactment, one convict had his death sentence commuted to life without parole based on racial bias in the selection of his jury. The Republican-led legislature responded by amending the NCRJA over the Democratic governor's veto. The amendments prohibited the use of statistics beyond the local jurisdiction. They also required more than statistical evidence to establish racial bias in the process resulting in the defendant's death sentence. The following year, a Republican governor signed the legislature's complete repeal of the NCRJA. Advocates of repeal argued that the law effectively precluded the state from carrying out the death penalty, while opponents of repeal said the law successfully revealed systemic racial bias in capital trials and sentencing. During the NCRJA's four-year existence, four death-row convicts out of 151 who made NCRJA challenges received sentence commutations to life without parole.

Other than these two states' reforms, proposed legislative remedies to meet the problems highlighted in *McCleskey* have had little success. Does this suggest the courts need to take a more active role in preventing racial bias in capital punishment or that the legislative process remains a more promising, though imperfect, avenue for a remedy?

5.   ***Problem: Your Justice Act.*** Assume that you work for an organization interested in addressing the racial disparities in the death penalty made evident by the Baldus study and studies with similar findings in other states. A United States Senator has approached your organization and agreed to support a bill if it would likely pass in both houses of Congress and be signed by the President. Assume that neither party has a significant majority in either house. Draft a law that would have a plausible chance of success. How would you garner political support for the reform? What back-up approaches would be worth considering if your proposed bill is unsuccessful?

6.   ***Race in Predicting Dangerousness.*** In a capital sentencing hearing, one factor that juries are sometimes asked to consider in deciding whether to impose the death penalty is the convicted defendant's future dangerousness to society. Consider *Buck v. Thaler*, 132 S.Ct. 32 (2011). In a statement supporting denial of certiorari, Justice Alito, joined by Justices Scalia and Breyer, laid out the facts of the underlying murder:

> One morning in July 1995, petitioner Duane E. Buck went to his ex-girlfriend's house with a rifle and a shotgun. After killing one person and wounding another, Buck chased his ex-girlfriend outside. Her children followed and witnessed Buck shoot and kill their mother as she attempted to flee. An arresting officer testified that Buck was laughing when he was arrested and said "[t]he bitch deserved what she got." 28 Tr. 51 (May 6, 1997).

132 S.Ct. at 32.

In a dissent from the denial of certiorari, Justice Sotomayor, joined by Justice Kagan, identified the factual basis of the constitutional challenge:

> Buck was convicted of capital murder in a Texas state court. During the penalty phase of Buck's trial, the defense called psychologist Walter Quijano as a witness. The defense sought Quijano's opinion as to whether Buck would pose a continuing threat to society—a fact that the jury was required to find in order to sentence Buck to death. Quijano testified that there were several "statistical factors we know to predict future dangerousness," and listed a defendant's past crimes, age, sex, race, socioeconomic status, employment stability, and substance abuse history. 28 Tr. 110–111 (May 6, 1997). As to race, Quijano said: "Race. It's a sad commentary that minorities, Hispanics and black people, are over represented in the Criminal Justice System." *Id.,* at 111. The defense then asked Quijano to "talk about environmental factors if [Buck were] incarcerated in prison." *Id.,* at 111–112. Quijano explained that, for example, Buck "has no assaultive incidents either at TDC or in jail," and that "that's a good sign that this person is controllable within a jail or prison setting." *Id.,* at 115. He also explained that Buck's "victim [was] not random" because "there [was] a pre-existing relationship," and that this reduced the probability that Buck would pose a future danger. *Id.,* at 112. Ultimately, when the defense asked Quijano whether Buck was likely to commit violent criminal acts if he were sentenced to life

imprisonment, Quijano replied, "The probability of that happening in prison would be low." *Id.,* at 115. The defense also offered into evidence, over the prosecutor's objection, a report containing Quijano's psychological evaluation of Buck, which substantially mirrored Quijano's trial testimony.

On cross-examination, the prosecutor began by asking Quijano about the financial compensation he received in return for his time and the methods he used to examine Buck. The prosecutor then said that she would "like to ask [Quijano] some questions from [his] report." *Id.,* at 155. After inquiring about the statistical factors of past crimes and age and how they might indicate future dangerousness in Buck's case, the prosecutor said: "You have determined that the sex factor, that a male is more violent than a female because that's just the way it is, and that the race factor, black, increases the future dangerousness for various complicated reasons; is that correct?" *Id.,* at 160. Quijano answered, "Yes." *Ibid.* After additional cross-examination and testimony from a subsequent witness, the prosecutor argued to the jury in summation that Quijano "told you that there was a probability that [Buck] would commit future acts of violence." *Id.,* at 260. The jury returned a verdict of death.

132 S.Ct. at 35–38 (Justice Sotomayor, with whom Justice Kagan joins, dissenting from denial of certiorari).

If expert testimony is based on sound statistical evidence that a defendant's race, combined with certain other factors, supports a finding of future dangerousness, should a jury be permitted to consider the defendant's race? Even if consideration of a defendant's race should have to satisfy strict scrutiny, is it not arguably necessary to advance the compelling interest of protecting society from a dangerous killer? If you believe the jury should not be permitted to hear evidence of race and future dangerousness, is it because you believe the government should always be color-blind, or is this circumstance different from others in which you would find race-conscious decision-making acceptable? Should it matter whether the testimony about the relevance of race in predicting the defendant's future dangerousness is presented by the defense attorney or the prosecutor?

In *Buck*, the Court denied certiorari, thereby letting his death sentence stand. The justices that explained their denial said it would have been reversible error for the prosecutor to elicit testimony about the defendant's race, but that, in this case, the testimony was elicited initially by the defense attorney. The justices dissenting from the denial of certiorari tacitly assumed that a defendant might not be able to complain if his own attorney elicited damaging testimony about the defendant's race, but that, in this case, the prosecutor compounded the defense attorney's actions by re-eliciting the racial testimony. If a defendant's race as a dangerousness factor is introduced exclusively by his own attorney, should a court permit the death sentence to stand even if it would have been improper for a prosecutor to introduce such evidence?

7. *Sentencing Factors with a Racially Disparate Impact.* Should sentencing judges consider factors that empirically predict future dangerousness? What if those factors correlate with race? A trend across the country permits or requires sentencing judges to consider factors that, according to statistical evidence, increase the risk that a defendant will commit future crime. The risk factors do not necessarily cause crime but they correlate with crime. Such factors include criminal history, unemployment, age, marital status, finances, education, neighborhood, and family background, including the criminal history of family members. For some defendants, such risk scores indicate a lower risk of crime than might otherwise be predicted, whereas for other defendants the score indicates a higher risk of crime. The risk factors also correlate with socioeconomic disadvantage and race. If scientifically reliable evidence indicates that certain factors correlate with a higher or lower risk of dangerousness, should sentencing judges take account of such factors? Would ignoring such factors be fair to low-risk defendants who would benefit from their consideration? Would ignoring such factors be fair to communities who would be harmed by defendants whose risk assessments would be high if such factors were considered? What factors should be considered in determining a defendant's sentence? For a critique of sentencing factors that correlate with race and socioeconomic status, *see* Sonja B. Starr, "Sentencing, by the Numbers," N.Y. Times, Aug. 11, 2014, at A17.

B. CRACK-POWDER SENTENCING DISPARITY

This chapter began with the question whether blacks are discriminatorily *prosecuted* for crack cocaine offenses. We conclude the chapter by asking whether blacks are discriminatorily *punished* for crack cocaine offenses. In 1986, Congress passed the Anti-Drug Abuse Act, Pub. L. No. 99–570, establishing a 100 to 1 differential between the amounts of powder cocaine versus crack that would trigger a given sentence. For example, it mandated a minimum of ten years for distributing fifty grams of crack but required distribution of 5000 grams of powder cocaine to receive the same penalty. In 1988, Congress further established a mandatory minimum of five years for possession of one to five grams of crack, making crack the only drug for which there was a mandatory minimum for a first offense of possession. In 1995, 2002, and 2007, the United States Sentencing Commission recommended eliminating or reducing the sentencing disparity between crack and powder cocaine. Each time, Congress rejected the proposal.

From the outset, the penalty disparity between crack and powder cocaine has had a disproportionate impact on blacks. In 1992, for example, of those convicted for crack cocaine offenses nationally, 92.6% were black and 4.7% were white. Conversely, of those convicted for powder cocaine offenses nationally, 45.2% were white, and 20.7% were black. A consequence of the high rates of arrest and conviction of black crack offenders is that the number of inmates, especially in federal prison, serving time for drug offenses is disproportionately black and male.

The legal debate over the crack-powder sentencing disparity has focused primarily on two issues: Is the sentencing disparity racially motivated and is it justified regardless. Consider the following court's response to these questions.

United States v. Clary

United States District Court, E.D. Missouri, Eastern Division, 1994.
846 F. Supp. 768.

■ CAHILL, DISTRICT JUDGE.

Defendant Edward Clary was arrested for possession with intent to distribute 67.76 grams of cocaine base. Clary pled guilty to possession with intent to distribute cocaine base ("crack cocaine"), pursuant to 21 U.S.C. § 841(b)(1)(A)(iii) (hereinafter referred to as the "crack statute"), punishable by a mandatory minimum sentence of 10 years imprisonment. Prior to sentencing, Clary, a black male, filed a motion challenging the constitutionality of the crack statute and contended, *inter alia,* that the sentence enhancement provisions contained in it and United States Sentencing Guidelines (U.S.S.G.) § 2D1.1 violated his equal protection rights guaranteed by the Fifth Amendment.

Specifically, defendant Clary asserts that the penalty differential of the "100 to 1" ratio of cocaine to cocaine base contained in both the crack statute and the United States Sentencing Guidelines has a disproportionate impact on blacks because blacks are more likely to possess cocaine base than whites who are more likely to possess cocaine powder. Therefore, defendant's argument continues, providing longer sentences for possession of cocaine base than for the identical amount of cocaine powder treats a similarly situated defendant in a dissimilar manner, which violates his right to equal protection under the law.

THE PROBLEM BEFORE THE COURT

Before this Court are two different sentencing provisions contained within the same statute for possession and distribution of different forms of the same drug. The difference—the key difference—is that possession and distribution of 50 grams of crack cocaine carries the same mandatory minimum sentence of 10 years imprisonment as possession and distribution of 5000 grams of powder cocaine. Both provisions punish the same drug, but penalize crack cocaine 100 times more than powder cocaine!

Congress tells us that the rationale for this sentencing dichotomy which produces harsher punishment for involvement with crack cocaine is because it is so much more dangerous than powder cocaine. As "proof," Congress relied upon endless media accounts of crack's increased threat to society. While Congress may have had well-intentioned concerns, the

Court is equally aware that this one provision, the crack statute, has been directly responsible for incarcerating nearly an entire generation of young black American men for very long periods, usually during the most productive time of their lives.

CRIME AND THE LEGISLATIVE RESPONSE

Crime!! The very word connotes fear and panic, resulting in a frenzied attempt to control and curtail criminal actions in today's violence-soaked world. Never before have Americans cringed at the thought of becoming victims of random, irrational assaults; never before has the fear and frustration of average citizens grown to such a level that a "lynch mob mentality" becomes the common emotional reaction to crime.

This Court recognizes that the control of crime is the most important goal of sentencing, and a firm and certain punishment must be the major goal in criminal justice. However, such punishment must be fair; it must fit the particulars of the offense and must acknowledge characteristics of individuals.

The "100 to 1" ratio, coupled with mandatory minimum sentencing provided by federal statute, has created a situation that reeks with inhumanity and injustice. The scales of justice have been turned topsy turvy so that those masterminds, the "kingpins" of drug trafficking, escape detection, while those whose role is minimal, even trivial, are hoisted on the spears of an enraged electorate and at the pinnacle of their youth are imprisoned for years while those most responsible for the evil of the day remain free.

THE CHALLENGE TO THE COURT

The Court is faced with the task of resolving whether the crack statute violated defendant Clary's equal protection rights. The equal protection component of the Fifth Amendment Due Process clause commands that similarly situated people must be treated alike. The Court's basic understanding of this constitutional rule is that when one group of people violates the same type of laws as other people similar to them, they should be punished in the same manner.

The difficult situation that a Court must face is to determine whether a statute which is facially neutral was enacted for racial reasons and would thereby have a disparate impact on a particular racial group. Whether or not racial discrimination was involved in legislative action that resulted in a law which, although facially neutral, still has a racially disparate impact "demands a sensitive inquiry into such circumstantial evidence of intent as may be available." *Arlington Heights v. Metropolitan Housing Development Corporation,* 429 U.S. 252, 266 (1977).

Under *Arlington,* the Supreme Court set forth key factors to evaluate whether a law was motivated by racial discrimination. These factors included the presence of disparate impact, the overall historical context of the legislation, the legislative history of the challenged law, and departures from the normal legislative process. Additional legal precedent has provided the Court with more criteria for its review, such as foreseeability of the consequences of the legislation; however, *Arlington* provides the Court with the major benchmark to discover the presence of racial influence in the legislative decision making process.

Today most legislation would not contain overtly racist referrals and, indeed, would eliminate the slightest allusion to racial factors in the words of the legislation itself. But today, despite the fact that a law may be racially neutral on its face, there still may be factors derived from unconscious racism that affect and infiltrate the legislative result.

A HISTORY OF RACISM IN CAPITAL PUNISHMENT

That black people have been punished more severely for violating the same law as whites is not a new phenomenon. A dual system of criminal punishment based on racial discrimination can be traced back to the time of slavery. In order to understand the role that racism has played in enacting the penalty enhancement for using crack cocaine, one must first take note of America's history of racially tainted criminal laws, particularly drug laws. Race has often served as a significant contributing factor to the enhancement of penalties for crime.

Early in our nation's history, legislatures were motivated by racial discrimination to differentiate between crimes committed by whites and crimes committed by blacks. For example, "An Act Against Stealing Hogs" provided a penalty of 25 lashes on a bare back or a 10 pound fine for white offenders, while nonwhites (slave and free) would receive 39 lashes, with no chance of paying a fine to avoid the whipping. In 1697, Pennsylvania passed death sentence legislation for black men who raped white women and castrated them for attempted rape. White men who committed the same offense would be fined, whipped, or imprisoned for one year.

In later decades cocaine became associated with exotic groups such as Hollywood entertainers and jazz musicians. It earned the moniker of the "rich man's drug." In the early 1960s and 1970s, cocaine began to move into mainstream society, and became the "drug of the eighties." Even with the widespread use of powder cocaine, no new drug laws were enacted to further criminalize or penalize cocaine possession. The "war on drugs" with respect to powder cocaine was concentrated on impeding international import of the drug or targeted large scale financiers. The social history is clear that so long as cocaine powder was a popular amusement among young, white professionals, law enforcement policy prohibiting cocaine was weakly enforced.

IMPACT OF THE 80S

The 1980s were times of cataclysmic economic change in America. The smoke-stack industries which furnished considerable highly paid employment to many persons with limited formal education were dead, dying, or moving elsewhere. Unemployment reached levels as high as 8 percent nationally but in the inner cities it hovered around 20 percent and in some cases soared to levels of 50 to 60 percent for young black men.

The 80s found many communities bereft of the assistance from institutions financed by the federal government, and with virtually no employment, many young residents of the inner cities lost hope and motivation. In their anger and frustration they turned to the most visible source of immediate financial reward—drug traffic. Because there were so few employment opportunities otherwise available, and because the immense drug market offered huge profits immediately, many persons were attracted to it.

Most important of all, those parts of a neighborhood believed to be immune to the spread of crime now found that the plague was spreading, first to the edges of the inner cities and then to the affluent suburbs and even to the distant rural towns and villages.

These portraits of misery and degradation are the daily world of the inner city resident and are all, part and parcel, products of unconscious racism. Is it any wonder that there is no motivation, no happiness, no hope? It is not strange to recognize that with such misery surrounding them they have lost the ambition to work and to fight, but only await the inevitable—death. The terror of long prison terms has little deterrence for them their life is already a prison of despair.

UNCONSCIOUS RACISM

Thus, the root of racism has been implanted in our collective unconscious and has biased the ideas that Americans accept about the significance of race. Racism goes beyond prejudicial discrimination and bigotry. It arises from outlooks, stereotypes, and fears of which we are vastly unaware. Our historical experience has made racism an integral part of our culture even though society has more recently embraced an ideal that rejects racism as immoral. When an individual experiences conflict between racist ideas and the social ethic that condemns those ideas, the mind excludes his racism from his awareness.

The illustration of unconscious racism is patently evident in the crack cocaine statutes. Had the same type of law been applied to powder cocaine, it would have sentenced droves of young whites to prison for extended terms. Before the enactment of such a law, it would have been much more carefully and deliberately considered. After all, in these days when "toughness on crime" is a political virtue, the simplest and fairest solution would have been to make the severe punishment for powder cocaine the same as for crack cocaine. But when the heavy punishment is inflicted only upon those in the weak and unpopular minority community, it is an example of benign neglect arising from unconscious racism.

Consequently, the focus on "purposeful" discrimination is inadequate as a response to more subtle and deeply buried forms of racism. In 1909, the United States Supreme Court acknowledged that "[racial] bias or prejudice is such an elusive condition of the mind that it is most difficult, if not impossible, to always recognize its existence." *Crawford v. United States,* 212 U.S. 183, 196 (1909). Eighty-three years later, *Crawford* holds: the inquiry to determine racial bias is still "difficult, if not impossible." Without consideration of the influences of unconscious racism, the standard of review set forth in *Davis* is a "crippling burden of proof." *Batson v. Kentucky,* 476 U.S. 79, 92 (1985).

The concomitant twin of racism is class oppression. On average, blacks experience significantly worse economic conditions than whites, and historically the criminal justice system has dealt more harshly with those who are economically weak. Black people constitute a disproportionate share of persons who exist in absolute poverty. In 1990, there were 33.6 million persons in poverty in the U.S. Although blacks comprise only 12% of the nation's population, 29% of those poverty stricken were black—2.4 times the rate of the general population. This mixture of race and economic discrimination has diminished the bright line of overt racism. "The . . . distorting effects of racial discrimination and poverty continue to be painfully visible" in decisions to mete out criminal punishment. *Godfrey v. Georgia,* 446 U.S. 420, 439 (1980) (Marshall, J. concurring).

It is against this background that the Court considers the merits of defendant's challenge.

EQUAL PROTECTION ANALYSIS

A current equal protection analysis must therefore take into account the unconscious predispositions of people, including legislators, who may sincerely believe that they are not making decisions on the basis of race. This predisposition is a pertinent factor in determining the existence of a racially discriminatory motive. Racial influences which unconsciously seeped into the legislative decision making process are no less injurious, reprehensible, or unconstitutional. Although intent *per se* may not have entered Congress' enactment of the crack statute, its failure to account for a foreseeable disparate impact which would affect black Americans in grossly disproportionate numbers would, nonetheless, violate the spirit and letter of equal protection.

A criminal defendant who alleges an equal protection violation must prove that the "invidious quality" of governmental action claimed to be racially discriminatory "must ultimately be traced to a racially discriminatory purpose." *Washington v. Davis,* 426 U.S. 229, 240 (1976). Absent direct evidence of intent to discriminate, the defendant can make a prima facie case "by showing [that] the totality of the relevant facts gives rise to an inference of discriminatory purpose." *Id.*

In *Arlington,* the Supreme Court listed circumstantial evidentiary sources for judicial review of legislative or executive motivation to determine whether a racially discriminatory purpose exists. The Court explicitly stated that the list of evidentiary sources was not exhaustive. Therefore, this Court will proceed with its examination by reviewing the circumstantial evidence, including the *Arlington* factors, to determine whether race influenced the legislature's actions.

ENACTMENT OF THE CRACK STATUTE

Crack cocaine eased into the mainstream of the drug culture about 1985 and immediately absorbed the media's attention. The media created a stereotype of a crack dealer as a young black male, unemployed, gang affiliated, gun toting, and a menace to society.

Legislators used these media accounts as informational support for the enactment of the crack statute. The *Congressional Record,* prior to enactment of the statute, is replete with news articles submitted by members for their colleagues' consideration which labeled crack dealers as black youths and gangs. Members of Congress also introduced into the record media reports containing language that was either overtly or subtly racist, and which exacerbated white fears that the "crack problem" would spill out of the ghettos.

These stereotypical images undoubtedly served as the touchstone that influenced racial perceptions held by legislators and the public as related to the "crack epidemic."

Arlington decided that departures from normal procedures are relevant in determining the existence of invidious influences. Defendant presented evidence that there were significant departures from prior substantive and procedural sequences, which point toward invidious discriminatory purpose.

The media reports associating blacks with the horrors of crack cocaine caused the Congress to react irrationally and arbitrarily. The evolution of the 100 to 1 crack to powder ratio mandatory minimum sentence was a direct result of a "frenzied" Congress that was moved to action based upon an unconscious racial animus. The "frenzied" state of Congress led members to depart from normal and substantive procedures that are *routinely* considered a part of the legislative process.

Few hearings were held in the House on the enhanced penalties for crack offenders. Despite the lack of fact-gathering about crack, "the 100:1 cocaine to crack ratio . . . was originally a 50:1 ratio in the Crime Subcommittee's bill, H.R. 5394, . . . arbitrarily doubled simply to symbolize redoubled Congressional seriousness." *Id.* at 4.

When the Senate considered the legislation, many Senators fruitlessly cautioned against undue haste in light of the House's abbreviated consideration of the bill, to little avail. Tossing caution to the wind, the Senate conducted a single hearing between 9:40 a.m. to 1:15

p.m., including recesses. Attendance was intermittent. *"Crack" Cocaine: Hearing Before the Permanent Subcommittee on Investigations of the Committee on Governmental Affairs,* United States Senate, 99th Cong. 2d Sess. (July 15, 1986) ("Crack Hearing").

Circumstantial evidence of invidious intent may include proof of disproportionate impact. *Davis,* 426 U.S. at 242. "impact of the official action—whether it 'bears more heavily on one race than another,'" id., is important evidence. . . . Defendant's evidence that the impact of the crack statute "bears more heavily" on blacks than whites is undisputed.

Objective evidence supports the belief that racial animus was a motivating factor in enacting the crack statute. Congress' decision was based, in large part, on the racial imagery generated by the media which connected the "crack problem" with blacks in the inner city. Congress deviated from procedural patterns, departed from a thorough, rational discussion of the "crack issue" and reacted to it in a "frenzy" initiated by the media and emotionally charged constituents. Under *Arlington,* all of these factors may be considered by the Court to infer intent.

PROSECUTORIAL AND LAW ENFORCEMENT DISCRETION

The crack statute in conjunction with the resultant mandatory minimum sentence, standing alone, may not have spawned the kind and degree of racially disparate impact that warrants judicial review but for the manner of its application by law enforcement agencies. The law enforcement practices, charging policies, and sentencing departure decisions by prosecutors constitute major contributing factors which have escalated the disparate outcome.

However, both national and local statistical data do not show that the prosecution is targeting the upper echelons in the drug trade. The Court notes that a close examination of many of the 57 files involving crack cocaine in this district shows that federal prosecution occurs with both state and federal law officers making the arrests. Generally, those arrested by state officers had very small amounts of crack cocaine. For example, nine of the 57 crack cocaine defendants were assigned to this Court and most of them had only tiny quantities of crack cocaine. All but one was black.

Without explanation, the logical inference to be drawn is that the prosecutors in the federal courts are selectively prosecuting black defendants who were involved with crack, no matter how trivial the amount, and ignoring or diverting whites when they do the same thing.

LEVEL OF JUDICIAL SCRUTINY

The totality of the facts in this case converge to support the conclusion that racial discriminatory influences, at least unconsciously, played an appreciable role in promulgating the enhanced statutory scheme for possession and distribution of crack. Legislators' unconscious racial aversion towards blacks, sparked by unsubstantiated reports of the effects of crack, reactionary media prodding, and an agitated constituency, motivated the legislators to enhance the punishment scheme to produce a dual system of punishment in the application of this statute.

To rebut defendant's claim that racial animus played a role in penalizing crimes involving cocaine base more severely than crimes involving powder cocaine, the Government offered evidence that members of Congress considered crack to be more dangerous because of its potency, its highly addictive nature, its affordability, and increasing prevalence. Ample evidence has been presented to this Court that contradicts many of Congress' claims. Congress had no hard evidence before it to support the contentions that crack was 100 times more potent or dangerous than powder cocaine. Crack's purported greater potency was not supported by the evidence. There is no evidence that the use of crack makes the user physiologically or psychologically more prone to violence or other antisocial behavior than does the use of powder cocaine. According to the market approach, crack cocaine can be distributed in small packets at a low unit price.

The record does not support the fact that Congress had a reasonable basis to make the harsh distinction between penalties for powder and crack cocaine. To the extent that the source dries up, the derivative must necessarily wither upon the vine. If any enhancement would be justified, it would be to penalize cocaine more severely. Hence, the absence of narrow tailoring corroborates the constitutional infirmity of the statute.

THE JUDICIARY

This Court fully realizes the difficulties facing a court when it must modify or vacate a legislative act especially when the Congress of the United States responds to the demands of its constituency to "do something" about the most pressing problem in America today—crime.

But judges, by their temperament, experience, and exposure, are expected to weigh more carefully both the long and short range effects of policies and laws. More importantly, the shield of the Constitution gives them the insulation to withstand the firestorm of uninformed public opinion on emotional subjects such as crime. The courts have only one yardstick to measure equality—the Constitution.

The reason why we cannot wait for the congressional modification and changes that the Court believes will occur in time is that the horror of continuing is so very destructive. There are many prisoners serving 10-year sentences for possessing with intent to distribute 50 grams of crack. They are usually between 18–30 years of age and about 90 percent are black. Their absence in such numbers, if continued, threatens the possibility of the ultimate extinction of the black race in America.

Even if appellate review points to a different path, the evaluation and reflection that this perplexing problem has occasioned is of great value. It will not have been in vain. The sequence of events which led to the enactment of the 1984 crack statute can be summarized as follows:

First, the historical precedent of imposing much more severe penalties against blacks than those placed upon whites for the same offense is evident, especially in drug cases. The crack statute of today follows that same pattern.

Second, the media engaged in a frenzy of reporting incidents involving crack cocaine and inner city blacks. Most of it was stereotypical of only a small portion of the black community.

Third, there was a furious and emotional demand for the Congress to do something at once. The greatest clamor came from suburbia (mostly white) with its mother lode of votes, while the proposed laws would affect the inner cities (mostly black) and with fewer votes.

Fourth, the Congress failed to follow its own customary procedural standards. Few hearings were held by the subcommittees, while the testimony adduced from the expert witnesses relied upon anecdotal incidents and was not based upon accepted scientific knowledge.

Fifth, the Senate raised the disproportionate punishment from 50 to 1 up to 100 to 1 for "symbolic" purposes.

Sixth, even if the government demonstrates a compelling interest in enacting adverse legislation regarding a suspect class, it must do so by narrow restrictions, not by arbitrary, irrational actions designed to curry political favor.

Seventh, the presumption that during the period 1989–92 the federal prosecutors may have permitted race to be a factor in their decisions to prosecute all blacks involved with crack and not to prosecute whites who were similarly involved is present because of the failure of the U.S. Attorney's Office in the Eastern District of Missouri to explain the principles which were followed to decide who would be prosecuted for crack offenses.

This Court further finds that while overt racism has largely disappeared as a result of the civil rights victories, racism still remains in its more subtle, covert form.

Thus it is easy to see the transition of de jure laws of the past dissolving into the de facto practices of today which portray the poor and undereducated blacks as criminals who must be imprisoned forever. If a white student with 50 grams of cocaine is only sentenced to 21 months of imprisonment, while his black counterpart must serve 10 years for the same amount of crack cocaine, we seem to be hearing a cowardly call to retreat.

FINDINGS AND CONCLUSIONS

In summary, the Court, after careful consideration, reluctantly concludes that the pertinent sections of 21 U.S.C. § 841 which mandate punishment to be 100 times greater for crack cocaine than for powder cocaine are constitutionally invalid, both generally and *as applied* in this case. The Court finds that there is no material difference between the chemical properties of crack and powder cocaine, and that they are one and the same drug. The Court further finds that this defendant has been denied equal protection of the laws when the punishment assessed against him is 100 times greater than the punishment assessed for the same violation but involving powder cocaine.

The Court further finds that the "symbolic" action of the Congress in raising the original 50 to 1 ratio to 100 to 1 is yet another indication of its irrational and arbitrary actions, and further evidences the failure of the Congress to narrowly tailor its provisions as required by law in suspect class cases.

The Court further finds that the Congress enacted this law in an arbitrary and irrational manner, without the testimony of adequate scientific and professional advice, and without providing sufficient time for subcommittee hearings and debate.

The Court further finds that the statistics offered by the defendant, both local and national, show that the disparate impact upon blacks is so great as to shock the conscience of the court.

INVALIDATION OF THE CRACK STATUTE

Therefore, this Court concludes that the disproportionate penalties for crack cocaine as specified in all of the pertinent sections of 21 U.S.C. § 841 violate the Equal Protection Clause of the U.S. Constitution generally and as applied in this case. The Court further holds that the prosecutorial selection of cases on the basis of race is constitutionally impermissible as applied to this defendant in this case.

Accordingly, the Court has sentenced the defendant to a prison term in conformity with this memorandum. [The court sentenced Clary to four years of incarceration rather than the ten-year minimum required by the federal crack statute that it ruled unconstitutional.]

NOTES AND QUESTIONS

1. ***Racially Discriminatory Purpose?*** Does the evidence discussed by Judge Cahill in *Clary* support a finding that Congress acted with a racially discriminatory purpose when it created the harsher penalty for crack offenses? Does the evidence he describes suggest that, subsequent to this case, Congress acted with racial bias when it repeatedly refused to reduce the disparity even when its racial impact became apparent? Judge Cahill found that, at the very least, Congress probably acted with *unconscious* racial bias when it enacted the sentencing disparity. Are his findings and conclusions persuasive? If Congress did act based on unconscious bias, should that be enough to invalidate the law or at least subject it to strict scrutiny, or should the "discriminatory purpose" that triggers strict scrutiny require conscious intention? What would the implications be for equal

protection analysis if claims could proceed based on allegations of unconscious bias?

Arguing that unconscious racism is a pervasive and problematic feature of modern society, Professor Charles Lawrence has argued,

> [R]equiring proof of conscious or intentional motivation as a prerequisite to constitutional recognition that a decision is race-dependent ignores much of what we understand about how the human mind works. It also disregards both the irrationality of racism and the profound effect that the history of American race relations has had on the individual and collective unconscious.

Charles R. Lawrence III, *The Id, the Ego, and Equal Protection: Reckoning with Unconscious Racism*, 39 Stanford L. Rev. 317, 323 (1987). Applying Lawrence's argument to the crack-powder sentencing context, one might argue that attempts to revise or overturn the sentencing disparity are doomed to fail as the disparity is based on unconscious racism.

Despite these arguments, every court except for the district court in *Clary*, has rejected claims that the crack-powder sentencing disparity was racially motivated. Cahill's ruling was itself promptly reversed by the Eighth Circuit, which held along with every other court of appeals that there is insufficient evidence of a racial motivation behind the federal crack statute's enactment to invalidate it under the Equal Protection Clause. *See United States v. Clary*, 34 F.3d 709 (8th Cir. 1994).

2.   *Racial Impact.* Even if the sentencing disparity was not motivated by a racial purpose, conscious or not, its racial impact is undeniable. Does that mean the disparity is unjustified? Answering this question should begin with asking whether the disparity is justified independent of its racial impact. Opponents of the sentencing disparity, in court and in the political arena, have argued it is not. They claim, for example, that at the pharmacological level, crack and powder cocaine are identical. Crack cocaine is cocaine turned into smokable form. It is the same drug and should be punished the same. Moreover, crack cocaine is downstream in the cocaine distribution market, which means that the "kingpins" that bring cocaine into the country are bringing it in powder form. Trafficking powder cocaine is thus the major cause of both crack and powder cocaine crime. There would be no crack without powder cocaine.

In support of the penalty differential, Congress heard testimony that crack is more dangerous to individuals and more harmful to communities than powder cocaine. It is more dangerous because its form is one that is more potent and addictive than powder cocaine. It is more harmful to communities for a number of reasons, including that its form is more easily marketed in small, cheap quantities and therefore spreads more rapidly in low-income populations.

Every federal court except Judge Cahill has analyzed the sentencing disparity by asking only whether the disparity has a rational basis and has concluded that it does. One state court found the rationales for a state law that punished crack offenses more severely than powder unjustified. The

Minnesota Supreme Court ruled, under a more searching form of rational basis scrutiny under its state constitution, that the purported differences between the effects of crack and powder cocaine are insufficient to justify a different penalty. *See State v. Russell*, 477 N.W.2d 886 (Minn. 1991).

Is the crack-powder sentencing disparity justified if it does not have a racial impact? If not, would a lesser disparity be justified or should the law treat crack and powder offenses the same? Now assume that it does have a racial impact. Does that change your analysis even if the impact is not based on any conscious or unconscious racial motivation? Which way does the racial impact cut? Do the more severe penalties disproportionately imposed on blacks and Latinos as a result of the sentencing disparity counsel against the disparity? Alternatively, given that the victims of the crack epidemic, including crack addicts and the victims of gang violence, are disproportionately black and Latino, does that justify punishing crack offenses *more severely* than powder cocaine in part *because of* its racial impact? Consider especially the most innocent victims in the crack epidemic . . . babies.

3.   ***Problem: Crack Babies and Hospital Policy.*** Gerald Carver, in the 1992 movie *Deep Cover*, paints a disturbing picture of crack babies. "Have you ever seen a crack baby? Newborn crack baby, six hours old, screaming its heart out, because it's going through withdrawal? Over the course of the next year, it doesn't learn to crawl or walk, or talk on time because it's got deformities, physical deformities, mental deformities." Deep Cover (New Line Productions 1992). What, if anything should be done to address this problem? Assume that you are an attorney in a big city with a major crack problem. In order to mitigate the harm caused to babies of crack-addicted mothers, one of the hospitals has set up a program with the police department to drug test pregnant women suspected of drug use. If a woman tests positive, a variety of counseling, health care, and prosecution programs are provided. A crack addicted black woman who was subjected to this program and a representative to the hospital both ask you to take their case, arguing against, and defending the program, respectively. Assuming neither potential client has given you enough information to create a conflict of interest, which case would you take? What would you argue? If you had to take the other side, what would you argue? *See Ferguson v. City of Charleston*, 532 U.S. 67 (2001) (holding that drug testing of pregnant women for law enforcement purposes violates the Fourth Amendment protection against unreasonable searches); *see also* Brian C. Spitzer, *A Response to "Cocaine Babies"—Amendment of Florida's Child Abuse and Neglect Laws to Encompass Infants Born Drug Dependent*, 15 FLA. ST. U.L. REV. 865 (1987). Note that recent research indicates that the fears of a crack baby epidemic turned out to be baseless and casts doubt on the supposed science behind the phenomenon. *See* Michael Winerip, *Revisiting the 'Crack Babies' Epidemic That Was Not*, N.Y. Times (May 20, 2013).

4.   ***Problem: Black Victims of Crack Versus Black Victims of Crack Punishment.*** Reflecting upon similar issues as those discussed in the previous Note, Dorothy Roberts has argued that punishing crack addicts who

have babies violates equal protection law because it perpetuates black subordination. *See* Dorothy Roberts, *Punishing Drug Addicts Who Have Babies: Women of Color, Equality, and the Right of Privacy*, 104 Harv. L. Rev. 1420 (1991). On the one hand, there may be a discriminatory element to targeting crack addicts, since black people disproportionately use crack. Why not, for example, equally target women who abuse powder cocaine or prescription drugs or alcohol? Fetal alcohol syndrome is a well-known problem. On the other hand, if no action were taken to try to protect crack babies (assuming such a phenomenon exists), one could argue that the system was discriminatory for failing to protect black victims. There is thus a racial trade-off between protecting babies from being born with crack-related problems and punishing or subordinating black women.

Police officers serve in both law enforcement and public safety roles. If you were a police officer, how would you balance these aspects of your job, particularly where you risk allegations of racism no matter what you do? Would you put more emphasis on equal justice for the child victims of mothers who are addicted to crack or other substances or on equal justice for mother victims of excessively harsh crack offense penalties?

5. *Collateral Consequences or "Invisible Punishment".* The negative consequences of a criminal conviction, and even of an arrest alone, go well beyond the scope of criminal punishment. Even after a defendant has completed a term of probation or incarceration and parole, he (or she) is typically subject to a broad range of "civil" disabilities or "collateral consequences." These include, depending on the state, the long-term or permanent loss of the right to vote, to serve on juries, to possess a gun, to work for the government, to live in government-subsidized housing, to be eligible for student loans, or to receive many kinds of welfare benefits, including nutrition assistance for people with a drug conviction. Indeed, an ex-convict may face arrest simply for visiting someone living in public housing, including a family member, who may in turn risk eviction for permitting such a visit. A non-citizen might also be deported as a result of a criminal conviction, even if the non-citizen is otherwise lawfully in the United States. Such consequences are legally termed "civil" or "collateral" to distinguish them from "criminal" punishment. Because they are not "criminal" consequences, they need not comply with due process requirements. For example, a defendant need not be informed of them when he is informed of the consequences of pleading guilty (although the Court has recently required informing defendants pleading guilty of the risk of deportation). A defendant may also be subject to consequences "ex post facto" (not legally authorized at the time of the crime); and the civil disabilities can be permanent without any determination as to whether they constitute cruel and unusual punishment. Even just an arrest record, without a subsequent conviction, can restrict a person's employment prospects when job applications ask for such information.

The question arises whether the kinds of collateral consequences imposed on often non-violent offenders is fair given that they have completed the sentence that the legislature deemed appropriate for the crime they committed. It is also questionable whether such consequences tend to further or impede the convict's successful re-entry into society. Such consequences, which often have a correlative or even causal relationship with race, arguably subject people with any kind of criminal record to second class citizenship, a twenty-first century "Jim Crow," as Professor Michele Alexander calls it. *See* Michele Alexander, *The New Jim Crow: Mass Incarceration in the Age of Colorblindness* (2012). The American Bar Association's Criminal Justice Section publishes an online database of collateral consequences at www.abacollateralconsequences.org.

6. *Jury Nullification?* This and the previous chapter have revealed major challenges to achieving racial justice in the criminal justice system. This has led some advocates of racial equality, most notably Professor Paul Butler, to encourage jury nullification, *i.e.,* acquitting a defendant believed to be guilty beyond reasonable doubt in light of some other more systemic injustice. Butler argues that it is unfair to punish black people for retributive reasons because societal racism is responsible for the social and economic conditions that produce black crime. Only utilitarian reasons can justify criminal punishment, Butler contends, such as the harm to the black community that could result from releasing a defendant who may commit violence. By contrast, blacks who commit "victimless" crimes, such as drug use, should not be convicted even if guilty because such defendants are likely more useful to the community free than in jail. Butler proposes a three-part framework for when black jurors should consider acquitting black defendants when the evidence of guilt is convincing:

> In cases involving violent *malum in se* crimes like murder, rape, and assault, jurors should consider the case strictly on the evidence presented, and, if they have no reasonable doubt that the defendant is guilty, they should convict. For nonviolent *malum in se* crimes such as theft or perjury, nullification is an option that the juror should consider, although there should be no presumption in favor of it. A juror might vote for acquittal, for example, when a poor woman steals from Tiffany's, but not when the same woman steals from her next-door neighbor. Finally, in cases involving nonviolent, *malum prohibitum* offenses, including "victimless" crimes like narcotics offenses, there should be a presumption in favor of nullification.

Paul Butler, *Racially Based Jury Nullification: Black Power in the Criminal Justice System*, 105 Yale L.J. 677, 715 (1995). Butler further defends his proposal by contending that black jurors already acquit black defendants out of frustration with the system but, he cautions, they sometimes acquit defendants who should not be acquitted, such as those who have committed serious crimes of violence. His proposal would help to sort out those that should be acquitted from those who should not.

What do you make of Butler's proposal? More generally, what do you think of jury nullification of black defendants? What about jury nullification of other-race defendants? Is race-based jury nullification a justified response to racial injustice or is it too extreme?

7. *Affirmative Action in the Criminal Justice System?* Professor Butler has also advocated an alternative to race-based jury nullification that he suggests would be less subversive, namely, affirmative action. *See* Paul Butler, *Affirmative Action and the Criminal Law*, 68 U. Colo. L. Rev. 841 (1997). The disproportionate rate of arrests, convictions, and punishment of black people, Butler contends, is likely the result of bias in the criminal justice system from the legislature down to police, prosecutors, juries, and judges. Moreover, even to the extent black people commit certain crimes more than other racial groups, the conditions that cause such higher crime rates are a product of white supremacy and racial oppression. Accordingly, prevailing justifications for affirmative action in employment and education, such as compensating for past and present discrimination, support preferential treatment for black people in the criminal justice system. The reforms he advocates include majority-black juries for black defendants and no capital punishment for black defendants accused of interracial homicide. He further contends, without elaboration, that the criminal justice system should make the rate of black arrests, convictions, and incarcerations mirror the percentage of blacks in the general population.

What do you think of Butler's proposals? Consider also other types of race-conscious remedies that the criminal justice system might employ. What if, for example, black defendants received a discount in sentencing, such as 80% of the sentence that would otherwise be imposed on a white defendant for the same crime? Or consider that even if black defendants or defendants accused of killing white victims were still eligible for capital punishment, the number of aggravating factors would have to be greater than for other defendants before the death penalty could be imposed? Are you more or less reluctant to support affirmative action in the criminal justice system than in other contexts? Why?

8. *Concluding Note on Political and Judicial Remedies for Racial Injustice.* Political activism eventually led Congress to reconsider the 100 to 1 crack-powder sentencing ratio. In 2010, Congress passed and President Barack Obama signed the Fair Sentencing Act of 2010, Pub. L. No. 111–220. The Act lowered the 100:1 sentencing disparity between crack and powder cocaine to a ratio of 18:1. It also increased the amount of crack cocaine that triggers a five-year minimum sentence for simple possession from 5 grams to 28 grams.

If you had concerns with the 100 to 1 disparity, were they adequately ameliorated by the shift to an 18 to 1 disparity in the Fair Sentencing Act? If so, does that demonstrate that activism is a promising avenue for achieving racial justice? If you continue to have concerns with the crack-powder sentencing differential, does that undermine the importance of activism or just reveal that it can only do so much in a society that is punitive toward drug crimes and under-concerned with the plight of people of color? Does the virtual impossibility of challenging the crack-powder differential under the Equal Protection Clause call into question the equal protection doctrine and proof standards we have examined in this chapter as a safeguard against racial injustice?

The extent to which the black and brown face of America's prison population has resulted from black and Latino crime rates versus a discriminatory criminal justice system remains subject to debate. What is clear is that the racial impact of the criminal justice system, especially the War on Drugs, is devastating to communities of color. Though we have focused on the law's role in generating this impact, there are economic, social, and political forces beyond the scope of our examination that influence the state of crime and its racial implications. We have, however, seen that the criminal justice process has a critically important role to play in how our society addresses crime and race. How should we as a legal system and as a society evaluate and address the problem of crime and its racial implications? More generally, how should we as a society, through our legislatures, executives, and courts, address issues that have a racially disparate impact, intentional or not? Let us continue to engage these questions in an effort to devise constructive strategies for resolving them.

CHAPTER 9

FREE EXPRESSION

I. INTRODUCTION

During September 2011, the American Freedom Defense Initiative (AFDI) submitted an ad to be placed on the exterior of New York City buses. The ad read, "in any war between the civilized man and the savage, support the civilized man. support Israel. defeat jihad." The Transit Authority refused to run the ad, citing its "no-demeaning standard," which prohibited ads that "demean an individual or group of individuals on account of race, color, religion, national origin, ancestry, gender, age, disability or sexual orientation." Even though it regarded the ad's message as constituting hate speech, the district court ordered the Transit Authority to run the ad and held the no-demeaning standard unconstitutional. Because the standard permitted such vitriolic statements as "Fat People are Slobs" and "Southerners are Bigots" but not those that demeaned on the basis of race or religion, the court held that the policy unconstitutionally distinguished speech on the basis of its content. *Am. Freedom Def. Initiative v. Metropolitan Transp. Authority,* 880 F.Supp.2d 456, 475 (S.D.N.Y. Jul. 20, 2012).

The AFDI approached the Metropolitan Washington Transit Authority to display the same ad in its subway stations only a few weeks after a YouTube video mocking the Prophet Muhammad sparked violent anti-American protests throughout the Arab World. The transit authority (WMATA) sought to delay the posting of the ad, citing recommendations of the Department of Homeland Security and concluding that, in the current volatile political climate, the ad might increase the likelihood that the subway system would become a target of terrorist activity. The D.C. Circuit held WMATA could not delay the posting despite its potential inflammatory effect. The opinion indicated that such offensive speech might even need greater protection than non-offensive speech. Am. Freedom Def. Initiative v. Wash. Metro. Area Transit Auth., No. 12–1564, 2012 U.S. Dist. Lexis 147052 (D.D.C. Oct. 12, 2012).

Although consistent with current First Amendment jurisprudence in the United States, this holding is inconceivable in many other countries. The American conception of free speech is more capacious than that of all other liberal democracies. Many countries, such as Austria, Belgium, Brazil, Canada, England, France, Germany, India, Israel, Italy, the Netherlands, and Switzerland have enacted laws that regulate racist or hate speech. Alexander Tesis, *Destructive Messages: How Hate Speech Paves the Way for Harmful Social Movements* 180, 192 (2002). As Professor Frederick Schauer, a leading authority on the First Amendment, has observed, "[t]he incitement to racial hatred and other verbal manifestations of race-based animosity are widely accepted as lying outside the boundaries of what a properly conceived freedom of expression encompasses." Frederick Schauer, *The Exceptional First Amendment* in AMERICAN EXCEPTIONALISM AND HUMAN RIGHTS 29 (MICHAEL IGNATIEFF ED., 2005).

The dominant understanding in U.S. jurisprudence is that hate speech must be tolerated as part of our recognition of dissenting and anti-orthodox voices in American culture. American jurisprudence recognizes only narrow exceptions to such protection; neither speech that advocates imminent violence nor obscenity, for example, is protected by the First Amendment. According to Harry Kalven, the oft-quoted First Amendment scholar: "Freedom of speech is indivisible; unless we protect it for all, we will have it for none." And so, even the most reviled speech is sometimes characterized as symbolic of free expression itself. First Amendment doctrine is often offered up as the quintessential example of American legal exceptionalism.

In contrast to free speech discourse in the United States, free speech debate in other jurisdictions weighs free expression against other competing values, including dignity, personal identity, and privacy. European free speech doctrine "rejects a conception of individuals as beings who merely should be left to their own devices to make up their own minds about the value of expression in the public domain, to be free to ignore it. Such an approach isolates human beings by forcing them to take the consequences of the painful conduct and ignores the particular susceptibility of certain groups to injury, especially when the offense of the speech seems to be targeted at such groups because of their identity. . . . Sometimes the state must act to show its solidarity with vulnerable minority groups and its commitment to equality." Sionaidh Douglas-Scott, *The Hatefulness of Protected Speech: A Comparison of the American and European Approaches*, 7 WM. & MARY BILL RTS. J. 305, 343–35 (1999). Speech is valued according to its promotion or inhibition of desirable social ends. Unlike the U.S. approach to speech, which scholars have described as characterized by "an emphasis on rule-based categorization," European law takes a "more flexible and open-ended balancing approach." Frederick Schauer, *The Exceptional First Amendment* in AMERICAN EXCEPTIONALISM AND HUMAN RIGHTS 29 (MICHAEL IGNATIEFF ED., 2005).

This chapter examines American free speech doctrine and its relationship to how we think about race, racial equality, and race relations in America. The central question raised by this chapter is whether racial equality is furthered or impeded by largely unfettered expression. In exploring this question, the chapter will raise a number of challenging inquiries. First, the chapter will ask what is harmful about hate speech or racist speech. The following epithets—Beaner, Camel Jockey, Ching Chong, Coon, Kike, Dago, Dink, Jap, Nigger, Raghead, Redskin, Sambo, Sand Nigger, Spic, Squaw, Towel Head, Wetback, Wop, and Yid, among other like words—are not generally accepted in polite company. Should they be excludable by law? What is the harm caused by these words? And do the benefits of prohibiting hate speech outweigh the costs of doing so?

Second, the chapter invites you to think about what we are calling the problem of racial asymmetry. It introduces two types of asymmetries related to disagreements that we as a society have about hate speech. First, can members of a group use words that would be viewed as denigrating if used by non-members of the group? For instance, should only people of Latino descent be allowed to use the word "spic"? Or should law prohibit hate speech categorically? Second, does hate speech have a greater, and more negative, impact on marginalized groups than privileged groups? Are whites equally harmed when labeled with a denigrating term as blacks are when referred to as a "nigger"? If a young man is beaten up because he is of Chinese descent are we all equally harmed or do Chinese-Americans experience this hate crime differently?

Third, the chapter inquires whether protecting hate speech undermines or promotes racial equality. Is unfettered speech a form of empowerment or a form of oppression? To what extent does the liberty that undergirds free expression empower people of color to improve their social and material conditions? Will changing how individuals speak or behave contribute to the achievement of racial justice? Or will we achieve racial equality only through the social engineering of material conditions? In the summer of 2015, President Barack Obama, the first African-American President, stated in an interview, "racism, we are not cured of it. And it's not just a matter of it not being polite to say nigger in public. That's not the measure of whether racism still exists or not. Societies don't, overnight, completely erase everything that happened 200 to 300 years prior. The legacy of slavery, Jim Crow, discrimination in almost every institution of our lives, that casts a long shadow and that's still part of our DNA that's passed on." http://www.wtfpod.com/pod cast/episodes/episode_613_-_president_barack_obama. Do you agree with the President? Does hate speech matter in a world of structural racial inequality, where, to name just one example, African Americans are incarcerated at a rate that is five times greater than whites? If you believe that structural inequality describes the problem of racial inequality in the 21st century, what role does free expression play, if at all, in reducing structural inequality?

Fourth, if we wish to proscribe racist speech, how much should we account for different institutional settings? Is the use of the word "nigger" always racist or does it matter if the word is being used in rap music or in the movies? What about the affectionate use of "nigger" in the workplace among multiracial co-workers? Or in the educational context used by Professor, of any race, who is teaching a class on the First Amendment? Does the institutional setting matter?

Lastly, the chapter invites you to think about the appropriate solution to racist speech. Is it legal prohibition or is it social sanction backed by protest politics? In the age of the Internet, social media, and Twitter activism, is hate speech best policed by awareness and social shunning or do we need the force of the law as well?

II. Racist Speech

A. The Harm of Racist Speech: The Victim's Perspective

Some commentators, in particular critical race theorists, have argued that racist hate speech can have severe impacts. They also argue that the harms of racist speech do not have the same effect on the majority as on the minority. Indeed, one of the most significant characteristics of racist speech is that its users intend it to have an asymmetric effect. Unlike personal attacks based on political or religious affiliation, for example, racist hate speech is based on an immutable personal trait of the victim. Further, the speaker chooses his or her target because of the intended victim's racial or ethnic characteristic. In this vein, consider the following account of the harm of racist speech from Professor Mari Matsuda:

> The negative effects of hate messages are real and immediate for the victims. Victims of vicious hate propaganda have experienced physiological symptoms and emotional distress ranging from fear in the gut, rapid pulse rate and difficulty in breathing, nightmares, post-traumatic stress disorder, hypertension, psychosis, and suicide.

> Victims are restricted in their personal freedom. In order to avoid receiving hate messages, victims have had to quit jobs, forgo education, leave their homes, avoid certain public places, curtail their own exercise of speech rights, and otherwise modify their behavior and demeanor. The recipient of hate messages struggles with inner turmoil. One subconscious response is to reject one's own identity as a victim-group member.

> As much as one may try to resist a piece of hate propaganda, the effect on one's self-esteem and sense of personal security is devastating. To be hated, despised, and alone is the ultimate fear of all human beings. However irrational racist speech may be, it hits right at the emotional place where we feel the most pain. The aloneness comes not only from the hate message itself, but also from the government response of tolerance. When hundreds of police officers are called out to protect racist marchers, when the courts refuse redress for racial insult, and when racist attacks are officially dismissed as pranks, the victim becomes a stateless person.

* * *

Research in psychosocial and psycholinguistic analysis of racism suggests a related effect of racist hate propaganda: at some level, no matter how much both victims and well-meaning dominant-group members resist it, racial inferiority is planted in our minds as an idea that may hold some truth. The idea is improbable and abhorrent, but it is there before us, because it is presented repeatedly. "Those people" are lazy, dirty, sexualized, money-grubbing, dishonest, inscrutable, we are told.

* * *

If the harm of racist hate messages is significant, and the truth value marginal, the doctrinal space for regulation of such speech is a possibility. An emerging international standard seizes this possibility.

Mari J. Matsuda, Public Response to Racist Speech: Considering the Victim's Story, 87 Mich. L. Rev. 2320, 2332–33, 2336–41 (1989).

How persuasive do you find Professor Matsuda's account? Professor Matsuda argues that racist speech causes both psychic harm, such as emotional distress, and physical harm, such as hypertension. Are these sufficiently compelling and pervasive to justify some type of protective regulation? Professor Matsuda also argues that hate speech imposes costs on minority groups as a whole, as well as on dominant group members. What do you think those costs might be? Which (if any) of these do you find the most worthy of a response through law?

Owen Fiss argues that the 1960s, oftentimes cited as illustrating the virtue of prioritizing free speech to achieve racial justice, actually gives us an illusory picture of the stakes of the First Amendment debate. In the Supreme Court's early and seminal civil rights cases that addressed the relationship between racial equality and speech, cases such as *NAACP v. Alabama*, 357 U.S. 449 (1958) and *NAACP v. Button*, 371 U.S. 415 (1963), the countervalues championed by the state, such as requiring disclosure of the membership of civil rights organizations, was "neither particularly alluring nor compelling, and for that reason the Court's decisions in favor of free speech generated widespread support." OWEN FISS, THE IRONY OF FREE SPEECH 7 (1996). In contrast, the dilemma of hate speech (like efforts to regulate pornography and enact campaign finance reform, according to Fiss) offers a strong and important countervalue against the absolutist liberal conception of speech. He argues that, in the wake of *Brown v. Board of Education*, liberal values were redefined such that they tempered the demand for limited government and came to balance liberty with the value of equality.

At the same time, according to Fiss, liberal values need not pit the values of liberty against the values of equality (the First versus the Fourteenth Amendments, as many writing on the issue have done).

Instead the regulation of hate speech can be done in the pursuit of First Amendment goals, in the name of liberty. He argues that "[s]ometimes we must lower the voices of some in order to hear the voices of others." *Id.* at 18. Even when championing First Amendment principles, Fiss argues we need to recognize the "silencing effect of speech" on disadvantaged groups, and ask whether hate speech really leads to more robust speech. Fiss at 26. Professor Richard Delgado affirms Fiss's contention that counterspeech is a myth and the most common response to hate speech is silence: "Victims of racial invective have few means of coping with the harms caused by the insults. Physical attacks are of course forbidden. 'More speech' frequently is useless because it may provoke only further abuse or because the insulter is in a position of authority over the victim." Richard Delgado, *Words that Wound: A Tort Action for Racial Insults, Epithets, and Name Calling* 146, *in* MARI MATSUDA, CHARLES R. LAWRENCE III, RICHARD DELGADO, AND KIMBERLE WILLIAMS CRENSHAW, WORDS THAT WOUND: CRITICAL RACE THEORY, ASSAULTIVE SPEECH, AND THE FIRST AMENDMENT 26 (1993). Only the law can help restore the position of helplessness that a person of color feels upon being confronted by one of these words. Are Fiss and Delgado right? Are the victims of hate speech silenced by such speech? Is unfettered free expression simply about power dynamics where targets of hate speech are only victims?

The dialectic between racial equality and free speech doctrine leads us to ask whether a different approach to speech might impact how we think about race and racial equality. What are the consequences of not recognizing race-based disparagement as substantively different from other forms of disparagement? How does this reflect how we think about race, racial identity, and racial equality? How has this relationship changed over time?

B. WHAT IS RACIST SPEECH?

Consider a first pass at a recurring problem: how sure are we that we can identify racist speech? Take a look at the following examples. Which ones count as racist speech and why?

- In 2008, Golf Channel host Kelly Tilghman, during a golf telecast discussing the golfer Tiger Woods, whose father is African American and mother Asian, stated that young golfers who wanted to keep up with the then-dominant Woods should "lynch him in a back alley." The civil rights activist Al Sharpton called for the Federal Communications Commission to levy a penalty on the Golf Channel and for the Golf Channel to fire Tilghman, who was subsequently suspended for two weeks.

- In April 2007, talk show host Don Imus referred to the Rutgers women's basketball team as "nappy-headed hoes."

Eight out of ten of the women on the basketball team at the *Racist* time were African American.[1]

- A black man found a noose hanging at his worksite; his supervisor said it was a joke. Three nooses were found *Racist* hanging from a tree in a school yard at a High School in Jena, Louisiana, the day after a black student asked to sit under the tree where normally only white students sat. A noose was found hanging on a tree on the Duke University campus. An undergraduate student eventually confessed to hanging the noose and maintained that his "purpose in hanging the noose was merely to take some pictures with my friends together with the noose, and then texting it to some others inviting them to come and 'hang out' with us— because it was such a nice day outside." He maintains that he was not aware of the meaning of the noose.

- A New Yorker cartoon in 2008 depicted Michelle Obama wearing a large Afro, carrying a machine gun, and fist- bumping then-Senator Obama, who is dressed in recognizably Muslim attire. A cartoon depicted then-Judge and Supreme Court nominee Sonia Sotomayor as a piñata *Racist* and President Obama wearing a sombrero asking Senate Republicans, "who wants to be first." A cartoon depicting President Obama as a pimp. A cartoon in which an immigrant family climbs through a white family's window during Thanksgiving dinner while the father of the white family states, "thanks to the President's immigration order

---

[1]   Imus's conversation with his producer, Bernard McGuirk, his co-host Charles McCord, and his sports announcer, Sid Rosenberg is reproduced below:

IMUS: So, I watched the basketball game last night between—a little bit of Rutgers and Tennessee, the women's final.

ROSENBERG: Yeah, Tennessee won last night—seventh championship for [Tennessee coach] Pat Summitt, I-Man. They beat Rutgers by 13 points.

IMUS: That's some rough girls from Rutgers. Man, they got tattoos and—

McGUIRK: Some hard-core hos.

IMUS: That's some nappy-headed hos there. I'm gonna tell you that now, man, that's some—woo. And the girls from Tennessee, they all look cute, you know, so, like—kinda like—I don't know.

McGUIRK: A Spike Lee thing.

IMUS: Yeah.

McGUIRK: The Jigaboos vs. the Wannabes—that movie that he had.

IMUS: Yeah, it was a tough—

McCORD: *Do The Right Thing*.

McGUIRK: Yeah, yeah, yeah.

IMUS: I don't know if I'd have wanted to beat Rutgers or not, but they did, right?

ROSENBERG: It was a tough watch. The more I look at Rutgers, they look exactly like the Toronto Raptors.

IMUS: Well, I guess, yeah.

RUFFINO: Only tougher.

McGUIRK: The [Memphis] Grizzlies would be more appropriate.

we'll be having extra guests this Thanksgiving." A cartoon depicting an intruder in the White House as the President is brushing his teeth in the bathroom. The intruder asks the President whether the President has tried the new watermelon-flavored toothpaste. New York Post cartoon depicting two officers shooting a chimp and one of the officers commenting "they'll have to find someone else to write the next stimulus bill."[2]

- If there is a single word that is synonymous with racist speech, it is the word *nigger*. The Ninth Circuit once characterized "nigger" as "the most noxious racial epithet in the contemporary American lexicon," as "uniquely provocative and demeaning" even as compared to other racial epithets. *Montiero v. Tempe Union High School District*, 158 F.3d 1022 (CA 9 1998). What is it that makes the "N-word" so powerful? Is it the unparalleled American historical atrocities committed during slavery? Or does its power come from the current social hierarchy? Nigger is derived from the Latin word Niger, which means black. As noted by an exhaustive study of the word and its usage, nigger did not originate as a racial insult, but by the "end of the first third of the nineteenth century, *nigger* had already become a familiar and influential insult." RANDALL KENNEDY, NIGGER: THE STRANGE CAREER OF A TROUBLESOME WORD 5 (2002). For some, nigger is the most insulting and derogatory word in the English language. Kennedy calls nigger the "paradigmatic slur." *Id*. at 27. He went on to observe: "It is the epithet that generates epithets. That is why Arabs are called sand niggers, Irish the niggers of Europe, and Palestinians the nigger of the Middle East; why black bowling balls have been called nigger eggs, games of craps nigger golf, watermelons nigger hams, rolls of one-dollar bills nigger rolls, bad luck nigger luck, gossip nigger news, and heavy boots nigger stompers." *Id* at 27–28. Consider the following controversies raised by the use of the word. How would you decide them?

  o Plaintiff is an African American woman who alleged that on two occasions within a twenty-four hour period her supervisor called her a "dumb nigger." Plaintiff filed suit alleging hostile work environment under Title VII. The question is whether calling someone a

---

[2] National Public Radio hosted a discussion of political caricatures of President Obama. A transcript can be found here: http://www.npr.org/templates/transcript/transcript.php?story Id=135770521.

severe & Penalis (handwritten)

"nigger" twice is sufficient to establish a hostile work environment.

o   Plaintiff is a white male who sued his employer, a news organization, after the employer fired the plaintiff for using the word "nigger." The plaintiff used the word during an editorial meeting in which journalists discussed the stories that would later air in the broadcasts. Plaintiff and his co-workers were discussing a story about a local NAACP that held a symbolic burial for the word nigger. During the course of the discussion, the plaintiff asked, "Does this mean we can finally say the word 'nigger'?" Up to this point, all of the participants had used the euphemism N-word instead of saying nigger. Plaintiff said "nigger" one more time during the course of the discussion. The plaintiff also used the word in subsequent discussions with his African American co-workers who were upset by his use of the word. Plaintiff was subsequently fired for using the word. Plaintiff filed a racial discrimination claim and hostile work environment claim under Title VII. He claimed that he used the word in a non-pejorative sense and that an African American co-worker used the word and was not fired for doing so. (The African American co-worker used nigger in describing the meeting that took place and the plaintiff's use of the word. On another occasion, an African American co-worker called a crime suspect a "dumb nigger.") Plaintiff also alleged that he was fired only because his African American co-workers demanded that he be fired. Would you have fired the plaintiff? Would you have fired the African American co-workers who used the word? Can a white person ever use the word nigger?

o   At the 2014 Motion Picture Awards, Michael Fassbender was nominated for an Oscar for his role as a white slave owner in the movie *12 Years a Slave*. In the broadcast presenting his nomination, the network played a video clip from the movie, but bleeped Fassbender's character when he said "nigger." Was the network correct in doing so?

o   Although there may have been a time when there was no question that the sole purpose of using the word was to express animus or demean, clearly this is no longer the case. Although oftentimes distinguished by its spelling ("nigga"), nigger or its variant has become a common term and particularly en vogue in some parts of black popular culture, particularly rap and hip-hop music. Nigger or nigga is sometimes used by and among some black people as a term of endearment; as a compliment meaning to work hard or to do something with tenacity; to show respect, etc. *See e.g.*, KENNEDY, *supra* at 36–37. The general aim by African Americans when they use the word nigger is to reappropriate the word—to redefine its meaning and to strip it of its racist potency. Reappropriation is a process by which a subordinated or out-group can take a "negatively evaluated label, and [by] revaluing it positively, a group can change the value of the label and thus, in at least some important ways, the value of the group." Adam Galinsky et al., *The Reappropriation of Stigmatizing Labels: Implications for Social Identity*, 5 RESEARCH ON MANAGING GROUPS AND TEAMS 221, 228 (2003). Can a word like nigger or nigga ever be reappropriated? Or should it be prohibited by social convention from use? For example, in 2016 at the White House Correspondents' Dinner, the event's host, comedian Larry Wilmore referred to President Obama as "my nigga." At the end of his speech, Wilmore stated: "Words alone do me no justice. So, Mr. President, if i'm going to keep it 100: Yo, Barry, you did it, my nigga. You did it." https://www.youtube.com/watch?v=1IDFt3BL 7FA; https://www.washingtonpost.com/news/reliable-source/wp/2016/05/01/the-complete-transcript-of-larry-wilmores-2016-white-house-correspondents-dinner-speech/. Wilmore, who is black, defended his use of the word as a show of black solidarity and reappropriation. Some criticized Wilmore for disrespecting the President and the presidency. Do you agree with the critics?

o   African-American filmmaker Spike Lee has very publicly criticized director Quentin Tarantino for his use of the word 'nigger' in his scripts consistently, as well as elements of Blaxploitation films in *Jackie Brown*. In particular, Lee vociferously criticized Tarantino's *Django Unchained*, a slave narrative told in the style of a spaghetti western in which "nigger" is used more than 100 times. When Lee himself was confronted by his use of the word nigger, he asserted that as an African-American, he had "more of a right" to do so. Luther Campbell of the music group 2LiveCrew rebuked Lee's criticisms, calling *Django* "a brilliant flick that more accurately depicts the African-

American experience than any of the 15 movies about black culture Lee's directed in his lifetime" and calling Lee "a conniving and scheming Uncle Tom." 80-year-old comedian and famed civil rights activist, Dick Gregory, also derided Lee's protest of the film, calling him a "thug" and a "punk." Who has the better of the argument here, Lee or his detractors?

- How should one draw the line between protected and racist speech in a university setting? On the one hand, one could argue that free inquiry is the raison d'être of a university and speech codes in a university setting are antagonistic to such free inquiry. On the other hand, universities have a distinctive educational mission that may be undermined by the prevalence of hate speech, and many arguable instances of hate speech have taken place on college campuses. Here are some incidents that have given rise to controversy:

  o At the University of Michigan, white students painted themselves black at "jungle parties." At Stanford University, Aryan Resistance literature was distributed among students. At Dartmouth College, a black professor was labeled a "cross between a welfare queen and a bathroom attendant." A student affairs director at one college sent an email to all students to avoid "racially inappropriate" costumes during the upcoming campus Halloween festivities. A member of the faculty then sent a follow up email, encouraging students to choose whichever costume they prefer and avoiding adherence to what she calls "over-politically-correctness." The email sparked a wave of student protest, especially by students identifying as racial and ethnic minorities, who were offended by the professor's email. The professor was summoned to a disciplinary hearing. What do you think about the professor's email? Should she have been fired for writing it? Are the students right to be offended by the email and protest against it?

  o Do incidents such as these demonstrate the need for legislative and judicial attention to the problem of racist speech, particularly on college campuses? Should universities adopt codes of conduct to police hate speech on college campuses? Michael Meyers, director of the New York Civil Rights coalition, has come out against campus speech codes as inhibiting the development of the next generation of radical resistance: "As a former student activist, and as a current black militant, [I] believe[ ] that free speech is the minority's strongest weapon. . . . [P]aternalism [and] censorship offer the college student a tranquilizer as the antidote to campus and societal racism. What we need is an alarm clock. . . . What we need is free speech . . . and more free speech." Do you think campus speech codes more likely to foster or suppress political agency?

C. PROMOTING CIVIL RIGHTS THROUGH THE FIRST AMENDMENT

From the current debates over hate or racist speech, the First Amendment might look to some as an obstacle to racial equality. Such a view would be too crude. It is not an exaggeration to say that the Civil Rights Movement was nurtured by a broad understanding of the First Amendment that favored the Movement's aims and goals.

Take, for example, *Beauharnais v. Illinois*, 343 U.S. 988 (1952). Joseph Beauharnais was president of the White Circle League of America, a racist organization that opposed miscegenation and integration. Beauharnais published and distributed a leaflet calling on the Mayor of Chicago to "halt the further encroachment, harassment and invasion of white people, their property, . . . by the Negro." He asked white people to unite to prevent whites from becoming "mongrelized by the Negro."

For producing and distributing the leaflet, Beauharnais was convicted of violating Illinois' group libel law. The statute prohibited, *inter alia*, the publication of any pictures, play, drama, or sketch that "portrays depravity, criminality, unchastity, or lack of virtue of a class of citizens of any race, color, creed . . . [that] exposes the citizens of any race, color, creed . . . to contempt, derision or obloquy or which is productive of breach of the peace or riots." In an opinion by Justice Frankfurter, a closely divided Court upheld the conviction. The majority concluded that in light of the history of racial and religious violence in Illinois, the legislature was justified in promulgating the statute. This is in part because "willful purveyors of falsehood concerning racial and religious groups promote strife and tend powerfully to obstruct the manifold adjustments required for free, ordered life in a metropolitan, polygot community." 343 U.S. at 259. The majority's decision in *Beauharnais* led Justice Black in dissent to complain that "Illinois inflicted criminal punishment on Beauharnais for causing the distribution of leaflets in the city of Chicago" and this is deeply inconsistent with the First Amendment. 343 U.S. at 267.

In *Beauharnais*, the Court upheld a state group libel law against a free speech challenge. In subsequent cases the Court used the First Amendment to protect the rights of African Americans to assemble, organize, and use the courts in defense of their civil liberties. We should add that free speech doctrine has moved considerably since *Beauharnais*, towards granting greater protection to speech. Thus, *Beauharnais*, which has been the subject of much criticism, is probably no longer good law.

A few years later, in *NAACP v. Alabama,* 357 U.S. 63 (1958), the NAACP challenged a subpoena for its membership list. The Court unanimously upheld the NAACP's right not to disclose its membership list under the freedom of association prong of First Amendment jurisprudence. Justice Harlan noted the "uncontroverted showing that on past occasions revelation of the identity of [the NAACP's] rank-and-file members has exposed these members to economic reprisal, loss of employment, threat of physical coercion, and other manifestations of public hostility." Though more recent cases have not preserved this First Amendment right to privacy of association, those cases have not involved the race-related harms implicated in *NAACP v. Alabama. See* e.g., *Doe v. Reed*, 561 U.S. 186 (2010), holding disclosure of the names on a referendum petition did not violate the First Amendment.

Only a few years after *NAACP v. Alabama*, the Court explicitly recognized freedom of speech as constitutive of political agency for the African American community. In *NAACP v. Button*, 371 U.S. 415 (1963), the Court held that litigation was a protected means of political speech and affirmed it as a mechanism for social change. The case, brought by the NAACP, challenged a Virginia statute that prohibited the improper solicitation of legal business. The Virginia Supreme Court of Appeals held that the prohibition applied to the NAACP, which would prohibit the NAACP from soliciting or identifying plaintiffs to challenge racial segregation in Virginia. The statute prohibited a third party from functioning as the intermediary between the client and the lawyer, or from inducing people who otherwise would not to sue. Justice Brennan, writing for the majority, held that "abstract discussion is not the only species of communication which the Constitution protects; the First Amendment also protects vigorous advocacy, certainly of lawful ends, against governmental intrusion." 371 U.S. at 429. He went on to note, "in the context of NAACP objectives, litigation is not a technique of resolving private differences; it is a means for achieving the lawful objectives of equality of treatment by all government, federal, state and local, for the members of the Negro community in this country. It is thus a form of political expression." *Id.* Brennan describes the statute at issue as the will of the majority attempting to silence the dissident minority:

> We cannot close our eyes to the fact that the militant Negro civil rights movement has engendered the intense resentment and opposition of the politically dominant white community of Virginia; litigation assisted by the NAACP has been bitterly fought. In such circumstances, a statute broadly curtailing group activity leading to litigation may easily become a weapon of oppression, however evenhanded its terms appear. Its mere existence could well freeze out of existence all such activity on behalf of the civil rights of Negro citizens. *Id.* 435–6.

In the landmark case of *New York Times v. Sullivan*, 376 U.S. 254 (1964), the Supreme Court again interpreted the First Amendment in a manner that would safeguard the Civil Rights Movement. The Court reversed a judgment awarding $500,000 to an elected official from Montgomery, Alabama, who filed an action for libel against the New York Times and a number of black clergy. The plaintiff claimed that he was libeled by an advertisement that the clergy placed in the New York Times to draw attention to the non-violent student protest movement and the movement for black suffrage in Alabama. The ad claimed that the protest movement was being met by a "wave of terror" from "police armed with shotguns" and "Southern violators." The ad appealed for funds to support the students, the movement for the right to vote, and a legal defense fund for Dr. Martin Luther King Jr.

In reversing the monetary award, the Court stated that it is a "long . . . settled" "general proposition that freedom of expression upon public questions is secured by the First Amendment." The Court concluded that even where a public official was falsely defamed, the "constitutional guarantees require, we think, a federal rule that prohibits a public official from recovering damages for a defamatory falsehood relating to his official conduct unless he proves that the statement was made with 'actual malice'—that is, with knowledge that it was false or with reckless disregard of whether it was false or not." The First Amendment prohibits a state from awarding damages for libel actions brought by public officials for criticisms of their official conduct, unless the official can prove actual malice, a fairly high bar. The Court then went on to conclude that the facts did not support a finding of actual malice.

In *Brown v. Louisiana*, 383 U.S. 131 (1966), a case that addressed the peaceful sit-in of five African-American protesters who refused to leave the segregated reading room of a public library, the Court recognized the importance of symbolic speech:

> We are here dealing with an aspect of a basic constitutional right—the right under the First and Fourteenth Amendments guaranteeing freedom of speech and of assembly, and freedom to petition the Government for a redress of grievances. The Constitution of the State of Louisiana reiterates these guaranties. *See* Art. I, ss 3, 5. As this Court has repeatedly stated, these rights are not confined to verbal expression. They embrace appropriate types of action which certainly include the right in a peaceable and orderly manner to protest by silent and reproachful presence, in a place where the protestant has every right to be, the unconstitutional segregation of public facilities. *Id.* at 141–42.

These cases show that the Court has interpreted the First Amendment pragmatically to further racial equality and in support of the Civil Rights Movement. As important, the relationship between the

First Amendment and the Civil Rights Movement has been mutually constitutive. Many credit the Movement and the cases of the era for expanding the scope of the First Amendment. For example, Professor Randall Kennedy has observed that the Civil Rights Movement germinated a "blossoming of libertarian themes in First Amendment jurisprudence," and that the free speech doctrines now being used against the interests of people of color were once championed by them. Randall Kennedy, Martin Luther King's Constitution: A Legal History of the Montgomery Bus Boycott, 98 Yale L.J. 999 (1989). *See also* HARRY KALVEN, THE NEGRO AND THE FIRST AMENDMENT (1965).

The First Amendment remains a tool that can be used to promote equality for disadvantaged groups. Perhaps the best contemporary example of its potential has been its use to curb the reach of English-only laws. The United States has never had an official language. And though English is the de facto lingua franca and the exclusive language spoken by the vast majority of Americans, linguistic diversity has been persistent because of ongoing immigration. The public perception that immigrants refuse to assimilate linguistically has fueled English-only movements throughout our history. Today, approximately 24 states have declared English their official language, and periodically members of Congress introduce bills to make English the official language of the United States. Many of these official language laws are just hortatory, but others preclude government officials from functioning in any language other than English, except under limited circumstances— prohibitions that obviously have an impact on the ability of non-English speakers, predominantly immigrants, to interact with public officials and take advantage of government programs. In the case excerpted below, the Ninth Circuit held that Arizona's constitutional amendment making English the official language of the state violated the First Amendment right of public employees. As you read it, consider which interests are most salient in the case.

Yñiguez v. Arizonans for Official English

United States Court of Appeals, Ninth Circuit, 1995.
69 F.3d 920, *vacated on other grounds by* 520 U.S. 43 (1997).

■ REINHARDT, CIRCUIT JUDGE:

Specifically at issue in this case is the constitutionality of Article XXVIII of the Arizona Constitution. Article XXVIII provides, *inter alia,* that English is the official language of the state of Arizona, and that the state and its political subdivisions—including all government officials and employees performing government business—must "act" only in English.

This case raises troubling questions regarding the constitutional status of language rights and, conversely, the state's power to restrict such rights. There are valid concerns on both sides. In our diverse and pluralistic society, the importance of establishing common bonds and a common language between citizens is clear. Equally important, however, is the American tradition of tolerance, a tradition that recognizes a critical difference between encouraging the use of English and repressing the use of other languages. Arizona's rejection of that tradition has severe consequences not only for its public officials and employees, but for the many thousands of Arizonans who would be precluded from receiving essential information from their state and local governments if the drastic prohibition contained in the provision were to be implemented.

We conclude that Article XXVIII constitutes a prohibited means of promoting the English language and affirm the district court's ruling that it violates the First Amendment.

A three-judge panel of this court issued an opinion reaching this same conclusion last year. *Yñiguez v. Arizonans for Official English*, 42 F.3d 1217 (9th Cir. 1994). We then decided to reconsider the question en banc. Having done so, we conclude that our opinion was correct. Because the opinion was withdrawn when we went en banc, we re-publish it now, with only a few changes that discuss the applicability of intervening Supreme Court cases or expand on points that warrant further explanation.

I.

In October 1987, Arizonans for Official English initiated a petition drive to amend Arizona's constitution to prohibit the government's use of languages other than English. The drive culminated in the 1988 passage by ballot initiative of Article XXVIII of the Arizona Constitution, entitled "English as the Official Language." The measure passed by a margin of one percentage point, drawing the affirmative votes of 50.5% of Arizonans casting ballots in the election. Under Article XXVIII, English is "the official language of the State of Arizona": "the language of . . . all government functions and actions." The provision declares that the "State and all [of its] political subdivisions"—defined as including "all government officials and employees during the performance of government business"—"shall act in English and no other language."

At the time of the passage of the article, Yñiguez, a Latina, was employed by the Arizona Department of Administration, where she handled medical malpractice claims asserted against the state. She was bilingual—fluent and literate in both Spanish and English. Prior to the article's passage, Yñiguez communicated in Spanish with monolingual Spanish-speaking claimants, and in a combination of English and Spanish with bilingual claimants.

State employees who fail to obey the Arizona Constitution are subject to employment sanctions. For this reason, immediately upon passage of Article XXVIII, Yñiguez ceased speaking Spanish on the job. She feared that because of Article XXVIII her use of Spanish made her vulnerable to discipline.

Although eighteen states have adopted "official-English" laws, Arizona's Article XXVIII is "by far the most restrictively worded official-English law to date." Besides declaring English "the official language of the State of Arizona," Article XXVIII states that English is "the language of . . . all government functions and actions." The article further specifies that the state and its subdivisions—defined as encompassing "all government officials and employees during the performance of government business"—"shall act in English and no other language." Its broad coverage is punctuated by several exceptions permitting, for example, the use of non-English languages as required by federal law, and in order to protect the rights of criminal defendants and victims of crime.

Yñiguez contends that Article XXVIII unlawfully prevented her from speaking Spanish with the Spanish-speaking claimants that came to her Department of Administration office. Yñiguez, however, challenges far more than Article XXVIII's ban on her own use of Spanish in the performance of her own particular job. She also contends that the speech rights of innumerable employees, officials, and officers in all departments and at all levels of Arizona's state and local governments are chilled by Article XXVIII's expansive reach. At least as important, she contends that the interests of many thousands of non-English-speaking Arizonans in receiving vital information would be drastically and unlawfully limited. For those reasons, she challenges Article XXVIII as overbroad on its face and invalid in its entirety.

Article XXVIII's ban on the use of languages other than English by persons in government service could hardly be more inclusive. The provision plainly states that it applies to "the legislative, executive, and judicial branches" of both state and local government, and to "all government officials and employees during the performance of government business." This broad language means that Article XXVIII on its face applies to speech in a seemingly limitless variety of governmental settings, from ministerial statements by civil servants at the office to teachers speaking in the classroom, from town-hall discussions between constituents and their representatives to the translation of judicial proceedings in the courtroom. Under the article, the Arizona state universities would be barred from issuing diplomas in Latin, and judges performing weddings would be prohibited from saying "Mazel Tov" as part of the official marriage ceremony. Accordingly, it is self-evident that Article XXVIII's sweeping English-only mandate limits the speech of governmental actors serving in a wide range of work-related contexts that differ significantly from that in which Yñiguez performed her daily tasks. The speech rights of all of Arizona's state and local employees, officials, and officers are thus adversely affected in a potentially unconstitutional manner by the breadth of Article XXVIII's ban on non-English governmental speech. Similarly, the interests of non-

English-speaking Arizonans in receiving all kinds of essential information are severely burdened.

[Analysis of overbreadth doctrine and severability omitted.— Eds.]

Arizonans for Official English argues vehemently that First Amendment scrutiny should be relaxed in this case because the decision to speak a non-English language does not implicate pure speech rights. Rather, the group suggests, "choice of language . . . is a mode of conduct"—a "*nonverbal* expressive activity." Accordingly, it compares this case to those involving only "expressive conduct" or "symbolic speech." In such cases, the government generally has a wider latitude in regulating the conduct involved, but only when the regulation is not directed at the communicative nature of that conduct.

We find the analysis employed in the above cases to be inapplicable here, as we are entirely unpersuaded by the comparison between speaking languages other than English and burning flags. * * *

As we have noted, it is frequently the need to convey information to members of the public that dictates the decision to speak in a different tongue. If all state and local officials and employees are prohibited from doing so, Arizonans who do not speak English will be unable to receive much essential information concerning their daily needs and lives. To call a prohibition that precludes the conveying of information to thousands of Arizonans in a language they can comprehend a mere regulation of "mode of expression" is to miss entirely the basic point of First Amendment protections.

Arizonans for Official English next contends, incorrectly, that Yñiguez seeks an affirmative right to have government operations conducted in foreign tongues. Because the organization misconceives Yñiguez's argument, it relies on a series of cases in which non-English-speaking plaintiffs have unsuccessfully tried to require the government to provide them with services in their own language. These cases, however, hold only that (at least under the circumstances there involved) non-English speakers have no affirmative right to compel state government to provide information in a language that they can comprehend. The cases are inapplicable here.

In the case before us, there is no claim of an affirmative right to compel the state to provide multilingual information, but instead only a claim of a negative right: that the state cannot, consistent with the First Amendment, gag the employees currently providing members of the public with information and thereby effectively preclude large numbers of persons from receiving information that they have previously received.

Accordingly, the argument of the amendment's sponsor is irrelevant to the right we consider in this case. For while the state may not be under any obligation to *provide* multilingual services and information, it is an entirely different matter when it deliberately sets out to *prohibit* the languages customarily employed by public employees. In this connection, we note that here, unlike in the affirmative right cases, there is no contention that "harried taxpayers" will be "saddled" with additional costs, or that the state will be subjected to a "patently unreasonable burden." All that the state must do to comply with the Constitution in this case is to refrain from terminating normal and cost-free services for reasons that are invidious, discriminatory, or, at the very least, wholly insufficient.

If this case involved a statewide ban on all uses of languages other than English within the geographical jurisdiction of the state of Arizona, the constitutional outcome would be clear. A state cannot simply prohibit all persons within its borders from speaking in the tongue of their choice. Such a restriction on private speech obviously could not stand. However, Article XXVIII's restraint on speech is of more limited scope. Its ban is restricted to speech by persons performing services for the government. Thus, we must look beyond first principles of First Amendment doctrine and consider the question of what limitations may constitutionally be placed on the speech of government servants.

For nearly half-a-century, it has been axiomatic in constitutional law that government employees do not simply forfeit their First Amendment rights upon entering the public workplace.

The employee speech banned by Article XXVIII is unquestionably of public import. It pertains to the provision of governmental services and information. Unless that speech is delivered in a form that the intended recipients can comprehend, they are likely to be deprived of much needed data as well as of substantial public and private benefits. The speech at issue is speech that members of the public desire to hear. Indeed, it is most often the recipient, rather than the public employee, who initiates the dialogue in a language other than English.

The practical effects of Article XXVIII's *de facto* bar on communications by or with government employees are numerous and varied. For example, monolingual Spanish-speaking residents of Arizona cannot, consistent with the article, communicate effectively with employees of a state or local housing office about a landlord's wrongful retention of a rental deposit, nor can they learn from clerks of the state court about how and where to file small claims court complaints. They cannot obtain information regarding a variety of state and local social services, or adequately inform the service-givers that the governmental employees involved are not performing their duties properly or that the government itself is not operating effectively or honestly. Those with a limited command of English will face commensurate difficulties in obtaining or providing such information. Moreover, as we suggested earlier, the restrictions that Article XXVIII imposes severely limit the ability of state legislators to communicate with their constituents concerning official matters. For example, the provision would preclude a legislative committee from convening on a reservation and questioning a tribal leader in his native language concerning the problems of his community. A state senator of Navajo extraction would be precluded from inquiring directly of his Navajo-speaking constituents regarding problems they sought to bring to his attention. So would his staff. The legislative fact-finding function would, in short, be directly affected.

Because Article XXVIII bars or significantly restricts communications by and with government officials and employees, it significantly interferes with the ability of the non-English-speaking populace of Arizona " 'to receive information and ideas.' "

Article XXVIII obstructs the free flow of information and adversely affects the rights of many private persons by requiring the incomprehensible to replace the intelligible. Under its provisions, bilingual public employees will be aware that in many instances the only speech they may lawfully offer may be of no value. The article effectively requires that these employees remain mute before members of the non-English speaking public who seek their assistance. At such moments of awkward silence between government employees and those they serve, it will be strikingly clear to all concerned that vital speech that individuals desire both to provide and to hear has been stifled by the state.

[W]e note that Arizonans for Official English's assertion that government inefficiency and "chaos" will result from Article XXVIII's invalidation is not only directly contrary to the stipulated facts but is predicated upon a wholly erroneous assumption as to the nature of Yñiguez's claim. The group contends that appellees seek the right to speak another language at will and regardless of whether the intended recipient of the speech primarily speaks that language or is even able to comprehend it. However, such a "right" would be of a far different order than the right at issue here. As the facts show, Yñiguez spoke Spanish with Spanish-speaking claimants and English with English-speaking claimants. She does not claim any right to "choose" to speak Spanish with claimants who would not understand her, nor would this or any other court uphold such a right. Accordingly, in the interests of clarity, we emphasize that by ruling that the state cannot unreasonably limit the use of non-English languages, we do not imply that the state is therefore forced to allow inappropriate or burdensome language uses. In short, we do not suggest that a public employee has a "right" to speak in another language when to do so would hinder job performance. We merely consider here the lawfulness of speech in languages other than English that *furthers* the state's traditional interest in efficiency and effectiveness.

Arizonans for Official English claims, as it and others did when the initiative was on the ballot, that Article XXVIII promotes significant state interests. The organization enumerates these interests as:

protecting democracy by encouraging "unity and political stability"; encouraging a common language; and protecting public confidence.

There is no basis in the record to support the proponents' assertion that any of the broad societal interests on which they rely are served by the provisions of Article XXVIII.

We also reject the justifications for even more basic reasons. Our conclusions are influenced primarily by two Supreme Court cases from the 1920s in which nearly identical justifications were asserted in support of laws restricting language rights. *Meyer* involved a Nebraska statute that prohibited the teaching of non-English languages to children under the eighth grade level; *Tokushige,* similarly, involved a Hawaii statute that singled out "foreign language schools," such as those in which Japanese was taught, for stringent government control.

In defending the statute at issue in *Meyer,* the state of Nebraska explained that "[t]he object of the legislation . . . [is] to create an enlightened American citizenship in sympathy with the principles and ideals of this country." More recently, the Court explicitly characterized the language restriction in *Meyer* as designed "to promote civic cohesiveness by encouraging the learning of English." Despite these worthy goals, the Court ruled that the repressive means adopted to further them were "arbitrary" and invalid.

Similarly, the provision at issue in *Tokushige* had the specific purpose of regulating language instruction "in order that the Americanism of the students may be promoted." As in *Meyer,* the *Tokushige* Court recognized the validity of the interests asserted in defense of the statute. Nonetheless, citing *Meyer*'s invalidation of the Nebraska law, it found that the statute's promotion of these interests was insufficient to justify infringing on the constitutionally protected right to educate one's children to become proficient in one's mother tongue.

Like the Court in *Meyer* and *Tokushige,* we recognize the importance of (1) promoting democracy and national unity and (2) encouraging a common language as a means of encouraging such unity. The two primary justifications relied on by the article's proponents are indeed closely linked. We cannot agree, however, that Article XXVIII is in any way a fair, effective, or appropriate means of promoting those interests, or that even under a more deferential analysis its severely flawed effort to advance those goals outweighs its substantial adverse effect on first amendment rights. As we have learned time and again in our history, the state cannot achieve unity by prescribing orthodoxy. Notwithstanding this lesson, the provision at issue here "promotes" English only by means of proscribing other languages and is, thus, wholly coercive. Moreover, the goals of protecting democracy and encouraging unity and stability are at most indirectly related to the repressive means selected to achieve them. Next, the measure inhibits rather than advances the state's interest in the efficient and effective performance of its duties. Finally, the direct effect of the provision is not only to restrict the rights of all state and local government servants in Arizona, but also to severely impair the free speech interests of a portion of the populace they serve.

We should add that we are entirely unmoved by the third justification—that allowing government employees to speak languages other than English when serving the public would undermine public confidence and lead to "disillusionment and concern." To begin with, it is clear that the non-English speaking public of Arizona would feel even greater disillusionment and concern if their communications with public employees and, effectively, their access to many government services, were to be barred by Article XXVIII. Moreover, numerous cases support the notion that the interest in avoiding public hostility does not justify infringements upon constitutional rights. In short, the "concern" that some members of the Arizona public may feel over the use of non-English languages provides no basis for prohibiting their use no matter the degree of scrutiny we apply.

As President Franklin D. Roosevelt once remarked, "all of our people all over the country, all except the pure-blooded Indians, are immigrants or descendants of immigrants, including those who came over on the Mayflower." N.Y. Times, Nov. 5, 1944, at 38. Many and perhaps most immigrants arrived in the United States speaking a language other than English. Nonetheless, this country has historically prided itself on welcoming immigrants with a spirit of tolerance and freedom—and it is this spirit, embodied in the Constitution, which, when it flags on occasion, courts must be vigilant to protect.

In closing, we note that tolerance of difference—whether difference in language, religion, or culture more generally—does not ultimately exact a cost. To the contrary, the diverse and multicultural character of our society is widely recognized as being among our greatest strengths. Recognizing this, we have not, except for rare repressive statutes such as those struck down in *Meyer, Bartels, Yu Cong Eng,* and *Farrington,* tried to compel immigrants to give up their native language; instead, we have encouraged them to learn English. The Arizona restriction on language provides no encouragement, however, only compulsion: as such, it is unconstitutional.

NOTES AND QUESTIONS

1.   *Rights of Employees or the Public?* Throughout the opinion, the Court highlights the negative consequences of Arizona's official English law for the non-English-speaking public. Why, then, was its holding based on the First Amendment rights of Arizona's public employees?

2.   *State's Interests.* Does the Court give short shrift to the State's interests? If a public worker is bilingual, why is it coercive to require her to interact with the public in English? If, as the court recognizes, there is no affirmative right to have government services provided in a language other than English, what's wrong with Arizona's language restriction?

3.   *The Limits of the First Amendment Analysis.* Consider this hypothetical Judge Kozinski poses in dissent (*see* 69 F.3d at 961): A City adopts a bilingual policy in order to provide non-English-speaking residents better access to government services. A bilingual employee nonetheless refuses to speak any language other than English. Would it be a violation of his First Amendment rights to require him to speak Spanish, his other language?

4.   *Assimilation or Pluralism?* Does any state, or the United States for that matter, have a legitimate interest in encouraging immigrants to learn and speak English in order to facilitate their integration into American society? A 1997 Report to Congress of the U.S. Commission on Immigration Reform notes Congress' interest in the "cultivation of a shared commitment to the American values of liberty, democracy and equal opportunity." U.S. Comm'n on Immigration Reform, Becoming an American: Immigration and Immigrant Policy 26 (1997). Does that interest include encouraging immigrants to learn common practices and values central to American heritage, culture, and identity? To that end, should Congress and the courts tolerate English-only policies that are not intended to discriminate on the basis of race or national origin, in order to encourage "Americanization"? In your view, should the goal of American society be the cultural assimilation of racial, ethnic, and immigrant groups, or should it be cultural pluralism fostered by affirmative government policies designed to encourage, or at least enable, the preservation of cultural differences? Does the answer to this question bear on the outcome of the court's First Amendment analysis in *Yñiguez?*

5.   *Subsequent Developments.* Another law recently enacted in Arizona seemingly puts the weight of the state behind the assimilationist vision. HB 2281, passed by the Arizona legislature in 2010, bans courses that promote the overthrow of the U.S. government, foster racial resentment, are designed for students of a particular ethnic group, or that advocate ethnic solidarity. The law was aimed at an experimental Tucson curriculum, offered to students in some local elementary, middle, and high schools, that emphasized critical thinking and focused on Mexican-American literature and perspectives. While supporters lauded the program, pointing to increased graduation rates, high student achievement, and a state-commissioned independent audit that recommended expanding the classes, conservative opponents accused the teachers of encouraging students to adopt left-wing ideas and resent white people. When the constitutionality of the law was challenged before the Ninth Circuit, Judge Wallace Tashima largely upheld the law. Cindy Carcamo, "Judge Upholds Arizona Law Banning Ethnic Studies Classes," L.A. Times (Mar. 12, 2013). Do you think there are potential costs to ethnic studies programs? What are the potential consequences, good or bad, of HB 2281?

D. CUSTOM, SOCIAL SANCTION, AND HATE SPEECH

Regulating hate speech by law need not be the only way to limit racist speech. We can and do address such speech through social sanction. In twenty-first century America, it is often socially and economically costly to engage in racist speech. Consider some prominent examples.

- Donald Sterling was the longtime owner of the NBA franchise the Los Angeles Clippers until someone released audiotapes purportedly recording Sterling making racist remarks to his girlfriend. Following the release of the tapes, many leading figures in the NBA, including Hall of Famer Earvin "Magic" Johnson, LeBron James, Michael Jordan, and many others called for the NBA Commissioner to swiftly punish Sterling. The Clippers' players, who were in the middle of the NBA playoffs, protested Sterling by throwing their warm-up jackets, wearing black socks and black wristbands on their left arms, and purportedly planning a boycott of the next playoff game. Many celebrities and fans vowed to boycott the Clippers so long as Sterling remained the owner. The team's head coach, Glenn "Doc" Rivers, who is African American, intimated that he would not coach the team beyond the current season if Sterling continued to own it. A number of the team's commercial sponsors began to withdraw their support. A few days later, NBA Commissioner Adam Silver announced that Donald Sterling was suspended indefinitely, would be forced to sell the team, and would be banned for life by the NBA. By almost all accounts, the Commissioner was moved to take such drastic action because of the social backlash against Sterling's racist comments. First Amendment doctrine did not have to be altered. Individuals and institutions simply reacted strongly and negatively, and they vowed to shun the Clippers and by extension the NBA.

- Recall the Don Imus episode mentioned earlier. Imus was once a very prominent radio host on CBS. During one of his shows, Imus made derogatory comments about some members of the Rutgers Women's Basketball team. Many interpreted the comments as racist and sexist and called for CBS to fire Imus. Commercial sponsors also began to withdraw their ads from Imus' show. A week later, CBS fired Imus, notwithstanding the fact that Imus' show reportedly made a lot of money for CBS.

- Food celebrity maven Paula Deen was fired, and her show was canceled on the Food Network, after reports surfaced that she had used racial epithets on multiple occasions and that she often told racist jokes. Paula Deen attempted to avoid the public backlash by posting numerous apologies. But one week after the reports surfaced, the Food Network fired her.

What do these examples and others like them tell us about the power of social sanction to limit or even eliminate racist and hate speech?

Online communication and the rise of social media provide contexts with which to think about how hate speech might be regulated without legal sanction. While the ubiquity of the Internet in daily life and public debate has brought with it many benefits, from increased access to information and learning opportunities, to diverse social connections across the globe, online forums have also provided an easily accessible, often anonymous, public space for the proliferation of racist speech. While most American online content providers cooperate extensively with law enforcement to address hate crimes and other criminal activity, multi-jurisdictional issues tied to the global nature of such content complicate the status of racist speech online. Many sites attempt to address the issue through heavy monitoring of content, according to terms and policies. As described below, these policies vary greatly in their treatment and acknowledgment of racist speech as an unfortunate feature of online communication.

Twitter, for example, may be one of the least intrusive platforms in terms of monitoring speech. It does not moderate or filter content, styling itself as a neutral platform. The site has a set of rules and policies intended to promote good behavior, which proscribe a relatively narrow range of speech including violence and threats, unlawful use, and targeted abuse. Racist speech is not mentioned in Twitter's policies, but may fall into one of these general categories. The company does not proactively monitor content, but reviews reports of violations and acts on a case-by-case basis. Twitter is a social media platform that African Americans in particular have used to disseminate ideas, ruminate on the issues of the day, and bring issues that matter to that community into the national consciousness, giving rise to the phenomenon of "Black Twitter." http://www.thedailybeast.com/articles/2015/07/06/the-power-of -black-twitter.html.

Facebook provides much more detailed guidance in its community standards, which include a section addressing hate speech. If reported, Facebook will remove content that directly attacks people based on their race, ethnicity, national origin, religious affiliation, sexual orientation, sex, gender, or gender identity, or serious disabilities or diseases. Facebook's policies clarify that the presence of content containing hate speech is not per se grounds for removal; content clearly intended to raise awareness or educate others about hate speech is permitted. Facebook also allows humor, satire, or social commentary related to these topics. Facebook also enables users to control what they see when visiting the site, providing a tool for users to remove users and content they find offensive from their own accounts.

Reddit, which in many ways mirrors the unstructured landscape of listservs during the Internet's early years, has comparatively few restrictions on content. Reddit self-consciously views itself as a place that promotes as much speech as possible. The site's policies proscribe illegal content, including involuntary pornography, encouragement or incitements to violence, threats and harassment, the impersonation of others, and spam. While the policies make no mention of racist speech, they indicate that further moderation may occur within individual "communities" or "subreddits" on the site. Reddit has had a significant problem dealing with hate speech. One commentator described Reddit as "a cesspool of hate in dire need of repair." Reddit developed a new policy of banning racist and hate-filled subreddits, such as "rcoontown." The new policy has been met with mixed success as racist users and groups have simply dispersed to other communities. Cf. http://www.wired.com/2015/08/reddit-mods-handle-hate-speech/. For another example of hate speech policies on social media, *see* YouTube's policy: https://support.google.com/youtube/answer/2801939.

Internet Service Providers also can play an important role in limiting racist speech on the Internet by requiring content providers to sign terms of service that enable ISPs to remove offensive content. For example, America Online removed a neo-Nazi website, the Nationalist Online, for violating the prohibition in its terms of service agreement of racially or ethnically offensive content. Is there reason to be skeptical of ISPs playing this role? Is the best response to racist speech publicity, especially online and in social media? What are the advantages and disadvantages of relying on the rules and customs of social media and the Internet to address the problem of racist speech?

III. WHY FREE SPEECH: THE DOCTRINE AND ITS JUSTIFICATIONS

What is the doctrinal context within which the discussion about hate speech takes place? In *Brandenburg v. Ohio*, 395 U.S. 444 (1969), the defendant invited a television reporter to a rally at which one speaker announced that, "the nigger should be returned to Africa," while another stated that " . . . [the] nigger will have to fight for every inch he gets from now on." The question was whether the racist speech was criminally actionable, and the Supreme Court held that it was not. In *Collin v. Smith*, 578 F.2d 1197 (7th Cir. 1978), neo-Nazis challenged a set of local ordinances, including an ordinance that prevented the dissemination of materials that would incite hatred on the basis of race and an ordinance forbidding members of political parties from assembling while wearing military-style uniforms. The neo-Nazis wanted to march in Skokie, Illinois, a village with a significant concentration of Jews and Holocaust survivors. The Seventh Circuit affirmed the lower court's decision, which found the ordinances unconstitutional. The Supreme Court, which had previously denied the petitioner's motion to stay the judgment of the Seventh Circuit, summarily denied the petitioner's writ of certiorari. *Brandenburg* and *Collin* are quintessential examples of the courts' resistance to making exceptions to the protections of the First Amendment for hate speech. As one scholar has observed: "That even in 1978 the United States Supreme Court deemed the march of the Nazis in Skokie so plainly protected as not even to warrant a full opinion speaks volumes about the First Amendment's unwillingness to treat Nazis differently from Socialists, to treat Klansmen differently from Republicans, or to treat intimidation on grounds of race, religion, or ethnicity differently from any other form of intimidation." Frederick Schauer, *The Exceptional First Amendment*, in Michael Ignatieff, ed., American Exceptionalism and Human Rights (2005).

What is the justification for protecting racist speech directed toward a recognized and oppressed minority group? Commentators over the centuries have offered a wide variety of justifications, including that speech provides a check on government and nurtures a culture of tolerance. But three justifications stand as central to the American speech tradition. Perhaps the most prominent valorizes the marketplace of ideas and the search-for-truth therein. In his 1859 *On Liberty*, John Stuart Mill presented a highly influential defense of this idea, arguing that the suppression of ideas is undesirable because the "opinion which it is attempted to suppress [may] be true. Those who desire to suppress it [are] not infallible. They have no authority to decide the question for all mankind, and exclude every other person from the means of judging." Six decades after Mill wrote, Justice Holmes endorsed the search-for-truth rationale for robust speech protection while dissenting in *Abrams v. United States*: "[T]he best test for truth is the power of the thought to get itself accepted in the competition of the market." 250 U.S. 616, 630 (1919) (Holmes, J., dissenting). Justice Brandeis endorsed a similar and influential rationale for broad speech protections in his concurrence in *Whitney v. California* (1927): "If there be time to expose through discussion the falsehoods and fallacies, to avert the evil by the process of education, the remedy to be applied is *more speech*, not enforced silence." 274 U.S. 357, 377 (Brandeis, J., concurring) (emphasis added).

A second prominent justification for free speech is that it is necessary for self-governance, a rationale generally credited to Alexander Meiklejohn and considered by some scholars to be the justification given the highest currency by the Supreme Court. This rationale proceeds from the proposition that that freedom of speech is "a deduction from the basic American agreement that public issues shall be decided by universal suffrage." As such, Meiklejohn argues in *Free Speech and Its Relation to Self-Government* (1948), "equality of status in the field of ideas lies deep in the very foundation of the self-governing process. When men govern themselves, it is they—and no one else—who must pass judgment upon unwisdom and unfairness and danger." ALEXANDER MEIKLEJOHN, FREE SPEECH AND ITS RELATION TO SELF-GOVERNMENT (1948). In the libel case *New York Times Co. v. Sullivan*, Justice Black endorsed Meiklejohn's approach: "freedom to discuss public affairs and public officials is unquestionably . . . the kind of speech the First Amendment was primarily designed to keep within the area of free discussion." 376 U.S. 254, 296–97 (1964) (Black J., concurring).

The third major justification found in commentary and doctrine is that freedom of speech promotes self-fulfillment and autonomy. If people cannot freely enjoy access to ideas, they cannot imagine the full range of possibility in their lives. Thus, because they are not making free choices, they are not truly autonomous. As David Richards has argued, "[The] value of free expression, in this view, rests on its deep relation to self-respect arising from autonomous self-determination without which the life of the spirit is meager and slavish." David A.J. Richards, *Free Speech and Obscenity Law: Toward a Moral Theory of the First Amendment*, 123 U. Pa. L. Rev. 45, 62 (November 1974).

Despite the broad framing of free speech doctrine, the First Amendment does not protect every kind of speech. A defendant accused of conspiracy to commit murder does not have a First Amendment defense. First Amendment jurisprudence has distinguished political speech as the "core" of its protections. Other kinds of speech, including fighting words, libel, obscenity, and fraudulent speech, are sometimes characterized as "outside" the scope of the First Amendment, though over time some of these exceptions have been defined narrowly.

Consider the "fighting words" doctrine, enunciated in *Chaplinsky v. New Hampshire,* and often thought to provide another exception to protected free speech. As the Court stated in *Chaplinsky*, "it is well understood that the right of free speech is not absolute at all times and under all circumstance." *Chaplinsky v. State of New Hampshire*, 315 U.S. 568, 571 (1942). Speech such as fighting words have not been protected, in part because they take on qualities beyond expression, allowing for their characterization as conduct, which the government can broadly regulate. In *Chaplinsky*, the Court defined fighting words as words "which by their very utterance inflict injury or tend to incite an immediate breach of the peace." 315 U.S. at 572. One could argue that many forms of verbal hate speech should be banned and punished under the fighting words doctrine if they are judged to be sufficiently likely to incite an immediate breach of the peace. Since *Chaplinsky*, however, the fighting words doctrine has been repeatedly narrowed and the Court has not upheld a single conviction under the doctrine.

As you read the cases below, consider which, if any, of the theoretical justifications of free speech discussed above support the Court's decisions.

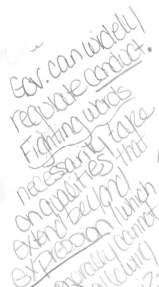

Gov. can widely regulate conduct. Fighting words necessarily take on qualities that extend beyond which expression which gov. generally cannot regulate allowing regulation of a character for which gov. can regulate

Brandenburg v. Ohio

Supreme Court of the United States, 1969.
395 U.S. 444.

■ PER CURIAM.

The appellant, a leader of a Ku Klux Klan group, was convicted under the Ohio Criminal Syndicalism statute for 'advocat(ing) . . . the duty, necessity, or propriety of crime, sabotage, violence, or unlawful methods of terrorism as a means of accomplishing industrial or political reform' and for 'voluntarily assembl(ing) with any society, group, or assemblage of persons formed to teach or advocate the doctrines of criminal syndicalism.' Ohio Rev. Code Ann. s 2923.13. He was fined $1,000 and sentenced to one to 10 years' imprisonment. The appellant challenged the consitutionality of the criminal syndicalism statute under the First and Fourteenth Amendments to the United States Constitution, but the intermediate appellate court of Ohio affirmed his conviction without opinion. The Supreme Court of Ohio dismissed his appeal, sua sponte, 'for the reason that no substantial constitutional question exists herein.' It did not file an opinion or explain its conclusions. Appeal was taken to this Court, and we noted probable jurisdiction. We reverse.

The record shows that a man, identified at trial as the appellant, telephoned an announcer-reporter on the staff of a Cincinnati television station and invited him to come to a Ku Klux Klan 'rally' to be held at a farm in Hamilton County. With the cooperation of the organizers, the reporter and a cameraman attended the meeting and filmed the events. Portions of the films were later broadcast on the local station and on a national network.

The prosecution's case rested on the films and on testimony identifying the appellant as the person who communicated with the reporter and who spoke at the rally. The State also introduced into evidence several articles appearing in the film, including a pistol, a rifle, a shotgun, ammunition, a Bible, and a red hood worn by the speaker in the films.

One film showed 12 hooded figures, some of whom carried firearms. They were gathered around a large wooden cross, which they burned. No one was present other than the participants and the newsmen who made the film. Most of the words uttered during the scene were incomprehensible when the film was projected, but scattered phrases could be understood that were derogatory of Negroes and, in one instance, of Jews.[3] Another scene on the same film showed the appellant, in Klan regalia, making a speech. The speech, in full, was as follows:

---

[3]   The significant portions that could be understood were:

'How far is the nigger going to-yeah.'

'This is what we are going to do to the niggers.'

'A dirty nigger.'

'This is an organizers' meeting. We have had quite a few members here today which are—we have hundreds, hundreds of members throughout the State of Ohio. I can quote from a newspaper clipping from the Columbus, Ohio Dispatch, five weeks ago Sunday morning. The Klan has more members in the State of Ohio than does any other organization. We're not a revengent organization, but if our President, our Congress, our Supreme Court, continues to suppress the white, Caucasian race, it's possible that there might have to be some revengeance taken.

'We are marching on Congress July the Fourth, four hundred thousand strong. From there we are dividing into two groups, one group to march on St. Augustine, Florida, the other group to march into Mississippi. Thank you.'

The second film showed six hooded figures one of whom, later identified as the appellant, repeated a speech very similar to that recorded on the first film. The reference to the possibility of 'revengeance' was omitted, and one sentence was added: 'Personally, I believe the nigger should be returned to Africa, the Jew returned to Israel.' Though some of the figures in the films carried weapons, the speaker did not.

The Ohio Criminal Syndicalism Statute was enacted in 1919. From 1917 to 1920, identical or quite similar laws were adopted by 20 States and two territories. E. Dowell, A History of Criminal Syndicalism Legislation in the United States 21 (1939). In 1927, this Court sustained the constitutionality of California's Criminal Syndicalism Act, the text of which is quite similar to that of the laws of Ohio. *Whitney v. California,* 274 U.S. 357 (1927). The Court upheld the statute on the ground that, without more, 'advocating' violent means to effect political and economic change involves such danger to the security of the State that the State may outlaw it. But Whitney has been thoroughly discredited by later decisions. *See Dennis v. United States,* 341 U.S. 494, at 507 (1951). These later decisions have fashioned the principle that the constitutional guarantees of free speech and free press do not permit a State to forbid or proscribe advocacy of the use of force or of law violation except where such advocacy is directed to inciting or producing imminent lawless action and is likely to incite or produce such action. As we said in *Noto v. United States,* 367 U.S. 290, 297–298 (1961), 'the mere abstract teaching

---

'Send the Jews back to Israel.'
'Let's give them back to the dark garden.'
'Save America.'
'Let's go back to constitutional betterment.'
'Bury the niggers.'
'We intend to do our part.'
'Give us our state rights.'
'Freedom for the whites.'
'Nigger will have to fight for every inch he gets from now on.'

. . . of the moral propriety or even moral necessity for a resort to force and violence, is not the same as preparing a group for violent action and steeling it to such action.' A statute which fails to draw this distinction impermissibly intrudes upon the freedoms guaranteed by the First and Fourteenth Amendments. It sweeps within its condemnation speech which our Constitution has immunized from governmental control.

Measured by this test, Ohio's Criminal Syndicalism Act cannot be sustained. The Act punishes persons who 'advocate or teach the duty, necessity, or propriety' of violence 'as a means of accomplishing industrial or political reform'; or who publish or circulate or display any book or paper containing such advocacy; or who 'justify' the commission of violent acts 'with intent to exemplify, spread or advocate the propriety of the doctrines of criminal syndicalism'; or who 'voluntarily assemble' with a group formed 'to teach or advocate the doctrines of criminal syndicalism.' Neither the indictment nor the trial judge's instructions to the jury in any way refined the statute's bald definition of the crime in terms of mere advocacy not distinguished from incitement to imminent lawless action.[4]

Accordingly, we are here confronted with a statute which, by its own words and as applied, purports to punish mere advocacy and to forbid, on pain of criminal punishment, assembly with others merely to advocate the described type of action. Such a statute falls within the condemnation of the First and Fourteenth Amendments.

NOTES AND QUESTIONS

1.   *Racist Speech or Violent Speech?* One lesson from *Brandenburg* is the doctrinal, if not practical or moral, importance of differentiating between racist speech and racist speech that advocates violence. The appellant's speech in *Brandenburg* was clearly racist, but didn't he also advocate violence? What are the facts that would support an argument that the speech also advocated or threatened violence? Was it the presence of guns? The burning of the cross? The words of the participants such as "bury the niggers?"

2.   *Doctrinal Framework.* Whether Brandenburg's speech advocated violence or not, the Court concluded that the state cannot prosecute an individual simply because he or she advocates violence. Racist and/or violent speech can be punished only when (a) it is express advocacy that is (b) directed toward producing lawless action and (c) is likely to produce such action. What are the justifications for the *Brandenburg* framework, especially if a speaker is explicitly advocating violence against an individual

---

[4]   The first count of the indictment charged that appellant 'did unlawfully by word of mouth advocate the necessity, or propriety of crime, violence, or unlawful methods of terrorism as a means of accomplishing political reform . . .' The second count charged that appellant 'did unlawfully voluntarily assemble with a group or assemblage of persons formed to advocate the doctrines of criminal syndicalism. . . .' The trial judge's charge merely followed the language of the indictment. No construction of the statute by the Ohio courts has brought it within constitutionally permissible limits. The Ohio Supreme Court has considered the statute in only one previous case, where the constitutionality of the statute was sustained.

or a group because of their race or ethnicity? The per curiam opinion states that Ohio's attempt to prosecute Brandenburg's speech "impermissibly intrudes upon the freedoms guaranteed by the First and Fourteenth Amendments." But the Court does not tell us what those guarantees are and how they are intruded upon. What arguments would you make in favor of the Court's position? Are theories of free expression, replicated above, helpful?

3. *Balancing Speech and Equality?* Can you think of a better way of balancing speech and equality than the approach adopted by the Court in Brandenburg? Why should we as a society tolerate any advocacy of violent racist speech whether expressly advocated or not? Moreover, if a person expressly advocates racist speech why should it matter whether that speech is likely to produce violent action? Put differently, if you think equality values ought to modify speech values, how would you modify the doctrinal framework to take equality values into account?

Collin v. Smith
Court of Appeals, Seventh Circuit, 1978.
578 F.2d 1197.

■ PELL, CIRCUIT JUDGE.

Plaintiff-appellee, the National Socialist Party of America (NSPA) is a political group described by its leader, plaintiff-appellee Frank Collin, as a Nazi party. Among NSPA's more controversial and generally unacceptable beliefs are that black persons are biologically inferior to white persons, and should be expatriated to Africa as soon as possible; that American Jews have "inordinate . . . political and financial power" in the world and are "in the forefront of the international Communist revolution." NSPA members affect a uniform reminiscent of those worn by members of the German Nazi Party during the Third Reich, and display a swastika thereon and on a red, white, and black flag they frequently carry.

The Village of Skokie, Illinois, a defendant-appellant, is a suburb north of Chicago. It has a large Jewish population,[5] including as many as several thousand survivors of the Nazi holocaust in Europe before and during World War II. Other defendants-appellants are Village officials.

When Collin and NSPA announced plans to march in front of the Village Hall in Skokie on May 1, 1977, Village officials responded by obtaining in state court a preliminary injunction against the demonstration. After state courts refused to stay the injunction pending appeal, the United States Supreme Court ordered a stay. The injunction was subsequently reversed first in part and then in its entirety. On May 2, 1977, the Village enacted three ordinances to prohibit demonstrations

---

[5] In 1974, 40,500 of the Village's 70,000 population were Jewish.

such as the one Collin and NSPA had threatened.[6] This lawsuit seeks declaratory and injunctive relief against enforcement of the ordinances.

Village Ordinance No. 77–5–N–994 (hereinafter designated, for convenience of reference, as 994) is a comprehensive permit system for all parades or public assemblies of more than 50 persons. It requires permit applicants to obtain $300,000 in public liability insurance and $50,000 in property damage insurance. One of the prerequisites for a permit is a finding by the appropriate official(s) that the assembly will not portray criminality, depravity or lack of virtue in, or incite violence, hatred, abuse or hostility toward a person or group of persons by reason of reference to religious, racial, ethnic, national or regional affiliation.

Another is a finding that the permit activity will not be conducted "for an unlawful purpose," None of this ordinance applies to activities of the Village itself or of a governmental agency and any provision of the ordinance may be waived by unanimous consent of the Board of Trustees of the Village. To parade or assemble without a permit is a crime, punishable by fines from $5 to $500.

Village Ordinance No. 77–5–N–995 (995) prohibits, "(t)he dissemination of any materials within the Village of Skokie which promotes and incites hatred against persons by reason of their race, national origin, or religion, and is intended to do so." "Dissemination of materials" includes publication or display or distribution of posters, signs, handbills, or writings and public display of markings and clothing of symbolic significance. Violation is a crime punishable by fine of up to $500, or imprisonment of up to six months. Village Ordinance No. 77–5–N–996 (996) prohibits public demonstrations by members of political parties while wearing "military-style" uniforms, s 28.42.1, and violation is punishable as in 995.

Collin and NSPA applied for a permit to march on July 4, 1977, which was denied on the ground the application disclosed an intention to violate 996. The Village apparently applies 994 so that an intention to violate 995 or 996 establishes an "unlawful purpose" for the march or assembly. The permit application stated that the march would last about a half hour, and would involve 30 to 50 demonstrators wearing uniforms including swastikas and carrying a party banner with a swastika and placards with statements thereon such as "White Free Speech," "Free Speech for the White Man," and "Free Speech for White America." A single file sidewalk march that would not disrupt traffic was proposed, without speeches or the distribution of handbills or literature. Counsel for the Village advises us that the Village does not maintain that Collin and NSPA will behave other than as described in the permit application(s).

---

[6] The district court herein found as a matter of legislative intent that the ordinances in question were designed to cover Nazi marches. The appellants do not attack the finding.

The district court, after considering memoranda, exhibits, depositions, and live testimony, issued a comprehensive and thorough opinion granting relief to Collin and NSPA. The insurance requirements of 994 were invalidated as insuperable obstacles to free speech in Skokie, and ss 27–56(c) & (i) (the latter when used to deny permits on the basis of anticipated violations of 995 or 996) were adjudged impermissible prior restraints. Ordinance 995 was determined to be fatally vague and overbroad, and 996 was invalidated as overbroad and patently unjustified.

On its appeal, the Village concedes the invalidity of the insurance requirements as applied to these plaintiffs and of the uniform prohibition of 996.

I.

The conflict underlying this litigation has commanded substantial public attention, and engendered considerable and understandable emotion. We would hopefully surprise no one by confessing personal views that NSPA's beliefs and goals are repugnant to the core values held generally by residents of this country, and, indeed, to much of what we cherish in civilization. As judges sworn to defend the Constitution, however, we cannot decide this or any case on that basis. Ideological tyranny, no matter how worthy its motivation, is forbidden as much to appointed judges as to elected legislators.

[O]ur task here is to decide whether the First Amendment protects the activity in which appellees wish to engage, not to render moral judgment on their views or tactics. No authorities need be cited to establish the proposition, which the Village does not dispute, that First Amendment rights are truly precious and fundamental to our national life. Nor is this truth without relevance to the saddening historical images this case inevitably arouses. It is, after all, in part the fact that our constitutional system protects minorities unpopular at a particular time or place from governmental harassment and intimidation, that distinguishes life in this country from life under the Third Reich.

Before undertaking specific analysis of the clash between the Village ordinances and appellees' desires to demonstrate in Skokie, it will be helpful to establish some general principles of pertinence to the decision required of us. Putting to one side for the moment the question of whether the content of appellees' views and symbols makes a constitutional difference here, we find we are unable to deny that the activities in which the appellees wish to engage are within the ambit of the First Amendment.

These activities involve the "cognate rights" of free speech and free assembly. *See Thomas v. Collins,* 323 U.S. 516, 530 (1945). "(T)he wearing of an armband for the purpose of expressing certain views is the type of symbolic act that is within the Free Speech Clause of the First Amendment." *Tinker v. Des Moines Independent Community School*

District, 393 U.S. 503, 505 (1969). Standing alone, at least, it is "closely akin to 'pure speech' which, we have repeatedly held, is entitled to comprehensive protection under the First Amendment."[7] The same thing can be said of NSPA's intended display of a party flag, *See Stromberg v. California,* 283 U.S. 359 (1931), and of the messages intended for the placards party members would carry. *See, e.g., Cohen v. California,* 403 U.S. 15, 18 (1971). Likewise, although marching, parading, and picketing, because they involve conduct implicating significant interests in maintaining public order, are less protected than pure speech, they are nonetheless subject to significant First Amendment protection. Indeed, an orderly and peaceful demonstration, with placards, in the vicinity of a seat of government, is "an exercise of (the) basic constitutional rights of (speech, assembly, and petition) in their most pristine and classic form." *Edwards v. South Carolina,* 372 U.S. 229, 235 (1963).

II.

We first consider ordinance 995, prohibiting the dissemination of materials which would promote hatred towards persons on the basis of their heritage. The Village would apparently apply this provision to NSPA's display of swastikas, their uniforms, and, perhaps, to the content of their placards.

The ordinance cannot be sustained on the basis of some of the more obvious exceptions to the rule against content control. While some would no doubt be willing to label appellees' views and symbols obscene, the constitutional rule that obscenity is unprotected applies only to material with erotic content. *Cohen, supra,* 403 U.S. at 20. Furthermore, although the Village introduced evidence in the district court tending to prove that some individuals, at least, might have difficulty restraining their reactions to the Nazi demonstration, the Village tells us that it does not rely on a fear of responsive violence to justify the ordinance, and does not even suggest that there will be any physical violence if the march is held. This confession takes this case out of the scope of Brandenburg, *supra.*

The concession also eliminates any argument based on the fighting words doctrine of *Chaplinsky v. New Hampshire,* 315 U.S. 568 (1942). The Court in Chaplinsky affirmed a conviction under a statute that, as authoritatively construed, applied only to words with a direct tendency to cause violence by the persons to whom, individually, the words were addressed. A conviction for less than words that at least tend to incite an immediate breach of the peace cannot be justified under Chaplinsky.

Four basic arguments are advanced by the Village to justify the content restrictions of 995. First, it is said that the content criminalized

---

[7]   Because the armbands are to be worn during a group demonstration, their display cannot stand entirely alone. On the other hand, it is worth noting that the display of tiepins, armbands, or a flag here, is not an example of pure conduct that is asserted to have expressive value, which may be somewhat more easily regulated. See *United States v. O'Brien,* 391 U.S. 367 (1968).

by 995 is "totally lacking in social content," and that it consists of "false statements of fact" in which there is "no constitutional value." *Gertz v. Robert Welch, Inc.,* 418 U.S. 323, 340 (1974). We disagree that, if applied to the proposed demonstration, the ordinance can be said to be limited to "statements of fact," false or otherwise. No handbills are to be distributed; no speeches are planned. To the degree that the symbols in question can be said to assert anything specific, it must be the Nazi ideology, which cannot be treated as a mere false "fact."

We may agree with the district court:

> Under the First Amendment there is no such thing as a false idea. However pernicious an opinion may seem, we depend for its correction not on the conscience of judges and juries but on the competition of other ideas. The asserted falseness of Nazi dogma, and, indeed, its general repudiation, simply do not justify its suppression.

Gertz. The asserted falseness of Nazi dogma, and, indeed, its general repudiation, simply do not justify its suppression.

The Village's second argument, and the one on which principal reliance is placed, centers on *Beauharnais v. Illinois,* 343 U.S. 250 (1952). There a conviction was upheld under a statute prohibiting, in language substantially (and perhaps not unintentionally) similar to that used in the ordinance here, the dissemination of materials promoting racial or religious hatred.

In our opinion Beauharnais does not support ordinance 995, for two independent reasons. First, the rationale of that decision turns quite plainly on the strong tendency of the prohibited utterances to cause violence and disorder.

[T]he Village, as we have indicated, does not assert appellees' possible violence, an audience's possible responsive violence, or possible violence against third parties by those incited by appellees, as justifications for 995. The rationale of Beauharnais, then, simply does not apply here.

Further, when considering the application of Beauharnais to the present litigation, we cannot be unmindful of the "package" aspects of the ordinances and that the "insulting" words are to be made public only after a 30-day permit application waiting period. Violence occurring under such a circumstance would have such indicia of premeditation as to seem inconsistent with calling into play any remaining vitality of the Beauharnais rationale.

The Village's third argument is that it has a policy of fair housing, which the dissemination of racially defamatory material could undercut. We reject this argument without extended discussion.

The Village's fourth argument is that the Nazi march, involving as it does the display of uniforms and swastikas, will create a substantive evil that it has a right to prohibit: the infliction of psychic trauma on resident holocaust survivors and other Jewish residents. The Village points out that Illinois recognizes the "new tort" of intentional infliction of severe emotional distress, the coverage of which may well include personally directed racial slurs. Assuming that specific individuals could proceed in tort under this theory to recover damages provably occasioned by the proposed march, and that a First Amendment defense would not bar the action, it is nonetheless quite a different matter to criminalize protected First Amendment conduct in anticipation of such results.

It would be grossly insensitive to deny, as we do not, that the proposed demonstration would seriously disturb, emotionally and mentally, at least some, and probably many of the Village's residents. The problem with engrafting an exception on the First Amendment for such situations is that they are indistinguishable in principle from speech that "invite(s) dispute. . . . induces a condition of unrest, creates dissatisfaction with conditions as they are, or even stirs people to anger." *Terminiello v. Chicago,* 337 U.S. 1, 4 (1949). Yet these are among the "high purposes" of the First Amendment. It is perfectly clear that a state many not "make criminal the peaceful expression of unpopular views." *Edwards v. South Carolina.* Likewise, "mere public intolerance or animosity cannot be the basis for abridgement of these constitutional freedoms." *Coates v. City of Cincinnati,* 402 U.S. 611, 615 (1971). Where, as here, a crime is made of a silent march, attended only by symbols and not by extrinsic conduct offensive in itself, we think the words of the Court in Street v. New York, are very much on point:

> (A)ny shock effect . . . must be attributed to the content of the ideas expressed. It is firmly settled that under our Constitution the public expression of ideas may not be prohibited merely because the ideas are themselves offensive to some of their hearers.

This case does not involve intrusion into people's homes. There need be no captive audience, as Village residents may, if they wish, simply avoid the Village Hall for thirty minutes on a Sunday afternoon, which no doubt would be their normal course of conduct on a day when the Village Hall was not open in the regular course of business. Absent such intrusion or captivity, there is no justifiable substantial privacy interest to save 995 from constitutional infirmity, when it attempts, by fiat, to declare the entire Village, at all times, a privacy zone that may be sanitized from the offensiveness of Nazi ideology and symbols.

We conclude that 995 may not be applied to criminalize the conduct of the proposed demonstration. Because it is susceptible to such an application, we also conclude that it suffers from substantial overbreadth, even if some of the purposes 995 is said to serve might constitutionally be protectible by an appropriate and narrower ordinance. *See* Cox v. Louisiana, *supra.* The latter conclusion is also supported by the fact that the ordinance could conceivably be applied to criminalize dissemination of The Merchant of Venice or a vigorous discussion of the merits of reverse racial discrimination in Skokie. Although there is reason to think, as the district court concluded, that the ordinance is fatally vague as well, because it turns in part on subjective reactions to prohibited conduct, we do not deem it necessary to rest our decision on that ground.

The preparation and issuance of this opinion has not been an easy task, or one which we have relished. Recognizing the implication that often seems to follow over-protestation, we nevertheless feel compelled once again to express our repugnance at the doctrines which the appellees desire to profess publicly. Indeed, it is a source of extreme regret that after several thousand years of attempting to strengthen the often thin coating of civilization with which humankind has attempted to hide brutal animal-like instincts, there would still be those who would resort to hatred and vilification of fellow human beings because of their racial background or their religious beliefs, or for that matter, because of any reason at all.

Retaining meaning in civil rights, particularly those many of the founding fathers believed sufficiently important as to delay the approval of the Constitution until they could be included in the Bill of Rights, seldom seems to be accomplished by the easy cases, however, and it was not so here.

Although we would have thought it unnecessary to say so, it apparently deserves emphasis in the light of the dissent's reference to this court apologizing as to the result, that our regret at the use appellees plan to make of their rights is not in any sense an apology for upholding the First Amendment. The result we have reached is dictated by the fundamental proposition that if these civil rights are to remain vital for all, they must protect not only those society deems acceptable, but also those whose ideas it quite justifiably rejects and despises.

The judgment of the district court is affirmed.

NOTES AND QUESTIONS

1. *Understanding the Harm.* What is the harm suffered by those objecting to the Nazis marching through Skokie? Should the law be used to ameliorate the harms experienced by survivors of the Holocaust exposed to anti-Semitic marchers wearing swastikas and Nazi paraphernalia? Do the Jewish residents of Skokie suffer greater harm than non-Jewish residents?

2. *The Relationship Between Speech-Suppression and Violence?* Search-for-truth proponents argue that suppressing racist speech will not eliminate hateful ideas, but instead will lead groups like the Ku Klux Klan to seek out more violent methods of broadcasting their ideas. What do you think about this argument? Would preventing the Nazis from marching in Skokie have led to greater violence?

3. *Matsuda's Approach.* Professor Matsuda argues that racist speech should be prosecuted when the speech: (a) communicates a message of racial inferiority; (b) is directed toward groups that have been historically oppressed; and (c) the speech is persecutory, hateful, and degrading. Matsuda, *supra* at 2357. How would you go about applying her argument in the *Skokie* case? Are you persuaded that free speech should yield to a state statute prohibiting hate speech where the speech is directed to a particular group, selected on the basis of that group's identity? Should we draw a distinction between *Brandenburg* (speech not directed at any group in particular) and *Collin* (speech directed at a particular group)? Notice the Court's answer in *Collin*: anyone likely to be offended can leave town for thirty minutes.

4. *Considering the Victim's Perspective.* As race relations have transformed in the United States, and as we have moved into the post-Civil Rights Era, scholars of race and law have questioned whether the libertarian approach to free speech doctrine continues to serve the goal of racial equality. Critical race theory scholars, in particular, have argued that a specific exception for racist hate speech should be carved out of the general protection of speech under the First Amendment. To support this position, scholars point to the fact that courts have privileged other values in certain contexts, such as reputation in libel law, while still advancing First Amendment values. Proponents of the regulation of racist hate speech argue that the interests of the victims of such speech, who suffer unique and grave harms, must be placed above society's general interest in freedom of speech in certain circumstances. They point to the fact that the international community, including the United Nations and numerous Western allies of the United States, have succeeded in taking measures to directly regulate racist hate speech. The United States is thus alone in refusing to recognize that the harms caused by racist hate speech justify a partial retreat from an absolute allegiance to First Amendment values. Mari Matsuda, *Public Response to Racist Speech: Considering the Victim's Story, in* MARI MATSUDA, CHARLES R. LAWRENCE III, RICHARD DELGADO, AND KIMBERLE WILLIAMS CRENSHAW, WORDS THAT WOUND: CRITICAL RACE THEORY, ASSAULTIVE SPEECH, AND THE FIRST AMENDMENT 26 (1993). Do you think the interests of the targets of racist hate speech should be incorporated into free speech doctrine? What are the advantages/ disadvantages of such approach?

IV. HATE CRIMES

The enactment of hate crimes laws is generally less complicated and raises fewer constitutional issues than regulating hate speech, since speech is normally a protected action, but assault is not. But this distinction is arguably misleading. Some critics argue that, since the action underlying a hate crime (such as assault) is already being punished, any increase in punishment condemns the perpetrator for her thoughts or speech, and it is a fundamental tenet of criminal law that one cannot be punished for one's thoughts. That said, state of mind can affect the reach of criminal law (e.g., the distinction between murder and manslaughter). As a result, hate crime legislation is oftentimes justified on the ground that the government is punishing the offender's motivation.

Given our nation's history of racial conflict, crimes motivated by racial prejudice have existed since the founding of the Republic. The term "hate crime," however, did not enter the American lexicon until the 1980's. While some scholars attribute this to an apparent increase in the number and severity of bias-motivated crimes during that decade, others have argued that the increased attention to such crimes resulted instead from a growth of societal concern for racial prejudice during that period. JAMES B. JACOBS & KIMBERLY POTTER, HATE CRIMES: CRIMINAL LAW & IDENTITY POLITICS 3 (1998). Although reported instances of hate crimes seem to have increased in the 1980's, selective and uneven reporting, as well as differences in the definitions of hate crimes in various locales, make it difficult to analyze and understand trends in hate crimes in any specific period. The government's efforts to mitigate this problem through the Hate Crime Statistic Act, passed in 1990, proved to be only partly successful. Participation by law enforcement agencies was voluntary, and many agencies abstained from reporting hate crimes. FREDERICK M. LAWRENCE, PUNISHING HATE: BIAS CRIMES UNDER AMERICAN LAW 20 (1999).

Despite these inconsistencies in reporting, numerous occurrences of hate crimes have captured the nation's attention in recent years. One startling incident took place in 1995, when a white man, after attacking and stabbing an Asian man in the parking lot of a grocery store, stated to police that he "woke up . . . [and] figured, what the f——, I'm gonna go kill me a Chinaman." In another incident, a black man on a crowded train killed six people and injured nineteen others, all of them either white or Asian-American. These incidents are labeled hate crimes in part because the victims would have been unharmed were it not for their race or ethnicity. FREDERICK M. LAWRENCE, PUNISHING HATE: BIAS CRIMES UNDER AMERICAN LAW 10 (1999).

Although hate crimes of the type described above, involving individual victimizers targeting and attacking victims because of their race or other identifying characteristic, are said to be the most common type of hate crime and are perhaps most closely associated with the term hate crime in the minds of the public, there are other, similar crimes that also fall into the category. Assassinations of well-known minorities are considered hate crimes but can be distinguished because the victim is not chosen at random. The assassination of civil rights leader Medgar Evers at the hands of a member of the Ku Klux Klan, as well as the killing of Jewish radio host Alan Berg by members of the neo-Nazi group "the Silent Brotherhood," are examples. JACOBS & POTTER, supra, at 22 (1998). These crimes are further distinguishable from the most common type of hate crime by the fact that they are carried out by members of hate groups acting in line with the ideology of the group, rather than unaffiliated individuals, who may also be influenced by those ideologies. Hate crimes can also take the form of vandalism, particularly through the use of graffiti to convey hateful messages. Reported incidents of such vandalism include the scribbling of swastikas on Jewish tombs and campus buildings and the painting of "KKK" on African-American homes.

The Court has addressed the issue of hate crimes in three cases. In *R.A.V. v. City of St. Paul*, and in *Virginia v. Black*, decided a decade apart, the Court asked whether the government may criminalize cross burnings motivated by bias. In *Wisconsin v. Mitchell*, which the Court decided between *R.A.V.* and *Black*, the Court asked whether the government may punish bias-motivated acts more severely than the same act where bias is not present. As you read these cases, presented chronologically, consider whether regulating bias is a sensible enterprise and whether the First Amendment is the proper vehicle for reining in the government when it has gone too far.

R.A.V. v. City of St. Paul

Supreme Court of the United States, 1992.
505 U.S. 377.

■ JUSTICE SCALIA delivered the opinion of the Court.

In the predawn hours of June 21, 1990, petitioner and several other teenagers allegedly assembled a crudely made cross by taping together broken chair legs. They then allegedly burned the cross inside the fenced yard of a black family that lived across the street from the house where petitioner was staying. Although this conduct could have been punished under any of a number of laws, one of the two provisions under which respondent city of St. Paul chose to charge petitioner (then a juvenile) was the St. Paul Bias-Motivated Crime Ordinance, which provides:

> "Whoever places on public or private property a symbol, object, appellation, characterization or graffiti, including, but not limited to, a burning cross or Nazi swastika, which one knows or has reasonable grounds to know arouses anger, alarm or resentment in others on the basis of race, color, creed, religion or gender commits disorderly conduct and shall be guilty of a misdemeanor."

Petitioner moved to dismiss this count on the ground that the St. Paul ordinance was substantially overbroad and impermissibly content based and therefore facially invalid under the First Amendment. The trial court granted this motion, but the Minnesota Supreme Court reversed. That court rejected petitioner's overbreadth claim because, as construed in prior Minnesota cases, the modifying phrase "arouses anger, alarm or resentment in others" limited the reach of the ordinance to conduct that amounts to "fighting words," i.e., "conduct that itself inflicts injury or tends to incite immediate violence . . . ," (citing *Chaplinsky v.*

New Hampshire, 315 U.S. 568 (1942)), and therefore the ordinance reached only expression "that the first amendment does not protect." The court also concluded that the ordinance was not impermissibly content based because, in its view, "the ordinance is a narrowly tailored means toward accomplishing the compelling governmental interest in protecting the community against bias-motivated threats to public safety and order."

[As an authoritative interpretation of state law, the Minnesota Supreme Court's interpretation of the statute is binding on the U.S. Supreme Court. –Eds.]

The First Amendment generally prevents government from proscribing speech, or even expressive conduct, because of disapproval of the ideas expressed. Content-based regulations are presumptively invalid. From 1791 to the present, however, our society, like other free but civilized societies, has permitted restrictions upon the content of speech in a few limited areas, which are "of such slight social value as a step to truth that any benefit that may be derived from them is clearly outweighed by the social interest in order and morality." *Chaplinsky*. We have recognized that "the freedom of speech" referred to by the First Amendment does not include a freedom to disregard these traditional limitations. [These exceptions include defamation, obscenity, and fighting words. –Eds.]

We have sometimes said that these categories of expression are "not within the area of constitutionally protected speech," or that the "protection of the First Amendment does not extend" to them. Such statements must be taken in context, however, and are no more literally true than is the occasionally repeated shorthand characterizing obscenity "as not being speech at all." What they mean is that these areas of speech can, consistently with the First Amendment, be regulated because of their constitutionally proscribable content (obscenity, defamation, etc.)— not that they are categories of speech entirely invisible to the Constitution, so that they may be made the vehicles for content discrimination unrelated to their distinctively proscribable content. Thus, the government may proscribe libel; but it may not make the further content discrimination of proscribing only libel critical of the government.

In other words, the exclusion of "fighting words" from the scope of the First Amendment simply means that, for purposes of that Amendment, the unprotected features of the words are, despite their verbal character, essentially a "nonspeech" element of communication. Fighting words are thus analogous to a noisy sound truck: Each is, as Justice Frankfurter recognized, a "mode of speech," both can be used to convey an idea; but neither has, in and of itself, a claim upon the First Amendment. As with the sound truck, however, so also with fighting words: The government may not regulate use based on hostility—or favoritism—towards the underlying message expressed.

Even the prohibition against content discrimination that we assert the First Amendment requires is not absolute. It applies differently in the context of proscribable speech than in the area of fully protected speech.

When the basis for the content discrimination consists entirely of the very reason the entire class of speech at issue is proscribable, no significant danger of idea or viewpoint discrimination exists. Such a reason, having been adjudged neutral enough to support exclusion of the entire class of speech from First Amendment protection, is also neutral enough to form the basis of distinction within the class. To illustrate: A State might choose to prohibit only that obscenity which is the most patently offensive in its prurience—i.e., that which involves the most lascivious displays of sexual activity. But it may not prohibit, for example, only that obscenity which includes offensive political messages.

Another valid basis for according differential treatment to even a content-defined subclass of proscribable speech is that the subclass happens to be associated with particular "secondary effects" of the speech, so that the regulation is "justified without reference to the content of the . . . speech," *Renton v. Playtime Theatres, Inc.*, 475 U.S. 41 (1986). A State could, for example, permit all obscene live performances except those involving minors. [. . .] Thus, for example, sexually derogatory "fighting words," among other words, may produce a violation of Title VII's general prohibition against sexual discrimination in employment practices. Where the government does not target conduct on the basis of its expressive content, acts are not shielded from regulation merely because they express a discriminatory idea or philosophy.

These bases for distinction refute the proposition that the selectivity of the restriction is "even arguably 'conditioned upon the sovereign's agreement with what a speaker may intend to say.' " There may be other such bases as well. Indeed, to validate such selectivity (where totally proscribable speech is at issue) it may not even be necessary to identify any particular "neutral" basis, so long as the nature of the content discrimination is such that there is no realistic possibility that official suppression of ideas is afoot. (We cannot think of any First Amendment interest that would stand in the way of a State's prohibiting only those obscene motion pictures with blue-eyed actresses.) Save for that limitation, the regulation of "fighting words," like the regulation of noisy speech, may address some offensive instances and leave other, equally offensive, instances alone.

Applying these principles to the St. Paul ordinance, we conclude that, even as narrowly construed by the Minnesota Supreme Court, the ordinance is facially unconstitutional. Although the phrase in the ordinance, "arouses anger, alarm or resentment in others," has been limited by the Minnesota Supreme Court's construction to reach only those symbols or displays that amount to "fighting words," the remaining, unmodified terms make clear that the ordinance applies only to "fighting words" that insult, or provoke violence, "on the basis of race, color, creed, religion or gender." Displays containing abusive invective, no matter how vicious or severe, are permissible unless they are addressed to one of the specified disfavored topics. Those who wish to use "fighting words" in connection with other ideas—to express hostility, for example, on the basis of political affiliation, union membership, or homosexuality—are not covered. The First Amendment does not permit St. Paul to impose special prohibitions on those speakers who express views on disfavored subjects.

In its practical operation, moreover, the ordinance goes even beyond mere content discrimination, to actual viewpoint discrimination. Displays containing some words—odious racial epithets, for example— would be prohibited to proponents of all views. But "fighting words" that do not themselves invoke race, color, creed, religion, or gender-aspersions upon a person's mother, for example—would seemingly be usable ad libitum in the placards of those arguing in favor of racial, color, etc., tolerance and equality, but could not be used by those speakers' opponents. One could hold up a sign saying, for example, that all "anti-Catholic bigots" are misbegotten; but not that all "papists" are, for that would insult and provoke violence "on the basis of religion." St. Paul has no such authority to license one side of a debate to fight freestyle, while requiring the other to follow Marquis of Queensberry rules.

Let there be no mistake about our belief that burning a cross in someone's front yard is reprehensible. But St. Paul has sufficient means at its disposal to prevent such behavior without adding the First Amendment to the fire.

The judgment of the Minnesota Supreme Court is reversed, and the case is remanded for proceedings not inconsistent with this opinion.

■ JUSTICE WHITE, with whom JUSTICE BLACKMUN and JUSTICE O'CONNOR join, and with whom JUSTICE STEVENS joins [in part], concurring in the judgment.

It is inconsistent to hold that the government may proscribe an entire category of speech because the content of that speech is evil, but that the government may not treat a subset of that category differently without violating the First Amendment; the content of the subset is by definition worthless and undeserving of constitutional protection.

The majority's observation that fighting words are "quite expressive indeed," is no answer. Fighting words are not a means of exchanging views, rallying supporters, or registering a protest; they are directed against individuals to provoke violence or to inflict injury. Therefore, a ban on all fighting words or on a subset of the fighting words category would restrict only the social evil of hate speech, without creating the danger of driving viewpoints from the marketplace.

[Justice White disagreed with the Court's reasoning but agreed that the ordinance was invalid because it was "overbroad." –Eds.]

In construing the St. Paul ordinance, the Minnesota Supreme Court drew upon the definition of fighting words that appears in *Chaplinsky*— words "which by their very utterance inflict injury or tend to incite an immediate breach of the peace." However, the Minnesota court was far from clear in identifying the "injur[ies]" inflicted by the expression that St. Paul sought to regulate. Indeed, the Minnesota court emphasized (tracking the language of the ordinance) that "the ordinance censors only those displays that one knows or should know will create anger, alarm or resentment based on racial, ethnic, gender or religious bias." I therefore understand the court to have ruled that St. Paul may constitutionally prohibit expression that "by its very utterance" causes "anger, alarm or resentment."

Our fighting words cases have made clear, however, that such generalized reactions are not sufficient to strip expression of its constitutional protection. The mere fact that expressive activity causes hurt feelings, offense, or resentment does not render the expression unprotected.

In the First Amendment context, "[c]riminal statutes must be scrutinized with particular care; those that make unlawful a substantial amount of constitutionally protected conduct may be held facially invalid even if they also have legitimate application." The St. Paul antibias ordinance is such a law. Although the ordinance reaches conduct that is unprotected, it also makes criminal expressive conduct that causes only hurt feelings, offense, or resentment, and is protected by the First Amendment. The ordinance is therefore fatally overbroad and invalid on its face.

■ [JUSTICE BLACKMUN's opinion concurring in the judgment is omitted.]

■ JUSTICE STEVENS, with whom JUSTICE WHITE and JUSTICE BLACKMUN join as to Part I, concurring in the judgment.

Conduct that creates special risks or causes special harms may be prohibited by special rules. Lighting a fire near an ammunition dump or a gasoline storage tank is especially dangerous; such behavior may be punished more severely than burning trash in a vacant lot. Threatening someone because of her race or religious beliefs may cause particularly severe trauma or touch off a riot, and threatening a high public official may cause substantial social disruption; such threats may be punished more severely than threats against someone based on, say, his support of a particular athletic team. There are legitimate, reasonable, and neutral justifications for such special rules.

This case involves the constitutionality of one such ordinance. Because the regulated conduct has some communicative content—a message of racial, religious, or gender hostility—the ordinance raises two quite different First Amendment questions. Is the ordinance "overbroad" because it prohibits too much speech? If not, is it "underbroad" because it does not prohibit enough speech?

In answering these questions, my colleagues today wrestle with two broad principles: first, that certain "categories of expression [including 'fighting words'] are 'not within the area of constitutionally protected speech,'" and second, that "[c]ontent-based regulations [of expression] are presumptively invalid." Although in past opinions the Court has repeated both of these maxims, it has—quite rightly—adhered to neither with the absolutism suggested by my colleagues. Thus, while I agree that the St. Paul ordinance is unconstitutionally overbroad . . . , I write separately to suggest how the allure of absolute principles has skewed the analysis of both the majority and Justice WHITE's opinions.

Just as Congress may determine that threats against the President entail more severe consequences than other threats, so St. Paul's City Council may determine that threats based on the target's race, religion, or gender cause more severe harm to both the target and to society than other threats. This latter judgment—that harms caused by racial, religious, and gender-based invective are qualitatively different from that caused by other fighting words—seems to me eminently reasonable and realistic.

In sum, the central premise of the Court's ruling—that "[c]ontent-based regulations are presumptively invalid"—has simplistic appeal, but lacks support in our First Amendment jurisprudence.

NOTES AND QUESTIONS

1. **R.A.V.'s *Immediate Impact*.** The Court's decision in *R.A.V.* received mixed reactions from different sectors of society. While *The Nation*, a popular liberal publication, worried that the case had "fostered the impression that hate crimes now enjoy the protection of the Constitution" and characterized Scalia's majority opinion as "frightening," its more centrist counterpart, *The New Republic*, observed that the Court had "repelled the most serious threat to open debate that the current generation of students has experienced" and characterized Scalia's opinion as "genius." TERRY EASTLAND, FREEDOM OF EXPRESSION IN THE SUPREME COURT: THE DEFINING CASES 331 (2000). Despite mixed reactions by the media and the public, the case sent a very clear message: statutes that directly criminalized racist speech were not constitutional. As a result, states such as Virginia and Michigan acted preemptively and struck down their own cross-burning laws. The decision had a similar effect on anti-racist speech efforts of various universities throughout the country. In *Doe v. University of Michigan*, a district court struck down's Michigan's anti-bias policy. Similarly, a University of Wisconsin regulation stating that students would be guilty of a violation if

they "intentionally made demeaning remarks to an individual based on that person's ethnicity" was invalidated. Akhil Reed Amar, The Supreme Court: 1991 Term—Comment: *The Case of the Missing Amendments*: R.A.V. v. City of St. Paul, 106 Harv. L. Rev. 124 (1992). Even Stanford University's hate speech statute, which had been carefully drafted to include only fighting words, was struck. DANIEL FARBER, THE FIRST AMENDMENT 113 (2003). Further evidence of the monumental effect of *R.A.V.* on hate speech regulation is the fact that, after the decision was issued, the FBI found it necessary to contact more than 16,000 local law enforcement agencies to inform them that the case did not change their data-collection duties under the Hate Crimes Statistics Act of 1990. FREDERICK M. LAWRENCE, PUNISHING HATE: BIAS CRIMES UNDER AMERICAN LAW 22 (1999).

2. ***Skeptical Reception.*** Among legal observers, the Court's opinion was received with a fair amount of skepticism. One scholar criticized the fact that, in a case so fraught with racial tension, the Court should have at least mentioned the Fourteenth Amendment to inform the interpretation of the First Amendment. *See e.g.*, Cedric Merlin Powell, *The Mythological Marketplace of Ideas:* R.A.V., Mitchell, *and Beyond*, 12 HARV. BLACKLETTER L.J. 1 (1995); Akhil Reed Amar, *The Case of the Missing Amendments*: R.A.V. v. City of St. Paul, 106 HARV. L. REV. 124 (1992). Another scholar found Justice Scalia's approach in the case to be "thoroughly flawed," and felt that the Justice "misconceive[d] the requirements of the content-neutrality doctrine." FREDERICK M. LAWRENCE, PUNISHING HATE: BIAS CRIMES UNDER AMERICAN LAW 87 (1999).

3. ***Cross Burnings as Fighting Words.*** In his opinion, Justice Scalia acknowledges that the Court had previously recognized the state's ability to regulate speech in certain categories because of the speech's content, such as fighting words, obscenity, or defamation. What makes the ordinance in *R.A.V.* different? Why can't the statute fit into the exception for fighting words, especially given that the Minnesota Supreme Court limited the St. Paul ordinance to reach only fighting words?

4. ***R.A.V.'s Analytical Coherence.*** In response to Justice Scalia's opinion, Justice White argues that if the government can limit a category of speech, it necessarily follows that it can limit a subset of that category. Justice Stevens laments that Justice Scalia's framework is inconsistent with the Court's past First Amendment jurisprudence. Who has the better of the argument here? What do you think of Justice Stevens's point that fighting words targeting individuals or groups on the basis of their race, gender, or religion are more harmful than threats on the basis of other categories, such as political identity?

5. ***Understanding the Case.*** Consider the following justification of the majority's approach: Cross burning communicates multiple messages. A burning cross may be expressive of religious identity, it may be expressive of white supremacy, it may be an artistic representation, or it may communicate a threat of racial violence. The state can proscribe that last message, but not the others. A critical component of First Amendment doctrine is distrust of the state. We do not trust the state when it tells us

that it is regulating pursuant to a legitimate objective. Justice Scalia's framework is premised on the view that St. Paul is regulating cross burning not because of the threat that it communicates, which would be permissible, but because of the message of white supremacy that it communicates, which is impermissible. His framework is an attempt to smoke out that illegitimate motive. Do you find this justification persuasive?

6.   *Advising Exercise.* You are City Counsel to the City of St. Paul, Minnesota. You have been asked to rewrite the St. Paul ordinance to make it consistent with the Court's opinion in R.A.V. What would you include in the revised ordinance? Do you include any protections against racial hate speech? Do you proscribe cross burning motivated by the desire to intimidate on the basis of race? Do you proscribe cross burning generally?

———————

In the wake of *R.A.V.*, the Supreme Court of Wisconsin struck down a hate-crimes sentencing enhancement as unconstitutional, holding that the statute could have an impermissible chilling effect on speech insofar as it sought to punish motivation alone:

> [I]f A strikes B in the face he commits criminal battery. However, should A add a word such as *nigger, honkey, jew, mick, kraut, spic,* or *queer*, the crime becomes a felony, and A will be punished not for his conduct alone—a misdemeanor—but for using the spoken word. . . . [T]he necessity to use speech to prove this intentional selection threatens to chill free speech."

State v. Mitchell, 485 N.W.2d 807, 816 (Wis. 1992), *rev'd*, 508 U.S. 476 (1993).

The state of Wisconsin, which had carefully drafted its hate crime statute to avoid its invalidation, appealed the decision to the Supreme Court of the United States.

Wisconsin v. Mitchell

Supreme Court of the United States, 1993.
508 U.S. 476.

■ CHIEF JUSTICE REHNQUIST delivered the opinion of the Court.

Respondent Todd Mitchell's sentence for aggravated battery was enhanced because he intentionally selected his victim on account of the victim's race. The question presented in this case is whether this penalty enhancement is prohibited by the First and Fourteenth Amendments. We hold that it is not.

On the evening of October 7, 1989, a group of young black men and boys, including Mitchell, gathered at an apartment complex in Kenosha, Wisconsin. Several members of the group discussed a scene from the motion picture "Mississippi Burning," in which a white man beat a young black boy who was praying. The group moved outside and Mitchell asked

them: " 'Do you all feel hyped up to move on some white people?' " Shortly
thereafter, a young white boy approached the group on the opposite side
of the street where they were standing. As the boy walked by, Mitchell
said: " 'You all want to fuck somebody up? There goes a white boy; go get
him.' " Mitchell counted to three and pointed in the boy's direction. The
group ran toward the boy, beat him severely, and stole his tennis shoes.
The boy was rendered unconscious and remained in a coma for four days.

[The Wisconsin Supreme Court's opinion overturned the lower
court's holding that the defendant's sentence should be increased in
accordance with a Wisconsin statute that enhances the maximum
penalty for an offense whenever the defendant "[i]ntentionally selects the
person against whom the crime . . . is committed . . . because of the race,
religion, color, disability, sexual orientation, national origin or ancestry
of that person. . . .", increasing Mitchell's sentence from two to seven
years. Relying on *R.A.V. v. St. Paul*, the Wisconsin Supreme Court held
the Wisconsin statute violated the First Amendment because it punished
not the conduct of selection, but the *motive* or *reason* behind the
selection.]

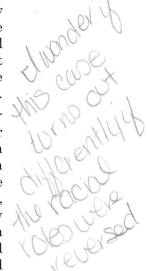

We granted certiorari because of the importance of the question
presented and the existence of a conflict of authority among state high
courts on the constitutionality of statutes similar to Wisconsin's penalty
enhancement provision. We reverse.

Mitchell argues that we are bound by the Wisconsin Supreme
Court's conclusion that the statute punishes bigoted thought and not
conduct. There is no doubt that we are bound by a state court's
construction of a state statute. . . . But here the Wisconsin Supreme
Court did not, strictly speaking, construe the Wisconsin statute in the
sense of defining the meaning of a particular statutory word or phrase.
Rather, it merely characterized the "practical effect" of the statute for
First Amendment purposes. . . . This assessment does not bind us. Once
any ambiguities as to the meaning of the statute are resolved, we may
form our own judgment as to its operative effect.

The State argues that the statute does not punish bigoted thought,
as the Supreme Court of Wisconsin said, but instead punishes only
conduct. While this argument is literally correct, it does not dispose of
Mitchell's First Amendment challenge. To be sure, our cases reject the
"view that an apparently limitless variety of conduct can be labeled
'speech' whenever the person engaging in the conduct intends thereby to
express an idea." Thus, a physical assault is not by any stretch of the
imagination expressive conduct protected by the First Amendment.

But the fact remains that under the Wisconsin statute the same
criminal conduct may be more heavily punished if the victim is selected
because of his race or other protected status than if no such motive
obtained. Thus, although the statute punishes criminal conduct, it
enhances the maximum penalty for conduct motivated by a

discriminatory point of view more severely than the same conduct engaged in for some other reason or for no reason at all. Because the only reason for the enhancement is the defendant's discriminatory motive for selecting his victim, Mitchell argues (and the Wisconsin Supreme Court held) that the statute violates the First Amendment by punishing offenders' bigoted beliefs.

Traditionally, sentencing judges have considered a wide variety of factors in addition to evidence bearing on guilt in determining what sentence to impose on a convicted defendant. The defendant's motive for committing the offense is one important factor. Thus, in many States the commission of a murder, or other capital offense, for pecuniary gain is a separate aggravating circumstance under the capital sentencing statute.

But it is equally true that a defendant's abstract beliefs, however obnoxious to most people, may not be taken into consideration by a sentencing judge. *Dawson v. Delaware*, 503 U.S. 159 (1992). In *Dawson*, the State introduced evidence at a capital sentencing hearing that the defendant was a member of a white supremacist prison gang. Because "the evidence proved nothing more than [the defendant's] abstract beliefs," we held that its admission violated the defendant's First Amendment rights. In so holding, however, we emphasized that "the Constitution does not erect a per se barrier to the admission of evidence concerning one's beliefs and associations at sentencing simply because those beliefs and associations are protected by the First Amendment." Thus, in *Barclay v. Florida*, 463 U.S. 939 (1983), we allowed the sentencing judge to take into account the defendant's racial animus towards his victim. The evidence in that case showed that the defendant's membership in the Black Liberation Army and desire to provoke a "race war" were related to the murder of a white man for which he was convicted. Because "the elements of racial hatred in [the] murder" were relevant to several aggravating factors, we held that the trial judge permissibly took this evidence into account in sentencing the defendant to death.

Mitchell suggests that *Dawson* and *Barclay* are inapposite because they did not involve application of a penalty enhancement provision. But in *Barclay* we held that it was permissible for the sentencing court to consider the defendant's racial animus in determining whether he should be sentenced to death, surely the most severe "enhancement" of all. And the fact that the Wisconsin Legislature has decided, as a general matter, that bias motivated offenses warrant greater maximum penalties across the board does not alter the result here. For the primary responsibility for fixing criminal penalties lies with the legislature.

Mitchell argues that the Wisconsin penalty enhancement statute is invalid because it punishes the defendant's discriminatory motive, or reason, for acting. But motive plays the same role under the Wisconsin statute as it does under federal and state antidiscrimination laws, which we have previously upheld against constitutional challenge. Title VII of the Civil Rights Act of 1964, for example, makes it unlawful for an employer to discriminate against an employee "because of such individual's race, color, religion, sex, or national origin."

Nothing in our decision last Term in *R.A.V.* compels a different result here. That case involved a First Amendment challenge to a municipal ordinance prohibiting the use of " 'fighting words' that insult, or provoke violence, 'on the basis of race, color, creed, religion or gender.' " Because the ordinance only proscribed a class of "fighting words" deemed particularly offensive by the city, i.e., those "that contain . . . messages of 'bias-motivated' hatred," we held that it violated the rule against content-based discrimination. But whereas the ordinance struck down in *R.A.V.* was explicitly directed at expression (i.e., "speech" or "messages"), the statute in this case is aimed at conduct unprotected by the First Amendment.

Moreover, the Wisconsin statute singles out for enhancement bias inspired conduct because this conduct is thought to inflict greater individual and societal harm. For example, according to the State and its amici, bias-motivated crimes are more likely to provoke retaliatory crimes, inflict distinct emotional harms on their victims, and incite community unrest. The State's desire to redress these perceived harms provides an adequate explanation for its penalty-enhancement provision over and above mere disagreement with offenders' beliefs or biases. As Blackstone said long ago, "it is but reasonable that among crimes of different natures those should be most severely punished, which are the most destructive of the public safety and happiness."

Finally, there remains to be considered Mitchell's argument that the Wisconsin statute is unconstitutionally overbroad because of its "chilling effect" on free speech. Mitchell argues (and the Wisconsin Supreme Court agreed) that the statute is "overbroad" because evidence of the defendant's prior speech or associations may be used to prove that the defendant intentionally selected his victim on account of the victim's protected status. Consequently, the argument goes, the statute impermissibly chills free expression with respect to such matters by those concerned about the possibility of enhanced sentences if they should in the future commit a criminal offense covered by the statute. We find no merit in this contention.

The sort of chill envisioned here is far more attenuated and unlikely than that contemplated in traditional "overbreadth" cases. We must conjure up a vision of a Wisconsin citizen suppressing his unpopular bigoted opinions for fear that if he later commits an offense covered by the statute, these opinions will be offered at trial to establish that he selected his victim on account of the victim's protected status, thus qualifying him for penalty enhancement. To stay within the realm of rationality, we must surely put to one side minor misdemeanor offenses covered by the statute, such as negligent operation of a motor vehicle; for it is difficult, if not impossible, to conceive of a situation where such offenses would be racially motivated. We are left, then, with the prospect of a citizen suppressing his bigoted beliefs for fear that evidence of such beliefs will be introduced against him at trial if he commits a more serious offense against person or property. This is simply too speculative a hypothesis to support Mitchell's overbreadth claim.

The First Amendment, moreover, does not prohibit the evidentiary use of speech to establish the elements of a crime or to prove motive or intent. Evidence of a defendant's previous declarations or statements is commonly admitted in criminal trials subject to evidentiary rules dealing with relevancy, reliability, and the like. Nearly half a century ago, in *Haupt v. United States*, 330 U.S. 631 (1947), we rejected a contention similar to that advanced by Mitchell here. Haupt was tried for the offense of treason, which, as defined by the Constitution (Art. III, s 3), may depend very much on proof of motive. To prove that the acts in question were committed out of "adherence to the enemy" rather than "parental solicitude," the Government introduced evidence of conversations that had taken place long prior to the indictment, some of which consisted of statements showing Haupt's sympathy with Germany and Hitler and hostility towards the United States. We rejected Haupt's argument that this evidence was improperly admitted. While "[s]uch testimony is to be scrutinized with care to be certain the statements are not expressions of mere lawful and permissible difference of opinion with our own government or quite proper appreciation of the land of birth," we held that "these statements . . . clearly were admissible on the question of intent and adherence to the enemy."

For the foregoing reasons, we hold that Mitchell's First Amendment rights were not violated by the application of the Wisconsin penalty enhancement provision in sentencing him. The judgment of the Supreme Court of Wisconsin is therefore reversed, and the case is remanded for further proceedings not inconsistent with this opinion.

NOTES AND QUESTIONS

1. **Mitchell *and* R.A.V.** Does the Court persuasively distinguish the Wisconsin statute from the ordinance it invalidated in *R.A.V.*? The Court argued that the ordinance in *R.A.V.* was aimed at expression, whereas the Wisconsin statute was aimed at conduct. *Mitchell* and *R.A.V.* arguably can be distinguished on the ground that the behavior in the two cases was not equivalent. An assault is criminal behavior, whereas cross burning is not necessarily so. Should that distinction have made a differences as a matter of First Amendment law?

2. ***Because of Race.*** What does it mean to select a victim "because of race"? This question of selectivity is particularly vexing when race potentially correlates with other characteristics. Suppose that the perpetrators in *Wisconsin v. Mitchell* selected their victims based on the

likelihood that they would fight back. Thus, if two black kids decided to rob a white kid because he would be less likely to fight back, is that a hate crime? Similarly, what if the perpetrators robbed only white people because they believed that whites were more likely to carry cash?

3.   *Two Models.* Due to the many instances of hate crimes that have taken place in the United States, legislators across the nation have enacted statutes to battle the problem. Aside from the Hate Crime Statistics Act of 1990, which was passed in the hope of shedding more light on the extent of the problem, numerous laws have been passed that have enhanced the penalties for hate crimes. Generally speaking, most of these laws can be separated into two distinct, yet sometimes overlapping categories, which have been termed the "discriminatory selection model" and the "racial animus model."

Laws that fit into the discriminatory selection model focus on whether the perpetrator chose his victim in any part because of the victim's race, without regard to whether the victim was chosen because of racial prejudice or because of some less hostile reason, such as the belief that a certain race is an easier or more profitable target. On the other hand, the racial animus model focuses on the role played by racial prejudice or hostility in the victimizer's motivation for committing the crime. To demonstrate the difference between these two models, consider the hypothetical case of a criminal who chooses only white victims because he believes that, on average, they are more likely to carry large amounts of money and expensive electronic gadgets. Under the discriminatory selection model, this criminal would be guilty of a hate crime because he selected his victims based on race, even if there was no animus towards that race. However, the lack of animus would take the crime out of the scope of racial animus model hate crime laws. JACOBS & POTTER, *supra*, at 22 (1998).

Several states that have enacted hate crimes legislation follow the racial animus model. New Jersey, for example, punishes criminal conduct motivated, at least in part, by "ill will, hatred, or bias due to race, color, religion, sexual orientation, or ethnicity." Various other states, including Connecticut, Florida, Maryland, New Hampshire, and Pennsylvania, have hate crime laws that require some level of animus towards the victim. Also, the Hate Crime Statistics Act of 1990 defines a hate crime as a criminal act motivated at least in part by a "pre-formed negative opinion or attitude toward a group of persons based on their race, religion, ethnicity/national origin, or sexual orientation." JACOBS & POTTER, *supra* at 22.

The majority of states, however, have passed hate crime laws that fit under the discriminatory selection model. California's law, for example, makes it a crime to commit certain conduct "because of the [victim's] race, color, religion, ancestry, national origin, or sexual orientation." While numerous other states have statutes nearly identical to the California statute, some states also introduce an element of malicious intent to the equation. The Washington statute, for example, provides that a person is guilty of a hate crime if he "maliciously and with the intent to intimidate or harass another person because of, or in a way that is reasonably related to, associated with, or directed toward, that person's race, color, religion, ancestry, national origin, or mental, physical, or sensory handicap." Although one could make a case that such statutes are a hybrid of the racial animus and discriminatory selection models, some perceive them to fit wholly under the latter model. The Washington Supreme Court interpreted the statute mentioned above, for example, as a purely discriminatory selection model statute, because "the statute is triggered by victim selection regardless of the actor's motives or beliefs." JACOBS & POTTER, *supra*, at 22.

Among the "because of" laws that fit under the discriminatory selection model, Wisconsin's hate crime statute is unique. Under the statute, conduct is considered to be a hate crime if the victimizer "intentionally selects the [victim] because of the race, religion, color, disability, sexual orientation, national origin or ancestry of that person." The statue is unique as it includes the language "intentionally selects," which is not found in other hate crime laws that are largely identical to the Wisconsin statute. Thus, it may be safe to assume that the drafters of the Wisconsin statute acted deliberately in including this language in their hate crime law.

4.   *Harm or Intent?* What are some of the possible ramifications of looking at the harms instead of the intent? Does the state take this approach in any other areas of criminal law? Professor Frederick Lawrence argues against the approach taken by the *Mitchell* Court. He says that, although in the civil context it is appropriate to look at harm, criminal law cannot embrace this model because the perpetrator could be completely devoid of racial motivation but convicted by the (mis)perceptions of the minority community. Lawrence argues that, despite the difficulty of proving intent, it must remain the standard by which these crimes are judged. Lawrence, PUNISHING HATE 64–65. Do you agree?

5.   *Black Defendants and White Victims.* The fact that the Court affirmed the constitutionality of bias-crime legislation in a case involving the prosecution of a black teenager for a crime committed against a white kid is telling. In fact, the statistics indicate that blacks in particular are overrepresented among persons charged with hate crimes, at 21 percent of prosecutions, though they comprise only 14 percent of the general U.S. population. *See* http://www.fbi.gov/news/pressrel/press-releases/fbi-releases–2011–hate-crime-statistics.

Therefore, although hate speech and hate crimes laws are normally advocated for in the name of substantive equality, there is at least some indication that whites more often than non-whites claim the benefit of hate crime legislation. This of course exacerbates the already unequal treatment of minorities in the criminal justice system. Does hate crime legislation promote racial equality? Consider the following account:

> The number of black offender/white victim crimes has made some strong proponents of hate crime laws uncomfortable. Some argue that black offenders who attack white victims are motivated by economics not prejudice. A few have proposed removing crimes based upon anti-white prejudice from the definition of hate crime. After the shootings (black perpetrator, white victims) and arson at

Freddy's clothing store in Harlem in 1995, which resulted in the death of eight people, a number of politicians argued that the crime should not be seen as a racial incident, but rather as a business dispute over a lease between the owner of Freddy's, who was Jewish and the owner of the adjacent store, who was black. The crime was committed by a black man, who previously had participated in demonstrations outside Freddy's that involved racial insults against customers, and threats against the owner and employees.

Jill Tregor, executive director of San Francisco's Intergroup Clearinghouse, which provides legal services and counseling to hate crime victims, claims that white crime victims are using hate crime laws to enhance penalties against minorities, who already experience prejudice within the criminal justice system. One law review author proposes that in cases of interracial assault by a white offender, prejudice should be presumed, and the burden placed on the defendant to prove the absence of a prejudiced motivation. No such presumption would apply in interracial attacks by black perpetrators.

JACOBS & POTTER, *supra*, at 17. Does the fact that people of color are disproportionately charged with perpetrating a hate crime and whites are disproportionately viewed as victims of hate crimes give you pause about hate crime legislation?

Virginia v. Black

Supreme Court of the United States, 2003.
538 U.S. 343.

■ JUSTICE O'CONNOR announced the judgment of the Court and delivered the opinion of the Court with respect to Parts I, II, and III, and an opinion with respect to Parts IV and V, in which THE CHIEF JUSTICE, JUSTICE STEVENS, and JUSTICE BREYER join.

In this case we consider whether the Commonwealth of Virginia's statute banning cross burning with "an intent to intimidate a person or group of persons" violates the First Amendment. Va.Code Ann. § 18.2–423 (1996). We conclude that while a State, consistent with the First Amendment, may ban cross burning carried out with the intent to intimidate, the provision in the Virginia statute treating any cross burning as prima facie evidence of intent to intimidate renders the statute unconstitutional in its current form.

I

Respondents Barry Black, Richard Elliott, and Jonathan O'Mara were convicted separately of violating Virginia's cross-burning statute, [which] provides:

"It shall be unlawful for any person or persons, with the intent of intimidating any person or group of persons, to burn, or cause to be burned, a cross on the property of another, a highway or other public place. Any person who shall violate any provision of this section shall be guilty of a Class 6 felony.

"Any such burning of a cross shall be prima facie evidence of an intent to intimidate a person or group of persons."

On August 22, 1998, Barry Black led a Ku Klux Klan rally in Carroll County, Virginia. Twenty-five to thirty people attended this gathering, which occurred on private property with the permission of the owner, who was in attendance. The property was located on an open field just off Brushy Fork Road (State Highway 690) in Cana, Virginia.

When the sheriff of Carroll County learned that a Klan rally was occurring in his county, he went to observe it from the side of the road. During the approximately one hour that the sheriff was present, about 40 to 50 cars passed the site, a "few" of which stopped to ask the sheriff what was happening on the property. Eight to ten houses were located in the vicinity of the rally. Rebecca Sechrist, who was related to the owner of the property where the rally took place, "sat and watched to see wha[t][was] going on" from the lawn of her in-laws' house. She looked on as the Klan prepared for the gathering and subsequently conducted the rally itself.

During the rally, Sechrist heard Klan members speak about "what they were" and "what they believed in." The speakers "talked real bad about the blacks and the Mexicans." One speaker told the assembled gathering that "he would love to take a .30/.30 and just random[ly] shoot the blacks." The speakers also talked about "President Clinton and Hillary Clinton," and about how their tax money "goes to . . . the black people." Sechrist testified that this language made her "very . . . scared."

At the conclusion of the rally, the crowd circled around a 25- to 30-foot cross. The cross was between 300 and 350 yards away from the road. According to the sheriff, the cross "then all of a sudden . . . went up in a flame." As the cross burned, the Klan played Amazing Grace over the loudspeakers. Sechrist stated that the cross burning made her feel "awful" and "terrible."

On May 2, 1998, respondents Richard Elliott and Jonathan O'Mara, as well as a third individual, attempted to burn a cross on the yard of James Jubilee. Jubilee, an African-American, was Elliott's next-door neighbor in Virginia Beach, Virginia. Four months prior to the incident, Jubilee and his family had moved from California to Virginia Beach. Before the cross burning, Jubilee spoke to Elliott's mother to inquire about shots being fired from behind the Elliott home. Elliott's mother explained to Jubilee that her son shot firearms as a hobby, and that he used the backyard as a firing range.

On the night of May 2, respondents drove a truck onto Jubilee's property, planted a cross, and set it on fire. Their apparent motive was to "get back" at Jubilee for complaining about the shooting in the backyard. Respondents were not affiliated with the Klan. The next morning, as Jubilee was pulling his car out of the driveway, he noticed the partially burned cross approximately 20 feet from his house. After seeing the cross, Jubilee was "very nervous" because he "didn't know what would be the next phase," and because "a cross burned in your yard . . . tells you that it's just the first round."

[Part II of the opinion is devoted to a review of the history of cross burning. It concludes: "In sum, while a burning cross does not inevitably convey a message of intimidation, often the cross burner intends that the recipients of the message fear for their lives. And when a cross burning is used to intimidate, few if any messages are more powerful."]

III

A

"True threats" encompass those statements where the speaker means to communicate a serious expression of an intent to commit an act of unlawful violence to a particular individual or group of individuals. The speaker need not actually intend to carry out the threat. Rather, a prohibition on true threats "protect[s] individuals from the fear of violence" and "from the disruption that fear engenders," in addition to protecting people "from the possibility that the threatened violence will occur." Intimidation in the constitutionally proscribable sense of the word is a type of true threat, where a speaker directs a threat to a person or group of persons with the intent of placing the victim in fear of bodily harm or death. Respondents do not contest that some cross burnings fit within this meaning of intimidating speech, and rightly so. As noted in Part II, *supra*, the history of cross burning in this country shows that cross burning is often intimidating, intended to create a pervasive fear in victims that they are a target of violence.

B

The Supreme Court of Virginia ruled that in light of *R.A.V. v. City of St. Paul*, even if it is constitutional to ban cross burning in a content-neutral manner, the Virginia cross-burning statute is unconstitutional because it discriminates on the basis of content and viewpoint. It is true, as the Supreme Court of Virginia held, that the burning of a cross is symbolic expression. The reason why the Klan burns a cross at its rallies, or individuals place a burning cross on someone else's lawn, is that the burning cross represents the message that the speaker wishes to communicate. Individuals burn crosses as opposed to other means of communication because cross burning carries a message in an effective and dramatic manner.[8]

The fact that cross burning is symbolic expression, however, does not resolve the constitutional question. The Supreme Court of Virginia relied upon *R.A.V. v. City of St. Paul* to conclude that once a statute discriminates on the basis of this type of content, the law is unconstitutional. We disagree.

We did not hold in *R.A.V.* that the First Amendment prohibits all forms of content-based discrimination within a proscribable area of speech. Rather, we specifically stated [in *R.A.V.*] that some types of content discrimination did not violate the First Amendment:

> "When the basis for the content discrimination consists entirely of the very reason the entire class of speech at issue is proscribable, no significant danger of idea or viewpoint discrimination exists. Such a reason, having been adjudged neutral enough to support exclusion of the entire class of speech from First Amendment protection, is also neutral enough to form the basis of distinction within the class."

> Indeed, we noted that it would be constitutional to ban only a particular type of threat: "[T]he Federal Government can criminalize only those threats of violence that are directed against the President . . . since the reasons why threats of violence are outside the First Amendment . . . have special force when applied to the person of the President." And a State may "choose to prohibit only that obscenity which is the most patently offensive *in its prurience*—i.e., that which involves the most lascivious displays of sexual activity." Consequently, while the holding of *R.A.V.* does not permit a State to ban only obscenity based on "offensive *political* messages," or "only those threats against the President that mention his policy on aid to inner cities," the First Amendment permits content discrimination "based on the very reasons why the particular class of speech at issue . . . is proscribable."

Similarly, Virginia's statute does not run afoul of the First Amendment insofar as it bans cross burning with intent to intimidate. Unlike the statute at issue in *R.A.V.*, the Virginia statute does not single out for opprobrium only that speech directed toward "one of the specified disfavored topics." It does not matter whether an individual burns a cross with intent to intimidate because of the victim's race, gender, or religion, or because of the victim's "political affiliation, union membership, or homosexuality." Moreover, as a factual matter it is not true that cross

---

[8] Justice THOMAS argues in dissent that cross burning is "conduct, not expression." While it is of course true that burning a cross is conduct, it is equally true that the First Amendment protects symbolic conduct as well as pure speech. As Justice THOMAS has previously recognized, a burning cross is a "symbol of hate," and "a symbol of white supremacy."

burners direct their intimidating conduct solely to racial or religious minorities. Indeed, in the case of Elliott and O'Mara, it is at least unclear whether the respondents burned a cross due to racial animus. *See* [dissenting opinion by Justice Hassell in the Supreme Court of Virginia] (noting that "these defendants burned a cross because they were angry that their neighbor had complained about the presence of a firearm shooting range in the Elliott's yard, not because of any racial animus").

The First Amendment permits Virginia to outlaw cross burnings done with the intent to intimidate because burning a cross is a particularly virulent form of intimidation. Instead of prohibiting all intimidating messages, Virginia may choose to regulate this subset of intimidating messages in light of cross burning's long and pernicious history as a signal of impending violence. Thus, just as a State may regulate only that obscenity which is the most obscene due to its prurient content, so too may a State choose to prohibit only those forms of intimidation that are most likely to inspire fear of bodily harm. A ban on cross burning carried out with the intent to intimidate is fully consistent with our holding in *R.A.V.* and is proscribable under the First Amendment.

[In Parts IV and V of her plurality opinion, Justice O'Connor concluded that the state's prima facie evidence provision was facially unconstitutional because of its indiscriminate coverage. Since the instruction was given in Black's case, the plurality voted to reverse his conviction, but it remanded the convictions of Elliott and O'Mara to determine whether the prima facie evidence provision was severable or whether it was subject to a narrowing construction. In a partial concurrence, Justice Scalia (joined by Justice Thomas) argued that the provision had such a modest potential impact on prosecutions that it should not be subject to a facial attack.]

■ JUSTICE SCALIA, with whom JUSTICE THOMAS joins as to Parts I and II, concurring in part, concurring in the judgment in part, and dissenting in part.

I agree with the Court that, under our decision in *R.A.V.*, a State may, without infringing the First Amendment, prohibit cross burning carried out with the intent to intimidate. Accordingly, I join Parts I–III of the Court's opinion. I also agree that we should vacate and remand the judgment of the Virginia Supreme Court so that that court can have an opportunity authoritatively to construe the prima-facie-evidence provision of Va.Code Ann. § 18.2–423 (1996). I write separately, however, to describe what I believe to be the correct interpretation of § 18.2–423, and to explain why I believe there is no justification for the plurality's apparent decision to invalidate that provision on its face.

I

Section 18.2–423 provides that the burning of a cross in public view "shall be prima facie evidence of an intent to intimidate." In order to determine whether this component of the statute violates the Constitution, it is necessary, first, to establish precisely what the presentation of prima facie evidence accomplishes.

Typically, "prima facie evidence" is defined as:

> "Such evidence as, in the judgment of the law, is sufficient to establish a given fact . . . and which if not rebutted or contradicted, will remain sufficient. [Such evidence], if unexplained or uncontradicted, is sufficient to sustain a judgment in favor of the issue which it supports, but [it] may be contradicted by other evidence." Black's Law Dictionary 1190 (6th ed.1990).

The Virginia Supreme Court has, in prior cases, embraced this canonical understanding of the pivotal statutory language.

The established meaning in Virginia, then, of the term "prima facie evidence" appears to be perfectly orthodox: It is evidence that suffices, on its own, to establish a particular fact. But it is hornbook law that this is true only to the extent that the evidence goes unrebutted. "Prima facie evidence of a fact is such evidence as, in judgment of law, is sufficient to establish the fact; and, *if not rebutted,* remains sufficient for the purpose."

To be sure, Virginia is entirely free, if it wishes, to discard the canonical understanding of the term "prima facie evidence." In this case, however, the Virginia Supreme Court has done nothing of the sort. To the extent that tribunal has spoken to the question of what "prima facie evidence" means for purposes of § 18.2–423, it has not deviated a whit from its prior practice and from the ordinary legal meaning of these words. Rather, its opinion explained that under § 18.2–423, "the act of burning a cross alone, with no evidence of intent to intimidate, will . . . suffice for arrest and prosecution and will insulate the Commonwealth from a motion to strike the evidence at the end of its case-in-chief." Put otherwise, where the Commonwealth has demonstrated through its case in chief that the defendant burned a cross in public view, this is sufficient, at least until the defendant has come forward with rebuttal evidence, to create a jury issue with respect to the intent element of the offense.

It is important to note that the Virginia Supreme Court did not suggest (as did the trial court's jury instructions in respondent Black's case, *see infra,* at 1557) that a jury may, in light of the prima-facie-evidence provision, ignore any rebuttal evidence that has been presented and, solely on the basis of a showing that the defendant burned a cross, find that he intended to intimidate. Nor, crucially, did that court say that the presentation of prima facie evidence is always sufficient to get a case to a jury, *i.e.,* that a court may never direct a verdict for a defendant who has been shown to have burned a cross in public view, even if, by the end of trial, the defendant has presented rebuttal evidence. Instead, according to the Virginia Supreme Court, the effect of the prima-facie-evidence provision is far more limited. It suffices to "insulate the Commonwealth from a motion to strike the evidence *at the end of its case-in-chief*," but it does nothing more. That is, presentation of evidence that a defendant burned a cross in public view is automatically sufficient, on its own, to support an inference that the defendant intended to intimidate *only until* the defendant comes forward with some evidence in rebuttal.

II

The question presented, then, is whether, given this understanding of the term "prima facie evidence," the cross-burning statute is constitutional. The Virginia Supreme Court answered that question in the negative. It stated that "§ 18.2–423 sweeps within its ambit for arrest and prosecution, both protected and unprotected speech." "The enhanced probability of prosecution under the statute chills the expression of protected speech sufficiently to render the statute overbroad."

This approach toward overbreadth analysis is unprecedented. We have never held that the mere threat that individuals who engage in protected conduct will be subject to arrest and prosecution suffices to render a statute overbroad. Rather, our overbreadth jurisprudence has consistently focused on whether *the prohibitory terms* of a particular statute extend to protected conduct; that is, we have inquired whether individuals who engage in protected conduct can be *convicted* under a statute, not whether they might be subject to arrest and prosecution.

Unwilling to embrace the Virginia Supreme Court's novel mode of overbreadth analysis, today's opinion properly focuses on the question of who may be convicted, rather than who may be arrested and prosecuted, under § 18.2–423. Thus, it notes that "[t]he prima facie evidence provision permits a jury *to convict* in every cross-burning case in which defendants exercise their constitutional right not to put on a defense." In such cases, the plurality explains, "[t]he provision permits the Commonwealth to arrest, prosecute, *and convict* a person based solely on the fact of cross burning itself." And this, according to the plurality, is constitutionally problematic because "a burning cross is not always intended to intimidate," and nonintimidating cross burning cannot be prohibited. In particular, the opinion notes that cross burning may serve as "a statement of ideology" or "a symbol of group solidarity" at Ku Klux Klan rituals, and may even serve artistic purposes as in the case of the film Mississippi Burning.

The plurality is correct in all of this—and it means that some individuals who engage in protected speech may, because of the prima-facie-evidence provision, be subject to conviction. Such convictions, assuming they are unconstitutional, could be challenged on a case-by-case basis. The plurality, however, with little in the way of explanation, leaps to the conclusion that the *possibility* of such convictions justifies facial invalidation of the statute.

In deeming § 18.2–423 facially invalid, the plurality presumably means to rely on some species of overbreadth doctrine. But it must be a rare species indeed. We have noted that "[i]n a facial challenge to the overbreadth and vagueness of a law, a court's first task is to determine whether the enactment reaches a substantial amount of constitutionally protected conduct." If one looks only to the core provision of § 18.2–423— "[i]t shall be unlawful for any person or persons, with the intent of intimidating any person or group of persons, to burn, or cause to be burned, a cross . . . "—it appears *not* to capture any protected conduct; that language is limited in its reach to conduct which a State is, under the Court's holding, *ante,* at 1549–1550, allowed to prohibit. In order to identify *any* protected conduct that is affected by Virginia's cross-burning law, the plurality is compelled to focus not on the statute's core prohibition, but on the prima-facie-evidence provision, and hence on *the process* through which the prohibited conduct may be found by a jury. And even in that context, the plurality cannot claim that improper convictions will result from the operation of the prima-facie-evidence provision *alone.* As the plurality concedes, the only persons who might impermissibly be convicted by reason of that provision are those who adopt a particular trial strategy, to wit, abstaining from the presentation of a defense.

The plurality is thus left with a strikingly attenuated argument to support the claim that Virginia's cross-burning statute is facially invalid. The class of persons that the plurality contemplates could impermissibly be convicted under § 18.2–423 includes only those individuals who (1) burn a cross in public view, (2) do not intend to intimidate, (3) are nonetheless charged and prosecuted, and (4) refuse to present a defense

Conceding (quite generously, in my view) that this class of persons exists, it cannot possibly give rise to a viable facial challenge, not even with the aid of our First Amendment overbreadth doctrine. For this Court has emphasized repeatedly that "where a statute regulates expressive conduct, the scope of the statute does not render it unconstitutional unless its overbreadth is not only real, but *substantial* as well, judged in relation to the statute's plainly legitimate sweep."

Perhaps more alarming, the plurality concedes that its understanding of the prima-facie-evidence provision is premised on the jury instructions given in respondent Black's case. This would all be well and good were it not for the fact that the plurality *facially invalidates* § 18.2–423. I am aware of no case—and the plurality cites none—in which we have facially invalidated an *ambiguous* statute on the basis of a constitutionally troubling jury instruction. And it is altogether unsurprising that there is no precedent for such a holding. For where state law is ambiguous, treating jury instructions as binding interpretations would cede an enormous measure of power over state law to trial judges. A single judge's idiosyncratic reading of a state statute could trigger its invalidation. In this case, the troubling instruction—

"The burning of a cross, by itself, is sufficient evidence from which you may infer the required intent," was taken verbatim from Virginia's Model Jury Instructions. But these Model Instructions have been neither promulgated by the legislature nor formally adopted by the Virginia Supreme Court. And it is hornbook law, in Virginia as elsewhere, that "[p]roffered instructions which do not correctly state the law . . . are erroneous and should be refused."

The plurality's willingness to treat this jury instruction as binding (and to strike down § 18.2–423 on that basis) would be shocking enough had the Virginia Supreme Court offered no guidance as to the proper construction of the prima-facie-evidence provision. For ordinarily we would decline to pass upon the constitutionality of an ambiguous state statute until that State's highest court had provided a binding construction. If there is any exception to that rule, it is the case where one of two possible interpretations of the state statute would clearly render it unconstitutional, and the other would not. In that situation, applying the maxim *"ut res magis valeat quam pereat"* we would do *precisely the opposite* of what the plurality does here—that is, we would adopt the alternative reading that renders the statute constitutional rather than unconstitutional. The plurality's analysis is all the more remarkable given the dissonance between the interpretation of § 18.2–423 implicit in the jury instruction and the one suggested by the Virginia Supreme Court. That court's opinion did not state that, once proof of public cross burning is presented, a jury is permitted to infer an intent to intimidate *solely* on this basis and regardless of whether a defendant has offered evidence to rebut any such inference. To the contrary, in keeping with the black-letter understanding of "prima facie evidence," the Virginia Supreme Court explained that such evidence suffices only to "insulate the Commonwealth from a motion to strike the evidence at the end of its case-in-chief."

As its concluding performance, in an apparent effort to paper over its unprecedented decision facially to invalidate a statute in light of an errant jury instruction, the plurality states:

"We recognize that the Supreme Court of Virginia has not authoritatively interpreted the meaning of the prima facie evidence provision. . . . We also recognize the theoretical possibility that the court, on remand, could interpret the provision in a manner different from that so far set forth in order to avoid the constitutional objections we have described. We leave open that possibility."

Now this is truly baffling. Having declared, in the immediately preceding sentence, that § 18.2–423 is "unconstitutional *on its face*," the plurality holds out the possibility that the Virginia Supreme Court will offer some saving construction of the statute. It should go without saying that if a saving construction of § 18.2–423 is possible, then facial invalidation is inappropriate. So, what appears to have happened is that the plurality has facially invalidated not § 18.2–423, but its own hypothetical interpretation of § 18.2–423, and has then remanded to the Virginia Supreme Court to learn the *actual* interpretation of § 18.2–423. Words cannot express my wonderment at this virtuoso performance.

III

As the analysis in Part I, *supra,* demonstrates, I believe the prima-facie-evidence provision in Virginia's cross-burning statute is constitutionally unproblematic. Nevertheless, because the Virginia Supreme Court has not yet offered an authoritative construction of § 18.2–423, I concur in the Court's decision to vacate and remand the judgment with respect to respondents Elliott and O'Mara. I also agree that respondent Black's conviction cannot stand. As noted above, the jury in Black's case was instructed that "[t]he burning of a cross, *by itself,* is sufficient evidence from which you may infer the required intent." Where this instruction has been given, it is impossible to determine whether the jury has rendered its verdict (as it must) in light of the entire body of facts before it—*including* evidence that might rebut the presumption that the cross burning was done with an intent to intimidate—or, instead, has chosen to ignore such rebuttal evidence and focused exclusively on the fact that the defendant burned a cross. Still, I cannot go along with the Court's decision to affirm the judgment with respect to Black. In that judgment, the Virginia Supreme Court, having erroneously concluded that § 18.2–423 is overbroad, not only vacated Black's conviction, but dismissed the indictment against him as well. Because I believe the constitutional defect in Black's conviction is rooted in a jury instruction and not in the statute itself, I would not dismiss the indictment and would permit the Commonwealth to retry Black if it wishes to do so.

■ [The opinion of JUSTICE STEVENS, concurring, is omitted.]

■ JUSTICE SOUTER, with whom JUSTICE KENNEDY and JUSTICE GINSBURG join, concurring in the judgment in part and dissenting in part.

I

The issue is whether the statutory prohibition restricted to this symbol falls within one of the exceptions to *R.A.V.*'s general condemnation of limited content-based proscription within a broader category of expression proscribable generally. Because of the burning cross's extraordinary force as a method of intimidation, the *R.A.V.* exception most likely to cover the statute is the first of the three mentioned there, which the *R.A.V.* opinion called an exception for content discrimination on a basis that "consists entirely of the very reason the entire class of speech at issue is proscribable." This is the exception the majority speaks of here as covering statutes prohibiting "particularly virulent" proscribable expression.

I do not think that the Virginia statute qualifies for this virulence exception as *R.A.V.* explained it. The statute fits poorly with the illustrative examples given in *R.A.V.*, none of which involves communication generally associated with a particular message, and in fact, the majority's discussion of a special virulence exception here moves that exception toward a more flexible conception than the version in *R.A.V.* I will reserve judgment on that doctrinal development, for even on a pragmatic conception of *R.A.V.* and its exceptions the Virginia statute could not pass muster, the most obvious hurdle being the statute's prima facie evidence provision. That provision is essential to understanding why the statute's tendency to suppress a message disqualifies it from any rescue by exception from *R.A.V.*'s general rule.

II

R.A.V. defines the special virulence exception to the rule barring content-based subclasses of categorically proscribable expression this way: prohibition by subcategory is nonetheless constitutional if it is made "entirely" on the "basis" of "the very reason" that "the entire class of speech at issue is proscribable" at all. The Court explained that when the subcategory is confined to the most obviously proscribable instances, "no significant danger of idea or viewpoint discrimination exists," and the explanation was rounded out with some illustrative examples. None of them, however, resembles the case before us.

The first example of permissible distinction is for a prohibition of obscenity unusually offensive "in its prurience." [But] distinguishing obscene publications on this basis does not suggest discrimination on the basis of the message conveyed. The opposite is true, however, when a general prohibition of intimidation is rejected in favor of a distinct proscription of intimidation by cross burning. The cross may have been selected because of its special power to threaten, but it may also have been singled out because of disapproval of its message of white supremacy, either because a legislature thought white supremacy was a pernicious doctrine or because it found that dramatic, public espousal of it was a civic embarrassment. Thus, there is no kinship between the cross-burning statute and the core prurience example.

Nor does this case present any analogy to the statute prohibiting threats against the President, the second of *R.A.V.*'s examples of the virulence exception and the one the majority relies upon. The content discrimination in that statute relates to the addressee of the threat and reflects the special risks and costs associated with threatening the President. Again, however, threats against the President are not generally identified by reference to the content of any message that may accompany the threat, let alone any viewpoint, and there is no obvious correlation in fact between victim and message. Millions of statements are made about the President every day on every subject and from every standpoint; threats of violence are not an integral feature of any one subject or viewpoint as distinct from others. Differential treatment of threats against the President, then, selects nothing but special risks, not special messages. A content-based proscription of cross burning, on the other hand, may be a subtle effort to ban not only the intensity of the intimidation cross burning causes when done to threaten, but also the particular message of white supremacy that is broadcast even by nonthreatening cross burning.

I thus read *R.A.V.*'s examples of the particular virulence exception as covering prohibitions that are not clearly associated with a particular viewpoint, and that are consequently different from the Virginia statute. On that understanding of things, I necessarily read the majority opinion as treating *R.A.V.*'s virulence exception in a more flexible, pragmatic manner than the original illustrations would suggest. Actually, another way of looking at today's decision would see it as a slight modification of *R.A.V.*'s third exception, which allows content-based discrimination within a proscribable category when its "nature" is such "that there is no realistic possibility that official suppression of ideas is afoot." The majority's approach could be taken as recognizing an exception to *R.A.V.* when circumstances show that the statute's ostensibly valid reason for punishing particularly serious proscribable expression probably is not a ruse for message suppression, even though the statute may have a greater (but not exclusive) impact on adherents of one ideology than on others.

III

My concern here, in any event, is not with the merit of a pragmatic doctrinal move. For whether or not the Court should conceive of exceptions to *R.A.V.*'s general rule in a more practical way, no content-based statute should survive even under a pragmatic recasting of *R.A.V.* without a high probability that no "official suppression of ideas is afoot," I believe the prima facie evidence provision stands in the way of any finding of such a high probability here.

To the extent the prima facie evidence provision skews prosecutions, then, it skews the statute toward suppressing ideas. Thus, the appropriate way to consider the statute's prima facie evidence term, in my view, is not as if it were an overbroad statutory definition amenable to severance or a narrowing construction. The question here is not the permissible scope of an arguably overbroad statute, but the claim of a clearly content-based statute to an exception from the general prohibition of content-based proscriptions, an exception that is not warranted if the statute's terms show that suppression of ideas may be afoot. Accordingly, the way to look at the prima facie evidence provision is to consider it for any indication of what is afoot. And if we look at the provision for this purpose, it has a very obvious significance as a mechanism for bringing within the statute's prohibition some expression that is doubtfully threatening though certainly distasteful.

■ JUSTICE THOMAS, dissenting.

I

Although I agree with the majority's conclusion that it is constitutionally permissible to "ban . . . cross burning carried out with the intent to intimidate," I believe that the majority errs in imputing an expressive component to the activity in question. In my view, whatever expressive value cross burning has, the legislature simply wrote it out by banning only intimidating conduct undertaken by a particular means. A conclusion that the statute prohibiting cross burning with intent to intimidate sweeps beyond a prohibition on certain conduct into the zone of expression overlooks not only the words of the statute but also reality.

That in the early 1950's the people of Virginia viewed cross burning as creating an intolerable atmosphere of terror is not surprising: Although the cross took on some religious significance in the 1920's when the Klan became connected with certain southern white clergy, by the postwar period it had reverted to its original function "as an instrument of intimidation."

It strains credulity to suggest that a state legislature that adopted a litany of segregationist laws self-contradictorily intended to squelch the segregationist message. Even for segregationists, violent and terroristic conduct, the Siamese twin of cross burning, was intolerable. The ban on cross burning with intent to intimidate demonstrates that even segregationists understood the difference between intimidating and terroristic conduct and racist expression. It is simply beyond belief that, in passing the statute now under review, the Virginia Legislature was concerned with anything but penalizing conduct it must have viewed as particularly vicious.

Accordingly, this statute prohibits only conduct, not expression. And, just as one cannot burn down someone's house to make a political point and then seek refuge in the First Amendment, those who hate cannot terrorize and intimidate to make their point. In light of my conclusion that the statute here addresses only conduct, there is no need to analyze it under any of our First Amendment tests.

[In the rest of Justice THOMAS's opinion, he dissents from the plurality's position on the statute's jury inference, stating that "the fact that the statute permits a jury to draw an inference of intent to intimidate from the cross burning itself presents no constitutional problems."]

NOTES AND QUESTIONS

1. *Distinguishing* R.A.V. How does Justice O'Connor navigate around *R.A.V.*? She purports to follow Justice Scalia's reasoning in *R.A.V.* that a state can regulate a proscribable category if it is regulating because "the basis for the content discrimination consists entirely of the very reason the entire class of speech at issue is proscribable." True threats are a

proscribable category, and cross burnings with the intent to intimidate can be prohibited because they are "most likely to inspire fear of bodily harm." Are you persuaded that *Black* is distinguishable from *R.A.V.*? As you consider this question, think about Justice White's argument in *R.A.V.* and Justice Souter's partial concurrence on this point in *Black*.

2. *The Meaning of Cross Burning.* One of the more interesting splits of the Court in *Black* is over the meaning of cross burning. Justice Thomas argues in his concurrence that the cross burning prohibited by the statute is intimidating terroristic conduct. Consider Justice Thomas' question at oral argument in the case to Deputy Solicitor General Michael Dreeben, who was arguing in favor of the constitutionality of the statute. By some accounts, the following exchange changed the nature of the oral arguments and may have altered the outcome of the case:

> [Justice Thomas]: Mr. Dreeben, aren't you understating the— the effects of—of the burning cross?
>
> [Justice Thomas]: Now it's my understanding that we had almost 100 years of lynching and activity in the South by the Knights of Camellia and—and the Ku Klux Klan, and this was a reign of terror and the cross was a symbol of that reign of terror. Was—isn't that significantly greater than intimidation or a threat?
>
> Answer: Well, I think they're coextensive, Justice Thomas, because it is—
>
> [Justice Thomas]: Well, my fear is, Mr. Dreeben, that you're actually understating the symbolism on—of and the effect of the cross, the burning cross. I—I indicated, I think, in the Ohio case that the cross was not a religious symbol and that it has—it was intended to have a virulent effect. And I—I think that what you're attempting to do is to fit this into our jurisprudence rather than stating more clearly what the cross was intended to accomplish and, indeed, that is unlike any symbol in our society.
>
> [M]y fear is that the—there was no other purpose to the cross. There was no communication of a particular message. It was intended to cause fear . . . and to terrorize a population.

Now consider this exchange, later in the oral arguments between Justice Scalia, who described cross burning as "reprehensible" in *R.A.V.*, with former law school Dean, Rodney Smolla, the lawyer for the respondents:

> Smolla: If I see a burning cross, my stomach may churn. I may feel a sense of loathing, disgust, a vague sense of . . . being intimidated.
>
> Question: How about a cross—how about a cross—
>
> Smolla: But that's not fear of bodily harm.
>
> Question: How about a cross on your lawn?
>
> [Justice Scalia]: Yes. I dare say that you would rather see a man with a—with a rifle on your front lawn—If you were a black

man at night, you'd rather see a man with a rifle than see a burning cross on your front lawn.

> Smolla: Your Honor, I concede that.

If Justices Thomas and Scalia are right about the meaning of the burning cross, how do we explain Justice Scalia's opinion in *R.A.V.* and Justice Thomas' willingness to join that opinion? If you were a black man at night, would you rather see a man with a rifle or a burning cross on your front lawn?

3.   *Epistemic Disputes.* Not all members of the Court agreed with Justices Thomas and Scalia. Though Justice O'Connor thought the primary message of cross burning was intimidation, she did not think it was invariably the case. Justice Souter seemed to think that cross burning communicated as much a message about white supremacy as intimidation, which led him to find the prima facie evidence component of the statute constitutionally problematic.

4.   *Asymmetry of Harm.* Related to the dispute about the meaning of cross burning is a worry about the asymmetry of harm. In the oral argument exchange quoted above, Justice Scalia considers the harm of cross burning on a lawn from the perspective of a black man. Is a burning cross more intimidating if you are a black man rather than a white man, or a white woman, or a black woman, or an Asian man? What if you are a black man from Jamaica or Sweden? Justice O'Connor claims, "as a factual matter it is not true that cross burners direct their intimidating conduct solely to racial and religious minorities." From her perspective, anyone can reasonably be a target of cross burning. Are whites likely targets of racist speech or likely victims of cross burnings? Is it reasonable to assume that there will be an asymmetry in the harm caused by a cross burning?

V.   RACIST SYMBOLS

The First Amendment's protections extend beyond speech communicated through the spoken or written word to encompass both "symbolic speech" conveyed through symbols and conduct, as well as "expression." The meanings of symbols are often historically contingent and are understood differently by different people. A central question we will confront in this section is whether it is possible for judges or lawmakers to determine which meanings ought to be proscribed and those that ought to be promoted.

What happens when meaning correlates with race? Take, for example, the confederate flag. Some claim that the flag represents southern heritage, pride, and resistance. For others, it stands for white supremacy. A recent CNN poll found that 57% of Americans see the flag as a symbol of southern pride rather than a symbol of racism. Not surprisingly, there is a sharp racial divide on this question. Among African Americans, 72% see the flag as a symbol of racism and only 17% view it as a symbol of southern pride. In contrast, 66% of white

Americans view the flag as a symbol of southern pride and only 25% as a symbol of racism. The question is whose meaning the law ought to privilege when the two meanings clash. What role should the First Amendment play in these disputes? Consider the following case.

Walker v. Texas Division, Sons of Confederate Veterans, Inc.

Supreme Court of the United States, 2015.
576 U.S. ___, 135 S.Ct. 2239.

■ JUSTICE BREYER delivered the opinion of the Court.

Texas offers automobile owners a choice between ordinary and specialty license plates. Those who want the State to issue a particular specialty plate may propose a plate design, comprising a slogan, a graphic, or (most commonly) both. If the Texas Department of Motor Vehicles Board approves the design, the State will make it available for display on vehicles registered in Texas.

In this case, the Texas Division of the Sons of Confederate Veterans proposed a specialty license plate design featuring a Confederate battle flag. The Board rejected the proposal. We must decide whether that rejection violated the Constitution's free speech guarantees. We conclude that it did not.

I

A

Texas law requires all motor vehicles operating on the State's roads to display valid license plates. And Texas makes available several kinds of plates. Drivers may choose to display the State's general-issue license plates. In the alternative, drivers may choose from an assortment of specialty license plates. Finally, Texas law provides for personalized plates (also known as vanity plates). Pursuant to the personalization program, a vehicle owner may request a particular alphanumeric pattern for use as a plate number, such as "BOB" or "TEXPL8."

Here we are concerned only with the second category of plates, namely specialty license plates, not with the personalization program. Texas offers vehicle owners a variety of specialty plates, generally for an annual fee. And Texas selects the designs for specialty plates through three distinct processes.

First, the state legislature may specifically call for the development of a specialty license plate. The legislature has enacted statutes authorizing, for example, plates that say "Keep Texas Beautiful" and "Mothers Against Drunk Driving."

Second, the Board may approve a specialty plate design proposal that a state-designated private vendor has created at the request of an individual or organization. Among the plates created through the private-vendor process are plates promoting the "Keller Indians" and plates with the slogan "Get it Sold with RE/MAX."

Third, the Board "may create new specialty license plates on its own initiative or on receipt of an application from a" nonprofit entity seeking to sponsor a specialty plate. And Texas law vests in the Board authority to approve or to disapprove an application. Specialty plates that the Board has sanctioned through this process include plates featuring the words "The Gator Nation," together with the Florida Gators logo, and plates featuring the logo of Rotary International and the words "SERVICE ABOVE SELF."

B

In 2009, the Sons of Confederate Veterans, Texas Division (a nonprofit entity), applied to sponsor a specialty license plate through this last-mentioned process. SCV's application included a draft plate design. The Board's predecessor denied this application.

In 2010, SCV renewed its application before the Board. The Board invited public comment on its website and at an open meeting. After considering the responses, including a number of letters sent by elected officials who opposed the proposal, the Board voted unanimously against issuing the plate. The Board explained that it had found "it necessary to deny th[e] plate design application, specifically the confederate flag portion of the design, because public comments ha[d] shown that many members of the general public find the design offensive, and because such comments are reasonable." The Board added "that a significant portion of the public associate the confederate flag with organizations advocating expressions of hate directed toward people or groups that is demeaning to those people or groups."

In 2012, SCV and two of its officers (collectively SCV) brought this lawsuit against the chairman and members of the Board (collectively Board). SCV argued that the Board's decision violated the Free Speech Clause of the First Amendment, and it sought an injunction requiring the Board to approve the proposed plate design. The District Court entered judgment for the Board. A divided panel of the Court of Appeals for the Fifth Circuit reversed.

We granted the Board's petition for certiorari, and we now reverse.

II

When government speaks, it is not barred by the Free Speech Clause from determining the content of what it says. *Pleasant Grove City v. Summum,* 555 U.S. 460, 467–468 (2009). That freedom in part reflects the fact that it is the democratic electoral process that first and foremost provides a check on government speech. Thus, government statements (and government actions and programs that take the form of speech) do not normally trigger the First Amendment rules designed to protect the marketplace of ideas.

Were the Free Speech Clause interpreted otherwise, government would not work. How could a city government create a successful recycling program if officials, when writing householders asking them to recycle cans and bottles, had to include in the letter a long plea from the local trash disposal enterprise demanding the contrary?

That is not to say that a government's ability to express itself is without restriction. Constitutional and statutory provisions outside of the Free Speech Clause may limit government speech.

III

In our view, specialty license plates issued pursuant to Texas's statutory scheme convey government speech. Our reasoning rests primarily on our analysis in *Summum,* a recent case that presented a similar problem.

A

In Summum, we considered a religious organization's request to erect in a 2.5-acre city park a monument setting forth the organization's religious tenets. In the park were 15 other permanent displays. At least 11 of these—including a wishing well, a September 11 monument, a historic granary, the city's first fire station, and a Ten Commandments monument—had been donated to the city by private entities. The religious organization argued that the Free Speech Clause required the city to display the organization's proposed monument because, by accepting a broad range of permanent exhibitions at the park, the city had created a forum for private speech in the form of monuments.

We held that the city had not "provid[ed] a forum for private speech" with respect to monuments. Rather, the city, even when "accepting a privately donated monument and placing it on city property," had "engage[d] in expressive conduct." The speech at issue, this Court decided, was "best viewed as a form of government speech" and "therefore [was] not subject to scrutiny under the Free Speech Clause."

We based our conclusion on several factors. First, history shows that "[g]overnments have long used monuments to speak to the public."

Second, we noted that it "is not common for property owners to open up their property for the installation of permanent monuments that convey a message with which they do not wish to be associated." As a result, "persons who observe donated monuments routinely—and reasonably—interpret them as conveying some message on the property owner's behalf."

Third, we found relevant the fact that the city maintained control over the selection of monuments. We thought it "fair to say that throughout our Nation's history, the general government practice with respect to donated monuments has been one of selective receptivity." And we observed that the city government in Summum " 'effectively controlled' the messages sent by the monuments in the [p]ark by exercising 'final approval authority' over their selection."

In light of these and a few other relevant considerations, the Court concluded that the expression at issue was government speech.

B

Our analysis in *Summum* leads us to the conclusion that here, too, government speech is at issue. First, the history of license plates shows that, insofar as license plates have conveyed more than state names and vehicle identification numbers, they long have communicated messages from the States.

In 1928, Idaho became the first State to include a slogan on its plates. The 1928 Idaho plate proclaimed "Idaho Potatoes" and featured an illustration of a brown potato, onto which the license plate number was superimposed in green. States have used license plate slogans to urge action, to promote tourism, and to tout local industries.

Texas, too, has selected various messages to communicate through its license plate designs. By 1919, Texas had begun to display the Lone Star emblem on its plates. In 1936, the State's general-issue plates featured the first slogan on Texas license plates: the word "Centennial." *Id.,* at 20. This kind of state speech has appeared on Texas plates for decades.

Second, Texas license plate designs "are often closely identified in the public mind with the [State]." Each Texas license plate is a government article serving the governmental purposes of vehicle registration and identification. The governmental nature of the plates is clear from their faces: The State places the name "TEXAS" in large letters at the top of every plate. Moreover, the State requires Texas vehicle owners to display license plates, and every Texas license plate is issued by the State. Texas also owns the designs on its license plates, including the designs that Texas adopts on the basis of proposals made by private individuals and organizations. And Texas dictates the manner in which drivers may dispose of unused plates.

Texas license plates are, essentially, government IDs. And issuers of ID "typically do not permit" the placement on their IDs of "message[s] with which they do not wish to be associated." Consequently, "persons who observe" designs on IDs "routinely—and reasonably—interpret them as conveying some message on the [issuer's] behalf."

Indeed, a person who displays a message on a Texas license plate likely intends to convey to the public that the State has endorsed that message. If not, the individual could simply display the message in question in larger letters on a bumper sticker right next to the plate. But the individual prefers a license plate design to the purely private speech expressed through bumper stickers. That may well be because Texas's license plate designs convey government agreement with the message displayed.

Third, Texas maintains direct control over the messages conveyed on its specialty plates. Texas law provides that the State "has sole control over the design, typeface, color, and alphanumeric pattern for all license plates." The Board must approve every specialty plate design proposal before the design can appear on a Texas plate. And the Board and its predecessor have actively exercised this authority. Texas asserts, and SCV concedes, that the State has rejected at least a dozen proposed designs.

This final approval authority allows Texas to choose how to present itself and its constituency. Thus, Texas offers plates celebrating the many educational institutions attended by its citizens. But it need not issue plates deriding schooling. Texas offers plates that pay tribute to the Texas citrus industry. But it need not issue plates praising Florida's oranges as far better. And Texas offers plates that say "Fight Terrorism." But it need not issue plates promoting al Qaeda.

These considerations, taken together, convince us that the specialty plates here in question are similar enough to the monuments in *Summum* to call for the same result.

For the reasons stated, we hold that Texas's specialty license plate designs constitute government speech and that Texas was consequently entitled to refuse to issue plates featuring SCV's proposed design. Accordingly, the judgment of the United States Court of Appeals for the Fifth Circuit is

Reversed.

■ JUSTICE ALITO, with whom THE CHIEF JUSTICE, JUSTICE SCALIA, and JUSTICE KENNEDY join, dissenting.

The Court's decision passes off private speech as government speech and, in doing so, establishes a precedent that threatens private speech that government finds displeasing. Under our First Amendment cases, the distinction between government speech and private speech is critical.

Here is a test. Suppose you sat by the side of a Texas highway and studied the license plates on the vehicles passing by. You would see, in addition to the standard Texas plates, an impressive array of specialty plates. (There are now more than 350 varieties.)

As you sat there watching these plates speed by, would you really think that the sentiments reflected in these specialty plates are the views of the State of Texas and not those of the owners of the cars? If a car with a plate that says "Rather Be Golfing" passed by at 8:30 am on a Monday morning, would you think: "This is the official policy of the State—better to golf than to work?" If you did your viewing at the start of the college football season and you saw Texas plates with the names of the University of Texas's out-of-state competitors in upcoming games—Notre

Dame, Oklahoma State, the University of Oklahoma, Kansas State, Iowa State—would you assume that the State of Texas was officially (and perhaps treasonously) rooting for the Longhorns' opponents?

The Court says that all of these messages are government speech. It is essential that government be able to express its own viewpoint, the Court reminds us, because otherwise, how would it promote its programs, like recycling and vaccinations? So when Texas issues a "Rather Be Golfing" plate, but not a "Rather Be Playing Tennis" or "Rather Be Bowling" plate, it is furthering a state policy to promote golf but not tennis or bowling.

This capacious understanding of government speech takes a large and painful bite out of the First Amendment. Specialty plates may seem innocuous. They make motorists happy, and they put money in a State's coffers. But the precedent this case sets is dangerous. While all license plates unquestionably contain *some* government speech (*e.g.,* the name of the State and the numbers and/or letters identifying the vehicle), the State of Texas has converted the remaining space on its specialty plates into little mobile billboards on which motorists can display their own messages. And what Texas did here was to reject one of the messages that members of a private group wanted to post on some of these little billboards because the State thought that many of its citizens would find the message offensive.

That is blatant viewpoint discrimination.

B

The [SCV] applied for a Texas specialty license plate in 2009 and again in 2010. Their proposed design featured a controversial symbol, the Confederate battle flag, surrounded by the words "Sons of Confederate Veterans 1896" and a gold border. The Texas Department of Motor Vehicles Board (or Board) invited public comments and considered the plate design at a meeting in April 2011. At that meeting, one board member was absent, and the remaining eight members deadlocked on whether to approve the plate. The Board thus reconsidered the plate at its meeting in November 2011. This time, many opponents of the plate turned out to voice objections. The Board then voted unanimously against approval.

At the same meeting, the Board approved a Buffalo Soldiers plate design by a 5-to-3 vote. Proceeds from fees paid by motorists who select that plate benefit the Buffalo Soldier National Museum in Houston, which is "dedicated primarily to preserving the legacy and honor of the African American soldier." "Buffalo Soldiers" is a nickname that was originally given to black soldiers in the Army's 10th Cavalry Regiment, which was formed after the Civil War, and the name was later used to describe other black soldiers. The original Buffalo Soldiers fought with distinction in the Indian Wars, but the "Buffalo Soldiers" plate was opposed by some Native Americans. One leader commented that he felt

" 'the same way about the Buffalo Soldiers' " as African-Americans felt about the Confederate flag. " 'When we see the U.S. Cavalry uniform,' " he explained, " 'we are forced to relive an American holocaust.' "

III

What Texas has done by selling space on its license plates is to create what we have called a limited public forum. It has allowed state property (*i.e.,* motor vehicle license plates) to be used by private speakers according to rules that the State prescribes. Under the First Amendment, however, those rules cannot discriminate on the basis of viewpoint. But that is exactly what Texas did here. The Board rejected Texas SCV's design, "specifically the confederate flag portion of the design, because public comments have shown that many members of the general public find the design offensive, and because such comments are reasonable." These statements indisputably demonstrate that the Board denied Texas SCV's design because of its viewpoint.

The Confederate battle flag is a controversial symbol. To the Texas Sons of Confederate Veterans, it is said to evoke the memory of their ancestors and other soldiers who fought for the South in the Civil War. To others, it symbolizes slavery, segregation, and hatred. Whatever it means to motorists who display that symbol and to those who see it, the flag expresses a viewpoint. The Board rejected the plate design because it concluded that many Texans would find the flag symbol offensive. That was pure viewpoint discrimination.

If the Board's candid explanation of its reason for rejecting the SCV plate were not alone sufficient to establish this point, the Board's approval of the Buffalo Soldiers plate at the same meeting dispels any doubt. The proponents of both the SCV and Buffalo Soldiers plates saw them as honoring soldiers who served with bravery and honor in the past. To the opponents of both plates, the images on the plates evoked painful memories. The Board rejected one plate and approved the other.

Like these two plates, many other specialty plates have the potential to irritate and perhaps even infuriate those who see them. Texas allows a plate with the words "Choose Life," but the State of New York rejected such a plate because the message " '[is] so incredibly divisive,' " and the Second Circuit recently sustained that decision. Allowing States to reject specialty plates based on their potential to offend is viewpoint discrimination.

Messages that are proposed by private parties and placed on Texas specialty plates are private speech, not government speech. Texas cannot forbid private speech based on its viewpoint. That is what it did here. Because the Court approves this violation of the First Amendment, I respectfully dissent.

NOTES AND QUESTIONS

1. *Government Speech or Private Speech?* Justice Breyer, in his majority opinion, holds that Texas did not violate the First Amendment because messages on specialty license plates constitute government speech. By contrast, Justice Alito in dissent contends that the majority's analysis is absurd. Who has the better argument here?

2. As a doctrinal matter, this case is not about the confederate flag but about the circumstances pursuant to which the government can engage in viewpoint discrimination. But do you think the case would have come out the same way if it hadn't been about arguably racist speech?

3. *Government Speech or Private Speech?* Below is the license plate proposed by the Sons of Confederate Veterans. If you saw this plate on a vehicle, would you think the government was speaking, or would you regard it as private speech? How should a court make this determination?

4. *Confederate Battle Flag.* Though initially introduced to address battlefield confusion between the almost-identical American flag and confederate national flag, the confederate battle flag has become a symbol of much more in contemporary American culture. The flag's popularity surged among both state actors and private individuals during the civil rights era of the 1950s and 1960s and became a symbol of opposition to *Brown v. Board of Education* and subsequent civil rights advances. Following *Brown*, the Georgia state legislature changed its state flag to prominently include the Confederate battle flag, while South Carolina and Alabama chose to raise the flag itself above their state capitol buildings. Private groups, such as the KKK and neo-Nazis also adopted the flag as a symbol of their radically racist values. While apologists for the flag's appearance in modern society emphasize its historical meaning as a symbol of southern identity, opponents feel strongly that the flag symbolizes both historical and contemporary racism. *See* "The Stars and Bars Is Not a Racist Symbol," WASH. POST, Feb. 13, 1988, at A17, and David Treadwell, "Symbol of Racism?," L.A. Times, Mar. 9, 1987, at A1. For more discussion, *see* generally James Forman Jr.,

Driving Dixie Down: Removing the Confederate Flag from Southern State Capitols, 101 Yale L.J. 505 (1991).

On June 17, 2015, a white supremacist murdered nine African-American parishioners who were attending a prayer meeting at the Emmanuel African Methodist Episcopal Church. The shooting triggered a debate on the confederate flag after pictures surfaced of the shooter posing with it. In the aftermath of the shooting, South Carolina Governor Nikki Haley, an American of Asian Indian descent, declared that she could no longer justify flying the flag on state grounds. Soon thereafter, the state's lawmakers voted to remove the flag from state grounds and display it in a state military museum. On July 10, 2015, the flag was removed from state grounds.

5.   ***Cultural Reappropriation Redux.*** As evident in the cases above, a symbol's multiple meanings create interpretive difficulties for the courts. When one meaning arises from the processes of cultural appropriation and reappropriation, the issue becomes even more complicated. Cultural reappropriation is the process through which a cultural minority attempts to reclaim a derogatory symbol by trying to disrupt or displace the power of the pejorative meaning, in order to use the symbol to convey a positive meaning. Think, for instance, of African Americans' attempts to reappropriate the word nigger. Can whites reappropriate the confederate flag by changing its meaning from a symbol of racism to a symbol of valor? Those who view the confederate flag as a symbol of southern pride might argue that they are an oppressed minority, whose views are out of favor or marginalized. Does that matter if the overwhelming majority of black Americans see the flag as an expression of hate?

6.   ***Harvard Law School Crest.*** For over 80 years, Harvard Law School has used an insignia consisting of a blue and crimson shield with three sheaves of golden wheat and the law school's motto, "Veritas," emblazoned inside it. The shield recalls the family crest of Isaac Royall Jr., whose family derived a significant portion of its wealth from slave labor. Mr. Royall, through a bequest in 1871, also endowed the first professorship at the Law School. Indeed, the law school owes its genesis to the first person to hold the Royall Professorship, Isaac Parker. Mr. Parker convinced the University to create a "law department," which eventually became the modern Harvard Law School. The shield was designed in 1936, its association with slavery did not come to public attention until 2000, through the research of Professor Daniel Coquillette. In the fall of 2015, a group of Harvard law students called for the law school to abandon its use of the shield, on the ground that it symbolized slavery and evoked past oppression and current racial discrimination. The Law School's Dean appointed a committee to study the issue, and it ultimately recommended that the Law School abandon the shield because of its connection to slavery. Professor Annette Gordon-Reed, the distinguished legal historian and Harvard Law Professor, as a member of the committee, dissented from its recommendation:

[F]rom the moment I learned, some years ago, about the wheat sheaves' connection to the Royall Plantation and the plantation's connection to the Law School, the burning question for me has been, "What would be the best and easiest way to keep alive the memory of the people whose labor gave Isaac Royall the resources to purchase the land whose sale helped found Harvard Law School?" And when I say, "keep alive," I do not mean keep the Royall connection as a story that we tell just amongst ourselves when students first enter the Law School—although we should obviously continue to do that. "Keep alive" means to be *unrelentingly frank and open with the whole world, now and into the future, about an important thing that went into making this institution.* Maintaining the current shield, and tying it to a historically sound interpretive narrative about it, would be the most honest and forthright way to insure that the true story of our origins, and connection to the people whom we should see as our progenitors (the enslaved people at Royall's plantations, not Isaac Royall), is not lost.

Why do I think the current shield can—and should—be made to carry forward the story of, and our connection to, those enslaved at the Royall Plantation? For nearly its entire existence, the shield has sent no singular public message or had any function besides announcing the "arrival" of the Harvard Law School, generally viewed positively as one of the premier educational institutions in the world. Therefore, the shield is not, as I have heard it said in formal conversations about this issue and in informal ones, in any way akin to the Confederate flag or the Nazi flag. Individuals can say they feel it is, but if they do they ought to think seriously about, and associate themselves with, the problematic implications of that position.

The Confederate Flag came into existence as part of a clear and unambiguous project: it was a battle standard flown against the United States of America in order to protect African-American chattel slavery by means of a war that took half a million lives. In the years since the Civil War, that flag has been hauled out to intimidate black people and to serve, at key moments, as a symbol of opposition to racial equality. By this point in our history, these associations are too strong to totally divest that flag of its original meaning, and the very public meaning it has been given in the decades after the war. On the Nazi flag, I should not have to belabor why an image of wheat, an image that has appeared on many shields and crests for centuries, and was even on America's penny, cannot be equated with a flag that sent armies marching across Europe, provoking a conflagration that killed over 60 million people worldwide.

The shield, it should be added, contains no physical representation of Royall, which would be an unambiguous celebration of the man himself. . . . Until Dan Coquillette's excellent work on the history of HLS, most people did not know of the connection between the Royalls, the sheaves, and the Law School. Since the shield's adoption in the 1930s, any HLS graduates who have paid attention to the shield (and I am one) have been forced, by the obscurity of the shield's origins, to make their own internal meaning of the image. It has carried no *one* specific and dominant association. This is nothing like the situation with the more famous symbols mentioned above.

Whatever the shield has (or has not) meant personally to thousands of HLS students and graduates, those students and alums have made the school's modern public reputation in the decades since the shield was adopted. Current students and faculty benefit from what the Law School's graduates have done in the 20th and 21st centuries. Many of our graduates have been at the forefront of movements for justice and equality, and have exhibited a profound commitment to public service. They did this without any knowledge of the sheaves' provenance or any intent to countenance Isaac Royall's way of life. What they have done over the past 80 years, particularly in very recent decades when the shield has been the most visible symbol of HLS, certainly creates a stronger source for defining what the shield means than whatever the Royall family may have been thinking about the sheaves centuries ago. By their accomplishments, actions, and work, HLS students and alums have made a new thing of the shield, and their efforts should not come second place to Royall and his family.

The enslaved at the Royall Plantation and the graduates of Harvard Law School should be tied together as they have been without our knowledge for so many years, and as they always will be whether we choose to hide that connection from the world or not. Disaggregating the benefit achieved from the labor of the enslaved—the money accrued from the sale of Royall land—from the "burdens" of being constantly reminded of from whence that money came, and of letting people outside the community know from whence it came, would be an abdication of our responsibility to the enslaved and a missed opportunity to educate. . . .

So, what is to be done? I understand that getting rid of the shield altogether may seem less confrontational and the more conservative option. But this is a moment for daring and creativity. We are in the midst of an explosion of interest in and scholarship about slavery in New England. As an educational institution, HLS should be among the leaders of the effort to explicate this history. We should be at the forefront of this, using our own history as a guide. We are coming upon our 200th anniversary. This would be a perfect time to re-dedicate the Law School and the shield—making explicit our debt to the enslaved and our commitment, in their memory, to the cause of justice. Though this could be accomplished without changing the shield, if it is to be changed, perhaps the word *"iustitia"* (justice) could be placed directly beneath the tablets spelling out "Veritas", and the sheaves made slightly smaller to accommodate the added word. This would tie the past to the present and to the future. Referencing how the law school began would be combined with the spirit that has motivated HLS since the adoption of the shield.

http://www.thecrimson.com/article/2016/3/4/law-school-seal-report/.

Professor Gordon-Reed raises a number of interesting objections to the committee's decision to recommend removal of the shield. Which objection do you find most compelling? Is it the argument that in order to come to terms with the truth of the past one must keep alive racist symbols? What do you make of the argument that shield is not a racist symbol because most people did not even know about the relationship between the shield and the Royalls? Similarly, are you convinced that it is not the shield that defines the Harvard Law School but the work of its alumni? Is she correct that a racist symbol and racist past should not be suppressed but be used to educate? How would you vote if you were a member of this committee?

7.   ***Cultural Critique and Free Expression.*** The agency fostered by the First Amendment does not always take the form of political protest; people of color have also fought for racial justice through the cultural liberties afforded by the First Amendment to critique the dominant culture narrative that presents itself as colorblind or non-racialized. In the face of these claims of neutrality, First Amendment protection has allowed artists of color to challenge prevailing social norms. One avenue afforded by the First Amendment for cultural activism/agency is the doctrine of fair use. Fair use emerged as a common law doctrine balancing the property rights of authors with the Constitutional purpose of "promot[ing] the Progress of Science and the Useful Arts" and the First Amendment. It was codified in the 1976 Copyright Act as the reproduction of a copyright work "for purposes such as criticism, comment, news reporting, teaching (including multiple copies for classroom use), scholarship or research." This legal doctrine allows for people of color to comment directly on the dominant forms of culture, exposing their racialized realities. Consider two examples.

The most famous fair use music case, and a landmark case in Copyright Law generally, vindicated 2 Live Crew's bawdy parody of the prosaic vision of love in Roy Orbison's "Pretty Woman." The "parody exception" it established has been invoked in every fair use music case since.

> [The] words of 2 Live Crew's song copy the original's first line, but then "quickly degenerat[e] into a play on words, substituting predictable lyrics with shocking ones . . . [that] derisively demonstrat[e] how bland and banal the Orbison song seems to them." 754 F.Supp., at 1155 (footnote omitted). Judge Nelson, dissenting below, came to the same conclusion, that the 2 Live Crew song "was clearly intended to ridicule the white-bread original" and "reminds us that sexual congress with nameless streetwalkers is not necessarily the stuff of romance and is not necessarily without

its consequences. The singers (there are several) have the same thing on their minds as did the lonely man with the nasal voice, but here there is no hint of wine and roses." 972 F.2d, at 1442.

[Whether], going beyond that, parody is in good taste or bad does not and should not matter to fair use. As Justice Holmes explained, "[i]t would be a dangerous undertaking for persons trained only to the law to constitute themselves final judges of the worth of [a work], outside of the narrowest and most obvious limits. At the one extreme some works of genius would be sure to miss appreciation. Their very novelty would make them repulsive until the public had learned the new language in which their author spoke." *Bleistein v. Donaldson Lithographing Co.,* 188 U.S. 239, 25 (1903) (circus posters have copyright protection); cf. *Yankee Publishing Inc. v. News America Publishing, Inc.,* 809 F.Supp. 267, 280 (SDNY 1992) (Leval, J.) ("First Amendment protections do not apply only to those who speak clearly, whose jokes are funny, and whose parodies succeed") (trademark case).

While we might not assign a high rank to the parodic element here, we think it fair to say that 2 Live Crew's song reasonably could be perceived as commenting on the original or criticizing it, to some degree. 2 Live Crew juxtaposes the romantic musings of a man whose fantasy comes true, with degrading taunts, a bawdy demand for sex, and a sigh of relief from paternal responsibility. The later words can be taken as a comment on the naiveté of the original of an earlier day, as a rejection of its sentiment that ignores the ugliness of street life and the debasement that it signifies. It is this joinder of reference and ridicule that marks off the author's choice of parody from the other types of comment and criticism that traditionally have had a claim to fair use protection as transformative works.

Campbell v. Acuff-Rose Music Inc., 510 U.S. 560, 573–4 (1994).

More recently, following the path carved out by 2 Live Crew's invocation of fair use, is a mash-up by hip-hop duo, the Legendary K.O., which James Boyle describes in his book *The Public Domain. See* James Boyle's *The Public Domain: Enclosing the Commons of the Mind* (2008). Following in a long tradition of appropriation in African American music, the Legendary K.O. sampled Kanye West's statement in the wake of Katrina, that "George Bush doesn't care about black people" and overlaid it over one of West's own songs, "Gold Digger." Legendary K.O. used Kanye's hooks to reflect on race relations and comment on a national tragedy.

In her novel, *The Wind Done Gone*, Alice Randall retells the narrative of *Gone With the Wind* from the perspective of a slave child on the O'Hara plantation. Although legally held to be a parody, Randall's work is not funny, but an incisive critique of the persistent romantic myths of the Old South and race relations. In *Suntrust Bank v. Houghton Mifflin*, the 11th Circuit held:

Alice Randall's [*The Wind Done Gone*] is more than an abstract, pure fictional work. It is principally and purposefully a critical statement that seeks to rebut and destroy the perspective, judgments, and mythology of [*Gone With the Wind*]. Randall's literary goal is to explode the romantic, idealized portrait of the antebellum South during and after the Civil War. In the world of [*Gone With the Wind*], the white characters comprise a noble aristocracy whose idyllic existence is upset only by the intrusion of Yankee soldiers, and, eventually, by the liberation of the black slaves. Through her characters as well as through direct narration, Mitchell describes how both blacks and whites were purportedly better off in the days of slavery: "The more I see of emancipation the more criminal I think it is. It's just ruined the darkies," says Scarlett O'Hara. *GWTW* at 639. Free blacks are described as "creatures of small intelligence . . . [l]ike monkeys or small children turned loose among treasured objects whose value is beyond their comprehension, they ran wild—either from perverse pleasure in destruction or simply because of their ignorance." *Id.* at 654. Blacks elected to the legislature are described as spending "most of their time eating goobers and easing their unaccustomed feet into and out of new shoes." *Id.* at 904.

As the district court noted: "The earlier work is a third-person epic, whereas the new work is told in the first-person as an intimate diary of the life of Cynara. Thematically, the new work provides a different viewpoint of the antebellum world." 136 F.Supp.2d at 1367. While told from a different perspective, more critically, the story is transformed into a very different tale, albeit much more abbreviated. Cynara's very language is a departure from Mitchell's original prose; she acts as the voice of Randall's inversion of [*Gone With the Wind*]. She is the vehicle of parody; she is its means—not its end. It is clear within the first fifty pages of Cynara's fictional diary that Randall's work flips [*Gone With the Wind*]'s traditional race roles, portrays powerful whites as stupid or feckless, and generally sets out to demystify [*Gone With the Wind*] and strip the romanticism from Mitchell's specific account of this period of our history. Approximately the last half of [*The Wind Done Gone*] tells a completely new story that, although involving characters based on [*Gone With the Wind*] characters, features plot elements found nowhere within the covers of [*Gone With the Wind*].

Where Randall refers directly to Mitchell's plot and characters, she does so in service of her general attack on [*Gone With the Wind*]. In [*Gone With the Wind*], Scarlett O'Hara often expresses disgust with and condescension towards blacks; in [*The Wind Done Gone*], Other, Scarlett's counterpart, is herself of mixed descent. In [*Gone With the Wind*], Ashley Wilkes is the initial object of Scarlett's affection; in [*The Wind Done Gone*], he is homosexual. In [*Gone With the Wind*], Rhett Butler does not consort with black female characters and is portrayed as the captain of his own destiny. In [*The Wind Done Gone*], Cynara ends her affair with Rhett's counterpart, R., to begin a relationship with a black Congressman; R. ends up a washed out former cad. In [*The Wind Done Gone*], nearly every black character is given some redeeming quality—whether depth, wit, cunning, beauty, strength, or courage—that their [*Gone With the Wind*] analogues lacked.

Suntrust Bank v. Houghton Mifflin Co., 268 F.3d 1257, 1270–71 (11th Cir. 2001).

8.   *The Washington Redskins and Other Native People Images.* Many sports teams around the country use Native American images and Native American names as sports mascots. High school, college, and professional sports organizations have been criticized for using images and names considered disparaging by many Native Americans and which promote negative and harmful stereotypes of Native Americans in the media and popular culture. Perhaps the most prominent example of this phenomenon is the Washington, D.C. professional football team, the Redskins. Along with attempts to bring awareness of the issue of the team's name, opponents to the use of the Redskins name and Native American mascot have sought out creative legal avenues to address the issue. Most notably, a 2014 decision of the Trademark Trial and Appeal Board granted a petition to cancel the "Redskins" trademarks under a rarely-used provision of the Lanham Act that allows a registered trademark to be cancelled if it is perceived to be disparaging to a substantial composite of the referenced group (i.e., Native Americans). In July 2015, this decision was affirmed by a federal judge in the District of D.C., who clarified that the denial of trademark protection for the "Redskins" trademarks did not prohibit the use of the term or images. Thus, despite this decision, which may reflect and subsequently influence public opinion, the football team and many others continue to use Native American images and references. In a poll of Native Americans by the Washington Post, 9 out of 10 Native Americans said that the name "Redskins" did not disparage Indians. Additionally, 80% of the respondents reported that they would not be offended if a non-Native person called them a "redskin." Should the football team be allowed to use the name if most Native Americans do not find it offensive? Should the views of Native Americans be dispositive of the issue?

Similarly, many towns and municipalities include Native American imagery (examples included below). Many local governments have voted to change their logos, while others retain the use of Native American images, raising questions about the use of potentially disparaging imagery by state actors. Consider the symbols below. Do you find them both appropriate, both offensive, one appropriate and the other offensive? If so, why?

9. *Navigating Linguistic Ambiguity.* Issues of appropriation, ambiguity of meaning, and in-group vs. out-group politics are difficult terrains to navigate. There are real debates over the meaning of words— linguistic ambiguity. And yet courts and constitutional doctrine may not have the flexibility necessary to deal with the nuance and context required to truly assess the ramifications of hate speech. In the context of adjudication, the results have to be binary and do not allow for shades of meaning. But what elements of the context should courts even consider? Could courts really determine whether a word uttered constituted hate speech by the color of the speaker's skin? As processes of appropriation and reappropriation become more prevalent, will there be another approach that makes sense? Does the difficulty of the task justify not addressing the prevalence of hate speech and hate crimes in our society?

Furthermore, do we trust ourselves to "know it when we see it"? Do we trust judges to know hate speech when they see it? Especially if one moves away from a model of animus/intent and focuses on the harm to the victim, can we really claim the harm is different based on who the speaker or victim is? Would distinguishing between in-group and out-group uses constitute viewpoint discrimination or violate the Fourteenth Amendment? Or is it just another instance of using race as a proxy that many fighting for racial justice want to disrupt?

In his book *Nigger: The Strange Career of a Troublesome Word*, Randall Kennedy relates the story of David Howard, which highlights the dangers of focusing exclusively on the victim. David Howard was the white director of a municipal agency in Washington D.C., forced to resign after telling his employees he would have to be "niggardly" with the money at his disposal due to recent budget cuts. After a public outcry, Howard submitted his resignation, which the Mayor of Washington D.C. accepted, stating that Howard had shown poor judgment. Even after clarification that the word niggardly, meaning 'miserly,' was not etymologically related to the racial slur, many remained highly critical of Howard. Columnist Debra Dickerson wrote that "[i]t matters here that anyone like Howard, involved in D.C. politics and putatively well-intentioned toward blacks, would use an obscure word that incorporates the hated slur, rather than one of its many synonyms." Is this a fair indictment?

VI. CONCLUSION

Are hate speech laws necessary and beneficial in an increasingly multicultural contemporary context? Is First Amendment doctrine too wooden to properly take account of the harms of hate speech? Or would we be better off handling the problem of hate speech by addressing its underlying causes rather than trying to regulate it?

Not too long after he became the first African American Attorney General of the United States, Eric Holder gave a speech in which he said that even though "race-related issues continue to occupy a significant portion of our political discussion, and though there remain many unresolved racial issues in this nation, we, average Americans, simply do not talk enough with each other about things racial." More controversial, Mr. Holder went on to say "in things racial we have always been and continue to be, in too many ways, essentially a nation of cowards." As we conclude this chapter, we invite you to reflect on two issues. First, do we need to talk more about race? If so, how do we do that? Many white Americans often complain that they risk being labelled racist whenever they talk about race. Many people of color complain that many white Americans are unwilling to confront difficult racial issues and talk about race, at least when people of color are present. Is either view justified? Are both? How often do you talk about race with someone of a different race?

The second question is whether talking about race will change racial attitudes and reduce material racial inequality. What is the relationship between racial discourse and structural discrimination or material inequalities: is it indicative of them, derive its power to wound from them, or merely distract one from them? There are two forms of the materialist critique of the current debate around racist speech. The first is that the focus on social constructs and speech distracts us from the important structural and material inequalities—without changing these fundamental power relations, the problem of hate speech can never truly be overcome. Professor Henry Louis Gates, Jr., advocates this position: "The problem may be that the continuing economic and material inequality between black and white America—and, more pointedly, the continuing immiseration of large segments of black America—cannot be erased simply through better racial attitudes." Henry Louis Gates, Jr., *Critical Race Theory and the First Amendment* in SPEAKING OF RACE, SPEAKING OF SEX 56 (1993). But can the material inequalities ever be erased without a change in racial attitudes? Should we be arguing about words that wound when people of color suffer from material inequality in housing, schooling, education, criminal justice, etc.?

The second materialist position argues the opposite side of Gates's point: it is precisely because there are material inequalities between the majority and minority groups that racial discourse is helpful and racist expression so harmful. Hate speech enables the persistence of these inequalities. Racial discourse reveals them. Which position do you incline toward and why?

CHAPTER 10

VOTING RIGHTS AND ELECTORAL PARTICIPATION

I. INTRODUCTION

The right to vote is both symbolic and instrumental. Voting expresses one's membership in the polity, and it provides a means through which to shape the laws and practices that govern one's life. Typically, only citizens are allowed to participate in the project of self-governance, though for much of our history, not all citizens. In the early Republic, only propertied white males were permitted to vote. Women, poor people, the illiterate, adherents of disfavored religions, and people convicted of certain crimes all have been disenfranchised, and some still are today.

Throughout American history, the right to vote has been denied on the basis of race, if not formally, then at least in practice. Slaves, of course, were not permitted to vote, and by the 1800s (after a time of greater openness during the colonial period) most states denied to the right to vote to free black people. ALEXANDER KEYSSAR, THE RIGHT TO VOTE: THE CONTESTED HISTORY OF DEMOCRACY IN THE UNITED STATES 44 (2009). By 1855, only five states, Massachusetts, Vermont, New Hampshire, Maine, and Rhode Island, did not formally deny the right to vote to free blacks. *Id.* The majority of states prohibited non-citizens from voting, and naturalization and the concomitant access to the franchise were denied to certain groups on the basis of race, including to Native peoples and Chinese immigrants. The circumscribing of the right to vote was a means of, in the words of historian Eric Foner, "defin[ing] a collective national identity." ERIC FONER, RECONSTRUCTION: AMERICA'S UNFINISHED REVOLUTION 1863–1877 278 (2005). Restrictions on voting were also a means of shaping the outcomes of the democratic process. As Harold Lasswell has put it, voting helps to determine who gets what, when, and how. *See* HAROLD LASSWELL, POLITICS, WHO GETS WHAT, WHEN, AND HOW (1936). Thus, racial restrictions on voting not only defined the polity by reference to the exclusion of African Americans, Native peoples, Chinese Americans, and other people of color, they also precluded people of color from asserting their interests in the political process—from influencing who gets what, when and how.

The Reconstruction Amendments were intended in part to free African Americans from racial discrimination in the political process. As a condition of their readmission to the Union, the Military Reconstruction Act required the former states of the Confederacy to include in their constitutions a provision that granted the right to vote without racial discrimination. As a means of overruling *Dred Scott v. Sanford*, 60 U.S. 393 (1857), the first section of Fourteenth Amendment of 1868 accorded both state and national citizenship to the freed slaves and prohibited the denial of equal protection of the laws. The second section penalized states for denying the right to vote to any adult male citizens in the state. The Fifteenth Amendment, ratified in 1870, went further, declaring: "The right of citizens of the United States to vote shall not be denied or abridged by the United States or by any State on account of race, color, or previous condition of servitude." Both Amendments granted Congress the power to enforce their protections through appropriate legislation.

In the years after the Civil War, the Reconstruction Amendments made real the right to vote for African-American men only for a brief period. During Reconstruction, the federal government supervised the electoral process in the Southern states, and Congress passed three Enforcement Acts between 1870 and 1871 that sought to limit racial discrimination in voting. "At the high point of southern black voting during Reconstruction, about two-thirds of eligible black males cast ballots in presidential and gubernatorial contests." Chandler Davidson, *The Voting Rights Act: A Brief History, in* Controversies in Minority Voting 7, 10 (Bernard Grofman & Chandler Davidson eds., 1992). Hundreds of African Americans were elected to national and state offices from the former Confederate states. J. Morgan Kousser, Colorblind Injustice: Minority Voting Rights and the Undoing of the Second Reconstruction 19 (1999).

The end of Reconstruction in 1877, barely a decade after the reestablishment of the Union, effectively ended most African Americans' opportunity to cast a vote. Officials in southern states employed all manner of schemes to prevent African Americans from voting. When whites regained control of the state legislatures, in what become known as "Redemption," they disenfranchised black voters through violence and intimidation, manipulating the size and shape of legislative districts, mandating that party primaries (which were necessary to reach the general election) be all white, and through poll taxes and literacy requirements. Rejecting the non-discrimination provisions that they had previously been forced to include in their constitutions, Southern states amended their constitutions for the precise purpose of disenfranchising black voters. *See* J. Morgan Kousser, *The Undermining of the First Reconstruction: Lessons for the Second, in* Minority Vote Dilution 30 (Chandler Davidson ed., 1989). By the early 1900s, many of the former confederate states had disenfranchised the vast majority of black citizens. *See* Chandler Davidson, *The Recent Evolution of Voting Rights Law Affecting Racial and Language Minorities, in* Quiet Revolution in the South: The Impact of the Voting Rights Act, 1965–1990 21 (Chandler Davidson and Bernard Grofman eds., 1994).

Piecemeal efforts to protect African Americans' right to vote were ineffective. Congressional legislation that allowed for case-by-case litigation by the Attorney General and the Department of Justice was no match for wily southern officials who quickly passed new discriminatory procedures to replace ones that were struck down. Into the early 1960s, black voter registration still lagged far behind that of whites, with less than 20% of blacks registered to vote in Alabama, and less than 7% in Mississippi. *See Shelby Cty. v. Holder*, 133 S.Ct. 2612, 2624 (2013). As the Supreme Court has concluded, "[t]he first century of congressional enforcement of the [Fifteenth] Amendment . . . can only be regarded as a failure." *Northwest Austin Municipal Util. Dist. No. One v. Holder*, 557 U.S. 193, 197 (2009).

It was not until 1965 that our nation began to make real for African Americans the promise of the right to vote. President Lyndon Johnson signed the Voting Rights Act (VRA) on August 6, 1965, and a new era began. The Act was a direct product of the Civil Rights Movement, spurred in part by the violence and terrorism with which some southerners met non-violent protest. The Act was a watershed development that aimed both to protect individuals' right to vote and enable African Americans as a group to influence the political process. Congress enacted the statute pursuant to its authority to enforce the Fifteenth Amendment. As you will see in detail below, the Act imposed a variety of federal restrictions on what had long been a state managed process. The Act was and remains controversial as a result, and some critics contend that Congress illegitimately put the states in a sort of federal receivership, in violation of the Constitution.

This chapter begins with the Voting Rights Act to engage three broad questions related to voting rights and political participation. First, how can and should the law regulate state efforts to restrict or burden individuals' right to vote? Second, how can and should the law facilitate the efforts of minorities as groups to play a meaningful role in the process of self-governance? Voters of color desire not simply to vote but also to advance their interests and policy preferences and to hold political leaders accountable. The grant of the right to vote, by itself, does not necessarily accomplish that group-oriented goal. Electoral structures— the drawing of legislative districts, for example—can bolster or thwart a group's ability to influence the political process. Third, and most generally, this chapter considers the extent and nature of the role that race should play in the political process. Should we accept race as a basis for political identity and mobilization? And enforce such self-understandings through law? Or should we aspire to a colorblind politics, and use law to move us toward that ideal? The chapter also touches on the continued efforts by states to make it harder for individuals to vote. Despite legal prohibitions and the formal protection of the right to vote, states continue to make voting difficult or impossible for some people. Can modern practice be reconciled with the ostensible formal legal right?

II. PROTECTING VOTING AS AN INDIVIDUAL RIGHT

As you read *South Carolina v. Katzenbach*, below, consider three key questions. First, could Congress have designed the VRA differently? Second, does the VRA sacrifice federalism values to the cause of racial equality? If so, was that sacrifice necessary? Third, to what extent is the Civil Rights Movement that made the VRA possible a model for social and racial change?

A. REMEDYING RACIAL DISCRIMINATION IN VOTING

South Carolina v. Katzenbach
Supreme Court of the United States, 1966.
383 U.S. 301.

■ MR. CHIEF JUSTICE WARREN delivered the opinion of the Court.

South Carolina has filed a bill of complaint, seeking a declaration that selected provisions of the Voting Rights Act of 1965 violate the Federal Constitution, and asking for an injunction against enforcement of these provisions by the Attorney General.

Recognizing that the questions presented were of urgent concern to the entire country, we invited all of the States to participate in this proceeding as friends of the Court. A majority responded by submitting or joining in briefs on the merits, some supporting South Carolina and others the Attorney General. Seven of these States also requested and received permission to argue the case orally at our hearing. Without exception, despite the emotional overtones of the proceeding, the briefs and oral arguments were temperate, lawyerlike and constructive. All viewpoints on the issues have been fully developed, and this additional assistance has been most helpful to the Court.

The Voting Rights Act was designed by Congress to banish the blight of racial discrimination in voting, which has infected the electoral process in parts of our country for nearly a century. The Act creates stringent new remedies for voting discrimination where it persists on a pervasive scale, and in addition the statute strengthens existing remedies for pockets of voting discrimination elsewhere in the country. Congress assumed the power to prescribe these remedies from § 2 of the Fifteenth Amendment, which authorizes the National Legislature to effectuate by 'appropriate' measures the constitutional prohibition against racial discrimination in voting. We hold that the sections of the Act which are properly before us are an appropriate means for carrying out Congress' constitutional responsibilities and are consonant with all other provisions of the Constitution. We therefore deny South Carolina's request that enforcement of these sections of the Act be enjoined.

I.

The constitutional propriety of the Voting Rights Act of 1965 must be judged with reference to the historical experience which it reflects. Before enacting the measure, Congress explored with great care the problem of racial discrimination in voting. The House and Senate Committees on the Judiciary each held hearings for nine days and received testimony from a total of 67 witnesses. More than three full days were consumed discussing the bill on the floor of the House, while the debate in the Senate covered 26 days in all. At the close of these deliberations, the verdict of both chambers was overwhelming. The House approved the bill by a vote of 328–74, and the measure passed the Senate by a margin of 79–18.

Two points emerge vividly from the voluminous legislative history of the Act contained in the committee hearings and floor debates. First: Congress felt itself confronted by an insidious and pervasive evil which had been perpetuated in certain parts of our country through unremitting and ingenious defiance of the Constitution. Second: Congress concluded that the unsuccessful remedies which it had prescribed in the past would have to be replaced by sterner and more elaborate measures in order to satisfy the clear commands of the Fifteenth Amendment. We pause here to summarize the majority reports of the House and Senate Committees, which document in considerable detail the factual basis for these reactions by Congress.

The Fifteenth Amendment to the Constitution was ratified in 1870. Promptly thereafter Congress passed the Enforcement Act of 1870, which made it a crime for public officers and private persons to obstruct exercise of the right to vote. The statute was amended in the following year to provide for detailed federal supervision of the electoral process, from registration to the certification of returns. As the years passed and fervor for racial equality waned, enforcement of the laws became spotty and ineffective, and most of their provisions were repealed in 1894. The remnants have had little significance in the recently renewed battle against voting discrimination.

Meanwhile, beginning in 1890, the States of Alabama, Georgia, Louisiana, Mississippi, North Carolina, South Carolina, and Virginia enacted tests still in use which were specifically designed to prevent Negroes from voting.[1] Typically, they made the ability to read and write

---

[1] The South Carolina Constitutional Convention of 1895 was a leader in the widespread movement to disenfranchise Negroes. Key, Southern Politics, 537–539. Senator Ben Tillman frankly explained to the state delegates the aim of the new literacy test: '(T)he only thing we can do as patriots and as statesmen is to take from (the 'ignorant blacks') every ballot that we can under the laws of our national government.' He was equally candid about the exemption from the literacy test for persons who could 'understand' and 'explain' a section of the state constitution: 'There is no particle of fraud or illegality in it. It is just simply showing partiality, perhaps, (laughter,) or discriminating.' He described the alternative exemption for persons paying state property taxes in the same vein: 'By means of the $300 clause you simply reach out and take in some more white men and a few more colored men.' Journal of the Constitutional

a registration qualification and also required completion of a registration form. These laws were based on the fact that as of 1890 in each of the named States, more than two-thirds of the adult Negroes were illiterate while less than one-quarter of the adult whites were unable to read or write. At the same time, alternate tests were prescribed in all of the named States to assure that white illiterates would not be deprived of the franchise. These included grandfather clauses, property qualifications, 'good character' tests, and the requirement that registrants 'understand' or 'interpret' certain matter.

The course of subsequent Fifteenth Amendment litigation in this Court demonstrates the variety and persistence of these and similar institutions designed to deprive Negroes of the right to vote. Grandfather clauses were invalidated in Guinn v. United States, and Myers v. Anderson. Procedural hurdles were struck down in Lane v. Wilson. The white primary was outlawed in Smith v. Allwright, and Terry v. Adams. Improper challenges were nullified in United States v. Thomas. Racial gerrymandering was forbidden by Gomillion v. Lightfoot. Finally, discriminatory application of voting tests was condemned in Schnell v. Davis; Alabama v. United States, and Louisiana v. United States.

According to the evidence in recent Justice Department voting suits, the latter stratagem is now the principal method used to bar Negroes from the polls. Discriminatory administration of voting qualifications has been found in all eight Alabama cases, in all nine Louisiana cases, and in all nine Mississippi cases which have gone to final judgment. Moreover, in almost all of these cases, the courts have held that the discrimination was pursuant to a widespread 'pattern or practice.' White applicants for registration have often been excused altogether from the literacy and understanding tests or have been given easy versions, have received extensive help from voting officials, and have been registered despite serious errors in their answers.[2] Negroes, on the other hand, have typically been required to pass difficult versions of all the tests, without any outside assistance and without the slightest error. The good-morals requirement is so vague and subjective that it has constituted an open invitation to abuse at the hands of voting officials. Negroes obliged to obtain vouchers from registered voters have found it virtually impossible to comply in areas where almost no Negroes are on the rolls.

In recent years, Congress has repeatedly tried to cope with the problem by facilitating case-by-case litigation against voting discrimination. The Civil Rights Act of 1957 authorized the Attorney General to seek injunctions against public and private interference with

---

Convention of the State of South Carolina 464, 469, 471 (1895). Senator Tillman was the dominant political figure in the state convention, and his entire address merits examination.

   [2]   A white applicant in Louisiana satisfied the registrar of his ability to interpret the state constitution by writing, 'FRDUM FOOF SPETGH.' A white applicant in Alabama who had never completed the first grade of school was enrolled after the registrar filled out the entire form for him.

the right to vote on racial grounds. Perfecting amendments in the Civil Rights Act of 1960 permitted the joinder of States as parties defendant, gave the Attorney General access to local voting records, and authorized courts to register voters in areas of systematic discrimination. Title I of the Civil Rights Act of 1964 expedited the hearing of voting cases before three-judge courts and outlawed some of the tactics used to disqualify Negroes from voting in federal elections.

Despite the earnest efforts of the Justice Department and of many federal judges, these new laws have done little to cure the problem of voting discrimination. According to estimates by the Attorney General during hearings on the Act, registration of voting-age Negroes in Alabama rose only from 14.2% to 19.4% between 1958 and 1964; in Louisiana it barely inched ahead from 31.7% to 31.8% between 1956 and 1965; and in Mississippi it increased only from 4.4% to 6.4% between 1954 and 1964. In each instance, registration of voting-age whites ran roughly 50 percentage points or more ahead of Negro registration.

During the hearings and debates on the Act, Selma, Alabama, was repeatedly referred to as the pre-eminent example of the ineffectiveness of existing legislation. In Dallas County, of which Selma is the seat, there were four years of litigation by the Justice Department and two findings by the federal courts of widespread voting discrimination. Yet in those four years, Negro registration rose only from 156 to 383, although there are approximately 15,000 Negroes of voting age in the county. Any possibility that these figures were attributable to political apathy was dispelled by the protest demonstrations in Selma in the early months of 1965.

II.

The Voting Rights Act of 1965 reflects Congress' firm intention to rid the country of racial discrimination in voting. The heart of the Act is a complex scheme of stringent remedies aimed at areas where voting discrimination has been most flagrant. Section 4(a)–(d) lays down a formula defining the States and political subdivisions to which these new remedies apply. The first of the remedies, contained in § 4(a), is the suspension of literacy tests and similar voting qualifications for a period of five years from the last occurrence of substantial voting discrimination. Section 5 prescribes a second remedy, the suspension of all new voting regulations pending review by federal authorities to determine whether their use would perpetuate voting discrimination. The third remedy, covered in ss 6(b), 7, 9, and 13(a), is the assignment of federal examiners on certification by the Attorney General to list qualified applicants who are thereafter entitled to vote in all elections.

Other provisions of the Act prescribe subsidiary cures for persistent voting discrimination. Section 8 authorizes the appointment of federal poll-watchers in places to which federal examiners have already been assigned. Section 10(d) excuses those made eligible to vote in sections of the country covered by § 4(b) of the Act from paying accumulated past poll taxes for state and local elections. Section 12(e) provides for balloting by persons denied access to the polls in areas where federal examiners have been appointed.

The remaining remedial portions of the Act are aimed at voting discrimination in any area of the country where it may occur. Section 2 broadly prohibits the use of voting rules to abridge exercise of the franchise on racial grounds. Sections 3, 6(a), and 13(b) strengthen existing procedures for attacking voting discrimination by means of litigation. Section 4(e) excuses citizens educated in American schools conducted in a foreign language from passing English-language literacy tests. Section 10(a)–(c) facilitates constitutional litigation challenging the imposition of all poll taxes for state and local elections. Sections 11 and 12(a)–(d) authorize civil and criminal sanctions against interference with the exercise of rights guaranteed by the Act.

Coverage formula.

The remedial sections of the Act assailed by South Carolina automatically apply to any State, or to any separate political subdivision such as county or parish, for which two findings have been made: (1) the Attorney General has determined that on November 1, 1964, it maintained a "test or device," and (2) the Director of the Census has determined that less than 50% of its voting age residents were registered on November 1, 1964, or voted in the presidential election of November 1964. These findings are not reviewable in any court and are final upon publication in the Federal Register. § 4(b). As used throughout the Act, the phrase "test or device" means any requirement that a registrant or voter must "(1) demonstrate the ability to read, write, understand, or interpret any matter, (2) demonstrate any educational achievement or his knowledge of any particular subject, (3) possess good moral character, or (4) prove his qualifications by the voucher of registered voters or members of any other class." § 4(c).

South Carolina was brought within the coverage formula of the Act on August 7, 1965, pursuant to appropriate administrative determinations which have not been challenged in this proceeding. On the same day, coverage was also extended to Alabama, Alaska, Georgia, Louisiana, Mississippi, Virginia, 26 counties in North Carolina, and one county in Arizona. Two more counties in Arizona, one county in Hawaii, and one county in Idaho were added to the list on November 19, 1965. Thus far Alaska, the three Arizona counties, and the single county in Idaho have asked the District Court for the District of Columbia to grant a declaratory judgment terminating statutory coverage.

Suspension of tests.

In a State or political subdivision covered by § 4(b) of the Act, no person may be denied the right to vote in any election because of his failure to comply with a "test or device." § 4(a).

On account of this provision, South Carolina is temporarily barred from enforcing the portion of its voting laws which requires every applicant for registration to show that he:

> Can both read and write any section of (the State) Constitution submitted to (him) by the registration officer or can show that he owns, and has paid all taxes collectible during the previous year on, property in this State assessed at three hundred dollars or more.

The Attorney General has determined that the property qualification is inseparable from the literacy test, and South Carolina makes no objection to this finding. Similar tests and devices have been temporarily suspended in the other sections of the country listed above.

Review of new rules.

In a State or political subdivision covered by § 4(b) of the Act, no person may be denied the right to vote in any election because of his failure to comply with a voting qualification or procedure different from those in force on November 1, 1964.

Federal examiners.

In any political subdivision covered by § 4(b) of the Act, the Civil Service Commission shall appoint voting examiners whenever the Attorney General certifies either of the following facts: (1) that he has received meritorious written complaints from at least 20 residents alleging that they have been disenfranchised under color of law because of their race, or (2) that the appointment of examiners is otherwise necessary to effectuate the guarantees of the Fifteenth Amendment.

III.

These provisions of the Voting Rights Act of 1965 are challenged on the fundamental ground that they exceed the powers of Congress and encroach on an area reserved to the States by the Constitution. South Carolina and certain of the amici curiae also attack specific sections of the Act for more particular reasons. They argue that the coverage formula prescribed in § 4(a)–(d) violates the principle of the equality of States, denies due process by employing an invalid presumption and by barring judicial review of administrative findings, constitutes a forbidden bill of attainder, and impairs the separation of powers by adjudicating guilt through legislation. . . .

The ground rules for resolving this question are clear. The language and purpose of the Fifteenth Amendment, the prior decisions construing its several provisions, and the general doctrines of constitutional interpretation, all point to one fundamental principle. As against the reserved powers of the States, Congress may use any rational means to effectuate the constitutional prohibition of racial discrimination in voting.

Section 1 of the Fifteenth Amendment declares that "(t)he right of citizens of the United States to vote shall not be denied or abridged by the United States or by any State on account of race, color, or previous condition of servitude." This declaration has always been treated as self-executing and has repeatedly been construed, without further legislative specification, to invalidate state voting qualifications or procedures which are discriminatory on their face or in practice.

[Section]2 of the Fifteenth Amendment expressly declares that "Congress shall have power to enforce this article by appropriate legislation." By adding this authorization, the Framers indicated that Congress was to be chiefly responsible for implementing the rights created in § 1. "It is the power of Congress which has been enlarged. Congress is authorized to *enforce* the prohibitions by appropriate legislation. Some legislation is contemplated to make the Civil War amendments fully effective." Accordingly, in addition to the courts, Congress has full remedial powers to effectuate the constitutional prohibition against racial discrimination in voting.

Congress has repeatedly exercised these powers in the past, and its enactments have repeatedly been upheld. On the rare occasions when the Court has found an unconstitutional exercise of these powers, in its opinion Congress had attacked evils not comprehended by the Fifteenth Amendment.

The basic test to be applied in a case involving § 2 of the Fifteenth Amendment is the same as in all cases concerning the express powers of Congress with relation to the reserved powers of the States. Chief Justice Marshall laid down the classic formulation, 50 years before the Fifteenth Amendment was ratified:

> "Let the end be legitimate, let it be within the scope of the constitution, and all means which are appropriate, which are plainly adapted to that end, which are not prohibited, but consist with the letter and spirit of the constitution, are constitutional." McCulloch v. Maryland.

We therefore reject South Carolina's argument that Congress may appropriately do no more than to forbid violations of the Fifteenth Amendment in general terms—that the task of fashioning specific remedies or of applying them to particular localities must necessarily be left entirely to the courts.

IV.

Congress exercised its authority under the Fifteenth Amendment in an inventive manner when it enacted the Voting Rights Act of 1965. First: The measure prescribes remedies for voting discrimination which go into effect without any need for prior adjudication. This was clearly a legitimate response to the problem, for which there is ample precedent under other constitutional provisions. Congress had found that case-by-case litigation was inadequate to combat widespread and persistent discrimination in voting, because of the inordinate amount of time and energy required to overcome the obstructionist tactics invariably encountered in these lawsuits. After enduring nearly a century of systematic resistance to the Fifteenth Amendment, Congress might well decide to shift the advantage of time and inertia from the perpetrators of the evil to its victims. The question remains, of course, whether the specific remedies prescribed in the Act were an appropriate means of combatting the evil, and to this question we shall presently address ourselves.

Second: The Act intentionally confines these remedies to a small number of States and political subdivisions which in most instances were familiar to Congress by name. This, too, was a permissible method of dealing with the problem. Congress had learned that substantial voting discrimination presently occurs in certain sections of the country, and it knew no way of accurately forecasting whether the evil might spread elsewhere in the future. In acceptable legislative fashion, Congress chose to limit its attention to the geographic areas where immediate action seemed necessary. The doctrine of the equality of States, invoked by South Carolina, does not bar this approach, for that doctrine applies only to the terms upon which States are admitted to the Union, and not to the remedies for local evils which have subsequently appeared.

Coverage formula.

We now consider the related question of whether the specific States and political subdivisions within § 4(b) of the Act were an appropriate target for the new remedies. South Carolina contends that the coverage formula is awkwardly designed in a number of respects and that it disregards various local conditions which have nothing to do with racial discrimination. These arguments, however, are largely beside the point. Congress began work with reliable evidence of actual voting discrimination in a great majority of the States and political subdivisions affected by the new remedies of the Act. The formula eventually evolved to describe these areas was relevant to the problem of voting discrimination, and Congress was therefore entitled to infer a significant danger of the evil in the few remaining States and political subdivisions covered by § 4(b) of the Act. No more was required to justify the application to these areas of Congress' express powers under the Fifteenth Amendment.

The areas for which there was evidence of actual voting discrimination share two characteristics incorporated by Congress into the coverage formula: the use of tests and devices for voter registration, and a voting rate in the 1964 presidential election at least 12 points below the national average. Tests and devices are relevant to voting discrimination because of their long history as a tool for perpetrating the evil; a low voting rate is pertinent for the obvious reason that widespread disenfranchisement must inevitably affect the number of actual voters. Accordingly, the coverage formula is rational in both practice and theory. It was therefore permissible to impose the new remedies on the few remaining States and political subdivisions covered by the formula, at least in the absence of proof that they have been free of substantial voting discrimination in recent years.

Suspension of tests.

We now arrive at consideration of the specific remedies prescribed by the Act for areas included within the coverage formula. South Carolina assails the temporary suspension of existing voting qualifications, reciting the rule laid down by Lassiter v. Northampton County Bd. of Elections, that literacy tests and related devices are not in themselves contrary to the Fifteenth Amendment. In that very case, however, the Court went on to say, 'Of course a literacy test, fair on its face, may be employed to perpetuate that discrimination which the Fifteenth Amendment was designed to uproot.' The record shows that in most of the States covered by the Act, including South Carolina, various tests and devices have been instituted with the purpose of disenfranchising Negroes, have been framed in such a way as to facilitate this aim, and have been administered in a discriminatory fashion for many years. Under these circumstances, the Fifteenth Amendment has clearly been violated.

The Act suspends literacy tests and similar devices for a period of five years from the last occurrence of substantial voting discrimination. This was a legitimate response to the problem, for which there is ample precedent in Fifteenth Amendment cases. Underlying the response was the feeling that States and political subdivisions which had been allowing white illiterates to vote for years could not sincerely complain about 'dilution' of their electorates through the registration of Negro illiterates. Congress knew that continuance of the tests and devices in use at the present time, no matter how fairly administered in the future, would freeze the effect of past discrimination in favor of unqualified white registrants. Congress permissibly rejected the alternative of requiring a complete re-registration of all voters, believing that this would be too harsh on many whites who had enjoyed the franchise for their entire adult lives.

Review of new rules.

The Act suspends new voting regulations pending scrutiny by federal authorities to determine whether their use would violate the Fifteenth Amendment. This may have been an uncommon exercise of congressional power, as South Carolina contends, but the Court has recognized that exceptional conditions can justify legislative measures not otherwise appropriate. Congress knew that some of the States covered by § 4(b) of the Act had resorted to the extraordinary stratagem of contriving new rules of various kinds for the sole purpose of perpetuating voting discrimination in the face of adverse federal court decrees. Congress had reason to suppose that these States might try similar maneuvers in the future in order to evade the remedies for voting discrimination contained in the Act itself. Under the compulsion of these unique circumstances, Congress responded in a permissibly decisive manner.

After enduring nearly a century of widespread resistance to the Fifteenth Amendment, Congress has marshalled an array of potent weapons against the evil, with authority in the Attorney General to employ them effectively. Many of the areas directly affected by this development have indicated their willingness to abide by any restraints legitimately imposed upon them. We here hold that the portions of the Voting Rights Act properly before us are a valid means for carrying out the commands of the Fifteenth Amendment. Hopefully, millions of non-white Americans will now be able to participate for the first time on an equal basis in the government under which they live. We may finally look forward to the day when truly "[t]he right of citizens of the United States to vote shall not be denied or abridged by the United States or by any State on account of race, color, or previous condition of servitude."

■ MR. JUSTICE BLACK, concurring and dissenting.

I agree with substantially all of the Court's opinion sustaining the power of Congress under § 2 of the Fifteenth Amendment to suspend state literacy tests and similar voting qualifications and to authorize the Attorney General to secure the appointment of federal examiners to register qualified voters in various sections of the country.

Though . . . I dissent from its holding that every part of § 5 of the Act is constitutional.

(a) The Constitution gives federal courts jurisdiction over cases and controversies only. [It] it is hard for me to believe that a justiciable controversy can arise in the constitutional sense from a desire by the United States Government or some of its officials to determine in advance what legislative provisions a State may enact or what constitutional amendments it may adopt.

(b) My second and more basic objection to § 5 is that Congress has here exercised its power under § 2 of the Fifteenth Amendment through the adoption of means that conflict with the most basic principles of the Constitution. One of the most basic premises upon which our structure of government was founded was that the Federal Government was to have certain specific and limited powers and no others, and all other power was to be reserved either "to the States respectively, or to the people." Certainly if all the provisions of our Constitution, which limit the power of the Federal Government and reserve other power to the States are to mean anything, they mean at least that the States have power to pass laws and amend their constitutions without first sending their officials hundreds of miles away to beg federal authorities to approve them. Moreover, it seems to me that § 5 which gives federal officials power to veto state laws they do not like is in direct conflict with the clear command of our Constitution that "The United States shall guarantee to every State in this Union a Republican Form of Government."

I cannot help but believe that the inevitable effect of any such law which forces any one of the States to entreat federal authorities in faraway places for approval of local laws before they can become effective is to create the impression that the State or States treated in this way are little more than conquered provinces. It is inconceivable to me that such a radical degradation of state power was intended in any of the provisions of our Constitution or its Amendments. Of course I do not mean to cast any doubt whatever upon the indisputable power of the Federal Government to invalidate a state law once enacted and operative on the ground that it intrudes into the area of supreme federal power. But the Federal Government has heretofore always been content to exercise this power to protect federal supremacy by authorizing its agents to bring lawsuits against state officials once and operative state law has created an actual case and controversy. A federal law which assumes the power to compel the States to submit in advance any proposed legislation they have for approval by federal agents approaches dangerously near to wiping the States out as useful and effective units in the government of our country. I cannot agree to any constitutional interpretation that leads inevitably to such a result.

NOTES AND QUESTIONS

1. ***Understanding the VRA.*** To appreciate the issues in *Katzenbach* and why the VRA was and is controversial, one must understand the complex provisions of the Act. The Act attacked the problem of voting discrimination in a number of ways.

   a. The DOJ as watchdog. It made the Department of Justice the chief administrator of the Act and the entity responsible for enforcing the guarantees of the Fifteenth Amendment.

   b. Federal examiners and registrars. It provided a mechanism for courts to appoint federal examiners to monitor jurisdictions sued by the DOJ. The VRA also provided registrars to help register voters and make sure that legitimate voting qualifications were fairly applied.

   c. English literacy provision. It prohibited states or subdivisions from conditioning the right to vote on the ability to read or write English for individuals educated in territories under American control, such as Puerto Rico, who have completed the sixth grade and for whom the predominant language of instruction was other than English.

   d. Section 2 and racial discrimination. Section 2 of the Act applies nationwide and precludes any state or political subdivision from applying a voting qualification or prerequisite to voting that denies a voter the right to vote on the basis of race. Congress amended section 2 in 1982 to include a disparate impact requirement, which transformed it into an important regulatory tool.

[handwritten margin note: I recognized in VRA via 1982 amendment!]

e. The core of the Act. The core and most controversial part of the Act is the coverage formula-preclearance tandem contained in sections 4 and 5. Sections 4 and 5 of the VRA targeted the jurisdictions that were the worst offenders, almost all of which were in the South. Though Congress knew which jurisdictions had engaged in the most flagrant discrimination, it did not name them. Rather, it created a formula to determine which ones would be covered by the preclearance requirement, indirectly accomplishing the same result.

    i. Section 4(b) of the Act provides two criteria to determine which jurisdictions would be covered by the Act. Section 4(b) applies to (a) any state or political subdivision that used a "test or device" for voting and (b) had a voter registration rate of less than 50 percent or a voter turnout rate of less than 50 percent in the 1964 presidential election. A state or political subdivision meeting those two requirements was a "covered jurisdiction." The Act defined a "test or device" as any legal requirement that demanded a voter: (a) prove that they are literate, (b) demonstrate their educational achievement or knowledge of a particular subject matter, (c) prove that they are person of good moral character; or (d) have someone vouch for them that they are an eligible voter. A covered jurisdiction cannot deny a citizen the right to vote because the citizen has not complied with any test or device. Under the original formula, Alabama, Georgia, Louisiana, Mississippi, South Carolina, Virginia, and over 35 counties in North Carolina became covered jurisdictions.

    ii. Once a jurisdiction has been identified under section 4, section 5 freezes the jurisdiction's laws in place. Section 5 precludes covered jurisdictions from enforcing any new voting qualification, that is a voting rule that was not in place on November 1, 1964, unless they "preclear" the voting qualification first with the Attorney General. Covered jurisdictions can additionally or alternatively submit proposed voting changes to the United States District Court for the District of Columbia. The Attorney General has sixty days to review the submission. The burden of proof is on the covered jurisdiction. If the jurisdiction cannot prove the absence of discrimination, the Attorney General can object to the proposed changes,

[handwritten margin note: ? discrim? ? meaning intent or impact??]

which prevents the jurisdiction from implementing the voting change.

iii. Section 4 also suspended literacy tests, originally for five years and only in the covered jurisdictions. Congress made the ban permanent in 1970 and made it applicable nationwide.

iv. Sections 4 and 5 are temporary provisions and were first enacted for five years. Congress renewed section 5 for another five years in 1970. It also added a new trigger date, November 1968, as the date to determine if a jurisdiction used a test or device. This new date brought in parts of ten states as covered jurisdictions. Congress extended section 5 again for seven years in 1975 and also addressed voting discrimination against language minority groups by requiring certain jurisdictions to provide bilingual ballots. Congress also updated the trigger date to November 1972. It redefined the meaning of "test or device" to include jurisdictions that provided election information in English only. As a consequence of this change, Alaska, Arizona, and Texas were brought in as covered states, as were parts of California, Florida, Michigan, New York, and additional counties in North Carolina, and South Dakota. Congress extended section 5 in 1982 for 25 years, and in 2006 for another 25 years.

v. The Act also contains a provision that allows a covered jurisdiction to "bailout" from coverage. A jurisdiction seeking bailout cannot have used a forbidden test or device, failed to receive preclearance, or engaged in vote dilution in the ten years prior to seeking bailout.

2. Redesigning the VRA? The Court in *Katzenbach* admitted that the VRA contains stringent remedies. But the Court argued that the remedies were justified by the problems that Congress was trying to resolve—the sustained and systematic attempt by many states and jurisdictions to prevent African Americans from exercising their constitutional right to vote. Could Congress have designed the VRA differently? Take preclearance and consider four options: (a) administrative preclearance only; (b) judicial preclearance only; (c) both judicial and administrative preclearance; and (d) neither administrative nor judicial preclearance. Which option would you have chosen and why? What are the benefits and drawbacks of each approach? Now take the coverage formula and consider some options: (a) the current coverage formula; (b) a nationwide coverage formula; (c) a different coverage formula that covers jurisdictions in which less than 90% of eligible voters are registered to vote; and (d) instead of a coverage formula, a statutory provision that spells out an expedited mechanism for individual voters to obtain temporary and permanent injunctions of potentially discriminatory laws. Which option would you choose and why? Do you have any better ideas?

3.   *Costs of Racial Equality.* Justice Black dissents in *Katzenbach*, effectively on the ground that federalism is too important a value to sacrifice on the altar of racial equality. His honest dissent is premised upon the unstated assumption that racial equality is often in tension with other constitutional values that we may hold dear. If achieving racial equality requires curtailing federalism, which one would you choose and why? Do you think that achieving racial equality often comes at a cost to other important values? And if so, what principles or values would you be willing to sacrifice in order to have racial equality?

4.   *The VRA as a Formula for Racial Equality?* The VRA had close to an immediate impact on reducing voting discrimination in the South. In the 1940s, only 3% of African Americans in the South who were eligible to vote were registered to vote. By 1964, on the eve of the VRA, black registration in the South was at 43%. But these aggregate numbers did not paint an accurate picture of how bad things were in the Deep South and in the states with some of the largest black populations. Only 6.7% of eligible black voters were registered to vote in Mississippi, and only 25% in Alabama. Within three years after passage of the VRA, Black registration in Mississippi rose from 6.7% to 59.4%. In Alabama, by 1967, 52% of the black population was registered to vote. Between 1970 and 2000, black officeholding throughout the country rose from just under 2200 to over 9000. Latino officeholding rose from slightly over 3000 in 1984 to just over 5100 by 2007. Some have described the VRA as the most effective civil rights statute that Congress ever passed.

This success likely depended upon two critical factors. First, it emerged from a sweeping social movement that forged a profound political consensus, at least for a time. Second, the VRA's enactment and implementation have entailed cooperation by all three political branches of government. Congress took the lead in passing the VRA. But its amendments have often codified judicial interpretations, many of which have given it a broad reading and filled in gaps in the legislation. Finally, the Department of Justice was also instrumental in the early success of the Act. It interpreted the provisions of the VRA expansively, took its preclearance responsibilities seriously, and worked hand-in-hand with communities of color to understand the potential discriminatory effects of proposed local changes.

5.   *Post-Katzenbach Development.* In the 2013 case of *Shelby County v. Holder*, the United States Supreme Court once again addressed the constitutionality of the VRA but dramatically circumscribed it, holding that the section 4 preclearance formula was unconstitutional. We discuss *Shelby County* and its implications below.

B. CONSTITUTIONAL LIMITS

In Chapter 2, you were introduced to two different visions of racial equality, one that prioritizes anticlassification or colorblindness, and the other that seeks to eradicate racial subordination, even if race consciousness is required to do so. This dichotomy intersects with two other questions posed by this chapter: whether political participation is expressive or instrumental, and how law ought to remedy past discrimination in the political process. In *Rice v. Cayetano*, the United States and Hawaii sought to remedy a supposed past wrong by using a race-conscious mechanism to empower Native Hawaiians. Though the Court did not raise any objections to the government's goals, it objected strongly to the government's race-conscious means of achieving its objectives, on the theory that colorblindness is the Constitution's normative position and that the expressive conception of voting predominates over its instrumental conception. *Rice* exposes the uncertain boundary between race consciousness and race blindness. It also asks us to consider under what circumstances it is justified to use an assertion of formal equality to undo a political compromise designed to remedy a past racial wrong.

Rice v. Cayetano

Supreme Court of the United States, 2000.
528 U.S. 495.

■ JUSTICE KENNEDY delivered the opinion of the Court.

A citizen of Hawaii comes before us claiming that an explicit, race-based voting qualification has barred him from voting in a statewide election. The Fifteenth Amendment to the Constitution of the United States, binding on the National Government, the States, and their political subdivisions, controls the case.

The Hawaiian Constitution limits the right to vote for nine trustees chosen in a statewide election. The trustees compose the governing authority of a state agency known as the Office of Hawaiian Affairs, or OHA. Haw. Const., Art. XII, § 5. The agency administers programs designed for the benefit of two subclasses of the Hawaiian citizenry. The smaller class comprises those designated as "native Hawaiians," defined by statute, with certain supplementary language later set out in full, as descendants of not less than one-half part of the races inhabiting the Hawaiian Islands prior to 1778. Haw.Rev.Stat. § 10–2 (1993). The second, larger class of persons benefited by OHA programs is "Hawaiians," defined to be, with refinements contained in the statute we later quote, those persons who are descendants of people inhabiting the Hawaiian Islands in 1778. *Ibid.* The right to vote for trustees is limited to "Hawaiians," the second, larger class of persons, which of course includes the smaller class of "native Hawaiians." Haw. Const., Art. XII, § 5.

Petitioner Rice, a citizen of Hawaii and thus himself a Hawaiian in a well-accepted sense of the term, does not have the requisite ancestry even for the larger class. He is not, then, a "Hawaiian" in terms of the statute; so he may not vote in the trustee election. The issue presented by this case is whether Rice may be so barred. Rejecting the State's arguments that the classification in question is not racial or that, if it is, it is nevertheless valid for other reasons, we hold Hawaii's denial of petitioner's right to vote to be a clear violation of the Fifteenth Amendment.

I

When Congress and the State of Hawaii enacted the laws we are about to discuss and review, they made their own assessments of the events which intertwine Hawaii's history with the history of America itself. We will begin with a very brief account of that historical background.

The origins of the first Hawaiian people and the date they reached the islands are not established with certainty, but the usual assumption is that they were Polynesians who voyaged from Tahiti and began to settle the islands around A.D. 750. When England's Captain Cook made landfall in Hawaii on his expedition in 1778, the Hawaiian people had developed, over the preceding 1,000 years or so, a cultural and political structure of their own. They had well-established traditions and customs and practiced a polytheistic religion. Agriculture and fishing sustained the people, and, though population estimates vary, some modern historians conclude that the population in 1778 was about 200,000–300,000. The accounts of Hawaiian life often remark upon the people's capacity to find beauty and pleasure in their island existence, but life was not altogether idyllic. In Cook's time the islands were ruled by four different kings, and intra-Hawaiian wars could inflict great loss and suffering. Kings or principal chieftains, as well as high priests, could order the death or sacrifice of any subject. The society was one, however, with its own identity, its own cohesive forces, its own history.

The 1800's are a story of increasing involvement of westerners in the economic and political affairs of the Kingdom. Rights to land became a principal concern, and there was unremitting pressure to allow non-Hawaiians to use and to own land and to be secure in their title. Westerners were not the only ones with pressing concerns, however, for the disposition and ownership of land came to be an unsettled matter among the Hawaiians themselves.

The status of Hawaiian lands has presented issues of complexity and controversy from at least the rule of Kamehameha I to the present day. We do not attempt to interpret that history, lest our comments be thought to bear upon issues not before us. It suffices to refer to various of the historical conclusions that appear to have been persuasive to Congress and to the State when they enacted the laws soon to be discussed.

In 1898, President McKinley signed a Joint Resolution, sometimes called the Newlands Resolution, to annex the Hawaiian Islands as territory of the United States. According to the Joint Resolution, the Republic of Hawaii ceded all former Crown, government, and public lands to the United States. The resolution further provided that revenues from the public lands were to be "used solely for the benefit of the inhabitants of the Hawaiian Islands for educational and other public purposes." Two years later the Hawaiian Organic Act established the Territory of Hawaii, asserted United States control over the ceded lands, and put those lands "in the possession, use, and control of the government of the Territory of Hawaii . . . until otherwise provided for by Congress."

Before we turn to the relevant provisions two . . . important matters, which affected the demographics of Hawaii, must be recounted. The first is the tragedy inflicted on the early Hawaiian people by the introduction of western diseases and infectious agents. These mortal illnesses no doubt were an initial cause of the despair, disenchantment, and despondency some commentators later noted in descendants of the early Hawaiian people.

The other important feature of Hawaiian demographics to be noted is the immigration to the islands by people of many different races and cultures. Mostly in response to the demand of the sugar industry for arduous labor in the cane fields, successive immigration waves brought Chinese, Portuguese, Japanese, and Filipinos to Hawaii.

With this background we turn to the legislative enactments of direct relevance to the case before us.

II

Not long after the creation of the new Territory, Congress became concerned with the condition of the native Hawaiian people. Reciting its purpose to rehabilitate the native Hawaiian population, *see* H.R.Rep. No. 839, at 1–2, Congress enacted the Hawaiian Homes Commission Act, which set aside about 200,000 acres of the ceded public lands and created a program of loans and long-term leases for the benefit of native Hawaiians. The Act defined "native Hawaiian [s]" to include "any descendant of not less than one-half part of the blood of the races inhabiting the Hawaiian Islands previous to 1778."

Hawaii was admitted as the 50th State of the Union in 1959. With admission, the new State agreed to adopt the Hawaiian Homes Commission Act as part of its own Constitution. In addition, the United States granted Hawaii title to all public lands and public property within the boundaries of the State, save those which the Federal Government retained for its own use.

The legislation authorizing the grant recited that these lands, and the proceeds and income they generated, were to be held "as a public trust" to be "managed and disposed of for one or more of" five purposes:

> "[1] for the support of the public schools and other public educational institutions, [2] for the betterment of the conditions of native Hawaiians, as defined in the Hawaiian Homes Commission Act, 1920, as amended, [3] for the development of farm and home ownership on as widespread a basis as possible [,][4] for the making of public improvements, and [5] for the provision of lands for public use." Admission Act § 5(f), 73 Stat. 6.

In the first decades following admission, the State apparently continued to administer the lands that had been set aside under the Hawaiian Homes Commission Act for the benefit of native Hawaiians. The income from the balance of the public lands is said to have "by and large flowed to the department of education."

In 1978 Hawaii amended its Constitution to establish the Office of Hawaiian Affairs, which has as its mission "[t]he betterment of conditions of native Hawaiians . . . [and] Hawaiians." Members of the 1978 constitutional convention, at which the new amendments were drafted and proposed, set forth the purpose of the proposed agency:

> "Members [of the Committee of the Whole] were impressed by the concept of the Office of Hawaiian Affairs which establishes a public trust entity for the benefit of the people of Hawaiian ancestry. Members foresaw that it will provide Hawaiians the right to determine the priorities which will effectuate the betterment of their condition and welfare and promote the protection and preservation of the Hawaiian race, and that it will unite Hawaiians as a people."

Purpose of OHA

Implementing statutes and their later amendments vested OHA with broad authority to administer two categories of funds: a 20 percent share of the revenue from the 1.2 million acres of lands granted to the State pursuant to § 5(b) of the Admission Act, which OHA is to administer "for the betterment of the conditions of native Hawaiians" and any state or federal appropriations or private donations that may be made for the benefit of "native Hawaiians" and/or "Hawaiians." The Hawaiian Legislature has charged OHA with the mission of "[s]erving as the principal public agency . . . responsible for the performance, development, and coordination of programs and activities relating to native Hawaiians and Hawaiians," "[a]ssessing the policies and practices of other agencies impacting on native Hawaiians and Hawaiians," "conducting advocacy efforts for native Hawaiians and Hawaiians," "[a]pplying for, receiving, and disbursing, grants and donations from all sources for native Hawaiian and Hawaiian programs and services," and "[s]erving as a receptacle for reparations."

OHA is overseen by a nine-member board of trustees, the members of which "shall be Hawaiians" and—presenting the precise issue in this case—shall be "elected by qualified voters who are Hawaiians, as provided by law." The term "Hawaiian" is defined by statute:

> "'Hawaiian' means any descendant of the aboriginal peoples inhabiting the Hawaiian Islands which exercised sovereignty and subsisted in the Hawaiian Islands in 1778, and which peoples thereafter have continued to reside in Hawaii."

The statute defines "native Hawaiian" as follows:

> " 'Native Hawaiian' means any descendant of not less than one-half part of the races inhabiting the Hawaiian Islands previous to 1778, as defined by the Hawaiian Homes Commission Act, 1920, as amended; provided that the term identically refers to the descendants of such blood quantum of such aboriginal peoples which exercised sovereignty and subsisted in the Hawaiian Islands in 1778 and which peoples thereafter continued to reside in Hawaii." *Ibid.*

Petitioner Harold Rice is a citizen of Hawaii and a descendant of preannexation residents of the islands. He is not, as we have noted, a descendant of pre-1778 natives, and so he is neither "native Hawaiian" nor "Hawaiian" as defined by the statute. Rice applied in March 1996 to vote in the elections for OHA trustees. To register to vote for the office of trustee he was required to attest: "I am also Hawaiian and desire to register to vote in OHA elections." Affidavit on Application for Voter Registration, Lodging by Petitioner, Tab 2. Rice marked through the words "am also Hawaiian and," then checked the form "yes." The State denied his application.

Rice sued Benjamin Cayetano, the Governor of Hawaii, in the United States District Court for the District of Hawaii. (The Governor was sued in his official capacity, and the Attorney General of Hawaii defends the challenged enactments. We refer to the respondent as "the State.") Rice contested his exclusion from voting in elections for OHA trustees and from voting in a special election relating to native Hawaiian sovereignty which was held in August 1996. After the District Court rejected the latter challenge, the parties moved for summary judgment on the claim that the Fourteenth and Fifteenth Amendments to the United States Constitution invalidate the law excluding Rice from the OHA trustee elections.

The District Court granted summary judgment to the State.

The Court of Appeals affirmed.

We granted certiorari, 526 U.S. 1016, 119 S.Ct. 1248, 143 L.Ed.2d 346 (1999), and now reverse.

III

The purpose and command of the Fifteenth Amendment are set forth in language both explicit and comprehensive. The National Government and the States may not violate a fundamental principle: They may not deny or abridge the right to vote on account of race. Color and previous condition of servitude, too, are forbidden criteria or classifications, though it is unnecessary to consider them in the present case.

Enacted in the wake of the Civil War, the immediate concern of the Amendment was to guarantee to the emancipated slaves the right to vote, lest they be denied the civil and political capacity to protect their new freedom. Vital as its objective remains, the Amendment goes beyond it. Consistent with the design of the Constitution, the Amendment is cast in fundamental terms, terms transcending the particular controversy which was the immediate impetus for its enactment. The Amendment grants protection to all persons, not just members of a particular race.

The design of the Amendment is to reaffirm the equality of races at the most basic level of the democratic process, the exercise of the voting franchise. A resolve so absolute required language as simple in command as it was comprehensive in reach. Fundamental in purpose and effect and self-executing in operation, the Amendment prohibits all provisions denying or abridging the voting franchise of any citizen or class of citizens on the basis of race. "[B]y the inherent power of the Amendment the word white disappeared" from our voting laws, bringing those who had been excluded by reason of race within "the generic grant of suffrage made by the State." *Guinn v. United States*, 238 U.S. 347, 363 (1915). The Court has acknowledged the Amendment's mandate of neutrality in straightforward terms: "If citizens of one race having certain qualifications are permitted by law to vote, those of another having the same qualifications must be. Previous to this amendment, there was no constitutional guaranty against this discrimination: now there is." *United States v. Reese*, 92 U.S. 214, 218 (1876).

[T]he voting structure now before us is neither subtle nor indirect. It is specific in granting the vote to persons of defined ancestry and to no others. The State maintains this is not a racial category at all but instead a classification limited to those whose ancestors were in Hawaii at a particular time, regardless of their race. The State points to theories of certain scholars concluding that some inhabitants of Hawaii as of 1778 may have migrated from the Marquesas Islands and the Pacific Northwest, as well as from Tahiti. Furthermore, the State argues, the restriction in its operation excludes a person whose traceable ancestors were exclusively Polynesian if none of those ancestors resided in Hawaii in 1778; and, on the other hand, the vote would be granted to a person who could trace, say, one sixty-fourth of his or her ancestry to a Hawaiian inhabitant on the pivotal date. These factors, it is said, mean the restriction is not a racial classification. We reject this line of argument.

Ancestry can be a proxy for race. It is that proxy here. Even if the residents of Hawaii in 1778 had been of more diverse ethnic backgrounds and cultures, it is far from clear that a voting test favoring their descendants would not be a race-based qualification. But that is not this case. For centuries Hawaii was isolated from migration. The inhabitants shared common physical characteristics, and by 1778 they had a common culture. Indeed, the drafters of the statutory definition in question emphasized the "unique culture of the ancient Hawaiians" in explaining their work. ("Modern scholarship also identified such race of people as culturally distinguishable from other Polynesian peoples"). The provisions before us reflect the State's effort to preserve that commonality of people to the present day. In the interpretation of the Reconstruction era civil rights laws we have observed that "racial discrimination" is that which singles out "identifiable classes of persons . . . solely because of their ancestry or ethnic characteristics." *Saint Francis College v. Al-Khazraji*, 481 U.S. 604, 613 (1987). The very object of the statutory definition in question and of its earlier congressional counterpart in the Hawaiian Homes Commission Act is to treat the early Hawaiians as a distinct people, commanding their own recognition and respect. The State, in enacting the legislation before us, has used ancestry as a racial definition and for a racial purpose.

The history of the State's definition demonstrates the point. As we have noted, the statute defines "Hawaiian" as

> "any descendant of the aboriginal peoples inhabiting the Hawaiian Islands which exercised sovereignty and subsisted in the Hawaiian Islands in 1778, and which peoples thereafter have continued to reside in Hawaii." Haw.Rev.Stat. § 10–2 (1993).

A different definition of "Hawaiian" was first promulgated in 1978 as one of the proposed amendments to the State Constitution. As proposed, "Hawaiian" was defined as "any descendant of the races inhabiting the Hawaiian Islands, previous to 1778." 1 Proceedings of the Constitutional Convention of Hawaii of 1978, Committee of the Whole Rep. No. 13, at 1018. Rejected as not ratified in a valid manner, *see Kahalekai v. Doi*, 60 Haw. 324, 342 (1979), the definition was modified and in the end promulgated in statutory form as quoted above. *See* Hawaii Senate Journal, Standing Committee Rep. No. 784, at 1350, 1353–1354; *id.* Conf. Comm. Rep. No. 77, at 998. By the drafters' own admission, however, any changes to the language were at most cosmetic. Noting that "[t]he definitions of 'native Hawaiian' and 'Hawaiian' are changed to substitute 'peoples' for 'races,'" the drafters of the revised definition "stress[ed] that this change is non-substantive, and that 'peoples' does mean 'races.'" *Ibid.*

The next definition in Hawaii's compilation of statutes incorporates the new definition of "Hawaiian" and preserves the explicit tie to race:

> "'Native Hawaiian' means any descendant of not less than one-half part of the races inhabiting the Hawaiian Islands previous to 1778, as defined by the Hawaiian Homes Commission Act, 1920, as amended; provided that the term identically refers to the descendants of such blood quantum of such aboriginal peoples which exercised sovereignty and subsisted in the Hawaiian Islands in 1778 and which peoples thereafter continued to reside in Hawaii." Haw.Rev.Stat. § 10–2 (1993).

This provision makes it clear: "[T]he descendants . . . of [the] aboriginal peoples" means "the descendants . . . of the races." *Ibid.*

As for the further argument that the restriction differentiates even among Polynesian people and is based simply on the date of an ancestor's residence in Hawaii, this too is insufficient to prove the classification is nonracial in purpose and operation. Simply because a class defined by ancestry does not include all members of the race does not suffice to make the classification race neutral. Here, the State's argument is undermined by its express racial purpose and by its actual effects.

The ancestral inquiry mandated by the State implicates the same grave concerns as a classification specifying a particular race by name. One of the principal reasons race is treated as a forbidden classification is that it demeans the dignity and worth of a person to be judged by ancestry instead of by his or her own merit and essential qualities. An inquiry into ancestral lines is not consistent with respect based on the unique personality each of us possesses, a respect the Constitution itself secures in its concern for persons and citizens.

The ancestral inquiry mandated by the State is forbidden by the Fifteenth Amendment for the further reason that the use of racial classifications is corruptive of the whole legal order democratic elections seek to preserve. The law itself may not become the instrument for generating the prejudice and hostility all too often directed against persons whose particular ancestry is disclosed by their ethnic characteristics and cultural traditions. "Distinctions between citizens solely because of their ancestry are by their very nature odious to a free people whose institutions are founded upon the doctrine of equality." *Hirabayashi v. United States*, 320 U.S. 81, 100 (1943). Ancestral tracing of this sort achieves its purpose by creating a legal category which employs the same mechanisms, and causes the same injuries, as laws or statutes that use race by name. The State's electoral restriction enacts a race-based voting qualification.

IV

C

Hawaii's final argument is that the voting restriction does no more than ensure an alignment of interests between the fiduciaries and the beneficiaries of a trust. Thus, the contention goes, the restriction is based on beneficiary status rather than race.

As an initial matter, the contention founders on its own terms, for it is not clear that the voting classification is symmetric with the beneficiaries of the programs OHA administers. Although the bulk of the funds for which OHA is responsible appears to be earmarked for the benefit of "native Hawaiians," the State permits both "native Hawaiians" and "Hawaiians" to vote for the office of trustee. The classification thus appears to create, not eliminate, a differential alignment between the identity of OHA trustees and what the State calls beneficiaries.

Hawaii's argument fails on more essential grounds. The State's position rests, in the end, on the demeaning premise that citizens of a particular race are somehow more qualified than others to vote on certain matters. That reasoning attacks the central meaning of the Fifteenth Amendment. The Amendment applies to "any election in which public issues are decided or public officials selected." *Terry*, 345 U.S. at 468. There is no room under the Amendment for the concept that the right to vote in a particular election can be allocated based on race. Race cannot qualify some and disqualify others from full participation in our democracy. All citizens, regardless of race, have an interest in selecting officials who make policies on their behalf, even if those policies will affect some groups more than others. Under the Fifteenth Amendment, voters are treated not as members of a distinct race but as members of the whole citizenry. Hawaii may not assume, based on race, that petitioner or any other of its citizens will not cast a principled vote. To accept the position advanced by the State would give rise to the same indignities, and the same resulting tensions and animosities, the Amendment was designed to eliminate. The voting restriction under review is prohibited by the Fifteenth Amendment.

When the culture and way of life of a people are all but engulfed by a history beyond their control, their sense of loss may extend down through generations; and their dismay may be shared by many members of the larger community. As the State of Hawaii attempts to address these realities, it must, as always, seek the political consensus that begins with a sense of shared purpose. One of the necessary beginning points is this principle: The Constitution of the United States, too, has become the heritage of all the citizens of Hawaii.

In this case the Fifteenth Amendment invalidates the electoral qualification based on ancestry. The judgment of the Court of Appeals for the Ninth Circuit is reversed.

■ JUSTICE STEVENS, with whom JUSTICE GINSBURG joins as to Part II, dissenting.

The Court's holding today rests largely on the repetition of glittering generalities that have little, if any, application to the compelling history of the State of Hawaii. When that history is held up against the manifest purpose of the Fourteenth and Fifteenth Amendments, and against two centuries of this Court's federal Indian law, it is clear to me that Hawaii's election scheme should be upheld.

I

According to the terms of the federal Act by which Hawaii was admitted to the Union, and to the terms of that State's Constitution and laws, the Office of Hawaiian Affairs (OHA) is charged with managing vast acres of land held in trust for the descendants of the Polynesians who occupied the Hawaiian Islands before the 1778 arrival of Captain Cook. In addition to administering the proceeds from these assets, OHA is responsible for programs providing special benefits for native Hawaiians. Established in 1978 by an amendment to the State Constitution, OHA was intended to advance multiple goals: to carry out the duties of the trust relationship between the islands' indigenous peoples and the Government of the United States; to compensate for past wrongs to the ancestors of these peoples; and to help preserve the distinct, indigenous culture that existed for centuries before Cook's arrival. As explained by the senior Senator from Hawaii, Senator Inouye, who is not himself a native Hawaiian but rather (like petitioner) is a member of the majority of Hawaiian voters who supported the 1978 amendments, the amendments reflect "an honest and sincere attempt on the part of the people of Hawai'i to rectify the wrongs of the past, and to put into being the mandate [of] our Federal government—the betterment of the conditions of Native Hawaiians."

Today the Court concludes that Hawaii's method of electing the trustees of OHA violates the Fifteenth Amendment. In reaching that conclusion, the Court has assumed that the programs administered by OHA are valid. That assumption is surely correct. In my judgment, however, the reasons supporting the legitimacy of OHA and its programs in general undermine the basis for the Court's decision holding its trustee election provision invalid. The OHA election provision violates neither the Fourteenth Amendment nor the Fifteenth.

That conclusion is in keeping with three overlapping principles. First, the Federal Government must be, and has been, afforded wide latitude in carrying out its obligations arising from the special relationship it has with the aboriginal peoples, a category that includes the native Hawaiians, whose lands are now a part of the territory of the United States. In addition, there exists in this case the State's own fiduciary responsibility—arising from its establishment of a public trust—for administering assets granted it by the Federal Government in part for the benefit of native Hawaiians. Finally, even if one were to ignore the more than two centuries of Indian law precedent and practice on which this case follows, there is simply no invidious discrimination present in this effort to see that indigenous peoples are compensated for past wrongs, and to preserve a distinct and vibrant culture that is as much a part of this Nation's heritage as any.

II

Throughout our Nation's history, this Court has recognized both the plenary power of Congress over the affairs of Native Americans and the fiduciary character of the special federal relationship with descendants of those once sovereign peoples. The source of the Federal Government's responsibility toward the Nation's native inhabitants, who were subject to European and then American military conquest, has been explained by this Court in the crudest terms, but they remain instructive nonetheless.

As our cases have consistently recognized, Congress' plenary power over these peoples has been exercised time and again to implement a federal duty to provide native peoples with special " 'care and protection.' " Federal regulation in this area is not limited to the strictly practical but has encompassed as well the protection of cultural values; for example, the desecration of Native American graves and other sacred sites led to the passage of the Native American Graves Protection and Repatriation Act, 25 U.S.C. § 3001 et seq.

Critically, neither the extent of Congress' sweeping power nor the character of the trust relationship with indigenous peoples has depended on the ancient racial origins of the people, the allotment of tribal lands, the coherence or existence of tribal self-government, or the varying definitions of "Indian." Congress has chosen to adopt. Rather, when it comes to the exercise of Congress' plenary power in Indian affairs, this Court has taken account of the "numerous occasions" on which "legislation that singles out Indians for particular and special treatment" has been upheld, and has concluded that as "long as the special treatment can be tied rationally to the fulfillment of Congress' unique obligation towards the Indians, such legislative judgments will not be disturbed." *Morton v. Mancari*, 417 U.S. 535, 554–555 (1974). . . .

In the end, however, one need not even rely on this official apology to discern a well-established federal trust relationship with the native Hawaiians. Among the many and varied laws passed by Congress in carrying out its duty to indigenous peoples, more than 150 today expressly include native Hawaiians as part of the class of Native Americans benefited. By classifying native Hawaiians as "Native Americans" for purposes of these statutes, Congress has made clear that native Hawaiians enjoy many of "the same rights and privileges accorded to American Indian, Alaska Native, Eskimo, and Aleut communities."

Declining to confront the rather simple logic of the foregoing, the majority would seemingly reject the OHA voting scheme for a pair of different reasons. First, Congress' trust-based power is confined to dealings with tribes, not with individuals, and no tribe or indigenous sovereign entity is found among the native Hawaiians. Second, the elections are "elections of the State," not of a tribe, and upholding this law would be "to permit a State, by racial classification, to fence out whole classes of citizens from decision-making in critical state affairs." In my view, neither of these reasons overcomes the otherwise compelling similarity, fully supported by our precedent, between the once subjugated, indigenous peoples of the continental United States and the peoples of the Hawaiian Islands whose historical sufferings and status parallel those of the continental Native Americans.

Membership in a tribe, the majority suggests, rather than membership in a race or class of descendants, has been the *sine qua non* of governmental power in the realm of Indian law . . . [I]t is a painful irony indeed to conclude that native Hawaiians are not entitled to special benefits designed to restore a measure of native self-governance because they currently lack any vestigial native government—a possibility of which history and the actions of this Nation have deprived them.

Of greater concern to the majority is the fact that we are confronted here with a state constitution and legislative enactment—passed by a majority of the entire population of Hawaii—rather than a law passed by Congress or a tribe itself. But as our own precedent makes clear, this reality does not alter our analysis. As I have explained, OHA and its trustee elections can hardly be characterized simply as an "affair of the State" alone; they are the instruments for implementing the Federal Government's trust relationship with a once sovereign indigenous people. This Court has held more than once that the federal power to pass laws fulfilling the federal trust relationship with the Indians may be delegated to the States.

The state statutory and constitutional scheme here was without question intended to implement the express desires of the Federal Government. The Admissions Act in § 4 mandated that the provisions of the Hawaiian Homes Commission Act "shall be adopted," with its multiple provisions expressly benefiting native Hawaiians and not others. More, the Admissions Act required that the proceeds from the lands granted to the State "shall be held by said State as a public trust for . . . the betterment of the conditions of native Hawaiians," and that those proceeds "shall be managed and disposed of . . . in such manner as the constitution and laws of said State may provide, and their use for any other object shall constitute a breach of trust for which suit may be brought by the United States." § 5, id. at 6. The terms of the trust were clear, as was the discretion granted to the State to administer the trust as the State's laws "may provide." And Congress continues to fund OHA on the understanding that it is thereby furthering the federal trust obligation.

The sole remaining question under [the Court's prior precedents] is thus whether the State's scheme "rationally further[s] the purpose identified by the State." Under this standard, as with the BIA preferences in *Mancari*, the OHA voting requirement is certainly reasonably designed to promote "self-government" by the descendants of the indigenous Hawaiians, and to make OHA "more responsive to the needs of its constituent groups." *Mancari*, 417 U.S. at 554. OHA is thus "directed to participation by the governed in the governing agency." *Mancari*, 417 U.S. at 554. In this respect among others, the requirement is "reasonably and directly related to a legitimate, nonracially based goal." *Ibid.*

The foregoing reasons are to me more than sufficient to justify the OHA trust system and trustee election provision under the Fourteenth Amendment.

III

Although the Fifteenth Amendment tests the OHA scheme by a different measure, it is equally clear to me that the trustee election provision violates neither the letter nor the spirit of that Amendment.

As the majority itself must tacitly admit, the terms of the Amendment itself do not here apply. The OHA voter qualification speaks in terms of ancestry and current residence, not of race or color. OHA trustee voters must be "Hawaiian," meaning "any descendant of the aboriginal peoples inhabiting the Hawaiian Islands which exercised sovereignty and subsisted in the Hawaiian Islands in 1778, and which peoples have thereafter continued to reside in Hawaii." The ability to vote is a function of the lineal descent of a modern-day resident of Hawaii, not the blood-based characteristics of that resident, or of the blood-based proximity of that resident to the "peoples" from whom that descendant arises.

The distinction between ancestry and race is more than simply one of plain language. The ability to trace one's ancestry to a particular progenitor at a single distant point in time may convey no information about one's own apparent or acknowledged race today. Neither does it of necessity imply one's own identification with a particular race, or the exclusion of any others "on account of race." The terms manifestly carry distinct meanings, and ancestry was not included by the Framers in the Amendment's prohibitions.

Presumably recognizing this distinction, the majority relies on the fact that "[a]ncestry can be a proxy for race." That is, of course, true, but it by no means follows that ancestry is always a proxy for race.

Ancestry surely can be a proxy for race, or a pretext for invidious racial discrimination. But it is simply neither proxy nor pretext here. All of the persons who are eligible to vote for the trustees of OHA share two qualifications that no other person old enough to vote possesses: They are beneficiaries of the public trust created by the State and administered by OHA, and they have at least one ancestor who was a resident of Hawaii in 1778. A trust whose terms provide that the trustees shall be elected by a class including beneficiaries is hardly a novel concept.

The majority makes much of the fact that the OHA trust—which it assumes is legitimate—should be read as principally intended to benefit the smaller class of "native Hawaiians," who are defined as at least one-half descended from a native islander circa 1778, Haw.Rev.Stat. § 10–2 (1993), not the larger class of "Hawaiians," which includes "any descendant" of those aboriginal people who lived in Hawaii in 1778 and "which peoples thereafter have continued to reside in Hawaii," ibid. *See* ante, at 1060. It is, after all, the majority notes, the larger class of Hawaiians that enjoys the suffrage right in OHA elections. There is therefore a mismatch in interest alignment between the trust beneficiaries and the trustee electors, the majority contends, and it thus cannot be said that the class of qualified voters here is defined solely by beneficiary status.

While that may or may not be true depending upon the construction of the terms of the trust, there is surely nothing racially invidious about a decision to enlarge the class of eligible voters to include "any descendant" of a 1778 resident of the Islands. The broader category of eligible voters serves quite practically to ensure that, regardless how "dilute" the race of native Hawaiians becomes—a phenomenon also described in the majority's lavish historical summary, *ante*, at 1051— there will remain a voting interest whose ancestors were a part of a political, cultural community, and who have inherited through participation and memory the set of traditions the trust seeks to protect. The putative mismatch only underscores the reality that it cannot be purely a racial interest that either the trust or the election provision seeks to secure; the political and cultural interests served are—unlike racial survival—shared by both native Hawaiians and Hawaiians.

It thus becomes clear why the majority is likewise wrong to conclude that the OHA voting scheme is likely to "become the instrument for generating the prejudice and hostility all too often directed against persons whose particular ancestry is disclosed by their ethnic characteristics and cultural traditions." *Ante*, at 1057. The political and cultural concerns that motivated the nonnative majority of Hawaiian voters to establish OHA reflected an interest in preserving through the self-determination of a particular people ancient traditions that they value. The fact that the voting qualification was established by the entire electorate in the State—the vast majority of which is not native Hawaiian—testifies to their judgment concerning the Court's fear of "prejudice and hostility" against the majority of state residents who are not "Hawaiian," such as petitioner. Our traditional understanding of democracy and voting preferences makes it difficult to conceive that the majority of the State's voting population would have enacted a measure that discriminates against, or in any way represents prejudice and hostility toward, that self-same majority. Indeed, the best insurance against that danger is that the electorate here retains the power to revise its laws.

IV

The Court today ignores the overwhelming differences between the Fifteenth Amendment case law on which it relies and the unique history of the State of Hawaii. The former recalls an age of abject discrimination against an insular minority in the old South; the latter at long last yielded the "political consensus" the majority claims it seeks, *ante*, at

1060—a consensus determined to recognize the special claim to self-determination of the indigenous peoples of Hawaii.

Accordingly, I respectfully dissent.

NOTES AND QUESTIONS

1.   *What Is a Racial Classification?* Hawaii argued that its ancestry classification was distinct from a racial classification because ancestry does not map perfectly onto any racial or ethnic group. Justice Kennedy rejects Hawaii's argument, stating that even an ancestry classification that included "diverse ethnic backgrounds and cultures" could still be a race-based classification. In addition, Justice Kennedy asserts that, just "because a class defined by ancestry does not include all members of the race does not suffice to make the classification race neutral." Note Justice Stevens' rejoinder that the "classification here is . . . both too inclusive and not inclusive enough to fall strictly along racial lines." Who has the better of this argument? Is Justice Kennedy right that ancestry in this case is a proxy for race?

2.   *Integration, Assimilation, Separation, and Multiculturalism.* In almost poetic terms, Justice Kennedy expressed his sympathy with Native Hawaiians who may be dismayed by the decline of their culture and way of life. But he noted that the remedy is to "seek the political consensus that begins with a shared sense of purpose" and to embrace the principle that the "Constitution of the United States, too, has become the heritage of all the citizens of Hawaii." This belief about the Constitution is arguably a central message of the Reconstruction Amendments and is laudable in its aspirations. But what does it mean to say that the Constitution is the heritage of those who were previously disenfranchised because of their race? Or of a people who have a different cultural, racial, and ancestral heritage from those who founded the Constitution, and from those who occupied their territory? Or of a people who were forcibly conquered and whose legal and political traditions were cast aside? Is Justice Kennedy implicitly asking Native Hawaiians to assimilate into the larger American culture? Is there any room for separate Native Hawaiian culture, heritage, and self-governance to be protected by law?

3.   *Remedying a Racist Past.* Justice Stevens' dissent emphasizes the remedial aspect of the OHA voting scheme. He argues that the history of Native Hawaiians is similar to the history of native peoples on the continent, and just as Native peoples are allowed "a measure of native self-governance" as a remedy for prior discrimination and subjugation by the federal government, so too should Native Hawaiians be given "a measure of native self-government." The essence of Justice Stevens' argument is that Native Hawaiians were once self-governing, they once owned land and possessed a rich cultural heritage, all of which was taken away from them by conquest. The land trust and the OHA voting schemes are justifiable remedies for the deprivations that the descendants of the Native Hawaiians have suffered at the hands of the United States. Is law capable of being deployed to effectively remedy past political and societal discrimination against a racial or ethnic

group, or is it better for law to forget the past and focus on enforcing formal equality for all individuals in the present day?

4.   *What Is the Principle of* Rice v. Cayetano*?* Consider the following view from Professor Ellen Katz:

> *Rice* suggests that the primary value of political participation through voting lies not in the policies implemented by those elected, but in two distinct and related intrinsic benefits the vote produces: namely, the constitutive benefit an individual derives from political engagement with others and the expressive benefit derived from full membership in the political community. *Rice* posits, on the one hand, that a jurisdiction's use of race to define an electorate distorts these beneficial effects by imposing on voters a state-approved identity instead of leaving voters free to develop an identity on their own and by disseminating the message that racial identity represents a relevant criterion for entry into the political community. *Rice* presumes, on the other hand, that the constitutive and expressive aspects of voting provide a crucial element to a group identity that would otherwise not be viewed as "racial." This view of race confirms the idea that, at least within our constitutional practice, the concept of racial identity is a complex legal conclusion, not a pre-legal fact.

Ellen D. Katz, *Race and the Right to Vote after* Rice v. Cayetano, 96 MICH. L. REV. 491, 495 (2000). Professor Katz's analysis of *Rice* is arresting. First, she notes that the Court in *Rice* does not understand political participation to be about the consequential exercise of political power, but to be constitutive and expressive. Second, she argues that, for the majority in *Rice*, racial identity is a legal conclusion and not a pre-political fact. Do you read *Rice* the same way she does? If she is right that the Court understands political participation as non-consequential and racial identity as a legal term of art, what follows for voting rights law and policy, which seems to depart from the contrary premise that political participation is consequential and that racial identity is politically significant? Isn't the point of voting to acquire political power and improve one's material circumstances?

5.   *Developments Following* Rice. In the wake of *Rice*, the board of the OHA was forced to resign and hold an election without racial restrictions on either voters or candidates. The OHA manages 500 million dollars in assets and has a budget of 50 million dollars a year to benefit Native Hawaiians, who comprise approximately 10% of the population of Hawaii. Native Hawaiians have attempted to gain recognition by the Department of the Interior as an Indian tribe. But that process was halted when the Supreme Court issued an injunction that stopped the election to elect delegates to a convention that would structure the tribal government.

C.   THE END OF THE SECOND RECONSTRUCTION?

In 2006, Congress renewed the VRA for another 25 years. In 2008 a group of plaintiffs challenged the constitutionality of the renewal in

Northwest Austin Utility District No One v. Holder, 557 U.S. 193 (2009) ("*NAMUDNO*"). The Court avoided the constitutional challenge, choosing instead to resolve the issue on statutory grounds. But the Court warned that it thought section 5 was unconstitutional because the "blatantly discriminatory" behaviors by states and localities in the covered jurisdictions were now rare. In *Shelby County v. Holder*, the Court returned to the constitutional question that it left unresolved in *NAMUDNO*: whether sections 4 and 5 of the VRA remain necessary in light of the fact that voters of color can in fact exercise their formal right to vote.

Shelby County, Alabama v. Holder

Supreme Court of the United States, 2013.
570 U.S. ___, 133 S.Ct. 2612.

■ CHIEF JUSTICE ROBERTS delivered the opinion of the Court.

The Voting Rights Act of 1965 employed extraordinary measures to address an extraordinary problem. Section 5 of the Act required States to obtain federal permission before enacting any law related to voting—a drastic departure from basic principles of federalism. And § 4 of the Act applied that requirement only to some States—an equally dramatic departure from the principle that all States enjoy equal sovereignty. This was strong medicine, but Congress determined it was needed to address entrenched racial discrimination in voting, "an insidious and pervasive evil which had been perpetuated in certain parts of our country through unremitting and ingenious defiance of the Constitution." *South Carolina v. Katzenbach.* As we explained in upholding the law, "exceptional conditions can justify legislative measures not otherwise appropriate." *Id.* Reflecting the unprecedented nature of these measures, they were scheduled to expire after five years.

Nearly 50 years later, they are still in effect; indeed, they have been made more stringent, and are now scheduled to last until 2031. There is no denying, however, that the conditions that originally justified these measures no longer characterize voting in the covered jurisdictions. By 2009, "the racial gap in voter registration and turnout [was] lower in the States originally covered by § 5 than it [was] nationwide." *Northwest Austin Municipal Util. Dist. No. One v. Holder.* Since that time, Census Bureau data indicate that African-American voter turnout has come to exceed white voter turnout in five of the six States originally covered by § 5, with a gap in the sixth State of less than one half of one percent.

At the same time, voting discrimination still exists; no one doubts that. The question is whether the Act's extraordinary measures, including its disparate treatment of the States, continue to satisfy constitutional requirements. As we put it a short time ago, "the Act imposes current burdens and must be justified by current needs." *Northwest Austin.*

I

A

[Previously w]e explained that § 5 "imposes substantial federalism costs" and "differentiates between the States, despite our historic tradition that all the States enjoy equal sovereignty." [*Northwest Austin*, 557 U.S.] We also noted that "[t]hings have changed in the South. Voter turnout and registration rates now approach parity. Blatantly discriminatory evasions of federal decrees are rare. And minority candidates hold office at unprecedented levels." Finally, we questioned whether the problems that § 5 meant to address were still "concentrated in the jurisdictions singled out for preclearance."

B

Shelby County is located in Alabama, a covered jurisdiction. It has not sought bailout, as the Attorney General has recently objected to voting changes proposed from within the county. Instead, in 2010, the county sued the Attorney General in Federal District Court in Washington, D.C., seeking a declaratory judgment that sections 4(b) and 5 of the Voting Rights Act are facially unconstitutional, as well as a permanent injunction against their enforcement. The District Court ruled against the county and upheld the Act.

The Court of Appeals for the D.C. Circuit affirmed.

We granted certiorari.

II

In *Northwest Austin,* we stated that "the Act imposes current burdens and must be justified by current needs." And we concluded that "a departure from the fundamental principle of equal sovereignty requires a showing that a statute's disparate geographic coverage is sufficiently related to the problem that it targets." *Ibid.* These basic principles guide our review of the question before us.

A

The Constitution and laws of the United States are "the supreme Law of the Land." State legislation may not contravene federal law. The Federal Government does not, however, have a general right to review and veto state enactments before they go into effect. A proposal to grant such authority to "negative" state laws was considered at the Constitutional Convention, but rejected in favor of allowing state laws to take effect, subject to later challenge under the Supremacy Clause.

Outside the strictures of the Supremacy Clause, States retain broad autonomy in structuring their governments and pursuing legislative objectives. Indeed, the Constitution provides that all powers not specifically granted to the Federal Government are reserved to the States or citizens. Amdt. 10. This "allocation of powers in our federal system preserves the integrity, dignity, and residual sovereignty of the States."

Bond v. United States. But the federal balance "is not just an end in itself: Rather, federalism secures to citizens the liberties that derive from the diffusion of sovereign power."

More specifically, " 'the Framers of the Constitution intended the States to keep for themselves, as provided in the Tenth Amendment, the power to regulate elections.' " Of course, the Federal Government retains significant control over federal elections. For instance, the Constitution authorizes Congress to establish the time and manner for electing Senators and Representatives. Art. I, § 4, cl. 1; *see also Arizona v. Inter Tribal Council of Ariz., Inc.* But States have "broad powers to determine the conditions under which the right of suffrage may be exercised." *Carrington v. Rash.* Drawing lines for congressional districts is likewise "primarily the duty and responsibility of the State." *Perry v. Perez.*

Not only do States retain sovereignty under the Constitution, there is also a "fundamental principle of *equal* sovereignty" among the States. *Northwest Austin.* Over a hundred years ago, this Court explained that our Nation "was and is a union of States, equal in power, dignity and authority." *Coyle v. Smith.* Indeed, "the constitutional equality of the States is essential to the harmonious operation of the scheme upon which the Republic was organized." *Id. Coyle* concerned the admission of new States, and *Katzenbach* rejected the notion that the principle operated as a *bar* on differential treatment outside that context. At the same time, as we made clear in *Northwest Austin,* the fundamental principle of equal sovereignty remains highly pertinent in assessing subsequent disparate treatment of States.

The Voting Rights Act sharply departs from these basic principles. It suspends "*all* changes to state election law—however innocuous—until they have been precleared by federal authorities in Washington, D.C." States must beseech the Federal Government for permission to implement laws that they would otherwise have the right to enact and execute on their own, subject of course to any injunction in a § 2 action.

And despite the tradition of equal sovereignty, the Act applies to only nine States (and several additional counties). While one State waits months or years and expends funds to implement a validly enacted law, its neighbor can typically put the same law into effect immediately, through the normal legislative process. Even if a noncovered jurisdiction is sued, there are important differences between those proceedings and preclearance proceedings; the preclearance proceeding "not only switches the burden of proof to the supplicant jurisdiction, but also applies substantive standards quite different from those governing the rest of the nation."

All this explains why, when we first upheld the Act in 1966, we described it as "stringent" and "potent." *Katzenbach.* We recognized that it "may have been an uncommon exercise of congressional power," but concluded that "legislative measures not otherwise appropriate" could be justified by "exceptional conditions." *Id*. We have since noted that the Act "authorizes federal intrusion into sensitive areas of state and local policymaking," *Lopez*, and represents an "extraordinary departure from the traditional course of relations between the States and the Federal Government," *Presley v. Etowah County Comm'n*. As we reiterated in *Northwest Austin*, the Act constitutes "extraordinary legislation otherwise unfamiliar to our federal system."

C

Nearly 50 years [since the passage of the VRA], things have changed dramatically. Shelby County contends that the preclearance requirement, even without regard to its disparate coverage, is now unconstitutional. Its arguments have a good deal of force. In the covered jurisdictions, "[v]oter turnout and registration rates now approach parity. Blatantly discriminatory evasions of federal decrees are rare. And minority candidates hold office at unprecedented levels." *Northwest Austin*. The tests and devices that blocked access to the ballot have been forbidden nationwide for over 40 years.

Those conclusions are not ours alone. Congress said the same when it reauthorized the Act in 2006, writing that "[s]ignificant progress has been made in eliminating first generation barriers experienced by minority voters, including increased numbers of registered minority voters, minority voter turnout, and minority representation in Congress, State legislatures, and local elected offices." The House Report elaborated that "the number of African-Americans who are registered and who turn out to cast ballots has increased significantly over the last 40 years, particularly since 1982," and noted that "[i]n some circumstances, minorities register to vote and cast ballots at levels that surpass those of white voters." That Report also explained that there have been "significant increases in the number of African-Americans serving in elected offices"; more specifically, there has been approximately a 1,000 percent increase since 1965 in the number of African-American elected officials in the six States originally covered by the Voting Rights Act.

There is no doubt that these improvements are in large part *because of* the Voting Rights Act. The Act has proved immensely successful at redressing racial discrimination and integrating the voting process. *See* § 2(b)(1), 120 Stat. 577. During the "Freedom Summer" of 1964, in Philadelphia, Mississippi, three men were murdered while working in the area to register African-American voters. On "Bloody Sunday" in 1965, in Selma, Alabama, police beat and used tear gas against hundreds marching in support of African-American enfranchisement. Today both of those towns are governed by African-American mayors. Problems remain in these States and others, but there is no denying that, due to the Voting Rights Act, our Nation has made great strides.

Yet the Act has not eased the restrictions in § 5 or narrowed the scope of the coverage formula in § 4(b) along the way. Those extraordinary and unprecedented features were reauthorized—as if nothing had changed. In fact, the Act's unusual remedies have grown even stronger. When Congress reauthorized the Act in 2006, it did so for another 25 years on top of the previous 40—a far cry from the initial five-year period. Congress also expanded the prohibitions in § 5. We had previously interpreted § 5 to prohibit only those redistricting plans that would have the purpose or effect of worsening the position of minority groups. In 2006, Congress amended § 5 to prohibit laws that could have favored such groups but did not do so because of a discriminatory purpose . . . even though we had stated that such broadening of § 5 coverage would "exacerbate the substantial federalism costs that the preclearance procedure already exacts, perhaps to the extent of raising concerns about § 5's constitutionality." In addition, Congress expanded § 5 to prohibit any voting law "that has the purpose of or will have the effect of diminishing the ability of any citizens of the United States," on account of race, color, or language minority status, "to elect their preferred candidates of choice." In light of those two amendments, the bar that covered jurisdictions must clear has been raised even as the conditions justifying that requirement have dramatically improved.

We have also previously highlighted the concern that "the preclearance requirements in one State [might] be unconstitutional in another." *Northwest Austin*. Nothing has happened since to alleviate this troubling concern about the current application of § 5.

Respondents do not deny that there have been improvements on the ground, but argue that much of this can be attributed to the deterrent effect of § 5, which dissuades covered jurisdictions from engaging in discrimination that they would resume should § 5 be struck down. Under this theory, however, § 5 would be effectively immune from scrutiny; no matter how "clean" the record of covered jurisdictions, the argument could always be made that it was deterrence that accounted for the good behavior.

The provisions of § 5 apply only to those jurisdictions singled out by § 4. We now consider whether that coverage formula is constitutional in light of current conditions.

III

A

When upholding the constitutionality of the coverage formula in 1966, we concluded that it was "rational in both practice and theory." *Katzenbach*. The formula looked to cause (discriminatory tests) and effect (low voter registration and turnout), and tailored the remedy (preclearance) to those jurisdictions exhibiting both.

By 2009, however, we concluded that the "coverage formula raise[d] serious constitutional questions." *Northwest Austin*. As we explained, a statute's "current burdens" must be justified by "current needs," and any "disparate geographic coverage" must be "sufficiently related to the problem that it targets." *Id.* The coverage formula met that test in 1965, but no longer does so.

Coverage today is based on decades-old data and eradicated practices. The formula captures States by reference to literacy tests and low voter registration and turnout in the 1960s and early 1970s. But such tests have been banned nationwide for over 40 years. § 6. And voter registration and turnout numbers in the covered States have risen dramatically in the years since. Racial disparity in those numbers was compelling evidence justifying the preclearance remedy and the coverage formula. *See, e.g., Katzenbach.* There is no longer such a disparity.

In 1965, the States could be divided into two groups: those with a recent history of voting tests and low voter registration and turnout, and those without those characteristics. Congress based its coverage formula on that distinction. Today the Nation is no longer divided along those lines, yet the Voting Rights Act continues to treat it as if it were.

B

The Government's defense of the formula is limited. First, the Government contends that the formula is "reverse-engineered": Congress identified the jurisdictions to be covered and *then* came up with criteria to describe them. Under that reasoning, there need not be any logical relationship between the criteria in the formula and the reason for coverage; all that is necessary is that the formula happen to capture the jurisdictions Congress wanted to single out.

The Government suggests that *Katzenbach* sanctioned such an approach, but the analysis in *Katzenbach* was quite different. *Katzenbach* reasoned that the coverage formula was rational because the "formula . . . was relevant to the problem": "Tests and devices are relevant to voting discrimination because of their long history as a tool for perpetrating the evil; a low voting rate is pertinent for the obvious reason that widespread disenfranchisement must inevitably affect the number of actual voters."

Here, by contrast, the Government's reverse-engineering argument does not even attempt to demonstrate the continued relevance of the formula to the problem it targets. And in the context of a decision as significant as this one—subjecting a disfavored subset of States to "extraordinary legislation otherwise unfamiliar to our federal system," *Northwest Austin*—that failure to establish even relevance is fatal.

The Government falls back to the argument that because the formula was relevant in 1965, its continued use is permissible so long as any discrimination remains in the States Congress identified back then—regardless of how that discrimination compares to discrimination in States unburdened by coverage. This argument does not look to "current political conditions," *Northwest Austin,* but instead relies on a comparison between the States in 1965. That comparison reflected the different histories of the North and South. It was in the South that slavery was upheld by law until uprooted by the Civil War, that the reign of Jim Crow denied African-Americans the most basic freedoms, and that state and local governments worked tirelessly to disenfranchise citizens on the basis of race. The Court invoked that history—rightly so—in sustaining the disparate coverage of the Voting Rights Act in 1966. *See Katzenbach*, ("The constitutional propriety of the Voting Rights Act of 1965 must be judged with reference to the historical experience which it reflects.").

But history did not end in 1965. By the time the Act was reauthorized in 2006, there had been 40 more years of it. In assessing the "current need [ ]" for a preclearance system that treats States differently from one another today, that history cannot be ignored. During that time, largely because of the Voting Rights Act, voting tests were abolished, disparities in voter registration and turnout due to race were erased, and African-Americans attained political office in record numbers. And yet the coverage formula that Congress reauthorized in 2006 ignores these developments, keeping the focus on decades-old data relevant to decades-old problems, rather than current data reflecting current needs.

The Fifteenth Amendment commands that the right to vote shall not be denied or abridged on account of race or color, and it gives Congress the power to enforce that command. The Amendment is not designed to punish for the past; its purpose is to ensure a better future. *See Rice v. Cayetano*, ("Consistent with the design of the Constitution, the [Fifteenth] Amendment is cast in fundamental terms, terms transcending the particular controversy which was the immediate impetus for its enactment."). To serve that purpose, Congress—if it is to divide the States—must identify those jurisdictions to be singled out on a basis that makes sense in light of current conditions. It cannot rely simply on the past. We made that clear in *Northwest Austin*, and we make it clear again today.

D

The dissent proceeds from a flawed premise. It quotes the famous sentence from *McCulloch v. Maryland*, with the following emphasis: "Let the end be legitimate, let it be within the scope of the constitution, and *all means which are appropriate, which are plainly adapted to that end, which are not prohibited, but consist with the letter and spirit of the constitution, are constitutional.*" *Post*, at 2637 (emphasis in dissent). But this case is about a part of the sentence that the dissent does not emphasize—the part that asks whether a legislative means is "consist[ent] with the letter and spirit of the constitution." The dissent states that "[i]t cannot tenably be maintained" that this is an issue with regard to the Voting Rights Act, but four years ago, in an opinion joined by two of today's dissenters, the Court expressly stated that "[t]he Act's preclearance requirement and its coverage formula raise serious constitutional questions." *Northwest Austin*. The dissent does not explain how those "serious constitutional questions" became untenable in four short years.

There is no valid reason to insulate the coverage formula from review merely because it was previously enacted 40 years ago. If Congress had started from scratch in 2006, it plainly could not have enacted the present coverage formula. It would have been irrational for Congress to distinguish between States in such a fundamental way based on 40-year-old data, when today's statistics tell an entirely different story. And it would have been irrational to base coverage on the use of voting tests 40 years ago, when such tests have been illegal since that time. But that is exactly what Congress has done.

Striking down an Act of Congress "is the gravest and most delicate duty that this Court is called on to perform." We do not do so lightly. That is why, in 2009, we took care to avoid ruling on the constitutionality of the Voting Rights Act when asked to do so, and instead resolved the case then before us on statutory grounds. But in issuing that decision, we expressed our broader concerns about the constitutionality of the Act. Congress could have updated the coverage formula at that time, but did not do so. Its failure to act leaves us today with no choice but to declare § 4(b) unconstitutional. The formula in that section can no longer be used as a basis for subjecting jurisdictions to preclearance.

Our decision in no way affects the permanent, nationwide ban on racial discrimination in voting found in § 2. We issue no holding on § 5 itself, only on the coverage formula. Congress may draft another formula based on current conditions. Such a formula is an initial prerequisite to a determination that exceptional conditions still exist justifying such an "extraordinary departure from the traditional course of relations between the States and the Federal Government." *Presley*. Our country has changed, and while any racial discrimination in voting is too much, Congress must ensure that the legislation it passes to remedy that problem speaks to current conditions.

The judgment of the Court of Appeals is reversed.

It is so ordered.

■ JUSTICE THOMAS, concurring.

I join the Court's opinion in full but write separately to explain that I would find § 5 of the Voting Rights Act unconstitutional as well. The Court's opinion sets forth the reasons.

"The Voting Rights Act of 1965 employed extraordinary measures to address an extraordinary problem." In the face of "unremitting and ingenious defiance" of citizens' constitutionally protected right to vote, § 5 was necessary to give effect to the Fifteenth Amendment in particular regions of the country. *South Carolina v. Katzenbach*. Though § 5's preclearance requirement represented a "shar[p] depart[ure]" from "basic principles" of federalism and the equal sovereignty of the States, *ante*, at 2622, 2623, the Court upheld the measure against early constitutional challenges because it was necessary at the time to address "voting discrimination where it persist[ed] on a pervasive scale." *Katzenbach.*

Today, our Nation has changed. "[T]he conditions that originally justified [§ 5] no longer characterize voting in the covered jurisdictions."

In spite of these improvements, however, Congress *increased* the already significant burdens of § 5.

While the Court claims to "issue no holding on § 5 itself," *ante*, at 2631, its own opinion compellingly demonstrates that Congress has failed to justify " 'current burdens' " with a record demonstrating " 'current needs.' " *See ante*, at 2622 (quoting *Northwest Austin, supra*, at 203). By leaving the inevitable conclusion unstated, the Court needlessly prolongs the demise of that provision. For the reasons stated in the Court's opinion, I would find § 5 unconstitutional.

■ JUSTICE GINSBURG, with whom JUSTICE BREYER, JUSTICE SOTOMAYOR, and JUSTICE KAGAN join, dissenting.

In the Court's view, the very success of § 5 of the Voting Rights Act demands its dormancy. Congress was of another mind. Recognizing that large progress has been made, Congress determined, based on a voluminous record, that the scourge of discrimination was not yet extirpated. The question this case presents is who decides whether, as currently operative, § 5 remains justifiable, this Court, or a Congress charged with the obligation to enforce the post-Civil War Amendments "by appropriate legislation." With overwhelming support in both Houses, Congress concluded that, for two prime reasons, § 5 should continue in force, unabated. First, continuance would facilitate completion of the impressive gains thus far made; and second, continuance would guard against backsliding. Those assessments were well within Congress' province to make and should elicit this Court's unstinting approbation.

I

Although the VRA wrought dramatic changes in the realization of minority voting rights, the Act, to date, surely has not eliminated all vestiges of discrimination against the exercise of the franchise by minority citizens. Jurisdictions covered by the preclearance requirement continued to submit, in large numbers, proposed changes to voting laws that the Attorney General declined to approve, auguring that barriers to minority voting would quickly resurface were the preclearance remedy eliminated. *City of Rome v. United States.* Congress also found that as "registration and voting of minority citizens increas[ed], other measures may be resorted to which would dilute increasing minority voting strength." *Ibid.* Efforts to reduce the impact of minority votes, in contrast to direct attempts to block access to the ballot, are aptly described as "second-generation barriers" to minority voting.

Second-generation barriers come in various forms. One of the blockages is racial gerrymandering, the redrawing of legislative districts in an "effort to segregate the races for purposes of voting." Another is adoption of a system of at-large voting in lieu of district-by-district voting in a city with a sizable black minority.

After considering the full legislative record, Congress made the following findings: The VRA has directly caused significant progress in eliminating first-generation barriers to ballot access, leading to a marked increase in minority voter registration and turnout and the number of minority elected officials. But despite this progress, "second generation barriers constructed to prevent minority voters from fully participating in the electoral process" continued to exist, as well as racially polarized voting in the covered jurisdictions, which increased the political vulnerability of racial and language minorities in those jurisdictions. Extensive "[e]vidence of continued discrimination," Congress concluded, "clearly show[ed] the continued need for Federal oversight" in covered jurisdictions. The overall record demonstrated to the federal lawmakers that, "without the continuation of the Voting Rights Act of 1965 protections, racial and language minority citizens will be deprived of the opportunity to exercise their right to vote, or will have their votes diluted, undermining the significant gains made by minorities in the last 40 years."

Based on these findings, Congress reauthorized preclearance for another 25 years, while also undertaking to reconsider the extension after 15 years to ensure that the provision was still necessary and effective. The question before the Court is whether Congress had the authority under the Constitution to act as it did.

II

In answering this question, the Court does not write on a clean slate. It is well established that Congress' judgment regarding exercise of its power to enforce the Fourteenth and Fifteenth Amendments warrants substantial deference. The VRA addresses the combination of race discrimination and the right to vote, which is "preservative of all rights." *Yick Wo v. Hopkins.* When confronting the most constitutionally invidious form of discrimination, and the most fundamental right in our democratic system, Congress' power to act is at its height.

The basis for this deference is firmly rooted in both constitutional text and precedent. The Fifteenth Amendment, which targets precisely and only racial discrimination in voting rights, states that, in this domain, "Congress shall have power to enforce this article by appropriate legislation." In choosing this language, the Amendment's framers invoked Chief Justice Marshall's formulation of the scope of Congress' powers under the Necessary and Proper Clause:

"Let the end be legitimate, let it be within the scope of the constitution, and *all means which are appropriate, which are plainly adapted to that end,* which are not prohibited, but consist with the letter and spirit of the constitution, are constitutional." *McCulloch v. Maryland.*

It cannot tenably be maintained that the VRA, an Act of Congress adopted to shield the right to vote from racial discrimination, is inconsistent with the letter or spirit of the Fifteenth Amendment, or any provision of the Constitution read in light of the Civil War Amendments.

The stated purpose of the Civil War Amendments was to arm Congress with the power and authority to protect all persons within the Nation from violations of their rights by the States. In exercising that power, then, Congress may use "all means which are appropriate, which are plainly adapted" to the constitutional ends declared by these Amendments. *McCulloch.* So when Congress acts to enforce the right to vote free from racial discrimination, we ask not whether Congress has chosen the means most wise, but whether Congress has rationally selected means appropriate to a legitimate end. "It is not for us to review the congressional resolution of [the need for its chosen remedy]. It is enough that we be able to perceive a basis upon which the Congress might resolve the conflict as it did." *Katzenbach v. Morgan.*

Until today, in considering the constitutionality of the VRA, the Court has accorded Congress the full measure of respect its judgments in this domain should garner. *South Carolina v. Katzenbach* supplies the standard of review: "As against the reserved powers of the States, Congress may use any rational means to effectuate the constitutional prohibition of racial discrimination in voting." Faced with subsequent reauthorizations of the VRA, the Court has reaffirmed this standard. *E.g., City of Rome.* Today's Court does not purport to alter settled precedent establishing that the dispositive question is whether Congress has employed "rational means."

For three reasons, legislation *reauthorizing* an existing statute is especially likely to satisfy the minimal requirements of the rational-basis test. First, when reauthorization is at issue, Congress has already assembled a legislative record justifying the initial legislation. Congress is entitled to consider that preexisting record as well as the record before it at the time of the vote on reauthorization.

Second, the very fact that reauthorization is necessary arises because Congress has built a temporal limitation into the Act. It has pledged to review, after a span of years (first 15, then 25) and in light of contemporary evidence, the continued need for the VRA. Cf. *Grutter v. Bollinger*, (anticipating, but not guaranteeing, that, in 25 years, "the use of racial preferences [in higher education] will no longer be necessary").

Third, a reviewing court should expect the record supporting reauthorization to be less stark than the record originally made. Demand for a record of violations equivalent to the one earlier made would expose Congress to a catch-22. If the statute was working, there would be less evidence of discrimination, so opponents might argue that Congress should not be allowed to renew the statute. In contrast, if the statute was not working, there would be plenty of evidence of discrimination, but scant reason to renew a failed regulatory regime.

This is not to suggest that congressional power in this area is limitless. It is this Court's responsibility to ensure that Congress has used appropriate means. The question meet for judicial review is whether the chosen means are "adapted to carry out the objects the amendments have in view." *Ex parte Virginia*. The Court's role, then, is not to substitute its judgment for that of Congress, but to determine whether the legislative record sufficed to show that "Congress could rationally have determined that [its chosen] provisions were appropriate methods." *City of Rome*.

In summary, the Constitution vests broad power in Congress to protect the right to vote, and in particular to combat racial discrimination in voting. This Court has repeatedly reaffirmed Congress' prerogative to use any rational means in exercise of its power in this area. And both precedent and logic dictate that the rational-means test should be easier to satisfy, and the burden on the statute's challenger should be higher, when what is at issue is the reauthorization of a remedy that the Court has previously affirmed, and that Congress found, from contemporary evidence, to be working to advance the legislature's legitimate objective.

III

The 2006 reauthorization of the Voting Rights Act fully satisfies the standard stated in *McCulloch*: Congress may choose any means "appropriate" and "plainly adapted to" a legitimate constitutional end. As we shall see, it is implausible to suggest otherwise.

A

I begin with the evidence on which Congress based its decision to continue the preclearance remedy. The surest way to evaluate whether that remedy remains in order is to see if preclearance is still effectively preventing discriminatory changes to voting laws. *See City of Rome*.

All told, between 1982 and 2006, DOJ objections blocked over 700 voting changes based on a determination that the changes were discriminatory. Congress found that the majority of DOJ objections included findings of discriminatory intent, and that the changes blocked by preclearance were "calculated decisions to keep minority voters from fully participating in the political process." On top of that, over the same time period the DOJ and private plaintiffs succeeded in more than 100 actions to enforce the § 5 preclearance requirements.

In addition to blocking proposed voting changes through preclearance, DOJ may request more information from a jurisdiction proposing a change. In turn, the jurisdiction may modify or withdraw the proposed change. The number of such modifications or withdrawals provides an indication of how many discriminatory proposals are deterred without need for formal objection. Congress received evidence that more than 800 proposed changes were altered or withdrawn since the last reauthorization in 1982. Congress also received empirical studies finding that DOJ's requests for more information had a significant effect on the degree to which covered jurisdictions "compl[ied] with their obligatio[n]" to protect minority voting rights.

Congress also received evidence that litigation under § 2 of the VRA was an inadequate substitute for preclearance in the covered jurisdictions. Litigation occurs only after the fact, when the illegal voting scheme has already been put in place and individuals have been elected pursuant to it, thereby gaining the advantages of incumbency.

The number of discriminatory changes blocked or deterred by the preclearance requirement suggests that the state of voting rights in the covered jurisdictions would have been significantly different absent this remedy. Surveying the type of changes stopped by the preclearance procedure conveys a sense of the extent to which § 5 continues to protect minority voting rights. Set out below are characteristic examples of changes blocked in the years leading up to the 2006 reauthorization:

- In 1995, Mississippi sought to reenact a dual voter registration system, "which was initially enacted in 1892 to disenfranchise Black voters," and for that reason, was struck down by a federal court in 1987.

- Following the 2000 census, the City of Albany, Georgia, proposed a redistricting plan that DOJ found to be "designed with the purpose to limit and retrogress the increased black voting strength . . . in the city as a whole."

- In 2001, the mayor and all-white five-member Board of Aldermen of Kilmichael, Mississippi, abruptly canceled the town's election after "an unprecedented number" of African-American candidates announced they were running for office. DOJ required an election, and the town elected its first black mayor and three black aldermen.

- In 2006, this Court found that Texas' attempt to redraw a congressional district to reduce the strength of Latino voters bore "the mark of intentional discrimination that could give rise to an equal protection violation," and ordered the district redrawn in compliance with the VRA. *League of United Latin American Citizens v. Perry*). In response, Texas sought to undermine this Court's order by curtailing early voting in the district, but was blocked by an action to enforce the § 5 preclearance requirement.

- In 2003, after African-Americans won a majority of the seats on the school board for the first time in history, Charleston County, South Carolina, proposed an at-large voting mechanism for the board. The proposal, made without consulting any of the African-American members of the school board, was found to be an " 'exact replica' "of an earlier voting scheme that, a federal court had determined, violated the VRA.

- In 1993, the City of Millen, Georgia, proposed to delay the election in a majority-black district by two years, leaving that district without representation on the city council while the neighboring majority-white district would have three representatives. DOJ blocked the proposal. The county then sought to move a polling place from a predominantly black neighborhood in the city to an inaccessible location in a predominantly white neighborhood outside city limits.

- In 2004, Waller County, Texas, threatened to prosecute two black students after they announced their intention to run for office. The county then attempted to reduce the availability of early voting in that election at polling places near a historically black university.

- In 1990, Dallas County, Alabama, whose county seat is the City of Selma, sought to purge its voter rolls of many black voters. DOJ rejected the purge as discriminatory, noting that it would have disqualified many citizens from voting "simply because they failed to pick up or return a voter update form, when there was no valid requirement that they do so."

These examples, and scores more like them, fill the pages of the legislative record. The evidence was indeed sufficient to support Congress' conclusion that "racial discrimination in voting in covered jurisdictions [remained] serious and pervasive."

True, conditions in the South have impressively improved since passage of the Voting Rights Act. Congress noted this improvement and found that the VRA was the driving force behind it. But Congress also found that voting discrimination had evolved into subtler second-generation barriers, and that eliminating preclearance would risk loss of the gains that had been made.

B

I turn next to the evidence on which Congress based its decision to reauthorize the coverage formula in § 4(b). Because Congress did not alter the coverage formula, the same jurisdictions previously subject to preclearance continue to be covered by this remedy. The evidence just described, of preclearance's continuing efficacy in blocking constitutional violations in the covered jurisdictions, itself grounded Congress' conclusion that the remedy should be retained for those jurisdictions.

There is no question, moreover, that the covered jurisdictions have a unique history of problems with racial discrimination in voting. Consideration of this long history, still in living memory, was altogether appropriate. The Court criticizes Congress for failing to recognize that "history did not end in 1965." But the Court ignores that "what's past is prologue." W. Shakespeare, The Tempest, act 2, sc. 1. And "[t]hose who cannot remember the past are condemned to repeat it." 1 G. Santayana, The Life of Reason 284 (1905). Congress was especially mindful of the need to reinforce the gains already made and to prevent backsliding.

Of particular importance, even after 40 years and thousands of discriminatory changes blocked by preclearance, conditions in the covered jurisdictions demonstrated that the formula was still justified by "current needs." *Northwest Austin.*

Congress learned of these conditions through a report, known as the Katz study, that looked at § 2 suits between 1982 and 2004. Because the private right of action authorized by § 2 of the VRA applies nationwide, a comparison of § 2 lawsuits in covered and noncovered jurisdictions provides an appropriate yardstick for measuring differences between covered and noncovered jurisdictions.

Although covered jurisdictions account for less than 25 percent of the country's population, the Katz study revealed that they accounted for 56 percent of successful § 2 litigation since 1982. Impact and Effectiveness 974. Controlling for population, there were nearly *four* times as many successful § 2 cases in covered jurisdictions as there were in noncovered jurisdictions.

The evidence before Congress, furthermore, indicated that voting in the covered jurisdictions was more racially polarized than elsewhere in the country. While racially polarized voting alone does not signal a constitutional violation, it is a factor that increases the vulnerability of racial minorities to discriminatory changes in voting law.

Just as buildings in California have a greater need to be earthquake-proofed, places where there is greater racial polarization in voting have a greater need for prophylactic measures to prevent purposeful race discrimination. This point was understood by Congress and is well recognized in the academic literature.

Congress was satisfied that the VRA's bailout mechanism provided an effective means of adjusting the VRA's coverage over time. Nearly 200 jurisdictions have successfully bailed out of the preclearance requirement, and DOJ has consented to every bailout application filed by an eligible jurisdiction since the current bailout procedure became effective in 1984. The bail-in mechanism has also worked. Several jurisdictions have been subject to federal preclearance by court orders, including the States of New Mexico and Arkansas.

This experience exposes the inaccuracy of the Court's portrayal of the Act as static, unchanged since 1965. Congress designed the VRA to be a dynamic statute, capable of adjusting to changing conditions. True, many covered jurisdictions have not been able to bail out due to recent acts of noncompliance with the VRA, but that truth reinforces the congressional judgment that these jurisdictions were rightfully subject to preclearance, and ought to remain under that regime.

IV

B

The Court stops any application of § 5 by holding that § 4(b)'s coverage formula is unconstitutional. It pins this result, in large measure, to "the fundamental principle of equal sovereignty." In *Katzenbach*, however, the Court held, in no uncertain terms, that the principle "*applies only to the terms upon which States are admitted to the Union,* and not to the remedies for local evils which have subsequently appeared." (emphasis added).

Today's unprecedented extension of the equal sovereignty principle outside its proper domain—the admission of new States—is capable of much mischief. Federal statutes that treat States disparately are hardly novelties. Do such provisions remain safe given the Court's expansion of equal sovereignty's sway?

C

The Court has time and again declined to upset legislation of this genre unless there was no or almost no evidence of unconstitutional action by States. *See, e.g., City of Boerne v. Flores.*

Throwing out preclearance when it has worked and is continuing to work to stop discriminatory changes is like throwing away your umbrella in a rainstorm because you are not getting wet.

The sad irony of today's decision lies in its utter failure to grasp why the VRA has proven effective. The Court appears to believe that the VRA's success in eliminating the specific devices extant in 1965 means that preclearance is no longer needed. With that belief, and the argument derived from it, history repeats itself. The same assumption—that the problem could be solved when particular methods of voting discrimination are identified and eliminated—was indulged and proved wrong repeatedly prior to the VRA's enactment. Unlike prior statutes, which singled out particular tests or devices, the VRA is grounded in Congress' recognition of the "variety and persistence" of measures designed to impair minority voting rights. *Katzenbach.* In truth, the evolution of voting discrimination into more subtle second-generation barriers is powerful evidence that a remedy as effective as preclearance remains vital to protect minority voting rights and prevent backsliding.

Beyond question, the VRA is no ordinary legislation. It is extraordinary because Congress embarked on a mission long delayed and of extraordinary importance: to realize the purpose and promise of the Fifteenth Amendment. For a half century, a concerted effort has been made to end racial discrimination in voting. Thanks to the Voting Rights Act, progress once the subject of a dream has been achieved and continues to be made.

The record supporting the 2006 reauthorization of the VRA is also extraordinary. It was described by the Chairman of the House Judiciary Committee as "one of the most extensive considerations of any piece of legislation that the United States Congress has dealt with in the 27 & half; years" he had served in the House. After exhaustive evidence-gathering and deliberative process, Congress reauthorized the VRA, including the coverage provision, with overwhelming bipartisan support. It was the judgment of Congress that "40 years has not been a sufficient amount of time to eliminate the vestiges of discrimination following nearly 100 years of disregard for the dictates of the 15th amendment and to ensure that the right of all citizens to vote is protected as guaranteed by the Constitution." That determination of the body empowered to enforce the Civil War Amendments "by appropriate legislation" merits this Court's utmost respect. In my judgment, the Court errs egregiously by overriding Congress' decision.

For the reasons stated, I would affirm the judgment of the Court of Appeals.

NOTES AND QUESTIONS

1. *The End of Racism?* The central message of Chief Justice Roberts's majority opinion is that the United States no longer experiences the type of systematic racial discrimination that it did prior to 1965. He writes, "things have changed," "our nation has made great strides," "there have been improvements on the ground," "history did not end in 1965," and "our country has changed." From the Chief Justice's perspective, Congress had failed to change the VRA along with the country. Is he right that, in light of the fact that the majority of Americans can formally exercise their right to vote, the coverage formula and the preclearance requirement can no longer be justified? What about Justice Ginsburg's dissent, which points to the evidence that Congress amassed to show that voting discrimination remains a problem? Who has the better of the argument here?

2. *Catch-22.* Justice Ginsburg argues that the Court's decision places Congress in a catch-22. If racial discrimination in voting had not improved since 1965, the Court would likely have struck down the VRA on the ground that its costs did not justify its benefits. But because the VRA has significantly diminished racial discrimination in voting and thus has made it harder for Congress to come up with egregious instances of voting discrimination, the Court strikes down the VRA on the ground that its costs

outweigh its benefits. Does the Chief Justice have a convincing response to Justice Ginsburg's observation?

3. ***Equality of Citizens and Not States.*** Chief Justice Roberts argues that Congress cannot justify permitting one state's laws to go into effect immediately, while forcing another state with an identical law to wait for preclearance. Commentators have criticized Roberts's analysis for focusing on the equality of states and ignoring voting rights violations against citizens. But is it not the case that the unequal treatment of states also means the unequal treatment of citizens? Suppose we have two states, Ohio and Texas. Both pass strict voter photo identification laws that have a disparate impact on the basis of race. Why should voters in Texas be afforded a layer of protection by the federal government that is not afforded to voters of color in Ohio?

4. ***What About Section 5?*** The majority opinion applies its analysis only to the coverage formula and not the preclearance requirement. But the opinion notes that the "Federal Government does not . . . have a general right to review and veto state enactments before they go into effect." If Congress were to draft another coverage formula, do you think the Court would find the preclearance requirement unconstitutional? Of course, given the current polarization in Congress, few expect Congress to do anything soon to update the VRA, though some legislators have introduced bills attempting to address the Court's concerns. *See* Voting Rights Act Amendment Act, https:// www.congress.gov/bill/114th-congress/house-bill/885/all-info. Should the majority have taken into account the fact that Congress is unlikely to fix the VRA, either the coverage formula or the preclearance requirement, because Congress is hopelessly divided?

5. ***Voting Rights for Native Peoples.*** Voting rights challenges remain significant for Native peoples, particularly on Indian reservations. In 1975, Congress amended the VRA to require election officials to provide ballots in languages other than English to certain language minorities, including Native peoples within the definition of language minority. Registration rates for Native peoples still continue to lag significantly behind that of other racial and ethnic groups. In some jurisdictions, less than 10% of Native peoples are registered to vote. Why do you think the bilingual ballots provision might not have made a significant difference? For analysis and background on voting rights issues with respect to Native peoples *see*, *Securing Indian Voting Rights*, 129 HARV. L. REV. 1731 (2016); Laughlin McDonald, *The Voting Rights Act in Indian Country: South Dakota, a Case Study*, 29 AM. INDIAN L. REV. 43 (2005); *see also* https://www.aclu.org/files/ pdfs/votingrights/indiancountryreport.pdf.

6. ***Advising Exercise: Fixing the VRA.*** Prior to *Shelby County*, as well as in its wake, commentators made a number of suggestions to update the coverage formula. Some commentators argued that Congress should update the formula using data on polarized voting. Others argued that Congress should use data on jurisdictions that have been found to engage in vote dilution in violation of section 2. Others proposed using survey data on anti-black stereotypes as part of a new coverage formula, with jurisdictions that

evidenced the most anti-black stereotypes being covered. Others have argued that Congress should abandon the coverage formula approach altogether. If you were asked to advise Congress on how to update the VRA post *Shelby County*, what would you suggest?

7.   *End of the Second Reconstruction.* Following the Court's decision in *Shelby County*, a number of states and localities changed their voting laws in ways that arguably made it harder for voters to exercise their right to vote. For example, Texas announced the implementation of a strict voter photo identification requirement, as did other states, such as Virginia, Alabama, Mississippi, South Carolina, and North Carolina. North Carolina also cut back the hours available for early voting and ended same day registration. Alabama announced a plan to close down driver's license offices, which advocates argued would make it more difficult for black voters to acquire the identification required for voting. Many of these laws would have been subject to the preclearance requirement, and many of them have a disparate racial impact. From the perspective of many voting rights activists, *Shelby County* has reopened the door to racial discrimination in voting. Some commentators have even argued that the Court's decision in *Shelby County* reflects the end of the Second Reconstruction. It signifies the end of Court's and Congress's departure from their role as enforcers of racial equality in the political process. Do you agree? In what ways is the Court's decision in *Shelby County* similar or different to the Court's decision in the *Civil Rights Cases*?

III. VOTING AS A GROUP RIGHT

The Voting Rights Act and the courts have done tremendous work in securing the formal individual right to vote and eliminating what some scholars call first generation voting rights problems, such as obstacles to voting registration and casting a ballot. But voting is not just about securing the individual right. It also has a collective dimension. Voting is also a group right. It is the mechanism for harnessing and exercising political power by enabling like-minded voters to band together. This part explores the group dimensions of the right to vote.

A.   VOTE DILUTION

Almost as soon as black voters in the South were able to exercise their formal right to vote, state and local officials devised schemes to minimize black political power and make their ballot less effective. Those schemes did not focus on depriving black voters of the individual right to vote directly, but rather on manipulating electoral structures so as to diminish the electoral strength of blacks as a group. Chandler Davidson, *Minority Vote Dilution: An Overview* 4 *in* MINORITY VOTE DILUTION (Chandler Davidson ed. 1989). This vote dilution occurs through the interaction of voter behavior and legal rules. Even when every individual voter is allowed to register, vote, and have their vote counted equally, vote dilution is still possible, because groups have different preferences and vote as blocs. The law determines groups' effectiveness in a variety of ways, including by organizing them into voting districts. Vote dilution can occur through how the state draws these lines, and it is thus parasitic on choices made by both voters—private preferences—and the government—state action.

Southern officials have used a number of devices to dilute the votes of black voters. They sometimes have deployed the racial gerrymander, which can take one of two forms. The person drawing the district lines can gerrymander by "packing," which means putting or packing more black voters in the district than is necessary for them to elect the person that they want. By so doing, the line drawer removes black voters from the surrounding districts so that they cannot have any influence in those districts. Or the person drawing the lines can gerrymander by "cracking", which means breaking up majority-minority districts, or districts with a significant number of voters of color, and removing just enough of those voters from the district so that minorities can never elect the person of their choice.

A preferred tool of local and state officials in the South has been the at-large or multi-member district. In an at-large district there is more than one seat up for election, and the same voters can vote for all the seats. The at-large district worked beautifully because it enabled the numerical majority to elect all of the candidates and the minority to elect none. Suppose that you have a city, City, with one hundred inhabitants. Suppose that City is composed of two groups, Blues and Greens, and that both groups engage in bloc voting—the Blues vote for the same candidates and the Greens vote for the same candidates. City is inhabited by 51 Blues and 49 Greens. City is entitled to two council seats and is debating how to elect the two council members. There are two plans presented. Under Plan A, City is divided into two single-member districts of equal population (or as equally as practicable) and each district elects one council member. Plan B creates one district, an at-large district, that is coterminous with the City's geographic boundaries. Under Plan B, each voter votes for two candidates. The voters will all vote on which plan to choose. Which plan do you think will be chosen? Which plan do you think ought to be chosen and why? If you are a Green are you comforted by the fact that you have a formal right to vote and you can vote for the candidate of your choice?

In *Thornburg v. Gingles*, below, Congress and the Court used section 2 of the Voting Rights Act to address the problem of vote dilution in at-large districts. As you read *Gingles*, consider whether the Court properly interpreted the statute and identified the correct remedy.

Thornburg v. Gingles

Supreme Court of the United States, 1986.
478 U.S. 30.

■ JUSTICE BRENNAN announced the judgment of the Court and delivered the opinion of the Court with respect to Parts I, II, III-A, III-B, IV-A, and V, and an opinion with respect to Part III-C, in which JUSTICE MARSHALL, JUSTICE BLACKMUN, and JUSTICE STEVENS join, and an opinion with respect to Part IV-B, in which JUSTICE WHITE joins.

This case requires that we construe for the first time § 2 of the Voting Rights Act of 1965, as amended June 29, 1982. The specific question to be decided is whether the three-judge District Court, convened in the Eastern District of North Carolina pursuant to 28 U.S.C. § 2284(a) and 42 U.S.C. § 1973c, correctly held that the use in a legislative redistricting plan of multimember districts in five North Carolina legislative districts violated § 2 by impairing the opportunity of black voters "to participate in the political process and to elect representatives of their choice."

I
BACKGROUND

In April 1982, the North Carolina General Assembly enacted a legislative redistricting plan for the State's Senate and House of Representatives. Appellees, black citizens of North Carolina who are registered to vote, challenged seven districts, one single-member and six multimember districts, alleging that the redistricting scheme impaired black citizens' ability to elect representatives of their choice in violation of the Fourteenth and Fifteenth Amendments to the United States Constitution and of § 2 of the Voting Rights Act.

Section 2, as amended reads as follows:

"(a) No voting qualification or prerequisite to voting or standard, practice, or procedure shall be imposed or applied by any State or political subdivision in a manner which results in a denial or abridgement of the right of any citizen of the United States to vote on account of race or color, or in contravention of the guarantees set forth in section 4(f)(2), as provided in subsection (b).

"(b) A violation of subsection (a) is established if, based on the totality of circumstances, it is shown that the political processes leading to nomination or election in the State or political subdivision are not equally open to participation by members of a class of citizens protected by subsection (a) in that its members have less opportunity than other members of the electorate to participate in the political process and to elect representatives of their choice. The extent to which members of a protected class have been elected to office in the State or political subdivision is one circumstance which may be considered: Provided, That nothing in this section establishes a right to have members of a protected class elected in numbers equal to their proportion in the population."

The Senate Judiciary Committee majority Report accompanying the bill that amended § 2, elaborates on the circumstances that might be probative of a § 2 violation, noting the following "typical factors":

"1. the extent of any history of official discrimination in the state or political subdivision that touched the right of the members of the minority group to register, to vote, or otherwise to participate in the democratic process;

"2. the extent to which voting in the elections of the state or political subdivision is racially polarized;

"3. the extent to which the state or political subdivision has used unusually large election districts, majority vote requirements, anti-single shot provisions, or other voting practices or procedures that may enhance the opportunity for discrimination against the minority group;

"4. if there is a candidate slating process, whether the members of the minority group have been denied access to that process;

"5. the extent to which members of the minority group in the state or political subdivision bear the effects of discrimination in such areas as education, employment and health, which hinder their ability to participate effectively in the political process;

"6. whether political campaigns have been characterized by overt or subtle racial appeals;

"7. the extent to which members of the minority group have been elected to public office in the jurisdiction.

"Additional factors that in some cases have had probative value as part of plaintiffs' evidence to establish a violation are:

"whether there is a significant lack of responsiveness on the part of elected officials to the particularized needs of the members of the minority group.

"whether the policy underlying the state or political subdivision's use of such voting qualification, prerequisite to voting, or standard, practice or procedure is tenuous." S.Rep., at 28–29, U.S.Code Cong. & Admin.News 1982, pp. 206–207.

The District Court applied the "totality of the circumstances" test set forth in § 2(b) to appellees' statutory claim, and, relying principally on the factors outlined in the Senate Report, held that the redistricting scheme violated § 2 because it resulted in the dilution of black citizens' votes in all seven disputed districts. In light of this conclusion, the court did not reach appellees' constitutional claims.

Preliminarily, the court found that black citizens constituted a distinct population and registered-voter minority in each challenged district. The court noted that at the time the multimember districts were created, there were concentrations of black citizens within the boundaries of each that were sufficiently large and contiguous to constitute effective voting majorities in single-member districts lying wholly within the boundaries of the multimember districts. With respect to the challenged single-member district, Senate District No. 2, the court also found that there existed a concentration of black citizens within its boundaries and within those of adjoining Senate District No. 6 that was sufficient in numbers and in contiguity to constitute an effective voting majority in a single-member district. The District Court then proceeded to find that the following circumstances combined with the multimember districting scheme to result in the dilution of black citizens' votes.

First, the court found that North Carolina had officially discriminated against its black citizens with respect to their exercise of the voting franchise from approximately 1900 to 1970 by employing at different times a poll tax, a literacy test, a prohibition against bullet (single-shot) voting and designated seat plans for multimember districts. The court observed that even after the removal of direct barriers to black voter registration, such as the poll tax and literacy test, black voter registration remained relatively depressed; in 1982 only 52.7% of age-qualified blacks statewide were registered to vote, whereas 66.7% of whites were registered. The District Court found these statewide depressed levels of black voter registration to be present in all of the disputed districts and to be traceable, at least in part, to the historical pattern of statewide official discrimination.

Second, the court found that historic discrimination in education, housing, employment, and health services had resulted in a lower socioeconomic status for North Carolina blacks as a group than for whites. The court concluded that this lower status both gives rise to special group interests and hinders blacks' ability to participate effectively in the political process and to elect representatives of their choice.

Third, the court considered other voting procedures that may operate to lessen the opportunity of black voters to elect candidates of their choice. It noted that North Carolina has a majority vote requirement for primary elections and, while acknowledging that no black candidate for election to the State General Assembly had failed to win solely because of this requirement, the court concluded that it nonetheless presents a continuing practical impediment to the opportunity of black voting minorities to elect candidates of their choice. The court also remarked on the fact that North Carolina does not have a subdistrict residency requirement for members of the General Assembly elected from multimember districts, a requirement which the court found could offset to some extent the disadvantages minority voters often experience in multimember districts.

Fourth, the court found that white candidates in North Carolina have encouraged voting along color lines by appealing to racial prejudice. It noted that the record is replete with specific examples of racial appeals, ranging in style from overt and blatant to subtle and furtive, and in date from the 1890's to the 1984 campaign for a seat in the United States Senate. The court determined that the use of racial appeals in political campaigns in North Carolina persists to the present day and that its current effect is to lessen to some degree the opportunity of black citizens to participate effectively in the political processes and to elect candidates of their choice.

Fifth, the court examined the extent to which blacks have been elected to office in North Carolina, both statewide and in the challenged districts. It found, among other things, that prior to World War II, only one black had been elected to public office in this century. While recognizing that "it has now become possible for black citizens to be elected to office at all levels of state government in North Carolina," the court found that, in comparison to white candidates running for the same office, black candidates are at a disadvantage in terms of relative probability of success. It also found that the overall rate of black electoral success has been minimal in relation to the percentage of blacks in the total state population. For example, the court noted, from 1971 to 1982 there were at any given time only two-to-four blacks in the 120-member House of Representatives—that is, only 1.6% to 3.3% of House members were black. From 1975 to 1983 there were at any one time only one or two blacks in the 50-member State Senate—that is, only 2% to 4% of State Senators were black. By contrast, at the time of the District Court's opinion, blacks constituted about 22.4% of the total state population.

With respect to the success in this century of black candidates in the contested districts, the court found that only one black had been elected to House District 36—after this lawsuit began. Similarly, only one black had served in the Senate from District 22, from 1975–1980. Before the 1982 election, a black was elected only twice to the House from District 39 (part of Forsyth County); in the 1982 contest two blacks were elected. Since 1973 a black citizen had been elected each 2-year term to the House from District 23 (Durham County), but no black had been elected to the Senate from Durham County. In House District 21 (Wake County), a black had been elected twice to the House, and another black served two terms in the State Senate. No black had ever been elected to the House or Senate from the area covered by House District No. 8, and no black person had ever been elected to the Senate from the area covered by Senate District No. 2.

The court did acknowledge the improved success of black candidates in the 1982 elections, in which 11 blacks were elected to the State House of Representatives, including 5 blacks from the multimember districts at issue here. However, the court pointed out that the 1982 election was conducted after the commencement of this litigation. The court found the circumstances of the 1982 election sufficiently aberrational and the success by black candidates too minimal and too recent in relation to the long history of complete denial of elective opportunities to support the conclusion that black voters' opportunities to elect representatives of their choice were not impaired.

Finally, the court considered the extent to which voting in the challenged districts was racially polarized. Based on statistical evidence presented by expert witnesses, supplemented to some degree by the testimony of lay witnesses, the court found that all of the challenged districts exhibit severe and persistent racially polarized voting.

Based on these findings, the court declared the contested portions of the 1982 redistricting plan violative of § 2 and enjoined appellants from conducting elections pursuant to those portions of the plan. Appellants, the Attorney General of North Carolina and others, took a direct appeal to this Court, pursuant to 28 U.S.C. § 1253, with respect to five of the multimember districts—House Districts 21, 23, 36, and 39, and Senate District 22. Appellants argue, first, that the District Court utilized a legally incorrect standard in determining whether the contested districts exhibit racial bloc voting to an extent that is cognizable under § 2. Second, they contend that the court used an incorrect definition of racially polarized voting and thus erroneously relied on statistical evidence that was not probative of polarized voting. Third, they maintain that the court assigned the wrong weight to evidence of some black candidates' electoral success. Finally, they argue that the trial court erred in concluding that these multimember districts result in black citizens having less opportunity than their white counterparts to participate in the political process and to elect representatives of their choice. We noted probable jurisdiction, and now affirm with respect to all of the districts except House District 23. With regard to District 23, the judgment of the District Court is reversed.

II

B

Appellees contend that the legislative decision to employ multimember, rather than single-member, districts in the contested jurisdictions dilutes their votes by submerging them in a white majority, thus impairing their ability to elect representatives of their choice.

The essence of a § 2 claim is that a certain electoral law, practice, or structure interacts with social and historical conditions to cause an inequality in the opportunities enjoyed by black and white voters to elect their preferred representatives. This Court has long recognized that multimember districts and at-large voting schemes may " 'operate to minimize or cancel out the voting strength of racial [minorities in] the voting population.' " The theoretical basis for this type of impairment is that where minority and majority voters consistently prefer different candidates, the majority, by virtue of its numerical superiority, will regularly defeat the choices of minority voters. Multimember districts and at-large election schemes, however, are not per se violative of minority voters' rights. Minority voters who contend that the multimember form of districting violates § 2, must prove that the use of a multimember electoral structure operates to minimize or cancel out their ability to elect their preferred candidates.

While many or all of the factors listed in the Senate Report may be relevant to a claim of vote dilution through submergence in multimember districts, unless there is a conjunction of the following circumstances, the use of multimember districts generally will not impede the ability of minority voters to elect representatives of their choice. Stated succinctly, a bloc voting majority must usually be able to defeat candidates supported by a politically cohesive, geographically insular minority group. These circumstances are necessary preconditions for multimember districts to operate to impair minority voters' ability to elect representatives of their choice for the following reasons. First, the minority group must be able to demonstrate that it is sufficiently large and geographically compact to constitute a majority in a single-member district. If it is not, as would be the case in a substantially integrated district, the multi-member form of the district cannot be responsible for minority voters' inability to elect its candidates. Second, the minority group must be able to show that it is politically cohesive. If the minority group is not politically cohesive, it cannot be said that the selection of a multimember electoral structure thwarts distinctive minority group interests. Third, the minority must be able to demonstrate that the white majority votes sufficiently as a bloc to enable it—in the absence of special circumstances, such as the minority candidate running unopposed—usually to defeat the minority's preferred candidate. In establishing this last circumstance, the minority group demonstrates that submergence in a white multimember district impedes its ability to elect its chosen representatives.

Finally, we observe that the usual predictability of the majority's success distinguishes structural dilution from the mere loss of an occasional election.

III

RACIALLY POLARIZED VOTING

Having stated the general legal principles relevant to claims that § 2 has been violated through the use of multimember districts, we turn to the arguments of appellants and of the United States as amicus curiae addressing racially polarized voting. First, we describe the District

Court's treatment of racially polarized voting. Next, we consider appellants' claim that the District Court used an incorrect legal standard to determine whether racial bloc voting in the contested districts was sufficiently severe to be cognizable as an element of a § 2 claim. Finally, we consider appellants' contention that the trial court employed an incorrect definition of racially polarized voting and thus erroneously relied on statistical evidence that was not probative of racial bloc voting.

A

THE DISTRICT COURT'S TREATMENT OF RACIALLY POLARIZED VOTING

The investigation conducted by the District Court into the question of racial bloc voting credited some testimony of lay witnesses, but relied principally on statistical evidence presented by appellees' expert witnesses, in particular that offered by Dr. Bernard Grofman. Dr. Grofman collected and evaluated data from General Assembly primary and general elections involving black candidacies. These elections were held over a period of three different election years in the six originally challenged multimember districts. Dr. Grofman subjected the data to two complementary methods of analysis—extreme case analysis and bivariate ecological regression analysis—in order to determine whether blacks and whites in these districts differed in their voting behavior. These analytic techniques yielded data concerning the voting patterns of the two races, including estimates of the percentages of members of each race who voted for black candidates.

The court's initial consideration of these data took the form of a three-part inquiry: did the data reveal any correlation between the race of the voter and the selection of certain candidates; was the revealed correlation statistically significant; and was the difference in black and white voting patterns "substantively significant"? The District Court found that blacks and whites generally preferred different candidates and, on that basis, found voting in the districts to be racially correlated. The court accepted Dr. Grofman's expert opinion that the correlation between the race of the voter and the voter's choice of certain candidates was statistically significant. Finally, adopting Dr. Grofman's terminology, the court found that in all but 2 of the 53 elections the degree of racial bloc voting was "so marked as to be substantively significant, in the sense that the results of the individual election would have been different depending upon whether it had been held among only the white voters or only the black voters."

The court also reported its findings, both in tabulated numerical form and in written form, that a high percentage of black voters regularly supported black candidates and that most white voters were extremely reluctant to vote for black candidates. The court then considered the relevance to the existence of legally significant white bloc voting of the fact that black candidates have won some elections. It determined that in most instances, special circumstances, such as incumbency and lack of opposition, rather than a diminution in usually severe white bloc voting, accounted for these candidates' success. The court also suggested that black voters' reliance on bullet voting was a significant factor in their successful efforts to elect candidates of their choice. Based on all of the evidence before it, the trial court concluded that each of the districts experienced racially polarized voting "in a persistent and severe degree."

B

THE DEGREE OF BLOC VOTING THAT IS
LEGALLY SIGNIFICANT UNDER § 2

2

The Standard for Legally Significant Racial Bloc Voting

The Senate Report states that the "extent to which voting in the elections of the state or political subdivision is racially polarized" is relevant to a vote dilution claim. Further, courts and commentators agree that racial bloc voting is a key element of a vote dilution claim. Because, as we explain below, the extent of bloc voting necessary to demonstrate that a minority's ability to elect its preferred representatives is impaired varies according to several factual circumstances, the degree of bloc voting which constitutes the threshold of legal significance will vary from district to district. Nonetheless, it is possible to state some general principles and we proceed to do so.

The purpose of inquiring into the existence of racially polarized voting is twofold: to ascertain whether minority group members constitute a politically cohesive unit and to determine whether whites vote sufficiently as a bloc usually to defeat the minority's preferred candidates. Thus, the question whether a given district experiences legally significant racially polarized voting requires discrete inquiries into minority and white voting practices. A showing that a significant number of minority group members usually vote for the same candidates is one way of proving the political cohesiveness necessary to a vote dilution claim and, consequently, establishes minority bloc voting within the context of § 2. And, in general, a white bloc vote that normally will defeat the combined strength of minority support plus white "crossover" votes rises to the level of legally significant white bloc voting. The amount of white bloc voting that can generally "minimize or cancel" black voters' ability to elect representatives of their choice, however, will vary from district to district according to a number of factors, including the nature of the allegedly dilutive electoral mechanism; the presence or absence of other potentially dilutive electoral devices, such as majority vote requirements, designated posts, and prohibitions against bullet voting; the percentage of registered voters in the district who are members of the minority group; the size of the district; and, in multimember districts, the number of seats open and the number of candidates in the field.

Because loss of political power through vote dilution is distinct from the mere inability to win a particular election, a pattern of racial bloc voting that extends over a period of time is more probative of a claim that a district experiences legally significant polarization than are the results of a single election. Also for this reason, in a district where elections are shown usually to be polarized, the fact that racially polarized voting is not present in one or a few individual elections does not necessarily negate the conclusion that the district experiences legally significant bloc voting. Furthermore, the success of a minority candidate in a particular election does not necessarily prove that the district did not experience polarized voting in that election; special circumstances, such as the absence of an opponent, incumbency, or the utilization of bullet voting, may explain minority electoral success in a polarized contest.

As must be apparent, the degree of racial bloc voting that is cognizable as an element of a § 2 vote dilution claim will vary according to a variety of factual circumstances. Consequently, there is no simple doctrinal test for the existence of legally significant racial bloc voting. However, the foregoing general principles should provide courts with substantial guidance in determining whether evidence that black and white voters generally prefer different candidates rises to the level of legal significance under § 2.

3

Standard Utilized by the District Court

We conclude that the District Court's approach, which tested data derived from three election years in each district, and which revealed that blacks strongly supported black candidates, while, to the black candidates' usual detriment, whites rarely did, satisfactorily addresses each facet of the proper legal standard.

EVIDENCE OF RACIALLY POLARIZED VOTING

1

Appellants' Argument

North Carolina and the United States also contest the evidence upon which the District Court relied in finding that voting patterns in the challenged districts were racially polarized. They argue that the term "racially polarized voting" must, as a matter of law, refer to voting patterns for which the *principal cause* is race. They contend that the District Court utilized a legally incorrect definition of racially polarized voting by relying on bivariate statistical analyses which merely demonstrated a *correlation* between the race of the voter and the level of voter support for certain candidates, but which did not prove that race was the primary determinant of voters' choices. According to appellants and the United States, only multiple regression analysis, which can take account of other variables which might also explain voters' choices, such as "party affiliation, age, religion, income [,] incumbency, education, campaign expenditures," . . . can prove that race was the primary determinant of voter behavior.

2

Causation Irrelevant to Section 2 Inquiry

The first reason we reject appellants' argument that racially polarized voting refers to voting patterns that are in some way caused by race, rather than to voting patterns that are merely correlated with the race of the voter, is that the reasons black and white voters vote differently have no relevance to the central inquiry of § 2. By contrast, the correlation between race of voter and the selection of certain candidates is crucial to that inquiry.

Both § 2 itself and the Senate Report make clear that the critical question in a § 2 claim is whether the use of a contested electoral practice or structure results in members of a protected group having less opportunity than other members of the electorate to participate in the political process and to elect representatives of their choice. As we explained, multimember districts may impair the ability of blacks to elect representatives of their choice where blacks vote sufficiently as a bloc as to be able to elect their preferred candidates in a black majority, single-member district and where a white majority votes sufficiently as a bloc usually to defeat the candidates chosen by blacks. It is the difference between the choices made by blacks and whites—not the reasons for that difference—that results in blacks having less opportunity than whites to elect their preferred representatives. Consequently, we conclude that under the "results test" of § 2, only the correlation between race of voter and selection of certain candidates, not the causes of the correlation, matters.

The irrelevance to a § 2 inquiry of the reasons why black and white voters vote differently supports, by itself, our rejection of appellants' theory of racially polarized voting.

3

Race of Voter as Primary Determinant of Voter Behavior

Appellants and the United States contend that the legal concept of "racially polarized voting" refers not to voting patterns that are merely *correlated with the voter's race*, but to voting patterns that are *determined primarily by the voter's race*, rather than by the voter's other socioeconomic characteristics.

The first problem with this argument is that it ignores the fact that members of geographically insular racial and ethnic groups frequently share socioeconomic characteristics, such as income level, employment status, amount of education, housing and other living conditions, religion, language, and so forth.

Furthermore, under appellants' theory of racially polarized voting, even uncontrovertible evidence that candidates strongly preferred by black voters are *always* defeated by a bloc voting white majority would be dismissed for failure to prove racial polarization whenever the black and white populations could be described in terms of other socioeconomic characteristics.

Congress could not have intended that courts employ this definition of racial bloc voting. First, this definition leads to results that are inconsistent with the effects test adopted by Congress when it amended § 2 and with the Senate Report's admonition that courts take a "functional" view of the political process, and conduct a searching and practical evaluation of reality.

Second, appellants' interpretation of "racially polarized voting" creates an irreconcilable tension between their proposed treatment of socioeconomic characteristics in the bloc voting context and the Senate Report's statement that "the extent to which members of the minority group . . . bear the effects of discrimination in such areas as education, employment and health" may be relevant to a § 2 claim.

6

Summary

In sum, we would hold that the legal concept of racially polarized voting, as it relates to claims of vote dilution, refers only to the existence of a correlation between the race of voters and the selection of certain candidates. Plaintiffs need not prove causation or intent in order to prove a prima facie case of racial bloc voting and defendants may not rebut that case with evidence of causation or intent.

IV

THE LEGAL SIGNIFICANCE OF SOME
BLACK CANDIDATES' SUCCESS

A

Nothing in the statute or its legislative history prohibited the court from viewing with some caution black candidates' success in the 1982 election, and from deciding on the basis of all the relevant circumstances to accord greater weight to blacks' relative lack of success over the course of several recent elections. Consequently, we hold that the District Court did not err, as a matter of law, in refusing to treat the fact that some black candidates have succeeded as dispositive of appellees' § 2 claim. Where multimember districting generally works to dilute the minority vote, it cannot be defended on the ground that it sporadically and serendipitously benefits minority voters.

B

The District Court did err, however, in ignoring the significance of the sustained success black voters have experienced in House District 23.

In that district, the last six elections have resulted in proportional representation for black residents. This persistent proportional representation is inconsistent with appellees' allegation that the ability of black voters in District 23 to elect representatives of their choice is not equal to that enjoyed by the white majority.

In some situations, it may be possible for § 2 plaintiffs to demonstrate that such sustained success does not accurately reflect the minority group's ability to elect its preferred representatives, but appellees have not done so here. Appellees presented evidence relating to black electoral success in the last three elections; they failed utterly, though, to offer any explanation for the success of black candidates in the previous three elections. Consequently, we believe that the District Court erred, as a matter of law, in ignoring the sustained success black voters have enjoyed in House District 23, and would reverse with respect to that District.

V

ULTIMATE DETERMINATION OF VOTE DILUTION

Finally, appellants and the United States dispute the District Court's ultimate conclusion that the multimember districting scheme at issue in this case deprived black voters of an equal opportunity to participate in the political process and to elect representatives of their choice.

B

The District Court in this case carefully considered the totality of the circumstances and found that in each district racially polarized voting; the legacy of official discrimination in voting matters, education, housing, employment, and health services; and the persistence of campaign appeals to racial prejudice acted in concert with the multimember districting scheme to impair the ability of geographically insular and politically cohesive groups of black voters to participate equally in the political process and to elect candidates of their choice. It found that the success a few black candidates have enjoyed in these districts is too recent, too limited, and, with regard to the 1982 elections, perhaps too aberrational, to disprove its conclusion. Excepting House District 23, with respect to which the District Court committed legal error, we affirm the District Court's judgment. We cannot say that the District Court, composed of local judges who are well acquainted with the political realities of the State, clearly erred in concluding that use of a multimember electoral structure has caused black voters in the districts other than House District 23 to have less opportunity than white voters to elect representatives of their choice.

NOTES AND QUESTIONS

1.   *The Elements of a Racial Vote Dilution Claim.* In order to state a claim of vote dilution in the context of multimember districts, the Court held that a plaintiff must be able to prove three factors, which are usually called the *Gingles* factors or *Gingles* preconditions. First, the racial group must be large enough and geographically compact to be able to fit into a single-member district. Second, the racial group must be politically cohesive. Third, the plaintiffs must be able to show that the racial majority votes as bloc to defeat the electoral preferences of the racial minority. After meeting the *Gingles* preconditions, the plaintiffs must also show that, under the "totality of circumstances," they do not possess the same opportunities to participate in the political process and elect representatives of their choice enjoyed by other voters. Courts are guided in their "totality of circumstances" inquiry by the factors listed in the Senate Report. For many courts, the most important factors in the inquiry are the "extent to which minority group members have been elected to public office in the jurisdiction," and "the extent to which voting in the elections of the state or political subdivision is racially polarized." The factors listed in the Senate Report were intended to codify the elements of a vote dilution claim as articulated by the Supreme Court in *White v. Regester*, 412 U.S. 755 (1973), and the Fifth Circuit in *Zimmer v. McKeithen*, 485 F.2d 1297 (5th Cir. 1973).

2.   *Remedy.* If a court finds that the *Gingles* preconditions are met and the "totality of circumstances" inquiry is satisfied, the plaintiff has stated a vote dilution claim and is entitled to a remedy, which is usually a single-member majority-minority district. Majority-minority means that the racial minority group now constitutes the majority of voters in the district, which should presumably enable voters to elect the candidate of their choice.

3.   *Racial Bloc Voting and Causation.* The Court in *Gingles* made racial bloc voting the *sine qua non* of a vote dilution claim. But Justice Brennan refused to make causation—why voters vote as racial blocs—a part of the inquiry. Do you think causation should matter as part of the legal inquiry? In *Gingles*, it was pretty clear that white voters in North Carolina were unwilling to vote for black candidates because of racial prejudice. There was a strong history of racial discrimination in North Carolina that impacted African Americans in all facets of their lives. But what if white voters voted as a bloc because they had different ideological or partisan preferences than black voters? Or because of different socioeconomic status? Or because white voters and black voters have different preferences on the issues? Is correlation sufficient or should we inquire into causation?

In cases prior to *Gingles*, the Court had held that the Constitution protects voters of color when they are the victims of racial discrimination but not when they are the victims of political discrimination. In *Whitcomb v. Chavis*, 403 U.S. 124 (1971), black plaintiffs challenged an Indiana legislative plan that used multimember districts for legislative elections. They sought single-member districts as a remedy. The plaintiffs argued that the districts diluted their vote in violation of the Fourteenth Amendment. The Court rejected the challenge on the ground that the plaintiffs did not show that their votes were diluted because of race. The Court acknowledged that the plaintiffs' preferred candidates routinely lost at the polls. But the Court concluded that plaintiffs' candidates lost because the plaintiffs chose to align their political fortunes with those of the Democratic Party, which also routinely lost at the polls. The Court stated that "the failure of the [plaintiffs] to have legislative seats in proportion to [their] population emerges more as a function of losing elections than of built in bias against" them. The voting power of the plaintiffs may have been diluted, "but this seems a mere euphemism for political defeat at the polls." 403 U.S. at 153. By contrast, in *White v. Regester*, 412 U.S. 755 (1973), the Court upheld a challenge to multimember districts by Latino and African American plaintiffs who challenged a legislative redistricting plan in Texas. The Court agreed with the lower court's findings of a history of racial discrimination and that the plaintiffs were effectively excluded from the political process leading to the nomination and election of state representatives. Consequently, single-member districts were an appropriate remedy. 412 U.S. at 765. *Whitcomb v. Chavis* and *White v. Regester* have come to stand for the proposition that courts will intervene in the political process on behalf of voters of color to remedy racial discrimination but not to remedy political discrimination. *See* for example *LULAC v. Clements*, 999 F.2d 831 (5th Cir. 1993). Do you think the distinction makes sense? Is political discrimination unrelated to racial discrimination?

4.   *Exercise.* One of the factors listed in the Senate Report and noted by the Court in *Gingles* is "whether political campaigns have been characterized by overt or subtle racial appeals." Do you think it ought to be impermissible, either as a moral or legal matter, for campaigns to tread on racial fears for electoral advantage? Consider some examples of the different ways that political candidates have used race in their campaigns. Are any of these examples racist appeals? Do you find any of them problematic or objectionable?

> a.   In the 2016 Republican Presidential primary, Republican candidate Donald Trump made what many, including some Republicans, believed to be an electoral appeal to religious and ethnic bigotry. Following a shooting at a mental health facility in San Bernardino, California by a Muslim couple, Trump stated that all Muslims should be barred from entering the country until the government could figure out what was "going on." Trump also called for surveillance of Mosques and the creation of a database to keep track of all Muslims in the United States.

> b.   In the 2008 Democratic Primary, then-Senator Barack Obama's campaign accused then-Senator Hillary Clinton's campaign, his primary challenger, of appealing to racial fears and bigotry. The accusations of racism followed two campaign events. The first was Clinton's "3 am" ad. https://www.you tube.com/watch?v=aZ_z9Tpdl9A. The ad asked whether Obama was prepared to answer the phone call and make tough

calls to defend the country. The ad featured sleeping white children and a phone ringing in the background. The second event occurred after Barack Obama defeated Hillary Clinton in the South Carolina Democratic Primary. Downplaying Obama's win, Bill Clinton stated that the Reverend Jesse Jackson Sr., had also won South Carolina in two previous and unsuccessful runs for the Democratic Presidential nomination. Jackson is a black civil rights leader who had run unsuccessfully for the Democratic Party's nomination in 1984 and 1988 and whose campaigns did not have a strong appeal to white voters, though he was very popular with black voters.

c. In 2006, the Republican National Committee ran a television ad against Harold Ford Jr., a black Democrat who was running for the Senate in Tennessee. Ford would have been the first black Senator from Tennessee since Reconstruction. The ad featured an attractive and seductively dressed white woman who claimed that she met Ford at a "Playboy party." At the end of the ad, she looked into the camera, winked, and says, "Harold, call me." The ad was criticized for playing into white fears about miscegenation. https://www.youtube.com/watch?v=1smE1Es–8QA. Ford lost the race.

d. In 1990 in a very close Senatorial race in North Carolina, Jesse Helms, the incumbent, was running behind the Democratic challenger, Harvey Gantt, who is African American. In the last days of the campaign, Helms's camp ran an ad in which a pair of white hands held a letter and scrunched it up as a narrator intoned, "You needed that job. And you were the best qualified. But they had to give it to a minority because of a racial quota. Is that really fair?" https://www.youtube.com/watch?v=KIyewCdXMzk.

e. Willie Horton was a felon who was serving a life sentence for murder in Massachusetts. In 1986, he escaped and raped a woman after being released in connection with a weekend furlough program. The Governor of Massachusetts at the time was Michael Dukakis, who supported the furlough program. When Dukakis later ran for President against George H.W. Bush in 1988, a PAC aligned with the Bush campaign ran an ad against Dukakis accusing Dukakis of being soft on crime for his support of the furlough program. The ad mentioned Horton by name and featured his mug shot very prominently. Horton was black. https://www.youtube.com/watch?v=Io9KMSSEZ0Y.

f. Campaigns sometimes engage in covert racist appeals, or "dog whistle politics." Politicians might use code words such as "welfare queen" or "food stamp" or "strapping young bucks," meant to prime the racial identity of white voters but at the same time shield the politicians from accusations of racism.

For an analysis of these issues, *see* IAN HANEY LOPEZ, DOG WHISTLE POLITICS: HOW CODED RACIAL APPEALS HAVE REINVENTED RACISM AND WRECKED THE MIDDLE CLASS (2014).

5.   *Appealing to Racial Minorities.* It has now become standard practice for candidates of all ethnicities to reach out to various ethnic and racial groups to solicit their political support. For example, political candidates routinely target the Latino community by making Spanish language ads, appearing before Latino interest groups, and targeting issues that they think might interest the Latino community. Similarly, political candidates, especially national candidates of both parties, have long appeared before African American organizations as a way of signaling their support for that community. During the 2014 midterm elections, the Democratic National Committee placed an ad in black newspapers with a picture of President Obama and the text "GET HIS BACK" in large letters. The ad was part of an advertising campaign targeting voters of color during the 2014 midterm elections and built on a theme used by the Obama campaign when he was running for reelection in 2012. Referred to in the popular press as "Obama's Black radio ad," the Obama campaign targeted African Americans by producing a radio ad clearly meant to appeal to black listeners and voters. https://www.youtube.com/watch?v=2zZNEvj8DV4.   Some   commentators noted that when Obama talked to Black voters he changed his vocabulary and cadence to sound more stereotypically "black." Obama's campaign also made special appeals to the Latino community. Most memorably, he appropriated noted labor leader's Cesar Chavez's slogan, *si se puede* (yes we can). What do you think of these types of racial appeals? Do they differ from racist appeals? What do you make of the fact that not all ethnic or racial groups are likely to be the object of a racial appeal? For example, Arab-Americans or Muslims are less likely to be solicited on the basis of their ethnic or religious identity than are Asian Americans or African Americans. If a campaign does not make specialized appeals to voters of color, should the absence of specialized appeals be calculated in the section 2 calculus, perhaps as part of the totality of circumstances analysis?

B.   CONSTITUTIONAL LIMITS ON RACIAL REPRESENTATION

Following *Gingles*, voting rights plaintiffs successfully challenged the use of multimember districts at all levels of government and successfully sought the creation of majority-minority districts as a remedy. But even before *Gingles*, courts had held that at-large or multimember districts could violate the Constitution if they were adopted to cancel out the voting power of voters of color. Though these cases were interpreting the Constitution and not the VRA, and though the standard articulated by the courts may have been more stringent than section 2's results test, the fact that courts were accustomed to addressing these claims and invalidating at-large electoral structures in favor of single-member majority-minority districts provided a useful template for Congress, when it amended section 2, and the Court in

Gingles. In addition, the DOJ often used its preclearance power to refuse to preclear at-large or multimember districts.

Single-member, majority-minority districts are certainly an important remedy for vote dilution. They enable voters of color to have their political preferences taken into account. The penchant for majority-minority districts is explained by reality, or the perception that single-member majority-minority districts seem to be the most reliable mechanism for providing descriptive representation for racial minority groups. Descriptive representation is the idea that voters ought to be represented by people who look like them or share their descriptive characteristics—e.g., race, gender, religion, sexual orientation and the like. Descriptive representation is often contrasted to substantive representation, which is the proposition that voters ought to be represented by those who share the voters' substantive views. There is a strong body of political science research showing that the probability of electing a representative person of color increases with the size of the minority population in the district. Thus, the probability of electing a black or Latino representative increases with the size of the black or Latino population of the district.

One can then see why both communities of color and would-be representatives of color would relentlessly pursue a strategy of creating as many majority-minority districts as possible: if you're a candidate of color seeking office, your best probability of being elected to office is from a majority-minority district. But the pursuit of racial representation is not without constitutional or public policy costs. We will use the case below, *Shaw v. Reno*, to explore a number of questions regarding racial representation. Why does racial representation matter? What are the legal and public policy costs of pursuing a strategy of racial representation? What are the different ways for pursuing representation for voters of color?

Shaw v. Reno

Supreme Court of the United States, 1993.
509 U.S. 630.

■ JUSTICE O'CONNOR delivered the opinion of the Court.

This case involves two of the most complex and sensitive issues this Court has faced in recent years: the meaning of the constitutional "right" to vote, and the propriety of race-based state legislation designed to benefit members of historically disadvantaged racial minority groups. As a result of the 1990 census, North Carolina became entitled to a 12th seat in the United States House of Representatives. The General Assembly enacted a reapportionment plan that included one majority-black congressional district. After the Attorney General of the United States objected to the plan pursuant to § 5 of the Voting Rights Act of 1965, the General Assembly passed new legislation creating a second majority-black district. Appellants allege that the revised plan, which contains district boundary lines of dramatically irregular shape, constitutes an unconstitutional racial gerrymander. The question before us is whether appellants have stated a cognizable claim.

I

The voting age population of North Carolina is approximately 78% white, 20% black, and 1% Native American; the remaining 1% is predominantly Asian. The black population is relatively dispersed; blacks constitute a majority of the general population in only 5 of the State's 100 counties. Geographically, the State divides into three regions: the eastern Coastal Plain, the central Piedmont Plateau, and the western mountains. The largest concentrations of black citizens live in the Coastal Plain, primarily in the northern part.

The first of the two majority-black districts contained in the revised plan, District 1, is somewhat hook shaped. Centered in the northeast portion of the State, it moves southward until it tapers to a narrow band; then, with finger-like extensions, it reaches far into the southern-most part of the State near the South Carolina border. District 1 has been compared to a "Rorschach ink-blot test," and a "bug splattered on a windshield," WALL STREET JOURNAL.

The second majority-black district, District 12, is even more unusually shaped. It is approximately 160 miles long and, for much of its length, no wider than the I-85 corridor. It winds in snakelike fashion through tobacco country, financial centers, and manufacturing areas "until it gobbles in enough enclaves of black neighborhoods." Northbound and southbound drivers on I-85 sometimes find themselves in separate districts in one county, only to "trade" districts when they enter the next county. Of the 10 counties through which District 12 passes, 5 are cut into 3 different districts; even towns are divided. At one point the district remains contiguous only because it intersects at a single point with two other districts before crossing over them. One state legislator has remarked that " '[i]f you drove down the interstate with both car doors open, you'd kill most of the people in the district.' " WASHINGTON POST.

II

B

Our focus is on appellants' claim that the State engaged in unconstitutional racial gerrymandering. That argument strikes a powerful historical chord: It is unsettling how closely the North Carolina plan resembles the most egregious racial gerrymanders of the past.

An understanding of the nature of appellants' claim is critical to our resolution of the case. In their complaint, appellants did not claim that the General Assembly's reapportionment plan unconstitutionally "diluted" white voting strength. They did not even claim to be white. Rather, appellants' complaint alleged that the deliberate segregation of voters into separate districts on the basis of race violated their constitutional right to participate in a "color-blind" electoral process.

Despite their invocation of the ideal of a "color-blind" Constitution, appellants appear to concede that race-conscious redistricting is not always unconstitutional. That concession is wise: This Court never has held that race-conscious state decisionmaking is impermissible in all circumstances. What appellants object to is redistricting legislation that is so extremely irregular on its face that it rationally can be viewed only as an effort to segregate the races for purposes of voting, without regard for traditional districting principles and without sufficiently compelling justification. For the reasons that follow, we conclude that appellants have stated a claim upon which relief can be granted under the Equal Protection Clause.

III

A

The Equal Protection Clause provides that "[n]o State shall . . . deny to any person within its jurisdiction the equal protection of the laws." U.S. Const., Amdt. 14, § 1. Its central purpose is to prevent the States from purposefully discriminating between individuals on the basis of race. Laws that explicitly distinguish between individuals on racial grounds fall within the core of that prohibition.

No inquiry into legislative purpose is necessary when the racial classification appears on the face of the statute.

B

In some exceptional cases, a reapportionment plan may be so highly irregular that, on its face, it rationally cannot be understood as anything other than an effort to "segregat[e] . . . voters" on the basis of race. *Gomillion*. *Gomillion*, in which a tortured municipal boundary line was drawn to exclude black voters, was such a case. So, too, would be a case in which a State concentrated a dispersed minority population in a single district by disregarding traditional districting principles such as compactness, contiguity, and respect for political subdivisions. We emphasize that these criteria are important not because they are constitutionally required—they are not—but because they are objective factors that may serve to defeat a claim that a district has been gerrymandered on racial lines.

Put differently, we believe that reapportionment is one area in which appearances do matter. A reapportionment plan that includes in one district individuals who belong to the same race, but who are otherwise widely separated by geographical and political boundaries, and who may have little in common with one another but the color of their skin, bears an uncomfortable resemblance to political apartheid. It reinforces the perception that members of the same racial group—regardless of their age, education, economic status, or the community in which they live—

think alike, share the same political interests, and will prefer the same candidates at the polls. We have rejected such perceptions elsewhere as impermissible racial stereotypes. By perpetuating such notions, a racial gerrymander may exacerbate the very patterns of racial bloc voting that majority-minority districting is sometimes said to counteract.

The message that such districting sends to elected representatives is equally pernicious. When a district obviously is created solely to effectuate the perceived common interests of one racial group, elected officials are more likely to believe that their primary obligation is to represent only the members of that group, rather than their constituency as a whole. This is altogether antithetical to our system of representative democracy.

We conclude that a plaintiff challenging a reapportionment statute under the Equal Protection Clause may state a claim by alleging that the legislation, though race-neutral on its face, rationally cannot be understood as anything other than an effort to separate voters into different districts on the basis of race, and that the separation lacks sufficient justification. It is unnecessary for us to decide whether or how a reapportionment plan that, on its face, can be explained in nonracial terms successfully could be challenged. Thus, we express no view as to whether "the intentional creation of majority-minority districts, without more," always gives rise to an equal protection claim. We hold only that, on the facts of this case, appellants have stated a claim sufficient to defeat the state appellees' motion to dismiss.

C

V

Racial classifications of any sort pose the risk of lasting harm to our society. They reinforce the belief, held by too many for too much of our history, that individuals should be judged by the color of their skin. Racial classifications with respect to voting carry particular dangers. Racial gerrymandering, even for remedial purposes, may balkanize us into competing racial factions; it threatens to carry us further from the goal of a political system in which race no longer matters—a goal that the Fourteenth and Fifteenth Amendments embody, and to which the Nation continues to aspire. It is for these reasons that race-based districting by our state legislatures demands close judicial scrutiny.

Today we hold only that appellants have stated a claim under the Equal Protection Clause by alleging that the North Carolina General Assembly adopted a reapportionment scheme so irrational on its face that it can be understood only as an effort to segregate voters into separate voting districts because of their race, and that the separation lacks sufficient justification.

■ JUSTICE WHITE, with whom JUSTICE BLACKMUN and JUSTICE STEVENS join, dissenting.

. . . The notion that North Carolina's plan, under which whites remain a voting majority in a disproportionate number of congressional districts, and pursuant to which the State has sent its first black representatives since Reconstruction to the United States Congress, might have violated appellants' constitutional rights is both a fiction and a departure from settled equal protection principles. Seeing no good reason to engage in either, I dissent.

I

A

The grounds for my disagreement with the majority are simply stated: Appellants have not presented a cognizable claim, because they have not alleged a cognizable injury. To date, we have held that only two types of state voting practices could give rise to a constitutional claim. The first involves direct and outright deprivation of the right to vote, for example by means of a poll tax or literacy test. . . . The second type of unconstitutional practice is that which "affects the political strength of various groups" in violation of the Equal Protection Clause. As for this latter category, we have insisted that members of the political or racial group demonstrate that the challenged action have the intent and effect of unduly diminishing their influence on the political process. Although this severe burden has limited the number of successful suits, it was adopted for sound reasons.

The central explanation has to do with the nature of the redistricting process. As the majority recognizes, "redistricting differs from other kinds of state decisionmaking in that the legislature always is aware of race when it draws district lines, just as it is aware of age, economic status, religious and political persuasion, and a variety of other demographic factors." "Being aware," in this context, is shorthand for "taking into account," and it hardly can be doubted that legislators routinely engage in the business of making electoral predictions based on group characteristics—racial, ethnic, and the like.

Because extirpating such considerations from the redistricting process is unrealistic, the Court has not invalidated all plans that consciously use race, but rather has looked at their impact.

Redistricting plans also reflect group interests and inevitably are conceived with partisan aims in mind. To allow judicial interference whenever this occurs would be to invite constant and unmanageable intrusion. Moreover, a group's power to affect the political process does not automatically dissipate by virtue of an electoral loss. Accordingly, we have asked that an identifiable group demonstrate more than mere lack of success at the polls to make out a successful gerrymandering claim.

With these considerations in mind, we have limited such claims by insisting upon a showing that "the political processes . . . were not equally open to participation by the group in question—that its members had less opportunity than did other residents in the district to participate in the political processes and to elect legislators of their choice." *White v. Regester*. Indeed, as a brief survey of decisions illustrates, the Court's gerrymandering cases all carry this theme—that it is not mere suffering at the polls but discrimination in the polity with which the Constitution is concerned.

To distinguish a claim that alleges that the redistricting scheme has discriminatory intent and effect from one that does not has nothing to do with dividing racial classifications between the "benign" and the malicious—an enterprise which, as the majority notes, the Court has treated with skepticism. Rather, the issue is whether the classification based on race discriminates against *anyone* by denying equal access to the political process.

B

[I]t strains credulity to suggest that North Carolina's purpose in creating a second majority-minority district was to discriminate against members of the majority group by "impair[ing] or burden[ing their] opportunity . . . to participate in the political process." The State has made no mystery of its intent, which was to respond to the Attorney General's objections by improving the minority group's prospects of electing a candidate of its choice. I doubt that this constitutes a discriminatory purpose as defined in the Court's equal protection cases— i.e., an intent to aggravate "the unequal distribution of electoral power." But even assuming that it does, there is no question that appellants have not alleged the requisite discriminatory effects. Whites constitute roughly 76% of the total population and 79% of the voting age population in North Carolina. Yet, under the State's plan, they still constitute a voting majority in 10 (or 83%) of the 12 congressional districts. Though they might be dissatisfied at the prospect of casting a vote for a losing candidate—a lot shared by many, including a disproportionate number of minority voters—surely they cannot complain of discriminatory treatment.

II

. . . The logic of [the majority's] theory appears to be that race-conscious redistricting that "segregates" by drawing odd-shaped lines is qualitatively different from race-conscious redistricting that affects groups in some other way. The distinction is without foundation.

B

Lacking support in any of the Court's precedents, the majority's novel type of claim also makes no sense. As I understand the theory that is put forth, a redistricting plan that uses race to "segregate" voters by drawing "uncouth" lines is harmful in a way that a plan that uses race to distribute voters differently is not, for the former "bears an uncomfortable resemblance to political apartheid." The distinction is untenable.

Racial gerrymanders come in various shades: At-large voting schemes, the fragmentation of a minority group among various districts "so that it is a majority in none," otherwise known as "cracking," the "stacking" of "a large minority population concentration . . . with a larger white population," and, finally, the "concentration of [minority voters] into districts where they constitute an excessive majority," also called "packing." In each instance, race is consciously utilized by the legislature for electoral purposes; in each instance, we have put the plaintiff challenging the district lines to the burden of demonstrating that the plan was meant to, and did in fact, exclude an identifiable racial group from participation in the political process.

Not so, apparently, when the districting "segregates" by drawing odd-shaped lines.[3] In that case, we are told, such proof no longer is needed. Instead, it is the State that must rebut the allegation that race was taken into account, a fact that, together with the legislators' consideration of ethnic, religious, and other group characteristics, I had thought we practically took for granted. Part of the explanation for the majority's approach has to do, perhaps, with the emotions stirred by words such as "segregation" and "political apartheid." But their loose and imprecise use by today's majority has, I fear, led it astray. The consideration of race in "segregation" cases is no different than in other race-conscious districting; from the standpoint of the affected groups, moreover, the line-drawings all act in similar fashion. A plan that "segregates" being functionally indistinguishable from any of the other varieties of gerrymandering, we should be consistent in what we require from a claimant: proof of discriminatory purpose and effect.

The other part of the majority's explanation of its holding is related to its simultaneous discomfort and fascination with irregularly shaped districts. Lack of compactness or contiguity, like uncouth district lines, certainly is a helpful indicator that some form of gerrymandering (racial or other) might have taken place and that "something may be amiss." Disregard for geographic divisions and compactness often goes hand in hand with partisan gerrymandering.

But while district irregularities may provide strong indicia of a potential gerrymander, they do no more than that. In particular, they have no bearing on whether the plan ultimately is found to violate the

---

[3] I borrow the term "segregate" from the majority, but, given its historical connotation, believe that its use is ill advised. Nor is it a particularly accurate description of what has occurred. The majority-minority district that is at the center of the controversy is, according to the State, 54.71% African-American. Even if racial distribution was a factor, no racial group can be said to have been "segregated"—i.e., "set apart" or "isolate[d]." Webster's Collegiate Dictionary (9th ed. 1983).

Constitution. Given two districts drawn on similar, race-based grounds, the one does not become more injurious than the other simply by virtue of being snake-like, at least so far as the Constitution is concerned and absent any evidence of differential racial impact.

Limited by its own terms to cases involving unusually shaped districts, the Court's approach nonetheless will unnecessarily hinder to some extent a State's voluntary effort to ensure a modicum of minority representation. This will be true in areas where the minority population is geographically dispersed. It also will be true where the minority population is not scattered but, for reasons unrelated to race—for example incumbency protection—the State would rather not create the majority-minority district in its most "obvious" location. When, as is the case here, the creation of a majority-minority district does not unfairly minimize the voting power of any other group, the Constitution does not justify, much less mandate, such obstruction.

■ JUSTICE BLACKMUN, dissenting.

I agree that the conscious use of race in redistricting does not violate the Equal Protection Clause unless the effect of the redistricting plan is to deny a particular group equal access to the political process or to minimize its voting strength unduly. It is particularly ironic that the case in which today's majority chooses to abandon settled law and to recognize for the first time this "analytically distinct" constitutional claim is a challenge by white voters to the plan under which North Carolina has sent black representatives to Congress for the first time since Reconstruction. I dissent.

■ JUSTICE STEVENS, dissenting.

I add these comments to emphasize that the two critical facts in this case are undisputed: First, the shape of District 12 is so bizarre that it must have been drawn for the purpose of either advantaging or disadvantaging a cognizable group of voters; and, second, regardless of that shape, it was drawn for the purpose of facilitating the election of a second black representative from North Carolina.

These unarguable facts, which the Court devotes most of its opinion to proving, give rise to three constitutional questions: Does the Constitution impose a requirement of contiguity or compactness on how the States may draw their electoral districts? Does the Equal Protection Clause prevent a State from drawing district boundaries for the purpose of facilitating the election of a member of an identifiable group of voters? And, finally, if the answer to the second question is generally "No," should it be different when the favored group is defined by race? Since I have already written at length about these questions, my negative answer to each can be briefly explained.

The first question is easy. There is no independent constitutional requirement of compactness or contiguity, and the Court's opinion (despite its many references to the shape of District 12) does not suggest otherwise. The existence of bizarre and uncouth district boundaries is powerful evidence of an ulterior purpose behind the shaping of those boundaries—usually a purpose to advantage the political party in control of the districting process. Such evidence will always be useful in cases that lack other evidence of invidious intent. In this case, however, we know what the legislators' purpose was: The North Carolina Legislature drew District 12 to include a majority of African-American voters. Evidence of the district's shape is therefore convincing, but it is also cumulative, and, for our purposes, irrelevant.

As for the second question, I believe that the Equal Protection Clause is violated when the State creates the kind of uncouth district boundaries seen in . . . *Gomillion v. Lightfoot*, and this case, for the sole purpose of making it more difficult for members of a minority group to win an election. The duty to govern impartially is abused when a group with power over the electoral process defines electoral boundaries solely to enhance its own political strength at the expense of any weaker group. That duty, however, is not violated when the majority acts to facilitate the election of a member of a group that lacks such power because it remains underrepresented in the state legislature—whether that group is defined by political affiliation, by common economic interests, or by religious, ethnic, or racial characteristics. The difference between constitutional and unconstitutional gerrymanders has nothing to do with whether they are based on assumptions about the groups they affect, but whether their purpose is to enhance the power of the group in control of the districting process at the expense of any minority group, and thereby to strengthen the unequal distribution of electoral power. When an assumption that people in a particular minority group (whether they are defined by the political party, religion, ethnic group, or race to which they belong) will vote in a particular way is used to benefit that group, no constitutional violation occurs. Politicians have always relied on assumptions that people in particular groups are likely to vote in a particular way when they draw new district lines, and I cannot believe that anything in today's opinion will stop them from doing so in the future.[4]

Finally, we must ask whether otherwise permissible redistricting to benefit an underrepresented minority group becomes impermissible

---

[4] The majority does not acknowledge that we require such a showing from plaintiffs who bring a vote dilution claim under § 2 of the Voting Rights Act. Under the three-part test established by *Thornburg v. Gingles*, a minority group must show that it could constitute the majority in a single-member district, "that it is politically cohesive," and "that the white majority votes sufficiently as a bloc to enable it . . . usually to defeat the minority's preferred candidate." At least the latter two of these three conditions depend on proving that what the Court today brands as "impermissible racial stereotypes." Because *Gingles* involved North Carolina, which the Court admits has earlier established the existence of "pervasive racial bloc voting", its citizens and legislators—as well as those from other States—will no doubt be confused by the Court's requirement of evidence in one type of case that the Constitution now prevents reliance on in another. The Court offers them no explanation of this paradox.

when the minority group is defined by its race. The Court today answers this question in the affirmative, and its answer is wrong. If it is permissible to draw boundaries to provide adequate representation for rural voters, for union members, for Hasidic Jews, for Polish Americans, or for Republicans, it necessarily follows that it is permissible to do the same thing for members of the very minority group whose history in the United States gave birth to the Equal Protection Clause.[5] A contrary conclusion could only be described as perverse.

■ JUSTICE SOUTER, dissenting.

I

Until today, the Court has analyzed equal protection claims involving race in electoral districting differently from equal protection claims involving other forms of governmental conduct, and before turning to the different regimes of analysis it will be useful to set out the relevant respects in which such districting differs from the characteristic circumstances in which a State might otherwise consciously consider race. Unlike other contexts in which we have addressed the State's conscious use of race, electoral districting calls for decisions that nearly always require some consideration of race for legitimate reasons where there is a racially mixed population. As long as members of racial groups have the commonality of interest implicit in our ability to talk about concepts like "minority voting strength," and "dilution of minority votes, and as long as racial bloc voting takes place, legislators will have to take race into account in order to avoid dilution of minority voting strength in the districting plans they adopt. One need look no further than the Voting Rights Act to understand that this may be required, and we have held that race may constitutionally be taken into account in order to comply with that Act.

A second distinction between districting and most other governmental decisions in which race has figured is that those other decisions using racial criteria characteristically occur in circumstances in which the use of race to the advantage of one person is necessarily at the obvious expense of a member of a different race. Thus, for example, awarding government contracts on a racial basis excludes certain firms from competition on racial grounds. And when race is used to supplant seniority in layoffs, someone is laid off who would not be otherwise. The same principle pertains in nondistricting aspects of voting law, where race-based discrimination places the disfavored voters at the disadvantage of exclusion from the franchise without any alternative benefit.

---

[5]   The Court's opinion suggests that African-Americans may now be the only group to which it is unconstitutional to offer specific benefits from redistricting. Not very long ago, of course, it was argued that minority groups defined by race were the only groups the Equal Protection Clause protected in this context.

In districting, by contrast, the mere placement of an individual in one district instead of another denies no one a right or benefit provided to others.[6] All citizens may register, vote, and be represented. In whatever district, the individual voter has a right to vote in each election, and the election will result in the voter's representation. As we have held, one's constitutional rights are not violated merely because the candidate one supports loses the election or because a group (including a racial group) to which one belongs winds up with a representative from outside that group. It is true, of course, that one's vote may be more or less effective depending on the interests of the other individuals who are in one's district, and our cases recognize the reality that members of the same race often have shared interests. "Dilution" thus refers to the effects of districting decisions not on an individual's political power viewed in isolation, but on the political power of a group. This is the reason that the placement of given voters in a given district, even on the basis of race, does not, without more, diminish the effectiveness of the individual as a voter.

II

Our different approaches to equal protection in electoral districting and nondistricting cases reflect these differences. There is a characteristic coincidence of disadvantageous effect and illegitimate purpose associated with the State's use of race in those situations in which it has immediately triggered at least heightened scrutiny (which every Member of the Court to address the issue has agreed must be applied even to race-based classifications designed to serve some permissible state interest). Presumably because the legitimate consideration of race in a districting decision is usually inevitable under the Voting Rights Act when communities are racially mixed, however, and because, without more, it does not result in diminished political effectiveness for anyone, we have not taken the approach of applying the usual standard of such heightened "scrutiny" to race-based districting decisions. To be sure, as the Court says, it would be logically possible to apply strict scrutiny to these cases (and to uphold those uses of race that are permissible). But just because there frequently will be a constitutionally permissible use of race in electoral districting, as exemplified by the consideration of race to comply with the Voting Rights Act (quite apart from the consideration of race to remedy a violation of the Act or the Constitution), it has seemed more appropriate for the Court to identify impermissible uses by describing particular effects sufficiently serious to justify recognition under the Fourteenth Amendment. Under

---

[6]   The majority's use of "segregation" to describe the effect of districting here may suggest that it carries effects comparable to school segregation making it subject to like scrutiny. But a principal consequence of school segregation was inequality in educational opportunity provided, whereas use of race (or any other group characteristic) in districting does not, without more deny equality of political participation. And while *Bolling v. Sharpe* (1954) held that requiring segregation in public education served no legitimate public purpose, consideration of race may be constitutionally appropriate in electoral districting decisions in racially mixed political units.

our cases there is in general a requirement that in order to obtain relief under the Fourteenth Amendment, the purpose and effect of the districting must be to devalue the effectiveness of a voter compared to what, as a group member, he would otherwise be able to enjoy. Justice White describes the formulations we have used and the common categories of dilutive practice in his dissenting opinion.

A consequence of this categorical approach is the absence of any need for further searching "scrutiny" once it has been shown that a given districting decision has a purpose and effect falling within one of those categories. If a cognizable harm like dilution or the abridgment of the right to participate in the electoral process is shown, the districting plan violates the Fourteenth Amendment. If not, it does not. Under this approach, in the absence of an allegation of such cognizable harm, there is no need for further scrutiny because a gerrymandering claim cannot be proven without the element of harm. Nor if dilution is proven is there any need for further constitutional scrutiny; there has never been a suggestion that such use of race could be justified under any type of scrutiny, since the dilution of the right to vote cannot be said to serve any legitimate governmental purpose.

There is thus no theoretical inconsistency in having two distinct approaches to equal protection analysis, one for cases of electoral districting and one for most other types of state governmental decisions. Nor, because of the distinctions between the two categories, is there any risk that Fourteenth Amendment districting law as such will be taken to imply anything for purposes of general Fourteenth Amendment scrutiny about "benign" racial discrimination, or about group entitlement as distinct from individual protection, or about the appropriateness of strict or other heightened scrutiny.

III

The Court appears to accept this, and it does not purport to disturb the law of vote dilution in any way. Instead, the Court creates a new "analytically distinct" cause of action, the principal element of which is that a districting plan be "so bizarre on its face" or "irrational on its face" or "extremely irregular on its face" that it "rationally cannot be understood as anything other than an effort to segregate citizens into separate voting districts on the basis of race without sufficient justification." Pleading such an element, the Court holds, suffices without a further allegation of harm, to state a claim upon which relief can be granted under the Fourteenth Amendment.

It may be that the terms for pleading this cause of action will be met so rarely that this case will wind up an aberration. The shape of the district at issue in this case is indeed so bizarre that few other examples are ever likely to carry the unequivocal implication of impermissible use of race that the Court finds here. It may therefore be that few electoral districting cases are ever likely to employ the strict scrutiny the Court holds to be applicable on remand if appellants' allegations are "not contradicted."

Nonetheless, in those cases where this cause of action is sufficiently pleaded, the State will have to justify its decision to consider race as being required by a compelling state interest, and its use of race as narrowly tailored to that interest. Meanwhile, in other districting cases, specific consequential harm will still need to be pleaded and proven, in the absence of which the use of race may be invalidated only if it is shown to serve no legitimate state purpose.

The Court offers no adequate justification for treating the narrow category of bizarrely shaped district claims differently from other districting claims.[7] Since there is no justification for the departure here from the principles that continue to govern electoral districting cases generally in accordance with our prior decisions, I would not respond to the seeming egregiousness of the redistricting now before us by untethering the concept of racial gerrymander in such a case from the concept of harm exemplified by dilution. In the absence of an allegation of such harm, I would affirm the judgment of the District Court. I respectfully dissent.

NOTES AND QUESTIONS

1. *What Is the Constitutional Harm in* **Shaw?** Consider some possibilities:

    a. Race consciousness. All of the Justices agree, including the Justices in the majority, that race consciousness is inevitable in redistricting. At the very least, race consciousness is necessary if the government does not want to dilute the votes of voters of color, in violation of the VRA.

    b. Individualized treatment. All of the Justices agree that the problem is not the failure of the government to treat the voters as individuals. Redistricting is about group aggregation, and a lawsuit alleging that the state failed to treat voters as individuals would not be sensible in this context. Voters are not entitled to individualized treatment in redistricting.

    c. Vote dilution. Justice O'Connor writes that the constitutional problem is not racial vote dilution under the Fourteenth

---

[7] The Court says its new cause of action is justified by what I understand to be some ingredients of stigmatic harm and by a "threat to . . . our system of representative democracy," both caused by the mere adoption of a districting plan with the elements I have described in the text. To begin with, the complaint nowhere alleges any type of stigmatic harm. Putting that to one side, it seems utterly implausible to me to presume, as the Court does, that North Carolina's creation of this strangely shaped majority-minority district "generates" within the white plaintiffs here anything comparable to "a feeling of inferiority as to their status in the community that may affect their hearts and minds in a way unlikely ever to be undone." *Brown v. Board of Education.* As for representative democracy, I have difficulty seeing how it is threatened (indeed why it is not, rather, enhanced) by districts that are not even alleged to dilute anyone's vote.

Amendment. To prove racial vote dilution under the Fourteenth Amendment, the plaintiffs would have had to show that there was an intent and effect to dilute their political power. They did not claim vote dilution, and it is not clear that they could sustain a claim for vote dilution.

2.   *What Is the Best Understanding of the Constitutional Problem?*
In an influential article, Professors Richard Pildes and Richard Niemi argued that *Shaw* gives rise to a different conception of constitutional harm, an expressive harm. As they explain:

> In the Court's view, the process of designing election districts violates the Constitution not when race-conscious lines are drawn, but when race consciousness dominates the process too extensively. . . . When race becomes the single dominant value to which the process subordinates all others, however, it triggers *Shaw*. For the Court, what distinguishes "bizarre" race-conscious districts is the signal they send out that, to government officials, race has become paramount and dwarfed all other, traditionally relevant criteria. . . . One can only understand *Shaw*, we believe, in terms of a view that what we call expressive harms are constitutionally cognizable. An expressive harm is one that results from the ideas or attitudes expressed through a governmental action, rather than from the more tangible or material consequences the action brings about.

Richard Pildes & Richard Niemi, Expressive Harms, "Bizarre Districts," And Voting Rights: Evaluating Election-District Appearances after *Shaw v. Reno*, 92 Mich. L. Rev. 483, 500–01, 506–07 (1993). The argument advanced by Professor Pildes and Niemi is that bizarre districts may unconstitutionally communicate the message that racial representation is all that matters in the political process. Is the expressive harms explanation of *Shaw* a persuasive one?

3.   *Racial Identity and Racial Districting.* Justice O'Connor objects to the *Shaw* districts in part because she worries that racial districting is based upon a racial stereotype: that voters of color think alike, share the same political interests, and prefer the same candidates at the polls, even though they may have nothing in common but the color of their skin. She worries that using racial identity as a proxy for political identity will either reify race, and therefore create a relationship between racial and political identity, or will reinforce an existing link between racial and political identity. Do you think it is a stereotype to believe that voters who share a racial identity will also share the same political identity? Do you think it is rational to draw districts or to vote for a candidate based on the belief that people who share the same racial identity will also share the same political identity?

4.   *Linked Fate.* Political scientist Michael C. Dawson argues that, notwithstanding the fact of social and economic heterogeneity in the African American community, African Americans share a common political identity because they have a sense of linked fate, or a belief that individual well being is tried to the well being of the group. This concept of linked fate may explain why African Americans may share a political identity even though they may share nothing else other than a racial identity. When African Americans are evaluating which candidates, policies, or parties are best for them individually, they substitute the group utility for their individual utility when making political decisions. Professor Dawson calls this the racial utility heuristic. *See* MICHAEL C. DAWSON, BEHIND THE MULE: RACE AND CLASS IN AFRICAN-AMERICAN POLITICS (1984). For Dawson, linked fate is a function of shared history of racial subjugation and exclusion. *Id.* at 77. Thus, "as long as African-Americans' life chances are powerfully shaped by race, it is efficient for individual African Americans to use their perceptions of the interests of African Americans as a group as a proxy for their own interests." *Id.* at 61. Political scientists have found that linked fate also explains the political identity of other racial groups, including Latinos, *see* for example Gabriel Sanchez, *The Role of Group Consciousness in Political Participation among Latinos in the United States*, 34 AMERICAN POLITICS RESEARCH 427 (2006) and Gabriel Sanchez and Natalie Masuoka, *Brown-Utility Heuristic? The Presence and Contributing Factors of Latino Linked Fate*, 32 HISPANIC JOURNAL OF BEHAVIORAL SCIENCES 519 (2010), and Asian Americans, *see* for example, PEI-TE M. LIEN, MARGARET CONWAY, AND JANELLE WONG, THE POLITICS OF ASIAN-AMERICANS: DIVERSITY AND COMMUNITY (2004) and Jane Junn, and Natalie Masuoka, *Asian American Identity: Shared Racial Status and Political Context*, 6 PERSPECTIVES ON POLITICS 729 (2008). Do you think the conception of linked fate provides a sufficient justification for grouping racial and ethnic groups into districts simply on the basis of their group identity?

5.   *Racial Representation.* Justice O'Connor also objected to the *Shaw* districts because of a concern that racial districting would communicate to the polity that political representation ought to be racial—that Asian Americans ought to be represented by Asian Americans, Latinos voters ought to be represented by Latino representatives, and so on. Justice O'Connor is engaged in an implicit critique of descriptive representation, the proposition that people are best represented by people who look like them. Why might we care about descriptive representation for its own sake? Note that descriptive representation might be important for non-instrumental reasons. The African American NY Times columnist, Charles M. Blow, reflecting on President Barack Obama's presidency at its twilight, writes that Obama's presidency was significant, aside from its material accomplishments, because "[h]e has opened yet another door of possibility, erased yet another myth of inadequacy, expanded yet another plane on which children can dream." http://www.nytimes.com/2016/01/14/opinion/the-other-obama-legacy.html?ref=opinion&_r=0. How much should we value the expressive dimensions of descriptive representation?

When is it appropriate for voters can take race into account when choosing their political representatives? Consider some possibilities. Which of the following do you think would violate a moral commitment to nondiscrimination and why: (a) a voter who is always aware of the race of the candidates but is never motivated to vote for a candidate on the basis of race no matter the circumstances; (b) a voter who is always motivated to vote in favor of candidates because of the candidates' race; (c) a voter who is always motivated to vote against candidates because of the candidates' race; (d) a voter who sometimes votes for a candidate because the candidate share's the voter's racial identity; (e) a voter who uses race as a proxy for political identity; and (f) a voter who uses race as a proxy for political competence.

In the 2008 Democratic Presidential Primary, which featured a contest between then-Senators Hillary Clinton and Barack Obama, about 85% of black voters who voted in the various state primaries were estimated to have voted for Barack Obama. By contrast, 56% of white voters who voted in various state primaries voted for Hillary Clinton. John Lewis, the legendary Congressman and civil rights hero, who had initially backed Hillary Clinton, was compelled to publicly switch his support because voters in his majority-black district voted 3–1 for Obama in Georgia's Democratic primary election. Barack Obama would not have won the Democratic presidential nomination in 2008 were it not for the fact that black voters voted en bloc for him. Were black voters engaged in a type of odious racial politics by overwhelmingly preferring their same-race candidate? Or were they being rational voters acting in their own best interest? Some commentators argued that there was not much of a policy difference between Obama and Clinton. If this is true, what is the best justification for the fact that black voters voted overwhelmingly for Obama? Does your explanation also justify the majority of white voters who voted for Clinton? How should white women view white women candidates, such as Carly Fiorina and Hillary Clinton? What about Latinos or Cuban-Americans and candidates Ted Cruz and Marco Rubio?

6. *Asymmetry of Preferences.* There is some empirical evidence that voters have asymmetrical preferences for descriptive representation. In particular, white voters have a stronger preference for a same-race representative than voters of color. Moreover, white voters are more likely to contact and evaluate favorably white representatives. *See* Claudine Gay, *Spirals of Trust? The Effect of Descriptive Representation on the Relationship Between Citizens and Their Government*, 46 Am. J. Pol. Sci. 717 (2002). Does this asymmetry of preferences for descriptive representation make you more or less likely to support the creation of majority-minority districts?

7. *Descriptive Representation and Turnout.* Some political science research has found that majority-minority districts mobilize voters of color and increase the probability that they will turn out to vote, because voters of color in these districts pay more attention to politics, trust the political process more, and perhaps feel more effective. Scholars have also found that voters, of all races, prefer voting for someone of their own race and therefore are more likely to turn out to vote for a "co-ethnic," a candidate who shares the voter's racial or ethnic background. These turnout effects have been found for both Latino and African American voters. *See* Lawrence Bobo and Frank D. Gilliam, *Race, Sociopolitical Participation and Black Empowerment*, 84 Amer. Pol. Sci. Rev. 377 (1990); Rene R. Roch et al., *Race and Turnout: Does Descriptive Representation in State Legislatures Increase*

Minority Voting?, 63 Pol. Research Q. 890 (2010); Bernard L. Fraga, *Redistricting and the Causal Impact on Voter Turnout* (forthcoming 2016). The literature is not unequivocal. Other studies have found limited or no effect on turnout. *See, e.g.*, Kimball Brace et al., *Minority Turnout and the Creation of Majority-Minority Districts*, 23 Am. Pol. Q. 190 (1995). Additionally, one study of congressional districts concluded that, not only were whites who were represented by an African American representative less likely to turn out to vote, African Americans in those districts were not much more likely to turn out to vote than African Americans represented by a white representative. *See* Claudine Gay, *The Effect of Black Congressional Representation on Political Participation*, 95 Am. Pol. Sci. Rev. 585 (2001). Do you think the empirical facts should have any bearing on the constitutional question of whether these types of districts are consistent with our understanding of constitutional equality?

8.   *Racial Districting and Substantive Representation.* Though there is not much disagreement that majority-minority districts increase descriptive representation, there is significant disagreement as to whether they increase substantive representation. That is, whether those districts make it more likely that voters of color will be able to get the substantive policies that they want. *See*, e.g., David Lublin, The Paradox of Representation: Racial Gerrymandering and Minority Interests in Congress 93–97 (1997); Carol Swain, Black Faces, Black Interests: The Representation of African Americans in Congress 232 (1993); Charles Cameron, David Epstein, and Sharyn O'Halloran, *Do Majority-Minority Districts Maximize Substantive Black Representation in Congress?*, 90 Am. Pol. Sci. Rev. 794 (1996); David Lubin, *Racial Redistricting and African-American Representation: A Critique of "Do Majority-Minority Districts Maximize Substantive Black Representation in Congress?*, 93 Am. Pol. Sci. Rev. 183 (1999). If majority-minority districts do not increase substantive representation for voters of color, should we limit their use either as a matter of policy and law, or is it enough that majority-minority districts increase descriptive representation?

9.   *Trading Off Race Against Party.* Some political scientists have argued that racial gerrymandering tends to benefit the Republican Party at the expense of the Democratic Party. *See, e.g.*, Lublin, The Paradox of Representation, *supra*: Swain, *supra*; Kevin A. Hill, *Does the Creation of Majority Black Districts Aid Republicans? An Analysis of the 1992 Congressional Elections in Eight Southern States*, 57 J. Pol. 384, 391 (1995). Gerrymandered districts remove voters of color, who are often the most reliable Democrats, especially in the South, from surrounding districts, making those districts more conservative. Majority-minority districts also may pit white Democratic aspirants to office against black and brown aspirants to office. Scholars, such as Professor Carol Swain, have argued that white Democrats can represent the interests of black voters as well as black Democrats. If the empirical data are true, do you think these data should factor into the constitutional analysis? As an additional consideration, Professor Lani Guinier has argued that representatives of color elected from majority-minority districts become politically and racially isolated at the legislative level—municipal, county, or state—because they are deprived of the ideological and racial allies necessary to build coalitions and pass legislation that is in the best interest of the communities that elected them.

10. *Cumulative Voting.* Some scholars have advocated replacing majority-minority districts with a different method of vote aggregation, such as cumulative voting. Professor Guinier has been particularly thoughtful proponent of this approach. *See* Guinier, *supra* at 14. Other scholars have advocated in favor of alternative voting systems where it is not possible to draw a compact majority-minority district. *See* Pamela S. Karlan, *Maps and Misreadings: The Role of Geographic Compactness in Racial Vote Dilution Litigation*, 24 Harv. C.R.-C.L. L. Rev. 173 (1989). Single-member district systems are majoritarian systems; whoever gets more than 50% of the vote captures the seat. Cumulative voting systems are proportional systems where voters get as many votes as there are seats, and the vote-to-seat share is proportionally distributed. Cumulative voting allows voters not just to express their preferences but also to express the intensity of their preferences. If you want really like Candidate A and you want her to be elected, you can give her all five of your votes. Cumulative voting also facilitates the ability of voters to build coalitions with like-minded others and self-select their identities. It is the primary method of voting used by corporate boards. Corporations like cumulative voting as a method of vote aggregation because it facilitates representation for minority shareholders. Imagine a jurisdiction that we will call Split, which has 100 voters, 70 of whom are Devils and 30 of whom are Angels. Assume that Split has a legislative body that has five representatives. Instead of dividing Split into five single-member districts of equal population, we are going to give each resident of Split five votes and permits them to distribute those votes in whatever way they want. They can "plump" all five votes on one candidate, vote for five different candidates, or otherwise split their vote between the candidates. If you want to use cumulative voting a method of vote aggregation, your first step will be to calculate what the experts call the threshold of exclusion or threshold of representation, which is the minimum share of the vote that a group needs to have in order to secure representation. In our example above, the Angels need to first think about what is the minimum percentage of the vote that they need in order to secure one seat. In a cumulative system, the threshold of exclusion is usually calculated as follows 1/1+ the number of seats. As there are five seats in our example the threshold of exclusion is, 1/6 or 17%. Our Angels can easily capture at least one seat. This means that the Angels have to capture 17% of the total vote cast to be guaranteed one seat. Given that our Angels are 30% of the population, if they vote as a bloc, they will very easily capture one seat. Notice that district lines do not need to be drawn here. The second step is to figure out the optimal strategy for voting. For example, our Angels wouldn't want to plump all of their votes on one candidate because they would be wasting votes. They can maximize the possibility of capturing more than one seat by forming a coalition with some Devils who might be sympathetic to their cause. If our Angels attract a small percentage of Devils to their side, the Angels might be able to easily capture two seats. Cumulative voting can encourage coalition building among voters, though it requires some ex ante strategic thinking.

11. *Partisanship.* The major political parties in the United States have become racially identifiable. On average, voters of color generally identify with the Democratic Party. On average, white voters, especially in the South, identify with the Republican Party. Some scholars have concluded that that development is a byproduct of the Civil Rights Movement, the civil rights statutes that were passed in the late 60s, and the VRA in particular. The VRA undermined the hold that the Democratic Party had on the South by opening the door for the Republican Party to compete for white voters. African Americans became attached to and identified with the Democratic Party because that Party delivered on civil rights. In the last decade or so, Latinos and Asian Americans have increased their identification with the Democratic Party, and more whites have increased their identification with the Republican Party. As some researchers have argued, it is race and racial issues that have transformed our political parties into racially identifiable parties. *See* Edward G. Carmines and James A. Stimson, Issue Evolution: Rae and the Transformation of American Politics (1989). Additionally, researchers have concluded that racial bloc voting remains a problem in American politics. In two studies of the 2008 and 2012 Presidential election, Stephen Ansolabehere and his colleagues concluded that, in states covered by section 5 of the VRA, fewer white voters voted for Barack Obama in 2008 and 2012 than voted for John Kerry in 2004. These results held after controlling for partisanship and ideology. *See* Stephen Ansolabehere, Nathaniel Persily, Charles Stewart III, *Regional Differences in Racial Polarization in the 2012 Presidential Election: Implications for the Constitutionality of Section 5 of the Voting Rights Act*, 126 Harv. L. Rev. Forum, 205 (2013); Stephen Ansolabehere, Nathaniel Persily, Charles Stewart III, *Race, Region, and Vote Choice in the 2008 Election: Implications for the Future of the Voting Rights Act*, 123 Harv. L. Rev. 1385 (2010). Do you find these developments troubling? Can we build a multiracial democracy if we have segregated political parties? If you think that it is wrong that the electorate is segregating itself on the basis of partisan identification, is there anything that can be done about this self-segregation? For example, should we advocate for more non-partisan primaries? What else would you suggest?

12. *Coalition and Influence Districts: A Different Way Forward?* In *Georgia v. Ashcroft*, 539 U.S. 461 (2003), the Court examined whether § 5 requires a State to concentrate minority voters into a few "safe" districts where it is highly likely that "minority voters will be able to elect the candidate of their choice," or whether states can "create a greater number of [coalition or influence] districts in which it is likely, although perhaps not quite as likely as under the benchmark plan, that minority voters will be able to elect candidates of their choice." The case presented a tradeoff among three different types of electoral structures: majority-minority districts, coalition districts, and influence districts. You considered the costs and benefits of majority-minority districts in the notes above.

Coalition districts are districts in which voters of color form a coalition with like-minded white voters and jointly determine the representative of choice. The benefit of a coalition district is that minority voters can elect a candidate of their choice even though they may not be a majority of the voters in the district. Yet voters of color may sometimes not be able to elect *the* candidate of their choice because they have to compromise with the rest of their coalition; they do not control the district the way they would if it were a majority-minority district. Moreover, there need to be white voters willing to form a coalition with voters of color.

Influence districts are districts in which voters of color can influence the outcome of the election. In an influence district, though voters of color are a numerical minority of voters in the district, they are large enough that their preferences cannot be completely ignored. The drawback of influence districts is that voters of color are unlikely to elect their candidates of choice and may have minimal, if any, impact on the electoral process.

Speaking for the majority in *Georgia v. Ashcroft*, Justice O'Connor stated that § 5 does not require a certain choice and that "State[s] may choose . . . that it is better to risk having fewer minority representatives in order to achieve greater overall representation of a minority group by increasing the number of representatives sympathetic to the interests of minority voters." Further, the Court established a more holistic approach to examining the possibility of backsliding, or "retrogression," saying that the District Court must look to the increases of minority voting age populations outside of the "safe" districts, and the legislative influence of representatives of majority-minority districts. In dissent, Justice Souter wrote that the State should also have to prove that nonminority voters would vote along with the minority, because the purpose of section 5 is to protect the political power of racial minorities.

13. *Doctrinal Developments After* Shaw. Two years after *Shaw*, in *Miller v. Johnson*, 515 U.S. 900 (1995), the Supreme Court clarified the basis of a *Shaw* claim. The plaintiffs in *Miller* challenged a majority-minority district created by the State of Georgia. The Court stated that the essence of a *Shaw* claim is not that a district is bizarrely shaped, but that the state used race to separate voters into districts. The Court admitted that the state can be aware of race when it redistricts and that a plaintiff must "show, either through circumstantial evidence of a district's shape and demographics or more direct evidence going to legislative purpose, that race was the predominant factor motivating the legislature's decision to place a significant number of voters within or without a particular district. To make this showing, a plaintiff must prove that the legislature subordinated traditional race-neutral districting principles, including but not limited to compactness, contiguity, and respect for political subdivisions or communities defined by actual shared interests, to racial considerations." *Id.* at 916. The Court went on to hold the district at issue unconstitutional on the ground that race was the predominant factor that motivated the drawing of the district. Is the predominant factor test consistent with the way the

Court thinks about race in other contexts such as affirmative action in higher education?

In *Easley v. Cromartie*, 532 U.S. 234 (2000), the Court addressed for the fourth time the district that was at issue in *Shaw v. Reno*. The Court reversed, finding the district court's factual findings clearly erroneous. The Court concluded that politics, not race (as the district court concluded), was the predominant explanation for the district's shape.

More recently a group of plaintiffs of color, including political organizations in Alabama that represent black legislators and Democrats, filed a *Shaw* claim against the State of Alabama, challenging its state legislative districts. *See Alabama Legislative Black Caucus v. Alabama*, 135 S. Ct. 1257 (2015). *Shaw* claims are often filed by white voters seeking to invalidate majority-minority districts on the theory that these districts violate the Fourteenth Amendment, but the plaintiffs in this lawsuit argue that the state diluted the votes of black voters by packing more black voters than necessary to create majority-minority districts. The lower court ruled for Alabama on the ground that the plaintiffs did not prove that race was the predominant factor in the districting plan. The Supreme Court reversed the lower court opinion for technical errors.

14. *Advising Exercise.* You are advising a city council rethinking its electoral system. The City is multiracial and equally divided between Whites, Latinos, and African Americans. There are also small but growing populations of Asian Americans and Native peoples. You are not constrained by any legal requirements that would prevent you from diluting the votes of any racial group. What would you advise? An at-large electoral structure? Single-member districts? Influence or coalition districts? Or cumulative voting?

C. INTER-MINORITY CONFLICT AND COALITION

As we become an increasingly multiracial society, we will increasingly confront the problem of how to allocate political power among various minority groups. Where minority groups have different political preferences, this process is likely to be zero-sum. No system of organizing electoral power can represent the preferences of all groups in a diverse and multicultural democratic society. So, some tradeoffs will have to be made. *Johnson v. De Grandy* provides an initial look at how the Court has navigated this very thorny problem.

Johnson v. De Grandy
Supreme Court of the United States, 1994.
512 U.S. 997.

■ JUSTICE SOUTER delivered the opinion of the Court.

These consolidated cases are about the meaning of vote dilution and the facts required to show it, when § 2 of the Voting Rights Act of 1965 is applied to challenges to single-member legislative districts. We hold that no violation of § 2 can be found here, where, in spite of continuing discrimination and racial bloc voting, minority voters form effective voting majorities in a number of districts roughly proportional to the minority voters' respective shares in the voting-age population. While such proportionality is not dispositive in a challenge to single-member districting, it is a relevant fact in the totality of circumstances to be analyzed when determining whether members of a minority group have "less opportunity than other members of the electorate to participate in the political process and to elect representatives of their choice."

I

On the first day of Florida's 1992 legislative session, a group of Hispanic voters including Miguel De Grandy (De Grandy plaintiffs) complained in the United States District Court against the speaker of Florida's House of Representatives, the president of its Senate, the Governor, and other state officials (State). The complainants alleged that the districts from which Florida voters had chosen their state senators and representatives since 1982 were malapportioned, failing to reflect changes in the State's population during the ensuing decade. The State Conference of NAACP Branches and individual black voters (NAACP plaintiffs) filed a similar suit, which the three-judge District Court consolidated with the De Grandy case.

Several months after the first complaint was filed, on April 10, 1992, the state legislature adopted Senate Joint Resolution 2-G (SJR 2-G), providing the reapportionment plan currently at issue. The plan called for dividing Florida into 40 single-member Senate, and 120 single-member House, districts based on population data from the 1990 census. As the Constitution of Florida required, the state attorney general then petitioned the Supreme Court of Florida for a declaratory judgment that the legislature's apportionment plan was valid under federal and state law. The court so declared, while acknowledging that state constitutional time constraints precluded full review for conformity with § 2 of the Voting Rights Act and recognizing the right of any interested party to bring a § 2 challenge to the plan in the Supreme Court of Florida.

The De Grandy and NAACP plaintiffs responded to SJR 2-G by amending their federal complaints to charge the new reapportionment plan with violating § 2. They claimed that SJR 2-G " 'unlawfully fragments cohesive minority communities and otherwise impermissibly submerges their right to vote and to participate in the electoral process,' " and they pointed to areas around the State where black or Hispanic populations could have formed a voting majority in a politically cohesive, reasonably compact district (or in more than one), if SJR 2-G had not fragmented each group among several districts or packed it into just a few.

The Department of Justice filed a similar complaint, naming the State of Florida and several elected officials as defendants and claiming that SJR 2-G diluted the voting strength of blacks and Hispanics in two parts of the State in violation of § 2. The Government alleged that SJR 2-G diluted the votes of the Hispanic population in an area largely covered by Dade County (including Miami) and the black population in an area covering much of Escambia County (including Pensacola). The District Court consolidated this action with the other two and held a 5-day trial, followed immediately by an hours-long hearing on remedy.

At the end of the hearing, on July 1, 1992, the District Court ruled from the bench. It held the plan's provisions for state House districts to be in violation of § 2 because "more than [SJR 2-G's] nine Hispanic districts may be drawn without having or creating a regressive effect upon black voters," and it imposed a remedial plan offered by the De Grandy plaintiffs calling for 11 majority-Hispanic House districts. As to the Senate, the court found that a fourth majority-Hispanic district could be drawn in addition to the three provided by SJR 2-G, but only at the expense of black voters in the area. The court was of two minds about the implication of this finding, once observing that it meant the legislature's plan for the Senate was a violation of § 2 but without a remedy, once saying the plan did not violate § 2 at all.5 In any event, it ordered elections to be held using SJR 2-G's senatorial districts.

In a later, expanded opinion the court reviewed the totality of circumstances as required by § 2 and Thornburg v. Gingles. In explaining Dade County's "tripartite politics," in which "ethnic factors . . . predominate over all other[s] . . . ," the court found political cohesion within each of the Hispanic and black populations but none between the two, and a tendency of non-Hispanic whites to vote as a bloc to bar minority groups from electing their chosen candidates except in a district where a given minority makes up a voting majority. The court further found that the nearly one million Hispanics in the Dade County area could be combined into 4 Senate and 11 House districts, each one relatively compact and with a functional majority of Hispanic voters, whereas SJR 2-G created fewer majority-Hispanic districts; and that one more Senate district with a black voting majority could have been drawn. Noting that Florida's minorities bore the social, economic, and political effects of past discrimination, the court concluded that SJR 2-G impermissibly diluted the voting strength of Hispanics in its House districts and of both Hispanics and blacks in its Senate districts. The findings of vote dilution in the senatorial districts had no practical effect, however, because the court held that remedies for the blacks and the Hispanics were mutually exclusive; it consequently deferred to the state legislature's work as the "fairest" accommodation of all the ethnic communities in south Florida.

We stayed the judgment of the District Court and noted probable jurisdiction.

III

On the merits of the vote dilution claims covering the House districts, the crux of the State's argument is the power of Hispanics under SJR 2-G to elect candidates of their choice in a number of districts that mirrors their share of the Dade County area's voting-age population (i.e., 9 out of 20 House districts); this power, according to the State, bars any finding that the plan dilutes Hispanic voting strength. The District Court is said to have missed that conclusion by mistaking our precedents to require the plan to maximize the number of Hispanic-controlled districts.

The dispute in this litigation centers on two quite different questions: whether Hispanics are sufficiently numerous and geographically compact to be a majority in additional single-member districts, as required by the first Gingles factor; and whether, even with all three Gingles conditions satisfied, the circumstances in totality support a finding of vote dilution when Hispanics can be expected to elect their chosen representatives in substantial proportion to their percentage of the area's population.

A

When applied to a claim that single-member districts dilute minority votes, the first Gingles condition requires the possibility of creating more than the existing number of reasonably compact districts with a sufficiently large minority population to elect candidates of its choice. The District Court found the condition satisfied by contrasting SJR 2-G with the De Grandy plan for the Dade County area, which provided for 11 reasonably compact districts, each with a voting-age population at least 64 percent Hispanic. While the percentage figures are not disputed, the parties disagree about the sufficiency of these super-majorities to allow Hispanics to elect representatives of their choice in all 11 districts. The District Court agreed with plaintiffs that the supermajorities would compensate for the number of voting-age Hispanics who did not vote, most commonly because they were recent immigrants who had not become citizens of the United States. The State protests that fully half of the Hispanic voting-age residents of the region are not citizens, with the result that several districts in the De Grandy plan lack enough Hispanic voters to elect candidates of their choice without cross-over votes from other ethnic groups. On these assumptions, the State argues that the condition necessary to justify tinkering with the State's plan disappears.

We can leave this dispute without a winner. The parties' ostensibly factual disagreement raises an issue of law about which characteristic of minority populations (e.g., age, citizenship) ought to be the touchstone for proving a dilution claim and devising a sound remedy. These cases may be resolved, however, without reaching this issue or the related question whether the first Gingles condition can be satisfied by proof that a so-called influence district may be created (that is, by proof that plaintiffs can devise an additional district in which members of a minority group are a minority of the voters, but a potentially influential one). As in the past, we will assume without deciding that even if Hispanics are not an absolute majority of the relevant population in the additional districts, the first Gingles condition has been satisfied in these cases.

B

We do, however, part company from the District Court in assessing the totality of circumstances. The District Court found that the three Gingles preconditions were satisfied, and that Hispanics had suffered historically from official discrimination, the social, economic, and political effects of which they generally continued to feel. Without more, and on the apparent assumption that what could have been done to create additional Hispanic supermajority districts should have been done, the District Court found a violation of § 2. But the assumption was erroneous, and more is required, as a review of Gingles will show.

1

Thornburg v. Gingles prompted this Court's first reading of § 2 of the Voting Rights Act of 1965 after its 1982 amendment.

Gingles provided some structure to the statute's "totality of circumstances" test in a case challenging multimember legislative districts.

The Court thus summarized the three now-familiar Gingles factors (compactness/numerousness, minority cohesion or bloc voting, and majority bloc voting) as "necessary preconditions," for establishing vote dilution by use of a multimember district.

But if Gingles so clearly identified the three as generally necessary to prove a § 2 claim, it just as clearly declined to hold them sufficient in combination, either in the sense that a court's examination of relevant circumstances was complete once the three factors were found to exist, or in the sense that the three in combination necessarily and in all circumstances demonstrated dilution. This was true not only because bloc voting was a matter of degree, with a variable legal significance depending on other facts, but also because the ultimate conclusions about equality or inequality of opportunity were intended by Congress to be judgments resting on comprehensive, not limited, canvassing of relevant facts. Lack of electoral success is evidence of vote dilution, but courts must also examine other evidence in the totality of circumstances, including the extent of the opportunities minority voters enjoy to participate in the political processes. To be sure, some § 2 plaintiffs may have easy cases, but although lack of equal electoral opportunity may be readily imagined and unsurprising when demonstrated under circumstances that include the three essential Gingles factors, that conclusion must still be addressed explicitly, and without isolating any other arguably relevant facts from the act of judgment.

2

If the three Gingles factors may not be isolated as sufficient, standing alone, to prove dilution in every multimember district challenge, a fortiori they must not be when the challenge goes to a series of single-member districts, where dilution may be more difficult to grasp. Plaintiffs challenging single-member districts may claim, not total submergence, but partial submergence; not the chance for some electoral success in place of none, but the chance for more success in place of some. When the question thus comes down to the reasonableness of drawing a series of district lines in one combination of places rather than another, judgments about inequality may become closer calls. As facts beyond the ambit of the three Gingles factors loom correspondingly larger, factfinders cannot rest uncritically on assumptions about the force of the Gingles factors in pointing to dilution.

The cases now before us, of course, fall on this more complex side of the divide, requiring a court to determine whether provision for somewhat fewer majority-minority districts than the number sought by the plaintiffs was dilution of the minority votes. The District Court was accordingly required to assess the probative significance of the Gingles factors critically after considering the further circumstances with arguable bearing on the issue of equal political opportunity. We think that in finding dilution here the District Court misjudged the relative importance of the Gingles factors and of historical discrimination, measured against evidence tending to show that in spite of these facts, SJR 2-G would provide minority voters with an equal measure of political and electoral opportunity.

The District Court did not, to be sure, commit the error of treating the three Gingles conditions as exhausting the enquiry required by § 2. Consistently with Gingles, the court received evidence of racial relations outside the immediate confines of voting behavior and found a history of discrimination against Hispanic voters continuing in society generally to the present day. But the District Court was not critical enough in asking whether a history of persistent discrimination reflected in the larger society and its bloc-voting behavior portended any dilutive effect from a newly proposed districting scheme, whose pertinent features were majority-minority districts in substantial proportion to the minority's share of voting-age population. The court failed to ask whether the totality of facts, including those pointing to proportionality, showed that the new scheme would deny minority voters equal political opportunity.

Treating equal political opportunity as the focus of the enquiry, we do not see how these district lines, apparently providing political effectiveness in proportion to voting-age numbers, deny equal political opportunity. The record establishes that Hispanics constitute 50 percent of the voting-age population in Dade County and under SJR 2-G would make up supermajorities in 9 of the 18 House districts located primarily within the county. Likewise, if one considers the 20 House districts located at least in part within Dade County, the record indicates that Hispanics would be an effective voting majority in 45 percent of them (i.e., nine), and would constitute 47 percent of the voting-age population in the area. In other words, under SJR 2-G Hispanics in the Dade County area would enjoy substantial proportionality. On this evidence, we think the State's scheme would thwart the historical tendency to exclude Hispanics, not encourage or perpetuate it. Thus in spite of that history and its legacy, including the racial cleavages that characterize Dade County politics today, we see no grounds for holding in these cases that SJR 2-G's district lines diluted the votes cast by Hispanic voters.

The De Grandy plaintiffs urge us to put more weight on the District Court's findings of packing and fragmentation, allegedly accomplished by the way the State drew certain specific lines: "[T]he line of District 116 separates heavily Hispanic neighborhoods in District 112 from the rest of the heavily Hispanic Kendall Lakes area and the Kendall area," so that the line divides "neighbors making up the . . . same housing development in Kendall Lakes," and District 114 "packs" Hispanic voters, while Districts 102 and 109 "fragmen[t]" them. We would agree that where a State has split (or lumped) minority neighborhoods that would have been grouped into a single district (or spread among several) if the State had employed the same line-drawing standards in minority neighborhoods as it used elsewhere in the jurisdiction, the inconsistent treatment might be significant evidence of a § 2 violation, even in the face of proportionality. The district court, however, made no such finding. Indeed, the propositions the Court recites on this point are not even phrased as factual findings, but merely as recitations of testimony offered by plaintiffs' expert witness. While the District Court may well have credited the testimony, the court was apparently wary of adopting the witness's conclusions as findings. But even if one imputed a greater significance to the accounts of testimony, they would boil down to findings that several of SJR 2-G's district lines separate portions of Hispanic neighborhoods, while another district line draws several Hispanic neighborhoods into a single district. This, however, would be to say only that lines could have been drawn elsewhere, nothing more. But some dividing by district lines and combining within them is virtually inevitable and befalls any population group of substantial size. Attaching the labels "packing" and "fragmenting" to these phenomena, without more, does not make the result vote dilution when the minority group enjoys substantial proportionality.

3

It may be that the significance of the facts under § 2 was obscured by the rule of thumb apparently adopted by the District Court, that anything short of the maximum number of majority-minority districts consistent with the Gingles conditions would violate § 2, at least where societal discrimination against the minority had occurred and continued to occur. But reading the first Gingles condition in effect to define dilution as a failure to maximize in the face of bloc voting (plus some other incidents of societal bias to be expected where bloc voting occurs) causes its own dangers, and they are not to be courted.

One may suspect vote dilution from political famine, but one is not entitled to suspect (much less infer) dilution from mere failure to guarantee a political feast. However prejudiced a society might be, it would be absurd to suggest that the failure of a districting scheme to provide a minority group with effective political power 75 percent above its numerical strength13 indicates a denial of equal participation in the political process. Failure to maximize cannot be the measure of § 2.

4

While, for obvious reasons, the State agrees that a failure to leverage minority political strength to the maximum possible point of power is not definitive of dilution in bloc-voting societies, it seeks to impart a measure of determinacy by applying a definitive rule of its own: that as a matter of law no dilution occurs whenever the percentage of single-member districts in which minority voters form an effective majority mirrors the minority voters' percentage of the relevant population. Proportionality so defined would thus be a safe harbor for any districting scheme.

It is enough to say that, while proportionality in the sense used here is obviously an indication that minority voters have an equal opportunity, in spite of racial polarization, "to participate in the political process and to elect representatives of their choice," the degree of probative value assigned to proportionality may vary with other facts. No single statistic provides courts with a shortcut to determine whether a set of single-member districts unlawfully dilutes minority voting strength.

5

While the United States concedes the relevance of proportionality to a § 2 claim, it would confine proportionality to an affirmative defense, and one to be made only on a statewide basis in cases that challenge districts for electing a body with statewide jurisdiction. In this litigation, the United States would have us treat any claim that evidence of proportionality supports the State's plan as having been waived because the State made no argument in the District Court that the proportion of districts statewide in which Hispanics constitute an effective voting majority mirrors the proportion of statewide Hispanic population.

The argument has two flaws. There is, first, no textual reason to segregate some circumstances from the statutory totality, to be rendered insignificant unless the defendant pleads them by way of affirmative defense. Second, and just as importantly, the argument would recast these cases as they come to us, in order to bar consideration of proportionality except on statewide scope, whereas up until now the dilution claims have been litigated on a smaller geographical scale. It is, indeed, the plaintiffs themselves, including the United States, who passed up the opportunity to frame their dilution claim in statewide terms. While the United States points to language in its complaint alleging that the redistricting plans dilute the votes of "Hispanic citizens and black citizens in the State of Florida," the complaint identifies "several areas of the State" where such violations of § 2 are said to occur, and then speaks in terms of Hispanics in the Dade County area (and blacks in the area of Escambia County). Nowhere do the allegations indicate that claims of dilution "in the State of Florida" are not to be considered in terms of the areas specifically mentioned. The complaint alleges no facts at all about the contours, demographics, or voting patterns of any districts outside the Dade County or Escambia County areas, and neither the evidence at trial nor the opinion of the District Court addressed white bloc voting and political cohesion of minorities statewide. The De Grandy plaintiffs even voluntarily dismissed their claims of Hispanic vote dilution outside the Dade County area. Thus we have no occasion to decide which frame of reference should have been used if the parties had not apparently agreed in the District Court on the appropriate geographical scope for analyzing the alleged § 2 violation and devising its remedy.

6

In sum, the District Court's finding of dilution did not address the statutory standard of unequal political and electoral opportunity, and reflected instead a misconstruction of § 2 that equated dilution with failure to maximize the number of reasonably compact majority-minority districts. Because the ultimate finding of dilution in districting for the Florida House was based on a misreading of the governing law, we hold it to be clearly erroneous. *See* Gingles.

IV

Having found insufficient evidence of vote dilution in the drawing of House districts in the Dade County area, we look now to the comparable districts for the state Senate. As in the case of House districts, we understand the District Court to have misapprehended the legal test for vote dilution when it found a violation of § 2 in the location of the Senate district lines. Because the court did not modify the State's plan, however, we hold the ultimate result correct in this instance.

SJR 2-G creates 40 single-member Senate districts, 5 of them wholly within Dade County. Of these five, three have Hispanic supermajorities of at least 64 percent, and one has a clear majority of black voters. Two more Senate districts crossing county lines include substantial numbers of Dade County voters, and in one of these, black voters, although not close to a majority, are able to elect representatives of their choice with the aid of cross-over votes.

Within this seven-district Dade County area, both minority groups enjoy rough proportionality. The voting-age population in the seven-district area is 44.8 percent Hispanic and 15.8 percent black. Hispanics predominate in 42.9 percent of the districts (three out of seven), as do blacks in 14.3 percent of them (one out of seven). While these numbers indicate something just short of perfect proportionality (42.9 percent against 44.8; 14.3 percent against 15.8), the opposite is true of the five districts located wholly within Dade County.

The District Court concentrated not on these facts but on whether additional districts could be drawn in which either Hispanics or blacks would constitute an effective majority. The court found that indeed a fourth senatorial district with a Hispanic supermajority could be drawn, or that an additional district could be created with a black majority, in each case employing reasonably compact districts. Having previously established that each minority group was politically cohesive, that each labored under a legacy of official discrimination, and that whites voted as a bloc, the District Court believed it faced "two independent, viable Section 2 claims." Because the court did not, however, think it was possible to create both another Hispanic district and another black district on the same map, it concluded that no remedy for either violation was practical and, deferring to the State's plan as a compromise policy, imposed SJR 2-G's senatorial districts.

We affirm the District Court's decision to leave the State's plan for Florida State Senate districts undisturbed. As in the case of the House districts, the totality of circumstances appears not to support a finding of vote dilution here, where both minority groups constitute effective voting majorities in a number of state Senate districts substantially proportional to their share in the population, and where plaintiffs have not produced evidence otherwise indicating that under SJR 2-G voters in either minority group have "less opportunity than other members of the electorate to participate in the political process and to elect representatives of their choice."

V

There being no violation of the Voting Rights Act shown, we have no occasion to review the District Court's decisions going to remedy. The judgment of the District Court is accordingly affirmed in part and reversed in part.

[Justice O'Connor, concurring, omitted]

[Justice Thomas, with whom Justice Scalia joins, dissenting, omitted]

NOTES AND QUESTIONS

1. *Understanding* **Johnson v. DeGrandy.** *DeGrandy* is a vote dilution case under section 2 and similar to *Thornburg v. Gingles.* But unlike *Gingles,* which challenged at-large or multi-member districts, *DeGrandy* challenges

single-member districts. The plaintiffs in *DeGrandy* argued that the state legislative redistricting plan diluted their votes by failing to create adequate majority-minority districts where they could have naturally have been created. The Supreme Court interpreted the plaintiffs' complaint as stating a claim of maximization. That is, the Court understood the plaintiffs to argue that the State failed to maximize the number of majority-minority districts it could have created on the plaintiffs' behalf. The Court concluded that the plaintiffs could not maintain a vote dilution claim because the plaintiffs constituted majorities in a sufficient number of districts in proportion to their share of the relevant geographical population.

2. ***Beyond the Black-White Paradigm***. *Gingles* and the VRA were developed in a context of black exclusion and white supremacy. But voting rights controversies have changed. They are increasingly about apportioning political power among various racial groups. In the 21st century, in a multiracial and multiethnic America, the problem of voting discrimination includes a growing and diverse Latino population, which is now the largest minority group in the country; a growing and diverse Asian American population, which includes people of Chinese, Japanese, Korean, and Indian descent; and an African American community that includes black Americans who are descendants of slaves as well as immigrants from Africa, the Caribbean, and Latin and Central America. How is political power to be apportioned among those groups and subgroups that are all making claims for belonging and self-determination? Was Justice O'Connor right in *Shaw* that we risk becoming a racially balkanized polity? Are the *Gingles* preconditions and totality of circumstances inquiry simply unsuited for a multiracial context?

3. ***Building Cross-Racial Coalitions Under Section 2***. There are at least two possibilities for minimizing the zero-sum nature of voting disputes. One possibility is to draw district lines that do not force voters to essentialize their racial identity as the price of representation. We have already explored the possibilities of cumulative voting in the context of *Gingles*. Another option is to encourage coalition building among various racial groups within the single-member districting structure. To state a claim for vote dilution, a racial group must be able to meet the three *Gingles* preconditions: that the group is sufficiently large and geographically compact that it can fit in a single-member district; that the group is politically cohesive; and that the racial majority engages in racial bloc voting. Coalitions of multiple racial and ethnic groups have sought to aggregate their populations where aggregation is necessary to meet the numbers requirement of the first *Gingles* precondition.

In *Concerned Citizens of Hardee County v. Hardee County Board of Commissioners*, 906 F.2d 524 (11th Cir. 1990), a panel from the Eleventh Circuit stated in passing that the black and Latino plaintiffs "may be a single section 2 minority if they can establish that they behave in a politically cohesive manner." *Id.* at 526. The court dismissed the case because the plaintiffs failed to prove that they voted cohesively. In *Campos v. Baytown*, 840 F.2d 1240 (5th Cir. 1988), the Fifth Circuit addressed a similar question.

The Court stated: "There is nothing in the law that prevents plaintiffs from identifying the protected aggrieved minority to include both Blacks and Hispanics. . . . If together they are of such numbers residing geographically so as to constitute a majority in a single member district, they cross the *Gingles* threshold as potentially disadvantaged voters." 840 F.2d at 1244. The court went on to note that the two groups must show that they "actually vote together and are impeded in their ability to elect their own candidates by all of the circumstances, including especially the bloc voting of a white majority that usually defeats the candidate in the minority." *Id.* On the other hand, in *Nixon v. Kent County*, 76 F.3d 1381 (6th Cir. 1996), the Sixth Circuit refused to permit cross-racial coalitions on the ground that Congress had not authorized it. The court held that "[n]othing in the clear, unambiguous language of § 2 allows or even recognizes the application of the Voting Rights Act to coalitions." 76 F.3d at 1386. What do you think? Should cross-racial coalition districts be permitted under section 2?

4.   *Antagonism Among Minority Racial Groups.* One impediment to cross-racial coalitions is the fact that minority racial groups sometimes harbor racial antagonisms against one another. The sad is truth is that both Latinos and Asian Americans harbor anti-black prejudice and African Americans harbor negative stereotypes against Asian Americans and Latinos. In some circumstances, antagonisms could even exist within ethnic groups, between people of different national origins. Indeed, why should we expect people of color to form coalitions across racial groups, ethnic identity, or country-of-origin background, rather than trying to maximize representation and public policy benefits for their respective groups? What might the benefits be of intra-ethnic or cross-racial coalitions?

D.   RACE AND POLITICAL STRUCTURE

Democracy and democratic politics are committed to two principles that sometimes come into conflict: the principles of majority rule and minority participation. As you saw with the Voting Rights Act and particularly *Thornburg v. Gingles*, electoral participation by people of color does not simply mean the ability to vote. People of color also ought to be able to elect candidates of their choice and secure the public policies they prefer, at least some of the time. But what if the state or a majority of white voters makes it harder for voters of color to secure those policies, not by preventing voters of color from voting or by diluting their votes, but by changing the structure of the political process? Legal actors might change the level of government at which political decisions are made— from cities to counties or from counties to the state as whole—in turn making it harder for voters of color, who are political minorities, to enact their preferences into policy. The case below addresses this potential problem.

Schuette v. Coalition to Defend Affirmative Action

Supreme Court of the United States, 2014.
572 U.S. ___, 134 S.Ct. 1623.

■ JUSTICE KENNEDY announced the judgment of the Court and delivered an opinion, in which THE CHIEF JUSTICE and JUSTICE ALITO join.

The Court in this case must determine whether an amendment to the Constitution of the State of Michigan, approved and enacted by its voters, is invalid under the Equal Protection Clause of the Fourteenth Amendment to the Constitution of the United States.

In 2003 the Court reviewed the constitutionality of two admissions systems at the University of Michigan, one for its undergraduate class and one for its law school. The undergraduate admissions plan was addressed in *Gratz v. Bollinger*. The law school admission plan was addressed in *Grutter v. Bollinger*. Each admissions process permitted the explicit consideration of an applicant's race. In *Gratz*, the Court invalidated the undergraduate plan as a violation of the Equal Protection Clause. In *Grutter*, the Court found no constitutional flaw in the law school admission plan's more limited use of race-based preferences.

In response to the Court's decision in *Gratz*, the university revised its undergraduate admissions process, but the revision still allowed limited use of race-based preferences. After a statewide debate on the question of racial preferences in the context of governmental decisionmaking, the voters, in 2006, adopted an amendment to the State Constitution prohibiting state and other governmental entities in Michigan from granting certain preferences, including race-based preferences, in a wide range of actions and decisions. Under the terms of the amendment, race-based preferences cannot be part of the admissions process for state universities. That particular prohibition is central to the instant case.

The ballot proposal was called Proposal 2 and, after it passed by a margin of 58 percent to 42 percent, the resulting enactment became Article I, § 26, of the Michigan Constitution. As noted, the amendment is in broad terms. Section 26 states, in relevant part, as follows:

> "The University of Michigan, Michigan State University, Wayne State University, and any other public college or university, community college, or school district shall not discriminate against, or grant preferential treatment to, any individual or group on the basis of race, sex, color, ethnicity, or national origin in the operation of public employment, public education, or public contracting.

> "The state shall not discriminate against, or grant preferential treatment to, any individual or group on the basis of race, sex, color, ethnicity, or national origin in the operation of public employment, public education, or public contracting.

"For the purposes of this section 'state' includes, but is not
necessarily limited to, the state itself, any city, county, any
public college, university, or community college, school district,
or other political subdivision or governmental instrumentality
of or within the State of Michigan not included in sub-section 1."

Section 26 was challenged in two cases. Among the plaintiffs in the suits
were the Coalition to Defend Affirmative Action, Integration and
Immigrant Rights and Fight for Equality By Any Means Necessary
(BAMN); students; faculty; and prospective applicants to Michigan public
universities.

In 2008, the District Court granted summary judgment to Michigan,
thus upholding Proposal 2. *BAMN v. Regents of Univ. of Mich.* The
District Court denied a motion to reconsider the grant of summary
judgment. A panel of the United States Court of Appeals for the Sixth
Circuit reversed the grant of summary judgment. Judge Gibbons
dissented from that holding. *Id.* The panel majority held that Proposal 2
had violated the principles elaborated by this Court in *Washington v.
Seattle School Dist. No. 1*, and in the cases that *Seattle* relied upon.

The Court of Appeals, sitting en banc, agreed with the panel
decision. The majority opinion determined that *Seattle* "mirrors the
[case] before us." *Id.* Seven judges dissented in a number of opinions. The
Court granted certiorari.

Before the Court addresses the question presented, it is important
to note what this case is not about. It is not about the constitutionality,
or the merits, of race-conscious admissions policies in higher education.
The consideration of race in admissions presents complex questions, in
part addressed last Term in *Fisher v. University of Texas at Austin.* In
Fisher, the Court did not disturb the principle that the consideration of
race in admissions is permissible, provided that certain conditions are
met.

In Michigan, the State Constitution invests independent boards of
trustees with plenary authority over public universities, including
admissions policies. Mich. Const., Art. VIII, § 5; *see also Federated
Publications, Inc. v. Board of Trustees of Mich. State Univ.* Although the
members of the boards are elected, some evidence in the record suggests
they delegated authority over admissions policy to the faculty. But
whether the boards or the faculty set the specific policy, Michigan's public
universities did consider race as a factor in admissions decisions before
2006.

In holding § 26 invalid in the context of student admissions at state
universities, the Court of Appeals relied in primary part on *Seattle,* which
it deemed to control the case. But that determination extends *Seattle's*
holding in a case presenting quite different issues to reach a conclusion
that is mistaken here. Before explaining this further, it is necessary to

consider the relevant cases that preceded *Seattle* and the background against which *Seattle* itself arose.

Though it has not been prominent in the arguments of the parties, this Court's decision in *Reitman v. Mulkey*, is a proper beginning point for discussing the controlling decisions. In *Mulkey,* voters amended the California Constitution to prohibit any state legislative interference with an owner's prerogative to decline to sell or rent residential property on any basis. Two different cases gave rise to *Mulkey*. In one a couple could not rent an apartment, and in the other a couple were evicted from their apartment. Those adverse actions were on account of race. In both cases the complaining parties were barred, on account of race, from invoking the protection of California's statutes; and, as a result, they were unable to lease residential property. This Court concluded that the state constitutional provision was a denial of equal protection. The Court agreed with the California Supreme Court that the amendment operated to insinuate the State into the decision to discriminate by encouraging that practice. The Court noted the "immediate design and intent" of the amendment was to "establis[h] a purported constitutional right to privately discriminate." *Id.* The Court agreed that the amendment "expressly authorized and constitutionalized the private right to discriminate." *Id.* The effect of the state constitutional amendment was to "significantly encourage and involve the State in private racial discriminations." *Id.* In a dissent joined by three other Justices, Justice Harlan disagreed with the majority's holding. *Id.* The dissent reasoned that California, by the action of its voters, simply wanted the State to remain neutral in this area, so that the State was not a party to discrimination. *Id.* That dissenting voice did not prevail against the majority's conclusion that the state action in question encouraged discrimination, causing real and specific injury.

The next precedent of relevance, *Hunter v. Erickson*, is central to the arguments the respondents make in the instant case. In *Hunter*, the Court for the first time elaborated what the Court of Appeals here styled the "political process" doctrine. There, the Akron City Council found that the citizens of Akron consisted of "people of different race[s], . . . many of whom live in circumscribed and segregated areas, under sub-standard unhealthful, unsafe, unsanitary and overcrowded conditions, because of discrimination in the sale, lease, rental and financing of housing." *Id.* To address the problem, Akron enacted a fair housing ordinance to prohibit that sort of discrimination. In response, voters amended the city charter to overturn the ordinance and to require that any additional antidiscrimination housing ordinance be approved by referendum. But most other ordinances "regulating the real property market" were not subject to those threshold requirements. *Id.* The plaintiff, a black woman in Akron, Ohio, alleged that her real estate agent could not show her certain residences because the owners had specified they would not sell to black persons.

Central to the Court's reasoning in *Hunter* was that the charter amendment was enacted in circumstances where widespread racial discrimination in the sale and rental of housing led to segregated housing, forcing many to live in "unhealthful, unsafe, unsanitary and overcrowded conditions." *Id.* The Court stated: "It is against this background that the referendum required by [the charter amendment] must be assessed." *Ibid.* Akron attempted to characterize the charter amendment "simply as a public decision to move slowly in the delicate area of race relations" and as a means "to allow the people of Akron to participate" in the decision. *Id.* The Court rejected Akron's flawed "justifications for its discrimination," justifications that by their own terms had the effect of acknowledging the targeted nature of the charter amendment. *Ibid.* The Court noted, furthermore, that the charter amendment was unnecessary as a general means of public control over the city council; for the people of Akron already were empowered to overturn ordinances by referendum. *Id.* The Court found that the city charter amendment, by singling out antidiscrimination ordinances, "places special burden on racial minorities within the governmental process," thus becoming as impermissible as any other government action taken with the invidious intent to injure a racial minority. *Id.* Justice Harlan filed a concurrence. He argued the city charter amendment "has the clear purpose of making it more difficult for certain racial and religious minorities to achieve legislation that is in their interest." *Id.* But without regard to the sentence just quoted, *Hunter* rests on the unremarkable principle that the State may not alter the procedures of government to target racial minorities.

Seattle is the third case of principal relevance here. There, the school board adopted a mandatory busing program to alleviate racial isolation of minority students in local schools. Voters who opposed the school board's busing plan passed a state initiative that barred busing to desegregate. The Court first determined that, although "white as well as Negro children benefit from" diversity, the school board's plan "inures primarily to the benefit of the minority." The Court next found that "the practical effect" of the state initiative was to "remov[e] the authority to address a racial problem—and only a racial problem—from the existing decisionmaking body, in such a way as to burden minority interests" because advocates of busing "now must seek relief from the state legislature, or from the statewide electorate." *Id.* The Court therefore found that the initiative had "explicitly us[ed] the racial nature of a decision to determine the decisionmaking process." *Id.*

Seattle is best understood as a case in which the state action in question (the bar on busing enacted by the State's voters) had the serious risk, if not purpose, of causing specific injuries on account of race, just as had been the case in *Mulkey* and *Hunter*. Although there had been no judicial finding of *de jure* segregation with respect to Seattle's school district, it appears as though school segregation in the district in the

1940's and 1950's may have been the partial result of school board policies that "permitted white students to transfer out of black schools while restricting the transfer of black students into white schools." *Parents Involved in Community Schools v. Seattle School Dist. No. 1* (BREYER, J., dissenting). In 1977, the National Association for the Advancement of Colored People (NAACP) filed a complaint with the Office for Civil Rights, a federal agency. The NAACP alleged that the school board had maintained a system of *de jure* segregation. Specifically, the complaint alleged "that the Seattle School Board had created or perpetuated unlawful racial segregation through, *e.g.,* certain school-transfer criteria, a construction program that needlessly built new schools in white areas, district line-drawing criteria, the maintenance of inferior facilities at black schools, the use of explicit racial criteria in the assignment of teachers and other staff, and a general pattern of delay in respect to the implementation of promised desegregation efforts." *Id.* As part of a settlement with the Office for Civil Rights, the school board implemented the "Seattle Plan," which used busing and mandatory reassignments between elementary schools to reduce racial imbalance and which was the subject of the state initiative at issue in *Seattle.*

In all events we must understand *Seattle* as *Seattle* understood itself, as a case in which neither the State nor the United States "challenge[d] the propriety of race-conscious student assignments for the purpose of achieving integration, even absent a finding of prior *de jure* segregation." In other words the legitimacy and constitutionality of the remedy in question (busing for desegregation) was assumed, and *Seattle* must be understood on that basis. *Ibid. Seattle* involved a state initiative that "was carefully tailored to interfere only with desegregative busing." *Id.* The *Seattle* Court, accepting the validity of the school board's busing remedy as a predicate to its analysis of the constitutional question, found that the State's disapproval of the school board's busing remedy was an aggravation of the very racial injury in which the State itself was complicit.

The broad language used in *Seattle,* however, went well beyond the analysis needed to resolve the case. The Court there seized upon the statement in Justice Harlan's concurrence in *Hunter* that the procedural change in that case had "the clear purpose of making it more difficult for certain racial and religious minorities to achieve legislation that is in their interest." That language, taken in the context of the facts in *Hunter,* is best read simply to describe the necessity for finding an equal protection violation where specific injuries from hostile discrimination were at issue. The *Seattle* Court, however, used the language from the *Hunter* concurrence to establish a new and far-reaching rationale. *Seattle* stated that where a government policy "inures primarily to the benefit of the minority" and "minorities . . . consider" the policy to be " 'in their interest,' " then any state action that "place[s] effective decisionmaking authority over" that policy "at a different level of government" must be reviewed under strict scrutiny. In essence, according to the broad reading of *Seattle*, any state action with a "racial focus" that makes it "more difficult for certain racial minorities than for other groups" to "achieve legislation that is in their interest" is subject to strict scrutiny. It is this reading of *Seattle* that the Court of Appeals found to be controlling here. And that reading must be rejected.

The broad rationale that the Court of Appeals adopted goes beyond the necessary holding and the meaning of the precedents said to support it; and in the instant case neither the formulation of the general rule just set forth nor the precedents cited to authenticate it suffice to invalidate Proposal 2. The expansive reading of *Seattle* has no principled limitation and raises serious questions of compatibility with the Court's settled equal protection jurisprudence. To the extent *Seattle* is read to require the Court to determine and declare which political policies serve the "interest" of a group defined in racial terms, that rationale was unnecessary to the decision in *Seattle*; it has no support in precedent; and it raises serious constitutional concerns. That expansive language does not provide a proper guide for decisions and should not be deemed authoritative or controlling. The rule that the Court of Appeals elaborated and respondents seek to establish here would contradict central equal protection principles.

In cautioning against "impermissible racial stereotypes," this Court has rejected the assumption that "members of the same racial group— regardless of their age, education, economic status, or the community in which they live—think alike, share the same political interests, and will prefer the same candidates at the polls." *Shaw v. Reno*; *see also Metro Broadcasting, Inc. v. FCC* (KENNEDY, J., dissenting) (rejecting the "demeaning notion that members of . . . defined racial groups ascribe to certain 'minority views' that must be different from those of other citizens"). It cannot be entertained as a serious proposition that all individuals of the same race think alike. Yet that proposition would be a necessary beginning point were the *Seattle* formulation to control, as the Court of Appeals held it did in this case. And if it were deemed necessary to probe how some races define their own interest in political matters, still another beginning point would be to define individuals according to race. But in a society in which those lines are becoming more blurred, the attempt to define race-based categories also raises serious questions of its own. Government action that classifies individuals on the basis of race is inherently suspect and carries the danger of perpetuating the very racial divisions the polity seeks to transcend. *Cf. Ho v. San Francisco Unified School Dist.* (school district delineating 13 racial categories for purposes of racial balancing).

Even assuming these initial steps could be taken in a manner consistent with a sound analytic and judicial framework, the court would next be required to determine the policy realms in which certain groups—

groups defined by race—have a political interest. That undertaking, again without guidance from any accepted legal standards, would risk, in turn, the creation of incentives for those who support or oppose certain policies to cast the debate in terms of racial advantage or disadvantage. Thus could racial antagonisms and conflict tend to arise in the context of judicial decisions as courts undertook to announce what particular issues of public policy should be classified as advantageous to some group defined by race. This risk is inherent in adopting the *Seattle* formulation.

There would be no apparent limiting standards defining what public policies should be included in what *Seattle* called policies that "inur[e] primarily to the benefit of the minority" and that "minorities ... consider" to be " 'in their interest.' " ... Racial division would be validated, not discouraged, were the *Seattle* formulation, and the reasoning of the Court of Appeals in this case, to remain in force.

Perhaps, when enacting policies as an exercise of democratic self-government, voters will determine that race-based preferences should be adopted. The constitutional validity of some of those choices regarding racial preferences is not at issue here. The holding in the instant case is simply that the courts may not disempower the voters from choosing which path to follow. In the realm of policy discussions the regular give-and-take of debate ought to be a context in which rancor or discord based on race are avoided, not invited. And if these factors are to be interjected, surely it ought not to be at the invitation or insistence of the courts.

One response to these concerns may be that objections to the larger consequences of the *Seattle* formulation need not be confronted in this case, for here race was an undoubted subject of the ballot issue. But a number of problems raised by *Seattle*, such as racial definitions, still apply. And this principal flaw in the ruling of the Court of Appeals does remain: Here there was no infliction of a specific injury of the kind at issue in *Mulkey* and *Hunter* and in the history of the Seattle schools. Here there is no precedent for extending these cases to restrict the right of Michigan voters to determine that race-based preferences granted by Michigan governmental entities should be ended.

By approving Proposal 2 and thereby adding § 26 to their State Constitution, the Michigan voters exercised their privilege to enact laws as a basic exercise of their democratic power. In the federal system States "respond, through the enactment of positive law, to the initiative of those who seek a voice in shaping the destiny of their own times." *Bond*. Michigan voters used the initiative system to bypass public officials who were deemed not responsive to the concerns of a majority of the voters with respect to a policy of granting race-based preferences that raises difficult and delicate issues.

The freedom secured by the Constitution consists, in one of its essential dimensions, of the right of the individual not to be injured by the unlawful exercise of governmental power. The mandate for segregated schools, a wrongful invasion of the home, or punishing a protester whose views offend others, and scores of other examples teach that individual liberty has constitutional protection, and that liberty's full extent and meaning may remain yet to be discovered and affirmed. Yet freedom does not stop with individual rights. Our constitutional system embraces, too, the right of citizens to debate so they can learn and decide and then, through the political process, act in concert to try to shape the course of their own times and the course of a nation that must strive always to make freedom ever greater and more secure. Here Michigan voters acted in concert and statewide to seek consensus and adopt a policy on a difficult subject against a historical background of race in America that has been a source of tragedy and persisting injustice. That history demands that we continue to learn, to listen, and to remain open to new approaches if we are to aspire always to a constitutional order in which all persons are treated with fairness and equal dignity. Were the Court to rule that the question addressed by Michigan voters is too sensitive or complex to be within the grasp of the electorate; or that the policies at issue remain too delicate to be resolved save by university officials or faculties, acting at some remove from immediate public scrutiny and control; or that these matters are so arcane that the electorate's power must be limited because the people cannot prudently exercise that power even after a full debate, that holding would be an unprecedented restriction on the exercise of a fundamental right held not just by one person but by all in common. It is the right to speak and debate and learn and then, as a matter of political will, to act through a lawful electoral process.

The respondents in this case insist that a difficult question of public policy must be taken from the reach of the voters, and thus removed from the realm of public discussion, dialogue, and debate in an election campaign. Quite in addition to the serious First Amendment implications of that position with respect to any particular election, it is inconsistent with the underlying premises of a responsible, functioning democracy. One of those premises is that a democracy has the capacity—and the duty—to learn from its past mistakes; to discover and confront persisting biases; and by respectful, rationale deliberation to rise above those flaws and injustices. That process is impeded, not advanced, by court decrees based on the proposition that the public cannot have the requisite repose to discuss certain issues. It is demeaning to the democratic process to presume that the voters are not capable of deciding an issue of this sensitivity on decent and rational grounds. The process of public discourse and political debate should not be foreclosed even if there is a risk that during a public campaign there will be those, on both sides, who seek to use racial division and discord to their own political advantage. An informed public can, and must, rise above this. The idea of democracy is that it can, and must, mature. Freedom embraces the right, indeed the duty, to engage in a rational, civic discourse in order to determine how best to form a consensus to shape the destiny of the Nation and its people. These First Amendment dynamics would be disserved if this Court were to say that the question here at issue is beyond the capacity of the voters to debate and then to determine.

These precepts are not inconsistent with the well-established principle that when hurt or injury is inflicted on racial minorities by the encouragement or command of laws or other state action, the Constitution requires redress by the courts. *Cf. Johnson v. California* ("[S]earching judicial review . . . is necessary to guard against invidious discrimination"); *Edmonson v. Leesville Concrete Co.* ("Racial discrimination" is "invidious in all contexts"). As already noted, those were the circumstances that the Court found present in *Mulkey, Hunter,* and *Seattle.* But those circumstances are not present here.

This case is not about how the debate about racial preferences should be resolved. It is about who may resolve it. There is no authority in the Constitution of the United States or in this Court's precedents for the Judiciary to set aside Michigan laws that commit this policy determination to the voters. *See Sailors v. Board of Ed. of County of Kent* ("Save and unless the state, county, or municipal government runs afoul of a federally protected right, it has vast leeway in the management of its internal affairs"). Deliberative debate on sensitive issues such as racial preferences all too often may shade into rancor. But that does not justify removing certain court-determined issues from the voters' reach. Democracy does not presume that some subjects are either too divisive or too profound for public debate.

The judgment of the Court of Appeals for the Sixth Circuit is reversed.

It is so ordered.

■ JUSTICE KAGAN took no part in the consideration or decision of this case.

■ CHIEF JUSTICE ROBERTS, concurring.

The dissent devotes 11 pages to expounding its own policy preferences in favor of taking race into account in college admissions, while nonetheless concluding that it "do[es] not mean to suggest that the virtues of adopting race-sensitive admissions policies should inform the legal question before the Court." (opinion of SOTOMAYOR, J.). The dissent concedes that the governing boards of the State's various universities could have implemented a policy making it illegal to "discriminate against, or grant preferential treatment to," any individual on the basis of race. On the dissent's view, if the governing boards conclude that drawing racial distinctions in university admissions is undesirable or counterproductive, they are permissibly exercising their policymaking authority. But others who might reach the same conclusion are failing to take race seriously.

The dissent states that "[t]hc way to stop discrimination on the basis of race is to speak openly and candidly on the subject of race." And it urges that "[r]ace matters because of the slights, the snickers, the silent judgments that reinforce that most crippling of thoughts: 'I do not belong here.' " *Ibid.* But it is not "out of touch with reality" to conclude that racial preferences may themselves have the debilitating effect of reinforcing precisely that doubt, and—if so—that the preferences do more harm than good. To disagree with the dissent's views on the costs and benefits of racial preferences is not to "wish away, rather than confront" racial inequality. People can disagree in good faith on this issue, but it similarly does more harm than good to question the openness and candor of those on either side of the debate.

■ JUSTICE SCALIA, with whom JUSTICE THOMAS joins, concurring in the judgment.

It has come to this. Called upon to explore the jurisprudential twilight zone between two errant lines of precedent, we confront a frighteningly bizarre question: Does the Equal Protection Clause of the Fourteenth Amendment *forbid* what its text plainly *requires*? Needless to say (except that this case obliges us to say it), the question answers itself. "The Constitution proscribes government discrimination on the basis of race, and state-provided education is no exception." *Grutter v. Bollinger* (SCALIA, J., concurring in part and dissenting in part). It is precisely this understanding—the correct understanding—of the federal Equal Protection Clause that the people of the State of Michigan have adopted for their own fundamental law. By adopting it, they did not simultaneously *offend* it.

Even taking this Court's sorry line of race-based-admissions cases as a given, I find the question presented only slightly less strange: Does the Equal Protection Clause forbid a State from banning a practice that the Clause barely—and only provisionally—permits? Reacting to those race-based-admissions decisions, some States—whether deterred by the prospect of costly litigation; aware that *Grutter*'s bell may soon toll; or simply opposed in principle to the notion of "benign" racial discrimination—have gotten out of the racial-preferences business altogether. And with our express encouragement: "Universities in California, Florida, and Washington State, where racial preferences in admissions are prohibited by state law, are currently engaging in experimenting with a wide variety of alternative approaches. Universities in other States can *and should* draw on the most promising aspects of these race-neutral alternatives as they develop." *Id.* Respondents seem to think this admonition was merely in jest. The experiment, they maintain, is not only over; it never rightly began. Neither the people of the States nor their legislatures ever had the option of directing subordinate public-university officials to cease considering the race of applicants, since that would deny members of those minority groups the option of enacting a policy designed to further their interest, thus denying them the equal protection of the laws. Never mind that it is hotly disputed whether the practice of race-based admissions is *ever* in a racial minority's interest. *Cf. id.* (THOMAS, J., concurring in part and dissenting in part). And never mind that, were a public university to stake its defense of a race-based-admissions policy on the ground that it was *designed* to benefit primarily minorities (as opposed to all students, regardless of color, by enhancing diversity), *we would hold the policy unconstitutional. See id.*

But the battleground for this case is not the constitutionality of race-based admissions—at least, not quite. Rather, it is the so-called political-process doctrine, derived from this Court's opinions in *Washington v. Seattle School Dist. No. 1*, and *Hunter v. Erickson.* I agree with those parts of the plurality opinion that repudiate this doctrine. But I do not agree with its reinterpretation of *Seattle* and *Hunter*, which makes them stand in part for the cloudy and doctrinally anomalous proposition that whenever state action poses "the serious risk ... of causing specific injuries on account of race," it denies equal protection. I would instead reaffirm that the "ordinary principles of our law [and] of our democratic heritage" require "plaintiffs alleging equal protection violations" stemming from facially neutral acts to "prove intent and causation and not merely the existence of racial disparity." *Freeman v. Pitts* (SCALIA, J., concurring) (citing *Washington v. Davis*). I would further hold that a law directing state actors to provide equal protection is (to say the least) facially neutral, and cannot violate the Constitution. Section 26 of the Michigan Constitution (formerly Proposal 2) rightly stands.

I

C

Taken to the limits of its logic, *Hunter-Seattle* is the gaping exception that nearly swallows the rule of structural state sovereignty. If indeed the Fourteenth Amendment forbids States to "place effective decisionmaking authority over" racial issues at "different level[s] of government," then it must be true that the Amendment's ratification in 1868 worked a partial ossification of each State's governing structure, rendering basically irrevocable the power of any subordinate state official who, the day *before* the Fourteenth Amendment's passage, happened to enjoy legislatively conferred authority over a "racial issue." Under the Fourteenth Amendment, that subordinate entity (suppose it is a city council) could itself take action on the issue, action either favorable or unfavorable to minorities. It could even reverse itself later. What it could not do, however, is redelegate its power to an even lower level of state government (such as a city-council committee) without forfeiting it, since the necessary effect of wresting it back would be to put an additional obstacle in the path of minorities. Likewise, no entity or official higher up the state chain (*e.g.,* a county board) could exercise authority over the issue. Nor, even, could the state legislature, or the people by constitutional amendment, revoke the legislative conferral of power to the subordinate, whether the city council, its subcommittee, or the county board. *Seattle*'s logic would create affirmative-action safe havens wherever subordinate officials in public universities (1) traditionally have enjoyed "effective decisionmaking authority" over admissions policy but (2) have not yet used that authority to prohibit race-conscious admissions decisions. The mere existence of a subordinate's discretion over the matter would work a kind of reverse pre-emption. It is "a strange notion—alien to our system—that local governmental bodies can forever pre-empt the ability of a State—the sovereign power—to address a matter of compelling concern to the State." (Powell, J., dissenting). But that is precisely what the political-process doctrine contemplates.

II

I part ways with *Hunter, Seattle*, and (I think) the plurality for an additional reason: Each endorses a version of the proposition that a facially neutral law may deny equal protection solely because it has a disparate racial impact. Few equal-protection theories have been so squarely and soundly rejected. "An unwavering line of cases from this Court holds that a violation of the Equal Protection Clause requires state action motivated by discriminatory intent," *Hernandez v. New York* (O'Connor, J., concurring in judgment), and that "official action will not be held unconstitutional solely because it results in a racially disproportionate impact," *Arlington Heights v. Metropolitan Housing Development Corp.* Indeed, we affirmed this principle the same day we decided *Seattle*: "[E]ven when a neutral law has a disproportionately adverse effect on a racial minority, the Fourteenth Amendment is violated only if a discriminatory purpose can be shown." *Crawford v. Board of Ed. of Los Angeles.*

As Justice Harlan observed over a century ago, "[o]ur Constitution is color-blind, and neither knows nor tolerates classes among citizens." *Plessy v. Ferguson* (dissenting opinion). The people of Michigan wish the same for their governing charter. It would be shameful for us to stand in their way.

■ JUSTICE BREYER, concurring in the judgment.

I agree with the plurality that the amendment is consistent with the Federal Equal Protection Clause. U.S. Const., Amdt. 14. But I believe this for different reasons.

First, we do not address the amendment insofar as it forbids the use of race-conscious admissions programs designed to remedy past exclusionary racial discrimination or the direct effects of that discrimination. Application of the amendment in that context would present different questions which may demand different answers. Rather, we here address the amendment only as it applies to, and forbids, programs that, as in *Grutter v. Bollinger*, rest upon "one justification":

using "race in the admissions process" solely in order to "obtai[n] the educational benefits that flow from a diverse student body," *id*.

Second, dissenting in *Parents Involved in Community Schools v. Seattle School Dist. No. 1*, I explained why I believe race-conscious programs of this kind are constitutional, whether implemented by law schools, universities, high schools, or elementary schools. I concluded that the Constitution does not "authorize judges" either to forbid or to require the adoption of diversity-seeking race-conscious "solutions" (of the kind at issue here) to such serious problems as "how best to administer America's schools" to help "create a society that includes all Americans." *Id*.

I continue to believe that the Constitution permits, though it does not require, the use of the kind of race-conscious programs that are now barred by the Michigan Constitution. The serious educational problems that faced Americans at the time this Court decided *Grutter* endure.

Third, cases such as *Hunter v. Erickson* and *Washington v. Seattle School Dist. No. 1* reflect an important principle, namely, that an individual's ability to participate meaningfully in the political process should be independent of his race. Although racial minorities, like other political minorities, will not always succeed at the polls, they must have the same opportunity as others to secure through the ballot box policies that reflect their preferences. In my view, however, neither *Hunter* nor *Seattle* applies here. And the parties do not here suggest that the amendment violates the Equal Protection Clause if not under the *Hunter-Seattle* doctrine.

This case . . . does not involve a reordering of the *political* process; it does not in fact involve the movement of decisionmaking from one political level to another. Rather, here, Michigan law delegated broad policymaking authority to elected university boards, *see* Mich. Const., Art. VIII, § 5, but those boards delegated admissions-related decisionmaking authority to unelected university faculty members and administrators. . . . The amendment took decisionmaking authority away from these unelected actors and placed it in the hands of the voters.

Why does this matter? For one thing, considered conceptually, the doctrine set forth in *Hunter* and *Seattle* does not easily fit this case. In those cases minorities had participated in the political process and they had won. The majority's subsequent reordering of the political process repealed the minority's successes and made it more difficult for the minority to succeed in the future. The majority thereby diminished the minority's ability to participate meaningfully in the electoral process. But one cannot as easily characterize the movement of the decisionmaking mechanism at issue here—from an administrative process to an electoral process—as diminishing the minority's ability to participate meaningfully in the *political* process. There is no prior electoral process in which the minority participated.

Finally, the principle that underlies *Hunter* and *Seattle* runs up against a competing principle, discussed above. This competing principle favors decisionmaking though the democratic process. Just as this principle strongly supports the right of the people, or their elected representatives, to adopt race-conscious policies for reasons of inclusion, so must it give them the right to vote not to do so.

As I have said, my discussion here is limited to circumstances in which decisionmaking is moved from an unelected administrative body to a politically responsive one, and in which the targeted race-conscious admissions programs consider race solely in order to obtain the educational benefits of a diverse student body. We need now decide no more than whether the Federal Constitution permits Michigan to apply its constitutional amendment in those circumstances. I would hold that it does. Therefore, I concur in the judgment of the Court.

■ JUSTICE SOTOMAYOR, with whom JUSTICE GINSBURG joins, dissenting.

We are fortunate to live in a democratic society. But without checks, democratically approved legislation can oppress minority groups. For that reason, our Constitution places limits on what a majority of the people may do. This case implicates one such limit: the guarantee of equal protection of the laws. Although that guarantee is traditionally understood to prohibit intentional discrimination under existing laws, equal protection does not end there. Another fundamental strand of our equal protection jurisprudence focuses on process, securing to all citizens the right to participate meaningfully and equally in self-government. That right is the bedrock of our democracy, for it preserves all other rights.

Yet to know the history of our Nation is to understand its long and lamentable record of stymieing the right of racial minorities to participate in the political process. At first, the majority acted with an open, invidious purpose. Notwithstanding the command of the Fifteenth Amendment, certain States shut racial minorities out of the political process altogether by withholding the right to vote. This Court intervened to preserve that right. The majority tried again, replacing outright bans on voting with literacy tests, good character requirements, poll taxes, and gerrymandering. The Court was not fooled; it invalidated those measures, too. The majority persisted. This time, although it allowed the minority access to the political process, the majority changed the ground rules of the process so as to make it more difficult for the minority, and the minority alone, to obtain policies designed to foster racial integration. Although these political restructurings may not have been discriminatory in purpose, the Court reaffirmed the right of minority members of our society to participate meaningfully and equally in the political process.

This case involves this last chapter of discrimination: A majority of the Michigan electorate changed the basic rules of the political process in that State in a manner that uniquely disadvantaged racial minorities.[8] Prior to the enactment of the constitutional initiative at issue here, all of the admissions policies of Michigan's public colleges and universities— including race-sensitive admissions policies—were in the hands of each institution's governing board. The members of those boards are nominated by political parties and elected by the citizenry in statewide elections. After over a century of being shut out of Michigan's institutions of higher education, racial minorities in Michigan had succeeded in persuading the elected board representatives to adopt admissions policies that took into account the benefits of racial diversity. And this Court twice blessed such efforts—first in *Regents of Univ. of Cal. v. Bakke* and again in *Grutter v. Bollinger*, a case that itself concerned a Michigan admissions policy.

In the wake of *Grutter*, some voters in Michigan set out to eliminate the use of race-sensitive admissions policies. Those voters were of course free to pursue this end in any number of ways. For example, they could have persuaded existing board members to change their minds through individual or grassroots lobbying efforts, or through general public awareness campaigns. Or they could have mobilized efforts to vote uncooperative board members out of office, replacing them with members who would share their desire to abolish race-sensitive admissions policies. When this Court holds that the Constitution permits a particular policy, nothing prevents a majority of a State's voters from choosing not to adopt that policy. Our system of government encourages—and indeed, depends on—that type of democratic action.

But instead, the majority of Michigan voters changed the rules in the middle of the game, reconfiguring the existing political process in Michigan in a manner that burdened racial minorities. They did so in the 2006 election by amending the Michigan Constitution to enact Art. I, § 26, which provides in relevant part that Michigan's public universities "shall not discriminate against, or grant preferential treatment to, any individual or group on the basis of race, sex, color, ethnicity, or national origin in the operation of public employment, public education, or public contracting."

As a result of § 26, there are now two very different processes through which a Michigan citizen is permitted to influence the admissions policies of the State's universities: one for persons interested in race-sensitive admissions policies and one for everyone else. A citizen who is a University of Michigan alumnus, for instance, can advocate for an admissions policy that considers an applicant's legacy status by meeting individually with members of the Board of Regents to convince them of her views, by joining with other legacy parents to lobby the

---

[8]   I of course do not mean to suggest that Michigan's voters acted with anything like the invidious intent of those who historically stymied the rights of racial minorities. But like earlier chapters of political restructuring, the Michigan amendment at issue in this case changed the rules of the political process to the disadvantage of minority members of our society.

Board, or by voting for and supporting Board candidates who share her position. The same options are available to a citizen who wants the Board to adopt admissions policies that consider athleticism, geography, area of study, and so on. The one and only policy a Michigan citizen may not seek through this long-established process is a race-sensitive admissions policy that considers race in an individualized manner when it is clear that race-neutral alternatives are not adequate to achieve diversity. For that policy alone, the citizens of Michigan must undertake the daunting task of amending the State Constitution.

Our precedents do not permit political restructurings that create one process for racial minorities and a separate, less burdensome process for everyone else. This Court has held that the Fourteenth Amendment does not tolerate "a political structure that treats all individuals as equals, yet more subtly distorts governmental processes in such a way as to place special burdens on the ability of minority groups to achieve beneficial legislation." *Washington v. Seattle School Dist. No. 1.* Such restructuring, the Court explained, "is no more permissible than denying [the minority] the [right to] vote, on an equal basis with others." *Hunter v. Erickson.* In those cases—*Hunter* and *Seattle*—the Court recognized what is now known as the "political-process doctrine": When the majority reconfigures the political process in a manner that burdens only a racial minority, that alteration triggers strict judicial scrutiny.

[T]his case is about *how* the debate over the use of race-sensitive admissions policies may be resolved, contra—that is, it must be resolved in constitutionally permissible ways. While our Constitution does not guarantee minority groups victory in the political process, it does guarantee them meaningful and equal access to that process. It guarantees that the majority may not win by stacking the political process against minority groups permanently, forcing the minority alone to surmount unique obstacles in pursuit of its goals—here, educational diversity that cannot reasonably be accomplished through race-neutral measures. Today, by permitting a majority of the voters in Michigan to do what our Constitution forbids, the Court ends the debate over race-sensitive admissions policies in Michigan in a manner that contravenes constitutional protections long recognized in our precedents.

Like the plurality, I have faith that our citizenry will continue to learn from this Nation's regrettable history; that it will strive to move beyond those injustices towards a future of equality. And I, too, believe in the importance of public discourse on matters of public policy. But I part ways with the plurality when it suggests that judicial intervention in this case "impede[s]" rather than "advance[s]" the democratic process and the ultimate hope of equality. I firmly believe that our role as judges includes policing the process of self-government and stepping in when necessary to secure the constitutional guarantee of equal protection. Because I would do so here, I respectfully dissent.

II

. . . Together, *Hunter* and *Seattle* recognized a fundamental strand of this Court's equal protection jurisprudence: the political-process doctrine.

B

Hunter and *Seattle* vindicated a principle that is as elementary to our equal protection jurisprudence as it is essential: The majority may not suppress the minority's right to participate on equal terms in the political process. Under this doctrine, governmental action deprives minority groups of equal protection when it (1) has a racial focus, targeting a policy or program that "inures primarily to the benefit of the minority," *Seattle*; and (2) alters the political process in a manner that uniquely burdens racial minorities' ability to achieve their goals through that process. A faithful application of the doctrine resoundingly resolves this case in respondents' favor.

1

Section 26 has a "racial focus." *Seattle*. That is clear from its text, which prohibits Michigan's public colleges and universities from "grant[ing] preferential treatment to any individual or group on the basis of race." Mich. Const., Art. I, § 26. Like desegregation of public schools, race-sensitive admissions policies "inur[e] primarily to the benefit of the minority," as they are designed to increase minorities' access to institutions of higher education.

2

Section 26 restructures the political process in Michigan in a manner that places unique burdens on racial minorities. It establishes a distinct and more burdensome political process for the enactment of admissions plans that consider racial diversity.

Long before the enactment of § 26, the Michigan Constitution granted plenary authority over all matters relating to Michigan's public universities, including admissions criteria, to each university's eight-member governing board.

The boards are indisputably a part of the political process in Michigan. Each political party nominates two candidates for membership to each board, and board members are elected to 8-year terms in the general statewide election. Prior to § 26, board candidates frequently included their views on race-sensitive admissions in their campaigns. For example, in 2005, one candidate pledged to "work to end so-called 'Affirmative-Action,' a racist, degrading system."

Before the enactment of § 26, Michigan's political structure permitted both supporters and opponents of race-sensitive admissions policies to vote for their candidates of choice and to lobby the elected and politically accountable boards. Section 26 reconfigured that structure.

After § 26, the boards retain plenary authority over all admissions criteria *except* for race-sensitive admissions policies. To change admissions policies on this one issue, a Michigan citizen must instead amend the Michigan Constitution. That is no small task. To place a proposed constitutional amendment on the ballot requires either the support of two-thirds of both Houses of the Michigan Legislature or a vast number of signatures from Michigan voters—10 percent of the total number of votes cast in the preceding gubernatorial election. *See* Mich. Const., Art. XII, §§ 1, 2. Since more than 3.2 million votes were cast in the 2010 election for Governor, more than 320,000 signatures are currently needed to win a ballot spot.

Michigan's Constitution has only rarely been amended through the initiative process. Between 1914 and 2000, voters have placed only 60 statewide initiatives on the Michigan ballot, of which only 20 have passed. Minority groups face an especially uphill battle. *See* Donovan 106 ("[O]n issues dealing with racial and ethnic matters, studies show that racial and ethnic minorities do end up more on the losing side of the popular vote"). In fact, "[i]t is difficult to find even a single statewide initiative in any State in which voters approved policies that explicitly favor racial or ethnic minority groups."

III

The political-process doctrine not only resolves this case as a matter of *stare decisis*; it is correct as a matter of first principles.

A

Under our Constitution, majority rule is not without limit. Our system of government is predicated on an equilibrium between the notion that a majority of citizens may determine governmental policy through legislation enacted by their elected representatives, and the overriding principle that there are nonetheless some things the Constitution forbids even a majority of citizens to do. The political-process doctrine, grounded in the Fourteenth Amendment, is a central check on majority rule.

The Fourteenth Amendment instructs that all who act for the government may not "deny to any person . . . the equal protection of the laws." We often think of equal protection as a guarantee that the government will apply the law in an equal fashion—that it will not intentionally discriminate against minority groups. But equal protection of the laws means more than that; it also secures the right of all citizens to participate meaningfully and equally in the process through which laws are created.

This right was hardly novel at the time of *Hunter* and *Seattle*. For example, this Court focused on the vital importance of safeguarding minority groups' access to the political process in *United States v. Carolene Products Co.*, a case that predated *Hunter* by 30 years. In a now-famous footnote, the Court explained that while ordinary social and economic legislation carries a presumption of constitutionality, the same may not be true of legislation that offends fundamental rights or targets minority groups.

The values identified in *Carolene Products* lie at the heart of the political-process doctrine. Indeed, *Seattle* explicitly relied on *Carolene Products*. . . . These values are central tenets of our equal protection jurisprudence.

Our cases recognize at least three features of the right to meaningful participation in the political process. Two of them, thankfully, are uncontroversial. First, every eligible citizen has a right to vote. *See Shaw v. Reno.* Second, the majority may not make it more difficult for the minority to exercise the right to vote. The third feature, the one the plurality dismantles today, is that a majority may not reconfigure the existing political process in a manner that creates a two-tiered system of political change, subjecting laws designed to protect or benefit discrete and insular minorities to a more burdensome political process than all other laws. This is the political-process doctrine of *Hunter* and *Seattle*.

My colleagues would stop at the second. The plurality embraces the freedom of "self-government" without limits.

That view drains the Fourteenth Amendment of one of its core teachings. Contrary to today's decision, protecting the right to meaningful participation in the political process must mean more than simply removing barriers to participation. It must mean vigilantly policing the political process to ensure that the majority does not use other methods to prevent minority groups from partaking in that process on equal footing. Why? For the same reason we guard the right of every citizen to vote. If "[e]fforts to reduce the impact of minority votes, in contrast to direct attempts to block access to the ballot," were "second-generation barriers" to minority voting, *Shelby County v. Holder* (GINSBURG, J., dissenting), efforts to reconfigure the political process in ways that uniquely disadvantage minority groups who have already long been disadvantaged are third-generation barriers. For as the Court recognized in *Seattle*, "minorities are no less powerless with the vote than without it when a racial criterion is used to assign governmental power in such a way as to exclude particular racial groups 'from effective participation in the political proces[s].' "

B

The political-process doctrine also follows from the rest of our equal protection jurisprudence—in particular, our reapportionment and vote dilution cases. In those cases, the Court described the right to vote as "the essence of a democratic society." *Shaw.* It rejected States' use of ostensibly race-neutral measures to prevent minorities from exercising their political rights. *See id.* And it invalidated practices such as at-large electoral systems that reduce or nullify a minority group's ability to vote as a cohesive unit, when those practices were adopted with a discriminatory purpose. *Id.* These cases, like the political-process doctrine, all sought to preserve the political rights of the minority.

IV

B

My colleagues are of the view that we should leave race out of the picture entirely and let the voters sort it out. We have seen this reasoning before. *See Parents Involved* ("The way to stop discrimination on the basis of race is to stop discriminating on the basis of race"). It is a sentiment out of touch with reality, one not required by our Constitution, and one that has properly been rejected as "not sufficient" to resolve cases of this nature. *Id.* While "[t]he enduring hope is that race should not matter[,] the reality is that too often it does." *Id.* "[R]acial discrimination . . . [is] not ancient history." *Bartlett v. Strickland*, 556 U.S. 1, 25, 129 S.Ct. 1231, 173 L.Ed.2d 173 (2009) (plurality opinion).

Race matters. Race matters in part because of the long history of racial minorities' being denied access to the political process. And although we have made great strides, "voting discrimination still exists; no one doubts that." *Shelby County.*

Race also matters because of persistent racial inequality in society—inequality that cannot be ignored and that has produced stark socioeconomic disparities.

And race matters for reasons that really are only skin deep, that cannot be discussed any other way, and that cannot be wished away. Race matters to a young man's view of society when he spends his teenage years watching others tense up as he passes, no matter the neighborhood where he grew up. Race matters to a young woman's sense of self when she states her hometown, and then is pressed, "No, where are you *really* from?", regardless of how many generations her family has been in the country. Race matters to a young person addressed by a stranger in a foreign language, which he does not understand because only English was spoken at home. Race matters because of the slights, the snickers, the silent judgments that reinforce that most crippling of thoughts: "I do not belong here."

In my colleagues' view, examining the racial impact of legislation only perpetuates racial discrimination. This refusal to accept the stark reality that race matters is regrettable. The way to stop discrimination on the basis of race is to speak openly and candidly on the subject of race, and to apply the Constitution with eyes open to the unfortunate effects of centuries of racial discrimination. As members of the judiciary tasked with intervening to carry out the guarantee of equal protection, we ought not sit back and wish away, rather than confront, the racial inequality that exists in our society. It is this view that works harm, by perpetuating the facile notion that what makes race matter is acknowledging the simple truth that race *does* matter.

The Constitution does not protect racial minorities from political defeat. But neither does it give the majority free rein to erect selective barriers against racial minorities. The political-process doctrine polices the channels of change to ensure that the majority, when it wins, does so without rigging the rules of the game to ensure its success. Today, the Court discards that doctrine without good reason.

Today's decision eviscerates an important strand of our equal protection jurisprudence. For members of historically marginalized groups, which rely on the federal courts to protect their constitutional rights, the decision can hardly bolster hope for a vision of democracy that preserves for all the right to participate meaningfully and equally in self-government.

I respectfully dissent.

NOTES AND QUESTIONS

1. *The Constitutional Harm.* How would you articulate the supposed constitutional harm suffered by the plaintiffs in *Schuette*? The plaintiffs are not claiming that they were denied the right to vote or to formally or practically participate in the political process. The plaintiffs do not gainsay that a majority of citizens have the right to use the political process to enact their preferred policies into account. Though everyone agrees that a voting majority is constrained by recognized constitutional limits, such as the prohibition against intentional racial discrimination, the plaintiffs are not arguing that an anti-affirmative action measure is per se discriminatory. So what is the constitutional harm?

Do you think Justice Sotomayor's opinion is helpful in explaining the harm? What do you make of her claim that the constitutional harm is based upon the fact that a "majority of the Michigan electorate changed the basic rules of the political process in that State in a manner that uniquely disadvantaged racial minorities" by creating two political processes, one "for racial minorities and a separate, less burdensome process for everyone else"? From this perspective, Michigan rendered the plaintiffs' participation in the political process superfluous by targeting an issue that benefited them as racial minorities, changing the level of government at which decision on issues of particular concern to them would be made by requiring an amendment to the state constitution to advance those objectives.

2. *The Standard of Review.* *Schuette* raises another very difficult problem: is there a standard that judges can apply reliably and consistently to adjudicate political process claims? Are there limits on majoritarian decision-making as applied to racial minorities, other than the traditional tools of equal protection scrutiny? Justices Scalia and Thomas think not. Justice Scalia argues in his concurrence, which Justice Thomas joined, that the Constitution does not impose any political process limits on what majorities can do to minorities, as long as the law in question is facially neutral and it is not motivated by a discriminatory intent. Justice Scalia's position means that racial minorities can theoretically always lose in the political process as long as the racial majority and the minority have different preferences. Seven Justices disagreed in some way with this position. The case offers three additional approaches: one by Justice Kennedy, one by Justice Breyer, and one by Justice Sotomayor.

Justice Breyer argues that the Court's political structure doctrine applies only when a victory secured by racial minorities in the political process has been undone by moving the decision-making about the underlying issue from one level to a higher one. Breyer argues that the political process doctrine is not implicated in *Schuette* because the "decisionmaking [ ] moved from an unelected body to a politically responsive one." But is Justice Breyer right as a matter of fact? The University trustees are elected, but they delegated decision-making authority to University administrators and faculty. Does delegation to an unelected body vitiate what seems otherwise to be a very political process? How would you defend Justice Breyer's position? To what extend does Justice Breyer's approach seem tailor-made to decide this case and this case alone?

Justice Sotomayor would apply the political structure doctrine whenever the government changes the political process to make it harder for minority voters to enact their public policy preferences on a matter with a racial focus. Presumably the restructuring of the political process offends the Constitution only when the majority targets laws benefiting a discrete and insular minority because such laws would be of some benefit to the minority and inimical to the interests of the majority. Using Justice Sotomayor's approach, we might say that a political process claim has three elements: (a) the government reconfigured the political process; (b) the government targeted a discrete and insular minority; and (c) the law that was affected by the reconfiguration benefitted the discrete and insular minority. How confident are you that judges can apply this framework? Are African Americans in Michigan discrete and insular minorities? Do you think courts have the institutional competence to determine which public policy issues advantage or disadvantage racial groups? Must the issue have a clear racial valence, or are certain issues inherently racial? Consider the following issues and try to define which groups they advantage and disadvantage: (a) welfare reform; (b) earned income tax credit; (c) immigration reform; (d) LGBT rights; (e) religious liberty issues; (f) criminal justice reform; (g) education reform; (e) voting rights; (f) health care reform; (g) affirmative action; (h) minimum wage; (i) unionization. What about public policies that benefit one minority group but burden another racial minority group? For example, some Asian Americans believe that race-based affirmative action benefits Latinos and African Americans at the expense of Asian Americans.

Justice Kennedy would apply a modified version of the political process doctrine whenever "the state action in question . . . had the serious risk, if not purpose, of causing specific injuries on account of race." Do you find Justice Kennedy's approach more workable than Justice Sotomayor's? What counts as a specific injury? Is a specific injury one that would be judicially cognizable under the Equal Protection Clause of the Fourteenth Amendment? If so, does Justice Kennedy's approach differ from Justice

Scalia's in any way? If a specific injury is one that goes beyond what the Court would recognize under its equal protection jurisprudence, is it not the case that Justice Kennedy's approach suffers from the same problems as Justice Sotomayor's? Which of the three approaches do you find most compelling and why?

3.   *Stopping Discrimination.* The plurality opinion and the primary dissenting opinion disavow the claim that their approach to the political process doctrine is influenced by their views of the underlying merits of the case—the constitutionality of affirmative action, which was not at issue in *Schuette.* But one cannot help but see the influence of their views of affirmative action on the way in which they approach the political process question. Consider in this vein the dispute between Chief Justice Roberts and Justice Sotomayor on the best way to stop racial discrimination. Responding to Chief Justice Roberts's opinion in *Parents Involved in Community Schools v. Seattle*, Justice Sotomayor in *Schuette* observes that the way to stop racial discrimination is not to stop discriminating on the basis of race but to "speak openly and candidly on the subject of race, and to apply the Constitution with eyes open to the unfortunate effects of centuries of racial discrimination." Why might she have included this language in her opinion?

4.   *Civility and Division.* In his plurality opinion, Justice Kennedy frets that the plaintiffs' position would exacerbate racial divisiveness in the political process. He observes that, if the Supreme Court were to adopt the position of the Court of Appeals, "[r]acial division would be validated, not discouraged." Moreover, in the "realm of policy discussion the regular give-and-take of debate ought to be a context in which rancor or discord based on race are avoided not invited." Is civility a legitimate goal of antidiscrimination law? Should antidiscrimination law strive to avoid divisiveness, or should racial equality be pursued no matter the costs? Whose offense counts?

IV. WHO STILL CAN'T VOTE

The United States is unique among many democracies in that its Constitution does not contain a formal right to vote. The Fifteenth Amendment contains a negative prohibition; it precludes interference with the right to vote on the basis of race. But it does not grant a universal or positive right to vote. Moreover, the Constitution divides authority over voting between the Federal government and the States. Article I, section 2 states, with respect to the voting qualifications for members of the House, that the "Electors in each State shall have the Qualifications requisite for Electors of the most numerous Branch of the State of the Legislature." The Seventeenth Amendment provides similarly for the election of Senators. Finally, Article I, section 4 states, the "times, places, and manner of holding elections for Senators and Representatives shall be prescribed in each State by the Legislature thereof; but the Congress may at any time by Law make or alter such

Regulations. . . ." Much is left to the discretion of the states, which can regulate voting via their constitutions or statutes. Many of today's state laws and practices related to voting may seem inconsistent with the commitment to broad political participation and racial equality. Some of these practices are historically rooted in a time when the country's conceptions of political rights and racial equality were not as robust as they are today. This section looks at three sets of laws and practice that arguably contradict the commitment to equal political participation.

A. EX-FELON DISENFRANCHISEMENT

In many states in the United States, an individual convicted of a crime loses his or her right to vote as a collateral consequence of a criminal conviction. Forty eight states and the District of Columbia prohibit inmates from voting while incarcerated for a felony offense. Maine and Vermont are the 2 exceptions. Felons lose their right to vote permanently in 11 states. In 20 states felons are allowed to regain their right after they have served their sentence, finished parole, and are no longer on probation. In four states, felons may vote after they have served their prison term and are no longer on parole. Thirteen states and the District of Columbia allow felons to vote after they have served their sentence.   http://felonvoting.procon.org/view.resource.php?resourceID= 000286. Sentencing Project 2008 Report: Felony Disenfranchisement Laws in the U.S.

Ex-felon disenfranchisement statutes are one of most controversial contemporary limitations on the right to vote. Almost six million voters, and 1 in 13 African-American voters, are prohibited from voting because they were convicted for committing a felony. Some voting rights advocates argue that ex-felon disenfranchisement laws are inconsistent with the constitutional conception of the right to vote and the right to political participation. Because many ex-felons are people of color, these statutes have a significant impact on communities of color and voters of color. In *Richardson v. Ramirez*, below, the Court addressed a constitutional challenge to California's disenfranchising constitutional provision.

Richardson v. Ramirez
Supreme Court of the United States, 1974.
418 U.S. 24.

■ MR. JUSTICE REHNQUIST delivered the opinion of the Court.

The three individual respondents in this case were convicted of felonies and have completed the service of their respective sentences and paroles. They filed a petition for a writ of mandate in the Supreme Court of California to compel California county election officials to register them as voters. They claimed, on behalf of themselves and others similarly situated, that application to them of the provisions of the California Constitution and implementing statutes which disenfranchised persons convicted of an 'in-famous crime' denied them the right to equal protection of the laws under the Federal Constitution. We granted certiorari.

Article XX, § 11, of the California Constitution has provided since its adoption in 1879 that "[laws] shall be made" to exclude from voting persons convicted of bribery, perjury, forgery, malfeasance in office, "or other high crimes." At the time respondents were refused registration, former Art, II, § 1, of the California Constitution provided in part that "no alien ineligible to citizenship, no idiot, no insane person, no person convicted of any infamous crime, no person hereafter convicted of the embezzlement or misappropriation of public money, and no person who shall not be able to read the Constitution in the English language and write his or her name, shall ever exercise the privileges of an elector in this State."

Each of the individual respondents was convicted of one or more felonies, and served some time in jail or prison followed by a successfully terminated parole. Respondent Ramirez was convicted in Texas; respondents Lee and Gill were convicted in California. When Ramirez applied to register to vote in San Luis Obispo County, the County Clerk refused to allow him to register. The Monterey County Clerk refused registration to respondent Lee, and the Stanislaus County Registrar of Voters (hereafter also included in references to clerks) refused registration to respondent Gill. All three respondents were refused registration because of their felony convictions.

II

Unlike most claims under the Equal Protection Clause, for the decision of which we have only the language of the Clause itself as it is embodied in the Fourteenth Amendment, respondents' claim implicates not merely the language of the Equal Protection Clause of § 1 of the Fourteenth Amendment, but also the provisions of the less familiar § 2 of the Amendment:

> Representatives shall be apportioned among the several States according to their respective numbers, counting the whole number of persons in each State, excluding Indians not taxed. But when the right to vote at any election for the choice of electors for President and Vice President of the United States, Representatives in Congress, the Executive and Judicial officers of a State, or the members of the Legislature thereof, is denied to any of the male inhabitants of such State, being twenty-one years of age, and citizens of the United States, or in any way abridged, except for participation in rebellion, or other crime, the basis of representation therein shall be reduced in the proportion which the number of such male citizens shall bear to

the whole number of male citizens twenty-one years of age in such State.

Petitioner contends that the italicized language of § 2 expressly exempts from the sanction of that section disenfranchisement grounded on prior conviction of a felony. She goes on to argue that those who framed and adopted the Fourteenth Amendment could not have intended to prohibit outright in § 1 of that Amendment that which was expressly exempted from the lesser sanction of reduced representation imposed by § 2 of the Amendment. This argument seems to us a persuasive one unless it can be shown that the language of § 2, 'except for participation in rebellion, or other crime,' was intended to have a different meaning than would appear from its face.

The problem of interpreting the 'intention' of a constitutional provision is, as countless cases of this Court recognize, a difficult one. Not only are there deliberations of congressional committees and floor debates in the House and Senate, but an amendment must thereafter be ratified by the necessary number of States. The legislative history bearing on the meaning of the relevant language of § 2 is scant indeed; the framers of the Amendment were primarily concerned with the effect of reduced representation upon the States, rather than with the two forms of disenfranchisement which were exempted from that consequence by the language with which we are concerned here. Nonetheless, what legislative history there is indicates that this language was intended by Congress to mean what it says.

We do know that the particular language of § 2 upon which petitioner relies was first proposed by Senator Williams of Oregon to a meeting of the Joint Committee on April 28, 1866. Senator Williams moved to strike out what had been § 3 of the earlier version of the draft, and to insert in place thereof the following:

> 'Representatives shall be apportioned among the several states which may be included within this Union according to their respective numbers, counting the whole number of persons in each State excluding Indians not taxed. But whenever in any State the elective franchise shall be denied to any portion of its male citizens, not less than twenty-one years of age, or in any way abridged, except for participation in rebellion or other crime, the basis of representation in such State shall be reduced in the proportion which the number of such male citizens shall bear to the whole number of male citizens not less than twenty-one years of age.'

The Joint Committee approved this proposal by a lopsided margin, and the draft Amendment was reported to the House floor with no change in the language of § 2.

Throughout the floor debates in both the House and the Senate, in which numerous changes of language in § 2 were proposed, the language 'except for participation in rebellion, or other crime' was never altered. The language of § 2 attracted a good deal of interest during the debates, but most of the discussion was devoted to its foreseeable consequences in both the Northern and Southern States, and to arguments as to its necessity or wisdom. What little comment there was on the phrase in question here supports a plain reading of it.

Congressman Bingham of Ohio, who was one of the principal architects of the Fourteenth Amendment and an influential member of the Committee of Fifteen, commented with respect to § 2 as follows during the floor debates in the House:

> 'The second section of the amendment simply provides for the equalization of representation among all the States of the Union, North, South, East, and West. It makes no discrimination. New York has a colored population of fifty thousand. By this section, if that great State discriminates against her colored population as to the elective franchise, (except in cases of crime,) she loses to that extent her representative power in Congress. So also will it be with every other State.' Cong. Globe, 39th Cong., 1st Sess., 2543 (1866).

Two other Representatives who spoke to the question made similar comments. Representative Eliot of Massachusetts commented in support of the enactment of § 2 as follows:

> 'Manifestly no State should have its basis of national representation enlarged by reason of a portion of citizens within its borders to which the elective franchise is denied. If political power shall be lost because of such denial, not imposed because of participation in rebellion or other crime, it is to be hoped that political interests may work in the line of justice, and that the end will be the impartial enfranchisement of all citizens not disqualified by crime.'

Representative Eckley of Ohio made this observation:

> 'Under a congressional act persons convicted of a crime against the laws of the United States, the penalty for which is imprisonment in the penitentiary, are now and always have been disfranchised, and a pardon did not restore them unless the warrant of pardon so provided.

> ' . . . But suppose the mass of the people of a State are pirates, counterfeiters, or other criminals, would gentlemen be willing to repeal the laws now in force in order to give them an opportunity to land their piratical crafts and come on shore to assist in the election of a President or members of Congress because they are numerous? And let it be borne in mind that these latter offenses are only crimes committed against

property; that of treason is against the nation, against the whole people—the highest known to the law.'

The debates in the Senate did not cover the subject as exhaustively as did the debates in the House, apparently because many of the critical decisions were made by the Republican Senators in an unreported series of caucuses off the floor. Senator Saulsbury of Delaware, a Democrat who was not included in the majority caucus, observed:

> 'It is very well known that the majority of the members of this body who favor a proposition of this character have been in very serious deliberation for several days in reference to these amendments, and have held some four or five caucuses on the subject.'

Nonetheless, the occasional comments of Senators on the language in question indicate an understanding similar to that of the House members. Senator Johnson of Maryland, one of the principal opponents of the Fourteenth Amendment, made this argument:

> 'Now it is proposed to deny the right to be represented of a part, simply because they are not permitted to exercise the right of voting. You do not put them upon the footing of aliens, upon the footing of rebels, upon the footing of minors, upon the footing of the females, upon the footing of those who may have committed crimes of the most heinous character. Murderers, robbers, houseburners, counterfeiters of the public securities of the United States, all who may have committed any crime, at any time, against the laws of the United States or the laws of a particular State, are to be included within the basis; but the poor black man, unless he is permitted to vote, is not to be represented, and is to have no interest in the Government.'

Senator Henderson of Missouri, speaking in favor of the version of § 2 which had been reported by the Joint Committee in April, as opposed to the earlier provision of the proposal which had been defeated in the Senate, said this:

> 'The States under the former proposition (the corresponding provision of the original Amendment reported by the Committee of Fifteen, which passed the House of Representatives but was defeated in the Senate) might have excluded the negroes under an educational test and yet retained their power in Congress. Under this they cannot. For all practical purposes, under the former proposition loss of representation followed the disfranchisement of the negro only; under this it follows the disfranchisement of white and black, unless excluded on account of 'rebellion or other crime.'

Further light is shed on the understanding of those who framed and ratified the Fourteenth Amendment, and thus on the meaning of § 2, by the fact that at the time of the adoption of the Amendment, 29 States had provisions in their constitutions which prohibited, or authorized the legislature to prohibit, exercise of the franchise by persons convicted of felonies or infamous crimes.

More impressive than the mere existence of the state constitutional provisions disenfranchising felons at the time of the adoption of the Fourteenth Amendment is the congressional treatment of States readmitted to the Union following the Civil War. For every State thus readmitted, affirmative congressional action in the form of an enabling act was taken, and as a part of the readmission process the State seeking readmission was required to submit for the approval of the Congress its proposed state constitution. In March 1867, before any State was readmitted, Congress passed 'An act to provide for the more efficient Government of the Rebel States,' the so-called Reconstruction Act. Section 5 of the Reconstruction Act established conditions on which the former Confederate States would be readmitted to representation in Congress. It provided:

> That when the people of any one of said rebel States shall have formed a constitution of government in conformity with the Constitution of the United States in all respects, framed by a convention of delegates elected by the male citizens of said State, twenty-one years old and upward, of whatever race, color, or previous condition, who have been resident in said State for one year previous to the day of such election, except such as may be disenfranchised for participation in the rebellion or for felony at common law, ... said State shall be declared entitled to representation in Congress, and senators and representatives shall be admitted therefrom on their taking the oath prescribed by law, and then and thereafter the preceding sections of this act shall be inoperative in said State.

The phrase 'under laws equally applicable to all the inhabitants of said State' was introduced as an amendment to the House bill by Senator Drake of Missouri. Senator Drake's explanation of his reason for introducing his amendment is illuminating. He expressed concern that without that restriction, Arkansas might misuse the exception for felons to disenfranchise Negroes:

> There is still another objection to the condition as expressed in the bill, and that is in the exception as to the punishment for crime. The bill authorizes men to be deprived of the right to vote 'as a punishment for such crimes as are now felonies at common law, whereof they shall have been duly convicted.' There is one fundamental defect in that, and that is that there is no requirement that the laws under which men shall be duly convicted of these crimes shall be equally applicable to all the inhabitants of the State. It is a very easy thing in a State to

make one set of laws applicable to white men, and another set of laws applicable to colored men.

This convincing evidence of the historical understanding of the Fourteenth Amendment is confirmed by the decisions of this Court which have discussed the constitutionality of provisions disenfranchising felons. Although the Court has never given plenary consideration to the precise question of whether a State may constitutionally exclude some or all convicted felons from the franchise, we have indicated approval of such exclusions on a number of occasions. In two cases decided toward the end of the last century, the Court approved exclusions of bigamists and polygamists from the franchise under territorial laws of Utah and Idaho. Much more recently we have strongly suggested in dicta that exclusion of convicted felons from the franchise violates no constitutional provision. In *Lassiter v. Northampton County Board of Elections*, 360 U.S. 45 (1959), where we upheld North Carolina's imposition of a literacy requirement for voting, the Court said, 'Residence requirements, age, previous criminal record are obvious examples indicating factors which a State may take into consideration in determining the qualifications of voters.'

Still more recently, we have summarily affirmed two decisions of three-judge District Courts rejecting constitutional challenges to state laws disenfranchising convicted felons. Despite this settled historical and judicial understanding of the Fourteenth Amendment's effect on state laws disenfranchising convicted felons, respondents argue that our recent decisions invalidating other state-imposed restrictions on the franchise as violative of the Equal Protection Clause require us to invalidate the disenfranchisement of felons as well. They rely on such cases as *Dunn v. Blumstein*, 405 U.S. 330 (1972), *Bullock v. Carter*, 405 U.S. 134 (1972), *Kramer v. Union Free School District*, 395 U.S. 621 (1969), and *Cipriano v. City of Houma*, 395 U.S. 701 (1969), to support the conclusions of the Supreme Court of California that a State must show a "compelling state interest" to justify exclusion of ex-felons from the franchise and that California has not done so here.

As we have seen, however, the exclusion of felons from the vote has an affirmative sanction in § 2 of the Fourteenth Amendment, a sanction which was not present in the case of the other restrictions on the franchise which were invalidated in the cases on which respondents rely. We hold that the understanding of those who adopted the Fourteenth Amendment, as reflected in the express language of § 2 and in the historical and judicial interpretation of the Amendment's applicability to state laws disenfranchising felons, is of controlling significance in distinguishing such laws from those other state limitations on the franchise which have been held invalid under the Equal Protection Clause by this Court. We do not think that the Court's refusal to accept Mr. Justice Harlan's position in his dissents in *Reynolds v. Sims*, 377

U.S. 533, 589 (1964*)*, and *Carrington v. Rash,* 380 U.S. 89, 97 (1965), that § 2 is the only part of the Amendment dealing with voting rights, dictates an opposite result. We need not go nearly so far as Mr. Justice Harlan would to reach our conclusion, for we may rest on the demonstrably sound proposition that § 1, in dealing with voting rights as it does, could not have been meant to bar outright a form of disenfranchisement which was expressly exempted from the less drastic sanction of reduced representation which § 2 imposed for other forms of disenfranchisement. Nor can we accept respondents' argument that because § 2 was made part of the Amendment "largely through the accident of political exigency rather than through the relation which it bore to the other sections of the Amendment," we must not look to it for guidance in interpreting § 1. It is as much a part of the Amendment as any of the other sections, and how it became a part of the Amendment is less important than what it says and what it means.

Pressed upon us by the respondents, and by amici curia, are contentions that these notions are outmoded, and that the more modern view is that it is essential to the process of rehabilitating the ex-felon that he be returned to his role in society as a fully participating citizen when he has completed the serving of his term. We would by no means discount these arguments if addressed to the legislative forum which may properly weigh and balance them against those advanced in support of California's present constitutional provisions. But it is not for us to choose one set of values over the other. If respondents are correct, and the view which they advocate is indeed the more enlightened and sensible one, presumably the people of the State of California will ultimately come around to that view. And if they do not do so, their failure is some evidence, at least, of the fact that there are two sides to the argument.

We therefore hold that the Supreme Court of California erred in concluding that California may no longer, consistent with the Equal Protection Clause of the Fourteenth Amendment, exclude from the franchise convicted felons who have completed their sentences and paroles. The California court did not reach respondents' alternative contention that there was such a total lack of uniformity in county election officials' enforcement of the challenged state laws as to work a separate denial of equal protection, and we believe that it should have an opportunity to consider the claim before we address ourselves to it. Accordingly, we reverse and remand for further proceedings not inconsistent with this opinion.

■ MR. JUSTICE MARSHALL, with whom MR. JUSTICE BRENNAN joins, dissenting.

The Court today holds that a State may strip ex-felons who have fully paid their debt to society of their fundamental right to vote without running afoul of the Fourteenth Amendment. This result is, in my view, based on an unsound historical analysis which already has been rejected by this Court. In straining to reach that result, I believe that the Court has also disregarded important limitations on its jurisdiction. For these reasons, I respectfully dissent.

II

The Court construes § 2 of the Fourteenth Amendment as an express authorization for the States to disenfranchise former felons. Section 2 does except disenfranchisement for 'participation in rebellion, or other crime' from the operation of its penalty provision. As the Court notes, however, there is little independent legislative history as to the crucial words 'or other crime'; the proposed § 2 went to a joint committee containing only the phrase 'participation in rebellion' and emerged with 'or other crime' inexplicably tacked on. In its exhaustive review of the lengthy legislative history of the Fourteenth Amendment, the Court has come upon only one explanatory reference for the 'other crimes' provision a reference which is unilluminating at best.

The historical purpose for § 2 itself is, however, relatively clear and, in my view, dispositive of this case. The Republicans who controlled the 39th Congress were concerned that the additional congressional representation of the Southern States which would result from the abolition of slavery might weaken their own political dominance. There were two alternatives available—either to limit southern representation, which was unacceptable on a long-term basis, or to insure that southern Negroes, sympathetic to the Republican cause, would be enfranchised; but an explicit grant of sufferage [sic] to Negroes was thought politically unpalatable at the time. Section 2 of the Fourteenth Amendment was the resultant compromise. It put Southern States to a choice—enfranchise Negro voters or lose congressional representation.

The political motivation behind § 2 was a limited one. It had little to do with the purposes of the rest of the Fourteenth Amendment. It is clear that § 2 was not intended and should not be construed to be a limitation on the other sections of the Fourteenth Amendment. Section 2 provides a special remedy—reduced representation—to cure a particular form of electoral abuse—the disenfranchisement of Negroes. There is no indication that the framers of the provisions intended that special penalty to be the exclusive remedy for all forms of electoral discrimination. This Court has repeatedly rejected that rationale. *See Reynolds v. Sims,* 377 U.S. 533 (1964); *Carrington v. Rash,* 380 U.S. 89 (1965).

Rather, a discrimination to which the penalty provision of § 2 is inapplicable must still be judged against the Equal Protection Clause of § 1 to determine whether judicial or congressional remedies should be invoked.

The Court's references to congressional enactments contemporaneous to the adoption of the Fourteenth Amendment, such as the Reconstruction Act and the readmission statutes, are inapposite.

They do not explain the purpose for the adoption of § 2 of the Fourteenth Amendment. They merely indicate that disenfranchisement for participation in crime was not uncommon in the States at the time of the adoption of the Amendment. Hence, not surprisingly, that form of disenfranchisement was excepted from the application of the special penalty provision of § 2. But because Congress chose to exempt one form of electoral discrimination from the reduction-of-representation remedy provided by § 2 does not necessarily imply congressional approval of this disenfranchisement. By providing a special remedy for disenfranchisement of a particular class of voters in § 2, Congress did not approve all election discriminations to which the § 2 remedy was inapplicable, and such discrimination thus are not forever immunized from evolving standards of equal protection scrutiny. There is no basis for concluding that Congress intended by § 2 to freeze the meaning of other clauses of the Fourteenth Amendment to the conception of voting rights prevalent at the time of the adoption of the Amendment. In fact, one form of disenfranchisement—one-year durational residence requirements—specifically authorized by the Reconstruction Act, one of the contemporaneous enactments upon which the Court relies to show the intendment of the framers of the Fourteenth Amendment, has already been declared unconstitutional by this Court in *Dunn v. Blumstein,* 405 U.S. 330 (1972).

Disenfranchisement for participation in crime, like durational residence requirements, was common at the time of the adoption of the Fourteenth Amendment. But 'constitutional concepts of equal protection are not immutably frozen like insects trapped in Devonian amber.' Accordingly, neither the fact that several States had ex-felon disenfranchisement laws at the time of the adoption of the Fourteenth Amendment, nor that such disenfranchisement was specifically excepted from the special remedy of § 2, can serve to insulate such disenfranchisement from equal protection scrutiny.

III

In my view, the disenfranchisement of ex-felons must be measured against the requirements of the Equal Protection Clause of § 1 of the Fourteenth Amendment. That analysis properly begins with the observation that because the right to vote "is of the essence of a democratic society, and any restrictions on that right strike at the heart of representative government," *Reynolds v. Sims,* 377 U.S. at 555, voting is a "fundamental" right. As we observed in *Dunn v. Blumstein, supra,* 405 U.S. at 336:

> 'There is no need to repeat now the labors undertaken in earlier cases to analyze (the) right to vote and to explain in detail the judicial role in reviewing state statutes that selectively distribute the franchise. In decision after decision, this Court has made clear that a citizen has a constitutionally

protected right to participate in elections on an equal basis with other citizens in the jurisdiction.

We concluded: '(I)f a challenge statute grants the right to vote to some citizens and denies the franchise to others, 'the Court must determine whether the exclusions are necessary to promote a compelling state interest.''

To determine that the compelling-state-interest test applies to the challenged classification is, however, to settle only a threshold question. 'Compelling state interest' is merely a shorthand description of the difficult process of balancing individual and state interests that the Court must embark upon when faced with a classification touching on fundamental rights. Our other equal protection cases give content to the nature of that balance. The State has the heavy burden of showing, first, that the challenged disenfranchisement is necessary to a legitimate and substantial state interest; second, that the classification is drawn with precision—that it does not exclude too many people who should not and need not be excluded; and third, that there are no other reasonable ways to achieve the State's goal with a lesser burden on the constitutionally protected interest.

I think it clear that the State has not met its burden of justifying the blanket disenfranchisement of former felons presented by this case. There is certainly no basis for asserting that ex-felons have any less interest in the democratic process than any other citizen.

It is argued that disenfranchisement is necessary to prevent vote frauds. Although the State has a legitimate and, in fact, compelling interest in preventing election fraud, the challenged provision is not sustainable on that ground. First, the disenfranchisement provisions are patently both overinclusive and underinclusive. The provision is not limited to those who have demonstrated a marked propensity for abusing the ballot by violating election laws. Rather, it encompasses all former felons and there has been no showing that ex-felons generally are any more likely to abuse the ballot than the remainder of the population. In contrast, many of those convicted of violating election laws are treated as misdemeanants and are not barred from voting at all. It seems clear that the classification here is not tailored to achieve its articulated goal, since it crudely excludes large numbers of otherwise qualified voters.

Another asserted purpose is to keep former felons from voting because their likely voting pattern might be subversive of the interests of an orderly society.

We have . . . explicitly held that such "differences of opinion cannot justify for excluding (any) group from . . . 'the franchise.' "

"[If] they are . . . residents, . . . they, as all other qualified residents, have a right to an equal opportunity for political representation. . . .

'Fencing out' from the franchise a sector of the population because of the way they way vote is constitutionally impermissible."

Although, in the last century, this Court may have justified the exclusion of voters from the electoral process for fear that they would vote to change laws considered important by a temporal majority, I have little doubt that we would not countenance such a purpose today. The process of democracy is one of change. Our laws are not frozen into immutable form, they are constantly in the process of revision in response to the needs of a changing society. The public interest, as conceived by a majority of the voting public, is constantly undergoing reexamination.

The public purposes asserted to be served by disenfranchisement have been found wanting in many quarters. When this suit was filed, 23 States allowed ex-felons full access to the ballot. Since that time, four more States have joined their ranks. Shortly after lower federal courts sustained New York's and Florida's disenfranchisement provisions, the legislatures repealed those laws. Congress has recently provided for the restoration of felons' voting rights at the end of sentence or parole in the District of. The National Conference on Uniform State Laws, the American Law Institute, the National Probation and Parole Association, the National Advisory Commission on Criminal Justice Standards and Goals, the President's Commission on Law Enforcement and the Administration of Justice, the California League of Women Voters, the National Democratic Party, and the Secretary of State of California have all strongly endorsed full suffrage rights for former felons.

The disenfranchisement of ex-felons had 'its origin in the fogs and fictions of feudal jurisprudence and doubtless has been brought forward into modern statutes without fully realizing either the effect of its literal significance or the extent of its infringement upon the spirit of our system of government.' I think it clear that measured against the standards of this Court's modern equal protection jurisprudence, the blanket disenfranchisement of ex-felons cannot stand.

I respectfully dissent.

■ MR. JUSTICE DOUGLAS, agreeing with Part I-A of this opinion, dissents from a reversal of the judgment below as he cannot say that it does not rest on an independent state ground. *See Hayakawa v. Brown,* 415 U.S. 1304 (Douglas, J., in chambers).

NOTES AND QUESTIONS

1. *The Court's Reasoning.* The majority, led by Chief Justice Rehnquist, performs a textual exegesis of sections 1 and 2 of the Fourteenth Amendment. The majority concludes: "[Section] 1, in dealing with the voting rights as it does, could not have been meant to bar outright a form of disenfranchisement which has expressly exempted from the less drastic sanction of reduced representation which [section] 2 imposed for other forms of disenfranchisement." Do you find this analysis persuasive?

2.   *Proportionality.* Should the Court have considered the proportionality of the sanction (a lifetime disenfranchisement as civil penalty) to the crime (conviction of an undefined infamous crime)?

3.   *An   Evolving   and   Progressive   Conception   of   Political Participation.* In his dissent, Justice Marshall offers two arguments in support of his point that these types of laws are unconstitutional. First, he argues that section 2 of the Fourteenth Amendment was not a remedy for electoral discrimination, but was instead designed strictly to limit the political power of Southern Democrats. Does Justice Marshall's historical analysis persuasively refute the Chief Justice's argument that section 2 is the only limitation on ex-felon disenfranchising laws? Justice Marshall also argues that the Court has articulated an evolving conception of the right to vote and political participation. From Justice Marshall's perspective, ex-felon disenfranchisement is inconsistent with this evolving conception, which is also represented by a growing number of states that have restored voting rights to ex-felons. Is Justice Marshall right that ex-felon disenfranchising laws are inconsistent with modern conceptions of political participation? Our concept of political rights and political participation has changed drastically since the Founding period, and even since the adoption of the Fourteenth Amendment. Why should we be bound by a nineteenth-century conception of political equality and political participation?

4.   *Is This Racial Discrimination?* In *Hunter v. Underwood*, 471 U.S. 222 (1985), the Supreme Court held that Alabama's felon disenfranchisement law violated the Fourteenth Amendment. The Court noted that, even though the law was neutral on its face, it was adopted with the intent to discriminate and had a discriminatory impact. But *Hunter* does not apply to laws that were not adopted with a discriminatory intent. Although not addressed in *Richardson*, one of the concerns with ex-felon disenfranchising laws is the disparate impact they have on communities of color. "One in seven black men is disfranchised for crime, and in ten states in America's decentralized system of suffrage, more than fifteen percent of blacks have lost the vote. No state disfranchises as many as ten percent of whites." J. Morgan Kousser, *Disenfranchisement Modernized*, 6 Elec. L. J. 104, 105–06 (2007).

5.   *The Lower Courts.* In *Farrakhan v. Gregoire,* 623 F.3d 990 (9th Cir. 2010), the Ninth Circuit, sitting en banc, reversed a prior panel opinion and concluded that Washington State's felon disenfranchisement law did not violate section 2 of the VRA. Washington's law disenfranchises both felons and ex-felons. In a relatively brief opinion, the en banc Court stated that Congress was aware of felon disenfranchisement laws when it passed and amended the VRA, "yet gave no indication that felon disenfranchisement was in any way suspect." *Id.* at 993. The Court also noted that the other two circuits that have examined the issue have concluded similarly. *See Hayden v. Pataki*, 449 F.3d 305 (2nd Cir. 2006) and *Simmons v. Galvin*, 575 F.3d 24 (1st Cir. 2009).

6.   *The United States as Outlier Among Post-Industrial Nations.* "No other democratic country in the world denies as many people—in absolute and proportional terms—the right to vote because of felony convictions." Jamie Fellner & Marc Mauer, *Losing the Vote: The Impact of Felony Disenfranchisement Laws in the United States*, Human Rights Watch and the Sentencing Project 4 (October 1998), *see also* Christopher Uggen & Jeff Manza, *Democratic Contraction? Political Consequences of Felon Disenfranchisement in the United States*, 67 Am. Soc. Rev. 777, 778 (2002) ("Among postindustrial democracies, the United States is virtually the only nation to permanently disenfranchise ex-felons as a class in many jurisdictions, and the only country to limit the rights of individuals convicted of offenses other than very rare treason or election-related crimes."). Do you think this American exceptionalism is related to America's racial history, or the fact that the felon disenfranchisement laws have such a disproportionate racial impact? Consider one explanation:

Felon disenfranchisement lies at the intersection of three distinct areas of law. First, while not regarded as "punishment" for due process purposes, it has a criminal law/sentencing component, as part of the package of sanctions automatically following criminal conviction. Accordingly, like loss of other rights (e.g., to possess a firearm; to obtain or retain public benefits, licenses or educational opportunities; and, for non-citizens, to live in this country), felon disenfranchisement just happens upon conviction. No one has to tell a defendant about it before pleading guilty, or to put it another way, before deciding whether it is really smarter to mortgage one's house and fight the case even though the prosecutor offered a walk-away deal. (It is the allegedly non-punitive nature of felon disenfranchisement that forecloses its legitimation on the ground that it is punishment for crime-if punishment, then the judge must disclose it at the time of the guilty plea.)

Second, felon disenfranchisement is part of race law. The disenfranchisement laws of several of the former Confederate states in particular bear the clear imprint of a purpose to maintain white supremacy. A remarkable example is the candid decision of a unanimous Mississippi Supreme Court which, in *Ratliff v. Beale*, explained the origins of the Mississippi Constitution of 1890, still in force today.

Third, felon disenfranchisement is part of election law and voting rights jurisprudence. Ideally, policies allowing some to vote and others not should be based on legitimate and justifiable reasons. A glance at, for example, the post-Civil War constitutional amendments shows that expanding access to the ballot was the single most important reason the Constitution-in-being was found to be unsatisfactory: The Fourteenth, Fifteenth, Seventeenth, Nineteenth, Twenty-third, Twenty-fourth and Twenty-sixth Amendments expanded the franchise to new groups, or, in the case of direct election of Senators, the ballot's value. If the unlamented demise of qualifications based on sex, race, and property begins to suggest an underlying principle of universal adult franchise, then the exclusion of a particular group, those with felony convictions, calls for a justification.

Gabriel J. Chin, *Felon Disenfranchisement and Democracy in the Late Jim Crow Era*, 5 Ohio St. J. Crim. L. 329, 330–331 (2007). It should be noted that a nascent recent trend may bring the United States much closer to the norm of post-industrialized nations. In 2016 both Maryland and Virginia made it possible for ex-felons to vote.

7. *Advising Exercise.* You are the law clerk to a judge deciding a challenge to your state's felony disenfranchisement law. The law was not enacted with a discriminatory purpose or intent, but it has a significant disparate racial impact. The plaintiffs have alleged a violation of section 2 of the VRA and the Fourteenth and Fifteenth Amendments. What do you recommend to your judge and why?

B. VOTER IDENTIFICATION REQUIREMENTS: THE NEW DENIAL OF THE VOTE?

Political activists and civil rights organizations have been preoccupied of late with the disproportionate impact that voter identification requirements might have on communities of color and poor white communities. These requirements have proliferated in the last decade, especially since the Court's decision in *Shelby County*. Polls show that they are very popular with voters. In the case below, the Court addressed the constitutionality of voter identification requirements. The case raises the question: are these laws modern equivalents of literacy tests or poll taxes—devices used to deny voters, particularly voters of color, access to the voting booth? Or, are they legitimate devices necessary to ensure the integrity of the political process?

Crawford v. Marion

Supreme Court of the United States, 2008.
553 U.S. 181.

■ JUSTICE STEVENS announced the judgment of the Court and delivered an opinion in which THE CHIEF JUSTICE and JUSTICE KENNEDY join.

At issue in these cases is the constitutionality of an Indiana statute requiring citizens voting in person on election day, or casting a ballot in person at the office of the circuit court clerk prior to election day, to present photo identification issued by the government.

Referred to as either the "Voter ID Law" or "SEA 483," the statute applies to in-person voting at both primary and general elections. The requirement does not apply to absentee ballots submitted by mail, and the statute contains an exception for persons living and voting in a state-licensed facility such as a nursing home. Ind.Code Ann. s 3–11–8–25.1(e) (West Supp.2007). A voter who is indigent or has a religious objection to being photographed may cast a provisional ballot that will be counted only if she executes an appropriate affidavit before the circuit court clerk within 10 days following the election. A voter who has photo identification but is unable to present that identification on election day may file a provisional ballot that will be counted if she brings her photo identification to the circuit county clerk's office within 10 days. No photo identification is required in order to register to vote, and the State offers free photo identification to qualified voters able to establish their residence and identity.

We are . . . persuaded that the District Court and the Court of Appeals correctly concluded that the evidence in the record is not sufficient to support a facial attack on the validity of the entire statute, and thus affirm.

I

In *Harper v. Virginia Bd. of Elections*, the Court held that Virginia could not condition the right to vote in a state election on the payment of a poll tax of $1.50. We rejected the dissenters' argument that the interest in promoting civic responsibility by weeding out those voters who did not care enough about public affairs to pay a small sum for the privilege of voting provided a rational basis for the tax. Applying a stricter standard, we concluded that a State "violates the Equal Protection Clause of the Fourteenth Amendment whenever it makes the affluence of the voter or payment of any fee an electoral standard." We used the term "invidiously discriminate" to describe conduct prohibited under that standard, noting that we had previously held that while a State may obviously impose "reasonable residence restrictions on the availability of the ballot," it "may not deny the opportunity to vote to a bona fide resident merely because he is a member of the armed services." Although the State's justification for the tax was rational, it was invidious because it was irrelevant to the voter's qualifications.

Thus, under the standard applied in *Harper*, even rational restrictions on the right to vote are invidious if they are unrelated to voter qualifications. In *Anderson v. Celebrezze*, however, we confirmed the general rule that "evenhanded restrictions that protect the integrity and reliability of the electoral process itself" are not invidious and satisfy the standard set forth in *Harper*. Rather than applying any "litmus test" that would neatly separate valid from invalid restrictions, we concluded that a court must identify and evaluate the interests put forward by the State as justifications for the burden imposed by its rule, and then make the "hard judgment" that our adversary system demands.

In later election cases we have followed *Anderson*'s balancing approach. Thus, in *Norman v. Reed*, after identifying the burden Illinois imposed on a political party's access to the ballot, we "called for the demonstration of a corresponding interest sufficiently weighty to justify the limitation," and concluded that the "severe restriction" was not justified by a narrowly drawn state interest of compelling importance.

Later, in *Burdick v. Takushi*, we applied *Anderson*'s standard for " 'reasonable, nondiscriminatory restrictions,' " and upheld Hawaii's prohibition on write-in voting despite the fact that it prevented a significant number of "voters from participating in Hawaii elections in a meaningful manner." We reaffirmed *Anderson*'s requirement that a court evaluating a constitutional challenge to an election regulation weigh the asserted injury to the right to vote against the " 'precise interests put forward by the State as justifications for the burden imposed by its rule.' "[9]

In neither *Norman* nor *Burdick* did we identify any litmus test for measuring the severity of a burden that a state law imposes on a political party, an individual voter, or a discrete class of voters. However slight that burden may appear, as *Harper* demonstrates, it must be justified by relevant and legitimate state interests "sufficiently weighty to justify the limitation." We therefore begin our analysis of the constitutionality of Indiana's statute by focusing on those interests.

II

The State has identified several state interests that arguably justify the burdens that SEA 483 imposes on voters and potential voters. While petitioners argue that the statute was actually motivated by partisan concerns and dispute both the significance of the State's interests and the magnitude of any real threat to those interests, they do not question the legitimacy of the interests the State has identified. Each is unquestionably relevant to the State's interest in protecting the integrity and reliability of the electoral process.

The first is the interest in deterring and detecting voter fraud. The State has a valid interest in participating in a nationwide effort to improve and modernize election procedures that have been criticized as antiquated and inefficient. The State also argues that it has a particular interest in preventing voter fraud in response to a problem that is in part the product of its own maladministration—namely, that Indiana's voter registration rolls include a large number of names of persons who are either deceased or no longer live in Indiana. Finally, the State relies on its interest in safeguarding voter confidence. Each of these interests merits separate comment.

Election Modernization

Two recently enacted federal statutes have made it necessary for States to reexamine their election procedures. Both contain provisions consistent with a State's choice to use government-issued photo

---

[9] Contrary to Justice SCALIA's suggestion, our approach remains faithful to *Anderson* and *Burdick*. The *Burdick* opinion was explicit in its endorsement and adherence to *Anderson*, and repeatedly cited *Anderson*. To be sure, *Burdick* rejected the argument that strict scrutiny applies to all laws imposing a burden on the right to vote; but in its place, the Court applied the "flexible standard" set forth in *Anderson*. *Burdick* surely did not create a novel "deferential 'important regulatory interests' standard."

identification as a relevant source of information concerning a citizen's eligibility to vote.

In the National Voter Registration Act of 1993 (NVRA), Congress established procedures that would both increase the number of registered voters and protect the integrity of the electoral process. The statute requires state motor vehicle driver's license applications to serve as voter registration applications. While that requirement has increased the number of registered voters, the statute also contains a provision restricting States' ability to remove names from the lists of registered voters. These protections have been partly responsible for inflated lists of registered voters.

Voter Fraud

The only kind of voter fraud that SEA 483 addresses is in-person voter impersonation at polling places. The record contains no evidence of any such fraud actually occurring in Indiana at any time in its history. Moreover, petitioners argue that provisions of the Indiana Criminal Code punishing such conduct as a felony provide adequate protection against the risk that such conduct will occur in the future. It remains true, however, that flagrant examples of such fraud in other parts of the country have been documented throughout this Nation's history by respected historians and journalists, that occasional examples have surfaced in recent years, and that Indiana's own experience with fraudulent voting in the 2003 Democratic primary for East Chicago Mayor—though perpetrated using absentee ballots and not in-person fraud—demonstrate that not only is the risk of voter fraud real but that it could affect the outcome of a close election.

There is no question about the legitimacy or importance of the State's interest in counting only the votes of eligible voters. Moreover, the interest in orderly administration and accurate recordkeeping provides a sufficient justification for carefully identifying all voters participating in the election process. While the most effective method of preventing election fraud may well be debatable, the propriety of doing so is perfectly clear.

Safeguarding Voter Confidence

Finally, the State contends that it has an interest in protecting public confidence "in the integrity and legitimacy of representative government." Brief for State Respondents, No. 07–25, p. 53. While that interest is closely related to the State's interest in preventing voter fraud, public confidence in the integrity of the electoral process has independent significance, because it encourages citizen participation in the democratic process.

III

States employ different methods of identifying eligible voters at the polls. Some merely check off the names of registered voters who identify themselves; others require voters to present registration cards or other documentation before they can vote; some require voters to sign their names so their signatures can be compared with those on file; and in recent years an increasing number of States have relied primarily on photo identification. A photo identification requirement imposes some burdens on voters that other methods of identification do not share. For example, a voter may lose his photo identification, may have his wallet stolen on the way to the polls, or may not resemble the photo in the identification because he recently grew a beard. Burdens of that sort arising from life's vagaries, however, are neither so serious nor so frequent as to raise any question about the constitutionality of SEA 483; the availability of the right to cast a provisional ballot provides an adequate remedy for problems of that character.

The burdens that are relevant to the issue before us are those imposed on persons who are eligible to vote but do not possess a current photo identification that complies with the requirements of SEA 483. The fact that most voters already possess a valid driver's license, or some other form of acceptable identification, would not save the statute under our reasoning in Harper, if the State required voters to pay a tax or a fee to obtain a new photo identification. But just as other States provide free voter registration cards, the photo identification cards issued by Indiana's BMV are also free. For most voters who need them, the inconvenience of making a trip to the BMV, gathering the required documents, and posing for a photograph surely does not qualify as a substantial burden on the right to vote, or even represent a significant increase over the usual burdens of voting.

Both evidence in the record and facts of which we may take judicial notice, however, indicate that a somewhat heavier burden may be placed on a limited number of persons. They include elderly persons born out-of-state, who may have difficulty obtaining a birth certificate; persons who because of economic or other personal limitations may find it difficult either to secure a copy of their birth certificate or to assemble the other required documentation to obtain a state-issued identification; homeless persons; and persons with a religious objection to being photographed. If we assume, as the evidence suggests, that some members of these classes were registered voters when SEA 483 was enacted, the new identification requirement may have imposed a special burden on their right to vote.

The severity of that burden is, of course, mitigated by the fact that, if eligible, voters without photo identification may cast provisional ballots that will ultimately be counted. To do so, however, they must travel to the circuit court clerk's office within 10 days to execute the required affidavit. It is unlikely that such a requirement would pose a constitutional problem unless it is wholly unjustified. And even assuming that the burden may not be justified as to few voters, that conclusion is by no means sufficient to establish petitioners' right to the relief they seek in this litigation.

IV

Balancing test for which Petitioners argue

Petitioners ask this Court, in effect, to perform a unique balancing analysis that looks specifically at a small number of voters who may experience a special burden under the statute and weighs their burdens against the State's broad interests in protecting election integrity. Petitioners urge us to ask whether the State's interests justify the burden imposed on voters who cannot afford or obtain a birth certificate and who must make a second trip to the circuit court clerk's office after voting. But on the basis of the evidence in the record it is not possible to quantify either the magnitude of the burden on this narrow class of voters or the portion of the burden imposed on them that is fully justified.

First, the evidence in the record does not provide us with the number of registered voters without photo identification; Judge Barker found petitioners' expert's report to be "utterly incredible and unreliable." Much of the argument about the numbers of such voters comes from extrarecord, postjudgment studies, the accuracy of which has not been tested in the trial court.

Further, the deposition evidence presented in the District Court does not provide any concrete evidence of the burden imposed on voters who currently lack photo identification. The record includes depositions of two case managers at a day shelter for homeless persons and the depositions of members of the plaintiff organizations, none of whom expressed a personal inability to vote under SEA 483. A deposition from a named plaintiff describes the difficulty the elderly woman had in obtaining an identification card, although her testimony indicated that she intended to return to the BMV since she had recently obtained her birth certificate and that she was able to pay the birth certificate fee.

The record says virtually nothing about the difficulties faced by either indigent voters or voters with religious objections to being photographed. While one elderly man stated that he did not have the money to pay for a birth certificate, when asked if he did not have the money or did not wish to spend it, he replied, "both." From this limited evidence we do not know the magnitude of the impact SEA 483 will have on indigent voters in Indiana. The record does contain the affidavit of one homeless woman who has a copy of her birth certificate, but was denied a photo identification card because she did not have an address. Id., at 67. But that single affidavit gives no indication of how common the problem is.

In sum, on the basis of the record that has been made in this litigation, we cannot conclude that the statute imposes "excessively burdensome requirements" on any class of voters. When we consider only the statute's broad application to all Indiana voters we conclude that it "imposes only a limited burden on voters' rights." The " 'precise interests'" advanced by the State are therefore sufficient to defeat petitioners' facial challenge to SEA 483.

Finally we note that petitioners have not demonstrated that the proper remedy—even assuming an unjustified burden on some voters— would be to invalidate the entire statute. When evaluating a neutral, nondiscriminatory regulation of voting procedure, "[w]e must keep in mind that '[a] ruling of unconstitutionality frustrates the intent of the elected representatives of the people.'"

V

[I]f a nondiscriminatory law is supported by valid neutral justifications, those justifications should not be disregarded simply because partisan interests may have provided one motivation for the votes of individual legislators. The state interests identified as justifications for SEA 483 are both neutral and sufficiently strong to require us to reject petitioners' facial attack on the statute. The application of the statute to the vast majority of Indiana voters is amply justified by the valid interest in protecting "the integrity and reliability of the electoral process."

The judgment of the Court of Appeals is affirmed.

It is so ordered.

■ JUSTICE SCALIA, with whom JUSTICE THOMAS and JUSTICE ALITO join, concurring in the judgment.

The lead opinion assumes petitioners' premise that the voter-identification law "may have imposed a special burden on" some voters, but holds that petitioners have not assembled evidence to show that the special burden is severe enough to warrant strict scrutiny. That is true enough, but for the sake of clarity and finality (as well as adherence to precedent), I prefer to decide these cases on the grounds that petitioners' premise is irrelevant and that the burden at issue is minimal and justified.

To evaluate a law respecting the right to vote—whether it governs voter qualifications, candidate selection, or the voting process—we use the approach set out in *Burdick v. Takushi,* 504 U.S. 428 (1992). This calls for application of a deferential "important regulatory interests" standard for nonsevere, nondiscriminatory restrictions, reserving strict scrutiny for laws that severely restrict the right to vote. The lead opinion resists the import of Burdick by characterizing it as simply adopting "the balancing approach" of Anderson v. Celebrezze. Although Burdick liberally quoted *Anderson, Burdick* forged *Anderson*'s amorphous "flexible standard" into something resembling an administrable rule. Since *Burdick*, we have repeatedly reaffirmed the primacy of its two-track approach. Thus, the first step is to decide whether a challenged law severely burdens the right to vote. Ordinary and widespread burdens,

[handwritten margin note: So incredibly problematic the court to allowing impermissible motivation to pass const. muster]

such as those requiring "nominal effort" of everyone, are not severe. Burdens are severe if they go beyond the merely inconvenient.

Not all of our decisions predating *Burdick* addressed whether a challenged voting regulation severely burdened the right to vote, but when we began to grapple with the magnitude of burdens, we did so categorically and did not consider the peculiar circumstances of individual voters or candidates.

A case-by-case approach naturally encourages constant litigation. Very few new election regulations improve everyone's lot, so the potential allegations of severe burden are endless. . . .

The lead opinion's record-based resolution of these cases, which neither rejects nor embraces the rule of our precedents, provides no certainty, and will embolden litigants who surmise that our precedents have been abandoned. There is no good reason to prefer that course.

■ JUSTICE SOUTER, with whom JUSTICE GINSBURG joins, dissenting.

Indiana's "Voter ID Law" threatens to impose nontrivial burdens on the voting right of tens of thousands of the State's citizens and a significant percentage of those individuals are likely to be deterred from voting. The statute is unconstitutional under the balancing standard of *Burdick v. Takushi*: a State may not burden the right to vote merely by invoking abstract interests, be they legitimate or even compelling, but must make a particular, factual showing that threats to its interests outweigh the particular impediments it has imposed. The State has made no such justification here, and as to some aspects of its law, it has hardly even tried. I therefore respectfully dissent from the Court's judgment sustaining the statute.

II

Under *Burdick*, "the rigorousness of our inquiry into the propriety of a state election law depends upon the extent to which a challenged regulation burdens First and Fourteenth Amendment rights," upon an assessment of the "character and magnitude of the asserted [threatened] injury," and an estimate of the number of voters likely to be affected.

A

The first set of burdens shown in these cases is the travel costs and fees necessary to get one of the limited variety of federal or state photo identifications needed to cast a regular ballot under the Voter ID Law. The travel is required for the personal visit to a license branch of the Indiana Bureau of Motor Vehicles (BMV), which is demanded of anyone applying for a driver's license or nondriver photo identification. The need to travel to a BMV branch will affect voters according to their circumstances, with the average person probably viewing it as nothing more than an inconvenience. Poor, old, and disabled voters who do not drive a car, however, may find the trip prohibitive, witness the fact that the BMV has far fewer license branches in each county than there are voting precincts. Marion County, for example, has over 900 active voting precincts, yet only 12 BMV license branches; in Lake County, there are 565 active voting precincts, to match up with only 8 BMV locations; and Allen County, with 309 active voting precincts, has only 3 BMV license branches. The same pattern holds in counties with smaller populations. Brown County has 12 active voter precincts, and only one BMV office; while there were 18 polling places available in Fayette County's 2007 municipal primary, there was only 1 BMV license branch; and Henry County, with 42 polling places approved for 2008 elections, has only 1 BMV office. Although making voters travel farther than what is convenient for most and possible for some does not amount to a "severe" burden under *Burdick*, that is no reason to ignore the burden altogether. It translates into an obvious economic cost (whether in work time lost, or getting and paying for transportation) that an Indiana voter must bear to obtain an ID.

For those voters who can afford the roundtrip, a second financial hurdle appears: in order to get photo identification for the first time, they need to present " 'a birth certificate, a certificate of naturalization, U.S. veterans photo identification, U.S. military photo identification, or a U.S. passport.' " Ante, at 1620, n.16 (lead opinion) (quoting Ind. Admin. Code, tit. 140, s 7–4–3 (2008)). As the lead opinion says, the two most common of these documents come at a price: Indiana counties charge anywhere from $3 to $12 for a birth certificate (and in some other States the fee is significantly higher), *see* ante, at 1620, n.16, and that same price must usually be paid for a first-time passport, since a birth certificate is required to prove U.S. citizenship by birth. The total fees for a passport, moreover, are up to about $100. So most voters must pay at least one fee to get the ID necessary to cast a regular ballot. As with the travel costs, these fees are far from shocking on their face, but in the Burdick analysis it matters that both the travel costs and the fees are disproportionately heavy for, and thus disproportionately likely to deter, the poor, the old, and the immobile.

B

To be sure, Indiana has a provisional-ballot exception to the ID requirement for individuals the State considers "indigent" as well as those with religious objections to being photographed, *see* ante, at 1621 (lead opinion), and this sort of exception could in theory provide a way around the costs of procuring an ID. But Indiana's chosen exception does not amount to much relief.

The law allows these voters who lack the necessary ID to sign the poll book and cast a provisional ballot. *See* 458 F.Supp.2d, at 786 (citing Ind.Code Ann. s 3–11–8–25.1 (West Supp.2007)). As the lead opinion recognizes, though, ante, at 1621, that is only the first step; to have the provisional ballot counted, a voter must then appear in person before the circuit court clerk or county election board within 10 days of the election, to sign an affidavit attesting to indigency or religious objection to being photographed (or to present an ID at that point), *see* 458 F.Supp.2d, at 786. Unlike the trip to the BMV (which, assuming things go smoothly, needs to be made only once every four years for renewal of nondriver photo identification, *see* id.), this one must be taken every time a poor person or religious objector wishes to vote, because the State does not allow an affidavit to count in successive elections. And unlike the trip to the BMV (which at least has a handful of license branches in the more populous counties), a county has only one county seat. Forcing these people to travel to the county seat every time they try to vote is particularly onerous for the reason noted already, that most counties in Indiana either lack public transportation or offer only limited coverage. *See supra*, at 1616.

That the need to travel to the county seat each election amounts to a high hurdle is shown in the results of the 2007 municipal elections in Marion County, to which Indiana's Voter ID Law applied. Thirty-four provisional ballots were cast, but only two provisional voters made it to the County Clerk's Office within the 10 days. *See* Brief for Respondents in No. 07–21, pp. 8–9. All 34 of these aspiring voters appeared at the appropriate precinct; 33 of them provided a signature, and every signature matched the one on file; and 26 of the 32 voters whose ballots were not counted had a history of voting in Marion County elections. *See* id., at 9.

All of this suggests that provisional ballots do not obviate the burdens of getting photo identification. And even if that were not so, the provisional-ballot option would be inadequate for a further reason: the indigency exception by definition offers no relief to those voters who do not consider themselves (or would not be considered) indigent but as a practical matter would find it hard, for nonfinancial reasons, to get the required ID (most obviously the disabled).

C

Indiana's Voter ID Law thus threatens to impose serious burdens on the voting right, even if not "severe" ones, and the next question under Burdick is whether the number of individuals likely to be affected is significant as well. Record evidence and facts open to judicial notice answer yes.

Tens of thousands of voting-age residents lack the necessary photo identification. A large proportion of them are likely to be in bad shape economically, *see* 472 F.3d 949, 951 (C.A.7 2007) ("No doubt most people who don't have photo ID are low on the economic ladder"); cf. *Bullock v. Carter,* 405 U.S. 134, 144 (1972) ("[W]e would ignore reality were we not to recognize that this system falls with unequal weight on voters . . . according to their economic status").

Petitioners, to be sure, failed to nail down precisely how great the cohort of discouraged and totally deterred voters will be, but empirical precision beyond the foregoing numbers has never been demanded for raising a voting-rights claim. . . . While of course it would greatly aid a plaintiff to establish his claims beyond mathematical doubt, he does enough to show that serious burden are likely.

Thus, petitioners' case is clearly strong enough to prompt more than a cursory examination of the State's asserted interests. And the fact that Indiana's photo identification requirement is one of the most restrictive in the country, *see* Brief for Current and Former State Secretaries of State as Amici Curiae 27–30 (compiling state voter-identification statutes); *see also* Brief for Texas et al. as Amici Curiae 10–13 (same), makes a critical examination of the State's claims all the more in order.

III

Because the lead opinion finds only "limited" burdens on the right to vote, *see* ante, at 1620, it avoids a hard look at the State's claimed interests. *See* ante, at 1616–1620. But having found the Voter ID Law burdens far from trivial, I have to make a rigorous assessment of " 'the precise interests put forward by the State as justifications for the burden imposed by its rule,' [and] 'the extent to which those interests make it necessary to burden the plaintiff's rights.' " *Burdick,* 504 U.S., at 434 (quoting Anderson, 460 U.S., at 789).

A

The lead opinion's discussion of the State's reasons begins with the State's asserted interests in "election modernization," ante, at 1617–1618, and in combating voter fraud, *see* ante, at 1618–1620. Although these are given separate headings, any line drawn between them is unconvincing; as I understand it, the "effort to modernize elections," Brief for Respondents in No. 07–25, p. 12, is not for modernity's sake, but to reach certain practical (or political) objectives. In any event, if a proposed modernization were in fact aimless, if it were put forward as change for change's sake, a State could not justify any appreciable burden on the right to vote that might ensue; useless technology has no constitutional value. And in fact that is not the case here. The State says that it adopted the ID law principally to combat voter fraud, and it is this claim, not the slogan of "election modernization," that warrants attention.

1

[R]equiring a voter to show photo identification before casting a regular ballot addresses only one form of voter fraud: in-person voter impersonation. The photo ID requirement leaves untouched the problems of absentee-ballot fraud, which (unlike in-person voter impersonation) is a documented problem in Indiana, *see* 458 F.Supp.2d, at 793; of registered voters voting more than once (but maintaining their own identities) in different counties or in different States; of felons and other disqualified individuals voting in their own names; of vote buying; or, for that matter, of ballot-stuffing, ballot miscounting, voter intimidation, or any other type of corruption on the part of officials administering elections. *See* Brief for Brennan Center for Justice et al. as Amici Curiae 7.

And even the State's interest in deterring a voter from showing up at the polls and claiming to be someone he is not must, in turn, be discounted for the fact that the State has not come across a single instance of in-person voter impersonation fraud in all of Indiana's history.

The State responds to the want of evidence with the assertion that in-person voter impersonation fraud is hard to detect. But this is like saying the "man who wasn't there" is hard to spot, and to know whether difficulty in detection accounts for the lack of evidence one at least has to ask whether in-person voter impersonation is (or would be) relatively harder to ferret out than other kinds of fraud (e.g., by absentee ballot) which the State has had no trouble documenting. The answer seems to be no; there is reason to think that "impersonation of voters is . . . the most likely type of fraud to be discovered." U.S. Election Assistance Commission.

The relative ease of discovering in-person voter impersonation is also owing to the odds that any such fraud will be committed by "organized groups such as campaigns or political parties" rather than by individuals acting alone. L. Minnite & D. Callahan, Securing the Vote: An Analysis of Election Fraud 14 (2003). It simply is not worth it for individuals acting alone to commit in-person voter impersonation, which is relatively ineffectual for the foolish few who may commit it.

NOTES AND QUESTIONS

1.   *Standard.* What is the standard that the Court applies in *Crawford*? Is it rational basis? Is it strict scrutiny? Is it an intermediate standard? The Court seems to speak of a "balancing approach" that weighs "the asserted injury to the right to vote against the precise interests put forward by the State as justifications for the burden imposed by its rule." The Court also said that there was no litmus test and that even slight burdens must be "justified by relevant and legitimate state interests sufficiently weighty to justify the limitation." Justice Scalia would seem to prefer applying a deferential standard in this case and would thus dismiss the plaintiffs' claim on the ground that the burden on the right to vote is not sufficiently severe. As between the majority's approach and Justice Scalia's approach, which one do you prefer and why?

2.   *Are Photo Voter Identification Requirements Necessary?* What is the best justification that you can think of for a law that requires voters to show a photo identification when they appear to vote at the polls? How compelling is your justification, and under what circumstances would you like to see such a law implemented?

3.   *Burdens.* In his dissenting opinion, Justice Souter focuses on how the law affects poor, elderly, and disabled voters and argues that their travel costs count as burdens. Of course, all election laws burden voters, and they do so differentially, depending upon the voters' circumstances. What do you think counts as a burden, and whose burden counts?

How should we balance a state's justifications for its election laws against any such burdens, especially voters of lower socio-economic means? In his opinion announcing the judgment of the Court (and joined by three Justices), Justice Stevens concludes that the state has a legitimate interest in protecting against voter fraud while acknowledging that there has never been any evidence of in person voter fraud in the history of the state. How should this lack of evidence be taken into account in weighing the state's interests? Given that voting constitutes a personal individual right, why shouldn't the state have to justify the law if it impedes even one voter from exercising her right to vote?

Justice Stevens also refuses to consider the burden placed upon voters who are unable to obtain a birth certificate or who cannot make additional trips to the clerk's office to obtain the photo identification the state issues for free, on the ground that the plaintiffs failed to identify accurately the number of voters that would fall in that category. Do you think it would be possible for plaintiffs to identify voters whose burdens would not be cured by either the free identification offered or the possibility of voting a provisional ballot?

4.   *Voter ID as Recent Development.* Voter identification requirements are part of a recent phenomenon in the United States. According to the National Conference of State Legislatures, about 1,000 voter identification bills have been introduced in state legislatures since 2001, *available at* http://www.ncsl.org/legislatures-elections/elections/voter-id.aspx#2012. In 2008, no state required identification as a prerequisite to voting. Today, a total of 36 states now legally require voters to show identification prior to voting. As *Crawford* underscores, these laws tend to be justified by the objective of preventing voter fraud. But what if these laws had little to do with whether voters believed that our electoral system was infected by fraud? *See* Nathaniel Persily and Stephen Ansolabehere, *Vote Fraud in the Eye of the Beholder: The Role of Public Opinion in the Challenge to Voter Identification Requirements*, 121 Harv. L. Rev. 1737 (2008) (concluding that voters' perception of voter fraud is not correlated with the likelihood that voters will turn out to vote, and voters' belief about fraud is not correlated with the presence or absence of a voter identification requirement).

Many civil rights activists object to voter identification laws on the ground that they are likely to have a disparate impact on minority voters, who are more likely to lack identification than white voters. According to one survey by the Government Accountability Office in 2014, 20% of African Americans lack valid identification. *See also* Robert Pastor, Robert Santos, Alison Prevost, and Vassia Stoilov, *Voting ID Requirements: A Survey of Registered Voters in Three States*, 40 Am. Rev. Pub. Admin. 461 (2010). But earlier studies have not found that voter identification statutes have had a disproportionate impact on voters of color, or that they have had an impact on voter turnout at all. By contrast, a more recent study by political scientists provides evidence that strict voter identification laws, such as those requiring photo identification, have a negative impact on the voter turnout of African-American and Latino voters. *See* Zoltan Hajnal, Nazita Lajevardi, and Lindsay Nielson, *Voter Identification Law and the Suppression of Minority Voters* (unpublished paper). How would you make sense of this conflicting evidence?

5.   *Race or Politics?* In March 2012, the state of Pennsylvania passed one the strictest voter identification laws in the country. In June of 2012, a top Republican politician in Pennsylvania, Mike Turzai, stated that the Pennsylvania voter identification law would help Governor Mitt Romney, the Republican nominee for President, unseat President Obama. Many in the civil rights community interpreted Mr. Turzai's comment as an admission that the purpose of the law was to make it harder for potential Obama voters, particularly African Americans, to vote. Many Republicans viewed the law as a remedy against voter fraud. In *Crawford*, the majority opinion wrote that where "a nondiscriminatory law is supported by neutral justifications, those justifications should not be disregarded simply because partisan interests may have provided one motivation for the votes of individual legislators." Assume that the Pennsylvania voter identification law was designed to make it harder for Obama voters to vote and not to combat voter fraud. Assume also that the law would have a disproportionate impact on voters of color, poor, and elderly voters. What follows under *Crawford*? Is this law meant to suppress the votes of Obama voters or black voters? Should the analysis turn on that distinction?

6.   *Voter Identification, the VRA, and* Shelby County. Some voter identification requirements, including those requiring photo identification, have been delayed or denied preclearance in jurisdictions that were required to preclear under the VRA. In particular, in *Texas v. Holder*, 888 F.Supp.2d 113 (D.D.C. 2012), a three-judge court blocked Texas' photo identification requirement on the ground that the law would have a retrogressive effect. The DOJ did not preclear photo identification laws in Alabama, Mississippi, and South Carolina. After the Court's decision in *Shelby County v. Holder*, the preclearance regime is no longer in effect. Consequently, many voter identification laws that would have failed preclearance were enacted post-*Shelby County*. Do you think that the proliferation of voter identification laws post-*Shelby County* demonstrates that the Court was wrong that racial discrimination in voting was a phenomenon of the past?

7.   *HAVA.* States are not the only entities imposing voter identification requirements. In 2002, the Help America Vote Act 2002 ("HAVA"), 42 U.S.C. § 15483, became law. HAVA required persons who vote by mail and are voting in person for the first time to present some kind of identification before they are permitted to vote. Specifically, HAVA requires "valid photo identification or . . . a copy of a current utility bill, bank statement, government check, paycheck, or other government document that shows the name and address of the voter." 42 U.S.C. § 15483(b). Does it matter to your analysis that a federal law imposes a voter identification requirement for

voting? What are the key characteristics that in your view might distinguish the HAVA voter identification requirement from the one at issue in *Crawford*?

8.   *Comparative Analysis.* Compare the voter identification statutes of Missouri and Indiana (excerpted below). Under the same facts presented in *Crawford*, do you think the Missouri statute would pass constitutional muster? Why?

* * *

Indiana Code § 3–5–2–40.5

(1)   The document shows the name of the individual to whom the document was issued, and the name conforms to the name in the individual's voter registration record.

(2)   The document shows a photograph of the individual to whom the document was issued.

(3)   The document includes an expiration date, and the document:

(A)   is not expired; or

(B)   expired after the date of the most recent general election.

(4)   The document was issued by the United States or the state of Indiana.

* * *

Missouri Statute § 115.427

1.   Before receiving a ballot, voters shall establish their identity and eligibility to vote at the polling place by presenting a form of personal identification. "Personal identification" shall mean only one of the following:

(1)   Nonexpired Missouri driver's license showing the name and a photograph or digital image of the individual; or

(2)   Nonexpired or nonexpiring Missouri nondriver's license showing the name and a photographic or digital image of the individual; or

(3)   A document that satisfies all of the following requirements:

(a)   The document contains the name of the individual to whom the document was issued, and the name substantially conforms to the most recent signature in the individual's voter registration record;

(b)   The document shows a photographic or digital image of the individual;

(c)   The document includes an expiration date, and the document is not expired, or if expired, expired not before the date of the most recent general election; and

(d)   The document was issued by the United States or the state of Missouri; or

(4)   Any identification containing a photographic or digital image of the individual which is issued by the Missouri National Guard, the United States armed forces, or the United States Department of Veteran Affairs to a member or former member of the Missouri National Guard or the United States armed forces and that does not have an expiration date.

* * *

The Supreme Court of Missouri struck down the Missouri voter identification statute as unconstitutional in *Weinschenk v. State*, 203 S.W. 3d 201, 217 (Mo. 2006). The Supreme Court of Missouri stated:

> Recognizing that the State does have compelling interests in preserving electoral integrity and combating voter fraud, the issue becomes whether the record shows that the type of Photo-ID Requirement enacted . . . "is necessary to accomplish a compelling state interest." Because, for the reasons set out above, this Court has found that the Photo-ID Requirement imposes a severe burden on the right to vote, it can survive strict scrutiny only by showing it is necessary to accomplish a compelling state interest or that it is "narrowly drawn to express the compelling state interest at stake." Yet, Appellants do not demonstrate that [the statute's] requirement of state or federally issued, non-expired photo IDs is strictly necessary or narrowly tailored to accomplish the State's asserted interests. To the contrary, Appellants concede that the only type of voter fraud that the Photo-ID Requirement prevents is in-person voter impersonation fraud at the polling place. It does not address absentee voting fraud or fraud in registration. While the Photo-ID Requirement may provide some additional protection against voter impersonation fraud, the evidence below demonstrates that the Photo-ID Requirement is not "necessary" to accomplish this goal. As the trial court found: "No evidence was presented that voter impersonation fraud exists to any substantial degree in Missouri. In fact, the evidence that was presented indicates that voter impersonation fraud is not a problem in Missouri.

C.   TERRITORIALITY AND CITIZENSHIP

In democratic societies, including the contemporary United States, the right to vote is generally limited to citizens, and universal suffrage among citizens has largely triumphed. There are, however, some remarkable exceptions. United States citizens living in the District of Columbia and in territories controlled by the United States do not have full voting rights. *Igartua De La Rosa v. United States* and the materials that follow it examine these limitations on the right to vote.

Igartua De La Rosa v. United States

United States Court of Appeals, First Circuit, 1994.
32 F. 3d 8.

■ Before TORRUELLA, CYR and BOUDIN, CIRCUIT JUDGES.

■ PER CURIAM.

Appellant residents of Puerto Rico allege that their inability to vote in the United States presidential election violates their constitutional rights. Some appellants, who previously voted in presidential elections while residing elsewhere but who are now ineligible to vote in those elections, also challenge the constitutionality of the Uniformed and Overseas Citizens Absentee Voting Act, 42 U.S.C. § 1973ff *et seq.* The district court dismissed appellants' request for declaratory and injunctive relief for failure to state a claim upon which relief could be granted. We summarily affirm.

I

While appellants are citizens of the United States, the Constitution does not grant citizens the right to vote directly for the President. Instead, the Constitution provides that the President is to be chosen by electors who, in turn, are chosen by "*each state . . .* in such manner as the Legislature thereof may direct." U.S. Const. art. II, § 1, cl. 2 (emphasis added). Pursuant to Article II, therefore, only citizens residing in *states* can vote for electors and thereby indirectly for the President. *See Attorney General of Guam on behalf of All U.S. Citizens Residing in Guam, etc. v. United States,* 738 F.2d 1017, 1019 (9th Cir.1984), *cert. denied,* 469 U.S. 1209, 105 S.Ct. 1174, 84 L.Ed.2d 323 (1985) ("The right to vote in presidential elections under Article II inheres not in citizens but in states; citizens vote indirectly for the President by voting for state electors."). Since Puerto Rico is concededly not a state, *see Trailer Marine Transport Corp. v. Rivera Vazquez,* 977 F.2d 1, 7 (1st Cir.1992) (status of Puerto Rico "is still not the same as that of a State in the Federal Union"), it is not entitled under Article II to choose electors for the President, and residents of Puerto Rico have no constitutional right to participate in that election. *See Attorney General of Guam,* 738 F.2d at 1019 ("Since Guam concededly is not a state, it can have no electors, and plaintiffs cannot exercise individual votes in a presidential election.").

The only jurisdiction, not a state, which participates in the presidential election is the District of Columbia, which obtained that right through the twenty-third amendment to the Constitution. Such a constitutional amendment was necessary precisely "because the Constitution ha[d] restricted th[e] privilege [of voting in national elections] to citizens who reside[d] in States." H.R.Rep. No. 1698, 86th Cong., 2d Sess. 2 (1960), *reprinted in* 1960 U.S.Code Cong. & Ad.News 1459, 1460. Only a similar constitutional amendment or a grant of statehood to Puerto Rico, therefore, can provide appellants the right to vote in the presidential election which they seek.

II

Some appellants, who previously voted in presidential elections while residing elsewhere, also assert that their constitutional rights to due process and equal protection have been violated by the Uniformed and Overseas Citizens Absentee Voting Act [Act]. The Act provides that United States citizens, including residents of Puerto Rico, *see* 42 U.S.C. § 1973ff–6(6) & (7), who reside outside the United States retain the right to vote via absentee ballot in their last place of residence in the United States, as long as these citizens otherwise qualify to vote under laws of the jurisdiction in which they last resided. 42 U.S.C. § 1973ff–1. It does not apply, however, to citizens who move from one jurisdiction to another within the United States. *See* 42 U.S.C. § 1973ff–6(5) (defining "overseas voter" as a person "who resides outside the United States").

Appellants claim that the Act illegally discriminates against citizens who have taken up residence in Puerto Rico rather than outside the United States, because the former are not entitled by the Act to vote in their prior state of residence. In fact, however, the Act does not distinguish between those who reside overseas and those who take up residence in Puerto Rico, but between those who reside overseas and those who move anywhere within the United States. Given that such a distinction neither affects a suspect class nor infringes a fundamental right, it need only have a rational basis to pass constitutional muster.

Without the Act, voters who move overseas could lose their right to vote in all federal elections. However, voters who move to a new residence within the United States are eligible to vote in a federal election in their new place of residence.[10] Hence, Congress had a rational basis for seeking to protect the absentee voting rights only of the former. While the Act does not guarantee that a citizen moving to Puerto Rico will be eligible to vote in a presidential election, this limitation is not a consequence of the Act but of the constitutional requirements discussed above.

Appellants' request for oral argument is *denied*. The dismissal of appellants' claims is *affirmed*.

NOTES AND QUESTIONS

1. *The Court's Analysis.* As the First Circuit recognized in *Igartua*, Puerto Ricans are United States citizens. In 1917, Congress passed the Jones Act, which granted United States citizenship to persons born in Puerto Rico. However, as the Court recognized, American citizens residing in Puerto Rico cannot participate in federal elections. Moreover, as the plaintiff argued, the

---

[10] For example, a citizen who moves to Puerto Rico would be eligible to vote in the federal election for the Resident Commissioner. *See* Puerto Rican Federal Relations Act, 48 U.S.C. § 891 (Resident Commissioner chosen by "[t]he qualified electors of Puerto Rico"); 42 U.S.C. § 1973ff–6(3) (defining "[f]ederal office" to include Resident Commissioner).

Uniformed and Overseas Citizens Absentee Voting Act protects the right of American citizens to vote by absentee ballot if they relocate to a foreign country but not if they are in Puerto Rico, an American territory. Notice the summary fashion with which the Court treated the plaintiff's claim. The opinion fails to wrestle with the difficult questions presented in the case. In particular, what does full citizenship mean if it does not permit one to participate in the most important decision made by a polity, the choice of its chief executive? The political theorist Judith Shklar writes that "[t]here is no notion more central in politics than citizenship, and none more variable in history, or contested in theory. . . . The ballot has always been a certificate of full membership in society, and its value depends primary on its capacity to confer a minimum of social dignity." JUDITH SHKLAR, AMERICAN CITIZENSHIP 1, 2 (1991). If Shklar is right, are Puerto Ricans really full citizens of the United States?

2.   *Is the Status of Puerto Rico Consistent with American Democratic Principles?* Puerto Ricans living in Puerto Rico do not have any representation in Congress or in the Electoral College. As one scholar has argued, this is inconsistent with both democratic theory and American democratic principles:

> This disenfranchisement places citizens of Puerto Rico in an unenviable and indefensible position, as they have no power to affect the very institution that holds full and complete discretionary powers over them. Neither democratic theory nor the modern voting rights revolution provides any support for this lack of representation. . . . How can one justify the disenfranchisement of millions of U.S. citizens on U.S. soil? . . . Citizens of Puerto Rico are grouped alongside felons and children in the voting rights hierarchy. . . . This circumstance is an embarrassment for American democracy. It is unseemly to hold onto territories in perpetuity, grant their inhabitants American citizenship, yet subject them to the full discretionary powers of congressional majorities. It is also inconsistent with American constitutional values.

Luis Fuentes-Rohwer, *The Land that Democratic Theory Forgot*, 83 Ind. L.J. 1525 (2008). Is Professor Fuentes-Rohwer correct that the status of Puerto Rico is inconsistent with American constitutional values?

3.   *Race and Colonialism. Igartua* reflects the consequences of American imperialism and territorial expansion, particularly toward the latter half of the nineteenth century and the early third of the twentieth century. During that period, the United States acquired a number of territories including Puerto Rico, American Samoa, Guam, and the United States Virgin Islands. Some scholars have argued that racism fueled America's colonial ambitions and the resultant unequal treatment of citizens within the acquired territory. Professor Juan Perea remarks that: "Race and racism have always played central roles in the ideology of United States conquest and United States citizenship. Racial difference or, more specifically, the racial inferiority attributed to the people targeted by American conquest has been

offered as the justification for this conquest." Juan F. Perea, *Fulfilling Manifest Destiny: Conquest, Race, and the Insular Cases* 140, *in* Foreign in a Domestic Sense Puerto Rico, American Expansion, and the Constitution (Christian Duffy Burnett & Burke Marshall eds., 2001). How would you determine whether the failure to grant federal voting rights to Puerto Ricans living on the Island constitutes a manifestation of racism? Recall here Justice Kennedy's opinion in *Rice v. Cateyano.* Is the status of Puerto Rico consistent with the ethos of the Fifteenth Amendment as articulated by Justice Kennedy in *Rice* and his argument that the Constitution is the heritage of all Americans?

4.   ***Subsequent Development.*** Gregorio Igartua De La Rosa, a lawyer and the plaintiff in *Igartua v. United States*, subsequently filed a second lawsuit challenging the denial of the right to vote in presidential elections to United States citizens living in Puerto Rico, *Igartua II*. In fact, Igartua De La Rosa filed many suits challenging the denial of his right to vote. In his second suit, the District Court agreed with him and held that United States citizens had a right to vote in presidential elections. The United States appealed to the First Circuit, which, in another per curiam opinion, reversed and affirmed its previous decision in *Igartua I*. But the Court's decision drew the following concurrence from Judge Torruella:

> As I did in Igartua I, I join the Court's opinion in this appeal because I believe it to be technically and, as the law now stands, legally correct in its conclusion that the Constitution does not guarantee United States citizens residing in Puerto Rico the right to vote in the national Presidential election. I also agree with the Court's indication that today's decision expresses no opinion with regard to the validity under Puerto Rico law of Law 403 of September 10, 2000, which is the subject of separate litigation and which I conclude is not properly before us. I am, however, compelled to write separately because I can no longer remain silent to the subjacent question, because from my perspective, there are larger issues at stake. . . .

> More than 100 years ago, at the conclusion of the Spanish-American War of 1898, Puerto Rico was ceded to the United States by Spain. Despite lofty rhetoric at the time extolling the virtues of American democracy,[11] the United States has since exercised almost unfettered power over Puerto Rico and the nearly 4,000,000 United States citizens who currently reside there. Although persons born in Puerto Rico are citizens of the United States at birth, and thereby "owe[ ] allegiance to the United States," *Kawakita v. United States,* 343 U.S. 717, 736 (1952), while residing in Puerto Rico they enjoy fewer rights than citizens of the United States that reside in the fifty States. *See United States v. Verdugo-*

---

[11]   It should be noted that, at the time of General Miles' arrival, and since the enactment of the Spanish Constitution of 1812, Puerto Ricans enjoyed Spanish citizenship and voting representation in the Spanish Parliament, rights which were confirmed in the Constitution of 1876 and in the Autonomic Charter of 1897.

Urquídez, 494 U.S. 259, 268, (1990). . . . Undoubtedly the most glaring evidence of this egregious disparity is the fact that they do not elect a single voting representative to a federal government that exercises almost absolute power over them. . . .

The United States citizens residing in Puerto Rico are caught in an untenable Catch-22. The national disenfranchisement of these citizens ensures that they will never be able, through the political processes, to rectify the denial of their civil rights in those very political processes. This uninterrupted condition clearly provides solid basis for judicial intervention at some point, one for which there is resounding precedent. *See* Brown v. Board of Education. . . .

In this 211th year of the United States Constitution, and 102nd year of United States presence in Puerto Rico, United States citizenship must mean more than merely the freedom to travel to and from the United States. This citizenship should not, cannot, be devalued to such a low scale.

After more than a century of United States possession of Puerto Rico, there continues to be tremendous debate over the status of the Island and the nature of its relationship with the United States. Certainly the citizens of Puerto Rico are divided on the issue, a condition which has permitted the federal government to externalize this question. What is established, for the time being at least, is that the federal courts continue to recognize the almost absolute power of Congress to unilaterally dictate the affairs of Puerto Rico and her people. So long as that is the case, the practicality of the matter is that Puerto Rico remains a colony with little prospect of exerting effective political pressure on the elected branches of government to take corrective action. . . .

The perpetuation of this colonial condition runs against the very principles upon which this Nation was founded. Indefinite colonial rule by the United States is not something that was contemplated by the Founding Fathers nor authorized per secula seculorum by the Constitution. And far from being a matter of local concern to the United States citizens in Puerto Rico only, the inequality to which these citizens are subjected is an injury to every American, because as surely as the current situation causes irreparable harm to United States citizens residing in Puerto Rico, it just as powerfully denigrates the entire Nation and the Constitution.

Although this is not the case, nor perhaps the time, for a federal court to take remedial action to correct what is a patently intolerable situation, it is time to serve notice upon the political branches of government that it is incumbent upon them, in the first instance, to take appropriate steps to correct what amounts to an outrageous disregard for the rights of a substantial segment of its citizenry. A failure to do so countenances corrective judicial action.

See Brown v. Board of Education, *supra*. It may be that the federal courts will be required to take extraordinary measures as necessary to protect discrete groups "completely under the sovereignty and dominion of the United States." *Cherokee Nation v. Georgia,* 30 U.S. (5 Pet.) 1, 17, 8 L.Ed. 25 (1831) (Marshall, C.J.).

My concurrence in today's decision, of course, indicates that I do not consider this the appropriate case for such intervention, largely because the particular issue of the presidential vote is governed by explicit language in the Constitution providing for the election of the President and Vice-President by the States, rather than by individual citizens. But I, for one, am of the view that my vote today is not equivalent to a carte blanche.

Igartua De La Rosa v. United States, 229 F.3rd 80, 85 (1st Cir. 2000) (Torruella concurring). Judge Torruella intended his concurrence as a shot across the bow to Congress. So far, Congress has not done anything to change the voting status of citizens living on the Island. Assuming further congressional inaction, is there anything the federal courts can do? What do you make of Judge Torruella's citations to *Brown v. Board*?

5. *Washington, D.C.* As you saw from *Igartua I*, the Twenty-Third Amendment, which was ratified in 1961, allows residents of the District of Columbia to vote in presidential elections. But D.C. residents, 49% of whom are African American, do not have the right to vote in congressional elections. In 2000, a number of residents of the District filed suit challenging the denial of the right to vote for Congress. They argued that the District should be considered a "state" for the purposes of congressional elections. A three-judge district court disagreed, concluding that the "text of the Constitution does not contemplate that the District may serve as a state for purposes of the apportionment of congressional representatives. That textual evidence is supported by historical evidence concerning the general understanding at the time of the District's creation." Is a constitutional amendment required to give residents of the District a right to vote in Congressional elections? Reviewing the constitutional history, Peter Raven-Hansen has argued:

> [T]he congressional disfranchisement wrought when the District was fully severed from Maryland and Virginia was unintended by both the constitutional framers and the parties to the cession legislation. The new government's purpose in creating the District was to gain exclusive police and judicial jurisdiction, thereby assuring the security of congressional deliberations. No federal purpose was asserted for, or served by, denying District residents participation in the national legislature equivalent to that exercised by state residents. Rather here, as in the diversity jurisdiction provisions, the framers proceeded in their drafting without considering the interests of the 'unborn citizens' of the 'hypothetical city' which was to become the District.
>
> In light of the limited purposes for which Congress was given complete jurisdiction over the District, and of the size to which they

'hypothetical city' has grown, a reconsideration of its claim to congressional representation is in order. Interpreting 'state' to include the District for purposes of congressional representation would remove a political disability which has no constitutional rationale. It would grant to District residents, who are in all other respects as much Americans as state residents, their proportionate influence in national decisions. It would correct the historical accident by which D.C. residents lost the shelter of state representation without gaining separate participation in the national legislature.

Peter Raven-Hansen, *Congressional Representation for the District of Columbia: A Constitutional Analysis*, 12 Harv. J. on Legis. 167, 184–85 (1975). Do you agree with Professor Raven-Hansen that courts should simply interpret "state" to include the District in light of his interpretation of the historical record?

6. *Noncitizens and Voting.* Generally speaking, lawful permanent residents, whose status means they may reside and work in the United States indefinitely (unless they engage in conduct that makes them deportable), cannot vote in local, state, or federal elections. These residents participate in society as Americans in many ways, including by serving in the armed forces, paying taxes, contributing to their communities, and working within the United States. While the Fifteenth Amendment only provides that "[t]he right of citizens of the United States to vote shall not be denied or abridged by the United States or by any State," U.S. CONST. amend. XV, § 1, some believe that permanent residents should be allowed to vote because these individuals functionally belong to the community in every way that counts. *See, e.g.*, Paul Tiao, Non-Citizen Suffrage: An Argument Based on the Voting Rights Act 25 Colum. Hum. Rts. L. Rev. 171, 171–73 (1993). Further, proponents of non-citizen voting argue that not allowing permanent residents to vote is essentially "taxation without representation." Many counter this argument by saying that, if non-citizens want to vote, they should become citizens. Commentators also emphasize that it is important to respect the formal demarcation between citizens and non-citizens, to give citizenship meaning. *See, e.g.*, http://thefederalist.com/2015/04/09/5–reasons-non-citizens-should-not-vote-in-new-york-city/ (explaining why New York City should not allow non-citizens to vote). What do you think? In the nineteenth century, many states permitted non-citizens to vote, including as a way of attracting inhabitants to their jurisdictions. Today, a small handful of localities enfranchise non-citizens, especially in school board elections. Why might the practice of non-citizen voting have fallen by the wayside? Do you think it is related to the racial composition of the country, especially of the non-citizen population? Is this yet another way in which race and law interact to determine electoral participation?

APPENDIX OF CONSTITUTIONAL AND STATUTORY LAW

Declaration of Independence
(1776).

We hold these truths to be self-evident, that all men are created equal, that they are endowed by their Creator with certain unalienable Rights, that among these are Life, Liberty and the pursuit of Happiness.

United States Constitution
(1788).

Excerpted below are the provisions of the original U.S. Constitution that related to or enshrined the institution of Slavery.

We the People of the United States of, in Order to form a more perfect union, establish Justice . . . promote the general Welfare, and secure the Blessings of Liberty to ourselves and our posterity.

Article 1, Section 2. Representatives and direct taxes shall be apportioned among several States which may be included within this Union, according to their respective numbers, which shall be determined by adding to the whole number of free persons, including those bound to service for a term of years, and including Indians not taxed, three-fifths of all other persons.

Article 1, Section 8. The Congress shall have Power. . . . To provide for calling forth the Militia to execute the Laws of the Union, suppress Insurrections and repel Invasions.

Article 1, Section 9. The migration or importation of any such persons as any of the States now existing shall think proper to admit, shall not be prohibited by Congress prior to the year one thousand eight hundred and eight; but a tax or duty may be imposed, not exceeding ten dollars each person.

Article 4, Section 2. No person held to service or labor in one State, escaping into another, shall in consequence of any law or regulation therein, be discharged from such service or labor, but shall be delivered up on claim of the party to whom such service or labor may be due.

Article 4, Section 4. The United States shall guarantee to every State in this Union a Republican form of Government; and shall protect each of them against invasion; and on application of the Legislature, or of the Executive, (when the Legislature cannot be convened,) against Domestic violence.

Article 5. The Congress, whenever two thirds of both Houses shall deem it necessary, shall propose Amendments to this Constitution. . . . Provided that no Amendment which may be made prior to the Year One thousand eight hundred and eight shall in any Manner affect the first . . . Clause . . . in the Ninth Section of the first Article.

Antebellum State Laws Regarding Slavery

The first slave laws were passed in the middle of the seventeenth century and by the beginning of the eighteenth century were widespread, in the north as well as the south. For example, consider this excerpt from the Virginia Slave Codes of 1705:

[A]ll servants imported and brought into this country, by sea or land, who were not Christians in their native country, (except Turks and Moors in amity with her majesty, and others that can make due proof of their being free in England, or any other Christian country, before they were shipped, in order to transportation hither) shall be accounted and be slaves, and as such be here bought and sold notwithstanding a conversion to Christianity afterwards. . . .

Here is an excerpt from South Carolina's 1740 slave code:

[A]ll Negroes and Indians, (free Indians in amity with this government, and degrees, mulattoes, and mustizoes, who are now free, excepted,) mulattoes or mustizoes who now are, or shall hereafter be, in this Province, and all their issue and offspring, born or to be born, shall be, and they are hereby declared to be, and remain forever hereafter, absolute slaves, and shall follow the condition of the mother, and shall be deemed, held, taken, reputed and adjudged in law, to be chattels personal, in the hands of their owners and possessors, and their executors, administrators, and assigns, to all intents, constructions and purposes whatsoever.

Corwin Amendment
12 Stat. 251 (1861).

No amendment shall be made to the Constitution which will authorize or give to Congress the power to abolish or interfere, within any State, with the domestic institutions thereof, including that of persons held to labor or service by the laws of said State.

Emancipation Proclamation
(1863).

By the President of the United States of America:

A Proclamation.

Whereas, on the twenty-second day of September, in the year of our Lord one thousand eight hundred and sixty-two, a proclamation was issued by the President of the United States, containing, among other things, the following, to wit:

"That on the first day of January, in the year of our Lord one thousand eight hundred and sixty-three, all persons held as slaves within any State or designated part of a State, the people whereof shall then be in rebellion against the United States, shall be then, thenceforward, and forever free; and the Executive Government of the United States, including the military and naval authority thereof, will recognize and maintain the freedom of such persons, and will do no act or acts to repress such persons, or any of them, in any efforts they may make for their actual freedom.

"That the Executive will, on the first day of January aforesaid, by proclamation, designate the States and parts of States, if any, in which the people thereof, respectively, shall then be in rebellion against the United States; and the fact that any State, or the people thereof, shall on that day be, in good faith, represented in the Congress of the United States by members chosen thereto at elections wherein a majority of the qualified voters of such State shall have participated, shall, in the absence of strong countervailing testimony, be deemed conclusive evidence that such State, and the people thereof, are not then in rebellion against the United States."

Now, therefore I, Abraham Lincoln, President of the United States, by virtue of the power in me vested as Commander-in-Chief, of the Army and Navy of the United States in time of actual armed rebellion against the authority and government of the United States, and as a fit and necessary war measure for suppressing said rebellion, do, on this first day of January, in the year of our Lord one thousand eight hundred and sixty-three, and in accordance with my purpose so to do publicly proclaimed for the full period of one hundred days, from the day first above mentioned, order and designate as the States and parts of States wherein the people thereof respectively, are this day in rebellion against the United States, the following, to wit:

Arkansas, Texas, Louisiana, (except the Parishes of St. Bernard, Plaquemines, Jefferson, St. John, St. Charles, St. James Ascension, Assumption, Terrebonne, Lafourche, St. Mary, St. Martin, and Orleans, including the City of New Orleans) Mississippi, Alabama, Florida,

Georgia, South Carolina, North Carolina, and Virginia, (except the forty-eight counties designated as West Virginia, and also the counties of Berkley, Accomac, Northampton, Elizabeth City, York, Princess Ann, and Norfolk, including the cities of Norfolk and Portsmouth[]], and which excepted parts, are for the present, left precisely as if this proclamation were not issued.

And by virtue of the power, and for the purpose aforesaid, I do order and declare that all persons held as slaves within said designated States, and parts of States, are, and henceforward shall be free; and that the Executive government of the United States, including the military and naval authorities thereof, will recognize and maintain the freedom of said persons.

And I hereby enjoin upon the people so declared to be free to abstain from all violence, unless in necessary self-defence; and I recommend to them that, in all cases when allowed, they labor faithfully for reasonable wages.

And I further declare and make known, that such persons of suitable condition, will be received into the armed service of the United States to garrison forts, positions, stations, and other places, and to man vessels of all sorts in said service.

And upon this act, sincerely believed to be an act of justice, warranted by the Constitution, upon military necessity, I invoke the considerate judgment of mankind, and the gracious favor of Almighty God.

In witness whereof, I have hereunto set my hand and caused the seal of the United States to be affixed.

Done at the City of Washington, this first day of January, in the year of our Lord one thousand eight hundred and sixty three, and of the Independence of the United States of America the eighty-seventh.

By the President: ABRAHAM LINCOLN

Freedmen's Bureau Bill

13 Stat. 507–509 (1865).

The North reacted to the spread of Black Codes by putting the South under military rule and establishing the so-called Freedmen's Bureau in 1865 (officially, the Bureau of Refugees, Freedmen, and Abandoned Lands). Established as part of Reconstruction to aid the freed slaves, the Freedman's Bureau operated until 1872. The Act provided in relevant part:

An Act to establish a Bureau for the Relief of Freedmen and Refugees.

Be it enacted by the Senate and House of Representatives of the United States of America in Congress assembled, That there is hereby established in the War Department, to continue during the present war of rebellion, and for one year thereafter, a bureau of refugees, freedmen, and abandoned lands, to which shall be committed, as hereinafter provided, the supervision and management of all abandoned lands, and the control of all subjects relating to refugees and freedmen from rebel states, or from any district of country within the territory embraced in the operations of the army, under such rules and regulations as may be prescribed by the head of the bureau and approved by the President. The said bureau shall be under the management and control of a commissioner to be appointed by the President, by and with the advice and consent of the Senate, whose compensation shall be three thousand dollars per annum, and such number of clerks as may be assigned to him by the Secretary of War, not exceeding one chief clerk, two of the fourth class, two of the third class, and five of the first class. And the commissioner and all persons appointed under this act, shall, before entering upon their duties, take the oath of office prescribed in an act entitled "An act to prescribe an oath of office, and for other purposes," approved July second, eighteen hundred and sixty-two. . . .

SEC. 2. And be it further enacted, That the Secretary of War may direct such issues of provisions, clothing, and fuel, as he may deem needful for the immediate and temporary shelter and supply of destitute and suffering refugees and freedmen and their wives and children, under such rules and regulations as he may direct.

SEC. 3. And be it further enacted, That the President may, by and with the advice and consent of the Senate, appoint an assistant commissioner for each of the states declared to be in insurrection, not exceeding ten in number, who shall, under the direction of the commissioner, aid in the execution of the provisions of this act. . . .

SEC. 4. And be it further enacted, That the commissioner, under the direction of the President, shall have authority to set apart, for the use of loyal refugees and freedmen, such tracts of land within the insurrectionary states as shall have been abandoned, or to which the United States shall have acquired title by confiscation or sale, or otherwise, and to every male citizen, whether refugee or freedman, as aforesaid, there shall be assigned not more than forty acres of such land, and the person to whom it was so assigned shall be protected in the use and enjoyment of the land for the term of three years at an annual rent not exceeding six per centum upon the value of such land, as it was appraised by the state authorities in the year eighteen hundred and sixty, for the purpose of taxation, and in case no such appraisal can be found, then the rental shall be based upon the estimated value of the land in said year, to be ascertained in such manner as the commissioner may by regulation prescribe. At the end of said term, or at any time during said term, the occupants of any parcels so assigned may purchase the land and receive such title thereto as the United States can convey, upon paying therefor the value of the land, as ascertained and fixed for the purpose of determining the annual rent aforesaid.

SEC. 5. And be it further enacted, That all acts and parts of acts inconsistent with the provisions of this act, are hereby repealed.

Second Freedmen's Bureau Bill

14 Stat. 173–177 (1866).

An Act to continue in force and to amend "An Act to establish a Bureau for the Relief of Freedmen and Refugees," and for other Purposes.

Be it enacted by the Senate and House of Representatives of the United States of America in Congress assembled, That the act to establish a bureau for the relief of freedmen and refugees, approved March third, eighteen hundred and sixty-five, shall continue in force for the term of two years from and after the passage of this act.

SEC. 2. And be it further enacted, That the supervision and care of said bureau shall extend to all loyal refugees and freedmen, so far as the same shall be necessary to enable them as speedily as practicable to become self-supporting citizens of the United States, and to aid them in making the freedom conferred by proclamation of the commander-in-chief, by emancipation under the laws of States, and by constitutional amendment, available to them and beneficial to the republic.

SEC. 3. And be it further enacted, That the President shall, by and with the advice and consent of the Senate, appoint two assistant commissioners, in addition to those authorized by the act to which this is an amendment, who shall give like bonds and receive the same annual salaries provided in said act, and each of the assistant commissioners of the bureau shall have charge of one district containing such refugees or freedmen, to be assigned him by the commissioner with the approval of the President. And the commissioner shall, under the direction of the President, and so far as the same shall be, in his judgment, necessary for the efficient and economical administration of the affairs of the bureau, appoint such agents, clerks, and assistants as may be required for the proper conduct of the bureau. Military officers or enlisted men may be detailed for service and assigned to duty under this act; and the President may, if in his judgment safe and judicious so to do, detail from the army all the officers and agents of this bureau; but no officer so assigned shall of pay or allowances. Each agent or clerk, not heretofore authorized by law, not being a military officer, shall have an annual salary of not less than five hundred dollars, nor more than twelve hundred dollars, according to the service required of him. And it shall be the duty of the commissioner, when it can be done consistently with public interest, to appoint, as assistant commissioners, agents, and clerks, such men as have proved their loyalty by faithful service in the armies of the Union during the rebellion. And all persons appointed to service under this act and the act to which this is an amendment, shall be so far deemed in the military service of the United States as to be under the military jurisdiction, and entitled to the military protection of the government while in discharge of the duties of their office.

SEC. 4. And be it further enacted, That officers of the veteran reserve corps or of the volunteer service, now on duty in the Freedmen's Bureau as assistant commissioners, agents. [sic] medical officers, or in other capacities, whose regiments or corps have been or may hereafter be mustered out of service, may be retained upon such duty as officers of said bureau, with the same compensation as is now provided by law for their respective grades; and the Secretary of War shall have power to fill vacancies until other officers can be detailed in their places without detriment to the public service.

SEC. 5. And be it further enacted, That the second section of the act to which this is an amendment shall be deemed to authorize the Secretary of War to issue such medical stores or other supplies and transportation, and afford such medical or other aid as here may be needful for the purposes named in said section. Provided, That no person shall be deemed "destitute," "suffering," or "dependent upon the government for support," within the meaning of this act, who is able to find employment, and could, by proper industry or exertion, avoid such destitution, suffering, or dependence.

SEC. 6. Whereas, by the provisions of an act approved February sixth, eighteen hundred and sixty-three, entitled "An act to amend an act entitled 'An act for the collection of direct taxes in insurrectionary districts within the United States, and for other purposes,' approved June seventh, eighteen hundred and sixty-two," certain lands in the parishes of St. Helena and Saint Luke, South Carolina, were bid in by the United States at public tax sales, and by the limitation of said act the time of redemption of said lands has expired; and whereas, in accordance with instructions issued by President Lincoln on the sixteenth day of September, eighteen hundred and sixty-three, to the United States direct tax commissioners for South Carolina, certain lands bid in by the United States in the parish of Saint Helena, in said State, were in part sold by the said tax commissioners to "heads of families of the African race," in parcels of not more than twenty acres to each purchaser; and whereas, under said instructions, the said tax commissioners did also set apart as "school farms" certain parcels of land in said parish, numbered on their plats from one to thirty-three, inclusive, making an aggregate of six thousand acres, more or less: Therefore, be it further enacted, That the sales made to "heads of families of the African race," under the instructions of President Lincoln to the United States direct tax commissioners for South Carolina, of date of September sixteenth, eighteen hundred and sixty-three, are hereby confirmed and established; and all leases which have been made to such "heads of families," by said direct tax commissioners, shall be changed into certificates of sale in all cases wherein the lease provides for such substitution; and all the lands now remaining unsold, which come within the same designation being eight thousand acres more or less, shall be disposed of according to said instructions.

SEC. 7. And be it further enacted, That all other lands bid in by the United States at tax sales being thirty-eight thousand acres more or less, and now in the bands of the said tax commissioners as the property of the United States, in the parishes of Saint Helena and Saint Luke, excepting the "school farms," as specified in the preceding section, and so much as may be necessary for military and naval purposes at Hilton Head, Bay Point, and Land's End, and excepting also the city of Port Royal, on Saint Helena Island, and the town of Beaufort, shall be disposed of in parcels of twenty acres, at one dollar and fifty cents per acre, to such persons and to such only as have acquired and are now occupying lands under and agreeably to the provisions of General Sherman's special field order, dated at Savannah, Georgia, January sixteenth, eighteen hundred and sixty-five; and the remaining lands, if any, shall be disposed of in like manner to such persons as had acquired lands agreeably to the said order of General Sherman, but who have been dispossessed by the restoration of the same to former owners: Provided, That the lands sold in compliance with the provisions of this and the preceding section shall not be alienated by their purchasers within six years from and after the passage of this act.

SEC. 8. And be it further enacted, That the "school farms" in the parish of Saint Helena, South Carolina, shall be sold, subject to any leases of the same, by the said tax commissioners, at public auction, on or before the first day of January, eighteen hundred and sixty-seven, at not less than ten dollars per acre; and the lots in the city of Port Royal, as laid down by the said tax commissioners, and the lots and houses in the Beaufort, which are still held in like manner, shall be sold at and houses in public auction; and the proceeds of said sales, after paying expenses of the surveys and sales, shall be invested in United States bonds, the interest of which shall be appropriated, under the direction of the commissioner, to the support of schools, without distinction of color or race, on the islands in the parishes of Saint Helena and Saint Luke.

SEC. 9. And be it further enacted, That the assistant commissioners for South Carolina and Georgia are hereby authorized to examine all claims to lands in their respective States which are claimed under the provisions of General Sherman's special field order, and to give each person a valid claim a warrant upon the direct tax commissioners for South Carolina for twenty acres of land; and the said direct tax commissioners shall issue to every person, or to his or her heirs, but in no case to any assigns, presenting such warrant, a lease of twenty acres of land, as provided for in section seven, for the term of six years; but at any time thereafter, upon the payment of a sum not exceeding one dollar and fifty cents per acre, the person holding such lease shall be entitled to a certificate of sale

of said tract of twenty acres from the direct tax commissioner or such officer as may be authorized to issue the same; but no warrant shall be held valid longer than two years after the issue of the same.

Sec. 10. And be it further enacted, That the direct tax commissioners for South Carolina are hereby authorized and required at the earliest day practicable to survey the lands designated in section seven into lots of twenty acres each, with proper metes and bounds distinctly marked, so that the several tracts shall be convenient in form, and as near as practicable have an average of fertility and woodland; and the expense of such surveys shall be paid from the proceeds of sales of said lands, or, if sooner required, out of any moneys received for other lands on these islands, sold by the United States for taxes, and now in the hands of the direct tax commissioners.

Sec. 11. And be it further enacted, That restoration of lands occupied by freedmen under General Sherman's field order dated at Savannah, Georgia, January sixteenth, eighteen hundred and sixty-five, shall not be made until after the crops of the present year shall have been gathered by the occupants of said lands, nor until a fair compensation shall have been made to them by the former owners of such lands, or their legal representatives, for all improvements or betterments erected or constructed thereon, and after due notice of the same being done shall have been given by the assistant commissioner.

Sec. 12. And be it further enacted, That the commissioner shall have power to seize, hold, use, lease, or sell all buildings and tenements, and any lands appertaining to the same, or otherwise, formerly held under color of title by the late so-called confederate states, and not heretofore disposed of by the United States, and any buildings or lands held in trust for the same by any person or persons, and to use the same or appropriate the proceeds derived therefrom to the education of the freed people; and whenever the bureau shall cease to exist, such of said so-called confederate states as shall have made provision for the education of their citizens without distinction of color shall receive the sum remaining unexpended of such sales or rentals, which shall be distributed among said states for educational purposes in proportion to their population.

Sec. 13. And be it further enacted, That the commissioner of this bureau shall at all times co-operate with private benevolent associations of citizens in aid of freedmen, and with agents and teachers, duly accredited and appointed by them, and shall hire or provide by lease buildings for purposes of education whenever such associations shall, without cost to the government, provide suitable teachers and means of instruction, and he shall furnish such protection as may be required for the safe conduct of such schools.

Sec. 14. And be it further enacted, That in every State or district where the ordinary course of judicial proceedings has been interrupted by the rebellion, and until the same shall be fully restored, and in every State or district whose constitutional relations to the government have been practically discontinued by the rebellion, and until such State shall have been restored in such relations, and shall be duly represented in the Congress of the United States, the right to make and enforce contracts. [sic] to sue, be parties, and give evidence, to inherit, purchase, lease, sell, hold, and convey real and personal property, and to have full and equal benefit of all laws and proceedings concerning personal liberty, personal security, and the acquisition, enjoyment, and disposition of estate, real and personal, including the constitutional right to bear arms, shall be secured to and enjoyed by all the citizens of such State or district without respect to race or color, or previous condition of slavery. And whenever in either of said States or districts the ordinary course of judicial proceedings has been interrupted by the rebellion, and until the same shall be fully restored, and until such State shall have been restored in its constitutional relations to the government, and shall be duly represented in the Congress of the United States, the President shall, through the commissioner and the officers of the bureau, and under such rules and regulations as the President, through the Secretary of War, shall prescribe, extend military protection and have military jurisdiction over all cases and questions conceiving the free enjoyment of such immunities and rights, and no penalty or punishment for any violation of law shall be imposed or permitted because of race or color, or previous condition of slavery, other or greater than the penalty or punishment to which white persons may be liable by law for the like offence. But the jurisdiction conferred by this section upon the officers of the bureau shall not exist in any State where the ordinary course of judicial proceedings has not been interrupted by the rebellion, and shall cease in every State when the courts of the State and the United States are not disturbed in the peaceable course of justice, and after such State shall be fully restored in its constitutional relations to the government, and shall be duly represented in the Congress of the United States.

SEC. 15. And be it further enacted, That all officers, agents, and employés of this bureau, before entering upon the duties of their office shall take the oath prescribed in the first section of the act to which this is an amendment; and all acts or parts of acts inconsistent with the provisions of this act are hereby repealed.

Civil Rights Act of 1866
14 Stat. 27–30.

In addition to creating the Freedman's Bureau, Congress passed the Civil Rights Act of 1866 (now codified as 42 U.S.C. §§ 1981–1985). The Act passed by one vote and over President Andrew Johnson's veto. The Act was the first civil rights statute ever passed by Congress and it represented the clearest legislative commitment to racial equality rivaled only by the

Civil Rights Act of 1964 and the Voting Rights Act of 1965. The Act contained ten sections and provided in part:

Be it enacted by the Senate and House of Representatives of the United States of America in Congress assembled,

That all persons born in the United States and not subject to any foreign power, excluding Indians not taxed, are hereby declared to be citizens of the United States; and such citizens, of every race and color, without regard to any previous condition of slavery or involuntary servitude, except as a punishment for crime whereof the party shall have been duly convicted, shall have the same right, in every State and Territory in the United States, to make and enforce contracts, to sue, be parties, and give evidence, to inherit, purchase, lease, sell, hold, and convey real and personal property, and to full and equal benefit of all laws and proceedings for the security of person and property, as is enjoyed by white citizens, and shall be subject to like punishment, pains, and penalties, and to none other, any law, statute, ordinance, regulation, or custom, to the contrary notwithstanding.

SEC. 2. And be it further enacted, That any person who, under color of any law, statute, ordinance, regulation, or custom, shall subject, or cause to be subjected, any inhabitant of any State or Territory to the deprivation of any right secured or protected by this act, or to different punishment, pains, or penalties on account of such person having at any time been held in a condition of slavery or involuntary servitude, except as a punishment for crime whereof the party shall have been duly convicted, or by reason of his color or race, than is prescribed for the punishment of white persons, shall be deemed guilty of a misdemeanor, and, on conviction, shall be punished by fine not exceeding one thousand dollars, or imprisonment not exceeding one year, or both, in the discretion of the court.

SEC. 3. And be it further enacted, That the district courts of the United States, within their respective districts, shall have, exclusively of the courts of the several States, cognizance of all crimes and offences committed against the provisions of this act, and also, concurrently with the circuit courts of the United States, of all causes, civil and criminal, affecting persons who are denied or cannot enforce in the courts or judicial tribunals of the State or locality where they may be any of the rights secured to them by the first section of this act; and if any suit or prosecution, civil or criminal, has been or shall be commenced in any State court, against any such person, for any cause whatsoever, or against any officer, civil or military, or other person, for any arrest or imprisonment, trespasses, or wrongs done or committed by virtue or under color of authority derived from this act or the act establishing a Bureau for the relief of Freedmen and Refugees, . . . such defendant shall have the right to remove such cause for trial to the proper district or circuit court in the manner prescribed by the "Act relating to habeas corpus and regulating judicial proceedings in certain cases," approved March three, eighteen hundred and sixty-three, and all acts amendatory thereof.

SEC. 4. And be it further enacted, That the district attorneys, marshals, and deputy marshals of the United States, the commissioners appointed by the circuit and territorial courts of the United States, with powers of arresting, imprisoning, or bailing offenders against the laws of the United States, the officers and agents of the Freedmen's Bureau, and every other officer who may be specially empowered by the President of the United States, shall be, and they are hereby, specially authorized and required, at the expense of the United States, to institute proceedings against all and every person who shall violate the provisions of this act. . . .

SEC. 5. And be it further enacted, That it shall be the duty of all marshals and deputy marshals to obey and execute all warrants and precepts issued under the provisions of this act. . . .

SEC. 6. And be it further enacted, That any person who shall knowingly and willfully obstruct, hinder, or prevent any officer, or other person charged with the execution of any warrant or process issued under the provisions of this act . . . shall, for either of said offences, be subject to a fine not exceeding one thousand dollars, and imprisonment not exceeding six months, by indictment and conviction before the district court of the United States for the district in which said offense may have been committed, or before the proper court of criminal jurisdiction, if committed within any one of the organized Territories of the United States.

SEC. 7. And be it further enacted, That the district attorneys, the marshals, their deputies, and the clerks of the said district and territorial courts shall be paid for their services the like fees as may be allowed to them for similar services in other cases. . . .

SEC. 8. And be it further enacted, That whenever the President of the United States shall have reason to believe that offences have been or are likely to be committed against the provisions of this act within any judicial district, it shall be lawful for him, in his discretion, to direct the judge, marshal, and district attorney of such district to attend at such place within the district, and for such time as he may designate, for the purpose of the more speedy arrest and trial of persons charged with a violation of this act; and it shall be the duty of every judge or other officer, when any such requisition shall be received by him, to attend at the place and for the time therein designated.

SEC. 9. And be it further enacted, That it shall be lawful for the President of the United States, or such person as he may empower for that purpose, to employ such part of the land or naval forces of the United States, or of the militia, as shall be necessary to prevent the violation and enforce the due execution of this act.

SEC. 10. And be it further enacted, That upon all questions of law arising in any cause under the provisions of this act a final appeal may be taken to the Supreme Court of the United States.

Reconstruction Amendments

Notwithstanding the fact that they voted to pass the Civil Rights Act of 1866, many of the Act's supporters doubted its constitutionality. To bolster the rights of the Freedman and provide a firmer foundation for federal civil rights legislation, Congress passed the Fourteenth Amendment, which was ratified only because its approval was made a condition of some former Confederate states' readmission to the Union. The Fifteenth Amendment followed. Both are reproduced below:

At the end of the Civil War, Congress passed, and the states ratified, the so-called **Reconstruction Amendments**, which provide as follows:

THIRTEENTH AMENDMENT (1865)

SEC. 1. Neither slavery nor involuntary servitude, except as a punishment for crime whereof the party shall have been duly convicted, shall exist within the United States, or any place subject to their jurisdiction.

SEC. 2. Congress shall have power to enforce this article by appropriate legislation.

FOURTEENTH AMENDMENT (1868)

SEC. 1. All persons born or naturalized in the United States, and subject to the jurisdiction thereof, are citizens of the United States and of the State wherein they reside. No State shall make or enforce any law which shall abridge the privileges or immunities of citizens of the United States; nor shall any State deprive any person of life, liberty, or property, without due process of law; nor deny to any person within its jurisdiction the equal protection of the laws.

SEC. 2. Representatives shall be apportioned among the several States according to their respective numbers, counting the whole number of persons in each State, excluding Indians not taxed. But when the right to vote at any election for the choice of electors for President and Vice President of the United States, Representatives in Congress, the Executive and Judicial officers of a State, or the members of the Legislature thereof, is denied to any of the male inhabitants of such State, being twenty-one years of age, and citizens of the United States, or in any way abridged, except for participation in rebellion, or other crime, the basis of representation therein shall be reduced in the proportion which the number of such male citizens shall bear to the whole number of male citizens twenty-one years of age in such State.

SEC. 3. No person shall be a Senator or Representative in Congress, or elector of President and Vice President, or hold any office, civil or military, under the United States, or under any State, who, having previously taken an oath, as a member of Congress, or as an officer of the United States, or as a member of any State legislature, or as an executive or judicial officer of any State, to support the Constitution of the United States, shall have engaged in insurrection or rebellion against the same, or given aid or comfort to the enemies thereof. But Congress may, by a vote of two-thirds of each House, remove such disability.

SEC. 4. The validity of the public debt of the United States, authorized by law, including debts incurred for payment of pensions and bounties for services in suppressing insurrection or rebellion, shall not be questioned. But neither the United States nor any State shall assume or pay any debt or obligation incurred in aid of insurrection or rebellion against the United States, or any claim for the loss or emancipation of any slave; but all such debts, obligations and claims shall be held illegal and void.

SEC. 5. The Congress shall have power to enforce, by appropriate legislation, the provisions of this article.

FIFTEENTH AMENDMENT (1870)

SEC. 1. The right of citizens of the United States to vote shall not be denied or abridged by the United States or by any State on account of race, color, or previous condition of servitude.

SEC. 2. The Congress shall have power to enforce this article by appropriate legislation.

Civil Rights Act of 1870
16 Stat. 140–146.

Be it enacted by the Senate and House of Representatives of the United States of America in Congress assembled, That all citizens of the United States who are or shall be otherwise qualified by law to vote at any election . . . shall be entitled and allowed to vote at all such elections, without distinction of race, color, or previous condition of servitude. . . .

SEC. 2. And be it further enacted, That if by or under the authority of the constitution or laws of any State, or the laws of any Territory, any act is or shall be required to be done as a prerequisite or qualification for voting, and by such constitution or laws persons or officers are or shall be charged with the performance of duties in furnishing to citizens an opportunity to perform such prerequisite, or to become qualified to vote, it shall be the duty of every such person and officer to give to all citizens of the United States the same and equal opportunity to perform such prerequisite, and to become qualified to vote without distinction of race, color, or previous condition of servitude; and if any such person or officer

shall refuse or knowingly omit to give full effect to this section, he shall, for every such offence, forfeit and pay the sum of five hundred dollars to the person aggrieved thereby, to be recovered by an action on the case, with full costs, and such allowance for counsel fees as the court shall deem just, and shall also, for every such offence, be deemed guilty of a misdemeanor, and shall, on conviction thereof, be fined not less than five hundred dollars, or be imprisoned not less than one month and not more than one year, or both, at the discretion of the court.

SEC. 6. And be it further enacted, That if two or more persons shall band or conspire together, or go in disguise upon the public highway, or upon the premises of another, with intent to violate any provision of this act, or to injure, oppress, threaten, or intimidate any citizen with intent to prevent or hinder his free exercise and enjoyment of any right or privilege granted or secured to him by the Constitution or laws of the United States, or because of his having exercised the same, such persons shall be held guilty of felony, and, on conviction thereof, shall be fined or imprisoned, or both, at the discretion of the court,-the fine not to exceed five thousand dollars, and the imprisonment not to exceed ten years,- and shall, moreover, be thereafter ineligible to, and disabled from holding, any office or place of honor, profit, or trust created by the Constitution or laws of the United States.

SEC 17. And be it further enacted, That any person who, under color of any law, statute, ordinance, regulation, or custom, shall subject, or cause to be subjected, any inhabitant of any State or Territory to the deprivation of any right secured or protected by the last preceding section [giving all persons the same rights as white citizens] of this act, or to different punishment, pains, or penalties on account of such person being an alien, or by reason of his color or race, than is prescribed for the punishment of citizens, shall be deemed guilty of a misdemeanor, and, on conviction, shall be punished by fine not exceeding one thousand dollars, or imprisonment not exceeding one year, or both, in the discretion of the court.

Civil Rights Act of 1871

17 Stat. 13–15.

An Act to enforce the Provisions of the Fourteenth Amendment to the Constitution of the United States, and for other Purposes.

Be it enacted by the Senate and House of Representatives of the United States of America in Congress assembled, That any person who, under color of any law, statute, ordinance, regulation, custom, or usage of any State, shall subject, or cause to be subjected, any person within the jurisdiction of the United States to the deprivation of any rights, privileges, or immunities secured by the Constitution of the United States, shall, any such law, statute, ordinance, regulation, custom, or usage of the State to the contrary notwithstanding, be liable to the party injured in any action at law, suit in equity, or other proper proceeding for redress; such proceeding to be prosecuted in the several district or circuit courts of the United States, with and subject to the same rights of appeal, review upon error, and other remedies provided in like cases in such courts, under the provisions of the act of the ninth of April, eighteen hundred and sixty-six, entitled "An act to protect all persons in the United States in their civil rights, and to furnish the means of their vindication"; and the other remedial laws of the United States which are in their nature applicable in such cases.

SEC. 2. That if two or more persons within any State or Territory of the United States shall conspire together to overthrow, or to put down, or to destroy by force the government of the United States, or to levy war against the United States, or to oppose by force the authority of the government of the United States, or by force, intimidation, or threat to prevent, hinder, or delay the execution of any law of the United States, or by force to seize, take, or possess any property of the United States contrary to the authority thereof, or by force, intimidation, or threat to prevent any person from accepting or holding any office or trust or place of confidence under the United States, or from discharging the duties thereof, or by force, intimidation, or threat to induce any officer of the United States to leave any State, district, or place where his duties as such officer might lawfully be performed, or to injure him in his person or property on account of his lawful discharge of the duties of his office, or to injure his person while engaged in the lawful discharge of the duties of his office, or to injure his property so as to molest, interrupt, hinder, or impede him in the discharge of his official duty, or by force, intimidation, or threat to deter any party or witness in any court of the United States from attending such court, or from testifying in any matter pending in such court fully, freely, and truthfully, or to injure any such party or witness in his person or property on account of his having so attended or testified, or by force, intimidation, or threat to influence the verdict, presentment, or indictment, of any juror or grand juror in any court of the United States, or to injure such juror in his person or property on account of any verdict, presentment, or indictment lawfully assented to by him, or on account of his being or having been such juror, or shall conspire together, or go in disguise upon the public highway or upon the premises of another for the purpose, either directly or indirectly, of depriving any person or any class of persons of the equal protection of the laws, or of equal privileges or immunities under the laws, or for the purpose of preventing or hindering the constituted authorities of any State from giving or securing to all persons within such State the equal protection of the laws, or shall conspire together for the purpose of in any manner impeding, hindering, obstructing, or defeating the due course of justice in any State or Territory, with intent to deny to any citizen of the United States the due and equal protection of the laws, or to injure any person in his person or his property for lawfully enforcing the right of any person or class of persons to the equal protection of the laws, or by force, intimidation, or threat to prevent any citizen of the United States lawfully entitled to vote from giving his support or advocacy in a lawful manner towards or in favor of the election of any lawfully qualified person as an elector of President or Vice-President of the United States, or as a member of the Congress of the United States, or to injure any such citizen in his person or property on account of such support or advocacy, each and every person so offending shall be deemed guilty of a high crime, and, upon conviction thereof in any district or circuit court of the United States or district or supreme court of any Territory of the United States having jurisdiction of similar offences, shall be punished by a fine not less than five hundred nor more than five thousand dollars, or by imprisonment, with or without hard labor, as the court may determine, for a period of not less than six months nor more than six years, as the court may determine, or by both such fine and imprisonment as the court shall determine. And if any one or more persons engaged in any such conspiracy shall do, or cause to be done, any act in furtherance of the object of such conspiracy, whereby any person shall be injured in his person or property, or deprived of having and exercising any right or privilege of a citizen of the United States, the person so injured or deprived of such rights and privileges may have and maintain an action for the recovery of damages occasioned by such injury or deprivation of rights and privileges against any one or more of the persons engaged in such conspiracy, such action to be prosecuted in the proper district or circuit court of the United States, with and subject to the same rights of appeal, review upon error, and other remedies provided in like cases in such courts under the provisions of the act of April ninth, eighteen hundred and sixty-six, entitled "An act to protect all persons in the United States in their civil rights, and to furnish the means of their vindication."

SEC. 3. That in all cases where insurrection, domestic violence, unlawful combinations, or conspiracies in any State shall so obstruct or hinder the execution of the laws thereof, and of the United States, as to deprive any portion or class of the people of such State of any of the rights, privileges, or immunities, or protection, named in the Constitution and secured by this act, and the constituted authorities of such State shall either be unable to protect, or shall, from any cause, fail in or refuse protection of the people in such rights, such facts shall be deemed a denial by such State of the equal protection of the laws to which they are entitled under the Constitution of the United States; and in all such cases, or whenever any such insurrection, violence, unlawful combination, or conspiracy shall oppose or obstruct the laws of the United States or the due execution thereof, or impede or obstruct the due course of justice under the same, it shall be lawful for the President, and it shall be his duty to take such measures, by the employment of the militia or the land and naval forces of the United States, or of either, or by other means, as he may deem necessary for the suppression of such insurrection, domestic violence, or combinations; and any person who shall be arrested under the provisions of this and the preceding section shall be delivered to the marshal of the proper district, to be dealt with according to law.

Sec. 4. That whenever in any State or part of a State the unlawful combinations named in the preceding section of this act shall be organized and armed, and so numerous and powerful as to be able, by violence, to either overthrow or set at defiance the constituted authorities of such State, and of the United States within such State, or when the constituted authorities are in complicity with, or shall connive at the unlawful purposes of, such powerful and armed combinations; and whenever, by reason of either or all of the causes aforesaid, the conviction of such offenders and the preservation of the public safety shall become in such district impracticable, in every such case such combinations shall be deemed a rebellion against the government of the United States, and during the continuance of such rebellion, and within the limits of the district which shall be so under the sway thereof, such limits to be prescribed by proclamation, it shall be lawful for the President of the United States, when in his judgment the public safety shall require it, to suspend the privileges of the writ of habeas corpus, to the end that such rebellion may be overthrown: Provided, That all the provisions of the second section of an act entitled "An act relating to habeas corpus, and regulating judicial proceedings in certain cases," approved March third, eighteen hundred and sixty-three, which relate to the discharge of prisoners other than prisoners of war, and to the penalty for refusing to obey the order of the court, shall be in full force so far as the same are applicable to the provisions of this section: Provided further, That the President shall first have made proclamation, as now provided by law, commanding such insurgents to disperse: And provided also, That the provisions of this section shall not be in force after the end of the next regular session of Congress.

Sec. 5. That no person shall be a grand or petit juror in any court of the United States upon any inquiry, hearing, or trial of any suit, proceeding, or prosecution based upon or arising under the provisions of this act who shall, in the judgment of the court, be in complicity with any such combination or conspiracy; and every such juror shall, before entering upon any such inquiry, hearing, or trial, take and subscribe an oath in open court that he has never, directly or indirectly, counselled, advised, or voluntarily aided any such combination or conspiracy; and each and every person who shall take this oath, and shall therein swear falsely, shall be guilty of perjury, and shall be subject to the pains and penalties declared against that crime, and the first section of the act entitled "An act defining additional causes of challenge and prescribing an additional oath for grand and petit jurors in the United States courts," approved

June seventeenth, eighteen hundred and sixty-two, be, and the same is hereby, repealed.

SEC. 6. That any person or persons, having knowledge that any of the wrongs conspired to be done and mentioned in the second section of this act are about to be committed, and having power to prevent or aid in preventing the same, shall neglect or refuse so to do, and such wrongful act shall be committed, such person or persons shall be liable to the person injured, or his legal representatives, for all damages caused by any such wrongful act which such first-named person or persons by reasonable diligence could have prevented; and such damages may be recovered in an action on the case in the proper circuit court of the United States, and any number of persons guilty of such wrongful neglect or refusal may be joined as defendants in such action: Provided, That such action shall be commenced within one year after such cause of action shall have accrued; and if the death of any person shall be caused by any such wrongful act and neglect, the legal representatives of such deceased person shall have such action therefor, and may recover not exceeding five thousand dollars damages therein, for the benefit of the widow of such deceased person, if any there be, or if there be no widow, for the benefit of the next of kin of such deceased person.

SEC. 7. That nothing herein contained shall be construed to supersede or repeal any former act or law except so far as the same may be repugnant thereto; and any offences heretofore committed against the tenor of any former act shall be prosecuted, and any proceeding already commenced for the prosecution thereof shall be continued and completed, the same as if this act had not been passed, except so far as the provisions of this act may go to sustain and validate such proceedings.

Civil Rights Act of 1875

18 Stat. 335–337.

Whereas, it is essential to just government we recognize the equality of all men before the law, and hold that it is the duty of the government in its dealings with the people to mete out equal and exact justice to all, of whatever nativity, race, color, or persuasion, religious or political; and it being the appropriate object of legislation to enact great fundamental principles into law: Therefore,

Be it enacted by the Senate and House of Representatives of the United States of America in Congress assembled, That all persons within the jurisdiction of the United States shall be entitled to the full and equal enjoyment of the accommodations, advantages, facilities, and privileges of inns, public conveyances on land or water, theaters, and other places of public amusement; subject only to the conditions and limitations established by law, and applicable alike to citizens of every race and color, regardless of any previous condition of servitude.

[Sec. 2–3 omitted]

Sec. 4. That no citizen possessing all other qualifications which are or may be prescribed by law shall be disqualified for service as grand or petit juror in any court of the United States, or of any State, on account of race, color, or previous condition of servitude; and any officer or other person charged with any duty in the selection or summoning of jurors who shall exclude or fail to summon any citizen for the cause aforesaid shall, on conviction thereof, be deemed guilty of a misdemeanor, and be fined not more than five thousand dollars.

Sec. 5. That all cases arising under the provisions of this act in the courts of the United States shall be reviewable by the Supreme Court of the United States, without regard to the sum in controversy, under the same provisions and regulations as are now provided by law for the review of other causes in said court.

Civil Rights Act of 1964 as Amended

P.L. 88–352, amended by P.L. 102–166.

An Act

To enforce the constitutional right to vote, to confer jurisdiction upon the district courts of the United States to provide injunctive relief against discrimination in public accommodations, to authorize the Attorney General to institute suits to protect constitutional rights in public facilities and public education, to extend the Commission on Civil Rights, to prevent discrimination in federally assisted programs, to establish a Commission on Equal Employment Opportunity, and for other purposes.

Be it enacted by the Senate and House of Representatives of the United States of America in Congress assembled, That this Act may be cited as the "Civil Rights Act of 1964".

[Title I omitted]

TITLE II—INJUNCTIVE RELIEF AGAINST DISCRIMINATION IN PLACES OF PUBLIC ACCOMMODATION

Sec. 201. (a) All persons shall be entitled to the full and equal enjoyment of the goods, services, facilities, and privileges, advantages, and accommodations of any place of public accommodation, as defined in this section, without discrimination or segregation on the ground of race, color, religion, or national origin.

(b) Each of the following establishments which serves the public is a place of public accommodation within the meaning of this title if its operations affect commerce, or if discrimination or segregation by it is supported by State action:

(1) any inn, hotel, motel, or other establishment which provides lodging to transient guests, other than an establishment located within a building which contains not more than five rooms for rent or hire and

which is actually occupied by the proprietor of such establishment as his residence;

(2) any restaurant, cafeteria, lunchroom, lunch counter, soda fountain, or other facility principally engaged in selling food for consumption on the premises, including, but not limited to, any such facility located on the premises of any retail establishment; or any gasoline station;

(3) any motion picture house, theater, concert hall, sports arena, stadium or other place of exhibition or entertainment; and

(4) any establishment (A)(i) which is physically located within the premises of any establishment otherwise covered by this subsection, or (ii) within the premises of which is physically located any such covered establishment, and (B) which holds itself out as serving patrons of such covered establishment.

(c) The operations of an establishment affect commerce within the meaning of this title if (1) it is one of the establishments described in paragraph (1) of subsection (b); (2) in the case of an establishment described in paragraph (2) of subsection (b), it serves or offers to serve interstate travelers or a substantial portion of the food which it serves, or gasoline or other products which it sells, has moved in commerce; (3) in the case of an establishment described in paragraph (3) of subsection (b), it customarily presents films, performances, athletic teams, exhibitions, or other sources of entertainment which move in commerce; and (4) in the case of an establishment described in paragraph (4) of subsection (b), it is physically located within the premises of, or there is physically located within its premises, an establishment the operations of which affect commerce within the meaning of this subsection. For purposes of this section, "commerce" means travel, trade, traffic, commerce, transportation, or communication among the several States, or between the District of Columbia and any State, or between any foreign country or any territory or possession and any State or the District of Columbia, or between points in the same State but through any other State or the District of Columbia or a foreign country.

(d) Discrimination or segregation by an establishment is supported by State action within the meaning of this title if such discrimination or segregation (1) is carried on under color of any law, statute, ordinance, or regulation; or (2) is carried on under color of any custom or usage required or enforced by officials of the State or political subdivision thereof; or (3) is required by action of the State or political subdivision thereof.

(e) The provisions of this title shall not apply to a private club or other establishment not in fact open to the public, except to the extent that the facilities of such establishment are made available to the customers or patrons of an establishment within the scope of subsection (b).

Sec. 202. All persons shall be entitled to be free, at any establishment or place, from discrimination or segregation of any kind on the ground of race, color, religion, or national origin, if such discrimination or segregation is or purports to be required by any law, statute, ordinance, regulation, rule, or order of a State or any agency or political subdivision thereof.

Sec. 203. No person shall (a) withhold, deny, or attempt to withhold or deny, or deprive or attempt to deprive, any person of any right or privilege secured by section 201 or 202, or (b) intimidate, threaten, or coerce, or attempt to intimidate, threaten, or coerce any person with the purpose of interfering with any right or privilege secured by section 201 or 202, or (c) punish or attempt to punish any person for exercising or attempting to exercise any right or privilege secured by section 201 or 202.

[SEC. 204–207 omitted]

[Title III–V omitted]

TITLE VI—NONDISCRIMINATION IN FEDERALLY ASSISTED PROGRAMS

SEC. 601. No person in the United States shall, on the ground of race, color, or national origin, be excluded from participation in, be denied the benefits of, or be subjected to discrimination under any program or activity receiving Federal financial assistance.

SEC. 602. Each Federal department and agency which is empowered to extend Federal financial assistance to any program or activity, by way of grant, loan, or contract other than a contract of insurance or guaranty, is authorized and directed to effectuate the provisions of section 601 with respect to such program or activity by issuing rules, regulations, or orders of general applicability which shall be consistent with achievement of the objectives of the statute authorizing the financial assistance in connection with which the action is taken. No such rule, regulation, or order shall become effective unless and until approved by the President. Compliance with any requirement adopted pursuant to this section may be effected (1) by the termination of or refusal to grant or to continue assistance under such program or activity to any recipient as to whom there has been an express finding on the record, after opportunity for hearing, of a failure to comply with such requirement, but such termination or refusal shall be limited to the particular political entity, or part thereof, or other recipient as to whom such a finding has been made and, shall be limited in its effect to the particular program, or part thereof, in which such non-compliance has been so found, or (2) by any other means authorized by law: Provided, however, That no such action shall be taken until the department or agency concerned has advised the appropriate person or persons of the failure to comply with the requirement and has determined that compliance cannot be secured by voluntary means. In the case of any action terminating, or refusing to grant or continue, assistance because of failure to comply with a requirement imposed pursuant to this section, the head of the federal department or agency shall file with the committees of the House and Senate having legislative jurisdiction over the program or activity involved a full written report of the circumstances and the grounds for such action. No such action shall become effective until thirty days have elapsed after the filing of such report.

SEC. 603. Any department or agency action taken pursuant to section 602 shall be subject to such judicial review as may otherwise be provided by law for similar action taken by such department or agency on other grounds. In the case of action, not otherwise subject to judicial review, terminating or refusing to grant or to continue financial assistance upon a finding of failure to comply with any requirement imposed pursuant to section 602, any person aggrieved (including any State or political subdivision thereof and any agency of either) may obtain judicial review of such action in accordance with section 10 of the Administrative Procedure Act, and such action shall not be deemed committed to unreviewable agency discretion within the meaning of that section.

SEC. 604. Nothing contained in this title shall be construed to authorize action under this title by any department or agency with respect to any employment practice of any employer, employment agency, or labor organization except where a primary objective of the Federal financial assistance is to provide employment.

SEC. 605. Nothing in this title shall add to or detract from any existing authority with respect to any program or activity under which Federal financial assistance is extended by way of a contract of insurance or guaranty.

TITLE VII—EQUAL EMPLOYMENT OPPORTUNITY

[SEC. 701–702 omitted]

SEC. 703. (a) It shall be an unlawful employment practice for an employer—

(1) to fail or refuse to hire or to discharge any individual, or otherwise to discriminate against any individual with respect to his compensation, terms, conditions, or privileges of employment, because of such individual's race, color, religion, sex, or national origin; or

(2) to limit, segregate, or classify his employees in any way which would deprive or tend to deprive any individual of employment opportunities or otherwise adversely affect his status as an employee, because of such individual's race, color, religion, sex, or national origin.

(b) It shall be an unlawful employment practice for an employment agency to fail or refuse to refer for employment, or otherwise to discriminate against, any individual because of his race, color, religion, sex, or national origin, or to classify or refer for employment any individual on the basis of his race, color, religion, sex, or national origin.

(c) It shall be an unlawful employment practice for a labor organization—

(1) to exclude or to expel from its membership, or otherwise to discriminate against, any individual because of his race, color, religion, sex, or national origin;

(2) to limit, segregate, or classify its membership, or to classify or fail or refuse to refer for employment any individual, in any way which would deprive or tend to deprive any individual of employment opportunities, or would limit such employment opportunities or otherwise adversely affect his status as an employee or as an applicant for employment, because of such individual's race, color, religion, sex, or national origin; or

(3) to cause or attempt to cause an employer to discriminate against an individual in violation of this section.

(d) It shall be an unlawful employment practice for any employer, labor organization, or joint labor-management committee controlling apprenticeship or other training or retraining, including on-the-job training programs to discriminate against any individual because of his race, color, religion, sex, or national origin in admission to, or employment in, any program established to provide apprenticeship or other training.

(e) Notwithstanding any other provision of this title, (1) it shall not be an unlawful employment practice for an employer to hire and employ employees, for an employment agency to classify, or refer for employment any individual, for a labor organization to classify its membership or to classify or refer for employment any individual, or for an employer, labor organization, or joint labor-management committee controlling apprenticeship or other training or retraining programs to admit or employ any individual in any such program, on the basis of his religion, sex, or national origin in those certain instances where religion, sex, or national origin is a bona fide occupational qualification reasonably necessary to the normal operation of that particular business or enterprise, and (2) it shall not be an unlawful employment practice for a school, college, university, or other educational institution or institution of learning to hire and employ employees of a particular religion if such school, college, university, or other educational institution or institution of learning is, in whole or in substantial part, owned, supported, controlled, or managed by a particular religion or by a particular religious corporation, association, or society, or if the curriculum of such school, college, university, or other educational institution or institution of learning is directed toward the propagation of a particular religion.

(f) As used in this title, the phrase "unlawful employment practice" shall not be deemed to include any action or measure taken by an employer, labor organization, joint labor-management committee, or employment agency with respect to an individual who is a member of the

Communist Party of the United States or of any other organization required to register as a Communist-action or Communist-front organization by final order of the Subversive Activities Control Board pursuant to the Subversive Activities Control Act of 1950.

(g) Notwithstanding any other provision of this title, it shall not be an unlawful employment practice for an employer to fail or refuse to hire and employ any individual for any position, for an employer to discharge any individual from any position, or for an employment agency to fail or refuse to refer any individual for employment in any position, or for a labor organization to fail or refuse to refer any individual for employment in any position, if—

(1) the occupancy of such position, or access to the premises in or upon which any part of the duties of such position is performed or is to be performed, is subject to any requirement imposed in the interest of the national security of the United States under any security program in effect pursuant to or administered under any statute of the United States or any Executive order of the President; and

(2) such individual has not fulfilled or has ceased to fulfill that requirement.

(h) Notwithstanding any other provision of this title, it shall not be an unlawful employment practice for an employer to apply different standards of compensation, or different terms, conditions, or privileges of employment pursuant to a bona fide seniority or merit system, or a system which measures earnings by quantity or quality of production or to employees who work in different locations, provided that such differences are not the result of an intention to discriminate because of race, color, religion, sex, or national origin, nor shall it be an unlawful employment practice for an employer to give and to act upon the results of any professionally developed ability test provided that such test, its administration or action upon the results is not designed, intended or used to discriminate because of race, color, religion, sex or national origin. It shall not be an unlawful employment practice under this title for any employer to differentiate upon the basis of sex in determining the amount of the wages or compensation paid or to be paid to employees of such employer if such differentiation is authorized by the provisions of section 6(d) of the Fair Labor Standards Act of 1938, as amended (29 U.S.C. 206(d)).

(i) Nothing contained in this title shall apply to any business or enterprise on or near an Indian reservation with respect to any publicly announced employment practice of such business or enterprise under which a preferential treatment is given to any individual because he is an Indian living on or near a reservation.

(j) Nothing contained in this title shall be interpreted to require any employer, employment agency, labor organization, or joint labor-management committee subject to this title to grant preferential treatment to any individual or to any group because of the race, color, religion, sex, or national origin of such individual or group on account of an imbalance which may exist with respect to the total number or percentage of persons of any race, color, religion, sex, or national origin employed by any employer, referred or classified for employment by any employment agency or labor organization, admitted to membership or classified by any labor organization, or admitted to, or employed in, any apprenticeship or other training program, in comparison with the total number or percentage of persons of such race, color, religion, sex, or national origin in any community, State, section, or other area, or in the available work force in any community, State, section, or other area.

(k)(1)(A) An unlawful employment practice based on disparate impact is established under this title only if—

(i) a complaining party demonstrates that a respondent uses a particular employment practice that causes a disparate impact on the basis of race, color, religion, sex, or national origin and the respondent fails to demonstrate that the challenged practice is job related for the position in question and consistent with business necessity; or

(ii) the complaining party makes the demonstration described in subparagraph (C) with respect to an alternative employment practice and the respondent refuses to adopt such alternative employment practice.

(B)(i) With respect to demonstrating that a particular employment practice causes a disparate impact as described in subparagraph (A)(i), the complaining party shall demonstrate that each particular challenged employment practice causes a disparate impact, except that if the complaining party can demonstrate to the court that the elements of a respondent's decisionmaking process are not capable of separation for analysis, the decisionmaking process may be analyzed as one employment practice.

(ii) If the respondent demonstrates that a specific employment practice does not cause the disparate impact, the respondent shall not be required to demonstrate that such practice is required by business necessity.

[SEC. 704–716 omitted]

[Titles VIII–XI omitted]

Voting Rights Act of 1965 as Amended

P.L. 89–110, amended by P.L. 91–285, P.L. 94–73, and P.L. 97–205.

AN ACT

To enforce the fifteenth amendment to the Constitution of the United States, and for other purposes.

Be it enacted by the Senate and House of Representatives of the United States of America in Congress assembled, That this Act shall be known as the "Voting Rights Act of 1965."

TITLE I—VOTING RIGHTS

SEC. 2. (a) No voting qualification or prerequisite to voting or standard, practice, or procedure shall be imposed or applied by any State or political subdivision in a manner which results in a denial or abridgment of the right of any citizen of the United States to vote on account of race or color, or in contravention of the guarantees set forth in section 4(f)(2), as provided in subsection (b).

(b) A violation of subsection (a) is established if, based on the totality of circumstances, it is shown that the political processes leading to nomination or election in the State or political subdivision are not equally open to participation by members of a class of citizens protected by subsection (a) in that its members have less opportunity than other members of the electorate to participate in the political process and to elect representatives of their choice. The extent to which members of a protected class have been elected to office in the State or political subdivision is one circumstance which may be considered: Provided, That nothing in this section establishes a right to have members of a protected class elected in numbers equal to their proportion in the population.

SEC. 4. (a)(1) To assure that the right of citizens of the United States to vote is not denied or abridged on account of race or color, or in contravention of the guarantees set forth in section 4(f) (2), no citizen shall be denied the right to vote in any Federal, State, or local election because of his failure to comply with any test or device in any State with respect to which the determinations have been made under the first to sentences of subsection (b) or in any political subdivision of such State (as such subdivision existed on the date such determinations were made with respect to such State), though such determinations were not made with respect to such subdivision as a separate unit, or in any political subdivision with respect to which such determinations have been made as a separate unit, unless the United States District Court for the District of Columbia issues a declaratory judgement under this section. No citizen shall be denied the right to vote in any Federal, State, or local election because of his failure to comply with any test or device in any State with respect to which the determinations have been made under the third sentence of subsection (b) of this section or in any political subdivision of such State (as such subdivision existed on the date such determinations were made with respect to such State), though such determinations were not made with respect to such subdivision as a separate unit, or in any political subdivision with respect to which such determinations have been made as a separate unit, unless the United States District Court for the District of Columbia issues a declaratory judgment under this section. A declaratory judgment under this section shall issue only if such court determines that during the ten years preceding the filing of the action, and during the pendency of such action—

(A) no such test or device has been used within such State or political subdivision for the purpose or with the effect of denying or abridging the right to vote on account of race or color or (in the case of a State or subdivision seeking a declaratory judgement under the second sentence of this subsection) in contravention of the guarantees of subsection (f)(2);

(B) no final judgment of any court of the United States, other than the denial of declaratory judgment under this section, has determined that denial or abridgements of the right to vote on account of race or color have occurred anywhere in the territory of such State or political subdivision or (in the case of a State or subdivision seeking a declaratory judgment under the second sentence of this subsection) that denials or abridgments of the right to vote in contravention of the guarantees of subsection (f)(2) have occurred anywhere in the territory of such or subdivision and no consent decree, settlement, or agreement has been entered into resulting in any abandonment of a voting practice challenged on such grounds; and no declaratory judgment under this section shall be entered during the pendency of an action commenced before the filing of an action under this section and alleging such denial or abridgments of the right to vote;

(C) no Federal examiners under this Act have been assigned to such State or political subdivision;

(D) such State or political subdivision and all governmental units within its territory have complied with section 5 of this Act, including compliance with the requirement that no change covered by section 5 has been enforced without preclearance under section 5, and have repealed all changes covered by section 5 to which the Attorney General has successfully objected or as to which the United States District Court for the District of Columbia has denied a declaratory judgment;

(E) the Attorney General has not interposed any objection (that has not been overturned by a final judgment of a court) and no declaratory judgment has been denied under section 5, with respect to any submission by or on behalf of the plaintiff or any governmental unit within its territory under section 5, and no such submissions or declaratory judgment actions are pending; and

(F) such State or political subdivision and all governmental units within its territory—

(i) have eliminated voting procedures and methods of election which inhibit or dilute equal access to the electoral process;

(ii) have engaged in constructive efforts to eliminate intimidation and harassment of persons exercising rights protected under this Act; and

(iii) have engaged in other constructive efforts, such as expanded opportunity for convenient registration and voting for every person of voting age and the appointment of minority persons as election officials throughout the jurisdiction and at all stages of the election and registration process.

(2) To assist the court in determining whether to issue a declaratory judgment under this subsection, the plaintiff shall present evidence of minority participation, including evidence of the levels of minority group registration and voting, changes in such levels over time, and disparities between minority-groups and non-minority-group participation.

(3) No declaratory judgment shall issue under this subsection with respect to such State or political subdivision is such plaintiff and governmental units within its territory have, during the period beginning ten years before the date the judgment is issued, engaged in violations of any provision of the Constitution or laws of the United States or any State or political subdivision with respect to discrimination in voting on account of race or color or (in the case of a State or subdivision seeking a declaratory judgment under the second sentence of this subsection) in contravention of the guarantees of subsection (f)(2) unless the plaintiff establishes that any such violations were trivial, were promptly corrected, and were not repeated.

(4) The State or political subdivision bringing such action shall publicize the intended commencement and any proposed settlement of such action in the media serving such State or political subdivision and in appropriate United States post offices. Any aggrieved party may as of right intervene at any stage in such action.

(5) An action pursuant to this subsection shall be heard and determined by a court of three judges in accordance with the provisions of section 2284 of title 28 of the United States Code and any appeal shall lie to the Supreme Court. The court shall retain jurisdiction of any action pursuant to this subsection for ten years after judgment and shall reopen the action upon motion of the Attorney General or any aggrieved person alleging that conduct has occurred which, had that conduct has occurred which, had that conduct occurred during the ten-year periods referred to in this subsection, would have precluded the issuance of a declaratory judgment under this subsection. The court, upon such reopening, shall vacate the declaratory judgment issued under this section if, after the issuance of such declaratory judgment was issued, a final judgment against the State of subdivision with respect to which such declaratory judgment was issued, or against any governmental unit within that State

or subdivision, determines that denials or abridgments of the right to vote on account of race or color have occurred anywhere in the territory of such State or political subdivision or (in the case of a State or subdivision which sought a declaratory judgment under the second sentence of this subsection) that denials or abridgments of the right to vote in contravention of the guarantees of subsection (f)(2) have occurred anywhere in the territory of such State or subdivision, or if, after the issuance of such declaratory judgment, a consent decree, settlement, or agreement has been entered into resulting in any abandonment of a voting practice challenged on such grounds.

(6) If, after two years from the date of the filing of a declaratory judgment under this subsection, no date has been set for a hearing in such action, and that delay has not been the result of an avoidable delay on the part of counsel for any party, the chief judge of the United States District Court for the District of Columbia may request the Judicial Council for the Circuit Court of the District of Columbia to provide the necessary judicial resources to expedite any action filed under this section. If such resources are unavailable within the circuit, the chief judge shall file a certificate of necessity in accordance with section 292(d) of title 28 of the United States Code.

(7) The Congress shall reconsider the provisions of this section at the end of the fifteen-year period following the effective date of the amendments made by the Voting Rights Act Amendments of 1982.

(8) The provisions of this section shall expire at the end of the twenty-five-year period following the effective date of the amendments made by the Voting Rights Act Amendments of 1982.

(9) Nothing in this section shall prohibit the Attorney General from consenting to an entry of judgment if based upon a showing of objective and compelling evidence by the plaintiff, and upon investigation, he is satisfied that the State or political subdivision has complied with the requirements of section 4(a)(1). Any aggrieved party may as of right intervene at any stage in such action.

(b) The provisions of subsection (a) shall apply in any State or in any political subdivision of a state which (1) the Attorney General determines maintained on November 1, 1964, any test or device, and with respect to which (2) the Director of the Census determines that less than 50 percentum of the persons of voting age residing therein were registered on November 1, 1964, or that less than 50 percentum of such persons voted in the presidential election of November 1964. On and after August 6, 1970, in addition to any State or political subdivision of a State determined to be subject to subsection (a) pursuant to the previous sentence, the provisions of subsection (a) shall apply in any State or any political subdivision of a State which (i) the Attorney General determines maintained on November 1, 1968, any test or device, and with respect to which (ii) the Director of the Census determines that less than 50 per centum of the persons of voting age residing therein were registered on November 1, 1968, or that less than 50 per centum of such persons voted in the presidential election of November 1968. On and after August 6, 1975, in addition to any State or political subdivision of a State determined to be subject to subsection (a) pursuant to the previous two sentences, the provisions of subsection (a) shall apply in any State or any political subdivision of a State which (i) the Attorney General determines maintained on November 1, 1972, any test or device, and with respect to which (ii) the Director of the Census determines that less than 50 per centum of the citizens of voting age were registered on November 1, 1972, or that less than 50 per centum of such persons voted in the presidential election of November 1972.

A determination or certification of the Attorney General or of the Director of the Census under this section or under section 6 or section 13 shall not be reviewable in any court and shall be effective upon publication in the Federal Register.[1]

(c) The phrase "test or device" shall mean any requirement that a person as a prerequisite for voting or registration for voting (1) demonstrate the ability to read, write, understand, or interpret any matter, (2) demonstrate any educational achievement or his knowledge of any particular subject, (3) possess good moral character, or (4) prove his qualifications by the voucher of registered voters or members of any other class.

(d) For purposes of this section no State or political subdivision shall be determined to have engaged in the use of tests or devices for the purpose or with the effect of denying or abridging the right to vote on account of race or color, or in contravention of the guarantees set forth in section 4(f) (2) if (1) incidents of such use have been few in number and have been promptly and effectively corrected by State or local action, (2) the continuing effect of such incidents has been eliminated, and (3) there is no reasonable probability of their recurrence in the future.

(e) (1) Congress hereby declares that to secure the rights under the fourteenth amendment of persons educated in American-flag schools in which the predominant classroom language was other than English, it is necessary to prohibit the States from conditioning the right to vote of such persons on ability to read, write, understand, or interpret any matter in the English language.

(2) No person who demonstrates that he has successfully completed the sixth primary grade in a public school in, or a private school accredited by, any State or territory, the District of Columbia, or the Commonwealth of Puerto Rico in which the predominant classroom language was other than English, shall be denied the right to vote in any Federal, State, or local election because of his inability to read, write,

---

[1]   Section 4(b) was found unconstitutional in *Shelby County v. Holder*, 570 U.S. ___ (2013).

understand, or interpret any matter in the English language, except that, in States in which State law provides that a different level of education is presumptive of literacy, he shall demonstrate that he has successfully completed an equivalent level of education in a public school in, or a private school accredited by, any State or territory, the District of Columbia, or the Commonwealth of Puerto Rico in which the predominant classroom language was other than English.

(f) (1) The Congress finds that voting discrimination against citizens of language minorities is pervasive and national in scope. Such minority citizens are from environments in which the dominant language is other than English. In addition they have been denied equal educational opportunities by State and local governments, resulting in severe disabilities and continuing illiteracy in the English language. The Congress further finds that, where State and local officials conduct elections only in English, language minority citizens are excluded from participating in the electoral process. In many areas of the country, this exclusion is aggravated by acts of physical, economic, and political intimidation. The Congress declares that, in order to enforce the guarantees of the fourteenth and fifteenth amendments to the United States Constitution, it is necessary to eliminate such discrimination by prohibiting English-only elections, and by prescribing other remedial devices.

(2) No voting qualifications or prerequisite to voting, or standard, practice, or procedure shall be imposed or applied by any State or political subdivision to deny or abridge the right of any citizen of the United States to vote because he is a member of a language minority group.

(3) In addition to the meaning given the term under section 4(c), the term 'test or device' shall also mean any practice or requirement by which any State or political subdivision provided any registration or voting notices, forms, instructions, assistance, or other materials or information relating to the electoral process, including ballots, only in the English language, where the Director of the Census determines that more than five per centum of the citizens of voting age residing in such State or political subdivision are members of a single language minority. With respect to section 4(b), the term 'test or device', as defined in this subsection, shall be employed only in making the determinations under the third sentence of that subsection.

(4) Whenever any State or political subdivision subject to the prohibitions of the second sentence of section 4(a) provides any registration or voting notices, forms, instructions, assistance, or other materials or information relating to the electoral process, including ballots, it shall provide them in the language of the applicable language minority group as well as in the English language: Provided, That where the language of the applicable minority group is oral or unwritten, or in the case of Alaskan Natives and American Indians, if the predominate

language is historically unwritten, the State or political subdivision is only required to furnish oral instructions, assistance, or other information relating to registration and voting.

SEC. 5. Whenever a State or political subdivision with respect to which the prohibitions set forth in section 4(a) based upon determinations made under the first sentence of section 4 (b) are in effect shall enact or seek to administer any voting qualification or prerequisite to voting, or standard, practice, or procedure with respect to voting different from that in force or effect on November 1, 1964, or whenever a State or political subdivision with respect to which the prohibitions set forth in section 4(a) based upon determinations made under the second sentence of section 4(b) are in effect shall enact or seek to administer any voting qualification or prerequisite to voting, or standard, practice, or procedure with respect to voting different from that in force or effect on November 1, 1968, or whenever a State or political subdivision with respect to which the prohibitions set forth in section 4(a) based upon determination made under the third sentence of section 4(b) are in effect shall enact or seek to administer any voting qualification or prerequisite to voting, or standard, practice, or procedure with respect to voting different from that in force or effect on November 1, 1972, such State or subdivision may institute an action in the United States District Court for the District of Columbia for a declaratory judgment that such qualification, prerequisite, standard, practice, or procedure does not have the purpose and will not have the effect of denying or abridging the right to vote on account of race or color, or in contravention of the guarantees set forth in section 4(f) (2), and unless and until the court enters such judgment no person shall be denied the right to vote for failure to comply with such qualification, prerequisite, standard, practice, or procedure: Provided, That such qualification, prerequisite, standard, practice, or procedure may be enforced without such proceeding if the qualification, prerequisite, standard, practice, or procedure has been submitted by the chief legal officer or other appropriate official of such State or subdivision to the Attorney General and the Attorney General has not interposed an objection within sixty days after such submission, except that neither the Attorney General's failure to object nor a declaratory judgment entered under this section shall bar a subsequent action to enjoin enforcement of such qualification, prerequisite, standard, practice, or procedure. Any action under this section shall be heard and determined by a court of three judges in accordance with the provisions of section 2284 of title 28 of the United States Code and any appeal shall lie to the Supreme Court.

TITLE II—SUPPLEMENTAL PROVISIONS

APPLICATION OF PROHIBITION TO OTHER STATES

SEC. 201. (a) No citizen shall be denied because of his failure to comply with any test or device, the right to vote in any Federal, State, or local election conducted in any State or political subdivision of a State.

(b) As used in this section, the term 'test or device' means any requirement that a person as a prerequisite for voting or registration for voting (1) demonstrate the ability to read, write, understand, or interpret any matter, (2) demonstrate any educational achievement or his knowledge of any particular subject, (3) possess good moral character, or (4) prove his qualifications by the voucher of registered voters or members of any other class.

RESIDENCE REQUIREMENTS FOR VOTING

SEC. 202. (a) The Congress hereby finds that the imprisonment and application of the durational residency requirement as a precondition to voting for the offices of President and Vice President, and the lack of sufficient opportunities for absentee registration and absentee balloting in presidential elections—

(1) denies or abridges the inherent constitutional right of citizens to vote for their president and Vice President;

(2) denies or abridges the inherent constitutional right of citizens to enjoy their free movement across State lines;

(3) denies or abridges the privileges and immunities guaranteed to the citizens of each State under article IV, section 2, clause 1, of the Constitution;

(4) in some instances has the impermissible purpose or effect of denying citizens the right to vote for such officers because of the way they may vote;

(5) has the effect of denying to citizens the equality of civil rights, and due process and equal protection of the laws that are guaranteed to them under the fourteenth amendment; and

(6) does not bear a reasonable relationship to any compelling State interest in the conduct of presidential elections.

(b) Upon the basis of these findings, Congress declares that in order to secure and protect the above-stated rights of citizens under the Constitution, to enable citizens to better obtain the enjoyment of such rights, and to enforce the guarantees of the fourteenth amendment, it is necessary (1) to completely abolish the durational residency requirement as a precondition to voting for President and Vice President, and (2) to establish nationwide, uniform standards relative to absentee registration and absentee balloting in presidential elections.

(c) No citizen of the United States who is otherwise qualified to vote in any election for President and Vice President shall be denied the right to vote for electors for President and Vice President, or for President and Vice President, in such election because of the failure of such citizen to comply with any durational residency requirement of such State or political subdivision; nor shall any citizen of the United States be denied the right to vote for electors for President and Vice President, or for

President and Vice President, in such elections because of failure of such citizen to be physically present in such State or political subdivision at the time of such election, if such citizen shall have complied with the requirements prescribed by the law of such State or political subdivision providing for the casting of absentee ballots in such election.

(d) For the purpose of this section, each State shall provide by law for the registration of other means of qualifications of a duly qualified residents of such State who apply, not later than thirty days immediately prior to any presidential election, for registration or qualification to vote for the choice of electors for President and Vice President or for President and Vice President in such election; and each State shall provide by law for the casting of absentee ballots for the choice of electors for President and Vice President, or for President and Vice President, by all duly qualifies residents of such State who may be absent from their election district or unit in such State on the day such election is held and who have applied therefor not later than seven days immediately prior to such election and have returned such ballots to the appropriate election official of such State not later than the time of closing of the polls in such State on the day of such election.

(e) If any citizen of the United States who is otherwise qualified to vote in any State or political subdivision in any election for President and Vice President has begun residence in such State or political subdivision after the thirtieth day next preceding such election and, for that reason, does not satisfy the registration requirements of such State or political subdivision he shall be allowed to vote for the choice of electors for President and Vice President, or for President and Vice President, in such election, (1) in person in the State or political subdivision in which he resided immediately prior to his removal if he had satisfied, as of the date of his change of residence, the requirements to vote in that State or political subdivision, or (2) by absentee ballot in the State or political subdivision in which he resides immediately prior to his removal if he satisfies, but for his nonresident status and the reason for his absence, the requirements for absentee voting in that State or political subdivision.

(f) No citizen of the United States who is otherwise qualified to vote by absentee ballot in any State or political subdivision in any election for President and Vice President shall be denied the right to vote for the choice of electors for President and Vice President, or for President and Vice President, in such election because of any requirement of registration that does not include a provision for absentee registration.

(g) Nothing in this section shall prevent any State or political subdivision from adopting less restrictive voting practices than those that are prescribed herein.

(h) The term 'State' as used in this section includes each of the several States and the District of Columbia.

(i) The provisions of section 11 (c) shall apply to false registration, and other fraudulent acts and conspiracies, committed under this section.

SEC. 207. (a) Congress hereby directs the Director of the Census forthwith to conduct a survey to compile registration and voting statistics: (i) in every State or political subdivision with respect to which the prohibitions of section 4(a) of the Voting Rights Act of 1965 are in effect, for every statewide general election for Members of the United States House of Representative after January 1, 1974; and (ii) in every State or political subdivision for any election designated by the United States Commission on Civil Rights. Such survey shall only include a count of citizens of voting age, race or color, and national origin, and a determination of the extent to which such persons are registered to vote and have in the elections surveyed.

(b) In any survey under subsection (a) of this section no person shall be compelled to disclose his race, color national origin, political party affiliation, or how he voted (or the reasons therefor), nor shall any penalty be imposed for his failure or refusal to make such disclosures. Every person interrogated orally, by written survey or questionnaire, or by any other mean with respect to such information shall be fully advised of his right to fail or refuse to furnish such information.

(c) The Director of the Census shall, at the earliest practicable time, report to the Congress the results of every survey conducted pursuant to the provisions of subsection (a) of this section.

(d) The provisions of section 9 and chapter 7 of title 13 of the United States Code shall apply to any survey, collection, or compilation of registration and voting statistics carried out under subsection (a) of this section.

Civil Rights Act of 1968 (Fair Housing Act)

P.L. 90–284, amended by P.L. 100–430.

TITLE VIII—FAIR HOUSING

DISCRIMINATION IN THE SALE OR RENTAL OF HOUSING AND OTHER PROHIBITED PRACTICES

SEC. 804. As made applicable by section 803 of this title and except as exempted by sections 803(b) and 807 of this title, it shall be unlawful—

(a) To refuse to sell or rent after the making of a bona fide offer, or to refuse to negotiate for the sale or rental of, or otherwise make unavailable or deny, a dwelling to any person because of race, color, religion, sex, familial status, or national origin.

(b) To discriminate against any person in the terms, conditions, or privileges of sale or rental of a dwelling, or in the provision of services or facilities in connection therewith, because of race, color, religion, sex, familial status, or national origin.

(c) To make, print, or publish, or cause to be made, printed, or published any notice, statement, or advertisement, with respect to the sale or rental of a dwelling that indicates any preference, limitation, or discrimination based on race, color, religion, sex, handicap, familial status, or national origin, or an intention to make any such preference, limitation, or discrimination.

(d) To represent to any person because of race, color, religion, sex, handicap, familial status, or national origin that any dwelling is not available for inspection, sale, or rental when such dwelling is in fact so available.

(e) For profit, to induce or attempt to induce any person to sell or rent any dwelling by representations regarding the entry or prospective entry into the neighborhood of a person or persons of a particular race, color, religion, sex, handicap, familial status, or national origin.

(f)(1) To discriminate in the sale or rental, or to otherwise make unavailable or deny, a dwelling to any buyer or renter because of a handicap of—

(A) that buyer or renter;

(B) a person residing in or intending to reside in that dwelling after it is so sold, rented, or made available; or

(C) any person associated with that buyer or renter.

(2) To discriminate against any person in the terms, conditions, or privileges of sale or rental of a dwelling, or in the provision of services or facilities in connection with such dwelling, because of a handicap of—

(A) that person; or

(B) a person residing in or intending to reside in that dwelling after it is so sold, rented, or made available; or

(C) any person associated with that person.

(3) For purposes of this subsection, discrimination includes—

(A) a refusal to permit, at the expense of the handicapped person, reasonable modifications of existing premises occupied or to be occupied by such person if such modifications may be necessary to afford such person full enjoyment of the premises, except that, in the case of a rental, the landlord may where it is reasonable to do so condition permission for a modification on the renter agreeing to restore the interior of the premises to the condition that existed before the modification, reasonable wear and tear excepted.

(B) a refusal to make reasonable accommodations in rules, policies, practices, or services, when such accommodations may be necessary to afford such person equal opportunity to use and enjoy a dwelling; or

(C) in connection with the design and construction of covered multifamily dwellings for first occupancy after the date that is 30 months after the date of enactment of the Fair Housing Amendments Act of 1988, a failure to design and construct those dwellings in such a manner that—

(i) the public use and common use portions of such dwellings are readily accessible to and usable by handicapped persons;

(ii) all the doors designed to allow passage into and within all premises within such dwellings are sufficiently wide to allow passage by handicapped persons in wheelchairs; and

(iii) all premises within such dwellings contain the following features of adaptive design:

(I) an accessible route into and through the dwelling;

(II) light switches, electrical outlets, thermostats, and other environmental controls in accessible locations;

(III) reinforcements in bathroom walls to allow later installation of grab bars; and

(IV) usable kitchens and bathrooms such that an individual in a wheelchair can maneuver about the space.

(4) Compliance with the appropriate requirements of the American National Standard for buildings and facilities providing accessibility and usability for physically handicapped people (commonly cited as "ANSI A117.1") suffices to satisfy the requirements of paragraph (3)(C)(iii).

(5)(A) If a State or unit of general local government has incorporated into its laws the requirements set forth in paragraph (3)(C), compliance with such laws shall be deemed to satisfy the requirements of that paragraph.

(B) A State or unit of general local government may review and approve newly constructed covered multifamily dwellings for the purpose of making determinations as to whether the design and construction requirements of paragraph (3)(C) are met.

(C) The Secretary shall encourage, but may not require, States and units of local government to include in their existing procedures for the review and approval of newly constructed covered multifamily dwellings, determinations as to whether the design and construction of such dwellings are consistent with paragraph (3)(C), and shall provide technical assistance to States and units of local government and other persons to implement the requirements of paragraph (3)(C).

(D) Nothing in this title shall be construed to require the Secretary to review or approve the plans, designs or construction of all covered multifamily dwellings, to determine whether the design and construction of such dwellings are consistent with the requirements of paragraph 3(C).

(6)(A) Nothing in paragraph (5) shall be construed to affect the authority and responsibility of the Secretary or a State or local public agency certified pursuant to section 810(f)(3) of this Act to receive and process complaints or otherwise engage in enforcement activities under this title.

(B) Determinations by a State or a unit of general local government under paragraphs (5) (A) and (B) shall not be conclusive in enforcement proceedings under this title.

(7) As used in this subsection, the term "covered multifamily dwellings" means—

(A) buildings consisting of 4 or more units if such buildings have one or more elevators; and

(B) ground floor units in other buildings consisting of 4 or more units.

(8) Nothing in this title shall be construed to invalidate or limit any law of a State or political subdivision of a State, or other jurisdiction in which this title shall be effective, that requires dwellings to be designed and constructed in a manner that affords handicapped persons greater access than is required by this title.

(9) Nothing in this subsection requires that a dwelling be made available to an individual whose tenancy would constitute a direct threat to the health or safety of other individuals or whose tenancy would result in substantial physical damage to the property of others.

DISCRIMINATION IN RESIDENTIAL REAL ESTATE-RELATED TRANSACTIONS

SEC. 805. (a) IN GENERAL.—It shall be unlawful for any person or other entity whose business includes engaging in residential real estate-related transactions to discriminate against any person in making available such a transaction, or in the terms or conditions of such a transaction, because of race, color, religion, sex, handicap, familial status, or national origin.

(b) DEFINITION.—As used in this section, the term "residential real estate-related transaction" means any of the following:

(1) The making or purchasing of loans or providing other financial assistance—

(A) for purchasing, constructing, improving, repairing, or maintaining a dwelling; or

(B) secured by residential real estate.

(2) The selling, brokering, or appraising of residential real property.

(c) APPRAISAL EXEMPTION.—Nothing in this title prohibits a person engaged in the business of furnishing appraisals of real property to take into consideration factors other than race, color, religion, national origin, sex, handicap, or familial status.

DISCRIMINATION IN PROVISION OF BROKERAGE SERVICES

SEC. 806. After December 31, 1968, it shall be unlawful to deny any person access to or membership or participation in any multiple-listing service, real estate brokers' organization or other service, organization, or facility relating to the business of selling or renting dwellings, or to discriminate against him in the terms or conditions of such access, membership, or participation, on account of race, color, religion, sex, handicap, familial status, or national origin.

RELIGIOUS ORGANIZATION OR PRIVATE CLUB EXEMPTION

SEC. 807. (a) Nothing in this title shall prohibit a religious organization, association, or society, or any nonprofit institution or organization operated, supervised or controlled by or in conjunction with a religious organization, association, or society, from limiting the sale, rental or occupancy of dwellings which it owns or operates for other than a commercial purpose to persons of the same religion, or from giving preference to such persons, unless membership in such religion is restricted on account of race, color, or national origin. Nor shall anything in this title prohibit a private club not in fact open to the public, which as an incident to its primary purpose or purposes provides lodgings which it owns or operates for other than a commercial purpose, from limiting the rental or occupancy of such lodgings to its members or from giving preference to its members.

(b)(1) Nothing in this title limits the applicability of any reasonable local, State, or Federal restrictions regarding the maximum number of occupants permitted to occupy a dwelling. Nor does any provision in this title regarding familial status apply with respect to housing for older persons.

(2) As used in this section, "housing for older persons" means housing—

(A) provided under any State or Federal program that the Secretary determines is specifically designed and operated to assist elderly persons (as defined in the State or Federal program); or

(B) intended for, and solely occupied by, persons 62 years of age or older; or

(C) intended and operated for occupancy by at least one person 55 years of age or older and—

(i) at least 80 percent of the occupied units are occupied by at least one person who is 55 years of age or older;

(ii) the housing facility or community publishes and adheres to policies and procedures that demonstrate the intent required under this subparagraph; and

(iii) the housing facility or community complies with rules issued by the Secretary for verification of occupancy, which shall—(I) provide for verification by reliable surveys and affidavits; and(II) include examples of the types of policies and procedures relevant to a determination of compliance with the requirement of clause (ii). Such surveys and affidavits shall be admissible in administrative and judicial proceedings for the purposes of such verification.

(3) Housing shall not fail to meet the requirements for housing for older persons by reason of:

(A) persons residing in such housing as of the date of enactment of this Act who do not meet the age requirements of subsections (2)(B) or (C): Provided, That new occupants of such housing meet the age requirements of subsections (2)(B) or (C); or

(B) unoccupied units: Provided, That such units are reserved for occupancy by persons who meet the age requirements of subsections (2)(B) or (C).

(4) Nothing in this title prohibits conduct against a person because such person has been convicted by any court of competent jurisdiction of the illegal manufacture or distribution of a controlled substance as defined in section 102 of the Controlled Substances Act (21 U.S.C. 802).

(5)(A) A person shall not be held personally liable for monetary damages for a violation of this title if such person reasonably relied, in good faith, on the application of the exemption under this subsection relating to housing for older persons.

(B) For the purposes of this paragraph, a person may only show good faith reliance on the application of the exemption by showing that—

(i) such person has no actual knowledge that the facility or community is not, or will not be, eligible for such exemption; and

(ii) the facility or community has stated formally, in writing, that the facility or community complies with the requirements for such exemption.

ENFORCEMENT BY PRIVATE PERSONS

SEC. 813. (a) CIVIL ACTION.—(1)(A) An aggrieved person may commence a civil action in an appropriate United States district court or State court not later than 2 years after the occurrence or the termination of an alleged discriminatory housing practice, or the breach of a conciliation agreement entered into under this title, whichever occurs last, to obtain appropriate relief with respect to such discriminatory housing practice or breach.

(B) The computation of such 2-year period shall not include any time during which an administrative proceeding under this title was pending with respect to a complaint or charge under this title based upon such discriminatory housing practice. This subparagraph does not apply to actions arising from a breach of a conciliation agreement.

(2) An aggrieved person may commence a civil action under this subsection whether or not a complaint has been filed under section 810(a) and without regard to the status of any such complaint, but if the Secretary or a State or local agency has obtained a conciliation agreement with the consent of an aggrieved person, no action may be filed under this subsection by such aggrieved person with respect to the alleged discriminatory housing practice which forms the basis for such complaint except for the purpose of enforcing the terms of such an agreement.

(3) An aggrieved person may not commence a civil action under this subsection with respect to an alleged discriminatory housing practice which forms the basis of a charge issued by the Secretary if an administrative law judge has commenced a hearing on the record under this title with respect to such charge.

(b) APPOINTMENT OF ATTORNEY BY COURT.—Upon application by a person alleging a discriminatory housing practice or a person against whom such a practice is alleged, the court may—

(1) appoint an attorney for such person; or

(2) authorize the commencement or continuation of a civil action under subsection (a) without the payment of fees, costs, or security, if in the opinion of the court such person is financially unable to bear the costs of such action.

(c) RELIEF WHICH MAY BE GRANTED.—(1) In a civil action under subsection (a), if the court finds that a discriminatory housing practice has occurred or is about to occur, the court may award to the plaintiff actual and punitive damages, and subject to subsection (d), may grant as relief, as the court deems appropriate, any permanent or temporary injunction, temporary restraining order, or other order (including an order enjoining the defendant from engaging in such practice or ordering such affirmative action as may be appropriate).

(2) In a civil action under subsection (a), the court, in its discretion, may allow the prevailing party, other than the United States, a reasonable attorney's fee and costs. The United States shall be liable for such fees and costs to the same extent as a private person.

(d) EFFECT ON CERTAIN SALES, ENCUMBRANCES, AND RENTALS.—Relief granted under this section shall not affect any contract, sale, encumbrance, or lease consummated before the granting of such relief and involving a bona fide purchaser, encumbrancer, or tenant, without actual notice of the filing of a complaint with the Secretary or civil action under this title.

(e) INTERVENTION BY ATTORNEY GENERAL.—Upon timely application, the Attorney General may intervene in such civil action, if the Attorney General certifies that the case is of general public importance. Upon such intervention the Attorney General may obtain such relief as would be available to the Attorney General under section 814(e) in a civil action to which such section applies.

ENFORCEMENT BY THE ATTORNEY GENERAL

SEC. 814. (a) PATTERN OR PRACTICE CASES.—Whenever the Attorney General has reasonable cause to believe that any person or group of persons is engaged in a pattern or practice of resistance to the full enjoyment of any of the rights granted by this title, or that any group of persons has been denied any of the rights granted by this title and such denial raises an issue of general public importance, the Attorney General may commence a civil action in any appropriate United States district court.

(b) ON REFERRAL OF DISCRIMINATORY HOUSING PRACTICE OR CONCILIATION AGREEMENT FOR ENFORCEMENT.—(1)(A) The Attorney General may commence a civil action in any appropriate United States district court for appropriate relief with respect to a discriminatory housing practice referred to the Attorney General by the Secretary under section 810(g).

(B) A civil action under this paragraph may be commenced not later than the expiration of 18 months after the date of the occurrence or the termination of the alleged discriminatory housing practice.

(2)(A) The Attorney General may commence a civil action in any appropriate United States district court for appropriate relief with respect to breach of a conciliation agreement referred to the Attorney General by the Secretary under section 810(c).

(B) A civil action may be commenced under this paragraph not later than the expiration of 90 days after the referral of the alleged breach under section 810(c).

(c) ENFORCEMENT OF SUBPOENAS.—The Attorney General, on behalf of the Secretary, or other party at whose request a subpoena is issued, under this title, may enforce such subpoena in appropriate proceedings in the United States district court for the district in which the person to whom the subpoena was addressed resides, was served, or transacts business.

(d) RELIEF WHICH MAY BE GRANTED IN CIVIL ACTIONS UNDER SUBSECTIONS (a) AND (b).—(1) In a civil action under subsection (a) or (b), the court—

(A) may award such preventive relief, including a permanent or temporary injunction, restraining order, or other order against the person responsible for a violation of this title as is necessary to assure the full enjoyment of the rights granted by this title;

(B) may award such other relief as the court deems appropriate, including monetary damages to persons aggrieved; and

(C) may, to vindicate the public interest, assess a civil penalty against the respondent—

(i) in an amount not exceeding $55,000, for a first violation; and

(ii) in an amount not exceeding $110,000, for any subsequent violation.

(2) In a civil action under this section, the court, in its discretion, may allow the prevailing party, other than the United States, a reasonable attorney's fee and costs. The United States shall be liable for such fees and costs to the extent provided by section 2412 of title 28, United States Code.

(e) INTERVENTION IN CIVIL ACTIONS.—Upon timely application, any person may intervene in a civil action commenced by the Attorney General under subsection (a) or (b) which involves an alleged discriminatory housing practice with respect to which such person is an aggrieved person or a conciliation agreement to which such person is a party. The court may grant such appropriate relief to any such intervening party as is authorized to be granted to a plaintiff in a civil action under section 813.

EFFECT ON STATE LAWS

SEC. 816. Nothing in this title shall be construed to invalidate or limit any law of a State or political subdivision of a State, or of any other jurisdiction in which this title shall be effective, that grants, guarantees, or protects the same rights as are granted by this title; but any law of a State, a political subdivision, or other such jurisdiction that purports to require or permit any action that would be a discriminatory housing practice under this title shall to that extent be invalid.

COOPERATION WITH STATE AND LOCAL AGENCIES ADMINISTERING

SEC. 817. The Secretary may cooperate with State and local agencies charged with the administration of State and local fair housing laws and, with the consent of such agencies, utilize the services of such agencies and their employees and, notwithstanding any other provision of law, may reimburse such agencies and their employees for services rendered to assist him in carrying out this title. In furtherance of such cooperative efforts, the Secretary may enter into written agreements with such State or local agencies. All agreements and terminations thereof shall be published in the Federal Register.

INTERFERENCE, COERCION, OR INTIMIDATION

SEC. 818. It shall be unlawful to coerce, intimidate, threaten, or interfere with any person in the exercise or enjoyment of, or on account of his having exercised or enjoyed, or on account of his having aided or encouraged any other person in the exercise or enjoyment of, any right granted or protected by section 803, 804, 805, or 806 of this title.

SEPARABILITY

SEC. 820. If any provision of this title or the application thereof to any person or circumstances is held invalid, the remainder of the title and the application of the provision to other persons not similarly situated or to other circumstances shall not be affected thereby.

TITLE IX—PREVENTION OF DISCRIMINATION IN FAIR HOUSING CASES

SEC. 901. Whoever, whether or not acting under color of law, by force or threat of force willfully injures, intimidates or interferes with, or attempts to injure, intimidate or interfere with—

(a) any person because of his race, color, religion, sex, handicap (as such term is defined in section 3602 of this title), familial status (as such term is defined in section 3602 of this title), or national origin and because he is or has been selling, purchasing, renting, financing, occupying, or contracting or negotiating for the sale, purchase, rental, financing or occupation of any dwelling, or applying for or participating in any service, organization, or facility relating to the business of selling or renting dwellings; or

(b) any person because he is or has been, or in order to intimidate such person or any other person or any class of persons from—

(1) participating, without discrimination on account of race, color, religion, sex, handicap (as such term is defined in section 3602 of this title), familial status (as such term is defined in section 3602 of this title), or national origin, in any of the activities, services, organizations or facilities described in subsection (a) of this section; or

(2) affording another person or class of persons opportunity or protection so to participate; or

(c) any citizen because he is or has been, or in order to discourage such citizen or any other citizen from lawfully aiding or encouraging other persons to participate, without discrimination on account of race, color, religion, sex, handicap (as such term is defined in section 3602 of this title), familial status (as such term is defined in section 3602 of this title), or national origin, in any of the activities, services, organizations or facilities described in subsection (a) of this section, or participating lawfully in speech or peaceful assembly opposing any denial of the opportunity to so participate—

shall be fined under title 18 or imprisoned no more than one year, or both; and if bodily injury results from the acts committed in violation of this section or if such acts include the use, attempted use, or threatened use of a dangerous weapon, explosives, or fire shall be fined under title 18 or imprisoned not more than ten years, or both; and if death results from the acts committed in violation of this section or if such acts include kidnapping or an attempt to kidnap, aggravated sexual abuse or an attempt to commit aggravated sexual abuse, or an attempt to kill, shall be fined under title 18 or imprisoned for any term of years or for life, or both.

INDEX

References are to Pages

WHITE FLIGHT, 262

WHITE SUPREMACY
Colorblindness and, 70
Historical background, 2
Ku Klux Klan era, 32
Persistence of, 1
USSC recognition, 179